GENERAL MOTORS

CELEBRITY / CENTURY / CUTLASS CIERA / 6000
1982-92 REPAIR MANUAL

CHILTON'S

Senior Vice President   Ronald A. Hoxter

Publisher   Kerry A. Freeman, S.A.E.
Editor-In-Chief   Dean F. Morgantini, S.A.E.
Director of Manufacturing   Mike D'Imperio
Production Manager   W. Calvin Settle, Jr., S.A.E.
Senior Editor   Richard J. Rivele, S.A.E.
Project Manager   Martin J. Gunther
Editor   Ken Grabowski, A.S.E.

CHILTON BOOK COMPANY

**ONE OF THE DIVERSIFIED PUBLISHING COMPANIES,
A PART OF CAPITAL CITIES/ABC, INC.**

Manufactured in USA
© 1992 Chilton Book Company
Chilton Way, Radnor, PA 19089
ISBN 0–8019–8252–9
Library of Congress Catalog Card No. 91–058818
1234567890   1098765432

Contents

Contents

Drive Train 7

Suspension and Steering 8

Brakes 9

Body 10

Glossary

Master Index

SAFETY NOTICE

Proper service and repair procedures are vital to the safe, reliable operation of all motor vehicles, as well as the personal safety of those performing repairs. This manual outlines procedures for servicing and repairing vehicles using safe, effective methods. The procedures contain many NOTES, CAUTIONS and WARNINGS which should be followed along with standard safety procedures to eliminate the possibility of personal injury or improper service which could damage the vehicle or compromise its safety.

It is important to note that the repair procedures and techniques, tools and parts for servicing motor vehicles, as well as the skill and experience of the individual performing the work vary widely. It is not possible to anticipate all of the conceivable ways or conditions under which vehicles may be serviced, or to provide cautions as to all of the possible hazards that may result. Standard and accepted safety precautions and equipment should be used when handling toxic or flammable fluids, and safety goggles or other protection should be used during cutting, grinding, chiseling, prying, or any other process that can caus material removal or projectiles.

Some procedures require the use of tools specially designed for a specific purpose. Before substituting another tool or procedure, you must be completely satisfied that neither your personal safety, nor the performance of the vehicle will be endangered.

Although information in this manual is based on industry sources and is complete as possible at the time of publication, the possibility exists that some car manufacturers made later changes which could not be included here. While striving for total accuracy, Chilton Book Company cannot assume responsibility for any errors, changes or omissions that may occur in the compilation of this data.

PART NUMBERS

Part numbers listed in this reference are not recommendations by Chilton for any product by brand name. They are references that can be used with interchange manuals and aftermarket supplier catalogs to locate each brand supplier's discrete part number.

SPECIAL TOOLS

Special tools are recommended by the vehicle manufacturer to perform their specific job. Use has been kept to a minimum, but where absolutely necessary, they are referred to in the text by the part number of the tool manufacturer. These tools can be purchased, under the appropriate part number, from your GM dealer or regional distributor, or an equivalent tool can be purchased locally from a tool supplier or parts outlet. Before substituting any tool for the one recommended, read the SAFETY NOTICE at the top of this page.

ACKNOWLEDGMENTS

The Chilton Book Company expresses appreciation to General Motors Corp., Detroit, Michigan for their generous assistance.

1

GENERAL INFORMATION AND MAINTENANCE

HOW TO USE THIS BOOK

This Chilton's Total Car Care manual for Celebrity, Century, Ciera and 6000 cars is designed to teach you some of the operating principles of your car, and guide you through maintenance and repair operations. You can perform many repairs yourself, as long as you have the time, initiative, patience, and proper assortment of tools.

A secondary purpose of this book is a reference for owners who want to understand their car and/or their mechanics better. In this case, no tools at all are required.

Sections 1 and 2 will probably be the most frequently used in the book. The first section contains all the information that may be required at a moment's notice — information such as the location of the various serial numbers and the proper towing instructions. It also contains all the information on basic day-to-day maintenance that you will need to ensure good performance and long component life. Section 2 covers tune-up procedures which will assist you not only in keeping the engine running properly and at peak performance levels, but also in restoring some of the more delicate components to operating condition in the event of a failure. Sections 3 through 10 cover repairs (rather than maintenance) for various portions of the car, with each section covering either one system or two related systems. The appendix then lists general information which may be useful in rebuilding the engine or performing some other operation on any car.

In using the Table of Contents, refer to the bold listings for the beginning of the section. See the smaller listings or the index for information on a particular component or specifications.

Before removing any bolts, read through the entire procedure. This will give you the overall view of what tools and supplies will be required. There is nothing more frustrating than having to walk to the bus stop on Monday morning because you were short one bolt on Sunday afternoon. So read ahead and plan ahead. Each operation should be approached logically and all procedures thoroughly understood before attempting any work.

Cautions and notes will be provided where appropriate to help prevent you from injuring yourself or damaging your car. Therefore, you should read through the entire procedure before beginning the work, and make sure that you are aware of the warnings. Since no number of warnings could cover every possible situation, you should work slowly and try to envision what is going to happen in each operation ahead of time.

When it comes to tightening things, there is generally a slim area between too loose to properly seal or resist vibration and so tight as to risk damage or warping. When dealing with major engine parts, or with any aluminum component, it pays to procure a torque wrench and go by the recommended figures.

When reference is made in this book to the right side or left side of the car, it should be understood that the positions are always to be viewed from the front seat. Thus, the left side of the car is always the driver's side and the right side is always the passenger's side, even when facing the car, as when working on the engine.

We have attempted to eliminate the use of special tools whenever possible, substituting more readily available hand tools. However, in some cases the special tools are necessary. These can be purchased from your General Motors dealer, or an automotive parts store.

Always be conscious of the need for safety in your work. Never get under the car unless it is firmly supported by jackstands or ramps. Never smoke near or allow flame to get near the battery or the fuel system. Keep your clothing, hands and hair clear of the fan and pulleys when working near the engine, if it is running. Most importantly, try to be patient; even in the midst of an argument with a stubborn bolt, reaching for the largest hammer in the garage is usually a cause for later regret and more extensive repair. As you gain confidence and experience, working on your car will become a source of pride and satisfaction.

When repair is not considered practical, we tell you how to remove the part and then how to install the new or rebuilt replacement. In this way, you at least save the labor costs.

TOOLS AND EQUIPMENT

It would be impossible to catalog each and every tool that you may need to perform all the operations included in this book. It would also not be wise for the amateur to rush out and buy an expensive set of tools on the theory that he may need one of them at some time. The best approach is to proceed slowly, gathering together a good quality set of those tools that are used most frequently. Don't be misled by the low cost of bargain tools. It is far better to spend a little more for quality, name brand tools. Forged wrenches, 12 point sockets and fine-tooth ratchets are a better investment than their less expensive counterparts. As any good mechanic can tell you, there are few worse experiences than trying to work on a car or truck with bad tools. Your monetary savings will be far outweighed by frustration and mangled knuckles.

Begin accumulating those tools that are used most frequently: those associated with routine maintenance and tune-up. In addition to the normal assortment of screwdrivers and pliers, you should have the following tools for routine maintenance jobs:

1. SAE (or Metric) or SAE/Metric wrenches-sockets and combination open end/box end wrenches in sizes from 1/8 in. (3mm) to 3/4 in. (19mm) and a spark plug socket (5/8 in.).

If possible, buy various length socket drive extensions. One break in this department is that the metric sockets available in the U.S. will all fit the ratchet handles and extensions you may already have (1/4 in., 3/8 in., and 1/2 in. drive);

2. Jackstands for support;
3. Oil filter wrench;
4. Oil filler spout for pouring oil;

5. Grease gun for chassis lubrication;
6. A container for draining oil;
7. Many rags for wiping up the inevitable mess.

In addition to the above items there are several others that are not absolutely necessary, but handy to have around. These include oil dry (oil-absorbent), a transmission funnel and the usual supply of lubricants, antifreeze and fluids, although these can be purchased as needed. This is a basic list for routine maintenance, but only your personal needs and desire can accurately determine your list of tools.

A more advanced set of tools, suitable for tune-up work, can be drawn up easily. While the tools are slightly more sophisticated, they need not be outrageously expensive. The key to these purchases is to make them with an eye towards

adaptability and wide range. A basic list of tune-up tools could include:

1. Tachometer;
2. Spark plug socket
3. Spark plug gauge and gapping tool
4. Timing light.

The choice of a timing light should be made carefully. A light which works on the DC current supplied by the car battery is the best choice; it should have a xenon tube for brightness. Since all these cars have an electronic ignition system, the timing light should have an inductive pickup which clamps around the No. 1 spark plug cable (the timing light illustrated has one of these pickups).

In addition to these basic tools, there are several other tools and gauges which, though not particularly necessary for basic tune-up work, you may find to be quite useful. These include:

1. A compression gauge. The screw-in type seals easily and eliminates the need for a remote starting switch during compression testing.
2. A manifold vacuum gauge;
3. A 12 VDC test light;
4. A combination volt/ohmmeter;
5. An induction meter, used to determine whether or not there is current flowing through a wire.

Finally, you will find a torque wrench necessary for all but the most basic of work. The

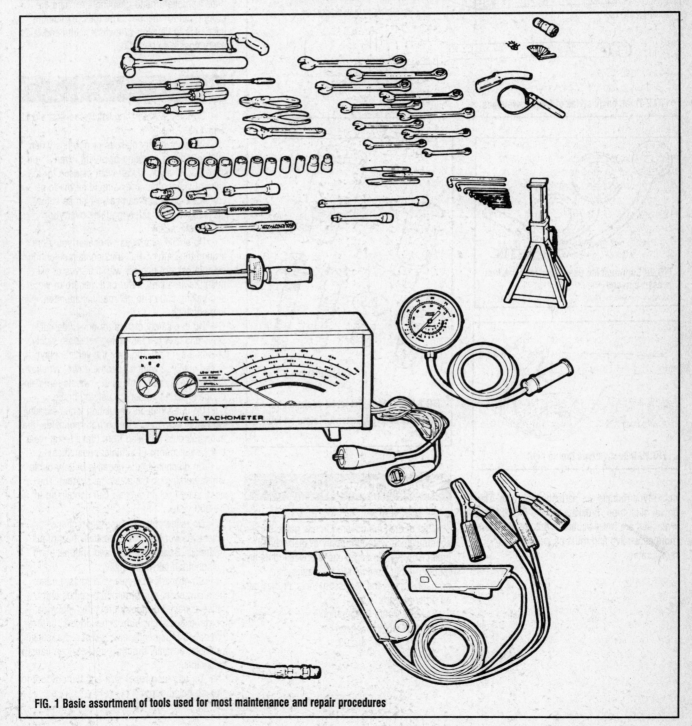

FIG. 1 Basic assortment of tools used for most maintenance and repair procedures

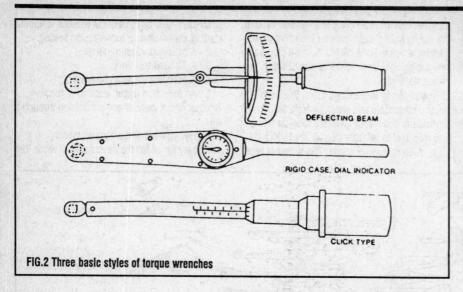

FIG.2 Three basic styles of torque wrenches

DEFLECTING BEAM

RIGID CASE, DIAL INDICATOR

CLICK TYPE

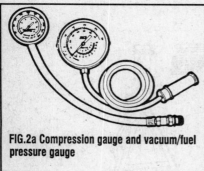

FIG.2a Compression gauge and vacuum/fuel pressure gauge

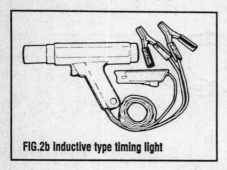

FIG.2b Inductive type timing light

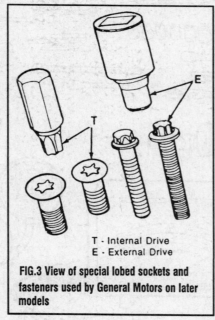

T - Internal Drive
E - External Drive

FIG.3 View of special lobed sockets and fasteners used by General Motors on later models

beam-type models are perfectly adequate. The newer click-type (breakaway) and digital torque wrenches are more accurate, but are also much more expensive and must be periodically recalibrated.

Special Tools

♦ SEE FIGS. 1 to 3

Most of the jobs covered in this guide can be accomplished with commonly available hand tools. However, in some cases special tools are required. Your General Motors dealer can probably supply the necessary tools, or they can be ordered from:

Kent-Moore Corporation
1501 South Jackson St.
Jackson, MI. 49203

SERVICING YOUR CAR SAFELY

It is virtually impossible to anticipate all of the hazards involved with automotive maintenance and service, but car and common sense will prevent most accidents.

The rules of safety for mechanics range from "don't smoke around gasoline", to "use the proper tool for the job". The trick to avoiding injuries is to develop safe work habits and take every possible precaution.

Do's

• Do keep a fire extinguisher and first aid kit within easy reach.

• Do wear safety glasses or goggles when cutting, drilling, grinding or prying, even if you have 20/20 vision. If you wear glasses for the sake of vision, then they should be made of hardened glass that can serve also as safety glasses, or wear safety goggles over your regular glasses.

• Do shield your eyes whenever you work around the battery. Batteries contain sulphuric acid; in case of contact with the eyes or skin, flush the area with water or a mixture of water and baking soda and get medical attention immediately.

• Do use safety stands for any undercar service. Jacks are for raising vehicles; safety stands are for making sure the vehicle stays raised until you want it to come down. Whenever the vehicle is raised, block the wheels remaining on the ground and set the parking brake.

• Do use adequate ventilation when working with any chemicals. Like carbon monoxide, the asbestos dust resulting from brake lining wear can be poisonous in sufficient quantities.

• Do disconnect the negative battery cable when working on the electrical system. The secondary ignition system can contain up to 40,000 volts.

• Do follow manufacturer's directions whenever working with potentially hazardous materials. Both brake fluid and antifreeze are poisonous if taken internally.

• Do properly maintain your tools. Loose hammerheads, mushroomed punches and chisels, frayed or poorly grounded electrical cords, excessively worn screwdrivers, spread wrenches (open end), cracked sockets, slipping ratchets, or faulty droplight sockets can cause accidents.

• Do use the proper size and type of tool for the job being done.

FIG.4 Always use jackstands when working under the vehicle

• Do when possible, pull on a wrench handle rather than push on it, and adjust your stance to prevent a fall.

• Do be sure that adjustable wrenches are tightly adjusted on the nut or bolt and pulled so that the face is on the side of the fixed jaw.

• Do select a wrench or socket that fits the nut or bolt. The wrench or socket should sit straight, not cocked.

• Do strike squarely with a hammer — avoid glancing blows.

• Do set the parking brake and block the drive wheels if the work requires that the engine be running.

Don't's

• Don't run an engine in a garage or anywhere else without proper ventilation — EVER! Carbon monoxide is poisonous; it takes a long time to leave the human body and you can build up a deadly supply of it in your system by simply breathing in a little ever day. You may not realize you are slowly poisoning yourself. Always use power vents, windows, fans or open the garage doors.

• Don;t work around moving parts while wearing a necktie or other loose clothing. Short sleeves are much safer than long, loose sleeves and hard-toed shoes with neoprene soles protect your toes and give a better grip on slippery surfaces. Jewelry such as watches, fancy belt buckles, beads or body adornment of any king is not safe working around a car. Long hair should be hidden under a hat or cap.

• Don't use pockets for toolboxes. A fall or bump can drive a screwdriver deep into your body. Even a wiping cloth hanging from the back pocket can wrap around a spinning shaft or fan.

• Don't smoke when working gasoline, cleaning solvent or other flammable material.

• Don't smoke when working around the battery. When the battery is being charged, it gives off explosive hydrogen gas.

• Don't use gasoline to wash your hands; there are excellent soaps available. Gasoline may contain lead, an lead can enter the body through a cut, accumulating in the body until you are very ill. Gasoline also removes all the natural oils from the skin so that bone dry hands will suck up oil and grease.

• Don't service the air conditioning system unless you are equipped with the necessary tools and training. The refrigerant, R-12, is extremely cold and when exposed to the air, will instantly freeze any surface it comes in contact with, including your eyes. Although the refrigerant is normally non-toxic, R-12 becomes a deadly poisonous gas in the presence of an open flame. One good whiff of the vapors from burning refrigerant can be fatal.

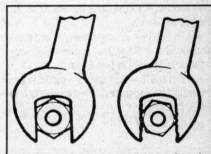

FIG.6 When using an open-end wrench, make certain it is the correct size

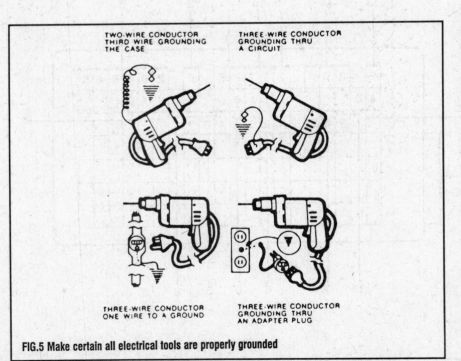

TWO-WIRE CONDUCTOR THIRD WIRE GROUNDING THE CASE

THREE-WIRE CONDUCTOR GROUNDING THRU A CIRCUIT

THREE-WIRE CONDUCTOR ONE WIRE TO A GROUND

THREE-WIRE CONDUCTOR GROUNDING THRU AN ADAPTER PLUG

FIG.5 Make certain all electrical tools are properly grounded

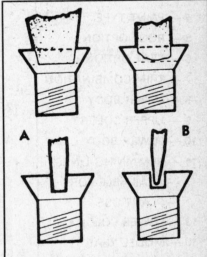

FIG.6a When using a screwdriver, make certain it is the correct size and the tip is in good condition. A) is a good screwdriver, B) needs to be replaced

SERIAL NUMBER IDENTIFICATION

Vehicle

♦ SEE FIG. 7

The vehicle identification number (V.I.N.) is a seventeen digit alpha/numeric sequence stamped on a plate which is located at the top, left hand side of the instrument panel.

As far as the car owner is concerned, many of the digits in the V.I.N. are of little or no value. At certain times, it may be necessary to refer to the V.I.N. to interpret certain information, such as when ordering replacement parts or determining if your vehicle is involved in a factory service campaign (recall). In either of these instances, the following information may be helpful:

• 1ST DIGIT — Indicates the place of manufacture. A **1** designates the U.S.A.; **2** designates Canada.

• 8TH DIGIT — Indicates the type and the manufacturer of the original engine which was installed in the vehicle (see Engine).

• 10TH DIGIT — Indicates the model year of the vehicle. **C** designates a 1982 model, **D** is for 1983, and so on.

• 11TH DIGIT — Indicates the specific plant at which the vehicle was assembled.

• 12TH–17TH DIGITS — This is the plant sequential number, which identifies the specific number of each vehicle within a production run. In the event of engineering change or a recall involving only a certain quantity of vehicles within a production run, the affected vehicles can be identified.

Body

♦ SEE FIG. 8

An identification plate for body-related items is attached to the front tie bar, just behind the passenger side headlamp. Information on the body identification plate would rarely be useful to the owner. An illustration of the plate is provided.

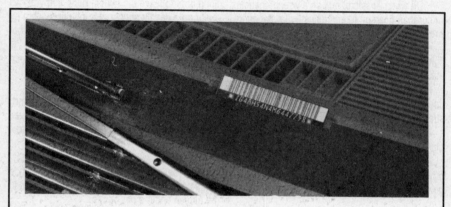

FIG. 7a General Motors vehicle identification number — Century shown

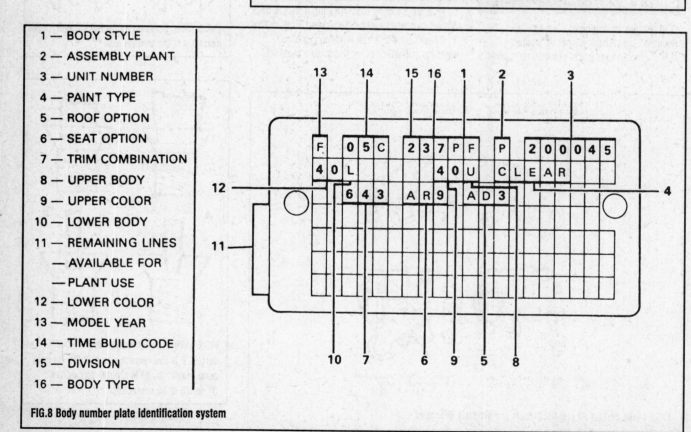

1 — BODY STYLE
2 — ASSEMBLY PLANT
3 — UNIT NUMBER
4 — PAINT TYPE
5 — ROOF OPTION
6 — SEAT OPTION
7 — TRIM COMBINATION
8 — UPPER BODY
9 — UPPER COLOR
10 — LOWER BODY
11 — REMAINING LINES
— AVAILABLE FOR
— PLANT USE
12 — LOWER COLOR
13 — MODEL YEAR
14 — TIME BUILD CODE
15 — DIVISION
16 — BODY TYPE

FIG.8 Body number plate identification system

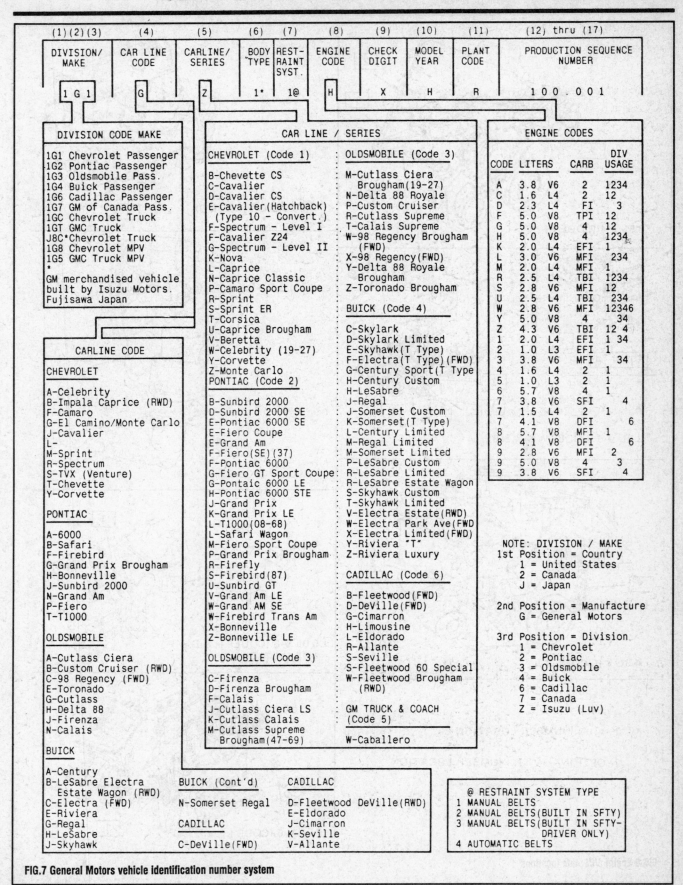

	(1)(2)(3)	(4)	(5)	(6)	(7)	(8)	(9)	(10)	(11)	(12) thru (17)
	DIVISION/ MAKE	CAR LINE CODE	CARLINE/ SERIES	BODY TYPE	RESTRAINT SYST.	ENGINE CODE	CHECK DIGIT	MODEL YEAR	PLANT CODE	PRODUCTION SEQUENCE NUMBER
	1 G 1	G	Z	1*	1@	H	X	H	R	1 0 0 . 0 0 1

DIVISION CODE MAKE

1G1 Chevrolet Passenger
1G2 Pontiac Passenger
1G3 Oldsmobile Pass.
1G4 Buick Passenger
1G6 Cadillac Passenger
1G7 GM of Canada Pass.
1GC Chevrolet Truck
1GT GMC Truck
J8C*Chevrolet Truck
1G8 Chevrolet MPV
1G5 GMC Truck MPV
*
GM merchandised vehicle
built by Isuzu Motors.
Fujisawa Japan

CARLINE CODE

CHEVROLET

A-Celebrity
B-Impala Caprice (RWD)
F-Camaro
G-El Camino/Monte Carlo
J-Cavalier
L-
M-Sprint
R-Spectrum
S-TVX (Venture)
T-Chevette
Y-Corvette

PONTIAC

A-6000
B-Safari
F-Firebird
G-Grand Prix Brougham
H-Bonneville
J-Sunbird 2000
N-Grand Am
P-Fiero
T-T1000

OLDSMOBILE

A-Cutlass Ciera
B-Custom Cruiser (RWD)
C-98 Regency (FWD)
E-Toronado
G-Cutlass
H-Delta 88
J-Firenza
N-Calais

BUICK

A-Century
B-LeSabre Electra
  Estate Wagon (RWD)
C-Electra (FWD)
E-Riviera
G-Regal
H-LeSabre
J-Skyhawk

CAR LINE / SERIES

CHEVROLET (Code 1)

B-Chevette CS
C-Cavalier
D-Cavalier CS
E-Cavalier(Hatchback)
 (Type 10 - Convert.)
F-Spectrum - Level I
F-Cavalier Z24
G-Spectrum - Level II
K-Nova
L-Caprice
N-Caprice Classic
P-Camaro Sport Coupe
R-Sprint
S-Sprint ER
T-Corsica
U-Caprice Brougham
V-Beretta
W-Celebrity (19-27)
Y-Corvette
Z-Monte Carlo

PONTIAC (Code 2)

B-Sunbird 2000
D-Sunbird 2000 SE
E-Pontiac 6000 SE
E-Fiero Coupe
E-Grand Am
F-Fiero(SE)(37)
F-Pontiac 6000
G-Fiero GT Sport Coupe
G-Pontiac 6000 LE
H-Pontiac 6000 STE
J-Grand Prix
K-Grand Prix LE
L-T1000(08-68)
L-Safari Wagon
M-Fiero Sport Coupe
P-Grand Prix Brougham
R-Firefly
S-Firebird(87)
U-Sunbird GT
V-Grand Am LE
W-Grand AM SE
W-Firebird Trans Am
X-Bonneville
Z-Bonneville LE

OLDSMOBILE (Code 3)

C-Firenza
D-Firenza Brougham
F-Calais
J-Cutlass Ciera LS
K-Cutlass Calais
M-Cutlass Supreme
  Brougham(47-69)

OLDSMOBILE (Code 3)

M-Cutlass Ciera
  Brougham(19-27)
N-Delta 88 Royale
P-Custom Cruiser
R-Cutlass Supreme
T-Calais Supreme
W-98 Regency Brougham
  (FWD)
X-98 Regency(FWD)
Y-Delta 88 Royale
  Brougham
Z-Toronado Brougham

BUICK (Code 4)

C-Skylark
D-Skylark Limited
E-Skyhawk(T Type)
F-Electra(T Type)(FWD)
G-Century Sport(T Type
H-Century Custom
J-Regal
J-Somerset Custom
K-Somerset(T Type)
L-Century Limited
M-Regal Limited
M-Somerset Limited
P-LeSabre Custom
R-LeSabre Limited
R-LeSabre Estate Wagon
S-Skyhawk Custom
T-Skyhawk Limited
V-Electra Estate(RWD)
W-Electra Park Ave(FWD)
X-Electra Limited(FWD)
Y-Riviera "T"
Z-Riviera Luxury

CADILLAC (Code 6)

B-Fleetwood(FWD)
D-DeVille(FWD)
G-Cimarron
H-Limousine
L-Eldorado
R-Allante
S-Seville
S-Fleetwood 60 Special
W-Fleetwood Brougham
  (RWD)

**GM TRUCK & COACH
(Code 5)**

W-Caballero

ENGINE CODES

CODE	LITERS		CARB	DIV USAGE
A	3.8	V6	2	1234
C	1.6	L4	2	12
D	2.3	L4	FI	3
F	5.0	V8	TPI	12
G	5.0	V8	4	12
H	5.0	V8	4	1234
K	2.0	L4	EFI	1
L	3.0	V6	MFI	234
M	2.0	L4	MFI	1
R	2.5	L4	TBI	1234
S	2.8	V6	MFI	12
U	2.5	L4	TBI	234
W	2.8	V6	MFI	12346
Y	5.0	V8	4	34
Z	4.3	V6	TBI	12 4
1	2.0	L4	EFI	1 34
2	1.0	L3	EFI	1
3	3.8	V6	MFI	34
4	1.6	L4	2	1
5	1.0	L3	2	1
6	5.7	V8	4	1
7	3.8	V6	SFI	4
7	1.5	L4	2	1
7	4.1	V8	DFI	6
8	5.7	V8	MFI	1
8	4.1	V8	DFI	6
9	2.8	V6	MFI	2
9	5.0	V8	4	3
9	3.8	V6	SFI	4

NOTE: DIVISION / MAKE
1st Position = Country
1 = United States
2 = Canada
J = Japan

2nd Position = Manufacture
G = General Motors

3rd Position = Division
1 = Chevrolet
2 = Pontiac
3 = Oldsmobile
4 = Buick
6 = Cadillac
7 = Canada
Z = Isuzu (Luv)

BUICK (Cont'd)

N-Somerset Regal

CADILLAC

C-DeVille(FWD)

CADILLAC

D-Fleetwood DeVille(RWD)
E-Eldorado
J-Cimarron
K-Seville
V-Allante

@ RESTRAINT SYSTEM TYPE
1 MANUAL BELTS
2 MANUAL BELTS(BUILT IN SFTY)
3 MANUAL BELTS(BUILT IN SFTY-
               DRIVER ONLY)
4 AUTOMATIC BELTS

FIG.7 General Motors vehicle identification number system

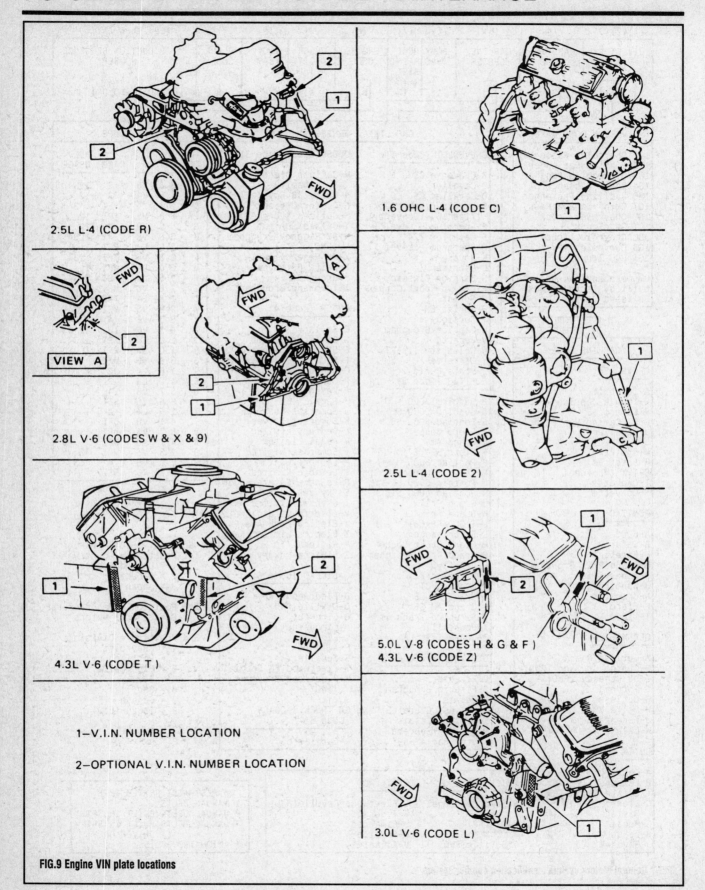

2.5L L-4 (CODE R)

VIEW A

2.8L V-6 (CODES W & X & 9)

4.3L V-6 (CODE T)

1.6 OHC L-4 (CODE C)

2.5L L-4 (CODE 2)

5.0L V-8 (CODES H & G & F)
4.3L V-6 (CODE Z)

3.0L V-6 (CODE L)

1—V.I.N. NUMBER LOCATION

2—OPTIONAL V.I.N. NUMBER LOCATION

FIG.9 Engine VIN plate locations

FIG. 9a Engine identification and emission label

Engine

The engine identification code will sometimes be required to order replacement engine parts. The code is stamped in different locations, depending upon the size of the engine. Refer to the accompanying illustrations to determine the code location for your engine.

ENGINE IDENTIFICATION

Year	Model	Engine Displacement Cu. In. (liter)	Engine Series Identification (VIN)	Fuel System	No. of Cylinders	Engine Type
1982	Celebrity	151 (2.5)	R	TBI	4	OHV
	Celebrity	151 (2.5)	5	2 bbl	4	OHV
	Celebrity	173 (2.8)	X	2 bbl	6	OHV
	Celebrity	260 (4.3)	T	DFI	6	OHV
	Century	151 (2.5)	R	TBI	4	OHV
	Century	173 (2.8)	X	2 bbl	6	OHV
	Century	183 (3.0)	E	2 bbl	6	OHV
	Century	260 (4.3)	T	DFI	6	OHV
	Cutlass Ciera	151 (2.5)	R	TBI	4	OHV
	Cutlass Ciera	173 (2.8)	X	2 bbl	6	OHV
	Cutlass Ciera	183 (3.0)	E	2 bbl	6	OHV
	Cutlass Ciera	260 (4.3)	T	DFI	6	OHV
	6000	151 (2.5)	R	TBI	4	OHV
	6000	173 (2.8)	X	2 bbl	6	OHV
	6000	260 (4.3)	T	DFI	6	OHV
1983	Celebrity	151 (2.5)	R	TBI	4	OHV
	Celebrity	151 (2.5)	5	2 bbl	4	OHV
	Celebrity	173 (2.8)	X	2 bbl	6	OHV
	Celebrity	260 (4.3)	T	DFI	6	OHV
	Century	151 (2.5)	R	TBI	4	OHV
	Century	173 (2.8)	X	2 bbl	6	OHV
	Century	183 (3.0)	E	2 bbl	6	OHV
	Century	260 (4.3)	T	DFI	6	OHV
	Cutlass Ciera	151 (2.5)	R	TBI	4	OHV
	Cutlass Ciera	173 (2.8)	X	2 bbl	6	OHV
	Cutlass Ciera	183 (3.0)	E	2 bbl	6	OHV
	Cutlass Ciera	260 (4.3)	T	DFI	6	OHV
	6000	151 (2.5)	R	TBI	4	OHV
	6000	173 (2.8)	X	2 bbl	6	OHV
	6000	260 (4.3)	T	DFI	6	OHV

ENGINE IDENTIFICATION

Year	Model	Engine Displacement Cu. In. (liter)	Engine Series Identification (VIN)	Fuel System	No. of Cylinders	Engine Type
1984	Celebrity	151 (2.5)	R	TBI	4	OHV
	Celebrity	151 (2.5)	5	2 bbl	4	OHV
	Celebrity	173 (2.8)	X	2 bbl	6	OHV
	Celebrity	260 (4.3)	T	DFI	6	OHV
	Century	151 (2.5)	R	TBI	4	OHV
	Century	173 (2.8)	X	2 bbl	6	OHV
	Century	183 (3.0)	E	2 bbl	6	OHV
	Century	231 (3.8)	3	MFI	6	OHV
	Century	260 (4.3)	T	DFI	6	OHV
	Cutlass Ciera	151 (2.5)	R	TBI	4	OHV
	Cutlass Ciera	231 (3.8)	3	MFI	6	OHV
	Cutlass Ciera	183 (3.0)	E	2 bbl	6	OHV
	Cutlass Ciera	260 (4.3)	T	DFI	6	OHV
	6000	151 (2.5)	R	TBI	4	OHV
	6000	173 (2.8)	X	2 bbl	6	OHV
	6000	173 (2.8) HO	Z	2 bbl	6	OHV
	6000	260 (4.3)	T	DFI	6	OHV
1985	Celebrity	151 (2.5)	R	TBI	4	OHV
	Celebrity	173 (2.8)	X	2 bbl	6	OHV
	Celebrity	173 (2.8) HO	W	MFI	6	OHV
	Celebrity	260 (4.3)	T	DFI	6	OHV
	Century	151 (2.5)	R	TBI	4	OHV
	Century	183 (3.0)	E	2 bbl	6	OHV
	Century	231 (3.8)	3	MFI	6	OHV
	Century	260 (4.3)	T	DFI	6	OHV
	Cutlass Ciera	151 (2.5)	R	TBI	4	OHV
	Cutlass Ciera	231 (3.8)	3	MFI	6	OHV
	Cutlass Ciera	183 (3.0)	E	2 bbl	6	OHV
	Cutlass Ciera	260 (4.3)	T	DFI	6	OHV
	6000	151 (2.5)	R	TBI	4	OHV
	6000	173 (2.8)	X	2 bbl	6	OHV
	6000	173 (2.8) HO	Z	2 bbl	6	OHV
	6000	260 (4.3)	T	DFI	6	OHV
1986	Celebrity	151 (2.5)	R	TBI	4	OHV
	Celebrity	173 (2.8)	X	2 bbl	6	OHV
	Celebrity	173 (2.8) HO	W	MFI	6	OHV
	Century	151 (2.5)	R	TBI	4	OHV
	Century	173 (2.8)	X	2 bbl	6	OHV
	Century	231 (3.8)	3	SFI	6	OHV
	Cutlass Ciera	151 (2.5)	R	TBI	4	OHV
	Cutlass Ciera	173 (2.8)	X	2 bbl	6	OHV
	Cutlass Ciera	173 (2.8)	W	MFI	6	OHV
	Cutlass Ciera	231 (3.8)	3	SFI	6	OHV
	Cutlass Ciera	231 (3.8)	B	SFI	6	OHV

ENGINE IDENTIFICATION

Year	Model	Engine Displacement Cu. In. (liter)	Engine Series Identification (VIN)	Fuel System	No. of Cylinders	Engine Type
1986	6000	151 (2.5)	R	TBI	4	OHV
	6000	173 (2.8)	X	2 bbl	6	OHV
	6000	173 (2.8)	W	MFI	6	OHV
1987	Celebrity	151 (2.5)	R	TBI	4	OHV
	Celebrity	173 (2.8)	W	MFI	6	OHV
	Century	151 (2.5)	R	TBI	4	OHV
	Century	173 (2.8)	W	MFI	6	OHV
	Century	231 (3.8)	3	SFI	6	OHV
	Cutlass Ciera	151 (2.5)	R	TBI	4	OHV
	Cutlass Ciera	173 (2.8)	W	MFI	6	OHV
	Cutlass Ciera	231 (3.8) HO	3	SFI	6	OHV
	6000	151 (2.5)	R	TBI	4	OHV
	6000	173 (2.8)	W	MFI	6	OHV
1988	Celebrity	151 (2.5)	R	TBI	4	OHV
	Celebrity	173 (2.8)	W	MFI	6	OHV
	Century	151 (2.5)	R	TBI	4	OHV
	Century	173 (2.8)	W	MFI	6	OHV
	Century	231 (3.8)	3	SFI	6	OHV
	Cutlass Ciera	151 (2.5)	R	TBI	4	OHV
	Cutlass Ciera	173 (2.8)	W	MFI	6	OHV
	Cutlass Ciera	231 (3.8)	3	SFI	6	OHV
	6000	151 (2.5)	R	TBI	4	OHV
	6000	173 (2.8)	W	MFI	6	OHV
1989–90	Celebrity	151 (2.5)	R	TBI	4	OHV
	Celebrity	173 (2.8)	W	MFI	6	OHV
	Century	151 (2.5)	R	TBI	4	OHV
	Century	173 (2.8)	W	MFI	6	OHV
	Century	204 (3.3)	N	MFI	6	OHV
	Cutlass Ciera	151 (2.5)	R	TBI	4	OHV
	Cutlass Ciera	173 (2.8)	W	MFI	6	OHV
	Cutlass Ciera	204 (3.3)	N	MFI	6	OHV
	6000	151 (2.5)	R	TBI	4	OHV
	6000	173 (2.8)	W	MFI	6	OHV
	6000	192 (3.1)	T	MFI	6	OHV
1990	Celebrity	151 (2.5)	R	TBI	4	OHV
	Celebrity	192 (3.1)	T	MFI	6	OHV
	Century	151 (2.5)	R	TBI	4	OHV
	Century	204 (3.3)	N	MFI	6	OHV
	Cutlass ①	151 (2.5)	R	TBI	4	OHV
	Cutlass ①	204 (3.3)	N	MFI	6	OHV
	6000	151 (2.5)	R	TBI	4	OHV
	6000	192 (3.1)	T	MFI	6	OHV

ENGINE IDENTIFICATION

Year	Model	Engine Displacement Cu. In. (liter)	Engine Series Identification (VIN)	Fuel System	No. of Cylinders	Engine Type
1991	Century	151 (2.5)	R	TBI	4	OHV
	Century	204 (3.3)	N	MFI	6	OHV
	Cutlass ①	151 (2.5)	R	TBI	4	OHV
	Cutlass ①	204 (3.3)	N	MFI	6	OHV
	6000	151 (2.5)	R	TBI	4	OHV
	6000	192 (3.1)	T	MFI	6	OHV
1992	Century	151 (2.5)	R	TBI	4	OHV
	Century	204 (3.3)	N	MFI	6	OHV
	Cutlass ①	151 (2.5)	R	TBI	4	OHV
	Cutlass ①	204 (3.3)	N	MFI	6	OHV
	6000	151 (2.5)	R	TBI	4	OHV
	6000	192 (3.1)	T	MFI	6	OHV

TBI—Throttle Body Injection
MFI—Multiport Fuel Injection
SFI—Sequential Fuel Injection
HO—High Output
OHV—Overhead Valves
① Ciera & Cruiser

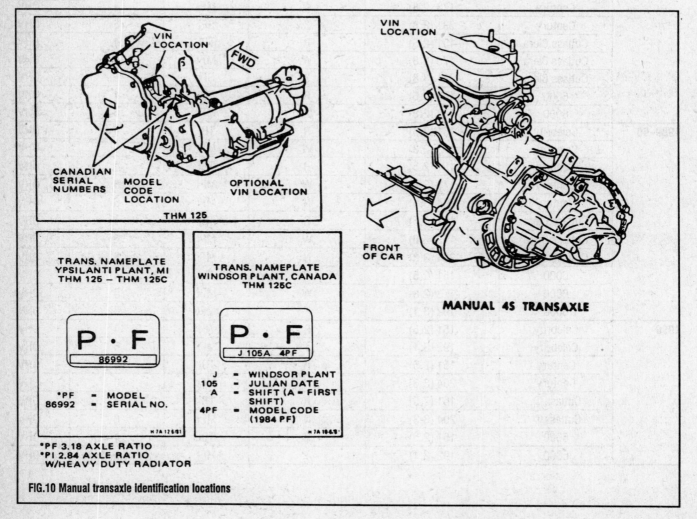

FIG.10 Manual transaxle identification locations

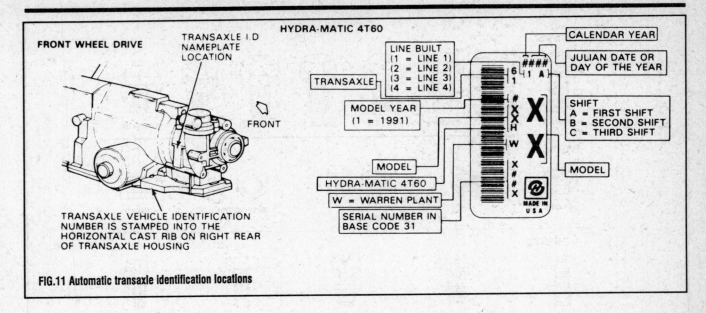

HYDRA-MATIC 4T60

FRONT WHEEL DRIVE

TRANSAXLE I.D NAMEPLATE LOCATION

FRONT

TRANSAXLE VEHICLE IDENTIFICATION NUMBER IS STAMPED INTO THE HORIZONTAL CAST RIB ON RIGHT REAR OF TRANSAXLE HOUSING

LINE BUILT
(1 = LINE 1)
(2 = LINE 2)
(3 = LINE 3)
(4 = LINE 4)

TRANSAXLE

MODEL YEAR
(1 = 1991)

MODEL

HYDRA-MATIC 4T60

W = WARREN PLANT

SERIAL NUMBER IN BASE CODE 31

CALENDAR YEAR

JULIAN DATE OR DAY OF THE YEAR

SHIFT
A = FIRST SHIFT
B = SECOND SHIFT
C = THIRD SHIFT

MODEL

MADE IN USA

FIG.11 Automatic transaxle identification locations

Transaxle

The transaxle code serves the same purpose as the engine identification code. Transaxle code locations may be determined by referring to the accompanying illustration.

Drive Axle

The drive axle code is stamped onto the axle shaft near the CV boot.

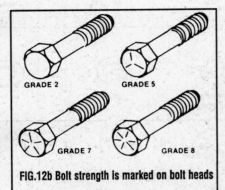

GRADE 2 GRADE 5

GRADE 7 GRADE 8

FIG.12b Bolt strength is marked on bolt heads

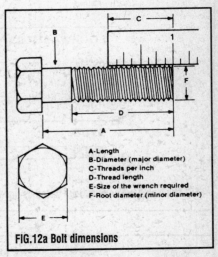

A-Length
B-Diameter (major diameter)
C-Threads per inch
D-Thread length
E-Size of the wrench required
F-Root diameter (minor diameter)

FIG.12a Bolt dimensions

ROUTINE MAINTENANCE

Proper maintenance of any vehicle is the key to long and trouble-free vehicle life. As a conscientious car owner, set aside a Saturday morning, say once a month, to check or replace items which could cause major problems later. keep your own personal log to jot down which services you performed, how much parts cost you, the date, and the exact odometer reading at the time. Keep all receipts for such items as engine oil and filters, so that they may be referred to in case of related problems or to determine operating expenses. As a do-it-yourselfer, these receipts are the only proof you have that the required maintenance was performed. In the event of a warranty problem, these receipts will be invaluable.

The literature provided with your car when it was originally delivered includes the factory recommended maintenance schedule. If you do not have the factory schedule, we have provided a mirror image of the GM schedule which should be used. No matter which schedule is used, follow it to the letter. Even if your car was previously owned, it is important that the maintenance be performed. The effects of poor maintenance can at least be halted by initiating a regular maintenance program.

Air Cleaner

▶ SEE FIG. 12

Regular air cleaner element replacement is a must, since a partially clogged element will cause a performance loss, decreased fuel mileage, and engine damage if enough dirt gets into the cylinders and contaminates the engine oil.

The air cleaner element must be checked periodically. Replacement of the element is simply a matter of removing the wing nut(s) from the air cleaner lid, lifting off the lid, and removing the old filter element. Wipe the inside of the housing with a damp cloth before placing the

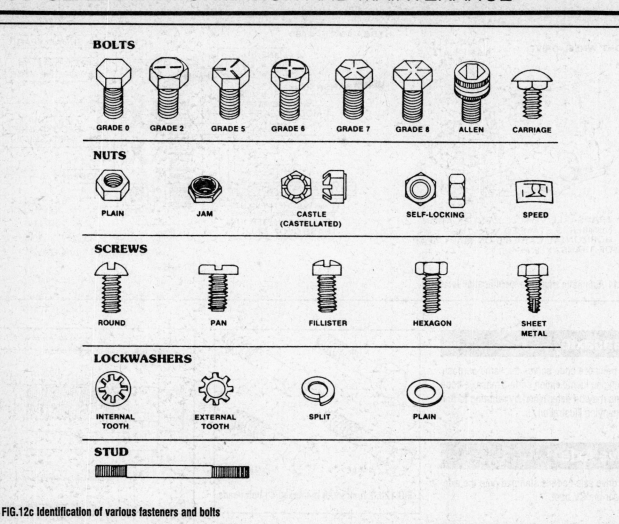

BOLTS

GRADE 0   GRADE 2   GRADE 5   GRADE 6   GRADE 7   GRADE 8   ALLEN   CARRIAGE

NUTS

PLAIN   JAM   CASTLE (CASTELLATED)   SELF-LOCKING   SPEED

SCREWS

ROUND   PAN   FILLISTER   HEXAGON   SHEET METAL

LOCKWASHERS

INTERNAL TOOTH   EXTERNAL TOOTH   SPLIT   PLAIN

STUD

FIG.12c Identification of various fasteners and bolts

FIG. 12d Moving back the air cleaner assembly — 3.3L Century shown

new element into the housing. When tightening the wing nut(s), just snug it down with moderate finger pressure. Excessive tightening of the wing nut(s) will damage components.

➡ **Never attempt to clean or soak the element in gasoline, oil, or cleaning solvent. The element is designed to be a throw-away item.**

Fuel Filter

REMOVAL & INSTALLATION

◆ SEE FIGS. 13 to 15

Gasoline Engines

INTERNAL

The internal filter is located in the inlet fitting of

FIG. 12e Releasing the clips on air cleaner assembly — 3.3L Century shown

FIG. 12f Removing the air cleaner filter — 3.3L Century shown

all carburetors. The elements are spring loaded and are held against the inlet fitting gasket surface.

1. Disconnect the fuel line connection at the fuel inlet filter nut. Remove the inlet filter nut, the filter and the spring.

2. Install a new filter (with the check valve end facing the fuel line), the spring, the gasket and the fuel line nut.

3. Torque the fuel filter nut to 18 ft. lbs. (24 Nm.), then install the fuel line and check for leaks.

THREADED FITTING

The filter is an inline unit located just ahead of the TBI unit or to the left of the fuel tank.

1. Ensure the engine is cold, then unclamp and remove the fuel hose.

2. Unscrew the filter from the fuel line.

To Install:

3. Place the new filter into position and connect the fuel lines.

4. Tighten the retaining clamp.

5. Start the engine and check for fuel leaks.

QUICK-CONNECT FITTING

1. Disconnect the negative battery cable.

2. Relieve the fuel system pressure.

3. Raise and safely support the vehicle.

4. Remove the filter bracket attaching screw and filter bracket.

5. Grasp the filter and 1 fuel line fitting. Twist the quick-connect fitting 1/4 turn in each direction to loosen any dirt within the fitting. Repeat for the other fuel line fitting.

6. Use compressed air, blow out dirt from the quick-connect fittings at both ends of the fuel filter.

7. To disconnect the fuel line fittings, squeeze the plastic tabs of the male end of the connector and pull the connector apart. Repeat for the other fitting.

8. Remove the fuel filter.

Diesel Engines

The fuel filter is located on the left fender front wheel house.

1. Disconnect the fuel lines from the inlet and the outlet ports. Disconnect the drain hose and, if equipped, the electrical connector harness at the filter.

2. Remove the filter assembly clamp-to-bracket bolts and the clamp. Rotate the filter assembly to disengage it from the bracket, then remove the filter assembly.

3. Cover the assembly with a cloth and clamp it in a vise, using the line openings and the flat on the opposite side.

4. Remove the filter and clean the gasket mounting surface.

5. Coat the new filter gasket with engine oil or diesel fuel. Install the filter on the cover and tighten it to 2/3 turn beyond the gasket contact.

6. Place the assembly into the bracket and engage the bracket lock tab into the bracket. Install new O-rings and loosely assemble the fuel lines to the assembly.

7. To complete the installation, reverse the removal procedures.

8. Open the air bleed screw, turn the ignition switch to the Run position (the pump will run) and close the air bleed screw when fuel flows from the opening.

9. Start the engine and check for leaks.

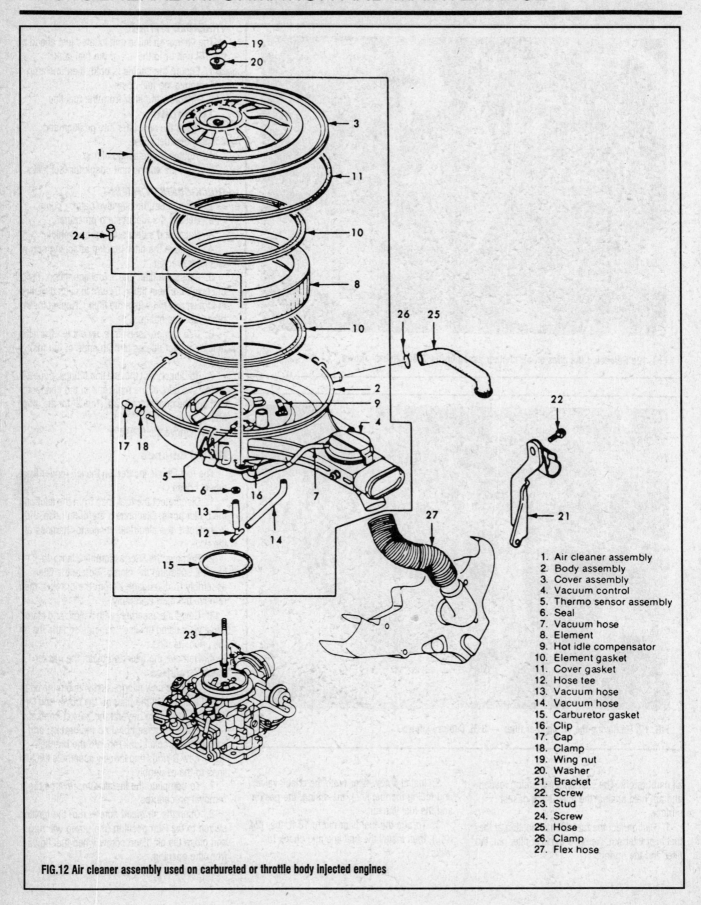

1. Air cleaner assembly
2. Body assembly
3. Cover assembly
4. Vacuum control
5. Thermo sensor assembly
6. Seal
7. Vacuum hose
8. Element
9. Hot idle compensator
10. Element gasket
11. Cover gasket
12. Hose tee
13. Vacuum hose
14. Vacuum hose
15. Carburetor gasket
16. Clip
17. Cap
18. Clamp
19. Wing nut
20. Washer
21. Bracket
22. Screw
23. Stud
24. Screw
25. Hose
26. Clamp
27. Flex hose

FIG.12 Air cleaner assembly used on carbureted or throttle body injected engines

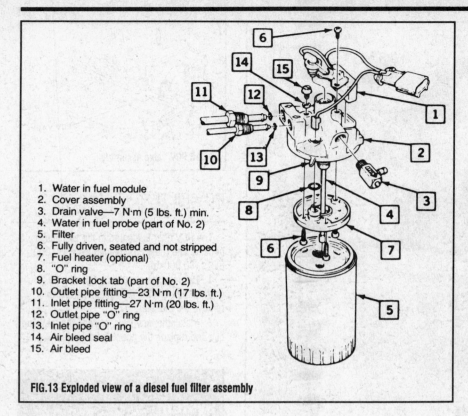

1. Water in fuel module
2. Cover assembly
3. Drain valve—7 N·m (5 lbs. ft.) min.
4. Water in fuel probe (part of No. 2)
5. Filter
6. Fully driven, seated and not stripped
7. Fuel heater (optional)
8. "O" ring
9. Bracket lock tab (part of No. 2)
10. Outlet pipe fitting—23 N·m (17 lbs. ft.)
11. Inlet pipe fitting—27 N·m (20 lbs. ft.)
12. Outlet pipe "O" ring
13. Inlet pipe "O" ring
14. Air bleed seal
15. Air bleed

FIG.13 Exploded view of a diesel fuel filter assembly

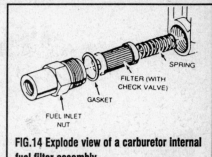

FIG.14 Explode view of a carburetor internal fuel filter assembly

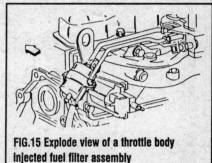

FIG.15 Explode view of a throttle body injected fuel filter assembly

➡ The inline filter should be changed when changing the fuel filter.

PCV Valve

The Positive Crankcase Ventilation (PCV) valve regulated crankcase ventilation during various engine running conditions. At high vacuum (idle speed and partial load range) it will open slightly and at low vacuum (full throttle) it will open fully. This causes vapors to be drawn from the crankcase by engine vacuum and then sucked into the combustion chamber where they are dissipated.

The PCV valve must be replaced every 30,000 miles (48,300km). Details on the PCV system, including system tests, are given in Section 4.

The valve is located in a rubber grommet in the valve cover, connected to the air cleaner housing by a large diameter rubber hose. To replace the valve:

1. Pull the valve (with the hose attached) from the rubber grommet in the valve cover.
2. Remove the valve from the hose.
3. Install a new valve into the hose.
4. Press the valve back into the rubber grommet in the valve cover.

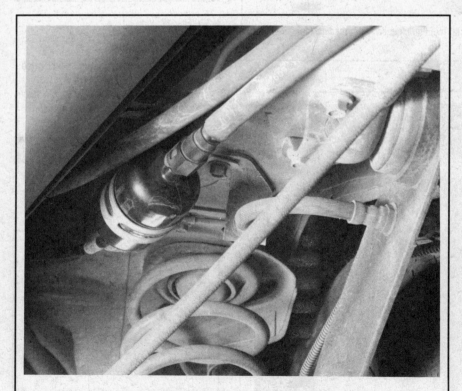

FIG. 15a The fuel filter on multi-port fuel injection is located under the car near the rear spring mount — 3.3L Century shown

FIG. 15b Use care when disconnecting the special fuel line clips on high pressure fuel inlines — 3.3L Century shown

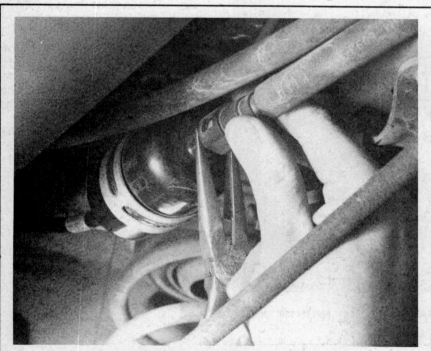

FIG. 15c Removing fuel filter on multi-port fuel injection — 3.3L Century shown

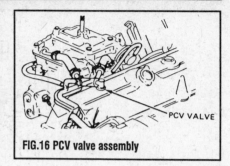

FIG.16 PCV valve assembly

PCV FILTER

The PCV filter is located in the air cleaner housing and must be replaced every 50,000 miles (80,000km).

1. Remove the air cleaner housing lid.
2. Slide back the filter retaining clip and remove the old filter.
3. Install the new filter, replace the retaining clip and replace the housing lid.

Evaporative Emissions System

◆ SEE FIG. 17

Check the fuel vapor lines and the vacuum hoses for proper connections and correct routing, as well as condition. Replace clogged, damaged or deteriorated parts as necessary.

For more details on the evaporative emissions system, please refer to Section 4.

Battery

The single battery used in models equipped with gasoline engines is located at the drivers side front corner of the engine compartment.

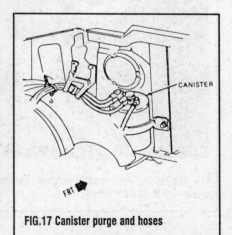

FIG.17 Canister purge and hoses

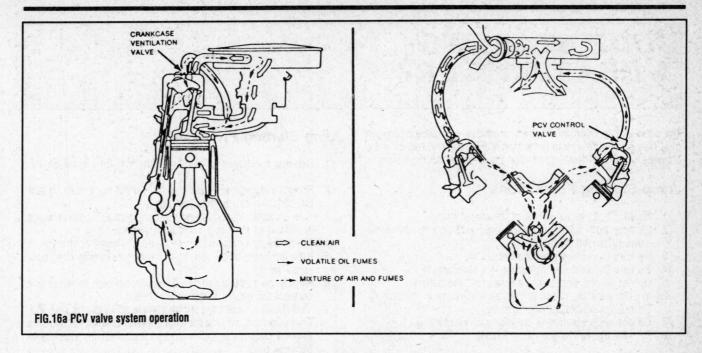

FIG.16a PCV valve system operation

CLEAN AIR

VOLATILE OIL FUMES

MIXTURE OF AIR AND FUMES

Because of the added cranking loads, diesel models use two batteries; one in each front corner of the engine compartment. All models use a Delco Freedom II battery. Though this battery is considered to be maintenance free due to the fact that it will never need water added, the battery should be given some attention once in a while.

GENERAL MAINTENANCE

The major cause of slow engine cranking or a no-start condition is battery terminals which are loose, dirty, or corroded. Every 3 months or so,

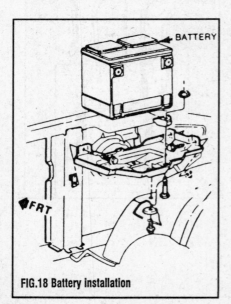

FIG.18 Battery installation

disconnect the battery and clean the terminals of both the battery and the cables. Cleaning tools for this purpose are available at most any auto parts store. When you buy a cleaning tool, be sure to specify whether you have a top terminal or side terminal battery, as the type of tool differs depending upon the style of battery.

> ☀ **CAUTION**
>
> **When loosening or tightening the positive battery cable screw(s) at the battery, DO NOT touch the wrench to any metal surface. Personal injury and/or component damage will result.**
>
> ➡ **To use a terminal cleaning tool on the battery(ies), it will probably be necessary to remove the windshield washer bottle (all models) or the coolant recovery tank (diesel only) to gain the necessary clearance.**

CABLES

◆ SEE FIG. 19

Check the battery cables for signs of wear or chafing. If corrosion is present on the cable or if the cable is visible through the cable jacket, the cable assembly should be replaced. If cable replacement is necessary, it is best to purchase a high quality cable that has the cable jacket sealed to the terminal ends.

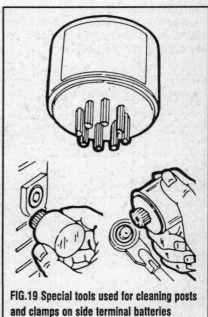

FIG.19 Special tools used for cleaning posts and clamps on side terminal batteries

Batteries themselves can be cleaned using a solution of baking soda and water. Surface coatings on battery cases can actually conduct electricity which will cause a slight voltage drain, so make sure the battery case is clean. To remove the battery(ies):

JUMP STARTING A DEAD BATTERY

The chemical reaction in a battery produces explosive hydrogen gas. This is the safe way to jump start a dead battery, reducing the chances of an accidental spark that could cause an explosion.

Jump Starting Precautions

1. Be sure both batteries are of the same voltage.
2. Be sure both batteries are of the same polarity (have the same grounded terminal).
3. Be sure the vehicles are not touching.
4. Be sure the vent cap holes are not obstructed.
5. Do not smoke or allow sparks around the battery.
6. In cold weather, check for frozen electrolyte in the battery. Do not jump start a frozen battery.
7. Do not allow electrolyte on your skin or clothing.
8. Be sure the electrolyte is not frozen.

CAUTION: Make certin that the ignition key, in the vehicle with the dead battery, is in the OFF position. Connecting cables to vehicles with on-board computers will result in computer destruction if the key is not in the OFF position.

Jump Starting Procedure

1. Determine voltages of the two batteries; they must be the same.
2. Bring the starting vehicle close (they must not touch) so that the batteries can be reached easily.
3. Turn off all accessories and both engines. Put both vehicles in Neutral or Park and set the handbrake.
4. Cover the cell caps with a rag—do not cover terminals.
5. If the terminals on the run-down battery are heavily corroded, clean them.
6. Identify the positive and negative posts on both batteries and connect the cables in the order shown.
7. Start the engine of the starting vehicle and run it at fast idle. Try to start the car with the dead battery. Crank it for no more than 10 seconds at a time and let it cool for 20 seconds in between tries.
8. If it doesn't start in 3 tries, there is something else wrong.
9. Disconnect the cables in the reverse order.
10. Replace the cell covers and dispose of the rags.

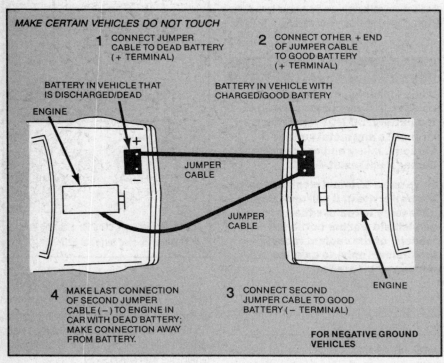

MAKE CERTAIN VEHICLES DO NOT TOUCH

1 CONNECT JUMPER CABLE TO DEAD BATTERY (+ TERMINAL)

2 CONNECT OTHER + END OF JUMPER CABLE TO GOOD BATTERY (+ TERMINAL)

BATTERY IN VEHICLE THAT IS DISCHARGED/DEAD

BATTERY IN VEHICLE WITH CHARGED/GOOD BATTERY

ENGINE

JUMPER CABLE

JUMPER CABLE

ENGINE

4 MAKE LAST CONNECTION OF SECOND JUMPER CABLE (–) TO ENGINE IN CAR WITH DEAD BATTERY; MAKE CONNECTION AWAY FROM BATTERY.

3 CONNECT SECOND JUMPER CABLE TO GOOD BATTERY (– TERMINAL)

FOR NEGATIVE GROUND VEHICLES

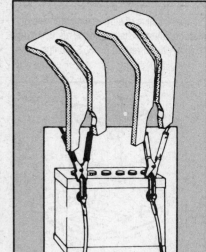

Side terminal batteries occasionally pose a problem when connecting jumper cables. There frequently isn't enough room to clamp the cables without touching sheet metal. Side terminal adaptors are available to alleviate this problem and should be removed after use

TESTING

The quickest test of a battery, without expensive tools, is a by using voltmeter set on the 15 volt dc scale. Attach the leads across the battery terminals it should read about 13 volts with the engine and lights off. If turning the headlights and defogger on lowers the reading below 10.5 volts the battery is too low. Before replacing the battery, charge the battery on a low ampere charger over for several hours, and repeat the test. The voltmeter should not drop below 10.5 volts when cranking the engine with the starter either, but caution must be used to prevent injury and the test could be misleading if the starter is defective causing a greater voltage drop.

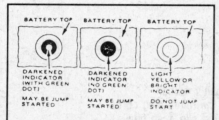

FIG.20 Maintenance free batteries may contain a built in hydrometer

Charging Rate Amps	Time
75	40 min
50	1 hr
25	2 hr
10	5 hr

Battery	Test Load (Amps)
83–50	150
83-60	180
85A-60	170
87A-60	230
89A-60	270
1981103	200
1981104	250
1981105	270
1981577	260

Temperature (°F)	Minimum Voltage
70 or above	9.6
60	9.5
50	9.4
40	9.3
30	9.1
20	8.9
10	8.7
0	8.5

FIG.21 Proper charging rates for a battery

➡ **If the car engine cranks over normally when cold, but cranks slowly when hot the problem is mostly NOT the battery. The starter and battery cables should be the first items suspected.**

CHARGING

Any time the engine won't crank, check the color of the battery condition indicator (which is actually a built-in hydrometer). If the indicator is green, the battery is sufficiently charged and in good condition. A complete check of the starter and related wiring should be performed. If the indicator is darkened, the battery is discharged. In this case, the reason for the discharge should be determined (e.g. low alternator output, voltage draw, etc.) then the battery itself should be tested and recharged. If the indicator is light without a green dot visible or if it is yellow in color, the battery must be replaced — DO NOT attempt to test or recharge a battery with this indicator condition. Test the electrical system after the battery has been replaced.

REPLACEMENT

1. Raise the hood and remove the front end diagonal brace(s) from above the battery(ies).
2. Disconnect the battery cables from the battery(ies). It may be necessary to use a small box end wrench or a 1/4 in. drive ratchet to sneak in between the battery and the windshield washer (or coolant recovery) tank. Avoid using an open-end wrench for the cable bolts. See the previous CAUTION.
3. Loosen and remove the battery holddown bolt and block. The use of a long extension which places the ratchet above the battery makes it very easy to get to the holddown bolt.
4. Carefully lift the battery from the engine compartment. It may be necessary to remove the air cleaner intake duct (except 4-cyl.) or the intake resonator (4-cyl. only) for clearance.
5. Clean the battery and the battery tray thoroughly with the baking soda/water solution. Don't allow the solution to get into the small vent holes of the battery.
6. Rinse the battery with clear water and wipe it dry with a couple of clean paper towels. Don't use the towels for anything else — they probably have traces of sulfuric acid on them. Dispose of the paper towels.

7. Thoroughly flush the battery tray and the surrounding area with clear water. Using a wire brush, remove any rust which may be on the tray. Clear away the rust and dry the tray.
8. Coat the battery tray liberally with anti-rust paint. Thoroughly clean the battery and cable terminals BEFORE installing the battery.
9. Install the battery in the reverse of steps 1-4. Tighten the holddown bolt snugly — don't overtighten it.

After you clean the terminals and reconnect the battery, apply a corrosion inhibitor to the terminals. Stay away from using any substance which is not meant specifically for this purpose. Do not apply the corrosion inhibitor to the mating surfaces of the terminals unless specified by the chemical manufacturer.

Drive Belts

INSPECTION

Every 12 months or 15,000 miles (24,100km) — every 5,000 miles (8,000km) on diesel engines, not dependent upon a period in months — check the drive belts for proper tension. Also look for signs of wear, fraying, separation, glazing and so on, and replace the belts as required.

ADJUSTMENT

Belt tension should be checked with a gauge made for that purpose. If a gauge is not available, tension can be checked with moderate thumb pressure applied to the belt at its longest span midway between pulleys. If the belt has a free span less than 12 in. (305mm), it should deflect approximately 1/8–1/4 in. (3–6mm). If the span is longer than 12 in. (305mm), deflection can range between 1/8 in. (3mm) and 3/8 in.(10mm).

➡ **Models with a serpentine belt which is automatically adjusted by a spring loaded belt tensioner. Adjustments are not normally required.**

1. Loosen the driven accessory's pivot and mounting bolts.
2. Move the accessory toward or away from the engine until the tension is correct. You can use a wooden hammer handle or a broomstick as a lever, but do not use anything metallic.

HOW TO SPOT WORN V-BELTS

V—Belts are vital to efficient engine operation—they drive the fan, water pump and other accessories. They require little maintenance (occasional tightening) but they will not last forever. Slipping or failure of the V—belt will lead to overheating. If your V—belt looks like any of these, it should be replaced.

Cracking or Weathering

This belt has deep cracks, which cause it to flex. Too much flexing leads to heat build—up and premature failure. These cracks can be caused by using the belt on a pulley that is too small. Notched belts are available for small diameter pulleys.

Softening (Grease and Oil)

Oil and grease on a belt can cause the belt's rubber compounds to soften and separate from the reinforcing cords that hold the belt together. The belt will first slip, then finally fail altogether.

Glazing

Glazing is caused by a belt that is slipping. A slipping belt can cause a run-down battery, erratic power steering, overheating or poor accessory performance. The more the belt slips, the more glazing will be built up on the surface of the belt. The more the belt is glazed, the more it will slip. If the glazing is light, tighten the belt.

Worn Cover

The cover of this belt is worn off and is peeling away. The reinforcing cords will begin to wear and the belt will shortly break. When the belt cover wears in spots or has a rough jagged appearance, check the pulley grooves for roughness.

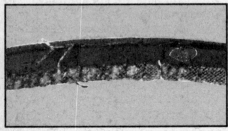

Separation

This belt is on the verge of breaking and leaving you stranded. The layers of the belt are separating and the reinforcing cords are exposed. It's just a matter of time before it breaks completely.

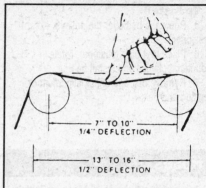

FIG.22 Checking belt deflection without the use of a gauge

3. Tighten the bolts and recheck the tension. If new bolts have been installed, run the engine for a few minutes, then recheck and readjust as necessary.

It is better to have belts too loose than too tight, because overtight belts will lead to bearing failure, particularly in the water pump and alternator. However, loose belts place an extremely high impact load on the driven component due to the whipping action of the belt.

REMOVAL & INSTALLATION

Except Serpentine Belt

1. Loosen the driven accessory's pivot and mounting bolts.

2. Move the accessory toward or away from the engine until there is enough slack in the belt to slip it over the pulley of the driven accessory.

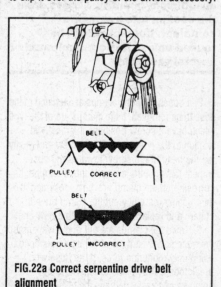

FIG.22a Correct serpentine drive belt alignment

FIG. 22b Release tension on serpentine drive belt by turning tensioner

FIG. 22c Check the belt routing diagram, before and after removal for proper routing through pulleys

3. Install the new belt and move the accessory toward or away from the engine until the tension is correct. You can use a wooden hammer handle or a broomstick as a lever, but do not use anything metallic.

4. Tighten the bolts and adjust the belt tension as explained above.

Serpentine Belt

1. Place a tool over the tensioner pulley axis bolt.

2. Rotate the tool counterclockwise.

3. Remove the drive belt.

4. Remove the tool.

FIG. 22d Hold wrench on tension to release tension while installing the belt making certain belt is positioned correctly

To install:

5. Route the belt over the pulleys, except tensioner.

6. Place tool over tensioner, rotate counterclockwise and install belt.

7. Remove belt and check alignment of tension and belt.

Hoses

The upper and lower radiator hoses and the heater hoses should be checked periodically for deterioration, leaks, and loose clamps. G.M. recommends that this be done every 12 months, or 15,000 miles (24,100km). For your own peace of mind, it may be wise to check these items at least every spring and fall, since the summer and winter months wreak the most havoc with your cooling system. Expect to replace the hoses about every 24 months or 30,000 miles (48,300km). To replace the hoses:

REMOVAL & INSTALLATION

1. Drain the cooling system.

✳ CAUTION

When draining the coolant, keep in mind that cats and dogs are attracted by the ethylene glycol antifreeze, and are quite likely to drink any that is left in an uncovered container or in puddles on the ground. This will prove fatal in sufficient quantity. Always drain the coolant into a sealable container. Coolant should be reused unless it is contaminated or several years old.

2. Loosen the hose clamps at each end of the hose to be removed. If the clamps are of the type which have a screw positioned vertically in relation to the hose, loosen the screw and gently tap the head of the screw towards the hose. Repeat this until the clamp is loose enough. If corrosion on the clamp prevents loosening in this manner, carefully cut the clamp off with cutters and replace the clamp with a new one.

3. Once the clamps are out of the way, grasp the hose and twist it off of the tube connection using only moderate force. If the hose won't break loose, DON'T use excessive force — doing so can easily damage the heater core and/

FIG. 22f Before removing any hoses or wires tag them for reassembly

HOW TO SPOT BAD HOSES

Both the upper and lower radiator hoses are called upon to perform difficult jobs in an inhospitable environment. They are subject to nearly 18 psi at under hood temperatures often over 280°F, and must circulate nearly 7500 gallons of coolant an hour—3 good reasons to have good hoses.

Swollen Hose

A good test for any hose is to feel it for soft or spongy spots. Frequently these will appear as swollen areas of the hose. The most likely cause is oil soaking. This hose could burst at any time, when hot or under pressure.

Cracked Hose

Cracked hoses can usually be seen but feel the hoses to be sure they have not hardened; a prime cause of cracking. This hose has cracked down to the reinforcing cords and could split at any of the cracks.

Frayed Hose End (Due to Weak Clamp)

Weakened clamps frequently are the cause of hose and cooling system failure. The connection between the pipe and hose has deteriorated enough to allow coolant to escape when the engine is hot.

Debris In Cooling System

Debris, rust and scale in the cooling system can cause the inside of a hose to weaken. This can usually be felt on the outside of the hose as soft or thinner areas.

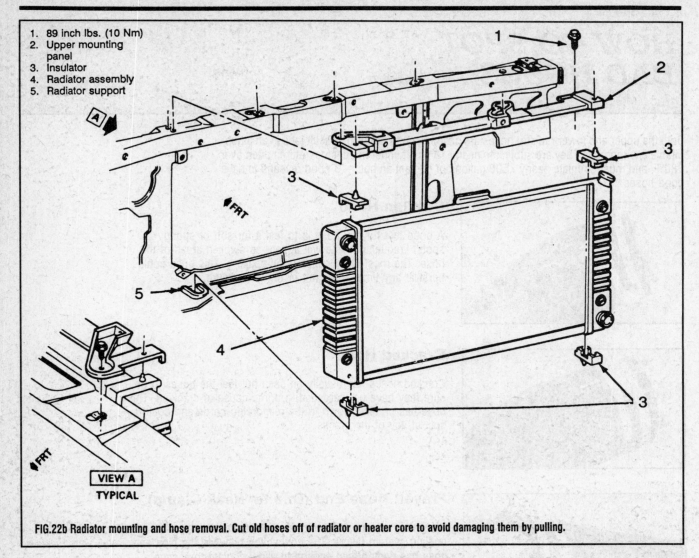

1. 89 inch lbs. (10 Nm)
2. Upper mounting panel
3. Insulator
4. Radiator assembly
5. Radiator support

VIEW A
TYPICAL

FIG.22b Radiator mounting and hose removal. Cut old hoses off of radiator or heater core to avoid damaging them by pulling.

or radiator tubes. Using a razor blade, carefully slit the portion of the hose which covers the connection point, peel the hose off of the connection and disconnect the hose.

4. If so equipped, disconnect the hose routing clamps from the hose.

5. Remove the hose and clean the hose connection points.

6. Slip the (loosened) hose clamps onto the hose ends and install the new hose, being careful to position the hose so that no interference is encountered.

7. Position the clamps at the ends of the hoses, beyond the sealing bead, and centered on the clamping surface. Tighten the hose clamps with a screwdriver — don't use a wrench on the screw heads to tighten them, as overtightening can damage the hose and/or connections points.

8. Refill the cooling system (detailed later) and check for leakage.

Air Conditioning System

GENERAL SERVICING PROCEDURES

The most important aspect of air conditioning service is the maintenance of a pure and adequate charge of refrigerant in the system. A refrigeration system cannot function properly if a significant percentage of the charge is lost. Leaks are common because the severe vibration encountered in an automobile can easily cause a sufficient cracking or loosening of the air conditioning fittings; as a result, the extreme operating pressures of the system force refrigerant out.

The problem can be understood by considering what happens to the system as it is operated with a continuous leak. Because the expansion valve regulates the flow of refrigerant to the evaporator, the level of refrigerant there is fairly constant. The receiver/drier stores any excess of refrigerant, and so a loss will first appear there as a reduction in the level of liquid. As this level nears the bottom of the vessel, some refrigerant vapor bubbles will begin to appear in the stream of liquid supplied to the expansion valve. This vapor decreases the capacity of the expansion valve very little as the valve opens to compensate for its presence. As the quantity of liquid in the condenser decreases, the operating pressure will drop there and throughout the high side of the system. As the R-12 continues to be expelled, the pressure available to force the liquid through the expansion valve will continue to decrease, and, eventually, the valve's orifice will prove to be too much of a restriction for adequate flow even with the needle fully withdrawn.

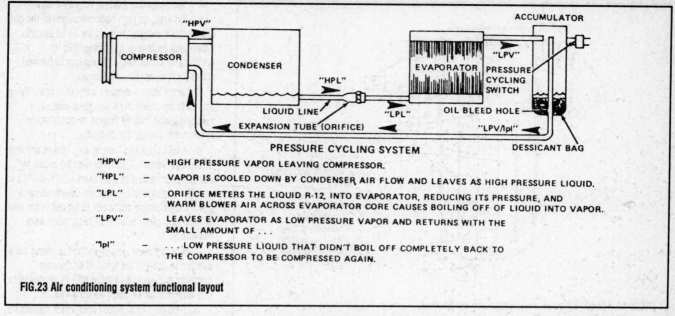

"HPV" – HIGH PRESSURE VAPOR LEAVING COMPRESSOR.

"HPL" – VAPOR IS COOLED DOWN BY CONDENSER AIR FLOW AND LEAVES AS HIGH PRESSURE LIQUID.

"LPL" – ORIFICE METERS THE LIQUID R-12 INTO EVAPORATOR, REDUCING ITS PRESSURE, AND WARM BLOWER AIR ACROSS EVAPORATOR CORE CAUSES BOILING OFF OF LIQUID INTO VAPOR.

"LPV" – LEAVES EVAPORATOR AS LOW PRESSURE VAPOR AND RETURNS WITH THE SMALL AMOUNT OF . . .

"lpl" – . . . LOW PRESSURE LIQUID THAT DIDN'T BOIL OFF COMPLETELY BACK TO THE COMPRESSOR TO BE COMPRESSED AGAIN.

FIG.23 Air conditioning system functional layout

At this point, low side pressure will start to drop, and severe reduction in cooling capacity, marked by freeze-up of the evaporator coil, will result. Eventually, the operating pressure of the evaporator will be lower than the pressure of the atmosphere surrounding it, and air will be drawn into the system wherever there are leaks in the low side.

Because all atmospheric air contains at least some moisture, water will enter the system and mix with the R-12 and the oil. Trace amounts of moisture will cause slugging of the oil, and corrosion of the system. Saturation and clogging of the filter/drier, and freezing of the expansion valve orifice will eventually result. As air fills the system to a greater and greater extent, it will interfere more and more with the normal flows of refrigerant and heat.

From this description, it should be obvious that much of the repairman's time will be spent detecting leaks, repairing them, and then restoring the purity and quantity of the refrigerant charge. A list of general precautions that should be observed while doing this follows:

1. Keep all tools as clean and dry as possible.
2. Thoroughly purge the service gauges and hoses of air and moisture before connecting them to the system. Keep them capped when not in use.
3. Thoroughly clean any refrigerant fitting before disconnecting it, in order to minimize the entrance of dirt into the system.
4. Plan any operation that requires opening the system beforehand, in order to minimize the length of time it will be exposed to open air. Cap or seal the open ends to minimize the entrance of foreign material.

5. When adding oil, pour it through an extremely clean and dry tube or funnel. Keep the oil capped whenever possible. Do not use oil that has not been kept tightly sealed.
6. Use only refrigerant R-12. Purchase refrigerant intended for use in only automatic air conditioning systems. Avoid the use of refrigerant R-12 that may be packaged for another use, such as cleaning, or powering a horn, as it is impure.
7. Completely evacuate any system that has been opened to replace a component, or that has leaked sufficiently to draw in moisture and air. This requires evacuating air and moisture with a good vacuum pump for at least one hour. If a system has been open for a considerable length of time it may be advisable to evacuate the system for up to 12 hours (overnight).
8. Use a wrench on both halves of a fitting that is to be disconnected, so as to avoid placing torque on any of the refrigerant lines.

9. When overhauling a compressor, pour some of the oil into a clean glass and inspect it. If there is evidence of dirt or metal particles, or both, flush all refrigerant components with clean refrigerant before evacuating and recharging the system. In addition, if metal particles are present, the compressor should be replaced.
10. Schrader valves may leak only when under full operating pressure. Therefore, if leakage is suspected but cannot be located, operate the system with a full charge of refrigerant and look for leaks from all Schrader valves. Replace any faulty valves.

Additional Preventive Maintenance Checks

ANTIFREEZE

In order to prevent heater core freeze-up during A/C operation, it is necessary to maintain permanent type antifreeze protection of +15°F

ORIFICE (EXPANSION) TUBE

1. LONG SCREEN END (INLET)
2. "O" RING
3. SHORT SCREEN END (OUTLET)

INSTALL WITH SHORTER SCREEN END IN EVAPORATOR INLET PIPE (TOWARDS EVAPORATOR) USE NEW "O" RINGS.

FIG.24 Air conditioning system orifice tube

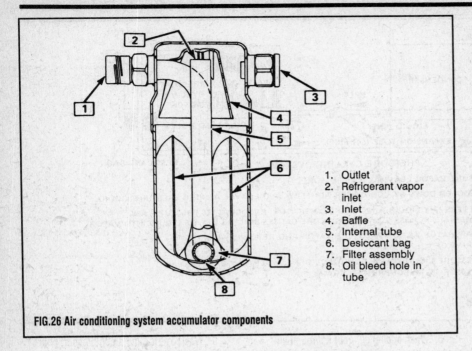

1. Outlet
2. Refrigerant vapor inlet
3. Inlet
4. Baffle
5. Internal tube
6. Desiccant bag
7. Filter assembly
8. Oil bleed hole in tube

FIG.26 Air conditioning system accumulator components

(–9°C), or lower. A reading of –15°F (–26°C) is ideal since this protection also supplies sufficient corrosion inhibitors for the protection of the engine cooling system.

➡ **The same antifreeze should not be used longer than the manufacturer specifies.**

RADIATOR CAP

For efficient operation of an air conditioned car's cooling system, the radiator cap should have a holding pressure which meets manufacturer's specifications. A cap which fails to hold these pressures should be replaced.

CONDENSER

Any obstruction of or damage to the condenser configuration will restrict the air flow which is essential to its efficient operation. It is therefore a good rule to keep this unit clean and in proper physical shape.

➡ **Bug screens are regarded as obstructions.**

CONDENSATION DRAIN TUBE

This single molded drain tube expels the condensation, which accumulates on the bottom of the evaporator housing, into the engine compartment. If this tube is obstructed, the air conditioning performance can be restricted and condensation buildup can spill over onto the vehicle's floor.

SAFETY WARNINGS

Because of the importance of the necessary safety precautions that must be exercised when working with air conditioning systems and R-12 refrigerant, a recap of the safety precautions are outlined.

1. Avoid contact with a charged refrigeration system, even when working on another part of the air conditioning system or vehicle. If a heavy tool comes into contact with a section of copper tubing or a heat exchanger, it can easily cause the relatively soft material to rupture.

2. When it is necessary to apply force to a fitting which contains refrigerant, as when checking that all system couplings are securely tightened, use a wrench on both parts of the fitting involved, if possible. This will avoid putting torque on refrigerant tubing. (It is advisable, when possible, to use tube or line wrenches when tightening these flare nut fittings.)

3. Do not attempt to discharge the system by merely loosening a fitting, or removing the service valve caps and cracking these valves. Precise control is possible only when using the service gauges. Place a rag under the open end of the center charging hose while discharging the system to catch any drops of liquid that might escape. Wear protective gloves when connecting or disconnecting service gauge hoses.

➡ **A proper recycling machine that meets SAE standards should be employed when discharging the system. Discharging Freon into the air should be avoided.**

4. Discharge the system only in a well ventilated area, as high concentrations of the gas can exclude oxygen and act as an anesthetic. When leak testing or soldering, this is particularly important, as toxic gas is formed when R-12 contacts any flame.

5. Never start a system without first verifying that both service valves are back-seated, if equipped, and that all fittings throughout the system are snugly connected.

6. Avoid applying heat to any refrigerant line or storage vessel. Charging may be aided by using water heated to less than 125°F (52°C) to warm the refrigerant container. Never allow a refrigerant storage container to sit out in the sun, or near any other source of heat, such as a radiator.

7. Always wear goggles when working on a system to protect the eyes. If refrigerant contacts the eyes, it is advisable in all cases to see a physician as soon as possible.

8. Frostbite from liquid refrigerant should be treated by first gradually warming the area with cool water, and then gently applying petroleum jelly. A physician should be consulted.

9. Always keep refrigerant drum fittings capped when not in use. Avoid sudden shock to the drum, which might occur from dropping it, or from banging a heavy tool against it. Never carry a drum in the passenger compartment of a car.

10. Always completely discharge the system before painting the vehicle (if the paint is to be baked on), or before welding anywhere near refrigerant lines.

SYSTEM INSPECTION

The air conditioning system should be checked periodically for worn hoses, loose connections, low refrigerant, leaks, dirt and bugs. If any of these conditions exist, they must be corrected or they will reduce the efficiency of your air conditioning system.

Keep the Condenser Clear

Periodically inspect the front of the condenser for bent fins or foreign material (dirt, bugs, leaves, etc.) If any cooling fins are bent, straighten them carefully with needlenosed pliers. You can remove any debris with a stiff bristle brush or hose.

Operate the A/C System Periodically

A lot of A/C problems can be avoided by simply running the air conditioner at least once a week, regardless of the season. Let the system run for at least 5 minutes a week (even in the

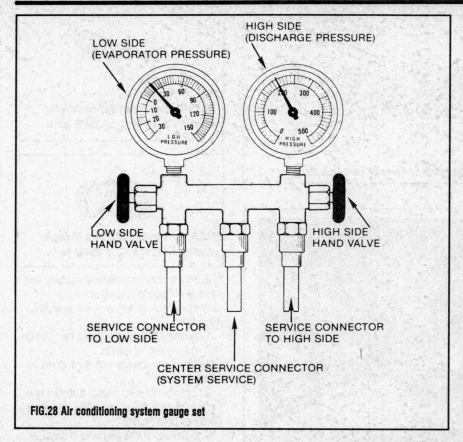

LOW SIDE
(EVAPORATOR PRESSURE)

HIGH SIDE
(DISCHARGE PRESSURE)

LOW SIDE
HAND VALVE

HIGH SIDE
HAND VALVE

SERVICE CONNECTOR
TO LOW SIDE

SERVICE CONNECTOR
TO HIGH SIDE

CENTER SERVICE CONNECTOR
(SYSTEM SERVICE)

FIG.28 Air conditioning system gauge set

winter), and you'll keep the internal parts lubricated as well as preventing the hoses from hardening.

REFRIGERANT LEVEL CHECK

The factory installed air conditioning unit has no sight glass for system checks. It is recommended that all air conditioning service work be entrusted to a qualified mechanic. The system is a potentially hazardous one.

GAUGE SETS

Most of the service work performed in air conditioning requires the use of two gauges, one for the high (head) pressure side of the system, the other for the low (suction).

The low side gauge records both pressure and vacuum. Vacuum readings are calibrated from 0 to no less than 60 psi (413.7kpa).

The high side gauge measures pressure from 0 to at least 600 psi (4137kpa). Both gauges are threaded into a manifold that contains two hand shut off valves. Proper manipulation of these

valves and the use of the attached test hoses allow the user to perform the following services:
1. Test high and low side pressures.
2. Remove air, moisture, and contaminated refrigerant.
3. Purge the system of refrigerant.
4. Charge the system with refrigerant.

The manifold valves are designed so they have no direct effect on gauge readings, but serve only to provide for, or cut off, flow of refrigerant through the manifold. During all testing and hook-up operations, the valves are kept in a closed position to avoid disturbing the refrigeration system. The valves are opened only to purge the system of refrigerant or to charge it. When purging the system, the center hose is uncapped at the lower end, and both valves are cracked open slightly. This allows refrigerant pressure to force the entire contents of the system out through the center hose. During charging, the valve on the high side of the manifold is closed, and the valve on the low side is cracked open. Under these conditions, the low pressure in the evaporator will draw refrigerant from the relatively warm refrigerant storage container into the system.

DISCHARGING THE SYSTEM

❋❋ CAUTION

Perform in a well ventilated area. The compressed refrigerant used in the air conditioning system expands and evaporates into the atmosphere at a temperature of –21.7°F (–29.8°C) or less. This will freeze any surface (including your eyes) that it contacts. In addition, the refrigerant decomposes into a poisonous gas in the presence of flame.

➡ **R-12 refrigerant is a chlorofluorocarbon which, when released into the atmosphere, can contribute to the depletion of the ozone layer in the upper atmosphere. Ozone filters out the harmful radiation from the sun. If possible, an approved R-12 Recovery Recycling machine that meets SAE standards should be employed when discharging the system. Follow the operating instruction provided with the approved equipment exactly to the properly discharge the system.**
1. Operate the air conditioner for at least 10 minutes.
2. Attach the gauges, shut off the engine, and the air conditioner.
3. Connect the center hose of the gauge set to the proper recovery system for the used R-12. The refrigerant will be discharged there and this precaution will control its uncontrolled exposure.
4. Open the low side hand valve on the gauge slightly.
5. Open the high side hand valve slightly.

➡ **If not discharged into a recovery system, too rapid a purging process will be identified by the appearance of an oily foam. If this occurs, close the hand valves a little more until this condition stops.**

6. Close both hand valves on the gauge set when the pressures read 0 and all the refrigerant has left the system.

➡ **The system should always be discharged before attempting to remove any hoses or component parts of the air conditioning system.**

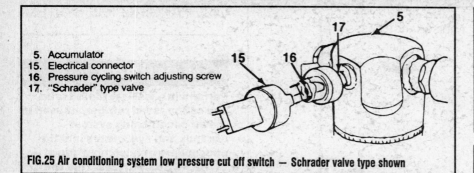

5. Accumulator
15. Electrical connector
16. Pressure cycling switch adjusting screw
17. "Schrader" type valve

FIG.25 Air conditioning system low pressure cut off switch — Schrader valve type shown

FIG.29 Air conditioning system straight adapter. J–5420 for ⁷⁄₁₆; J–25498 for ³⁄₈

FIG.30 Air conditioning system 90 degree adapter. J–9459 for ⁷⁄₁₆; J–25499 for ³⁄₈

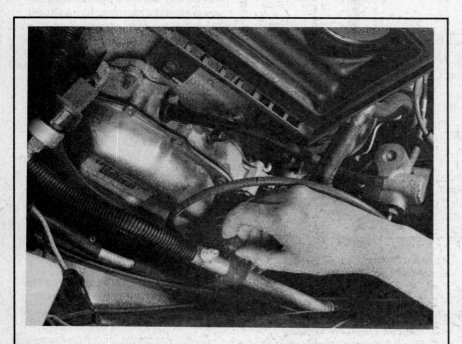

FIG. 25a Air conditioning pressure switch and remove Schrader valve cap — 3.3L Century shown

to do so will result in ineffective charging and possible damage to the system.

Use this hook-up for the proper evacuation procedure:

1. Connect both service gauge hoses to the high and low service outlets.
2. Open high and low side hand valves on gauge manifold.
3. Open both service valves a slight amount (from back seated position), allow refrigerant to discharge from system.
4. Install center charging hose of gauge set to vacuum pump.
5. Operate vacuum pump for at least one hour. (If the system has been subjected to open conditions for a prolonged period of time it may be necessary to "pump the system down" overnight. Refer to "System Sweep" procedure.)

➡ **If low pressure gauge does not show at least 28 in.Hg within 5 minutes, check the system for a leak or loose gauge connectors.**

6. Close hand valves on gauge manifold.
7. Shut off pump.
8. Observe low pressure gauge to determine if vacuum is holding. A vacuum drop may indicate a leak.

EVACUATING THE SYSTEM

Before charging any system it is necessary to purge the refrigerant and draw out the trapped moisture with a suitable vacuum pump. Failure

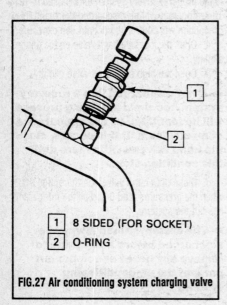

1 8 SIDED (FOR SOCKET)
2 O-RING

FIG.27 Air conditioning system charging valve

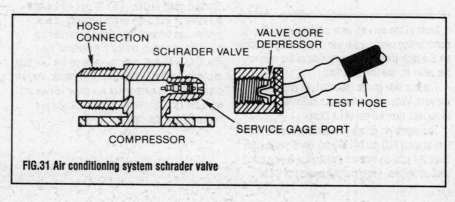

HOSE CONNECTION
SCHRADER VALVE
VALVE CORE DEPRESSOR
TEST HOSE
COMPRESSOR
SERVICE GAGE PORT

FIG.31 Air conditioning system schrader valve

SYSTEM SWEEP

An efficient vacuum pump can remove all the air contained in a contaminated air conditioning system very quickly, because of its vapor state. Moisture, however, is far more difficult to remove because the vacuum must force the liquid to evaporate before it will be able to remove it from the system. If a system has become severely contaminated, as, for example, it might become after all the charge was lost in conjunction with vehicle accident damage, moisture removal is extremely time consuming. A vacuum pump could remove all of the moisture only if it were operated for 12 hours or more.

Under these conditions, sweeping the system with refrigerant will speed the process of moisture removal considerably. To sweep, follow the following procedure:

1. Connect vacuum pump to gauges, operate it until vacuum ceases to increase, then continue operation for ten more minutes.
2. Charge system with 50% of its rated refrigerant capacity.
3. Operate system at fast idle for ten minutes.
4. Discharge the system.
5. Repeat twice the process of charging to 50% capacity, running the system for ten minutes, and discharging it, for a total of three sweeps.
6. Replace drier.
7. Pump system down as in Step 1.
8. Charge system.

CHARGING THE SYSTEM

Refrigerant enters the suction side of the system as a vapor while the compressor is running. Before proceeding, the system should be in a partial vacuum after adequate evacuation. Both hand valves on the gauge manifold should be closed.

1. Attach both test hoses to their respective service valve ports. Mid-position manually operated service valves, if present.

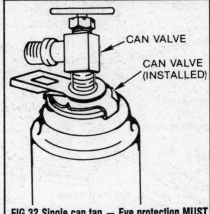

FIG.32 Single can tap — Eye protection MUST be worn at all times by all in the area

2. Install the dispensing valve (closed position) on the refrigerant container. Single and multiple refrigerant manifolds are available to accommodate one to four 15 oz. (0.425kg) cans.
3. Attach the center charging hose to the refrigerant container valve.
4. Open dispensing valve on the refrigerant valve.
5. Loosen the center charging hose coupler where it connects to the gauge manifold to allow the escaping refrigerant to purge the hose of contaminants.
6. Tighten the center charging hose connector.
7. Purge the low pressure test hose at the gauge manifold.
8. Start the engine, roll down the windows and adjust the air conditioner to maximum cooling. The engine should be at normal operating temperature before proceeding. The heated environment helps the liquid vaporize more efficiently.

➡ Placing the refrigerant can in a container of warm water (no hotter than 125°F [52°C]) will speed the charging process. Slight agitation of the can is helpful too, but be careful not to turn the can upside down.

9. Crack open the low side hand valve on the manifold. Manipulate the valve so that the refrigerant that enters the system does not cause the low side pressure to exceed 40 psi (275.8kpa). Too sudden a surge may permit the entrance of unwanted liquid to the compressor. Since liquids cannot be compressed, the compressor will suffer damage if compelled to attempt it. If the suction side of the system remains in a vacuum the system is blocked. Locate and correct the condition before proceeding any further.

LEAK TESTING

Refrigerant leaks show up as oily areas on the various components because the compressor oil is transported around the entire system along with the refrigerant. Look for oily spots on all the hoses and lines, and especially on the hose and tubing connections. If there are oily deposits, the system may have a leak, and you should have it checked by a qualified repairman.

➡ A small area of oil on the front of the compressor is normal and no cause for alarm.

Leak Testing the System

There are several methods of detecting leaks in an air conditioning system; among them, the two most popular are (1) halide leak-detection or the "open flame method," and (2) electronic leak-detection.

The halide leak detection is a torch like device which produces a yellow-green color when refrigerant is introduced into the flame at the burner. A purple or violet color indicates the presence of large amounts of refrigerant at the burner.

In electronic leak detector is a small portable electronic device with an extended probe. With the unit activated the probe is passed along those components of the system which contain refrigerant. If a leak is detected, the unit will sound an alarm signal or activate a display signal depending on the manufacturer's design. It is advisable to follow the manufacturer's instructions as the design and function of the detection may vary significantly.

Windshield Wipers

Each exposed windshield wiper is divided basically into four segments:

1. Wiper arm connected to the pivot at the base of the windshield.
2. Wiper blade connected at the opposite end of the wiper arm and hoes the yokes.

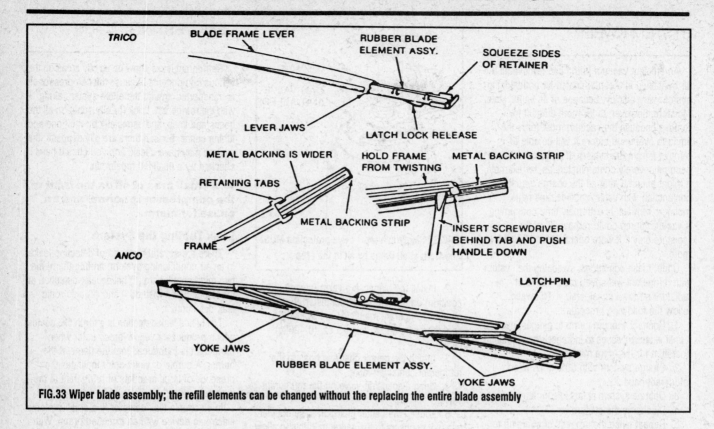

TRICO

BLADE FRAME LEVER

RUBBER BLADE ELEMENT ASSY.

SQUEEZE SIDES OF RETAINER

LEVER JAWS

LATCH LOCK RELEASE

METAL BACKING IS WIDER

HOLD FRAME FROM TWISTING

METAL BACKING STRIP

RETAINING TABS

METAL BACKING STRIP

INSERT SCREWDRIVER BEHIND TAB AND PUSH HANDLE DOWN

FRAME

ANCO

LATCH-PIN

YOKE JAWS

RUBBER BLADE ELEMENT ASSY.

YOKE JAWS

FIG.33 Wiper blade assembly; the refill elements can be changed without the replacing the entire blade assembly

3. Wiper yokes hold the element in a manner which distributed the pressure load across the element.

4. Wiper element flexible rubber element which contacts the windshield glass and actually performs the cleaning function.

For maximum effectiveness and longest life, the windshield and wiper elements should be kept clean. Dirt, tree sap, road tar, etc., will cause streaking, smearing, and wiper element deterioration. Hardening of the elements will cause the elements to chatter as they wipe the windshield. Wash the windshield thoroughly with a glass cleaner at least once a month. Wipe off the rubber element with a wet rag afterwards.

Obviously, the item most frequently requiring replacement is the element. It is very rarely necessary to replace the blade or arm unless they become accidentally bent or damaged in some other manner.

Your car can use one of three types of elements: the first type is commonly referred to as the Anco® style; the second type is the Trico® style; and the third is the plastic style which uses a plastic blade assembly. Replacement of any element type is very simple and requires only a few minutes to do.

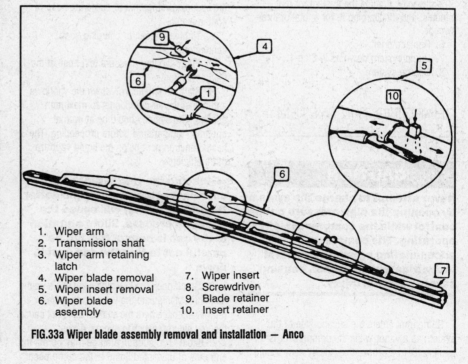

1. Wiper arm
2. Transmission shaft
3. Wiper arm retaining latch
4. Wiper blade removal
5. Wiper insert removal
6. Wiper blade assembly
7. Wiper insert
8. Screwdriver
9. Blade retainer
10. Insert retainer

FIG.33a Wiper blade assembly removal and installation — Anco

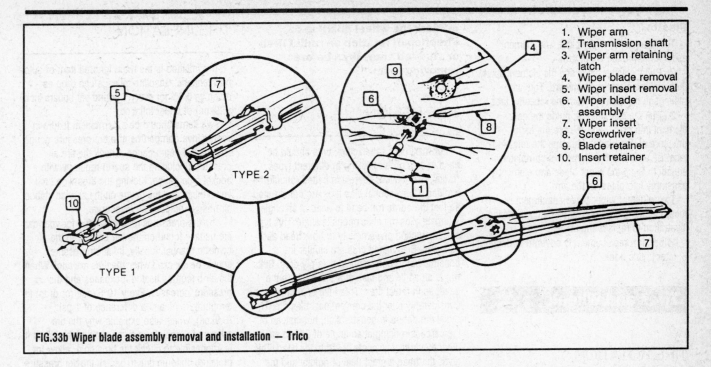

FIG.33b Wiper blade assembly removal and installation — Trico

1. Wiper arm
2. Transmission shaft
3. Wiper arm retaining latch
4. Wiper blade removal
5. Wiper insert removal
6. Wiper blade assembly
7. Wiper insert
8. Screwdriver
9. Blade retainer
10. Insert retainer

REPLACEMENT

ANCO® Style Element

1. Locate the red release button at the top of one of the yokes (free yoke), push the button, and separate the free yoke from the blade.

2. Pull the element out of the other yoke (attached yoke).

3. Transfer the free yoke to the new element, being sure to engage the element into all of the yoke jaws.

4. Feed the other end of the element into the attached yoke, again being sure that the element is fully engaged.

5. Push the button and snap the free yoke into place on the blade. Release the button and double-check that the element is fully engaged into all of the yoke jaws.

Trico® Style Element

1. Squeeze the sides of the element retainer (located on only one side of the element) and pull the element out of the blade/yoke assembly.

2. To install the new element, guide the new element into all of the blade/yoke jaws. The element must be positioned in the same manner as the one which was removed. When the retainer comes in contact with the end of the blade, make sure that each side of the retainer is positioned on the inside of the jaws, then snap the element into place.

3. Check that the element is fully engaged to all of the jaws before operating the wipers.

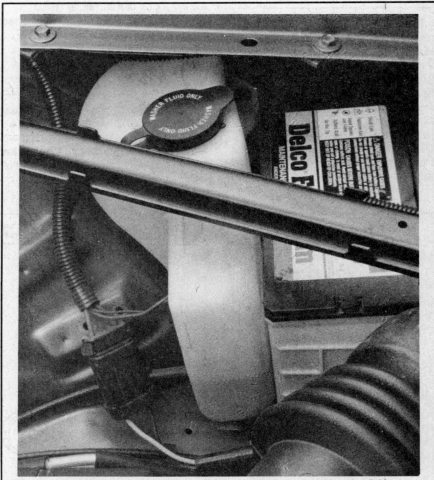

FIG. 33c Make certain not to confuse the coolant bottle with the windshield washer fluid. Even a little anti-freeze here would impair vision.

Plastic

1. Remove the wiper blade and element assembly from the wiper arm.

2. Pull the wiper blade and the element apart, then pull the element downward. This will disengage the element from the retaining tabs.

3. Pull the element out, guide the new element into place, and release the hand pressure on the blade to engage the retaining tabs. Be sure that the element is completely engaged. Snap the wiper blade and element assembly into place on the arm.

Two different wiper blade attachment methods are used. Refer to the accompanying illustration to replace the blades.

Wiper arm replacement is covered in Section 6, later in this book.

Tires and Wheels

TIRE ROTATION

Tire rotation is recommended every 6,000 miles (9,655km) or so, to obtain maximum tire wear. The pattern you use depends on whether or not your car has a usable spare. Radial tires should not be cross-switched (from one side of the car to the other). They last longer if their direction of rotation is not changed. Snow tires sometimes have directional arrows molded into the side of the carcass. The arrow shows the direction of rotation. They will wear very rapidly if the rotation is reversed. Studded tires will lose their studs if their rotational direction is reversed.

➡ **Mark the wheel position or direction of rotation on radial tires or studded snow tires before removing them.**

TIRE DESIGN

For maximum satisfaction, tires should be used in sets of five. Mixing of different types (radial, bias-belted, fiberglass belted) should be avoided. Conventional bias tires are constructed so that the cords run bead to bead at an angle. Alternate plies run at an opposite angle. This type of construction gives rigidity to both tread and side wall. Bias belted tires are similar in construction to conventional bias ply tires. Belts run at an angle and also at a 90° angle to the bead, as in radial tires. Tread life is improved considerably over the conventional bias tire. The radial tire differs in construction, but instead of the carcass running at an angle of 90á to each other they run at an angle of 90° to the bead. This gives the tread a great deal of rigidity and the side wall a great deal of flexibility (which accounts for the characteristic bulge associated with radial tires).

TIRE STORAGE

Store the tires at the proper inflation pressure if they are mounted on wheels. Keep them in a cool dry place, laid on their sides. If the tires are stored in the garage or basement, do not let them stand on a concrete floor. Set them on strips of wood.

TIRE INFLATION

Tire inflation is the most ignored item of auto maintenance. Gasoline mileage can drop as much as 0.8% for every 1 pound per square inch (6.9kpa) of under inflation.

Two items should be a permanent fixture in every glove compartment: a tire pressure gauge and a tread depth gauge. Check the tire air pressure (including the spare) regularly with a pocket type gauge. Kicking the tires won't tell you a thing, and the gauge on the service station air hose is notoriously inaccurate.

The tire pressures recommended for your car are usually found on the left door or in the owner's manual. Ideally, inflation pressure should be checked when the tires are cool. When the air becomes heated it expands and the pressure increases. Every 10°F (rise (or drop) in temperature means a difference of 1 psi (6.9kpa), which also explains why the tire appears to lose air on a very cold night. When it is impossible to check the tires cold, allow for pressure build-up due to heat. If the hot pressure exceeds the cold pressure by more than 15 psi (103.4kpa), reduce your speed, load or both. Otherwise internal heat is created in the tire. When the heat approaches the temperature at which the tire was cured, during manufacture, the tread can separate from the body.

❈❈❈ CAUTION

Never counteract excessive pressure build-up by bleeding off air pressure (letting some air out). This will only further raise the tire operating temperature.

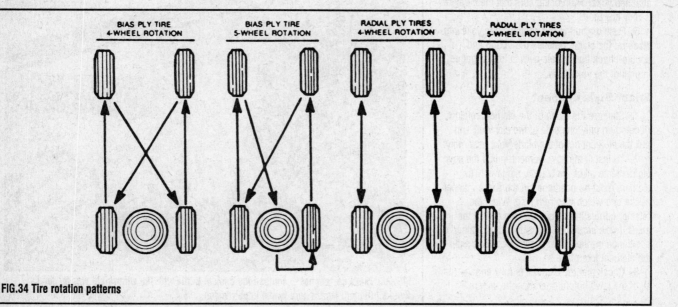

FIG.34 Tire rotation patterns

Before starting a long trip with lots of luggage, you can add about 2–4 psi (13.8–27.6kpa) to the tires to make them run cooler, but never exceed the maximum inflation pressure on the side of the tire.

CARE OF SPECIAL WHEELS

If you have invested money in magnesium, aluminum alloy or sport wheels, special precautions should be taken to make sure your investment is not wasted, and that your special wheels look good for the lifetime of the car.

Special wheels are easily scratched and/or damaged. Occasionally check the rim for cracks, damage or air leaks. If any of these conditions are found, replace the wheel. In order to prevent this type of damage, and the costly replacement of a special wheel, observe the following precautions:

• Take special care not to damage the wheels during removal, installation, balancing etc. After removal of the wheels from the car, place them on a rubber mat or other protective surface.

• While the vehicle is being driven, be careful not to drive over sharp obstacles or allow the wheels to contact the shoulder of the road.

• When washing, use a mild detergent and water. Avoid using cleansers with abrasives, or hard brushes. And a little polish after washing will help your wheels keep that new look.

• If possible, remove your special wheels from the car during the winter months, and replace them with regular steel rims. Salt and sand that is applied to the roadways for snow removal during these months can do severe damage to special wheels.

• Make sure that the recommended lug nut torque is never exceeded, or you may crack your wheels. And never use snow chains with special wheels.

• If you intend to store the wheels, lay them flat on a protective surface and cover them. Do not stack them on top of each other and do not place anything else, except a protective cover, on them.

FIG.35 Tread wear indicators; showing tread wear

FIG.36 Checking tread wear using a tread depth gauge

TREAD DEPTH

All tires made since 1968, have 7 built-in tread wear indicator bars that show up as ½ in. (13mm) wide smooth bands across the tire when 1/32 in. (0.8mm) of tread remains. The appearance of tread wear indicators means that the tires should be replaced. In fact, many states have laws prohibiting the use of tires with less than 1/32 in. (0.8mm) tread.

You can check your own tread depth with an inexpensive gauge or by using a Lincoln head penny. Slip the Lincoln penny into several tread grooves. If you can see the top of Lincoln's head in 2 adjacent grooves, the tires have less than 1/32 in. (0.8mm) tread left and should be

FIG.37 Checking tread wear using Lincoln's head on a penny as a gauge

replaced. You can measure snow tires in the same manner by using the tails side of the Lincoln penny. If you can see the top of the Lincoln memorial, it's time to replace the snow tires.

BUYING NEW TIRES

When buying new tires, give some though to the following points, especially if you are considering a switch to larger tires or a different profile series:

1. All four tires must be of the same construction type. This rule cannot be violated. Radial, bias, and bias-belted tires must not be mixed.

2. The wheels should be the correct width for the tire. Tire dealers have charts of tire and rim compatibility. A mismatch will cause sloppy handling and rapid tire wear. The tread width should match the rim width (inside bead to inside bead) within an inch. For radial tires, the rim width should be 80% or less of the tire (not tread) width.

3. The height (mounted diameter) of the new tires can change speedometer accuracy, engine speed at a given road speed, fuel mileage, acceleration, and ground clearance. Tire manufacturers furnish full measurement specifications.

4. The spare tire should be usable, at least for short distance and low speed operation, with the new tires.

5. There shouldn't be any body interference when loaded, on bumps, or in turns.

FLUIDS AND LUBRICANTS

Fuel and Engine Oil Recommendations

FUEL RECOMMENDATIONS

Gasoline

All these cars must use unleaded fuel. The use of leaded fuel will plug the catalyst rendering it imperative, and will increase the exhaust back pressure to the point where engine output will be severely reduced. The minimum octane for all engines is 87 RON. All unleaded fuels sold in the U.S. are required to meet this minimum octane rating.

Use of a fuel too low in octane (a measurement of anti-knock quality) will result in spark knock. Since many factors affect operating efficiency, such as altitude, terrain, air temperature and humidity, knocking may result even though the recommended fuel is being sued. If persistent knocking occurs, it may be necessary to switch to a slightly higher grade of unleaded gasoline. Continuous or heavy knocking may result in serious engine damage, for which the manufacturer is not responsible.

➡ **Your car's engine fuel requirement can change with time, due to carbon buildup, which changes the compression ratio. If your car's engine knocks, pings, or runs on, switch to a higher grade of fuel, if possible, and check the ignition timing. Sometimes changing brands of gasoline will cure the problem. If it is necessary to retard timing from specifications, don't change it more than a few degrees. Retarded timing will reduce power output and fuel mileage, and will increase engine temperature.**

	Anticipated Temperature Range	SAE Viscosity
Multi-grade	Above 32°F	10W—40 10W—50 20W—40 20W—50 10W—30
	May be used as low as −10°F	10W—30 10W—40
	Consistently below 10°F	5W—20 5W—30
Single-grade	Above 32°F	30
	Temperature between +32°F and −10°F	10W

FIG.38a Oil viscosity selection chart — vehicle since 1987 are designed to use 5W–30 all year

Diesel

✳✳ WARNING

Failure to use fuels specified below will result in engine damage for which the manufacturer is not responsible. Use of fuel additives is NOT recommended.

At any outside temperature above 20°F (−7°C), Number 2-D diesel fuel should be used, since it will give better fuel economy then Number 1-D. When the outside temperature is below 20°F (−7°C), use either Number 1-D fuel (preferred if available) or a blended Number 2-D. The blended Number 2-D has 1-D fuel in it, but will usually be called just Number 2-D. Check with the service station operator to be sure you get the proper fuel.

➡ **Diesel fuel may foam during filling, which is normal. The foam may cause the automatic pump nozzle to turn off before the tank is actually filled. The foaming effect can be reduced by slowing the fill rate.**

OPERATING IN COLD WEATHER

All types of diesel fuel have a certain paraffin content. The paraffin components are high in energy content and help to improve fuel economy. Below about 20°F (−7°C), the trouble with paraffin begins. At this temperature, the paraffin components begin turning to wax flakes.

Depending upon the temperature, the wax flakes can block wither or both of the two fuel filters (tank or engine) and stop fuel from reaching the engine.

Since Number 2-D fuel has more paraffin components than Number 1-D (or blended Number 2-D), Number 2-D would be more apt to cause waxing problems (See Fuel Recommendations).

If the fuel tank filter plugs due to waxing, a check valve inside of the fuel tank will open and allow fuel to flow to the engine. Because of the check valve location, not all of the fuel in the tank can be used if the filter remains clogged (check valve open). About 4 gallons of fuel will remain in the tank when you run out of fuel. When driving in temperatures below 20°F (−7°C), be sure to keep the tank more than 1/4 full to help prevent running out of fuel if the filter plugs.

If equipped, the fuel line heater should be used when temperatures are expected to be below 10°F (−12°C) and you have Number 2-D fuel in the tank.

WATER IN THE FUEL

Diesel fuel should be purchased from a reputable dealer, since the majority of the water found in a diesel fuel system gets into the system during refueling. Water can cause extensive (and expensive) damage to the diesel fuel system.

These cars have a water separator system in the fuel tank and a Water-In-Fuel indicator on the instrument panel. The indicator is designed to illuminate when starting the engine (as a bulb check), or when water is detected in the tank. If the light comes on at any other time, there is

probably a fault in the detector circuit. If the engine loses power and begins to run rough without the detector light on, there is probably water in the system. Both the fuel system and the detector circuit should be checked.

If the indicator light comes on immediately after refueling, a large amount of water was pumped into the tank — DON'T run the engine; the fuel system must be purged right away.

If the indicator lights after braking, cornering, etc., a moderate amount of water is in the system. In this case, the water should be removed within one or two days.

OIL RECOMMENDATIONS

Gasoline Engine

Under normal conditions, the engine oil and the filter should be changed at the first 7500 miles (12,000km) or once a year (1982–86 models), or every 3,000 miles (4,800km) or 3 months (1987–92 models) or whichever comes first. G.M. recommends that the oil filter be changed at every other oil change thereafter on the 1982–86 models. On 1987 and later models G.M. recommends that the oil filter be changed at every oil change. For the small price of an oil filter, it's cheap insurance to replace the filter at every oil change on the 1982–86 models as well. One of the larger filter manufacturers points out in its advertisements that not changing the filter leaves one quart of dirty oil in the engine. This claim is true and should be kept in mind when changing your oil.

Under severe conditions, such as: a) driving in dusty areas. b) trailer towing. c) frequent idling or idling for extended periods. or d) frequently driving short distances — 4 miles (6km) or so — in freezing weather, the engine oil and filter should be changed every 3 months or 3000 miles (4,800km), whichever comes first. If dust storms are ever encountered in your area, change the oil and filter as soon as possible after the storm.

The A.P.I. (American Petroleum Institute) designation (printed on the oil container) indicates the classification of engine oil for use under certain operating conditions. Oils having an A.P.I. service designation of SG should be used in your car. The SG rating designates the highest quality oil meant for passenger car usage. It is okay to use an SG oil having a combination rating such as SG/CC or SG/CD for gasoline powered engines. In addition, G.M. recommends the use of SG/Energy Conserving oil. Oils labeled, Energy Conserving (or Saving); Fuel (Gas or Gasoline) Saving, etc., are recommended due to their superior lubricating

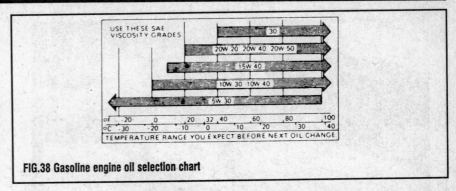

FIG.38 Gasoline engine oil selection chart

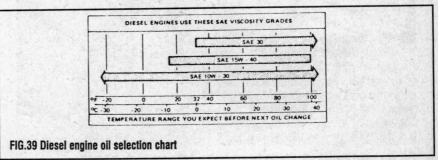

FIG.39 Diesel engine oil selection chart

qualities (less friction = easier and more efficient engine operation) and fuel saving characteristics. Use of engine oil additives is not recommended, because if the correct oil is purchased to begin with, the additives will be of no value.

➡ **Use of engine oils without an SG rating, or failing to change the oil and filter at the recommended intervals will cause excessive engine wear and could affect your warranty.**

Diesel Engines

The engine oil requirements for diesel engines are more stringent than those for gasoline engines, since contaminant build-up in the engine oil occurs much faster in the diesel engine. Also, the diesel contaminants are more damaging to the engine oil.

Under normal operating conditions, the engine oil and filter MUST be changed every 5000 miles (8,000km), regardless of the time period involved.

Under severe operating conditions, such as those mentioned previously under Gasoline Engines, the oil and filter must be changed every 2500 miles (4,000km) or 3 months, whichever comes first.

In the diesel equipped car, ONLY an engine oil having one of the two following A.P.I. designations should be used: SG/CC or SG/CD. Period! Don't use any other type of oil.

✳✳✳ CAUTION

Failure to use an SG/CC or SG/CD oil will result in excessive engine wear and will probably void the engine warranty. Failure to change the oil and filter at the recommended intervals will have the same results.

In diesel engines, the use of oil in regard to its viscosity is limited. With a diesel, you only have three choices: 10W–30, 15W–40, or straight 30W. Refer to the accompanying chart to choose the engine oil viscosity according to the expected outside air temperature.

OIL LEVEL CHECK

The engine oil level may be checked either when the engine is cold or warm, though the latter is preferred. If you check the level while the engine is cold, DO NOT start the engine first, since the cold oil won't drain back to the engine oil pan fast enough to give an accurate reading. Even when the engine is warm, wait a couple of minutes after turning it off to let the oil drain back to the pan.

1. Raise the hood, pull the dipstick out and wipe it clean.

2. Reinsert the dipstick, being sure that you push it back in completely.

FIG. 40a Insert dipstick into tube as far as possible, being careful not to bent it

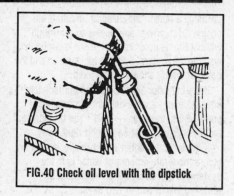

FIG.40 Check oil level with the dipstick

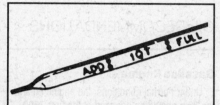

FIG.41 The oil level should be between the ADD and FULL marks on the dipstick

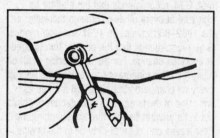

FIG.42 Loosen the drain plug and get the drain pan ready

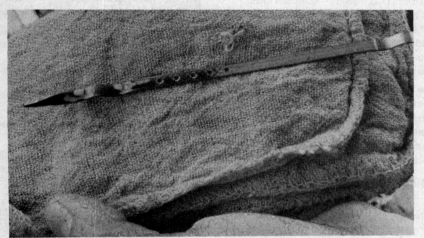

FIG. 41a Oil should appear clean and not dark in color, Dirt in oil or on dipstick are signs of needed oil change

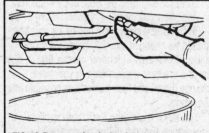

FIG.43 Remove the drain plug, be careful if the oil is hot

3. Pull the dipstick back out, hold it horizontally, and check the level at the end of the dipstick. Some dipsticks are marked with **ADD** and **FULL** lines, others with **ADD 1 QT** and **OPERATING RANGE**. In either case, the level must be above the **ADD** line. Reinsert the dipstick completely.

4. If oil must be added, it can be poured in through the rocker (valve) cover after removing the filler cap on the cover. Recheck the level a few minutes after adding oil.

5. Be sure that the dipstick and oil filler cap are installed before closing the hood.

OIL AND FILTER CHANGE

◆ SEE FIGS. 42 to 47

1. Drive the car until the engine is at normal operating temperature. A run to the parts store for oil and a filter should accomplish this. If the engine is not hot when the oil is changed, most of the acids and contaminants will remain inside the engine.

2. Shut off the engine, and slide a pan of at least six quarts capacity under the oil pan.

3. Remove the drain plug from the engine oil pan, after wiping the plug area clean. The drain plug is the bolt inserted at an angle into the lowest point of the oil pan.

4. The oil from the engine will be HOT. It will probably not be possible to hold onto the drain plug. You may have to let it fall into the pan and fish it out later. Allow all the oil to drain completely. This will take a few minutes.

FIG.44 Loosen the oil filter, move the drain pan under the filter then remove it. Take care as there is still oil in the filter.

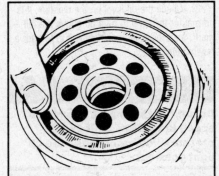

FIG.45 Wipe clean oil on the new filter seal before installing it

FIG.46 Install the new oil filter and hand tighten it.

FIG.47 Make certain the drain plug and filter are installed properly before adding the new oil

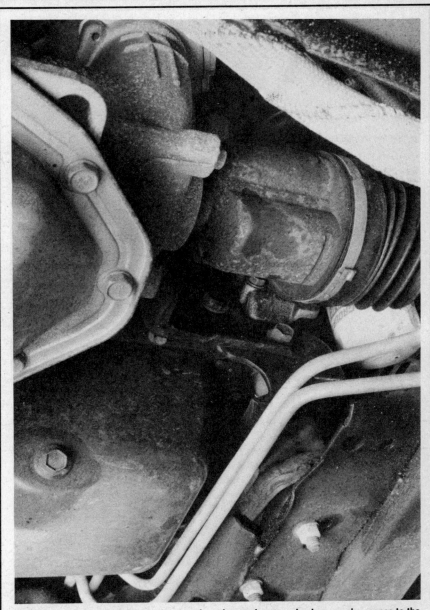

FIG. 47a Placing the vehicle on safety stands and removing one wheel may make access to the oil filter easier on some models

5. Wipe off the drain plug, removing any traces of metal particles. Check the condition of the plastic drain plug gasket. If it is cracked or distorted in any way, replace it. Reinstall the drain plug and gasket. Tighten the drain plug snugly.

6. The oil filter for the V6 gasoline engine is right up front, just behind the radiator. The four cylinder oil filter is at the back of the engine. It is impossible to reach from above, and almost as inaccessible from below. It may be easiest to remove the right front wheel and reach through the fender opening to get at the four cylinder oil filter. The oil filter of the diesel V6 engine is located on the passenger side face of the engine block. Use an oil strap wrench to loosen the oil filter; these are available at auto parts stores. It is recommended that you purchase one with as thin a strap as possible, to get into tight areas. Place the drain pan on the ground, under the filter. Unscrew and discard the old filter. It will be VERY HOT, so be careful.

7. If the oil filter is on so tightly that it collapses under pressure from the wrench, drive a long punch or a nail through it, across the diameter and as close to the base as possible, and use this as a lever to unscrew it. Make sure you are turning it counterclockwise.

FIG. 47b Make certain to add the correct type oil to the engine

8. Clean off the oil filter mounting surface with a rag. Apply a thin film of clean engine oil to the filter gasket.

9. Screw the filter on by hand until the gasket makes contact. Then tighten it by hand an additional 1/2 to 3/4 of a turn. Do not overtighten.

10. Remove the filler cap on the rocker (valve) cover, after wiping the area clean.

11. Add the correct number of quarts of oil specified in the Capacities chart. If you don't have an oil can spout, you will need a funnel. Be certain you do not overfill the engine, which can cause serious damage. Replace the cap.

12. Check the oil level on the dipstick. It is normal for the level to be a bit above the full mark. Start the engine and allow it to idle for a few minutes.

✳✳ CAUTION

Do not run the engine above idle speed until it has built up oil pressure, indicated when the oil light goes out.

Check around the filter and and drain plug for any leaks.

13. Shut off the engine, allow the oil to drain for a minute, and check the oil level.

After completing this job, you will have several quarts of oil to dispose of. The best thing to do with it is to funnel it into old plastic milk containers or bleach bottles. Then, you can locate a service station with a recycling barrel. Disposing of oil in drain systems pollutes the environment and violates federal law.

Manual Transaxle

FLUID RECOMMENDATIONS

Under normal conditions, the lubricant used in the manual transaxle does not require periodic

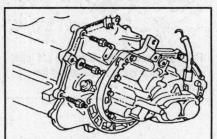

FIG.48 Some models may use a dipstick to check the manual transaxle lubricant

FIG. 47c Using a funnel, even with the newer type bottles, can help keep the engine clean by avoiding the drips and spills

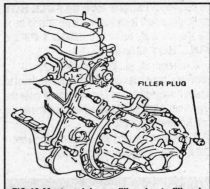

FIG.49 Most models use filler plug to fill and check the manual transaxle lubricant

changing. The fluid level in the transaxle should be checked every 12 months or 7500 miles (12,000km), whichever comes first. The manual transaxle is designed for use with Dexron®II automatic transmission. Don't use standard manual transmission lubricant in the transaxle.

LEVEL CHECK

1. Park the car on a level surface. Before proceeding, the transaxle case must be cool to the touch. Due to the expansion characteristics of the Dexron®II fluid, it will be above the level of the filler plug when the transmission is hot.

2. Slowly remove the filler plug from the driver's side of the transaxle (see the illustration). The lubricant level should be right at the bottom of the filler plug hole. If the fluid trickles out as the plug is removed, or if you can just touch the fluid through the filler plug hole, the level is correct.

3. If you cannot feel the fluid level with your finger through the filler plug hole, add Dexron®II automatic transmission through the hole until the fluid begins to trickle out of the hole.

4. When the level is correct, install the filler plug and tighten it snugly.

DRAIN AND REFILL

1. Park the car on a level surface, turn off engine and apply the parking brake.

2. Place a container of adequate capacity beneath the drain plug which is located underneath the car, on the bottom of the transaxle housing.

3. Use the proper size wrench to loosen the drain plug slowly, while maintaining a slight upward pressure, to keep the oil from leaking out around the plug.

4. Allow all of the lubricant to drain from the transaxle, then install the drain plug and gasket (if so equipped).

5. Remove the transaxle dipstick and fill the transaxle to the capacity shown in the Capacities chart. Do not overfill.

6. Check the oil level as outlined above.

Automatic Transaxle

FLUID RECOMMENDATIONS

Under normal operating conditions, the automatic transmission fluid only needs to be changed every 100,000 miles (161,000km), according to G.M. If one or more of the following driving conditions is encountered, the fluid and filter should be changed every 15,000 miles (24,100km): a) driving in heavy city traffic when the outside temperature regularly reached 90°F (32°C), b) driving regularly in hilly or mountainous areas, c)towing a trailer, or d) using the vehicle as a taxi or police car, or for delivery purposes. Remember, these are the factory recommendations, and in this case are considered to be the minimum. You must determine a change interval which fits your driving habits. If your vehicle is never subjected to these conditions, a 100,000 mile (161,000km) change interval is adequate. If you are a normal driver, a two-year/30,000 mile (48,300km) interval will be more than sufficient to maintain the long life for which your automatic transaxle was designed.

When replacing or adding fluid, use only fluid labeled Dexron®II. Use of other fluids could cause erratic shifting and transmission damage.

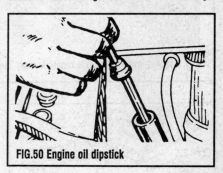

FIG.50 Engine oil dipstick

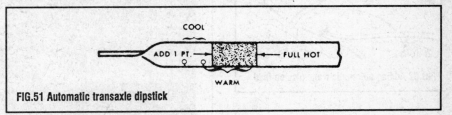

FIG.51 Automatic transaxle dipstick

FIG. 51a Automatic transaxle dipstick — 3.3L Century shown

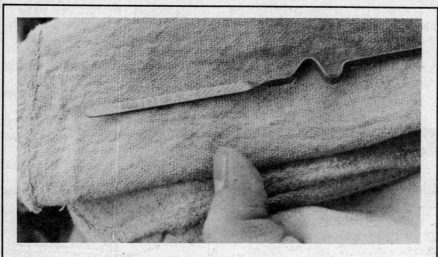

FIG. 51b Automatic transaxle dipsticks only require a pint at the add mark. Never over fill.

be between the dimples above the **FULL HOT** mark. If the fluid feels hot, the level should be in the hatched area, between the **ADD 1 PT** and **FULL HOT** marks.

8. If required, add just enough Dexron®II automatic transmission fluid to bring the level to where it should be. One pint of fluid will raise the level from **ADD** to **FULL** when the transaxle is hot. Recheck the level.

9. Reinsert the dipstick, again making sure that it is fully seated. Lower the hood.

❋ WARNING

NEVER overfill the transaxle, as fluid foaming and subsequent transaxle damage will occur!

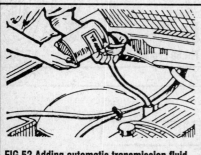

FIG.52 Adding automatic transmission fluid

LEVEL CHECK

The fluid level may be checked with the transaxle code, warm, or hot, as this is accounted for on the dipstick graduations.

➡ **If the vehicle has just been driven in extreme conditions, allow the fluid to cool for about 30 minutes.**

1. Park the car on a level surface and set the parking brake.

2. Start the engine, apply the regular brakes, and move the shift lever through all of the gear ranges, ending up in Park.

3. Let the engine idle for at least 5 minutes with the transaxle in Park.

4. The dipstick is located on the driver's side of the engine compartment, ahead of the engine.

5. Raise the hood, pull the dipstick out and wipe it off with a clean cloth.

6. Reinsert the dipstick, being sure that it is fully seated.

7. Again, remove the dipstick. Hold it horizontally and read the fluid level. Touch the fluid — if it feels cold or warm, the level should

FIG. 52a Special long neck funnels are available for adding automatic transmission fluid, they must be kept clean

DRAIN, FILTER SERVICE AND REFILL

➡ **Some transaxle use RTV sealer In place of a gasket. Do not attempt to replace the sealer with a gasket.**

1. Jack up the front of your vehicle and support it with jackstands.

2. Remove the front and side pan bolts.

3. Loosen the rear bolts about 4 turns.

4. Carefully pry the oil pan loose, allowing the fluid to drain.

5. Remove the remaining bolts, the pan, and the gasket or RTV. Discard the gasket.

6. Clean the pan with solvent and dry thoroughly, with compressed air.

7. Remove the strainer and O-ring seal.

8. Install new strainer and new O-ring seal locating the strainer against the dipstick stop.

9. Install a new gasket or RTV. Tighten the pan bolts to 12 ft. lbs. S
▶ SEE FIG. 53.

10. Lower the car. Add about 4 quarts of Dexron®II transmission fluid.

11. Start the engine; let it idle. Block the wheels and apply the parking brake.

12. Move the shift lever through the ranges.

13. With the lever in park check the fluid level. Add fluid if necessary.

➡ **Always replace the filter with a new one, don't attempt to clean the old filter. The transmission fluid currently being used may appear to be darker and have a strong odor. This is normal and not a sign of required maintenance or transmission failure.**

FIG.53 Installing a new pan gasket

Cooling System

Every 12 months or 15,000 miles (24,100km), the following services should be performed:

1. Wash and inspect the radiator cap and the filler neck.

2. Check the coolant level and the degree of freezing protection.

3. If a pressure tester is available, pressure test the system and the radiator cap.

4. Inspect the hoses of the cooling system. Expect to replace the hoses at 24 months/ 30,000 miles (48,300km).

5. Check the fins of the radiator (or air conditioning condenser, if equipped as such) for blockage.

RADIATOR CAP

Before removing the cap. squeeze the upper radiator hose. If it compresses easily (indicating little or no pressure in the system), the cap may be removed by turning it counterclockwise until it reaches the stop. If any hissing is noted at this point (indicating the release of pressure), wait until the hissing stops before you remove the cap. To completely remove the cap, press downward and turn it counterclockwise.

✳✳ CAUTION

To avoid personal Injury, DO NOT ATTEMPT to remove the radiator cap while the engine is hot.

If the upper radiator hose is hard, pressure is indicated within the system. In this case, a greater degree of caution should be used in removing the cap. Cover the radiator cap with a thick cloth, and while wearing a heavy glove, carefully turn the cap to the stop. This will allow the pressure to be relieved from the system.

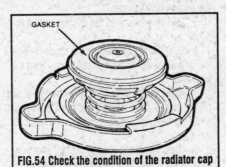

FIG.54 Check the condition of the radiator cap and gaskets

After the hissing stops, completely remove the cap (press and turn counterclockwise).

Check the condition of the radiator cap gasket and the seal inside of the cap. The radiator cap is designed to seal the cooling system under normal operating conditions which allows the system to build-up a certain amount of pressure (this pressure rating is stamped or printed on the cap). The pressure in the system raises the boiling point of the coolant to help prevent overheating. If the radiator cap does not seal, the boiling point of the coolant is lowered and overheating will occur. If the cap must be replaced, purchase the new cap according to the pressure rating which is specified for your vehicle.

Prior to installing the cap, inspect and clean the radiator filler neck. If you are reusing the old cap, clean it thoroughly with clear water. After turning the cap on, make sure that the arrows on the cap align with the overflow hose.

FLUID RECOMMENDATIONS

The coolant used in any General Motors engine must:

a. Be a high quality ethylene glycol-based solution. Do not use alcohol or methanol-based solutions at any time.

b. Have built-in rust inhibitors.

c. Be designed for year-round use.

d. Offer complete protection for a minimum of 1 years/30,000 miles (48,300km), without replacement, as long as the proper concentration is maintained.

e. Meet G.M. Specification 1825-M (as specified on the container). This point is critical for diesel engines; coolant meeting other specifications could result in cooling system damage and engine damage due to overheating.

f. Be mixed in the proper proportions: 50% coolant/50% water for gasoline engines; 64% Coolant/36% water for diesel engines.

➡ **On diesels, this proportion can be accurately attained only when refilling the system entirely. See Draining and Refilling.**

The use of self-sealing coolants is not recommended. Also, the use of a coolant meeting the above requirements negates the need for supplemental additives. Use of such supplemental products is an unnecessary expense and may cause less than optimum cooling system performance.

LEVEL AND CONDITION CHECK

Any time the hood is raised, check the level of the coolant in the see-through plastic coolant recovery tank. With the engine cold, the coolant level should be near the **ADD** mark on the tank. At normal engine operating temperature, the level should be at the **FULL** mark on the bottle. If coolant must be added to the tank, use a 50/50 mix of coolant/water to adjust the fluid level on models with gasoline engines. On models with diesel engines, use straight, undiluted coolant to adjust the level in the tank.

An inexpensive tester may be purchased to test the freezing protection of the coolant. Follow the instructions provided with the tester. The coolant used in models with gasoline engines should protect to –37°F (–38°C); diesels must have protection to –75°F (–59°C).

DRAINING AND REFILLING

At least every 2 years or 30,000 miles (48,300km) — whichever comes first — the

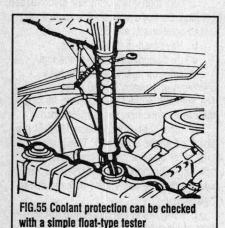

FIG.55 Coolant protection can be checked with a simple float-type tester

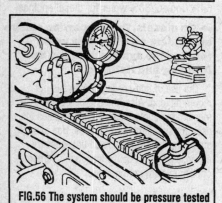

FIG.56 The system should be pressure tested at least once a year

cooling system should be completely drained and refilled with the proper mixture of coolant and water. Many mechanics recommend that this be done once a year for extra protection against corrosion and subsequent overheating.

Though most coolants are labeled permanent, this only means that the coolant will retain its anti-freezing characteristics. The required rust inhibitors and other chemicals which were added to the coolant during its manufacture will become less effective over a period of time. The following procedure covers the factory recommended procedure for draining and refilling the system.

➡ **If you are only replacing the hoses, perform steps 1–3, and 11–16 as required.**

1. Remove the radiator cap.
2. Raise the front of the vehicle and support it safely with jackstands.
3. Open the radiator fitting (located at the bottom of the radiator) by turning it counterclockwise. It may be wise to coat the fitting with penetrating lubricant before you attempt to turn it. Allow the coolant to drain from the radiator.

❄ CAUTION

When draining the coolant, keep in mind that cats and dogs are attracted by the ethylene glycol antifreeze, and are quite likely to drink any that is left in an uncovered container or in puddles on the ground. This will prove fatal in sufficient quantity. Always drain the coolant into a sealable container. Coolant should be reused unless it is contaminated or several years old.

4. Remove the drain plug(s) from the engine block (located on the engine block, above the engine oil pan) and allow the coolant to drain.
5. Close the radiator drain fitting and reinstall the engine block plugs.
6. Add clear water to the system until it is filled.
7. Start the engine and repeat steps 3–6 until the drained water is almost colorless. Turn the engine OFF.
8. Allow the system to drain completely and repeat step 5. Remove the cap from the coolant recovery tank, leaving the hoses connected to the cap.
9. Unbolt and remove the coolant recovery tank, drain it, and flush it with clear water. Reinstall the tank.

10. Fill the radiator to the base of the radiator filler neck with a 50/50 mixture of coolant/water. Remember, on diesel equipped models, add a gallon of undiluted coolant first, then add the 50/50 solution.

➡ **If only the radiator was drained, use a 50/50 solution to refill it, then check the freezing protection after the level stabilizes.**

11. Fill the coolant recovery tank to the **FULL** mark with the 50/50 solution.
12. With the radiator cap still removed, start the engine and allow it to idle until the upper radiator hose becomes hot, indicating that the thermostat has opened.
13. With the engine still idling, fill the radiator to the base of the filler neck with the 50/50 solution.
14. Install the radiator cap, being sure to align the arrows on the cap with the overflow tube.
15. Turn the engine Off, check for leakage, and double check that the radiator drain is closed and the drain plug(s) is tighten.

CLEAN RADIATOR OF DEBRIS

Periodically clean any debris — leaves, paper, insects, etc. — from the radiator fins. Pick the large pieces off by hand. The smaller pieces can be washed away with water pressure from a hose.

Carefully straighten any bent radiator fins with a pair of needle nose pliers. Be careful — the fins are very soft. Don't wiggle the fins back and forth too much. Straighten them once and try not to move them again.

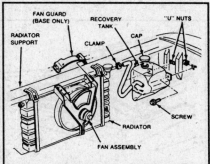

FIG.57 The coolant recovery tank is at the side of the radiator

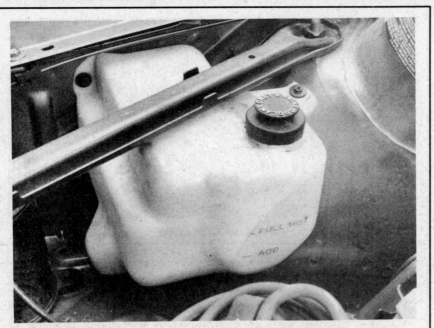

FIG. 57a Fill the coolant system recovery tank to between the add and full hot marks with a mixture of anti-freeze and water

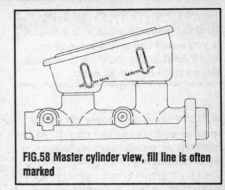

FIG.58 Master cylinder view, fill line is often marked

2. Wipe off the master cylinder cover before you remove it, to prevent contaminating the fluid with dirt.

➡ **On most models, a see-through reservoir is used, eliminating the need of removing the cylinder cover.**

3. The cover is snapped into place on the master cylinder. To remove the cover, just press up on the two tabs on the side of the cover, tilt it, then remove it. Be careful not to damage the rubber seal under the cover.

FLUSHING AND CLEANING THE SYSTEM

Several aftermarket radiator flushing and cleaning kits can be purchased at your local auto parts store. It is recommended that the radiator be cleaned and flushed of sludge and any rust build-up once a year. Manufacturers directions for proper use, and safety precautions, come in each kit.

Master Cylinder

FLUID RECOMMENDATIONS

Only extra-heavy duty fluid meeting DOT 3 specifications must be used. Using an inferior fluid will result in component damage and reduced braking capabilities.

LEVEL CHECK

About once a month, the fluid level in the master cylinder should be checked.

1. Park the car on a level surface, turn it off and raise the hood.

FIG. 58a Before removing the cap to the master cylinder clean the area so no dirt can fall into the fluid

❊❊ CAUTION

If you value the paint on your car, don't spill brake fluid on the finish. Brake fluid destroys paint.

➡ **Don't leave the cover off of the master cylinder or the cap off of the brake fluid container any longer than necessary.**

4. The fluid level in each master cylinder reservoir should be 1/4 in. (6mm) below the lowest edge of the filler opening. Use fresh brake fluid to adjust the level if necessary.

It is normal for the master cylinder fluid level to drop as the brake linings wear — 1/8 in. (3mm) drop about every 10,000 miles (16,100km). If the fluid level is constantly low, the system should be checked for leaks.

5. Carefully seat the cover seal into the cover, then snap the cover into place on the master cylinder. Be sure that all four snaps latch completely.

Power Steering Pump

FLUID RECOMMENDATIONS

When adding power steering fluid use G.M. part #1050017 or its equal. Dexron®II automatic transmission fluid is an acceptable substitute.

FIG. 59a The power steering fluid cap has a built in dipstick

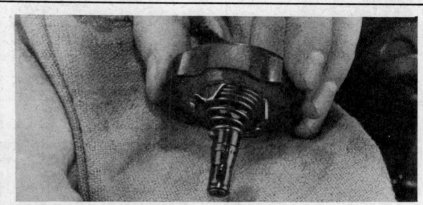

FIG. 59b Proper level for power steering fluid is between the lines on the dipstick. Always check the power steering fluid warm

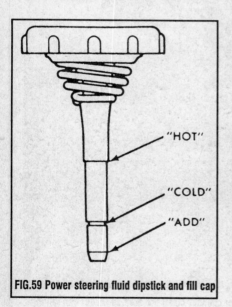

FIG.59 Power steering fluid dipstick and fill cap

"HOT"

"COLD"

"ADD"

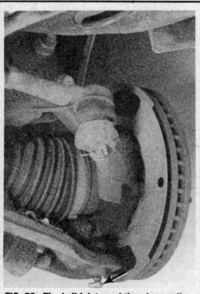

FIG. 59c The ball joints and tierods usually have grease fittings

LEVEL CHECK

The power steering fluid level should be checked at every oil change. On models with gasoline engines, the power steering pump and reservoir are integrated into one unit bolted to the front of the engine. On models with diesel engines, the pump is mounted on the engine, and a separate, translucent reservoir is attached to the firewall in the engine compartment.

To check the fluid level, run the engine until it reaches normal operating temperature, then turn the engine off. Remove the reservoir filler cap and check the oil level on the dipstick. The fluid level must be between the HOT and COLD marks on the filler cap indicator. Add power steering fluid as required then reinstall the cap.

Steering Gear

FLUID RECOMMENDATIONS AND LEVEL CHECK

All models use integral rack and pinion power steering. The power steering pump delivers hydraulic pressure through two hoses to the steering gear itself. Refer to the power steering pump fluid recommendation and level check procedures above to check the steering gear fluid level.

Chassis Greasing

Front Suspension and Steering Linkage

These parts should be greased every 12 months or 7,500 miles (12,000km) with an EP grease meeting G.M. specification 6031M.

If you choose to do this job yourself, you will need to purchase a hand operated grease gun, if you do not own one already, and a long flexible extension hose to reach the various grease fittings. You will also need a cartridge of the appropriate grease.

Press the fitting of the grease gun hose onto the grease fitting of the suspension or steering linkage component. Pump a few shots of grease into the fitting, until the rubber boot on the joint begins to expand, indicating that the joint is full. Remove the gun from the fitting. Be careful not to overfill the joints, which will rupture the rubber boots, allowing the entry of dirt. You can keep the grease fittings clean by covering them with a small square of tin foil.

Transaxle Shift Linkage

Lubricate the manual transaxle shift linkage contact points with the EP grease used for chassis greasing, which should meet G.M. specification 6031M. The automatic transaxle linkage should be lubricated with clean engine oil.

Body Lubrication

Clean the latch surfaces and apply clean engine oil to the latch pilot bolts and the spring anchor. Use the engine oil to lubricate the hood hinges as well. Use a chassis grease to lubricate all the pivot points in the latch release mechanism.

DOOR HINGES

The gas tank filler door, car door, and rear hatch or trunk lid hinges should be wiped clean and lubricated with clean engine oil. Silicone spray also works well on these parts, but must be applied more often. Use engine oil to lubricate the trunk or hatch lock mechanism and the lock bolt and striker. The door lock cylinders can be lubricated easily with a shot of silicone spray or one of the many dry penetrating lubricants commercially available.

PARKING BRAKE LINKAGE

Use chassis grease on the parking brake cable where is contacts the guides, links, levers, and pulleys. The grease should be a water resistant one for durability under the car.

ACCELERATOR LINKAGE

Lubricate the carburetor stud, carburetor lever, and the accelerator pedal lever at the support inside the car with clean engine oil.

Rear Wheel Bearings

The bearing assembly used on these vehicles doesn't need normal grease service, the following procedures can be used if a problem with the rear bearing assembly is suspected.

REMOVAL & INSTALLATION

1. Raise and support the car on a hoist.
2. Remove the wheel and brake drum.

✳✳ CAUTION

Do not hammer on the brake drum as damage to the bearing could result.

3. Remove the hub and bearing assembly to rear axle attaching bolts and remove the rear axle.

➡ **The bolts which attach the hub and bearing assembly also support the brake assembly. When removing these bolts, support the brake assembly with a wire or other means. Do not let the brake line support the brake assembly.**

4. Install the hub and bearing assembly to the rear axle and torque the hub and bearing bolts to 45 ft. lbs.
5. Install the brake drum, tire and wheel assembly and lower the car.

ADJUSTMENT

There is no necessary adjustment to the rear wheel bearing and hub assembly.

TRAILER TOWING

Your car is designed and intended to be used mainly to carry people. Towing a trailer will affect handling, durability and economy.

Your safety and satisfaction depend upon proper use and correct equipment. You should also avoid overloads and other abusive use.

Information on trailer towing ability, special equipment required and optional equipment available should be obtained from your dealer.

PUSHING AND TOWING

DO NOT attempt to start your car by pushing or towing as damage to the catalytic convertor or other components may result. If the battery is weak, the vehicle may be jump started, using the procedure found after this section.

As long as the driveline and steering are normally operable, your car may be towed on all four wheels. If this is done, don't exceed 35 mph or travel further than 50 miles (80km). The steering wheel must be unlocked, the transaxle in Neutral, and the parking brake released. Never attach towing equipment to the bumpers or bumper brackets — the equipment must be attached to the main structural members of the car.

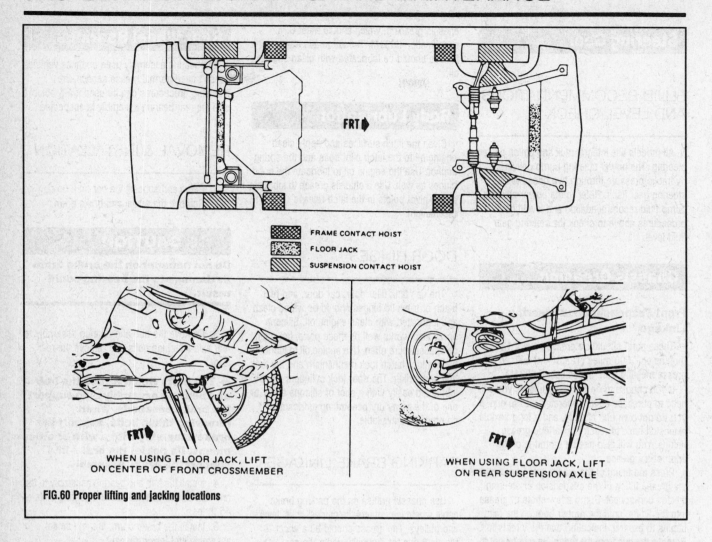

FRAME CONTACT HOIST
FLOOR JACK
SUSPENSION CONTACT HOIST

WHEN USING FLOOR JACK, LIFT
ON CENTER OF FRONT CROSSMEMBER

WHEN USING FLOOR JACK, LIFT
ON REAR SUSPENSION AXLE

FIG.60 Proper lifting and jacking locations

➡ **Remember that there will be no power assist for brakes and steering with the engine Off. Also, be sure to check into state and local towing laws before flat-towing your vehicle.**

If the car is to be towed by a wrecker, instructions supplied by the wrecker manufacturer should be followed. Because of the front wheel drive, towing on the rear wheels is preferred. If absolutely necessary, the car may be towed on the front wheels as long as the speed does not exceed 25 mph and the towing distance does not exceed 10 miles (16km).

✳✳ CAUTION

Don't exceed the speed or distance limits which are outlined here. Severe transaxle damage could result.

JACKING

Precautions

•NEVER use the jack supplied with the vehicle for anything but changing tire and wheel assemblies.

•NEVER crawl underneath the vehicle while it is supported by the factory supplied jack.

•NEVER start or run the engine while the car is supported by only a jack.

•ALWAYS secure the spare tire, jack, etc., to prevent loose parts from causing personal injury during hard braking.

Instructions (Factory supplied Jack Only)

Please refer to the accompanying illustrations for detailed jacking instructions and spare tire/jack stowage instructions.

The accompanying illustrations depict the preferred jacking and jack stand support points underneath the vehicle. When using a floor jack, either the center of the engine cradle crossmember or the center of the rear axle bar can be used as jacking points in addition to the previous hoisting points.

FIG. 61 The proper lifting location for front of car

FIG. 62 The proper lifting location for rear of car

FIG. 63 The proper safety stand location for the front of car. Be careful take stand doesn't touch painted body panel

FIG. 64 The proper safety stand location for the rear of car. Be careful take stand doesn't touch painted body panel

PREVENTIVE MAINTENANCE CHART

Item No.	To Be Serviced	When to Perform Miles or Months, Whichever Occurs First Miles (000)	The services shown in this schedule up to 60,000 miles are to be performed after 60,000 miles at the same intervals							
			7.5	15	22.5	30	37.5	45	52.5	60
1	Engine Oil Change	Every 7,500 Miles or 12 Months	•	•	•	•	•	•	•	•
	Oil Filter Change	At First and Every Other Oil Change or 12 Months	•		•		•		•	
2	Chassis Lubrication	Every oil change	•	•	•	•	•	•	•	•
3	Carburetor Choke and Hoses Inspection	At 6 Months or 7,500 Miles and at 60,000 Miles	•		•					•
4	Carburetor or T.B.I. Mounting Bolt Torque Check	At 6 Months or 7,500 Miles and at 60,000 Miles	•							•
5	Engine Idle Speed Adjustment	At 6 Months or 7,500 Miles and at 60,000 Miles	•							•
6	Engine Accessory Drive Belts Inspection	Every 24 Months or 30,000 Miles				•				•
7	Cooling System Service	Every 24 Months or 30,000 Miles				•				•
8	Front Wheel Bearing Repack	Every 30,000 Miles				•				•
9	Transmission Service	30,000 Miles				•				•
10	Vacuum Advance System Inspection	Check at 6 Months or 7,500 Miles, then at 30,000 Miles, and then at 15,000 Mile intervals.	•			•		•		•
11	Spark Plugs and Wire Service	Every 30,000 Miles				•				•
12	PCV System Inspection	Every 30,000 Miles				•				•
13	ERG System Check	Every 30,000 Miles				•				•
14	Air Cleaner and PCV Filter Replacement	Every 30,000 Miles				•				•
15	Engine Timing Check	Every 30,000 Miles				•				•
16	Fuel Tank, Cap and Lines Inspection	Every 24 Months or 30,000 Miles				•				•
17	Early Fuel Evaporation System Inspection	At 7,500 Miles and at 30,000 Miles then at 30,000 Mile intervals.	•			•				•
18	Evaporative Control System Inspection	Every 30,000 Miles				•				•
19	Fuel Filter Replacement	Every 30,000 Miles				•				•
20	Valve Lash Adjustment	Every 15,000 Miles		•		•		•		•
21	Thermostatically Controlled Air Cleaner Inspection	Every 30,000 Miles				•				•

CAPACITIES

Year	Model	Engine VIN	Engine Displacement cu. in. (liter)	Engine Crankcase with filter	Transmission (pts.)			Fuel Tank (gals.)	Cooling System (qts.)
					4	5	Auto.		
1982	Celebrity	R	151 (2.5)	3.5	—	—	10①	16.0	9.6
	Celebrity	X	173 (2.8)	4.5	—	—	10①	16.0	12.5
	Celebrity	T	260 (4.3)	6.5	—	—	10	16.0	13.1
	Century	R	151 (2.5)	3.5	6	6	8①	15.7	9.7②
	Century	X	173 (2.8)	4.5	—	—	10①	16.0	12.5
	Cutlass Ciera	R	151 (2.5)	3.5	6	6	8①	15.7	9.5
	Cutlass Ciera	X	173 (2.8)	4.5	6	6	8①	16.5	11.7
	6000	R	151 (2.5)	3.5	6	—	8①	15.7	9.4
	6000	X	173 (2.8)	4.5	6	—	8①	16.4	11.3
1983	Celebrity	R	151 (2.5)	3.5	—	—	10①	16.0	9.6
	Celebrity	5	151 (2.5)	3.5	—	—	10①	16.0	9.6
	Celebrity	X	173 (2.8)	4.5	—	—	10①	16.0	12.5
	Celebrity	T	260 (4.3)	6.5	—	—	10①	16.0	13.1
	Century	R	151 (2.5)	3.5	6	6	8①	15.7	9.7②
	Century	X	173 (2.8)	4.5	—	—	10①	16.0	12.5
	Century	E	183 (3.0)	4.5	6	6	8①	15.7	13.1
	Century	T	260 (4.3)	6.5	—	—	8①	16.4	12.6
	Cutlass Ciera	R	151 (2.5)	3.5	6	6	8①	15.7	9.5
	Cutlass Ciera	X	173 (2.8)	4.5	6	6	8①	16.5	11.7
	Cutlass Ciera	E	183 (3.0)	4.5	6	6	8①	15.7	12.5
	Cutlass Ciera	T	260 (4.3)	6.5	—	—	8①	16.5	13.2
	6000	R	151 (2.5)	3.5	6	—	8①	15.7	9.4
	6000	X	173 (2.8)	4.5	6	—	8①	16.4	11.3
	6000	T	260 (4.3)	6.5	—	—	8①	16.5	13.2
1984	Celebrity	R	151 (2.5)	3.5	—	—	10	16.0	9.6
	Celebrity	5	151 (2.5)	3.5	—	—	10	16.0	9.6
	Celebrity	X	173 (2.8)	4.5	—	—	10	16.0	12.5
	Celebrity	T	260 (4.3)	6.5	—	—	10	16.0	13.1
	Century	R	151 (2.5)	3.5	6	6	8①	15.7	9.7②
	Century	X	173 (2.8)	4.5	—	—	10	16.4	12.5
	Century	E	183 (3.0)	4.5	6	6	8①	15.7	13.1
	Century	3	231 (3.8)	4.5	6	6	8①	16.6③	12.6
	Century	T	260 (4.3)	6.5	—	—	8①	16.4	12.6
	Cutlass Ciera	R	151 (2.5)	3.5	6	6	①	15.7	9.5
	Cutlass Ciera	3	231 (3.8)	4.5	6	6	①	15.7	12.8
	Cutlass Ciera	E	183 (3.0)	4.5	6	6	①	15.7	12.8
	Cutlass Ciera	T	260 (4.3)	6.5	—	—	①	16.6	12.8
	6000	R	151 (2.5)	3.5	6	—	8①	15.7	9.4
	6000	X	173 (2.8)	4.5	6	—	8①	16.4	11.3
	6000	Z	173 (2.8)	4.5	6	—	8①	16.4	11.3
	6000	T	260 (4.3)	6.5	—	—	①	16.5	13.2

CAPACITIES

Year	Model	Engine VIN	Engine Displacement cu. in. (liter)	Engine Crankcase with filter	Transmission (pts.)			Fuel Tank (gals.)	Cooling System (qts.)
					4	5	Auto.		
1985	Celebrity	R	151 (2.5)	3.5	6	—	①	15.7	9.7
	Celebrity	X	173 (2.8)	4.5	6	—	①	16.4	12.6
	Celebrity	W	173 (2.8)	4.5	6	—	①	15.7	12.6
	Celebrity	T	260 (4.3)	6.5	—	—	①	16.6	13.1
	Century	R	151 (2.5)	3.5	6	6	①	15.7	9.7②
	Century	E	183 (3.0)	4.5	6	6	①	15.7	13.1
	Century	3	231 (3.8)	4.5	6	6	①	16.6	12.6
	Century	T	260 (4.3)	6.5	—	—	①	16.4	12.6
	Cutlass Ciera	R	151 (2.5)	3.5	6	6	①	15.7	9.5
	Cutlass Ciera	3	231 (3.8)	4.5	6	6	①	15.7	12.8
	Cutlass Ciera	E	183 (3.0)	4.5	6	6	①	15.7	12.8
	Cutlass Ciera	T	260 (4.3)	6.5	—	—	①	16.6	12.8
	6000	R	151 (2.5)	3.5	6	—	①	15.7	9.4
	6000	X	173 (2.8)	4.5	6	—	①	16.4	11.3
	6000	Z	173 (2.8)	4.5	6	—	①	16.4	11.3
	6000	T	260 (4.3)	6.5	—	—	①	16.5	13.2
1986	Celebrity	R	151 (2.5)	3.5	6	—	①	15.7	9.6
	Celebrity	X	173 (2.8)	4.5	6	—	①	16.4	12.6
	Celebrity	W	173 (2.8)	4.5	6	—	①	15.7③	12.6
	Century	R	151 (2.5)	3.5	6	6	①	16.6③	9.7
	Century	X	173 (2.8)	4.5	6	6	①	16.6③	11.8
	Century	3	231 (3.8)	4.5	6	6	①	16.6③	12.6
	Cutlass Ciera	R	151 (2.5)	3.5	6	6	①	15.7	9.7
	Cutlass Ciera	X	173 (2.8)	4.5	6	6	①	16.4	12.7
	Cutlass Ciera	W	173 (2.8)	4.5	6	6	①	15.7	12.7
	Cutlass Ciera	3	231 (3.8)	4.5	6	6	①	15.7	12.7
	Cutlass Ciera	B	231 (3.8)	4.5	6	6	①	15.7	12.7
	6000	R	151 (2.5)	3.5	—	—	①	15.7	9.7
	6000	X	173 (2.8)	4.5	—	—	①	16.4	12.7
	6000	W	173 (2.8)	4.5	—	—	①	16.4	12.7
1987	Celebrity	R	151 (2.5)	3.5	6	—	①	15.7	9.6
	Celebrity	W	173 (2.8)	4.5	6	—	①	15.7	12.6
	Century	R	151 (2.5)	3.5	—	—	①	15.5	9.7②
	Century	W	173 (2.8)	4.0	—	—	①	15.5	12.5
	Century	3	231 (3.8)	4.5	—	—	①	15.5	12.6
	Cutlass Ciera	R	151 (2.5)	3.5	6	6	①	15.7	12.0
	Cutlass Ciera	W	173 (2.8)	4.5	6	6	①	15.7	13.5
	Cutlass Ciera	3	231 (3.8)	4.5	6	6	①	15.7	12.7
	6000	R	151 (2.5)	3.5	—	4	①	15.7	9.7②
	6000	W	173 (2.8)	4.5	—	4	①	16.4	12.9

CAPACITIES

Year	Model	Engine VIN	Engine Displacement cu. in. (liter)	Engine Crankcase with filter	Transmission (pts.) 4	5	Auto.	Fuel Tank (gals.)	Cooling System (qts.)
1988	Celebrity	R	151 (2.5)	3.5	—	4	①	15.7	9.7②
	Celebrity	W	173 (2.8)	4.0	—	4	①	15.7	13.5
	Century	R	151 (2.5)	3.5	—	—	①	15.7	9.7②
	Century	W	173 (2.8)	4.5	—	—	①	15.7	13.5
	Century	3	231 (3.8)	4.5	—	—	①	15.7	12.7
	Cutlass Ciera	R	151 (2.5)	3.5	6	6	①	15.7	12.0
	Cutlass Ciera	W	173 (2.8)	4.5	6	6	①	15.7	13.5
	Cutlass Ciera	3	231 (3.8)	4.5	6	6	①	15.7	12.7
	6000	R	151 (2.5)	4.5	—	—	①	15.7	9.7②
	6000	W	173 (2.8)	4.5	—	—	①	15.7	13.5
1989	Celebrity	R	151 (2.5)	4.5	—	—	①	15.7	9.7
	Celebrity	W	173 (2.8)	4.5	—	—	①	15.7	13.2
	Century	R	151 (2.5)	4.5	—	—	①	15.7	9.7
	Century	W	173 (2.8)	4.5	—	—	①	15.7	13.2
	Century	N	204 (3.3)	4.5	—	—	①	15.7	15.7
	Cutlass Ciera	R	151 (2.5)	4.5	—	—	①	15.7	9.7
	Cutlass Ciera	W	173 (2.8)	4.5	—	—	①	15.7	13.2
	Cutlass Ciera	N	204 (3.3)	4.5	—	—	①	15.7	12.7
	6000	R	151 (2.5)	4.5	—	—	①	15.7	9.7
	6000	W	173 (2.8)	4.5	—	—	①	15.7	13.2
	6000	T	192 (3.1)	4.5	—	—	①	15.7	12.6
1990	Celebrity	R	151 (2.5)	4.5	—	—	①	15.7	9.7
	Celebrity	T	192 (3.1)	4.5	—	—	①	15.7	12.8
	Century	R	151 (2.5)	4.5	—	—	①	15.7	9.7
	Century	N	204 (3.3)	4.5	—	—	①	15.7	15.7
	Cutlass	R	151 (2.5)	4.5	—	—	①	15.7	9.7
	Cutlass	N	204 (3.3)	4.5	—	—	①	15.7	13.2
	6000	R	151 (2.5)	4.5	—	—	①	15.7	9.7
	6000	T	192 (3.1)	4.5	—	—	①	15.7	12.6
1991	Century	R	151 (2.5)	4.5	—	—	①	15.7	9.7
	Century	N	204 (3.3)	4.5	—	—	①	15.7	15.7
	Cutlass	R	151 (2.5)	4.5	—	—	①	15.7	9.7
	Cutlass	N	204 (3.3)	4.5	—	—	①	15.7	13.2
	6000	R	151 (2.5)	4.5	—	—	①	15.7	9.7
	6000	T	192 (3.1)	4.5	—	—	①	15.7	12.6
1992	Century	R	151 (2.5)	4.5	—	—	①	15.7	9.7
	Century	N	204 (3.3)	4.5	—	—	①	15.7	15.7
	Cutlass	R	151 (2.5)	4.5	—	—	①	15.7	9.7
	Cutlass	N	204 (3.3)	4.5	—	—	①	15.7	13.2
	6000	R	151 (2.5)	4.5	—	—	①	15.7	9.7
	6000	T	192 (3.1)	4.5	—	—	①	15.7	12.6

① 125C 8pts—Overhaul 12pts;
   440T4—13pts—Overhaul 20pts.
② 12 qts. with heavy duty system
③ Wagon 15.7 gals.

Troubleshooting Basic Air Conditioning Problems

Problem	Cause	Solution
There's little or no air coming from the vents (and you're sure it's on)	• The A/C fuse is blown • Broken or loose wires or connections • The on/off switch is defective	• Check and/or replace fuse • Check and/or repair connections • Replace switch
The air coming from the vents is not cool enough	• Windows and air vent wings open • The compressor belt is slipping • Heater is on • Condenser is clogged with debris • Refrigerant has escaped through a leak in the system • Receiver/drier is plugged	• Close windows and vent wings • Tighten or replace compressor belt • Shut heater off • Clean the condenser • Check system • Service system
The air has an odor	• Vacuum system is disrupted • Odor producing substances on the evaporator case • Condensation has collected in the bottom of the evaporator housing	• Have the system checked/repaired • Clean the evaporator case • Clean the evaporator housing drains
System is noisy or vibrating	• Compressor belt or mountings loose • Air in the system	• Tighten or replace belt; tighten mounting bolts • Have the system serviced

Sight glass condition
  Constant bubbles, foam or oil streaks
  Clear sight glass, but no cold air
  Clear sight glass, but air is cold
  Clouded with milky fluid
	• Undercharged system
	
	• No refrigerant at all
	• System is OK
	• Receiver drier is leaking dessicant
		• Charge the system
		
		• Check and charge the system
		
		• Have system checked

Large difference in temperature of lines	• System undercharged	• Charge and leak test the system
Compressor noise	• Broken valves • Overcharged • Incorrect oil level • Piston slap • Broken rings • Drive belt pulley bolts are loose	• Replace the valve plate • Discharge, evacuate and install the correct charge • Isolate the compressor and check the oil level. Correct as necessary. • Replace the compressor • Replace the compressor • Tighten with the correct torque specification
Excessive vibration	• Incorrect belt tension • Clutch loose • Overcharged • Pulley is misaligned	• Adjust the belt tension • Tighten the clutch • Discharge, evacuate and install the correct charge • Align the pulley
Condensation dripping in the passenger compartment	• Drain hose plugged or improperly positioned • Insulation removed or improperly installed	• Clean the drain hose and check for proper installation • Replace the insulation on the expansion valve and hoses

Troubleshooting Basic Air Conditioning Problems (cont.)

Problem	Cause	Solution
Frozen evaporator coil	• Faulty thermostat • Thermostat capillary tube improperly installed • Thermostat not adjusted properly	• Replace the thermostat • Install the capillary tube correctly • Adjust the thermostat
Low side low—high side low	• System refrigerant is low • Expansion valve is restricted	• Evacuate, leak test and charge the system • Replace the expansion valve
Low side high—high side low	• Internal leak in the compressor—worn	• Remove the compressor cylinder head and inspect the compressor. Replace the valve plate assembly if necessary. If the compressor pistons, rings or
Low side high—high side low (cont.)	• Cylinder head gasket is leaking • Expansion valve is defective • Drive belt slipping	cylinders are excessively worn or scored replace the compressor • Install a replacement cylinder head gasket • Replace the expansion valve • Adjust the belt tension
Low side high—high side high	• Condenser fins obstructed • Air in the system • Expansion valve is defective • Loose or worn fan belts	• Clean the condenser fins • Evacuate, leak test and charge the system • Replace the expansion valve • Adjust or replace the belts as necessary
Low side low—high side high	• Expansion valve is defective • Restriction in the refrigerant hose	• Replace the expansion valve • Check the hose for kinks—replace if necessary
Low side low—high side high	• Restriction in the receiver/drier • Restriction in the condenser	• Replace the receiver/drier • Replace the condenser
Low side and high normal (inadequate cooling)	• Air in the system • Moisture in the system	• Evacuate, leak test and charge the system • Evacuate, leak test and charge the system

Troubleshooting Basic Wheel Problems

Problem	Cause	Solution
The car's front end vibrates at high speed	• The wheels are out of balance • Wheels are out of alignment	• Have wheels balanced • Have wheel alignment checked/adjusted
Car pulls to either side	• Wheels are out of alignment • Unequal tire pressure • Different size tires or wheels	• Have wheel alignment checked/adjusted • Check/adjust tire pressure • Change tires or wheels to same size
The car's wheel(s) wobbles	• Loose wheel lug nuts • Wheels out of balance • Damaged wheel • Wheels are out of alignment • Worn or damaged ball joint • Excessive play in the steering linkage (usually due to worn parts) • Defective shock absorber	• Tighten wheel lug nuts • Have tires balanced • Raise car and spin the wheel. If the wheel is bent, it should be replaced • Have wheel alignment checked/adjusted • Check ball joints • Check steering linkage • Check shock absorbers
Tires wear unevenly or prematurely	• Incorrect wheel size • Wheels are out of balance • Wheels are out of alignment	• Check if wheel and tire size are compatible • Have wheels balanced • Have wheel alignment checked/adjusted

Troubleshooting Basic Tire Problems

Problem	Cause	Solution
The car's front end vibrates at high speeds and the steering wheel shakes	• Wheels out of balance • Front end needs aligning	• Have wheels balanced • Have front end alignment checked
The car pulls to one side while cruising	• Unequal tire pressure (car will usually pull to the low side) • Mismatched tires • Front end needs aligning	• Check/adjust tire pressure • Be sure tires are of the same type and size • Have front end alignment checked
Abnormal, excessive or uneven tire wear See "How to Read Tire Wear"	• Infrequent tire rotation • Improper tire pressure • Sudden stops/starts or high speed on curves	• Rotate tires more frequently to equalize wear • Check/adjust pressure • Correct driving habits
Tire squeals	• Improper tire pressure • Front end needs aligning	• Check/adjust tire pressure • Have front end alignment checked

Tire Size Comparison Chart

"Letter" sizes			Inch Sizes	Metric-inch Sizes		
"60 Series"	"70 Series"	"78 Series"	1965–77	"60 Series"	"70 Series"	"80 Series"
		Y78-12	5.50-12, 5.60-12 6.00-12	165/60-12	165/70-12	155-12
		W78-13	5.20-13	165/60-13	145/70-13	135-13
		Y78-13	5.60-13	175/60-13	155/70-13	145-13
			6.15-13	185/60-13	165/70-13	155-13, P155/80-13
A60-13	A70-13	A78-13	6.40-13	195/60-13	175/70-13	165-13
B60-13	B70-13	B78-13	6.70-13	205/60-13	185/70-13	175-13
			6.90-13			
C60-13	C70-13	C78-13	7.00-13	215/60-13	195/70-13	185-13
D60-13	D70-13	D78-13	7.25-13			
E60-13	E70-13	E78-13	7.75-13			195-13
			5.20-14	165/60-14	145/70-14	135-14
			5.60-14	175/60-14	155/70-14	145-14
			5.90-14			
A60-14	A70-14	A78-14	6.15-14	185/60-14	165/70-14	155-14
	B70-14	B78-14	6.45-14	195/60-14	175/70-14	165-14
	C70-14	C78-14	6.95-14	205/60-14	185/70-14	175-14
D60-14	D70-14	D78-14				
E60-14	E70-14	E78-14	7.35-14	215/60-14	195/70-14	185-14
F60-14	F70-14	F78-14, F83-14	7.75-14	225/60-14	200/70-14	195-14
G60-14	G70-14	G77-14, G78-14	8.25-14	235/60-14	205/70-14	205-14
H60-14	H70-14	H78-14	8.55-14	245/60-14	215/70-14	215-14
J60-14	J70-14	J78-14	8.85-14	255/60-14	225/70-14	225-14
L60-14	L70-14		9.15-14	265/60-14	235/70-14	
	A70-15	A78-15	5.60-15	185/60-15	165/70-15	155-15
B60-15	B70-15	B78-15	6.35-15	195/60-15	175/70-15	165-15
C60-15	C70-15	C78-15	6.85-15	205/60-15	185/70-15	175-15
	D70-15	D78-15				
E60-15	E70-15	E78-15	7.35-15	215/60-15	195/70-15	185-15
F60-15	F70-15	F78-15	7.75-15	225/60-15	205/70-15	195-15
G60-15	G70-15	G78-15	8.15-15/8.25-15	235/60-15	215/70-15	205-15
H60-15	H70-15	H78-15	8.45-15/8.55-15	245/60-15	225/70-15	215-15
J60-15	J70-15	J78-15	8.85-15/8.90-15	255/60-15	235/70-15	225-15
	K70-15		9.00-15	265/60-15	245/70-15	230-15
L60-15	L70-15	L78-15, L84-15	9.15-15			235-15
	M70-15	M78-15				255-15
		N78-15				

NOTE: Every size tire is not listed and many size comaprisons are approximate, based on load ratings. Wider tires than those supplied new with the vehicle should always be checked for clearance

TORQUE SPECIFICATIONS

Component	English	Metric
Automatic Transaxle		
Oil pan retaining nuts		
1982-88:	15 ft. lbs	20 Nm
1989-92:	8 ft. lbs.	11 Nm
Fuel Line Fittings:	22 ft. lbs.	30 Nm
Oil Pan Plug		
2.5L engine:	25 ft. lbs.	34 Nm
3.3L engine:	30 ft. lbs.	40 Nm
3.8L engine:	30 ft. lbs.	40 Nm
Except above:		
M6 bolt:	8 ft. lbs.	11 Nm
M8 bolt:	18 ft. lbs.	25 Nm
Oil Filter Access Plug		
2.5L engine:	Hand tighten + ¼ turn	Hand tighten + ¼ turn
Belt tensioner bolt		
2.5L engine:	37 ft. lbs.	50 Nm
2.8L engine:	40 ft. lbs.	54 Nm
3.1L engine:	40 ft. lbs.	54 Nm
3.3L engine:	38 ft. lbs.	52 Nm
Spark plugs:		
Except 2.8L carburated	20 ft. lbs.	27 Nm
2.8L carburated	15 ft. lbs.	17 Nm
Starter through bolts:	32 ft. lbs.	43 Nm
Wheel lug nuts:	100 ft. lbs.	138 Nm

2

ENGINE PERFORMANCE AND TUNE-UP

GASOLINE ENGINE TUNE-UP SPECIFICATIONS

Year	Engine VIN	Engine Displacement cu. in. (liter)	Spark Plugs Gap (in.)	Ignition Timing (deg.)		Fuel Pump (psi)	Idle Speed (rpm)		Valve Clearance	
				MT	AT		MT	AT	In.	Ex.
1982	R	4-151 (2.5)	0.060	8B	8B	6.0–8.0	950	750	Hyd.	Hyd.
	X	6-173 (2.8)	0.045	10B	10B	6.0–7.5	800	600	Hyd.	Hyd.
	Z①	6-173 (2.8)	0.045	6B	10B	6.0–7.5	850③	750	Hyd.	Hyd.
	E	6-181 (3.0)	0.080	—	15B	6.0–8.0	—	⑤	Hyd.	Hyd.
1983	R	4-151 (2.5)	0.060	8B	8B	6.0–8.0	950	750	Hyd.	Hyd.
	X	6-173 (2.8)	0.045	10B	10B	6.0–7.5	800	600	Hyd.	Hyd.
	Z①	6-173 (2.8)	0.045	6B	10B	6.0–7.5	850③	750	Hyd.	Hyd.
	E	6-181 (3.0)	0.080	—	15B	6.0–8.0	—	⑤	Hyd.	Hyd.
1984	R	4-151 (2.5)	0.060	8B	8B	6.0–8.0	950	750	Hyd.	Hyd.
	X	6-173 (2.8)	0.045	10B	10B	6.0–7.5	800	600	Hyd.	Hyd.
	Z①	6-173 (2.8)	0.045	6B	10B	6.0–7.5	850③	750	Hyd.	Hyd.
	E	6-181 (3.0)	0.080	—	15B	6.0–8.0	—	⑤	Hyd.	Hyd.
1985	R	4-151 (2.5)	0.060	④	④	6.0–7.0	④	④	Hyd.	Hyd.
	X	6-173 (2.8)	0.045	④	④	6.0–7.0	④	④	Hyd.	Hyd.
	W	6-173 (2.8)	0.045	④	④	9.0–13.0	④	④	Hyd.	Hyd.
	E	6-181 (3.0)	0.060	①	①	4.0–6.5	④	④	Hyd.	Hyd.
	3	6-231 (3.8)	0.080	④	④	34.0–40.0	④	④	Hyd.	Hyd.
1986	R	4-151 (2.5)	0.060	④	④	6.0–7.0	④	④	Hyd.	Hyd.
	X	6-173 (2.8)	0.045	④	④	6.0–7.0	④	④	Hyd.	Hyd.
	W	6-173 (2.8)	0.045	④	④	40.0–46.0	④	④	Hyd.	Hyd.
	3	6-231 (3.8)	0.080	④	④	34.0–40.0	④	④	Hyd.	Hyd.
	B	6-231 (3.8)	0.045	①	①	34.0–40.0	④	④	Hyd.	Hyd.
1987	R	4-151 (2.5)	0.060	④	④	6.0–7.0	④	④	Hyd.	Hyd.
	W	6-173 (2.8)	0.045	④	④	40.0–46.0	④	④	Hyd.	Hyd.
	3	6-231 (3.8)	0.080	④	④	34.0–40.0	④	④	Hyd.	Hyd.
1988	R	4-151 (2.5)	0.060	④	④	6.0–7.0	④	④	Hyd.	Hyd.
	W	6-173 (2.8)	0.045	④	④	40.0–46.0	④	④	Hyd.	Hyd.
	3	6-231 (3.8)	0.080	④	④	34.0–40.0	④	④	Hyd.	Hyd.
1989	R	4-151 (2.5)	0.060	④	④	6.0–7.0	④	④	Hyd.	Hyd.
	W	6-173 (2.8)	0.045	④	④	40.0–46.0	④	④	Hyd.	Hyd.
	T	6-192 (3.1)	0.045	④	④	34.0–47.0	④	④	Hyd.	Hyd.
	N	6-204 (3.3)	0.060	④	④	37.0–43.0	④	④	Hyd.	Hyd.
1990	R	4-151 (2.5)	0.060	④	④	6.0–7.0	④	④	Hyd.	Hyd.
	T	6-192 (3.1)	0.045	④	④	34.0–47.0	④	④	Hyd.	Hyd.
	N	6-204 (3.3)	0.060	④	④	41.0–47.0	④	④	Hyd.	Hyd.
1991	R	4-151 (2.5)	0.060	④	④	9.0–13.0	④	④	Hyd.	Hyd.
	T	6-192 (3.1)	0.045	④	④	40.5–47.0	④	④	Hyd.	Hyd.
	N	6-204 (3.3)	0.060	④	④	41.0–47.0	④	④	Hyd.	Hyd.

GASOLINE ENGINE TUNE-UP SPECIFICATIONS

Year	Engine VIN	Engine Displacement cu. in. (liter)	Spark Plugs Gap (in.)	Ignition Timing (deg.) MT	AT	Fuel Pump (psi)	Idle Speed (rpm) MT	AT	Valve Clearance In.	Ex.
1992	R	4-151 (2.5)	0.060	④	④	9.0–13.0	④	④	Hyd.	Hyd.
	T	6-192 (3.1)	0.045	④	④	40.5–47.0	④	④	Hyd.	Hyd.
	N	6-204 (3.3)	0.060	④	④	41.0–47.0	④	④	Hyd.	Hyd.

NOTE: The lowest cylinder pressure should be within 75% of the highest cylinder pressure reading. For example, if the highest cylinder is 134 psi, the lowest should be 101. Engine should be at normal operating temperature with throttle valve in the wide open position.

The underhood specifications sticker often reflects tune-up specification changes in production. Sticker figures must be used if they disagree with those in this chart.

① High Output
② With A/C: 900
③ California: 750
④ Refer to underhood specifications sticker
⑤ See text

DIESEL ENGINE TUNE-UP SPECIFICATIONS

Year	Engine VIN	Engine Displacement cu. in. (liter)	Valve Clearance Intake (in.)	Exhaust (in.)	Intake Valve Opens (deg.)	Injection Pump Setting (deg.)	Injection Nozzle Pressure (psi) New	Used	Idle Speed (rpm)	Cranking Compression Pressure (psi)
1983	T	6-263 (4.3)	Hyd.	Hyd.	16	①	1000	850	650	300
1984	T	6-263 (4.3)	Hyd.	Hyd.	16	①	1000	850	650	300
1985	T	6-263 (4.3)	Hyd.	Hyd.	16	①	1000	850	650	300

① Refer to the underhood sticker

TUNE-UP PROCEDURES

In order to extract the full measure of performance and economy from your car's engine it is essential that it be properly tuned at regular intervals. Although the tune-up intervals for these cars have been stretched to limits which would have been thought impossible a few years ago, periodic maintenance is still required. A regularly scheduled tune-up will keep your car's engine running smoothly and will prevent the annoying minor breakdowns and poor performance associated with an untuned engine.

A complete tune-up should be performed at the interval specified in the Maintenance Intervals chart in Section 1. This interval should be halved if the car is operated under severe conditions, such as trailer towing, prolonged idling, continual stop-and-start driving, or if starting and running problems are noticed. It is assumed that the routine maintenance described in the first section has been kept up, as this will have a decided effect on the results of a tune-up. All of the applicable steps should be followed in order, as the result is a cumulative one.

If the specifications on the tune-up label in the engine compartment of your A-Body disagree with the Tune-Up Specifications chart in this section, the figures on the sticker must be used. The label often reflects changes made during the production run.

Spark Plugs

➡ SEE FIGS. 1 to 6

Spark plugs ignite the air and fuel mixture in the cylinder as the piston reaches the top of the compression stroke. The controlled explosion that results forces the piston down, turning the crankshaft and the rest of the drive train.

The average life of a spark plug 30,000 miles (48,300km). Part of the reason for this extraordinarily long life is the exclusive use of unleaded fuel, which reduces the amount of deposits within the combustion chamber and on the spark plug electrodes themselves, compared with the deposits left by the leaded gasoline used in the past. An additional contribution to long life is made by the HEI (High Energy Ignition) System, which fires the spark plugs with over 35,000 volts of electricity. The high voltage serves to keep the electrodes clear, and because it is a cleaner blast of electricity than that produced by breaker points ignitions, the electrodes suffer less pitting and wear.

Nevertheless, the life of a spark plug is dependent on a number of factors, including the mechanical condition of the engine, driving conditions, and the driver's habits.

When you remove the plugs, check the condition of the electrodes, they are a good indicator of the internal state of the engine. Since the spark plug wires must be checked every

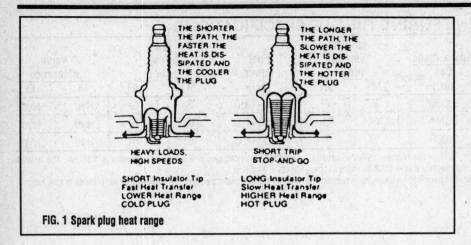

FIG. 1 Spark plug heat range

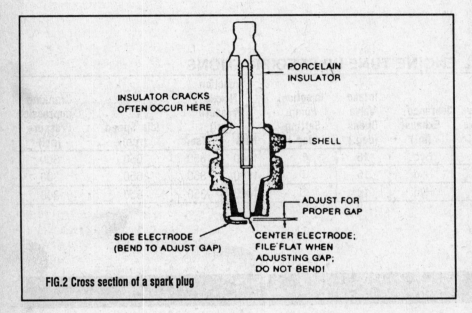

FIG.2 Cross section of a spark plug

deposits, but the electrodes will burn away quickly and, in some cases, pre-ignition may result. Pre-ignition occurs when the spark plug tips get so hot that they ignite the fuel/mixture before the actual spark fires. This premature ignition will usually cause a pinging sound under conditions of low speed and heavy load. In severe cases, the heat may become high enough to start the fuel/air mixture burning throughout the combustion chamber rather than just to the front of the plug. In this case, the resultant explosion (detonation) will be strong enough to damage pistons, rings, and valves.

In most cases, the factory recommended heat range is correct; it is chosen to perform well under a wide range of operating conditions. However, if most of your driving is long distance, high speed travel, you may want to install a spark plug one range colder than standard. If most of your driving is of the short trip variety, when the engine may not always reach operating temperature, a hotter plug may help burn off the deposits normally accumulated under those conditions.

REMOVAL

1. Number the wires with pieces of adhesive tape so that you won't cross them when you replace them.

2. The spark plug boots have large grips to aid in removal. Grasp the wire by the rubber boot and twist the boot 1/2 turn in either direction to break the tight seal between the boot and the plug. Then twist and pull on the boot to remove the wire from the spark plug. Do not pull on the wire itself or you will damage the carbon cord conductor.

3. Use a 5/8 in. spark plug socket to loosen all of the plugs about two turns. A universal joint installed at the socket end of the extension will ease the process.

If removal of the plugs is difficult, apply a few drops of penetrating oil or silicone spray to the area around the base of the plug, and allow it a few minutes to work.

4. If compressed air is available, apply it to the area around the spark plug holes. Otherwise, use a rag or a brush to clean the area. Be careful not to allow any foreign material to drop into the spark plug holes.

5. Remove the plugs by unscrewing them the rest of the way.

15,000 miles (24,000km), the spark plugs can be removed and examined at the same time. This will allow you to keep an eye on the mechanical status of the engine.

A small deposit of light tan or rust/red material on a spark plug that has been used for any period of time is to be considered normal. Any other color, or abnormal amounts of wear or deposits, indicates that there is something amiss in the engine.

The gap between the center electrode and the side or ground electrode can be expected to increase not more than 0.001 in. (0.025mm) every 1,000 miles (1609km) under normal conditions.

When a spark plug is functioning normally or, more accurately, when the plug is installed in an engine that is functioning properly, the plugs can be taken out, cleaned, regapped, and reinstalled in the engine without doing the engine any harm.

When, and if, a plug fouls and begins to

misfire, you will have to investigate, correct the cause of the fouling, and either clean or replace the plug.

There are several reasons why a spark plug will foul and you can learn which is at fault by just looking at the plug. A few of the most common reasons for plug fouling, and a description of the fouled plug's appearance, are listed in the color insert section.

Spark plugs suitable for use in your car's engine are offered in a number of different heat ranges. The amount of heat which the plug absorbs is determined by the length of the lower insulator. The longer the insulator, the hotter the plug will operate; the shorter the insulator, the cooler it will operate. A spark plug that absorbs (or retains) little heat and remains too cool will accumulate deposits of oil and carbon, because it is not hot enough to burn them off. This leads to fouling and consequent misfiring. A spark plug that absorbs too much heat will have no

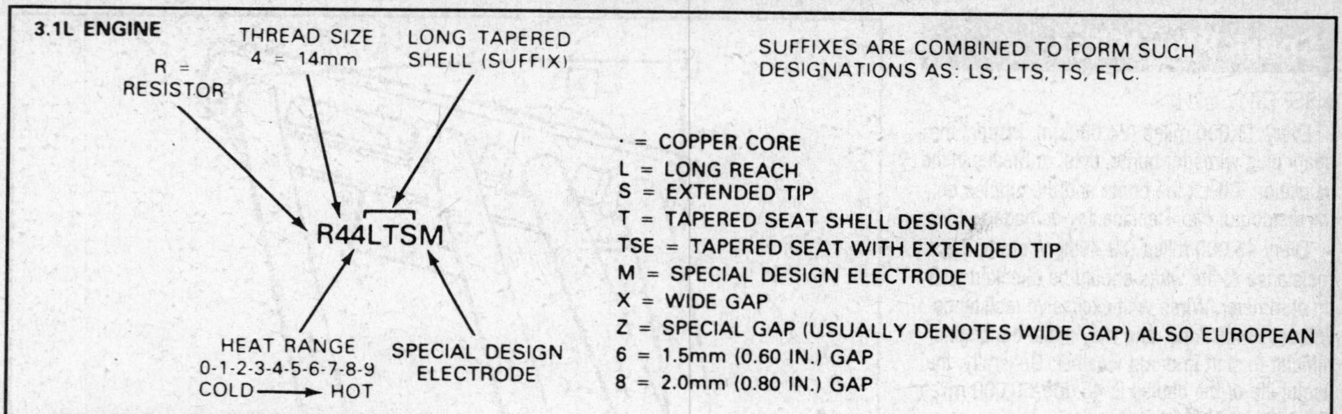

3.1L ENGINE

R = RESISTOR

THREAD SIZE 4 = 14mm

LONG TAPERED SHELL (SUFFIX)

R44LTSM

HEAT RANGE
0-1-2-3-4-5-6-7-8-9
COLD ⟶ HOT

SPECIAL DESIGN ELECTRODE

SUFFIXES ARE COMBINED TO FORM SUCH DESIGNATIONS AS: LS, LTS, TS, ETC.

· = COPPER CORE
L = LONG REACH
S = EXTENDED TIP
T = TAPERED SEAT SHELL DESIGN
TSE = TAPERED SEAT WITH EXTENDED TIP
M = SPECIAL DESIGN ELECTRODE
X = WIDE GAP
Z = SPECIAL GAP (USUALLY DENOTES WIDE GAP) ALSO EUROPEAN
6 = 1.5mm (0.60 IN.) GAP
8 = 2.0mm (0.80 IN.) GAP

FIG.3 Heat range example for 3.1L engine

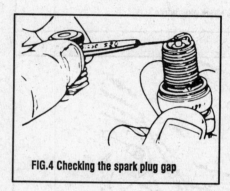

FIG.4 Checking the spark plug gap

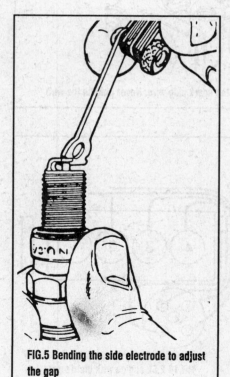

FIG.5 Bending the side electrode to adjust the gap

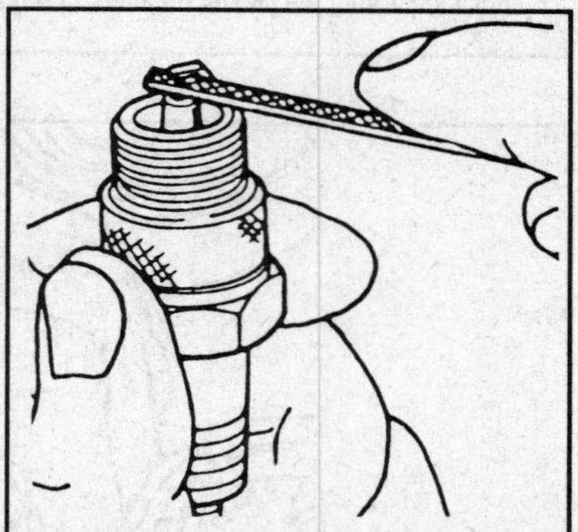

FIG.6 Plugs that are in good condition can be cleaned and reused

INSPECTION

Check the plugs for deposits and wear. If they are not going to be replaced, clean the plugs thoroughly. Remember that any kind of deposit will decrease the efficiency of the plug. Plugs can be cleaned on a spark plug cleaning machine, which can sometimes be found in service stations, or you can do an acceptable job of cleaning with a stiff brush. If the plugs are cleaned, the electrodes must be filed flat. Use an ignition points file, not an emery board or the like, which will leave deposits. The electrodes must be filed perfectly flat with sharp edges; rounded edges reduce the spark plug voltage by as much as 50%.

Check the spark plug gap before installation. The ground electrode must be parallel to the center electrode and the specified size wire gauge should pass through the gap with a slight drag. Always check the gap on new plugs, too; they are not always correctly set at the factory.

Do not use a flat feeler gauge when measuring the gap, because the reading will be inaccurate. Wire gapping tools usually have a bending tool attached. Use that to adjust the side electrode until the proper distance is obtained. Also, be careful not to bend the side electrode too far or too often; it may weaken and break off within the engine, requiring removal of the cylinder head to retrieve it.

INSTALLATION

1. Lubricate the threads of the spark plugs with a drop of oil or a shot of silicone spray. Install the plugs and tighten them handtight. Take care not to crossthread them.

2. Tighten the spark plugs with the socket. Do not apply the same amount of force you would use for a bolt; just snug them in. These spark plugs do not use gaskets, and over-tightening will make future removal difficult. If a torque wrench is available, tighten to 10-20 ft. lbs.

➡ **While over-tightening the spark plug is to be avoided, under-tightening is just as bad. If combustion gases leak past the threads, the spark plug will overheat and rapid electrode wear will result.**

3. Install the wires on their respective plugs. Make sure the wires are firmly connected. You will be able to feel them click into place. Spark plug wiring diagrams are in this section if you get into trouble.

Spark Plug Wires

♦ SEE FIG. 7 and 8

Every 15,000 miles (24,000km), inspect the spark plug wires for burns, cuts, or breaks in the insulation. Check the boots and the nipples on the distributor cap. Replace any damaged wiring.

Every 45,000 miles (72,400km) or so, the resistance of the wires should be checked with an ohmmeter. Wires with excessive resistance will cause misfiring, and may make the engine difficult to start in damp weather. Generally, the useful life of the cables is 45,000-60,000 miles (72,400–96,500km).

To check resistance, remove the distributor cap, leaving the wires in place. Connect one lead of an ohmmeter to an electrode within the cap; connect the other lead to the corresponding spark plug terminal (remove it from the spark plug for this test). Replace any wire which shows a resistance over 30,000Ω. The following chart gives resistance values as a function of length. Generally speaking, however, resistance should not be considered the outer limit of acceptability.

- 0-15 in. (0–38cm): 3,000-10,000Ω
- 15-25 in. (38–64cm): 4,000-15,000Ω
- 25-35 in. (64–89cm): 6,000-20,000Ω
- Over 35 in. (89cm): 25,000Ω

It should be remembered that resistance is also a function of length; the longer the wire, the greater the resistance. Thus, if the wires on your car are longer than the factory originals, resistance will be higher, quite possibly outside these limits.

When installing new wires, replace them one at a time to avoid mixups. Start by replacing the longest one first. Install the boot firmly over the spark plug. Route the wire over the the same path as the original. Insert the nipple firmly onto the tower on the distributor cap, then install the cap cover and latches to secure the wires.

Firing Orders

➡ **To avoid confusion, remove and tag the wires one at a time, for replacement**

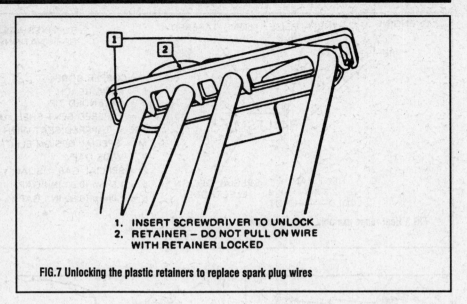

1. INSERT SCREWDRIVER TO UNLOCK
2. RETAINER – DO NOT PULL ON WIRE WITH RETAINER LOCKED

FIG.7 Unlocking the plastic retainers to replace spark plug wires

FIG.8 Twist and pull the rubber boot to remove the spark plug wire. Never plug on the wire

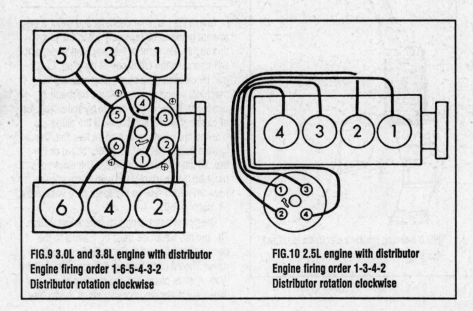

FIG.9 3.0L and 3.8L engine with distributor
Engine firing order 1-6-5-4-3-2
Distributor rotation clockwise

FIG.10 2.5L engine with distributor
Engine firing order 1-3-4-2
Distributor rotation clockwise

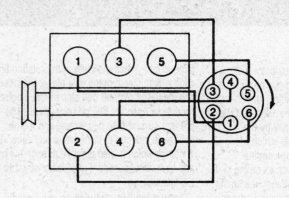

FIG.11 2.8L engine with distributor
Engine firing order 1-2-3-4-5-6
Distributor rotation clockwise

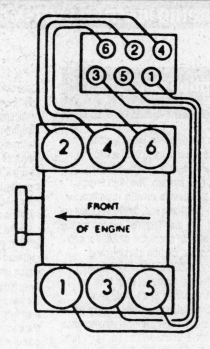

FIG.12 3.8L engine without distributor
Engine firing order 1-6-5-4-3-2
Distributorless ignition

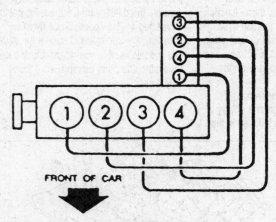

FRONT OF CAR

FIG.13 2.5L engine without Distributor
Engine firing order 1-3-4-2
Distributorless ignition

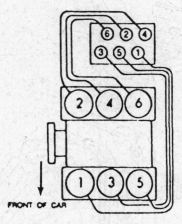

FRONT OF CAR

FIG.15 3.3L engine without Distributor
Engine firing order 1-6-5-4-3-2
Distributorless ignition

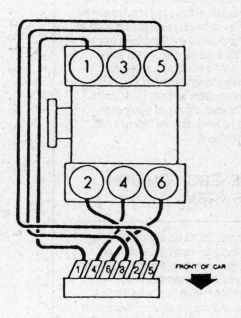

FRONT OF CAR

FIG.14 3.1L engine without Distributor
Engine firing order 1-2-3-4-5-6
Distributorless ignition

ELECTRONIC IGNITION SYSTEMS

Description and Operation

General Motors uses two basic ignition systems on these vehicles. A high energy distributor type system or a high energy distributorless type system. The High Energy Ignition (H.E.I.) system is virtually maintenance free, since it is electronic and, therefore, uses no breaker points. The only required service for the H.E.I. distributor is to check the distributor cap and rotor for cracks, carbon tracking, and corrosion every 30,000 miles (48,300km).

On distributorless systems, even less maintenance is required. Since there is no distributor, there is also no distributor cap or rotor to wear out. The only normal maintenance required on these systems will be the spark plug wires. Diagnosis of no start conditions may require testing the ignition module or coil assemblies, these items are not much different than the ignition module or coil used on HEI systems.

The distributorless ignition systems used by General Motors go by two names, either DIS or C³I. DIS simple stands for distributorless ignition system while C³I stands for computer controlled coil ignition. Both of these systems function the same way; by connecting a several coil packs to a pairs of spark plugs and firing the proper coil each time the a specific plug should spark, instead of using a distributor cap and rotor.

The distributorless systems is a far better ignition system. More accurate spark control, less parts to wear, capable of higher spark output and hotter spark at the high rpm that newer engine run at.

HIGH ENERGY IGNITION (HEI) SYSTEM

The General Motors HEI system is a pulse-triggered, transistor-controlled, inductive discharge ignition system. The entire HEI system is contained within the distributor cap.

The distributor, in addition to housing the mechanical and vacuum advance mechanisms, contains the ignition coil, the electronic control module, and the magnetic pick-up assembly contains a permanent magnet, a pole piece with internal teeth, and a pick-up coil (not to be confused with the ignition coil).

For 1982 and later an HEI distributor with Electronic Spark Timing is used (for more information on EST, refer to Section 4).

All spark timing changes in the 1982 and later distributors are done electronically by the Electronic Control Module (ECM) which monitors information from various engine sensors, computes the desired spark timing and then signals the distributor to change the timing accordingly. No vacuum or mechanical advance systems are used whatsoever.

In the HEI system, as in other electronic ignition systems, the breaker points have been replaced with an electronic switch, a transistor, which is located within the control module. This switching transistor performs the same function the points did in a conventional ignition system; it simply turns coil primary current on and off at the correct time. Essentially then, electronic and conventional ignition systems operate on the same principle.

The module which houses the switching transistor is controlled (turned on and off) by a magnetically generated impulse induced in the pick-up coil. When the teeth of the rotating timer align with the teeth of the pole piece, the induced voltage in the pick-up coil signals the electronic module to open the coil primary circuit. The primary current then decreases, and a high voltage is induced in the ignition coil secondary windings which is then directed through the rotor and high voltage leads. (spark plug wires) to fire the spark plugs.

In essence then, the pick-up coil module system simply replaces the conventional breaker points and condenser. The condenser found within the distributor is for radio suppression purposes only and has nothing to do with the ignition process. The module automatically controls the dwell period, increasing it with increasing engine speed. Since dwell is automatically controlled, it cannot be adjusted. The module itself is non-adjustable and non-repairable and must be replaced if found defective.

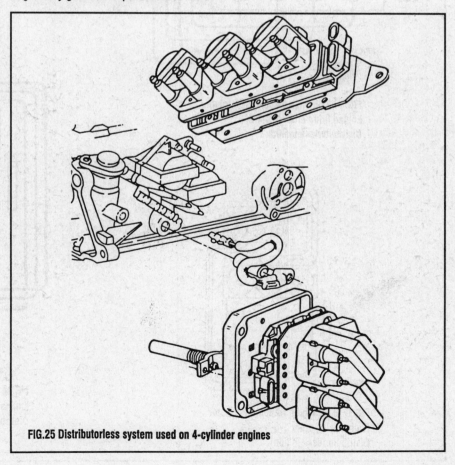

FIG.25 Distributorless system used on 4-cylinder engines

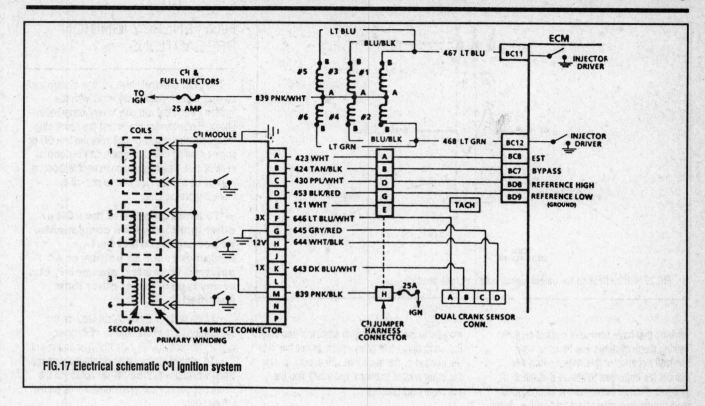

FIG.17 Electrical schematic C³I ignition system

COMPUTER CONTROLLED COIL IGNITION (C³I) SYSTEM

Starting in 1987, some models of the A-body cars came with 4 and 6 cylinder engines equipped with Computer Controlled Coil Ignition (C³I) or Distributorless Ignition System (DIS), which eliminates the distributor. The C³I ignition system consists of a coil pack, ignition module, camshaft and crankshaft sensor. There are two types of C³I coils used. Type 1 coils have three plug wires on each side of the coil assembly; Type 2 coils have all six wires connected on one side of the coil. When troubleshooting or replacing components, it is important to determine which C³I system is installed on the engine.

Both DIS and C³I system consists of the coil pack, ignition module, crankshaft sensor, interrupter rings and electronic control module (ECM). All components are serviced as complete assemblies, although individual coils are available for Type 2 coil packs. Since the ECM controls the ignition timing, no timing adjustments are necessary or possible.

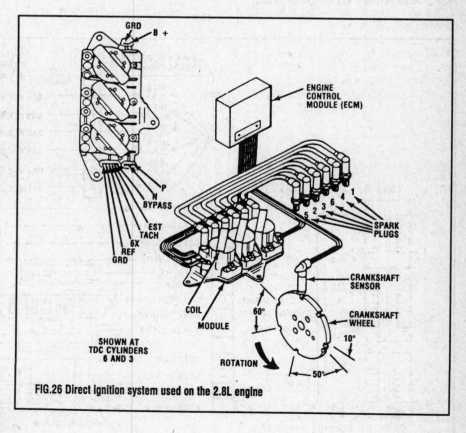

FIG.26 Direct ignition system used on the 2.8L engine

Diagnosis and Testing

The ignition, fuel, electrical and emission systems are all interrelated on the newer

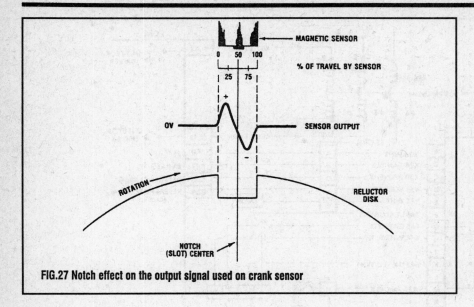

FIG.27 Notch effect on the output signal used on crank sensor

HIGH ENERGY IGNITION PRECAUTIONS

This is an extremely high voltage system and contact with the spark plug wires with the ignition switch ON can give a very dangerous shock. Never service the or test the spark plug wires, distributor cap or coil with the key ON or engine running unless instructed to perform a specific test. Before going on to troubleshooting, it might be a good idea to take note of the following precautions:

➡ **To avoid damage to the ECM or other ignition system components, do not use electrical test equipment such as battery or AC powered voltmeter, ohmmeter, etc. or any type of tester other than specified.**

• When performing electrical tests on the system, use a high impedance multimeter, digital voltmeter (DVM) J-34029-A or equivalent.
• To prevent electrostatic discharge damage, when working with the ECM, do not touch the connector pins or soldered components on the circuit board.

vehicles that have computer control engines. Testing these systems has become very involved because of this. When using this manual it's important to realize that these systems overlap. Some testing or component replacement that may effect the ignition system may be in the fuel or engine electrical sections. If a component test or symptom is not found in the section of the book that you expect, check the other related sections and you'll find the necessary procedures.

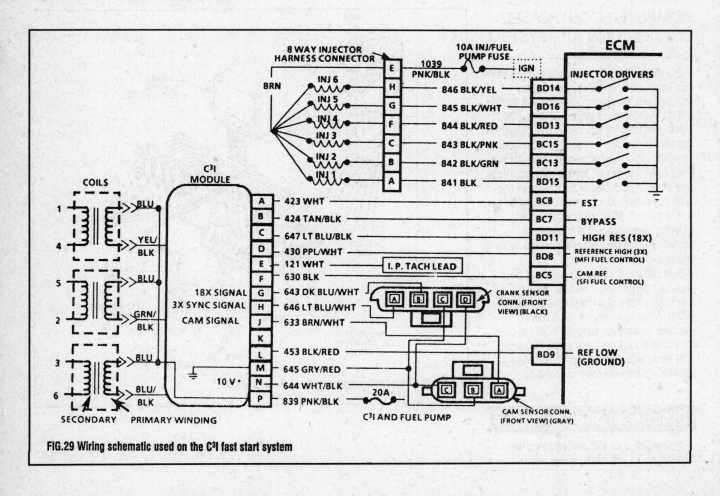

FIG.29 Wiring schematic used on the C³I fast start system

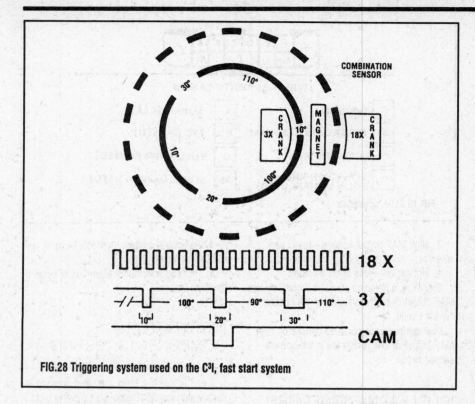

FIG.28 Triggering system used on the C³I, fast start system

• When handling a PROM, CAL-PAK or MEM-CAL, do not touch the component leads. Also, do not remove the integrated circuit from the carrier.

• When performing electrical tests on the system, use a high impedance multimeter, digital voltmeter (DVM) J-34029-A or equivalent.

• Never pierce a high tension lead or boot for any testing purpose; otherwise, future problems are guaranteed.

• Leave new components and modules in the shipping package until ready to install them.

• Never disconnect any electrical connection with the ignition switch **ON** unless instructed to do so in a test.

Timing Light Use

Inductive pick-up timing lights are the best kind of use with HEI. Timing light which connect between the spark plug and the spark plug wire occasionally (not always) give false readings.

Spark Plug Wires

The plug wires used with HEI systems are of a different construction than conventional wires. When replacing them, make sure you get the correct wires, since conventional wires won't carry the voltage. Also, handle them carefully to avoid cracking or splitting them and never pierce them.

Tachometer Use

Not all tachometers will operate or indicate correctly when used on a HEI system. While some tachometers may give a reading, this does not necessarily mean the reading is correct. In addition, some tachometers hook up differently from others. If you can't figure out whether or not your tachometer will work on your car, check with the tachometer manufacturer. Dwell readings, or course, have no significance at all.

HEI System Testers

Instruments designed specifically for testing HEI systems are available from several tool manufacturers. Some of these will even test the module itself.

If the engine cranks but doesn't start additional tests are in section 4. Use the A-Charts especially Charts A-2 to A-7. These charts provide step by step instruction for testing for spark and fuel.

TROUBLESHOOTING THE IGNITION SYSTEM

The symptoms of a defective component within the electronic ignition system are exactly the same as those you would encounter in a conventional system. Some of these symptoms are:

• Hard or no Starting
• Rough Idle
• Poor Fuel Economy
• Engine misses under load or while accelerating

If you suspect a problem in your ignition system, there are certain preliminary checks which you should carry out before you begin to check the electronic portions of the system. First, it is extremely important to make sure the vehicle battery is in a good state of charge. A defective or poorly charged battery will cause the various components of the ignition system to read incorrectly when they are being tested. Second, Make sure all wiring connections are clean and tight, not only at the battery, but also at the distributor cap, ignition coil, and at the electronic control module.

Since the only change between electronic and conventional ignition systems is in the distributor component area, it is imperative to check the secondary ignition circuit first. If the secondary circuit checks out properly, then the engine condition is probably not the fault of the ignition system. To check the secondary ignition system, perform a simple spark test. Remove one of the plug wires and insert some sort of extension in the plug socket. An old spark plug with the ground electrode removed makes a good extension. Hold the wire and extension about ¼ in. (6mm) away from the block and crank the engine. If a normal spark occurs, then the problem is most likely not in the ignition system. Check for fuel system problems, or fouled spark plugs.

If, however, there is no spark or a weak spark, then further ignition system testing will have to be done. Troubleshooting techniques fall into two categories, depending on the nature of the problem. The categories are (1) Engine cranks, but won't start or (2) Engine runs, but runs rough or cuts out. To begin with, let's consider the first case.

Engine Fail to Start

If the engine won't start, perform a spark test as described earlier. This will narrow the problem area down considerably. If no spark occurs, check for the presence of normal battery voltage of the battery (BAT) terminal in the distributor cap. The ignition switch must be in the ON position for this test. Either a voltmeter or a test light may be used for this test. Connect the test light wire to ground and probe end to the BAT terminal at the distributor. If the light comes on, you have voltage on the distributor. If the light fails to come on, this indicates an open circuit in the ignition primary wiring leading to the distributor. In this case, you will have to check wiring continuity back to the ignition switch using a test light. If there is battery voltage at the BAT terminal, but no spark at the plugs, then the problem lies within the distributor assembly.

Engine Runs, But Runs Rough or Cuts Out

1. Make sure the plug wires are in good shape first. There should be no obvious cracks or breaks. You can check the plug wires with an ohmmeter, but do not pierce the wires with a probe. Check the chart for the correct plug wire resistance.

2. If the plug wires are OK, remove the cap assembly and check of moisture, cracks, ships, or carbon tracks, or any other high voltage leaks or failures. Replace the cap if any defects are found. Make sure the timer wheel rotates when the engine is cranked.

READING CODES

♦ SEE FIG. 16

Assembly Line Diagnostic Link (ALDL) connector is used for communicating with the ECM. It is usually located under the instrument panel and is sometimes covered by a plastic cover labeled DIAGNOSTIC CONNECTOR. Codes stored in the ECM's memory can be read through a handheld diagnostic scanner plugged into the ALDL connector. Codes can also be read by connecting terminal A to B of the ALDL connector and counting the number of flashes of the Service Engine Soon light, with the ignition switch turned **ON**.

CLEARING CODES

To clear codes from the ECM memory, the ECM power feed must be disconnected for at least 30 seconds. Depending on the vehicle, the ECM power feed can be disconnected at the positive battery terminal pigtail, the inline fuseholder that originates at the positive connection at the battery or the ECM fuse in the fuse block. The negative battery cable may also be disconnected; however, other on-board memory data, such as preset radio tuning, will also be lost.

SYMPTOM DIAGNOSIS

The ECM uses information from the MAP and coolant sensor, in addition to rpm to calculate spark advance as follows:

1. Low MAP output voltage—more spark advance

2. Cold engine—more spark advance

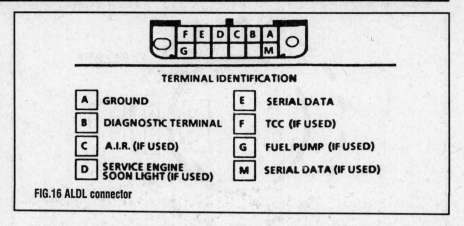

TERMINAL IDENTIFICATION

A GROUND	**E** SERIAL DATA
B DIAGNOSTIC TERMINAL	**F** TCC (IF USED)
C A.I.R. (IF USED)	**G** FUEL PUMP (IF USED)
D SERVICE ENGINE SOON LIGHT (IF USED)	**M** SERIAL DATA (IF USED)

FIG.16 ALDL connector

3. High MAP output voltage—less spark advance

4. Hot engine—less spark advance

Therefore, detonation could be caused by low MAP output or high resistance in the coolant sensor circuit.

Poor performance could be caused by high MAP output or low resistance in the coolant sensor circuit.

IDLE LEARN PROCEDURE

This procedure allows the ECM memory to be updated with the correct IAC valve pintle position. The Idle Learn procedure must be performed on the 3.1L engine as follows:

1. Place the transaxle in **P** or **N**.

2. Install the Tech 1 scan tool or equivalent.

3. Turn the ignition switch **ON**, engine OFF.

4. Select IAC system, then Idle Learn in the MISC Test mode.

5. Proceed with the Idle Learn as directed by the scan tool.

DISTRIBUTOR COMPONENTS TESTING

If the trouble has been narrowed down to the units within the distributor, the following tests can help pinpoint the defective component. An ohmmeter with both high and low ranges should be used. These tests are made with the cap assembly removed and the battery wire disconnected. If a tachometer is connected to the TACH terminal, disconnect it before making these tests.

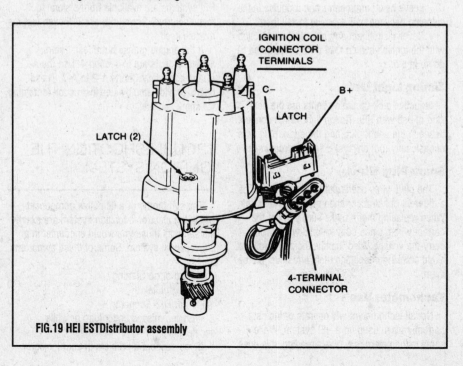

FIG.19 HEI EST Distributor assembly

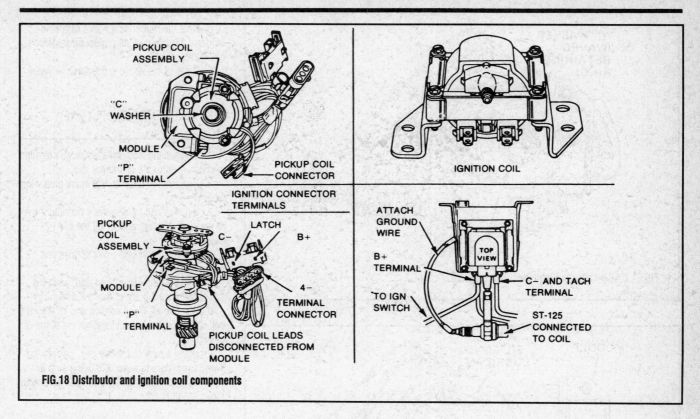

FIG.18 Distributor and ignition coil components

Tachometer Hookup

There is a terminal marked TACH on the distributor cap. Connect one tachometer lead to this terminal and the other lead to a ground. On some tachometer, the leads must be connected to the TACK terminal and to the battery positive terminal.

⁂ CAUTION

Never ground the TACH terminal; serious module and ignition coil damage will result. If there is any doubt as to the correct tachometer hookup, check with the tachometer manufacturer.

---

1. Connect an ohmmeter between the TACH and BAT terminals in the distributor cap. The primary coil resistance should be less than 1Ω.

2. To check the coil secondary resistance, connect an ohmmeter between the rotor button and BAT terminal. Note the reading. Connect the ohmmeter between the rotor button and the TACH terminal. Note the reading. The resistance in both cases should be between 6,000 and 30,000Ω. Be sure to test between the rotor button and both the BAT and TACH terminals.

3. Replace the coil only if the readings in Step 1 and Step 2 are infinite.

➠ **These resistance checks will not disclose shorted could windings. This condition can only be detected with scope analysis or a suitably designed coil tester. If these instruments are unavailable, replace the coil with a known good coil as a final coil test.**

4. To test the pick-up coil, first disconnect the white and green module leads. Set the ohmmeter on the high scale and connect it between a ground and either the white or green lead. Any resistance measurement less than infinity requires replacement of the pick-up coil.

5. Pick-up coil continuity is tested by connecting the ohmmeter (on low range)

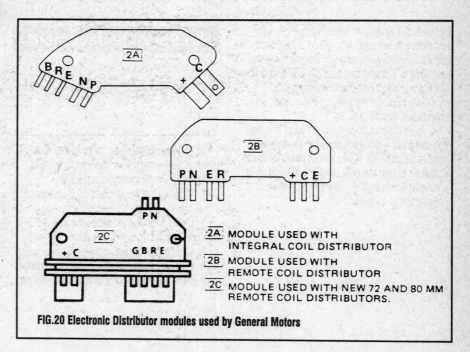

FIG.20 Electronic Distributor modules used by General Motors

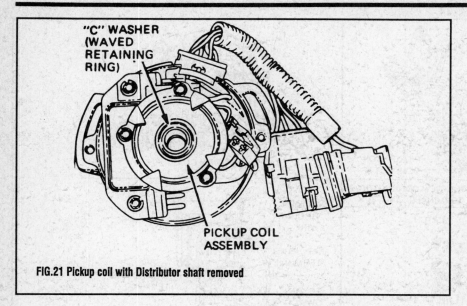

FIG.21 Pickup coil with Distributor shaft removed

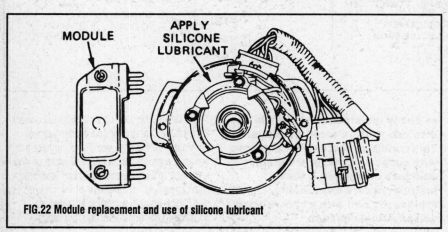

FIG.22 Module replacement and use of silicone lubricant

between the white and green leads. Normal resistance is between 800–1500 ohms. Move the vacuum advance arm while performing this test. This will detect any break in coil continuity. Such a condition can cause intermittent misfiring. Replace the pick-up if the reading is outside the specified limits.

6. If no defects have been found at this time, you still have a problem, then the module will have to be checked. If you do not have access to a module tester, the only possible alternative is a substitution test. If the module fails the substitution test, replace it.

HEI Parts Replacement

HEI INTEGRAL IGNITION COIL

1. Disconnect the feed and module wire terminal connectors from the distributor cap.
2. Remove the ignition set retainer.
3. Remove the 4 coil cover-to-distributor cap screws.
5. Using a blunt drift, press the coil wire spade terminals up out of the distributor cap.
6. Lift the coil up out of the distributor cap.
7. Remove and clean the coil spring, rubber seal washer and coil cavity of the distributor cap.

8. Coat the rubber seal with a dielectric lubricant furnished in the replacement ignition coil package.
9. Reverse the above procedures to install.

HEI DISTRIBUTOR CAP

1. Remove the feed and module wire terminal connectors from the distributor cap.
2. Remove the retainer and spark plug wires from the cap.
3. Depress and release the 4 distributor cap-to-housing retainers and lift off the cap assembly.
4. Remove the 4 coil cover screws and cover.
5. Using a finger or a blunt drift, push the spade terminals up out of the distributor cap.
6. Remove all 4 coil screws and lift the coil, coil spring and rubber seal washer out of the cap coil cavity.
7. Using a new distributor cap, reverse the above procedure to assemble being sure to clean and lubricate the rubber seal washer with dielectric lubricant.

HEI ROTOR

1. Disconnect the feed and module wire connector from the distributor.
2. Depress and release the 4 distributor cap-to-housing retainers and lift off the cap assembly.
3. Remove the two rotor attaching screws and rotor.
4. Reverse the above procedure to install.

HEI MODULE

1. Remove the distributor cap and rotor as previously described.
2. Disconnect the harness connector and pick-up coil spade connectors from the module. Be careful not to damage the wires when removing the connector.
3. Remove the two screws and module from the distributor housing.
4. Coat the bottom of the new module with dielectric lubricant supplied with the new module. Reverse the above procedure to install.

DISTRIBUTOR DISASSEMBLY
TEST AND REASSEMBLY
(SEPARATELY MOUNTED COIL)

HEI/EST DISTRIBUTOR

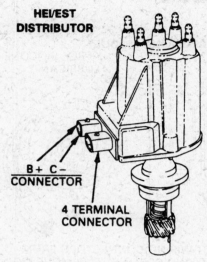

B+ C−
―――――
CONNECTOR

4 TERMINAL CONNECTOR

1. A TYPICAL DISTRIBUTOR USED WITH A SEPARATELY MOUNTED COIL IS SHOWN.

TESTING PICKUP COIL

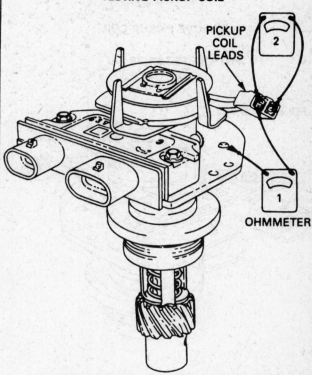

PICKUP COIL LEADS

OHMMETER

3. REMOVE ROTOR AND PICKUP COIL LEADS FROM MODULE.

4. CONNECT OHMMETER PART 1 AND PART 2.

5. OBSERVE OHMMETER. FLEX LEADS BY HAND TO CHECK FOR INTERMITTENT OPENS.

   STEP 1 — SHOULD READ INFINITE AT ALL TIMES. IF NOT, PICKUP COIL IS DEFECTIVE.

   STEP 2 — SHOULD READ ONE STEADY VALUE BETWEEN 500-1500 OHMS AS LEADS ARE FLEXED BY HAND. IF NOT, PICKUP COIL IS DEFECTIVE.

TESTING IGNITION COIL

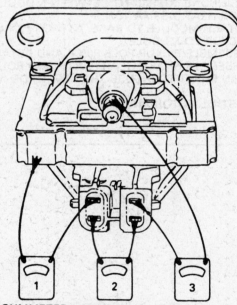

OHMMETER   OHMMETER   OHMMETER

2. CHECK IGNITION COIL WITH OHMMETER FOR OPENS AND GROUNDS:

   STEP 1. — USE HIGH SCALE. SHOULD READ VERY HIGH (INFINITE). IF NOT, REPLACE COIL.

   STEP 2. — USE LOW SCALE. SHOULD READ VERY LOW OR ZERO. IF NOT, REPLACE COIL.

   STEP 3. — USE HIGH SCALE. SHOULD NOT READ INFINITE. IF IT DOES, REPLACE COIL.

DRIVING PIN FROM SHAFT

ROLL PIN

6. DRIVE ROLL PIN FROM GEAR AND REMOVE SHAFT ASSEMBLY. MARK GEAR AND SHAFT FOR CORRECT REASSEMBLY.

DISTRIBUTOR DISASSEMBLY TEST AND REASSEMBLY (SEPARATELY MOUNTED COIL)

REMOVE PICKUP COIL

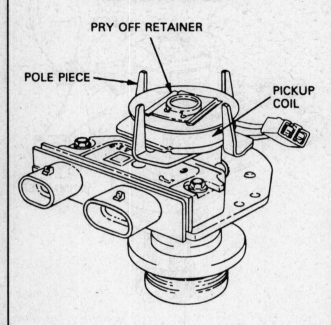

PRY OFF RETAINER

POLE PIECE

PICKUP COIL

7. TO REMOVE PICKUP COIL, REMOVE RETAINER.
8. LIFT PICKUP COIL ASSEMBLY STRAIGHT UP TO REMOVE FROM DISTRIBUTOR.

REMOVING MODULE

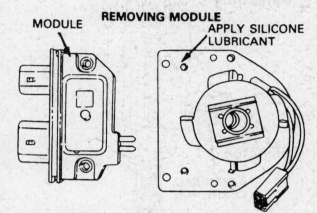

MODULE

APPLY SILICONE LUBRICANT

9. DISCONNECT WIRING CONNECTORS FROM MODULE. REMOVE TWO SCREWS TO REMOVE MODULE TEST MODULE WITH AN APPROVED MODULE TESTER.

REASSEMBLY

10. WIPE DISTRIBUTOR BASE AND MODULE CLEAN, APPLY SILICONE LUBRICANT BETWEEN MODULE AND BASE FOR HEAT DISSIPATION.
11. ATTACH MODULE TO BASE. ATTACH PICKUP CONNECTOR TO MODULE.
12. ASSEMBLE PICKUP POLE PIECE AND RETAINER.
13. ASSEMBLE SHAFT, GEAR PARTS AND ROLL PIN.
14. SPIN SHAFT TO INSURE THAT TEETH DO NOT TOUCH.
15. INSTALL ROTOR AND CAP.

DISTRIBUTOR DISASSEMBLY TEST AND REASSEMBLY (COIL IN CAP)

"COIL IN CAP" DISTRIBUTOR

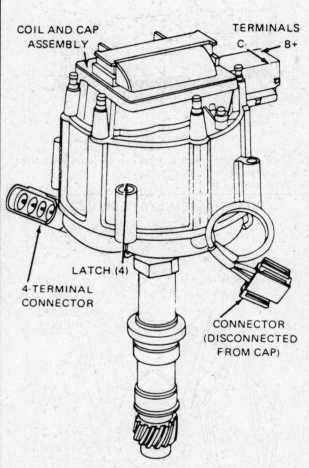

COIL AND CAP ASSEMBLY

TERMINALS
C B+

LATCH (4)

4-TERMINAL CONNECTOR

CONNECTOR (DISCONNECTED FROM CAP)

1. A 6-cyl. EST distributor with coil-in-cap is illustrated.
2. Detach wiring connector from cap, as shown.
3. Turn four latches and remove cap and coil assembly from lower housing.

TESTING IGNITION COIL

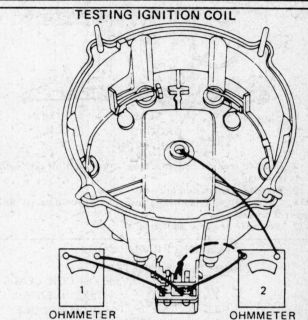

1 OHMMETER

2 OHMMETER

4. Connect ohmmeter. Test 1.
5. Reading should be zero, or nearly zero. If not, replace coil, Step 8.
6. Connect ohmmeter both ways. Test 2. Use high scale. Replace coil only if both readings are infinite. Step 8.
7. If coil is good, go to Step 13.

IGNITION COIL ATTACHING SCREWS

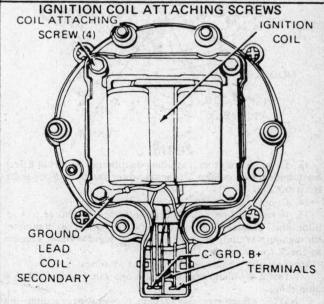

COIL ATTACHING SCREW (4)

IGNITION COIL

GROUND LEAD COIL SECONDARY

C- GRD. B+ TERMINALS

8. Remove coil-cover attaching screws and lift off cover.

IGNITION COIL REMOVED FROM CAP

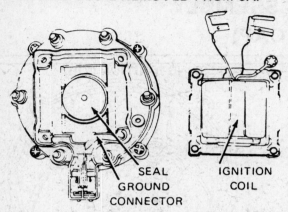

SEAL GROUND CONNECTOR

IGNITION COIL

9. Remove ignition coil attaching screws and lift coil with leads from cap.

10. Remove ignition coil arc seal.

11. Clean with soft cloth and inspect cap for defects. Replace, if needed.

12. Assemble new coil and cover to cap.

TESTING PICKUP COIL

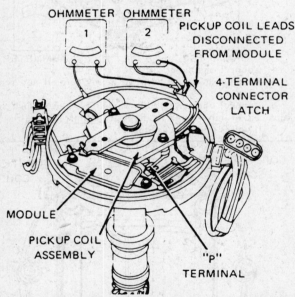

OHMMETER 1   OHMMETER 2   PICKUP COIL LEADS DISCONNECTED FROM MODULE

4-TERMINAL CONNECTOR LATCH

MODULE

PICKUP COIL ASSEMBLY

"P" TERMINAL

13. On all distributors, including distributors with Hall Effect Switch identified in Step 27, remove rotor and pickup coil leads from module.

14. Connect ohmmeter Test 1 and then Test 2.

15. If vacuum unit is used, connect vacuum source to vacuum unit. Replace unit if inoperative. Observe ohmmeter throughout vacuum range; flex leads by hand without vacuum to check for intermittent opens.

16. Test 1 — should read infinite at all times.

Test 2 — should read steady at one value within 500-1500 ohm range.

NOTE: Ohmmeter may deflect if operating vacuum unit causes teeth to align. This is not a defect.

17. If pickup coil is defective, go to Step 18. If okay, go to Step 23.

DRIVING PIN FROM SHAFT

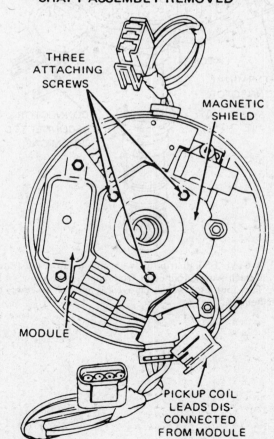

ROLL PIN

18. Mark distributor shaft and gear so they can be reassembled in same position.

19. Drive out roll pin.

SHAFT ASSEMBLY REMOVED

THREE ATTACHING SCREWS

MAGNETIC SHIELD

MODULE

PICKUP COIL LEADS DISCONNECTED FROM MODULE

20. Remove gear and pull shaft assembly from distributor.

ALUMINUM NON-MAGNETIC SHIELD REMOVED

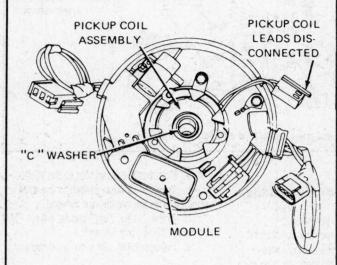

PICKUP COIL ASSEMBLY

PICKUP COIL LEADS DIS-CONNECTED

"C" WASHER

MODULE

21. Remove three attaching screws and remove magnetic shield.

PICKUP COIL REMOVED AND DISASSEMBLED

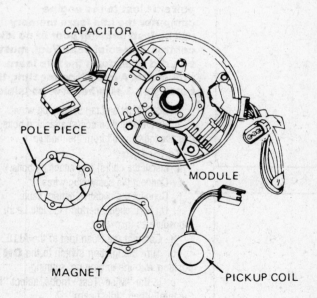

CAPACITOR

POLE PIECE

MODULE

MAGNET

PICKUP COIL

22. Remove retaining ring and remove pickup coil, magnet and pole piece.

MODULE REMOVED

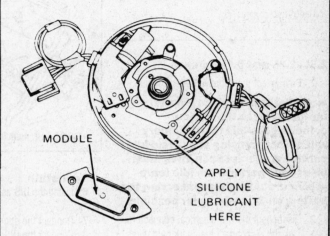

MODULE

APPLY SILICONE LUBRICANT HERE

23. Remove two module attaching screws, and capacitor attaching screw. Lift module, capacitor and harness assembly from base.

24. Disconnect wiring harness from module.

25. Check module with an approved module tester.

26. Install module, wiring harness, and capacitor assembly. Use silicone lubricant on housing under module.

REASSEMBLY

27. Assemble pickup and thin "C" washer.
28. Assemble shaft, gear parts and roll pin.
29. Spin shaft to insure that teeth do not touch.
30. Loosen, then re-tighten pickup coil teeth to eliminate contact.
31. Install rotor and cap.

DIS Parts Replacement

DIS ASSEMBLY

2.5L, 2.8L and 3.1L Engines

1. Disconnect the negative battery cable.

➡ **On the 3.1L engines if battery power is lost to the engine computer the idle learn memory will be lost, causing poor or no idle control. A special Scan Tool, must be used to perform the idle learn procedure. Avoid disconnecting the battery on 3.1L whenever possible.**

2. Disconnect the DIS electrical connectors.
3. Tag and disconnect the spark plug wires.
4. Remove the DIS assembly attaching bolts.
5. Remove the DIS assembly from the engine.

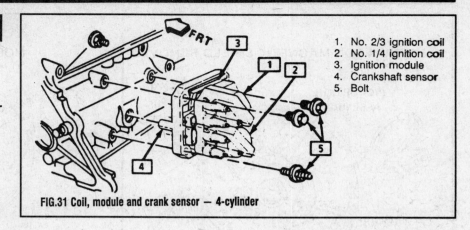

1. No. 2/3 ignition coil
2. No. 1/4 ignition coil
3. Ignition module
4. Crankshaft sensor
5. Bolt

FIG.31 Coil, module and crank sensor — 4-cylinder

To install:

6. Install the DIS assembly and attaching bolts.
7. Connect the spark plug wires.
8. Connect the DIS electrical connectors.
9. Connect the negative battery cable.
10. On 3.1L engine, perform the Idle Learn Procedure as follows:

a. Connect the Scan tool to the ALDL.
b. Turn the ignition switch to the **ON** position with the engine not running.
c. In the "Misc. Test" mode, select "IAC System", then "Idle Learn".
d. Proceed with idle learn as directed.

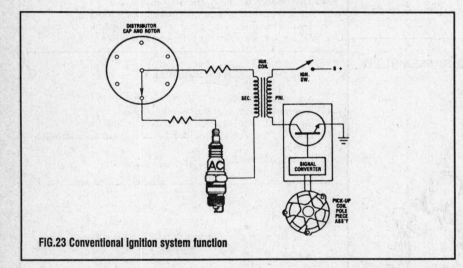

FIG.23 Conventional ignition system function

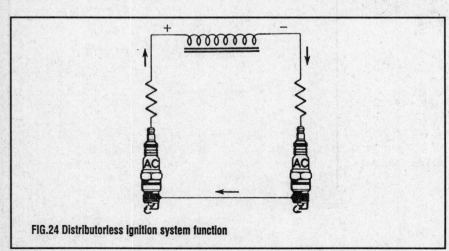

FIG.24 Distributorless ignition system function

IGNITION COIL(S)

2.5L, 2.8L and 3.1L Engines

1. Disconnect the negative battery cable.

➡ **On the 3.1L engines if battery power is lost to the engine computer the idle learn memory will be lost, causing poor or no idle control. A special Scan Tool, must be used to perform the idle learn procedure. Avoid disconnecting the battery on 3.1L whenever possible.**

2. Disconnect and tag spark plug wires.
3. Remove ignition coil(s) attaching bolts, then the ignition coil from the module.

To install:

4. Install the coil(s) and attaching bolts.
5. Connect the spark plug wires.
6. Connect the negative battery cable.
7. On 3.1L engine perform the Idle Learn Procedure as follows:

a. Connect the Scan tool to the ALDL.
b. Turn the ignition switch to the **ON** position with the engine not running.
c. In the "Misc. Test" mode, select "IAC System", then "Idle Learn".
d. Proceed with idle learn as directed.

IGNITION MODULE

2.5L, 2.8L and 3.1L Engines

1. Disconnect the negative battery cable.

➡ **On the 3.1L engines if battery power is lost to the engine computer the idle learn memory will be lost, causing poor or no idle control. A special Scan Tool, must be used to perform the idle learn procedure. Avoid disconnecting the battery on 3.1L whenever possible.**

2. Remove the DIS assembly from the engine.

3. Remove the coils from the assembly.

4. Remove DIS module from the assembly plate.

To install:

5. Install the DIS module to the assembly plate.

6. Install the coils to the assembly.

7. Install the DIS assembly to the engine.

8. Connect the negative battery cable.

9. On 3.1L engine perform the Idle Learn Procedure as follows:

   a. Connect the Scan tool to the ALDL.

   b. Turn the ignition switch to the **ON** position with the engine not running.

   c. In the "Misc. Test" mode, select "IAC System", then "Idle Learn".

   d. Proceed with idle learn as directed.

CRANKSHAFT SENSOR

2.5L, 2.8L and 3.1L Engines

1. Disconnect the negative battery cable.

➡ **On the 3.1L engines if battery power is lost to the engine computer the idle learn memory will be lost, causing poor or no idle control. A special Scan Tool, must be used to perform the idle learn procedure. Avoid disconnecting the battery on 3.1L whenever possible.**

2. Disconnect crankshaft sensor electrical connector.

3. Remove the crankshaft sensor attaching bolt, then remove the crankshaft sensor from the vehicle.

To install:

4. Inspect the sensor O-ring for wear, cracks or leakage. Replace as necessary. Lubricate the new O-ring with engine oil prior to installation.

5. Install the sensor into the hole in the engine block and install retaining bolt.

6. Connect the electrical connector.

7. Connect the negative battery cable.

8. On 3.1L engine perform the Idle Learn Procedure as follows:

   a. Connect the Scan tool to the ALDL.

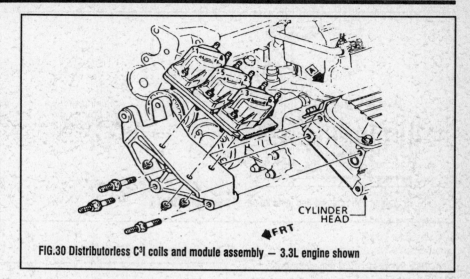

FIG.30 Distributorless C³I coils and module assembly — 3.3L engine shown

FIG.36 Camshaft sensor used on 3.8L (VIN C) engine with C³I system

   b. Turn the ignition switch to the **ON** position with the engine not running.

   c. In the "Misc. Test" mode, select "IAC System", then "Idle Learn".

   d. Proceed with idle learn as directed.

C³I System Parts Replacement

C³I MODULE

3.3L and 3.8L Engine

1. Disconnect the negative battery cable.

2. Disconnect the 14-way connector at the ignition module.

3. Tag and disconnect the spark plug wires at the coil assembly.

4. Remove the nuts and washers securing the C³I module assembly to the bracket.

5. Remove the 6 bolts attaching the coil assemblies to the ignition module.

To install:

6. Install the coil assemblies to the ignition module and install the 6 attaching bolts.

7. Install the nuts and washers attaching the assembly to the bracket.

8. Connect the spark plug wires.

9. Connect the 14-way connector to the module.

10. Connect the negative battery cable.

IGNITION COIL(S)

3.3L and 3.8L Engine

1. Disconnect the negative battery cable.

2. Tag and disconnect spark plug wires.

3. Remove ignition coil(s) attaching bolts, then the ignition coil from the module.

To install:

4. Install the coil(s) and attaching bolts.

5. Connect the spark plug wires.

6. Connect the negative battery cable.

DUAL CRANKSHAFT SENSOR

◆ SEE FIG. 34

3.3L and 3.8L Engine

1. Disconnect battery negative cable.

2. Disconnect serpentine belt from crankshaft pulley.

3. Raise and safely support the vehicle.

4. Remove right front tire and wheel assembly, then the inner access cover.

5. Remove crankshaft harmonic balancer retaining bolt and crankshaft harmonic balancer.

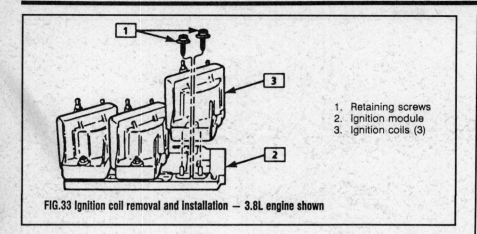

1. Retaining screws
2. Ignition module
3. Ignition coils (3)

FIG.33 Ignition coil removal and installation — 3.8L engine shown

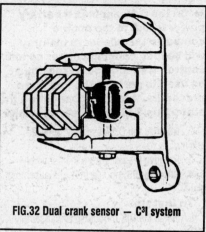

FIG.32 Dual crank sensor — C³I system

6. Disconnect electrical connector from sensor and remove the crankshaft sensor from the vehicle.

To install:

7. Loosely install the crankshaft sensor on the pedestal.

8. Position the sensor with the pedestal attached on special tool J–37089.

9. Position the tool on the crankshaft.

10. Install the bolts to hold the pedestal to the block face. Tighten to 14–28 ft. lbs. (20–40 Nm).

11. Tighten the pedestal pinch bolt to 30–35 inch lbs. (3–4 Nm).

12. Remove special tool J–37089.

13. Place special tool J–37089 on the harmonic balancer and turn. If any vane of the harmonic balancer touches the tool, replace the balancer assembly.

➡ **A clearance of 0.025 inch is required on either side of the interrupter ring. Be certain to obtain the correct clearance. Failure to do so will damage the sensor. A misadjusted sensor of bent interrupter ring could cause rubbing of the sensor, resulting in potential driveability problems, such as rough idle, poor performance, or a no start condition.**

14. Install the balancer on the crankshaft and install the crankshaft balancer bolt. Tighten to 200–239 ft. lbs. (270–325 Nm).

15. Install the inner fender shield.

16. Install the tire and wheel assembly. Tighten to 100 ft. lbs. (140 Nm).

17. Lower the vehicle.

18. Install the serpentine belt.

19. Connect the negative battery cable.

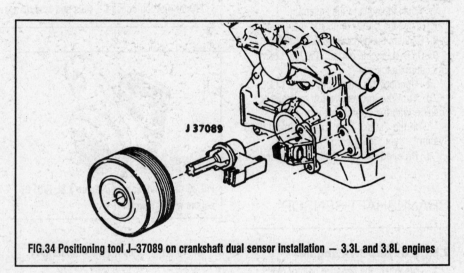

J 37089

FIG.34 Positioning tool J–37089 on crankshaft dual sensor installation — 3.3L and 3.8L engines

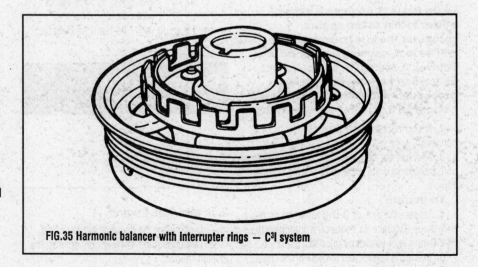

FIG.35 Harmonic balancer with interrupter rings — C³I system

IGNITION TIMING

♦ SEE FIGS. 37–40

Ignition timing is the point at which each spark plug fires in relation to its respective piston, during the compression stroke of the engine.

As far as ignition timing is concerned, the position of the piston can be related (in degrees) to the following reference terms: Top Dead Center (TDC), After Top Dead Center (ATDC), and Before Top Dead Center (BTDC). The movement of the piston is expressed in degrees due to the rotation of the crankshaft. Even though the crankshaft turns 720° to complete one entire 4-stroke cycle, all we're concerned about here is the compression stroke, since this is when the ignition of the air/fuel mixture takes place (or more accurately, should take place).

Because it takes a fraction of a second for the spark (at the spark plug) to ignite the air/fuel mixture and for the mixture to burn completely, the spark should ideally occur just before the piston reaches TDC. If the spark didn't occur until exactly TDC or ATDC, the piston would already be on its way down before the mixture explosion would not exert as much downward force on the piston as it would if the ignition timing was properly set. The result of this would be reduced power and fuel economy.

Should ignition of the air/fuel mixture occur too far BTDC (advanced), the mixture explosion will try to force the piston downward before it can mechanically do so. This contest between the explosion forcing the piston downward and the crankshaft forcing the piston upward will result in a pinging sound if you're lucky; severe engine damage if you're not so lucky. If you experience pinging, check with a trusted mechanic to determine if the pinging is mild or severe. Only a trained car mechanic can safely determine this.

➡ **Pinging can also be caused by inferior gasoline, since lower octane gas burns at a faster, more uncontrolled rate than a higher octane fuel.**

In order to compensate for low quality gas, the ignition timing may be retarded a couple of degrees, though this is not recommended since performance and fuel economy will suffer.

On United States engines, after the initial (base) timing is set, the emission control computer and related components electronically determine and adjust the degree of spark advance under all conditions. On 1982-85 Canadian models, total ignition timing advance is determined by three things: initial timing setting, distributor vacuum control and distributor mechanical control.

ADJUSTMENT

DIS and C³I Systems

All vehicles that equipped with either the Direct Ignition System (DIS) or the Computer Controlled Coil Ignition (C³I) system. The systems consist of a coil pack, ignition module, crankshaft reluctor or interrupter ring(s), magnetic sensor and an Electronic Control Module (ECM). Timing advance and retard are accomplished through the ECM with the Electronic Spark Timing (EST) and Electronic Spark Control (ESC) circuitry. No ignition timing adjustment is required or possible.

HEI System

To check the timing before and after adjustment, a timing light is used. The timing light will visually show you a) when the spark is sent to the spark plug, and b) the position of the crankshaft when the spark occurs.

There are three basic types of timing light available. The first is a simple neon bulb with two wire connections (one for the spark plug and one for the plug wire, connecting the light in series). This type of light is quite dim, and must be held closely to the marks to be seen, but it is quite inexpensive. The second type of light operates

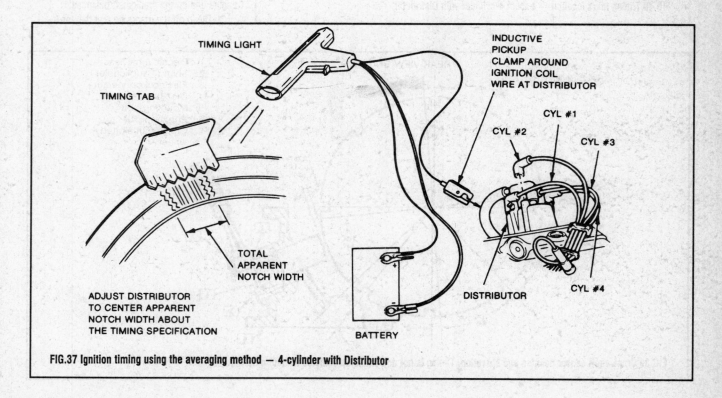

FIG.37 Ignition timing using the averaging method — 4-cylinder with Distributor

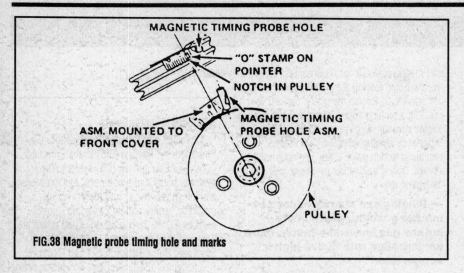

FIG.38 Magnetic probe timing hole and marks

MAGNETIC TIMING PROBE HOLE

"O" STAMP ON POINTER

NOTCH IN PULLEY

MAGNETIC TIMING PROBE HOLE ASM.

ASM. MOUNTED TO FRONT COVER

PULLEY

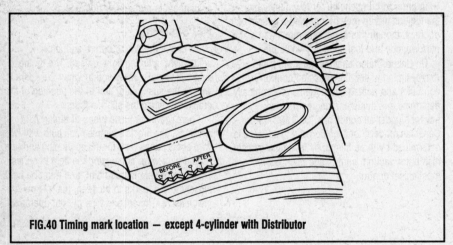

FIG.40 Timing mark location — except 4-cylinder with Distributor

BEFORE   AFTER

form the car's battery. Two alligator clips connect to the battery terminals, while a third wire connects to the spark plug with an adapter. This type of light is more expensive, but the xenon bulb provides a nice bright flash which can even be seen in sunlight. The third type replaces the battery source with 110 volt house current. Some timing lights have other functions built into them, such as dwell meters, tachometers, or remote starting switches. These are convenient, in that they reduce the tangle of wires under the hood, but may duplicate the functions of tools you already have.

Because your car has electronic ignition, you should use a timing light which has an inductive pick-up. This type of pick-up merely clamps around the No. 1 spark plug wire, eliminating any kind of adapter. Other types of timing lights may cause false timing readings when used with H.E.I. systems.

✷✷ CAUTION

NEVER use a timing light which requires piercing of the spark plug wire.

---

1. Refer to the instructions listed on the emission control label inside the engine compartment. Follow all instructions on the label.
2. Locate the timing marks on the front of the engine and on the crankshaft balances.
3. Clean off the marks so that they are

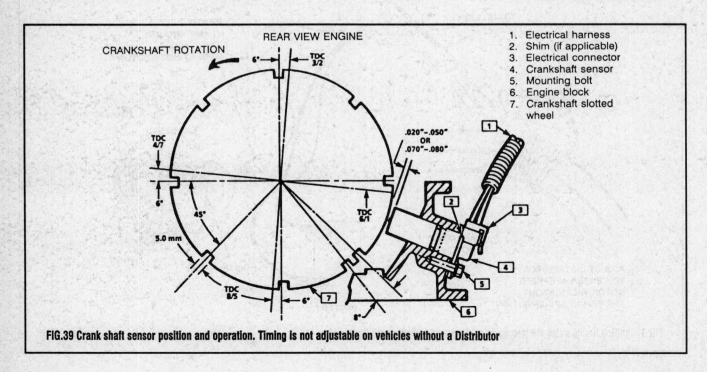

CRANKSHAFT ROTATION

REAR VIEW ENGINE

TDC 3/2

TDC 4/7

45°

5.0 mm

TDC 8/5

6°

8°

TDC 6/1

.020"-.050" OR .070"-.080"

1. Electrical harness
2. Shim (if applicable)
3. Electrical connector
4. Crankshaft sensor
5. Mounting bolt
6. Engine block
7. Crankshaft slotted wheel

FIG.39 Crank shaft sensor position and operation. Timing is not adjustable on vehicles without a Distributor

readable. Chalk or white paint on the balancer mark (line) and at the correct point on the timing scale will make the marks much easier to accurately align.

4. If specified on the emissions label, attach a tachometer to the engine according to the tachometer manufacturer's instructions.

➡ **On 4-cylinder engines, the TACH terminal is at the brown wire Connection at the ignition coil; on V6's, it is next to the BAT connector on the distributor cap.**

5. Attach a timing light according to the timing light manufacturer's instructions. Remember that the inductive pick-up is clamped around the No. 1 spark plug wire.

6. Check that all wiring is clear of the fan, then start the engine. Allow the engine to reach normal operating temperature.

7. Aim the timing light at the timing marks. The line on the crankshaft balancer will line up at a timing mark. If the line is within 1° of where it should be, no adjustment is necessary.

8. If adjustment is necessary, loosen the distributor holddown bolt slightly. Slowly rotate the distributor until the proper setting is attained.

9. Tighten the holddown bolt, recheck the timing and readjust if required.

10. Turn the engine off and disconnect the timing light (and tachometer, if in use).

➡ **Disregard the short tube which may be integral with the timing scale on some engines. This tube is used to connect magnetic timing equipment which is marketed to professional shops.**

VALVE LASH

Adjustment

EXCEPT 2.8L ENGINE

All models utilize an hydraulic valve lifter system to obtain zero lash. No adjustment is necessary. An initial adjustment is required anytime that the lifters are removed or the valve train is disturbed, this procedure is covered in Section 3.

2.8L (173CID) ENGINE
◆ SEE FIG. 42

Anytime the V6 valve train is disturbed, the valve lash must be adjusted. Crank the engine until the timing mark aligns with the **O** mark on the timing scale, and both valves in the No. 1 cylinder are closed. If the valves are moving as the timing marks align, the engine is in the No. 4 firing position. Turn the crankshaft one more revolution. With the engine in the No. 1 firing position, adjust the following valves:

- exhaust—1,2,3
- intake—1,5,6

Rotate the crankshaft one full revolution, until it is in the No. 4 firing position. Adjust the following valves:

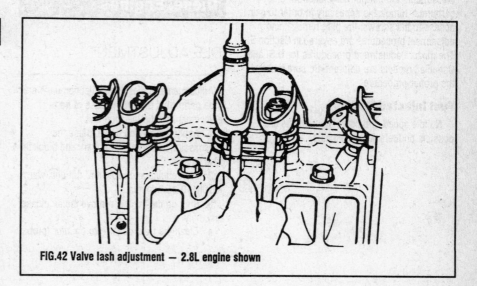

FIG.42 Valve lash adjustment — 2.8L engine shown

- Exhaust—4,5,6
- Intake—2,3,4

Adjustment is made by backing off the rocker arm adjusting nut until there is play in the pushrod. Tighten the nut to remove the pushrod clearance (this can be determined by rotating the pushrod with your fingers while tightening the adjusting nut). When the pushrod cannot be freely turned, tighten the nut 1½ additional turns to place the hydraulic lifter in the center of its travel. No further adjustment is required.

IDLE SPEED AND MIXTURE ADJUSTMENTS

Gasoline Engines

IDLE SPEED

U.S. Carbureted Models

On non-A/C models not equipped with ISC, the idle speed is adjusted at the idle speed screw on the carburetor. Before adjusting, check the underhood sticker for any preparations required. On A/C equipped models which do not have an ISC motor, an idle speed solenoid is used. This solenoid is adjusted at the solenoid screw. Consult the underhood specifications sticker for special instructions.

Canadian Models

The idle speed may be adjusted on Canadian models, though this is not part of a normal tune-up. Be sure to follow the instructions on the underhood emissions label to the letter in order to properly perform this adjustment.

Fuel Injected Models

No idle speed or mixture adjustments are possible on fuel injected engines.

MIXTURE ADJUSTMENT

Carbureted Models

Mixture adjustments are a function of the Computer Command Control (CCC) system. The idle speed on models equipped with an Idle Speed Control (ISC) motor is also automatically adjusted by the Computer Command Control System, making manual adjustment unnecessary. The underhood specifications sticker will indicate ISC motor use. We strongly recommend that mixture adjustments be referred to a qualified, professional technician.

As on U.S. models, the idle mixture screws are concealed under hardened plugs and mixture adjustments are not normally required. Since carburetor removal is necessary in order to gain access to the screws, the plug removal and adjustment procedures are covered in Section 5. The mixture adjustment procedures for U.S. and Canadian models are different. Be sure to follow the proper procedure.

Fuel Injected Models

No idle speed or mixture adjustments are possible on fuel injected engines.

FIG.41 Diesel fuel injection tachometer

Diesel Engines

IDLE ADJUSTMENT

Adjustments to diesel fuel injection units are to be performed only in the case of parts replacement on the injection unit.

1. Apply the parking brake, place the transmission selector lever in Park and block the drive wheels.
2. Start engine and allow it to run until warm, usually 10-15 minutes.
3. Shut off the engine, remove the air cleaner assembly.
4. Clean the front cover rpm counter (probe holder) and the crankshaft balancer rim.
5. Install the magnetic pick-up probe of tool J-26925 fully into the rpm counter. Connect the battery leads; red to positive (+) and black to negative (–).
6. Disconnect the two-lead connector at the generator.
7. Turn off all electrical accessories.
8. Allow no one to touch either the steering wheel or service brake pedal.
9. Start the engine and place the transmission selector lever in Drive.
10. Check the slow idle speed reading against the one given on the underhood emission control sticker. Reset if required.
11. Unplug the connector from the fast idle cold advance (engine temp.) switch and install a jumper between the connector terminals. Do not allow the jumper to touch ground.
12. Check the fast idle solenoid speed against the one given on the underhood sticker and reset if required.
13. Remove the jumper and reconnect the connector to the temperature switch.
14. Recheck and reset the slow idle speed if necessary.
15. Shut off the engine.
16. Reconnect the lead at the generator.
17. Disconnect and remove the tachometer.
18. If equipped with cruise control adjust the servo throttle cable to minimum slack then install the clip on the servo stud.

Diagnosis of Spark Plugs

Problem	Possible Cause	Correction
Brown to grayish-tan deposits and slight electrode wear.	• Normal wear.	• Clean, regap, reinstall.
Dry, fluffy black carbon deposits.	• Poor ignition output.	• Check distributor to coil connections.
Wet, oily deposits with very little electrode wear.	• "Break-in" of new or recently overhauled engine. • Excessive valve stem guide clearances. • Worn intake valve seals.	• Degrease, clean and reinstall the plugs. • Refer to Section 3. • Replace the seals.
Red, brown, yellow and white colored coatings on the insulator. Engine misses intermittently under severe operating conditions.	• By-products of combustion.	• Clean, regap, and reinstall. If heavily coated, replace.
Colored coatings heavily deposited on the portion of the plug projecting into the chamber and on the side facing the intake valve.	• Leaking seals if condition is found in only one or two cylinders.	• Check the seals. Replace if necessary. Clean, regap, and reinstall the plugs.
Shiny yellow glaze coating on the insulator.	• Melted by-products of combustion.	• Avoid sudden acceleration with wide-open throttle after long periods of low speed driving. Replace the plugs.
Burned or blistered insulator tips and badly eroded electrodes.	• Overheating.	• Check the cooling system. • Check for sticking heat riser valves. Refer to Section 1. • Lean air-fuel mixture. • Check the heat range of the plugs. May be too hot. • Check ignition timing. May be over-advanced. • Check the torque value of the plugs to ensure good plug-engine seat contact.
Broken or cracked insulator tips.	• Heat shock from sudden rise in tip temperature under severe operating conditions. Improper gapping of plugs.	• Replace the plugs. Gap correctly.

TORQUE SPECIFICATIONS

Component	U.S.	Metric
C3I Ignition module:	19 ft. lbs.	25 Nm
C3I Crankshaft sensor:	71 inch lbs.	8 Nm
Crankshaft bolt		
3.3L engine:	220 ft. lbs.	300 Nm
3.8L engine:	220 ft. lbs.	300 Nm
DIS Coil pack:	40 inch lbs.	4.5 Nm
DIS Crankshaft sensor:	20 inch lbs.	2.3 Nm
Spark plugs:		
Except 2.8L carburated	20 ft. lbs.	27 Nm
2.8L carburated	15 ft. lbs.	17 Nm

3

ENGINE AND ENGINE OVERHAUL

Troubleshooting the Cooling System

Problem	Cause	Solution
High temperature gauge indication—overheating	• Coolant level low	• Replenish coolant
	• Fan belt loose	• Adjust fan belt tension
	• Radiator hose(s) collapsed	• Replace hose(s)
	• Radiator airflow blocked	• Remove restriction (bug screen, fog lamps, etc.)
	• Faulty radiator cap	• Replace radiator cap
	• Ignition timing incorrect	• Adjust ignition timing
	• Idle speed low	• Adjust idle speed
	• Air trapped in cooling system	• Purge air
	• Heavy traffic driving	• Operate at fast idle in neutral intermittently to cool engine
	• Incorrect cooling system component(s) installed	• Install proper component(s)
	• Faulty thermostat	• Replace thermostat
	• Water pump shaft broken or impeller loose	• Replace water pump
	• Radiator tubes clogged	• Flush radiator
	• Cooling system clogged	• Flush system
	• Casting flash in cooling passages	• Repair or replace as necessary. Flash may be visible by removing cooling system components or removing core plugs.
	• Brakes dragging	• Repair brakes
	• Excessive engine friction	• Repair engine
	• Antifreeze concentration over 68%	• Lower antifreeze concentration percentage
	• Missing air seals	• Replace air seals
	• Faulty gauge or sending unit	• Repair or replace faulty component
	• Loss of coolant flow caused by leakage or foaming	• Repair or replace leaking component, replace coolant
	• Viscous fan drive failed	• Replace unit
Low temperature indication—undercooling	• Thermostat stuck open	• Replace thermostat
	• Faulty gauge or sending unit	• Repair or replace faulty component
Coolant loss—boilover	• Overfilled cooling system	• Reduce coolant level to proper specification
	• Quick shutdown after hard (hot) run	• Allow engine to run at fast idle prior to shutdown
	• Air in system resulting in occasional "burping" of coolant	• Purge system
	• Insufficient antifreeze allowing coolant boiling point to be too low	• Add antifreeze to raise boiling point
	• Antifreeze deteriorated because of age or contamination	• Replace coolant
	• Leaks due to loose hose clamps, loose nuts, bolts, drain plugs, faulty hoses, or defective radiator	• Pressure test system to locate source of leak(s) then repair as necessary

Troubleshooting the Cooling System (cont.)

Problem	Cause	Solution
Coolant loss—boilover	• Faulty head gasket • Cracked head, manifold, or block • Faulty radiator cap	• Replace head gasket • Replace as necessary • Replace cap
Coolant entry into crankcase or cylinder(s)	• Faulty head gasket • Crack in head, manifold or block	• Replace head gasket • Replace as necessary
Coolant recovery system inoperative	• Coolant level low • Leak in system • Pressure cap not tight or seal missing, or leaking • Pressure cap defective • Overflow tube clogged or leaking • Recovery bottle vent restricted	• Replenish coolant to FULL mark • Pressure test to isolate leak and repair as necessary • Repair as necessary • Replace cap • Repair as necessary • Remove restriction
Noise	• Fan contacting shroud • Loose water pump impeller • Glazed fan belt • Loose fan belt • Rough surface on drive pulley • Water pump bearing worn • Belt alignment	• Reposition shroud and inspect engine mounts • Replace pump • Apply silicone or replace belt • Adjust fan belt tension • Replace pulley • Remove belt to isolate. Replace pump. • Check pulley alignment. Repair as necessary.
No coolant flow through heater core	• Restricted return inlet in water pump • Heater hose collapsed or restricted • Restricted heater core • Restricted outlet in thermostat housing • Intake manifold bypass hole in cylinder head restricted • Faulty heater control valve • Intake manifold coolant passage restricted	• Remove restriction • Remove restriction or replace hose • Remove restriction or replace core • Remove flash or restriction • Remove restriction • Replace valve • Remove restriction or replace intake manifold

NOTE: *Immediately after shutdown, the engine enters a condition known as heat soak. This is caused by the cooling system being inoperative while engine temperature is still high. If coolant temperature rises above boiling point, expansion and pressure may push some coolant out of the radiator overflow tube. If this does not occur frequently it is considered normal.*

THE ENGINE ELECTRICAL SYSTEM

The engine electrical system can be broken down into three separate and distinct systems:

1. The starting system
2. The charging system
3. The ignition system.

HEI Ignition Coil

TESTING

◆ SEE FIGS. 1 to 3

An ohmmeter with both high and low ranges should be used for these test. Tests are made with the cap assembly removed and the battery wire disconnected. If a tachometer is connected to the TACH terminal, disconnect it before making these test.

1. Connect an ohmmeter between the TACH and BAT terminals in the distributor cap. The primary coil resistance should be less than 1Ω.

2. To check the coil secondary resistance, connect an ohmmeter between the rotor button and the BAT terminal. Note the reading. Connect an ohmmeter between the rotor button and the TACH terminal. Note the reading. The resistance in both cases should be between 6,000 and 30,000 ohms. Be sure to test between the rotor button and both the BAT and TACH terminals.

3. Replace the coil ONLY if the readings in Step 1 and Step 2 are infinite.

➡ **These resistance checks will not disclose shorted coil windings. This condition can only be detected with scope analysis or a suitably designed coil tester. If these instruments are not available, replace the coil with a known good coil as a final coil test.**

REMOVAL & INSTALLATION

1. Disconnect the feed and module wire terminal connectors from the distributor cap.
2. Remove the ignition set retainer.
3. Remove the 4 coil cover-to-distributor cap screws.
5. Using a blunt drift, press the coil wire spade terminals up out of the distributor cap.
6. Lift the coil up out of the distributor cap.

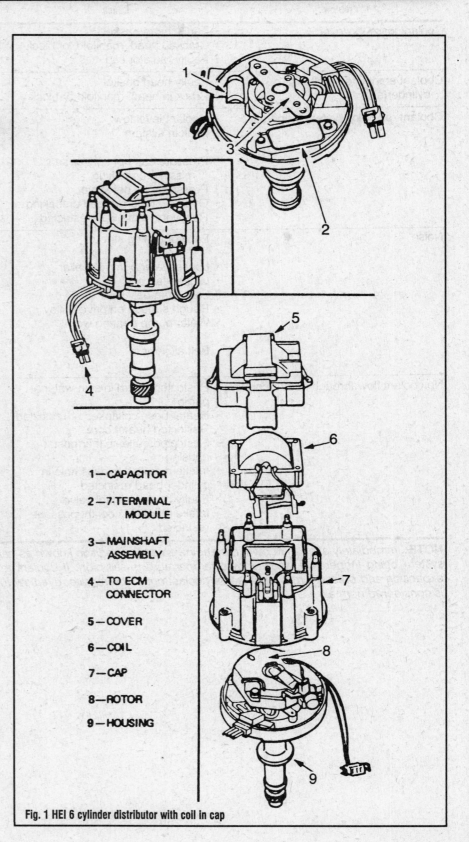

1 — CAPACITOR

2 — 7-TERMINAL MODULE

3 — MAINSHAFT ASSEMBLY

4 — TO ECM CONNECTOR

5 — COVER

6 — COIL

7 — CAP

8 — ROTOR

9 — HOUSING

Fig. 1 HEI 6 cylinder distributor with coil in cap

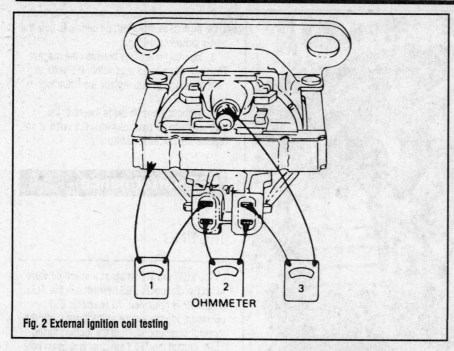

Fig. 2 External ignition coil testing

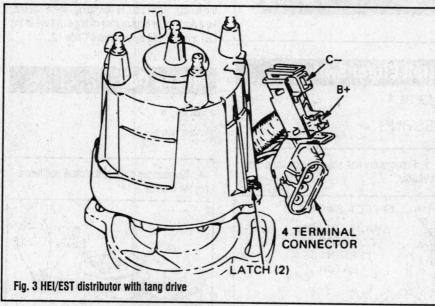

Fig. 3 HEI/EST distributor with tang drive

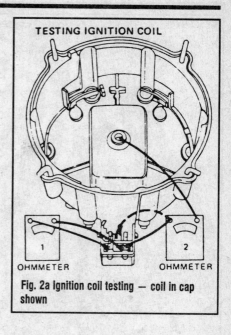

Fig. 2a ignition coil testing — coil in cap shown

Follow the engine cranks but won't run charts in the fuel system section of this manual.

REMOVAL & INSTALLATION

2.5L, 2.8L and 3.1L Engines

1. Disconnect the negative battery cable.

➡ On the 3.1L engines if battery power is lost to the engine computer the idle learn memory will be lost, causing poor or no idle control. A special Scan Tool, must be used to perform the idle learn procedure. Avoid disconnecting the battery on 3.1L whenever possible.

2. Disconnect and tag spark plug wires.
3. Remove ignition coil(s) attaching bolts, then the ignition coil from the module.

To install:

4. Install the coil(s) and attaching bolts.
5. Connect the spark plug wires.
6. Connect the negative battery cable.
7. On 3.1L engine perform the Idle Learn Procedure as follows:

    a. Connect the Scan tool to the ALDL.
    b. Turn the ignition switch to the **ON** position with the engine not running.
    c. In the "Misc. Test" mode, select "IAC System", then "Idle Learn".
    d. Proceed with idle learn as directed.

7. Remove and clean the coil spring, rubber seal washer and coil cavity of the distributor cap.
8. Coat the rubber seal with a dielectric lubricant furnished in the replacement ignition coil package.
9. Reverse the above procedures to install.

DIS and C³I Ignition Coils

TESTING

Since the ignition and fuel system are both controlled by the same computer and the computer bases it's ignition and timing on sensors these systems must be tested together.

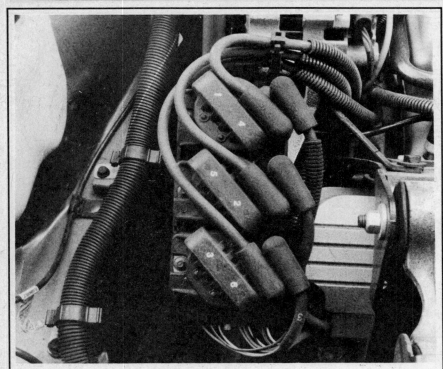

Fig. 3a Coil pack assembly used on the 3.3L engine

3.3L Engine

1. Disconnect the negative battery cable.
2. Tag and disconnect spark plug wires.
3. Remove ignition coil(s) attaching bolts, then the ignition coil from the module.

To install:

4. Install the coil(s) and attaching bolts.
5. Connect the spark plug wires.
6. Connect the negative battery cable.

Hall Effect Switch

▶ SEE FIG. 4

TESTING

1. Remove the hall effect switch from the distributor.

2. Connect a 12 volts battery and a voltmeter to the switch, as indicated. Be certain to note the proper polarity markings.

3. Insert a knife blade between the magnet. The voltmeter should read within 0.5 volts of battery voltage. If not, replace the hall effect switch.

4. Without the knife blade inserted, the voltmeter should read less than 0.5 volts. If not, replace the hall effect switch.

EST Performance

TESTING

The ECM will set timing at a specified value when the diagnostic TEST terminal in the ALDL connector is grounded. To check for EST operation, run the engine at 2000 rpm with the terminal ungrounded. Note the ignition timing. Then, ground the TEST terminal and again note the timing. If the EST is operating, there should be a noticeable engine rpm change. A fault in the EST system will set a trouble Code 42.

Pickup Coil

▶ SEE FIG. 5

TESTING

1. Remove the rotor and pickup coil leads from the module.

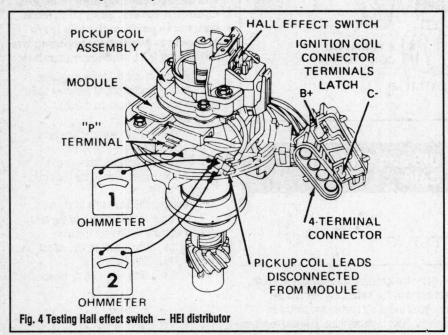

Fig. 4 Testing Hall effect switch — HEI distributor

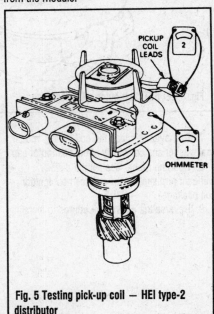

Fig. 5 Testing pick-up coil — HEI type-2 distributor

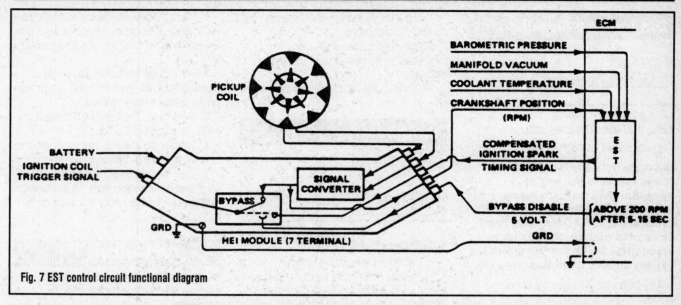

Fig. 7 EST control circuit functional diagram

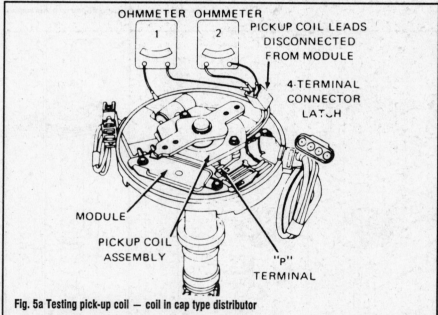

Fig. 5a Testing pick-up coil — coil in cap type distributor

2. Using an ohmmeter, test as follow:

a. Connect 1 lead of the ohmmeter between the distributor housing and 1 of the pickup coil lead. Meter should read infinity. Flex the leads by hand while observing the ohmmeter, to check for intermittent opens.

b. Connect the ohmmeter between leads between both of the pickup coil leads. Meter should read a steady value between 500–1500 ohms.

3. If the readings are not as specified, the pickup coil is defective and should be replaced.

HEI Module

SEE FIG. 8

REMOVAL & INSTALLATION

1. Remove the distributor cap and rotor as previously described.

2. Disconnect the harness connector and pickup coil spade connectors from the module. Be careful not to damage the wires when removing the connector.

3. Remove the two screws and module from the distributor housing.

4. Coat the bottom of the new module with dielectric lubricant supplied with the new module. Reverse the above procedure to install.

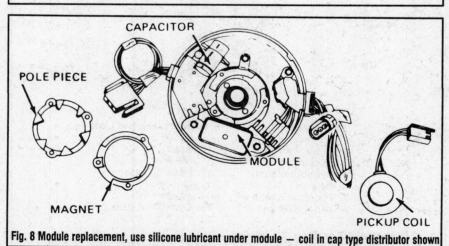

Fig. 8 Module replacement, use silicone lubricant under module — coil in cap type distributor shown

DIS Ignition Module

REMOVAL & INSTALLATION

2.5L, 2.8L and 3.1L Engines

1. Disconnect the negative battery cable.

➡ **On the 3.1L engines if battery power is lost to the engine computer the idle learn memory will be lost, causing poor or no idle control. A special Scan Tool, must be used to perform the idle learn procedure. Avoid disconnecting the battery on 3.1L whenever possible.**

2. Remove the DIS assembly from the engine.
3. Remove the coils from the assembly.
4. Remove DIS module from the assembly plate.

To install:

5. Install the DIS module to the assembly plate.
6. Install the coils to the assembly.
7. Install the DIS assembly to the engine.
8. Connect the negative battery cable.
9. On 3.1L engine perform the Idle Learn Procedure as follows:

   a. Connect the Scan tool to the ALDL.

   b. Turn the ignition switch to the **ON** position with the engine not running.

   c. In the "Misc. Test" mode, select "IAC System", then "Idle Learn".

   d. Proceed with idle learn as directed.

C³I Ignition Module

REMOVAL & INSTALLATION

3.3L Engine

1. Disconnect the negative battery cable.
2. Disconnect the 14-way connector at the ignition module.
3. Tag and disconnect the spark plug wires at the coil assembly.
4. Remove the nuts and washers securing the Cúl module assembly to the bracket.
5. Remove the 6 bolts attaching the coil assemblies to the ignition module.

To install:

6. Install the coil assemblies to the ignition module and install the 6 attaching bolts.

7. Install the nuts and washers attaching the assembly to the bracket.
8. Connect the spark plug wires.
9. Connect the 14-way connector to the module.
10. Connect the negative battery cable.

Distributor

REMOVAL

4-Cylinder Engines

1. Disconnect the negative battery cable.
2. Raise the front of the vehicle and support is safely with jackstands. DO NOT place the jackstands under the engine cradle.

3. Place a jack under the engine cradle then extend the jack so that it just touches the cradle. The jack must not block any of the engine cradle bolts.
4. Remove the two rear engine cradle attaching bolts and lower the cradle just enough to gain access to the distributor.
5. Remove the five screws which attach the brake line support to the floorpan.
6. Remove the coil wire from the distributor.
7. Remove the distributor cap.
8. Mark the position of the rotor firing tip on the distributor body, then mark the relationship between the distributor body and some on the engine.

✳✳✳ WARNING

DO NOT attempt to crank the engine while the distributor is removed.

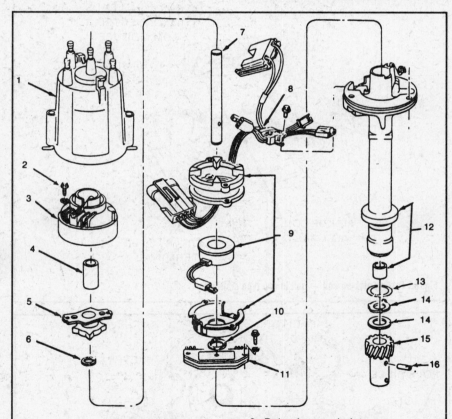

1. Distributor cap	9. Pole piece and plate assy. (pick-up coil)
2. Screw	10. Seal
3. Rotor	11. Module
4. Bushing	12. Housing assembly
5. Distributor shaft	13. O-ring
6. Retainer	14. Washer
7. Distributor shaft	15. Distributor gear
8. Wiring harness	16. Pin

Fig. 6 Exploded view of 4 cylinder distributor

9. Loosen the distributor holddown clamp bolt and slide the holddown clamp aside to clear the distributor body.

10. Lift the distributor out of the engine and mark the point at which the rotor stops turning while you're pulling upward. The rotor will have to be positioned at this same spot in order to install the distributor correctly.

V6 Engines

1. Disconnect the negative battery cable at the battery.

2. Release the distributor and ignition coil electrical connections at the distributor cap.

3. Follow steps 8 through 10 of the previous procedure to complete the removal of the distributor.

INSTALLATION — ENGINE NOT DISTURBED

1. Align the ignition rotor with the mark made during the previous step 10.

2. Install the distributor into the engine, noting that the marks made during the previous step 8 must align. If they don't line up the first time, remove the distributor and try again.

3. Reposition the holddown clamp on the distributor body and tighten the bolt until the distributor is snug, but can be moved with a little effort.

4. Connect all wiring to the distributor, and on four cylinder models, jack the engine cradle back into place, install the engine cradle bolts and the brake line support bolts.

5. Connect the battery cable and lower the vehicle if necessary.

6. Adjust the ignition timing as previously outlined.

INSTALLATION — ENGINE DISTURBED WITH DISTRIBUTOR REMOVED

1. Remove the spark plug from the No. 1 cylinder.

2. Place your thumb over the spark plug hole and turn the crankshaft by hand with a wrench until pressure is felt at the plug hole.

3. Look at the timing marks on the front of the engine and check to see if the balancer slash is aligned with the **0** on the timing scale. If necessary, turn the crankshaft until it does align.

4. On the four cylinder engine, turn the rotor until the rotor firing tip is positioned between the Nos. 1 and 3 spark plug towers of the distributor

cap. On the V6, position the firing tip between the Nos.1 and 6 towers of the cap.

5. Install the distributor and follow steps 3 through 6 of the first (previous) installation procedure to complete the installation.

The Charging System

The automobile charging system provides electrical power for operation of the vehicle's ignition and starting systems and all the electrical accessories. The battery serves as an electrical surge or storage tank, storing (in chemical form) the energy originally produced by the engine driven A.C. (alternator). The system also provides a means of regulating alternator output to protect the battery from being overcharged and to avoid excessive voltage to the accessories.

The storage battery is a chemical device incorporating parallel lead plates in a tank containing a sulfuric acid/water solution. Adjacent plates are slightly dissimilar, and the chemical reaction of the two dissimilar plates produces electrical energy when the battery is connected to a load such as the starter motor. The chemical reaction is reversible, so that when the alternator is producing a voltage (electrical pressure) greater than that produced by the battery, electricity is forced into the battery, and the battery is returned to its fully charged state.

The vehicle's alternator is driven mechanically, through belts, by the engine crankshaft. It consists of two coils of fine wire, cone stationary (the stator), and one movable (the rotor). The rotor may also be known as the armature, and consists of fine wire wrapped around an iron core which is mounted on a shaft. The electricity which flows through the two coils of wire (provided initially by the battery in some cases) creates an intense magnetic field around both rotor and stator, and the interaction between the two fields creates voltage, allowing the generator to power the accessories and charges the battery.

Newer automobiles, including your car, use alternating current alternators because they are efficient, can be rotated at high speeds, and have few brush problems. In an alternator, the field rotates while all the current produced passes only through the stator windings. The brushes bear against continuous slip rings rather than a commutator. This causes the current produced to periodically reverse the direction of its flow. Diodes (electrical one-way switches) block the flow of current from traveling in the wrong direction. A series of diodes is wired together to permit the alternating flow of the stator to be converted to a pulsating, but unidirectional flow

at the alternator output. the alternator's field is wired in series with the voltage regulator. Alternators are self-limiting as far as maximum current is concerned.

SAFETY PRECAUTIONS

Observing these precautions will ensure safe handling of the electrical system components, and will avoid damage to the vehicle's electrical system:

a. Be absolutely sure of the polarity of a booster battery before making connections. Connect the cables positive to positive, and negative to negative. Connect positive cables first and then make the last connection to a ground on the body of the booster vehicle so that arcing cannot ignite hydrogen gas that may have accumulated near the battery. Even momentary connection of a booster battery with the polarity reserved will damage alternator diodes.

b. Disconnect both vehicle battery cables before attempting to charge a battery.

c. Never ground the alternator output or battery terminal. Be cautious when using metal tools around a battery to avoid creating a short circuit between the terminals.

d. Never run an alternator or generator without load unless the field circuit is disconnected.

e. Never attempt to polarize an alternator.

Alternator

Two of the serviceable models are the SI series alternator are used. The 10 SI, 12SI, 15 SI and 17 SI are of similar construction; the 15 SL and 17 SI are slightly larger, use different stator windings, and produce more current. The new CS series, CS 130, require no periodic maintenance. The CS series can only be serviced as a complete unit, no internal repair parts are available.

The procedures for overhaul included in this manual only cover the the older style alternators used before 1987 that General Motors recommended servicing. General Motors does not advise servicing the newer type alternator and does not provide parts for them. Before attempting to service or disassemble any electrical component always check on the cost and availability of replacement parts. A complete rebuilt or new unit may be more cost effective than trying the safe the defective part.

FIG. 9a Disconnecting the BATT lead from the alternator

PRECAUTIONS

1. When installing a battery, make sure that the positive and negative cables are not reversed.

2. When jump-starting the car, be sure that like terminals are connected. This also applies to using a battery charger. Reverse polarity will burn out the alternator and regulator in a matter of seconds.

3. Never operate the alternator with the battery disconnected or on an otherwise uncontrolled open circuit.

4. Do not short across or ground any alternator or regulator terminals.

5. Do not try to polarize the alternator.

6. Do not apply full battery voltage to the field (brown) connector.

7. Always disconnect the battery ground cable before disconnecting the alternator lead.

8. Always disconnect the battery (negative cable first) when charging it.

9. Never subject the alternator to excessive

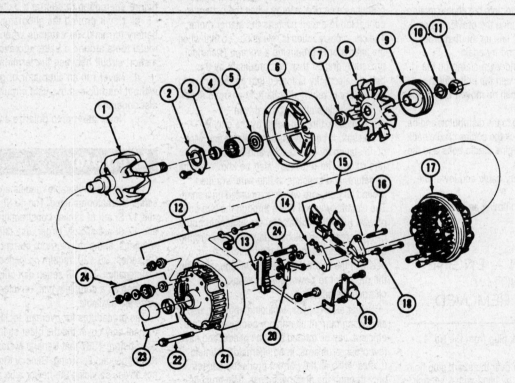

1. Rotor	9. Pulley
2. Front bearing retainer	10. Lockwasher
3. Inner collar	11. Pulley nut
4. Bearing	12. Terminal assembly
5. Washer	13. Rectifier bridge
6. Front housing	14. Regulator
7. Outer collar	15. Brush assembly
8. Fan	16. Screw

17. Stator
18. Insulating washer
19. Capacitor
20. Diode trio
21. Rear housing
22. Through bolt
23. Bearing and seal assembly
24. Terminal assembly

Fig. 9 Exploded view of the 10-SI alternator

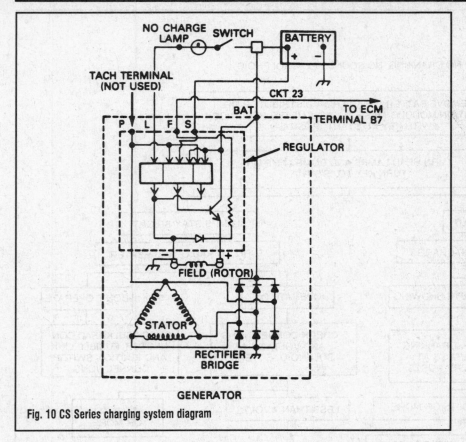

Fig. 10 CS Series charging system diagram

plates held a short distance apart in a solution of sulfuric acid and water. The two types of plates are of dissimilar metals. This causes a chemical reaction to set up, and it is this reaction which produces current flow from the battery when its positive and negative terminals are connected to an electrical appliance such as a lamp or motor. The continued transfer of electrons would eventually convert the sulfuric acid in the electrolyte to water, and make the two plates identical in chemical composition. As electrical energy is removed from the battery, its voltage output tends to drop. Thus, measuring battery voltage and battery electrolyte composition are two ways of checking the ability of the unit to supply power. During the starting of the engine, electrical energy is removed from the battery. However, if the charging circuit is in good condition and the operating conditions are normal, the power removed from the battery will be replaced by the generator (or alternator) which will force electrons back through the battery, reversing the normal flow, and restoring the battery to its original chemical state.

The battery and starting motor are linked by very heavy electrical cables designed to minimize resistance to the flow of current. The major power supply cable that leaves the battery goes directly to the starter, while other electrical system needs are supplied by a smaller cable. During the starter operation, power flows from the battery to the starter and is grounded through the car's frame and the battery's negative ground strap.

heat or dampness. If you are steam cleaning the engine, cover the alternator.

10. Never use arc-welding equipment on the car with the alternator connected.

REMOVAL & INSTALLATION

1. Disconnect the negative battery cable.
2. Remove the two-terminal plug and the battery leads from the rear of the alternator.
3. Remove the adjusting bolt from the alternator on gasoline engined models. The adjusting bolt is the one within the slotted hole.
4. On diesel equipped models, fit the end of a ratchet extension into the square hole of the belt tensioner bracket, then attach a ratchet to the extension. Lever the tensioner towards the firewall side of the engine compartment and remove the serpentine drive belt from the alternator.
5. On gasoline engined models, move the alternator to loosen the drive belt, then remove the belt.
6. On four cylinder models, remove the upper alternator bracket.
7. On diesel models, remove the alternator brace bolt from the rear of the alternator.

8. On gasoline engined models, remove the alternator pivot bolt and remove the alternator.
9. On diesel models, remove both alternator attaching bolts and remove the alternator.
10. Installation is the reverse of removal. Be sure to adjust the tension of the drive belt properly, then tighten the adjusting bolt(s) (on gasoline engined models).

Regulator

A solid regulator is mounted within the alternator. All regulator components are enclosed in a solid mold. The regulator is non-adjustable and requires no maintenance.

Battery

The battery is the first link in the chain of mechanisms which work together to provide cranking of the automobile engine. In most modern cars, the battery is a lead-acid electro-chemical device consisting of six two-volt (2V) subsections connected in series so the unit is capable of producing approximately 12 volts of electrical pressure. Each subsection, or cell, consists of a series of positive and negative

REMOVAL & INSTALLATION

1. Raise the hood and remove the front end diagonal brace(s) from above the battery(ies).
2. Disconnect the battery cables from the battery(ies). It may be necessary to use a small box end wrench or a $1/4$ in. drive ratchet to sneak in between the battery and the windshield washer (or coolant recovery) tank. Avoid using an open-end wrench for the cable bolts.
3. Loosen and remove the battery holddown bolt and block. The use of a long extension which places the ratchet above the battery makes it very easy to get to the holddown bolt.
4. Carefully lift the battery from the engine compartment. It may be necessary to remove the air cleaner intake duct (except 4-cyl.) or the intake resonator (4-cyl. only) for clearance.

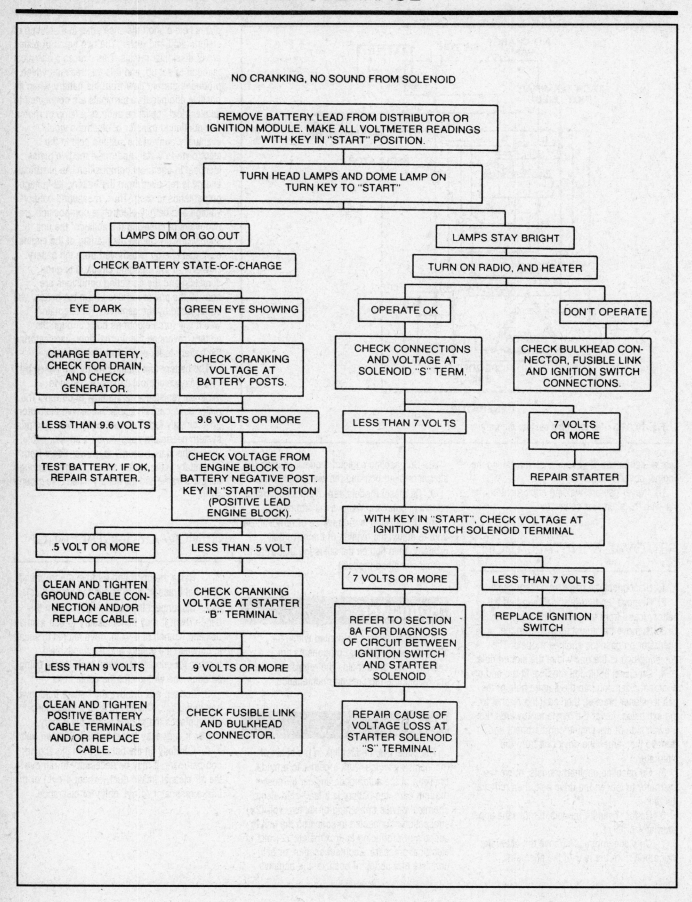

NO CRANKING, NO SOUND FROM SOLENOID

REMOVE BATTERY LEAD FROM DISTRIBUTOR OR IGNITION MODULE. MAKE ALL VOLTMETER READINGS WITH KEY IN "START" POSITION.

TURN HEAD LAMPS AND DOME LAMP ON TURN KEY TO "START"

LAMPS DIM OR GO OUT

CHECK BATTERY STATE-OF-CHARGE

EYE DARK

CHARGE BATTERY, CHECK FOR DRAIN, AND CHECK GENERATOR.

LESS THAN 9.6 VOLTS

TEST BATTERY. IF OK, REPAIR STARTER.

GREEN EYE SHOWING

CHECK CRANKING VOLTAGE AT BATTERY POSTS.

9.6 VOLTS OR MORE

CHECK VOLTAGE FROM ENGINE BLOCK TO BATTERY NEGATIVE POST. KEY IN "START" POSITION (POSITIVE LEAD ENGINE BLOCK).

.5 VOLT OR MORE

CLEAN AND TIGHTEN GROUND CABLE CONNECTION AND/OR REPLACE CABLE.

LESS THAN 9 VOLTS

CLEAN AND TIGHTEN POSITIVE BATTERY CABLE TERMINALS AND/OR REPLACE CABLE.

LESS THAN .5 VOLT

CHECK CRANKING VOLTAGE AT STARTER "B" TERMINAL

9 VOLTS OR MORE

CHECK FUSIBLE LINK AND BULKHEAD CONNECTOR.

LAMPS STAY BRIGHT

TURN ON RADIO, AND HEATER

OPERATE OK

CHECK CONNECTIONS AND VOLTAGE AT SOLENOID "S" TERM.

LESS THAN 7 VOLTS

WITH KEY IN "START", CHECK VOLTAGE AT IGNITION SWITCH SOLENOID TERMINAL

7 VOLTS OR MORE

REFER TO SECTION 8A FOR DIAGNOSIS OF CIRCUIT BETWEEN IGNITION SWITCH AND STARTER SOLENOID

REPAIR CAUSE OF VOLTAGE LOSS AT STARTER SOLENOID "S" TERMINAL.

LESS THAN 7 VOLTS

REPLACE IGNITION SWITCH

DON'T OPERATE

CHECK BULKHEAD CONNECTOR, FUSIBLE LINK AND IGNITION SWITCH CONNECTIONS.

7 VOLTS OR MORE

REPAIR STARTER

Starter

◆ SEE FIGS. 11 to 17

The starting motor is a specially designed, direct current electric motor capable of producing a very great amount of power for its size. One thing that allows the motor to produce a great deal of power is its tremendous rotating speed. It drives the engine through a tiny pinion gear (attached to the starter's armature), which drives the very large flywheel ring gear at a greatly reduced speed. Another factor allowing it to produce so much power is that only intermittent operation is required of it. Thus, little allowance for air circulation is required, and the windings can be built into a very small space.

The starter solenoid is a magnetic device which employs the small current supplied by the starting switch circuit of the ignition switch. This magnetic action moves a plunger which mechanically engages the starter and electrically closes the heavy switch which connects it to the battery. The starting switch circuit consists of the starting switch contained within the ignition switch, a transmission neutral safety switch or clutch pedal switch, and the wiring necessary to connect these with the starter solenoid or relay.

A pinion, which is a small gear, is mounted to a one-way drive clutch. This clutch is splined to the starter armature shaft. When the ignition switch is moved to the start position, the solenoid plunger slides the pinion toward the flywheel ring gear via a collar and spring. If the teeth on the pinion and flywheel match properly, the pinion will engage the flywheel immediately. If the gear teeth butt one another, the spring will be compressed and will force the gears to mesh as soon as the starter turns far enough to allow them to do so. As the solenoid plunger reaches the end of its travel, it closes the contacts that connect the battery and starter and then the engine is cranked.

As soon as the engine starts, the flywheel ring gear begins turning fast enough to drive the pinion at an extremely high rate of speed. At this point, the one-way clutch begins allowing the pinion to spin faster than the starter shaft so that the starter will not operate at excessive speed. When the ignition switch is released from the start position, the solenoid is de-energized, and a spring contained within the solenoid assembly pulls the gear out of mesh and interrupts the current flow to the starter.

REMOVAL & INSTALLATION

Diesel Engine

1982

1. Disconnect the negative battery cable(s).
2. Raise the front of the vehicle and support it safely with jackstands.
3. Remove the lower starter shield nut and flex the starter shield for access during removal.
4. Mark and disconnect the wires from the starter.
5. Remove the front starter attaching bolt.
6. Loosen the rear starter attaching bolt and remove the starter assembly, leaving the rear bolt in the starter housing.
7. Installation is the reverse of removal.

1983–85

1. Disconnect the negative battery cable(s) from the battery(s).
2. Install tool J–28467 to the engine, then raise the vehicle on a hoist.
3. Remove the left and the center engine mounting stud nuts.
4. Move the intermediate shaft seal upwards, then remove the intermediate shaft-to-stud shaft pinch bolt and disconnect the shaft from the gear.

✳✳ CAUTION

It is necessary to disconnect the intermediate shaft from the rack and pinion stud shaft; otherwise, damage to the steering gear and/or the intermediate shaft can occur, which may result in the loss of steering control.

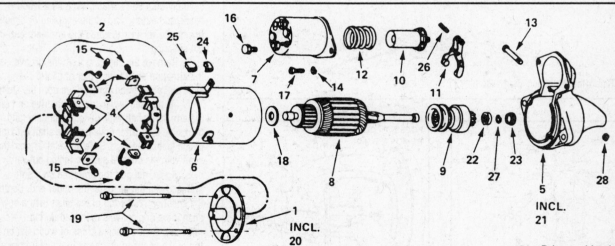

1. Frame, commutator end
2. Brush and holder pkg.
3. Brush
4. Brush holder
5. Housing, drive end
6. Frame and field assembly
7. Solenoid Switch
8. Armature
9. Drive assembly
10. Plunger
11. Shift lever
12. Plunger return spring
13. Shift lever shaft
14. Lock washer
15. Brush attaching screw
16. Field lead screw
17. Switch attaching screw
18. Brake washer
19. Bolt
20. Commutator end bushing
21. Drive end bushing
22. Pinion stop collar
23. Trust collar
24. Grommet
25. Grommet
26. Plunger pin
27. Pinion stop retainer ring
28. Lever shaft retaining ring

FIG. 11 Exploded view of the 5MT starter

FIG. 14c Make sure that all wiring is tightened properly to the starter before connecting the battery

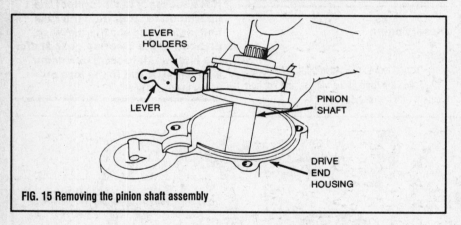

LEVER HOLDERS

LEVER

PINION SHAFT

DRIVE END HOUSING

FIG. 15 Removing the pinion shaft assembly

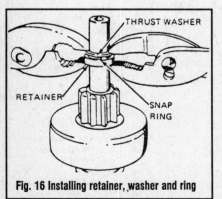

THRUST WASHER

RETAINER

SNAP RING

Fig. 16 Installing retainer, washer and ring

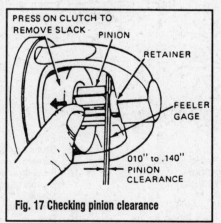

PRESS ON CLUTCH TO REMOVE SLACK

PINION

RETAINER

FEELER GAGE

.010" to .140" PINION CLEARANCE

Fig. 17 Checking pinion clearance

Diesel Aluminum Starter (Type 2)

After the field coil connector nut and the two solenoid attaching screws are removed, pull the solenoid upward and forward to remove it. Installation is simply a matter of bolting the solenoid into place, fastening the field coil connector and reinstalling the starter. It is recommended by G.M., however, to check the pinion position as outline (Step 35a–35e of the Diesel Type 2 assembly procedure).

STARTER OVERHAUL — GASOLINE ENGINES

Drive Replacement

1. Disconnect the field coil straps from the solenoid.
2. Remove the through-bolts, and separate the commutator end frame, field frame assembly, drive housing, and armature assembly from each other.
3. Slide the thrust washer off the end of the armature shaft.
4. Slide a suitably metal cylinder, such as a standard half-inch pipe coupling, or an old pinion, on the shaft so that the end of the coupling or pinion butts up against the edge of the pinion retainer.
5. Support the lower end of the armature securely on a soft surface, such as a wood block, and tap the end of the coupling or pinion, driving the retainer towards the armature end of the snapring.
6. Remove the snapring from the groove in the armature shaft with a pair of pliers. Then, slide the retainer and starter drive from the shaft.
7. To reassemble, lubricate the drive end of the armature shaft with silicone lubricant, and then slide the starter drive onto the shaft with the pinion facing outward. Slide the retainer onto the shaft with the cupped surface facing outward.
8. Again, support the armature on a soft surface, with the pinion at the upper end. Center the snapring on the top of the shaft (use a new snap if the original was damaged during removal). Gently place a block of wood flat on top of the snapring so as not to move it from a centered position. Tap the wooden block with a hammer in order to force the snapring around the shaft. Then, slide the ring down into the snapring groove.
9. Lay the armature down flat on the surface you're working on. Slide the retainer up on to the shaft and position it and the thrust collar next to the snapring. Using two pairs of pliers on opposite sides of the shaft, squeeze the thrust

collar and the retainer together until the snapring is forced into the retainer.

10. Lube the drive housing bushing with a silicone lubricant. Then, install the armature and clutch assembly into the drive housing, engaging the solenoid shift lever with the clutch, and positioning the front end of armature shaft into the bushing.

11. Apply a sealing compound approved for this application onto the drive housing; then position the field frame around the armature shaft and against the drive housing. Work slowly and carefully to prevent damaging the starter brushes.

12. Lubricate the bushing in the commutator end frame with a silicone lubricant, place the leather brake washer onto the armature shaft, and then slide the commutator end frame over the shaft and into position against the field frame. Line up the bolt holes, and then install and tighten the through-bolts.

13. Reconnect the field coil straps to the **motor** terminal of the solenoid.

➡ **If replacement of the starter drive fails to cure the improper engagement of the starter pinion to the flywheel, there are probably defective parts in the solenoid and/ or shift lever. The best procedure would probably be to take the assembly to a shop where a pinion clearance check can be made by energizing the solenoid on a test bench. If the pinion clearance is incorrect, disassemble the solenoid and the shift lever, inspect, and replace worn parts.**

Brush Replacement

1. After removing the starter from the engine, disconnect the field coil from the motor solenoid terminal.

2. Remove the starter through-bolts and remove the commutator end frame and washer.

3. Remove the field frame and the armature assembly from the drive housing.

4. Remove the brush holder pivot pin which positions one insulated and one grounded brush.

5. Remove the brush springs.

6. Remove the brushes.

7. Installation is in the reverse order of removal.

STARTER OVERHAUL — DIESEL TYPE ONE

➡ **The Type One diesel starter is identified by having a cast iron housing, whereas the Type Two unit covered later, has an aluminum housing.**

Drive Replacement

1. Remove the starter from the vehicle as previously outlined.

2. Remove the screw from the field coil connector strap at the solenoid.

3. Separate the field frame assembly from the drive gear assembly.

4. Remove the solenoid mounting screws, turn the solenoid 90° and remove the solenoid.

5. Remove the shift lever shaft retaining ring, lever shaft, and the housing through-bolts in order to separate the drive assembly, drive housing and gear housing.

6. Remove the thrust washer or collar from the drive shaft, in front of the drive assembly.

7. Slide a 5/8 in. deep socket (or a piece of suitably sized pipe) over the shaft and against the retainer.

8. Tap the socket (or pipe) to move the retainer off the snapring.

9. Remove the snapring from the groove in the shaft. If the ring becomes distorted during removal, it must be replaced with a new ring during assembly.

10. Remove the starter drive assembly from the shaft.

11. Slide the new drive assembly onto the drive shaft, then place the snapring retainer over the shaft with the cupped side of the retainer facing away from the gear of the drive unit.

12. Position the armature upright (drive unit facing upward), resting the lower end on a block of wood.

13. Center the snapring on the top of the shaft. Remember that a new ring should be used if the old one was damaged during removal.

14. Carefully place a block of wood on the ring then tap on the block of wood (using a light hammer) to force the ring onto the shaft. Slide the ring down into the snapring groove.

15. Place the thrust collar onto the drive shaft, then squeeze the thrust collar and retainer together, which will force the retainer over the snapring.

16. Assemble the plunger and shift lever into the drive housing with the lever shaft and the retaining ring.

17. Place the drive shaft washer over the drive shaft on the side of the gear opposite the drive assembly. Lubricate the gear teeth with G.M. #1960954 lubricant or its equivalent.

18. Assemble the gear housing with the attaching screws.

19. Assemble the solenoid to the drive housing.

20. Lubricate the bushing in the commutator end frame with the same lubricant mentioned previously.

21. Assemble the armature, field frame and the commutator end frame to the gear housing with the through-bolts.

22. Attach the field coil connector to the solenoid terminal. Install the starter assembly as previously outlined.

Brush Replacement

1. Please follow steps 1–5 of the last Drive Replacement procedure in order to separate the field coil and frame assembly from the armature.

2. Remove the commutator end frame in order to gain access to the brushes.

3. Remove the brush holder pivot pin which positions one insulated and one grounded brush.

4. Remove the brush spring.

5. Replace the brushes as required, then reinstall the brush spring and the pivot pin.

6. Repeat steps 3, 4, and 5 for the remaining pair of brushes.

7. Re-assemble the remaining starter components in the reverse of removal.

STARTER OVERHAUL — DIESEL TYPE TWO

➡ **The Type Two diesel starter is identified by having an aluminum housing.**

Drive and Brush Replacement

➡ **G.M. special tool #J–22888 and a dial indicator will be needed to properly assemble the starter.**

1. Remove the starter assembly from the vehicle as previously outlined.

2. Remove the nut from the field coil connector at the solenoid.

3. Remove the two solenoid mounting screws then remove the solenoid by pulling it upward and forward.

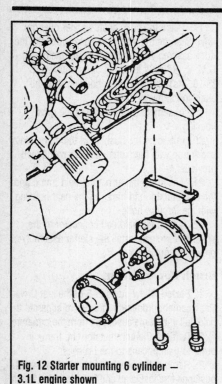

Fig. 12 Starter mounting 6 cylinder — 3.1L engine shown

5. Remove the 2 front cradle mounting bolts, then lower the cradle at the front to gain access to the flywheel cover bolts.

6. Remove the flywheel cover bolts and the cover.

7. Remove the starter shield nut from the starter and the flex shield.

8. Mark and disconnect the wires from the starter. Remove the starter mounting bolts and the starter.

9. To install, reverse the removal procedures. Torque the stub shaft pinch bolt to 45 ft. lbs. (62 Nm.) and the starter-to-engine bolts to 32 ft. lbs. (43 Nm.).

1982–85 Except Diesel Engines

1. Disconnect the negative battery cable.
2. Raise the front of the vehicle and support it safely with jackstands.
3. From underneath the vehicle, remove the two starter motor-to-engine bolts and carefully lower the starter. Note the location of shims (if so equipped).
4. On the four cylinder engine, remove the nut that holds the starter bracket to the rear of the starter.
5. Mark and disconnect all wiring at the starter.
6. Installation is the reverse of removal.

1986–92

2.5L AND 2.8L ENGINES

1. Disconnect the negative battery cable.
2. Raise and safely support the vehicle.
3. Disconnect the solenoid wires and battery cable from the starter.
4. Remove the bolt from the engine cross brace.
5. Place a prybar tool between the upper engine mount and engine to pry rearward and support the engine.

6. Remove the 4 bolts holding the dust covers. Remove the dust covers.
7. Remove the 2 bolts attaching the starter.
8. On the 2.5L engine, remove the bolt attaching the starter bracket to the engine.
9. Remove the starter and any shims.

To install:

➡ **If replacing the starter, transfer the starter bracket to the new starter.**

10. Install the starter and any shims.
11. Install the 2 starter attaching bolts.
12. On the 2.5L engine, install the bolt attaching the starter bracket to the engine.
13. Install the dust cover and 4 attaching bolts.
14. Connect the battery cable and solenoid wires.
15. Lower the vehicle.
16. Roll the engine forward and replace the engine brace bolts.
17. Connect the negative battery cable.

3.1L ENGINE

1. Disconnect the negative battery cable.
2. Raise and safely support the vehicle.
3. If equipped, remove the nut from the brace at the air conditioning compressor.
4. If equipped, remove the nuts from the starter-to-engine brace.
5. Remove the drain pan under the engine oil pan.
6. Disconnect the oil pressure sending unit electrical connector. Remove the oil pressure sending unit.
7. Remove the oil filter.
8. Remove the bolts from the flywheel inspection cover. Remove the inspection cover.
9. Remove the bolts from the starter motor.
10. Remove the starter motor and any shims.
11. Disconnect the starter motor electrical connectors.

To install:

12. Connect the starter motor electrical connectors.
13. Install the starter motor and any shims.
14. Install the starter motor attaching bolts. Tighten to 32 ft. lbs. (43 Nm).
15. Install the flywheel inspection cover and attaching bolts.
16. Install the oil filter.
17. Install the oil pressure sending unit. Connect the electrical connector.
18. Install the drain pan.
19. Install the nuts to the starter-to-engine brace.
20. Install the nut to brace at the air conditioner compressor.
21. Lower the vehicle.
22. Connect the negative battery cable.

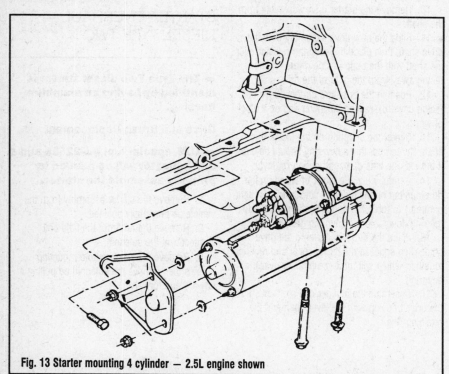

Fig. 13 Starter mounting 4 cylinder — 2.5L engine shown

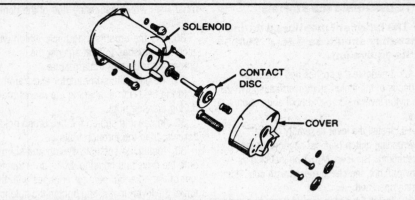

Fig. 14 Removing a cover to access the starter will be necessary on some models like this 3.3L engine

Fig. 14a There is not much room for tools. Make certain to use the correct size wrench, for the starter solenoid wiring

Fig. 14b To remove the starter bolts a long extension is almost always necessary

23. Check the engine oil level, add as required.

3.3L ENGINE

1. Disconnect the negative battery cable.
2. Properly discharge the air conditioning system.
3. On 3.3L engine, remove the cooling fan assembly.
4. Remove the front exhaust manifold.
5. Raise and support the vehicle safely.
6. Remove the bolts from the flywheel inspection cover and remove the cover.
7. Disconnect the air conditioner condenser hose from the compressor and position aside.
8. Disconnect the starter motor electrical connectors.
9. Remove the 2 bolts attaching the starter.
10. Remove the starter and any shims.

To Install:

11. Install the starter motor and any shims.
12. Install the 2 bolts attaching the starter. Tighten to 30 ft. lbs. (40 Nm).
13. Connect the starter motor electrical connectors.
14. Replace the condenser O-ring. Lubricate with refrigerant oil. Connect the air conditioner condenser hose to the compressor.
15. Install the flywheel inspection cover and attaching bolts.
16. Lower the vehicle.
17. Install the front exhaust manifold.
18. On 3.3L engine, install the cooling fan assembly.
19. Evacuate, recharge and leak test the air conditioning system.
20. Connect the negative battery cable.

SOLENOID REMOVAL AND INSTALLATION

Except Diesel Aluminum Starter

1. Remove the starter and solenoid assembly as previously outlined.
2. Remove the screw and washer from the motor connector strap terminal.
3. Remove the two screws which retain the solenoid housing to the end frame assembly.
4. Twist the solenoid clockwise to remove the flange key from the keyway slot in the housing.
5. Remove the solenoid assembly.
6. With the solenoid return spring installed on the plunger, position the solenoid body on the drive housing and turn it counterclockwise to engage the flange key in the key way slot.
7. Install the two screws which retain the solenoid housing to the end frame.

➡ **In some cases, shims will be present between the solenoid and the drive end housing. These shims are used to set the drive pinion position.**

4. Remove the two through bolts and the two brush holder retaining screws. Remove the commutator end frame from the armature and bearing assembly.

5. Remove the field frame assembly and the armature from the center housing.

6. Carefully pry each brush spring back so that each brush can be backed away from the armature about 1/4 in. (6mm). Release the spring to hold the brushes in the backed out position, then remove the armature from the field frame and brush holder.

7. Remove the cover retaining screws, cover, C-washer and plate from the armature side of the center housing.

8. Remove the two center housing bolts, the center housing and the shim thrust washers.

9. Remove the reduction gear, spring holder and two lever springs.

10. Slide a 5/8 in. socket or suitably sized piece of pipe over the nose of the pinion shaft, against the drive pinion stopper.

11. Tap on the socket (or pipe) to drive the stopper off of the snapring. Using a pair of snapring pliers, remove the drive pinion snapring from the groove in the pinion shaft.

➡ **If the ring becomes distorted during removal, it must be replaced with a new ring during assembly.**

12. Remove the stopper, drive pinion gear and spring.

13. Remove the pinion shaft/overrunning clutch from the drive end housing.

To replace the brushes:

14. Remove the brush holder and the negative brush assembly from the field frame by removing the positive brushes from the brush holder.

15. Cut the old positive brush leads from the field coil bar as close to the brush connection point as possible; cut the negative brush leads from the brush holder plate.

16. Connection tangs are provided for installation of new brushes. Clean the connection tangs then solder the new brush leads on the tangs. Use only high temperature solder to connect the new brushes, and make sure that the positive brush connections are made properly in order to prevent grounding of the brush connection.

17. Reinstall the positive and the negative brushes in the brush holder assembly. Position the brushes in the backed-out position as described earlier.

To assemble the starter:

➡ **The lubricant mentioned during assembly should be G.M. #1960954 or its equivalent.**

18. Lubricate the splines and bearing surfaces of the pinion shaft/overrunning clutch, the nylon lever holders and both ends of the lever.

19. Install the lever assembly on the overrunning clutch (see the accompanying illustration). The lever MUST be installed as shown; if not, the clutch mechanism could lock during operation.

20. Install the pinion shaft/overrunning clutch and lever assembly into the drive end housing.

21. Slide the spring, drive pinion and stopper (in that order) over the pinion shaft, making sure that the cupped side of the stopper faces the end of the shaft.

22. Press the drive pinion and stopper towards the drive end housing and install the snapring into the groove of the pinion shaft.

23. Using tool J–22888, force the drive pinion towards the end of the pinion shaft, which will force the stopper over the snapring. It may be necessary to tap the ring with a drift pin to seat the ring in the groove of the stopper.

24. Install the two lever springs and the spring holder into the drive end housing.

25. Lubricate the reduction gear teeth, then install the gear and shim thrust washer(s) onto the pinion shaft assembly.

26. Position the center housing to the drive end housing and install the two attaching bolts.

27. Check the end-play of the pinion shaft as follows:

a. Install the plate and the C-shaped washer onto the pinion shaft.

b. With the drive end housing suitably supported, insert an appropriately sized feeler gauge between the C-washer and the cover plate. Using a screwdriver, move the pinion shaft axially to determine the total end play. Try different sized feeler gauges until the thickest gauge fits the clearance. Total end-play should be 0.004–0.020 in. (0.10–0.50mm). Replace or remove the shim thrust washers as required to bring the clearance within specification.

c. Remove the cover plate (if it is not already removed) and fill the cover 1/2 full with lubricant.

d. Reinstall the cover and install and tighten the two cover bolts.

28. Install the armature by carefully engaging the splines of the shaft with the reduction gear.

29. Position the field frame and brush holder assembly on the center housing, noting that the rubber grommet for the field coil lead

must align with the locating ribs of the center housing.

30. Pry the brush spring back, which will allow the brushes to seat against the commutator bars of the armature.

31. Position the commutator end frame onto the field frame, aligning the marks made during disassembly.

32. Install and tighten the two brush holder screws, then the through bolts.

33. Install the solenoid switch and shims onto the drive end housing. Make sure that the slot of the solenoid plunger engages with the top of the lever. Install and tighten the solenoid retaining bolts.

34. Connect the field coil connector to the solenoid switch terminal.

35. Because the starter has been disassembled, it is necessary to check the pinion position as follows:

a. Connect one 12V lead of a battery to the terminal marked **S** on the solenoid. Momentarily touch the other 12V lead to the starter frame. This action will shift the drive pinion into its cranking position until one of the battery leads is disconnected. DO NOT leave the pinion in the cranking position for more than 30 seconds at a time.

b. With the pinion in the cranking position, set up a dial indicator as shown, then zero the indicator needle.

c. Push the pinion shaft back by hand and record the amount of movement indicated by the indicator needle. Detach one of the battery leads to bring the drive pinion back to its off position.

d. The indicator reading should have been between 0.020–0.080 in. (0.50–2.00mm). The clearance is adjusted by adding or removing shims between the solenoid and the front bracket. Shims are available in 0.010 in. (0.25mm) and 0.020 in. (0.50mm) thicknesses.

e. If a shim thickness adjustment was required, reinstall the solenoid with the new shims and repeat the clearance check.

Sending Units and Sensors

◆ SEE FIGS. 18 to 23

REMOVAL & INSTALLATION

Crankshaft Sensor

2.5L, 2.8L AND 3.1L ENGINES

1. Disconnect the negative battery cable.

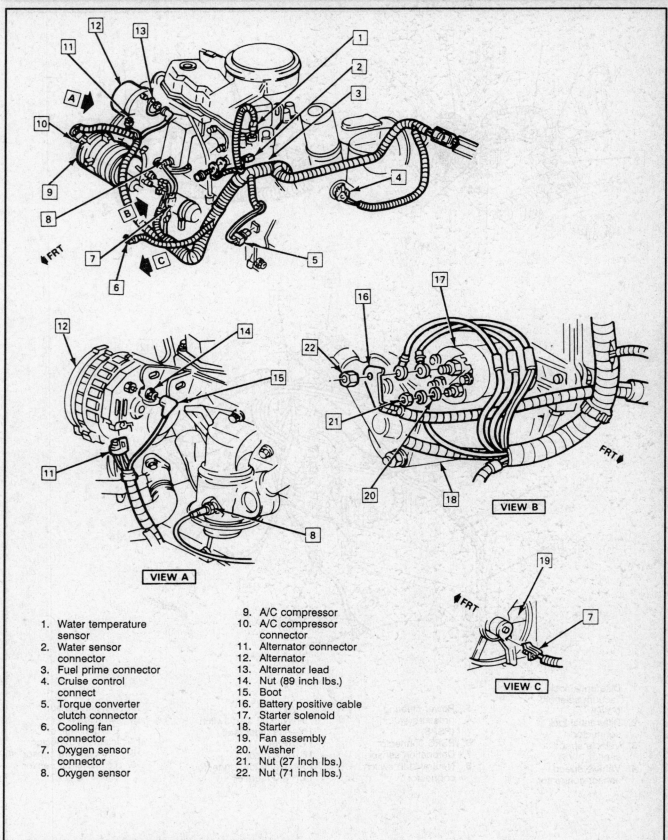

1. Water temperature sensor
2. Water sensor connector
3. Fuel prime connector
4. Cruise control connect
5. Torque converter clutch connector
6. Cooling fan connector
7. Oxygen sensor connector
8. Oxygen sensor
9. A/C compressor
10. A/C compressor connector
11. Alternator connector
12. Alternator
13. Alternator lead
14. Nut (89 inch lbs.)
15. Boot
16. Battery positive cable
17. Starter solenoid
18. Starter
19. Fan assembly
20. Washer
21. Nut (27 inch lbs.)
22. Nut (71 inch lbs.)

Fig. 18 Sensor locations 4 cylinder engine — 2.5L engine shown

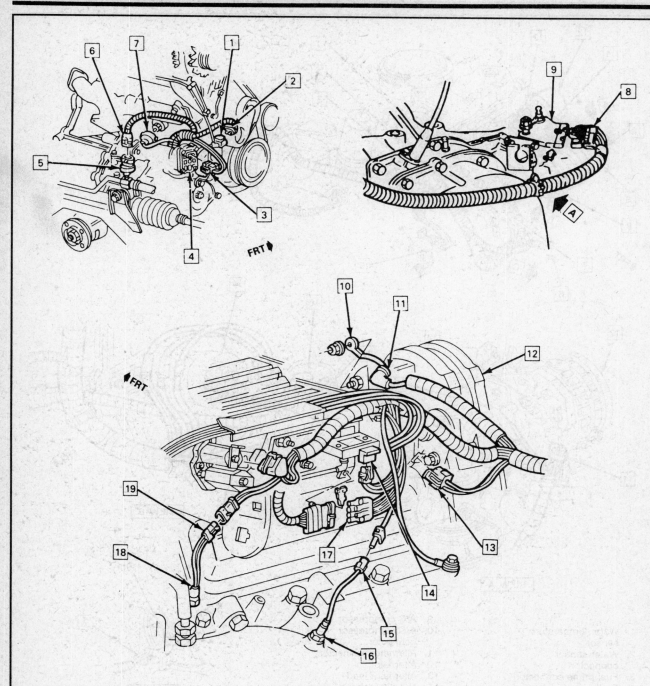

1. Differential lock
   vacuum solenoid
   (AWD)
2. Differential lock
   connector
3. Vehicle speed
   sensor (VVS)
4. Vehicle speed
   sensor connector
5. Power steering
   pressure switch
   (PSPS)
6. PSPS connector
7. Detonation sensor
8. Neutral start switch
   connector
9. Neutral start switch
10. Alternator lead
11. Boot
12. Alternator
13. Alternator connector
14. MAP sensor
15. Oxygen sensor
   connector
16. Oxygen sensor
17. Injector connector
18. Temperature sensor
19. Temperature sensor
   connector

Fig. 18a Sensor locations 6 cylinder engine — 3.1L engine shown

2. Disconnect crankshaft sensor electrical connector.

3. Remove the crankshaft sensor attaching bolt, then remove the crankshaft sensor from the vehicle.

To install:

4. Inspect the sensor O-ring for wear, cracks or leakage. Replace as necessary. Lubricate the new O-ring with engine oil prior to installation.

5. Install the sensor into the hole in the engine block and install retaining bolt.

6. Connect the electrical connector.

7. Connect the negative battery cable.

8. On 3.1L engine perform the Idle Learn Procedure as follows:

   a. Connect the Scan tool to the ALDL.

   b. Turn the ignition switch to the **ON** position with the engine not running.

   c. In the "Misc. Test" mode, select "IAC System", then "Idle Learn".

   d. Proceed with idle learn as directed.

Dual Crankshaft Sensor

3.3L AND 3.8L ENGINES

1. Disconnect battery negative cable.

2. Disconnect serpentine belt from crankshaft pulley.

3. Raise and safely support the vehicle.

4. Remove right front tire and wheel assembly, then the inner access cover.

5. Remove crankshaft harmonic balancer retaining bolt and crankshaft harmonic balancer.

6. Disconnect electrical connector from sensor and remove the crankshaft sensor from the vehicle.

To install:

7. Loosely install the crankshaft sensor on the pedestal.

8. Position the sensor with the pedestal attached on special tool J-37089.

9. Position the tool on the crankshaft.

10. Install the bolts to hold the pedestal to the block face. Tighten to 14–28 ft. lbs. (20–40 Nm).

11. Tighten the pedestal pinch bolt to 30–35 inch lbs. (3–4 Nm).

12. Remove special tool J-37089.

13. Place special tool J-37089 on the harmonic balancer and turn. If any vane of the harmonic balancer touches the tool, replace the balancer assembly.

14. Install the balancer on the crankshaft and install the crankshaft balancer bolt. Tighten to 200–239 ft. lbs. (270–325 Nm).

15. Install the inner fender shield.

16. Install the tire and wheel assembly. Tighten to 100 ft. lbs. (140 Nm).

17. Lower the vehicle.

18. Install the serpentine belt.

19. Connect the negative battery cable.

Coolant Temperature Sensor

Most engine functions are effected by the coolant temperature. Determining whether the engine is hot or cold is largely dependent on the temperature of the coolant. An accurate temperature signal to the ECM is supplied by the coolant temperature sensor. The coolant temperature sensor is a thermistor mounted in the engine coolant stream. A thermistor is an electrical device that varies its resistance in relation to changes in temperature. Low coolant temperature produces a high resistance (100,000 ohms at –40°F/–40°C) and high coolant temperature produces low resistance (70 ohms at 266°F/130°C). The ECM supplies a signal of 5 volts to the coolant temperature sensor through a resistor in the ECM and measures the voltage. The voltage will be high when the engine is cold and low when the engine is hot.

1. Disconnect the negative battery cable.

2. Drain the cooling system into a clean container for reuse.

3. Disconnect the electrical connector from the coolant temperature sensor.

4. Remove the coolant temperature sensor.

To install:

5. Install the coolant temperature sensor.

6. Connect the electrical connector.

7. Fill the cooling system.

8. Connect the negative battery cable.

9. Start the engine and check for leaks.

Manifold Absolute Pressure (MAP) Sensor

The MAP sensor measures the changes in intake manifold pressure, which result from engine load and speed changes and converts this information to a voltage output. The MAP sensor reading is the opposite of a vacuum gauge reading: when manifold pressure is high, MAP sensor value is high and vacuum is low. A MAP sensor will produce a low output on engine coastdown with a closed throttle while a wide open throttle will produce a high output. The high output is produced because the pressure inside the manifold is the same as outside the manifold, so 100 percent of the outside air pressure is measured.

The MAP sensor is also used to measure barometric pressure under certain conditions, which allows the ECM to automatically adjust for different altitudes.

The MAP sensor changes the 5 volt signal supplied by the ECM, which reads the change and uses the information to control fuel delivery and ignition timing.

1. Disconnect the negative battery cable.

2. Disconnect the vacuum harness assembly.

3. Release the electrical connector locking tab.

4. Remove the bolts or release the MAP sensor locking tabs and remove the sensor.

To install:

5. Install the bolts or snap sensor onto the bracket.

6. Connect the MAP sensor electrical connector.

7. Connect the MAP sensor vacuum harness connector.

8. Connect the negative battery cable.

Manifold Air Temperature (MAT) Sensor

The MAT sensor is a thermistor which supplies manifold air temperature information to the ECM. The MAT sensor produces high resistance (100,000 ohms at –40°F/–40°C) at low temperatures and low resistance of 70 ohms at 266°F (130°C) at high temperatures. The ECM supplies a 5 volt signal to the MAT sensor and measures MAT sensor output voltage. The voltage signal will be high when the air is cold and low when the air is hot.

1. Disconnect the negative battery cable.

2. Disconnect the MAT sensor electrical connector locking tab.

3. Remove the MAT sensor.

To install:

4. Install the MAT sensor.

5. Connect the electrical connector.

6. Connect the negative battery cable.

Oxygen Sensor

The exhaust oxygen sensor or O_2 sensor is mounted in the exhaust stream where it monitors oxygen content in the exhaust gas. The oxygen content in the exhaust is a measure of the air/fuel mixture going into the engine. The oxygen in the exhaust reacts with the oxygen sensor to produce a voltage which is read by the ECM. The voltage output is very low, ranging from 0.1 volt in a high oxygen-lean mixture condition to 0.9 volt in a low oxygen-rich mixture condition.

PRECAUTIONS:

• Careful handling of the oxygen sensor is essential.

• The electrical pigtail and connector are permanently attached and should not be removed from the oxygen sensor.

• The inline electrical connector and louvered end of the oxygen sensor must be kept free of grease, dirt and other contaminants.

• Avoid using cleaning solvents of any type on the oxygen sensor.

• Do not drop or roughly handle the oxygen sensor.

• The oxygen sensor may be difficult to remove if the engine temperature is below 120°F

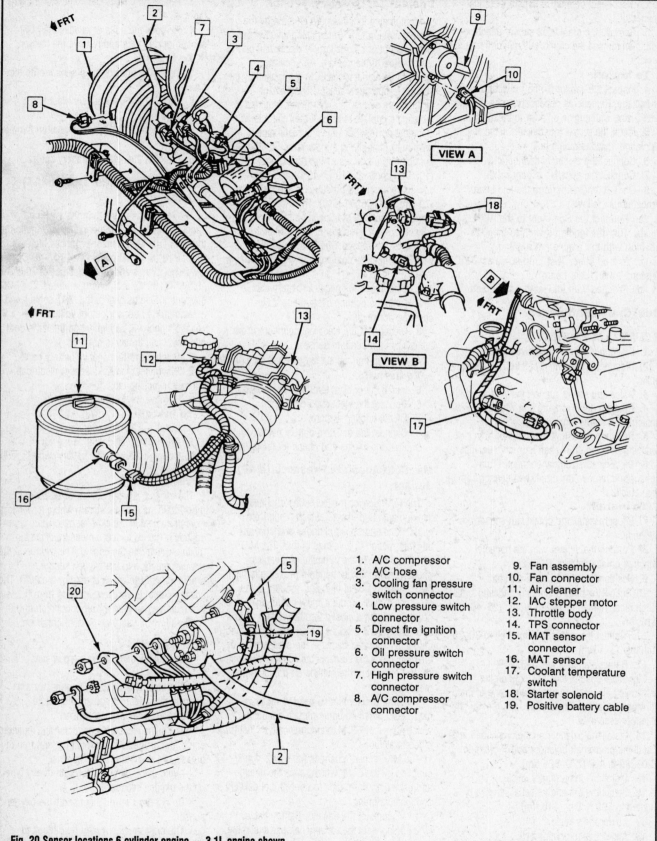

1. A/C compressor
2. A/C hose
3. Cooling fan pressure switch connector
4. Low pressure switch connector
5. Direct fire ignition connector
6. Oil pressure switch connector
7. High pressure switch connector
8. A/C compressor connector
9. Fan assembly
10. Fan connector
11. Air cleaner
12. IAC stepper motor
13. Throttle body
14. TPS connector
15. MAT sensor connector
16. MAT sensor
17. Coolant temperature switch
18. Starter solenoid
19. Positive battery cable

Fig. 20 Sensor locations 6 cylinder engine — 3.1L engine shown

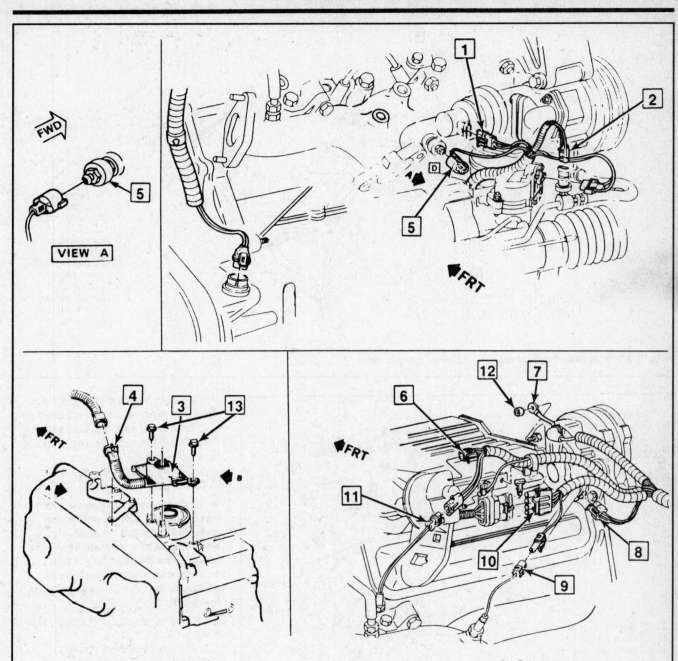

Fig. 21 Sensor locations 6 cylinder engine — 2.8L (VIN W) engine shown

1. Air control connector
2. PSPS switch
3. Neutral start switch
4. Neutral start switch connector
5. Knock sensor
6. EGR solenoid connector
7. Alternator lead
8. Alternator connector
9. Oxygen sensor connector
10. Injector connector
11. Temperature sensor connector
12. Nut (5.5 ft. lbs)
13. Bolt (20 ft. lbs)

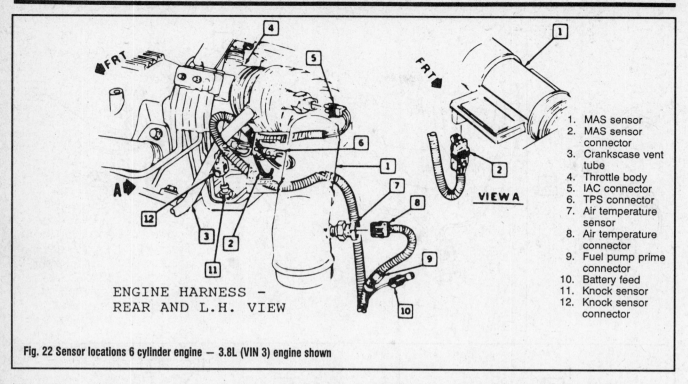

1. MAS sensor
2. MAS sensor connector
3. Crankscase vent tube
4. Throttle body
5. IAC connector
6. TPS connector
7. Air temperature sensor
8. Air temperature connector
9. Fuel pump prime connector
10. Battery feed
11. Knock sensor
12. Knock sensor connector

Fig. 22 Sensor locations 6 cylinder engine — 3.8L (VIN 3) engine shown

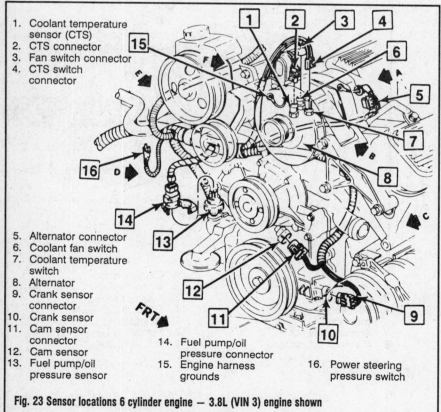

1. Coolant temperature sensor (CTS)
2. CTS connector
3. Fan switch connector
4. CTS switch connector
5. Alternator connector
6. Coolant fan switch
7. Coolant temperature switch
8. Alternator
9. Crank sensor connector
10. Crank sensor
11. Cam sensor connector
12. Cam sensor
13. Fuel pump/oil pressure sensor
14. Fuel pump/oil pressure connector
15. Engine harness grounds
16. Power steering pressure switch

Fig. 23 Sensor locations 6 cylinder engine — 3.8L (VIN 3) engine shown

(48°C). Excessive force may damage the threads in the exhaust manifold or exhaust pipe.

1. Disconnect the negative battery cable.
2. Release the electrical connector locking tab and disconnect.
3. Carefully remove the oxygen sensor.

To Install:

➡ **Replacement oxygen sensors will have a coating of an anti-seize compound on the threads. If, for any reason, the original sensor is being reinstalled, apply a thin coating of a suitable anti-seize compound to the threads prior to installation.**

4. Install the oxygen sensor and tighten to 30 ft. lbs. (41 Nm).
5. Connect the electrical connector.
6. Connect the negative battery cable.

Throttle Position Sensor (TPS)

The TPS is mounted to the throttle body, opposite the throttle lever and is connected to the throttle shaft. Its function is to sense the current throttle valve position and relay that information to the ECM. Throttle position information allows the ECM to generate the required injector control signals. The TPS consists of a potentiometer which alters the flow of voltage according to the position of a wiper on the variable resistor windings, in proportion to the movement of the throttle shaft.

1. Disconnect the negative battery cable.
2. Disconnect the TPS electrical connector.

FIG. 19 Oxygen sensor location. A long socket extension will be needed

3. Remove the 2 mounting screws.
4. Remove the TPS and, if equipped, TPS seal from the throttle body.

To Install:

5. Place the TPS in position. Align the TPS lever with the TPS drive lever on the throttle body.

6. Install the 2 TPS mounting screws.
7. Connect the electrical connector.
8. Connect the negative battery cable.

Vehicle Speed Sensor (VSS)

The VSS is located on the transmission or behind the dash at the speedometer, and sends a pulsing voltage signal to the ECM which is converted to miles per hour. This sensor mainly controls the operation of the TCC system, shift light, cruise control and activation of the EGR system. The following procedures are for the transmission mounted unit. Follow the instrument panel procedures for the VSS mounted to the back of the speedometer.

1. Disconnect the negative battery cable.
2. Raise and safely support the vehicle.
3. Disconnect the VSS electrical connector.
4. Remove the retaining bolt.
5. Have a clean container to catch the transmission fluid and remove the VSS.
6. Remove and discard the O-ring.

To Install:

7. Lubricate a new O-ring with a thin film of transmission fluid. Install the O-ring and VSS.
8. Install the retaining bolt.
9. Connect the electrical connector.
10. Lower the vehicle.
11. Connect the negative battery cable.
12. Refill transmission to proper level.

ENGINE MECHANICAL

Engine Overhaul Tips

Most engine overhaul procedures are fairly standard. In addition to specific parts replacement procedures and complete specifications for your individual engine, this Section also is a guide to accept rebuilding procedures. Examples of standard rebuilding practice are shown and should be used along with specific details concerning your particular engine.

Competent and accurate machine shop services will ensure maximum performance, reliability and engine life.

In most instances it is more profitable for the do-it-yourself mechanic to remove, clean and inspect the component, buy the necessary parts and deliver these to a shop for actual machine work.

On the other hand, much of the rebuilding work (crankshaft, block, bearings, piston rods, and other components) is well within the scope of the do-it-yourself mechanic.

TOOLS

The tools required for an engine overhaul or parts replacement will depend on the depth of your involvement. With a few exceptions, they will be the tools found in a mechanic's tool kit (see Section 1). More in-depth work will require any or all of the following:

- a dial indicator (reading in thousandths) mounted on a universal base
- micrometers and telescope gauges
- jaw and screw-type pullers
- scraper
- valve spring compressor
- ring groove cleaner
- piston ring expander and compressor
- ridge reamer
- cylinder hone or glaze breaker
- Plastigage®
- engine stand

Use of most of these tools is illustrated in this Section. Many can be rented for a one-time use

from a local parts jobber or tool supply house specializing in automotive work.

Occasionally, the use of special tools is called for. See the information on Special Tools and Safety Notice in the front of this book before substituting another tool.

INSPECTION TECHNIQUES

Procedures and specifications are given in this Section for inspecting, cleaning and assessing the wear limits of most major components. Other procedures such as Magnaflux® and Zyglo® can be used to locate material flaws and stress cracks. Magnaflux® is a magnetic process applicable only to ferrous materials. The Zyglo® process coats the material with a fluorescent dye penetrant and can be used on any material Check for suspected surface cracks can be more readily made using spot check dye. The dye is sprayed onto the

suspected area, wiped off and the area sprayed with a developer. Cracks will show up brightly.

OVERHAUL TIPS

Aluminum has become extremely popular for use in engines, due to its low weight. Observe the following precautions when handling aluminum parts:
• Never hot tank aluminum parts (the caustic hot tank solution will eat the aluminum.
• Remove all aluminum parts (identification tag, etc.) from engine parts prior to the tanking.
• Always coat threads lightly with engine oil or antiseize compounds before installation, to prevent seizure.
• Never over-torque bolts or spark plugs especially in aluminum threads.

Stripped threads in any component can be repaired using any of several commercial repair kits (Heli-Coil®, Microdot®, Keenserts®, etc.).

When assembling the engine, any parts that will be frictional contact must be prelubed to provide lubrication at initial start-up. Any product specifically formulated for this purpose can be used, but engine oil is not recommended as a prelube.

When semi-permanent (locked, but removable) installation of bolts or nuts is desired, threads should be cleaned and coated with Loctite® or other similar, commercial non-hardening sealant.

REPAIRING DAMAGED THREADS

◆ SEE FIGS. 24 to 28
Several methods of repairing damaged threads are available. Heli-Coil® (shown here), Keenserts® and Microdot® are among the most widely used. All involve basically the same principle — drilling out stripped threads, tapping the hole and installing a prewound insert — making welding, plugging and oversize fasteners unnecessary.

Two types of thread repair inserts are usually supplied — a standard type for most Inch Coarse, Inch Fine, Metric Course and Metric Fine thread sizes and a spark lug type to fit most spark plug port sizes. Consult the individual manufacturer's catalog to determine exact applications. Typical thread repair kits will contain a selection of prewound threaded inserts, a tap (corresponding to the outside diameter threads of the insert) and an installation tool. Spark plug inserts usually differ because

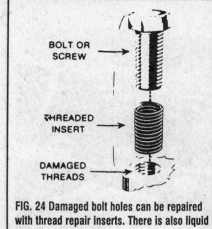

FIG. 24 Damaged bolt holes can be repaired with thread repair inserts. There is also liquid thread maker available.

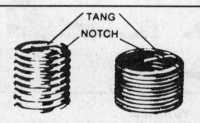

Fig. 25 standard thread repair insert (left) and spark plug threat repair insert (right)

Fig. 26 Use a specific drill to remove damage threads

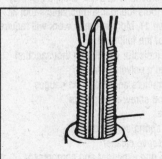

Fig. 27 With a tap supplied, tap the hole to receive the thread insert. Keep the tap well oiled and back it out often to avoid cracking the treads

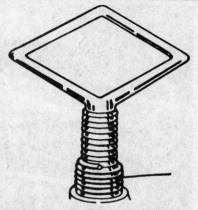

Fig. 28 Screw the threaded insert onto the installation tool until the tang engages the slot. Screw the insert into the tapped hole until it is 1/4 to 1/2 turn below the top of the surface. After installation break off the tang with a hammer and a punch

they require a tap equipped with pilot threads and a combined reamer/tap section. Most manufacturers also supply blister-packed thread repair inserts separately in addition to a master kit containing a variety of taps and inserts plus installation tools.

Before effecting a repair to a threaded hole, remove any snapped, broken or damaged bolts or studs. Penetrating oil can be used to free frozen threads; the offending item can be removed with locking pliers or with a screw or stud extractor. After the hole is clear, the thread can be repaired, as follows:

Checking Engine Compression

◆ SEE FIGS. 29 and 31
A noticeable lack of engine power, excessive oil consumption and/or poor fuel mileage measured over an extended period are all indicators of internal engine war. Worn piston rings, scored or worn cylinder bores, blown head gaskets, sticking or burnt valves and worn valve seats are all possible culprits here. A check of each cylinder's compression will help you locate the problems.

As mentioned in the Tools and Equipment section of Section 1, a screw-in type compression gauge is more accurate that the type you simply hold against the spark plug hole, although it takes slightly longer to use. It's worth it to obtain a more accurate reading. Follow the procedures below for gasoline and diesel engines.

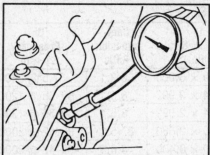

Fig. 29 The screw in type compression gauge is more accurate

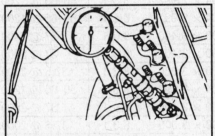

Fig. 30 Diesel engines require a special compression gauge adaptor

GASOLINE ENGINES

1. Warm up the engine to normal operating temperature.
2. Remove all spark plugs.

3. Disconnect the high tension lead from the ignition coil.

4. On fully open the throttle either by operating the carburetor throttle linkage by hand or by having an assistant floor the accelerator pedal.

5. Screw the compression gauge into the no.1 spark plug hole until the fitting is snug.

➡ **Be careful not to crossthread the plug hole. On aluminum cylinder heads use extra care, as the threads in these heads are easily ruined.**

6. Ask an assistant to depress the accelerator pedal fully on both carbureted and fuel injected vehicles. Then, while you read the compression gauge, ask the assistant to crank the engine two or three times in short bursts using the ignition switch.

7. Read the compression gauge at the end of each series of cranks, and record the highest of these readings. Repeat this procedure for each of the engine's cylinders. Compare the highest reading of each cylinder to the compression pressure specification in the Tune-Up Specifications chart in Section 2. The specs in this chart are maximum values. A cylinder's compression pressure is usually acceptable if it is not less than 80% of maximum. The difference between each cylinder should be no more than 12–14 pounds.

8. If a cylinder is unusually low, pour a tablespoon of clean engine oil into the cylinder through the spark plug hole and repeat the compression test. If the compression comes up after adding the oil, it appears that the cylinder's piston rings or bore are damaged or worn. If the pressure remains low, the valves may not be seating properly (a valve job is needed), or the head gasket may be blown near that cylinder. If compression in any two adjacent cylinders is low, and if the addition of oil doesn't help the compression, there is leakage past the head gasket. Oil and coolant water in the combustion chamber can result from this problem. There may be evidence of water droplets on the engine dipstick when a head gasket has blown.

Diesel Engines

Checking cylinder compression on diesel engines is basically the same procedure as on gasoline engines except for the following:

1. A special compression gauge adaptor suitable for diesel engines (because these engines have much greater compression pressures) must be used.

2. Remove the injector tubes and remove the injectors from each cylinder.

➡ **Don't forget to remove the washer underneath each injector; otherwise, it may get lost when the engine is cranked.**

3. When fitting the compression gauge adaptor to the cylinder head, make sure the bleeder of the gauge (if equipped) is closed.

4. When reinstalling the injector assemblies, install new washers underneath each injector.

GENERAL ENGINE SPECIFICATIONS

Year	Engine VIN	Engine Displacement cu. in. (liter)	Fuel System Type	Net Horsepower @ rpm	Net Torque @ rpm (ft. lbs.)	Bore × Stroke (in.)	Compression Ratio	Oil Pressure @ rpm
1982–84	R	4-151 (2.5)	TBI	92 @ 4000	134 @ 2800	4.000 × 3.000	8.2:1	37.5 @ 2000
	X	6-173 (2.8)	2 bbl	112 @ 4800	145 @ 2100	3.500 × 3.000	8.5:1	50–65 @ 1200
	Z	6-173 (2.8) ②	2 bbl	135 @ 5400	145 @ 2400	3.500 × 3.000	8.9:1	50–65 @ 1200
	E	6-181 (3.0)	2 bbl	110 @ 4800	145 @ 2600	3.800 × 2.660	8.45:1	35–42 @ 2000
1983	R	4-151 (2.5)	TBI	92 @ 4000	134 @ 2800	4.000 × 3.000	8.2:1	37.5 @ 2000
	X	6-173 (2.8)	2 bbl	112 @ 4800	145 @ 2100	3.500 × 3.000	8.5:1	50–65 @ 1200
	Z	6-173 (2.8) ②	2 bbl	135 @ 5400	145 @ 2400	3.500 × 3.000	8.9:1	50–65 @ 1200
	E	6-181 (3.0)	2 bbl	110 @ 4800	145 @ 2600	3.800 × 2.660	8.45:1	35–42 @ 2000
	T	6-263 (4.3)	Diesel	85 @ 3600	165 @ 1600	4.057 × 3.385	21.6:1	40–45 @ 2000
1984	R	4-151 (2.5)	TBI	92 @ 4000	134 @ 2800	4.000 × 3.000	8.2:1	37.5 @ 2000
	X	6-173 (2.8)	2 bbl	112 @ 4800	145 @ 2100	3.500 × 3.000	8.5:1	50–65 @ 1200
	Z	6-173 (2.8) ②	2 bbl	135 @ 5400	145 @ 2400	3.500 × 3.000	8.9:1	50–65 @ 1200
	E	6-181 (3.0)	2 bbl	110 @ 4800	145 @ 2600	3.800 × 2.660	8.45:1	35–42 @ 2000
	T	6-263 (4.3)	Diesel	85 @ 3600	165 @ 1600	4.057 × 3.385	21.6:1	40–45 @ 2000

GENERAL ENGINE SPECIFICATIONS

Year	Engine VIN	Engine Displacement cu. in. (liter)	Fuel System Type	Net Horsepower @ rpm	Net Torque @ rpm (ft. lbs.)	Bore × Stroke (in.)	Compression Ratio	Oil Pressure @ rpm
1985	R	4-151 (2.5)	TBI	92 @ 4000	134 @ 2800	4.000 × 3.000	8.2:1	37.5 @ 2000
	X	6-173 (2.8)	2 bbl	112 @ 4800	145 @ 2100	3.504 × 2.992	8.5:1	50–65 @ 1200
	W	6-173 (2.8)	MFI	130 @ 4800	155 @ 3600	3.504 × 2.992	8.5:1	50–65 @ 1200
	E	6-181 (3.0)	2 bbl	110 @ 4800	145 @ 2600	3.800 × 2.660	8.45:1	35–42 @ 2000
	3	6-231 (3.8)	MFI	125 @ 4800	195 @ 2000	3.800 × 3.400	8.0:1	35–42 @ 2000
	T	6-263 (4.3)	Diesel	85 @ 3600	165 @ 1600	4.057 × 3.385	21.6:1	40–45 @ 2000
1986	R	4-151 (2.5)	TBI	92 @ 4000	134 @ 2800	4.000 × 3.000	8.2:1	37.5 @ 2000
	X	6-173 (2.8)	2 bbl	112 @ 4800	145 @ 2100	3.504 × 2.992	8.5:1	50–65 @ 1200
	W	6-173 (2.8)	MFI	130 @ 4800	155 @ 3600	3.504 × 2.992	8.5:1	50–65 @ 1200
	3	6-231 (3.8)	SFI	150 @ 4400	200 @ 2000	3.800 × 3.400	8.0:1	37 @ 2400
	B	6-231 (3.8)	SFI	150 @ 4400	200 @ 2000	3.800 × 3.400	8.0:1	37 @ 2400
1987	R	4-151 (2.5)	TBI	92 @ 4000	134 @ 2800	4.000 × 3.000	8.2:1	37.5 @ 2000
	W	6-173 (2.8)	MFI	130 @ 4800	155 @ 3600	3.504 × 2.992	8.5:1	50–65 @ 1200
	3	6-231 (3.8)	SFI	150 @ 4400	200 @ 2000	3.800 × 3.400	8.0:1	37 @ 2400
1988	R	4-151 (2.5)	TBI	92 @ 4000	134 @ 2800	4.000 × 3.000	8.3:1	37.5 @ 2000
	W	6-173 (2.8)	PFI	130 @ 4800	155 @ 3600	3.503 × 2.992	8.9:1	50–65 @ 1200
	3	6-231 (3.8)	SFI	150 @ 4400	200 @ 2000	3.800 × 3.400	8.0:1	37 @ 2400
1989	R	4-151 (2.5)	TBI	92 @ 4000	134 @ 2800	4.000 × 3.000	8.3:1	37.5 @ 2000
	W	6-173 (2.8)	PFI	130 @ 4800	155 @ 3600	3.503 × 2.992	8.9:1	50–65 @ 1200
	T	6-192 (3.1)	PFI	120 @ 4200	175 @ 2200	3.503 × 3.312	8.8:1	50–65 @ 2400
	N	6-204 (3.3)	PFI	160 @ 5200	185 @ 2000	3.700 × 3.160	9.0:1	45 @ 2000
1990	R	4-151 (2.5)	TBI	92 @ 4400	134 @ 2800	4.000 × 3.000	8.3:1	37.5 @ 2000
	T	6-192 (3.1)	PFI	120 @ 4200	175 @ 2200	3.503 × 3.312	8.8:1	50–65 @ 2400
	N	6-204 (3.3)	PFI	160 @ 5200	185 @ 2000	3.700 × 3.160	9.0:1	45 @ 2000
1991	R	4-151 (2.5)	TBI	92 @ 4400	134 @ 2800	4.000 × 3.000	8.3:1	37.5 @ 2000
	T	6-192 (3.1)	PFI	120 @ 4200	175 @ 2200	3.503 × 3.312	8.8:1	50–65 @ 2400
	N	6-204 (3.3)	PFI	160 @ 5200	185 @ 2000	3.700 × 3.160	9.0:1	45 @ 2000

NOTE: Due to manufacturing tolerance variations, figures given for bore and stroke are reference values only. Always use actual piston, bore and crankshaft measurements prior to any machine work.
TBI—Throttle Body Injection
PFI—Port Fuel Injection
SFI—Sequential Multi-port Fuel Injection
① California
② HO—High Output

VALVE SPECIFICATIONS

Year	Engine VIN	Engine Displacement cu. in. (liter)	Seat Angle (deg.)	Face Angle (deg.)	Spring Test Pressure (lbs. @ in.)	Spring Installed Height (in.)	Stem-to-Guide Clearance (in.)		Stem Diameter (in.)	
							Intake	Exhaust	Intake	Exhaust
1982–84	R	4-151 (2.5)	46	45	176 @ 1.254	1.660	0.0010–0.0027	0.0010–0.0027	0.3418–0.3425	0.3418–0.3425
	X, Z	6-173 (2.8)	46	45	155 @ 1.160	1.610	0.0010–0.0027	0.0010–0.0027	0.3410–0.3416	0.3410–0.3416
	E	6-181 (3.0)	45	45	220 @ 1.340	1.727	0.0015–0.0035	0.0015–0.0035	0.3401–0.3412	0.3402–0.3415
1983	R	4-151 (2.5)	46	45	176 @ 1.254	1.660	0.0010–0.0027	0.0010–0.0027	0.3418–0.3425	0.3418–0.3425
	X, Z	6-173 (2.8)	46	45	155 @ 1.160	1.610	0.0010–0.0027	0.0010–0.0027	0.3410–0.3416	0.3410–0.3416
	E	6-181 (3.0)	45	45	220 @ 1.340	1.727	0.0015–0.0035	0.0015–0.0035	0.3401–0.3412	0.3402–0.3415
	T	6-263 (4.3)	①	②	210 @ 1.220	1.670	0.0010–0.0027	0.0015–0.0032	0.3425–0.3432	0.3420–0.3427
1984	R	4-151 (2.5)	46	45	176 @ 1.254	1.660	0.0010–0.0027	0.0010–0.0027	0.3418–0.3425	0.3418–0.3425
	X, Z	6-173 (2.8)	46	45	155 @ 1.160	1.610	0.0010–0.0027	0.0010–0.0027	0.3410–0.3416	0.3410–0.3416
	E	6-181 (3.0)	45	45	220 @ 1.340	1.727	0.0015–0.0035	0.0015–0.0035	0.3401–0.3412	0.3402–0.3415
	T	6-263 (4.3)	①	②	210 @ 1.220	1.670	0.0010–0.0027	0.0015–0.0032	0.3425–0.3432	0.3420–0.3427
1985	R	4-151 (2.5)	46	45	176 @ 1.254	1.660	0.0010–0.0027	0.0010–0.0027	0.3418–0.3425	0.3418–0.3425
	X, W	6-173 (2.8)	46	45	155 @ 1.160	1.610	0.0010–0.0027	0.0010–0.0027	0.3410–0.3416	0.3410–0.3416
	E	6-181 (3.0)	45	45	220 @ 1.340	1.727	0.0015–0.0035	0.0015–0.0035	0.3401–0.3412	0.3402–0.3415
	T	6-263 (4.3)	①	②	210 @ 1.220	1.670	0.0010–0.0027	0.0015–0.0032	0.3425–0.3432	0.3420–0.3427
1986	R	4-151 (2.5)	46	45	176 @ 1.260	1.690	0.0010–0.0027	0.0010–0.0027	0.3420–0.3430	0.3420–0.3430
	3	6-231 (3.8)	45	45	220 @ 1.340	1.727	0.0015–0.0032	0.0015–0.0032	0.3405–0.3412	0.3412
	B	6-231 (3.8)	45	45	220 @ 1.340	1.727	0.0015–0.0032	0.0015–0.0032	0.3405–0.3412	0.3412
1987	R	4-151 (2.5)	46	45	176 @ 1.254	1.690	0.0010–0.0027	0.0010–0.0032	0.3410–0.3140	0.3410–0.3130
	W	6-173 (2.8)	46	45	215 @ 1.291	1.727	0.0015–0.0027	0.0015–0.0027	0.3412–0.3416	0.3412–0.3416
	3	6-231 (3.8)	45	45	195 @ 1.340	1.727	0.0015–0.0032	0.0015–0.0032	0.3412–0.3405	0.3412–0.3405
1988	R	4-151 (2.5)	46	46	176 @ 1.254	1.440	0.0010–0.0028	0.0013–0.0041	0.3130–0.3140	0.3120–0.3130
	W	6-173 (2.8)	46	45	215 @ 1.291	1.727	0.0010–0.0027	0.0010–0.0027	0.3412–0.3416	0.3412–0.3416
	3	6-231 (3.8)	45	45	195 @ 1.340	1.727	0.0015–0.0035	0.0015–0.0032	0.3405–0.3412	0.3405–0.3412

VALVE SPECIFICATIONS

Year	Engine VIN	Engine Displacement cu. in. (liter)	Seat Angle (deg.)	Face Angle (deg.)	Spring Test Pressure (lbs. @ in.)	Spring Installed Height (in.)	Stem-to-Guide Clearance (in.)		Stem Diameter (in.)	
							Intake	Exhaust	Intake	Exhaust
1989	R	4-151 (2.5)	46	46	176 @ 1.254	1.440	0.0010–0.0028	0.0013–0.0041	0.3130–0.3140	0.3120–0.3130
	W	6-173 (2.8)	46	45	215 @ 1.291	1.727	0.0010–0.0027	0.0010–0.0027	0.3412–0.3416	0.3412–0.3416
	T	6-192 (3.1)	46	45	215 @ 1.291	1.575	0.0010–0.0027	0.0010–0.0027	NA	NA
	N	6-204 (3.3)	46	45	215 @ 1.291	1.701	0.0010–0.0027	0.0010–0.0027	NA	NA
1990	R	4-151 (2.5)	46	46	176 @ 1.254	1.440	0.0010–0.0028	0.0013–0.0041	NA	NA
	T	6-192 (3.1)	46	45	215 @ 1.291	1.575	0.0010–0.0027	0.0010–0.0027	NA	NA
	N	6-204 (3.3)	46	45	215 @ 1.291	1.701	0.0010–0.0027	0.0010–0.0027	NA	NA
1991	R	4-151 (2.5)	46	45	173 @ 1.240	1.680	0.0010–0.0028	0.0013–0.0041	NA	NA
	T	6-192 (3.1)	46	45	215 @ 1.291	1.5758	0.0010–0.0027	0.0010–0.0027	NA	NA
	N	6-204 (3.3)	45	45	210 @ 1.315	1.690–1.720	0.0015–0.0035	0.0015–0.0032	NA	NA
1992	R	4-151 (2.5)	46	45	173 @ 1.240	1.680	0.0010–0.0028	0.0013–0.0041	NA	NA
	T	6-192 (3.1)	46	45	215 @ 1.291	1.5758	0.0010–0.0027	0.0010–0.0027	NA	NA
	N	6-204 (3.3)	45	45	210 @ 1.315	1.690–1.720	0.0015–0.0035	0.0015–0.0032	NA	NA

NA—Not available
① Intake: 45
   Exhaust: 31
② Intake: 44
   Exhaust: 30

CAMSHAFT SPECIFICATIONS

All measurements given in inches.

Year	Engine VIN	Engine Displacement cu. in. (liter)	Journal Diameter					Elevation		Bearing Clearance	Camshaft End Play
			1	2	3	4	5	In.	Ex.		
1982	R	4-151 (2.5)	1.869	1.869	1.869	—	—	0.398	0.398	0.0007–0.0027	0.0015–0.0050
	X	6-173 (2.8)	1.869	1.869	1.869	1.869	—	0.231	0.263	0.0010–0.0040	—
	Z	6-173 (2.8)	1.869	1.869	1.869	1.869	—	0.231	0.263	0.0010–0.0040	—
	E	6-181 (3.0)	1.786	1.786	1.786	1.786	1.786	0.406	0.406	①	—

CAMSHAFT SPECIFICATIONS

All measurements given in inches.

Year	Engine VIN	Engine Displacement cu. in. (liter)	Journal Diameter					Elevation		Bearing Clearance	Camshaft End Play
			1	2	3	4	5	In.	Ex.		
1983	R	4-151 (2.5)	1.869	1.869	1.869	—	—	0.398	0.398	0.0007–0.0027	0.0015–0.0050
	X	6-173 (2.8)	1.869	1.869	1.869	1.869	—	0.231	0.263	0.0010–0.0040	—
	Z	6-173 (2.8)	1.869	1.869	1.869	1.869	—	0.231	0.263	0.0010–0.0040	—
	E	6-181 (3.0)	1.786	1.786	1.786	1.786	1.786	0.406	0.406	①	—
	T	6-263 (4.3)	②	2.205	2.185	2.165	—	NA	NA	0.0020–0.0059	0.0008–0.0228
1984	R	4-151 (2.5)	1.869	1.869	1.869	—	—	0.398	0.398	0.0007–0.0027	0.0015–0.0050
	X	6-173 (2.8)	1.869	1.869	1.869	1.869	—	0.231	0.263	0.0010–0.0040	—
	Z	6-173 (2.8)	1.869	1.869	1.869	1.869	—	0.231	0.263	0.0010–0.0040	—
	E	6-181 (3.0)	1.786	1.786	1.786	1.786	1.786	0.406	0.406	①	—
	T	6-263 (4.3)	②	2.205	2.185	2.165	—	NA	NA	0.0020–0.0059	0.0008–0.0228
1985	R	4-151 (2.5)	1.869	1.869	1.869	—	—	0.398	0.398	0.0007–0.0027	0.0015–0.0050
	X	6-173 (2.8)	1.869	1.869	1.869	1.869	—	0.231	0.263	0.0010–0.0040	—
	Z	6-173 (2.8)	1.869	1.869	1.869	1.869	—	0.231	0.263	0.0010–0.0040	—
	E	6-181 (3.0)	1.786	1.786	1.786	1.786	1.786	0.406	0.406	①	—
	3	6-231 (3.8)	1.786	1.786	1.786	1.786	1.786	0.406	0.406	①	—
	T	6-263 (4.3)	②	2.205	2.185	2.165	—	NA	NA	0.0020–0.0059	0.0008–0.0228
1986	R	4-151 (2.5)	1.869	1.869	1.869	—	—	0.398	0.398	0.0007–0.0027	0.0015–0.0050
	X	6-173 (2.8)	1.869	1.869	1.869	1.869	—	0.263	0.273	0.0010–0.0040	—
	W	6-173 (2.8)	1.869	1.869	1.869	1.869	—	0.263	0.273	0.0010–0.0040	—
	3	6-231 (3.8)	1.786	1.786	1.786	1.786	1.786	0.397	0.397	①	—
	B	6-231 (3.8)	1.786	1.786	1.786	1.786	1.786	0.397	0.397	①	—
1987	R	4-151 (2.5)	1.869	1.869	1.869	—	—	0.398	0.398	0.0007–0.0027	0.0015–0.0050
	W	6-173 (2.8)	1.869	1.869	1.869	1.869	—	0.263	0.273	0.0010–0.0040	—
	3	6-231 (3.8)	1.786	1.786	1.786	1.786	1.786	0.397	0.397	①	—
1988	R	4-151 (2.5)	1.8690	1.8690	1.8690	—	—	0.232	0.232	0.0007–0.0027	0.0015–0.0050
	W	6-173 (2.8)	1.8678–1.8815	1.8678–1.8815	1.8678–1.8815	1.8678–1.8815	—	0.262	0.273	0.0010–0.0040	NA
	3	6-231 (3.8)	1.7850–1.7860	1.7850–1.7860	1.7850–1.7860	1.7850–1.7860	—	0.245	0.245	0.0005–0.0035	NA

CAMSHAFT SPECIFICATIONS

All measurements given in inches.

Year	Engine VIN	Engine Displacement cu. in. (liter)	Journal Diameter 1	2	3	4	5	Elevation In.	Ex.	Bearing Clearance	Camshaft End Play
1989	R	4-151 (2.5)	1.8690	1.8690	1.8690	—	—	0.232	0.232	0.0007–0.0027	0.0015–0.0050
	W	6-173 (2.8)	1.8678–1.8815	1.8678–1.8815	1.8678–1.8815	1.8678–1.8815	—	0.262	0.273	0.0010–0.0040	NA
	T	6-192 (3.1)	1.8678–1.8815	1.8678–1.8815	1.8678–1.8815	1.8678–1.8815	—	0.263	0.273	0.0010–0.0040	NA
	N	6-204 (3.3)	1.7850–1.7860	1.7850–1.7860	1.7850–1.7860	1.7850–1.7860	—	0.250	0.255	0.0005–0.0035	NA
1990	R	4-151 (2.5)	1.8690	1.8690	1.8690	—	—	0.248	0.248	0.0007–0.0027	0.0015–0.0050
	T	6-192 (3.1)	1.8678–1.8815	1.8678–1.8815	1.8678–1.8815	1.8678–1.8815	—	0.263	0.273	0.0010–0.0040	NA
	N	6-204 (3.3)	1.7850–1.7860	1.7850–1.7860	1.7850–1.7860	1.7850–1.7860	—	0.250	0.255	0.0005–0.0035	NA
1991	R	4-151 (2.5)	1.8690	1.8690	1.8690	—	—	0.248	0.248	0.0007–0.0027	0.0015–0.0050
	T	6-192 (3.1)	1.8678–1.8815	1.8678–1.8815	1.8678–1.8815	1.8678–1.8815	—	0.263	0.273	0.0010–0.0040	NA
	N	6-204 (3.3)	1.7850–1.7860	1.7850–1.7860	1.7850–1.7860	1.7850–1.7860	—	0.250	0.255	0.0005–0.0035	NA
1992	R	4-151 (2.5)	1.8690	1.8690	1.8690	—	—	0.248	0.248	0.0007–0.0027	0.0015–0.0050
	T	6-192 (3.1)	1.8678–1.8815	1.8678–1.8815	1.8678–1.8815	1.8678–1.8815	—	0.263	0.273	0.0010–0.0040	NA
	N	6-204 (3.3)	1.7850–1.7860	1.7850–1.7860	1.7850–1.7860	1.7850–1.7860	—	0.250	0.255	0.0005–0.0035	NA

NA—Not available
① No. 1: 0.0005–0.0025
No. 2–5: 0.0005–0.0035

② No. 1 bearing is not boreable, but must be replaced separately

CRANKSHAFT AND CONNECTING ROD SPECIFICATIONS

All measurements are given in inches.

Year	Engine VIN	Engine Displacement cu. in. (liter)	Crankshaft Main Brg. Journal Dia.	Main Brg. Oil Clearance	Shaft End-play	Thrust on No.	Connecting Rod Journal Diameter	Oil Clearance	Side Clearance
1982	R	4-151 (2.5)	2.2995–2.3005	0.0005–0.0022	0.0035–0.0085	5	1.9995–2.0005	0.0005–0.0026	0.006–0.022
	X, Z	6-173 (2.8)	2.4397–2.4946	0.0017–0.0030	0.0020–0.0067	3	1.9984–1.9994	0.0014–0.0036	0.006–0.017
	E	6-181 (3.0)	2.4990–2.5000	0.0003–0.0018	0.0030–0.0090	2	2.2487–2.2495	0.0005–0.0026	0.023–0.022
1983	R	4-151 (2.5)	2.2995–2.3005	0.0005–0.0022	0.0035–0.0085	5	1.9995–2.0005	0.0005–0.0026	0.006–0.022
	X, Z	6-173 (2.8)	2.4397–2.4946	0.0017–0.0030	0.0020–0.0067	3	1.9984–1.9994	0.0014–0.0036	0.006–0.017
	E	6-181 (3.0)	2.4990–2.5000	0.0003–0.0018	0.0030–0.0090	2	2.2487–2.2495	0.0005–0.0026	0.023–0.022
	T	6-263 (4.3)	2.9993–3.0003	①	0.0035–0.0135	4	2.2490–2.2510	0.0003–0.0025	0.008–0.021

CRANKSHAFT AND CONNECTING ROD SPECIFICATIONS

All measurements are given in inches.

Year	Engine VIN	Engine Displacement cu. in. (liter)	Crankshaft				Connecting Rod		
			Main Brg. Journal Dia.	Main Brg. Oil Clearance	Shaft End-play	Thrust on No.	Journal Diameter	Oil Clearance	Side Clearance
1984	R	4-151 (2.5)	2.2995–2.3005	0.0005–0.0022	0.0035–0.0085	5	1.9995–2.0005	0.0005–0.0026	0.006–0.022
	X, Z	6-173 (2.8)	2.4397–2.4946	0.0017–0.0030	0.0020–0.0067	3	1.9984–1.9994	0.0014–0.0036	0.006–0.017
	E	6-181 (3.0)	2.4990–2.5000	0.0003–0.0018	0.0030–0.0090	2	2.2487–2.2495	0.0005–0.0026	0.023–0.022
	T	6-263 (4.3)	2.9993–3.0003	①	0.0035–0.0135	4	2.2490–2.2510	0.0003–0.0025	0.008–0.021
1985	R	4-151 (2.5)	2.2995–2.3005	0.0005–0.0022	0.0035–0.0085	5	1.9995–2.0005	0.0005–0.0026	0.006–0.022
	X, W	6-173 (2.8)	2.4397–2.4946	0.0017–0.0030	0.0020–0.0067	3	1.9984–1.9994	0.0014–0.0036	0.006–0.017
	E	6-181 (3.0)	2.4990–2.5000	0.0003–0.0018	0.0030–0.0090	2	2.2487–2.2495	0.0005–0.0026	0.023–0.022
	T	6-263 (4.3)	2.9993–3.0003	①	0.0035–0.0135	4	2.2490–2.2510	0.0003–0.0025	0.008–0.021
1986	R	4-151 (2.5)	2.2995–2.3005	0.0005–0.0022	0.0035–0.0085	5	1.9995–2.0005	0.0005–0.0026	0.006–0.022
	X, W	6-173 (2.8)	2.4397–2.4946	0.0017–0.0030	0.0020–0.0067	3	1.9984–1.9994	0.0014–0.0036	0.006–0.017
	3	6-231 (3.8)	2.4995	0.0003–0.0018	0.003–0.011	2	2.2487–2.2495	0.0005–0.0026	0.006–0.023
	B	6-231 (3.8)	2.4995	0.0003–0.0018	0.003–0.011	2	2.2487–2.2495	0.0005–0.0026	0.006–0.023
1987	R	4-151 (2.5)	2.2995–2.3005	0.0005–0.0022	0.0035–0.0085	5	1.9995–2.0005	0.0005–0.0026	0.006–0.022
	W	6-173 (2.8)	2.6473–2.6483	0.0016–0.0033	0.002–0.008	3	1.9983–1.9993	0.0013–0.0026	0.006–0.017
	3	6-231 (3.8)	2.4995	0.0003–0.0018	0.003–0.011	2	2.2487–2.2495	0.0005–0.0026	0.006–0.023
1988	R	4-151 (2.5)	2.3000	0.0005–0.0022	0.003–0.008	5	1.9995–2.0005	0.0005–0.0026	0.006–0.022
	W	6-173 (2.8)	2.6473–2.6483	0.0016–0.0033	0.002–0.008	3	1.9983–1.9993	0.0013–0.0026	0.006–0.017
	3	6-231 (3.8)	2.4988–2.4998	0.0003–0.0018	0.003–0.011	2	2.2487–2.2495	0.0005–0.0026	0.006–0.023
1989	R	4-151 (2.5)	2.3000	0.0005–0.0022	0.003–0.008	5	1.9995–2.0005	0.0005–0.0026	0.006–0.022
	W	6-173 (2.8)	2.6473–2.6483	0.0016–0.0033	0.002–0.008	3	1.9983–1.9993	0.0013–0.0026	0.006–0.017
	T	6-192 (3.1)	2.6473–2.6483	0.0012–0.0027	0.002–0.008	3	1.9983–1.9994	0.0013–0.0031	0.014–0.027
	N	6-204 (3.3)	2.4988–2.4998	0.0003–0.0018	0.003–0.011	3	2.2487–2.2499	0.0003–0.0026	0.003–0.015

CRANKSHAFT AND CONNECTING ROD SPECIFICATIONS

All measurements are given in inches.

Year	Engine VIN	Engine Displacement cu. in. (liter)	Crankshaft				Connecting Rod		
			Main Brg. Journal Dia.	Main Brg. Oil Clearance	Shaft End-play	Thrust on No.	Journal Diameter	Oil Clearance	Side Clearance
1990	R	4-151 (2.5)	2.3000	0.0005–0.0022	0.003–0.008	5	1.9995–2.0005	0.0005–0.0026	0.006–0.022
	T	6-192 (3.1)	2.6473–2.6483	0.0012–0.0027	0.002–0.008	3	1.9983–1.9994	0.0013–0.0031	0.014–0.027
	N	6-204 (3.3)	2.4988–2.4998	0.0003–0.0018	0.003–0.011	3	2.2487–2.2499	0.0003–0.0026	0.003–0.015
1991	R	4-151 (2.5)	2.3000	0.0005–0.0022	0.005–0.001	5	2.0000	0.0005–0.0030	0.006–0.024
	T	6-192 (3.1)	2.6473–2.6483	0.0012–0.0030	0.002–0.008	3	1.9983–1.9994	0.0011–0.0034	0.014–0.027
	N	6-204 (3.3)	2.4988–2.4998	0.0003–0.0018	0.003–0.011	3	2.2487–2.2499	0.0003–0.0026	0.003–0.015
1992	R	4-151 (2.5)	2.3000	0.0005–0.0022	0.005–0.001	5	2.0000	0.0005–0.0030	0.006–0.024
	T	6-192 (3.1)	2.6473–2.6483	0.0012–0.0030	0.002–0.008	3	1.9983–1.9994	0.0011–0.0034	0.014–0.027
	N	6-204 (3.3)	2.4988–2.4998	0.0003–0.0018	0.003–0.011	3	2.2487–2.2499	0.0003–0.0026	0.003–0.015

NOTE: Due to manufacturing tolerance variations, figures given are reference values only. Always use actual piston, bore and crankshaft measurements prior to any machine work.
① No. 1, 2, 3: 0.0005–0.0021
  No. 4: 0.0020–0.034

PISTON AND RING SPECIFICATIONS

All measurements are given in inches.

Year	Engine VIN	Engine Displacement cu. in. (liter)	Piston Clearance	Ring Gap			Ring Side Clearance		
				Top Compression	Bottom Compression	Oil Control	Top Compression	Bottom Compression	Oil Control
1982	R	4-151 (2.5)	0.0025–0.0033	0.010–0.022	0.010–0.027	0.0015–0.0055	0.0015–0.0030	0.0015–0.0030	Snug
	X, Z	6-173 (2.8)	0.0017–0.0027	0.010–0.020	0.010–0.020	0.020–0.055	0.0012–0.0028	0.0016–0.0037	0.008
	E	6-181 (3.0)	0.0008–0.0020	0.013–0.023	0.013–0.023	0.015–0.035	0.0030–0.0050	0.0030–0.0050	0.0035
1983	R	4-151 (2.5)	0.0025–0.0033	0.010–0.022	0.010–0.027	0.0015–0.0055	0.0015–0.0030	0.0015–0.0030	Snug
	X, Z	6-173 (2.8)	0.0017–0.0027	0.010–0.020	0.010–0.020	0.020–0.055	0.0012–0.0028	0.0016–0.0037	0.008
	E	6-181 (3.0)	0.0008–0.0020	0.013–0.023	0.013–0.023	0.015–0.035	0.0030–0.0050	0.0030–0.0050	0.0035
	T	6-263 (4.3)	0.0030–0.0040	0.015–0.025	0.015–0.025	0.015–0.055	0.0050–0.0070	0.0030–0.0070	0.001–0.005
1984	R	4-151 (2.5)	0.0025–0.0033	0.010–0.022	0.010–0.027	0.0015–0.0055	0.0015–0.0030	0.0015–0.0030	Snug
	X, Z	6-173 (2.8)	0.0017–0.0027	0.010–0.020	0.010–0.020	0.020–0.055	0.0012–0.0028	0.0016–0.0037	0.008
	E	6-181 (3.0)	0.0008–0.0020	0.013–0.023	0.013–0.023	0.015–0.035	0.0030–0.0050	0.0030–0.0050	0.0035
	T	6-263 (4.3)	0.0030–0.0040	0.015–0.025	0.015–0.025	0.015–0.055	0.0050–0.0070	0.0030–0.0070	0.001–0.005

PISTON AND RING SPECIFICATIONS

All measurements are given in inches.

Year	Engine VIN	Engine Displacement cu. in. (liter)	Piston Clearance	Ring Gap			Ring Side Clearance		
				Top Compression	Bottom Compression	Oil Control	Top Compression	Bottom Compression	Oil Control
1985	R	4-151 (2.5)	0.0014–0.0022 ①	0.010–0.020	0.010–0.020	0.020–0.060	0.002–0.003	0.001–0.003	0.015–0.055
	X, W	6-173 (2.8)	0.0017–0.0027	0.010–0.020	0.010–0.020	0.020–0.055	0.0012–0.0028	0.0016–0.0037	0.008
	E	6-181 (3.0)	0.0008–0.0020	0.013–0.023	0.013–0.023	0.015–0.035	0.0030–0.0050	0.0030–0.0050	0.0035
	3	6-231 (3.8)	0.0008–0.0020	0.010–0.020	0.010–0.020	0.015–0.055	0.003–0.005	0.003–0.005	0.0035
	T	6-263 (4.3)	0.0035–0.0045	0.019–0.027	0.013–0.021	0.015–0.055	0.005–0.007	0.003–0.007	0.001–0.005
1986	R	4-151 (2.5)	0.0014–0.0022 ①	0.010–0.020	0.010–0.020	0.020–0.060	0.002–0.003	0.001–0.003	0.015–0.055
	X, W	6-173 (2.8)	0.0017–0.0027	0.010–0.020	0.010–0.020	0.020–0.055	0.0012–0.0028	0.0016–0.0037	0.008
	3, B	6-231 (3.8)	0.001–0.002	0.013–0.023	0.013–0.023	0.015–0.035	0.003–0.005	0.003–0.005	0.0035
1987	R	4-151 (2.5)	0.0014–0.0022 ①	0.010–0.020	0.010–0.020	0.020–0.060	0.002–0.003	0.001–0.003	0.015–0.055
	W	6-173 (2.8)	0.0020–0.0028	0.010–0.020	0.010–0.020	0.020–0.055	0.001–0.003	0.001–0.003	0.008–0.005
	3	6-231 (3.8)	0.001–0.002	0.013–0.023	0.013–0.023	0.015–0.035	0.003–0.005	0.003–0.005	0.0035
1988	R	4-151 (2.5)	0.0014–0.0022 ①	0.010–0.020	0.010–0.020	0.020–0.060	0.002–0.003	0.001–0.003	0.015–0.055
	W	6-173 (2.8)	0.0020–0.0028	0.010–0.020	0.010–0.020	0.020–0.055	0.001–0.003	0.001–0.003	0.005–0.008
	3	6-231 (3.8)	0.0010–0.0020	0.013–0.023	0.013–0.023	0.015–0.035	0.003–0.005	0.003–0.005	0.003
1989	R	4-151 (2.5)	0.0014–0.0022 ①	0.010–0.020	0.010–0.020	0.020–0.060	0.002–0.003	0.001–0.003	0.015–0.055
	W	6-173 (2.8)	0.0020–0.0028	0.010–0.020	0.010–0.020	0.020–0.055	0.001–0.003	0.001–0.003	0.005–0.008
	T	6-192 (3.1)	0.0022–0.0028	0.010–0.020	0.010–0.020	0.010–0.050	0.002–0.004	0.002–0.004	0.008 ②
	N	6-204 (3.3)	0.0004–0.0022 ③	0.010–0.025	0.010–0.025	0.010–0.040	0.001–0.003	0.001–0.003	0.001 0.008
1990	R	4-151 (2.5)	0.0014–0.0022 ①	0.010–0.020	0.010–0.020	0.020–0.060	0.002–0.003	0.001–0.003	0.015–0.055
	T	6-192 (3.1)	0.0022–0.0028	0.010–0.020	0.010–0.020	0.010–0.050	0.002–0.004	0.002–0.004	0.008 ②
	N	6-204 (3.3)	0.0004–0.0022 ③	0.010–0.025	0.010–0.025	0.010–0.040	0.001–0.003	0.001–0.003	0.001 0.008
1991	R	4-151 (2.5)	0.0014–0.0022	0.010–0.020	0.010–0.020	0.020–0.060	0.002–0.003	0.001–0.003	0.015–0.055
	T	6-192 (3.1)	0.0009–0.0022	0.010–0.020	0.010–0.028	0.010–0.030	0.0020–0.0035	0.0020–0.0035	0.008 ②
	N	6-204 (3.3)	0.0004–0.0022 ③	0.010–0.025	0.010–0.025	0.010–0.040	0.0013–0.0031	0.0013–0.0031	0.0011–0.0081

PISTON AND RING SPECIFICATIONS

All measurements are given in inches.

Year	Engine VIN	Engine Displacement cu. in. (liter)	Piston Clearance①	Ring Gap			Ring Side Clearance		
				Top Compression	Bottom Compression	Oil Control	Top Compression	Bottom Compression	Oil Control
1992	R	4-151 (2.5)	0.0014–0.0022	0.010–0.020	0.010–0.020	0.020–0.060	0.002–0.003	0.001–0.003	0.015–0.055
	T	6-192 (3.1)	0.0009–0.0022	0.010–0.020	0.010–0.028	0.010–0.030	0.0020–0.0035	0.0020–0.0035	0.008②
	N	6-204 (3.3)	0.0004–0.0022③	0.010–0.025	0.010–0.025	0.010–0.040	0.0013–0.0031	0.0013–0.0031	0.0011–0.0081

① Measured ⅛ in. down from piston top
② Maximum clearance
③ 44 mm from top of piston

TORQUE SPECIFICATIONS

All readings in ft. lbs.

Year	VIN	No. Cylinder Displacement cu. in. (liter)	Cylinder Head Bolts	Main Bearing Bolts	Rod Bearing Bolts	Crankshaft Pulley Bolts	Flywheel Bolts	Manifold		Spark Plugs
								Intake	Exhaust	
1982	R	4-151 (2.5)	92	70	32	200	44	29	44	NA
	X,Z	6-173 (2.8)	70	68	37	75	50	23	25	7–15
	E	6-181 (3.0)	80	100	40–45	225	60	32	25–37	13
1983	R	4-151 (2.5)	92	70	32	200	44	29	44	NA
	X,Z	6-173 (2.8)	70	68	37	75	50	23	25	7–15
	E	6-181 (3.0)	80	100	40–45	225	60	32	25–37	13
	T	6-263 (4.3)	⑪	107	42	200	76	41	29	—
1984	R	4-151 (2.5)	92	70	32	200	44	29	44	NA
	X,Z	6-173 (2.8)	70	68	37	75	50	23	25	7–15
	E	6-181 (3.0)	80	100	40–45	225	60	32	25–37	13
	T	6-263 (4.3)	⑪	107	42	200	76	41	29	—
1985	R	4-151 (2.5)	92	70	32	200	44	29	③	15
	X,W	6-173 (2.8)	70	68	37	75	50	23	25	15
	E	6-181 (3.0)	80	100	40–45	200	60	47	25–37	13
	3	6-231 (3.8)	80	100	40	200	60	47	25	13
	T	6-263 (4.3)	⑪	107	42	200	76	41	29	—
1986	R	4-151 (2.5)	92	70	32	200	44	25	③	15
	X,W	6-173 (2.8)	65–90	68	37	75	50	23	25	7–15
	3,B	6-231 (3.8)	⑤	100	40	200	60	32	37	20
1987	R	4-151 (2.5)	①	70	32	162	⑫	25	③	15
	W	6-173 (2.8)	②	68	37	75	⑬	25	15–23	10–25
	3	6-231 (3.8)	⑤	100	45	219	60	32	37	20
1988	R	4-151 (2.5)	①	70	32	162	55	25	③	15
	W	6-173 (2.8)	②	73	39	76	52	⑨	15–23	10–25
	3	6-231 (3.8)	⑤	100	45	219	60	32	37	20
1989	R	4-151 (2.5)	①	70	32	162	55	25	③	15
	W	6-173 (2.8)	②	73	39	76	52	⑨	15–23	10–25
	T	6-192 (3.1)	②	73	34–40	76	52	⑨	19	10–25
	N	6-204 (3.3)	⑥	⑦	⑧	219	④	88⑩	41	20

TORQUE SPECIFICATIONS

All readings in ft. lbs.

Year	VIN	No. Cylinder Displacement cu. in. (liter)	Cylinder Head Bolts	Main Bearing Bolts	Rod Bearing Bolts	Crankshaft Pulley Bolts	Flywheel Bolts	Manifold		Spark Plugs
								Intake	Exhaust	
1990	R	4-151 (2.5)	①	65	29	162	55	25	③	15
	T	6-192 (3.1)	②	73	39	76	52	⑨	19	10–25
	N	6-204 (3.3)	⑥	⑦	⑧	219	④	88⑩	41	20
1991	R	4-151 (2.5)	①	65	29	162	55	25	③	20
	T	6-192 (3.1)	②	73	39	76	52	⑨	19	18
	N	6-204 (3.3)	⑥	⑦	⑧	219	④	89⑩	41	20
1992	R	4-151 (2.5)	①	65	29	162	55	25	③	20
	T	6-192 (3.1)	②	73	39	76	52	⑨	19	18
	N	6-204 (3.3)	⑥	⑦	⑧	219	④	89⑩	41	20

① Step 1: All bolts to 18 ft. lbs.
Step 2: Except position "I or 9" to 26 ft. lbs.
Step 3: Retorque position "I or 9" to 18 ft. lbs.
Step 4: All bolts +90° turn
② Step 1: 33 ft. lbs.
Step 2: +90° turn
③ Inner bolts: 37 ft. lbs.
Outer bolts: 28 ft. lbs.
④ Step 1: 89 inch lbs.
Step 2: +90° turn

⑤ Step 1: 25 ft. lbs.
Step 2: +90° turn
Step 3: +90° turn
NOTE: If at any time 60 ft. lbs. is reached during the sequence, STOP! Do not continue turning the bolt
⑥ Step 1: 35 ft. lbs.
Step 2: +130° turn
Step 3: +30° turn on 4 center bolts only
⑦ Step 1: 26 ft. lbs.
Step 2: +45° turn

⑧ Step 1: 20 ft. lbs.
Step 2: +50° turn
⑨ Manifold-to-cylinder head: 24 ft. lbs.
Manifold-to-plenum: 16 ft. lbs.
⑩ Inch lbs.
⑪ All exc. No. 5, 6, 11, 12, 13, 14: 142 ft. lbs.
No. 5, 6, 11, 12, 13, 14: 59 ft. lbs.
⑫ Manual Trans.: 69 ft. lbs.
Automatic Trans.: 55 ft. lbs.
⑬ Manual Trans.: 52 ft. lbs.
Automatic Trans.: 46 ft. lbs.

Engine

REMOVAL & INSTALLATION

✳✳ CAUTION

When draining the coolant, keep in mind that cats and dogs are attracted by the ethylene glycol antifreeze, and are quite likely to drink any that is left in an uncovered container or in puddles on the ground. This will prove fatal in sufficient quantity. Always drain the coolant into a sealable container. Coolant should be reused unless it is contaminated or several years old.

2.5L Engine with Manual Transaxle

➡ **Relieve the pressure in the fuel system.**

1. Disconnect battery cables at battery.
2. Hoist car.

3. Remove front mount-to-cradle nuts.
4. Remove forward exhaust pipe.
5. Remove starter assembly (wires attached and swing to side).
6. Remove flywheel inspection cover.
7. Lower car.
8. Remove air cleaner.
9. Remove all bell housing bolts.
10. Remove forward torque reaction rod from engine and core support.
11. If equipped with air conditioning, remove air conditioning belt and compressor and swing to side.
12. Remove emission hoses at canister.
13. Remove power steering hose (if so equipped).
14. Remove vacuum hoses and electrical connectors at solenoid.
15. Remove heater blower motor.
16. Disconnect throttle cable.
17. Drain heater hose.
18. Disconnect heater hose.
19. Disconnect radiator hose.
20. Disconnect engine harness at bulkhead connector.
21. With engine lifting tool, hoist engine (remove heater hose at intake manifold and disconnect fuel line).

To install:

22. Lower the engine into the engine compartment.

23. Connect engine harness at bulkhead connector.
24. Connect radiator hose.
25. Connect heater hose.
26. Connect the throttle cable
27. Install the heater blower motor.
28. Install the vacuum hoses and electrical connectors at the solenoid.
29. Install the power steering hose.
30. Install the emission hoses at the canister.
31. Install the air conditioning compressor and belt.
32. Install the forward torque reaction rod to the engine and core support.
33. Install all bell housing bolts.
34. Install the air cleaner.
35. Raise the vehicle.
36. Install the flywheel inspection cover.
37. Install the starter assembly.
38. Connect the forward exhaust pipe.
39. Install the front mount-to-cradle nuts.
40. Lower the vehicle and install the battery.

2.5L Engine with Automatic Transaxle

➡ **Relieve the pressure in the fuel system.**

1. Disconnect battery cables at battery.
2. Drain cooling system.
3. Remove air cleaner and pre-heat tube.

4. Disconnect engine harness connector.

5. Disconnect all external vacuum hose connections.

6. Remove throttle and transaxle linkage at E.F.I. assembly and intake manifold.

7. Remove upper radiator hose.

8. If equipped with air conditioning, remove air conditioning compressor from mounting brackets and set aside. Do not disconnect hoses.

9. Remove the front engine strut assembly.

10. Disconnect heater hose at intake manifold.

11. Remove transaxle to engine bolts leaving upper two bolts in place.

12. Remove front mount-to-cradle nuts.

13. Remove forward exhaust pipe.

14. Remove flywheel inspection cover and remove starter motor.

15. Remove torque converter to flywheel bolts.

16. Remove power steering pump and bracket and move to one side.

17. Remove heater hose and lower radiator hose.

18. Remove two rear transaxle support bracket bolts.

19. Remove fuel supply line at fuel filter.

20. Using a floor jack and a block of wood placed under the transaxle, raise engine and transaxle until engine front mount studs clear cradle.

21. Connect engine lift equipment and put tension on engine.

22. Remove two remaining transaxle bolts.

23. Slide engine forward and lift from car.

To Install:

24. Lower the engine into the vehicle. Do not completely lower the engine with a jack supporting the transaxle.

25. Install two transaxle bolts.

26. Remove the floor jack and lower the engine completely into the vehicle.

27. Connect the fuel supply line and install the filter.

28. Install the two transaxle rear support bracket bolts.

29. Install the heater and lower radiator hoses.

30. Connect the power steering bracket and pump.

31. Install the torque converter-to-flywheel bolts.

32. Install the starter motor and the flywheel inspection cover.

33. Connect the forward exhaust pipe.

34. Install the front mount-to-cradle nuts.

35. Install the transaxle to engine bolts.

36. Connect the heater hose at intake manifold.

37. Install the front engine strut assembly.

38. Install the air conditioning compressor mounting brackets and the compressor.

39. Install the upper radiator hose.

40. Connect the throttle and transaxle linkage at the E.F.I. assembly and intake manifold.

41. Connect all external vacuum hose connections.

42. Connect the engine harness connector.

43. Install the air cleaner and pre-heat tube.

44. Fill the cooling system.

45. Connect battery cables at battery.

2.8L Engine with Manual Transaxle

1. Disconnect cables from battery.

2. Remove air cleaner.

3. Drain cooling system.

4. Disconnect vacuum hosing to all non-engine mounted components.

5. Disconnect accelerator linkage from carburetor.

6. Disconnect engine harness connector from the ECM and pull the connector through the front of the dash.

7. Disconnect radiator hoses from radiator.

8. Disconnect heater hoses from engine.

9. If equipped, remove power steering pump and bracket assembly from engine.

10. Disconnect clutch cable from transaxle.

11. Disconnect shift linkage from transaxle shift levers. Remove cables from transaxle bosses.

12. Disconnect speedometer cable from transaxle.

13. Raise and support the vehicle on jack stands.

14. Remove exhaust crossover.

15. Remove all but one of the transaxle to engine retaining bolts.

16. Remove side and crossmember assembly.

17. Disconnect exhaust pipe.

18. Remove all power train mount to cradle attachments.

19. Disconnect the engine harness from the junction block at the left side of the dash.

20. Lower vehicle. If equipped with MFI, disconnect the throttle, the T.V. and the cruise control cables at the throttle body.

21. Install engine support fixture. Raise engine until weight is relieved from mount assembled.

22. Lower left side of engine/transaxle assembly by loosening tool J–22825.

23. Place jack under transaxle.

24. Remove the final transaxle to engine attaching bolt and separate transaxle from engine and lower.

25. Lower vehicle.

26. Install engine lifting fixture.

27. If air conditioning equipped, remove compressor from mounting bracket and swing aside.

28. Disconnect forward strut bracket from radiator support. Swing aside.

29. Lift engine out of vehicle.

To Install:

30. Lower the engine into the vehicle.

31. Connect forward strut bracket to radiator support.

32. Install the air conditioning compressor and mounting bracket.

33. Raise the vehicle and place the transaxle jack under the transaxle.

34. Raise the transaxle flush with the engine and install the engine-to-transaxle attaching bolts.

35. Remove the transaxle jack and lower the vehicle just enough to install the engine support fixture.

36. Raise engine until weight is relieved from mount assemblies.

37. Connect all power train mount to cradle attachments.

38. Connect exhaust pipe.

39. Install the side and crossmember assembly. Connect the engine harness to the junction block at the left side of the dash.

40. Install all remaining transaxle to engine retaining bolts.

41. Install the exhaust crossover.

42. Remove the engine support fixture.

43. Lower the vehicle.

44. Connect the speedometer cable to the transaxle.

45. Install the cables to the transaxle bosses.

46. Connect the transaxle shift linkage.

47. Connect the clutch cable.

48. Install the power steering bracket and pump assembly.

49. Connect the heater hoses to the engine.

50. Install the radiator hoses to the radiator.

51. Feed the engine harness connector through the front of the dash and connect it to the ECM.

52. Connect the throttle, the T.V. and the cruise control cables at the throttle body.

53. Connect the accelerator linkage to the carburetor.

54. Connect vacuum hosing to all non-engine mounted components.

55. Fill the cooling system.

56. Install the air cleaner.

58. Connect the battery cables.

2.8L Engine with Automatic Transaxle

1. Disconnect battery cables from battery.

2. Remove air cleaner.

3. Drain cooling system.

4. Disconnect vacuum hosing to all non-engine mounted components.

5. Disconnect detent cable from carburetor lever.

6. Disconnect accelerator linkage. If equipped with MFI, disconnect the throttle at the T.V. and the cruise control cables at the throttle body.

7. Disconnect engine harness connector from the ECM and pull the connector through the front of the dash, then disconnect it from the junction block at the left side of the dash.

8. Disconnect ground strap from engine at engine forward strut.

9. Disconnect radiator hoses from radiator.

10. Disconnect heater hoses from engine.

11. Remove power steering pump and bracket assembly from engine, if equipped.

12. Raise vehicle.

13. Disconnect exhaust pipe.

14. Disconnect fuel lines at rubber hose connections at right side of engine.

15. Remove engine front mount to cradle retaining nuts (right side of vehicle).

16. Disconnect battery cables from engine (Starter and transaxle housing bolt).

17. Remove flex plate cover and disconnect torque convertor from flex plate.

18. Remove transaxle case to cylinder case support bracket bolts.

19. Lower vehicle. Place a support under the transaxle rear extension.

20. Remove engine strut bracket from radiator support and swing rearward.

21. Remove exhaust crossover pipe.

22. Remove transaxle to cylinder case retaining bolts. Make note of ground stud location.

23. If air conditioning equipped, remove compressor from mounting bracket and lay aside.

24. Install lift fixture to engine and remove engine from vehicle.

To Install:

25. Lower the engine into the vehicle.

26. Install the compressor mounting bracket and the compressor.

27. Install the transaxle to cylinder case retaining bolts and the ground stud.

28. Install the exhaust crossover pipe.

29. Install the engine stud bracket to the radiator support.

30. Raise the vehicle and remove the support from the transaxle rear extension.

31. Install the transaxle case to cylinder case support bracket bolts.

32. Connect the torque converter to the flex plate and install the flex plate cover.

33. Connect the battery cables to the engine (Starter and transaxle housing bolt).

34. Install the engine front mount to cradle retaining nuts (right side of vehicle).

35. Connect fuel lines at rubber hose connections at right side of engine.

36. Connect exhaust pipe.

37. Lower the vehicle.

38. Install the power steering pump and bracket assembly to the engine.

39. Connect the heater hoses to the engine.

40. Connect the radiator hoses to the radiator.

41. Connect the ground strap to the engine at the engine forward strut.

42. Connect the engine harness connector to the junction block at the left side of the dash then push the connector through the front of the dash and connect it to the ECM.

43. Connect accelerator linkage. If equipped with MFI, connect the throttle at the T.V. and the cruise control cables at the throttle body.

44. Connect detent cable from carburetor lever.

45. Connect vacuum hosing to all non-engine mounted components.

46. Fill the cooling system.

47. Install the air cleaner.

48. Connect battery cables.

3.0L Engine

1. Disconnect battery cables from battery.

2. Remove air cleaner.

3. Drain cooling system.

4. Disconnect vacuum hosing to all non-engine mounted components.

5. Disconnect detent cable from carburetor lever.

6. Disconnect accelerator linkage.

7. Disconnect engine harness connector.

8. Disconnect ground strap from engine at engine forward strut.

9. Disconnect radiator hoses from radiator.

10. Disconnect heater hoses from engine.

11. Remove power steering pump and bracket assembly from engine.

12. Raise vehicle.

13. Disconnect exhaust pipe at manifold.

14. Disconnect fuel lines at rubber hose connections.

15. Remove engine front mount to cradle retaining nuts (right side of vehicle).

16. Disconnect battery cables from engine (Starter and transaxle housing bolt).

17. Remove flex plate cover and disconnect torque converter from flex plate.

18. Remove transaxle case to cylinder case support bracket bolts.

19. Lower vehicle. Place a support under the transaxle rear extension.

20. Remove engine strut bracket from radiator support and swing rearward.

21. Remove transaxle to cylinder case retaining bolts. Make note of ground stud location.

22. If air conditioning equipped, remove compressor from mounting bracket and lay aside.

23. Install a lift fixture to the engine.

24. Remove the engine from the vehicle.

To Install:

25. Lower the engine into the vehicle.

26. Install the compressor mounting bracket and the compressor.

27. Install the transaxle to cylinder case retaining bolts and the ground stud.

28. Install the exhaust crossover pipe.

29. Install the engine stud bracket to the radiator support.

30. Raise the vehicle and remove the support from the transaxle rear extension.

31. Install the transaxle case to cylinder case support bracket bolts.

32. Connect the torque converter to the flex plate and install the flex plate cover.

33. Connect the battery cables to the engine (Starter and transaxle housing bolt).

34. Install the engine front mount to cradle retaining nuts (right side of vehicle).

35. Connect fuel lines at rubber hose connections at right side of engine.

36. Connect exhaust pipe.

37. Lower the vehicle.

38. Install the power steering pump and bracket assembly to the engine.

39. Connect the heater hoses to the engine.

40. Connect the radiator hoses to the radiator.

41. Connect the ground strap to the engine at the engine forward strut.

42. Connect the engine harness connector to the junction block at the left side of the dash then push the connector through the front of the dash and connect it to the ECM.

43. Connect the accelerator linkage.

44. Connect detent cable from carburetor lever.

45. Connect vacuum hosing to all non-engine mounted components.

46. Fill the cooling system.

47. Install the air cleaner.

48. Connect battery cables.

3.1L Engine

1. Relieve the fuel system pressure.

2. Disconnect the negative battery cable. Scribe reference marks at the hood supports and remove the hood. Install covers on both fenders.

3. Remove the airflow tube at the air cleaner and throttle valve.

4. Drain the cooling system.

5. Disconnect vacuum hoses from all non-engine mounted components.

6. Disconnect the accelerator linkage and TV cable. Disconnect the cruise control cable, if equipped.

7. Disconnect the engine harness connector from the ECM and pull the connector through the front of dash. Disconnect the engine harness from the junction block at the dash panel.

8. Remove the engine strut bracket from the radiator support and position aside, as required.

9. Disconnect the radiator hoses from radiator and heater hoses from engine. Disconnect and plug the transaxle cooler lines.

10. Remove the serpentine belt cover and belt.

11. On vehicles with the air conditioning compressor mounted on the upper portion of the engine, remove the AIR pump and bracket. Then, remove the air conditioning compressor from the mounting bracket and position aside.

12. If equipped, remove power steering pump from engine and set it aside.

13. Disconnect and plug the fuel lines.

14. Disconnect the EGR at the exhaust, as required.

15. Raise and safely support the vehicle.

16. On vehicles with the air conditioning compressor mounted on the lower portion of the engine, remove the air conditioning compressor from the engine. Do not discharge the air conditioning system.

17. Remove the engine front mount-to-cradle and mount-to-engine bracket retaining nuts, as required.

18. Disconnect and tag all electrical wiring at the starter. Remove the starter retaining bolts and remove the starter.

19. If equipped with automatic transaxle, remove the transaxle inspection cover and disconnect the torque converter from the flexplate.

20. Disconnect the exhaust pipe.

21. Remove the 1 transaxle-to-engine bolt from the back side of the engine.

22. Disconnect the power steering cut-off switch, if equipped.

23. Lower the vehicle.

24. Remove the exhaust crossover pipe.

25. Remove the remaining transaxle-to-engine bolts.

26. Support the transaxle by positioning a floor jack and a block of wood under the transaxle. Install an engine lift tool and remove the engine from the vehicle.

To install:

27. Position the engine in the vehicle while aligning the transaxle. Install the transaxle-to-engine bolts.

28. Position the front engine mount studs in the cradle and engine bracket.

29. Remove the engine lift tool. Raise and support the vehicle safely.

30. Install the engine mount retaining nuts.

31. If equipped, connect the power steering cut-off switch.

32. Install the 1 transaxle-to-engine bolt from the back side of the engine.

33. Connect the exhaust pipe.

34. If equipped with automatic transaxle, connect the torque converter to the flexplate and install the transaxle inspection cover.

35. Install the starter and retaining bolts. Connect the starter electrical connectors.

36. Install the engine front mount-to-cradle and mount-to-engine bracket retaining nuts.

37. On vehicles with the air conditioning compressor mounted on the lower portion of the engine, install the air conditioning compressor.

38. Lower the vehicle.

39. Connect the EGR at the exhaust, if removed.

40. Connect the fuel lines.

41. If equipped, install power steering pump.

42. On vehicles with the air conditioning compressor mounted on the upper portion of the engine, install the air conditioner compressor. Install the AIR pump and bracket.

43. Install the serpentine belt cover and belt.

44. Connect the radiator and heater hoses. Connect the transaxle cooler lines.

45. Install the engine strut bracket to the radiator support.

46. Connect the engine harness connector to the ECM.

47. Connect the accelerator linkage and TV cable. Connect the cruise control cable, if equipped.

48. Connect vacuum hoses to all non-engine mounted components.

49. Install the airflow tube at the air cleaner and throttle valve.

50. Install the hood using the reference marks made upon removal.

51. Connect the negative battery cable.

52. Fill cooling system and check for leaks. Start the engine and allow to come to normal operating temperature. Check for leaks and refill the cooling system.

3.3L Engine

1. Disconnect the negative battery cable. Scribe reference marks at the hood supports and remove the hood. Install covers on both fenders.

2. Relieve the fuel system pressure.

3. Disconnect the negative battery cable.

4. Drain the cooling system. Disconnect the radiator and heater hoses. Disconnect and plug the transaxle cooler lines.

5. Remove the upper engine strut and engine cooling fan.

6. Remove the intake duct from the throttle body. Disconnect vacuum hoses from all non-engine mounted components. Disconnect all electrical connections.

7. Remove the cable bracket and cables from the throttle body.

8. Remove the serpentine belt. If equipped, remove the power steering pump and locate to the side.

9. Remove the upper transaxle-to-engine retaining bolts.

10. Raise and support the vehicle safely.

11. Remove the air conditioning compressor and locate to the side.

12. Remove the engine mount-to-frame nuts, flywheel dust cover and flywheel-to-converter bolts.

13. Remove the lower engine-to-transaxle bolts; 1 bolt is located behind the transaxle case and engine block.

14. Lower the vehicle. Install an engine lift tool and remove the engine from the vehicle.

To install:

15. Install the engine in the engine compartment. Install the upper engine-to-transaxle bolts. Remove the engine lift tool.

16. Raise and safely support the vehicle.

17. Install the lower engine-to-transaxle bolts; 1 bolt is located behind the transaxle case and engine block.

18. Install the flywheel-to-converter bolts, flywheel dust cover and engine mount-to-frame nuts.

19. Install the air conditioning compressor.

20. Lower the vehicle.

21. If equipped, install the power steering pump. Install the serpentine belt.

22. Install the cable bracket and cables to the throttle body.

23. Install the intake duct to the throttle body. Connect vacuum hoses to all non-engine mounted components. Connect all electrical connections.

24. Install the upper engine strut and engine cooling fan.

25. Connect the radiator and heater hoses. Connect the transaxle cooler lines.

26. Install the hood.

27. Connect the negative battery cable.

28. Fill cooling system and check for leaks. Start the engine and allow to come to normal operating temperature. Recheck for leaks and fill the cooling system.

3.8L Engine

1. Disconnect the negative battery cable. Scribe reference marks at the hood supports and remove the hood. Install covers on both fenders.

2. Remove the air cleaner assembly and drain the cooling system.

3. Disconnect vacuum hoses to all non-engine mounted components.

4. Disconnect the detent cable and accelerator linkage.

5. Disconnect the engine electrical harness and ground strap.

6. Disconnect the heater hoses from the engine and radiator hoses from the radiator. Disconnect the transaxle cooler lines, if equipped.

7. If equipped, remove the power steering pump and bracket assembly.

8. Raise and safely support the vehicle.

9. Disconnect the exhaust pipe from the manifold.

10. Disconnect the fuel lines.

11. Remove the engine front mount-to-cradle retaining nuts.

12. Disconnect and tag all electrical wiring at the starter. Remove the starter retaining bolts and remove the starter.

13. If equipped with automatic transaxle, remove the flexplate cover and disconnect the flexplate from the torque converter.

14. Remove the retaining bolts from the transaxle rear support bracket.

15. Lower the vehicle and place a support under the transaxle rear extension.

16. Remove the engine strut bracket from the radiator support and position aside.

17. Remove the transaxle-to-engine retaining bolts.

18. If equipped with air conditioning, remove the air conditioning compressor from the mounting bracket and lay aside.

19. Install an engine lift tool and remove the engine from the vehicle.

To Install:

20. Position the engine in the vehicle and align the engine front mount studs. Align the transaxle and install the transaxle-to-engine retaining bolts.

21. Remove the engine lift tool.

22. If equipped, install the air conditioning compressor to the mounting bracket.

23. Raise and safely support the vehicle. Install the retaining bolts to the transaxle rear support bracket.

24. If equipped with automatic transaxle, connect the flexplate to the torque converter and install the flexplate cover.

25. Install the starter and retaining bolts. Connect the starter electrical connectors.

26. Install the engine front mount-to-cradle retaining nuts.

27. Connect the fuel lines.

28. Connect the exhaust pipe to the manifold.

29. Lower the vehicle.

30. If equipped, install the power steering bracket assembly and pump.

31. Connect the heater and radiator hoses. Connect the transaxle cooler lines, if equipped.

32. Connect the engine electrical harness and ground strap.

33. Connect the detent cable and accelerator linkage.

34. Connect vacuum hoses to all non-engine mounted components.

35. Install the air cleaner assembly.

36. Install the hood.

37. Connect the negative battery cable.

38. Fill cooling system and check for leaks. Start the engine and allow to come to normal operating temperature. Check for leaks and refill the cooling system.

4.3L Diesel Engine

1. Drain the cooling system. Remove the serpentine drive belt (and vacuum pump drive belt, if air conditioning equipped).

2. Remove air cleaner and install cover J-26996.

3. Disconnect battery negative cable(s) at batteries and ground wires at inner fender panel. Disconnect engine ground strap, rear (right) head to cowl.

4. Hoist car.

5. Remove the flywheel cover.

6. Remove the flywheel to torque converter bolts.

7. Disconnect the exhaust pipe from the rear exhaust manifold.

8. Remove the engine to transaxle brace.

9. Remove the engine mount to cradle retaining nuts and washers.

10. Disconnect the leads to the starter motor, #2 cylinder glow plug and battery ground cable at transaxle to engine bolt.

11. Disconnect the lower oil cooler hose and cap the openings.

12. Remove the accessible power steering pump bracket fasteners.

13. Lower the car.

14. Remove the remaining power steering pump bracket/brace fasteners and lower the power steering pump with hoses out of the way.

15. Remove heater water return pipe.

16. Disconnect all remaining glow plug leads at the glow plugs.

17. Disconnect all other leads at the engine, disconnect the engine harness at the cowl connector and body mounted relays and position the engine harness aside.

18. If air conditioning equipped, disconnect the compressor with brackets and lines attached and position aside.

19. Disconnect the fuel and vacuum hoses, cap all fuel line openings.

20. Disconnect the throttle and T.V. cables at the injection pump and cable bracket. Position cables aside.

21. Disconnect the upper oil cooler hose and cap the openings.

22. Remove the exhaust crossover pipe heat shield.

23. Disconnect and move aside the transaxle filler tube.

24. Remove the exhaust crossover pipe.

25. Remove the engine mounting strut and strut brackets.

26. Install a suitable engine lifting device. Make certain that when installing chains to the cylinder heads that washers are used under the chains and bolt heads and that the bolts are torqued to 20 ft. lbs.

❋❋ CAUTION

Failure to properly secure the engine lift to the aluminum cylinder heads can result in personal injury.

27. Position a support under the transaxle rear extension. It may be necessary to raise the support as the engine is being removed.

28. Remove the engine to transaxle bolts and remove the engine.

29. To install, reverse the removal process noting the following:

   a. Before installing the flex plate-to-converter bolts, make sure that the weld nuts on the converter are flush with the flex plate, and the converter rotates freely by hand.

   b. Use only new O-rings at all connections.

   c. Adjust the throttle valve cable as outlined in the Section 7.

Valve Cover(s)

REMOVAL & INSTALLATION

❋❋ CAUTION

When draining the coolant, keep in mind that cats and dogs are attracted by the ethylene glycol antifreeze, and are quite likely to drink any that is left in an uncovered container or in puddles on the ground. This will prove fatal

in sufficient quantity. Always drain the coolant into a sealable container. Coolant should be reused unless it is contaminated or several years old.

2.5L Engine

1. Remove the air cleaner assembly, being sure to tag all disconnected hoses for reassembly purposes.

2. Remove the P.C.V. valve and hose from the valve cover grommet.

3. Remove the valve cover retaining bolts.

4. Remove the spark plug wires from the spark plugs and the locating clips. Be sure to tag the wires so that they may be attached properly.

5. Remove the cover retaining bolts, then the valve cover by tapping it with a rubber mallet. This must be done to break the R.T.V. seal. DON'T attempt to pry the cover off, as it is easily damaged.

6. Remove the valve cover retaining bolts then remove the valve cover. If the cover sticks, tap it loose with a rubber mallet. DON'T attempt to pry it off of the head, as the cover may be easily damaged.

7. Refer to steps 6–8 of the previous 4–2.5L procedure to prepare and seal the valve cover during installation.

8. The remainder of the installation is performed in the reverse of removal. Torque the front engine strut bracket bolts to 35 ft. lbs.

2.8L Engine

1. Disconnect the negative battery cable at the battery.

2. Remove the air cleaner assembly, being sure to tag all disconnected hoses for reassembly purposes.

➡ **If equipped with an MFI system, remove any component which will interfere with the valve cover removal.**

3. Remove the spark plug wires from the spark plugs and the locating clips. Be sure to tag the wires so that they may be attached properly.

4. Disconnect the accelerator linkage and springs from the carburetor.

5. If your vehicle has an automatic transaxle, disconnect the T.V. (throttle valve) linkage at the carburetor.

6. If your vehicle has cruise control remove the diaphragm actuator mounting bracket.

7. Remove the air management valve and the necessary hoses (see Section 4).

8. Remove the valve cover retaining bolts, then remove the valve cover. If the cover sticks, tap it loose with a rubber mallet. DON'T attempt to pry it off of the head, as the cover may be easily damaged.

9. Refer to steps 6–8 of the previous 4–2.5L procedure to prepare and seal the valve cover during installation. The valve cover retaining bolts must be torqued to 11 ft. lbs.

10. The remainder of the installation is performed in the reverse order of removal.

3.0L, and 3.8L Engines

FRONT COVER

1. Disconnect the negative battery cable.

2. Remove the crankcase breather tube.

3. Remove the spark plug wire harness cover and disconnect the spark plug wires at the spark plugs.

4. Remove the valve cover nuts, washers, seals and valve cover.

5. Using a putty knife, clean the gasket mounting surfaces.

6. To install, use a new gasket and reverse the removal procedures. Torque the valve cover nuts to 7 ft. lbs. (10 Nm.).

REAR COVER

1. Disconnect the negative battery cable.

2. Remove the C3I ignition coil module, the spark plug cables, the wiring connectors, the EGR solenoid wiring and vacuum hoses.

➡ **If equipped with an MFI system, remove any component which will interfere with the valve cover removal.**

3. Remove the serpentine drive belt.

4. Remove the alternator's wiring connectors, then the mounting bolt and swing the alternator toward the front of the vehicle.

5. Remove the power steering pump from the belt tensioner (move it aside) and the belt tensioner assembly.

6. Remove the engine lift bracket and the rear alternator brace.

7. Drain the cooling system below the level of the heater hose, then disconnect the throttle body heater hoses.

8. Remove the valve cover nuts, the washers, the seals, the valve cover and the gasket.

9. Using a putty knife, clean the gasket mounting surfaces.

10. To install, use a new gasket and reverse the removal procedures. Torque the valve cover nuts to 7 ft. lbs. (10 Nm.).

3.1L Engine

➡ **On the 3.1L engines if battery power is lost to the engine computer the idle learn memory will be lost, causing poor or no idle control. A special Scan Tool, should be used to perform the idle learn procedure. Avoid disconnecting the battery on 3.1L whenever possible.**

FRONT COVER

1. Release fuel system pressure and disconnect the negative battery cable.

2. Remove the air cleaner assembly.

3. Drain the cooling system.

4. Disconnect the ignition wire clamps from the coolant tube.

5. Remove the coolant tube mount at head and coolant tube from each end.

6. Remove the coolant tube at the coolant pump and remove the tube.

7. Remove the ignition wire guide.

8. Remove the spark plug wire harness cover and disconnect the spark plug wires at the spark plugs, as needed.

9. Remove the valve cover nuts, washers, seals and valve cover.

10. Using a putty knife, clean the gasket mounting surfaces.

11. To install, use a new gasket and reverse the removal procedures. Torque the valve cover nuts to 7 ft. lbs. (10 Nm.).

REAR COVER

1. Release fuel system pressure and disconnect the negative battery cable.

2. Drain the cooling system below the level of the heater hose.

3. Remove the hoses at the intake plenum.

4. Remove the airflow tube.

5. Remove the EGR valve crossover pipe.

6. Remove the ignition wire guide.

7. Tag and remove the ignition wires.

8. Disconnect the coolant hoses at the throttle body.

9. Tag and disconnect all electrical connectors to throttle body and that will ease the operation by moving asside.

10. Disconnect the throttle body cables.

11. Remove the bracket at the right side of the intake plenum.

12. Remove the power brake booster supply hose.

13. Remove the serpentine belt.

14. Remove the coolant recovery bottle.

15. Remove the exhaust crossover pipe.

16. Remove the alternator and support it out of the way.

17. Remove the PCV valve from the valve cover.

18. Remove the valve cover nuts, the washers, the seals, the valve cover and the gasket.

19. Using a putty knife, clean the gasket mounting surfaces.

To install:

20. Use a new gasket and reverse the removal procedures. Torque the valve cover nuts to 7 ft. lbs. (10 Nm).

21. Install the PCV valve.

22. Install the alternator, exhaust crossover and coolant recovery tank.

23. Install the serpentine drive belt.

24. Install the brake booster hose.

25. Install the bracket to the right side of the intake plenum.

26. Connect the throttle body cables, electrical connectors and hoses.

27. Install the ignition wires and guides.

28. Install the EGR valve crossover pipe and the airflow tube.

29. Install the vacuum hoses.

30. Fill the radiator and check for leaks.

31. Connect the negative battery cable, install air cleaner and perform the Idle Learn Procedure on 3.1L engines. Tighten the air cleaner bolt to 11 ft. lbs. (15 Nm).

3.3L Engine

FRONT COVER

1. Disconnect the negative battery cable.

2. Remove the serpentine drive belt.

3. Remove the alternator brace bolt and brace.

4. Remove the spark plug wire harness cover and disconnect the spark plug wires at the spark plugs.

5. Remove the valve cover nuts, washers, seals and valve cover.

6. Using a putty knife, clean the gasket mounting surfaces.

7. To install, use a new gasket and reverse the removal procedures. Torque the valve cover nuts to 7 ft. lbs. (10 Nm).

REAR COVER

1. Disconnect the negative battery cable.

2. Remove the serpentine drive belt.

3. Loosen the power steering pump bolts and slide the pump forward. Remove the pump braces.

4. Remove the power steering pump from the belt tensioner (move it aside) and the belt tensioner assembly.

5. Remove the valve cover nuts, the washers, the seals, the valve cover and the gasket.

6. Remove the valve cover nuts, the washers, the seals, the valve cover and the gasket.

7. Using a putty knife, clean the gasket mounting surfaces.

8. To install, use a new gasket and reverse the removal procedures. Torque the valve cover nuts to 7 ft. lbs. (10 Nm).

9. Reinstall the power steering pump and install the serpentine drive belt.

10. Install the negative battery cable, start engine and check for leaks.

4.3L Diesel Engine

1. Disconnect the negative battery cable.

2. Remove the fuel injection lines.

3. Remove the forward engine support strut, which is bolted to the radiator support strut and an engine bracket.

4. Unbolt and remove the strut bracket from the engine.

5. If necessary, remove any additional piece(s) which may interfere with removal of the cover.

6. Unbolt and remove the cover. If the cover sticks, tap it loose with a rubber mallet. DON'T attempt to pry it off of the head, as the cover may be easily damaged.

7. Raise the jack until it just starts to lift the vehicle.

8. Remove the two front body mount bolts from the cradle, along with the cushions and the retainers. Remove the cushions from the bolts.

9. Thread the body mount bolts (with the retainers) back into place, making sure to turn them at least three full turns each.

10. Carefully and slowly lower the jack until the cradle contacts the retainers. While you are lowering the jack, be sure to watch for any component interference and correct as required.

✳✳ CAUTION

DO NOT attempt to lower the cradle without the bolts and retainers in place, as this could cause damage of various underhood components.

11. Unbolt and remove the cover. If the cover sticks, tap it loose with a rubber mallet. DON'T attempt to pry it off of the head, as the cover may be easily damaged.

12. Refer to steps 6–8 of the previous 4–2.5L procedure to prepare and seal the valve cover during installation.

13. To install reverse steps 1 through 12.

Rocker Arm and Pushrod

REMOVAL & INSTALLATION

2.5L Engine

1. Remove the valve cover.

2. On fuel injected engines, see the fuel pump section to relieve pressure, in the fuel system before disconnecting any fuel lines.

3. If only the pushrod is being removed, loosen the rocker arm bolt and swing the rocker arm aside.

4. Remove the rocker arm nut and ball.

5. Lift the rocker arm off the stud, keeping rocker arms in order for installation.

6. To install reverse steps 1 through 5. Tighten the rocker arm bolt to 20 ft. lbs.; the rocker cover to 5 ft. lbs.

2.8L Engine

Rocker arms are removed by removing the adjusting nut. Be sure to adjust valve lash after replacing rocker arms.

➡ **When replacing an exhaust rocker, move an old intake rocker arm to the exhaust rocker arm stud and install the new rocker arm on the intake stud.**

Cylinder heads use threaded rocker arm studs. If the threads in the head are damaged or stripped, the head can be retapped and a helical type insert installed.

➡ **If engine is equipped with the A.I.R. exhaust emission control system, the interfering components of the system must be removed. Disconnect the lines at the air injection nozzles in the exhaust manifolds.**

3.0L and 3.8L Engine

1. Remove the rocker arm cover(s).

2. Remove the rocker arm shaft(s).

3. Place the shaft on a clean surface.

4. Remove the nylon rocker arm retainers. A pair of slip joint pliers is good for this.

5. Slide the rocker arms off the shaft and inspect them for wear or damage. Keep them in order!

6. To install reverse steps 1 through 5. If new rocker arms are being installed, note that they are stamped R (right) or L (left), meaning that they be used on the right or left of each cylinder,

NOT right and left cylinder banks. Each rocker arm must be centered over its oil hole. New nylon retainers must be used.

3.1L Engine

1. Release fuel pressure and disconnect the negative battery cable.

➡ **On the 3.1L engines if battery power is lost to the engine computer the idle learn memory will be lost, causing poor or no idle control. A special Scan Tool, should be used to perform the idle learn procedure. Avoid disconnecting the battery on 3.1L whenever possible.**

2. Remove the valve covers.
3. Remove the rocker arm nuts.
4. Remove rocker are pivot ball and arms.

➡ **Keep all components separated, if old parts are to be reinstalled they must be installed in the same locations.**

5. Remove the pushrods.

➡ **Keep all components separated. The pushrods are not the same length. Intake pushrods are 6 in. (152mm) long and mark orange, while the exhaust pushrods are 6³/₈ in. (162mm) long and marked blue. To install:**

6. Install the pushrods taking care they are in the proper locations.
7. Make sure the pushrods are seated in the lifters.
8. Install the rocker arms, pivots and nuts. They should be coated with prelube GM 1052365 or equivalent.
9. Torque the rocker arm nuts to 18 ft. lbs. (25 Nm).
10. Install the valve covers. Install the battery cable.
11. On 3.1L engine perform the Idle Learn Procedure as follows:
   a. Connect the Scan tool to the ALDL.
   b. Turn the ignition switch to the **ON** position with the engine not running.
   c. In the "Misc. Test" mode, select "IAC System", then "Idle Learn".
   d. Proceed with idle learn as directed, by the Scan Tool.

3.3L Engine

1. Release fuel pressure and disconnect the negative battery cable.
2. Remove the valve covers.
3. Remove the rocker arm pedestal bolts.
4. Remove rocker arm and pedestal assembly.

➡ **Keep all components separated, if old parts are to be reinstalled they must be installed in the same locations.**

5. Remove the pushrods.
To Install:
6. Install the pushrods taking care they are in the proper locations.
7. Make sure the pushrods are seated in the lifters.
8. Install the rocker arm assembly. Coat threads with lock compound GM 12345493 or equivalent.
9. Torque the rocker arm bolts to 28 ft. lbs. (38Nm).
10. Install the valve covers. Install the battery cable.

4.3L Diesel Engine

➡ **This procedure requires that the valve lifters be bled!**

1. Remove the valve cover(s). See the Valve Cover procedure.
2. Remove the rocker arm nuts, pivot and rocker arms.
3. If rocker arms are being replaced, they must be replaced in cylinder sets. Never replace just one rocker arm per cylinder! If a stud was replaced, coat the threads with locking compound and torque it to 11 ft. lb.
4. To installation reverse the above process. See the section on Valve lifter bleed-down. This is absolutely necessary! If lifters are not bled, engine damage will be unavoidable! Torque the rocker arm nuts to 28 ft. lbs.; the cover to 5 ft. lbs.

Thermostat

REMOVAL & INSTALLATION

All Models

1. Disconnect the negative battery cable.
2. Drain the cooling system.

❄ CAUTION

When draining the coolant, keep in mind that cats and dogs are attracted by the ethylene glycol antifreeze, and are quite likely to drink any that is left in an uncovered container or in puddles on the ground. This will prove fatal in sufficient quantity. Always drain the coolant into a sealable container. Coolant should be reused unless it is contaminated or several years old.

3. Some models with cruise control have a vacuum modulator attached to the thermostat housing with a bracket. It your vehicle is equipped as such, remove the bracket from the housing.
4. On the 4-cyl. engines, unbolt the water outlet from the thermostat housing, remove the outlet from the housing and lift the thermostat out of the housing. On all other models, unbolt the water outlet from the intake manifold, remove the outlet and lift the thermostat out of the manifold.

To install:
5. Clean both of the mating surfaces and run a ¹/₈ in. (3mm) bead of R.T.V.(room temperature vulcanizing) sealer in the groove of the water outlet.
6. Install the thermostat (spring towards engine) and bolt the water outlet into place while the R.T.V. sealer is still wet. Torque the bolts to 21 ft. lbs. The remainder of the installation is the reverse of removal. Check for leaks after the car is started and correct as required.

Intake Manifold

▶ SEE FIGS. 33 to 38

REMOVAL & INSTALLATION

❄ CAUTION

When draining the coolant, keep in mind that cats and dogs are attracted by the ethylene glycol antifreeze, and are quite likely to drink any that is left in an uncovered container or in puddles on the ground. This will prove fatal in sufficient quantity. Always drain the coolant into a sealable container. Coolant should be reused unless it is contaminated or several years old.

2.5L Engine

> ### ❋❋ CAUTION
>
> **If throttle body injected, bleed pressure from the fuel system, before servicing. See Section 5.**

1. Remove the air cleaner and the PCV valve.
2. Drain the cooling system into a clean container.
3. Disconnect the fuel and vacuum lines and the electrical connections at the carburetor and manifold.
4. Disconnect the throttle linkage at the EFI unit and disconnect the transaxle downshift linkage and cruise control linkage.
5. Remove the carburetor and the spacer.
6. Remove the bell crank and the throttle linkage. Position to the side for clearance.
7. Remove the heater hose at the intake manifold.
8. Remove the pulse air check valve bracket from the manifold.
9. Remove the manifold attaching bolt and remove the manifold.

2.8L Engine

CARBURETED ENGINE

1. Remove the rocker covers.
2. Drain the cooling system.
3. If equipped, remove the AIR pump and bracket.
4. Remove the distributor cap. Mark the position of the ignition rotor in relation to the distributor body, and remove the distributor. Do not crank the engine with the distributor removed.
5. Remove the heater and radiator hoses from the intake manifold.
6. Remove the power brake vacuum hose.
7. Disconnect and label the vacuum hoses. Remove the EFE pipe from the rear of the manifold.

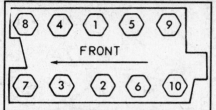

Fig. 34 Intake manifold bolt torque sequence — 2.8L (VIN X) engine

8. Remove the carburetor linkage. Disconnect and plug the fuel line.

➡ **If equipped with an MFI system, remove any component which will interfere with the intake manifold removal.**

9. Remove the manifold retaining bolts and nuts.
10. Remove the intake manifold. Remove and discard the gaskets, and scrape off the old silicone seal from the front and rear ridges.

To Install:

1. The gaskets are marked for right and left side installation; do not interchange them. Clean the sealing surface of the engine block, and apply a $\frac{3}{16}$ in. (5mm) bead of silicone sealer to each ridge.
2. Install the new gaskets onto the heads. The gaskets will have to be cut slightly to fit past the center pushrods. Do not cut any more material than necessary. Hold the gaskets in place by extending the ridge bead of sealer $\frac{1}{4}$ in. (6mm) onto the gasket ends.
3. Install the intake manifold. The area between the ridges and the manifold should be completely sealed.
4. Install the retaining bolts and nuts, and tighten in sequence to 23 ft. lbs. Do not overtighten; the manifold is made from aluminum, and can be warped or cracked with excessive force.
5. The rest of installation is the reverse of removal. Adjust the ignition timing after installation, and check the coolant level after the engine has warmed up.

FUEL INJECTED

1. Relieve the pressure in the fuel system before disconnecting any fuel line connections.
2. Disconnect the negative battery cable.
3. Disconnect the accelerator and TV cable bracket at the intake plenum.
4. Disconnect the throttle body at the intake plenum.
5. Disconnect the EGR valve at the intake plenum.
6. Remove the intake plenum.
7. Disconnect the fuel inlet and return pipes at the fuel rail.
8. Remove the serpentine belt.
9. Remove the power steering pump and lay it aside.
10. Disconnect the alternator and lay it aside.
11. Loosen the alternator bracket.
12. Disconnect the idle air vacuum hose at the throttle body.
13. Disconnect the wires at the injectors.
14. Disconnect the fuel rail.
15. Remove the breather tube.
16. Remove both rocker covers.
17. Drain the cooling system.
18. Disconnect the radiator hose at the thermostat housing.
19. Disconnect the wires at the coolant sensor and the oil sending switch.
20. Remove the coolant sensor.
21. Disconnect the bypass hose at the fill neck and head.
22. Loosen the rocker arms and remove the pushrods.
23. Remove the intake manifold bolts and remove the intake manifold.

To Install:

24. Place a $\frac{3}{16}$ in. (5mm) diameter bead GM sealer 1052917 or equivalent, on each ridge.
25. Position a new intake manifold gasket.
26. Install the pushrods and tighten the rocker arm nuts to 14–20 ft. lbs. (19–27 Nm).
27. Install the intake manifold and torque the bolts to specifications.
28. Connect the bypass hose to the filler neck and head.
29. Install the coolant sensor.
30. Connect the wires to the coolant sensor and the oil sending switch.
31. Connect the radiator hose to the thermostat housing.
32. Install both rocker covers.
33. Install the breather tube.
34. Connect the fuel rail.
35. Connect the wires to the injectors.
36. Connect the idle air vacuum hose to the throttle body.
37. Tighten the alternator bracket.
38. Connect the alternator electrical connectors.
39. Install the power steering pump.

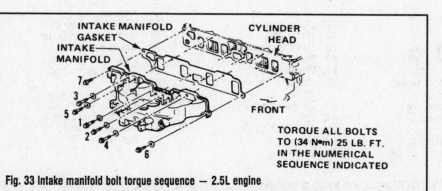

INTAKE MANIFOLD GASKET
INTAKE MANIFOLD
CYLINDER HEAD
FRONT
TORQUE ALL BOLTS TO (34 N•m) 25 LB. FT. IN THE NUMERICAL SEQUENCE INDICATED

Fig. 33 Intake manifold bolt torque sequence — 2.5L engine

1. Piston ring
2. Piston
3. Piston pin
4. Connecting rod
5. Connecting rod bolt
6. Connecting rod bearing
7. Connecting rod nut
8. Pushrod cover
9. Pushrod cover stud
10. Cylinder head dowel pin
11. Trans line up pin
12. Camshaft rear bearing plug
13. Cylinder and case oil gallery plug
14. Oil level indicator tube
15. Oil level indicator
16. Oil level indicator tube seal
17. Engine block heater
18. Engine block heater bolt
19. Flywheel to crankshaft bolt
20. Flywheel
21. Flywheel to crankshaft spacer
22. Crankshaft insert
23. Crankshaft rear oil seal
24. Coolant drain bolt
25. Engine
26. Crankshaft rear bearing
27. Crankshaft bearing
28. Crankshaft
29. Crankshaft gear key
30. Crankshaft sprocket
31. Bearing cap
32. Crankshaft bearing cap
33. Gear
34. Spring pin
35. Oil pressure regulator spring
36. Oil pressure regulator valve
37. Bolt
38. Oil pump screw
39. Oil pump cover
40. Internal oil filter
41. Starter
42. Starter bolt
43. Starter bolt
44. Washer
45. Starter bracket
46. Nut
47. Bolt
48. Oil pan
49. Oil pan drain adn filter gasket
50. Oil pan and filter plug
51. Drain plug
52. Gasket
53. Bolt
54. Pump screen

55. Oil pump gear
56. Balancer bolt
57. Balancer bolt
58. Screw
59. Balancer pump shaft
60. Baffle
61. Bushing
62. Balancer housing
63. Housing dow pin
64. Bolt
65. Seal
66. Pully
67. Washer
68. Bolt
69. Front cover seal
70. Crankshaft pulley bolt
71. Drive belt tensioner
72. Oil gallery plug
73. Coil and module
74. Module studs
75. Bolt
76. Switch/sensor

77. Coolant plug
78. Roller lifter
79. Valve lifter guide
80. Bolt
81. Washer
82. Camshaft timing chain
83. Camshaft sprocket
84. Bolt
85. Camshaft thrust bearing

86. Camshaft sprocket key
87. Camshaft
88. Camshaft bearing
89. Valve lifter guide retainer
90. Push rod cover stud
91. Coolant pump pulley
92. Coolant pump
93. Bolt
94. Coolant pump bolt
95. Bolt
96. Coolant pump inlet
97. Bolt/Screw
98. Fuel feed and return pipe clip bracket
99. Nut

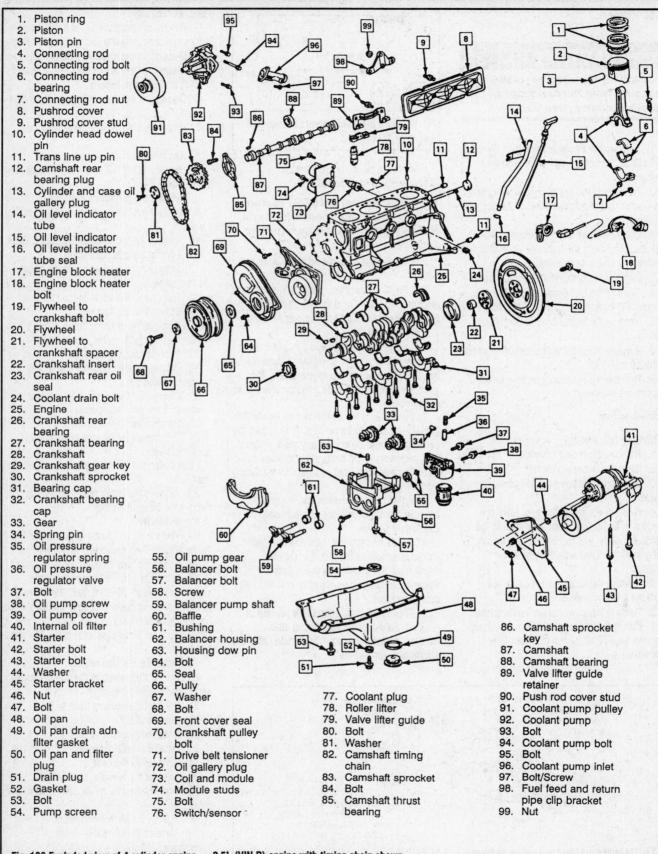

Fig. 106 Exploded view of 4 cylinder engine — 2.5L (VIN R) engine with timing chain shown

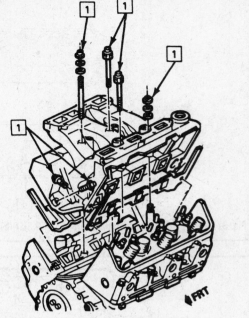

1 | 22 N·m (16 LB. FT.)
THEN 32 N·m (23 LB. FT.)
RETORQUE 32 N·m
(23 LB. FT.) IN SEQUENCE

⑦ ④ ③ ⑥
⑧ ① ② ⑤

Fig. 35 Intake manifold bolt torque sequence — 2.8L (VIN W) and 3.1L (VIN T) engines

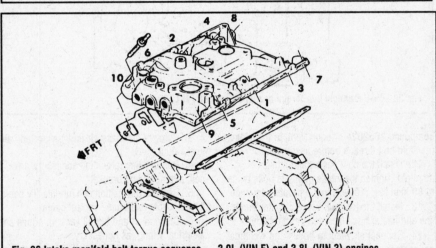

Fig. 36 Intake manifold bolt torque sequence — 3.0L (VIN E) and 3.8L (VIN 3) engines

40. Install the serpentine belt.

41. Connect the fuel inlet and return pipes to the fuel rail.

42. Install the intake plenum.

43. Connect the EGR valve to the intake plenum.

44. Connect the throttle body to the intake plenum.

45. Connect the accelerator and TV cable bracket to the intake plenum.

46. Connect the negative battery cable.

47. Fill cooling system and check for leaks. Start the engine and allow to come to normal operating temperature. Check for leaks and top off the coolant.

48. Adjust the valve, as required.

3.0L Engine

1. Disconnect the battery ground.

2. Drain the cooling system.

3. Remove the air cleaner.

4. Disconnect all hoses and wiring from the manifold.

5. Disconnect the accelerator linkage and cruise control chain.

➡ **If equipped with an MFI system, remove any component which will interfere with the intake manifold removal.**

6. Disconnect the fuel line.

7. Remove the distributor cap and rotor and remove the Torx® head bolt from the left side of the manifold.

8. Unbolt and remove the manifold.

9. To install reverse steps 1 through 8. When installing the front and rear seals, make sure that the ends of the seals fit snugly against the block and head. Install nos. 1 & 2 bolts first and tighten them until snug, then install the other bolts in order.

3.1L ENGINE

1. Relieve the pressure in the fuel system before disconnecting any fuel line connections.

2. Disconnect the negative battery cable.

➡ **On the 3.1L engines if battery power is lost to the engine computer the idle learn memory will be lost, causing poor or no idle control. A special Scan Tool, should be used to perform the Idle Learn procedure.**

3. Disconnect the accelerator and TV cable bracket at the intake plenum.

4. Disconnect the throttle body at the intake plenum.

5. Disconnect the EGR valve at the intake plenum.

6. Remove the intake plenum.

7. Disconnect the fuel inlet and return pipes at the fuel rail.

8. Remove the serpentine belt.

9. Remove the power steering pump and lay it aside.

10. Disconnect the alternator and lay it aside.

11. Loosen the alternator bracket.

12. Disconnect the idle air vacuum hose at the throttle body.

13. Disconnect the wires at the injectors.

14. Disconnect the fuel rail.

15. Remove the breather tube.

16. Remove both rocker covers.

17. Drain the cooling system.

18. Disconnect the radiator hose at the thermostat housing.

19. Disconnect the wires at the coolant sensor and the oil sending switch.

20. Remove the coolant sensor.

21. Disconnect the bypass hose at the fill neck and head.

22. Loosen the rocker arms and remove the pushrods.

23. Remove the intake manifold bolts and remove the intake manifold.

To install:

24. Place a 3/16 in. (5mm) diameter bead GM sealer 1052917 or equivalent, on each ridge.

25. Position a new intake manifold gasket.

26. Install the pushrods and tighten the rocker arm nuts to 14–20 ft. lbs. (19–27 Nm).

27. Install the intake manifold and torque the bolts to specifications.

28. Connect the bypass hose to the filler neck and head.

29. Install the coolant sensor.

30. Connect the wires to the coolant sensor and the oil sending switch.

31. Connect the radiator hose to the thermostat housing.

32. Install both rocker covers.

33. Install the breather tube.

34. Connect the fuel rail.

35. Connect the wires to the injectors.

36. Connect the idle air vacuum hose to the throttle body.

37. Tighten the alternator bracket.

38. Connect the alternator electrical connectors.

39. Install the power steering pump.

40. Install the serpentine belt.

41. Connect the fuel inlet and return pipes to the fuel rail.

42. Install the intake plenum.

43. Connect the EGR valve to the intake plenum.

44. Connect the throttle body to the intake plenum.

45. Connect the accelerator and TV cable bracket to the intake plenum.

46. Connect the negative battery cable.

47. Fill cooling system and check for leaks. Start the engine and allow to come to normal operating temperature. Recheck for leaks. Top-up coolant.

48. Adjust the valve, as required.

3.3L Engine

1. Relieve the pressure in the fuel system before disconnecting any fuel line connections.

2. Disconnect the negative battery cable.

3. Drain the cooling system.

4. Remove the serpentine belt, alternator and braces and power steering pump braces.

5. Remove the coolant bypass hose, heater pipe and upper radiator hose.

6. Remove the air inlet duct, throttle cable bracket and cables.

7. Disconnect and tag all vacuum hoses and electrical connectors, as necessary.

8. Remove the fuel rail, vapor canister purge line and heater hose from the throttle body.

9. Remove the intake manifold retaining bolts and intake manifold.

To install:

10. Clean the cylinder head and intake manifold surfaces from any foreign matter, nicks or heavy scratches.

11. Apply sealer 12345336 or equivalent, to the ends of the manifold seals. Clean the intake manifold bolts and bolt holes. Apply thread lock

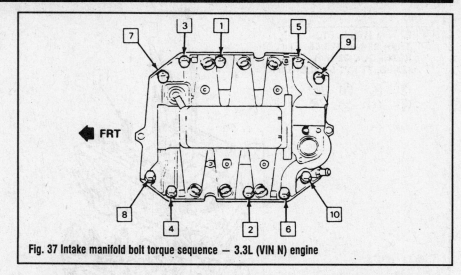

FRT

Fig. 37 Intake manifold bolt torque sequence — 3.3L (VIN N) engine

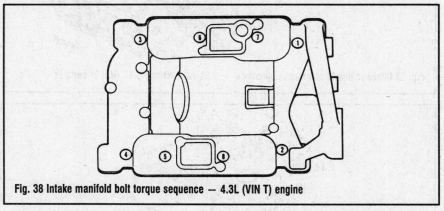

Fig. 38 Intake manifold bolt torque sequence — 4.3L (VIN T) engine

compound 1052624 or equivalent, to the intake manifold bolt threads before assembly.

12. Install the new gasket and intake manifold. Tighten the intake manifold bolts twice to 88 inch lbs. (10 Nm) in the proper sequence.

13. Install the fuel rail, vapor canister purge line and heater hose from the throttle body.

14. Connect all vacuum hoses and electrical connectors.

15. Install the air inlet duct, throttle cable bracket and cables.

16. Install the coolant bypass hose, heater pipe and upper radiator hose.

17. Install the serpentine belt, alternator and braces and power steering pump braces.

18. Connect the negative battery cable.

19. Fill cooling system and check for leaks. Start the engine and allow to come to normal operating temperature. Recheck for leaks. Top-up coolant.

3.8L Engine

1. Relieve the pressure in the fuel system before disconnecting any fuel line connections.

2. Disconnect the negative battery cable.

3. Remove the mass air flow sensor and air intake duct.

4. Remove the serpentine accessory drive belt, alternator and bracket.

5. Remove the ignition coil module, TV cable, throttle cable and cruise control cable.

6. Disconnect and tag all vacuum hoses and electrical wiring, as necessary.

7. Drain the cooling system. Remove the heater hoses from the throttle body and upper radiator hose.

8. Disconnect the fuel lines from the fuel rail and injectors.

9. Remove the intake manifold retaining bolts and remove the intake manifold and gasket.

To install:

10. Clean the cylinder head and intake manifold surfaces from any foreign matter, nicks or heavy scratches.

11. Install the intake manifold gasket and rubber seals. Apply sealer 1050026 or equivalent, on the gasket. Apply sealer/lubricant 1052080 or equivalent, to all pipe thread fitting.

12. Carefully install the intake manifold to cylinder block. Install the intake manifold bolts and torque in sequence to the specified value.

13. Connect the fuel lines to the fuel rail and injectors.

14. Install the heater hoses to the throttle body and upper radiator hose.

15. Connect all vacuum hoses and electrical wiring.

16. Install the ignition coil module, TV cable, throttle cable and cruise control cable.

17. Install the bracket, alternator and serpentine belt.

18. Install the mass air flow sensor and air intake duct.

19. Connect the negative battery cable.

20. Fill cooling system and check for leaks. Start the engine and allow to come to normal operating temperature. Recheck for leaks. Top-up coolant.

6–4.3L Diesel Engine

➡ **This procedure requires the removal, disassembly draining and reassembly of the valve lifters. Read that procedure, below, before continuing.**

1. Remove the air cleaner assembly.

2. Drain the radiator, then disconnect the upper radiator hose from the water outlet.

3. Disconnect the heater inlet hose from the outlet on intake manifold and disconnect the heater outlet pipe from the intake manifold attachments and move it aside.

4. Remove air crossover and the fuel injection pump.

5. Disconnect wiring as necessary at the generator (and air conditioning compressor) and switches (if so equipped).

6. Remove the cruise control servo if so equipped.

7. Remove the air conditioning compressor bracket and brace bolts and position the compressor (if so equipped) with lines attached out of the way.

8. Remove the generator assembly.

9. Disconnect the engine mounting strut.

10. Remove the fuel lines, filter and brackets. Cap all openings.

11. Disconnect the electrical leads to the glow plug controller and sending units.

12. Disconnect the exhaust crossover pipe heat shield.

13. Remove the left (forward) injection lines and cap all openings. Use backup wrench on the nozzles.

14. Disconnect the throttle and T.V. cables from the bracket.

15. Remove the drain tube.

16. Remove the intermediate pump adapter.

17. Remove pump adapter and seal.

18. Remove the intake manifold.

19. Clean the machined surfaces of cylinder head and intake manifold with a putty knife. Use care not to gouge or scratch the machined surfaces. Clean all bolts and bolt holes.

20. Coat both sides of gasket sealing surface that seal the intake manifold to the head with 1050026 sealer or equivalent and position intake manifold gasket. Install end seals, making sure that ends are positioned under the cylinder heads. The seals and mating surfaces must be dry. Any liquid, including sealer will act as a lubricant and cause the seal to move during assembly. Use RTV sealer only on each end of the seal.

21. Position intake manifold on engine. Lubricate the entire intake manifold bolt (all) with lubricant 1052080 or equivalent.

22. Torque the bolts in sequence shown to 20 ft. lbs. Then retorque to 41 ft. lbs.

23. Install the drain tube.

24. Install the pump adapter.

25. Apply chassis lube to seal area of intake manifold and pump adapter.

26. Apply chassis lube to inside and outside diameter of seal and seal area of tool J–28425.

27. Install seal on tool and install the seal.

28. Install intermediate pump adapter.

29. Reverse the order of removal and install all other removed parts except the air crossover.

30. Fill the cooling system.

31. Install manifold covers, J–29657.

32. Start engine and check for leaks.

33. Check and if necessary, reset the injection pump timing.

34. Remove screen covers from manifold.

35. Install air crossover.

36. Install the air cleaner.

37. Road test car and inspect for leaks.

Diesel Engine Valve Lifter Bleed–Down

If the intake manifold and valve rocker arms have been removed, it will be necessary to remove, disassemble, drain and reassemble the lifters on that side. If the rocker arms have been loosened or removed, but the intake manifold was not removed, skip down to the Bleed–Down procedure.

REMOVAL

Keep lifters and pushrods in order! This is absolutely necessary for installation, since these parts have differences which could result in engine damage if not installed in their original positions!

1. Remove intake manifold. Refer to Intake Manifold.

2. Remove valve covers, rocker arm assemblies and pushrods.

3. Remove the valve lifter guide retainer bolts.

4. Remove the retainer guides and valve lifters.

DISASSEMBLY

1. Remove the retainer ring with a small screwdriver.

2. Remove pushrod seat and oil metering valve.

3. Remove plunger and plunger spring.

4. Remove check valve retainer from plunger, then remove valve and spring.

CLEANING AND INSPECTION

After lifters are disassembled, all parts should be cleaned in clean solvent. A small particle of foreign material under the check valve will cause malfunctioning of the lifter. Close inspection should be made for nicks, burrs or scoring of parts. If either the roller body or plunger is defective, replace with a new lifter assembly. Whenever lifters are removed, check as follows:

1. Roller should rotate freely, but without excessive play.

2. Check for missing or broken needle bearings.

3. Roller should be free of pits or roughness. If present, check camshaft for similar condition. If pits or roughness are evident replace lifter and camshaft.

ASSEMBLY

1. Coat all lifter parts with a coating of clean kerosene or diesel fuel.

2. Assemble the ball check, spring and retainer into the plunger.

3. Install plunger spring over check retainer.

4. Hold plunger with spring up and insert into lifter body. Hold plunger vertically to prevent cocking spring.

5. Submerge the lifter in clean kerosene or diesel fuel.

6. Install oil metering valve and pushrod seat into lifter and install retaining ring.

INSTALLATION

Prime new lifters by working lifter plunger while submerged in clean kerosene or diesel fuel. Lifter could be damaged when starting engine if dry.

1. When a rocker arm is loosened or removed, valve lifter bleed down is required. Lifters must be bled down as possible valve to piston interference due to the close tolerances could exist. Before installing a new or used lifter in the engine, lubricate the roller and bearings of the lifter with No. 1052365 lubricant or equivalent.

2. Install lifters and pushrods into original position in cylinder block. See note under Removal.

3. Install manifold gaskets and manifold.

4. Position rocker arms, pivots and bolts on cylinder head.

5. Install valve covers.

6. Install intake manifold assembly.

BLEED-DOWN

1. Before installing any removed rocker arms, rotate the engine crankshaft to a position of number 1 cylinder being 32° before top dead center. This is a 50mm (2 in.) counterclockwise from the **O** pointer. If only the right valve cover was removed, remove No. 1 cylinder's glow plug to determine if the position of the piston is the correct one. The compression pressure will tell you that you are in the right position. If the left valve cover was removed, rotate the crankshaft until the number 5 cylinder intake valve pushrod ball is 7.0mm (0.28 in.) above the number 5 cylinder exhaust valve pushrod ball.

➡ **Use only hand wrenches to torque the rocker arm pivot nuts to avoid engine damage.**

2. If removed, install the No. 5 cylinder pivot and rocker arms. Torque the nuts alternately between the intake and exhaust valves until the intake valve begins to open, then stop.

3. Install remaining rocker arms except No. 3 exhaust valve. (If this rocker arm was removed).

4. If removed, install but do not torque No. 3 valve pivots beyond the point that the valve would be fully open. This is indicated by strong resistance while still turning the pivot retaining bolts. Going beyond this would bend the pushrod. Torque the nuts SLOWLY allowing the lifter to bleed down.

5. Finish torquing No. 5 cylinder rocker arm pivot nut SLOWLY. Do not go beyond the point that the valve would be fully open. This is

indicated by strong resistance while still turning the pivot retaining bolts. Going beyond this would bend the pushrod.

6. DO NOT turn the engine crankshaft for at least 45 minutes.

7. Finish reassembling the engine as the lifters are being bled.

➡ **Do not rotate the engine until the valve lifters have been bleed down, or damage to the engine will occur.**

Exhaust Manifold

◆ SEE FIGS. 39 and 40

REMOVAL & INSTALLATION

2.5L Engine

1. Disconnect the negative battery cable. Remove the air cleaner and the TBI preheat tube.

2. Remove the manifold strut bolts from the radiator support panel and the cylinder head.

3. Remove the air conditioning compressor bracket to one side. Do not disconnect any of the refrigerant lines.

4. If necessary, remove the dipstick tube attaching bolt and the engine mount bracket from the cylinder head.

5. Raise the vehicle and support safely. Disconnect the exhaust pipe from the manifold.

6. Remove the manifold attaching bolts and remove the manifold.

To Install:

7. Install the exhaust manifold and gasket to the cylinder head. Torque all bolts in sequence to the specified torque value.

8. Connect the exhaust pipe to the manifold. Lower the vehicle.

9. Install the dipstick tube attaching bolt and the engine mount bracket to the cylinder head.

10. Install the air conditioning compressor bracket.

11. Install the manifold strut bolts to the radiator support panel and the cylinder head.

12. Install the air cleaner and the TBI preheat tube.

13. Connect the negative battery cable.

2.8L Engine

LEFT SIDE

1. Remove the air cleaner. Remove the exhaust crossover pipe.

2. Remove the air supply plumbing from the exhaust manifold, if equipped.

3. Raise and support the car. Unbolt and remove the exhaust pipe at the manifold.

4. Unbolt and remove the manifold.

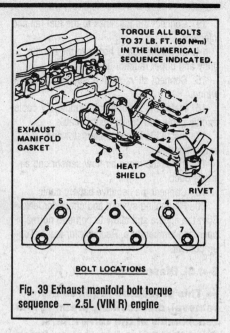

Fig. 39 Exhaust manifold bolt torque sequence — 2.5L (VIN R) engine

To install:

5. Clean the mating surfaces of the cylinder head and manifold. Install the manifold onto the head, and install the retaining bolts finger tight.

6. Tighten the manifold bolts in a circular pattern, working from the center to the ends, to 25 ft. lbs. in two stages.

7. Connect the exhaust pipe to the manifold.

8. The remainder of installation is the reverse of removal.

RIGHT SIDE

1. Disconnect the negative battery cable.

2. Raise and safely support the vehicle.

3. Disconnect the exhaust pipe and lower the vehicle.

4. Remove the air cleaner assembly, breather, mass air flow sensor and heat shield.

5. Remove the crossover at the manifold.

6. Remove the accelerator and TV cables and brackets, as required.

7. Remove the exhaust manifold retaining bolts and remove the manifold.

To install:

8. Install the exhaust manifold and retaining bolts. Tighten to 15–22 ft. lbs. (20–30 Nm).

9. If removed, install the accelerator, TV cables and brackets.

10. Install the crossover at the manifold.

11. Install the air cleaner assembly, breather, mass air flow sensor and heat shield.

12. Raise and safely support the vehicle.

13. Connect the exhaust pipe and lower the vehicle.

14. Connect the negative battery cable.

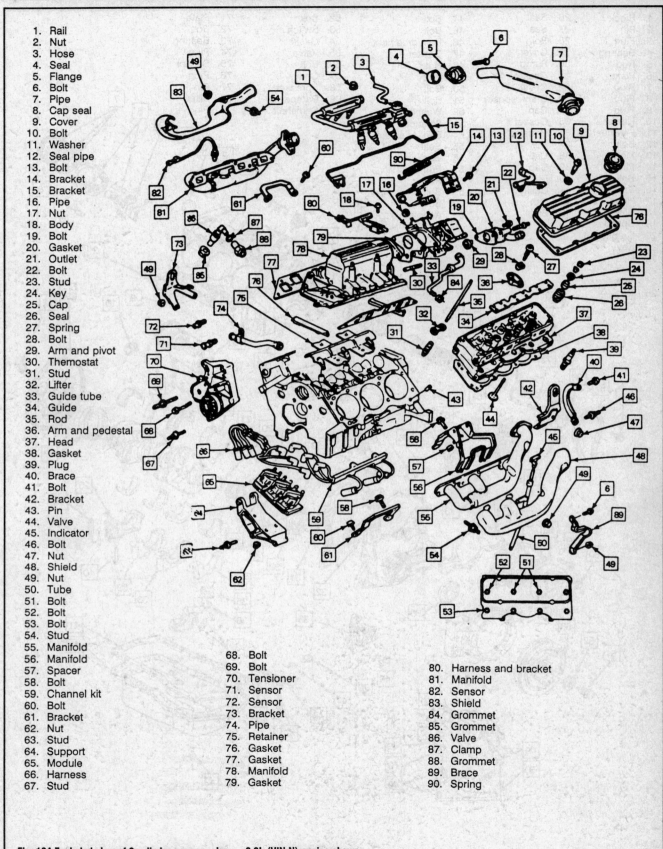

1. Rail
2. Nut
3. Hose
4. Seal
5. Flange
6. Bolt
7. Pipe
8. Cap seal
9. Cover
10. Bolt
11. Washer
12. Seal pipe
13. Bolt
14. Bracket
15. Bracket
16. Pipe
17. Nut
18. Body
19. Bolt
20. Gasket
21. Outlet
22. Bolt
23. Stud
24. Key
25. Cap
26. Seal
27. Spring
28. Bolt
29. Arm and pivot
30. Themostat
31. Stud
32. Lifter
33. Guide tube
34. Guide
35. Rod
36. Arm and pedestal
37. Head
38. Gasket
39. Plug
40. Brace
41. Bolt
42. Bracket
43. Pin
44. Valve
45. Indicator
46. Bolt
47. Nut
48. Shield
49. Nut
50. Tube
51. Bolt
52. Bolt
53. Bolt
54. Stud
55. Manifold
56. Manifold
57. Spacer
58. Bolt
59. Channel kit
60. Bolt
61. Bracket
62. Nut
63. Stud
64. Support
65. Module
66. Harness
67. Stud
68. Bolt
69. Bolt
70. Tensioner
71. Sensor
72. Sensor
73. Bracket
74. Pipe
75. Retainer
76. Gasket
77. Gasket
78. Manifold
79. Gasket
80. Harness and bracket
81. Manifold
82. Sensor
83. Shield
84. Grommet
85. Grommet
86. Valve
87. Clamp
88. Grommet
89. Brace
90. Spring

Fig. 104 Exploded view of 6 cylinder upper engine — 3.3L (VIN N) engine shown

1. Block
2. Pin
3. Plug
4. Bearing
5. Rod
6. Piston
7. Ring
8. Plug
9. Plug
10. Heater
11. Flywheel
12. Bolt
13. Motor
14. Pin
15. Bolt
16. Spring
17. Hose
18. Clamp
19. Sprocket
20. Crankshaft
21. Key
22. Bearing
23. Bolt
24. Bolt
25. Cap

26. Seal
27. Seal
28. Bolt
29. Cover
30. Pump
31. Gasket
32. Cover
33. Crank sensor
34. Cap
35. Gasket
36. Housing
37. Bolt
38. Cap
39. Cap
40. Bolt
41. Gasket
42. Pan
43. Bolt

44. Bolt
45. Bolt
46. Reinforcement
47. Gasket
48. Nut
49. Bolt
50. Bolt
51. Bolt
52. Washer
53. Balancer
54. Sensor shield
55. Seal
56. Gasket
57. Pump kit
58. Pulley
59. Bolt
60. Bolt
61. Adapter

62. Bolt
63. Switch
64. Gasket
65. Valve
66. Bolt
67. Chain
68. Sprocket
69. Damperner
70. Camshaft

71. Plate
72. Bolt
73. Bearing
74. Plug
75. Sensor
76. Plug
77. Pin
78. Filter
79. Plug

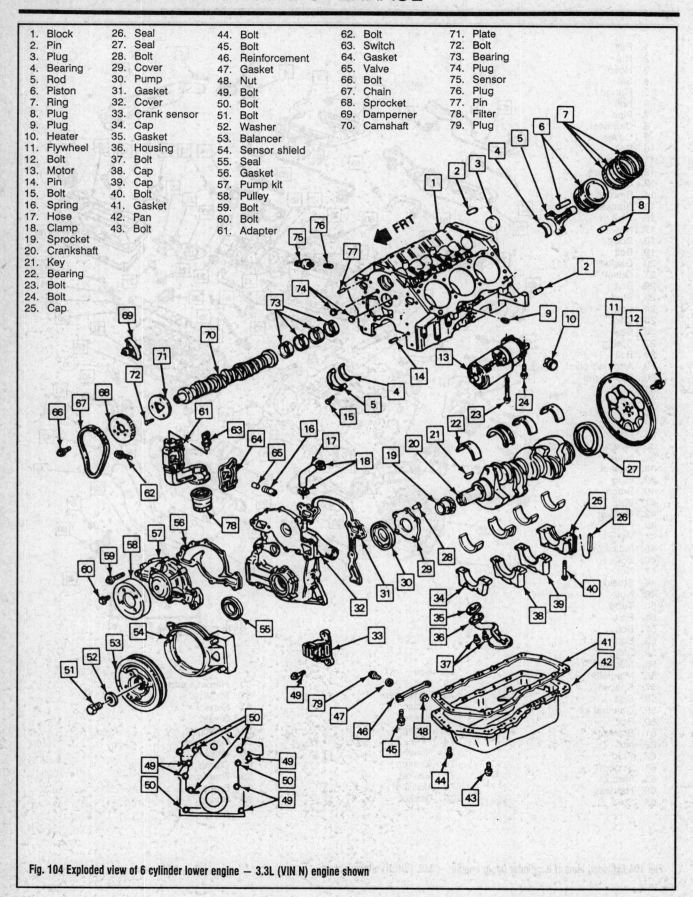

Fig. 104 Exploded view of 6 cylinder lower engine — 3.3L (VIN N) engine shown

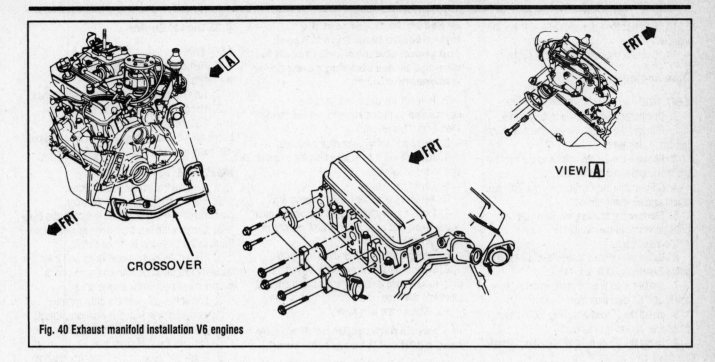

Fig. 40 Exhaust manifold installation V6 engines

3.0L Engine

LEFT SIDE

1. Disconnect the battery ground.
2. Unbolt and remove the crossover pipe.
3. Remove the upper engine support strut.
4. Unbolt and remove the manifold.
5. To install reverse steps 1 through 4.

RIGHT SIDE

1. Disconnect the negative battery cable.
2. Remove the intermediate shaft pinch bolt and separate the intermediate shaft from the stub shaft.

> **✳✳ CAUTION**
>
> **Failure to disconnect the intermediate shaft from the rack and pinion stub shaft can result in damage to the steering gear and/or the intermediate shaft. This damage can cause loss of steering control.**

3. Raise the support the vehicle on jackstands.
4. Remove the exhaust pipe-to-manifold bolts, then lower the vehicle.
5. Place a jack under the front crossmember of the cradle, then raise the jack until it starts to raise the vehicle and remove the two front body mount bolts.
6. With the cushions removed, thread the body mount bolts and retainers at least three turns into the cage nuts, then slowly release the jack.
7. Remove the power steering pump and bracket, then move it aside.
8. Disconnect the oxygen sensor connector.
9. Remove the crossover pipe-to-manifold nuts, the exhaust manifold bolts and the manifold.
10. To install, reverse the removal procedures.

3.1L ENGINES

LEFT SIDE

1. Disconnect the negative battery cable.
2. Remove the air supply plumbing from the exhaust manifold, as required.
3. Remove the coolant recovery bottle, if necessary.
4. Remove the serpentine belt cover and belt, as required.
5. Remove the air conditioning compressor and lay aside, if necessary.
6. Remove the right side torque strut, air conditioning and torque strut mounting bracket, as required.
7. Remove the heat shield, if equipped.
8. Remove the exhaust crossover pipe at the manifold.
9. Remove the exhaust manifold retaining bolts and manifold.

To install:

10. Install the exhaust manifold and retaining bolts. Tighten to 15–22 ft. lbs. (20–30).
11. Install the exhaust crossover pipe at the manifold.
12. Install the heat shield, if equipped.
13. If removed, install the right side torque strut, air conditioning and torque strut mounting bracket.
14. If removed, install the air conditioning compressor.
15. If removed, install the serpentine belt and cover.
16. If removed, install the coolant recovery bottle.
17. Install the air supply plumbing to the exhaust manifold.
18. Connect the negative battery cable.

RIGHT SIDE

1. Disconnect the negative battery cable.
2. Raise and safely support the vehicle.
3. Disconnect the exhaust pipe and lower the vehicle.
4. Remove the air cleaner assembly, breather, mass air flow sensor and heat shield.
5. Remove the crossover at the manifold.
6. Remove the accelerator and TV cables and brackets, as required.
7. Remove the exhaust manifold retaining bolts and remove the manifold.

To install:

8. Install the exhaust manifold and retaining bolts. Tighten to 15–22 ft. lbs. (20–30 Nm).
9. If removed, install the accelerator, TV cables and brackets.
10. Install the crossover at the manifold.
11. Install the air cleaner assembly, breather, mass air flow sensor and heat shield.
12. Raise and safely support the vehicle.

13. Connect the exhaust pipe and lower the vehicle.

14. Connect the negative battery cable.

3.3L Engine

LEFT SIDE

1. Disconnect the negative battery cable.

2. Remove the air cleaner inlet ducting. Install the spark plug wires.

3. Remove the 2 bolts attaching the exhaust crossover pipe to the manifold.

4. Remove the engine lift hook, manifold heat shield and oil level indicator.

5. Remove the exhaust manifold retaining bolts and remove the manifold.

To install:

6. Install the exhaust manifold and retaining bolts. Tighten to 30 ft. lbs. (41 Nm).

7. Install the engine lift hook, manifold heat shield and oil level indicator.

8. Install the 2 bolts attaching the exhaust crossover pipe to the manifold.

9. Install the air cleaner inlet ducting. Install the spark plug wires.

10. Connect the negative battery cable.

RIGHT SIDE

1. Disconnect the negative battery cable.

2. Remove the spark plug wires, oxygen sensor connector, throttle cable bracket and cables.

3. Remove the brake booster hose from the manifold.

4. Remove the 2 bolts attaching the exhaust crossover pipe to the manifold.

5. Remove the exhaust pipe-to-manifold bolts, engine lift hook and transaxle oil level indicator tube.

6. Remove the manifold heat shield. Remove the exhaust manifold retaining bolts and remove the manifold.

To install:

7. Install the exhaust manifold and retaining bolts. Tighten to 30 ft. lbs. (41 Nm). Install the manifold heat shield.

8. Install the exhaust pipe-to-manifold bolts, engine lift hook and transaxle oil level indicator tube.

9. Install the 2 bolts attaching the exhaust crossover pipe to the manifold.

10. Install the brake booster hose to the manifold.

11. Install the spark plug wires, oxygen sensor connector, throttle cable bracket and cables.

12. Connect the negative battery cable.

3.8L ENGINE

1. Disconnect the negative battery cable.

➡ **Failure to disconnect the intermediate shaft from the rack and pinion stub shaft may result in damage to the steering gear and/or intermediate shaft.**

2. Remove the pinch bolt from the intermediate shaft and separate the intermediate shaft from the stub shaft.

3. Raise and safely support the vehicle.

4. Remove the 2 bolts attaching the exhaust pipe to the manifold.

5. Lower the vehicle.

6. Remove the upper engine support strut.

7. Place a jack under the front crossmember of the cradle and raise the jack until it starts to raise the vehicle.

8. Remove the 2 front body mount bolts.

9. With the cushions removed, thread the body mount bolts and retainers a minimum of 3 turns into the cage nuts.

10. Release the jack slowly.

➡ **To avoid damage, do not lower the cradle without it being restrained.**

11. Remove the power steering pump and bracket from the cylinder head and exhaust manifold.

12. Disconnect the oxygen sensor.

13. If removing the left side exhaust manifold, remove the upper engine support strut.

14. Remove the 2 nuts retaining the crossover pipe to the exhaust manifold.

15. Remove the 6 bolts attaching the manifold to the cylinder head.

16. Remove the exhaust manifold.

To install:

17. Carefully, clean the gasket sealing surfaces of old gasket material.

18. Install the exhaust manifold and the manifold-to-cylinder head bolts. Tighten to 37 ft. lbs. (50 Nm).

19. If the left side exhaust manifold was removed, install the crossover pipe to the manifold.

20. If the right side exhaust manifold was removed, install the upper engine support strut.

21. Connect the oxygen sensor wire.

22. Install the power steering pump and bracket.

23. Support the cradle with the jack. Remove the 2 body mount bolts and install the cushions.

24. Raise the cradle into position and install the 2 body mount bolts.

25. Remove the jack.

26. Connect the intermediate shaft to the stub shaft and install the pinch bolt.

27. Raise and safely support the vehicle.

28. Install the exhaust pipe-to-manifold bolts.

29. Lower the vehicle.

30. Connect the negative battery cable.

4.3L Diesel Engine

LEFT SIDE

1. Remove the crossover pipe from the manifolds.

2. Raise and support the car on jackstands.

3. Unbolt and remove the manifold.

4. Installation is the reverse of removal. Lubricate the entire length of each manifold bolt with lubricant 1052080 or its equivalent.

RIGHT SIDE

1. Remove the engine support strut.

2. Place a floor jack under the front crossmember and take up the weight of the car.

3. Remove the two front body mount bolts. Remove the cushions from the bolts.

4. Thread the body mount bolts with their retainers into the cage nuts so that the bolts restrict movement of the engine cradle.

5. Lower the jack until the crossmember contacts the body mount bolt retainers. Check for any hose or wire interference.

6. Remove the crossover pipe.

7. Raise and support the car on jackstands.

8. Disconnect the exhaust pipe from the manifold.

9. Lower the car.

10. Unbolt and remove the manifold.

11. Installation is the reverse of removal. Lubricate the entire length of each manifold bolt with lubricant 1052080 or its equivalent.

Radiator

REMOVAL & INSTALLATION

All Models

1. Disconnect the negative battery cable. On 3.1L and 3.3L engines remove the air cleaner assembly.

2. Drain the cooling system.

❄❄ CAUTION

When draining the coolant, keep in mind that cats and dogs are attracted by the ethylene glycol antifreeze, and are quite likely to drink any that is left in an uncovered container or in puddles on the ground. This will prove fatal in sufficient quantity. Always drain the coolant into a sealable container. Coolant should be reused unless it is contaminated or several years old.

3. Remove the forward strut brace for the engine at the radiator. Loosen the bolt to prevent shearing the rubber bushing, then swing the strut rearward.

4. On 2.5L engine, remove the resonator mounting and resonator. Disconnect the headlamp wiring harness from the fan frame. Unplug the fan electrical connector.

5. Remove the attaching bolts for the fan.

6. Scribe the hood latch location on the radiator support, then remove the latch.

7. Disconnect the coolant hoses from the radiator. Remove the coolant recovery tank hose from the radiator neck. Disconnect and plug the automatic transmission fluid cooler lines from the radiator, if so equipped. On the diesel engine, disconnect the engine oil cooler hoses.

8. Remove the radiator attaching bolts and remove the radiator. If the car has air conditioning, if first may be necessary to raise the left side of the radiator so that the radiator neck will clear the compressor.

To install:

➡ **If a new radiator is going to be installed, check that all the fittings and brackets from the old radiator are removed, you'll need them on the new one.**

9. Install the radiator in the car, tightening the mounting bolts to 7 inch lbs. Connect the transmission cooler lines and hoses. Install the coolant recovery hose.

10. Install the hood latch. Tighten to 6 ft. lbs.

11. Install the fan, making sure the bottom leg of the frame fits into the rubber grommet at the lower support.

12. Install the fan wires and the headlamp wiring harness. Swing the strut and brace forward, tightening to 11 ft. lbs.

13. Connect the engine ground strap to the strut brace. Install the negative battery cable, fill the cooling system, and check for leaks.

Electric Cooling Fan

REMOVAL & INSTALLATION

1. Disconnect the negative battery cable.

2. Tag and disconnect the electrical connector from the fan motor and fan frame.

3. Remove the fan frame-to-radiator support bolts.

4. Remove the fan and frame assembly from the vehicle.

To install:

5. Install the fan and frame assembly to the vehicle.

6. Install the fan frame-to-radiator support bolts.

7. Connect the electrical connector to the fan motor.

8. Connect the negative battery cable.

Water Pump

REMOVAL & INSTALLATION

❊❊❊ CAUTION

When draining the coolant, keep in mind that cats and dogs are attracted by the ethylene glycol antifreeze, and are quite likely to drink any that is left in an uncovered container or in puddles on the ground. This will prove fatal in sufficient quantity. Always drain the coolant into a sealable container. Coolant should be reused unless it is contaminated or several years old.

2.5L Engine

1. Disconnect battery negative cable.

2. Drain the cooling system.

3. Remove serpentine belt, removal of the alternator and/or bracket may help give more room for easier access.

4. Remove water pump attaching bolts and nut and remove pump.

To install:

5. Clean the sealing surfaces and place a $\frac{3}{32}$ in. (2mm) bead of RTV sealant or equivalent on the water pump sealing surface.

6. Coat bolt threads with pipe sealant 1052080 or equivalent.

7. Install pump and torque bolts to 10 ft. lbs.

8. Connect the negative battery cable.

9. Fill cooling system and check for leaks. Start the engine and allow to come to normal operating temperature. Recheck for leaks. Top-up coolant.

2.8L Engine

1. Disconnect battery negative cable.

2. Drain cooling system and remove heater hose.

3. Remove water pump attaching bolts and nut and remove pump.

4. With the sealant surfaces cleaned, place a 2mm ($\frac{3}{32}$ in.) bead of sealant #1052357 or equivalent on the water pump sealing surface.

5. Clean old sealant from pump.

6. Coat bolt threads with pipe sealant #1052080 or equivalent.

7. Install pump and torque bolts to 10 ft. lbs.

8. Connect battery negative battery cable.

➡ **When replacing the water pump on a car equipped with the V6 engine, the timing cover must be clamped to the cylinder block PRIOR TO removing the water pump bolts. Certain bolts holding the water pump pass through the front cover and when removed, may allow the front cover to pull away from the cylinder block, breaking the seal. This may or may not be readily apparent and if left undetected, could allow coolant to enter the crankcase. To prevent this possible separation during water pump removal, Special Tool #J29176 will have to be installed.**

3.0L Engine

1. Disconnect the negative battery cable and drain the coolant.

2. Remove accessory drive belts. Removed the radiator and the heater hoses from the water pump.

3. Remove water pump attaching bolts.

4. Remove the engine support strut.

5. Place a floor jack under the front crossmember of the cradle and raise the jack until the jack just starts to raise the car.

6. Remove the front two body mount bolts with the lower cushions and retainers.

7. Remove the cushions from the bolts.

8. Thread the body mount bolts with retainers a minimum of three (3) turns into the cage nuts so that the bolts restrain cradle movement.

9. Release the floor jack slowly until the crossmember contacts the body mount bolts retainers. As the jack is being lowered watch and correct any interference with hoses, lines, pipes and cables.

➡ **Do not lower the cradle without its being restrained as possible damage can occur to the body and underhood items.**

10. Remove water pump from engine.

11. Reverse removal procedure.

12. Install pump and torque to 25 ft. lbs.

13. Connect negative battery cable.

14. Fill with coolant and check for leaks.

3.1L Engine

1. Disconnect the negative battery cable.

➡ On the 3.1L engines if battery power is lost to the engine computer the idle learn memory will be lost, causing poor or no idle control. A special Scan Tool, should be used to perform the Idle Learn procedure. Avoid disconnecting the battery on 3.1L whenever possible.

2. Drain cooling system in to a drain pan.

3. Remove the serpentine belt.

4. Remove the heater hose and radiator hose.

5. Remove the water pump cover attaching bolts and remove the cover.

6. Remove the water pump attaching bolts and remove the water pump. Notice that the water pump has a vacuum line attached that must be reattached when installing.

To install:

7. Position the water pump on the engine and install the attaching bolts. Torque bolts to 89 inch lbs. (10 Nm).

8. Install the water pump cover and attaching bolts.

9. Install the heater hose and radiator hose.

10. Install the serpentine belt.

11. Connect the negative battery cable.

12. Fill cooling system and check for leaks. Start the engine and allow to come to normal operating temperature. Recheck for leaks. Top-up coolant.

3.3L Engine

1. Disconnect the negative battery cable.

2. Drain cooling system.

3. Remove the serpentine drive belt.

4. Remove the coolant hose at the water pump.

5. Remove the water pump pulley bolts. The long bolt should be removed through the access hole provided in the body side rail. Remove the pulley.

6. Remove the water pump attaching bolts and remove the water pump.

To install:

7. Install the water pump attaching bolts and install the water pump.

8. Install the pulley. Install the water pump pulley bolts. The long bolt should be installed through the access hole provided in the body side rail.

9. Install the coolant hose at the water pump.

10. Install the serpentine drive belt.

11. Connect the negative battery cable.

12. Fill cooling system and check for leaks. Start the engine and allow to come to normal operating temperature. Recheck for leaks. Top-up coolant.

3.8L Engine

1. Disconnect the negative battery cable.

2. Drain cooling system.

3. Remove the serpentine drive belt.

4. Disconnect the radiator and heater hoses at the water pump.

5. Remove the water pump pulley bolts, long bolt removed through access hole provided in the body side rail. Remove the pulley.

6. Remove the water pump attaching bolts. Remove the water pump.

To install:

7. Clean all gasket mating surfaces.

8. Using a new gasket, install the water pump to the engine.

9. Install the water pump pulley.

10. Connect the radiator and heater hoses to the water pump.

11. Install the serpentine drive belt.

12. Connect the negative battery cable.

13. Fill cooling system and check for leaks. Start the engine and allow to come to normal operating temperature. Check for leaks and top-off the coolant.

4.3L Diesel Engine

1. Drain radiator. Remove the negative battery cable.

2. Disconnect lower radiator hose at water pump.

3. Disconnect the heater return hose at the water pump, remove the bolt retaining the heater water return pipe to the intake manifold and position the pipe out-of-the-way.

4. If equipped with AC, remove the vacuum pump drive belt.

5. Remove the serpentine drive belt.

6. Remove the generator, air conditioning compressor or vacuum pump brackets.

7. Remove the water pump attaching bolts and remove the water pump assembly.

8. Using tools J-29785 and J-29786, remove the water pump pulley.

9. Clean gasket material from engine block.

10. Apply a thin coat of 1050026 sealer or equivalent to the water pump housing to retain the gasket, then position new gasket on the housing. Also apply sealer to water pump mounting bolts. Torque bolts to 12–15 ft. lbs.

Cylinder Head

♦ SEE FIGS. 41 to 46

REMOVAL & INSTALLATION

❋❋ CAUTION

When draining the coolant, keep in mind that cats and dogs are attracted by the ethylene glycol antifreeze, and are quite likely to drink any that is left in an uncovered container or in puddles on the ground. This will prove fatal in sufficient quantity. Always drain the coolant into a sealable container. Coolant should be reused unless it is contaminated or several years old.

2.5L Engine

❋❋ CAUTION

On fuel injected engines, relieve the pressure in the fuel system before disconnecting any fuel line connections.

➡ The engine should be not be warm, it is best to leave engine sit overnight to cool before removing the cylinder head.

1. Drain the cooling system into a clean container.

2. Remove the air cleaner, the negative battery cable, the oil indicator tube, the ignition coil, the engine-to-upper strut rod bolt and the power steering pump bracket.

3. Remove the intake and exhaust manifolds as previously outlined.

4. Remove the alternator bracket bolts.

5. Remove the air conditioning compressor bracket bolts and position the compressor to one side. Do not disconnect any of the refrigerant lines.

6. Disconnect all vacuum and electrical connections from the cylinder head.

7. Disconnect the upper radiator hose.

8. Disconnect the spark plug wires and remove the plugs.

9. Remove the rocker arm cover, rocker arms, and pushrods.

10. Unbolt and remove the cylinder head.

11. Clean the gasket surfaces thoroughly.

12. Install a new gasket over the dowels and position the cylinder head.

13. Coat the head bolt threads with sealer and install finger tight.

14. Tighten the bolts in sequence, in three equal steps to the specified torque.

15. Install all parts in the reverse of removal.

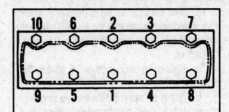

**Fig. 41 Cylinder head bolt torque sequence —
2.5L (VIN R) engine**

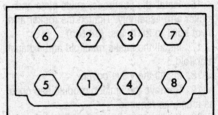

**Fig. 42 Cylinder head bolt torque sequence —
2.8L (VIN X) engine**

2.8L Engine

LEFT SIDE

1. Raise and support the car.
2. Drain the coolant from the block and lower the car.
3. Remove the intake manifold.
4. Remove the crossover.
5. Remove the alternator and AIR pump brackets.
6. Remove the dipstick tube.
7. Loosen the rocker arm bolts and remove the pushrods. Keep the pushrods in the same order as removed.
8. Remove the cylinder head bolts in stages and in the reverse order of the tightening sequence.
9. Remove the cylinder head. Do not pry on the head to loosen it.
10. Installation is the reverse of removal.

➡ **The words This Side Up on the new cylinder head gasket should face upward. Coat the cylinder head bolts with sealer and torque to specifications in the sequence shown. Make sure the pushrods seat in the lifter seats and adjust the valves.**

RIGHT SIDE

1. Raise the car and drain the coolant from the block.
2. Disconnect the exhaust pipe and lower the car.
3. If equipped, remove the cruise control servo bracket.
4. Remove the air management valve and hose.

5. Remove the intake manifold.
6. Remove the exhaust crossover.
7. Loosen the rocker arm nuts and remove the pushrods. Keep the pushrods in the order in which they were removed.
8. Remove the cylinder head bolts in stages and in the reverse order of the tightening sequence.
9. Remove the cylinder head. Do not pry on the cylinder head to loosen it.

➡ **The words This Side Up on the new cylinder head gasket should face upwards. Coat the cylinder head bolts with sealer and tighten them to specifications in the sequence shown. Make sure the lower ends of the pushrods seat in the lifter seats and adjust the valves.**

3.0L Engine

1. Disconnect negative battery cable.
2. Remove intake manifold.
3. Loosen the remove belt(s).
4. When removing LEFT cylinder head;
   a. Remove oil dipstick.
   b. Remove air and vacuum pumps with mounting bracket if present, and move out of the way with hoses attached.
5. When removing RIGHT cylinder head:
   a. Remove alternator.
   b. Disconnect power steering gear pump and brackets attached to cylinder head.
6. Disconnect wires from spark plugs, and remove the spark plug wire clips from the rocker arm cover studs.
7. Remove exhaust manifold bolts from head being removed.
8. With air hose and cloths, clean dirt off cylinder head and adjacent area to avoid getting dirt into engine. It is extremely important to avoid getting dirt into the hydraulic valve lifters.
9. Remove rocker arm cover and rocker

arm and shaft assembly from cylinder head. Lift out pushrods.

➡ **If lifters are to be serviced, remove them at this time and place them in a container with numbered holes or a similar device, to keep them identified as to engine position. If they are not to be removed, protect lifters and camshaft from dirt by covering area with a clean cloth.**

10. Loosen all cylinder head bolts, then remove bolts and lift off the cylinder head.
11. With cylinder head on bench, remove all spark plugs for cleaning and to avoid damaging them during work on the head.
12. Installation is the reverse of removal. Clean all gasket surfaces thoroughly. Always use a new head gasket. The head gasket is installed with the bead downward. Coat the head bolt threads with heavy-bodied thread sealer. Torque the head bolts in three equal stages. Recheck head bolt torque after the engine has been warmed to operating temperature.

3.1L Engine

LEFT SIDE

1. Relieve the pressure in the fuel system before disconnecting any fuel line connections. Disconnect the fuel lines.
2. Disconnect the negative battery cable. Raise and safely support the vehicle.
3. Drain the cylinder block and lower the vehicle.
4. Remove the oil level indicator tube, rocker arm cover, intake manifold and plenum, as required.
5. Remove the exhaust crossover, alternator bracket, AIR pump and brackets.
6. Disconnect and tag all electrical wiring and vacuum hoses that may interfere with the removal of the left cylinder head.
7. Loosen the rocker arm until the pushrods

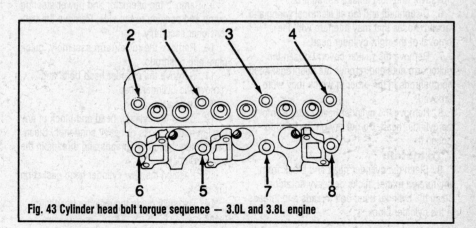

Fig. 43 Cylinder head bolt torque sequence — 3.0L and 3.8L engine

can be removed. Remove the pushrods. Keep the pushrods in the same order as removed.

8. Remove the cylinder head bolts. Remove the cylinder head. Do not pry on the head to loosen it.

To install:

9. Clean the cylinder head and block from any foreign matter, nicks or heavy scratches. Clean the cylinder head bolt threads and threads in the cylinder block.

10. Position the new cylinder head gasket over the dowel pins with the words "This Side Up" facing upwards. Carefully guide the cylinder head into place.

11. Install the cylinder head bolts and tighten in sequence to 33 ft. lbs. (45 Nm). Turn an additional 90° in sequence.

12. Install the pushrods. Make sure the lower ends of the pushrods are in the lifter seats. Install the rocker arm nuts and torque the nuts to 14–20 ft. lbs. (20–27 Nm).

13. Install the intake manifold.

14. Connect all electrical wiring and vacuum hoses.

15. Install the exhaust crossover, alternator and AIR pump brackets, alternator and AIR pump.

16. If removed, install the oil level indicator tube, rocker arm cover, intake manifold and plenum.

17. Connect the fuel lines.

18. Connect the negative battery cable.

19. Adjust the valve lash, as required.

RIGHT SIDE

1. Relieve the pressure in the fuel system before disconnecting any fuel line connections.

2. Disconnect the negative battery cable. Raise the vehicle and support it safely.

3. Drain the cylinder block and lower the vehicle.

4. If equipped, remove the cruise control servo bracket, the air management valve and hose and the intake manifold.

5. Remove the exhaust pipe at crossover, crossover and heat shield, as required.

6. Disconnect and tag all electrical wiring and vacuum hoses that may interfere with the removal of the right cylinder head.

7. Remove the rocker cover. Loosen the rocker arm nuts and remove the pushrods. Keep the pushrods in the order in which they were removed.

8. Remove the cylinder head bolts. Remove the cylinder head. Do not pry on the head to loosen it.

To install:

9. Clean the cylinder head and block from any foreign matter, nicks or heavy scratches. Clean the cylinder head bolt threads and threads in the cylinder block.

10. Position the new cylinder head gasket over the dowel pins with the words "This Side Up" facing upwards. Carefully guide the cylinder head into place. Install the pushrods and loosely retain with the rocker arms.

11. Install the cylinder head bolts and tighten in sequence to 33 ft. lbs. (45 Nm). Turn an additional 90° in sequence.

12. Install the pushrods. Make sure the lower ends of the pushrods are in the lifter seats. Install the rocker arm nuts and torque the nuts to 14–20 ft. lbs. (20–27 Nm).

13. Install the intake manifold.

14. Install the rocker cover.

15. Connect all electrical wiring and vacuum hoses.

16. If removed, install the crossover exhaust pipe and heat shield.

17. If equipped, install the cruise control servo bracket, the air management valve and hose.

18. Connect the negative battery cable.

19. Fill cooling system and check for leaks. Start the engine and allow to come to normal operating temperature. Recheck for leaks. Top-up coolant.

20. Adjust the valve lash, as required.

3.3L Engine

1. Relieve the pressure in the fuel system before disconnecting any fuel line connections.

2. Disconnect the negative battery cable. Raise the vehicle and support it safely.

3. Drain the cylinder block and lower the vehicle.

4. Remove the intake manifold and exhaust manifold.

5. Remove the valve cover.

6. Remove the ignition module and coils as a unit.

7. Disconnect and tag all electrical wiring and vacuum hoses, as necessary.

8. If equipped with air conditioning, remove the air conditioning compressor and position to the side.

9. Remove the alternator and power steering pump and position to the side. Remove the belt tensioner assembly.

10. Remove the rocker arm assembly, guide plate and pushrods.

11. Remove the cylinder head bolts and remove the cylinder head.

To install:

12. Clean the cylinder head and block of any foreign matter, nicks or heavy scratches. Clean the cylinder head bolt threads and threads in the cylinder block.

13. Position the new cylinder head gasket on the block.

14. Carefully guide the cylinder head into place.

15. Coat the cylinder head bolts with sealing compound and install into the head. Tighten the cylinder head bolts according to the following procedure:

   a. Tighten in sequence to 35 ft. lbs. (47 Nm).

   b. Using an appropriate torque angle gauge, rotate each bolt in sequence an additional 130°.

   c. Rotate the center 4 bolts an additional 30° in sequence.

16. Install the pushrods, guide plate and rocker arm assembly. Tighten the rocker arm pivot bolts to 28 ft. lbs. (38 Nm).

17. Install the intake manifold and exhaust manifold.

18. Install the valve cover.

19. Remove the ignition module and coils as a unit, as required.

20. Connect all electrical wiring and vacuum hoses.

21. If equipped with air conditioning, install the air conditioning compressor.

22. Install the alternator and power steering pump. Remove the belt tensioner assembly.

23. Connect the negative battery cable.

24. Fill cooling system and check for leaks. Start the engine and allow to come to normal operating temperature. Recheck for leaks. Top-up coolant.

3.8L Engine

1. Relieve the pressure in the fuel system before disconnecting any fuel line connections.

2. Disconnect the negative battery cable. Raise the vehicle and support it safely.

3. Drain the cylinder block and lower the vehicle.

4. Remove the serpentine belt.

5. Remove the alternator, AIR pump, oil indicator and power steering pump, as required. Position to the side.

6. Remove the throttle cable. Remove the cruise control cable, if equipped.

7. Disconnect the fuel lines and fuel rail, as required.

8. Remove the heater hoses and radiator hoses.

9. Disconnect and tag all vacuum and electrical wiring.

10. Remove the radiator and cooling fan, if necessary.

11. Remove the intake manifold and valve cover.

12. Remove the exhaust manifold(s).

13. Remove the rocker arm assembly and pushrods.

14. Remove the cylinder head bolts and remove the cylinder head.

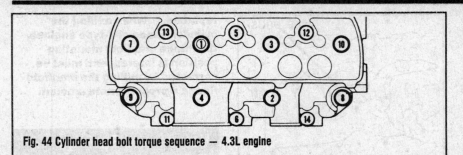

Fig. 44 Cylinder head bolt torque sequence — 4.3L engine

To install:

15. Clean the cylinder head and block from any foreign matter, nicks or heavy scratches. Clean the cylinder head bolt threads and threads in the cylinder block.

16. Position the new cylinder head gasket on the block.

17. Carefully guide the cylinder head into place. Coat the cylinder head bolts with sealing compound and install.

18. Tighten the cylinder head bolts according to the following procedure:

a. Tighten the cylinder head bolts in sequence to 25 ft. lbs. (34 Nm).

b. Do not exceed 60 ft. lbs. (81 Nm) at any point during the next 2 steps.

c. Using a torque angle gauge, tighten each bolt an additional 90° in sequence.

d. Tighten each bolt an additional 90° in sequence.

19. Install the exhaust manifold.

20. Install the intake manifold, pushrods and rocker arm assembly.

21. Install the valve cover.

22. Install the radiator and cooling fan, as required.

23. Connect all vacuum and electrical wiring.

24. Install the heater hoses and radiator hoses.

25. Connect the fuel lines and fuel rail.

26. Install the throttle cable. Install the cruise control cable, if equipped.

27. Install the alternator, AIR pump, oil indicator and power steering pump.

28. Install the serpentine belt.

29. Connect the negative battery cable.

30. Fill cooling system and check for leaks. Start the engine and allow to come to normal operating temperature. Check for leaks and top off the coolant.

4.3L Diesel Engine

➡ **This procedure requires the complete disassembly of the valve lifters as explained under Diesel Engine Valve Lifter Bleed-Down.**

1. Remove intake manifold.

2. Remove valve cover. Loosen or remove any accessory brackets or pipe clamps which interfere.

➡ **If removing the left cylinder head, remove the oil level indicator guide.**

3. Disconnect glow plug wiring (and block heater lead if so equipped on rear bank).

4. Remove the ground strap from the rear cylinder head. Remove the fuel lines at the injector nozzles.

5. Remove rocker arm nuts, pivots, rocker arms and pushrods. Scribe pivots and keep rocker arms separated so they can be installed in their original locations.

6. Disconnect the exhaust crossover pipe from the exhaust manifold on the side being worked on and loosen it on the other.

7. Remove engine block drain plug, from side of the block where head is being removed.

8. Remove the pipe plugs covering the upper cylinder head bolts.

9. Remove all the cylinder head bolts and remove the cylinder head.

10. If necessary to remove the prechamber, remove the glow plug and injection nozzle, then tap out with a small blunt 1/8 in. (3mm) drift. Do NOT use a tapered drift.

11. Installation is the reverse of removal. Do not use sealer on the head gasket. If a prechamber was replaced, measure the chamber height and grind the new one to within 0.001 in. (0.025mm) of the old chamber's height, using #80 grit wet sandpaper to polish it. Coat the head bolts with sealer, preventing coolant leakage.

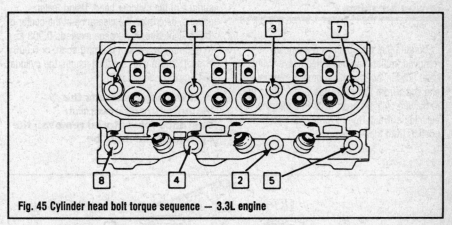

Fig. 45 Cylinder head bolt torque sequence — 3.3L engine

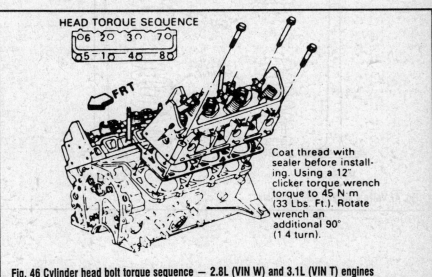

Coat thread with sealer before installing. Using a 12" clicker torque wrench torque to 45 N·m (33 Lbs. Ft.). Rotate wrench an additional 90° (1 4 turn).

Fig. 46 Cylinder head bolt torque sequence — 2.8L (VIN W) and 3.1L (VIN T) engines

12. Torque the cylinder head bolts, except No. 5, 6, 11, 12, 13 and 14, to 100 ft. lbs. (135 Nm.); No. 5, 6, 11, 12, 13 and 14 bolts to 41 ft. lbs. (55 Nm.). Retorque the cylinder head bolts, except No. 5, 6, 11, 12, 13 and 14, to 142 ft. lbs. (193 Nm.); No. 5, 6, 11, 12, 13 and 14 bolts to 59 ft. lbs. (80 Nm.).

CLEANING AND INSPECTION

Chip carbon away from the valve heads, combustion chambers, and ports, using a chisel made of hardwood. Remove the remaining deposits with a stiff wire brush.

✳✳ WARNING

DO NOT use a steel wire brush to clean an aluminum cylinder head. Special brushes are sold just for use on aluminum. Always wear eye protection when grinding chipping or wire brushing.

Be sure that the deposits are actually removed, rather than burnished. Have cylinder head hot-tanked to remove grease, corrosion, and scale from the water passages. Clean the remaining cylinder head parts in an engine cleaning solvent. Do not remove the protective coating from the springs.

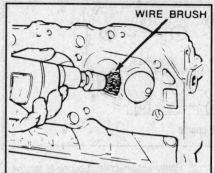

Fig. 48 Remove the carbon from the cylinder head with a wire brush and drill. Always wear eye protection

RESURFACING

➡ **All machine work should be performed by a competent, professional machine shop.**

Place a straightedge across the gasket surface of the cylinder head. Using feeler gauges, determine the clearance at the center of the straightedge. If warpage exceeds 0.003 in. (0.076mm) in a 6 in. (152mm) span, or 0.006 in. (0.152mm) over the total length, the cylinder head must be resurfaced.

➡ **If warpage exceeds the manufacturer's maximum tolerance for material removal, the cylinder head must be**

replaced. **When milling the cylinder heads of V-type engines, the intake manifold mounting position is latered, and must be corrected by milling the manifold flange a proportionate amount.**

Valves and Springs

ADJUSTMENT

➡ **This procedure must be performed with the engine COLD.**

1. Remove the valve cover and the No. 1 spark plug.
2. Rotate the engine until the **O** mark on the crankshaft pulley aligns with the timing tab and the No. 1 cylinder is on the TDC of the compression stroke.
3. With the engine in this position, adjust the exhaust valves of No. 1, 2 and 3 and the intake valves of N. 1, 5 and 6. Back out the adjusting nut until lash is felt at the push rod, then turn the nut to remove the lash. With the lash removed, turn the nut an additional 1½ turns.
4. Rotate the engine 1 complete revolution until the **O** mark on the crankshaft pulley aligns with the timing tab and the No. 4 piston is on the TDC of the compression stroke.
5. With the engine in this position, adjust the exhaust valves of No. 2, 3 and 4; adjust the valves the same way as in Step No. 3.
6. Install the valve covers and the spark plugs.

REMOVAL & INSPECTION

1. Remove the cylinder head(s) from the vehicle as previously outlined.
2. Using a suitable valve spring compressor, compress the valve spring and remove the valve keys using a magnetic retrieval tool.
3. Slowly release the compressor and remove the valve spring caps (or rotators) and the valve springs.
4. Fabricate a valve arrangement board to use when you remove the valves, which will indicate the port in which each valve was originally installed (and which cylinder head on V6 models). Also note that the valve keys, rotators, caps, etc. should be arranged in a manner which will allow you to reinstall them on the valve on which they were originally used.

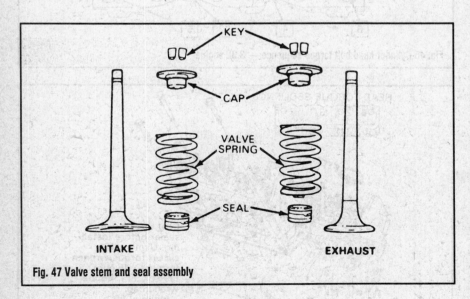

Fig. 47 Valve stem and seal assembly

5. Remove and discard the valve seals. On models using the umbrella type seals, note the location of the large and small seals for assembly purposes.

6. Thoroughly clean the valves on the wire wheel of a bench grinder, then clean the cylinder head mating surface with a) a soft wire wheel, b) a soft wire brush, or c) a wooden scraper. Avoid using a metallic scraper, since this can cause damage to the cylinder head mating surface, especially on models with aluminum heads.

7. Using a valve guide cleaner chucked into a drill, clean all of the valve guides.

8. Reinstall each valve into its respective port (guide) of the cylinder head.

9. Mount a dial indicator so that the stem is at 90° to the valve stem, as close to the valve guide as possible.

10. Move the valve off its seat, and measure the valve guide-to-stem clearance by rocking the stem back and forth to actuate the dial indicator.

11. Measure the valve stems using a micrometer, and compare to specifications, to determine whether stem or guide wear is responsible for excessive clearance.

➡ **Consult the Specifications tables earlier in this Section.**

REFACING

Using a valve grinder, resurface the valves according to specifications in this Section. All machine work should be performed by a competent, professional machine shop.

➡ **Valve face angle is not always identical to valve seat angle.**

A minimum margin of $\frac{1}{32}$ in. (0.8mm) should remain after grinding the valve. The valve stem top should also be squared and resurfaced, by placing the stem in the V-block of the grinder, and turning it while pressing lightly against the grinding wheel. Be sure to chamfer the edge of the tip so that the squared edges don't dig into the rocker arm.

Fig. 50 Lapping valves by hand

LAPPING

This procedure should be performed after the valves and seats have been machined, to insure that each valve mates to each seat precisely.

1. Invert the cylinder head, lightly lubricate the valve stems, and install the valves in the head as numbered.

2. Coat valve seats with fine grinding compound, and attach the lapping tool suction cup to a valve head.

➡ **Moisten the suction cup.**

3. Rotate the tool between the palms, changing position and lifting the tool often to prevent grooving.

4. Lap the valve until a smooth, polished seat is evident.

5. Remove the valve and tool, and rinse away all traces of grinding compound.

VALVE SEALS

The valve seals can be replaced with the cylinder head on or off the engine. But great care and skill must be used to perform this procedure with the cylinder head on the engine. With the

cylinder head off the engine compress the valve spring using tool J26513 or equivalent, remove the keeper, spring and seal. All parts must be return to their original locations.

If the cylinder head is on the vehicle, 60 psi or more of compressed air must be used. The procedure will require bringing the piston of the cylinder to be service up to top dead center on compression stoke. Then apply compressed air through the spark plug hole using a compressor gauge fitting. The valve spring and seal can now be remove.

➡ **If the air pressure is too low or drops during this procedure the valve will fall into the engine, requiring complete disassembly of the cylinder head assembly. Also if the valve is pressed downward at all pressure will be lost and the valve will fall in.**

Valve Spring Testing

Place the spring on a flat surface next to a square. Measure the height of the spring and rotate it against the edge of the square to measure distortion. If spring height varies (by comparison) by more than $\frac{1}{16}$ in. (1.6mm) or if distortion exceeds $\frac{1}{16}$ in. (1.6mm), replace the spring. In addition to evaluating the spring as above, test the spring pressure at the installed and compressed (installed height minus valve lift) height using a valve spring tester. Spring pressure should be ± 1 lb. (0.45kg) of all other springs in either position.

Valve Seat Service

The valve seats are integral with the cylinder head on all engines except the V6 diesel with aluminum cylinder heads. On all engines except

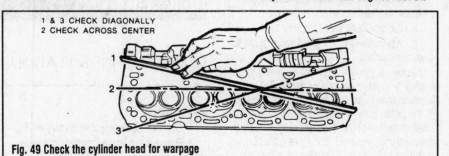

1 & 3 CHECK DIAGONALLY
2 CHECK ACROSS CENTER

Fig. 49 Check the cylinder head for warpage

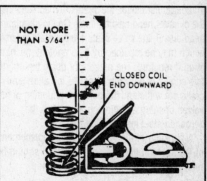

NOT MORE THAN 5/64''

CLOSED COIL END DOWNWARD

Fig. 51 Check the valve spring free length and squareness. Replace if not square or same length as other springs

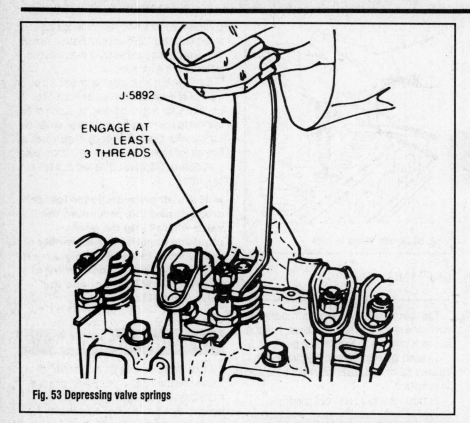

J-5892

ENGAGE AT LEAST 3 THREADS

Fig. 53 Depressing valve springs

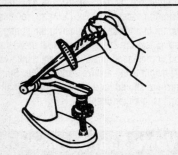

Fig. 52 Check the valve spring tension. Replace if not within specification or less than the other springs

that particular diesel, the seats are machined into the cylinder head casting itself. On the aluminum head diesel, the valve seats are separate inserts, which may be replaced by a competent machine shop if required. The reason for using inserts on this engine is basically because the aluminum could not withstand the constant pounding of the valves opening and closing as well as the hardened steel insert which is used.

Machining of the valve seats, or replacement of the seats in the case of the diesel, should be referred to a professional machine shop.

Valve Guide Service

The valve guides used in these engines are integral with the cylinder head, that is, they cannot be replaced.

➥ **Refer to the previous Valves Removal and Installation to check the valve guides for wear.**

Valve guides are most accurately repaired using the bronze wall rebuilding method. In this operation, threads are cut into the bores of the valve guide and bronze wire is turned into the threads. The bronze wall is then reamed to the proper diameter. This method is well received for a number of reasons:

    a. It is relatively inexpensive

    b. It offers better valve lubrication (the wire forms channels which retain oil)

    c. It offers less valve friction

    d. It preserves the original valve guide-to-seat relationship.

Another popular method of repairing valve guides is to have the guides knurled. The knurling entails cutting action raises metal off of the guide bore which actually narrows the inner diameter of the bore, thereby reducing the clearance between the valve guide bore and the valve stem. This method offers the same advantages as the bronze wall method, but will generally wear faster.

Another method of repairing the guides is to ream the bores and install oversize valves.

Either of the above services must be performed by a professional machine shop which has the specialized knowledge and tools necessary to perform the service.

Valve and Spring Installation

➥ **Be sure that all traces of lapping compound have been cleaned off before the valves are installed.**

1. Lubricate all of the valve stems with a light coating of engine oil, then install the valves into the proper ports/guides.

2. If umbrella-type valve seals are used, install them at this time. Be sure to use a seal protector to prevent damage to the seals as they are pushed over the valve keeper grooves.

➥ **If O-ring seals are used, don't install them yet.**

3. Install the valve springs and the spring retainers (or rotators), and using the valve compressing tool, compress the springs.

4. If umbrella-type seals are used, just install the valve keepers (white grease may be used to hold them in place) and release the pressure on the compressing tool. If O-ring type seals are used, carefully work the seals into the second groove of the valve (closest to the head), install the valve keepers and release the pressure on the tool.

➥ **If the O-ring seals are installed BEFORE the springs and retainers are compressed, the seal will be destroyed.**

5. After all of the valves are installed and retained, tap each valve spring retainer with a rubber mallet to seat the keepers in the retainer.

Valve Lifters

REMOVAL & INSTALLATION

2.5L Engine

1. Disconnect the negative battery cable.

2. Remove the intake manifold and valve cover.

3. Loosen the rocker arms and rotate to clear the pushrods.

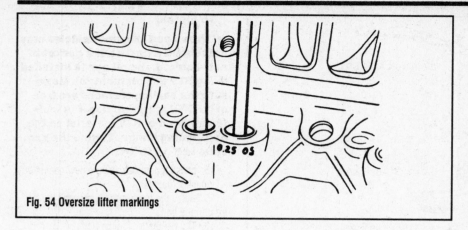

Fig. 54 Oversize lifter markings

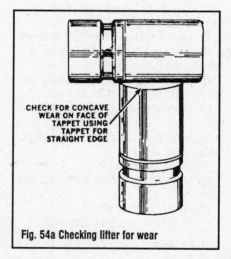

CHECK FOR CONCAVE WEAR ON FACE OF TAPPET USING TAPPET FOR STRAIGHT EDGE

Fig. 54a Checking lifter for wear

4. Remove the pushrods, retainer and guide.
5. Remove the lifters. Keep all components separated so they may be reinstalled in the same location.

To Install:

6. Lubricate the lifters with engine oil and install the lifters in their bore.
7. Install the guides, retainers and pushrods.
8. With the lifter on the base circle of the camshaft, tighten the rocker arm bolts to 24 ft. lbs. (32 Nm).
9. Install the intake manifold and valve cover.
10. Connect battery negative cable.

Except 2.5L Engine

1. Disconnect the negative battery cable.
2. Drain the cooling system.
3. Remove the valve cover and the intake manifold.
4. If the engine is equipped with individual rocker arms, loosen the rocker arm adjusting nut and rotate the arm so as to clear the pushrod.
5. If the engine is equipped with a rocker shaft assembly, remove the rocker shaft retaining bolts/nuts and remove the shaft assembly.

➡ **Be sure to keep all valve train parts in order so they may be reinstalled in their original locations and with the same mating surfaces as when removed.**

6. Remove the pushrods and valve lifters using tool J–3049 or equivalent.

To Install:

7. Lubricate the bearing surfaces with Molykote® or equivalent.
8. Install the lifters in their original locations.
9. With the lifter on the base circle of the camshaft, tighten the rocker arm bolts to 14–20 ft. lbs. (20–27 Nm).
10. Connect the negative battery cable.
11. Adjust the valves, as required.

Oil Pan

▶ SEE FIGS. 55 to 57

REMOVAL & INSTALLATION

❈ CAUTION

The EPA warns that prolonged contact with used engine oil may cause a number of skin disorders, including cancer! You should make every effort to minimize your exposure to used engine oil. Protective gloves should be worn when changing the oil. Wash your hands and any other exposed skin areas as soon as possible after exposure to used engine oil. Soap and water, or waterless hand cleaner should be used.

2.5L Engine

1. Raise and support the car. Drain the oil.
2. Remove the engine cradle-to-front engine mounts.
3. Disconnect the exhaust pipe at both the exhaust manifold and at the front of the converter.
4. Disconnect and remove the starter. Remove the flywheel housing or torque converter cover.
5. Remove the alternator upper bracket. Remove the splash shield.
6. Install an engine lifting chain and raise the engine. If equipped, remove the power steering pump and bracket and move it aside.
7. Remove the lower alternator bracket. Remove the engine support bracket.
8. Remove the oil pan retaining bolts and remove the pan.
9. Reverse the procedure to install. Clean all gasket surfaces thoroughly. Install the rear oil pan gasket into the rear main bearing cap, then apply a thin bead of silicone sealer to the pan gasket depressions. Install the front pan gasket into the timing cover. Install the side gaskets onto the pan, not the block. They can be retained in place with grease. Apply a thin bead of silicone seal to the mating joints of the gaskets. Install the oil pan; install the timing gear bolts last, after the other bolts have been snugged down.

2.8L Engine

1. Disconnect the battery ground.

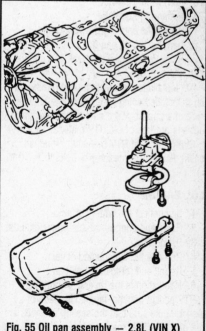

Fig. 55 Oil pan assembly — 2.8L (VIN X) engine shown

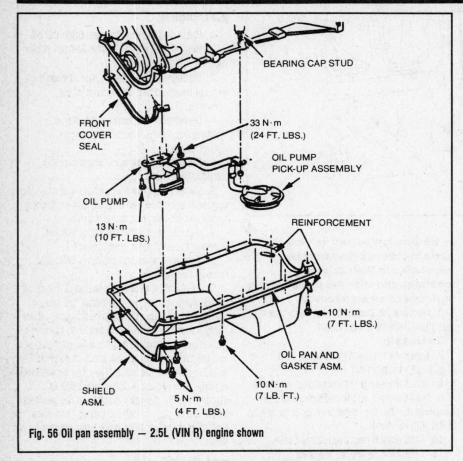

FRONT COVER SEAL

BEARING CAP STUD

33 N·m (24 FT. LBS.)

OIL PUMP PICK-UP ASSEMBLY

OIL PUMP

13 N·m (10 FT. LBS.)

REINFORCEMENT

10 N·m (7 FT. LBS.)

OIL PAN AND GASKET ASM.

SHIELD ASM.

5 N·m (4 FT. LBS.)

10 N·m (7 LB. FT.)

Fig. 56 Oil pan assembly — 2.5L (VIN R) engine shown

2. Raise and support the car on jackstands.
3. Drain the oil.
4. Remove the bellhousing cover.
5. Remove the starter.
6. Support the engine.
7. Unbolt the engine from its mounts.
8. Remove the oil pan bolts.
9. Raise the engine with a jack, just enough to remove the oil pan.
10. Installation is the reverse of removal. The pan is installed using RTV gasket material in place of a gasket. Make sure that the sealing surfaces are free of old RTV material. Use a ⅛ in. (3mm) bead of RTV material on the pan sealing flange. Torque the pan bolts to 8–10 ft. lbs.

3.0L Engine

1. Disconnect the battery ground.
2. Raise and support the car on jackstands.
3. Drain the oil.
4. Remove the bellhousing cover.
5. Unbolt and remove the oil pan.
6. Installation is the reverse of removal. RTV gasket material is used in place of a gasket. Make sure that the sealing surfaces are free of all old RTV material. Use a ⅛ in. (3mm) bead of RTV material on the oil pan sealing flange. Torque the pan bolts to 10 ft. lbs.

3.1L Engine

1. Disconnect the battery ground.
2. Remove the serpentine belt cover, belt and tensioner.
3. Support the engine with tool J–28467–A or equivalent, using an extra support leg.
4. Raise and safely support the vehicle.
5. Drain the oil.
6. Remove the right tire and wheel assembly. Remove the splash shield.
7. Remove the steering gear pinch bolt, as required.
8. Remove the transaxle mount retaining nuts and engine-to-frame mount retaining nuts, as required.
9. Remove the front engine horse collar bracket from the block, as required.
10. Remove the bellhousing cover and remove the starter.
11. Position a jackstand under the frame front center crossmember.
12. Loosen but do not remove the rear frame bolts.
13. Remove the front frame bolts and lower the front frame.
14. Remove the oil pan retaining bolts and remove the oil pan.

To install:

➡ The oil pan on some vehicles may not require a gasket. If a gasket is not required, the oil pan is installed using RTV gasket material. Make sure the sealing surfaces are free of old RTV material. Use a ⅛ inch (3mm) bead of RTV material on the pan sealing flange. Torque the pan bolts to 8–10 ft. lbs.

15. Install the oil pan using a new gasket or RTV gasket material.
16. Raise the front frame and install the the front frame bolts.
17. Tighten the rear frame bolts.
18. Remove the jackstand from the front center crossmember.
19. Install the starter and bellhousing cover.
20. If removed, install the front engine horse collar bracket from the block.
21. Install the transaxle mount retaining nuts and engine to frame mount retaining nuts.
22. If removed, install the steering gear pinch bolt.
23. Install the splash shield. Install the right tire and wheel assembly.
24. Lower the vehicle.
25. Install the tensioner, serpentine belt and cover.
26. Fill the crankcase with oil.
27. Connect the negative battery cable.

3.3L Engine

1. Disconnect the negative battery cable.
2. Raise and support the vehicle safely.

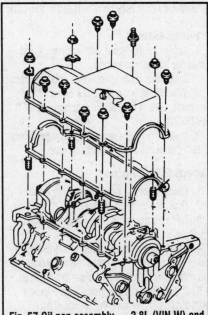

Fig. 57 Oil pan assembly — 2.8L (VIN W) and 3.1 (VIN T) engines shown

3. Drain the engine oil.

4. Remove the transaxle converter cover and starter motor.

5. Remove the oil filter, oil pan retaining bolts and oil pan assembly.

To install:

6. Clean the oil pan and cylinder block mating surfaces.

7. Install a new oil pan gasket to the oil pan flange.

8. Install the oil pan and torque the retaining bolts 8–10 ft. lbs.

9. Lower the vehicle.

10. Fill the crankcase with oil.

11. Connect the negative battery cable.

3.8L Engine

1. Disconnect the battery ground cable.

2. Raise and safely support the vehicle.

3. Drain the oil.

4. Remove the bellhousing cover.

5. Unbolt and remove the oil pan.

To install:

6. RTV gasket material is used in place of a gasket. Make sure the sealing surfaces are free of all old RTV material. Use a 1/8 inch (3mm) bead of RTV material on the oil pan sealing flange. Torque the pan bolts to 10–14 ft. lbs.

7. Install the bellhousing cover.

8. Lower the vehicle.

9. Fill the crankcase with oil.

10. Connect the negative battery cable.

4.3L Diesel Engine

> ※※ **CAUTION**
>
> **The following procedure will be personally hazardous unless the procedures are followed exactly.**

1. Install the engine support fixture tool J–28467. Be certain to arrange washers on the fixture so that the bolt securing the chain to the cylinder head can be torqued to 20 ft. lbs. THIS IS ABSOLUTELY NECESSARY!

2. Raise the front and rear of the car and support it on jackstands with the rear slightly lower than the front. The front jackstands should be located at the front lift points shown in your owner's manual.

3. Turn the intermediate steering shaft so that the steering gear stub shaft clamp bolt is in the UP position. Remove the clamp bolt and disconnect the two shafts. Drain the oil.

4. Remove the left side steering gear cradle bolt and loosen the right side cradle bolt.

5. Remove the front stabilizer bar.

6. Using a 1/2 in. (13mm) drill bit, drill through the spot weld located between the rear holes at the left front stabilizer bar mounting.

7. Remove the nuts securing the engine and transaxle to its cradle.

8. Disconnect the left lower ball joint from the knuckle.

9. Place a wood block on a floor jack and raise the transaxle under the pan until the mount studs clear the cradle.

10. Remove the bolts securing the front crossmember to the right side of the cradle.

11. Remove the bolts from the left side front body mounts.

12. Remove the left side and front crossmember assemblies. It will be necessary to lower the rear crossmember below the left side of the body through the careful use of a large pry bar.

13. Remove the bellhousing cover.

14. Remove the starter.

15. Remove the engine from mount bracket.

16. Unbolt and remove the oil pan.

17. Installation is the reverse of removal. Apply sealer to both sides of the oil pan gasket and make sure that the tabs on the gaskets are installed in the seal notches. Apply RTV sealer to the front cover oil pan seal retainer, and to each seal where it contacts the block. Wipe the seal area of the pan with clean engine oil before installing the pan. Torque the pan bolts to 10 ft. lbs. and the steering clamp bolt to 40 ft. lbs.

Oil Pump

▶ SEE FIGS. 58 and 59

REMOVAL & INSTALLATION

> ※※ **CAUTION**
>
> **The EPA warns that prolonged contact with used engine oil may cause a number of skin disorders, including cancer! You should make every effort to minimize your exposure to used engine oil. Protective gloves should be worn when changing the oil. Wash your hands and any other exposed skin areas as soon as possible after exposure to used engine oil. Soap and water, or waterless hand cleaner should be used.**

2.5L ENGINE

1. Disconnect the negative battery cable.

2. Raise and support the vehicle safely.

3. Drain the engine oil and remove the oil pan.

4. Remove the 2 flange mounting bolts and nut from the main bearing cap bolt.

5. Remove the pump and screen as an assembly.

To install:

6. Remove the 4 cover attaching screws and cover from the oil pump assembly.

7. Pack the space around the oil pump gears completely full of petroleum jelly. There must be no air space left inside the pump. If the pump is not packed, it may not begin to pump oil as soon as the engine is started and engine damage may result.

8. Align the oil pump shaft to match with the oil pump drive shaft tang, then install the oil pump to the block positioning the flange over the oil pump driveshaft lower bushing. Do not use any gasket. Torque the bolts to 20 ft. lbs. (30 Nm).

9. Install the oil pan using a new gasket and seals.

10. Install the 2 flange mounting bolts and nut to the main bearing cap bolt.

11. Lower the vehicle.

12. Fill the crankcase with oil.

13. Connect the negative battery cable.

2.8L Engine

1. Disconnect the negative battery cable.

2. Raise and support the vehicle safely.

3. Drain the engine oil and remove the oil pan.

4. Remove the pump-to-rear main bearing cap bolt and remove the pump and extension shaft.

To install:

5. Remove the 4 cover attaching screws and cover from the oil pump assembly.

6. Pack the space around the oil pump gears completely full of petroleum jelly. There must be no air space left inside the pump. If the pump is not packed, it may not begin to pump oil as soon as the engine is started and engine damage may result.

7. Assemble the pump and extension shaft with retainer to rear main bearing cap, aligning the top end of the extension shaft with the lower end of the drive gear.

8. Install the pump-to-the rear bearing cap bolt. Tighten to 30 ft. lbs. (40 Nm).

9. Install the oil pan.

10. Lower the vehicle.

11. Fill the crankcase with oil.

12. Connect the negative battery cable.

3.0L Engines

1. Remove the oil filter.
2. Unbolt the oil pump cover from the timing chain cover.
3. Slide out the oil pump gears. Clean all parts thoroughly in solvent and check for wear. Remove the oil pressure relief valve cap, spring and valve.
4. Installation is the reverse of removal. Torque the pressure relief valve cap to 35 ft. lbs. Install the pump gears and check their clearances:
   - End clearance: 0.002–0.006 in. (0.05–0.15mm)
   - Side clearance: 0.002–0.005 in. (0.05–0.13mm)

Place a straightedge across the face of the pump cover and check that it is flat to within 0.001 in. (0.025mm). Pack the oil pump cavity with petroleum jelly so that there is no air space. Install the cover and torque the bolts to 10 ft. lbs.

3.1 Engine

1. Disconnect the negative battery cable.
2. Raise and support the vehicle safely.
3. Drain the engine oil and remove the oil pan.
4. Remove the pump-to-rear main bearing cap bolt and remove the pump and extension shaft.

To install:

5. Remove the 4 cover attaching screws and cover from the oil pump assembly.
6. Pack the space around the oil pump gears completely full of petroleum jelly. There must be no air space left inside the pump. If the pump is not packed, it may not begin to pump oil as soon as the engine is started and engine damage may result.
7. Assemble the pump and extension shaft

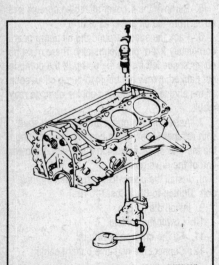

Fig. 58 Oil pump assembly — 2.8L (VIN W) and 3.1 (VIN T) engines shown

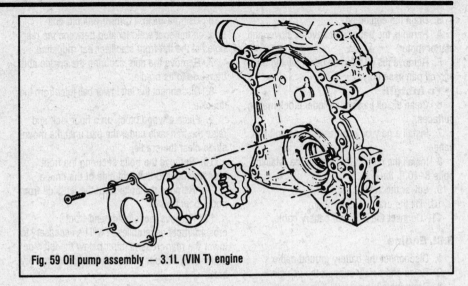

Fig. 59 Oil pump assembly — 3.1L (VIN T) engine

with retainer to rear main bearing cap, aligning the top end of the extension shaft with the lower end of the drive gear.

8. Install the pump-to-the rear bearing cap bolt. Tighten to 30 ft. lbs. (40 Nm).
9. Install the oil pan.
10. Lower the vehicle.
11. Fill the crankcase with oil.
12. Connect the negative battery cable.

3.3L And 3.8L Engines

1. Disconnect the negative battery cable.
2. Drain the engine oil.
3. Remove the oil filter adapter, pressure regulator valve and spring.
4. Remove the oil pump cover attaching screws and cover.
5. Remove the gears.

To install:

6. Lubricate the gears with petroleum jelly.
7. Assemble the gears in the housing.
8. Pack the gear cavity with petroleum jelly.
9. Install the oil pump cover and screws. Tighten to 97 inch lbs. (11 Nm).
10. Install the pressure regulator and spring valve.
11. Install the oil filter adapter with a new gasket. Tighten the oil filter adapter bolts to 24 ft. lbs. (33 Nm).
12. Install the front cover on the engine.
13. Fill the crankcase with oil.
14. Connect the negative battery cable.

4.3L Diesel Engine

1. Remove the oil pan.
2. Unbolt and remove the oil pump and drive extension.
3. Installation is the reverse of removal. Torque the pump bolts to 18 ft. lbs.

Crankshaft Damper

REMOVAL & INSTALLATION

2.5L, 3.3L and 3.8L Engine

1. Disconnect the negative battery cable, and remove the serpentine belt.
2. Raise and safely support the vehicle.
3. Remove the flywheel or torque converter cover.
4. Right front tire and wheel assembly.
5. Remove the right front engine splash shield.
6. Use a suitable tool on the flywheel to keep engine from rotating and remove the bolt and washer from the damper.
7. Remove the balancer and the key.

To install:

8. Install the key and balancer.
9. Install the bolt and washer, torque the bolt to 162 ft. lbs. (220 Nm).
10. Install the engine splash shield.
11. Install the tire and wheel assembly.
12. Install the flywheel or torque converter cover.
13. Lower the vehicle.
14. Install the serpentine belt.
15. Connect the negative battery cable.

2.8L Engine

1. Disconnect the negative battery cable, and remove the serpentine belt.
2. Raise and safely support the vehicle.
3. Remove the flywheel or torque converter cover.
4. Right front tire and wheel assembly.

5. Remove the right front engine splash shield.

6. Remove the AIR pump, if equipped.

7. Use a suitable tool on the flywheel to keep engine from rotating and remove the bolt and washer from the damper.

8. With tool J29113, or equivalent, installed on the damper, turn the puller screw.

→ **The inertia weight section of the damper is assembled to the hub with a rubber sleeve. A proper puller must be used to avoid damaging the damper assembly.**

9. Remove the damper.

To install:

10. Coat the cover seal with clean engine oil before installing the damper using tool J 29113 or equivalent.

11. Apply sealant to the key and keyway.

12. Place the damper into position and pull into place with tool.

13. Install the retaining bolt and torque to 110 ft. lbs. (80 Nm).

14. Install the AIR pump, inner splash shield and lower the vehicle.

15. Install the serpentine drive belt.

16. Install the negative battery cable.

3.1L Engine

1. Disconnect the negative battery cable, and remove the serpentine belt.

2. Raise and safely support the vehicle.

3. Remove the flywheel or torque converter cover.

4. Right front tire and wheel assembly.

5. Remove the right front engine splash shield.

6. Use a suitable tool on the flywheel to keep engine from rotating and remove the bolt and washer from the damper.

7. Remove the balancer and the key. With tool J 24420–B and turn puller screw to remove the balancer.

To install:

8. Install the key and balancer.

9. Install the bolt and washer, torque the bolt to 76 ft. lbs. (103 Nm).

10. Install the engine splash shield.

11. Install the tire and wheel assembly.

12. Install the flywheel or torque converter cover.

13. Lower the vehicle.

14. Install the serpentine belt.

15. Connect the negative battery cable and perform Idle Learn procedure.

Timing Gear Cover

♦ SEE FIGS. 60 to 64

REMOVAL & INSTALLATION

✱✱✱ CAUTION

When draining the coolant, keep in mind that cats and dogs are attracted by the ethylene glycol antifreeze, and are quite likely to drink any that is left in an uncovered container or in puddles on the ground. This will prove fatal in sufficient quantity. Always drain the coolant into a sealable container. Coolant should be reused unless it is contaminated or several years old.　The EPA warns that prolonged contact with used engine oil may cause a number of skin disorders, including cancer! You should make every effort to minimize your exposure to used engine oil. Protective gloves should be worn when changing the

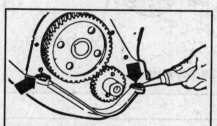

Fig. 60 Apply sealant where shown — 2.5L engine

oil. Wash your hands and any other exposed skin areas as soon as possible after exposure to used engine oil. Soap and water, or waterless hand cleaner should be used.

2.5L Engine

1. Relieve the pressure in the fuel system before disconnecting any fuel line connections.

2. Disconnect the negative battery cable.

3. Remove the inner fender splash shield. Remove the crankshaft pulley.

4. Remove the alternator lower bracket and the front engine mounts.

5. Using a floor jack, raise the engine.

6. Remove the engine mount mounting bracket-to-cylinder block bolts. Remove the bracket and mount as an assembly.

7. Remove the oil pan-to-front cover screws and front cover-to-block screws.

8. Pull the cover slightly forward, just enough to allow cutting of the oil pan front seal flush with the block on both sides.

9. Remove the front cover and attached portion of the pan seal.

10. Clean the gasket surfaces thoroughly.

To install:

11. Cut the tabs from the new oil pan front seal.

12. Install the seal on the front cover pressing the tips into the holes provided.

13. Coat the new gasket with sealer and position it on the front cover.

14. Apply a 1/8 in. (3mm) bead of silicone sealer to the joint formed at the oil pan and stock.

15. Align the front cover seal with a centering tool and install the front cover. Tighten the screws. Install the pulley and connect the battery negative cable.

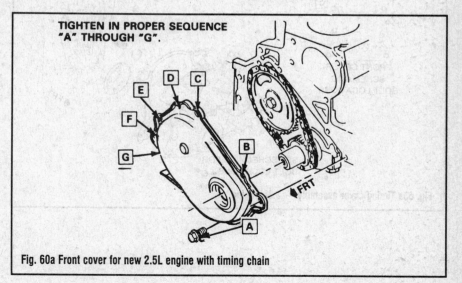

TIGHTEN IN PROPER SEQUENCE "A" THROUGH "G".

Fig. 60a Front cover for new 2.5L engine with timing chain

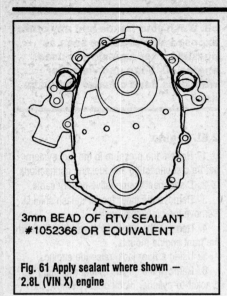

3mm BEAD OF RTV SEALANT
#1052366 OR EQUIVALENT

Fig. 61 Apply sealant where shown —
2.8L (VIN X) engine

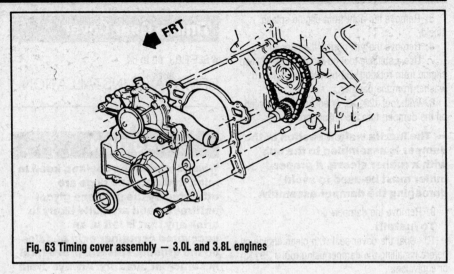

Fig. 63 Timing cover assembly — 3.0L and 3.8L engines

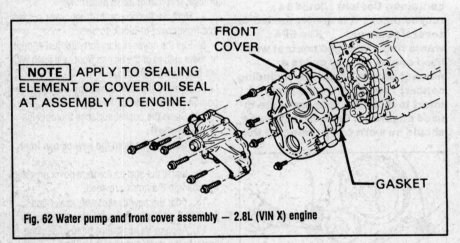

NOTE APPLY TO SEALING
ELEMENT OF COVER OIL SEAL
AT ASSEMBLY TO ENGINE.

FRONT
COVER

GASKET

Fig. 62 Water pump and front cover assembly — 2.8L (VIN X) engine

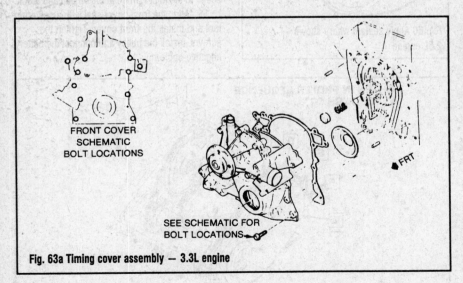

FRONT COVER
SCHEMATIC
BOLT LOCATIONS

SEE SCHEMATIC FOR
BOLT LOCATIONS

Fig. 63a Timing cover assembly — 3.3L engine

2.8L and 3.1L Engine

> ❄ **CAUTION**
>
> **The engines use a harmonic balancer. Breakage may occur as the balancer is hammered back onto the crankshaft. A press or special installation tool is necessary.**

1. Relieve the pressure in the fuel system before disconnecting any fuel line connections. Disconnect the negative battery cable.
2. Drain the cooling system.
3. Remove the serpentine belt and tensioner.
4. Remove the alternator and power steering pump. Locate and support these accessories to the side, remove the AIR pump and hoses, as needed.
5. Remove the A/C compressor without disconnecting any air conditioning lines and lay it aside. If equipped, remove the A.I.R. pump. Raise and support the vehicle safely.
6. Remove the inner splash shield. Remove the torsion damper using tool J–24420–B or equivalent.
7. Remove the flywheel cover at the transaxle and starter.
8. Remove the serpentine belt idler pulley.

➡ **The outer ring (weight) of the harmonic balancer is bonded to the hub with rubber. The balancer must be removed with a puller which acts on the inner hub only. Pulling on the outer portion of the balancer will break the rubber bond or destroy the tuning of the torsional damper.**

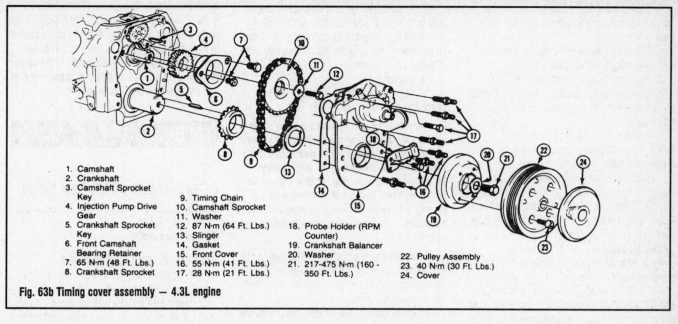

1. Camshaft
2. Crankshaft
3. Camshaft Sprocket Key
4. Injection Pump Drive Gear
5. Crankshaft Sprocket Key
6. Front Camshaft Bearing Retainer
7. 65 N·m (48 Ft. Lbs.)
8. Crankshaft Sprocket
9. Timing Chain
10. Camshaft Sprocket
11. Washer
12. 87 N·m (64 Ft. Lbs.)
13. Slinger
14. Gasket
15. Front Cover
16. 55 N·m (41 Ft. Lbs.)
17. 28 N·m (21 Ft. Lbs.)
18. Probe Holder (RPM Counter)
19. Crankshaft Balancer
20. Washer
21. 217-475 N·m (160 - 350 Ft. Lbs.)
22. Pulley Assembly
23. 40 N·m (30 Ft. Lbs.)
24. Cover

Fig. 63b Timing cover assembly — 4.3L engine

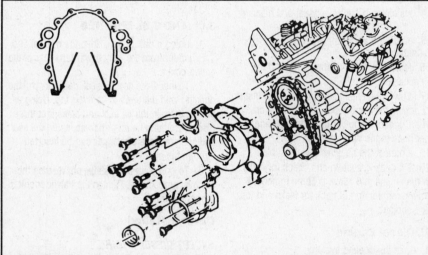

Fig. 64 Timing cover assembly, apply sealant where shown — 2.8L (VIN W) and 3.1L (VIN T) engines

9. Drain the engine oil. Remove the oil pan and lower front cover bolts.

10. Lower the vehicle.

11. Remove the radiator hose at the water pump. Remove the heater hose at fill pipe.

12. Remove the bypass hose and overflow hoses. Remove the canister purge hose.

13. Remove the upper front cover retaining bolts and remove the front cover.

14. After removing the timing cover, pry oil seal from front of cover. Lubricate the seal lip and install new lip seal with lip, open side of seal, facing toward the cylinder block. Carefully drive or press seal into place.

To Install:

15. Clean the mating surfaces of the front cover and cylinder block.

16. Install a new gasket. Make sure not to damage the sealing surfaces. Apply sealer 1052080 or equivalent, to the sealing surface of the front cover.

17. Position the front cover on the engine block and install the upper cover bolt.

18. Raise and safely support the vehicle. Install the oil pan and lower cover bolts.

19. Install the serpentine belt idler pulley.

20. Install the flywheel cover to the transaxle. Install the starter.

21. Install the torsion damper. Install the inner splash shield.

22. Lower the vehicle.

23. Install the bypass hose and overflow hoses. Install the canister purge hose.

24. Connect the radiator hose to the water pump. Connect the heater hose to fill pipe.

25. Install the alternator and power steering pump.

26. Install the tensioner serpentine belt.

27. Connect the negative battery cable.

3.0L Engine

1. Drain the cooling system.

2. Disconnect the radiator hoses and the heater hose at the water pump.

3. Remove the water pump pulley and all drive belts. Remove the front engine mount-to-cradle bolts and raise the engine.

4. Remove the alternator and brackets.

5. Remove the distributor. Remove the front and using a puller, remove the balancer.

6. Remove the balancer bolt and washer, and using a puller, remove the balancer.

7. Remove the cover-to-block bolts. Remove the two oil pan-to-cover bolts.

8. Remove the cover and gasket.

9. Installation is the reverse of removal. Always use a new gasket coated with sealer. Remove the oil pump cover and pack the area around the gears with petroleum jelly so that no air space is left within the pump. Apply sealer to the cover bolt threads.

3.3L Engine

1. Relieve the pressure in the fuel system before disconnecting any fuel line connections. Disconnect the negative battery cable.

2. Drain the cooling system.

3. Remove the serpentine belt.

4. Remove the heater pipes. Remove the coolant bypass hose and lower radiator hose from cover.

5. Raise and support the vehicle safely.

6. Remove the inner splash shield.

7. Remove the crankshaft balancer.

8. Disconnect all electrical connectors at the camshaft sensor, crankshaft sensor and oil pressure sender.

9. Remove the oil pan-to-front cover retaining bolts, front cover retaining bolts and remove the front cover.

10. After removing the timing cover, pry oil seal from front of cover. Lubricate the seal lip and install new lip seal with lip, open side of seal, facing toward the cylinder block. Carefully drive or press seal into place.

To install:

11. Clean the mating surfaces of the front cover and cylinder block.

12. Install a new gasket on the cylinder block. Install the front cover. Apply sealer to the threads of the cover retaining bolts and secure the cover. Tighten the bolts to 22 ft. lbs. (30 Nm).

13. Install the oil pan-to-front cover bolts. Tighten the bolts to 88 inch lbs. (10 Nm).

14. Reconnect the camshaft sensor, crankshaft sensor and oil pressure sender electrical connectors. Adjust the crankshaft sensor using tool J–37087 or equivalent.

15. Install the crankshaft balancer.

16. Install the inner splash shield.

17. Lower the vehicle.

18. Install the heater pipes. Install the coolant bypass hose and lower radiator hose from cover.

19. Install the serpentine belt.

20. Connect the negative battery cable.

21. Fill cooling system and check for leaks. Start the engine and allow to come to normal operating temperature. Recheck for leaks. Top-up coolant.

3.8L Engine

1. Relieve the pressure in the fuel system before disconnecting any fuel line connections. Disconnect the negative battery cable.

2. Drain the cooling system.

3. Disconnect the lower radiator hose and the heater hose from the water pump.

4. Remove the 2 nuts from the front engine mount from the cradle and raise the engine using a suitable lifting device.

5. Remove the water pump pulley and the serpentine belt.

6. Remove the alternator and brackets.

7. Remove the balancer bolt and washer. Using a puller, remove the balancer.

8. Remove the cover-to-block bolts. Remove the 2 oil pan-to-cover bolts.

9. Remove the cover and gasket.

10. After removing the timing cover, pry oil seal from front of cover. Lubricate the seal lip and install new lip seal with lip, open side of seal, facing toward the cylinder block. Carefully drive or press seal into place.

To install:

11. Clean the mating surfaces of the front cover and cylinder block.

➡ **Remove the oil pump cover and pack the space around the oil pump gears completely with petroleum jelly. There must be no air space left inside the pump. If the pump is not packed, it may not begin to pump oil as soon as the engine is started and engine damage may result.**

12. Install a new gasket to the oil pan and cylinder block. Install the front cover. Apply sealer to the threads of the cover retaining bolts and secure the cover.

13. Install the cover-to-block bolts. Install the 2 oil pan-to-cover bolts.

14. Install the balancer, washer and balancer bolt.

15. Install the alternator brackets and install the alternator.

16. Install the water pump pulley and the serpentine belt.

17. Lower the engine into position and install the 2 nuts to the front engine mount at the cradle.

18. Connect the lower radiator hose and the heater hose to the water pump.

19. Connect the negative battery cable.

20. Fill cooling system and check for leaks. Start the engine and allow to come to normal operating temperature. Check for leaks and top off the coolant.

4.3L Diesel Engine

1. Drain the cooling system.

2. Disconnect the radiator hoses and the heater hoses at the water pump. Disconnect the heater outlet pipe at the manifold.

3. Disconnect the power steering pump, vacuum pump, belt tensioner, air conditioning compressor and alternator brackets.

✳✳ CAUTION

Do not disconnect any refrigerant lines.

---

4. Remove the crankshaft balancer using a puller.

5. Unbolt and remove the front cover and gasket.

6. Installation is the reverse of removal. Grind a chamfer on the end of each dowel pin to aid in cover installation. Trim 1/8 in. (3mm) from the ends of the new front pan seal. Apply RTV sealer to the oil pan seal retainer. After the cover gasket is in place, apply sealer to the junction of the pan, gasket and block. When installing the cover, rotate it right and left while guiding the pan seal into place with a small screwdriver.

Oil Seal

REMOVAL & INSTALLATION

Cover Removed

EXCEPT 3.0L AND 3.8L ENGINES

1. After removing the timing cover, pry oil seal out of front of cover.

2. Install new lip seal with lip (open side of seal) inside and drive or press seal carefully into place.

3.0L AND 3.8L ENGINES

1. Using a drift punch, drive the oil seal and the shedder from the front toward the rear of the timing cover.

2. To install the new oil seal, coil it around the opening with the ends toward the top. Using a punch, drive in the oil seal and stake it at three places. Rotate a hammer handle inside the seal until the crankshaft balancer can be inserted through the opening.

3. To complete the installation, reverse the removal procedures. Tighten the balancer bolt to proper torque.

Cover Installed

EXCEPT DIESEL ENGINE

The oil seal may be removed from the timing cover without removing the cover. To do this, remove the damper pulley and pry the oil seal from the timing cover, using a small pry bar.

Place a Seal Installation Tool J–34995 on the crankshaft (to prevent damaging the seal) when installing the new oil seal or the front cover. To install the new oil seal, place the seal's open end toward the inside of the cover and drive it into cover. Tighten the damper pulley bolt to proper torque.

4.3L DIESEL ENGINE

1. Refer to the Timing Cover, Removal and Installation procedures in the section and remove the crankshaft balancer from the crankshaft.

2. Using tools J–1859–03 and J–23129, press the oil seal from the timing cover.

3. Lubricate the seal lip with engine oil and the outer edge with sealant No. 1050026. Using tool J–29659, press the new oil seal into the timing cover until it seats.

4. To complete the installation, reverse the removal procedures. Torque the crankshaft balancer bolt to 203–350 ft. lbs.

Timing Gear and/or Chain

♦ SEE FIGS. 65 to 69

REMOVAL & INSTALLATION

2.5L Engine

➡ **On the 2.5L engine that does not use a timing chain, the camshaft gear is press fitted on the camshaft. If replacement of the camshaft gear is necessary, the engine must be removed from the vehicle and the camshaft and gear removed from the engine.**

GEAR DRIVEN

1. Relieve the pressure in the fuel system before disconnecting any fuel line connections.
2. Disconnect the negative battery cable.
3. Remove the engine from the vehicle.
4. Remove the camshaft and gear assembly from the engine block.
5. Using an arbor press and adapter, remove the gear from the camshaft. Position the thrust plate to avoid damage by interference with the Woodruff® key as the gear is removed.

To install:

6. Support the camshaft at the back of the front journal in the arbor press using press plate adapters.
7. Position the spacer ring thrust plate over the end of the shaft and Woodruff® key in keyway.
8. Press the gear on the shaft with the bottom against the spacer ring. Measure the end clearance at the thrust plate. Clearance should be within 0.0015–0.0050 in. (0.0381–1.270mm).
9. If the clearance is less than 0.0015 in. (0.0381mm), replace the spacer ring.
2. 10. If more than 0.0050 in. (1.270mm), make certain the gear is seated properly against the spacer. If the clearance is still excessive, replace the thrust plate.

11. Measure the backlash at position outside the 2 retainer plate access holes and at 2 other areas 90° from these holes. If the backlash is not within specifications, replace the camshaft and crankshaft gears.

12. Lubricate the camshaft journals with a high quality engine oil supplement. Install the camshaft and gear into the engine block.

13. Rotate the camshaft and crankshaft so the timing marks on the gear teeth align. The engine is now in No. 4 cylinder firing position.

14. Install the camshaft thrust plate-to-block screws and tighten to 90 inch lbs. (10 Nm).

15. Install the engine in the vehicle.
16. Connect the negative battery cable.

CHAIN DRIVEN

In some 1990 cars, General Motors started using a camshaft driven by a chain rather than gears. Most of the repair procedures for these newer design engines are the same. The main difference is the procedure needed to service the timing chain. Limited working space still makes service difficult, but the engine no longer needs to be removed to service the chain or gears.

1. Relieve the pressure in the fuel system before disconnecting any fuel line connections. Disconnect the negative battery cable.
2. Remove the crankcase front cover.
3. Place the No. 1 piston at TDC with the

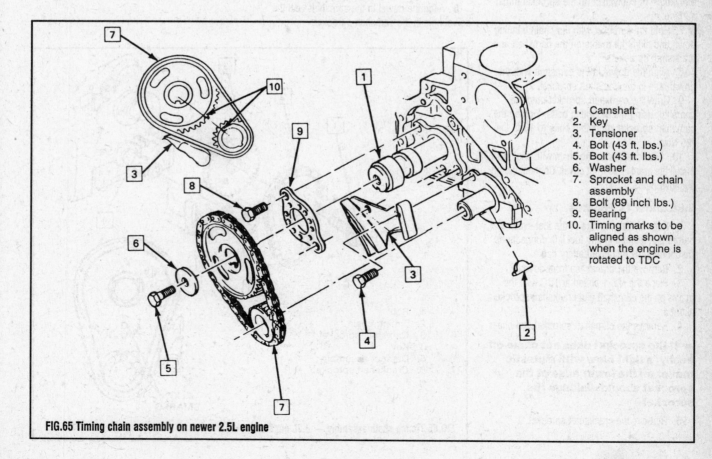

1. Camshaft
2. Key
3. Tensioner
4. Bolt (43 ft. lbs.)
5. Bolt (43 ft. lbs.)
6. Washer
7. Sprocket and chain assembly
8. Bolt (89 inch lbs.)
9. Bearing
10. Timing marks to be aligned as shown when the engine is rotated to TDC

FIG. 65 Timing chain assembly on newer 2.5L engine

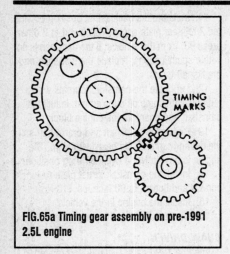

FIG.65a Timing gear assembly on pre-1991 2.5L engine

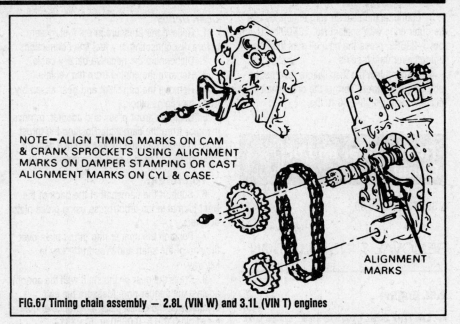

NOTE—ALIGN TIMING MARKS ON CAM & CRANK SPROCKETS USING ALIGNMENT MARKS ON DAMPER STAMPING OR CAST ALIGNMENT MARKS ON CYL & CASE.

ALIGNMENT MARKS

FIG.67 Timing chain assembly — 2.8L (VIN W) and 3.1L (VIN T) engines

marks on the camshaft and crankshaft sprockets aligned.

4. Remove the camshaft sprocket and chain.

➡ **If the sprocket does not come off easily, a light blow with a plastic mallet on the lower edge of the sprocket should dislodge the sprocket.**

5. Remove the crankshaft sprocket.

To install:

6. Install the crankshaft sprocket. Apply Molykote® or equivalent, to the sprocket thrust surface.

7. Hold the sprocket with the chain hanging down and align the marks on the camshaft and crankshaft sprockets.

8. Align the dowel in the camshaft with the dowel hole in the camshaft sprocket.

9. Draw the camshaft sprocket onto the camshaft using the mounting bolts. Tighten the camshaft sprocket mounting bolts to 18 ft. lbs. (25 Nm).

10. Lubricate the timing chain with engine oil. Install the crankcase front cover. Connect battery negative cable.

2.8L and 3.1L Engines

1. Relieve the pressure in the fuel system before disconnecting any fuel line connections. Disconnect the negative battery cable.

2. Remove the crankcase front cover.

3. Place the No. 1 piston at TDC with the marks on the camshaft and crankshaft sprockets aligned.

4. Remove the camshaft sprocket and chain.

➡ **If the sprocket does not come off easily, a light blow with a plastic mallet on the lower edge of the sprocket should dislodge the sprocket.**

5. Remove the crankshaft sprocket.

To install:

6. Install the crankshaft sprocket. Apply Molykote® or equivalent, to the sprocket thrust surface.

7. Hold the sprocket with the chain hanging down and align the marks on the camshaft and crankshaft sprockets.

8. Align the dowel in the camshaft with the dowel hole in the camshaft sprocket.

9. Draw the camshaft sprocket onto the camshaft using the mounting bolts. Tighten the camshaft sprocket mounting bolts to 18 ft. lbs. (25 Nm).

10. Lubricate the timing chain with engine oil. Install the crankcase front cover. Connect battery negative cable.

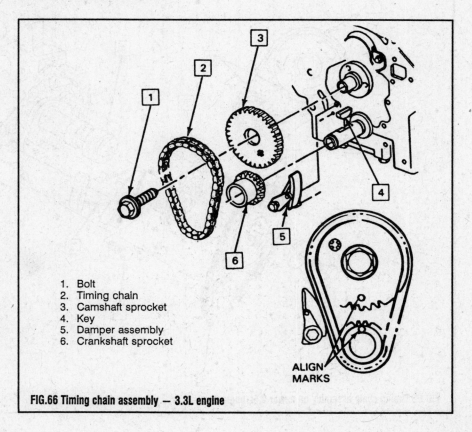

1. Bolt
2. Timing chain
3. Camshaft sprocket
4. Key
5. Damper assembly
6. Crankshaft sprocket

ALIGN MARKS

FIG.66 Timing chain assembly — 3.3L engine

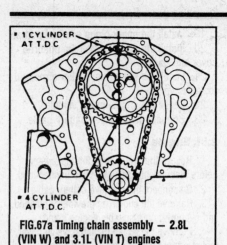

FIG.67a Timing chain assembly — 2.8L (VIN W) and 3.1L (VIN T) engines

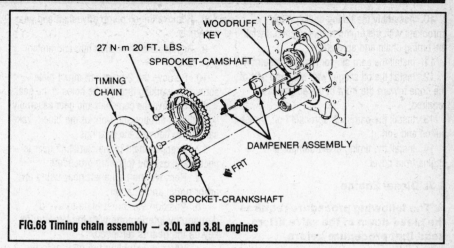

FIG.68 Timing chain assembly — 3.0L and 3.8L engines

3.0L Engine

1. Remove the timing chain cover.
2. Turn the crankshaft so that the timing marks are aligned.
3. Remove the crankshaft oil slinger.
4. Remove the camshaft sprocket bolts.
5. Use two prybars to alternately pry the camshaft and crankshaft sprocket free along with the chain.
6. Installation is the reverse of removal. If the engine was turned, make sure that the #1 cylinder is at TDC.

3.3L Engine

1. Relieve the pressure in the fuel system before disconnecting any fuel line connections. Disconnect the negative battery cable.

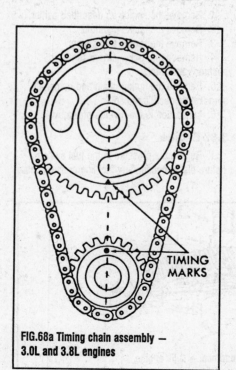

FIG.68a Timing chain assembly — 3.0L and 3.8L engines

2. Remove the crankcase front cover and camshaft thrust bearing.
3. Turn the crankshaft so the timing marks are aligned.
4. Remove the timing chain damper and camshaft sprocket bolts.
5. Remove the camshaft sprocket and chain. Remove the crankshaft sprocket.

To Install:

6. Make sure the crankshaft is positioned so No. 1 piston is at TDC on compression stroke.
7. Rotate the camshaft with the sprocket temporarily installed, so the timing mark is straight down.
8. Assembly the timing chain on the sprockets with the timing marks aligned. Install the timing chain and sprocket.
9. Install the camshaft sprocket bolts. Torque the bolts to 27 ft. lbs. (37 Nm).
10. Install the timing chain damper and engine front cover. Connect battery negative cable.

3.8L Engine

1. Relieve the pressure in the fuel system before disconnecting any fuel line connections. Disconnect the negative battery cable.
2. Remove the crankcase front cover.
3. Turn the crankshaft so the timing marks are aligned.
4. Remove the crankshaft oil slinger, as required.
5. Remove the camshaft sprocket bolts.
6. Remove the cam sensor magnet assembly.
7. Use 2 prybars to alternately pry the camshaft and crankshaft sprocket free along with the chain.

To Install:

8. Make sure the crankshaft is positioned so No. 1 piston is at TDC.
9. Rotate the camshaft with the sprocket temporarily installed, so the timing mark is straight down.

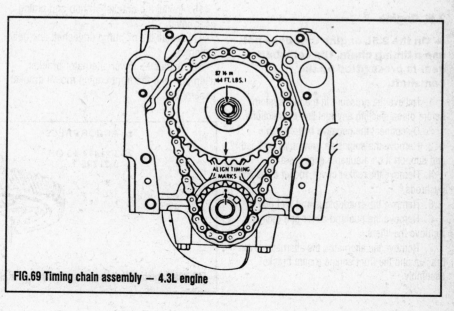

FIG.69 Timing chain assembly — 4.3L engine

10. Assembly the timing chain on the sprockets with the timing marks aligned. Install the timing chain and sprocket.

11. Install the cam sensor magnet assembly.

12. Install the oil slinger with the large part of the cone toward the front of the engine, as required.

13. Install the camshaft sprocket bolt, thrust button and spring.

14. Install the timing chain damper and engine front cover.

4.3L Diesel Engine

➡ **The following procedure requires the bleed-down of the valve lifters. Read that procedure before proceeding.**

1. Remove the front cover.

2. Loosen all the rocker arms. See Rocker Arm Removal and Installation.

3. Remove the crankshaft oil slinger.

4. Remove the camshaft sprocket bolt.

5. Using two prybars, work the camshaft and crankshaft sprockets alternately off their shafts along with the chain. It may be necessary to remove the crankshaft sprocket with a puller.

6. Installation is the reverse of removal. If the engine was turned, make sure that the #1 piston is at TDC. Bleed the lifters following the procedure under Diesel Engine Valve Lifter Bleed-Down.

Camshaft

REMOVAL & INSTALLATION

2.5L Engine

➡ **On the 2.5L engine that does not use a timing chain, the camshaft gear is press fitted on the camshaft.**

1. Relieve the pressure in the fuel system before disconnecting any fuel line connections.

2. Disconnect the negative battery cable.

3. Remove the engine as previously outlined, and support it on a suitable engine stand.

4. Remove the rocker cover, rocker arms and pushrods.

5. Remove the spark plugs and fuel pump.

6. Remove the pushrod cover and gasket. Remove the lifters.

7. Remove the alternator, the alternator lower bracket and the front engine mount bracket assembly.

8. Remove the oil pump driveshaft and gear assembly.

9. Remove the crankshaft hub and timing gear cover.

10. Remove the 2 camshaft thrust plate screws by working through the holes in the gear.

11. Remove the camshaft and gear assembly by pulling it through the front of the block. Take care not to damage the bearings.

12. If replacement of the camshaft gear is necessary, use the following procedure:

a. Remove the camshaft gear using an arbor press and adapter.

b. Position the thrust plate to avoid damage by interference with the Woodruff® key as the gear is removed.

c. When assembling the gear onto the camshaft, support the camshaft at the back of the front journal in the arbor press using press plate adapters.

d. Press the gear on the shaft until it bottoms against the spacer ring.

e. Measure the end clearance of the thrust plate. End clearance should be 0.0015–0.0050 in. (0.0381–0.1270mm).

f. If clearance is less than 0.0015 in. (0.0381mm) , replace the spacer ring.

g. If clearance is more than 0.0050 in. (0.127mm), replace the thrust plate.

To install:

13. Lubricate the camshaft journals with a high quality engine oil supplement and carefully install the camshaft and gear into the cylinder block.

14. Rotate the camshaft and crankshaft so the timing marks on the gear teeth align. The engine is now in No. 4 cylinder firing position.

15. Install the camshaft thrust plate-to-block screw. Torque the screw to 90 inch lbs. (10 Nm).

16. Install the crankshaft hub and timing gear cover.

17. Install the oil pump driveshaft and gear assembly.

18. Install the lower alternator bracket, alternator and the front engine mount bracket assembly.

19. Install the spark plugs and fuel pump.

20. Install the lifters. Install the pushrod cover and gasket.

21. Install the pushrods, rocker arms and rocker cover.

22. Install the engine in the vehicle.

23. Connect the negative battery cable.

2.8L Engine

1. Relieve the pressure in the fuel system before disconnecting any fuel line connections.

2. Disconnect the negative battery cable.

3. Remove the engine as previously outlined, and support it on a suitable engine stand.

4. Remove the intake manifold, valve cover, rocker arms, pushrods and valve lifters.

5. Remove the crankshaft balancer and front cover.

6. Remove the timing chain and sprockets.

7. Carefully remove the camshaft. Avoid marring the camshaft bearing surfaces.

To install:

8. Coat the camshaft with lubricant 1052365 or equivalent, and install the camshaft.

9. Install the timing chain and sprocket.

10. Install the camshaft thrust button and front cover.

11. Install the crankshaft balancer.

12. Install the intake manifold, valve cover, rocker arms, pushrods and valve lifters.

13. Install the engine in the vehicle.

14. Connect the negative battery cable.

15. Adjust the valves, as required.

3.0L Engine

1. Remove the engine as described earlier.

2. Remove the intake manifold.

3. Remove the rocker arm covers.

4. Remove the rocker arm assemblies, pushrods and lifters.

5. Remove the timing chain and camshaft sprocket as described earlier.

6. Installation is the reverse of removal.

3.8L Engine

1. Relieve the pressure in the fuel system before disconnecting any fuel line connections.

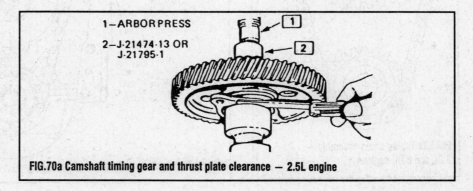

1—ARBOR PRESS

2—J-21474-13 OR J-21795-1

FIG.70a Camshaft timing gear and thrust plate clearance — 2.5L engine

2. Disconnect the negative battery cable.

3. Remove the engine as previously outlined, and support it on a suitable engine stand.

4. Remove the intake manifold.

5. Remove the rocker arm covers.

6. Remove the rocker arm assemblies, pushrods and lifters.

7. Remove the timing chain cover.

➡ **Align the timing marks of the camshaft and crankshaft sprockets to avoid burring the camshaft journals by the crankshaft.**

8. Remove the timing chain, camshaft sensor magnet assembly and sprockets.

To install:

9. Coat the camshaft with lubricant 1052365 or equivalent, and install the camshaft.

10. Install the timing chain, camshaft sensor magnet assembly and sprockets.

11. Install the camshaft thrust button and front cover.

12. Complete installation by reversing the removal procedure. Connect battery negative cable.

4.3L Diesel Engine

➡ **This procedure requires the removal, disassembly, cleaning, reassembly and bleed-down of all the valve lifters. Read that procedure, described earlier, before proceeding.**

1. Remove the engine as described earlier.

2. Remove the intake manifold.

3. Remove the oil pump drive assembly.

4. Remove the timing chain cover.

5. Align the timing marks.

6. Remove the rocker arms, pushrods and lifters, keeping them in order for reassembly.

7. Remove the timing chain and camshaft lifters, keeping them in order for reassembly.

8. Remove the camshaft bearing retainer.

9. Remove the cam sprocket key.

10. Remove the injection pump drive gear.

11. Remove the injection pump driven gear, intermediate pump adapter and pump adapter. Remove the snapring and selective washer. Remove the driven gear and spring.

12. Carefully slide the camshaft out of the block.

13. If the camshaft bearings are being replaced, you'll have to remove the oil pan.

14. Installation is the reverse of removal. Perform the complete valve lifter bleed-down procedure mentioned earlier.

Camshaft Bearings

REMOVAL & INSTALLATION

2.5L Engine

1. Remove the engine from the vehicle as previously outlined.

2. Remove the camshaft from the engine as previously outlined.

3. Unbolt and remove the engine flywheel.

4. Drive the rear camshaft expansion plug out of the engine block from the inside.

5. Using a camshaft bearing service tool, J–21473–1 (1982–84) or J–33049 (1985 and later), drive the front camshaft bearing towards the rear and the rear bearing towards the front.

6. Install the appropriate extension tool J–21054–1 on the service tool and drive the center bearing out towards the rear.

7. Drive all of the new bearings into place in the opposite direction of which they were removed, making sure to align the oil holes of each bearing with each of the feed holes in the engine block bores.

➡ **The front camshaft bearing must be driven approximately $\frac{1}{8}$ in. (3mm) behind the front of the cylinder block to uncover the oil hole to the timing gear oiling nozzle.**

8. Install the camshaft into the engine then reinstall the engine as previously outlined.

2.8L Engine

Camshaft bearings can be replaced with engine completely or partially disassembled. To replace bearings without complete disassembly remove the camshaft and crankshaft leaving cylinder heads attached and pistons in place. Before removing crankshaft, tape threads of connecting rod bolts to prevent damage to crankshaft. Fasten connecting rods against sides of engine so they will not be in the way while replacing camshaft bearings.

1. Remove the camshaft rear cover.

2. Using Tool J–6098 (1982–84) or J–33049 (1985–88 and later) or its equivalent, with nut and thrust washer installed to end of threads, index pilot in camshaft front bearing and install puller screw through pilot.

3. Install remover and installer tool with shoulder toward bearing, making sure a sufficient amount of threads are engaged.

4. Using two wrenches, hold puller screw while turning nut. When bearing has been pulled from bore, remove remover and installer tool and bearing from puller screws.

5. Remove remaining bearings (except front and rear) in the same manner. It will be necessary to index pilot in camshaft rear bearing to remove the rear intermediate bearing.

6. Assemble remover and installer tool on driver handle and remove camshaft front and rear bearings by driving towards center of cylinder block.

The camshaft front and rear bearings should be installed first. These bearings will act as guides for the pilot and center the remaining bearings being pulled into place.

1. Assemble remover and installer tool on driver handle and install camshaft front and rear bearings by driving towards center of cylinder block.

2. Using Tool Set J–6098 (1982–84) or J–33049 (1985 and later), or its equivalent with nut then thrust washer installed to end of threads, index pilot in camshaft front bearing and install puller screw through pilot.

3. Index camshaft bearing in bore (with oil hole aligned as outlined below), then install remover and installer tool on puller screw with shoulder toward bearing.

• The rear and intermediate bearing oil holes must be aligned at 2:30 o'clock.

• The front bearing oil holes must be aligned at 1:00 and 2:30 o'clock (two holes).

4. Using two wrenches, hold puller screw while turning nut. After bearing has been pulled into bore, remove the remover and installer tool from puller screw and check alignment of oil hole in camshaft bearing.

5. Install remaining bearings in the same

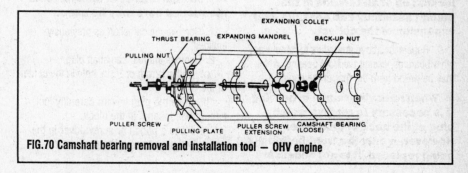

FIG.70 Camshaft bearing removal and installation tool — OHV engine

manner. It will be necessary to index pilot in the camshaft rear bearing to install the rear intermediate bearing. Clean the rear cover mating surfaces and bolt holes then apply a $\frac{1}{8}$ in. (3mm) bead of R.T.V. to the cover. Install the cover.

3.1L and 3.3L Engine

1. Remove the engine from the vehicle as previously outlined.
2. Remove the camshaft from the engine as previously outlined.
3. Remove the camshaft rear plug.
4. Assembly the removal tool. Using care and follow proper tool instructions remove camshaft bearings.
5. Select the proper pilot, nut and thrust washer.
6. Assemble to J–33–49. Make certain the puller engages a sufficient number of threads and pull the bearing.
7. Install the appropriate extension tool J–21054–1 on the service tool and drive the center bearing out towards the rear.

3.0L and 3.8L Engines

Care must be exercised during bearing removal and installation, not to damage bearings that are not being replaced.
1. Remove camshaft as previously outlined.
2. Assemble puller screw to required length.
3. Select proper size expanding collect and back-up nut.
4. Install expanding collect on expanding mandrel. Install back-up nut.
5. Insert this assembly into camshaft bearing to be removed. Tighten back-up nut to expand collect to fit I.D. of bearing.
6. Thread end of puller screw assembly into end of expanding mandrel and collect assembly.
7. Install pulling plate, thrust bearing, and pulling nut on threaded end of puller screw.
8. Bearing can then be removed by turning pulling nut.

➡ **Make certain to grip the $\frac{5}{8}$ in. hex end of the puller screw with a wrench to keep it from rotating when the pulling nut is turned. Failure to do this will result in the locking up of all threads in the pulling assembly and possible over expansion of the collect.**

9. Repeat the above procedure to remove any other bearings, except the front bearing, which may be pulled from the rear of the engine.

➡ **When removing rear cam bearing, it is necessary to remove welch plug at the back of cam bore. However, if only the front bearing is being replaced, it is not necessary**

to remove the engine or welch plug. The front bearing can be removed by using a spacer between the pulling plate and the cylinder block.

To install the bearings:
10. Assemble puller screw to required length.
11. Select proper size expanding collect and back-up nut.
12. Install expanding collect on expanding mandrel.
13. Install back-up nut.
14. Place new camshaft bearing on collect and GENTLY hand tighten back-up nut to expand collect to fit bearing. Do not over tighten back-up nut. A loose sliding fit between collect and bearing surface is adequate. This will provide just enough clearance to allow for the collapse which will occur when the new bearing is pulled into the engine block.
15. Slide mandrel assembly and bearing into bearing bore as far as it will go without force.
16. Thread end of puller screw onto the end of the mandrel. Make certain to align oil holes in bearing and block properly. One of the collect separation lines may be used as a reference point.
17. Install pulling plate, thrust bearing and pulling nut on threaded end of puller screw.
18. Install bearing in the same manner as described in Steps 8 and 9 under Bearing Removal.

➡ **When installing rear cam bearing, install new welch plug at back of cam bore. Coat O.D. of plug with non-hardening sealer before installation.**

4.3L Diesel Engine

The front camshaft bearing may be replaced separately but numbers 2, 3 and 4 must be replaced as a completed set. This is because it is necessary to remove the forward bearings to gain access to the rearward bearings.

Camshaft Bearing Remover and Installer Set BT–6409 and camshaft bearing pilot spacer BT–7817 are available tools. This set can be used to remove can bearings. To replace bearings with engine in car, proceed as follows:

➡ **The equivalents of special tools mentioned here may be used.**

1. Remove the camshaft as previously outlined.
2. Remove the rear camshaft plug:
   a. Drill a 12mm or $\frac{1}{2}$ in. hole in the center of the plug.
   b. Drive the plug inward carefully just enough to loosen it in the block.
   c. Place a punch or screwdriver in the drilled hole and remove the plug.

d. Remove all the metal particles that entered the block and all traces of the old sealer.

➡ **Failure to remove the metal particles will result in engine damage.**

3. Front bearing removal and installation:
   a. To remove the front (No. 1) camshaft bearing, support the retainer in a vise and drive the bearing out using BT–6409–2 with driver BT–6409–7.
   b. To install the bearing use the same tools but make certain that the oil hole in the bearing is in alignment with the oil hole in the retainer.
4. #2, 3, & 4 bearing removal and installation:
   a. Install tool BT–6409–2 on handle BT–6409–7 and drive out No. 2 cam bearing.
   b. Remove the No. 3 bearing in the same manner using BT–6409–3 on handle BT–6409–7.
   c. Remove the No. 4 bearing using puller BT–6409–8.

To aid aligning the bearings with the oil passages, place each bearing in the front of the bore with tapered edge toward the block and align the oil hole in the bearing with the center of the oil slot in the bore. Mark bottom of bearing. When installing the bearings, the mark will act as a guide.

Using pilot BT–6409–1 will aid in installing the No. 4 and 3 bearings by preventing cocking of the bearings.
   d. Install No. 4 bearing using tool BT–6409–4.

➡ **Drive the bearing in carefully, stopping to make certain that the oil holes are in alignment otherwise it is possible to drive the bearing in beyond the oil passage opening. Use a piece of $\frac{3}{32}$ in. (2.4mm) brass rod with a 90° bend at the end to check the oil hole opening.**

   e. Install the No. 3 bearing using tool BT–6409–3 until the oil holes are in alignment.
   f. Install the No. 2 bearing using tool BT–6409–2 carefully until the oil holes are in alignment.
   g. Use a piece of $\frac{3}{32}$ in. (2.4mm) brass rod with a 90° bend at the end to check all oil hole openings. Wire must enter hole or the bearing will not receive sufficient lubrication.
5. Install the rear plug:
   a. Coat the block with R.T.V. sealer.
   b. Drive the plug into the block until it is flush or no more than 0.5mm (0.020 in.) concave.

c. Install the camshaft and engine assembly. Road test the car and inspect for leaks.

CHECKING CAMSHAFT

Degrease the camshaft, using solvent, and clean out all oil holes. Visually inspect cam lobes and bearing journals for excessive wear. If a lobe is questionable, check all lobes as indicated below. If a journal or lobe is worn, the camshaft must be reground or replaced.

➡ **If a journal is worn, there is a good chance that the bushings are worn. If lobes and journals appear intact, place the front and rear journals in V-blocks, and rest a dial indicator on the center journal. Rotate the camshaft to check straightness. If deviation exceeds 0.001 in. (0.025mm), replace the camshaft. Check the camshaft lobes with a micrometer, by measuring the lobes from the nose to base and again at 90°. The lift is**

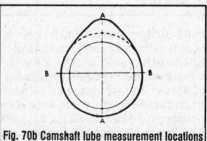

Fig. 70b Camshaft lube measurement locations

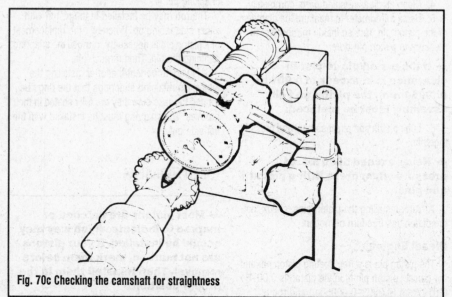

Fig. 70c Checking the camshaft for straightness

determined by subtracting the second measurement from the first. If all exhaust lobes and all intake lobes are not identical, the camshaft must be reground or replaced.

Pistons and Connecting Rods

✳✳ CAUTION

The EPA warns that prolonged contact with used engine oil may cause a number of skin disorders, including cancer! You should make every effort to minimize your exposure to used engine oil. Protective gloves should be worn when changing the oil. Wash your hands and any other exposed skin areas as soon as possible after exposure to used engine oil. Soap and water, or waterless hand cleaner should be used.

REMOVAL

1. Remove the engine assembly from the car, see Engine Removal and Installation.
2. Remove the intake manifold, cylinder head or heads.

3. Remove the oil pan.
4. Remove the oil pump assembly.
5. Stamp the cylinder number on the machined surfaces of the bolt bosses of the connecting rod and cap for identification when reinstalling. If the pistons are to be removed from the connecting rod, mark the cylinder number on the piston with a silver pencil or quick drying paint for proper cylinder identification and cap to rod location. The 2.5L engine is numbered 1–4 from front to back; on the 3.0L, 3.3L, 3.8L and 4.3L diesel V6s, the right (rear) bank is numbered 2–4–6, left (front) bank 1–3–5; the 2.8L and 3.1L engine are numbered 1–3–5 on the right bank, 2–4–6 on the left bank.
6. Examine the cylinder bore above the ring travel. If a ridge exists, remove the ridge with a ridge reamer before attempting to remove the piston and rod assembly.
7. Remove the rod bearing cap and bearing.
8. Install a guide hose over threads of rod bolts. This is to prevent damage to bearing journal and rod bolt threads.

➡ **All caps and rods are matched pairs and must be assembled together. They must also return to their original locations. Match mark all caps to rods, for both location and direction. Installing the caps on the wrong rod or facing the wrong way will cause perminate engine damage.**

9. Remove the rod and piston assembly through the top of the cylinder bore.
10. Remove any other rod and piston assemblies in the same manner, pistons must be marked for proper identification, too. If the piston are to be removed from the rods, mark the cylinder number on the piston with a silver pencil or paint for proper identification.

CLEANING AND INSPECTION

Pistons

Using a piston ring expansion tool, remove the rings from the piston. Removing the rings by any other method usually will damage the rings and could also scratch the piston requiring a new piston.

Clean varnish from piston skirts and pins with a cleaning solvent. DO NOT WIRE BRUSH ANY PART OF THE PISTON. Clean the ring grooves with a groove cleaner and make sure oil ring holes and slots are clean.

Inspect the piston for cracked ring lands, skirts or pin bosses, wavy or worn ring lands, scuffed or damaged skirts, eroded areas at top

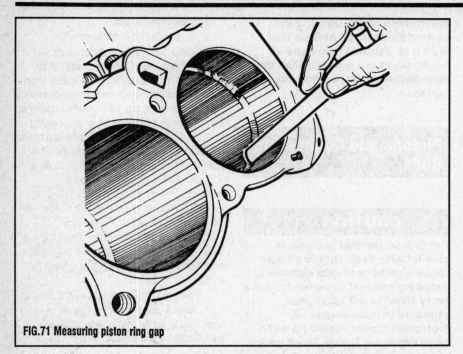

FIG.71 Measuring piston ring gap

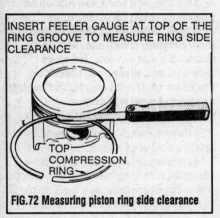

INSERT FEELER GAUGE AT TOP OF THE RING GROOVE TO MEASURE RING SIDE CLEARANCE

TOP COMPRESSION RING

FIG.72 Measuring piston ring side clearance

of the piston. Replace pistons that are damaged or show signs of excessive wear.

Inspect the grooves for nicks or burrs that might cause the rings to hang up.

Measure piston skirt (across center line of piston pin) and check piston clearance.

Connecting Rods

Wash connecting rods in cleaning solvent and dry with compressed air. Check for twisted or bent rods and inspect for nicks or cracks. Replace connecting rods that are damaged.

PISTON PIN REPLACEMENT

Gasoline Engines

Use care at all times when handling and servicing connecting rods and pistons To prevent possible damage to these units, do not clamp rod or piston is vise since they may become distorted. Do not allow pistons to strike against one another, against hard objects or bench surfaces, since distortion of piston contour or nicks in the soft aluminum material may result.

1. Remove piston rings using suitable piston ring remover.

2. Install guide bushing of piston pin removing and installing tool.

3. Install piston and connecting rod assembly on support and place assembly in an arbor press. Press pin out of connecting rod, using the appropriate piston pin tool.

4. Clean all disassembled parts completely.

5. Use a mircometer to measure the diameter of the piston pin. Use an inside mircometer to measure to piston pin bore.

➡ **If the piston pin-to-piston clearance is in excess of 0.001 in. (0.0254mm), the piston and pin assembly must be replaced.**

6. Lube piston and pin assembly and press fit together.

➡ **Never exceed 5000 lbs. of pressure when press fitting piston and pins.**

7. After installing the piston pins, check that the piston has freedom of motion.

Diesel Engines

The piston pin is a free floating piston pin and the correct piston pin fit in the piston is 0.0076–0.0127mm (0.0003–0.0005 in.) and rod is

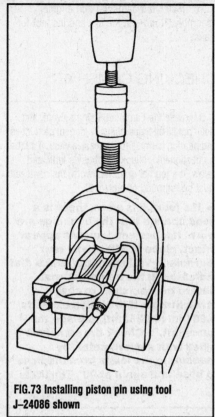

FIG.73 Installing piston pin using tool J–24086 shown

0.0076–0.033mm (0.003–0.0013 in.) loose. If the pin to piston clearance is to the high limit 0.0127–0.033mm (0.005 in. piston or 0.0013 in. rod), the pin can be inserted in the piston or rod with very little hand pressure and will fall through the piston or rod by its own weight. If the clearance is 0.0076mm (0.0003 in.), the pin will not fall through. It is important that the piston and rod pin hole be clean and free of oil when checking pin fit.

The rod may be installed in the piston with either side facing up. Whenever the replacement of a piston pin is necessary, remove the snapring retaining the pin. Then remove pin.

It is very important that after installing the piston pin retaining snaprings that the rings be rotated to make sure they are fully seated in their grooves. The snapring must be installed with the flat side out.

POSITIONING

➡ **Most pistons are notched or marked to indicate which way they should be installed. If your pistons are not marked, mark them before removal. Then reinstall them in the proper position.**

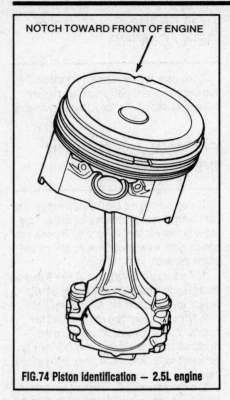

NOTCH TOWARD FRONT OF ENGINE

FIG.74 Piston identification — 2.5L engine

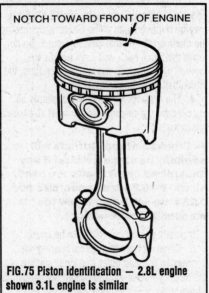

NOTCH TOWARD FRONT OF ENGINE

FIG.75 Piston identification — 2.8L engine shown 3.1L engine is similar

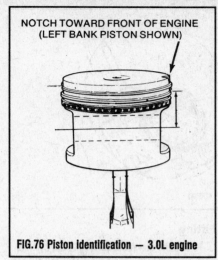

NOTCH TOWARD FRONT OF ENGINE (LEFT BANK PISTON SHOWN)

FIG.76 Piston identification — 3.0L engine

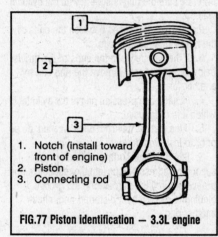

1. Notch (install toward front of engine)
2. Piston
3. Connecting rod

FIG.77 Piston identification — 3.3L engine

MEASURING THE OLD PISTONS

Check used piston to cylinder bore clearance as follows:

1. Measure the cylinder bore diameter with a telescope gage.

2. Measure the piston diameter. When measuring piston for size or taper, measurement must be made with the piston pin removed.

3. Subtract piston diameter from cylinder bore diameter to determine piston-to-bore clearance.

4. Compare piston-to-bore clearance obtained with those clearances recommended. Determine is piston-to-bore clearance is in acceptable range.

5. When measuring taper, the largest reading must be at the bottom of the skirt.

SELECTING NEW PISTONS

1. If the used piston is not acceptable, check service piston sizes and determine if a new piston can be selected. Service pistons are available in standard, high limit and standard 0.254mm (0.010 in.) oversize.

2. Occasionally during the honing operation, the cylinder bore should be thoroughly cleaned and the selected piston checked for correct fit.

3. When finish honing a cylinder bore, the hone should be moved up and down at a sufficient speed to obtain very fine uniform surface finish marks in a cross hatch pattern of approximately 45° to 65° included angle. The finish marks should be clean but not sharp, free from imbedded particles and torn or folded metal.

4. Permanently mark the piston for the cylinder to which it has been fitted and proceed to hone the remaining cylinders.

➡ **Handle pistons with care. Do not attempt to force pistons through cylinders through cylinders until the cylinders have been honed to correct size. Pistons can be distorted through careless handling.**

5. Thoroughly clean the bores with hot water and detergent. Scrub well with a stiff bristle brush and rinse thoroughly with hot water. It is extremely essential that a good cleaning operation be performed. If any of the abrasive material is allowed to remain in the cylinder bores, it will rapidly wear the new rings and cylinder bores. The bores should be swabbed several times with light engine oil and a clean

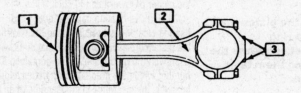

1. Notch on piston towards front of engine Left bank
2. No. 1, 3 and 5 has two bosses on rod towards rear of engine (not shown)
3. Chamfered corners on rod cap towards front of engine Right bank

2. No. 2, 4 and 6 has two bosses on rod towards the front of engine (not shown)
3. Chamfered corners on rod cap towards rear of engine

FIG.78 Piston identification — 3.8L engine

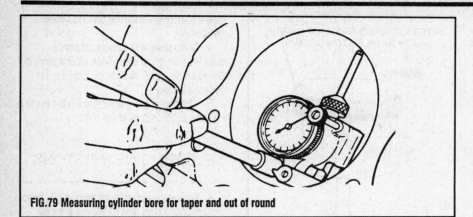

FIG.79 Measuring cylinder bore for taper and out of round

cloth and then wiped with a clean dry cloth. CYLINDERS SHOULD NOT BE CLEANED WITH KEROSENE OR GASOLINE. Clean the remainder of the cylinder block to remove the excess material spread during the honing operation.

CHECKING CYLINDER BORE

Cylinder bore size can be measured with inside micrometers or a cylinder gage. The most wear will occur at the top of the ring travel.

Reconditioned cylinder bores should be held to not more than 0.025mm (0.001 in.) out-of-round and 0.025mm (0.001 in.) taper.

If the cylinder bores are smooth, the cylinder walls should not be deglazed. If the cylinder walls are scored, the walls may have to be honed before installing new rings. It is important that reconditioned cylinder bores be thoroughly washed with a soap and water solution to remove all traces of abrasive material to eliminate premature wear.

PISTON RING REPLACEMENT

Using a ring expander, remove the rings from the piston.

Clean the ring grooves using an appropriate tool, exercising care to avoid cutting too deeply. Thoroughly clean all carbon and varnish from the piston with solvent.

✳✳ WARNING

Do not use a wire brush or caustic solvent on pistons.

Inspect the pistons for scuffing, scoring, cracks, pitting, or excessive ring groove wear. If wear is evident, the piston must be replaced.

Fitting

1. Slip the compression ring in the cylinder bore. Be sure the ring is square with the cylinder wall.

2. Measure the space between the ends of the ring with a feeler gauge.

3. If the gap between the ends of the ring is below specifications, remove the ring and try another for fit.

4. Fit each compression ring to the cylinder in which it is to be used.

5. If the pistons have not been cleaned, do so prior to installing them.

6. Slip the outer surface of the top and second compression ring into the respective ring groove and roll the ring around the groove. If binding is caused by a distorted ring, check another ring.

INSTALLATION

1. Install oil ring spacer in the groove being sure the ends are butted and not overlapped.

2. Hold the spacer ends butted and install lower steel oil ring rail.

3. Install upper steel oil ring rail with the gap staggered.

4. Flex the oil ring to make sure it is free. If binding occurs, determine the cause.

5. Install the second compression ring. Stagger the gap.

6. Install the top compression ring. Stagger the gap.

➡ **In order to install the piston and rings, you will need a ring compressor. This tool squeezes the rings thereby allowing them to fit into the cylinder bore.**

ROD BEARING REPLACEMENT

If you have already removed the connecting rod and piston assemblies from the engine, follow only steps 3–7 of the following procedure.

REMOVAL, INSPECTION, INSTALLATION

The connecting rod bearings are designed to have a slight projection above the rod and cap faces to insure a positive contact. The bearings can be replaced without removing the rod and piston assembly from the engine.

1. Remove the oil pan, see Oil Pan. It may be necessary to remove the oil pump to provide access to rear connecting rod bearings.

2. With the connecting rod journal at the bottom, stamp the cylinder number on the machined surfaces of connecting rod and cap for identification when reinstalling, then remove caps.

3. Inspect journals for roughness and wear. Slight roughness may be removed with a fine grit polishing cloth saturated with engine oil. Burrs may be removed with a fine oil stone by moving the stone on the journal circumference. Do not move the stone back and forth across the journal. If the journals are scored or ridged, the crankshaft must be replaced.

4. The connecting rod journals should be checked for out-of-round and correct size with a micrometer.

➡ **Crankshaft rod journals will normally be standard size. If any undersized crankshafts are used, all will be 0.254mm undersize and 0.254mm will be stamped the number 4 counterweight.**

If plastic gaging material is to be used:

5. Clean oil from the journal bearing cap, connecting rod and outer and inner surface of the bearing inserts. Position insert so that tang is properly aligned with notch in rod and cap.

6. Place a piece of plastic gaging material in the center of lower bearing shell.

7. Remove bearing cap and determine bearing clearances by comparing the width of the flattened plastic gaging material at its widest point with the graduation on the container. The number within the graduation on the envelopes indicates the clearance in thousandths of an inch or millimeters. If this clearance is excessive, replace the bearing and recheck clearance with plastic gaging material. Lubricate bearing with engine oil before installation. Repeat Steps 2

through 7 on remaining connecting rod bearings. All rods must be connected to their journals when rotating the crankshaft to prevent engine damage.

Piston and Connecting Rod

INSTALLATION

1. Install connecting rod bolt guide hose over rod bolt threads.
2. Apply engine oil to the rings and piston, then install piston ring compressing tool on the piston.
3. Install the assembly in its respective cylinder bore.
4. Lubricate the crankshaft journal with engine oil and install connecting rod bearing and cap, with bearing index tang in rod and capon same side.

➡ **When more than one rod and piston assembly is being installed, the connecting rod cap attaching nuts should only be tightened enough to keep each rod in position until all have been installed. This will aid installation of remaining piston assemblies.**

5. Torque the rod bolt nuts to specification.
6. Install all other removed parts.
7. Install the engine in the car, see Engine Removal and Installation.

Freeze Plugs

REMOVAL & INSTALLATION

1. Remove the negative battery cable.
2. Drain the cooling system.

❈ CAUTION

When draining the coolant, keep in mind that cats and dogs are attracted by the ethylene glycol antifreeze, and are quite likely to drink any that is left in an uncovered container or in puddles on the ground. This will prove fatal in sufficient quantity. Always drain

the coolant into a sealable container. Coolant should be reused unless it is contaminated or several years old.

3. If equipped with drain plugs on the engine remove them. They would be located at the bottom of the block near the oil pan.
4. Remove any components that restrict access to the freeze plugs, like the starter or motor mounts.
5. Wearing proper eye protection, tap the bottom edge of the freeze plug with a chisel. This should tilt the freeze plug, not cut it. Then use pliers to pull or pry the freeze plug from its bore. Another method is to drill the freeze plug and use a slide hammer, but more often there's not enough room to do that.
6. After the plug is removed clean the area completely. Coat the freeze plug and/or bore with gasket sealant.
7. Install the freeze plug into the hole, it must do in evenly or it will keep popping back out as you tap on it. Using a plug installer or socket that fits the edge of the plug can help keep it straight as you tap it in place.
8. Fill the engine with coolant, connect the battery cable. Start engine and check for leaks.

Block Heater

REMOVAL & INSTALLATION

Factory block heaters are not installed on these models. If an aftermarket heater has been installed the following procedure will most likely work. There are two basic types, one for the oil and one for the coolant. The oil heater usually just slips into the dipstick tube or replaces the oil drain plug. The following procedure is for the coolant type.
1. Remove the negative battery cable.
2. Drain the cooling system.

❈ CAUTION

When draining the coolant, keep in mind that cats and dogs are attracted by the ethylene glycol antifreeze, and are quite likely to drink any that is left in an uncovered container or in puddles on the ground. This will prove fatal in sufficient quantity. Always drain the coolant into a sealable

container. Coolant should be reused unless it is contaminated or several years old.

3. Remove the block heater in the same way as the freeze plugs. Some heater units have a bolt that must be loosened or a V-Clamp that must be removed to remove the heating element.
4. Disconnect the heater connector and remove the heater element.
5. Coat the new heater with sealant and install as removed.
6. Fill the engine with coolant, connect the battery cable. Start engine and check for leaks.

Rear Main Oil Seal

REMOVAL & INSTALLATION

2.5L Engine

1. Disconnect the negative battery cable.
2. Support the engine. Remove the transaxle and flywheel.
3. Being careful not to scratch the crankshaft, pry out the old seal with an suitable pry tool.
   To install:
4. Coat the new seal with clean engine oil and install it by hand or use seal installer tool J–34924 onto the crankshaft. The seal backing must be flush with the block opening.
5. Install the flywheel.
6. Install the transaxle.
7. Connect the negative battery cable.

2.8L Engine

2 PIECE THIN SEAL

1. Remove the oil pan and pump.
2. Remove the rear main bearing cap.

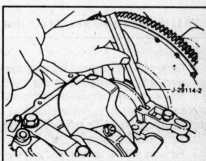

FIG.82 Installing the upper rear main seal on 2 piece seal engine — 2.8L (VIN X) engine shown

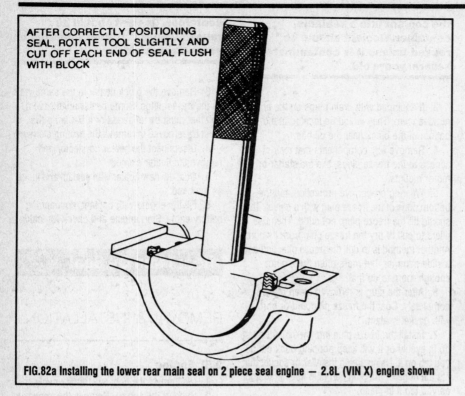

AFTER CORRECTLY POSITIONING SEAL, ROTATE TOOL SLIGHTLY AND CUT OFF EACH END OF SEAL FLUSH WITH BLOCK

FIG.82a Installing the lower rear main seal on 2 piece seal engine — 2.8L (VIN X) engine shown

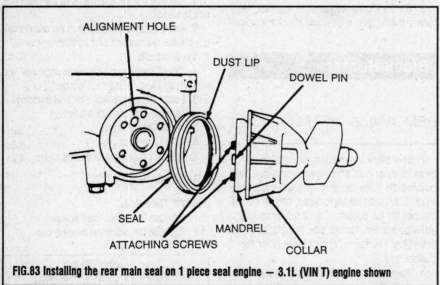

ALIGNMENT HOLE

DUST LIP

DOWEL PIN

SEAL

ATTACHING SCREWS

MANDREL

COLLAR

FIG.83 Installing the rear main seal on 1 piece seal engine — 3.1L (VIN T) engine shown

3. Gently pack the upper seal into the groove approximately 1/4 in. (6mm) on each side.

4. Measure the amount the seal was driven in on one side and add 1/16 in. (1.6mm). Cut this length from the old lower cap seal. Be sure to get a sharp cut. Repeat for the other side.

5. Place the piece of cut seal into the groove and pack the seal into the block. Do this for each side.

➡ G.M. makes a guide tool (J–29114–1) which bolts to the block via an oil pan bolt hole, and a packing tool (J–29114–2) which are machined to provide a built-in stop for the installation of the short cut pieces. Using the packing tool, work the short pieces of seal onto the guide tool, then pack them into the block with the packing tool.

6. Install a new lower seal in the rear main cap.

7. Install a piece of Plastigage® or the equivalent on the bearing journal. Install the rear cap and tighten to 70 ft. lbs. Remove the cap and check the gauge for bearing clearance. If out of specification, the ends of the seal may be frayed or not flush, preventing the cap from proper sealing. Correct as required.

8. Clean the journal, and apply a thin film of sealer to the mating surfaces of the cap and block. Do not allow any sealer to get onto the journal or bearing. Install the bearing cap and tighten to 70 ft. lbs. Install the pan and pump.

1 PIECE THICK SEAL

1. Remove the transaxle and the flexplate.

2. Using a small pry bar, pry the seal from the block.

❋❋ CAUTION

Be careful not to damage the crankshaft surface when removing the oil seal.

3. Clean and inspect the seal mounting surface for nicks and burrs.

4. Coat the new seal with engine oil. Using tool J–34686, press the seal into the block, until it seats.

5. To complete the installation, reverse the removal procedures. Start the engine and check for leaks.

3.0L and 4.3L Diesel Engines

LOWER OIL SEAL REPAIR

Braided fabric seals are pressed into grooves formed in crankcase and rear bearing cap to rear of the oil collecting groove, to seal against leakage of oil around the crankshaft.

A new braided fabric seal can be installed in crankcase only when crankshaft is removed, but it can be repaired while crankshaft is installed, as outlined under Rear Main Bearing Upper Oil Seal Repair. The seal can be replaced in cap whenever the cap is removed. Remove old seal and place new seal in groove with both ends projecting surface of cap. Force seal into groove rubbing down with hammer handle or smooth stick until seal projects above the groove not more than 1/16 in. (1.6mm). Cut ends off flush with surface of cap, using sharp knife or razor blade.

The engine must be operated at slow speed when first started after a new braided seal is installed.

Neoprene composition seals are placed in grooves in the sides of bearing cap to seal against leakage in the joints between cap and

crankcase. The neoprene composition swells in the presence of oil and heat. The seals are undersize when newly installed and may even leak for a short time until the seals have had time to swell and seal the opening.

The neoprene seals are slightly longer than the grooves in the bearing cap. The seals must not be cut to length. Before installation of seals, soak for 1 to 2 minutes in light oil or kerosene. After installation of bearing cap in crankcase, install seal in bearing cap.

To help eliminate oil leakage at the joint where the cap meets the crankcase, apply silastic sealer, or equivalent, to the rear main bearing cap split line. When applying sealer, use only a thin coat as an over abundance will not allow the cap to seat properly.

After seal is installed, force seals up into the cap with a blunt instrument to be sure of a seal at the upper parting line between the cap and case.

UPPER OIL SEAL REPAIR

1. Remove oil pan.
2. Insert packing tool (J–21526–2) against one end of the seal in the cylinder block. Drive the old seal gently into the groove until it is packed tight. This varies from 1/4 in. (6mm) to 3/4 in. (19mm) depending on the amount of pack required.
3. Repeat Step 2 on the other end of the seal in the cylinder block.
4. Measure the amount the seal was driven up on one side and add 1/16 in. (1.6mm). Using a single edge razor blade, cut that length from the old seal removed from the rear main bearing cap. Repeat the procedure for the other side. Use the rear main bearing cap as a holding fixture when cutting the seal.
5. Install Guide Tool (J–21526–1) onto cylinder block.
6. Using packing tool, work the short pieces cut in Step 4 into the guide tool and then pack into cylinder block. The guide tool and packing tool have been machined to provide a built-in stop. Use this procedure for both sides. It may help to use oil on the short pieces of the rope seal when packing into the cylinder block.
7. Remove the guide tool.
8. Install a new fabric seal in the rear main bearing cap. Install cap and torque to specifications.
9. Install oil pan.

3.1L Engine

1. Disconnect the negative battery cable.
2. Support the engine with tool J–28467–A or equivalent.
3. Remove the transaxle and flywheel.
4. Carefully remove the old seal by inserting a prying tool through the dust lip at an angle. Pry out the old seal with an suitable pry tool.

To install:

5. Coat the new seal with clean engine oil, and install it using seal installer tool J–34686 or equivalent.
6. Install the flywheel.
7. Install the transaxle.
8. Remove the engine support tool.
9. Connect the negative battery cable.

3.3L and 3.8L Engines

1. Disconnect the negative battery cable.
2. Raise and support the vehicle safely.
3. Drain the engine oil and remove the oil pan.
4. Remove the rear main bearing cap. Remove the oil seal from the bearing cap.

To install:

5. Insert a packing tool J–21526–2 or equivalent against one end of the seal in the cylinder block. Pack the old seal in until it is tight. Pack the other end of seal in the same manner.
6. Measure the amount the seal was driven up into the block on one side and add approximately 3/32 in. (2mm). With a single edge razor blade, cut this amount off of the old lower seal. The bearing cap can be used as a holding fixture.
7. Install the packing guide tool J–21526–1 or equivalent, onto the cylinder block.
8. Using the packing tool, work the short pieces of the seal into the guide tool and pack into the cylinder block until the tool hits the built in stop. Repeat this step on the other side. A small amount of oil on the pieces of seal may be helpful when packing into the cylinder block.
9. Remove the guide tool.
10. Install a new rope seal in the bearing cap and install the cap. Torque the retaining bolts to specifications.
11. Install the oil pan.
12. Fill the crankcase with oil.
13. Connect the negative battery cable.

Crankshaft

♦ SEE FIGS. 84 to 89

REMOVAL

1. Remove the engine assembly as previously outlined.
2. Remove the engine front cover.
3. Remove the timing chain and sprockets or gears.
4. Remove the oil pan.
5. Remove the oil pump.
6. Stamp the cylinder number on the machined surfaces of the bolt bosses of the connecting rods and caps for identification when reinstalling. If the pistons are to be removed from

the connecting rod, mark cylinder number on piston with a silver pencil or quick drying paint for proper cylinder identification and cap to rod location.

7. Remove the connecting rod caps and install thread protectors.
8. Mark the main bearing caps so that they can be reinstalled in their original positions.
9. Remove all the main bearing caps, mark all caps, main and rod for position. They all must go back to their original locations and they must all face the same direction. Any cap install incorrectly will cause engine damage when reassembled.
10. Note position of keyway in crankshaft so it can be installed in the same position.
11. Lift crankshaft out of block. Rods will pivot to the center of the engine when the crankshaft is removed.
12. Remove both halves of the rear main oil seal if two piece design, if one piece design remove the seal.

INSTALLATION

1. Measure the crankshaft journals with a micrometer to determine the correct size rod and main bearings to be used. Whenever a new or reconditioned crankshaft is installed, new connect rod bearings and main bearings should be installed. See Main Bearings and Rod Bearings.
2. Clean all oil passages in the block (and crankshaft if it is being reused.

➡ **A new rear main seal should be installed anytime the crankshaft is removed or replaced. If any engine repair is made any related seals or gaskets should be replaced. It's not worth the time lost to repeat a repair job due to an old seal or gasket leaking.**

3. Install sufficient oil pan bolts in the block to align with the connecting rod bolts. Use rubber bands between the bolts to position the connecting rods as required. Connecting rod position can be adjusted by increasing the tension on the rubber bands with additional turns around the pan bolts or thread protectors.
4. Position the upper half of main bearings in the block and lubricate with engine oil.
5. Position crankshaft keyway in the same position as removed and lower into block. The connecting rods will follow the crank pins into the correct position as the crankshaft is lowered.
6. Lubricate the thrust flanges with 1050169 Lubricant or equivalent. Install caps with lower half of bearings lubricated with engine oil.

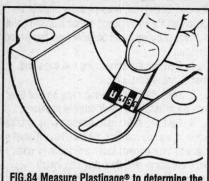

FIG.84 Measure Plastigage® to determine the main bearing clearance

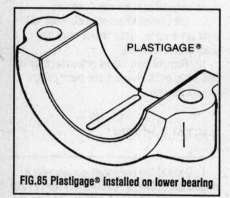

PLASTIGAGE®

FIG.85 Plastigage® installed on lower bearing

Lubricate cap bolts with engine oil and install, but do not tighten.

7. With a block of wood, bump shaft in each direction to align thrust flanges of main bearing. After bumping shaft in each direction, wedge the shaft to the front and hold it while torquing the thrust bearing cap bolts.

➡ **In order to prevent the possibility of cylinder block and/or main bearing cap damage, the main bearing caps are to be tapped into their cylinder block cavity using a brass or leather mallet before attaching bolts are installed. Do not use attaching bolts to pull main bearing caps into their seat. Failure to observe this information may damage the cylinder block or a bearing cap.**

8. Torque all main bearing caps to specification.

9. Remove the connecting rod bolt thread protectors and lubricate the connecting rod bearings with engine oil.

10. Install the connecting rod bearing caps in their original position. Torque the nuts to specification.

11. Complete the installation by reversing the removal steps.

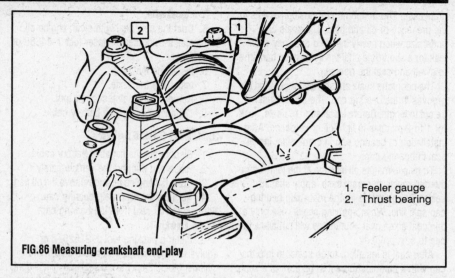

1. Feeler gauge
2. Thrust bearing

FIG.86 Measuring crankshaft end-play

Main Bearings

CHECKING BEARING CLEARANCE

1. Remove bearing cap and wipe oil from crankshaft journal and outer and inner surfaces of bearing shell.

2. Place a piece of plastic gaging material in the center of bearing.

3. Use a floor jack or other means to hold crankshaft against upper bearing shell. This is necessary to obtain accurate clearance readings when using plastic gaging material.

4. Reinstall bearing cap and bearing. Place engine oil on cap bolts and install Torque bolts to specification.

5. Remove bearing cap and determine bearing clearance by comparing the width of the flattened plastic gaging material at its widest point with graduations on the gaging material container. The number within the graduation on the envelope indicates the clearance in millimeters or thousandths of an inch. If the clearance is greater than allowed, REPLACE BOTH BEARING SHELLS AS A SET. Recheck clearance after replacing shells.

REPLACEMENT

Main bearing clearances must be corrected by the use of selective upper and lower shells. UNDER NO CIRCUMSTANCES should the use of shims behind the shells to compensate for wear be attempted. To install main bearing shells, proceed as follows:

1. Remove the oil pan as outlined. On some models, the oil pump may also have to be removed.

2. Loosen all main bearing caps.

3. Remove bearing cap and remove lower shell.

4. Insert a flattened cotter pin or roll out pin in the oil passage hole in the crankshaft in the direction opposite to cranking rotation. The pin will contact the upper shell and roll it out.

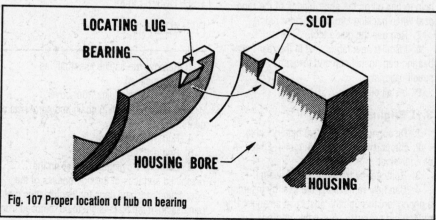

LOCATING LUG

BEARING

SLOT

HOUSING BORE

HOUSING

Fig. 107 Proper location of hub on bearing

FIG.87 Measuring connecting rod side clearance

5. The main bearing journals should be checked for roughness and wear. Slight roughness may be removed with a fine grit polishing cloth saturated with engine oil. Burrs may be removed with a fine oil stone. If the journals are scored or ridged, the crankshaft must be replaced.

➡ **The journals can be measured for out-of-round with the crankshaft installed by using a crankshaft caliper and inside micrometer or a main bearing micrometer. The upper bearing shell must be removed when measuring the crankshaft journals. Maximum out-of-round of the crankshaft journals must not exceed 0.037mm (0.0015 in.).**

6. Clean crankshaft journals and bearing caps thoroughly before installing new main bearings.

7. Apply special lubricant, No. 1050169 to the thrust flanges of bearing shells.

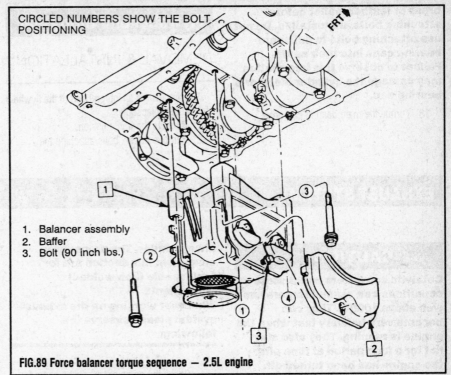

CIRCLED NUMBERS SHOW THE BOLT POSITIONING

1. Balancer assembly
2. Baffer
3. Bolt (90 inch lbs.)

FIG.89 Force balancer torque sequence — 2.5L engine

8. Place new upper shell on crankshaft journal with locating tang incorrect position and rotate shaft to turn it into place using cotter pin or roll out pin as during removal.

9. Place new bearing shell in bearing cap.

10. Install a new oil seal in the rear main bearing cap and block.

11. Lubricate the removed or replaced main bearings with engine oil. Lubricate the thrust surface with lubricant 1050169 or equivalent.

12. Lubricate the main bearing cap bolts with engine oil.

➡ **In order to prevent the possibility of cylinder block and/or main bearing cap damage, the main bearing caps are to be tapped into their cylinder block cavity using a**

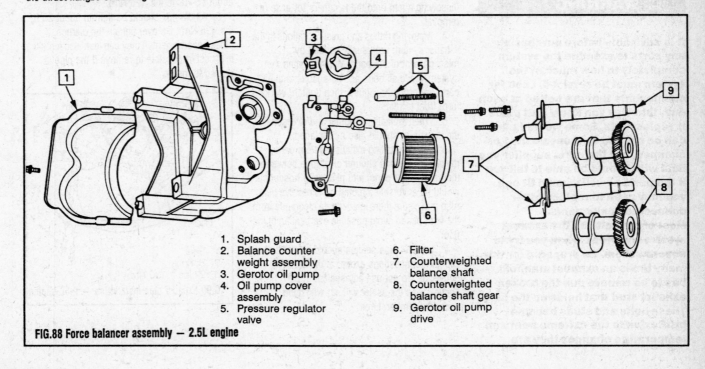

1. Splash guard
2. Balance counter weight assembly
3. Gerotor oil pump
4. Oil pump cover assembly
5. Pressure regulator valve
6. Filter
7. Counterweighted balance shaft
8. Counterweighted balance shaft gear
9. Gerotor oil pump drive

FIG.88 Force balancer assembly — 2.5L engine

brass or leather mallet before attaching bolts are installed. Do not use attaching bolts to pull main bearing caps into their seats. Failure to observe this information may damage the cylinder block or a bearing cap.

13. Torque the main bearing cap bolts.

Flywheel and Ring Gear

REMOVAL & INSTALLATION

The ring gear is an integral part of the flywheel and is not replaceable.
1. Remove the transmission.
2. Remove the six bolts attaching the flywheel to the crankshaft flange. Remove the flywheel.
3. Inspect the flywheel for cracks, and inspect the ring gear for burrs or worn teeth. Replace the flywheel if any damage is apparent. Remove burrs with a mill file.
4. Install the flywheel. The flywheel will only attach to the crankshaft in one position, as the bolt holes are unevenly spaced. Install the bolts and torque to specification.

EXHAUST SYSTEM

❄❄ CAUTION

Catalytic converters under some conditions can reach temperatures well above 1000°F. They can become very hot very fast when the engine is running. They also stay hot for a long period of time after the engine has been turned off.

Most factory new exhaust is a one piece welded system. This means that even though you can purchase just one piece of the system from an aftermarket supplier you may not be able to install it with out cutting and welding. Once the original system has been replaced, then most parts are serviceable separately.

❄❄ WARNING

It is advisable before purchasing any parts to examine the system completely to how much of the system must be serviced. Look for components that are bolted at each end, that way you know that piece is replaceable. Some welded parts can be cut and new ones bolted or clamped, but the parts supplier you deal with should be able to tell you if the parts he sells would fit or if you may need to replace other connected components.
Most of the bolts on the exhaust system will break when you try to unscrew them. Be prepared for this, many times an exhaust manifold has to be remove due the broken exhaust stud that holds on the pipe. These bolts and studs become brittle due to the extreme heat and temperature changes they are

always under. The procedures covered in this section are for replaceable (non-welded) components.
Whenever working on the exhaust system please observe the following:

1. Check the complete exhaust system for open seams, holes loose connections, or other deterioration which could permit exhaust fumes to seep into the passenger compartment.
2. The exhaust system is supported by free-hanging rubber mountings which permit some movement of the exhaust system, but do not permit transfer of noise and vibration into the passenger compartment.
3. Before removing any component of the exhaust system, ALWAYS squirt a liquid rust dissolving agent onto the fasteners for ease of removal.
4. Annoying rattles and noise vibrations in the exhaust system are usually caused by misalignment of the parts. When aligning the system, leave all bolts and nuts loose until all parts are properly aligned, then tighten, working from front to rear.
5. When replacing a muffler and/or resonator, the tailpipe(s) should also be replaced.
6. When installing exhaust system parts, make sure there is enough clearance between the hot exhaust parts, and pipes and hoses that would be adversely affected by excessive heat. Also make sure there is adequate clearance from the floor pan to avoid possible overheating of the floor.
7. Exhaust pipe sealers should be used at all slip joint connections except at the catalytic convertor. Do not use any sealers at the convertor as the sealer will not withstand convertor temperatures.

Front Pipe or Crossover Pipe

REMOVAL & INSTALLATION

1. Raise and support the front of the vehicle on jackstands.
2. Remove the exhaust pipe-to-manifold nuts.
3. Support the catalytic converter and disconnect the pipe from the converter. Remove the pipe.
4. To install, use a new gasket, add sealer to the connecting surfaces, assembly the system, check the clearance and tighten the bolts to about 15–18 ft. lbs. (25 Nm).
5. All clamps should be tight to about 25 ft. lbs. (35 Nm). Do over tighten the clamps, if pipes become dented they can leak also it makes it almost impossible to remove if the pipe is dented to much.

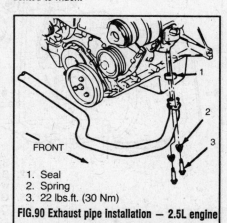

1. Seal
2. Spring
3. 22 lbs.ft. (30 Nm)

FIG.90 Exhaust pipe installation — 2.5L engine

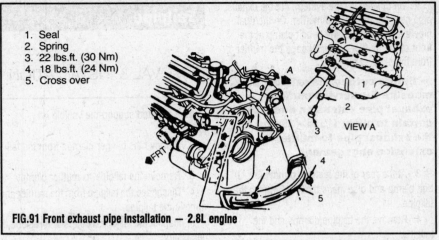

1. Seal
2. Spring
3. 22 lbs.ft. (30 Nm)
4. 18 lbs.ft. (24 Nm)
5. Cross over

VIEW A

FIG.91 Front exhaust pipe installation — 2.8L engine

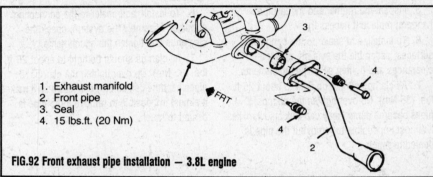

1. Exhaust manifold
2. Front pipe
3. Seal
4. 15 lbs.ft. (20 Nm)

FIG.92 Front exhaust pipe installation — 3.8L engine

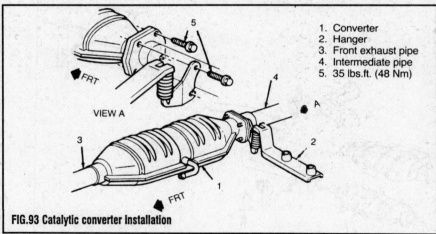

1. Converter
2. Hanger
3. Front exhaust pipe
4. Intermediate pipe
5. 35 lbs.ft. (48 Nm)

VIEW A

FIG.93 Catalytic converter installation

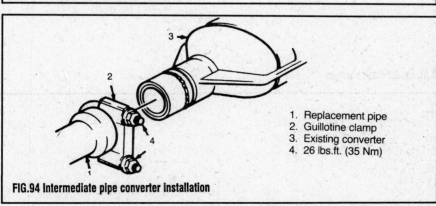

1. Replacement pipe
2. Guillotine clamp
3. Existing converter
4. 26 lbs.ft. (35 Nm)

FIG.94 Intermediate pipe converter installation

Intermediate Pipe

The intermediate pipe is the section between the catalytic converter and the muffler.

REMOVAL & INSTALLATION

1. Raise and support the front of the vehicle.
2. Disconnect the intermediate pipe from the catalytic converter. If the pipe is original you may have to cut the pipe from the catalytic converter. Before doing this it is advisable to check with the supplier you will purchase the new pipe from to see where to cut or even if the part will fit.
3. At the muffler, remove the clamp and the intermediate pipe.
4. To install, use a new clamp and nuts/bolts, assembly the system, check the clearances and tighten the connectors.
5. All clamps should be tight to about 25 ft. lbs. (35 Nm). Do over tighten the clamps, if pipes become dented they can leak also it makes it almost impossible to remove if the pipe is dented to much.

Catalytic Converter

REMOVAL & INSTALLATION

1. Raise and support the front of the vehicle on jackstands and place a support under the catalytic converter.
2. Remove the clamp at the front of the converter, then cut the pipe at the front of the converter. If the pipe is original you may have to cut the pipe from the catalytic converter. Before doing this it is advisable to check with the

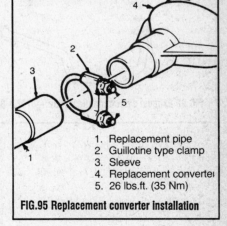

1. Replacement pipe
2. Guillotine type clamp
3. Sleeve
4. Replacement converter
5. 26 lbs.ft. (35 Nm)

FIG.95 Replacement converter installation

supplier you will purchase the new pipe from to see where to cut or even if the part will fit.

3. Remove the converter-to-intermediate pipe nuts/bolts.

4. Disconnect the converter-to-crossover pipe or front pipe.

6. To install, add sealer to the connecting surfaces, use new clamps and nuts/bolts, assemble the system, check the clearances and tighten all of the attachments.

7. All clamps should be tight to about 25 ft. lbs. (35 Nm). Do over tighten the clamps, if pipes become dented they can leak also it makes it almost impossible to remove if the pipe is dented to much.

Muffler

The exhaust system pipes rearward of the mufflers, must be replaced whenever a new muffler is installed.

REMOVAL & INSTALLATION

1. Raise and support the vehicle on jackstands.

2. On the single pipe system, cut the exhaust pipe near the front of the muffler. On the dual pipe system, remove the U-bolt clamp at the front of the muffler and disengage the muffler from the exhaust pipe.

➡ **Before cutting the exhaust pipe, measure the service muffler exhaust pipe extension and make certain to allow 1¹/₂ in. (38mm) for the exhaust pipe-to-muffler extension engagement.**

3. At the rear of the muffler, remove the U-bolt clamp and disengage the muffler from the tailpipe.

4. Remove the tailpipe clamps and the tailpipe.

5. Inspect the muffler and the tailpipe hangers; replace if necessary.

6. To install, add sealer to the connecting surfaces, assemble the system, check the clearances and tighten all of the attachments.

7. All clamps should be tight to about 25 ft. lbs. (35 Nm). Do over tighten the clamps, if pipes become dented they can leak also it makes it almost impossible to remove if the pipe is dented to much.

Tailpipe

REMOVAL & INSTALLATION

1. Raise and support the vehicle on jackstands.

2. Remove the hanger clamps from the tail pipe.

3. Remove the tailpipe-to-muffler clamp.

4. Disengage the tailpipe from the muffler and remove the tailpipe.

5. Inspect the tailpipe hangers and replace, if necessary.

6. To install, add sealer to the connecting surfaces, assemble the system, check the clearance and tighten the attachments.

7. All clamps should be tight to about 25 ft. lbs. (35 Nm). Do over tighten the clamps, if pipes become dented they can leak also it makes it almost impossible to remove if the pipe is dented to much.

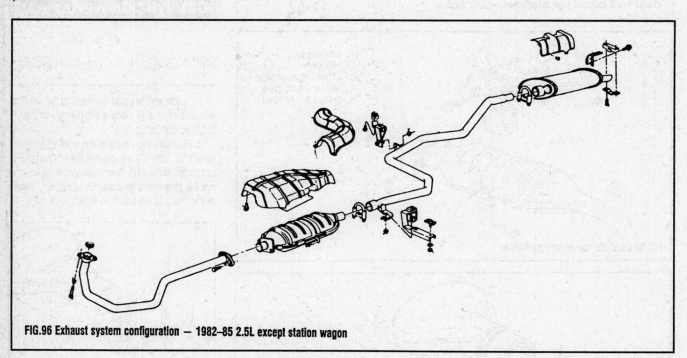

FIG.96 Exhaust system configuration — 1982–85 2.5L except station wagon

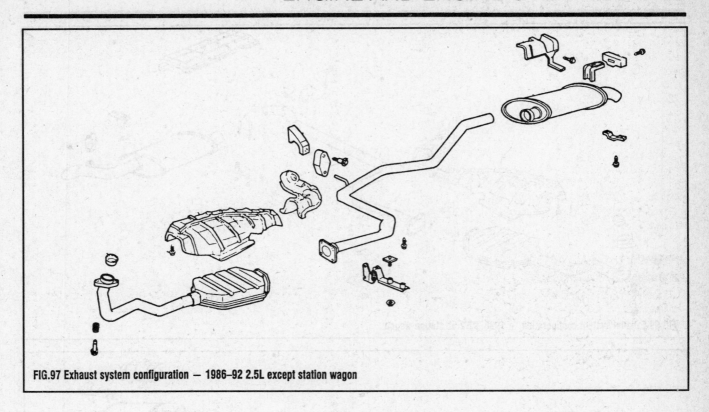

FIG.97 Exhaust system configuration — 1986–92 2.5L except station wagon

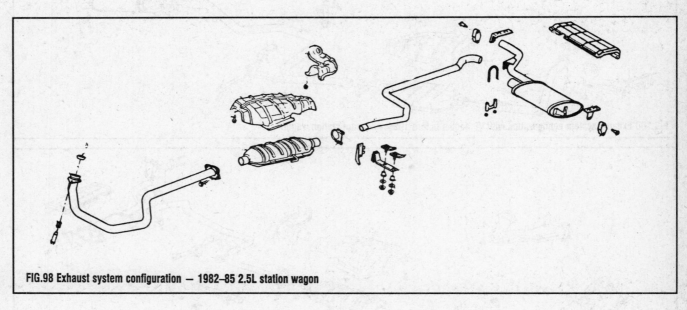

FIG.98 Exhaust system configuration — 1982–85 2.5L station wagon

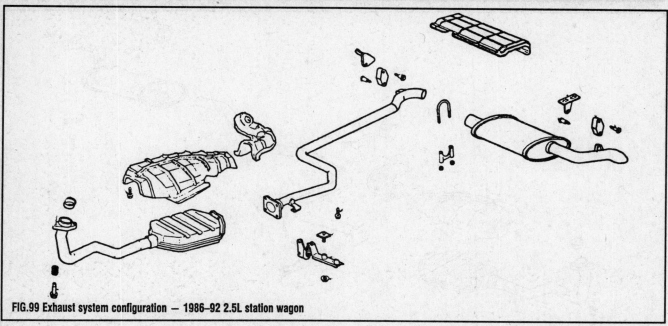

FIG.99 Exhaust system configuration — 1986–92 2.5L station wagon

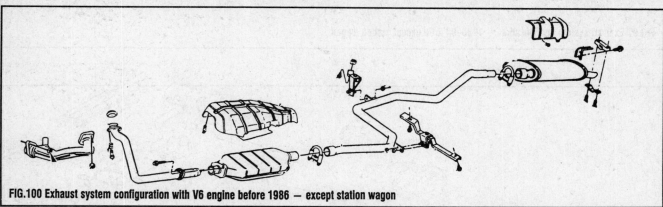

FIG.100 Exhaust system configuration with V6 engine before 1986 — except station wagon

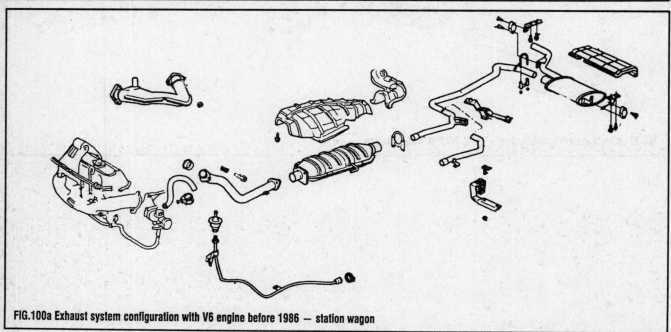

FIG.100a Exhaust system configuration with V6 engine before 1986 — station wagon

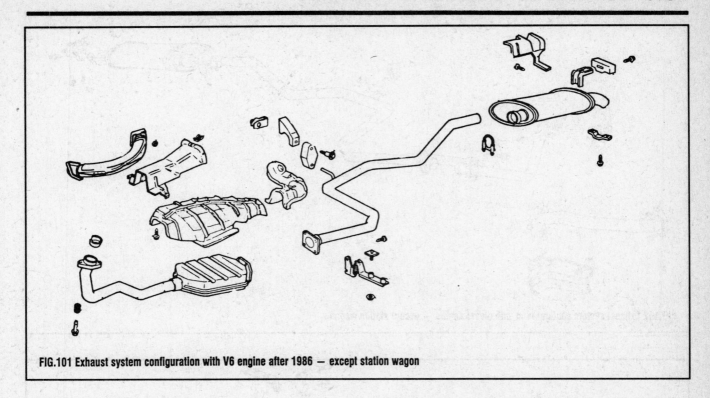

FIG.101 Exhaust system configuration with V6 engine after 1986 — except station wagon

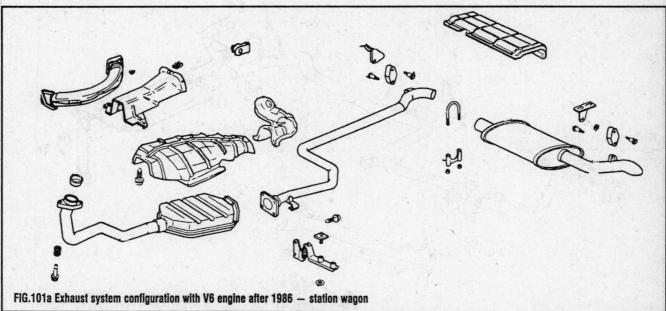

FIG.101a Exhaust system configuration with V6 engine after 1986 — station wagon

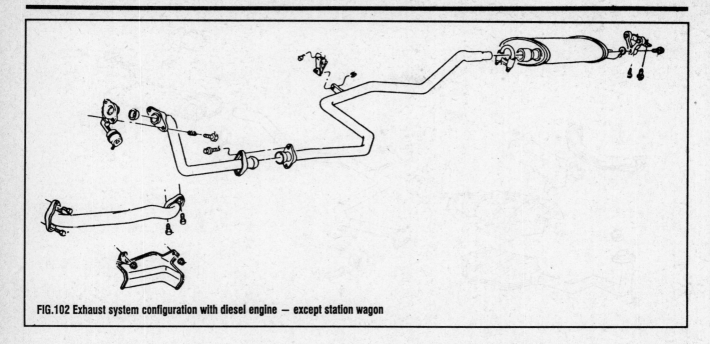

FIG.102 Exhaust system configuration with diesel engine — except station wagon

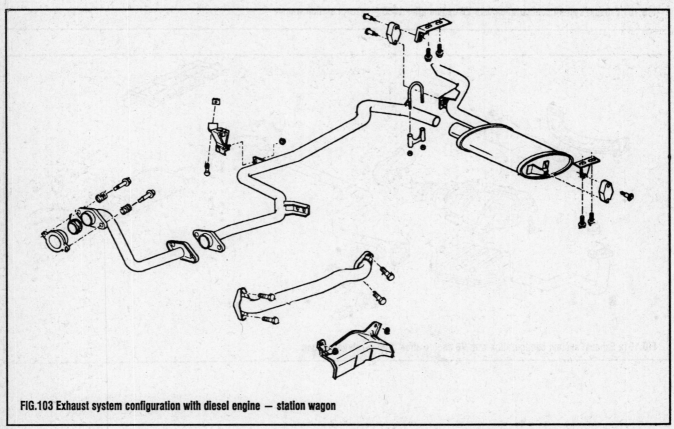

FIG.103 Exhaust system configuration with diesel engine — station wagon

Troubleshooting Basic Charging System Problems

Problem	Cause	Solution
Noisy alternator	• Loose mountings • Loose drive pulley • Worn bearings • Brush noise • Internal circuits shorted (High pitched whine)	• Tighten mounting bolts • Tighten pulley • Replace alternator • Replace alternator • Replace alternator
Squeal when starting engine or accelerating	• Glazed or loose belt	• Replace or adjust belt
Indicator light remains on or ammeter indicates discharge (engine running)	• Broken fan belt • Broken or disconnected wires • Internal alternator problems • Defective voltage regulator	• Install belt • Repair or connect wiring • Replace alternator • Replace voltage regulator
Car light bulbs continually burn out—battery needs water continually	• Alternator/regulator overcharging	• Replace voltage regulator/alternator
Car lights flare on acceleration	• Battery low • Internal alternator/regulator problems	• Charge or replace battery • Replace alternator/regulator
Low voltage output (alternator light flickers continually or ammeter needle wanders)	• Loose or worn belt • Dirty or corroded connections • Internal alternator/regulator problems	• Replace or adjust belt • Clean or replace connections • Replace alternator or regulator

Troubleshooting Basic Starting System Problems

Problem	Cause	Solution
Starter motor rotates engine slowly	• Battery charge low or battery defective • Defective circuit between battery and starter motor • Low load current • High load current	• Charge or replace battery • Clean and tighten, or replace cables • Bench-test starter motor. Inspect for worn brushes and weak brush springs. • Bench-test starter motor. Check engine for friction, drag or coolant in cylinders. Check ring gear-to-pinion gear clearance.
Starter motor will not rotate engine	• Battery charge low or battery defective • Faulty solenoid • Damage drive pinion gear or ring gear • Starter motor engagement weak • Starter motor rotates slowly with high load current • Engine seized	• Charge or replace battery • Check solenoid ground. Repair or replace as necessary. • Replace damaged gear(s) • Bench-test starter motor • Inspect drive yoke pull-down and point gap, check for worn end bushings, check ring gear clearance • Repair engine

Troubleshooting Basic Starting System Problems

Problem	Cause	Solution
Starter motor drive will not engage (solenoid known to be good)	• Defective contact point assembly	• Repair or replace contact point assembly
	• Inadequate contact point assembly ground	• Repair connection at ground screw
	• Defective hold-in coil	• Replace field winding assembly
Starter motor drive will not disengage	• Starter motor loose on flywheel housing	• Tighten mounting bolts
	• Worn drive end busing	• Replace bushing
	• Damaged ring gear teeth	• Replace ring gear or driveplate
	• Drive yoke return spring broken or missing	• Replace spring
Starter motor drive disengages prematurely	• Weak drive assembly thrust spring	• Replace drive mechanism
	• Hold-in coil defective	• Replace field winding assembly
Low load current	• Worn brushes	• Replace brushes
	• Weak brush springs	• Replace springs

Troubleshooting Engine Mechanical Problems

Problem	Cause	Solution
External oil leaks	• Fuel pump gasket broken or improperly seated	• Replace gasket
	• Cylinder head cover RTV sealant broken or improperly seated	• Replace sealant; inspect cylinder head cover sealant flange and cylinder head sealant surface for distortion and cracks
	• Oil filler cap leaking or missing	• Replace cap
External oil leaks	• Oil filter gasket broken or improperly seated	• Replace oil filter
	• Oil pan side gasket broken, improperly seated or opening in RTV sealant	• Replace gasket or repair opening in sealant; inspect oil pan gasket flange for distortion
	• Oil pan front oil seal broken or improperly seated	• Replace seal; inspect timing case cover and oil pan seal flange for distortion
	• Oil pan rear oil seal broken or improperly seated	• Replace seal; inspect oil pan rear oil seal flange; inspect rear main bearing cap for cracks, plugged oil return channels, or distortion in seal groove
	• Timing case cover oil seal broken or improperly seated	• Replace seal
	• Excess oil pressure because of restricted PCV valve	• Replace PCV valve
	• Oil pan drain plug loose or has stripped threads	• Repair as necessary and tighten
	• Rear oil gallery plug loose	• Use appropriate sealant on gallery plug and tighten
	• Rear camshaft plug loose or improperly seated	• Seat camshaft plug or replace and seal, as necessary
	• Distributor base gasket damaged	• Replace gasket

Troubleshooting Engine Mechanical Problems (cont.)

Problem	Cause	Solution
Excessive oil consumption	• Oil level too high	• Drain oil to specified level
	• Oil with wrong viscosity being used	• Replace with specified oil
	• PCV valve stuck closed	• Replace PCV valve
	• Valve stem oil deflectors (or seals) are damaged, missing, or incorrect type	• Replace valve stem oil deflectors
	• Valve stems or valve guides worn	• Measure stem-to-guide clearance and repair as necessary
	• Poorly fitted or missing valve cover baffles	• Replace valve cover
	• Piston rings broken or missing	• Replace broken or missing rings
	• Scuffed piston	• Replace piston
	• Incorrect piston ring gap	• Measure ring gap, repair as necessary
	• Piston rings sticking or excessively loose in grooves	• Measure ring side clearance, repair as necessary
	• Compression rings installed upside down	• Repair as necessary
	• Cylinder walls worn, scored, or glazed	• Repair as necessary
	• Piston ring gaps not properly staggered	• Repair as necessary
	• Excessive main or connecting rod bearing clearance	• Measure bearing clearance, repair as necessary
No oil pressure	• Low oil level	• Add oil to correct level
	• Oil pressure gauge, warning lamp or sending unit inaccurate	• Replace oil pressure gauge or warning lamp
	• Oil pump malfunction	• Replace oil pump
	• Oil pressure relief valve sticking	• Remove and inspect oil pressure relief valve assembly
	• Oil passages on pressure side of pump obstructed	• Inspect oil passages for obstruction
	• Oil pickup screen or tube obstructed	• Inspect oil pickup for obstruction
	• Loose oil inlet tube	• Tighten or seal inlet tube
Low oil pressure	• Low oil level	• Add oil to correct level
	• Inaccurate gauge, warning lamp or sending unit	• Replace oil pressure gauge or warning lamp
	• Oil excessively thin because of dilution, poor quality, or improper grade	• Drain and refill crankcase with recommended oil
	• Excessive oil temperature	• Correct cause of overheating engine
	• Oil pressure relief spring weak or sticking	• Remove and inspect oil pressure relief valve assembly
	• Oil inlet tube and screen assembly has restriction or air leak	• Remove and inspect oil inlet tube and screen assembly. (Fill inlet tube with lacquer thinner to locate leaks.)
	• Excessive oil pump clearance	• Measure clearances
	• Excessive main, rod, or camshaft bearing clearance	• Measure bearing clearances, repair as necessary

Troubleshooting Engine Mechanical Problems (cont.)

Problem	Cause	Solution
High oil pressure	• Improper oil viscosity	• Drain and refill crankcase with correct viscosity oil
	• Oil pressure gauge or sending unit inaccurate	• Replace oil pressure gauge
	• Oil pressure relief valve sticking closed	• Remove and inspect oil pressure relief valve assembly
Main bearing noise	• Insufficient oil supply	• Inspect for low oil level and low oil pressure
	• Main bearing clearance excessive	• Measure main bearing clearance, repair as necessary
	• Bearing insert missing	• Replace missing insert
	• Crankshaft end play excessive	• Measure end play, repair as necessary
	• Improperly tightened main bearing cap bolts	• Tighten bolts with specified torque
	• Loose flywheel or drive plate	• Tighten flywheel or drive plate attaching bolts
	• Loose or damaged vibration damper	• Repair as necessary
Connecting rod bearing noise	• Insufficient oil supply	• Inspect for low oil level and low oil pressure
	• Carbon build-up on piston	• Remove carbon from piston crown
	• Bearing clearance excessive or bearing missing	• Measure clearance, repair as necessary
	• Crankshaft connecting rod journal out-of-round	• Measure journal dimensions, repair or replace as necessary
	• Misaligned connecting rod or cap	• Repair as necessary
	• Connecting rod bolts tightened improperly	• Tighten bolts with specified torque
Piston noise	• Piston-to-cylinder wall clearance excessive (scuffed piston)	• Measure clearance and examine piston
	• Cylinder walls excessively tapered or out-of-round	• Measure cylinder wall dimensions, rebore cylinder
	• Piston ring broken	• Replace all rings on piston
	• Loose or seized piston pin	• Measure piston-to-pin clearance, repair as necessary
	• Connecting rods misaligned	• Measure rod alignment, straighten or replace
	• Piston ring side clearance excessively loose or tight	• Measure ring side clearance, repair as necessary
	• Carbon build-up on piston is excessive	• Remove carbon from piston

Troubleshooting Engine Mechanical Problems (cont.)

Problem	Cause	Solution
Valve actuating component noise	• Insufficient oil supply	• Check for: (a) Low oil level (b) Low oil pressure (c) Plugged push rods (d) Wrong hydraulic tappets (e) Restricted oil gallery (f) Excessive tappet to bore clearance
	• Push rods worn or bent	• Replace worn or bent push rods
	• Rocker arms or pivots worn	• Replace worn rocker arms or pivots
	• Foreign objects or chips in hydraulic tappets	• Clean tappets
	• Excessive tappet leak-down	• Replace valve tappet
	• Tappet face worn	• Replace tappet; inspect corresponding cam lobe for wear
	• Broken or cocked valve springs	• Properly seat cocked springs; replace broken springs
	• Stem-to-guide clearance excessive	• Measure stem-to-guide clearance, repair as required
	• Valve bent	• Replace valve
	• Loose rocker arms	• Tighten bolts with specified torque
	• Valve seat runout excessive	• Regrind valve seat/valves
	• Missing valve lock	• Install valve lock
	• Push rod rubbing or contacting cylinder head	• Remove cylinder head and remove obstruction in head
	• Excessive engine oil (four-cylinder engine)	• Correct oil level

Troubleshooting the Cooling System

Problem	Cause	Solution
High temperature gauge indication—overheating	• Coolant level low	• Replenish coolant
	• Fan belt loose	• Adjust fan belt tension
	• Radiator hose(s) collapsed	• Replace hose(s)
	• Radiator airflow blocked	• Remove restriction (bug screen, fog lamps, etc.)
	• Faulty radiator cap	• Replace radiator cap
	• Ignition timing incorrect	• Adjust ignition timing
	• Idle speed low	• Adjust idle speed
	• Air trapped in cooling system	• Purge air
	• Heavy traffic driving	• Operate at fast idle in neutral intermittently to cool engine
	• Incorrect cooling system component(s) installed	• Install proper component(s)
	• Faulty thermostat	• Replace thermostat
	• Water pump shaft broken or impeller loose	• Replace water pump
	• Radiator tubes clogged	• Flush radiator
	• Cooling system clogged	• Flush system
	• Casting flash in cooling passages	• Repair or replace as necessary. Flash may be visible by removing cooling system components or removing core plugs.
	• Brakes dragging	• Repair brakes
	• Excessive engine friction	• Repair engine
	• Antifreeze concentration over 68%	• Lower antifreeze concentration percentage
	• Missing air seals	• Replace air seals
	• Faulty gauge or sending unit	• Repair or replace faulty component
	• Loss of coolant flow caused by leakage or foaming	• Repair or replace leaking component, replace coolant
	• Viscous fan drive failed	• Replace unit
Low temperature indication—undercooling	• Thermostat stuck open	• Replace thermostat
	• Faulty gauge or sending unit	• Repair or replace faulty component
Coolant loss—boilover	• Overfilled cooling system	• Reduce coolant level to proper specification
	• Quick shutdown after hard (hot) run	• Allow engine to run at fast idle prior to shutdown
	• Air in system resulting in occasional "burping" of coolant	• Purge system
	• Insufficient antifreeze allowing coolant boiling point to be too low	• Add antifreeze to raise boiling point
	• Antifreeze deteriorated because of age or contamination	• Replace coolant
	• Leaks due to loose hose clamps, loose nuts, bolts, drain plugs, faulty hoses, or defective radiator	• Pressure test system to locate source of leak(s) then repair as necessary

Troubleshooting the Cooling System (cont.)

Problem	Cause	Solution
Coolant loss—boilover	• Faulty head gasket • Cracked head, manifold, or block • Faulty radiator cap	• Replace head gasket • Replace as necessary • Replace cap
Coolant entry into crankcase or cylinder(s)	• Faulty head gasket • Crack in head, manifold or block	• Replace head gasket • Replace as necessary
Coolant recovery system inoperative	• Coolant level low • Leak in system • Pressure cap not tight or seal missing, or leaking • Pressure cap defective • Overflow tube clogged or leaking • Recovery bottle vent restricted	• Replenish coolant to FULL mark • Pressure test to isolate leak and repair as necessary • Repair as necessary • Replace cap • Repair as necessary • Remove restriction
Noise	• Fan contacting shroud • Loose water pump impeller • Glazed fan belt • Loose fan belt • Rough surface on drive pulley • Water pump bearing worn • Belt alignment	• Reposition shroud and inspect engine mounts • Replace pump • Apply silicone or replace belt • Adjust fan belt tension • Replace pulley • Remove belt to isolate. Replace pump. • Check pulley alignment. Repair as necessary.
No coolant flow through heater core	• Restricted return inlet in water pump • Heater hose collapsed or restricted • Restricted heater core • Restricted outlet in thermostat housing • Intake manifold bypass hole in cylinder head restricted • Faulty heater control valve • Intake manifold coolant passage restricted	• Remove restriction • Remove restriction or replace hose • Remove restriction or replace core • Remove flash or restriction • Remove restriction • Replace valve • Remove restriction or replace intake manifold

NOTE: *Immediately after shutdown, the engine enters a condition known as heat soak. This is caused by the cooling system being inoperative while engine temperature is still high. If coolant temperature rises above boiling point, expansion and pressure may push some coolant out of the radiator overflow tube. If this does not occur frequently it is considered normal.*

Troubleshooting the Serpentine Drive Belt

Problem	Cause	Solution
Tension sheeting fabric failure (woven fabric on outside circumference of belt has cracked or separated from body of belt)	• Grooved or backside idler pulley diameters are less than minimum recommended • Tension sheeting contacting (rubbing) stationary object • Excessive heat causing woven fabric to age • Tension sheeting splice has fractured	• Replace pulley(s) not conforming to specification • Correct rubbing condition • Replace belt • Replace belt
Noise (objectional squeal, squeak, or rumble is heard or felt while drive belt is in operation)	• Belt slippage • Bearing noise • Belt misalignment • Belt-to-pulley mismatch • Driven component inducing vibration • System resonant frequency inducing vibration	• Adjust belt • Locate and repair • Align belt/pulley(s) • Install correct belt • Locate defective driven component and repair • Vary belt tension within specifications. Replace belt.
Rib chunking (one or more ribs has separated from belt body)	• Foreign objects imbedded in pulley grooves • Installation damage • Drive loads in excess of design specifications • Insufficient internal belt adhesion	• Remove foreign objects from pulley grooves • Replace belt • Adjust belt tension • Replace belt
Rib or belt wear (belt ribs contact bottom of pulley grooves)	• Pulley(s) misaligned • Mismatch of belt and pulley groove widths • Abrasive environment • Rusted pulley(s) • Sharp or jagged pulley groove tips • Rubber deteriorated	• Align pulley(s) • Replace belt • Replace belt • Clean rust from pulley(s) • Replace pulley • Replace belt
Longitudinal belt cracking (cracks between two ribs)	• Belt has mistracked from pulley groove • Pulley groove tip has worn away rubber-to-tensile member	• Replace belt • Replace belt
Belt slips	• Belt slipping because of insufficient tension • Belt or pulley subjected to substance (belt dressing, oil, ethylene glycol) that has reduced friction • Driven component bearing failure • Belt glazed and hardened from heat and excessive slippage	• Adjust tension • Replace belt and clean pulleys • Replace faulty component bearing • Replace belt
"Groove jumping" (belt does not maintain correct position on pulley, or turns over and/or runs off pulleys)	• Insufficient belt tension • Pulley(s) not within design tolerance • Foreign object(s) in grooves	• Adjust belt tension • Replace pulley(s) • Remove foreign objects from grooves

Troubleshooting the Serpentine Drive Belt (cont.)

Problem	Cause	Solution
"Groove jumping" (belt does not maintain correct position on pulley, or turns over and/or runs off pulleys)	• Excessive belt speed • Pulley misalignment • Belt-to-pulley profile mismatched • Belt cordline is distorted	• Avoid excessive engine acceleration • Align pulley(s) • Install correct belt • Replace belt
Belt broken (Note: identify and correct problem before replacement belt is installed)	• Excessive tension • Tensile members damaged during belt installation • Belt turnover • Severe pulley misalignment • Bracket, pulley, or bearing failure	• Replace belt and adjust tension to specification • Replace belt • Replace belt • Align pulley(s) • Replace defective component and belt
Cord edge failure (tensile member exposed at edges of belt or separated from belt body)	• Excessive tension • Drive pulley misalignment • Belt contacting stationary object • Pulley irregularities • Improper pulley construction • Insufficient adhesion between tensile member and rubber matrix	• Adjust belt tension • Align pulley • Correct as necessary • Replace pulley • Replace pulley • Replace belt and adjust tension to specifications
Sporadic rib cracking (multiple cracks in belt ribs at random intervals)	• Ribbed pulley(s) diameter less than minimum specification • Backside bend flat pulley(s) diameter less than minimum • Excessive heat condition causing rubber to harden • Excessive belt thickness • Belt overcured • Excessive tension	• Replace pulley(s) • Replace pulley(s) • Correct heat condition as necessary • Replace belt • Replace belt • Adjust belt tension

ENGINE SPECIFICATIONS

Component	U.S.	Metric
Camshaft		
2.5L (VIN R) engine		
End Play:	0.0015-0.005 in.	0.0381-0.127 mm
Bearing Diameter:	1.869 in.	47.4726 mm
Bearing Clearance:	0.0007-0.0027 in.	0.01778-0.0685 mm
Lobe Lift (1982-88)		
Intake:	0.398 in.	10.3124 mm
Exhaust:	0.398 in.	10.3124 mm
Lobe Lift (1989)		
Intake:	0.232 in.	5.8882 mm
Exhaust:	0.232 in.	5.8882 mm
Lobe Lift (1990–92)		
Intake:	0.248 in.	6.302 mm
Exhaust:	0.248 in.	6.302 mm
2.8L (VIN W) engine		
End Play:	NA	NA
Bearing Diameter:	1.8678-1.8815 in.	47.44-47.79 mm
Bearing Clearance:	0.001-0.004 in.	0.026-0.101 mm
Lobe Lift		
Intake:	0.2626 in.	6.67 mm
Exhaust:	0.2732 in.	6.94 mm

ENGINE SPECIFICATIONS

Component	U.S.	Metric
2.8L (VIN X) engine		
End Play:	NA	NA
Bearing Diameter:	1.8876-1.8996 in.	47.44-47.49 mm
Bearing Clearance:	0.001-0.004 in.	0.026-0.101 mm
Lobe Lift		
Intake:	0.2348 in.	5.87 mm
Exhaust:	0.2668 in.	6.67 mm
2.8L (VIN Z) engine		
End Play:	NA	NA
Bearing Diameter:	1.8876-1.8996 in.	47.44-47.49 mm
Bearing Clearance:	0.001-0.004 in.	0.026-0.101 mm
Lobe Lift		
Intake:	0.2348 in.	5.87 mm
Exhaust:	0.2668 in.	6.67 mm
3.0L (VIN E) engine		
End Play:	NA	NA
Bearing Diameter:	1.785-1.786 in.	45.339-45.364 mm
Bearing Clearance		
Number 1:	0.0005-0.0025 in.	0.0127-0.0635 mm
Numbers 2, 3, 4:	0.0005-0.0035 in.	0.0127-0.0889 mm
3.1L (VIN T) engine		
End Play:	NA	NA
Bearing Diameter:	1.8678-1.8815 in.	47.44-47.79 mm
Bearing Clearance:	0.001-0.004 in.	0.026-0.101 mm
Lobe Lift		
Intake:	0.2626 in.	6.67 mm
Exhaust:	0.2732 in.	6.94 mm
3.3L (VIN N) engine		
End Play:	NA	NA
Bearing Diameter:	1.7850-1.7860 in.	45.339-45.364 mm
Bearing Clearance:	0.0005-0.0035 in.	0.013-0.089 mm
Lobe Lift		
Intake:	0.250 in.	6.43 mm
Exhaust:	0.255 in.	6.48 mm
3.8L (VIN 3) engine		
End Play:	NA	NA
Bearing Diameter:	1.785-1.786 in.	45.339-45.364 mm
Bearing Clearance		
Number 1:	0.0005-0.0025 in.	0.0127-0.0635 mm
Numbers 2, 3, 4:	0.0005-0.0035 in.	0.0127-0.0889 mm
4.3L (VIN T) engine		
End Clearance:	0.0008-0.0228 0.02-0.58 mm	
Bearing Diameter		
Cam sprocket:	2.035-2.036 in.	51.707-51.727 mm
Number 2:	2.015-2.016 in.	51.219-51.199 mm
Number 3:	1.996-1.995 in.	50.71-50.60 mm
Number 4:	1.976-1.975 in.	50.20-50.18 mm
Bearing Clearance:	0.0020-0.0043 in.	0.05-0.11 mm
Lobe Lift		
Intake:	0.252 in.	6.40 mm
Exhaust:	0.279 in.	7.09 mm

ENGINE SPECIFICATIONS

Component	U.S.	Metric
Valves		
2.5L (VIN R) engine		
Face Angle:	45°	45°
Seat Angle:	46°	46°
Seat Runout:	0.002 in.	0.05 mm
Seat Width		
Intake:	0.035-0.075 in.	0.889-1.905 mm
Exhaust (1982-89):	0.058-0.097 in.	1.473-2.642 mm
Exhaust (1990-92):	0.058-0.105 in.	1.473-2.667 mm
Stem Clearance		
Intake:	0.001-0.0028 in.	0.028-0.071 mm
Exhaust (1982-89):	0.0013-0.0041 in.	0.033-0.1040 mm
Exhaust (1990-92):	0.0013-0.0041 in.	0.033-0.1040 mm
2.8L (VIN W) engine		
Face Angle:	45°	45°
Seat Angle:	46°	46°
Seat Runout:	0.001 in.	0.25 mm
Seat Width		
Intake:	0.061-0.073 in.	1.550-1.850 mm
Exhaust:	0.067-0.079 in.	1.70-2.0 mm
Stem Clearance		
Intake:	0.001-0.0027 in.	0.026-0.068 mm
Exhaust:	0.001-0.0027 in.	0.026-0.068 mm
2.8L (VIN X) engine		
Face Angle:	45°	45°
Seat Angle:	46°	46°
Seat Runout:	0.002 in.	0.05 mm
Seat Width		
Intake:	0.049-0.059 in.	1.250-1.50 mm
Exhaust:	0.049-0.059 in.	1.250-1.50 mm
Stem Clearance		
Intake:	0.001-0.0027 in.	0.026-0.068 mm
Exhaust:	0.001-0.0027 in.	0.026-0.068 mm
2.8L (VIN Z) engine		
Face Angle:	45°	45°
Seat Angle:	46°	46°
Seat Runout:	0.002 in.	0.05 mm
Seat Width		
Intake:	0.049-0.059 in.	1.250-1.50 mm
Exhaust:	0.049-0.059 in.	1.250-1.50 mm
Stem Clearance		
Intake:	0.001-0.0027 in.	0.026-0.068 mm
Exhaust:	0.001-0.0027 in.	0.026-0.068 mm
3.0L (VIN E) engine		
Face Angle:	45°	45°
Seat Angle:	46°	46°
Seat Runout:	0.002 in.	0.05 mm
Seat Diameter		
Intake:	0.3412-0.3401 in.	8.666-8.638 mm
Exhaust:	0.3412-0.3405 in.	8.666-8.649 mm
Stem Clearance		
Intake:	0.0015-0.0035 in.	0.038-0.089 mm
Exhaust:	0.0015-0.0032 in.	0.038-0.081 mm
3.1L (VIN T) engine		
Face Angle:	45°	45°
Seat Angle:	46°	46°
Seat Runout:	0.001 in.	0.25 mm
Seat Width		
Intake:	0.061-0.073 in.	1.550-1.850 mm
Exhaust:	0.067-0.079 in.	1.70-2.0 mm
Stem Clearance		
Intake:	0.001-0.0027 in.	0.026-0.068 mm
Exhaust:	0.001-0.0027 in.	0.026-0.068 mm

ENGINE SPECIFICATIONS

Component	U.S.	Metric
3.3L (VIN N) engine		
Face Angle:	45°	45°
Seat Angle:	45°	45°
Seat Runout:	0.002 in.	0.05 mm
Seat Width		
Intake:	0.060-0.080 in.	1.530-2.030 mm
Exhaust:	0.090-0.110 in.	2.29-2.79 mm
Stem Clearance		
Intake:	0.0015-0.0035 in.	0.038-0.089 mm
Exhaust:	0.0015-0.0032 in.	0.038-0.081 mm
3.8L (VIN 3) engine		
Face Angle:	45°	45°
Seat Angle:	46°	46°
Seat Runout:	0.002 in.	0.05 mm
Seat Diameter		
Intake:	0.3412-0.3401 in.	8.666-8.638 mm
Exhaust:	0.3412-0.3405 in.	8.666-8.649 mm
Stem Clearance		
Intake:	0.0015-0.0035 in.	0.038-0.089 mm
Exhaust:	0.0015-0.0032 in.	0.038-0.081 mm
4.3L (VIN T) engine		
Face Angle		
Intake:	44°	44°
Exhaust:	30°	30°
Seat Angle		
Intake:	45°	45°
Exhaust:	31°	31°
Overall Length		
Intake:	5.120 in.	130.048 mm
Exhaust:	5.029 in.	127.7366 mm
Seat Runout		
Intake:	0.004 in.	0.10 mm
Exhaust:	0.002 in.	0.05 mm
Head Diameter		
Internal EGR		
Intake:	1.875 in.	47.01 mm
Exhaust:	1.622 in.	41.20 mm
External EGR		
Intake:	1.750 in.	44.45 mm
Exhaust:	1.500 in.	38.20 mm
Stem Diameter		
Intake:	0.3425-0.3432 in.	8.6995-8.7376 mm
Exhaust:	0.3420-0.3428 in.	8.6870-8.7070 mm
Clearance in guide		
Intake:	0.0010-0.0027 in.	0.026-0.068 mm
Exhaust:	0.0015-0.0032 in.	0.038-0.081 mm
Seat Width		
Intake (cast):	0.0037-0.075 in.	0.94-1.9 mm
Intake (aluminum):	0.0032-0.077 in.	0.81-1.97 mm
Exhaust:	0.0046-0.0840 in.	1.17-2.14 mm
Valve Spring		
2.5L (VIN R) engine		
Free Length:	2.01 in.	51 mm
Installed Height:	1.68 in.	42.64 mm
2.8L (VIN W) engine		
Free Length:	1.91 in.	48.5 mm
Installed Height:	1.5748 in.	40.0 mm
2.8L (VIN X) engine		
Free Length:	1.91 in.	48.5 mm
2.8L (VIN Z) engine		
Free Length:	1.91 in.	48.5 mm

ENGINE SPECIFICATIONS

Component	U.S.	Metric
3.1L (VIN T) engine		
Free Length:	1.91 in.	48.5 mm
Installed Height:	1.5748 in.	40.0 mm
3.3L (VIN N) engine		
Free Length:	1.98 in.	50.32 mm
Installed Height:	1.69-1.720 in.	42.93-44.45 mm
4.3L (VIN T) engine		
Free Length:	2.09 in.	53.09 mm
Spring Load		
2.5L (VIN R) engine		
Closed:	75 ft.lbs. @ 1.68 in.	332 Nm @ 42.64 mm
Open:	173 ft.lbs. @ 1.24 in.	770 Nm @ 31.46 mm
2.8L (VIN W) engine		
Closed:	90 ft.lbs. @ 1.70 in.	400 Nm @ 43.0 mm
Open:	215 ft.lbs. @ 1.29 in.	956 Nm @ 33.0 mm
2.8L (VIN X) engine		
Closed:	88 lbs. @ 1.70 in.	40 Kg @ 40.0 mm
Open:	195 lbs. @ 1.57 in.	88 Kg @ 30.0 mm
2.8L (VIN Z) engine		
Closed:	88 lbs. @ 1.70 in.	40 Kg @ 40.0 mm
Open:	195 lbs. @ 1.57 in.	88 Kg @ 30.0 mm
3.0L (VIN E) engine		
Closed:	93 ft.lbs. @ 1.727 in.	413 Nm @ 43.9 mm
Open:	220 ft.lbs. @ 1.340 in.	978 Nm @ 34.0 mm
3.1L (VIN T) engine		
Closed:	90 ft.lbs. @ 1.701 in.	400 Nm @ 43.0 mm
Open:	215 ft.lbs. @ 1.291 in.	956 Nm @ 33.0 mm
3.3L (VIN N) engine		
Closed:	80 ft.lbs. @ 1.750 in.	356 Nm @ 43.7 mm
Open:	210 ft.lbs. @ 1.315 in.	935 Nm @ 33.4 mm
3.8L (VIN 3) engine		
Closed:	64 ft.lbs. @ 1.727 in.	285 Nm @ 43.9 mm
Open:	182 ft.lbs. @ 1.340 in.	810 Nm @ 34.0 mm
4.3L (VIN T) engine		
Closed:	90 ft.lbs. @ 1.670 in.	400 Nm @ 42.4 mm
Open:	208 ft.lbs. @ 1.220 in.	935 Nm @ 31.0 mm
Lifter		
2.5L (VIN R) engine		
Body Diameter:	0.841-0.843 in.	21.3668-21.4046 mm
Bore Diameter:	0.844-0.845 in.	21.425-21.450 mm
Bore Clearance:	0.002-0.0006 in.	0.06-0.016 mm
Plunger Travel:	0.022 in.	5.3 mm
2.8L (VIN W) engine	NA	NA
2.8L (VIN X) engine	NA	NA
2.8L (VIN Z) engine	NA	NA
3.0L (VIN E) engine		
Body Diameter:	0.820-0.8427 in.	21.3668-21.4046 mm
Bore Clearance:	0.008-0.0025 in.	0.0203-0.0635 mm
3.1L (VIN T) engine	NA	NA
3.3L (VIN N) engine	NA	NA
3.8L (VIN 3) engine		
Body Diameter:	0.820-0.8427 in.	21.3668-21.4046 mm
Bore Clearance:	0.008-0.0025 in.	0.0203-0.0635 mm
4.3L (VIN T) engine		
Body Diameter:	0.920-0.922 in.	23.39-23.41 mm
Bore Clearance:	0.0003-0.002 in.	0.009-0.054 mm
Length:	2.706 in.	68.73 mm

ENGINE SPECIFICATIONS

Component	U.S.	Metric
Oil Pump		
2.5L (VIN R) engine		
Gear Pocket Depth:	0.514-0.516 in.	13.05-13.10 mm
Gear Thickness:	0.511-0.512 in.	12.973-12.998 mm
2.8L (VIN W) engine	NA	NA
2.8L (VIN X) engine		
Gear Pocket Depth:	1.195-1.198 in.	30.36-30.44 mm
Gear Thickness:	1.503-1.506 in.	38.18-38.25 mm
Gear Length:	1.200-1.199 in.	30.48-30.45 mm
Gear Diameter:	1.498-1.500 in.	38.05-38.10 mm
Side Clearance:	0.003-0.004 in.	0.08-0.10 mm
End Clearance:	0.002-0.005 in.	0.05-0.13 mm
Valve to Bore:	0.0015-0.0035 in.	0.089-0.038 mm
2.8L (VIN Z) engine		
Gear Pocket Depth:	1.195-1.198 in.	30.36-30.44 mm
Gear Thickness:	1.503-1.506 in.	38.18-38.25 mm
Gear Length:	1.200-1.199 in.	30.48-30.45 mm
Gear Diameter:	1.498-1.500 in.	38.05-38.10 mm
Side Clearance:	0.003-0.004 in.	0.08-0.10 mm
End Clearance:	0.002-0.005 in.	0.05-0.13 mm
Valve to Bore:	0.0015-0.0035 in.	0.089-0.038 mm
3.0L (VIN E) engine	NA	NA
3.1L (VIN T) engine	NA	NA
3.3L (VIN N) engine		
Gear Pocket Depth:	0.461-0.4625 in.	11.71-11.75 mm
Gear Diameter:	3.508-3.512 in.	89.10-89.20 mm
Inner Gear		
Tip Clearance:	0.006 in.	0.152 mm
Outer Gear		
End Clearance:	0.001-00035 in.	0.025-0.089 mm
Diameter Clearance:	0.08-0.015 in.	0.203-0.381 mm
Valve to bore:	0.0015-0.0035 in.	0.089-0.038 mm
3.8L (VIN 3) engine	NA	NA
4.3L (VIN T) engine		
Gear Pocket Depth:	1.505-1.5090 in.	38.1-38.125 mm
Gear Diameter:	1.534-1.539 in.	38.960-39.096 mm
Gear		
Length:	1.505-1.5095 in.	38.29-38.341 mm
Diameter:	1.529-1.531 in.	38.887-38.836 mm
Side Clearance:	0.0015-0.0045 in.	0.04-0.12 mm
Valve to bore:	0.0025-0.0050 in.	0.063-0.127 mm
Cylinder Bore		
2.5L (VIN R) engine		
Diameter:	4.0 in.	101.6 mm
Out of Round:	0.001 in.	0.02 mm
Taper:	0.005 in.	0.13 mm
2.8L (VIN W) engine		
Diameter:	3.5046-3.5033 in.	89.016-89.034 mm
Out of Round:	0.0005 in.	0.13 mm
Taper:	0.0005 in.	0.13 mm
2.8L (VIN X) engine		
Diameter:	3.504-3.5067 in.	88.90-89.07 mm
Out of Round:	0.001 in.	0.02 mm
Taper:	0.001 in.	0.02 mm
2.8L (VIN Z) engine		
Diameter:	3.504-3.5067 in.	88.90-89.07 mm
Out of Round:	0.001 in.	0.02 mm
Taper:	0.001 in.	0.02 mm

ENGINE SPECIFICATIONS

Component	U.S.	Metric
3.0L (VIN E) engine		
Diameter:	3.8 in.	96.52 mm
Out of Round:	0.001 in.	0.02 mm
Taper:	0.001 in.	0.02 mm
3.1L (VIN T) engine		
Diameter:	3.5046-3.5033 in.	89.016-89-034 mm
Out of Round:	0.0005 in.	0.13 mm
Taper:	0.0005 in.	0.13 mm
3.3L (VIN N) engine		
Diameter:	3.7 in.	93.9 mm
Out of Round:	0.0004 in.	0.10 mm
Taper:	0.0005 in.	0.13 mm
3.8L (VIN 3) engine		
Diameter:	3.8 in.	96.52 mm
Out of Round:	0.001 in.	0.02 mm
Taper:	0.001 in.	0.02 mm
4.3L (VIN T) engine		
Diameter:	4.057 in.	103.05 mm
Out of Round:	0.001 in.	0.025 mm
Taper:	0.001 in.	0.025 mm
Piston		
2.5L (VIN R) engine		
Clearance:	0.0014-0.0022 in.	0.036-0.056 mm
2.8L (VIN W) engine		
Clearance:	0.00093-0.00222 in.	0.0235-0.0565 mm
2.8L (VIN X) engine		
Clearance:	0.0017-0.003 in.	0.043-0.069 mm
2.8L (VIN Z) engine		
Clearance:	0.0017-0.003 in.	0.043-0.069 mm
3.0L (VIN T) engine		
Clearance:	0.0008-0.0020 in.	0.020-0.051 mm
3.1L (VIN T) engine		
Clearance:	0.0022-0.0028 in.	0.057-0.072 mm
3.3L (VIN N) engine		
Clearance:	0.0004-0.0022 in.	0.010-0.056 mm
3.8L (VIN 3) engine		
Clearance:	0.0008-0.0020 in.	0.020-0.051 mm
4.3L (VIN T) engine		
Clearance:	0.0035-0.0045 in.	0.088-0.114 mm
Piston Rings		
2.5L (VIN R) engine		
Gap (top):	0.01-0.02 in.	0.30-0.50 mm
Gap (second):	0.01-0.02 in.	0.30-0.50 mm
Gap (oil):	0.02-0.06 in.	0.50-1.50 mm
Side Clearance		
Top:	0.002-0.003 in.	0.05-0.08 mm
Second:	0.001-0.003 in.	0.03-0.08 mm
Oil Control:	0.015-0.055 in.	0.38-1.40 mm
2.8L (VIN W) engine		
Gap (top):	0.01-0.02 in.	0.30-0.50 mm
Gap (second):	0.01-0.02 in.	0.30-0.50 mm
Gap (oil):	0.02-0.55 in.	0.50-1.40 mm
Side Clearance		
Top:	0.001-0.003 in.	0.03-0.08 mm
Second:	0.001-0.003 in.	0.03-0.08 mm
Oil Control:	0.008 in.	0.20 mm

ENGINE SPECIFICATIONS

Component	U.S.	Metric
2.8L (VIN X) engine		
Gap (top):	0.01-0.02 in.	0.30-0.50 mm
Gap (second):	0.02-0.55 in.	0.50-1.40 mm
Gap (oil):	NA	NA
Side Clearance		
Top:	0.001-0.003 in.	0.03-0.08 mm
Second:	0.001-0.003 in.	0.03-0.08 mm
Oil Control:	0.008 in.	0.20 mm
2.8L (VIN Z) engine		
Gap (top):	0.01-0.02 in.	0.30-0.50 mm
Gap (second):	0.02-0.55 in.	0.50-1.40 mm
Gap (oil):	NA	NA
Side Clearance		
Top:	0.001-0.003 in.	0.03-0.08 mm
Second:	0.001-0.003 in.	0.03-0.08 mm
Oil Control:	0.008 in.	0.20 mm
3.0L (VIN E) engine		
Gap (top):	0.01-0.020 in.	0.254-0.508 mm
Gap (second):	0.01-0.020 in.	0.254-0.508 mm
Gap (oil):	0.015-0.55 in.	0.381-0.397 mm
Groove Width		
Top:	0.0770-0.0780 in.	1.955-1.981 mm
Second:	0.0770-0.0780 in.	1.955-1.981 mm
Oil Control:	0.183-0.189 in.	4.684-4.80 mm
Ring Depth		
Top:	0.184-0.194 in.	4.674-4.928 mm
Second:	0.186-0.194 in.	4.724-4.928 mm
Oil Control:	0.188-0.196 in.	4.7752-4.978 mm
3.1L (VIN T) engine		
Gap (top):	0.01-0.02 in.	0.30-0.50 mm
Gap (second):	0.01-0.02 in.	0.30-0.50 mm
Gap (oil):	0.01-0.50 in.	0.25-1.27 mm
Side Clearance		
Top:	0.002-0.0035 in.	0.05-0.09 mm
Second:	0.002-0.0035 in.	0.05-0.09 mm
Oil Control:	0.008 in.	0.20 mm
3.3L (VIN N) engine		
Gap (top):	0.01-0.025 in.	0.30-0.63 mm
Gap (second):	0.01-0.025 in.	0.30-0.63 mm
Gap (oil):	0.01-0.40 in.	0.25-0.40 mm
Side Clearance		
Top:	0.0013-0.0031 in.	0.033-0.079 mm
Second:	0.0013-0.0031 in.	0.033-0.079 mm
Oil Control:	0.0011-0.0081 in.	0.28-0.206 mm
Ring Width		
Top:	0.0581-0.0589 in.	1.476-1.497 mm
Second:	0.0581-0.0589 in.	1.476-1.497 mm
Oil Control:	0.1122-0.1182 in.	2.850-3.002 mm
3.8L (VIN 3) engine		
Gap (top):	0.01-0.020 in.	0.254-0.508 mm
Gap (second):	0.01-0.020 in.	0.254-0.508 mm
Gap (oil):	0.015-0.55 in.	0.381-0.397 mm
Groove Width		
Top:	0.0770-0.0780 in.	1.955-1.981 mm
Second:	0.0770-0.0780 in.	1.955-1.981 mm
Oil Control:	0.183-0.189 in.	4.684-4.80 mm
Ring Depth		
Top:	0.184-0.194 in.	4.674-4.928 mm
Second:	0.186-0.194 in.	4.724-4.928 mm
Oil Control:	0.188-0.196 in.	4.7752-4.978 mm

ENGINE SPECIFICATIONS

Component	U.S.	Metric
4.3L (VIN T) engine		
Gap (top):	0.019-0.027 in.	0.4826-0.6858 mm
Gap (second):	0.013-0.021 in.	0.3302-0.5334 mm
Gap (oil):	0.015-0.55 in.	0.381-0.397 mm
Side Clearance		
Top:	0.005-0.007 in.	0.127-0.178 mm
Second:	0.003-0005 in.	0.077-0.134 mm
Oil Control:	0.001-0.005 in.	0.025-0.127 mm
Ring Width:	0.078-0.077 in.	1.958-1.981 mm
Piston Pins		
2.5L (VIN R) engine		
Diameter:	0.927-0.928 in.	23.546-23.561 mm
Fit in piston:	0.0003-0.0005 in.	0.008-0.013 mm
Fit in rod:	press fit	press fit
2.8L (VIN W) engine		
Diameter:	0.9052-0.9056 in.	22.937-23.001 mm
Clearance:	0.00025-0.0037 in.	0.0065-0.091 mm
Fit in rod:	0.00078-0.0021 in.	0.020-0.0515 mm
2.8L (VIN X) engine		
Diameter:	0.9052-0.9056 in.	22.937-23.001 mm
Fit in piston:	0.00026-0.0037 in.	0.0065-0.091 mm
Fit in rod:	0.00078-0.0021 in.	0.020-0.0515 mm
2.8L (VIN Z) engine		
Diameter:	0.9052-0.9056 in.	22.937-23.001 mm
Fit in piston:	0.00026-0.0037 in.	0.0065-0.091 mm
Fit in rod:	0.00078-0.0021 in.	0.020-0.0515 mm
3.0L (VIN E) engine		
Diameter:	0.9391-0.9394 in.	23.853-23.860 mm
Fit in piston:	0.0004-0.0007 in.	0.0100-0.0177 mm
Fit in rod:	0.00078-0.0017 in.	0.017-0.0432 mm
Pin off-set:	0.040 in. thrust side	1.016 thrust side mm
3.1L (VIN T) engine		
Diameter:	0.9052-0.9054 in.	22.937-22.964 mm
Clearance:	0.0004-0.0008 in.	0.0096-0.0215 mm
Fit in rod:	0.00078-0.0021 in.	0.020-0.0515 mm
3.3L (VIN N) engine		
Diameter:	0.9053-0.9055 in.	22.995-23.000 mm
Fit in piston:	0.0004-0.0008 in.	0.0096-0.0215 mm
Fit in rod:	0.0007-0.0017 in.	0.018-0.043 mm
3.8L (VIN 3) engine		
Diameter:	0.9391-0.9394 in.	23.853-23.860 mm
Fit in piston:	0.0004-0.0007 in.	0.0100-0.0177 mm
Fit in rod:	0.00078-0.0017 in.	0.017-0.0432 mm
Pin Off-set:	0.040 in. thrust side	1.016 mm thrust side
4.3L (VIN T) engine		
Diameter:	1.0949-1.0952 in.	27.81-27.82 mm
Fit in piston:	0.0003-0.0005 in.	0.0076-0.0127 mm
Fit in rod:	0.0003-0.0013 in.	0.076-0.0330 mm

ENGINE SPECIFICATIONS

Component	U.S.	Metric
Crankshaft		
2.5L (VIN R) engine		
Main Journal		
Diameter:	2.3 in.	58.399-58.400 mm
Taper:	0.0005 in.	0.013 mm
Out of Round:	0.0005 in.	0.013 mm
Clearance:	0.0005-0.0022 in.	0.013-0.056 mm
End-play:	0.0051-0.010 in.	0.13-0.26 mm
Crankpin		
Diameter:	2.0 in.	50.708-50.805 mm
Taper:	0.0005 in.	0.013 mm
Out of Round:	0.0005 in.	0.013 mm
Clearance		
Bearing:	0.0005-0.003 in.	0.013-0.07 mm
Side:	0.006-0.024in.	0.015-0.06 mm
2.8L (VIN W) engine		
Main Journal		
Diameter:	2.6473-2.6483 in.	67.241-67.265 mm
Taper:	0.0002 in.	0.005 mm
Out of Round:	0.0002 in.	0.005 mm
Clearance:	0.0012-0.0027 in.	0.032-0.069 mm
Thrust:	0.0016-0.0031 in.	0.042-0.079 mm
End-play:	0.0024-0.0083 in.	0.06-0.21 mm
Crankpin		
Diameter:	1.9994-1.9983 in.	50.784-50.758 mm
Taper:	0.0002 in.	0.005 mm
Out of Round:	0.0002 in.	0.005 mm
Clearance		
Bearing:	0.0015-0.0036 in.	0.038-0.083 mm
Side:	0.014-0.027in.	0.360-0.680 mm
2.8L (VIN X) engine		
Main Journal		
Diameter:	2.5850-2.5860 in.	63.340-63.364 mm
Taper:	0.0002 in.	0.005 mm
Out of Round:	0.0002 in.	0.005 mm
Clearance:	0.002-0.003 in.	0.05-0.08 mm
End-play:	0.002-0.007 in.	0.05-0.18 mm
Crankpin		
Diameter:	2.0713-2.0715 in.	50.784-50.758 mm
Taper:	0.0002 in.	0.005 mm
Out of Round:	0.0002 in.	0.005 mm
Clearance		
Bearing:	0.0014-0.0037 in.	0.040-0.083 mm
Side:	0.0065-0.018 in.	0.160-0.440 mm
2.8L (VIN Z) engine		
Main Journal		
Diameter:	2.5850-2.5860 in.	63.340-63.364 mm
Taper:	0.0002 in.	0.005 mm
Out of Round:	0.0002 in.	0.005 mm
Clearance:	0.002-0.003 in.	0.05-0.08 mm
End-play:	0.002-0.007 in.	0.05-0.18 mm
Crankpin		
Diameter:	2.0713-2.0715 in.	50.784-50.758 mm
Taper:	0.0002 in.	0.005 mm
Out of Round:	0.0002 in.	0.005 mm
Clearance		
Bearing:	0.0014-0.0037 in.	0.040-0.083 mm
Side:	0.0065-0.018 in.	0.160-0.440 mm

ENGINE SPECIFICATIONS

Component	U.S.	Metric
3.0L (VIN E) engine		
Main Journal		
Diameter:	2.4995 in.	63.4873 mm
Taper:	0.0002 in.	0.005 mm
Out of Round:	0.0002 in.	0.005 mm
Clearance:	0.003-0.0018 in.	0.08-0.0457 mm
End-play:	0.003-0.0011in.	0.08-0.2794 mm
Length		
Number 1, 3, 4:	0.864 in.	21.9456 mm
Number 2:	1.057 in.	26.8478 mm
Crankpin		
Diameter:	2.2487-2.2495 in.	57.1169-57.1373 mm
Taper:	0.0002 in.	0.005 mm
Out of Round:	0.0002 in.	0.005 mm
Clearance:	0.0005-0.0026 in.	0.0127-0.066 mm
End-play:	0.003-0.015 in.	0.0762-0.381 mm
Length:	0.654 in.	16.611 mm
3.1L (VIN T) engine		
Main Journal		
Diameter:	2.6473-2.6483 in.	67.241-67.265 mm
Taper:	0.0003 in.	0.008 mm
Out of Round:	0.0002 in.	0.005 mm
Clearance:	0.0012-0.0027 in.	0.032-0.069 mm
Thrust:	0.0012-0.0027 in.	0.032-0.069 mm
End-play:	0.0024-0.0083 in.	0.06-0.21 mm
Crankpin		
Diameter:	1.9994-1.9983 in.	50.784-50.758 mm
Taper:	0.0003 in.	0.008 mm
Out of Round:	0.0002 in.	0.005 mm
Clearance		
Bearing:	0.0013-0.0031 in.	0.032-0.079 mm
Side:	0.014-0.027in.	0.360-0.680 mm
3.3L (VIN N) engine		
Main Journal		
Diameter:	2.4988-2.4998 in.	63.47-63.495 mm
Taper:	0.0003 in.	0.008 mm
Out of Round:	0.0003 in.	0.008 mm
Clearance:	0.0003-0.0018 in.	0.008-0.045 mm
End-play:	0.003-0.0011 in.	0.076-0.279 mm
Crankpin		
Diameter:	2.2487-2.2499 in.	57.117-57.147 mm
Taper:	0.0003 in.	0.008 mm
Out of Round:	0.0003 in.	0.008 mm
Clearance		
Bearing:	0.0003-0.0026 in.	0.0076-0.071 mm
Side:	0.003-0.015 in.	0.076-0.381 mm
3.8L (VIN 3) engine		
Main Journal		
Diameter:	2.4995 in.	63.4873 mm
Taper:	0.0002 in.	0.005 mm
Out of Round:	0.0002 in.	0.005 mm
Clearance:	0.003-0.0018 in.	0.08-0.0457 mm
End-play:	0.003-0.0011in.	0.08-0.2794 mm
Length		
Number 1, 3, 4:	0.864 in.	21.9456 mm
Number 2:	1.057 in.	26.8478 mm
Crankpin		
Diameter:	2.2487-2.2495 in.	57.1169-57.1373 mm
Taper:	0.0002 in.	0.005 mm
Out of Round:	0.0002 in.	0.005 mm
Clearance:	0.0005-0.0026 in.	0.0127-0.066 mm
End-play:	0.003-0.015 in.	0.0762-0.381 mm
Length:	0.654 in.	16.611 mm

ENGINE SPECIFICATIONS

Component	U.S.	Metric
4.3L (VIN T) engine		
Main Journal		
Diameter:	2.9993-3.0003 in.	76.181-76.207 mm
Taper:	0.0005 in.	0.013 mm
Out of Round:	0.0005 in.	0.013 mm
Clearance		
No. 1, 2, 3:	0.0005-0.002 in.	0.0127-0.0533 mm
No. 4 (rear):	0.0020-0.0034 in.	0.051-0.086 mm
End-play:	0.003-0.0135 in	0.087-0.343 mm
Shell Width		
No. 1 & 2:	0.970-0.980 in.	21.9456 mm
No. 3:	1.193-1.195 in.	30.302-30.353 mm
No. 4:	1.27 in.	32.26 mm
Crankpin		
Diameter:	2.2498-2.2490 in.	57.120-57.146 mm
Diameter:	2.9993-3.0003 in.	76.181-76.207 mm
Taper:	0.0005 in.	0.013 mm
Clearance:	0.0004-0.0026 in.	0.010-0.066 mm
Side play:	0.008-0.0214 in.	0.21-0.545 mm

TORQUE SPECIFICATIONS

Component	U.S.	Metric
Alternator bracket		
2.5L (VIN R) engine		
Long bolt:	37 ft. lbs.	50 Nm
Short bolt:	18 ft. lbs.	25 Nm
Camshaft sprocket		
2.8L:	15-20 ft. lbs.	20-27 Nm
3.1L:	15-20 ft. lbs.	20-27 Nm
3.3L, 3.8L, 4.3L:	52 ft. lbs. + 110°	70 Nm + 110°
Camshaft thrust plate bolt		
2.5L, 2.8L, 3.0L, 3.1L:	89 inch lbs.	10 Nm
3.3L, 3.8L, 4.3L:	11 inch lbs.	15 Nm
Camshaft rear cover	6-9 ft. lbs.	8-12 Nm
Connecting rod cap nuts		
2.5L (VIN R) engine:	29 ft. lbs.	40 Nm
2.8L (VIN W) engine:	34-40 ft. lbs.	46-54 Nm
2.8L (VIN X) engine:	34-40 ft. lbs.	46-54 Nm
2.8L (VIN Z) engine:	34-40 ft. lbs.	46-54 Nm
3.0L (VIN E) engine:	40-45 ft. lbs.	54-61 Nm
3.1L (VIN T) engine:	34-40 ft. lbs.	46-54 Nm
3.3L (VIN N) engine:	20 ft. lbs. + 50°	27 Nm + 50°
3.8L (VIN 3) engine:	45 ft. lbs.	61 Nm
4.3L (VIN T) engine:	40-45 ft. lbs.	54-61 Nm
Crankshaft damper/balancer		
2.5L (VIN R) (1982-87) engine:	200 ft. lbs.	260 Nm
2.5L (VIN R) (1988-92) engine:	162 ft. lbs.	220 Nm
2.8L (VIN W) engine:	75 ft. lbs.	102 Nm
2.8L (VIN X) engine:	75 ft. lbs.	102 Nm
2.8L (VIN Z) engine:	75 ft. lbs.	102 Nm
3.0L (VIN E) engine:	200 ft. lbs.	260 Nm
3.1L (VIN T) engine:	75 ft. lbs.	102 Nm
3.3L (VIN N) engine:	105 ft. lbs. + 56°	140 Nm + 56°
3.8L (VIN 3) engine:	220 ft. lbs.	290 Nm
4.3L (VIN T) engine:	40-45 ft. lbs.	54-61 Nm
Engine mount to engine		
2.5L. 2.8L, 3.0L, 3.1L:	40 ft. lbs.	50 Nm
3.3L, 3.8L, 4.3L:	70 ft. lbs.	95 Nm

TORQUE SPECIFICATIONS

Component	U.S.	Metric
Engine mount to frame		
2.5L, 2.8L, 3.0L, 3.1L:	35 ft. lbs.	47 Nm
3.3L, 3.8L, 4.3L:	32 ft. lbs.	44 Nm
Exhaust manifold		
2.5L (VIN R) engine		
Inner bolt:	37 ft. lbs.	50 Nm
Outer bolt:	28 ft. lbs.	38 Nm
2.8L (VIN W) engine:	15-23 ft. lbs.	20-30 Nm
2.8L (VIN X) engine:	25 ft. lbs.	34 Nm
2.8L (VIN Z) engine:	25 ft. lbs.	34 Nm
3.0L (VIN E) engine:	25-37 ft. lbs.	34-50 Nm
3.1L (VIN T) engine:	15-23 ft. lbs.	20-30 Nm
3.3L (VIN N) engine:	41 ft. lbs.	55 Nm
3.8L (VIN 3) engine:	37 ft. lbs.	50 Nm
4.3L (VIN T) engine:	29 ft. lbs.	37 Nm
Exhaust pipe:	15-18 ft. lbs.	23-27 Nm
Exhaust pipe clamps:	25 ft. lbs.	35 Nm
Flywheel bolts		
2.5L (VIN R) engine:		
1982-86:	44 ft. lbs.	61 Nm
1987-92:	55 ft. lbs.	75 Nm
2.8L (VIN W) engine:	52 ft. lbs.	70 Nm
2.8L (VIN X) engine:	52 ft. lbs.	70 Nm
2.8L (VIN Z) engine:	52 ft. lbs.	70 Nm
3.0L (VIN E) engine:	60 ft. lbs.	80 Nm
3.1L (VIN T) engine:	76 ft. lbs.	108 Nm
3.3L (VIN N) engine:	89 inch lbs. + 90°	10 Nm + 90°
3.8L (VIN 3) engine:	60 ft. lbs.	80 Nm
4.3L (VIN T) engine:	76 ft. lbs.	108 Nm
Front cover		
2.5L, 2.8L, 3.0L, 3.1L:	89 inch lbs.	89 Nm
3.3L, 3.8L, 4.3L:	22 ft. lbs.	30 Nm
Intake Manifold		
2.5L (VIN R) engine:	25 ft. lbs.	32 Nm
2.8L (VIN W) engine:	25 ft. lbs.	32 Nm
2.8L (VIN X) engine:	23 ft. lbs.	30 Nm
2.8L (VIN Z) engine:	23 ft. lbs.	30 Nm
3.0L (VIN E) engine:	47 ft. lbs.	65 Nm
3.1L (VIN T) engine:	25 ft. lbs.	32 Nm
3.3L (VIN N) engine:	89 inch lbs.	10 Nm
3.8L (VIN 3) engine:	47 ft. lbs.	65 Nm
4.3L (VIN T) engine:	41 ft. lbs.	55 Nm
Lifter guide retainer stud	89 inch lbs.	10 Nm
Main bearing caps		
2.5L (VIN R) engine:		
1982-89:	70 ft. lbs.	95 Nm
1990-92:	65 ft. lbs.	88 Nm
2.8L (VIN W) engine:	63-83 ft. lbs.	85-112 Nm
2.8L (VIN X) engine:	68 ft. lbs.	90 Nm
2.8L (VIN Z) engine:	68 ft. lbs.	90 Nm
3.0L (VIN E) engine:	100 ft. lbs.	135 Nm
3.1L (VIN T) engine:	63-83 ft. lbs.	85-112 Nm
3.3L (VIN N) engine:	26 ft. lbs. + 45°	35 Nm + 45°
3.8L (VIN 3) engine:	100 ft. lbs.	135 Nm
4.3L (VIN T) engine:	107 ft. lbs.	145 Nm
Oil pan		
Except 3.3L (VIN N) engine:		
M6 size bolt:	6-9 ft. lbs.	8-12 Nm
M8 size bolt:	15-23 ft. lbs.	20-30 Nm
3.3L (VIN N) engine:	124 inch lbs.	14 Nm

TORQUE SPECIFICATIONS

Component	U.S.	Metric
Oil pump hold down	67-85 ft. lbs.	27-41 Nm
Oil cover to timing cover		
3.3L (VIN N) engine:	97 inch lbs.	11 Nm
Oxygen sensor:	30 ft. lbs.	41 Nm
Push rod cover	89 inch lbs.	10 Nm
Rocker arm covers		
2.5L (VIN R) engine:	80 inch lbs.	9 Nm
2.8L (VIN W) engine:	6-9 ft. lbs.	8-12 Nm
2.8L (VIN X) engine:	10 ft. lbs.	11 Nm
2.8L (VIN Z) engine:	10 ft. lbs.	11 Nm
3.0L (VIN E) engine:	14 ft. lbs.	19 Nm
3.1L (VIN T) engine:	6-9 ft. lbs.	8-12 Nm
3.3L (VIN N) engine:	14 ft. lbs.	19 Nm
3.8L (VIN 3) engine:	14-20 ft. lbs.	19-27 Nm
4.3L (VIN T) engine:	14-20 ft. lbs.	19-27 Nm
Rocker arm nuts/bolts		
2.5L (VIN R) engine:	20 ft. lbs.	27 Nm
except 2.5L engine:	10-25 ft. lbs.	14-34 Nm
Spark plugs		
2.5L:	10-25 ft. lbs.	14-34 Nm
2.8L (VIN W) engine:	10-25 ft. lbs.	14-34 Nm
2.8L (VIN X) & (VIN Z):	7-15 ft. lbs.	Nm
3.0L (VIN E) engine:	7-15 ft. lbs.	Nm
3.1L (VIN T) engine:	10-25 ft. lbs.	14-34 Nm
3.3L, 3.8L, 4.3L:	20 ft. lbs.	27 Nm
Starter mounting bolts:	32 ft. lbs.	43 Nm
Thermostat housing	15-23 ft. lbs.	20-30 Nm
Timing chain damper	14-19 ft. lbs.	18-24 Nm
Water pump		
2.5L (VIN R) (1982-86) engine:	25 ft. lbs.	30 Nm
2.5L (VIN R) (1987-92) engine:	10 ft. lbs.	11 Nm
V6 Gasoline engines		
M6 bolt:	6-9 ft. lbs.	8-12 Nm
M10 bolt:	25 ft. lbs.	34 Nm

4

EMISSION CONTROLS

AIR POLLUTION

The earth's atmosphere, at or near sea level, consists of 78% nitrogen, 21% oxygen and 1% other gases, approximately. If it were possible to remain in this state, 100% clean air would result. However, many varied causes allow other gases and particulates to mix with the clean air, causing the air to become unclean or polluted.

Certain of these pollutants are visible while others are invisible, with each having the capability of causing distress to the eyes, ears, throat, skin and respiratory system. Should these pollutants be concentrated in a specific area and under the right conditions, death could result due to the displacement or chemical change of the oxygen content in the air. These pollutants can cause much damage to the environment and to the many man made objects that are exposed to the elements.

To better understand the causes of air pollution, the pollutants can be categorized into 3 separate types, natural, industrial and automotive.

Natural Pollutants

Natural pollution has been present on earth before man appeared and is still a factor to be considered when discussing air pollution, although it causes only a small percentage of the present overall pollution problem existing in our country. It is the direct result of decaying organic matter, wind born smoke and particulates from such natural events as plains and forest fires (ignited by heat or lightning), volcanic ash, sand and dust which can spread over a large area of the countryside.

Such a phenomenon of natural pollution has been recent volcanic eruptions, with the resulting plume of smoke, steam and volcanic ash blotting out the sun's rays as it spreads and rises higher into the atmosphere, where the upper air currents catch and carry the smoke and ash, while condensing the steam back into water vapor. As the water vapor, smoke and ash traveled on their journey, the smoke dissipates into the atmosphere while the ash and moisture settle back to earth in a trail hundred of miles long. In many cases, lives are lost and millions of dollars of property damage result, and ironically, man can only stand by and watch it happen.

Industrial Pollution

Industrial pollution is caused primarily by industrial processes, the burning of coal, oil and natural gas, which in turn produces smoke and fumes. Because the burning fuels contain much sulfur, the principal ingredients of smoke and fumes are sulfur dioxide (SO_2) and particulate matter. This type of pollutant occurs most severely during still, damp and cool weather, such as at night. Even in its less severe form, this pollutant is not confined to just cities. Because of air movements, the pollutants move for miles over the surrounding countryside, leaving in its path a barren and unhealthy environment for all living things.

Working with Federal, State and Local mandated rules, regulations and by carefully monitoring the emissions, industries have greatly reduced the amount of pollutant emitted from their industrial sources, striving to obtain an acceptable level. Because of the mandated industrial emission clean up, many land areas and streams in and around the cities that were formerly barren of vegetation and life, have now begun to move back in the direction of nature's intended balance.

Automotive Pollutants

The third major source of air pollution is the automotive emissions. The emissions from the internal combustion engine were not an appreciable problem years ago because of the small number of registered vehicles and the nation's small highway system. However, during the early 1950's, the trend of the American people was to move from the cities to the surrounding suburbs. This caused an immediate problem in the transportation areas because the majority of the suburbs were not afforded mass transit conveniences. This lack of transportation created an attractive market for the automobile manufacturers, which resulted in a dramatic increase in the number of vehicles produced and sold, along with a marked increase in highway construction between cities and the suburbs. Multi-vehicle families emerged with much emphasis placed on the individual vehicle per family member. As the increase in vehicle ownership and usage occurred, so did the pollutant levels in and around the cities, as the suburbanites drove daily to their businesses and employment in the city and its fringe area,

returning at the end of the day to their homes in the suburbs.

It was noted that a fog and smoke type haze was being formed and at times, remained in suspension over the cities and did not quickly dissipate. At first this "smog", derived from the words "smoke" and "fog", was thought to result from industrial pollution but it was determined that the automobile emissions were largely to blame. It was discovered that as normal automobile emissions were exposed to sunlight for a period of time, complex chemical reactions would take place.

It was found the smog was a photo chemical layer and was developed when certain oxides of nitrogen (NOx) and unburned hydrocarbons (HC) from the automobile emissions were exposed to sunlight and was more severe when the smog would remain stagnant over an area in which a warm layer of air would settle over the top of a cooler air mass at ground level, trapping and holding the automobile emissions, instead of the emissions being dispersed and diluted through normal air flows. This type of air stagnation was given the name "Temperature Inversion".

Temperature Inversion

In normal weather situations, the surface air is warmed by the heat radiating from the earth's surface and the sun's rays and will rise upward, into the atmosphere, to be cooled through a convection type heat expands with the cooler upper air. As the warm air rises, the surface pollutants are carried upward and dissipated into the atmosphere.

When a temperature inversion occurs, we find the higher air is no longer cooler but warmer than the surface air, causing the cooler surface air to become trapped and unable to move. This warm air blanket can extend from above ground level to a few hundred or even a few thousand feet into the air. As the surface air is trapped, so are the pollutants, causing a severe smog condition. Should this stagnant air mass extend to a few thousand feet high, enough air movement with the inversion takes place to allow the smog layer to rise above ground level but the pollutants still cannot dissipate. This inversion can remain for days over an area, with only the smog level rising or lowering from ground level to a few hundred feet high. Meanwhile, the pollutant levels increases, causing eye irritation, respirator problems, reduced visibility, plant damage and in some cases, cancer type diseases.

This inversion phenomenon was first noted in the Los Angeles, California area. The city lies in a basin type of terrain and during certain weather conditions, a cold air mass is held in the basin while a warmer air mass covers it like a lid.

Because this type of condition was first documented as prevalent in the Los Angeles area, this type of smog was named Los Angeles Smog, although it occurs in other areas where a large concentration of automobiles are used and the air remains stagnant for any length of time.

Internal Combustion Engine Pollutants

Consider the internal combustion engine as a machine in which raw materials must be placed so a finished product comes out. As in any machine operation, a certain amount of wasted material is formed. When we relate this to the internal combustion engine, we find that by putting in air and fuel, we obtain power from this mixture during the combustion process to drive the vehicle. The by-product or waste of this power is, in part, heat and exhaust gases with which we must concern ourselves.

HEAT TRANSFER

The heat from the combustion process can rise to over 4000°F (2204°C). The dissipation of this heat is controlled by a ram air effect, the use of cooling fans to cause air flow and having a liquid coolant solution surrounding the combustion area and transferring the heat of combustion through the cylinder walls and into the coolant. The coolant is then directed to a thin-finned, multi-tubed radiator, from which the excess heat is transferred to the outside air by 1 or all of the 3 heat transfer methods, conduction, convection or radiation.

The cooling of the combustion area is an important part in the control of exhaust emissions. To understand the behavior of the combustion and transfer of its heat, consider the air/fuel charge. It is ignited and the flame front burns progressively across the combustion chamber until the burning charge reaches the cylinder walls. Some of the fuel in contact with the walls is not hot enough to burn, thereby snuffing out or Quenching the combustion process. This leaves unburned fuel in the combustion chamber. This unburned fuel is then forced out of the cylinder along with the exhaust gases and into the exhaust system.

Many attempts have been made to minimize the amount of unburned fuel in the combustion chambers due to the snuffing out or "Quenching", by increasing the coolant temperature and lessening the contact area of the coolant around the combustion area. Design limitations within the combustion chambers prevent the complete burning of the air/fuel charge, so a certain amount of the unburned fuel is still expelled into the exhaust system, regardless of modifications to the engine.

EXHAUST EMISSIONS

Composition Of The Exhaust Gases

The exhaust gases emitted into the atmosphere are a combination of burned and unburned fuel. To understand the exhaust emission and its composition review some basic chemistry.

When the air/fuel mixture is introduced into the engine, we are mixing air, composed of nitrogen (78%), oxygen (21%) and other gases (1%) with the fuel, which is 100% hydrocarbons (HC), in a semi-controlled ratio. As the combustion process is accomplished, power is produced to move the vehicle while the heat of combustion is transferred to the cooling system. The exhaust gases are then composed of nitrogen, a diatomic gas (N_2), the same as was introduced in the engine, carbon dioxide ($CO2$), the same gas that is used in beverage carbonation and water vapor (H_2O). The nitrogen (N_2), for the most part passes through the engine unchanged, while the oxygen (O_2) reacts (burns) with the hydrocarbons (HC) and produces the carbon dioxide (CO_2) and the water vapors (H_2O). If this chemical process would be the only process to take place, the exhaust emissions would be harmless. However, during the combustion process, other pollutants are formed and are considered dangerous. These pollutants are carbon monoxide (CO), hydrocarbons (HC), oxides of nitrogen (NOx) oxides of sulfur (SOx) and engine particulates.

Lead (Pb), is considered 1 of the particulates and is present in the exhaust gases whenever leaded fuels are used. Lead (Pb) does not dissipate easily. Levels can be high along roadways when it is emitted from vehicles and can pose a health threat. Since the increased usage of unleaded gasoline and the phasing out of leaded gasoline for fuel, this pollutant is gradually diminishing. While not considered a major threat lead is still considered a dangerous pollutant.

HYDROCARBONS

Hydrocarbons (HC) are essentially unburned fuel that have not been successfully burned during the combustion process or have escaped into the atmosphere through fuel evaporation. The main sources of incomplete combustion are rich air/fuel mixtures, low engine temperatures and improper spark timing. The main sources of hydrocarbon emission through fuel evaporation come from the vehicle's fuel tank and carburetor bowl.

To reduce combustion hydrocarbon emission, engine modifications were made to minimize dead space and surface area in the combustion chamber. In addition the air/fuel mixture was made more lean through improved carburetion, fuel injection and by the addition of external controls to aid in further combustion of the hydrocarbons outside the engine. Two such methods were the addition of an air injection system, to inject fresh air into the exhaust manifolds and the installation of a catalytic converter, a unit that is able to burn traces of hydrocarbons without affecting the internal combustion process or fuel economy.

To control hydrocarbon emissions through fuel evaporation, modifications were made to the fuel tank and carburetor bowl to allow storage of the fuel vapors during periods of engine shut-down, and at specific times during engine operation, to purge and burn these same vapors by blending them with the air/fuel mixture.

CARBON MONOXIDE

Carbon monoxide is formed when not enough oxygen is present during the combustion

process to convert carbon (C) to carbon dioxide (CO_2). An increase in the carbon monoxide (CO) emission is normally accompanied by an increase in the hydrocarbon (HC) emission because of the lack of oxygen to completely burn all of the fuel mixture.

Carbon monoxide (CO) also increases the rate at which the photo chemical smog is formed by speeding up the conversion of nitric oxide (NO) to nitrogen dioxide (NO_2). To accomplish this, carbon monoxide (CO) combines with oxygen (O_2) and nitrogen dioxide (NO_2) to produce carbon dioxide (CO_2) and nitrogen dioxide (NO_2). ($CO + O_2 + NO = CO_2 + NO_2$).

The dangers of carbon monoxide, which is an odorless, colorless toxic gas are many. When carbon monoxide is inhaled into the lungs and passed into the blood stream, oxygen is replaced by the carbon monoxide in the red blood cells, causing a reduction in the amount of oxygen being supplied to the many parts of the body. This lack of oxygen causes headaches, lack of coordination, reduced mental alertness and should the carbon monoxide concentration be high enough, death could result.

NITROGEN

Normally, nitrogen is an inert gas. When heated to approximately 2500°F (1371°C) through the combustion process, this gas becomes active and causes an increase in the nitric oxide (NOx) emission.

Oxides of nitrogen (NOx) are composed of approximately 97–98% nitric oxide ($NO2$). Nitric oxide is a colorless gas but when it is passed into the atmosphere, it combines with oxygen and forms nitrogen dioxide ($NO2$). The nitrogen dioxide then combines with chemically active hydrocarbons (HC) and when in the presence of sunlight, causes the formation of photo chemical smog.

OZONE

To further complicate matters, some of the nitrogen dioxide (NO_2) is broken apart by the sunlight to form nitric oxide and oxygen. (NO_2 + sunlight = NO + O). This single atom of oxygen then combines with diatomic (meaning 2 atoms) oxygen (O_2) to form ozone (O_3). Ozone is 1 of the smells associated with smog. It has a pungent and offensive odor, irritates the eyes and lung tissues, affects the growth of plant life and causes rapid deterioration of rubber products. Ozone can be formed by sunlight as well as electrical discharge into the air.

The most common discharge area on the automobile engine is the secondary ignition electrical system, especially when inferior quality spark plug cables are used. As the surge of high voltage is routed through the secondary cable, the circuit builds up an electrical field around the wire, acting upon the oxygen in the surrounding air to form the ozone. The faint glow along the cable with the engine running that may be visible on a dark night, is called the "corona discharge." It is the result of the electrical field passing from a high along the cable, to a low in the surrounding air, which forms the ozone gas. The combination of corona and ozone has been a major cause of cable deterioration. Recently, different types and better quality insulating materials have lengthened the life of the electrical cables.

Although ozone at ground level can be harmful, ozone is beneficial to the earth's inhabitants. By having a concentrated ozone layer called the 'ozonosphere', between 10 and 20 miles (16–32km) up in the atmosphere much of the ultra violet radiation from the sun's rays are absorbed and screened. If this ozone layer were not present, much of the earth's surface would be burned, dried and unfit for human life.

There is much discussion concerning the ozone layer and its density. A feeling exists that this protective layer of ozone is slowly diminishing and corrective action must be directed to this problem. Much experimenting is presently being conducted to determine if a problem exists and if so, the short and long term effects of the problem and how it can be remedied.

OXIDES OF SULFUR

Oxides of sulfur (SOx) were initially ignored in the exhaust system emissions, since the sulfur content of gasoline as a fuel is less than $\frac{1}{10}$ of 1%. Because of this small amount, it was felt that it contributed very little to the overall pollution problem. However, because of the difficulty in solving the sulfur emissions in industrial pollutions and the introduction of catalytic converter to the automobile exhaust systems, a change was mandated. The automobile exhaust system, when equipped with a catalytic converter, changes the sulfur dioxide (SO_2) into the sulfur trioxide (SO_3).

When this combines with water vapors (H_2O), a sulfuric acid mist (H_2SO_4) is formed and is a very difficult pollutant to handle and is extremely corrosive. This sulfuric acid mist that is formed, is the same mist that rises from the vents of an automobile storage battery when an active

chemical reaction takes place within the battery cells.

When a large concentration of vehicles equipped with catalytic converters are operating in an area, this acid mist will rise and be distributed over a large ground area causing land, plant, crop, paints and building damage.

PARTICULATE MATTER

A certain amount of particulate matter is present in the burning of any fuel, with carbon constituting the largest percentage of the particulates. In gasoline, the remaining percentage of particulates is the burned remains of the various other compounds used in its manufacture. When a gasoline engine is in good internal condition, the particulate emissions are low but as the engine wears internally, the particulate emissions increase. By visually inspecting the tail pipe emissions, a determination can be made as to where an engine defect may exist. An engine with light gray smoke emitting from the tail pipe normally indicates an increase in the oil consumption through burning due to internal engine wear. Black smoke would indicate a defective fuel delivery system, causing the engine to operate in a rich mode. Regardless of the color of the smoke, the internal part of the engine or the fuel delivery system should be repaired to a "like new" condition to prevent excess particulate emissions.

Diesel and turbine engines emit a darkened plume of smoke from the exhaust system because of the type of fuel used. Emission control regulations are mandated for this type of emission and more stringent measures are being used to prevent excess emission of the particulate matter. Electronic components are being introduced to control the injection of the fuel at precisely the proper time of piston travel, to achieve the optimum in fuel ignition and fuel usage. Other particulate after-burning components are being tested to achieve a cleaner particular emission.

Good grades of engine lubricating oils should be used, meeting the manufacturers specification. "Cut-rate" oils can contribute to the particulate emission problem because of their low "flash" or ignition temperature point. Such oils burn prematurely during the combustion process causing emissions of particulate matter.

The cooling system is an important factor in the reduction of particulate matter. With the cooling system operating at a temperature specified by the manufacturer, the optimum of combustion will occur. The cooling system must

be maintained in the same manner as the engine oiling system, as each system is required to perform properly in order for the engine to operate efficiently for a long time.

Other Automobile Emission Sources

Before emission controls were mandated on the internal combustion engines, other sources of engine pollutants were discovered, along with the exhaust emission. It was determined the engine combustion exhaust produced 60% of the total emission pollutants, fuel evaporation from the fuel tank and carburetor vents produced 20%, with the another 20% being produced through the crankcase as a by-product of the combustion process.

CRANKCASE EMISSIONS

Crankcase emissions are made up of water, acids, unburned fuel, oil fumes and particulates. The emissions are classified as hydrocarbons (HC) and are formed by the small amount of unburned, compressed air/fuel mixture entering the crankcase from the combustion area during the compression and power strokes, between the cylinder walls and piston rings. The head of the compression and combustion help to form the remaining crankcase emissions.

Since the first engines, crankcase emissions were allowed to go into the air through a road draft tube, mounted on the lower side of the engine block. Fresh air came in through an open oil filler cap or breather. The air passed through the crankcase mixing with blow-by gases. The motion of the vehicle and the air blowing past the open end of the road draft tube caused a low

pressure area at the end of the tube. Crankcase emissions were simply drawn out of the road draft tube into the air.

To control the crankcase emission, the road draft tube was deleted. A hose and/or tubing was routed from the crankcase to the intake manifold so the blow-by emission could be burned with the air/fuel mixture. However, it was found that intake manifold vacuum, used to draw the crankcase emissions into the manifold, would vary in strength at the wrong time and not allow the proper emission flow. A regulating type valve was needed to control the flow of air through the crankcase.

Testing, showed the removal of the blow-by gases from the crankcase as quickly as possible, was most important to the longevity of the engine. Should large accumulations of blow-by gases remain and condense, dilution of the engine oil would occur to form water, soots, resins, acids and lead salts, resulting in the formation of sludge and varnishes. This condensation of the blow-by gases occur more frequently on vehicles used in numerous starting and stopping conditions, excessive idling and when the engine is not allowed to attain normal operating temperature through short runs. The crankcase purge control or PCV system will be described in detail later in this section.

FUEL EVAPORATIVE EMISSIONS

Gasoline fuel is a major source of pollution, before and after it is burned in the automobile engine. From the time the fuel is refined, stored, pumped and transported, again stored until it is pumped into the fuel tank of the vehicle, the gasoline gives off unburned hydrocarbons (HC) into the atmosphere. Through redesigning of the storage areas and venting systems, the pollution factor has been diminished but not eliminated,

from the refinery standpoint. However, the automobile still remained the primary source of vaporized, unburned hydrocarbon (HC) emissions.

Fuel pumped form an underground storage tank is cool but when exposed to a warner ambient temperature, will expand. Before controls were mandated, an owner would fill the fuel tank with fuel from an underground storage tank and park the vehicle for some time in warm area, such as a parking lot. As the fuel would warm, it would expand and should no provisions or area be provided for the expansion, the fuel would spill out the filler neck and onto the ground, causing hydrocarbon (HC) pollution and creating a severe fire hazard. To correct this condition, the vehicle manufacturers added overflow plumbing and/or gasoline tanks with built in expansion areas or domes.

However, this did not control the fuel vapor emission from the fuel tank and the carburetor bowl. It was determined that most of the fuel evaporation occurred when the vehicle was stationary and the engine not operating. Most vehicles carry 5–25 gallons (19–95 liters) of gasoline. Should a large concentration of vehicles be parked in one area, such as a large parking lot, excessive fuel vapor emissions would take place, increasing as the temperature increases.

To prevent the vapor emission from escaping into the atmosphere, the fuel system is designed to trap the fuel vapors while the vehicle is stationary, by sealing the fuel system from the atmosphere. A storage system is used to collect and hold the fuel vapors from the carburetor and the fuel tank when the engine is not operating. When the engine is started, the storage system is then purged of the fuel vapors, which are drawn into the engine and burned with the air/fuel mixture.

The components of the fuel evaporative system will be described in detail later in this section.

EMISSION CONTROLS

You'll find emission controls, ignition controls and fuel system controls are interrelated systems on the newer cars. In this section of the manual you'll find emission components related to exhaust gas recirculation, crankcase fume venting, evaporative. The Electronic Engine Control portion of the section should be be used in conjunction with the Fuel System section of the manual.

Crankcase Ventilation System

OPERATION

All these gasoline vehicles are equipped with a positive crankcase ventilation (PCV) system to

control crankcase blow-by vapors. The system functions as follows:

When the engine is running, a small portion of the gases which are formed in the combustion chamber leak by the piston rings and enter the crankcase. Since these gases are under pressure, they tend to escape from the crankcase and enter the atmosphere. If these gases are allowed to remain in the crankcase for any period of time, they contaminate the engine oil and cause sludge to build up in the

crankcase. If the gases are allowed to escape into the atmosphere, they pollute the air with unburned hydrocarbons.

The job of the crankcase emission control equipment is to recycle these gases back into the engine combustion chamber where they are reburned.

The crankcase (blow-by) gases are recycled in the following way: as the engine is running, clean, filtered air is drawn through the air filter and into the crankcase. As the air passes through the crankcase, it picks up the combustion gases and carries them out of the crankcase, through the oil separator, through the PCV valve, and into the induction system. As they enter the intake manifold, they are drawn into the combustion chamber where they are reburned.

The most critical component in the system is the PCV valve. This valve controls the amount of gases which are recycled into the combustion chamber. At low engine speeds, the valve is partially closed, limiting the flow of gases into the intake manifold. As engine speed increases, the valve opens to admit greater quantities of gases into the intake manifold. If the valve should become blocked or plugged, the gases will be prevented from escaping from the crankcase by the normal route. Since these gases are under pressure, they will find their own way out of the crankcase. This alternate route is usually a weak oil seal or gasket in the engine. As the gas escapes by the gasket, it also creates an oil leak. Besides causing oil leaks, a clogged PCV valve also allows these gases to remain in the crankcase for an extended period of time, promoting the formation of sludge in the engine.

SERVICE

Inspect the PCV system hose and connections at each tune-up and replace any deteriorated hoses. Check the PCV valve at every tune-up and replace it at 30,000 mile intervals.

1. Remove the PCV valve from the rocker arm cover.

2. Start engine, allow to reach normal temperature and idle speed.

3. Place your thumb over the end of the valve to check for vacuum. If no vacuum, check the valve and hose. Most likely the hose is plugged up.

4. Newer computer controlled vehicles may no show much of a change in engine rpm when the valve is blocked or removed due to the computer compensating almost instantly to the vacuum change.

5. Remove the valve from the engine and

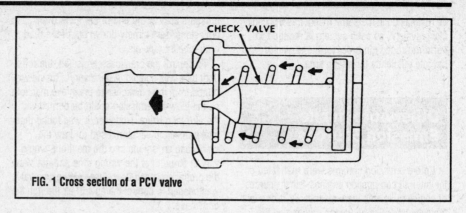

FIG. 1 Cross section of a PCV valve

hose. Shake the valve it should rattle. If not it's plugged up with dirt and must be replaced.

6. When replacing a PCV valve you MUST use the correct valve. Many valves look alike on the outside, but have different mechanical values. Putting an incorrect PCV valve on a vehicle can cause a great deal of driveability problems. The engine computer assumes the valve is the correct one and may over adjust ignition timing or fuel mixture.

REMOVAL & INSTALLATION

▶ SEE FIG. 1

In replacing the PCV valve, make sure it is fully inserted in the hose, that the clamp is moved over the ridge on the valve so that the valve will not slip out of the hose, and that the valve is fully inserted into the grommet in the valve cover.

1. Slide the rubber coupling that joins the tube coming from the valve cover to the filter off the filter nipple. Then, remove the top of the air cleaner. Slide the spring clamp off the filter, and remove the filter.

2. Inspect the rubber grommet in the valve cover and the rubber coupling for brittleness or cracking. Replace parts as necessary.

3. Insert the new PCV filter through the hole in the air cleaner with the open portion of the filter upward. Make sure that the square portion of filter behind the nipple fits into the (square) hole in the air cleaner.

4. Install a new spring clamp onto the nipple. Make sure the clamp goes under the ridge on the filter nipple all the way around. Then, reconnect the rubber coupling and install the air cleaner cover.

Diesel Crankcase Ventilation

▶ SEE FIG. 2

A crankcase depression regulator valve is used to regulate the flow of crankcase gases back into the engine. This valve is designed to limit vacuum in the crankcase. The gases are drawn from the valve cover through the CDRV and into the intake manifold.

1. Inlet port (2) (Gases from) crankcase
2. Mounting bracket
3. Cover diaphragm
4. Body
5. Spring
6. Outlet tube (Gases to intake manifold)

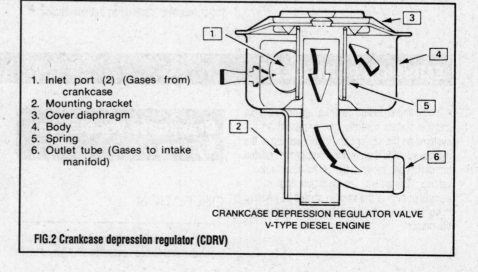

CRANKCASE DEPRESSION REGULATOR VALVE
V-TYPE DIESEL ENGINE

FIG.2 Crankcase depression regulator (CDRV)

Fresh air enters the engine through the combination filter, check valve, and oil fill cap. This air mixes with blow-by gases and enters the opposite valve cover. These gases pass through a filter on the valve cover and are drawn into the connected tubing.

Intake manifold vacuum acts against a spring loaded diaphragm to control the flow of crankcase gases. Higher vacuum levels pull the diaphragm closer to the top of the outlet tube. This reduces the amount of gases being drawn from the crankcase and decreases vacuum in the crankcase. As intake vacuum decreases, the spring pushes the diaphragm away from the top of the outlet tube allowing more gases into the manifold.

➡ **Do not allow solvent to come in contact with the diaphragm of the CDRV, as it will cause diaphragm damage.**

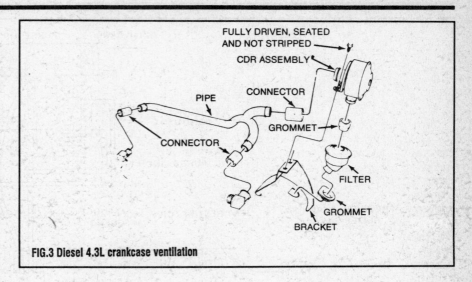

FIG.3 Diesel 4.3L crankcase ventilation

EVAPORATIVE EMISSION CONTROL SYSTEM

The basic Evaporative Emission Control System (EEC) used on all models is the carbon canister storage method. The system is used to reduce emissions of fuel vapors from the car's fuel system. Evaporated fuel vapors are stored for burning during combustion rather than being vented into the atmosphere when the engine is not running. To accomplish this, the fuel tank and the carburetor float bowl are vented through a vapor canister containing activated charcoal. The system utilizes a sealed fuel tank with a dome that collects fuel vapors and allows them to pass on into a line connected with the vapor canister. In addition, the vapors that form above the float chamber in the carburetor also pass into a line connected with the canister. The canister absorbs these vapors in a bed of activated charcoal and retains them until the canister is purged or cleared by air drawn through the filter at its bottom. The absorbing occurs when the car is not running, while the purging or cleaning occurs when the car is running. The amount of vapor being drawn into the engine at any given

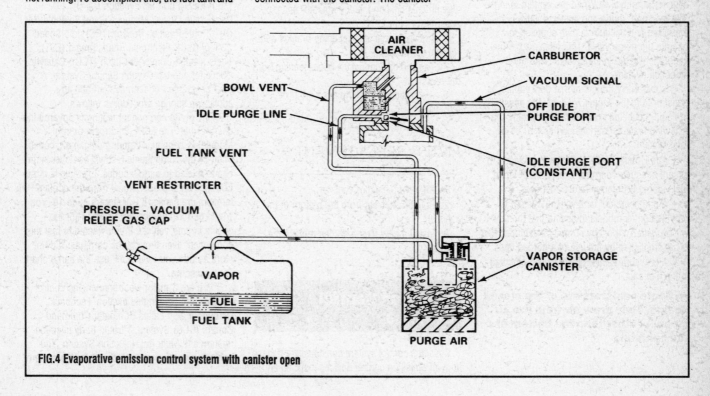

FIG.4 Evaporative emission control system with canister open

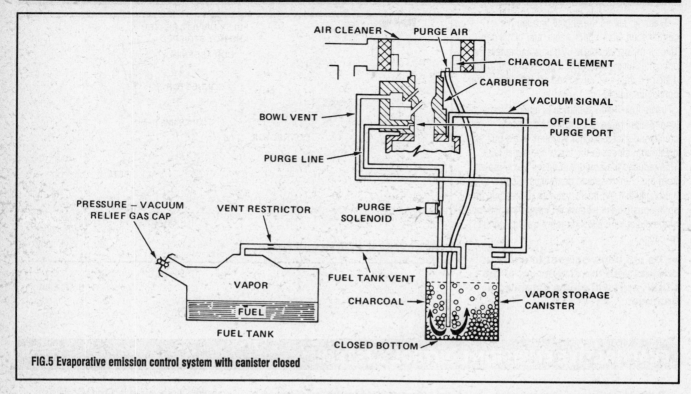

FIG.5 Evaporative emission control system with canister closed

time is too small to have an effect on either fuel economy or engine performance.

The Electronic Control Module (ECM) controls the vacuum to the canister purge valve by using an electrically operated solenoid valve. When the system is in the 'Open Loop' mode, the solenoid valve is energized and blocks all vacuum to the canister purge valve. When the system is in the 'Closed Loop' mode, the solenoid valve is de-energized and vacuum is then supplied to operate the purge valve. This releases the fuel vapors, collected in the canister, into the induction system.

It is extremely important that only vapors be transferred to the engine. To avoid the possibility of liquid fuel being drawn into the system, the following features are included as part of the total system:

• A fuel tank overfill protector is provided to assure adequate room for expansion of liquid fuel volume with temperature changes.

• A one point fuel tank venting system is provided on all models to assure that the tank will be vented under any normal car attitude. This is accomplished by the use of a domed tank.

• A pressure-vacuum relief valve is located in the fuel cap.

➡ **Some canisters are of the closed design. They draw air from the air cleaner rather than the bottom of the canister.**

VAPOR CANISTER REMOVAL & INSTALLATION

1. Loosen the screw holding the canister retaining bracket.
2. If equipped with A/C, loosen the attachments holding the accumulator and pipe assembly.
3. Rotate the canister retaining bracket and remove the canister.
4. Tag and disconnect the hoses leading from the canister.
5. Installation is in the reverse order of removal.

FILTER REPLACEMENT

1. Remove the vapor canister.
2. Pull the filter out from the bottom of the canister.
3. Install a new filter and then replace the canister.

Emission Control Systems

Emission control system constitute the largest body of emission control devices installed on A-

Body cars. Many of these systems are controlled by or engine control computer. Included in this category are: Thermostatic Air Cleaner (THERMAC); Air Management System; Early Fuel Evaporation System (EFE); Exhaust Gas Recirculation (EGR); Computer Command Control System (CCC); Throttle Body Injection (TBI); Multi-Port Fuel Injection (MPI); Deceleration Valve; Mixture Control Solenoid (M/C); Throttle Position Sensor (TPS); Idle Speed Control (ISC); Electronic Spark Timing (EST); Transmission Converter Clutch (TCC); Catalytic Converter and the Oxygen Sensor System. A brief description of each system and any applicable service procedures follows.

Many of the component testing is covered in chart format. The ECM (Electronic Control Module) is capable of storing diagnostic codes. Many of the components test will be cover in the charts related to certain codes. Example is if the ECM see an improper signal from the coolant temperature sensor it will store a code 14. You would perform the test for Code 14 for the engine in your vehicle. If you wanted to test this component even thought the computer did not store a code you would still use the same chart and procedure.

There are 3 major electronic engine control systems covered in this section. Feedback Carburetor also called Computer Command Control (CCC) System, Throttle Body Injection System and Multi-Port Injection System. You only need use the text and charts for the system

which your car uses. The Fuel Systems section of the book will cover must removal, installation and adjustments. This section will be used for general descriptions of systems and components and the testing charts needed to diagnosis them.

Thermostatic Air Cleaner (THERMAC)

All Feedback Carbureted, and Throttle Body Injected engines use the THERMAC system. This system is designed to warm the air entering the carburetor when underhood temperatures are low, and to maintain a controlled air temperature into the carburetor at all times. By allowing preheated air to enter the carburetor, the amount of time the choke is on is reduced, resulting in better fuel economy and lower emissions. Engine warm-up time is a also reduced.

The THERMAC system is composed of the air cleaner body, a filter, sensor unit, vacuum diaphragm, damper door, and associated hoses and connections. Heat radiating from the exhaust manifold is trapped by a heat stove and is ducted to the air cleaner to supply heated air to the carburetor. A movable door in the air cleaner case snorkel allows air to be drawn in from the heat stove (cold operation). The door position is controlled by the vacuum motor, which receives intake manifold vacuum as modulated by the temperature sensor.

SYSTEM CHECKS

1. Check the vacuum hoses for leaks, kinks, breaks, or improper connections and correct any defects.

2. With the engine off, check the position of the damper door within the snorkel. A mirror can be used to make this job easier. The damper door should be open to admit outside air.

3. Apply at least 7 in.Hg of vacuum to the damper diaphragm unit. The door should close. If it doesn't, check the diaphragm linkage for binding and correct hookup.

4. With the vacuum still applied and the door closed, clamp the tube to trap the vacuum. If the door doesn't remain closed, there is a leak in the diaphragm assembly.

Air Management System

The AIR management system, is used to provide additional oxygen to continue the combustion process after the exhaust gases leave the combustion chamber. Air is injected into either the exhaust port(s), the exhaust manifold(s) or the catalytic converter by an engine driven air pump. The system is in operation at all times and will bypass air only momentarily during deceleration and at high speeds. The bypass function is performed by the AIR Management Valve, while the check valve protects the air pump by preventing any backflow of exhaust gases.

The AIR management system helps reduce HC and CO content in the exhaust gases by injecting air into the exhaust ports during cold engine operation. This air injection also helps the catalytic converter to reach the proper temperature quicker during warmup. When the engine is warm (Closed Loop), the AIR system injects air into the beds of a three-way converter to lower the HC and the CO content in the exhaust.

The Air Management system utilizes the following components:

1. An engine driven AIR pump.
2. AIR management valves (Air Control, Air Switching).
3. Air flow and control hoses.
4. Check valves.

5. A dual-bed, three-way catalytic converter.

The belt driven, vane-type air pump is located at the front of the engine and supplies clean air to the AIR system for purposes already stated. When the engine is cold, the Electronic Control Module (ECM) energizes an AIR control solenoid. This allows air to flow to the AIR switching valve. The AIR switching valve is then energized to direct air to the exhaust ports.

When the engine is warm, the ECM de-energizes the AIR switching valve, thus directing the air between the beds of the catalytic converter. This provides additional oxygen for the oxidizing catalyst in the second bed to decrease HC and CO, while at the same time keeping oxygen levels low in the first bed, enabling the reducing catalyst to effectively decrease the levels of NOx.

If the AIR control valve detects a rapid increase in manifold vacuum (deceleration), certain operating modes (wide open throttle, etc.) or if the ECM self-diagnostic system detects any problem in the system, air is diverted to the air cleaner or directly into the atmosphere.

The primary purpose of the ECM's divert mode is to prevent backfiring. Throttle closure at the beginning of deceleration will temporarily create air/fuel mixtures which are too rich to burn completely. These mixtures become burnable when they reach the exhaust if combined with the injection air. The next firing of the engine will ignite this mixture causing an exhaust backfire. Momentary diverting of the injection air from the exhaust prevents this.

The AIR management system check valves and hoses should be checked periodically for any leaks, cracks or deterioration.

REMOVAL & INSTALLATION

Air Pump

1. Remove the AIR management valves and/or adapter at the pump.

2. Loosen the air pump adjustment bolt and remove the drive belt.

3. Unscrew the pump mounting bolts and then remove the pump pulley.

4. Unscrew the pump mounting bolts and then remove the pump.

5. Installation is in the reverse order of removal. Be sure to adjust the drive belt tension after installing it.

Check Valve

1. Release the clamp and disconnect the air hoses from the valve.

2. Unscrew the check valve from the air injection pipe.

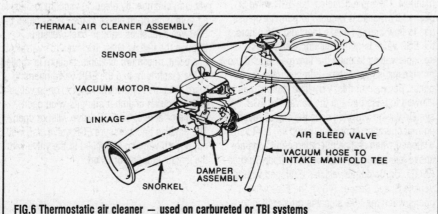

THERMAL AIR CLEANER ASSEMBLY

SENSOR

VACUUM MOTOR

LINKAGE

SNORKEL

DAMPER ASSEMBLY

AIR BLEED VALVE

VACUUM HOSE TO INTAKE MANIFOLD TEE

FIG.6 Thermostatic air cleaner — used on carbureted or TBI systems

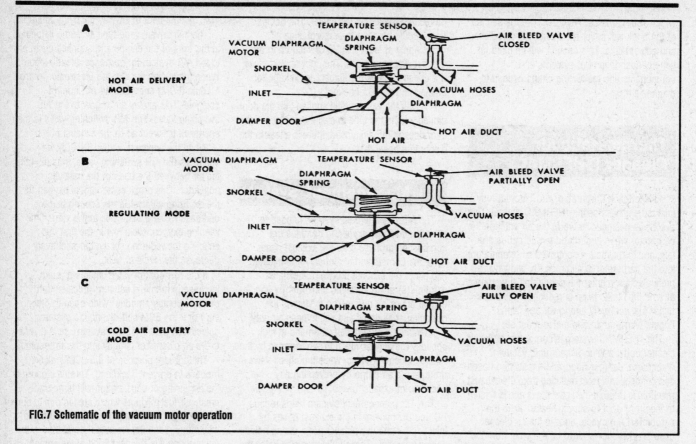

FIG.7 Schematic of the vacuum motor operation

3. Installation is in the reverse order of removal.

Air Management Valve

1. Disconnect the negative battery cable.

2. Remove the air cleaner.

3. Tag and disconnect the vacuum hose from the valve.

4. Tag and disconnect the air outlet hoses from the valve.

5. Bend back the lock tabs and then remove the bolts holding the elbow to the valve.

6. Tag and disconnect any electrical connections at the valve and then remove the valve from the elbow.

7. Installation is in the reverse order of removal.

Exhaust Gas Recirculation System

♦ SEE FIGS. 8 to 12

➡ **Not all vehicles are equipped with an EGR system.**

The EGR system is used to reduce oxides of nitrogen (NOx) emission levels caused by high combustion chamber temperatures. This is accomplished by the use of an EGR valve which opens, under specific engine operating conditions, to admit a small amount of exhaust gas into the intake manifold, below the throttle plate. The exhaust gas mixes with the incoming air charge and displaces a portion of the oxygen in the air/fuel mixture entering the combustion chamber. The exhaust gas does not support combustion of the air/fuel mixture but it takes up volume, the net effect of which is to lower the temperature of the combustion process. This lower temperature also helps control detonation.

The EGR valve is a mounted on the intake manifold and has an opening into the exhaust manifold. On some vehicles, the EGR valve is opened by manifold vacuum to permit exhaust gas to flow into the intake manifold. On others, the EGR valve is purely electrical and uses solenoid valves to open the flow passage. If too much exhaust gas enters, combustion will not occur. Because of this, very little exhaust gas is allowed to pass through the valve. The EGR system will be activated once the engine reaches normal operating temperature and the EGR valve will open when engine operating conditions are above idle speed and below Wide Open Throttle (WOT). On California vehicles equipped with a Vehicle Speed Sensor (VSS), the EGR valve opens when the VSS signal is greater than 2 mph. The EGR system is deactivated on vehicles equipped with a Transmission Converter Clutch (TCC) when the TCC is engaged. There are three basic types of systems as described below, differing in the way EGR flow is modulated.

POSITIVE BACKPRESSURE EGR VALVE

An air bleed valve, located inside the EGR valve assembly acts as a vacuum regulator. The bleed valve controls the amount of vacuum in the vacuum chamber by bleeding vacuum to outside air during the open phase of the cycle. When the EGR valve receives enough backpressure through the hollow shaft, it closes the valve. At this point, maximum available vacuum is applied to the diaphragm and the EGR valve opens. If there is a small amount of vacuum or no vacuum in the vacuum chamber such as wide open throttle or at idle, the EGR valve will not open. The positive backpressure EGR valve also will not open if vacuum is applied to the valve with the engine stopped or idling.

NEGATIVE BACKPRESSURE EGR VALVE

The negative backpressure EGR valve is similar to the positive backpressure EGR valve except that the bleed valve spring is moved from above the diaphragm to below and the bleed valve is normally closed. The negative backpressure EGR valve varies the amount of exhaust gas flow into the intake manifold depending on manifold vacuum and variations in exhaust backpressure. The diaphragm on the valve has an internal air bleed hole which is held closed by a small spring when there is no exhaust backpressure. Engine vacuum opens the EGR valve against the pressure of a spring. When manifold vacuum combines with negative exhaust backpressure, the vacuum bleed hole opens and the EGR valve closes. This valve will open if vacuum is applied with the engine not running.

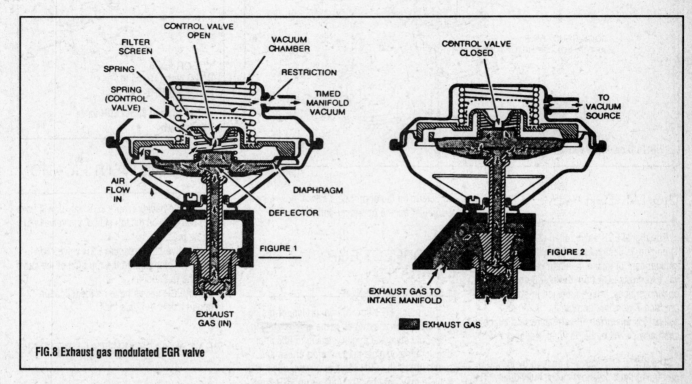

FIG.8 Exhaust gas modulated EGR valve

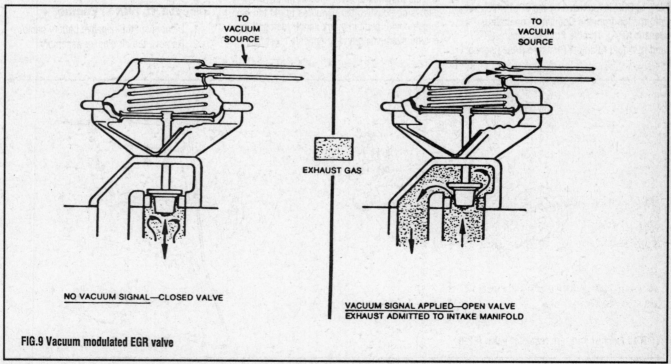

FIG.9 Vacuum modulated EGR valve

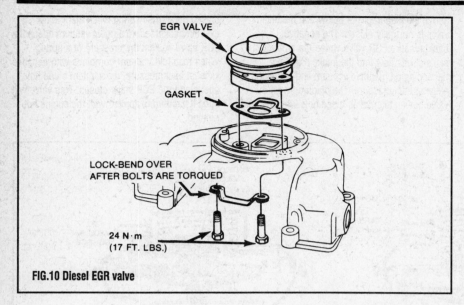

FIG.10 Diesel EGR valve

Labels in figure:
EGR VALVE
GASKET
LOCK-BEND OVER AFTER BOLTS ARE TORQUED
24 N·m (17 FT. LBS.)

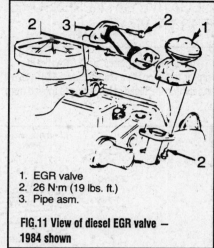

1. EGR valve
2. 26 N·m (19 lbs. ft.)
3. Pipe asm.

FIG.11 View of diesel EGR valve — 1984 shown

DIGITAL EGR VALVE

The digital EGR valve, used on the 3.1L (VIN T) engine, is designed to control the flow of EGR independent of intake manifold vacuum. The valve controls EGR flow through 3 solenoid-opened orifices, which increase in size, to produce 7 possible combinations. When a solenoid is energized, the armature with attached shaft and swivel pintle, is lifted, opening the orifice.

The digital EGR valve is opened by the ECM, grounding each solenoid circuit individually. The flow of EGR is regulated by the ECM which uses information from the Coolant Temperature Sensor (CTS), Throttle Position Sensor (TPS) and Manifold Absolute Pressure (MAP) sensor to determine the appropriate rate of flow for a particular engine operating condition.

INCORRECT EGR OPERATION

Too much EGR flow at idle, cruise, or during cold operation may result in the engine stalling after cold start, the engine stalling at idle after deceleration, vehicle surge during cruise and rough idle. If the EGR valve is always open, the vehicle may not idle. Too little or no EGR flow allows combustion temperatures to get too high which could result in spark knock (detonation), engine overheating and/or emission test failure.

EGR VALVE IDENTIFICATION

• Positive backpressure EGV valves will have a "P" stamped on the top side of the valve below the date built.
• Negative backpressure EGR valves will have a "N" stamped on the top side of the valve below the date built.
• Port EGR valves have no identification stamped below the date built.

REMOVAL & INSTALLATION

Except 3.1L (VIN T) Engine

1. Disconnect the negative battery cable.
2. Remove the air cleaner assembly.

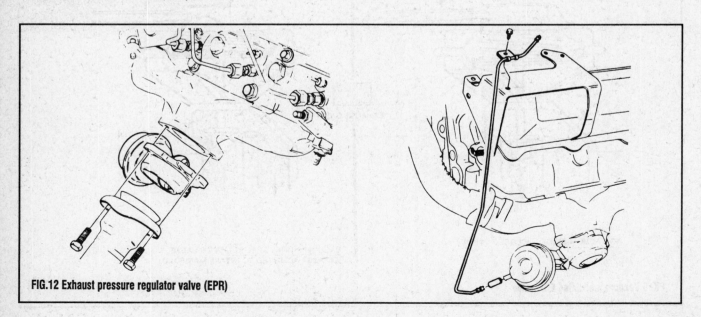

FIG.12 Exhaust pressure regulator valve (EPR)

3. Tag and disconnect the necessary hoses and wiring to gain access to the EGR valve.

4. Remove the EGR valve retaining bolts.

5. Remove the EGR valve. Discard the gasket.

6. Buff the exhaust deposits from the mounting surface and around the valve using a wire wheel.

7. Remove deposits from the valve outlet.

8. Clean the mounting surfaces of the intake manifold and valve assembly.

To Install:

9. Install a new EGR gasket.

10. Install the EGR valve to the manifold.

11. Install the retaining bolts and torque to 16 ft. lbs. (22 Nm).

12. Connect the wiring and hoses.

13. Install the air cleaner assembly.

14. Connect the negative battery cable.

3.1L (VIN T) Engine

1. Disconnect the negative battery cable.

2. Disconnect the electrical connector at the solenoid.

3. Remove the 2 base-to-flange bolts.

4. Remove the digital EGR valve.

To Install:

5. Install the digital EGR valve.

6. Install the 2 base-to-flange bolts. Tighten to 22 ft. lbs. (30 Nm).

7. Connect the negative battery cable.

EGR SOLENOID

REMOVAL & INSTALLATION

1. Disconnect the negative battery cable.

2. Remove the air cleaner, as required.

3. Disconnect the electrical connector at the solenoid.

4. Disconnect the vacuum hoses.

5. Remove the retaining bolts and the solenoid.

6. Remove the filter, as required.

To Install:

7. If removed, install the filter.

8. Install the solenoid and retaining bolts.

9. Connect the vacuum hoses.

10. Connect the electrical connector.

11. If removed, install the air cleaner.

12. Connect the negative battery cable.

Diesel EGR System

The diesel EGR systems work in the same basic manner as gasoline engine EGR systems: exhaust gases are introduced into the combustion chambers to reduce combustion temperatures, and thus lower the formation of nitrogen oxides (NOx).

Vacuum from the vacuum pump is modulated by the Vacuum Regulator Valve (VRV) mounted on the injection pump.

The amount of EGR valve opening is further modulated by a Vacuum Modulator Valve (VMV). The VMV allows for an increase in vacuum to the EGR valve as the throttle is closed, up to the switching point of the VMV. The system also employs an RVR valve.

In 1985, the EGR valve was moved to the rear of the engine and has become electronically controlled.

BASIC COMPONENT TESTING

Vacuum Regulator Valve (VRV)

The VRV is attached to the side of the injection pump and regulates vacuum in proportion to throttle angle. Vacuum from the vacuum pump is supplied to port A and vacuum at port **B** (see illustration) is reduced as the throttle is opened. At closed throttle the vacuum is 15 in.Hg; at half throttle, 6 in. (152mm); at wide open throttle there should be zero vacuum.

Exhaust Gas Recirculation Valve

Apply vacuum to the vacuum port. The valve should be fully open at 12 in.Hg and closed below 6 in. (152mm).

Response Vacuum Reducer (RVR)

Connect a vacuum gauge to the port marked To EGR valve or TCC solenoid. Connect a hand operated vacuum pump to the VRV port. Draw 15 in.Hg of vacuum on the pump and the reading on the vacuum gauge should be lower than the vacuum pump reading by 0.75 in..

Exhaust Pressure Regulator Valve

Apply vacuum to the vacuum port of the valve. The valve should be fully closed at 12 in.Hg and open below 6 in.

Vacuum Modulator Valve (VMV)

To test the VMV, block the drive wheels, and apply the parking brake. With the shift lever in Park, start the engine and run at a slow idle. Connect a vacuum gauge to the hose that connects to the port marked **MAN**. There

should be at least 14 in.Hg of vacuum. If not, check the vacuum pump, VRV, RVR, solenoid, and all connecting hoses. Reconnect the hose to the **MAN** port. Connect a vacuum gauge to the **DIST** port on the VMV. The vacuum reading should be 12 in.Hg except on High Altitude cars, which should be 9 in.Hg.

Emission Service Light

An emissions indicator flag may appear in the odometer window of the speedometer on some vehicles. The flag could say "Sensor", "Emissions" or "Catalyst" depending on the part or assembly that is scheduled for regular emissions maintenance replacement. The word "Sensor" indicates a need for oxygen sensor replacement and the words "Emissions" or "Catalyst" indicate the need for catalytic converter catalyst replacement.

RESETTING

1. Remove the instrument panel trim plate.

2. Remove the instrument cluster lens.

3. Locate the flag indicator reset notches at the drivers side of the odometer.

4. Use a pointed tool to apply light downward pressure on the notches, until the indicator is reset.

5. When the indicator is reset an alignment mark will appear in the left center of the odometer window.

Service Interval Reminder Light

RESETTING

If equipped, the SERVICE REMINDER section of the driver information center (DIC) display shows how many miles remain until service is needed. When the RESET button is pressed twice, a type of service and number of miles remaining until the service is needed will be displayed. Each time the RESET button is pressed, another type of service and mile remaining for it will be displayed.

With the ignition switch in the RUN, BULB, TEST or START position, voltage is applied from the ECM fuse through a pink/black wire to the ECM. As the vehicle moves the speed sensor

sends pulses to the ECM. The ECM then sends signals to the speed input of the DIC module. The DIC module converts these pulses to miles. The module then subtracts the miles travelled from the distance on the DIC display. All four types of service can be displayed at the same time.

To reset the service light ti will be necessary to subtract the mileage from the service interval light that is illuminated. The miles remaining for a certain type of service can be decreased by holding the RESET button, the miles remaining will be decreased in steps of 500 miles every 5 seconds. If the RESET button is held in and the miles remaining reach zero, the DIC display will show the service interval for the service selected. The service intervals are; oil change 7500 miles; oil filter 7500 miles, next filter 15,000 miles; rotate tires 7500 miles, next rotate 15,000 miles; tune-up 30,000 miles.

If the RESET button is still held down, the miles will decrease in steps of 500 miles from the service interval. When the RESET button is released, the mile display shown will be the new distance until the service should be performed.

When the service distance reaches zero, the service reminder item will be displayed. If the service interval is reset within 10 miles the display will go out immediately. If more than 10 miles passes before the service interval is reset, the item will remain displayed for another 10 miles after begin reset before going out.

➡ **On some models it may be necessary to depress the SYSTEM RECALL button in order to display the service interval light on the driver information center in order to be able to decrease mileage from to reset the interval light**

Service Engine Soon Light

RESETTING

The SES light or Check Engine light will light if an engine or emission problem is detected. If an emission problem is detected the computer will store a code for that fault. If the fault goes away or is repair the light will go out, but the code will remain in memory. If the problem returns or is not repair the light will not go out and can not be reset. When the problem goes away the light goes out.

Oxygen Sensor

The exhaust oxygen sensor or O2 sensor is mounted in the exhaust stream where it monitors oxygen content in the exhaust gas. The oxygen content in the exhaust is a measure of the air/fuel mixture going into the engine. The oxygen in the exhaust reacts with the oxygen sensor to produce a voltage which is read by the ECM. The voltage output is very low, ranging from 0.1 volt in a high oxygen-lean mixture condition to 0.9 volt in a low oxygen-rich mixture condition.

Testing the oxygen sensor without the use of special scan tools to observe its operation is difficult. The oxygen sensor should not be condemned because of a Code 44 or 45. These codes tell you the oxygen sensor is seeing a constant rich or leak mixture. This code is usually not due to a bad oxygen sensor. A rich mixture could be a dirty air filter, stuck choke, leaking injector, burn valve or other problems. A lean mixture could be a vacuum leak, low fuel pressure or even a bad spark plug wire. Follow the proper charts to test the components.

PRECAUTIONS

• Careful handling of the oxygen sensor is essential.

• The electrical pigtail and connector are permanently attached and should not be removed from the oxygen sensor.

• The in-line electrical connector and louvered end of the oxygen sensor must be kept free of grease, dirt and other contaminants.

• Avoid using cleaning solvents of any type on the oxygen sensor.

• Do not drop or roughly handle the oxygen sensor.

• The oxygen sensor may be difficult to remove if the engine temperature is below 120°F (48°C). Excessive force may damage the threads in the exhaust manifold or exhaust pipe.

REMOVAL & INSTALLATION

♦ SEE FIG. 13

The oxygen sensor must be replaced every 30,000 miles (48,000 km.). The sensor may be difficult to remove when the engine temperature is below 120°F (48°C). Excessive removal force may damage the threads in the exhaust manifold or pipe; follow the removal procedure carefully.

1. Locate the oxygen sensor. It protrudes from the center of the exhaust manifold at the front of the engine compartment (it looks somewhat like a spark plug).

2. Disconnect the electrical connector from the oxygen sensor.

3. Spray a commercial heat riser solvent onto the sensor threads and allow it to soak in for at least five minutes.

4. Carefully unscrew and remove the sensor.

5. To install, first coat the new sensor's threads with G.M. anti-seize compound No. 5613695 or the equivalent. This is not a conventional anti-seize paste. The use of a regular compound may electrically insulate the sensor, rendering it inoperative. You must coat the threads with an electrically conductive anti-seize compound.

6. Installation torque is 30 ft. lbs. (42 Nm.). Do not overtighten.

7. Reconnect the electrical connector. Be careful not to damage the electrical pigtail. Check the sensor boot for proper fit and installation.

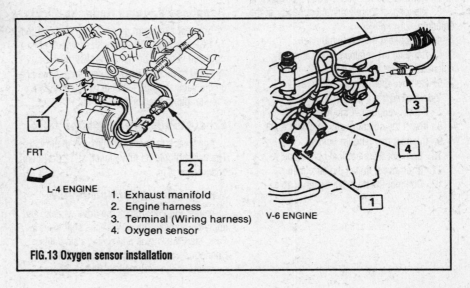

FRT

L-4 ENGINE

1. Exhaust manifold
2. Engine harness
3. Terminal (Wiring harness)
4. Oxygen sensor

V-6 ENGINE

FIG.13 Oxygen sensor installation

ELECTRONIC ENGINE CONTROL SYSTEMS

There are 3 basic fuel control systems used on the General Motors A-Body cars. The feedback carburetor vehicles use a system called Computer Command Control (CCC) System. The other two systems are fuel injection systems. One system is called Throttle Body Injection (TBI), this system uses an injected built into the throttle body. Throttle body injected vehicle appear very much like carbureted vehicles, but you'll notice there is no choke. The third system is Multi-Port Injected (MPI) Systems. This MPI system has an injector mounted in the intake manifold at each intake valve. There is one injector for each cylinder.

Feedback Carburetor and Computer Control (CCC) System

The CCC system monitors engine and vehicle operating conditions which it uses to control engine and emission control systems. This system controls engine operation and lowers the exhaust emissions while maintaining good fuel economy and driveability. The Electronic Control Module (ECM) is the brain of the CCC system. The ECM controls engine related systems constantly adjusting the engine operation. In addition to maintaining the ideal air/fuel ratio for the catalytic converter and adjusting ignition timing, the CCC system also controls the Air Management System so that the catalytic converter can operate at the highest efficiency possible. The system also controls the lockup on the transmission torque converter clutch, adjusts idle speed over a wide range of conditions, purges the evaporative emissions charcoal canister, controls the EGR valve operation and operates the Early Fuel Evaporative (EFE) system. Not all engines use all of the above sub-systems.

The CCC system is primarily an emission control system, designed to maintain a 14.7:1 air/fuel ratio under all operating conditions. When this ideal air/fuel ratio is maintained the catalytic converter can control oxides of nitrogen (NOx), hydrocarbon (HC) and carbon monoxide (CO) emissions.

There are 2 operation modes for CCC system: closed loop and open loop fuel control. Closed loop fuel control means the oxygen sensor is controlling the carburetor's air/fuel mixture ratio. Under open loop fuel control operating conditions (wide open throttle, engine and/or oxygen sensor cold), the oxygen sensor has no effect on the air/fuel mixture.

➡ **On some engines, the oxygen sensor will cool off while the engine is idling, putting the system into open loop operation. To restore closed loop operation, run the engine at part throttle and accelerate from idle to part throttle a few times.**

The basic system block diagram shows the catalytic converter located in the exhaust system close to the engine. It is ahead of the muffler and tailpipe. If the converter is to do its job effectively, the engine must receive an air/fuel mixture of approximately 14.7:1.

The carburetor mixes air and gasoline into a combustible mixture before delivering it to the engine. However, carburetors have reached a point where they can no longer control the air/fuel mixture sufficiently close to the ideal 14.7:1 ratio for most operating conditions. Therefore, a different type of control must be used on the carburetor, something that has never been used before.

An electric solenoid in the carburetor controls the air/fuel ratio. The solenoid is connected to an electronic module (ECM) which is an on board computer. The ECM provides a controlling signal to the solenoid. The solenoid controls the metering rod(s) and an idle air bleed valve to closely control the air/fuel ration throughout the operating range of the engine. However, since the engine operates under a wide variety of conditions, the computer must be told what those conditions are. This is so that it will know what to tell the carburetor solenoid to do.

A sensor is located in the exhaust stream close to the engine. It's known as an oxygen sensor or usually refer to as the oxygen (O_2) sensor. This sensor functions when the engine's exhaust temperature rises above 600°F (315°C). There is a direct relationship between the mixture delivered by the carburetor and the amount of oxygen left in the exhaust gases. The O_2 sensor can determine whether the exhaust is too rich or too lean. It sends a varying voltage signal to the ECM.

The ECM will then signal the mixture control solenoid to deliver richer or leaner mixture for the current engine operating conditions. As the carburetor makes a change, the O_2 sensor will sense that change and signal the ECM whether or not it's too rich or too lean. The ECM will then make a correction, if necessary. This goes on continually and is what we refer to as Closed

Loop operation. Closed loop conditions deliver a 14.7:1 air/fuel mixture to the engine. This makes it possible for the converter to act upon all 3 of the major pollutants in an efficient and effective manner. consider, however, what happens in the morning when it's cold and the vehicle is started. If the system where to keep the air/fuel mixture to the 14.7:1 air/fuel ratio when it's cold the chances are that the engine wouldn't run very well. When the engine is cold, it has to have a richer mixture. An automatic choke is used to give the engine a richer mixture until it is up to normal operating temperature. during this time, the O_2 sensor signals are ignored by the ECM.

A temperature sensor is located in the water jacket of the engine and connected to the electronic control module. When the engine is cold, the temperature sensor will tell the ECM to ignore the oxygen sensor signal, since the sensor is too cold to operate. The electronic control module then tells the carburetor to deliver a richer mixture based upon what has already been programmed into the ECM. The ECM will also use information from other sensors during cold start operation.

After the engine has been running for some time and has reached normal operating temperature, the temperature sensor will signal the ECM that the engine is warm and it can accept the oxygen sensor signal. If other system requirements are met, closed loop operations begins. The oxygen sensor will then influence the ECM as to what mixture it should deliver to the engine. In addition to these 2 conditions, there are 3 other conditions which affect the air/fuel mixture delivered to the engine. First is the load that is placed upon the engine. When an engine is working hard, such as pulling a heavy load up a long grade, it requires a richer air/fuel mixture. This is different from a vehicle that is operating in a cruise condition on a level highway at a constant rate of speed.

Manifold vacuum is used to determine engine load. A manifold pressure sensor is connected to the intake manifold. It detects changes in the manifold pressure which are signalled to the ECM. As changes occur, the load placed upon the engine varies. The ECM takes this varying signal into account when determining what mixture the carburetor should be delivering to the engine. The next condition in determining what air/fuel mixture should be is the amount of throttle opening. The more throttle opening at any given time, the richer the mixture required by the engine. On most applications a Throttle Position Sensor (TPS) in the carburetor sends a signal to the ECM. It tells the ECM the position of the

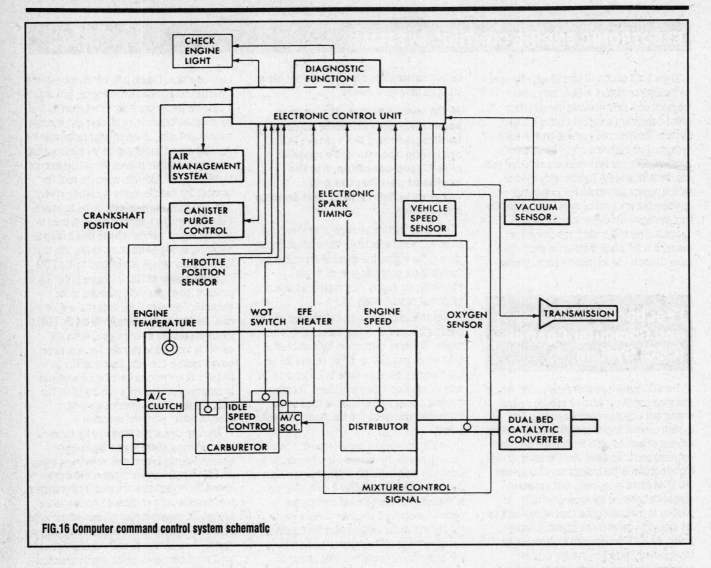

FIG.16 Computer command control system schematic

throttle, whether it it at idle, part throttle, wide open or whatever condition that exists in between.

The last condition, which has a bearing on the mixture that the engine would require, is the speed the engine is running. Certainly when an engine is operating at 600 rpm, it doesn't need as much gasoline as it does when it is operating at 4000 rpm. Therefore, a tachometer signal from the distributor is delivered to the ECM. This tells the ECM how fast the engine is running. This signal will also be taken into consideration when the ECM decides what mixture the carburetor should be delivering to the engine. In the typical CCC system, the ECM will use various inputs to make decisions that will best control the operation of the mixture control solenoid for maximum system efficiency.

CCC SYSTEM COMPONENTS

ELECTRONIC CONTROL MODULE (ECM)

The ECM is a reliable solid state computer, protected in a metal box. It is used to monitor and control all the functions of the CCC system and is located in on the passenger side kick panel. The ECM can perform several on-car functions at the same time and has the ability to diagnose itself as well as other CCC system circuits.

The ECM performs the functions of an on and off switch. It can send a voltage signal to a circuit or connect a circuit to ground at a precise time. Programmed into the ECM's memory are voltage and time values. These valves will differ from engine to engine. As an example then, if the ECM sees a proper voltage value for the correct length of time it will perform a certain function.

This could be turning the EGR system on as the engine warms up. If however, the voltage or the time interval is not correct, the ECM will also recognize this. It will not perform its function and in most cases turn the "CHECK ENGINE" or "SERVICE ENGINE SOON" light on.

The other CCC components include the oxygen sensor, an electronically controlled variable-mixture carburetor, a 3-way catalytic converter, throttle position and coolant sensors, a barometric pressure (BARO) sensor, a manifold absolute pressure (MAP) sensor, a "CHECK ENGINE" light on the instrument cluster and an Electronic Spark Timing (EST) distributor, which on some engines is equipped with an Electronic Spark Control (ESC) which retards ignition spark under some conditions (detonation, etc.).

Other components used by the CCC system include the Air Injection Reaction (AIR) Management System, charcoal canister purge solenoid, EGR valve control, vehicle speed

sensor (located in the instrument cluster), transmission torque converter clutch solenoid (automatic transmission models only), idle speed control and Early Fuel Evaporative (EFE) system.

The CCC system ECM, in addition to monitoring sensors and sending a control signal to the carburetor, also controls the charcoal canister purge, AIR Management System, fuel control, idle speed control, idle air control, automatic transmission converter clutch lockup, distributor ignition timing, EGR valve control, EFE control, air conditioner compressor clutch operation, electric fuel pump and the "CHECK ENGINE" light.

The AIR Management System is an emission control which provides additional oxygen either to the catalyst or the exhaust manifold. An AIR Management System, composed of an air switching valve and/or an air control valve, controls the air pump flow and is itself controlled by the ECM. The AIR system uses vacuum operated, ECM controlled (grounds to complete the circuit and energize the solenoids) valves to control the AIR switching. The 5.0L (VIN Y) engine uses an Electric Air Switching and Electric Divert Valve (EAS and EDV) 2 valve system, while the 5.7L (VIN H) and 5.0L (VINs 6 and G) use and Electric Divert/Air Switching Valve (EDES) system, that combines the functions of both valves.

The charcoal canister purge control is an electrically operated solenoid valve controlled by the ECM. When energized, the purge control solenoid blocks vacuum from reaching the canister purge valve. When the ECM de-energizes the purge control solenoid, vacuum is allowed to reach the canister and operate the purge valve. This releases the fuel vapors collected in the canister into the induction system.

The EGR valve control solenoid is activated by the ECM in similar fashion to the canister purge solenoid. When the engine is cold, the ECM energizes the solenoid, which blocks the vacuum signal to the EGR valve. When the engine is warm, the ECM de-energizes the solenoid and the vacuum signal is allowed to reach and activate the EGR valve.

The Transmission Converter Clutch (TCC) lock is controlled by the ECM through an electrical solenoid in the automatic transmission. When the vehicle speed sensor in the instrument panel signals the ECM that the vehicle has reached the correct speed, the ECM energizes the solenoid which allows the torque converter to mechanically couple the engine to the transmission. When the brake pedal is pushed or during deceleration, passing, etc., the ECM returns the transmission to fluid drive.

The idle speed control adjusts the idle speed

to load conditions and will lower the idle speed under no-load or low-load conditions to conserve gasoline.

The Early Fuel Evaporative (EFE) system is used on most engines to provide rapid heat to the engine induction system to promote smooth start-up and operation. There are 2 types of system: vacuum servo and electrically heated. They use different means to achieve the same end, which is to pre-heat the incoming air/fuel mixture. They may or may not be controlled by the ECM.

A/C Wide Open Throttle (WOT) Control, on this system the ECM controls the A/C compressor clutch to disengage the clutch during hard acceleration. On some engines, the ECM disengages the clutch during the engine start-up on a warm engine. The WOT control is not installed on all engines.

Electronic Spark Control (ESC), on this system the ECM controls the spark timing on certain engines to allow the engine to have maximum spark advance without spark knock. This improves the driveability and fuel economy. This system is not used on all engines.

Shift Light Control, on some vehicles, the ECM controls a shift light, to indicate the best manual transmission shift point for maximum fuel economy. This control is not used on all engines.

ROCHESTER FEEDBACK CARBURETORS

These carburetors are all basically the same except that the E2ME and E4ME uses an electrically heated choke and the E4MC uses an integral hot air choke. Both the E4ME and the E4MC are 4 barrel, 2 stage Quadrajet design. While the E2ME and E2MC are 2 barrel single stage design. All carburetors are used with the Computer Command Control (CCC) System of fuel control. All Rochester carburetors consist of 3 major assemblies: the air horn, the float bowl and the throttle body. They have 6 basic operating systems: float, idle, main metering, power, pump and choke.

A single float chamber supplies fuel to the 4 carburetor bores. A closed-cell rubber float, brass needle seat and a rubber tipped float valve with pull clip, are used to control fuel level in the float chamber. An electrically operated mixture control solenoid, mounted in the float bowl, is used to control the air and fuel mixture in the primary bores of the carburetor. The plunger in the solenoid is controlled (or pulsed) by electrical signals received from the Electronic Control Module (ECM).

The air valve and metering rods control the air/fuel metering in the secondary bores. A pair of tapered metering rods are attached to a hanger, which operates by cam action resulting from the air valve angle and provides the additional fuel flow necessary during increased engine air flow at wide open throttle.

The carburetor model identification number is stamped vertically on the float bowl, near the secondary throttle lever. The letters in the model name describe the specific features of the carburetor. For example:

1. E — It is electronically controlled.
2. 4M — It is a member of the Quadrajet carburetor family.
3. C — It has an integral hot air choke.

➡ **If the carburetor number has an "E" at the end (like E4ME) of it, that carburetor has an integral Electric Choke.**

For Carburetor repair, overhaul or adjustment, refer to procedures covered in Section 5 Fuel Systems.

DIAGNOSTIC AND TESTING

➡ **The following explains how to activate the trouble code signal light in the instrument cluster and gives an explanation of what each code means. This is not a full CCC system troubleshooting and isolation procedure.**

Before suspecting the CCC system or any of its components as faulty, check the ignition system including distributor, timing, spark plugs and wires. Check the engine compression, air cleaner and emission control components not controlled by the ECM. Also check the intake manifold, vacuum hoses and hose connectors for leaks and the carburetor bolts for tightness.

The following symptoms could indicate a possible problem with the CCC system.

1. Detonation
2. Stalls or rough idle — cold
3. Stalls or rough idle — hot
4. Missing
5. Hesitation
6. Surges
7. Poor gasoline mileage
8. Sluggish or spongy performance
9. Hard starting — cold
10. Objectionable exhaust odors (rotten egg smell)
11. Cuts out
12. Improper idle speed

As a bulb and system check, the "CHECK ENGINE" light will come on when the ignition switch is turned to the **ON** position but the engine is not started. The "CHECK ENGINE" light will also produce the trouble code or codes by a series of flashes which translate as follows. When the diagnostic test terminal under the dash is grounded, with the ignition in the **ON** position and the engine not running, the "CHECK ENGINE" light will flash once, pause, then flash twice in rapid succession. This is a code 12, which indicates that the diagnostic system is working. After a long pause, the code 12 will repeat itself 2 more times. The cycle will then repeat itself until the engine is **STARTED** or the ignition is turned **OFF**.

When the engine is started, the "CHECK ENGINE" light will remain on for a few seconds, then turn off. If the "CHECK ENGINE" light remains on, the self-diagnostic system has detected a problem. If the test terminal is then grounded, the trouble code will flash 3 times. If more than a single problem is found, each trouble code will flash 3 times. Trouble codes will flash in numerical order (lowest code number to highest). The trouble codes series will repeat as long as the test terminal is grounded.

A trouble code indicates a problem with a given circuit. For example, trouble code 14 indicates a problem in the cooling sensor circuit. This includes the coolant sensor, its electrical harness and the Electronic Control Module (ECM). Since the self-diagnostic system cannot diagnose every possible fault in the system, the absence of a trouble code does not mean the system is trouble-free. To determine problems within the system which do not activate a trouble code, a system performance check must be made.

In the case of an intermittent fault in the system, the "CHECK ENGINE" light will go out when the fault goes away, but the trouble code will remain in the memory of the ECM. Therefore, it a trouble code can be obtained even though the "CHECK ENGINE" light is not on, the trouble code must be evaluated. It must be determined if the fault is intermittent or if the engine must be at certain operating conditions (under load, etc.) before the "CHECK ENGINE" light will come on. Some trouble codes will not be recorded in the ECM until the engine has been operated at part throttle for about 5–18 minutes. On the CCC system, a trouble code will be stored until terminal **R** of the ECM has been disconnected from the battery for 10 seconds.

An easy way to erase the computer memory on the CCC system is to disconnect the battery terminals from the battery. If this method is used, don't forget to reset clocks and electronic preprogrammable radios. Another method is to remove the fuse marked ECM in the fuse panel.

Not all models have such a fuse.

CCC SYSTEM CIRCUIT DIAGNOSIS

To diagnosis CCC system circuits, use the same general troubleshooting approach that is used for other automotive electrical systems. Finding the fault in a CCC circuit will require the testing tools described in this section. these tools are used with the diagnostic charts for CCC system troubleshooting. Always use a digital voltmeter for accuracy of readings when using CCC diagnostic charts.

Testing the CCC System Performance with a Dwellmeter

The dwellmeter is used to analyze the operation of the M/C solenoid circuit. The operation of that circuit is controlled by the ECM, which used information from the sensors.

A chart called the "System Performance Check" is provided in the section. This chart provides step-by-step instructions to determine if the M/C control solenoid circuit, ECM and various sensors (M/C control system) are functioning properly. If they are not, the chart indicates the steps to take in order to locate and repair the source of the trouble.

Charts for the other systems, such as AIR, EST, EGR , EFE, TCC and canister purge are also provided in the section. Another chart called the "Diagnostic Circuit Check" follows the system performance check. This chart is the starting point for any diagnosis.

The dwellmeter is used to diagnose the M/C control system. Connect a dwellmeter to the pigtail connector in the M/C solenoid wiring harness. In the old contact point style ignition system, the dwellmeter read the period of time that the points were closed (dwell) and voltage flowed to the ignition coil.

In the CCC system the dwellmeter is used to read the time that the ECM closed the M/C solenoid circuit to ground, allowing voltage to operate the M/C solenoid. Dwell, as used in CCC system performance diagnosis, is the time that the M/C solenoid circuit is closed (or energized). The dwellmeter will translate this time into degrees. The 6 cylinder (0–60 degree) scale on the dwellmeter is used for this reading. The ability of the dwellmeter to perform this kind of conversion makes it an ideal tool to check the amount of time the ECM,'s internal switch is closed, thus energizing the M/C solenoid. The only difference is that the degree scale on the meter is more like the percent of solenoid ON time rather than actual degrees of dwell.

Connecting the Dwellmeter

First set the dwellmeter on the 6 cylinder position, then connect it to the M/C solenoid dwell lead to measure the output of the ECM. Do not allow the terminal to touch ground, this includes any hoses. The dwellmeter must be set to the 6 cylinder position when diagnosing all engines, whether working on is a 4, 6, or 8 cylinder engine.

➡ **Some older dwellmeters may not work properly on CCC. Don't use any dwellmeter which causes a change in engine operation when it is connected to the solenoid lead.**

The 6 cylinder scale on the dwellmeter provides evenly divided points, for example:
  a. 15 degrees = $1/4$ scale
  b. 30 degrees = midscale
  c. 45 degrees = $3/4$ scale

Connect the positive clip lead of the dwellmeter to the M/C solenoid pigtail connector shown in. Attach the other dwellmeter clip lead to ground. Do not allow the clip leads to contact other conductive cables or hoses which could interfere with accurate readings.

After connecting the dwellmeter to a warm, operating engine, the dwell at idle and part throttle will vary between 5–55 degrees. That is, the needle will move continuously up and down the scale. Needle movement indicates that the engine is in closed loop and that the dwell is being varied by signals from the ECM. However, if the engine is cold, has just been restarted, or the throttle is wide open, the dwell will be fixed and the needle will be steady. Those are signs that the engine is in open loop.

Diagnostic checks to find a condition without a trouble code are usually made on a warm engine (in closed loop) as indicated by a hot upper radiator hose. There are 3 ways of distinguishing open from closed loop operation.

1. A variation in dwell will occur only in closed loop.

2. Test for closed loop operation. Cause the mixture to become richer, by restricting the air flow through into the carburetor or manually closing the choke. If the dwellmeter moves up scale, that indicates closed loop.

3. If a large vacuum leak is created and the dwell drops down, that also indicates closed loop.

Reading the Dwellmeter

The M/C solenoid moves the metering rods up and down 10 times per second. This frequency was chosen to be slow enough to allow full stop-to-stop M/C solenoid travel, but fast enough to prevent any undesirable influence on vehicle response.

The duration of the on period determines whether the mixture is rich (mostly up) or lean (mostly down). When the metering rods are down for a longer period (54 degrees) than they are up (6 degrees), a lean mixture results.

As the solenoid on-time changes, the up time and down time of the metering rods also changes. When a lean mixture is desired, the M/C solenoid will restrict fuel flow through the metering jet 90% of the time, or, in other words, a lean mixture will be provided to the engine.

This lean command will read as 54 degrees on the dwellmeter (54 degrees is 90% of 60 degrees). This means the M/C solenoid has restricted fuel flow 90% of the time. A rich mixture is provided when the M/C solenoid restricts fuel flow only 10% of the time and allows a rich mixture to flow to the engine. A rich command will have a dwellmeter reading of 6 degrees (10% of 60 degrees); the M/C solenoid has restricted fuel flow 10% of the time.

On some engines dwellmeter readings can vary between 5–55 degrees, rather than between 6–54 degrees. The ideal mixture would be shown on the dwellmeter with the needle varying or swinging back and forth, anywhere between 10–50 degrees. Varying means the needle continually moves up and down the scale. The amount it moves does not matter, only the fact that it does move. The dwell is being varied by the signal sent to the ECM by the oxygen sensor in the exhaust manifold.

Under certain operating conditions such as Wide Open Throttle (WOT), or a cold engine, the dwell will remain fixed and the needle will be steady. Remember, a low dwellmeter reading (5–10 degrees) indicates the ECM signal to the M/C control solenoid is a rich command, while 55 degrees would indicate a lean command.

Open and Closed Loop Operation

Two terms are often used when referring to CCC system operation. They are closed loop and open loop.

Basically, closed loop indicates that the ECM is using information from the exhaust oxygen sensor to influence operation of the mixture control (M/C) solenoid. the ECM still considers other information, such as engine temperature, rpm, barometric and manifold pressure and throttle position, along with the exhaust oxygen sensor information.

During open loop, all information except the exhaust oxygen sensor input is considered by the ECM to control the M/C solenoid. The diagnostic charts are based on a warmed up engine (closed loop operation) and will generally state, run engine at part throttle for 3 minutes or until there is a varying dwellmeter indication before beginning diagnosis.

It is important to note that the exhaust oxygen sensor may cool below its operational temperature during prolonged idling. This will cause an open loop condition and make the diagnostic chart information not usable during diagnosis. Engine rpm must be increased to warm the exhaust oxygen sensor and re-establish closed loop. diagnosis should begin again at the first step on the chart after closed loop is resumed.

DIAGNOSTIC PROCEDURES

The following is a complete diagnosis sequence of the CCC system. In all cases, the sequence is begun with routine engine checks. Then the following:

1. System diagnostic circuit check
2. Code chart or chart for systems without codes
3. System performance check

This procedure must be followed each time the CCC system is suspected as the cause of a problem.

Diagnostic Charts

The section contains tree-type charts for locating the source of a fault in the CCC system circuits. When using a tree chart, always start at the first step and follow the sequence from top to bottom. Often there will be several branches of the tree to follow. Follow the branch that is applicable to the result obtained in that step. Several charts will be used during diagnosis and this procedure will be used in all cases.

➡ **The CCC system should not be considered as a possible source of poor engine performance, fuel economy, or excessive emissions until all the routine engine checks, such as ignition, plugs, air cleaner and vacuum hoses, have been made.**

SYSTEM DIAGNOSTIC CIRCUIT CHECK

Begin the Diagnostic Circuit Check by making sure that the diagnostic system itself is working. Turn the ignition to **ON** with the engine stopped. If the "CHECK ENGINE" or "SERVICE ENGINE SOON" light comes on, ground the diagnostic code terminal (test lead) under the dash. If the "CHECK ENGINE" or "SERVICE ENGINE SOON" light flashes Code 12, the self-diagnostic system is working and can detect a faulty circuit. If there is no Code 12, see the appropriate chart in this section. If any additional codes flash, record them for later use.

If a Code 51 flashes, use chart 51 to diagnose that condition before proceeding with the Diagnostic Circuit Check. A Code 51 means that the "CHECK ENGINE" or "SERVICE ENGINE SOON" light flashes 5 times, pauses, then flashes again once. After a longer pause, code 51 will flash again twice in this same way. To find out what diagnostic step to follow, look up the chart for Code 51 in this section. If there is not a Code 51, follow the "No Code 51" branch of the chart.

Clear the ECM memory by disconnecting the voltage lead either at the fuse panel or the ECM letter connector for 10 seconds. This clears any codes remaining from previous repairs, or codes for troubles not present at this time. Remember, even though a code is stored, if the trouble is not present the diagnostic charts cannot be used. The charts are designed only to locate present faults.

➡ **When erasing the computer memory on the CCC system the ignition switch must be turned OFF before removing any fuses, wire connectors or battery cables. If the battery cable is to disconnect from the battery, don't forget to reset clocks and electronic preprogrammable radios.**

Next, remove the TEST terminal ground, set the parking brake and put the transmission in **P**. Run the warm engine for several minutes, making sure it is run at the specified curb idle. Then, if the "CHECK ENGINE" or "SERVICE ENGINE SOON" light comes on while the engine is idling, ground the TEST lead again and observe (count) the flashing trouble code.

If the "CHECK ENGINE" or "SERVICE ENGINE SOON" light does not come on, check the codes which were recorded earlier. If there were no additional codes, road test the vehicle for the problem being diagnosed to make sure it still exists.

The purpose of the Diagnostic Circuit check is to make sure the "CHECK ENGINE" or "SERVICE SOON SOON" light works, that the ECM is operating and can recognize a fault and to determine if any trouble codes are stored in the ECM memory.

If trouble codes are stored, it also checks to see if they indicate an intermittent problem. This is the starting point of any diagnosis. If there are no codes stored, move on to the System Performance Check.

The codes obtained from the "CHECK ENGINE" or "SERVICE ENGINE SOON" light display method indicate which diagnostic charts provide in the section are to be used. For example, code 23 can be diagnosed by following the step-by-step procedures on chart 23.

➡ **If more than a single code is stored in the ECM, the lowest code number must be diagnosed first, then proceed to the next highest code. The only exception is when a 50 series flashes. 50 series code take precedence over all other trouble codes and must be dealt with first, since they point to a fault in the PROM unit or the ECM.**

SERVICE

Before suspecting the CCC system, or any of its components as being faulty, check the ignition system (distributor, timing, spark plugs and wires). Check the engine compression, the air cleaner and any of the emission control components that are not controlled by the ECM. Also check the intake manifold, the vacuum hoses and hose connectors for any leaks. Check the carburetor mounting bolts for tightness.

The following symptoms could indicate a possible problem area with the CCC system:
1. Detonation.
2. Stalling or rough idling when the engine is cold.
3. Stalling or rough idling when the engine is hot.
4. Missing.
5. Hesitation.
6. Surging.
7. Poor gasoline mileage.
8. Sluggish or spongy performance.
9. Hard starting when engine is cold.
10. Hard starting when the engine is hot.
11. Objectionable exhaust odors.
12. Engine cuts out.
13. Improper idle speed

As a bulb and system check, the Check Engine light will come on when the ignition switch is turned to the ON position but the engine is not started.

The Check Engine light will also produce the trouble code/codes by a series of flashes which translate as follows: When the diagnostic test terminal under the instrument panel is grounded, with the ignition in the ON position and the engine not running, the Check Engine light will flash once, pause, and then flash twice in rapid succession. This is a Code 12, which indicates that the diagnostic system is working. After a long pause, the Code 12 will repeat itself two more times. This whole cycle will then repeat itself until the engine is started or the ignition switch is turned OFF.

When the engine is started, the Check Engine light will remain on for a few seconds and then turn off. If the Check Engine light remains on, the self-diagnostic system has detected a problem. If the test terminal is then grounded, the trouble code will flash (3) three times. If more than one problem is found to be in existence, each trouble code will flash (3) three times and then change to the next one. Trouble codes will flash in numerical order (lowest code number to highest). The trouble code series will repeat themselves for as long as the test terminal remains grounded.

A trouble code indicates a problem with a given circuit. For example, trouble code 14 indicates a problem in the coolant sensor circuit. This includes the coolant sensor, its electrical harness and the Electronic Control Module (ECM).

Since the self-diagnostic system cannot diagnose every possible fault in the system, the absence of a trouble code does not necessarily mean that the system is trouble-free. To determine whether or not a problem with the system exists that does not activate a trouble code, a system performance check must be made. You can follow the symptom charts for the fuel system your car has. If the chart doesn't help you find the problem or instructs you to more involved testing using special tool you may wish to seek a qualified service technician. Guessing which component to test or testing a component incorrectly can be very expensive.

In the case of an intermittent fault in the system, the Check Engine light will go out when the fault goes away, but the trouble code will remain in the memory of the ECM. Therefore, if a trouble code can be obtained even though the Check Engine light is not on, it must still be evaluated. It must be determined if the fault is intermittent or if the engine must be operating under certain conditions (acceleration, deceleration, etc.) before the Check Engine light will come on. In some cases, certain trouble codes will not be recorded in the ECM until the engine has been operated at part throttle for at least 5 to 18 minutes.

On the CCC system, a trouble code will be stored until the terminal **R** at the ECM has been disconnected from the battery for at least 10 seconds, or the battery cable has be removed.

ACTIVATING THE TROUBLE CODE

On the CCC system, locate the test terminal under the instrument panel (see illustration). Use a jumper wire and ground only the lead.

➡ **Ground the test terminal according to the instructions given previously in the Basic Troubleshooting section.**

CARBURETOR COMPONENT TESTING

Electric Choke

Check the choke unloader and idle setting adjustments. The choke linkage and fast idle cam must operate freely. Bent, dirty or otherwise damaged linkage must be cleaned, repaired or replaced as necessary. Do not lubricate linkage since lubricant will collect dust and cause sticking.

1. Allow the choke to cool so that when the throttle is opened slightly, the choke blade fully closes.
2. Start the engine and determine the time for the choke blade to reach the full open position.
3. If the the choke blade fails to open fully within 3.5 minutes, proceed with Step 4 and 5 below.
4. Check the voltage at the choke heater connection (engine must be running):
   a. If the voltage is approximately 12–15 volts, replace the electric choke unit.
   b. If the voltage is low or zero, check all wires and connections. If any connections in the oil pressure switch circuitry are faulty, or if pressure switch is failed open, the oil warning light will be on with the engine running. Repair wires or connectors as required.
5. If Steps 4a and 4b do not correct the problem, replace oil pressure switch. No gasket is used between the choke cover and the choke housing due to grounding requirements.

Hot Air Choke

1. With the parking brake applied and the drive wheels blocked, place the transmission in **P** or **N**, start the engine and allow it to warm up. Visually check to be sure the choke valve fully opens.
2. If the choke fails to open fully , momentarily touch the choke housing and the hot air inlet pipe or hose, to determine if sufficient heat is reaching the choke stat.

✳✳✳ CAUTION

The choke housing and the hot air inlet pipe or hose will be HOT to the touch, use caution to prevent burning of hands.

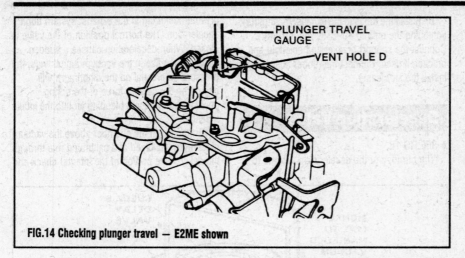

FIG.14 Checking plunger travel — E2ME shown

3. If the choke housing and or heat inlet are cool to the touch, check for a loss of vacuum to the housing, restricted heat inlet pipe in the choke housing or choke heat pipe, or restricted passages in the manifold choke heat stove.

4. Replace or correct as necessary.

Float Level

This is an external check procedure.

1. With engine idling and choke wide open, insert gauge J–34935–1, or equivalent, in vent slot or vent hole. Allow the gauge to float freely.

2. Observe the mark on the gauge that lines up with the top of the casting.

3. Setting should be within $\frac{1}{16}$ in. (1.6mm) of the specified float level setting.

4. If not within specified range, check fuel pressure.

5. If fuel pressure is correct, remove air horn and adjust float.

Mixture Control Solenoid

This is a mixture control solenoid travel test.

Before checking the mixture control solenoid travel, it may be necessary to modify the float gauge J–9789–130 or equivalent (used to externally check the float level).

This should be done by filing or grinding the sufficient material off the gauge to allow for insertion down the vertical D-shaped hole in the air horn casting (located next to the idle air bleed valve cover).

Check that the gauge freely enters the D-shaped vent hole and does not bind. The gauge will also be used to determine the total mixture control solenoid travel.

With the engine off and the air cleaner removed, measure the control solenoid travel as follows:

1. Insert a modified float gauge J–9789–130 or equivalent down the D-shaped vent hole. Press down on the gauge and release it.

2. Observe that the gauge moves freely and does not bind. With the gauge released (solenoid in the up position), be sure to read it at eye level and record the mark on the gauge that lines up with the top of the air horn casting (upper edge).

3. Lightly press down on the gauge until bottomed (solenoid in the down position). Record the mark on the gauge that lines up with the top of the air horn casting.

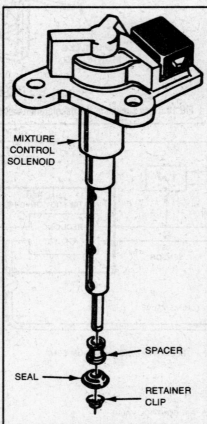

FIG.17 Mixture control solenoid is located in the carburetor. For poor idle or stalling check that the tip is not broken.

4. Subtract the gauge up dimension from gauge dimension. Record the difference. This difference is total solenoid travel.

5. If total solenoid travel is not within $\frac{1}{16}$–$\frac{1}{8}$ in. (1.6–3mm), perform the mixture control solenoid adjustments. If the difference is within $\frac{1}{16}$–$\frac{1}{8}$ in. (1.6–3mm), proceed to the idle air bleed valve adjustment.

➡ **If adjustment is required, it will be necessary to remove the air horn and drive out the mixture control solenoid screw plug from the under side of the air horn.**

Idle Load Compensator (ILC)

1. Inspect the condition of the tube cap covering the access to plunger travel adjustment screw. If missing or damaged, the diaphragm chamber will lose vacuum.

2. Hold throttle lever half open, to allow ILC to extend fully.

3. Apply finger pressure to the ILC plunger.

4. Apply 20 in. Hg of vacuum to the ILC, plunger should begin to retract. If not replace the ILC.

5. Observe vacuum gauge, vacuum should hold for at least 20 seconds, if not replace the ILC.

6. Release vacuum from the ILC. The plunger should extend, if not replace the ILC.

Pulse Air Injection (PULSAIR)

◆ SEE FIG. 15

All engines use the Pulsair air injection system, which uses exhaust system air pulses to siphon fresh air into the exhaust manifold. The injected air supports continued combustion of the hot exhaust gases in the exhaust manifold, reducing exhaust emissions. A secondary

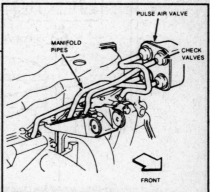

FIG.15 Pulsair installed on the four cylinder engine

purpose of the Pulsair system is to introduce more oxygen into the exhaust system upstream of the catalytic converter, to supply the converter with the oxygen required for the oxidation reaction.

Air is drawn into the Pulsair valve through a hose connected to the air cleaner. The air passes through a check valve (there is one check valve for each cylinder; all check valves are installed in the Pulsair valve), then through a manifold pipe to the exhaust manifold. All manifold pipes are the same length, to prevent uneven pulsation. The check valves open during pulses of negative exhaust back pressure, admitting air into the manifold pipe and the exhaust manifold. During pulses of positive exhaust back pressure, the check valves close, preventing backfiring into the Pulsair valve and air cleaner.

The Pulsair check valves, hoses and pipes should be checked occasionally for leaks, cracks, or breaks.

REMOVAL & INSTALLATION

1. Remove the air cleaner case. Disconnect the rubber hose(s) from the Pulsair valve(s).
2. Disconnect the support bracket, if present. Some V6 engines have a Pulsair solenoid and bracket, which must be removed.
3. Unscrew the attaching nuts and remove the Pulsair tubes from the exhaust manifold(s).
4. To install, first apply a light coat of clean oil to the ends of the Pulsair tubes.

5. Install the tubes to the exhaust manifold(s), tightening the nuts to 10-13 ft. lbs. (10Nm.). Connect the support bracket and solenoid and bracket, if used. Connect the rubber hose(s) and install the air cleaner.

Deceleration Valve

♦ SEE FIG 18

The purpose of the deceleration valve is to prevent backfiring in the exhaust system during deceleration. The normal position of the valve is closed. When deceleration causes a sudden vacuum increase in the vacuum signal lines, the pressure differential on the diaphragm will overcome the closing force of the spring, opening the valve and bleeding air into the intake manifold.

Air trapped in the chamber above the vacuum diaphragm will bleed at a calibrated rate through the delay valve portion of the integral check and

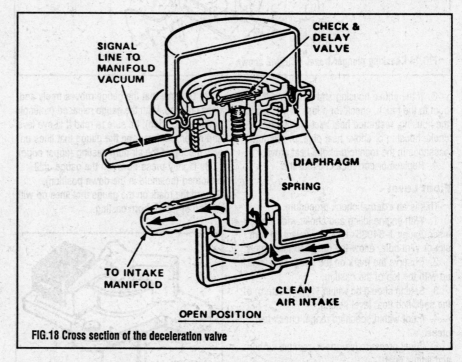

FIG.18 Cross section of the deceleration valve

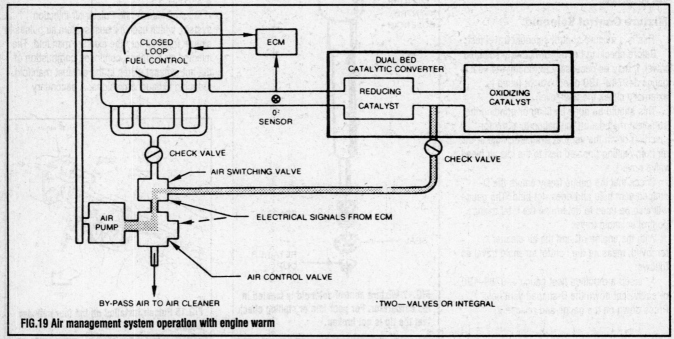

FIG.19 Air management system operation with engine warm

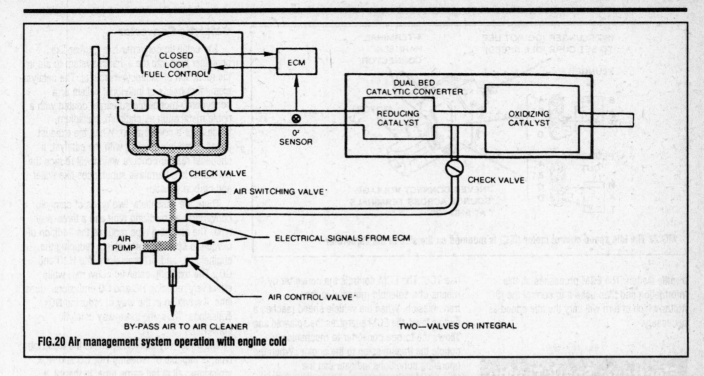

FIG.20 Air management system operation with engine cold

delay valve, reducing the vacuum acting on the diaphragm. When the vacuum load on the diaphragm and the spring load equalize, the valve assembly will close, shutting off the air flow into the intake manifold.

The check valve portion of the check and delay valve provides quick balancing of chamber pressure when a sudden decrease in vacuum is caused by acceleration rather than deceleration.

Mixture Control Solenoid (M/C)

The fuel flow through the carburetor idle main metering circuits is controlled by a mixture control (M/C) solenoid located in the carburetor. The M/C solenoid changes the air/fuel mixture to the engine by controlling the fuel flow through the carburetor. The ECM controls the solenoid by providing a ground. When the solenoid is energized, the fuel flow through the carburetor is reduced, providing a leaner mixture. When the ECM removes the ground, the solenoid is de-energized, increasing the fuel flow and providing a richer mixture. The M/C solenoid is energized and de-energized at a rate of 10 times per second.

Throttle Position Sensor (TPS)

◆ SEE FIG 21

The throttle position sensor is mounted in the carburetor body and is used to supply throttle position information to the ECM. The ECM memory stores an average of operating conditions with the ideal air/fuel ratios for each of those conditions. When the ECM receives a signal that indicates throttle position change, it immediately shifts to the last remembered set of operating conditions that resulted in an ideal air/fuel ratio control. The memory is continually being updated during normal operations.

Idle Speed Control (ISC)

◆ SEE FIG. 22

The idle speed control does just what its name implies-it controls the idle. The ISC is used to maintain low engine speeds while at the same time preventing stalling due to engine load changes. The system consists of a motor assembly mounted on the carburetor which moves the throttle lever so as to open or close the throttle blades.

The whole operation is controlled by the ECM. The ECM monitors engine load to determine the proper idle speed. To prevent stalling, it monitors the air conditioning compressor switch, the transmission, the park/neutral switch and the ISC

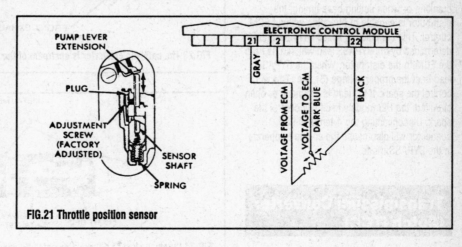

FIG.21 Throttle position sensor

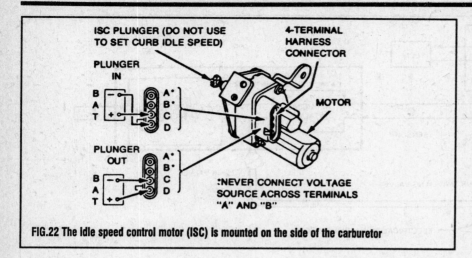

FIG.22 The idle speed control motor (ISC) is mounted on the side of the carburetor

throttle switch. The ECM processes all this information and then uses it to control the ISC motor which in turn will vary the idle speed as necessary.

Electronic Spark Timing (EST)

All models use EST. The EST distributor, as described in an earlier Section, contains no vacuum or centrifugal advance mechanism and uses a seven terminal HEI module. It has four wires going to a four terminal connector in addition to the connectors normally found on HEI distributors. A reference pulse, indicating engine rpm is sent to the ECM. The ECM determines the proper spark advance for the engine operating conditions and then sends an EST pulse back to the distributor.

Under most normal operating conditions, the ECM will control the spark advance. However, under certain operating conditions such as cranking or when setting base timing, the distributor is capable of operating without ECM control. This condition is called BYPASS and is determined by the BYPASS lead which runs from the ECM to the distributor. When the BYPASS lead is at the proper voltage (5), the ECM will control the spark. If the lead is grounded or open circuited, the HEI module itself will control the spark. Disconnecting the 4-terminal EST connector will also cause the engine to operate in the BYPASS mode.

Transmission Converter Clutch (TCC)

All models with an automatic transmission

use TCC. The ECM controls the converter by means of a solenoid mounted in the transmission. When the vehicle speed reaches a certain level, the ECM energizes the solenoid and allows the torque converter to mechanically couple the transmission to the engine. When the operating conditions indicate that the transmission should operate as a normal fluid coupled transmission, the ECM will de-energize the solenoid. Depressing the brake will also return the transmission to normal automatic operation.

Catalytic Converter

The catalytic converter is a muffler-like container built into the exhaust system to aid in the reduction of exhaust emissions. The catalyst element consists of individual pellets or a honeycomb monolithic substrate coated with a noble metal such as platinum, palladium, rhodium or a combination. When the exhaust gases come into contact with the catalyst, a chemical reaction occurs which will reduce the pollutants into harmless substances like water and carbon dioxide.

There are essentially two types of catalytic converters: an oxidizing type and a three-way type. The oxidizing type requires the addition of oxygen to spur the catalyst into reducing the engine's HC and CO emissions into H_2O and CO_2. The oxidizing catalytic converter, while effectively reducing HC and CO emissions, does little, if anything in the way of reducing NOx emissions. Thus, the three-way catalytic converter.

The three-way converter, unlike the oxidizing type, is capable of reducing HC, CO and NOx emissions; all at the same time. In theory, it seems impossible to reduce all three pollutants in one system since the reduction of HC and CO requires the addition of oxygen, while the reduction of NOx calls for the removal of oxygen.

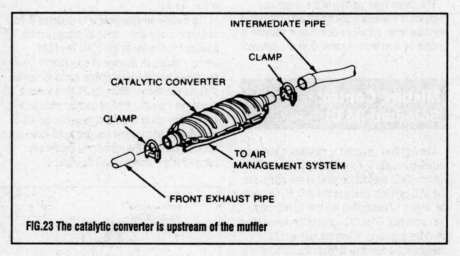

FIG.23 The catalytic converter is upstream of the muffler

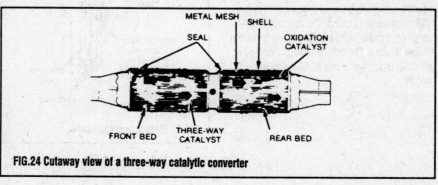

FIG.24 Cutaway view of a three-way catalytic converter

In actuality, the three-way system really can reduce all three pollutants, but only if the amount of oxygen in the exhaust system is precisely controlled. Due to this precise oxygen control requirement, the three-way converter system is used only in conjunction with an oxygen sensor system.

There are no service procedures required for the catalytic converter, although the converter body should be inspected occasionally for damage.

PRECAUTIONS

1. Use only unleaded fuel.
2. Avoid prolonged idling; the engine should run no longer than 20 min. at curb idle and no longer than 10 min. at fast idle.
3. Do not disconnect any of the spark plug leads while the engine is running.
4. Make engine compression checks as quickly as possible.

CATALYST TESTING

At the present time there is no known way to reliably test catalytic converter operation in the field. The only reliable test is a 12 hour and 40 min. soak test (CVS) which must be done in a laboratory.

An infrared HC/CO tester is not sensitive enough to measure the higher tailpipe emissions from a failing converter. Thus, a bad converter may allow enough emissions to escape so that the car is no longer in compliance with Federal or state standards, but will still not cause the needle on a tester to move off zero.

The chemical reactions which occur inside a catalytic converter generate a great deal of heat. Most converter problems can be traced to fuel or ignition system problems which cause unusually high emissions. As a result of the increased intensity of the chemical reactions, the converter literally burns itself up.

A completely failed converter might cause a tester to show a slight reading. As a result, it is occasionally possible to detect one of these.

As long as you avoid severe overheating and the use of leaded fuels it is reasonably safe to assume that the converter is working properly. If you are in doubt, take the car to a diagnostic center that has a tester.

Early Fuel Evaporation (EFE)

All models are equipped with this system to reduce engine warm-up time, improve

driveability and reduce emissions. The system is electric and uses a ceramic heater grid located underneath the primary bore of the carburetor as part of the carburetor insulator/gasket. When the ignition switch is turned on and the engine coolant temperature is low, voltage is applied to the EFE relay by the ECM. The EFE relay in turn energizes the heater grid. When the coolant temperature increases, the ECM de-energizes the relay which will then shut off the EFE heater.

REMOVAL & INSTALLATION

1. Remove the air cleaner and disconnect the negative battery cable.
2. Disconnect all electrical, vacuum and fuel connections from the carburetor.
3. Disconnect the EFE heater electrical lead.

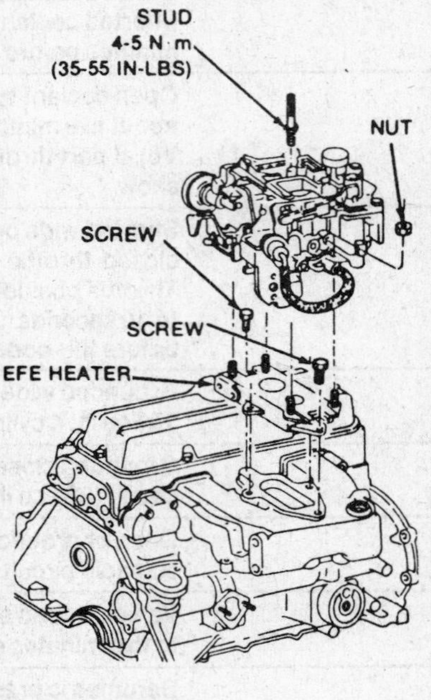

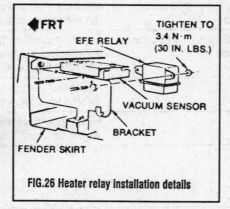

STUD
4-5 N·m
(35-55 IN-LBS)

NUT

SCREW

SCREW

EFE HEATER

FIG.25 EFE heater grid

◄FRT

EFE RELAY

TIGHTEN TO
3.4 N·m
(30 IN. LBS.)

VACUUM SENSOR

BRACKET

FENDER SKIRT

FIG.26 Heater relay installation details

4. Remove the carburetor as detailed later in this Section.
5. Lift off the EFE heater grid.
6. Installation is in the reverse order of removal.

EFE HEATER RELAY REPLACEMENT

1. Disconnect the negative battery cable.
2. Remove the retaining bracket.
3. Tag and disconnect all electrical connections.
4. Unscrew the retaining bolts and remove the relay.
5. Installation is in the reverse order of removal.

CCC SYSTEM DIAGNOSTIC CHARTS

To properly diagnosis driveability problems you need to use the following charts. Make certain the charts cover the engine your car has. If your check engine light is not lit, check for engine stored engine codes. If any codes are stored write them down for reference later. Clear the codes as described earlier. Road test the vehicle to see if any of the codes return. Never try to fix a code problem until you're sure that it comes back. It may have been a old code from years ago that was never cleared or a code that was set do to a rain storm, battery jump, etc.

After clearing any codes and checking that they do not return. If the car drives fine your finished. But if there are no codes and the car runs poorly you'll need to check the symptoms charts. The problem is most likely not the computer or the devices it controls but the ignition system or engine mechanical.

If you do have a code(s) that returns start with the lowest code and follow the proper chart. You must follow every step of the chart and not jump from test to test or you'll never be certain to find and fix the real problem.

Start with the lowest to highest code chart, making sure to use the charts for your engine. If you have a 50 series code, like code 54. Always check those out first. They are rare but usually indicate a problem with the computer itself or its ability to test itself properly.

➡ **For carburetor overhaul or service refer to Section 5 Fuel Systems.**

EXPLANATION OF TROUBLE CODES
GM C-4 AND CCC SYSTEMS
(Ground test lead or terminal AFTER engine is running.)

Trouble Code	Applicable System	Notes		Possible Problem Area
12	C-4, CCC			No tachometer or reference signal to computer (ECM). This code will only be present while a fault exists, and will not be stored if the problem is intermittent.
13	C-4, CCC			Oxygen sensor circuit. The engine must run for about five minutes (eighteen on C-4 equipped 231 cu in. V6) at part throttle (and under road load—CCC equipped cars) before this code will show.
13 & 14 (at same time)	C-4	Except cu in. V6	and 171	See code 43.
13 & 43 (at same time)	C-4		171 cu in. V6	See code 43.
14	C-4, CCC			Shorted coolant sensor circuit. The engine has to run 2 minutes before this code will show.
15	C-4, CCC			Open coolant sensor circuit. The engine has to operate for about five minutes (18 minutes for C-4 equipped 231 cu in. V6) at part throttle (some models) before this code will show.
21	C-4			Shorted wide open throttle switch and/or open closed-throttle switch circuit (when used).
	C-4, CCC			Throttle position sensor circuit. The engine must be run up to 10 seconds (25 seconds—CCC System) below 800 rpm before this code will show.
21 & 22 (at same time)	C-4			Grounded wide open throttle switch circuit (231 cu in. V6, 151 cu in. 4 cylinder).
22	C-4			Grounded closed throttle or wide open throttle switch circuit (231 cu in. V6, 151 cu in. 4 cylinder).
23	C-4, CCC			Open or grounded carburetor mixture control (M/C) solenoid circuit.
24	CCC			Vehicle speed sensor (VSS) circuit. The car must operate up to five minutes at road speed before this code will show.
32	C-4, CCC			Barometric pressure sensor (BARO) circuit output low.
32 & 55 (at same time)	C-4			Grounded +8V terminal or V(REF) terminal for barometric pressure sensor (BARO), or faulty ECM computer.
34	C-4	Except Cutlass	260 cu in.	Manifold absolute pressure (MAP) sensor output high (after ten seconds and below 800 rpm).
34	CCC	Including Cutlass	260 cu in.	Manifold absolute pressure (MAP) sensor circuit or vacuum sensor circuit. The engine must run up to five minutes below 800 R.P.M before this code will set.
35	CCC			Idle speed control (ISC) switch circuit shorted (over ½ throttle for over two seconds).
41	CCC			No distributor reference pulses to the ECM at specified engine vacuum. This code will store in memory.

EXPLANATION OF TROUBLE CODES
GM C-4 AND CCC SYSTEMS

(Ground test lead or terminal AFTER engine is running.)

Trouble Code	Applicable System	Notes	Possible Problem Area
42	CCC		Electronic spark timing (EST) bypass circuit grounded.
43	C-4		Throttle position sensor adjustment (on some models, engine must run at part throttle up to ten seconds before this code will set).
44	C-4, CCC		Lean oxygen sensor indication. The engine must run up to five minutes in closed loop (oxygen sensor adjusting carburetor mixture), at part throttle and under road load (drive car) before this code will set.
44 & 55 (at same time)	C-4, CCC		Faulty oxygen sensor circuit.
45	C-4, CCC	Restricted air cleaner can cause code 45	Rich oxygen sensor system indication. The engine must run up to five minutes in closed loop (oxygen sensor adjusting carburetor mixture), at part throttle under road load before this code will set.
51	C-4, CCC		Faulty calibration unit (PROM) or improper PROM installation in electronic control module (ECM). It takes up to thirty seconds for this code to set.
52 & 53	C-4		"Check Engine" light off: Intermittent ECM computer problem. "Check Engine" light on: Faulty ECM computer (replace).
52	C-4, CCC		Faulty ECM computer.
53	CCC	Including 1980 260 cu in. Cutlass	Faulty ECM computer.
54	C-4, CCC		Faulty mixture control solenoid circuit and/or faulty ECM computer.
55	C-4	Except 1980 260 cu. in. Cutlass	Faulty oxygen sensor, open manifold absolute pressure sensor or faulty ECM computer (231 cu in. V6). Faulty throttle position sensor or ECM computer (except 231 cu. in. V6). Faulty ECM computer (151 cu in. 4 cylinder)
55	CCC	Including 1980 260 cu in. Cutlass	Grounded + 8 volt supply (terminal 19 of ECM computer connector), grounded 5 volt reference (terminal 21 of ECM computer connector), faulty oxygen sensor circuit or faulty ECM computer.

Computer Controlled Catalytic Converter—C4

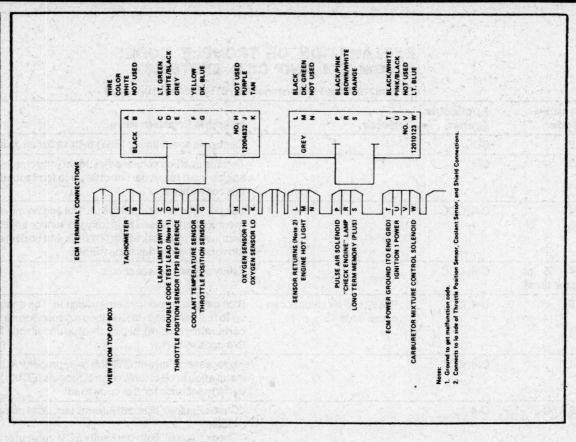

ECM TERMINAL CONNECTIONS

VIEW FROM TOP OF BOX

Terminal		WIRE COLOR
BLACK	A	BLACK
	B	WHITE
		NOT USED
	C	LT. GREEN
	D	WHITE/BLACK
	E	GREY
	F	YELLOW
	G	DK. BLUE
	H	NOT USED
NO. 12004832	J	PURPLE
	K	TAN
GREY	L	BLACK
	M	DK. GREEN
	N	NOT USED
	P	BLACK/PINK
	R	BROWN/WHITE
	S	ORANGE
	T	BLACK/WHITE
NO. 12010123	U	PINK/BLACK
	V	NOT USED
	W	LT. BLUE

TACHOMETER — A, B
LEAN LIMIT SWITCH — C
TROUBLE CODE TEST LEAD (Note 1) — D
THROTTLE POSITION SENSOR (TPS) REFERENCE — E
COOLANT TEMPERATURE SENSOR — F
THROTTLE POSITION SENSOR — G
OXYGEN SENSOR HI — H
OXYGEN SENSOR LO — J, K
SENSOR RETURNS (Note 2) — L, M
ENGINE HOT LIGHT — N
PULSE AIR SOLENOID — P
"CHECK ENGINE" LAMP — R
LONG TERM MEMORY (PLUS) — S
ECM POWER GROUND (TO ENG GRD) — T, U
IGNITION 1 POWER — V
CARBURETOR MIXTURE CONTROL SOLENOID — W

Notes:
1. Ground to get malfunction code.
2. Connects to lo side of Throttle Position Sensor, Coolant Sensor, and Shield Connections.

Computer Controlled Catalytic Converter—C4

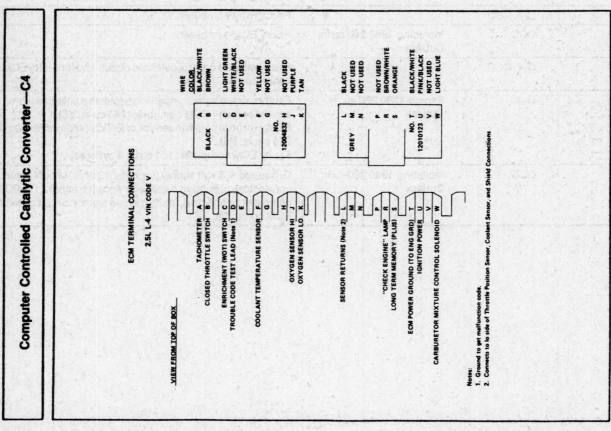

ECM TERMINAL CONNECTIONS

2.5L L-4 VIN CODE V

VIEW FROM TOP OF BOX

Terminal		WIRE COLOR
BLACK	A	BLACK/WHITE
	B	BROWN
	C	LIGHT GREEN
	D	WHITE/BLACK
	E	NOT USED
	F	YELLOW
	G	NOT USED
	H	NOT USED
NO. 12004832	J	PURPLE
	K	TAN
GREY	L	BLACK
	M	NOT USED
	N	NOT USED
	P	NOT USED
	R	BROWN/WHITE
	S	ORANGE
	T	BLACK/WHITE
NO. 12010123	U	PINK/BLACK
	V	NOT USED
	W	LIGHT BLUE

TACHOMETER — A, B
CLOSED THROTTLE SWITCH — C
ENRICHMENT (WOT) SWITCH — D
TROUBLE CODE TEST LEAD (Note 1) — E
COOLANT TEMPERATURE SENSOR — F, G
OXYGEN SENSOR HI — H
OXYGEN SENSOR LO — J, K
SENSOR RETURNS (Note 2) — L, M, N
"CHECK ENGINE" LAMP — P, R
LONG TERM MEMORY (PLUS) — S
ECM POWER GROUND (TO ENG GRD) — T
IGNITION POWER — U, V
CARBURETOR MIXTURE CONTROL SOLENOID — W

Notes:
1. Ground to get malfunction code.
2. Connects to lo side of Throttle Position Sensor, Coolant Sensor, and Shield Connections.

Computer Controlled Catalytic Converter—C4

DIAGNOSTIC ENGINE PERFORMANCE CHART

Preliminary Conditions: If the check engine light is not on, follow the procedures for checking a driveability complaint on any vehicle not equipped with a C4 system. When the generator or coolant light is on at the same time as the check engine light, check for a generator or coolant problem first. Inspect for poor connections at the coolant sensor, M/C solenoid and wiring. Check for loose vacuum hoses and connections and repair as needed.

Any time an engine is started, even a warm engine, it must be run at part throttle for 3 minutes or until the dwell starts to vary before proceeding with any checks.

Driver Complaint	Probable Cause	Correction or Additional Testing
Intermittent check engine light but no trouble code stored	1. Engine runs below 200 rpm	1. No correction—code not stored when caused by low rpm condition
	2. Poor electrical connection ⊕ at the distributor tach to ECM "A" terminal	2. Repair or tighten connections
	3. Poor connection from the ⊖ "1" ignition to the ECM "v" terminal	3. Repair or tighten connections
	4. Poor connection from the ⊖ ECM "T" to terminal to ground	4. Repair or tighten connections
	5. Tach filter defective or faulty. The filter should have 14,000–18,000 ohms when checked with an end disconnected and an open circuit to ground	5. Replace tach filter
	6. Low battery voltage (less than 9 volts)	6. Recharge battery/repair charging system
Loss of long term memory	1. Defective 20 amp ECS fuse	1. Replace 20 amp ECS fuse
	2. Defective Electronic Control Module—ECM Momentarily ground the dwell lead with engine idling and test lead disconnected. This should produce a code 23, which should be retained after the engine is stopped and restarted. If voltage is present at the long term memory terminal "S" of the ECM, but the code is not stored, the ECM is defective	2. Replace the ECM
Backfire during warmup	1. A.I.R. pump diverter valve not shifting air to air cleaner for 5 seconds after engine start up or on quick deceleration	1. Replace the diverter valve
Poor gas mileage	1. Air management switch not shifting air pump output to the catalytic converter upon TVS signal after engine warmup	1. Replace air switch valve.
Full throttle performance complaint	1. Follow TPS chart number 4	1. Repair as check out indicates
All other complaints	1. Make systems perform-check on warm engine	1. Repair as check out indicates

NOTE: System performance checks should be performed after any repairs to the C4 system have been completed. ⊖ On 3.8L V6 trace the circuit. Distributor module terminal "R" to terminal "C" and "R", and ECM terminal "10", Bat. to ECM terminal "U" to ground.

Computer Controlled Catalytic Converter—C4

V6 — Connector

View - Top of Box

Pin	
22	Not used
21	5V Reference
20	MAP Sensor
19	8V Supply
18	M/C Solenoid
17	Not Used
16	Not Used
15	WOT sw.
14	Oxygen Sensor-Lo
13	Dist. Ref. Pulse-Lo
12	EST

BLUE — 1 2 3 4 5 6 7 8 9 10 11 / 22 21 20 19 18 17 16 15 14 13 12 — BLUE

J K L M N P R S T U
H G F E D C B A

RED

- Not Used
- Not Used
- "CHECK ENGINE" Lamp
- Not Used
- Not Used
- Not Used
- Ign. 1 Power
- Not Used
- Air Select Sol.
- Not Used

View - Bottom of Box

- Baro Sensor Output
- TPS Sensor Output
- Coolant temp. Sensor
- Not Used
- Not Used
- Not Used
- Sensor Return
- Not Used
- Oxygen Sensor-Hi
- Dist. Ref. Pulse-Hi
- Ign. Module By Pass
- Trouble Code Test Lead
- Not Used
- Not Used
- Not Used
- Not Used
- Long Term Memory (PLUS)
- Not Used
- EGR-EFE Solenoid-(Turbo Only)
- Ground (To Engine)

Computer Controlled Catalytic Converter—C4

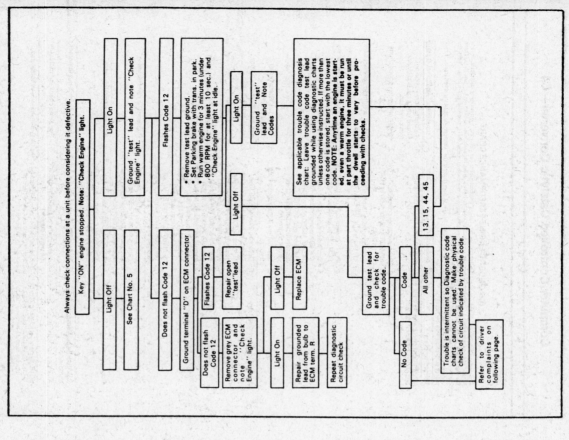

Always check connections at a unit before considering it defective.

Key "ON" engine stopped. Note: "Check Engine" light.

- Light Off → See Chart No. 5
- Light On → Ground "test" lead and note "Check Engine" light.
  - Flashes Code 12
    - Remove test lead ground.
    - Set Parking brake with trans. in park.
    - Run warm engine for 3 minutes (under 800 RPM for at least 10 sec.) and "Check Engine" light at idle.
    - Light On → Ground "test" lead and Note Codes
    - Light Off
      - See applicable trouble code diagnosis chart. Leave trouble code test lead grounded while using diagnostic charts unless otherwise instructed. If more then one code is stored, start with the lowest code. NOTE: Anytime an engine is started, even a warm engine, it must be run at part throttle for three minutes or until the dwell starts to vary before proceeding with checks.
  - Does not flash Code 12 → Ground terminal "D" on ECM connector
    - Flashes Code 12 → Remove grey ECM connector and note "Check Engine" light.
      - Light On → Repair grounded lead from bulb to ECM term. R
      - Light Off → Replace ECM
    - Does not flash Code 12 → Repair open "test" lead

Repeat diagnostic circuit check

Ground test lead and check for trouble code.
- No Code → Trouble is intermittent so Diagnostic code charts cannot be used. Make physical check of circuit indicated by trouble code.
- Code
  - 13, 15, 44, 45
  - All other → Refer to driver complaints on following page.

Computer Controlled Catalytic Converter—C4

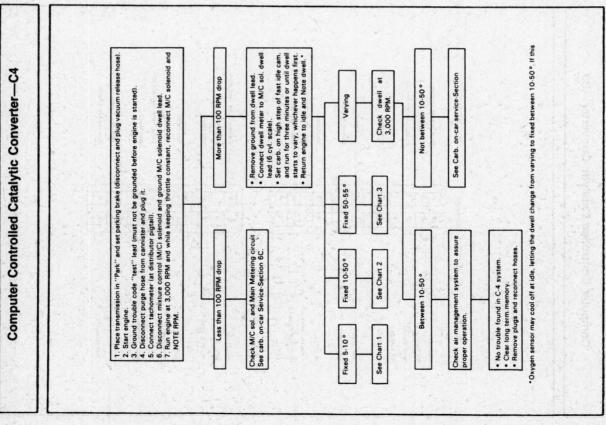

1. Place transmission in "Park" and set parking brake (disconnect and plug vacuum release hose).
2. Start engine.
3. Ground trouble code "test" lead (must not be grounded before engine is started).
4. Disconnect purge hose from cannister and plug it.
5. Connect tachometer (at distributor pigtail).
6. Disconnect mixture control (M/C) solenoid and ground M/C solenoid lead.
7. Run engine at 3,000 RPM and while keeping throttle constant, reconnect M/C solenoid and NOTE RPM.

- Less than 100 RPM drop → Check M/C sol. and Main Metering circuit See carb. on-car Service-Section 6C.
- More than 100 RPM drop
  - Remove ground from dwell lead.
  - Connect dwell meter to M/C sol. dwell lead (6 cyl. scale).
  - Set carb. on high step of fast idle cam. and run for three minutes or until dwell starts to vary, whichever happens first.
  - Return engine to idle and Note dwell.*

  - Fixed 5-10° → See Chart 1
  - Fixed 10-50° → See Chart 2
  - Fixed 50-55° → See Chart 3
  - Varying → Check dwell at 3,000 RPM.
    - Between 10-50° → Check air management system to assure proper operation.
      - No trouble found in C-4 system.
      - Clear long term memory.
      - Remove plugs and reconnect hoses.
    - Not between 10-50° → See Carb. on-car service-Section

*Oxygen sensor may cool off at idle, letting the dwell change from varying to fixed between 10-50°. If this

Computer Controlled Catalytic Converter—C4

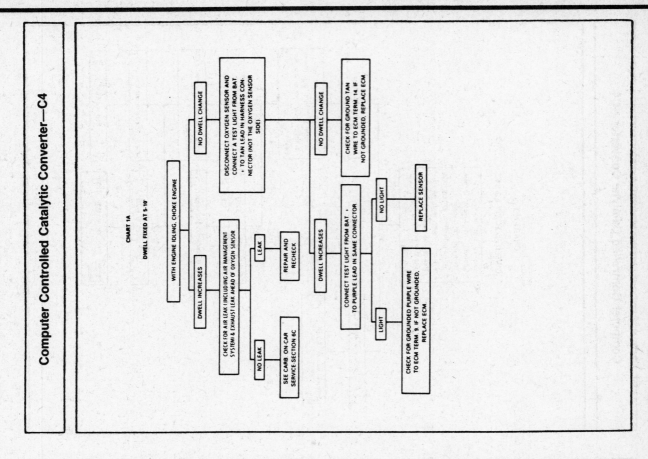

CHART 1A

DWELL FIXED AT 5-10°

WITH ENGINE IDLING, CHOKE ENGINE

DWELL INCREASES
- CHECK FOR AIR LEAK (INCLUDING AIR MANAGEMENT SYSTEM) & EXHAUST LEAK AHEAD OF OXYGEN SENSOR
  - LEAK → REPAIR AND RECHECK
  - NO LEAK → SEE CARB ON CAR SERVICE SECTION 6C

NO DWELL CHANGE
- DISCONNECT OXYGEN SENSOR AND CONNECT A TEST LIGHT FROM BAT. + TO TAN LEAD IN HARNESS CONNECTOR (NOT THE OXYGEN SENSOR SIDE)
  - DWELL INCREASES → CONNECT TEST LIGHT FROM BAT. + TO PURPLE LEAD IN SAME CONNECTOR
    - NO LIGHT → REPLACE SENSOR
    - LIGHT → CHECK FOR GROUNDED PURPLE WIRE TO ECM TERM. 9. IF NOT GROUNDED, REPLACE ECM.
  - NO DWELL CHANGE → CHECK FOR GROUND TAN WIRE TO ECM TERM. 14. IF NOT GROUNDED, REPLACE ECM.

Computer Controlled Catalytic Converter—C4

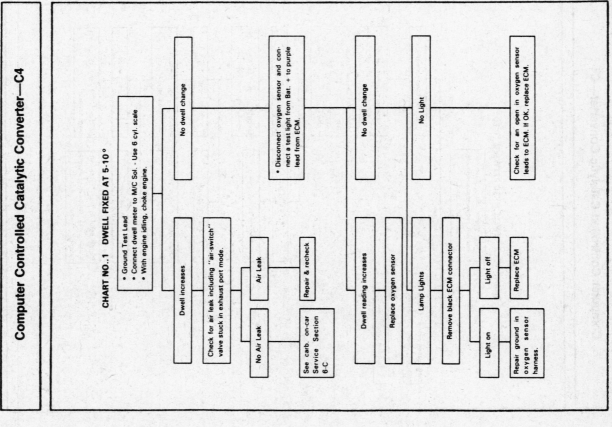

CHART NO..1 DWELL FIXED AT 5-10°
- Ground Test Lead
- Connect dwell meter to M/C Sol. - Use 6 cyl. scale
- With engine idling, choke engine.

Dwell increases
- Check for air leak including "air-switch" valve stuck in exhaust port mode.
  - Air Leak → Repair & recheck
  - No Air Leak → See carb. on-car Service Section 6-C

No dwell change
- Disconnect oxygen sensor and connect a test light from Bat. + to purple lead from ECM.
  - Dwell reading increases → Replace oxygen sensor
  - No dwell change → Lamp Lights
    - Remove black ECM connector
      - Light off → Replace ECM
      - Light on → Repair ground in oxygen sensor harness.
    - No Light → Check for an open in oxygen sensor leads to ECM. If OK, replace ECM.

Computer Controlled Catalytic Converter—C4

CHART NO. 3

DWELL FIXED AT 50-55°

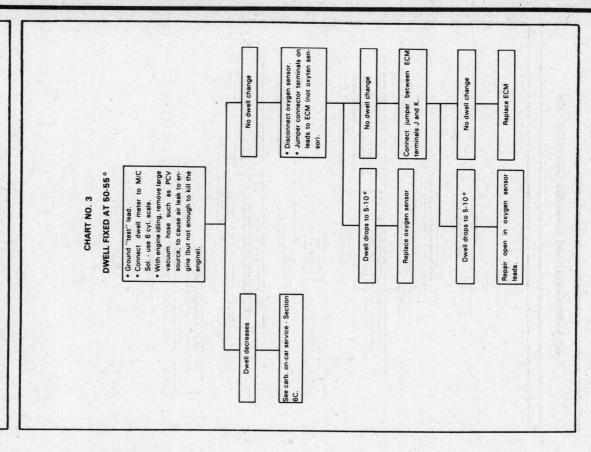

Computer Controlled Catalytic Converter—C4

CHART NO. 2 DWELL FIXED BETWEEN 10-50°

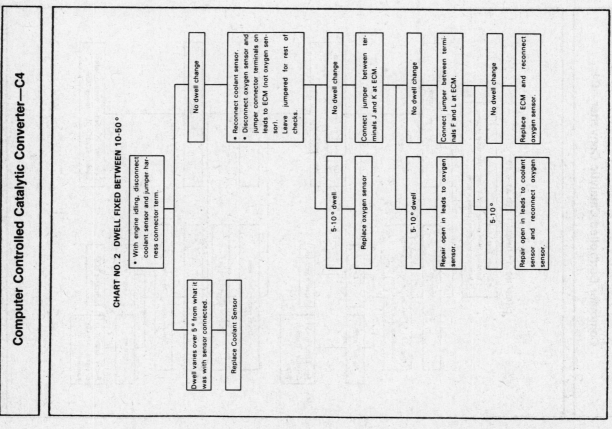

Computer Controlled Catalytic Converter—C4

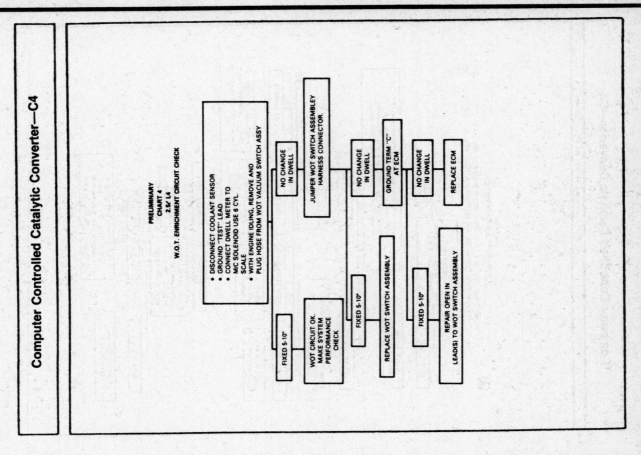

PRELIMINARY
CHART 4
2.5" L4
W.O.T. ENRICHMENT CIRCUIT CHECK

- DISCONNECT COOLANT SENSOR
- GROUND "TEST" LEAD
- CONNECT DWELL METER TO MIC SOLENOID USE 6 CYL. SCALE
- WITH ENGINE IDLING, REMOVE AND PLUG HOSE FROM WOT VACUUM SWITCH ASSY

Computer Controlled Catalytic Converter—C4

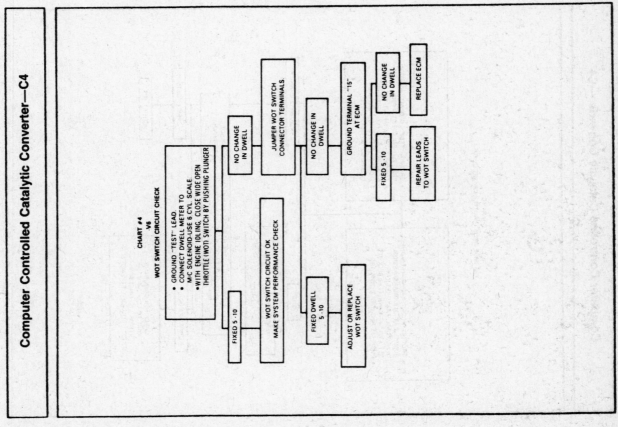

CHART #4
V6
WOT SWITCH CIRCUIT CHECK

- GROUND "TEST" LEAD
- CONNECT DWELL METER TO MIC SOLENOID-USE 6 CYL. SCALE.
- WITH ENGINE IDLING, CLOSE WIDE OPEN THROTTLE (WOT) SWITCH BY PUSHING PLUNGER

Computer Controlled Catalytic Converter—C4

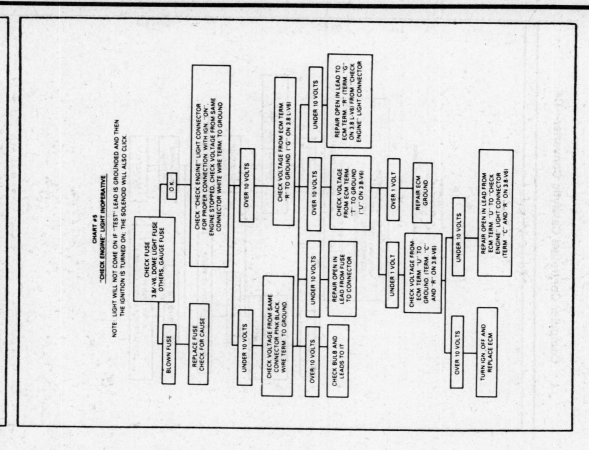

CHART #5

"CHECK ENGINE" LIGHT INOPERATIVE

NOTE: LIGHT WILL NOT COME ON IF "TEST" LEAD IS GROUNDED AND THEN THE IGNITION IS TURNED ON; THE SOLENOID WILL ALSO CLICK.

Computer Controlled Catalytic Converter—C4

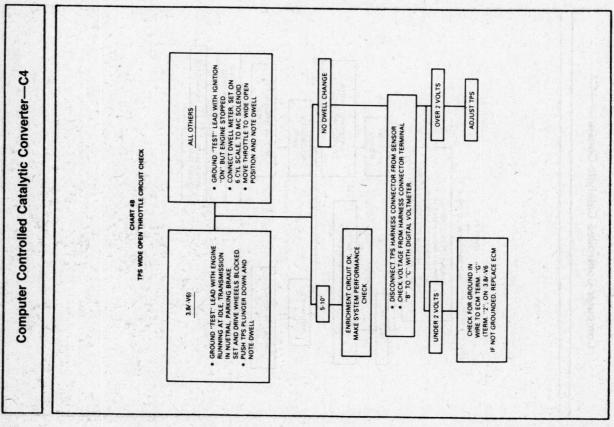

CHART 4B

TPS WIDE OPEN THROTTLE CIRCUIT CHECK

Computer Controlled Catalytic Converter—C4

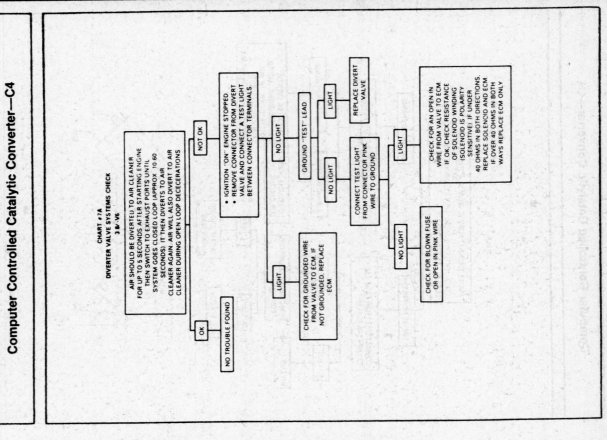

Computer Controlled Catalytic Converter—C4

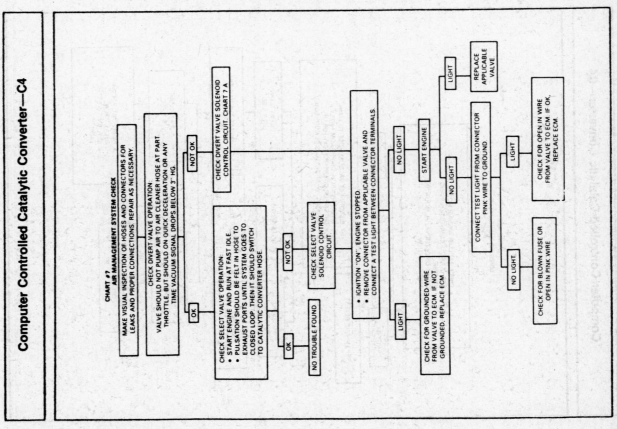

Computer Controlled Catalytic Converter—C4

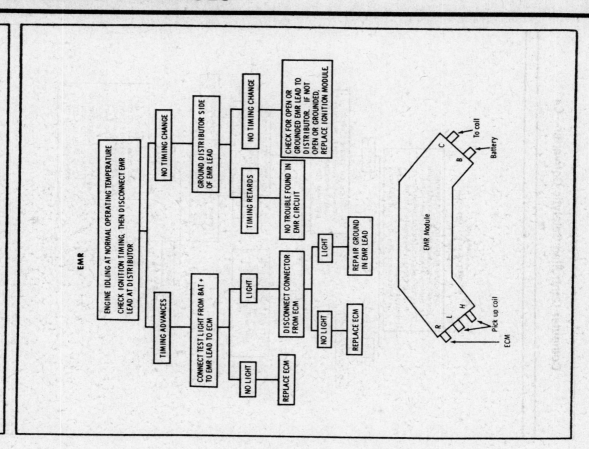

EMR

ENGINE IDLING AT NORMAL OPERATING TEMPERATURE
CHECK IGNITION TIMING, THEN DISCONNECT EMR LEAD AT DISTRIBUTOR

- TIMING ADVANCES
  - CONNECT TEST LIGHT FROM BAT + TO EMR LEAD TO ECM
    - NO LIGHT
      - REPLACE ECM
    - LIGHT
      - DISCONNECT CONNECTOR FROM ECM
        - NO LIGHT
          - REPLACE ECM
        - LIGHT
          - REPAIR GROUND IN EMR LEAD
- NO TIMING CHANGE
  - GROUND DISTRIBUTOR SIDE OF EMR LEAD
    - NO TIMING CHANGE
    - TIMING RETARDS
      - NO TROUBLE FOUND IN EMR CIRCUIT
      - CHECK FOR OPEN OR GROUNDED EMR LEAD TO DISTRIBUTOR. IF NOT OPEN OR GROUNDED, REPLACE IGNITION MODULE

EMR Module — To coil, Battery, Pick up coil, ECM, C, B, H, L, R

Computer Controlled Catalytic Converter—C4

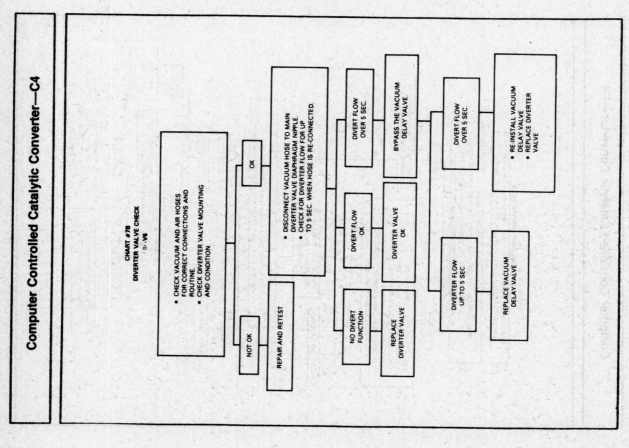

CHART #7B
DIVERTER VALVE CHECK
'81 - V6

- CHECK VACUUM AND AIR HOSES FOR CORRECT CONNECTIONS AND ROUTINE.
- CHECK DIVERTER VALVE MOUNTING AND CONDITION.
  - NOT OK
    - REPAIR AND RETEST
  - OK
    - DISCONNECT VACUUM HOSE TO MAIN DIVERTER VALVE DIAPHRAGM NIPPLE.
    - CHECK FOR DIVERTER FLOW FOR UP TO 5 SEC. WHEN HOSE IS RE-CONNECTED.
      - NO DIVERT FUNCTION
        - REPLACE DIVERTER VALVE
      - DIVERT FLOW OK
        - DIVERTER VALVE OK
      - DIVERT FLOW OVER 5 SEC.
        - BYPASS THE VACUUM DELAY VALVE.
          - DIVERTER FLOW UP TO 5 SEC.
            - REPLACE VACUUM DELAY VALVE
          - DIVERT FLOW OVER 5 SEC.
            - RE-INSTALL VACUUM DELAY VALVE
            - REPLACE DIVERTER VALVE

Computer Controlled Catalytic Converter—C4

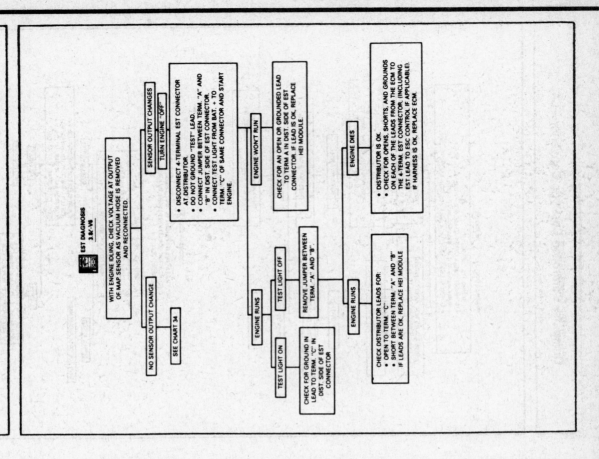

EST DIAGNOSIS
3.8· V6

WITH ENGINE IDLING, CHECK VOLTAGE AT OUTPUT OF MAP SENSOR AS VACUUM HOSE IS REMOVED AND RECONNECTED.

NO SENSOR OUTPUT CHANGE

SEE CHART 34

SENSOR OUTPUT CHANGES

TURN ENGINE "OFF"

- DISCONNECT 4-TERMINAL EST CONNECTOR AT DISTRIBUTOR.
- DO NOT GROUND "TEST" LEAD.
- CONNECT JUMPER BETWEEN TERM. "A" AND "B" IN DIST. SIDE OF EST CONNECTOR.
- CONNECT TEST LIGHT FROM BAT. + TO TERM. "C" OF SAME CONNECTOR AND START ENGINE.

ENGINE RUNS

TEST LIGHT ON

CHECK FOR GROUND IN LEAD TO TERM. "C" IN DIST. SIDE OF EST CONNECTOR

TEST LIGHT OFF

REMOVE JUMPER BETWEEN TERM. "A" AND "B"

ENGINE RUNS

CHECK DISTRIBUTOR LEADS FOR:
- OPEN TO TERM. "C"
- SHORT BETWEEN TERM. "A" AND "B"
IF LEADS ARE OK, REPLACE HEI MODULE

ENGINE WON'T RUN

CHECK FOR AN OPEN OR GROUNDED LEAD TO TERM A IN DIST. SIDE OF EST CONNECTOR. IF LEAD IS OK, REPLACE HEI MODULE.

ENGINE DIES

- DISTRIBUTOR IS OK.
- CHECK FOR OPENS, SHORTS, AND GROUNDS ON EACH OF THE LEADS FROM THE ECM TO THE 4-TERM. EST CONNECTOR, (INCLUDING EST LEAD TO ESC CONTROL IF APPLICABLE) IF HARNESS IS OK, REPLACE ECM.

Computer Controlled Catalytic Converter—C4

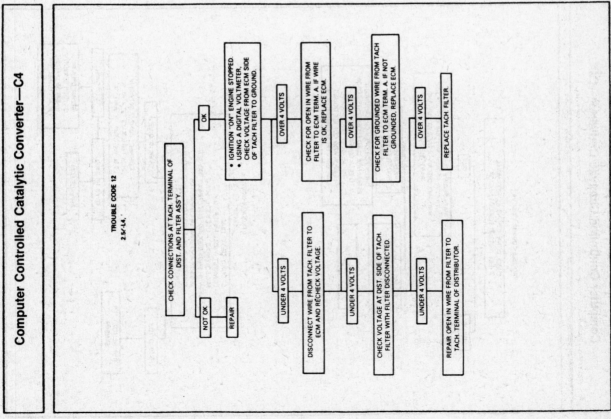

TROUBLE CODE 12
2.5/-1.4,

CHECK CONNECTIONS AT TACH. TERMINAL OF DIST. AND FILTER ASS'Y.

NOT OK

REPAIR

OK

- IGNITION "ON" ENGINE STOPPED.
- USING A DIGITAL VOLTMETER, CHECK VOLTAGE FROM ECM SIDE OF TACH FILTER TO GROUND.

UNDER 4 VOLTS

DISCONNECT WIRE FROM. FILTER TO ECM AND RECHECK VOLTAGE.

UNDER 4 VOLTS

CHECK VOLTAGE AT DIST. SIDE OF TACH FILTER WITH FILTER DISCONNECTED.

UNDER 4 VOLTS

REPAIR OPEN IN WIRE FROM FILTER TO TACH. TERMINAL OF DISTRIBUTOR.

OVER 4 VOLTS

CHECK FOR OPEN IN WIRE FROM FILTER TO ECM TERM. A. IF WIRE IS OK, REPLACE ECM.

OVER 4 VOLTS

CHECK FOR GROUNDED WIRE FROM TACH FILTER TO ECM TERM. A. IF NOT GROUNDED, REPLACE ECM.

OVER 4 VOLTS

REPLACE TACH. FILTER.

Computer Controlled Catalytic Converter—C4

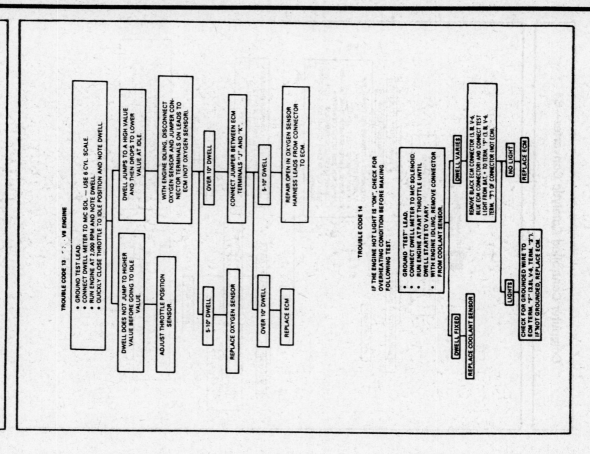

TROUBLE CODE 13   V8 ENGINE

- GROUND TEST LEAD.
- CONNECT DWELL METER TO M/C SOL. — USE 6 CYL. SCALE.
- RUN ENGINE AT 2,000 RPM AND NOTE DWELL.
- QUICKLY CLOSE THROTTLE TO IDLE POSITION AND NOTE DWELL.

DWELL JUMPS TO A HIGH VALUE AND THEN DROPS TO LOWER VALUE AT IDLE.

DWELL DOES NOT JUMP TO HIGHER VALUE BEFORE GOING TO IDLE VALUE.

ADJUST THROTTLE POSITION SENSOR.

WITH ENGINE IDLING, DISCONNECT OXYGEN SENSOR AND JUMPER CONNECTOR TERMINALS ON LEADS TO ECM (NOT OXYGEN SENSOR).

OVER 10° DWELL

5-10° DWELL

5-10° DWELL

REPLACE OXYGEN SENSOR

CONNECT JUMPER BETWEEN ECM TERMINALS "J" AND "K".

OVER 10° DWELL

REPLACE ECM

5-10° DWELL

REPAIR OPEN IN OXYGEN SENSOR HARNESS LEADS FROM CONNECTOR TO ECM.

TROUBLE CODE 14

IF THE ENGINE HOT LIGHT IS "ON", CHECK FOR OVERHEATING CONDITION BEFORE MAKING FOLLOWING TEST.

- GROUND "TEST" LEAD.
- CONNECT DWELL METER TO M/C SOLENOID.
- RUN ENGINE AT PART THROTTLE UNTIL DWELL STARTS TO VARY.
- WITH ENGINE IDLING, REMOVE CONNECTOR FROM COOLANT SENSOR.

DWELL VARIES

DWELL FIXED

REPLACE COOLANT SENSOR

REMOVE BLACK ECM CONNECTOR (3, 8L V4, BLUE ECM CONNECTOR) AND CONNECT TEST LIGHT FROM BAT. + TO TERM. "F" (3, 8L V4, TERM. "7") OF CONNECTOR (NOT ECM).

NO LIGHT

LIGHTS

REPLACE ECM

CHECK FOR GROUNDED WIRE TO ECM TERM. "F" (3,8L V4, TERM. "3"). IF NOT GROUNDED, REPLACE ECM.

Computer Controlled Catalytic Converter—C4

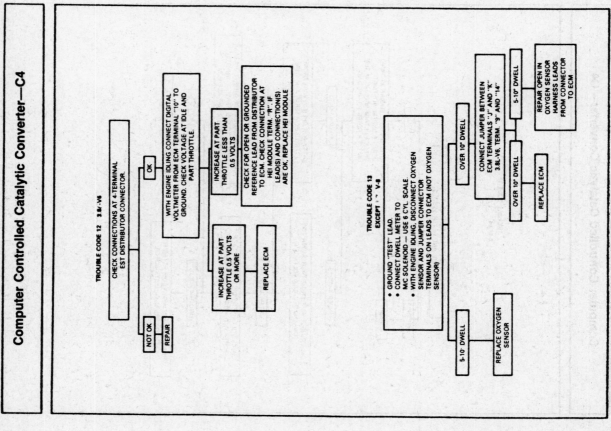

TROUBLE CODE 12   3.8L V6

CHECK CONNECTIONS AT 4-TERMINAL EST DISTRIBUTOR CONNECTOR.

OK

NOT OK

REPAIR

WITH ENGINE IDLING CONNECT DIGITAL VOLTMETER FROM ECM TERMINAL "10" TO GROUND. CHECK VOLTAGE AT IDLE AND PART THROTTLE.

INCREASE AT PART THROTTLE LESS THAN 0.5 VOLTS

INCREASE AT PART THROTTLE 0.5 VOLTS OR MORE

REPLACE ECM

CHECK FOR OPEN OR GROUNDED REFERENCE LEAD FROM DISTRIBUTOR TO ECM. CHECK CONNECTION AT HEI MODULE TERM. "R". IF LEAD(S) AND CONNECTION(S) ARE OK, REPLACE HEI MODULE

TROUBLE CODE 13   EXCEPT V-8

- GROUND "TEST" LEAD.
- CONNECT DWELL METER TO M/C SOLENOID — USE 6 CYL. SCALE.
- WITH ENGINE IDLING, DISCONNECT OXYGEN SENSOR AND JUMPER CONNECTOR TERMINALS ON LEADS TO ECM (NOT OXYGEN SENSOR)

OVER 10° DWELL

5-10° DWELL

REPLACE OXYGEN SENSOR

CONNECT JUMPER BETWEEN ECM TERMINALS "J" AND "K" 3.8L-V6, TERM. "9" AND "14"

OVER 10° DWELL

5-10° DWELL

REPLACE ECM

REPAIR OPEN IN OXYGEN SENSOR HARNESS LEADS FROM CONNECTOR TO ECM

Computer Controlled Catalytic Converter—C4

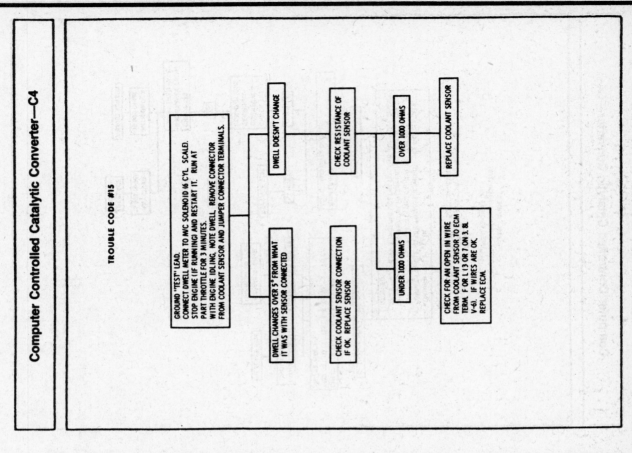

Computer Controlled Catalytic Converter—C4

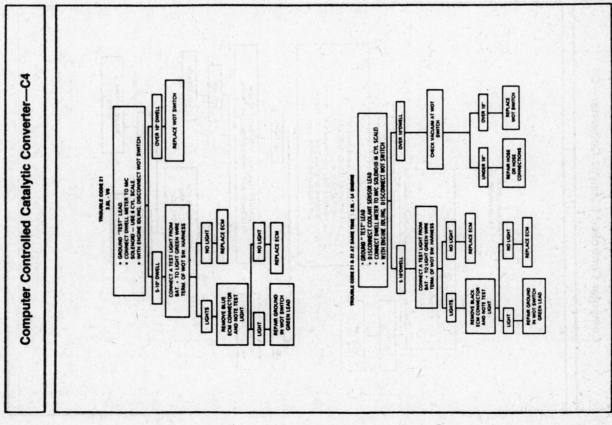

Computer Controlled Catalytic Converter—C4

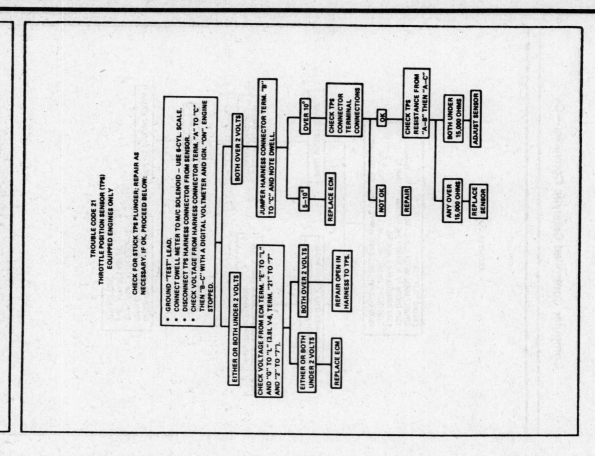

**TROUBLE CODE 21
THROTTLE POSITION SENSOR (TPS)
EQUIPPED ENGINES ONLY**

CHECK FOR STUCK TPS PLUNGER; REPAIR AS
NECESSARY. IF OK, PROCEED BELOW:

- GROUND "TEST" LEAD.
- CONNECT DWELL METER TO M/C SOLENOID — USE 6-CYL. SCALE.
- DISCONNECT TPS HARNESS CONNECTOR FROM SENSOR.
- CHECK VOLTAGE FROM HARNESS CONNECTOR TERM. "A" TO "C"
  THEN "B-C" WITH A DIGITAL VOLTMETER AND IGN. "ON", ENGINE
  STOPPED.

BOTH OVER 2 VOLTS → **JUMPER HARNESS CONNECTOR TERM. "B" TO "C" AND NOTE DWELL.**
- **OVER 10°** → **CHECK TPS CONNECTOR TERMINAL CONNECTIONS** → **OK** → **CHECK TPS RESISTANCE FROM "A–B" THEN "A–C"**
  - **BOTH UNDER 15,000 OHMS** → **ADJUST SENSOR**
  - **ANY OVER 15,000 OHMS** → **REPLACE SENSOR**
- **5–10°** → **REPLACE ECM**
- **NOT OK** → **REPAIR**

EITHER OR BOTH UNDER 2 VOLTS → **CHECK VOLTAGE FROM ECM TERM. "E" TO "L" AND "G" TO "L" (3.8L V-6, TERM. "21" TO "7" AND "Z" TO "7").**
- **BOTH OVER 2 VOLTS** → **REPAIR OPEN IN HARNESS TO TPS.**
- **EITHER OR BOTH UNDER 2 VOLTS** → **REPLACE ECM**

Computer Controlled Catalytic Converter—C4

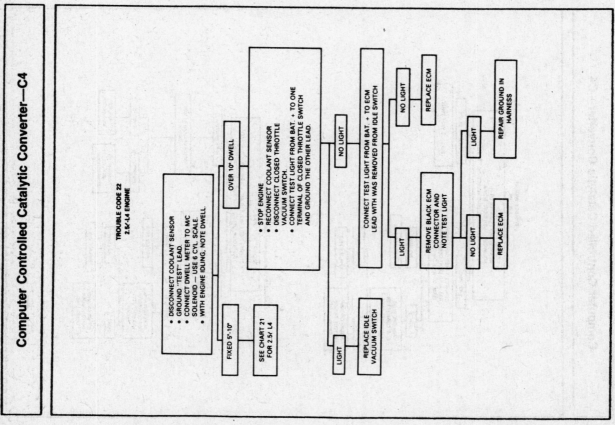

**TROUBLE CODE 22
2.5ℓ-L4 ENGINE**

- DISCONNECT COOLANT SENSOR
- GROUND "TEST" LEAD.
- CONNECT DWELL METER TO M/C
  SOLENOID — USE 6 CYL. SCALE.
- WITH ENGINE IDLING, NOTE DWELL.

FIXED 5°-10° → **SEE CHART 21 FOR 2.5ℓ L4**

OVER 10° DWELL →
- STOP ENGINE
- RECONNECT COOLANT SENSOR
- DISCONNECT CLOSED THROTTLE
  VACUUM SWITCH.
- CONNECT TEST LIGHT FROM BAT. + TO ONE
  TERMINAL OF CLOSED THROTTLE SWITCH
  AND GROUND THE OTHER LEAD.

- **LIGHT** → **REPLACE IDLE VACUUM SWITCH**
- **NO LIGHT** → **CONNECT TEST LIGHT FROM BAT. + TO ECM LEAD WITH WAS REMOVED FROM IDLE SWITCH**
  - **NO LIGHT** → **REPLACE ECM**
  - **LIGHT** → **REMOVE BLACK ECM CONNECTOR AND NOTE TEST LIGHT**
    - **NO LIGHT** → **REPLACE ECM**
    - **LIGHT** → **REPAIR GROUND IN HARNESS**

Computer Controlled Catalytic Converter—C4

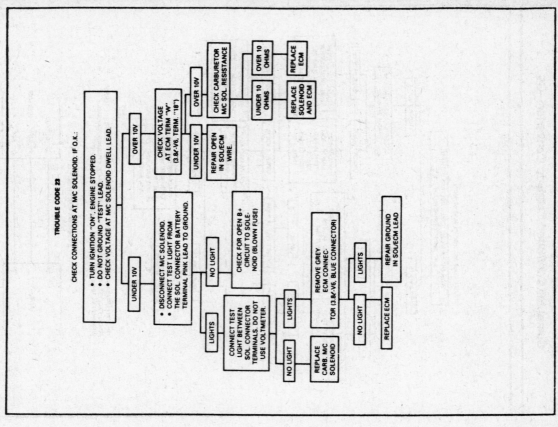

Computer Controlled Catalytic Converter—C4

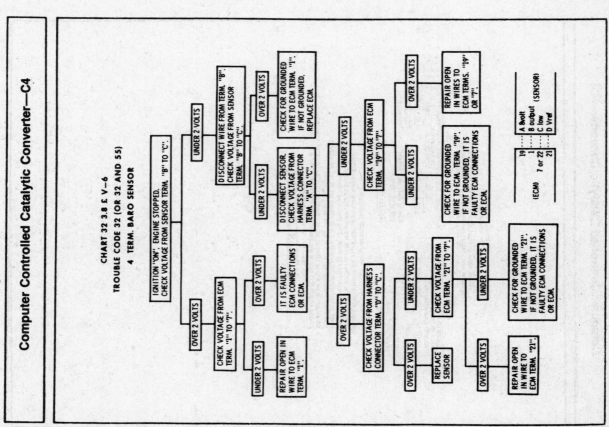

Computer Controlled Catalytic Converter—C4

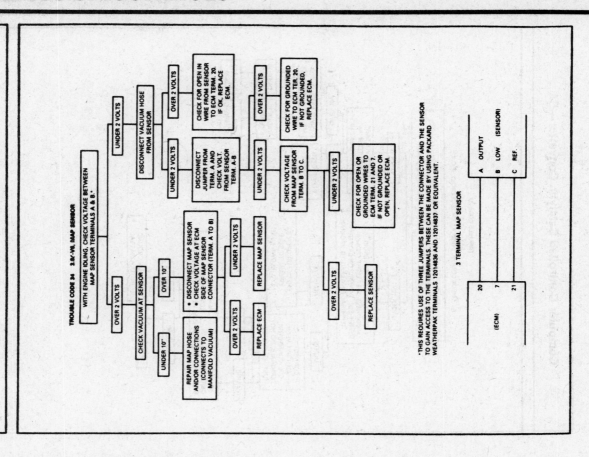

TROUBLE CODE 34   3.8L-V6, MAP SENSOR

WITH ENGINE IDLING, CHECK VOLTAGE BETWEEN MAP SENSOR TERMINALS A & B.*

- **OVER 2 VOLTS** → CHECK VACUUM AT SENSOR
  - **OVER 10"** → • DISCONNECT MAP SENSOR • CHECK VOLTAGE AT ECM SIDE OF MAP SENSOR CONNECTOR (TERM. A TO B)
    - **UNDER 2 VOLTS** → REPLACE MAP SENSOR
    - **OVER 2 VOLTS** → REPLACE ECM
  - **UNDER 10"** → REPAIR MAP HOSE AND/OR CONNECTIONS (CONNECTS TO MANIFOLD VACUUM)

- **UNDER 2 VOLTS** → DISCONNECT VACUUM HOSE FROM SENSOR
  - **OVER 2 VOLTS** → CHECK FOR OPEN IN WIRE FROM SENSOR TO ECM TERM. 20. IF OK, REPLACE ECM.
  - **UNDER 2 VOLTS** → DISCONNECT JUMPER FROM TERM. A AND CHECK VOLT. FROM SENSOR TERM. A-B
    - **OVER 2 VOLTS** → CHECK FOR GROUNDED WIRE TO ECM TER. 20. IF NOT GROUNDED, REPLACE ECM.
    - **UNDER 2 VOLTS** → CHECK VOLTAGE FROM MAP SENSOR TERM. B TO C.
      - **UNDER 2 VOLTS** → CHECK FOR OPEN OR GROUNDED WIRES TO ECM TERM. 21 AND 7. IF NOT GROUNDED OR OPEN, REPLACE ECM.
      - **OVER 2 VOLTS** → REPLACE SENSOR

*THIS REQUIRES USE OF THREE JUMPERS BETWEEN THE CONNECTOR AND THE SENSOR TO GAIN ACCESS TO THE TERMINALS. THESE CAN BE MADE BY USING PACKARD WEATHERPAK TERMINALS 12014836 AND 12014837 OR EQUIVALENT.

3 TERMINAL MAP SENSOR

(ECM)			
20		A	OUTPUT
7		B	LOW (SENSOR)
21		C	REF.

Computer Controlled Catalytic Converter—C4

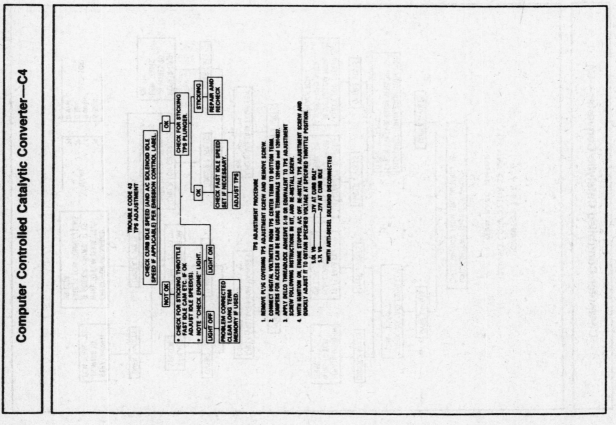

TROUBLE CODE 43   TPS ADJUSTMENT

CHECK CURB IDLE SPEED (AND A/C SOLENOID IDLE SPEED IF APPLICABLE) PER EMISSION CONTROL LABEL.

- **HOT OK** → • CHECK FOR STICKING THROTTLE FAST IDLE CAM ETC. IF OK ADJUST IDLE SPEED(S). • NOTE "CHECK ENGINE" LIGHT.
  - **LIGHT OFF** → PROBLEM CORRECTED CLEAR LONG TERM MEMORY IF USED.
  - **LIGHT ON**

- **OK** → CHECK FOR STICKING TPS PLUNGER.
  - **OK** → CHECK FAST IDLE SPEED SET IF NECESSARY.
    - ADJUST TPS
  - **STICKING** → REPAIR AND RECHECK

TPS ADJUSTMENT PROCEDURE

1. REMOVE PLUG COVERING TPS ADJUSTMENT SCREW AND REMOVE SCREW.
2. CONNECT DIGITAL VOLTMETER FROM TPS CENTER TERM TO BOTTOM TERM. JUMPERS FOR ACCESS CAN BE MADE USING TERMINALS 12014836 and 12014837.
3. APPLY WELD THREADLOCK ADHESIVE 2-10 OR EQUIVALENT TO TPS ADJUSTMENT SCREW FOLLOWING INSTRUCTIONS IN KIT, AND RE-INSTALL SCREW.
4. WITH IGNITION ON, ENGINE STOPPED, A/C OFF, RE-INSTALL TPS ADJUSTMENT SCREW AND QUICKLY ADJUST IT TO OBTAIN SPECIFIED VOLTAGE AT SPECIFIED THROTTLE POSITION.

3.0L V6........37V AT CURB IDLE*
3.7L V6........37V AT CURB IDLE
*WITH ANTI-DIESEL SOLENOID DISCONNECTED

Computer Controlled Catalytic Converter—C4

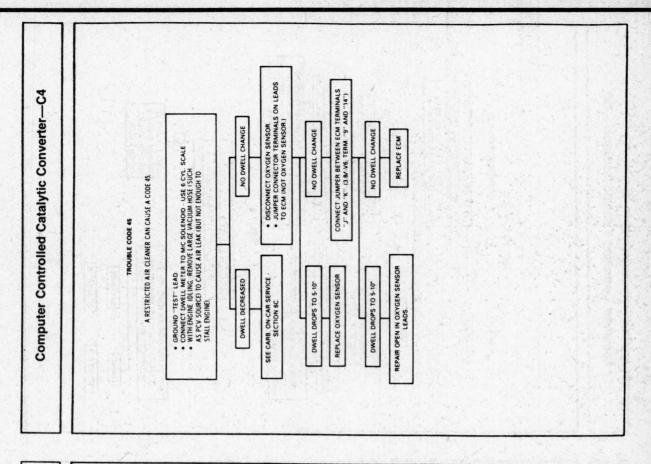

TROUBLE CODE 45

A RESTRICTED AIR CLEANER CAN CAUSE A CODE 45.

- GROUND "TEST" LEAD
- CONNECT DWELL METER TO M/C SOLENOID - USE 6 CYL. SCALE
- WITH ENGINE IDLING, REMOVE LARGE VACUUM HOSE (SUCH AS PCV SOURCE) TO CAUSE AIR LEAK (BUT NOT ENOUGH TO STALL ENGINE).

DWELL DECREASED
→ SEE CARB. ON-CAR SERVICE - SECTION 6C

NO DWELL CHANGE
→ DISCONNECT OXYGEN SENSOR. JUMPER CONNECTOR TERMINALS ON LEADS TO ECM (NOT OXYGEN SENSOR.)

DWELL DROPS TO 5-10°
→ REPLACE OXYGEN SENSOR

NO DWELL CHANGE
→ CONNECT JUMPER BETWEEN ECM TERMINALS "J" AND "K" (3 &/ V6, TERM. "9" AND "14")

DWELL DROPS TO 5-10°
→ REPAIR OPEN IN OXYGEN SENSOR LEADS.

NO DWELL CHANGE
→ REPLACE ECM

Computer Controlled Catalytic Converter—C4

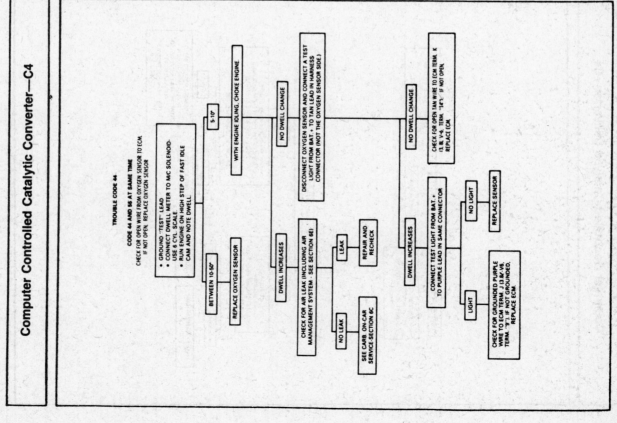

TROUBLE CODE 44

CODE 44 AND 55 AT SAME TIME

CHECK FOR OPEN WIRE FROM OXYGEN SENSOR TO ECM. IF NOT OPEN, REPLACE OXYGEN SENSOR

- GROUND "TEST" LEAD
- CONNECT DWELL METER TO M/C SOLENOID- USE 6 CYL. SCALE
- RUN ENGINE ON HIGH STEP OF FAST IDLE CAM AND NOTE DWELL

BETWEEN 10-50°
→ REPLACE OXYGEN SENSOR

5-10°
→ WITH ENGINE IDLING, CHOKE ENGINE.

DWELL INCREASES
→ CHECK FOR AIR LEAK (INCLUDING AIR MANAGEMENT SYSTEM - SEE SECTION 6E)

  NO LEAK
  → SEE CARB. ON-CAR SERVICE-SECTION 6C

  LEAK
  → REPAIR AND RECHECK

NO DWELL CHANGE
→ DISCONNECT OXYGEN SENSOR AND CONNECT A TEST LIGHT FROM BAT.+ TO TAN LEAD IN HARNESS CONNECTOR (NOT THE OXYGEN SENSOR SIDE.)

DWELL INCREASES
→ CONNECT TEST LIGHT FROM BAT.+ TO PURPLE LEAD IN SAME CONNECTOR

  LIGHT
  → CHECK FOR GROUNDED PURPLE WIRE TO ECM TERM. J (3.8/ V6, TERM. "9"). IF NOT GROUNDED, REPLACE ECM.

  NO LIGHT
  → REPLACE SENSOR

NO DWELL CHANGE
→ CHECK FOR OPEN TAN WIRE TO ECM TERM. K (3.8/ V6, TERM. "14"). IF NOT OPEN REPLACE ECM

Computer Controlled Catalytic Converter—C4

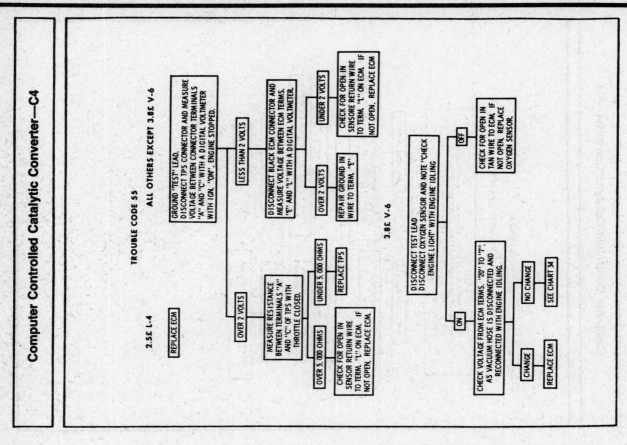

Computer Controlled Catalytic Converter—C4

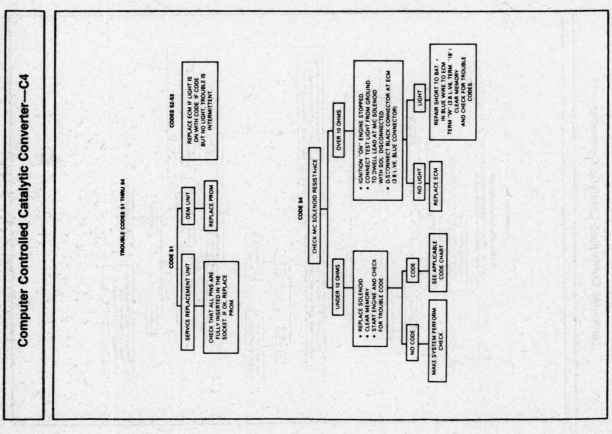

Computer Command Control (With EST)

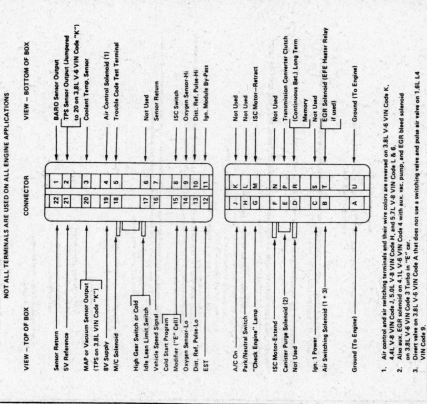

ECM TERMINAL IDENTIFICATION
NOT ALL TERMINALS ARE USED ON ALL ENGINE APPLICATIONS

VIEW – TOP OF BOX | **CONNECTOR** | **VIEW – BOTTOM OF BOX**

Top of box	Bottom of box
Sensor Return	BARO Sensor Output
5V Reference	TPS Sensor Output (Jumpered to 20 on 3.8L V-6 VIN Code "K")
MAP or Vacuum Sensor Output (TPS on 3.8L VIN Code "K")	Coolant Temp. Sensor
8V Supply	Air Control Solenoid (1)
M/C Solenoid	Trouble Code Test Terminal
High Gear Switch or Cold	Not Used
Idle Lean Limit Switch	Sensor Return
Vehicle Speed Signal	ISC Switch
Cold Start Program	Oxygen Sensor-Hi
Modifier ("E" Cell)	Dist. Ref. Pulse-Hi
Oxygen Sensor-Lo	Ign. Module By-Pass
Dist. Ref. Pulse-Lo	
EST	
A/C On	Not Used
Park/Neutral Switch	Not Used
"Check Engine" Lamp	ISC Motor–Retract
ISC Motor–Extend	Not Used
Canister Purge Solenoid (2)	Transmission Converter Clutch
Not Used	(Continuous Bat.) Long Term
Ign. 1 Power	Memory
Air Switching Solenoid (1 + 3)	Not Used
	EGR Solenoid (EFE Heater Relay if used)
Ground (To Engine)	Ground (To Engine)

1. Air control and air switching terminals and their wire colors are reversed on 3.8L V-6 VIN Code K, 4.4L V-8 VIN Code J, 5.0L V-8 VIN Code H, and 5.7L V-8 VIN Code L & 6.
2. Also aux. EGR solenoid on 4.1L V-6 VIN Code 4 with aux. vac. pump, and EGR bleed solenoid on 3.8L V-6 VIN Code 3 Turbo in "E" car.
3. Divert valve on 3.8L V-6 VIN Code A that does not use a switching valve and pulse air valve on 1.6L L4 VIN Code 9.

Computer Command Control (With EST)

DIAGNOSTIC CIRCUIT CHECK

ALWAYS CHECK PROM FOR CORRECT APPLICATION AND INSTALLATION BEFORE REPLACING AN ECM. ALSO, REMOVE TERMINAL(S) FROM ECM CONNECTOR FOR CIRCUIT INVOLVED, CLEAN TERMINAL CONTACT AND EXPAND IT SLIGHTLY TO INCREASE CONTACT PRESSURE AND RECHECK TO SEE IF PROBLEM IS CORRECTED.

- KEY 'ON' ENGINE STOPPED. 'TEST' TERM. UNGROUNDED.
- NOTE CHECK ENGINE LIGHT

LIGHT 'OFF' — SEE CHART 4

LIGHT 'ON' STEADY

GROUND 'TEST' TERM. AND NOTE CHECK ENGINE LIGHT

FLASHES CODE 12

DOES NOT FLASH CODE 12 — SEE CHART 7

CODE 51 — CHECK THAT ALL PROM PINS ARE FULLY SEATED IN SOCKET. IF OK, REPLACE PROM. CLEAR MEMORY AND RECHECK. IF IT REAPPEARS, REPLACE ECM.

NO CODE 51 — NOTE AND RECORD ANY ADDITIONAL CODES

- TURN IGNITION OFF
- CLEAR LONG TERM MEMORY
- REMOVE 'TEST' TERM. GROUND
- SET PARKING BRAKE WITH TRANS. IN PARK (A.T.), NEUTRAL (M.T.), AND BLOCK DRIVE WHEELS
- RUN WARM ENGINE AT SPECIFIED CURB IDLE FOR 2 MINUTES AND NOTE CHECK ENGINE LIGHT

LIGHT ON

LIGHT OFF — REFER TO THE ADDITIONAL CODES RECORDED ABOVE (NOT CODE 12)

NO ADDITIONAL CODES — TROUBLE IS INTERMITTENT SO CODE CHARTS CAN NOT BE USED. MAKE A PHYSICAL CHECK OF CIRCUIT INDICATED BY TROUBLE CODE

ADDITIONAL CODES: 12, 14, 21, 23, 24, 32, 34, 35 — 42, 51, 53, 54, 13, 15, 24, 44, 45, 55 — SEE APPLICABLE CODE CHART. IF MORE THAN ONE CODE IS STORED, START WITH LOWEST CODE. UNLESS ONE IS 50 OR 63 WITH 50 CODE, RE-PLACE THE ECM. LEAVE 'TEST' TERM. GROUNDED WHILE USING CHARTS UNLESS OTHERWISE INSTRUCTED

SEE DRIVER COMPLAINTS ON FOLLOWING PAGE

GROUND 'TEST' TERM. AND NOTE LIGHT

FLASHES CODE

FLASHES BUT NOT A CODE

LIGHT FLASHES (IN- TERMITTENTLY OR A CODE)

CHECK VOLT. AT ECM TERM. 21 TO GND — OVER 4V / UNDER 4V

CHECK FOR GN'DED CIR. CUIT TO ECM TERM. 16 IF USED, AND 21. IF NOT GN'DED, IT IS FAULTY ECM.

CHECK FOR GN'DED WIRE TO ECM TERM. 5. IF NOT GN'DED IT IS FAULTY ECM

CHECK VOLT. FROM ECM TERM. 21 TO GROUND — OVER 4V / UNDER 4V

CHECK FOR GROUNDED CIRCUIT TO ECM TERM. 21. IF NOT GROUNDED REPLACE ECM

REPLACE ECM

'TEST' TERM — GN'D

Computer Command Control (With EST)

DRIVER COMPLAINT

ENGINE PERFORMANCE PROBLEM (ODOR, SURGE, FUEL ECONOMY . . .)
EMISSION PROBLEM

IF THE "CHECK ENGINE" LIGHT IS NOT ON, NORMAL CHECKS THAT WOULD BE PERFORMED ON CARS WITHOUT THE SYSTEM SHOULD BE DONE FIRST.

IF GENERATOR OR COOLANT LIGHT IS ON WITH THE CHECK ENGINE LIGHT, THEY SHOULD BE DIAGNOSED FIRST.

INSPECT FOR POOR CONNECTIONS AT COOLANT SENSOR, M/C SOLENOID, ETC., AND POOR OR LOOSE VACUUM HOSES AND CONNECTIONS. REPAIR AS NECESSARY.

- Intermittent Check Engine light but no trouble code stored.
  Check for intermittent connection in circuit from:
  - Ignition coil to ground and arcing at spark plug wires or plugs.
  - Bat. to ECM Term. 'C' and 'R'.
  - ECM Terms. 'A' and 'U' to engine ground.
- Loss of long-term memory.
  Grounding dwell lead for "10 seconds with "test" lead ungrounded should give Code 23 which should be retained after engine is stopped and ignition turned to "RUN" position.
  If it is not, ECM is defective.
- EST wires should be kept away from spark plug wires, distributor housing, coil and generator. Wires from ECM Term. 13 to dist. and the shield around EST wires should be a good ground.
- Open diode across A/C compressor clutch.
- Stalling, Rough Idle, or Improper Idle Speed.
  See idle speed control.
- Detonation (spark knock)
  Check:
  - MAP or Vacuum Sensor output.
  - EGR operation.
  - TPS enrichment operation.
  - HEI operation.
- Poor Performance and/or Fuel Economy.
  See EST diagnosis.
- Poor Full Throttle Performance
  See Chart 4 if equipped with TPS.
- ALL OTHER COMPLAINTS
  Make system performance check on warm engine (upper radiator hose hot).

The system performance check should be performed after any repairs to the system has been made.

Computer Command Control (With EST)

SYSTEM PERFORMANCE CHECK

1. Start engine.
2. Ground "test" term. (Must not be grounded before engine is started.)
3. Disconnect purge hose from canister and plug it. On E2SE carburetors, disconnect bowl vent at carburetor.
4. Connect tachometer.
5. Disconnect Mixture Control (M/C) Solenoid and ground M/C Solenoid dwell term.
6. Run engine at 3,000 RPM and, while keeping throttle constant, reconnect M/C Solenoid and note RPM. If car is equipped with an electric cooling fan, it may lower RPM when it engages.
7. Remove ground from M/C Solenoid dwell term. before returning to idle.

Less than 100 RPM drop
- Check that pink wire is attached to right-hand term. of M/C Solenoid Connector, as viewed from harness end.
- Check evaporator canister for being loaded with fuel and related valves, such as purge and bowl vents for leaks which would cause richness. Also check for fuel in crankcase. If OK, see Carb. On-Car Service, Section 6C.

More than 100 RPM drop
- Connect dwell meter to M/C sol. dwell term. (6 cyl. scale).
- Set carb. on high step of fast idle cam. and run for one (1) minute or until dwell is starts to vary, whichever happens first.
- Return engine to idle and note dwell.*

Fixed under 10°	Fixed 10-50°	Fixed over 50°	Varying
See Chart #1	See Chart #2	See Chart #3	

Varying → Check dwell at 3,000 RPM (on 2.8L V-6, Auto Trans. Only, disconnect and plug hose to vacuum sensor during check.)

- Between 10-50° → Check air management system.
  - No trouble found in the "System."
  - Clear long term memory.**

- Not between 10-50° → See Carb. Calibration Procedure-including TPS adjust.

*Oxygen sensors may cool off at idle and the dwell change from varying to fixed. If this happens, running the engine at fast idle will warm it up again.
**See Code(s) Clearing Procedure.

Computer Command Control (With EST)

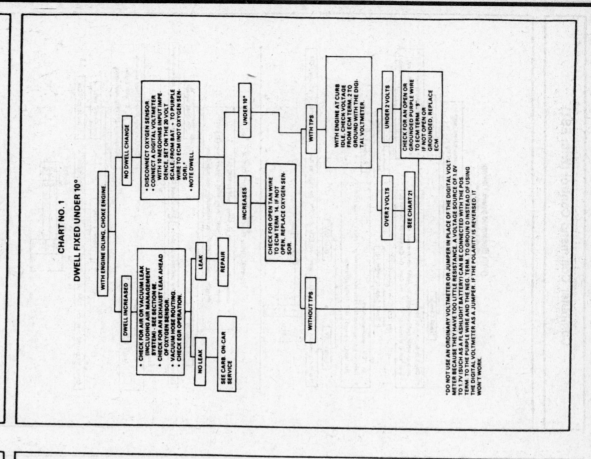

CHART NO. 1

DWELL FIXED UNDER 10°

Computer Command Control (With EST)

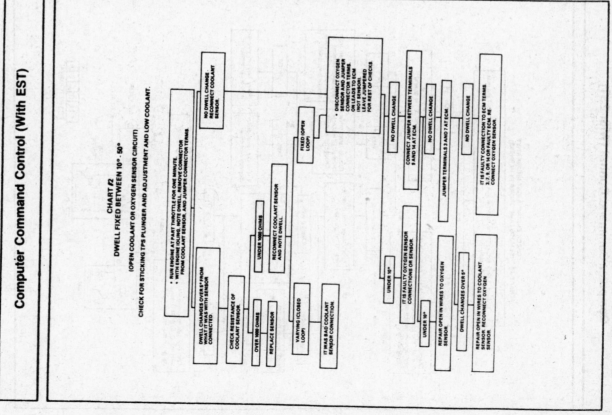

CHART #2

DWELL FIXED BETWEEN 10° - 50°

(OPEN COOLANT OR OXYGEN SENSOR CIRCUIT)

CHECK FOR STICKING TPS PLUNGER AND ADJUSTMENT AND LOW COOLANT.

Computer Command Control (With EST)

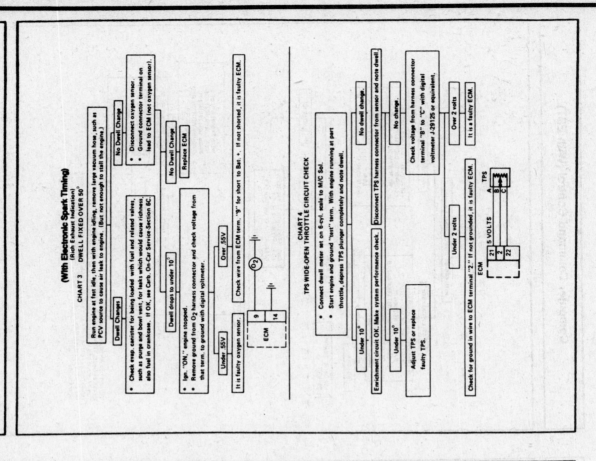

CHART 3

(With Electronic Spark Timing)
(Rich Exhaust Indication)
DWELL FIXED OVER 50°

Computer Command Control (With EST)

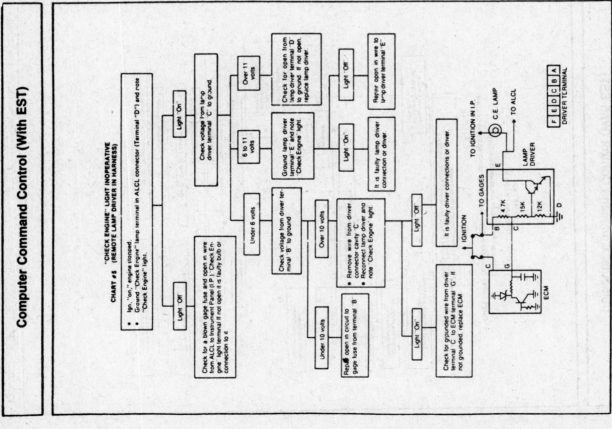

CHART #5

"CHECK ENGINE" LIGHT INOPERATIVE
(REMOTE LAMP DRIVER IN HARNESS)

Computer Command Control (With EST)

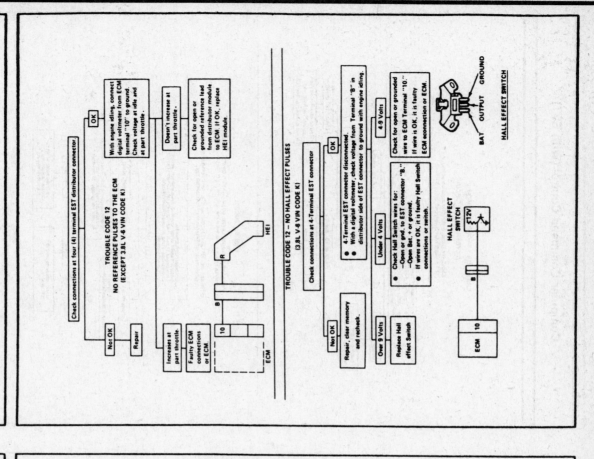

Computer Command Control (With EST)

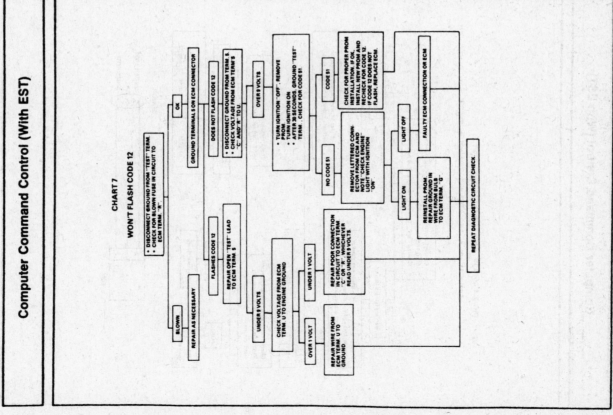

Computer Command Control (With EST)

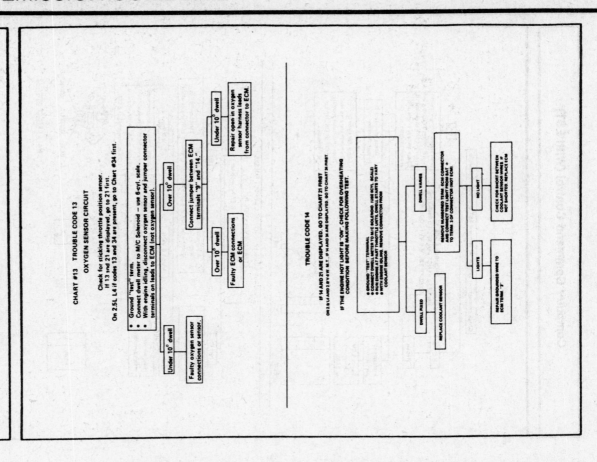

CHART #13   TROUBLE CODE 13

OXYGEN SENSOR CIRCUIT

Check for sticking throttle position sensor.
If 13 and 21 are displayed, go to 21 first.
On 2.5L L4 if codes 13 and 34 are present, go to Chart #34 first.

- Ground "test" term.
- Connect dwell meter to M/C Solenoid — use 6-cyl. scale.
- With engine idling, disconnect oxygen sensor and jumper connector terminals on leads to ECM (not oxygen sensor).

Under 10° dwell		Over 10° dwell

Faulty oxygen sensor connections or sensor.

Over 10° dwell	Under 10° dwell

Connect jumper between ECM terminals "9" and "14."

Faulty ECM connections or ECM.

Repair open in oxygen sensor harness leads from connector to ECM.

TROUBLE CODE 14

IF 14 AND 21 ARE DISPLAYED, GO TO CHART 21 FIRST
ON 2.5L L4 AND 2.8 V-6 W. M.T., IF 14 AND 34 ARE DISPLAYED, GO TO CHART 34 FIRST

IF THE ENGINE HOT LIGHT IS "ON", CHECK FOR OVERHEATING CONDITION BEFORE MAKING FOLLOWING TEST.

- GROUND "TEST" TERMINAL
- CONNECT DWELL METER TO M/C SOLENOID (USE 6CYL. SCALE)
- CONNECT AT PART THROTTLE IDLE UNTIL DWELL STARTS TO VARY
- WITH ENGINE IDLING, REMOVE CONNECTOR FROM COOLANT SENSOR

DWELL FIXED	DWELL VARIES

REPLACE COOLANT SENSOR

REMOVE NUMBERED TERM. - ECM CONNECTION AND CONNECT TEST LIGHT FROM BAT. + TO TERM. 3 OF CONNECTOR (NOT ECM).

LIGHTS	NO LIGHT

REPAIR GROUNDED WIRE TO ECM TERM. "3."

CHECK FOR SHORT BETWEEN COOLANT SENSOR WIRES. IF NOT SHORTED, REPLACE ECM.

Computer Command Control (With EST)

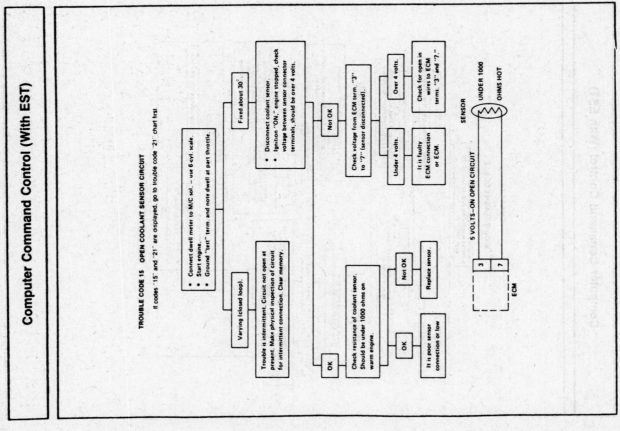

TROUBLE CODE 15   OPEN COOLANT SENSOR CIRCUIT

If codes "15" and "21" are displayed, go to trouble code "21" chart first

- Connect dwell meter to M/C sol. — use 6-cyl. scale.
- Start engine.
- Ground "test" term. and note dwell at part throttle.

Varying (closed loop).	Fixed about 30°.

Trouble is intermittent. Circuit not open at present. Make physical inspection of circuit for intermittent connection. Clear memory.

- Disconnect coolant sensor.
- Ignition "ON," engine stopped, check voltage between sensor connector terminals, should be over 4 volts.

OK	Not OK

Check resistance of coolant sensor. Should be under 1000 ohms on warm engine.

OK	Not OK

It is poor sensor connection or low

Replace sensor.

Check voltage from ECM term. "3" to "7" (sensor disconnected).

Under 4 volts.	Over 4 volts.

It is faulty ECM connection or ECM.

Check for open in wires to ECM terms. "3" and "7."

SENSOR

UNDER 1000 OHMS HOT

5 VOLTS—ON OPEN CIRCUIT

3	7

ECM

Computer Command Control (With EST)

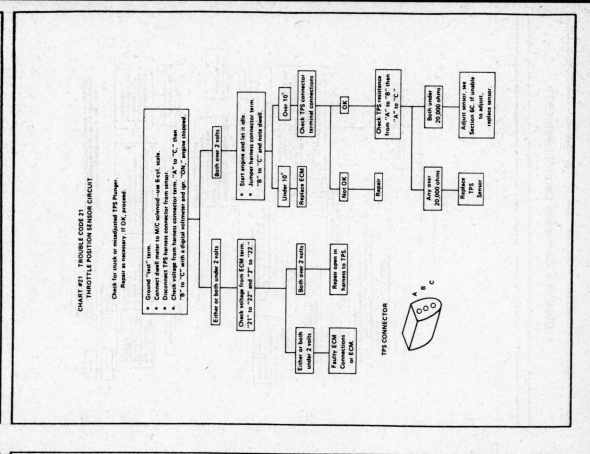

CHART #21   TROUBLE CODE 21
THROTTLE POSITION SENSOR CIRCUIT

Check for stuck or misadjusted TPS Plunger.
Repair as necessary. If O.K, proceed:

- Ground "test" term.
- Connect dwell meter to M/C solenoid—use 6-cyl. scale.
- Disconnect TPS harness connector from sensor.
- Check voltage from harness connector term. "A" to "C," then "B" to "C" with a digital voltmeter and ign. "ON," engine stopped.

TPS CONNECTOR

Computer Command Control (With EST)

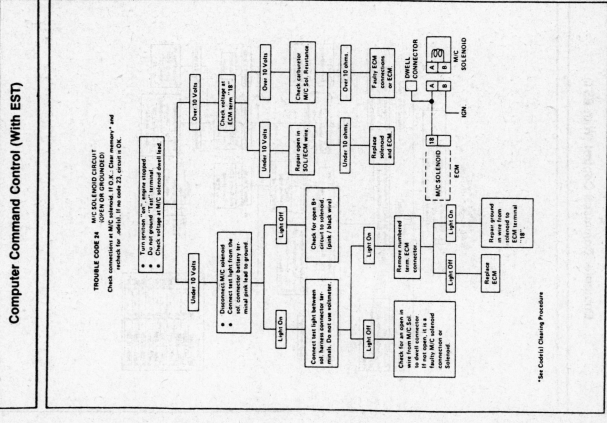

TROUBLE CODE 24   M/C SOLENOID CIRCUIT
(OPEN OR GROUNDED)

Check connections at M/C solenoid. If O.K.: Clear memory* and recheck for .ddeldt. If no code 23, circuit is OK.

- Turn ignition "on", engine stopped.
- Do not ground "Test" terminal.
- Check voltage at M/C solenoid dwell lead.

DWELL
CONNECTOR

M/C
SOLENOID

IGN.

M/C SOLENOID

ECM

*See Code(s) Clearing Procedure

Computer Command Control (With EST)

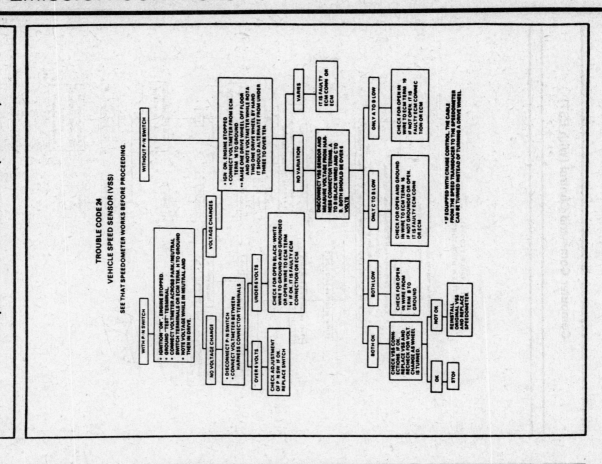

TROUBLE CODE 24

VEHICLE SPEED SENSOR (VSS)

SEE THAT SPEEDOMETER WORKS BEFORE PROCEEDING.

Computer Command Control (With EST)

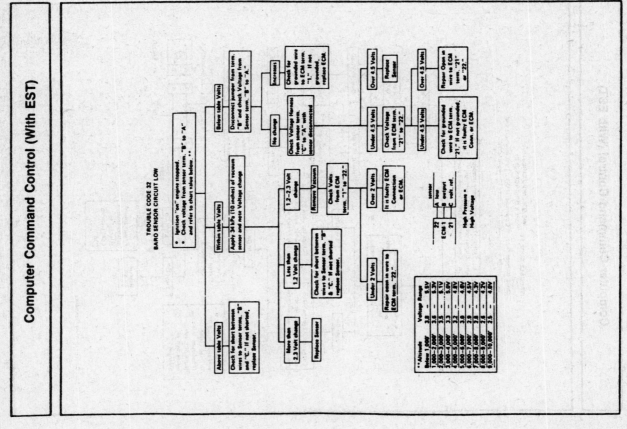

TROUBLE CODE 32

BARO SENSOR CIRCUIT LOW

Computer Command Control (With EST)

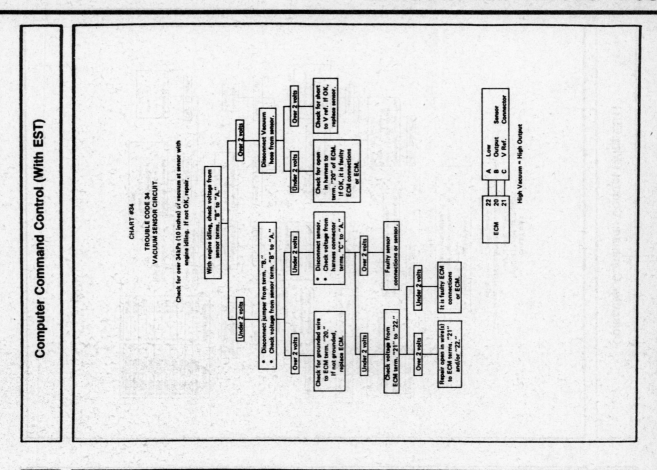

CHART #34

TROUBLE CODE 34
VACUUM SENSOR CIRCUIT

Check for over 34 kPa (10 inches) of vacuum at sensor with engine idling. If not OK, repair.

Computer Command Control (With EST)

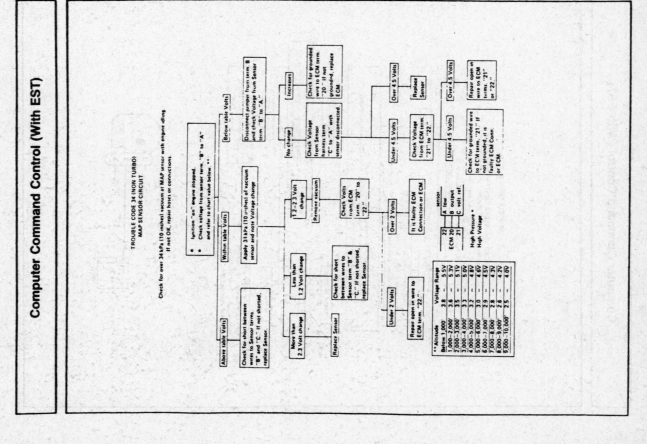

TROUBLE CODE 34 (NON TURBO)
MAP SENSOR CIRCUIT

Check for over 34 kPa (10 inches) vacuum at MAP sensor with engine idling. If not OK, repair hoses or connections.

Computer Command Control (With EST)

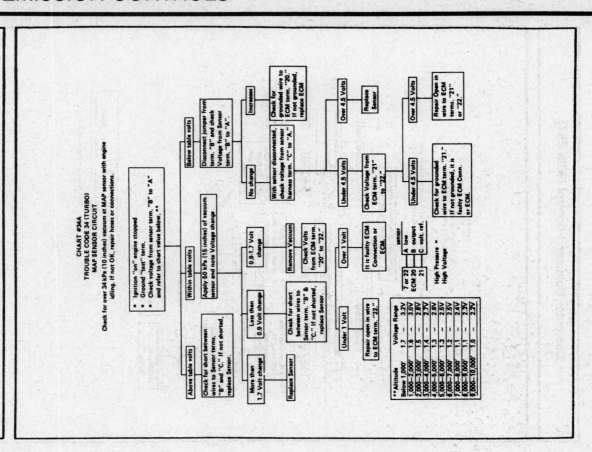

CHART #34A
TROUBLE CODE 34 (TURBO)
MAP SENSOR CIRCUIT

Check for over 34 kPa (10 inches) vacuum at MAP sensor with engine idling. If not OK, repair hoses or connections.

- Ignition "on" engine stopped
- Ground "test" term.
- Check voltage from sensor term. "B" to "A" and refer to chart value below. **

** Altitude	Voltage Range	
Below 1,000'	1.7 –	3.2V
1,000–2,000'	1.6 –	3.0V
2,000–3,000'	1.5 –	2.8V
3,000–4,000'	1.4 –	2.7V
4,000–5,000'	1.3 –	2.6V
5,000–6,000'	1.3 –	2.5V
6,000–7,000'	1.2 –	2.5V
7,000–8,000'	1.1 –	2.4V
8,000–9,000'	1.1 –	2.3V
9,000–10,000'	1.0 –	2.2V

sensor =
A low
B output
C volt. ref.

7 or 22
ECM 20
21

High Pressure = High Voltage

Computer Command Control (With EST)

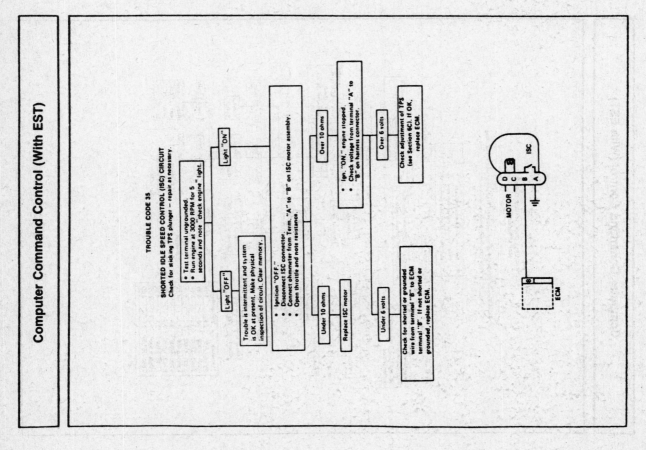

TROUBLE CODE 35

SHORTED IDLE SPEED CONTROL (ISC) CIRCUIT
Check for sticking TPS plunger — repair as necessary.

- Test terminal ungrounded.
- Run engine at 3000 RPM for 5 seconds and note "check engine" light.

Computer Command Control (With EST)

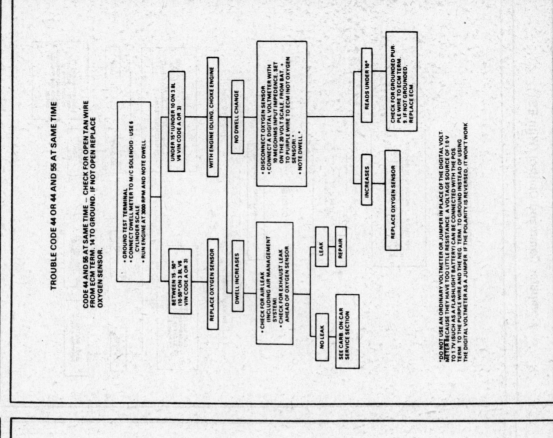

TROUBLE CODE 44 OR 44 AND 55 AT SAME TIME

CODE 44 AND 55 AT SAME TIME — CHECK FOR OPEN TAN WIRE FROM ECM TERM. 14 TO GROUND. IF NOT OPEN REPLACE OXYGEN SENSOR.

- GROUND TEST TERMINAL.
- CONNECT DWELL METER TO M/C SOLENOID. USE 6 CYLINDER SCALE
- RUN ENGINE AT 3000 RPM AND NOTE DWELL

BETWEEN 15, 50° (10-50° ON 3 BL V6 VIN CODE A OR 3)

UNDER 15° (UNDER 10 ON 3 BL V6 VIN CODE A OR 3)

REPLACE OXYGEN SENSOR

WITH ENGINE IDLING, CHOKE ENGINE

DWELL INCREASES

NO DWELL CHANGE

- CHECK FOR AIR LEAK (INCLUDING AIR MANAGEMENT SYSTEM)
- CHECK FOR EXHAUST LEAK AHEAD OF OXYGEN SENSOR

- DISCONNECT OXYGEN SENSOR
- CONNECT A DIGITAL VOLTMETER WITH 10 MEGOHMS INPUT IMPEDENCE. SET ON THE 20 VOLT SCALE. FROM BAT + TO PURPLE WIRE TO ECM (NOT OXYGEN SENSOR)
- NOTE DWELL *

NO LEAK

LEAK

REPAIR

SEE CARE ON CAR SERVICE SECTION

INCREASES

REPLACE OXYGEN SENSOR

READS UNDER 10*

CHECK FOR GROUNDED PURPLE WIRE TO ECM TERM. 9. IF NOT GROUNDED, REPLACE ECM.

*DO NOT USE AN ORDINARY VOLTMETER OR JUMPER IN PLACE OF THE DIGITAL VOLTMETER BECAUSE THEY MAY HAVE TOO LITTLE RESISTANCE. A VOLTAGE SOURCE OF 10V TO 1.7V (SUCH AS A FLASHLIGHT BATTERY) CAN BE CONNECTED WITH THE POS. TERM. TO THE PURPLE WIRE AND THE NEG. TERM. TO GROUND INSTEAD OF USING THE DIGITAL VOLTMETER AS A JUMPER. IF THE POLARITY IS REVERSED, IT WON'T WORK

Computer Command Control (With EST)

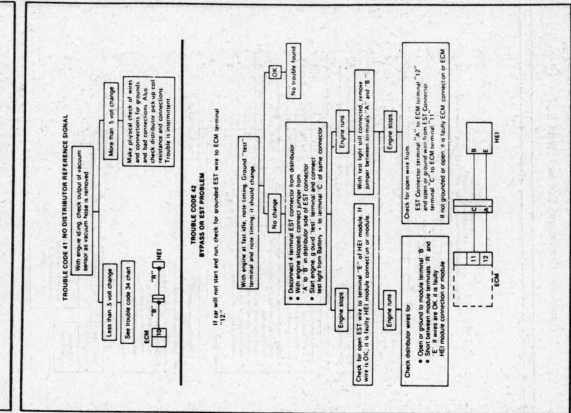

TROUBLE CODE 41 NO DISTRIBUTOR REFERENCE SIGNAL

With engine idling, check output of vacuum sensor as vacuum hose is removed

Less than 5 volt change

More than 5 volt change

See trouble code 34 chart

Make physical check of wires and connections for grounds and bad connections. Also check distributor pick-up coil resistance and connections. Trouble is intermittent

ECM
10 — "G" — "R" — HEI

TROUBLE CODE 42 BYPASS OR EST PROBLEM

If car will not start and run, check for grounded EST wire to ECM terminal "12."

With engine at fast idle, note timing. Ground "test" terminal and note timing: it should change

No change

OK

No trouble found

- Disconnect 4 terminal EST connector from distributor
- With engine stopped, connect jumper from "A" to "B" in distributor side of EST connector
- Start engine. g round "test" terminal and connect test light from Battery, + to terminal "C" of same connector

Engine stops

Engine runs

Check for open EST wire to terminal "E" of HEI module. If wire is OK, it is faulty HEI module connection or module.

With test light still connected, remove jumper between terminals "A" and "B."

Engine runs

Engine stops

Check for open wire from:
EST Connector terminal "A" to ECM terminal "12"
and open or ground wire from EST Connector terminal "C" to ECM terminal "11."

If not grounded or open, it is faulty ECM connection or ECM

Check distributor wires for:
- Open or ground to module terminal "B"
- Short between module terminals "R" and "E." If wires are OK, it is faulty HEI module connection or module

ECM
11
12

B
C A
E
HEI

Computer Command Control (With EST)

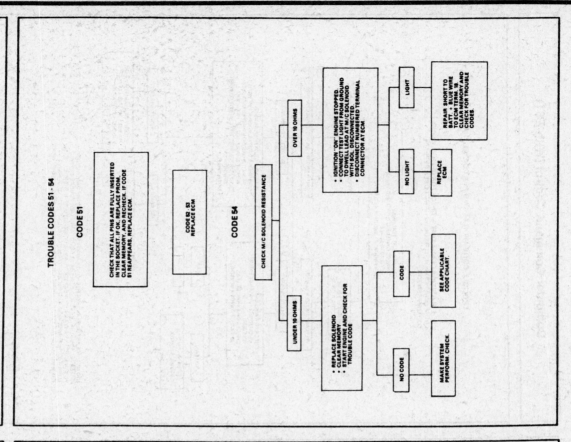

TROUBLE CODES 51 - 54

CODE 51

CHECK THAT ALL PINS ARE FULLY INSERTED IN THE SOCKET. IF OK, REPLACE PROM, CLEAR MEMORY, AND RECHECK. IF CODE 51 REAPPEARS, REPLACE ECM.

CODE 52 - 53
REPLACE ECM

CODE 54

CHECK M/C SOLENOID RESISTANCE

OVER 10 OHMS

• IGNITION "ON" ENGINE STOPPED
• CONNECT TEST LIGHT FROM GROUND TO DWELL LEAD AT M/C SOLENOID WITH SOL. DISCONNECTED
• DISCONNECT NO. 16 (RED) TERMINAL CONNECTOR AT ECM

LIGHT

REPAIR SHORT TO BAT + & BLUE WIRE TO ECM TERM. 16 CLEAR MEMORY AND CHECK FOR TROUBLE CODES.

NO LIGHT

REPLACE ECM

UNDER 10 OHMS

• REPLACE SOLENOID
• CLEAR MEMORY
• START ENGINE AND CHECK FOR TROUBLE CODE

CODE

SEE APPLICABLE CODE CHART.

NO CODE

MAKE SYSTEM PERFORM. CHECK.

Computer Command Control (With EST)

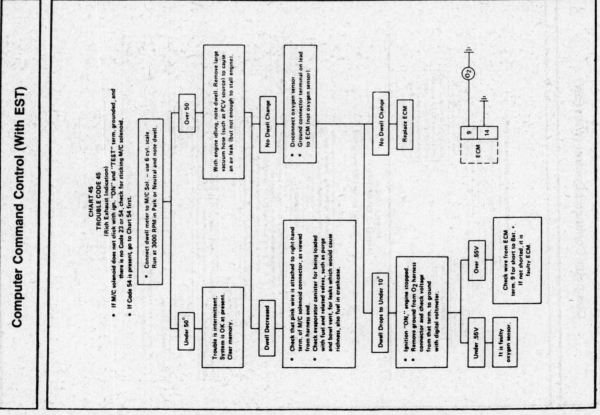

CHART 45
TROUBLE CODE 45
(Rich Exhaust Indication)
• If M/C solenoid does not click with ign. "ON" and "TEST" term. grounded, and there is no Code 23 or 54, check for sticking M/C solenoid.
• If Code 54 is present, go to Chart 54 first.

• Connect dwell meter to M/C Sol. – use 6 cyl. scale. Run at 3000 RPM in Park or Neutral and note dwell.

Over 50

With engine idling, note dwell. Remove large vacuum hose (such as PCV source) to cause an air leak (but not enough to stall engine).

No Dwell Change

• Disconnect oxygen sensor.
• Ground connector terminal on lead to ECM (not oxygen sensor).

No Dwell Change

Replace ECM

Under 50°

Trouble is intermittent. System is OK at present. Clear memory.

Dwell Decreased

• Check that pink wire is attached to right-hand term. of M/C solenoid connector, as viewed from harness end.
• Check evaporator canister for being loaded with fuel and related valves, such as purge and bowl vent, for leaks which would cause richness, also fuel in crankcase.

Dwell Drops to Under 10°

• Ignition "ON," engine stopped.
• Remove ground from O2 harness connector and check voltage from that term. to ground with digital voltmeter.

Over .55V

Check wire from ECM term. 9 for short to Bat. +. If not shorted, it is faulty ECM.

Under .55V

It is faulty oxygen sensor.

O2

ECM 9 14

Computer Command Control (With EST)

ENGINE CRANKS, BUT WILL NOT RUN (WITH INTEGRAL IGNITION COIL)

NOTE: Perform diagnostic circuit check before using this procedure. If a tachometer is connected to the tachometer terminal, disconnect it before proceeding with the test.

1. Check spark at plug with ST-125 while cranking (if no spark on one wire, check a second wire).
 - **Spark** → Check fuel, spark plugs, etc.
 - **No Spark (Without EST)**
2. Check voltage at distributor "bat" terminal while cranking.
 - **7 volts or more**
 - **Under 7 volts** → Repair primary circuit to ignition switch.
3. With ignition "on," check "tach" terminal voltage.
 - **10 Volts or More**
 - **1 to 10 Volts** → Replace module and check for spark from coil as in Step 6.
 - **Under 1 Volt** → It is faulty ign. coil connection or coil
4. Check for spark at coil output terminal with ST-125 while cranking.
 - **Spark** → Check color match of pick-up coil con-nector and ign. coil lead. Inspect cap for water, cracks, etc. If OK, replace rotor.
 - **No Spark**
5. Remove pick-up coil leads from module. Check tach. term. voltage with "ign" "on." Watch voltmeter as test light is momentarily (not more than five (5) seconds) connected from bat. + to module term.
 - 4 Term. Mod.—Term "G"
 - 5 Term. Mod.—Term. "D" or ESC—Term. "P"
 - 7 Term. Mod.—Term. "P"
 - **Voltage Drops**
 - **No Drop in Voltage** → Check module grnd. and for open in wires from cap to distributor. If OK, replace mod.
6. Check for spark from coil with ST-125 as test light is removed from module terminal.
 - **Spark** → It is pick-up coil or connections. Coil resistance should be 500-1500 ohms and not grounded.
 - **No Spark** → If no module tester is available. If module tester is available, test module. OK / Bad → Replace mod.
7. Check ign. coil ground circuit. If OK, replace ign. coil and repeat Step 6.
 - **Spark** → System OK
 - **No Spark** → Replace ign. coil. If OK, replace ign. coil.

Replace ign. coil. It, too, is faulty.

System OK

Coil removed is OK, reinstall original coil and replace module

PICK-UP COIL — GREEN WIRE — WHITE WIRE / YELLOW WIRE — CONNECTOR
IGN. COIL — YELLOW WIRE / RED WIRE — P/N 1875894
PICK-UP COIL — WHITE WIRE — GREEN WIRE / BLACK, BLUE CONNECTOR
IGN. COIL — RED WIRE — CLEAR, BLACK WIRE — P/N 1876209

Computer Command Control (With EST)

TROUBLE CODE 55 FAULTY OXYGEN SENSOR OR ECM

Check for corrosion at ECM edgeboard connectors and terms. If present, check for coolant sensor, windshield or heater core leaks. Repair leak, clean connector terms, and replace ECM. Also, check for 4 term. EST harness being too close to electrical signals, such as spark plug wires, distributor housing, generator, etc.

- Disconnect test terminal.
- Disconnect oxygen sensor and note "check engine" light with engine idling for less than one minute.
 - **Light Off**
 - **Light On**
 - Ignition "ON," engine stopped.
 - Check voltage from ECM Terminal "21" to "22."
 - **Over 6 Volts**
 - **4 to 6 Volts**
 - **Under 4 Volts**
 - Turn ign. "OFF."
 - Disconnect numbered connector from ECM.
 - Ign. "ON," check voltage from connector Term. "21" to "22."
 - **Voltage**
 - Check for short in B+ wire to Term. "21."
 - **0 Volts** → Replace ECM
 - Check for ground in circuit to ECM Terminal "21" (includes shorted or grounded TPS Vacuum or Vehicle Speed Sensors). If not grounded or shorted, replace ECM.
 - Disconnect O2 sensor.
 - Ign. "ON," engine stopped.
 - Check voltage from connector of purple wire disconnected from oxygen sensor.
 - **Over 1 Volt**
 - **Under 1 Volt**
 - Turn "OFF" ign., disconnect numbered ECM connector and then turn ign. "ON."
 - Check voltage from ECM harness connector Term. "9" to ground.
 - **Over 1 Volt**
 - **Under 1 Volt**
 - Check for short from wire to ECM Term. "9" to ground. If not open, replace ECM.
 - Check for open circuit to Term. "14" to ground. If not open, replace ECM.
 - Check for intermittent ground in circuit to ECM Terminal "21" (includes TPS, MAP, BARO, and Vacuum Sensors). Clear codes and check for reoccurrence of Code 55. If it reappears, it could be faulty oxygen sensor (except on 4.3L VIN Code "F" and 5.0 VIN Code "Y").

OXYGEN SENSOR — VACUUM SENSOR OR MAP — TPS — BARO SENSOR
O2 SENSOR 9 — C — GROUND 14 — A — 5 VOLT REF 21 — ECM

Computer Command Control (With EST)

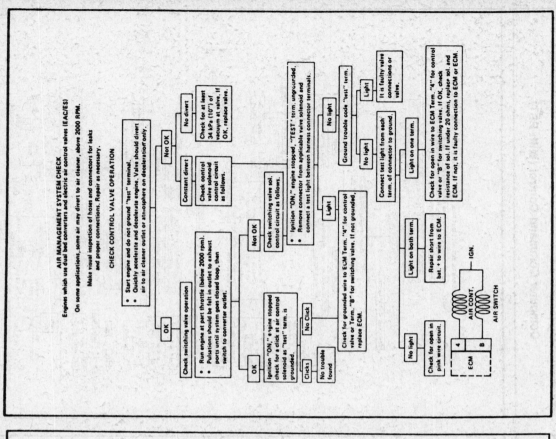

Computer Command Control (With EST)

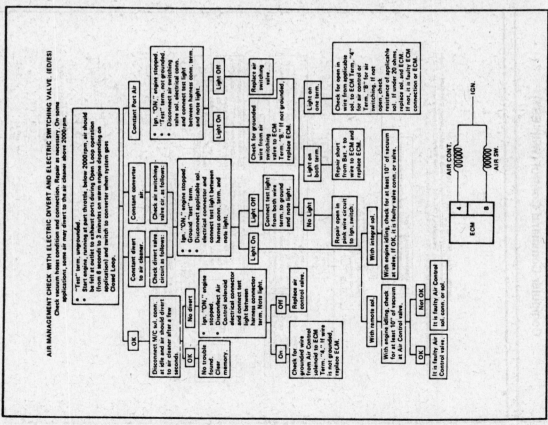

Computer Command Control (With EST)

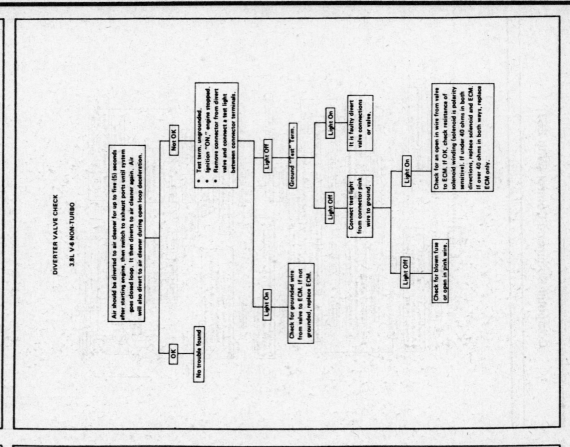

DIVERTER VALVE CHECK

3.8L V-6 NON-TURBO

Air should be diverted to air cleaner for up to five (5) seconds after starting engine, then switch to exhaust ports until system goes closed loop. It then diverts to air cleaner again. Air will also divert to air cleaner during open loop deceleration.

OK → No trouble found.

Not OK →
- Test term. ungrounded.
- Ignition "ON," engine stopped.
- Remove connector from divert valve and connect a test light between connector terminals.

Light On → Check for grounded wire from valve to ECM. If not grounded, replace ECM.

Light Off → Ground "test" term.

Light On → It is faulty divert valve connections or valve.

Light Off → Connect test light from connector pink wire to ground.

Light On → Check for an open in wire from valve to ECM. If OK, check resistance of solenoid winding (solenoid is polarity sensitive). If under 40 ohms in both directions, replace solenoid and ECM. If over 40 ohms in both ways, replace ECM only.

Light Off → Check for blown fuse or open in pink wire.

Computer Command Control (With EST)

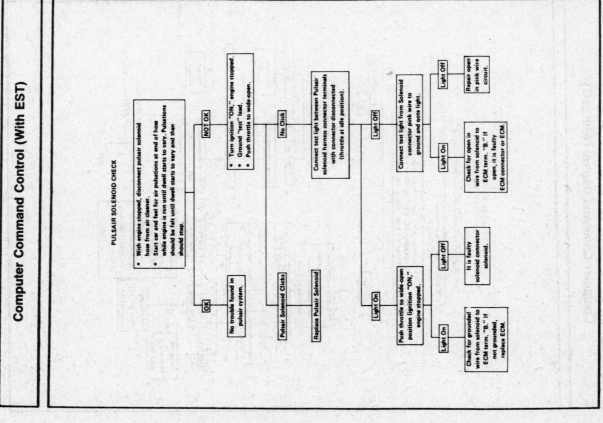

PULSAIR SOLENOID CHECK

- With engine stopped, disconnect pulsair solenoid hose from air cleaner.
- Start car and feel for air pulsations at end of hose while engine is run until dwell starts to vary. Pulsations should be felt until dwell starts to vary and then should stop.

OK → No trouble found in pulsair system.

NOT OK →
- Turn ignition "ON," engine stopped.
- Ground "test" lead.
- Push throttle to wide-open.

Pulsair Solenoid Clicks → Replace Pulsair Solenoid

No Click → Connect test light between Pulsair solenoid harness connector terminals with connector disconnected (throttle at idle position).

Light On → Push throttle to wide-open position (ignition "ON," engine stopped).

Light On → Check for grounded wire from solenoid to ECM term. "B." If not grounded, replace ECM.

Light Off → It is faulty solenoid connector solenoid.

Light Off → Connect test light from Solenoid connector pink wire to ground and note light.

Light On → Check for open in wire from solenoid to ECM term. "B." If open, it is faulty ECM connector or ECM.

Light Off → Repair open in pink wire circuit.

Computer Command Control (With EST)

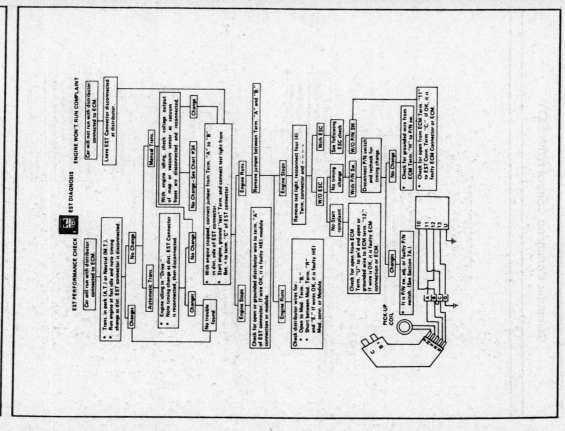

Computer Command Control (With EST)

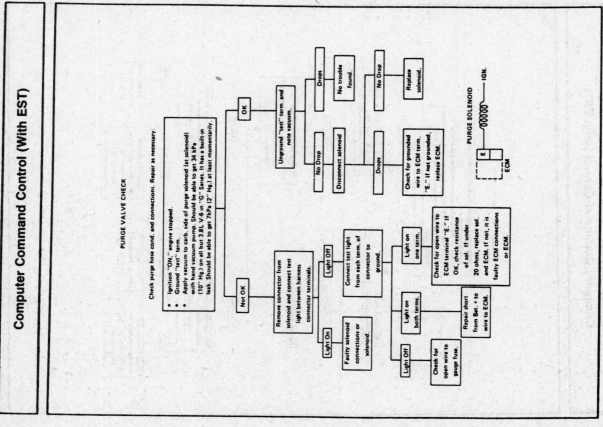

Computer Command Control (With EST)

ESC CHECK
(EST CHECK – CONTINUED)

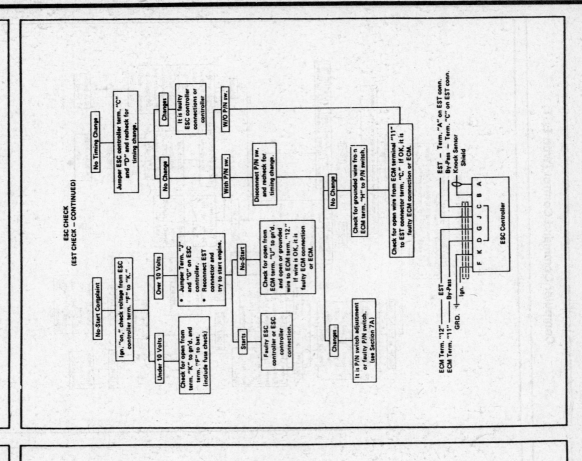

Computer Command Control (With EST)

ESC PERFORMANCE DIAGNOSTIC

This chart should only be used after other causes of knock have been checked, i.e., timing, lack of EGR, engine temp., etc.

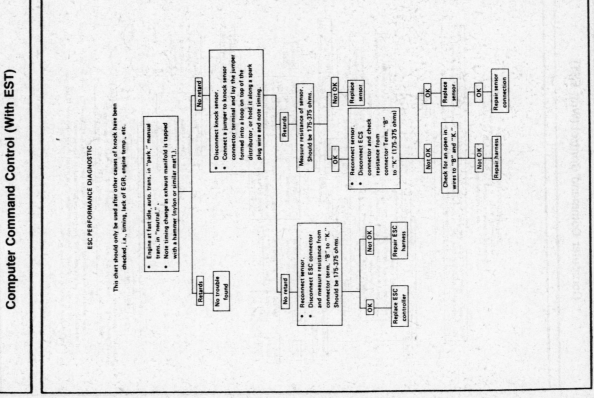

Computer Command Control (With EST)

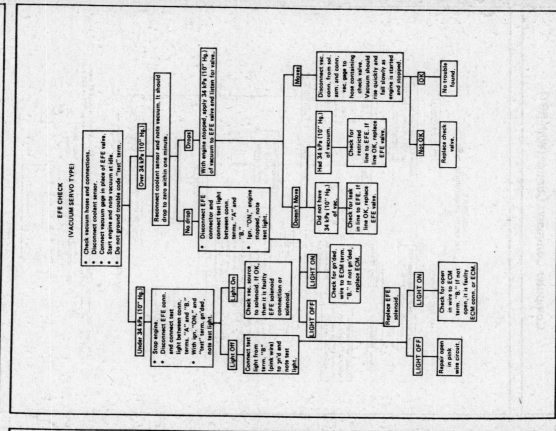

Computer Command Control (With EST)

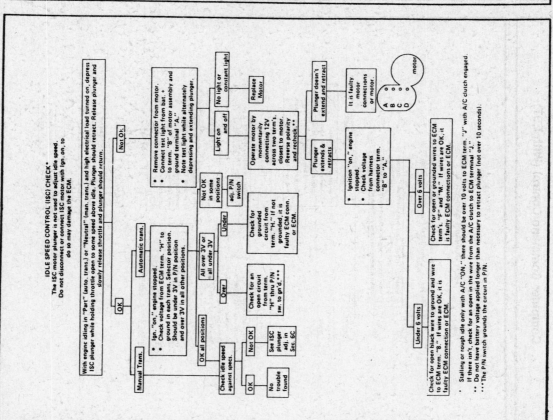

Computer Command Control (With EST)

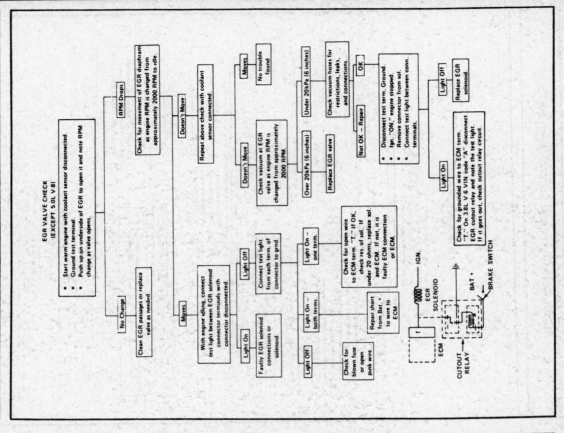

EGR VALVE CHECK
(EXCEPT 5.0L V8)

- Start warm engine with coolant sensor disconnected.
- Ground test terminal.
- Push up on underside of EGR to open it and note RPM change as valve opens.

Computer Command Control (With EST)

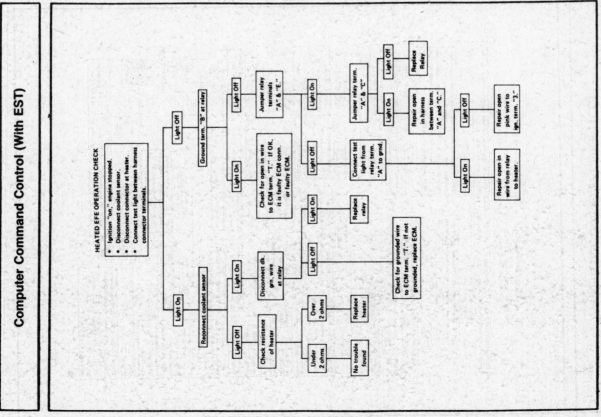

HEATED EFE OPERATION CHECK

- Ignition "on," engine stopped.
- Disconnect coolant sensor.
- Disconnect connector at heater.
- Connect test light between harness connector terminals.

Computer Command Control (With EST)

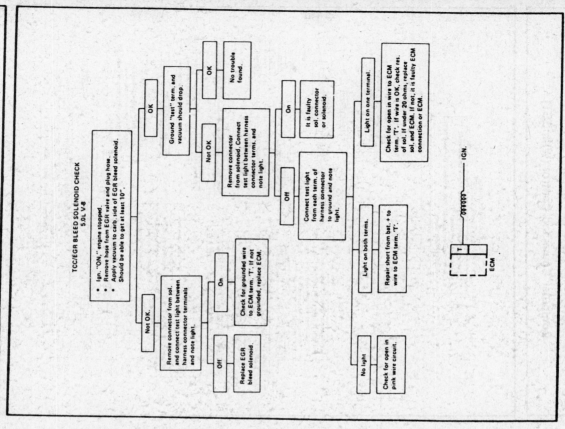

Transmission Converter Clutch (TCC)

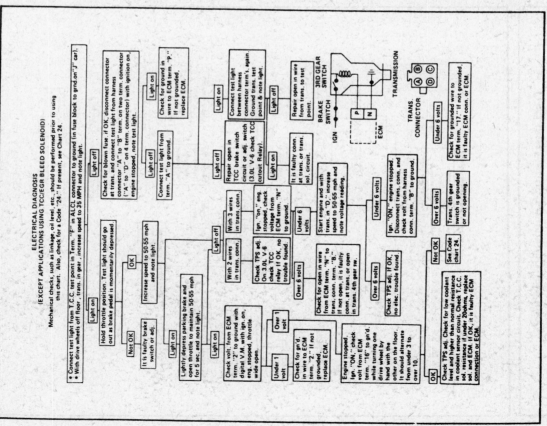

Throttle Body Fuel Injection (TBI)

The electronic throttle body fuel injection system is a fuel metering system with the amount of fuel delivered by the throttle body injector(s) (TBI) determined by an electronic signal supplied by the Electronic Control Module (ECM) or Powertrain Control Module (PCM). The ECM monitors various engine and vehicle conditions to calculate the fuel delivery time (pulse width) of the injector(s). The fuel pulse may be modified by the ECM to account for special operating conditions, such as cranking, cold starting, altitude, acceleration, and deceleration.

The Throttle Body Injection (TBI) system provides a means of fuel distribution for controlling exhaust emissions within legislated limits. The TBI system, by precisely controlling the air/fuel mixture under all operating conditions, provides as near as possible complete combustion.

This is accomplished by using an Electronic Control Module (ECM) (a small on-board microcomputer) that receives electrical inputs from various sensors about engine operating conditions. An oxygen sensor in the main exhaust stream functions to provide feedback information to the ECM as to the oxygen content, lean or rich, in the exhaust. The ECM uses this information from the oxygen sensor, and other sensors, to modify fuel delivery to achieve, as near as possible, an ideal air/fuel ratio of 14.7:1. This air/fuel ratio allows the 3-way catalytic converter to be more efficient in the conversion process of reducing exhaust emissions while at the same time providing acceptable levels of driveability and fuel economy.

ELECTRONIC CONTROL MODULE

The ECM program electronically signals the fuel injector in the TBI assembly to provide the correct quantity of fuel for a wide range of operating conditions. Several sensors are used to determine existing operating conditions and the ECM then signals the injector to provide the precise amount of fuel required.

The ECM used on EFI vehicles has a learning capability. If the battery is disconnected to clear diagnostic codes, or for repair, the learning process has to begin all over again. A change may be noted in vehicle performance. To teach the vehicle, make sure the vehicle is at operating temperature and drive at part throttle, under moderate acceleration and idle conditions, until performance returns.

With the EFI system, the TBI assembly is centrally located on the intake manifold where air and fuel are distributed through a single bore in the throttle body, similar to a carbureted engine. Air for combustion is controlled by a single throttle valve which is connected to the accelerator pedal linkage by a throttle shaft and lever assembly. A special plate is located directly beneath the throttle valve to aid in mixture distribution.

Fuel for combustion is supplied by 1 or 2 fuel injector(s), mounted on the TBI2 assembly, whose metering tip is located directly above the throttle valve. The injector is pulsed or timed open or closed by an electronic output signal received from the ECM. The ECM receives inputs concerning engine operating conditions from the various sensors (coolant temperature sensor, oxygen sensor, etc.). The ECM, using this information, performs high speed calculations of engine fuel requirements and pulses or times the injector, open or closed, thereby controlling fuel and air mixtures to achieve, as near as possible, ideal air/fuel mixture ratios.

When the ignition key is turned **ON**, the ECM will initialize (start program running) and energize the fuel pump relay. The fuel pump pressurizes the system to approximately 10 psi. If the ECM does not receive a distributor reference pulse (telling the ECM the engine is turning) within 2 seconds, the ECM will then de-energize the fuel pump relay, turning off the fuel pump. If a distributor reference pulse is later received, the ECM will turn the fuel pump back on.

The ECM controls the exhaust emissions by modifying fuel delivery to achieve, as near as possible, and air/fuel ratio of 14.7:1. The injector on-time is determined by various inputs to the ECM. By increasing the injector pulse, more fuel is delivered, enriching the air/fuel ratio. Decreasing the injector pulse, leans the air/fuel ratio. Pulses are sent to the injector in 2 different modes: synchronized and nonsynchronized.

Synchronized Mode

In synchronized mode operation, the injector is pulsed once for each distributor reference pulse. In dual injector throttle body systems, the injectors are pulse alternately.

Nonsynchronized Mode

In nonsynchronized mode operation, the injector is pulsed once every 12.5 milliseconds or 6.25 milliseconds depending on calibration. This pulse time is totally independent of distributor reference pulses. Nonsynchronized mode results only under the following conditions:

1. The fuel pulse width is too small to be delivered accurately by the injector (approximately 1.5 milliseconds)
2. During the delivery of prime pulses (prime pulses charge the intake manifold with fuel during or just prior to engine starting)
3. During acceleration enrichment
4. During deceleration leanout

The basic TBI unit is made up of 2 major casting assemblies: (1) a throttle body with a valve to control airflow and (2) a fuel body assembly with an integral pressure regulator and fuel injector to supply the required fuel. An

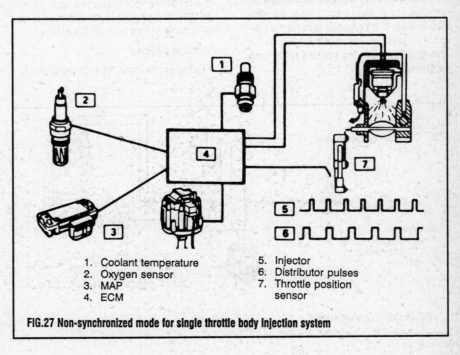

1. Coolant temperature
2. Oxygen sensor
3. MAP
4. ECM
5. Injector
6. Distributor pulses
7. Throttle position sensor

FIG.27 Non-synchronized mode for single throttle body injection system

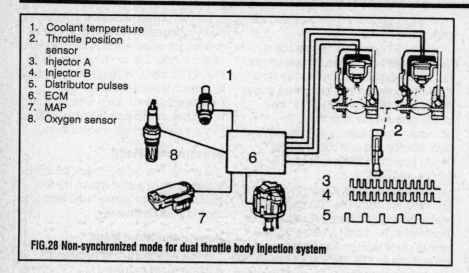

1. Coolant temperature
2. Throttle position
   sensor
3. Injector A
4. Injector B
5. Distributor pulses
6. ECM
7. MAP
8. Oxygen sensor

FIG.28 Non-synchronized mode for dual throttle body injection system

electronically operated device to control the idle speed and a device to provide information regarding throttle valve position are included as part of the TBI unit.

The fuel injector(s) is a solenoid-operated device controlled by the ECM. The incoming fuel is directed to the lower end of the injector assembly which has a fine screen filter surrounding the injector inlet. The ECM actuates the solenoid, which lifts a normally closed ball valve off a seat. The fuel under pressure is injected in a conical spray pattern at the walls of the throttle body bore above the throttle valve. The excess fuel passes through a pressure regulator before being returned to the vehicle's fuel tank.

The pressure regulator is a diaphragm-operated relief valve with injector pressure on one side and air cleaner pressure on the other. The function of the regulator is to maintain a constant pressure drop across the injector throughout the operating load and speed range of the engine.

The throttle body portion of the TBI may contain ports located at, above, or below the throttle valve. These ports generate the vacuum signals for the EGR valve, MAP sensor, and the canister purge system.

The Throttle Position Sensor (TPS) is a variable resistor used to convert the degree of throttle plate opening to an electrical signal to the ECM. The ECM uses this signal as a reference point of throttle valve position. In addition, an Idle Air Control (IAC) assembly, mounted in the throttle body s used to control idle speeds. A cone-shaped valve in the IAC assembly is located in an air passage in the throttle body that leads from the point beneath the air cleaner to below the throttle valve. The ECM monitors idle speeds and, depending on engine load, moves the IAC cone in the air passage to increase or decrease air bypassing the throttle valve to the intake manifold for control of idle speeds.

Cranking Mode

During engine crank, for each distributor

reference pulse the ECM will deliver an injector pulse (synchronized). The crank air/fuel ratio will be used if the throttle position is less than 80% open. Crank air fuel is determined by the ECM and ranges from 1.5:1 at –33°F (–36°C) to 14.7:1 at 201°F (94°C).

The lower the coolant temperature, the longer the pulse width (injector on-time) or richer the air/fuel ratio. The higher the coolant temperature, the less pulse width (injector on-time) or the leaner the air/fuel ratio.

Clear Flood Mode

If for some reason the engine should become flooded, provisions have been made to clear this condition. To clear the flood, the driver must depress the accelerator pedal enough to open to wide-open throttle position. The ECM then issues injector pulses at a rate that would be equal to an air/fuel ratio of 20:1. The ECM maintains this injector rate as long as the throttle remains wide open and the engine rpm is below 600. If the throttle position becomes less than 80%, the ECM then would immediately start issuing crank pulses to the injector calculated by the ECM based on the coolant temperature.

Run Mode

There are 2 different run modes. When the engine rpm is above 400, the system goes into open loop operation. In open loop operation, the ECM will ignore the signal from the oxygen (O_2) sensor and calculate the injector on-time based upon inputs from the coolant and manifold absolute pressure sensors.

During open loop operation, the ECM analyzes the following items to determine when the system is ready to go to the closed loop mode:

1. The oxygen sensor varying voltage output. (This is dependent on temperature).

2. The coolant sensor must be above specified temperature.

3. A specific amount of time must elapse after starting the engine. These values are stored in the PROM.

When these conditions have been met, the system goes into closed loop operation In closed loop operation, the ECM will modify the pulse width (injector on-time) based upon the signal from the oxygen sensor. The ECM will decrease the on-time if the air/fuel ratio is too rich, and will increase the on-time if the air/fuel ratio is too lean.

The pulse width, thus the amount of enrichment, is determined by manifold pressure change, throttle angle change, and coolant temperature. The higher the manifold pressure and the wider the throttle opening, the wider the pulse width. The acceleration enrichment pulses are delivered nonsynchronized.

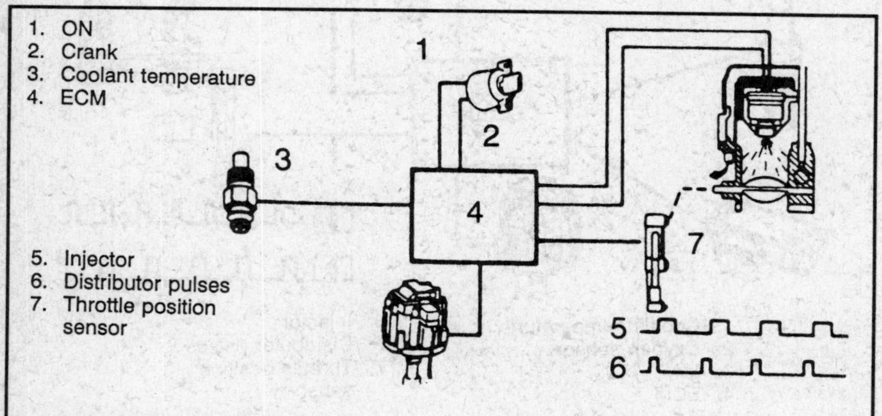

1. ON
2. Crank
3. Coolant temperature
4. ECM

5. Injector
6. Distributor pulses
7. Throttle position
   sensor

FIG.29 Cranking air/fuel ratio

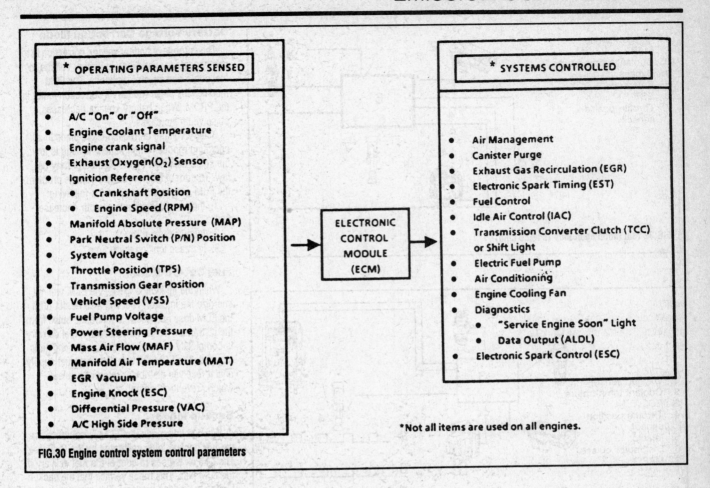

FIG.30 Engine control system control parameters

* **OPERATING PARAMETERS SENSED**

- A/C "On" or "Off"
- Engine Coolant Temperature
- Engine crank signal
- Exhaust Oxygen(O_2) Sensor
- Ignition Reference
  - Crankshaft Position
  - Engine Speed (RPM)
- Manifold Absolute Pressure (MAP)
- Park Neutral Switch (P/N) Position
- System Voltage
- Throttle Position (TPS)
- Transmission Gear Position
- Vehicle Speed (VSS)
- Fuel Pump Voltage
- Power Steering Pressure
- Mass Air Flow (MAF)
- Manifold Air Temperature (MAT)
- EGR Vacuum
- Engine Knock (ESC)
- Differential Pressure (VAC)
- A/C High Side Pressure

ELECTRONIC
CONTROL
MODULE
(ECM)

* **SYSTEMS CONTROLLED**

- Air Management
- Canister Purge
- Exhaust Gas Recirculation (EGR)
- Electronic Spark Timing (EST)
- Fuel Control
- Idle Air Control (IAC)
- Transmission Converter Clutch (TCC) or Shift Light
- Electric Fuel Pump
- Air Conditioning
- Engine Cooling Fan
- Diagnostics
  - "Service Engine Soon" Light
  - Data Output (ALDL)
- Electronic Spark Control (ESC)

*Not all items are used on all engines.

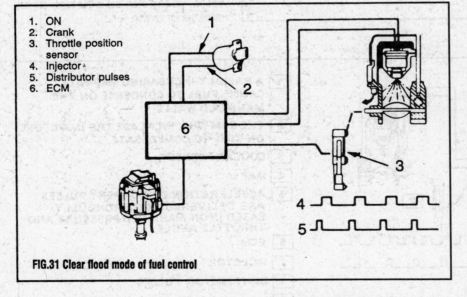

1. ON
2. Crank
3. Throttle position sensor
4. Injector
5. Distributor pulses
6. ECM

FIG.31 Clear flood mode of fuel control

Any reduction in throttle angle will cancel the enrichment pulses. This way, quick movements of the accelerator will not over-enrich the mixture.

Acceleration Enrichment Mode

When the engine is required to accelerate, the opening of the throttle valve(s) causes a rapid increase in Manifold Absolute Pressure (MAP). This rapid increase in the manifold pressure causes fuel to condense on the manifold walls.

The ECM senses this increase in throttle angle and MAP, and supplies additional fuel for a short period of time. This prevents the engine from stumbling due to too lean a mixture.

Deceleration Leanout Mode

Upon deceleration, a leaner fuel mixture is required to reduce emission of hydrocarbons (HC) and carbon monoxide (CO). To adjust the injection on-time, the ECM uses the decrease in manifold pressure and the decrease in throttle position to calculate a decrease in pulse width. To maintain an idle fuel ratio of 14.7:1, fuel output is momentarily reduced. This is done because of the fuel remaining in the intake manifold during deceleration.

Deceleration Fuel Cut-Off Mode

The purpose of deceleration fuel cut-off is to remove fuel from the engine during extreme deceleration conditions. Deceleration fuel cut-off is based on values of manifold pressure, throttle position, and engine rpm stored in the calibration PROM. Deceleration fuel cut-off overrides the deceleration enleanment mode.

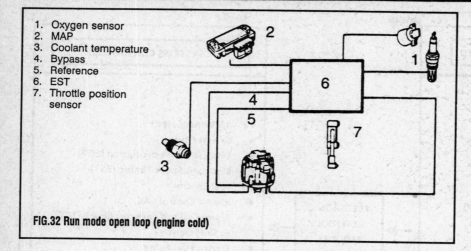

1. Oxygen sensor
2. MAP
3. Coolant temperature
4. Bypass
5. Reference
6. EST
7. Throttle position sensor

FIG.32 Run mode open loop (engine cold)

Battery Voltage Correction Mode

The purpose of battery voltage correction is to compensate for variations in battery voltage to fuel pump and injector response. The ECM modifies the pulse width by a correction factor in the PROM. When battery voltage decreases, pulse width increases.

Battery voltage correction takes place in all operating modes. When battery voltage is low, the spark delivered by the distributor may be low. To correct this low battery voltage problem, the ECM can do any or all of the following:

1. Increase injector pulse width (increase fuel)
2. Increase idle rpm
3. Increase ignition dwell time

Fuel Cut-Off Mode

When the ignition is **OFF**, the ECM will not energize the injector. Fuel will also be cut off if the ECM does not receive a reference pulse from the distributor. To prevent dieseling, fuel delivery is completely stopped as soon as the engine is stopped. The ECM will not allow any fuel supply until it receives distributor reference pulses which prevents flooding.

Backup Mode

When in this mode, the ECM is operating on the fuel backup logic calibrated by the CalPak. The CalPak is used to control the fuel delivery if the ECM fails. This mode verifies that the backup feature is working properly. The parameters that can be read on a scan tool in this mode are not much use for service.

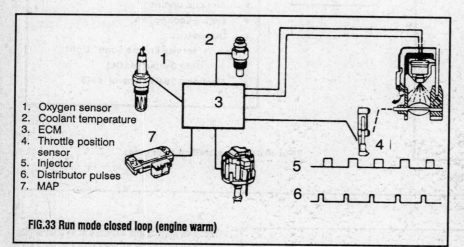

1. Oxygen sensor
2. Coolant temperature
3. ECM
4. Throttle position sensor
5. Injector
6. Distributor pulses
7. MAP

FIG.33 Run mode closed loop (engine warm)

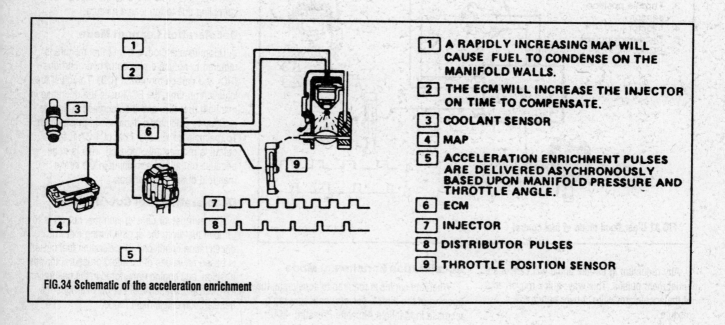

FIG.34 Schematic of the acceleration enrichment

1. A RAPIDLY INCREASING MAP WILL CAUSE FUEL TO CONDENSE ON THE MANIFOLD WALLS.
2. THE ECM WILL INCREASE THE INJECTOR ON TIME TO COMPENSATE.
3. COOLANT SENSOR
4. MAP
5. ACCELERATION ENRICHMENT PULSES ARE DELIVERED ASYCHRONOUSLY BASED UPON MANIFOLD PRESSURE AND THROTTLE ANGLE.
6. ECM
7. INJECTOR
8. DISTRIBUTOR PULSES
9. THROTTLE POSITION SENSOR

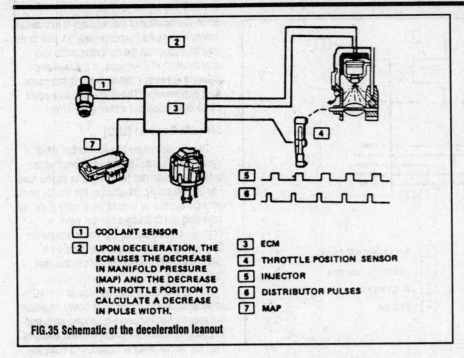

1 COOLANT SENSOR

2 UPON DECELERATION, THE ECM USES THE DECREASE IN MANIFOLD PRESSURE (MAP) AND THE DECREASE IN THROTTLE POSITION TO CALCULATE A DECREASE IN PULSE WIDTH.

3 ECM
4 THROTTLE POSITION SENSOR
5 INJECTOR
6 DISTRIBUTOR PULSES
7 MAP

FIG.35 Schematic of the deceleration leanout

Highway Mode

When driven at highway speeds the system may enter highway or semi-closed loop mode. This improves fuel economy by leaning out fuel mixture slightly. The ECM must see correct engine temperature, ignition timing, canister activity and a constant vehicle speed before if will enter this mode. The system will switch back to closed loop periodically to check all system functions.

A scan tool determines highway mode by looking at the integrator/block learn values and oxygen sensor voltage. Integrator and block learn will show very little change and the oxygen sensor voltage is be less than 100 millivolts.

ALCL/ALDL Connector

The Assembly Line Communication Link (ALCL) or Assembly Line Diagnostic Link (ALDL) is a diagnostic connector located in the passenger compartment. It has terminals which are used in the assembly plant to check that the engine is operating properly before it leaves the plant. This connector is a very useful tool in diagnosing EFI engines. Important information from the ECM is available at this terminal and can be read with one of the many popular scanner tools.

➡ **Some models refer to the ALCL as the Assembly Line Diagnostic Link (ALDL). Either way it is referred to, they both still perform the same function.**

FUEL INJECTION SUBSYSTEMS

Electronic Fuel Injection (EFI) is the name given to the entire fuel injection system. Various subsystems are combined to form the overall system. These subsystems are:

1. Fuel supply system
2. Throttle Body Injector (TBI) assembly
3. Idle Air Control (IAC)
4. Electronic Control Module (ECM)
5. Data sensors
6. Electronic Spark Timing (EST)
7. Emission controls

Fuel Supply System

Fuel, supplied by an electric fuel pump mounted in the fuel tank, passes through an in-line fuel filter to the TBI assembly. To control fuel pump operation, a fuel pump relay is used.

When the ignition switch is turned to the **ON** position, the fuel pump relay activates the electric fuel pump for 1.5–2.0 seconds to prime the injector. If the ECM does not receive reference pulses from the distributor after this time, the ECM signals the relay to turn the fuel pump off. The relay will once again activate the fuel pump when the ECM receives distributor reference pulses.

The oil pressure sender is the backup for the fuel pump relay. The sender has 2 circuits, 1 for the instrument cluster light or gauge, the other to activate the fuel pump if the relay fails. If the fuse relay has failed, the sender activates the fuel pump when oil pressure reaches 4 psi. Thus a failed fuel pump relay would cause a longer crank, especially in cold weather. If the fuel pump fails, a no start condition exists.

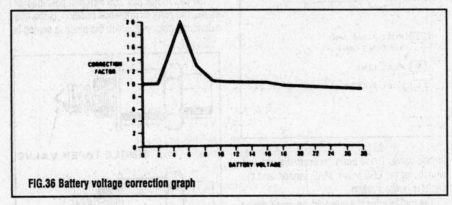

FIG.36 Battery voltage correction graph

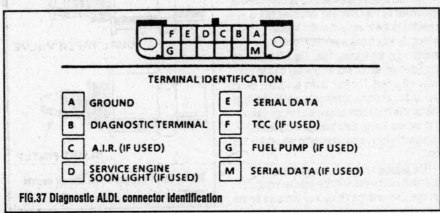

TERMINAL IDENTIFICATION

A GROUND	**E** SERIAL DATA
B DIAGNOSTIC TERMINAL	**F** TCC (IF USED)
C A.I.R. (IF USED)	**G** FUEL PUMP (IF USED)
D SERVICE ENGINE SOON LIGHT (IF USED)	**M** SERIAL DATA (IF USED)

FIG.37 Diagnostic ALDL connector identification

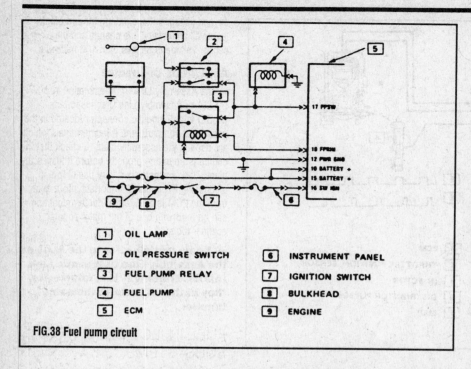

FIG.38 Fuel pump circuit

[1] OIL LAMP
[2] OIL PRESSURE SWITCH
[3] FUEL PUMP RELAY
[4] FUEL PUMP
[5] ECM
[6] INSTRUMENT PANEL
[7] IGNITION SWITCH
[8] BULKHEAD
[9] ENGINE

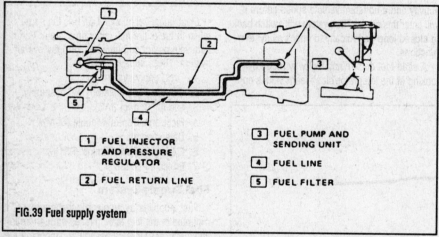

FIG.39 Fuel supply system

[1] FUEL INJECTOR AND PRESSURE REGULATOR
[2] FUEL RETURN LINE
[3] FUEL PUMP AND SENDING UNIT
[4] FUEL LINE
[5] FUEL FILTER

Throttle Body Injector (TBI) Assembly

The basic TBI model 700 is used on 4 cylinder engines, is made up of 2 major casting assemblies: (1) a throttle body with a valve to control airflow and (2) a fuel body assembly with an integral pressure regulator and fuel injector to supply the required fuel. A device to control idle speed (IAC) and a device to provide information about throttle valve position (TPS) are included as part of the TBI unit.

The model 220 is used on V6 and V8 engines, consists of 3 major castings. (1) fuel meter cover with pressure regulator, (2) Fuel meter body with injectors and (3) throttle body with IAC valve and TPS sensor.

The throttle body portion of the TBI unit may contain ports located at, above, or below the throttle valve. These ports generate the vacuum signals for the EGR valve, MAP sensor, and the canister purge system.

The fuel injector is a solenoid-operated device controlled by the ECM. The incoming fuel is directed to the lower end of the injector assembly which has a fine screen filter surrounding the injector inlet. The ECM turns on the solenoid, which lifts a normally closed ball valve off a seat. The fuel, under pressure, is injected in a conical spray pattern at the walls of the throttle body bore above the throttle valve. The excess fuel passes through a pressure regulator before being returned to the vehicle fuel tank.

The pressure regulator is a diaphragm-operated relief valve with the injector pressure on one side, and the air cleaner pressure on the other. The function of the regulator is to maintain constant pressure (approximately 11 psi) to the injector throughout the operating loads and speed ranges of the engine. If the regulator pressure is too low, below 9 psi, it can cause poor performance. Too high a pressure could cause detonation and a strong fuel odor.

Idle Air Control (IAC)

The purpose of the Idle Air Control (IAC) system is to control engine idle speed while preventing stalls due to changes in engine load. The IAC assembly, mounted on the throttle body, controls bypass air around the throttle plate. By extending or retracting a conical valve, a controlled amount of air can move around the throttle plate. If rpm is too low, more air is diverted around the throttle plate to increase rpm.

During idle, the proper position of the IAC valve is calculated by the ECM based on battery voltage, coolant temperature, engine load, and engine rpm. If the rpm drops below a specified rate, the throttle plate is closed. The ECM will then calculate a new valve position.

Three different designs are used for the IAC conical valve. The first design used is single 35 taper while the second design used is a dual taper. The third design is a blunt valve. Care should be taken to insure use of the correct design when service replacement is required.

The IAC motor has 255 different positions or steps. The zero, or reference position, is the fully extended position at which the pintle is seated in

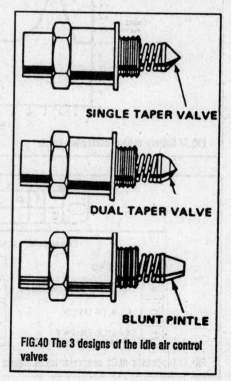

SINGLE TAPER VALVE

DUAL TAPER VALVE

BLUNT PINTLE

FIG.40 The 3 designs of the idle air control valves

the air bypass seat and no air is allowed to bypass the throttle plate. When the motor is fully retracted, maximum air is allowed to bypass the throttle plate. When the motor is fully retracted, maximum air is allowed to bypass the throttle plate.

The ECM always monitors how many steps it has extended or retracted the pintle from the zero or reference position; thus, it always calculates the exact position of the motor. Once the engine has started and the vehicle has reached approximately 40 mph, the ECM will extend the motor 255 steps from whatever position it is in. This will bottom out the pintle against the seat. The ECM will call this position 0 and thus keep its zero reference updated.

The IAC only affects the engine's idle characteristics. If it is stuck fully open, idle speed is too high (too much air enters the throttle bore) If it is stuck closed, idle speed is too low (not enough air entering). If it is stuck somewhere in the middle, idle may be rough, and the engine won't respond to load changes.

Idle Speed Control (ISC)

Incorrect diagnosis and/or misunderstanding of the idle speed control systems used on EFI engines may lead to unnecessary replacement of the IAC valve. Engine idle speed is controlled by the ECM which changes the idle speed by moving the IAC valve. The ECM adjusts idle speed in response to fluctuations in engine load (A/C, power steering, electrical loads, etc.) to maintain acceptable idle quality and proper exhaust emission performance.

The following is provided to assist the you to better understand the system. Asking yourself questions that a mechanic would ask you will help you narrow down the problem area.

1. Rough idle/low idle speed
2. High idle speed/warm-up idle speed; no kickdown

Rough Idle/Low Idle Speed

The ECM will respond to increases in engine load, which would cause a drop in idle speed, by moving the IAC valve to maintain proper idle speed. After the induced load is removed the ECM will return the idle speed to the proper level.

During A/C compressor operation (MAX, BI-LEVEL, NORM or DEFROST mode) the ECM will increase idle speed in response to an A/C-ON signal, thereby compensating for any drop in idle speed due to compressor load. On some vehicles, the ECM will also increase the idle speed in response to high power steering loads.

During periods of especially heavy loads (A/C-ON plus parking maneuvers) significant effects on idle quality may be experienced. These effects are more pronounced on 4-cylinder engines. Abnormally low idle, rough idle and idle

shake may occur if the ECM does not receive the proper signals from the monitored systems.

High Idle Speed/Warm-Up Idle Speed

(No Kickdown)

Engine idle speeds as high as 2100 rpm may be experienced during cold starts to quickly raise the catalytic converter to operating temperature for proper exhaust emissions performance. The idle speed attained after a cold start is ECM controlled and will not drop for 45 seconds regardless of driver attempts to kickdown.

It is important to recognize the EFI engines have no accelerator pump or choke. Idle speed during warm-up is entirely ECM controlled and cannot be changed by accelerator kickdown or pumping.

Abnormally low idle speeds are usually caused by an ECM system-controlled or monitored irregularity, while the most common cause for abnormally high idle speed is an induction (intake air) leak. The idle air control valve may occasionally lose its memory function, and it has an ECM programmed method of relearning the correct idle position. This reset, when required, will occur the next time the car exceeds 35 mph. At this time the ECM seats the pintle of the IAC valve in the throttle body to determine a reference point. Then it backs out a fixed distance to maintain proper idle speed.

DATA SENSORS

A variety of sensors provide information to the ECM regarding engine operating characteristics. These sensors and their functions are described below. Be sure to take note that not every sensor described is used with every engine application.

Engine Coolant Temperature

The Coolant Temperature Sensor (CTS) is a thermister (a resistor which changes value based on temperature) mounted on the engine coolant stream. As the temperature of the engine coolant changes, the resistance of the coolant sensor changes. Low coolant temperature produces a high resistance (100,000 ohms at –40°C/–40°F), while high temperature causes low resistance (70 ohms at 130°C/266°F).

The ECM supplies a 5 volt signal to the coolant sensor and measures the voltage that returns. By measuring the voltage change, the ECM determines the engine coolant temperature. The voltage will be high when the engine is cold and low when the engine is hot. This information is used to control fuel management, IAC, spark timing, EGR, canister purge and other engine operating conditions.

A failure in the coolant sensor circuit should either set a Code 14 or 15. These codes indicate a failure in the coolant temperature sensor circuit.

Oxygen Sensor

The exhaust oxygen sensor is mounted in the exhaust system where it can monitor the oxygen content of the exhaust gas stream. The oxygen content in the exhaust reacts with the oxygen sensor to produce a voltage output. This voltage ranges from approximately 100 millivolts (high oxygen — lean mixture) to 900 millivolts (low oxygen — rich mixture).

By monitoring the voltage output of the oxygen sensor, the ECM will determine what fuel mixture command to give to the injector (lean mixture — low voltage — rich command, rich mixture — high voltage — lean command).

Remember that oxygen sensor indicates to the ECM what is happening in the exhaust. It does not cause things to happen. It is a type of gauge: high oxygen content = lean mixture; low oxygen content = rich mixture. The ECM adjust fuel to keep the system working.

The oxygen sensor, if open should set a Code 13. A constant low voltage in the sensor circuit should set a Code 44 while a constant high voltage in the circuit should set a Code 45. Codes 44 and 45 could also be set as a result of fuel system problems.

Manifold Absolute Pressure Sensor

The Manifold Absolute Pressure (MAP) sensor measures the changes in the intake manifold pressure which result from engine load and speed changes. The pressure measured by the MAP sensor is the difference between barometric pressure (outside air) and manifold pressure (vacuum). A closed throttle engine coastdown would produce a relatively low MAP value (approximately 20–35 kPa), while wide-open throttle would produce a high value (100 kPa). This high value is produced when the pressure inside the manifold is the same as outside the manifold, and 100% of outside air (or 100 kPa) is being measured. This MAP output is the opposite of what you would measure on a vacuum gauge. The use of this sensor also allows the ECM to adjust automatically for different altitude.

The ECM sends a 5 volt reference signal to the MAP sensor. As the MAP changes, the electrical resistance of the sensor also changes. By monitoring the sensor output voltage the ECM can determine the manifold pressure. A higher pressure, lower vacuum (high voltage) requires more fuel, while a lower pressure, higher vacuum (low voltage) requires less fuel. The ECM uses the MAP sensor to control fuel

delivery and ignition timing. A failure in the MAP sensor circuit should set a Code 33 or Code 34.

Intake Air Temperature Sensor

The Intake Air Temperature (IAT) and Manifold Air Temperature (MAT) are the same sensor. This sensor is a thermistor mounted in the intake manifold or air intake. A thermistor is a resistor which changes resistance based on temperature. Low manifold air temperature produces a high resistance (100,000 ohms at −40°F/−40°C), while high temperature cause low resistance (70 ohms at 266°F/130°C).

The ECM supplies a 5 volt signal to the MAT/IAT sensor through a resistor in the ECM and monitors the voltage. The voltage will be high when the manifold air is cold and low when the air is hot. By monitoring the voltage, the ECM calculates the air temperature and uses this data to help determine the fuel delivery and spark advance. A failure in the MAT/IAT circuit should set either a Code 23 or Code 25.

Vehicle Speed Sensor

➡ **A vehicle equipped with a speed sensor, should not be driven without a the speed sensor connected, as idle quality may be affected. Also extreme poor gas mileage and a code will be stored in the computers memory.**

The Vehicle Speed Sensor (VSS) is mounted behind the speedometer in the instrument cluster or on the transmission/speedometer drive gear. It provides electrical pulses to the ECM from the speedometer head. The pulses indicate the road speed. The ECM uses this information to operate the IAC, canister purge, and TCC.

Some vehicles equipped with digital instrument clusters use a Permanent Magnet (PM) generator to provide the VSS signal. The

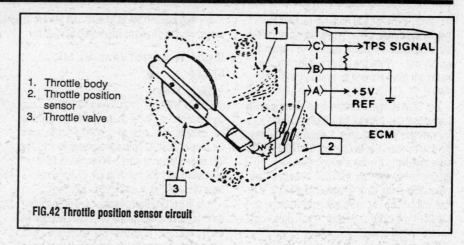

1. Throttle body
2. Throttle position sensor
3. Throttle valve

FIG.42 Throttle position sensor circuit

PM generator is located in the transmission and replaces the speedometer cable. The signal from the PM generator drives a stepper motor which drives the odometer. A failure in the VSS circuit should set a Code 24.

Throttle Position Sensor

The Throttle Position Sensor (TPS) is connected to the throttle shaft and is controlled by the throttle mechanism. A 5 volt reference signal is sent to the TPS from the ECM. As the throttle valve angle is changed (accelerator pedal moved), the resistance of the TPS also changes. At a closed throttle position, the resistance of the TPS is high, so the output voltage to the ECM will be low (approximately 0.5 volts). As the throttle plate opens, the resistance decreases so that, at wide open throttle, the output voltage should be approximately 5 volts. At closed throttle position, the voltage at the TPS should be less than 1.25 volts.

By monitoring the output voltage from the TPS, the ECM can determine fuel delivery based on throttle valve angle (driver demand). The TPS

can either be misadjusted, shorted, open or loose. Misadjustment might result in poor idle or poor wide-open throttle performance. An open TPS signals the ECM that the throttle is always closed, resulting in poor performance. This usually sets a Code 22. A shorted TPS gives the ECM a constant wide-open throttle signal and should set a Code 21. A loose TPS indicates to the ECM that the throttle is moving. This causes intermittent bursts of fuel from the injector and an unstable idle. On some vehicles, the TPS is adjustable and therefore can be adjusted to correct any complications caused by to high or to low of a voltage signal.

Crankshaft And Camshaft Sensor

These sensors are mounted on the engine block, near the engine crankshaft, and also near the camshaft on some engines. The sensors are used to send a signal through the Direct Ignition System (DIS) module to the ECM. The ECM uses this reference signal to calculate engine speed and crankshaft position.

In a typical 4 cylinder engine application, a sensor is mounted with the ignition module and 2 ignition coils to comprise the direct ignition assembly. When mounted on the engine block, the sensor tip is very close to a metal disk wheel with slots which is mounted on the crankshaft.

The sensor tip contains a small magnet and a small coil of wire. As the metal disk wheel with the slots rotates past the sensor tip, the magnetic field of the permanent magnet is changed and a voltage is induced into the coil. This voltage signal is sent to the ignition module. The ignition module is able to determine engine speed from the frequency of the voltage curve, which changes with engine speed.

A 6 cylinder engine may use a different type of sensor called a hall effect switch. With the direct ignition connected to the vehicle electrical system, the system voltage is applied to the hall effect switch located near the tip of the sensor.

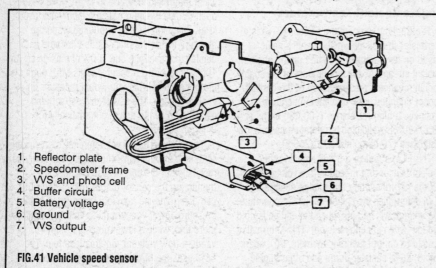

1. Reflector plate
2. Speedometer frame
3. VVS and photo cell
4. Buffer circuit
5. Battery voltage
6. Ground
7. VVS output

FIG.41 Vehicle speed sensor

A small permanent magnet creates a magnetic field in the hall 2. effect switch circuit. As the disc wheel with the slots rotates past the sensor2. tip, the magnetic field in the hall effect switch changes and a change in the voltage occurs at the hall effect switch output terminal.

Since this terminal is connect to the ignition module, the module senses this change in voltage and correlates the frequency of the voltage curve to determine the engine speed. The ignition module then uses this voltage input to help determine when to close and open the ignition coil primary circuit and fire the spark plug.

Park/Neutral Switch

➡ **Vehicle should not be driven with the park/neutral switch disconnected as idle quality may be affected in PARK or NEUTRAL and a Code 24 (VSS) may be set.**

This switch indicates to the ECM when the transmission is in **P** or **N**. The information is used by the ECM for control on the torque converter clutch, EGR, and the idle air control valve operation.

Air Conditioner Request Signal

This signal indicates to the ECM that an air conditioning mode is selected at the switch and that the A/C low pressure switch is closed. The ECM controls the A/C and adjusts the idle speed in response to this signal.

Torque Converter Clutch Solenoid

The purpose of the Torque Converter Clutch (TCC) system is designed to eliminate power loss by the converter (slippage) to increase fuel economy. By locking the converter clutch, a more effective coupling to the flywheel is achieved. The converter clutch is operated by the ECM controlled torque converter clutch solenoid.

Power Steering Pressure Switch

The Power Steering Pressure Switch (PSPS) is used so that the power steering oil pressure pump load will not effect the engine idle. Turning the steering wheel increase the power steering oil pressure and pump load on the engine. The power steering pressure switch will close before the load can cause an idle problem.

Oil Pressure Switch

The oil pressure switch is usually mounted on the back of the engine, just below the intake manifold. Some vehicles use the oil pressure switch as a parallel power supply, with the fuel pump relay and will provide voltage to the fuel pump, after approximately 4 psi (28 kPa) of oil pressure is reached. This switch will also help prevent engine seizure by shutting off the power to the fuel pump and causing the engine to stop when the oil pressure is lower than 4 psi.

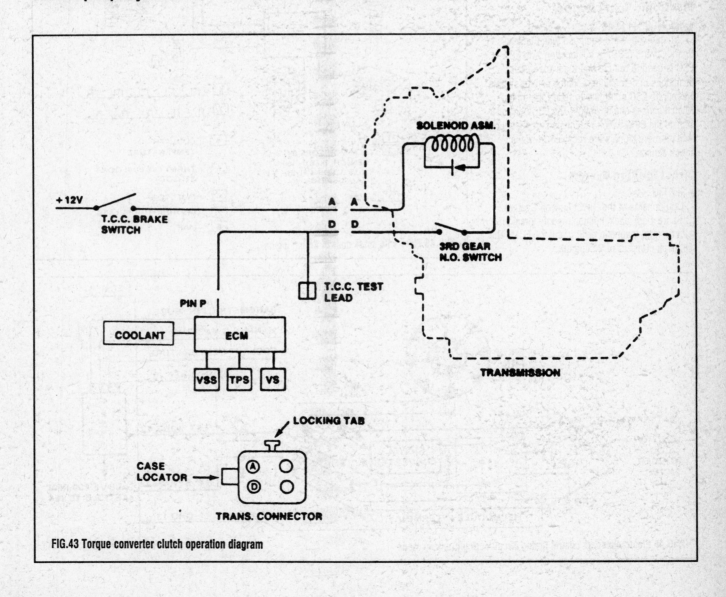

FIG.43 Torque converter clutch operation diagram

Electronic Spark Timing

Electronic Spark Timing (EST) is used on all engines. The EST distributor contains no vacuum or centrifugal advance and uses a 7-terminal distributor module. It also has 4 wires going to a 4-terminal connector in addition to the connectors normally found on HEI distributors. A reference pulse, indicating both engine rpm and crankshaft position, is sent to the ECM. The ECM determines the proper spark advance for the engine operating conditions and sends an EST pulse to the distributor.

The EST system is designed to optimize spark timing for better control of exhaust emissions and for fuel economy improvements. The ECM monitors information from various engine sensors, computes the desired spark timing and changes the timing accordingly. A backup spark advance system is incorporated in the module in case of EST failure.

Electronic Spark Control

▶ SEE FIGS. 44 to 48

When engines are equipped with Electronic Spark Control (ESC) in conjunction with EST, ESC is used to reduce spark advance under conditions of detonation. A knock sensor signals a separate ESC controller to retard the timing when it senses engine knock. The ESC controller signals the ECM which reduces spark advance until no more signals are received from the knock sensor.

Direct Ignition System

▶ SEE FIG. 49

Components of the Direct Ignition System (DIS) are a coil pack, ignition module, crankshaft reluctor ring, magnetic sensor and the ECM. The coil pack consists of 2 separate,

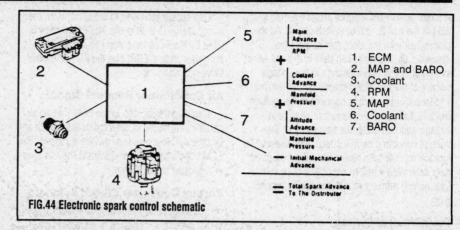

1. ECM
2. MAP and BARO
3. Coolant
4. RPM
5. MAP
6. Coolant
7. BARO

FIG.44 Electronic spark control schematic

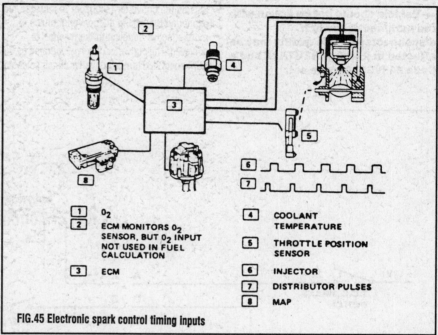

1	O₂
2	ECM MONITORS O₂ SENSOR, BUT O₂ INPUT NOT USED IN FUEL CALCULATION
3	ECM
4	COOLANT TEMPERATURE
5	THROTTLE POSITION SENSOR
6	INJECTOR
7	DISTRIBUTOR PULSES
8	MAP

FIG.45 Electronic spark control timing inputs

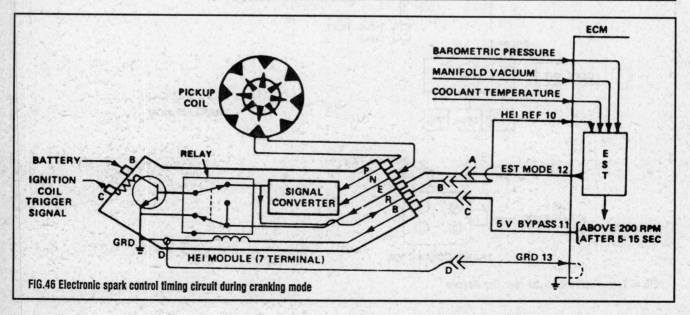

FIG.46 Electronic spark control timing circuit during cranking mode

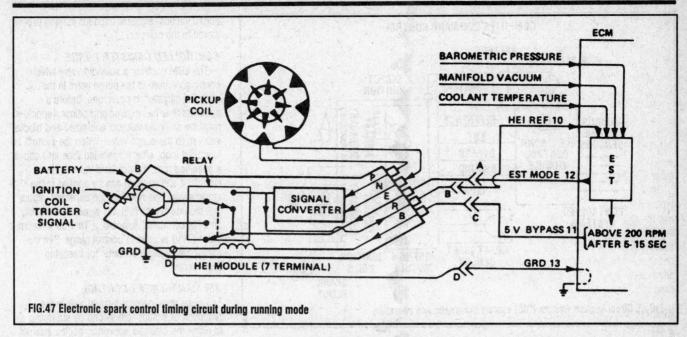

FIG.47 Electronic spark control timing circuit during running mode

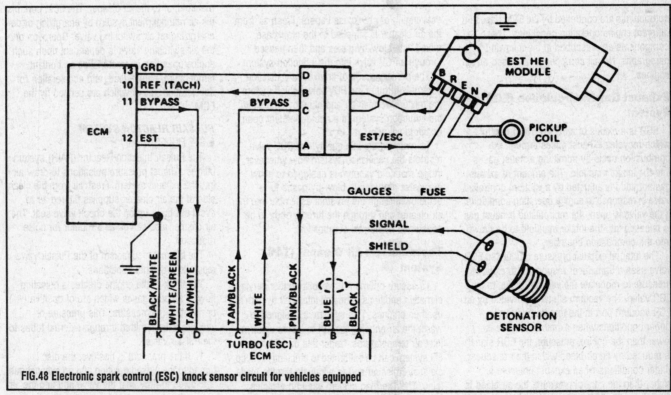

FIG.48 Electronic spark control (ESC) knock sensor circuit for vehicles equipped

interchangeable, ignition coils. These coils operate in the same manner as previous coils. Two coils are needed because each coil fires for 2 cylinders. The ignition module is located under the coil pack and is connected to the ECM by a 6 pin connector. The ignition module controls the primary circuits to the coils, turning them on and off and controls spark timing below 400 rpm and if the ECM bypass circuit becomes open or grounded.

The magnetic pickup sensor inserts through the engine block, just above the pan rail in proximity to the crankshaft reluctor ring. Notches in the crankshaft reluctor ring trigger the magnetic pickup sensor to provide timing information to the ECM. The magnetic pickup sensor provides a cam signal to identify correct firing sequence and crank signals to trigger each coil at the proper time.

This system uses EST and control wires from

the ECM, as with the distributor systems. The ECM controls the timing using crankshaft position, engine rpm, engine temperature and manifold absolute pressure sensing.

EMISSION CONTROL

Various components are used to control exhaust emissions from a vehicle. These

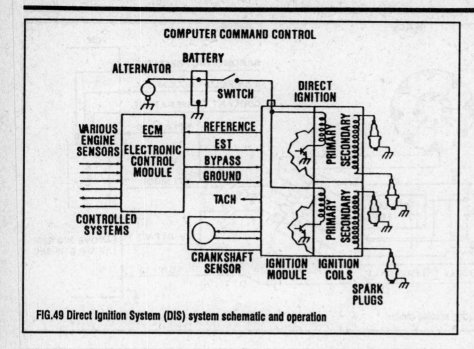

COMPUTER COMMAND CONTROL

FIG.49 Direct Ignition System (DIS) system schematic and operation

components are controlled by the ECM based on different engine operating conditions. These components are described in the following paragraphs. Not all components are used on all engines.

Exhaust Gas Recirculation (EGR) System

EGR is a oxides of nitrogen (NOx) control which recycles exhaust gases through the combustion cycle by admitting exhaust gases into the intake manifold. The amount of exhaust gas admitted is adjusted by a vacuum controlled valve in response to engine operating conditions. If the valve is open, the recirculated exhaust gas is released into the intake manifold to be drawn into the combustion chamber.

The integral exhaust pressure modulated EGR valve uses a transducer responsive to exhaust pressure to modulate the vacuum signal to the EGR valve. The vacuum signal is provided by an EGR vacuum port in the throttle body valve. Under conditions when exhaust pressure is lower than the control pressure, the EGR signal is reduced by an air bleed within the transducer. Under conditions when exhaust pressure is higher than the control pressure, the air bleed is closed and the EGR valve responds to an unmodified vacuum signal. Physical arrangement of the valve components will vary depending on whether the control pressure is positive or negative.

Positive Crankcase Ventilation (PCV) System

A closed Positive Crankcase Ventilation (PCV) system is used to provide more complete scavenging of crankcase vapors. Fresh air from the air cleaner is supplied to the crankcase, mixed with blow-by gases and then passed through a PCV valve into the induction system.

The primary mode of crankcase ventilation control is through the PCV valve which meters the mixture of fresh air and blow-by gases into the induction system at a rate dependent upon manifold vacuum.

To maintain the idle quality, the PCV valve restricts the ventilation system flow whenever intake manifold vacuum is designed to allow excessive amounts of blow-by gases to backflow through the breather assembly into the air cleaner and through the throttle body to be consumed by normal combustion.

Thermostatic Air Cleaner (TAC) System

To assure optimum driveability under varying climatic conditions, a heated intake air system is used on engines. This system is designed to warm the air entering the TBI to insure uniform inlet air temperatures. Under this condition, the EFI system can be calibrated to efficiently reduce exhaust emission and to eliminate throttle blade icing. The Thermac system used on vehicles equipped with EFI operates identical to other Thermac systems.

Evaporative Emission Control (EEC) Systems

The basic evaporative emission control system used on all vehicles uses the carbon canister storage method. This method transfers fuel vapor to an activated carbon storage device for retention when the vehicle is not operating. A ported vacuum signal is used for purging vapors stored in the canister.

CONTROLLED CANISTER PURGE

The ECM controls a solenoid valve which controls vacuum to the purge valve in the charcoal canister. In open loop, before a specified time has expired and below a specified rpm, the solenoid valve is energized and blocks vacuum to the purge valve. When the system is in closed loop, after a specified time and above a specified rpm, the solenoid valve is de-energized and vacuum can be applied to the purge valve. This releases the collected vapors into the intake manifold. On systems not using an ECM controlled solenoid, a Thermo Vacuum Valve (TVV) is used to control purge. See the appropriate vehicle sections for checking procedures.

AIR MANAGEMENT CONTROL

The air management system aids in the reduction of exhaust emissions by supplying air to either the catalytic converter, engine exhaust manifold, or to the air cleaner. The ECM controls the air management system by energizing or de-energizing an air switching valve. Operation of the air switching valve is dependent upon such engine operating characteristics as coolant temperature, engine load, and acceleration (or deceleration), all of which are sensed by the ECM.

PULSAIR REACTOR SYSTEM
▶ SEE FIG. 50

The Pulsair Injection Reactor (PAIR) system utilizes exhaust pressure pulsations to draw air into the exhaust system. Fresh air from the clean side of the air cleaner supplies filtered air to avoid dirt build-up on the check valve seat. The air cleaner also serves as a muffler for noise reduction.

The internal mechanism of the Pulsair valve reacts to 3 distinct conditions.

The firing of the engine creates a pulsating flow of exhaust gases which are of positive (+) or negative (−) pressure. This pressure or vacuum is transmitted through external tubes to the Pulsair valve.

1. If the pressure is positive, the disc is forced to the closed position and no exhaust gas is allowed to flow past the valve and into the air supply line.

2. If there is a negative pressure (vacuum) in the exhaust system at the valve, the disc will open, allowing fresh air to mix with the exhaust gases.

3. Due to the inertia of the system, the disc ceases to follow the pressure pulsations at high engine rpm. At this point, the disc remains closed, preventing any further fresh air flow.

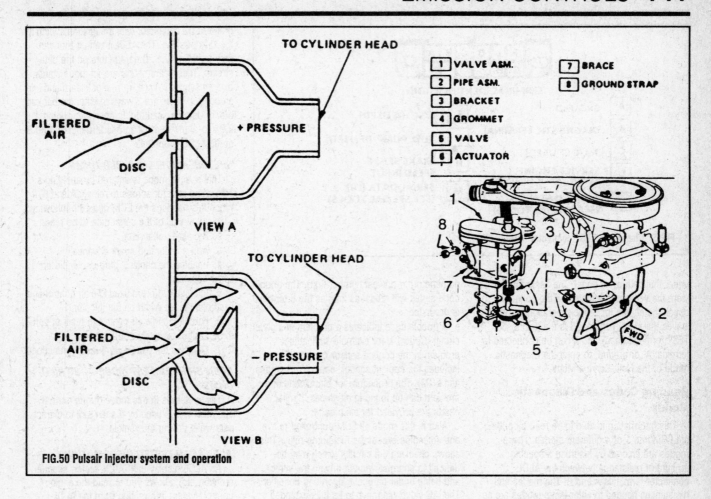

FIG.50 Pulsair injector system and operation

CATALYTIC CONVERTER

Of all emission control devices available, the catalytic converter is the most effective in reducing tailpipe emissions. The major tailpipe pollutants are hydrocarbons (HC), carbon monoxide (CO), and oxides of nitrogen (NOx).

SERVICE PRECAUTIONS

When working around any part of the fuel system, take precautionary steps to prevent fire and/or explosion:
• Disconnect negative terminal from battery (except when testing with battery voltage is required).
• When possible, use a flashlight instead of a drop light.
• Keep all open flame and smoking material out of the area.
• Use a shop cloth or similar to catch fuel when opening a fuel system.
• Relieve fuel system pressure before servicing.
• Use eye protection.

• Always keep a dry chemical (class B) fire extinguisher near the area.

➡ **Due to the amount of fuel pressure in the fuel lines, before doing any work to the fuel system, the fuel system should be depressurized.**

Electrostatic Discharge Damage

Electronic components used in the control system are often design to carry very low voltage and are very susceptible to damage caused by electrostatic discharge. It is possible for less than 100 volts of static electricity to cause damage to some electronic components. By comparison it takes as much as 4000 volts for a person to even feel the zap of a static discharge.

There are several ways for a person to become statically charged. The most common methods of charging are by friction and induction. An example of charging by friction is a person sliding across a car seat, in which a charge as much as 25000 volts can build up. Charging by induction occurs when a person with well insulated shoes stands near a highly charged object and momentarily touches ground. Charges of the same polarity are drained off, leaving the person highly charged with the opposite polarity. Static charges of either type can cause damage, therefore, it is important to use care when handling and testing electronic components.

➡ **To prevent possible electrostatic discharge damage to the ECM, do not touch the connector pins or soldered components on the circuit board. When handling a PROM, Mem-Cal or Cal-Pak, do not touch the component leads and remove the integrated circuit from the carrier.**

DIAGNOSTIC ENGINE COMPUTER CODES

ALCL/ALDL Connector

The Assembly Line Communication Link (ALCL) also known as the Assembly Line Diagnostic Link (ALDL) is a diagnostic connector located in the passenger compartment usually

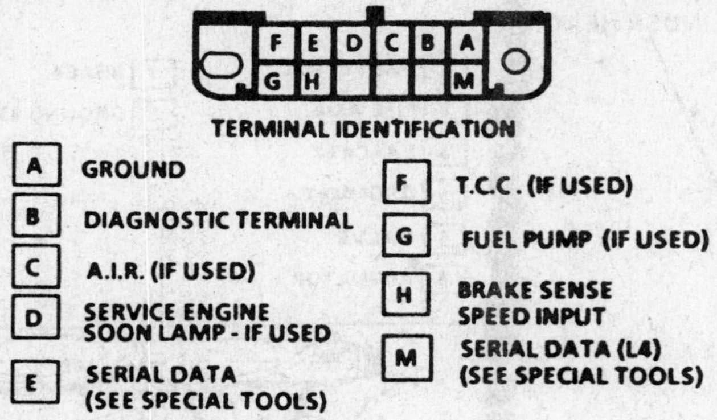

TERMINAL IDENTIFICATION

A	GROUND		F	T.C.C . (IF USED)
B	DIAGNOSTIC TERMINAL		G	FUEL PUMP (IF USED)
C	A.I.R. (IF USED)		H	BRAKE SENSE SPEED INPUT
D	SERVICE ENGINE SOON LAMP - IF USED		M	SERIAL DATA (L4) (SEE SPECIAL TOOLS)
E	SERIAL DATA (SEE SPECIAL TOOLS)			

FIG.51 Diagnostic ALDL connector identification

under the instrument panel. The assembly plant were the vehicles originate use the connector to check the engine for proper operation before it leaves the plant. Terminal B is the diagnostic TEST terminal (lead) and it can be connected to terminal A, or ground, to enter the Diagnostic mode or the Field Service Mode.

Reading Codes and Diagnostic Modes

This information is able to be read by putting the ECM into 1 of 4 different modes. These modes are entered by inserting a specific amount of resistance between the ALDL connector terminals A and B. The modes and resistances needed to enter these modes are as follows:

DIAGNOSTIC MODES — 0 OHMS

When 0 resistance is between terminals A and B of the ALDL connector, the diagnostic mode is entered. There are 2 positions to this mode. One with the engine **OFF**, but the ignition **ON**; the other is when the engine is running called Field Service Mode.

If the diagnostic mode is entered with the engine in the **OFF** position, trouble codes will flash and the idle air control motor will pulsate in and out. Also, the relays and solenoids are energized with the exception of the fuel pump and injector.

As a bulb and system check, the SERVICE ENGINE SOON light will come on with the ignition switch **ON** and the engine not running. When the engine is started, the SERVICE ENGINE SOON light will turn off. If the SERVICE ENGINE SOON light remains on, the self-diagnostic system has detected a problem.

If the B terminal is then grounded with the ignition **ON**, engine not running, each trouble code will flash and repeat 3 times. If more than 1 problem has been detected, each trouble code will flash 3 times. Trouble codes will flash in numeric order (lowest number first). The trouble code series will repeat as long as the B terminal is grounded.

A trouble code indicates a problem in a given circuit (Code 14, for example, indicates a problem in the coolant sensor circuit; this includes the coolant sensor, connector harness, and ECM). The procedure for pinpointing the problem can be found in diagnosis. Similar charts are provided for each code.

Also in this mode all ECM controlled relays and solenoids except the fuel pump relay. This allows checking the circuits which may be difficult to energize without driving the vehicle and being under particular operating conditions. The IAC valve will move to its fully extended position on most models, block the idle air passage. This is useful in checking the minimum idle speed.

FIELD SERVICE MODE — 0 OHMS

When the ALDL connector terminal B is grounded with the engine running, the ECM goes into the field service mode. In this mode, the SERVICE ENGINE SOON light flashes closed or open loop and indicates the rich/lean status of the engine. The ECM runs the engine at a fixed ignition timing advanced above the base setting.

The SERVICE ENGINE SOON light will show whether the system is in Open loop or Closed loop. In Open loop the SERVICE ENGINE SOON light flashes 2 times and one half times per second. In Closed loop the light flashes once per second. Also in closed loop, the light will stay OUT most of the time if the system is too lean. It will stay ON most of the time if the system is too rich. In either case the Field Service mode check, which is part of the Diagnostic circuit check, will lead you into choosing the correct diagnostic chart to refer to.

BACK-UP MODE — 3.9 KILO-OHMS

The backup mode is entered by applying 3.9 kilo-ohms resistance between terminals A and B of the ALDL connector with the ignition switch in the **ON** position. The ALDL scanner tool can now read 5 of the 20 parameters on the data stream. These parameters are as mode status, oxygen sensor voltage, rpm, block learn and idle air control. There are 2 ways to enter the backup mode. Using a scan tool is one way; putting a 3.9 kilo-ohms resistor across terminals A and B of the ALDL is another.

SPECIAL MODE — 10 KILO-OHMS

This special mode is entered by applying a 10K ohms resistor across terminals A and B. When this happens the ECM does the following:

1. Allows all of the serial data to be read.
2. Bypasses all timers.
3. Add a calibrated spark advance.
4. Enables the canister purge solenoid on some engines.
5. Idles at 1000 rpm fixed idle air control and fixed base pulse width on the injector.
6. Forces the idle air control to reset at part throttle (approximately 2000 rpm).
7. Disables the park/neutral restrict functions

OPEN OR ROAD TEST MODE — 20 KILO-OHMS

The system is in this mode during normal operation and is used by a scan tool to extract data while driving the vehicle.

ALDL SCAN TESTER INFORMATION

An ALDL display unit (ALDL tester, scanner, monitor, etc), allows you to read the engine control system information from the ALDL connector under the instrument panel. It can provide information faster than a digital voltmeter or ohmmeter can. The scan tool does not diagnose the exact location of the problem. The tool supplies information about the ECM, the information that it is receiving and the commands that it is sending plus special information such as integrator and block learn. To use an ALDL display tool you should understand thoroughly how an engine control system operates.

An ALDL scanner or monitor puts a fuel injection system into a special test mode. This mode commands an idle speed of 1000 rpm. The idle quality cannot be evaluated with a tester plugged in. Also the test mode commands a fixed spark with no advance. On vehicles with Electronic Spark Control (ESC), there will be a fixed spark, but it will be advanced. On vehicles with ESC, there might be a serious spark knock, this spark knock could be bad enough so as not being able to road test the vehicle in the ALDL test mode. Be sure to check the tool manufacturer for instructions on special test modes which should overcome these limitations.

When a tester is used with a fuel injected

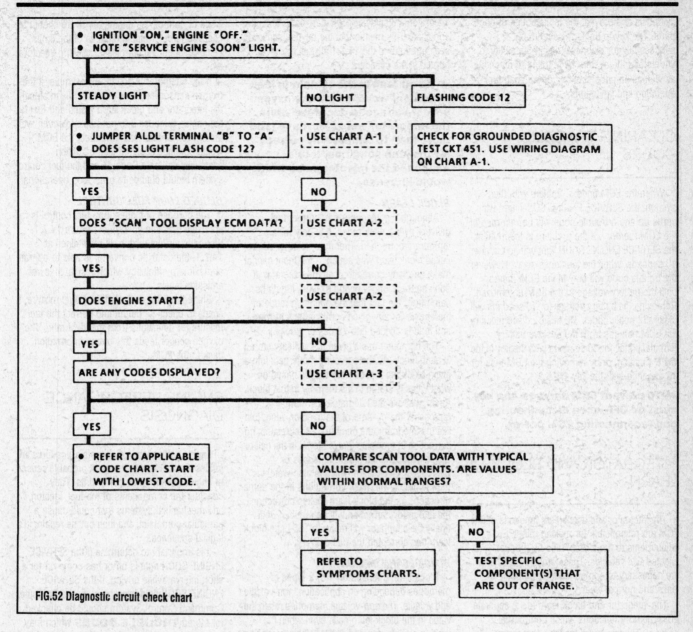

FIG.52 Diagnostic circuit check chart

engine, it bypasses the timer that keeps the system in Open loop for a certain period of time. When all Closed loop conditions are met, the engine will go into Closed loop as soon as the vehicle is started. This means that the air management system will not function properly and air may go directly to the converter as soon as the engine is started.

These tools cannot diagnose everything. They do not tell where a problem is located in a circuit. The diagnostic charts to pinpoint the problems must still be used. These tester's do not let you know if a solenoid or relay has been turned on. They only tell the ECM command. To find out if a solenoid has been turned on, check it with a suitable test light or digital voltmeter, or see if vacuum through the solenoid changes.

SCAN TOOLS FOR INTERMITTENTS

In some scan tool applications, the data update rate may make the tool less effective than a voltmeter, such as when trying to detect an intermittent problem which lasts for a very short time. Some scan tools have a snapshot function which stores several seconds or even minutes of operation to located an intermittent problem. Scan tools allow one to manipulate the wiring harness or components under the hood with the engine not running while observing the scan tool's readout.

The scan tool can be plugged in and observed while driving the vehicle under the condition when the SERVICE ENGINE SOON light turns on momentarily or when the engine driveability is momentarily poor. If the problem seems to be related to certain parameters that can be checked on the scan tool, they should be checked while driving the vehicle. If there does not seem to be any correlation between the problem and any specific circuit, the scan tool can be checked on each position. Watching for a period of time to see if there is any change in the reading that indicates intermittent operation.

The scan tool is also an easy way to compare the operating parameters of a poorly operating engine with typical scan data for the vehicle being serviced or those of a known good engine. For example, a sensor may shift in value but not set a trouble code. Comparing the sensor's reading with those of a known good parameters may uncover the problem.

The scan tool has the ability to save time in

diagnosis and prevent the replacement of good parts. The key to using the scan tool successfully for diagnosis lies in the ability to understand the system he is trying to diagnose as well as an understanding of the scan tool's operation and limitations.

CLEARING TROUBLE CODES

When the ECM finds a problem with the system, the SERVICE ENGINE SOON light will come on and a trouble code will be recorded in the ECM memory. If the problem is intermittent, the SERVICE ENGINE SOON light will go out after 10 seconds, when the fault goes away. However the trouble code will stay in the ECM memory until the battery voltage to the ECM is removed. Removing the battery voltage for 10 seconds will clear all trouble codes. Do this by disconnecting the ECM harness from the positive battery terminal pigtail for 10 seconds with the key in the **OFF** position, or by removing the ECM fuse for 10 seconds with the key **OFF**.

➡ **To prevent ECM damage, the key must be OFF when disconnecting and reconnecting ECM power.**

INTEGRATOR AND BLOCK LEARN

The integrator and block learn functions of the ECM are responsible for making minor adjustments to the air/fuel ratio on the fuel injected GM vehicles. These small adjustments are necessary to compensate for pinpoint air leaks and normal wear.

The integrator and block learn are 2 separate ECM memory functions which control fuel delivery. The integrator makes a temporary change and the block learn makes a more permanent change. Both of these functions apply only while the engine is in CLOSED LOOP. They represent the on-time of the injector. Also, integrator and block learn controls fuel delivery on the fuel injected engines as does the MC solenoid dwell on the CCC carbureted engines.

INTEGRATOR

Integrator is the term applied to a means of temporary change in fuel delivery. Integrator is displayed through the ALDL data line and monitored with a scanner as a number between 0 and 255 with an average of 128. The integrator monitors the oxygen sensor output voltage and adds and subtracts fuel depending on the lean or rich condition of the oxygen sensor. When the

integrator is displaying 128, it indicates a neutral condition. This means that the oxygen sensor is seeing results of the 14.7:1 air/fuel mixture burned in the cylinders.

➡ **An air leak in the system (a lean condition) would cause the oxygen sensor voltage to decrease while the integrator would increase (add more fuel) to temporarily correct for the lean condition. If this happened the injector pulse width would increase.**

BLOCK LEARN

Although the integrator can correct fuel delivery over a wide range, it is only for a temporary correction. Therefore, another control called block learn was added. Although it cannot make as many corrections as the integrator, it does so for a longer period of time. It gets its name from the fact that the operating range of the engine for any given combinations of rpm and load is divided into 16 cell or blocks.

The computer has a given fuel delivery stored in each block. As the operating range gets into a given block the fuel delivery will be based on what value is stored in the memory in that block. Again, just like the integrator, the number represents the on-time of the injector. Also, just like the integrator, the number 128 represents no correction to the value that is stored in the cell or block. When the integrator increases or decreases, block learn which is also watching the integrator will make corrections in the same direction. As the block learn makes corrections, the integrator correction will be reduced until finally the integrator will return to 128 if the block learn has corrected the fuel delivery.

BLOCK LEARN MEMORY

Block learn operates on 1 of 2 types of memories depending on application, non-volatile and volatile. The non-volatile memories retain the value in the block learn cells even when the ignition switch is turned **OFF**. When the engine is restarted, the fuel delivery for a given block will be based on information stored in memory.

The volatile memories lose the numbers stored in the block learn cells when the ignition is turned to the **OFF** position. Upon restarting, the block learn starts at 128 in every block and corrects from that point as necessary.

INTEGRATOR/BLOCK LEARN LIMITS

Both the integrator and block learn have limits which will vary from engine to engine. If the mixture is off enough so that the block learn reaches the limit of its control and still cannot correct the condition, the integrator would also go to its limit of control in the same direction and the engine would then begin to run poorly. If the integrators and block learn are close to or at their

limits of control, the engine hardware should be checked to determine the cause of the limits being reached, vacuum leaks, sticking injectors, etc.

If the integrator is lied to, for example, if the oxygen sensor lead was grounded (lean signal) the integrator and block learn would add fuel to the engine to cause it to run rich. However, with the oxygen sensor lead grounded, the ECM would continue seeing a lean condition eventually setting a Code 44 and the fuel control system would change to open loop operations.

CLOSED LOOP FUEL CONTROL

The purpose of closed loop fuel control is to precisely maintain an air/fuel mixture 14.7:1. When the air/fuel mixture is maintained at 14.7:1, the catalytic converter is able to operate at maximum efficiency which results in lower emission levels.

Since the ECM controls the air/fuel mixture, it needs to check its output and correct the fuel mixture for deviations from the ideal ratio. The oxygen sensor feeds this output information back to the ECM.

ENGINE PERFORMANCE DIAGNOSIS

Engine performance diagnosis procedures are guides that will lead to the most probable causes of engine performance complaints. They consider the components of the fuel, ignition, and mechanical systems that could cause a particular complaint, and then outline repairs in a logical sequence.

It is important to determine if the SERVICE ENGINE SOON light is on or has come on for a short interval while driving. If the SERVICE ENGINE SOON light has come on, the Computer Command Control System should be checked for stored **TROUBLE CODES** which may indicate the cause for the performance complaint.

All of the symptoms can be caused by worn out or defective parts such as spark plugs, ignition wiring, etc. If time and/or mileage indicate that parts should be replaced, it is recommended that it be done.

➡ **Before checking any system controlled by the Electronic Fuel Injection (EFI) system, the Diagnostic Circuit Check must be performed or misdiagnosis may occur. If the complaint involves the SERVICE ENGINE SOON light, go directly to the Diagnostic Circuit Check.**

Basic Troubleshooting

➡ **The following explains how to activate the trouble code signal light in the instrument cluster and gives an explanation of what each code means. This is not a full system troubleshooting and isolation procedure.**

Before suspecting the system or any of its components as faulty, check the ignition system including distributor, timing, spark plugs and wires. Check the engine compression, air cleaner, and emission control components not controlled by the ECM. Also check the intake manifold, vacuum hoses and hose connectors for leaks.

The following symptoms could indicate a possible problem with the system:

1. Detonation
2. Stalls or rough idle-cold
3. Stalls or rough idle-hot
4. Missing
5. Hesitation
6. Surges
7. Poor gasoline mileage
8. Sluggish or spongy performance
9. Hard starting-cold
10. Objectionable exhaust odors (that rotten egg smell)
11. Cuts out
12. Improper idle speed

As a bulb and system check, the SERVICE ENGINE SOON light will come on when the ignition switch is turned to the **ON** position but the engine is not started. The SERVICE ENGINE SOON light will also produce the trouble code or codes by a series of flashes which translate as follows. When the diagnostic test terminal under the dash is grounded, with the ignition in the **ON** position and the engine not running, the SERVICE ENGINE SOON light will flash once, pause, then flash twice in rapid succession. This is a Code 12, which indicates that the diagnostic system is working. After a long pause, the Code 12 will repeat itself 2 more times. The cycle will then repeat itself until the engine is started or the ignition is turned off.

When the engine is started, the SERVICE ENGINE SOON light will remain on for a few seconds, then turn off. If the SERVICE ENGINE SOON light remains on, the self-diagnostic system has detected a problem. If the test terminal is then grounded, the trouble code will flash 3 times. If more than 1 problem is found, each trouble code will flash 3 times. Trouble codes will flash in numerical order (lowest code number to highest). The trouble codes series will repeat as long as the test terminal is grounded.

A trouble code indicates a problem with a given circuit. For example, trouble Code 14

indicates a problem in the cooling sensor circuit. This includes the coolant sensor, its electrical harness, and the ECM. Since the self-diagnostic system cannot diagnose every possible fault in the system, the absence of a trouble code does not mean the system is trouble-free. To determine problems within the system which do not activate a trouble code, a system performance check must be made.

In the case of an intermittent fault in the system, the SERVICE ENGINE SOON light will go out when the fault goes away, but the trouble code will remain in the memory of the ECM. Therefore, it a trouble code can be obtained even though the SERVICE ENGINE SOON light is not on, the trouble code must be evaluated. It must be determined if the fault is intermittent or if the engine must be at certain operating conditions (under load, etc.) before the SERVICE ENGINE SOON light will come on. Some trouble codes will not be recorded in the ECM until the engine has been operated at part throttle for about 5–18 minutes.

Fuel System Pressure Testing

Due to the varied application of components, a general procedure is outlined. For the exact procedure for the vehicle being service use Chart A7 for the appropriate engine. A fuel system pressure test is part of several of the diagnostic charts and symptom checks.

1. Relieve the fuel pressure from the fuel system. Turn the ignition **OFF** and remove the air cleaner assembly (if necessary).

2. Plug the Thermac vacuum port if required on the TBI unit.

3. Uncouple the fuel supply flexible hose in the engine compartment and install fuel pressure gauge J29658/BT8205 or equivalent in the pressure line or install the fuel pressure gauge into the pressure line connector located near the left engine compartment frame rail. Connection of the fuel gauge will vary accordingly to all the different engine application.

4. Be sure to tighten the fuel line to the gauge to ensure that there no leaks during testing.

5. Start the engine and observe the fuel pressure reading. The fuel pressure should be 9–13 psi (62–90 kPa).

6. Relieve the fuel pressure. Remove the fuel pressure gauge and reinstall the fuel line. Be sure to install a new O-ring on the fuel feed line.

7. Start the engine and check for fuel leaks. Stop the engine and remove the plug covering the Thermac vacuum port on the TBI unit and install the air cleaner assembly.

➡ **Some vehicles will use more sensors than others. Also, a complete general diagnostic section is outlined. The steps and procedures can be altered as necessary according to the specific model being diagnosed and the sensors it is equipped with. If the battery power is disconnected for any reason, the volatile memory resets and the learning process begins again. A change may be noted in the performance of the vehicle. To teach the vehicle, ensure that the engine is at normal operating temperature. Then, the vehicle should be driven at part throttle, with moderate acceleration and idle conditions until normal performance returns.**

TBI SYSTEM DIAGNOSTIC CHARTS

To properly diagnosis driveability problems you need to use the following charts. Make certain the charts cover the engine your car has. If your check engine light is not lit, check for engine stored engine codes. If any codes are stored write them down for reference later. Clear the codes as described earlier. Road test the vehicle to see if any of the codes return. Never try to fix a code problem until you're sure that it comes back. It may have been a old code from years ago that was never cleared or a code that was set do to a rain storm, battery jump, etc.

After clearing any codes and checking that they do not return. If the car drives fine your finished. But if there are no codes and the car runs poorly you'll need to check the symptoms charts. The problem is most likely not the computer or the devices it controls but the ignition system or engine mechanical.

If you do have a code(s) that returns start with the lowest code and follow the proper chart. You must follow every step of the chart and not jump from test to test or you'll never be certain to find and fix the real problem.

Start with the lowest to highest code chart, making sure to use the charts for your engine. If you have a 50 series code, like code 54. Always check those out first. They are rare but usually indicate a problem with the computer itself or its ability to test itself properly.

➡ **Component repair and replacement are covered in Section 5 Fuel System, this section will only deal with the testing of the system for both driveablities and emission problems.**

THROTTLE BODY INJECTION DIAGNOSTIC CHARTS

RPO: LR8   VIN CODE: R   2.5L L4 TBI

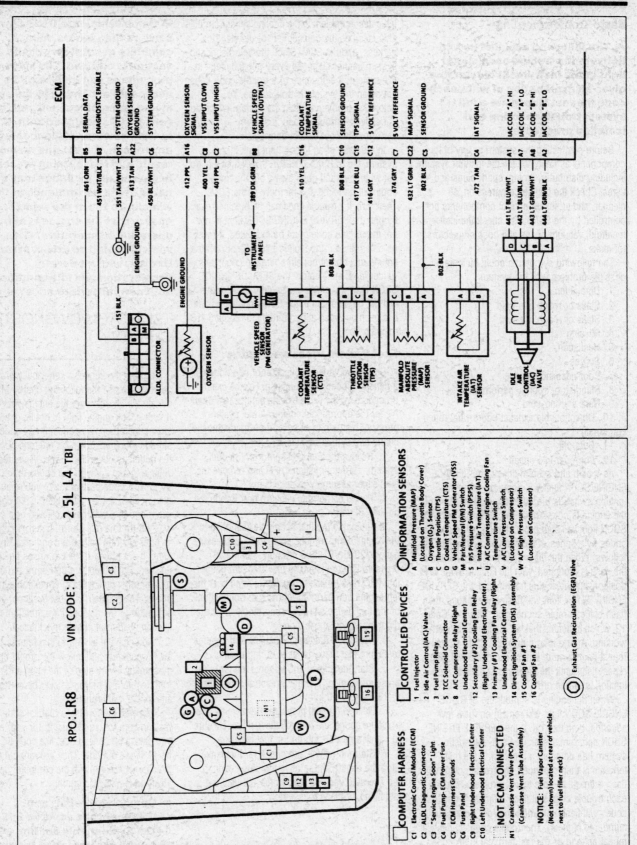

COMPUTER HARNESS

- C1 Electronic Control Module (ECM)
- C3 ALDL Diagnostic Connector
- C4 "Service Engine Soon" Light
- C5 Fuel Pump- ECM Power Fuse
- C6 ECM Harness Grounds
- C6 Fuse Panel
- C9 Right Underhood Electrical Center
- C10 Left Underhood Electrical Center

NOT ECM CONNECTED

- N1 Crankcase Vent Valve (PCV)
  (Crankcase Vent Tube Assembly)

NOTICE: Fuel Vapor Canister
(Not shown) located at rear of vehicle
next to fuel filler neck)

CONTROLLED DEVICES

- 1 Fuel Injector
- 2 Idle Air Control (IAC) Valve
- 3 Fuel Pump Relay
- 5 TCC Solenoid Connector
- 8 A/C Compressor Relay (Right Underhood Electrical Center)
- 12 Secondary (#2) Cooling Fan Relay (Right Underhood Electrical Center)
- 13 Primary (#1) Cooling Fan Relay (Right Underhood Electrical Center)
- 14 Direct Ignition System (DIS) Assembly
- 15 Cooling Fan #1
- 16 Cooling Fan #2

INFORMATION SENSORS

- A Manifold Pressure (MAP) (Located on Throttle Body Cover)
- B Oxygen (O₂) Sensor
- C Throttle Position (TPS)
- D Coolant Temperature (CTS)
- G Vehicle Speed PM Generator (VSS)
- M Park/Neutral (P/N) Switch
- S P/S Pressure Switch (PSPS)
- T Intake Air Temperature (IAT)
- U A/C Compressor/Engine Cooling Fan Temperature Switch
- V A/C Low Pressure Switch (Located on Compressor)
- W A/C High Pressure Switch (Located on Compressor)

Exhaust Gas Recirculation (EGR) Valve

THROTTLE BODY INJECTION DIAGNOSTIC CHARTS

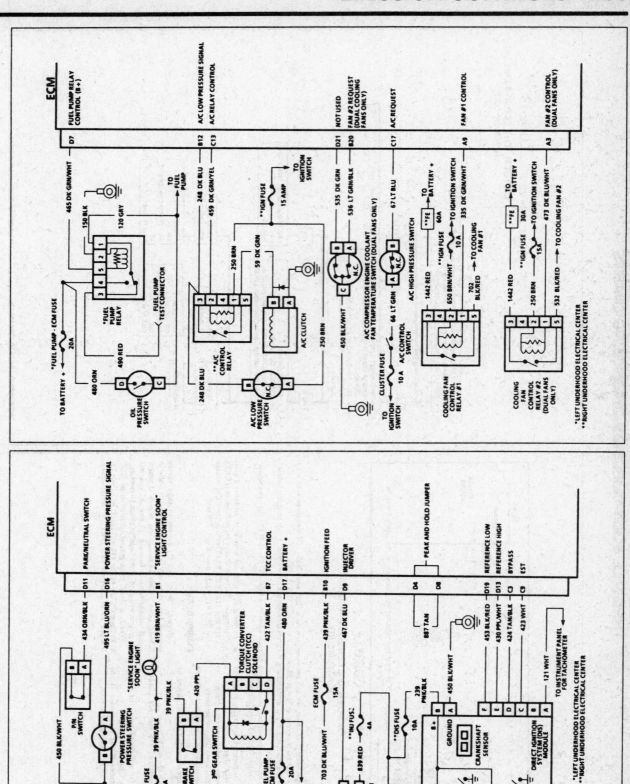

THROTTLE BODY INJECTION DIAGNOSTIC CHARTS

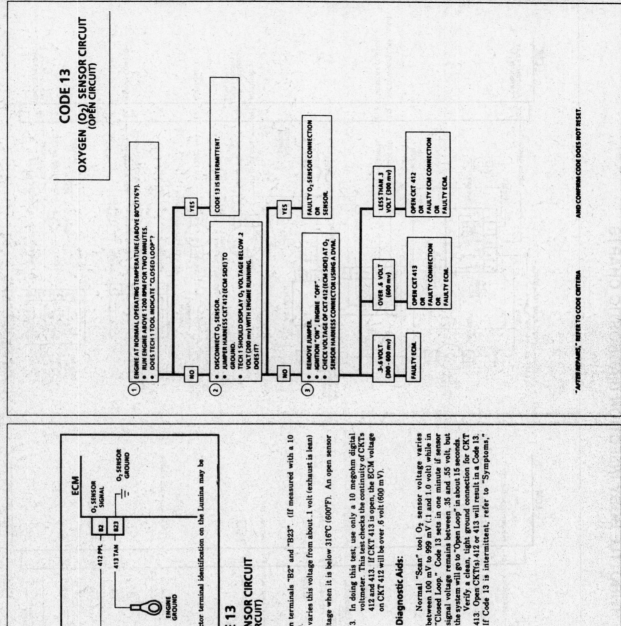

CODE 13
OXYGEN (O₂) SENSOR CIRCUIT
(OPEN CIRCUIT)

Circuit Description:

The ECM supplies a voltage of about .45 volt between terminals "B2" and "B23". (If measured with a 10 megohm digital voltmeter, this may read as low as .32 volt).

When the O₂ sensor reaches operating temperature, it varies this voltage from about .1 volt (exhaust is lean) to about .9 volt (exhaust is rich).

The sensor is like an open circuit and produces no voltage when it is below 316°C (600°F). An open sensor circuit, or cold sensor, causes "Open Loop" operation.

Test Description: Numbers below refer to circled numbers on the diagnostic chart.

1. Code 13 will set under the following conditions:
   - Engine at normal operating temperature.
   - At least 40 seconds have elapsed since engine start-up.
   - O₂ signal voltage is steady between .35 and .55 volt.
   - Throttle angle is above 7%.
   - All above conditions are met for about 4 seconds.

   If the conditions for a Code 13 exist, the system will not operate in "Closed Loop."

2. This test determines if the O₂ sensor is the problem or if the ECM and wiring are at fault.

3. In doing this test, use only a 10 megohm digital voltmeter. This test checks the continuity of CKTs 412 and 413. If CKT 413 is open, the ECM voltage on CKT 412 will be over .6 volt (600 mV).

Diagnostic Aids:

Normal "Scan" tool O₂ sensor voltage varies between 100 mV to 999 mV (.1 and 1.0 volt) while in "Closed Loop." Code 13 sets in one minute if sensor signal voltage remains between .35 and .55 volt, but the system will go to "Open Loop" in about 15 seconds.

Verify a clean, tight ground connection for CKT 413. Open CKT(s) 412 or 413 will result in a Code 13. If Code 13 is intermittent, refer to "Symptoms."

CODE 13
OXYGEN (O₂) SENSOR CIRCUIT
(OPEN CIRCUIT)

1.
   - ENGINE AT NORMAL OPERATING TEMPERATURE (ABOVE 80°C/176°F).
   - RUN ENGINE ABOVE 1200 RPM FOR TWO MINUTES.
   - DOES TECH 1 TOOL INDICATE "CLOSED LOOP"?

   NO → 2

   YES → CODE 13 IS INTERMITTENT.

2.
   - DISCONNECT O₂ SENSOR.
   - JUMPER HARNESS CKT 412 (ECM SIDE) TO GROUND.
   - TECH 1 SHOULD DISPLAY O₂ VOLTAGE BELOW .2 VOLT (200 mV) WITH ENGINE RUNNING. DOES IT?

   YES → FAULTY O₂ SENSOR CONNECTION OR SENSOR.

   NO → 3

3.
   - REMOVE JUMPER.
   - IGNITION "ON", ENGINE "OFF".
   - CHECK VOLTAGE OF CKT 412 (ECM SIDE) AT O₂ SENSOR HARNESS CONNECTOR USING A DVM.

   .3-.6 VOLT (300-600 mV) → FAULTY ECM.

   OVER .6 VOLT (600 mV) → OPEN CKT 413 OR FAULTY ECM CONNECTION OR FAULTY ECM.

   LESS THAN .3 VOLT (300 mV) → OPEN CKT 412 OR FAULTY ECM CONNECTION OR FAULTY ECM.

"AFTER REPAIRS," REFER TO CODE CRITERIA AND CONFIRM CODE DOES NOT RESET.

ECM

O₂ SENSOR SIGNAL — B2

O₂ SENSOR GROUND — B23

412 PPL

413 TAN

ENGINE GROUND

OXYGEN (O₂) SENSOR

EXHAUST

The connector terminal identification on the Lumina may be different.

THROTTLE BODY INJECTION DIAGNOSTIC CHARTS

CODE 14
COOLANT TEMPERATURE SENSOR (CTS) CIRCUIT
(HIGH TEMPERATURE INDICATED)

1. DOES TECH 1 DISPLAY COOLANT TEMPERATURE OF 130°C (266°F) OR HIGHER?

   NO → CODE 14 IS INTERMITTENT.

   YES → 2. DISCONNECT COOLANT TEMPERATURE SENSOR. TECH 1 SHOULD DISPLAY COOLANT TEMPERATURE BELOW -30°C (-22°F). DOES IT?

   YES → REPLACE COOLANT TEMPERATURE SENSOR.

   NO → CKT 410 SHORTED TO GROUND OR CKT 410 SHORTED TO SENSOR GROUND CIRCUIT OR FAULTY ECM.

DIAGNOSTIC AID

COOLANT SENSOR
TEMPERATURE VS. RESISTANCE VALUES
(APPROXIMATE)

°C	°F	OHMS
100	212	177
90	194	241
80	176	332
70	158	467
60	140	667
50	122	973
45	113	1188
40	104	1459
35	95	1802
30	86	2238
25	77	2796
20	68	3520
15	59	4450
10	50	5670
5	41	7280
0	32	9420
-5	23	12300
-10	14	16180
-15	5	21450
-20	-4	28680
-30	-22	52700
-40	-40	100700

"AFTER REPAIRS," REFER TO CODE CRITERIA AND CONFIRM CODE DOES NOT RESET.

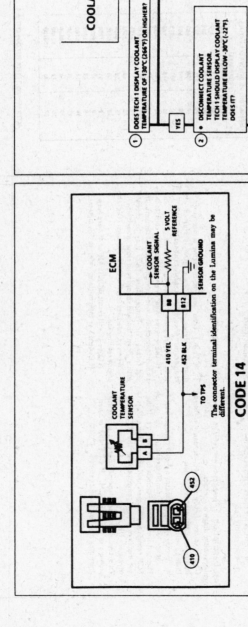

CODE 14
COOLANT TEMPERATURE SENSOR (CTS) CIRCUIT
(HIGH TEMPERATURE INDICATED)

ECM — COOLANT SENSOR SIGNAL — 5 VOLT REFERENCE — SENSOR GROUND — B8 — B12 — 410 YEL — 452 BLK — TO TPS — COOLANT TEMPERATURE SENSOR — A B

The connector terminal identification on the Lumina may be different.

Circuit Description:

The Coolant Temperature Sensor (CTS) uses a thermistor to control the signal voltage to the ECM. The ECM applies a reference voltage on CKT 410 to the sensor. When the engine is cold, the sensor (thermistor) resistance is high. The ECM will then sense a high signal voltage.

As the engine warms up, the sensor resistance decreases and the voltage drops. At normal engine operating temperature, the voltage will measure about 1.5 to 2.0 volts at ECM terminal "B8".

Coolant temperature is one of the inputs used to control the following:
- Fuel Delivery
- Electronic Spark Timing (EST)
- Cooling Fan
- Torque Converter Clutch (TCC)
- Idle Air Control (IAC)

Test Description: Numbers below refer to circled numbers on the diagnostic chart.

1. Checks to see if code was set as result of hard failure or intermittent condition.
Code 14 will set if:
- Signal voltage indicates a coolant temperature above 135°C (275°F) for 3 seconds.

2. This test simulates conditions for a Code 15. If the ECM recognizes the open circuit (high voltage) and displays a low temperature, the ECM and wiring are OK.

Diagnostic Aids:

A Tech 1 "Scan" tool reads engine temperature in degrees Celsius.

After the engine is started, the temperature should rise steadily to about 90°C (194°F), then stabilize when the thermostat opens.

If the engine has been allowed to cool to an ambient temperature (overnight), coolant temperature and Intake Air Temperature (IAT) may be checked with a "Scan" tool and should read close to each other. When a Code 14 is set, the ECM will turn "ON" the engine cooling fan.

A Code 14 will result if CKT 410 is shorted to ground.

If Code 14 is intermittent, refer to "Symptoms."

THROTTLE BODY INJECTION DIAGNOSTIC CHARTS

CODE 15
COOLANT TEMPERATURE SENSOR (CTS) CIRCUIT
(LOW TEMPERATURE INDICATED)

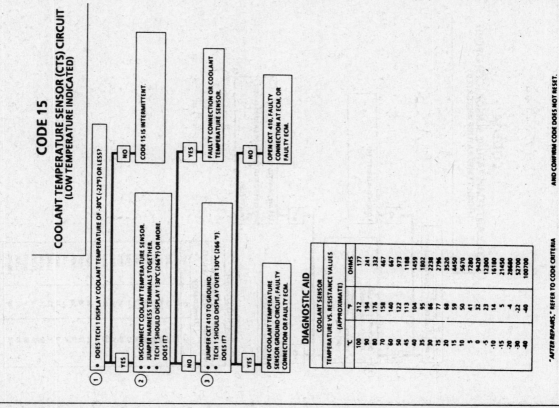

① • DOES TECH 1 DISPLAY COOLANT TEMPERATURE OF -30°C (-22°F) OR LESS?

YES → ②

NO → CODE 15 IS INTERMITTENT.

② • DISCONNECT COOLANT TEMPERATURE SENSOR.
• JUMPER HARNESS TERMINALS TOGETHER.
• TECH 1 SHOULD DISPLAY 130°C (266°F) OR MORE.
DOES IT?

YES → FAULTY CONNECTION OR COOLANT TEMPERATURE SENSOR.

NO → ③

③ • JUMPER CKT 410 TO GROUND.
• TECH 1 SHOULD DISPLAY OVER 130°C (266°F).
DOES IT?

YES → OPEN COOLANT TEMPERATURE SENSOR GROUND CIRCUIT, FAULTY CONNECTION OR FAULTY ECM.

NO → OPEN CKT 410, FAULTY CONNECTION AT ECM, OR FAULTY ECM.

DIAGNOSTIC AID

COOLANT SENSOR
TEMPERATURE VS. RESISTANCE VALUES
(APPROXIMATE)

°C	°F	OHMS
100	212	177
90	194	241
80	176	332
70	158	467
60	140	667
50	122	973
45	113	1188
40	104	1459
35	95	1802
30	86	2238
25	77	2796
20	68	3520
15	59	4450
10	50	5670
5	41	7280
0	32	9420
-5	23	12300
-10	14	16180
-15	5	21450
-20	-4	28680
-30	-22	52700
-40	-40	100700

"AFTER REPAIRS," REFER TO CODE CRITERIA AND CONFIRM CODE DOES NOT RESET.

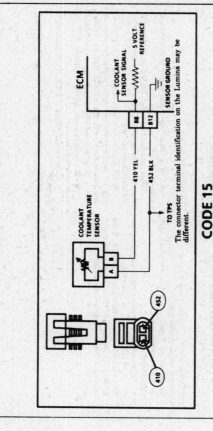

ECM

COOLANT SENSOR SIGNAL
5 VOLT REFERENCE
SENSOR GROUND
B8
B12
410 YEL
452 BLK
TO TPS

COOLANT TEMPERATURE SENSOR

The connector terminal identification on the Lumina may be different.

CODE 15
COOLANT TEMPERATURE SENSOR (CTS) CIRCUIT
(LOW TEMPERATURE INDICATED)

Circuit Description:

The Coolant Temperature Sensor (CTS) uses a thermistor to control the signal voltage to the ECM. The ECM applies a reference voltage on CKT 410 to the sensor. When the engine is cold, the sensor (thermistor) resistance is high. The ECM will then sense a high signal voltage.

As the engine warms up, the sensor resistance decreases and the voltage drops. At normal engine operating temperature, the voltage will measure about 1.5 to 2.0 volts at ECM terminal "B8".

Coolant temperature is one of the inputs used to control the following:
- Fuel Delivery
- Electronic Spark Timing (EST)
- Cooling Fan
- Torque Convertor Clutch (TCC)
- Idle Air Control (IAC)

Test Description: Numbers below refer to circled numbers on the diagnostic chart.

1. Checks to see if code was set as result of hard failure or intermittent condition. Code 15 will set if:
   - Signal voltage indicates a coolant temperature below -30°C (-22°F) for 60 seconds.
2. This test simulates conditions for a Code 14. If the ECM recognizes the grounded circuit (low voltage) and displays a high temperature, the ECM and wiring are OK.
3. This test will determine if there is a wiring problem or a faulty ECM. If CKT 452 is open, there may also be a Code 21 stored.

Diagnostic Aids:

A Tech 1 "Scan" tool reads engine temperature in degrees Celsius. After the engine is started, the temperature should rise steadily to about 90°C (194°F), then stabilize when the thermostat opens.

If the engine has been allowed to cool to an ambient temperature (overnight), coolant temperature and Intake Air Temperature (IAT) may be checked with a "Scan" tool and should read close to each other. When a Code 15 is set, the ECM will turn "ON" the engine cooling fan.

A Code 15 will result if CKTs 410 or 452 are open. If Code 15 is intermittent, refer to "Symptoms,"

THROTTLE BODY INJECTION DIAGNOSTIC CHARTS

CODE 21
THROTTLE POSITION SENSOR (TPS) CIRCUIT
(SIGNAL VOTAGE HIGH)

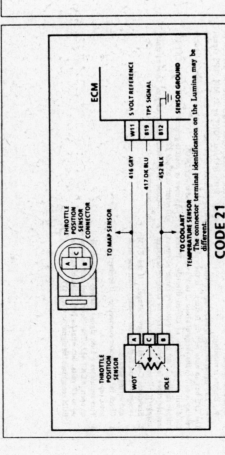

ECM

- W11 — 5 VOLT REFERENCE
- B19 — TPS SIGNAL
- B12 — SENSOR GROUND

- 416 GRY
- 417 DK BLU
- 452 BLK

THROTTLE POSITION SENSOR CONNECTOR

TO MAP SENSOR

TO COOLANT TEMPERATURE SENSOR
The connector terminal identification on the Lumina may be different.

THROTTLE POSITION SENSOR

WOT — IDLE

CODE 21
THROTTLE POSITION SENSOR (TPS) CIRCUIT
(SIGNAL VOLTAGE HIGH)

Circuit Description:
The Throttle Position Sensor (TPS) provides a voltage signal that changes relative to the throttle valve. Signal voltage will vary from about 3 to 1.3 volts at idle to about 5 volts at Wide Open Throttle (WOT).
The TPS signal is one of the most important inputs used by the ECM for fuel control and for many of the ECM controlled outputs

Test Description: Numbers below refer to circled numbers on the diagnostic chart.
1. This step checks to see if Code 21 is the result of a hard failure or an intermittent condition.
A Code 21 will set under the following conditions:
- TPS reading above 2.5 volts
- Engine speed less than 1800 rpm
- MAP reading below 60 kPa
- All of the above conditions present for at least 2 seconds.

The TPS has an auto zeroing feature. If the voltage reading is within the range of about 3 to 1.3 volts, the ECM will use that value as closed throttle. If the voltage reading is out of the auto zero range at closed throttle, check for a binding throttle cable or damaged linkage. If OK, continue with diagnosis.
2. This step simulates conditions for a Code 22. If the ECM recognizes the change of state, the ECM and CKTs 416 and 417 are OK.
3. This step isolates a faulty sensor, ECM, or an open CKT 452. If CKT 452 is open, there may also be a Code 15 stored.

Diagnostic Aids:
A Tech 1 "Scan" tool displays throttle position in volts. Closed throttle voltage should be 3 to 1.3 volts. TPS voltage should increase at a steady rate as throttle is moved toward WOT
A Code 21 will result if CKT 452 is open or CKT 417 is shorted to voltage. If Code 21 is intermittent, refer to "Intermittents" in "Symptoms."

---

① THROTTLE CLOSED.
DOES TECH 1 DISPLAY THROTTLE POSITION OVER 2.5 VOLTS?

- YES
- NO → CODE 21 IS INTERMITTENT.

② DISCONNECT THROTTLE POSITION SENSOR. TECH 1 SHOULD DISPLAY THROTTLE POSITION BELOW .2 VOLT (200mv). DOES IT?

- YES
- NO → TPS SIGNAL CIRCUIT SHORTED TO VOLTAGE OR FAULTY ECM.

③ PROBE SENSOR GROUND CIRCUIT WITH A TEST LIGHT CONNECTED TO BATTERY VOLTAGE.

- LIGHT "ON" → FAULTY CONNECTION OR THROTTLE POSITION SENSOR.
- LIGHT "OFF" → OPEN SENSOR GROUND CIRCUIT OR FAULTY ECM.

" AFTER REPAIRS," REFER TO CODE CRITERIA AND CONFIRM CODE DOES NOT RESET.

THROTTLE BODY INJECTION DIAGNOSTIC CHARTS

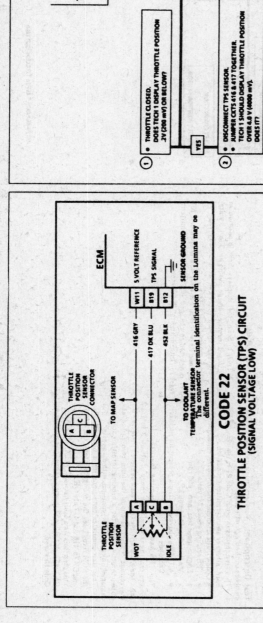

ECM

5 VOLT REFERENCE — W11 — 416 GRY
TPS SIGNAL — B19 — 417 DK BLU
SENSOR GROUND — B12 — 452 BLK

THROTTLE POSITION SENSOR CONNECTOR

TO MAP SENSOR

TO COOLANT TEMPERATURE SENSOR
The connector terminal identification on the Lumina may be different.

THROTTLE POSITION SENSOR

WOT   IDLE

CODE 22
THROTTLE POSITION SENSOR (TPS) CIRCUIT
(SIGNAL VOLTAGE LOW)

Circuit Description:

The Throttle Position Sensor (TPS) provides a voltage signal that changes relative to the throttle valve. Signal voltage will vary from about .3 to 1.3 volts at idle to about 5 volts at Wide Open Throttle (WOT).

The TPS signal is one of the most important inputs used by the ECM for fuel control and for many of the ECM controlled outputs.

Test Description: Numbers below refer to circled numbers on the diagnostic chart.

1. Code 22 will set if:
   • Engine is running
   • TPS signal voltage is less than .20 volt.

The TPS has an auto zeroing feature. If the voltage reading is within the range of about .3 to 1.3 volts, the ECM will use that value as closed throttle. If the voltage reading is out of the auto zero range at closed throttle, check for a binding throttle cable or damaged linkage, if OK, continue with diagnosis.

2. Simulates Code 21: (high voltage). If the ECM recognizes the high signal voltage then the ECM and wiring are OK.

3. Check for good sensor connection. If connection is good, replace TPS.

4. This simulates a high signal voltage to check for an open in CKT 417. The "Scan" tool will not read up to 12 volts, but what is important is that the ECM recognizes the signal on CKT 417.

Diagnostic Aids:

A Tech 1 "Scan" tool reads throttle position in volts. With ignition "ON" or at idle, TPS signal voltage should read from about .3 to 1.3 volts with the throttle closed and increase at a steady rate as throttle is moved toward WOT.

An open or short to ground in CKT 416 or CKT 417 will result in a Code 22.

If Code 22 is intermittent, refer to "Intermittents" in "Symptoms."

CODE 22
THROTTLE POSITION SENSOR (TPS) CIRCUIT
(SIGNAL VOLTAGE LOW)

① THROTTLE CLOSED. DOES TECH 1 DISPLAY THROTTLE POSITION .21V (200 mV) OR BELOW?

- YES →
- NO → • CODE 22 IS INTERMITTENT.

② DISCONNECT TPS SENSOR. JUMPER CKTS 416 & 417 TOGETHER. TECH 1 SHOULD DISPLAY THROTTLE POSITION OVER 4.8 V (4800 mV). DOES IT?

- YES →
- NO →

④ PROBE CKT 417 WITH A TEST LIGHT CONNECTED TO BATTERY VOLTAGE. TECH 1 SHOULD DISPLAY THROTTLE POSITION OVER 4.8V (4800 mV). DOES IT?

- YES → CKT 416 OPEN OR SHORTED TO GROUND OR FAULTY CONNECTION OR FAULTY ECM.
- NO → CKT 417 OPEN OR SHORTED TO GROUND, OR SHORTED TO THROTTLE POSITION SENSOR GROUND CIRCUIT OR FAULTY ECM CONNECTION OR FAULTY ECM.

"AFTER REPAIRS," REFER TO CODE CRITERIA AND CONFIRM CODE DOES NOT RESET.

THROTTLE BODY INJECTION DIAGNOSTIC CHARTS

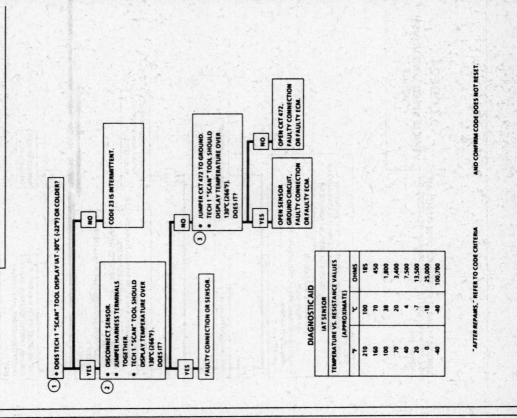

CODE 23
INTAKE AIR TEMPERATURE (IAT) SENSOR CIRCUIT
(LOW TEMPERATURE INDICATED)

① DOES TECH 1 "SCAN" TOOL DISPLAY IAT -30°C (-22°F) OR COLDER?

NO → CODE 23 IS INTERMITTENT.

YES ↓

② • DISCONNECT SENSOR.
• JUMPER HARNESS TERMINALS TOGETHER.
• TECH 1 "SCAN" TOOL SHOULD DISPLAY TEMPERATURE OVER 130°C (266°F).
DOES IT?

YES → FAULTY CONNECTION OR SENSOR.

NO ↓

③ • JUMPER CKT 472 TO GROUND.
• TECH 1 "SCAN" TOOL SHOULD DISPLAY TEMPERATURE OVER 130°C (266°F).
DOES IT?

YES → OPEN SENSOR GROUND CIRCUIT, FAULTY CONNECTION OR FAULTY ECM.

NO → OPEN CKT 472, FAULTY CONNECTION OR FAULTY ECM.

DIAGNOSTIC AID

IAT SENSOR
TEMPERATURE VS. RESISTANCE VALUES
(APPROXIMATE)

°F	°C	OHMS
210	100	185
160	70	450
100	38	1,800
70	20	3,400
40	4	7,500
20	-7	13,500
0	-18	25,000
-40	-40	100,700

"AFTER REPAIRS," REFER TO CODE CRITERIA AND CONFIRM CODE DOES NOT RESET.

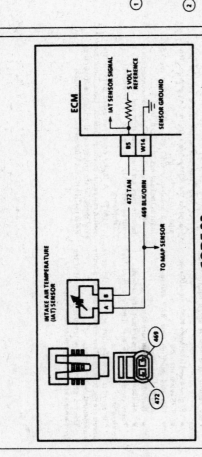

ECM

IAT SENSOR SIGNAL
5 VOLT REFERENCE
SENSOR GROUND

B5
W14

472 TAN
469 BLK/ORN

TO MAP SENSOR

INTAKE AIR TEMPERATURE (IAT) SENSOR

469
472

CODE 23
INTAKE AIR TEMPERATURE (IAT) SENSOR CIRCUIT
(LOW TEMPERATURE INDICATED)

Circuit Description:

The Intake Air Temperature (IAT) sensor, located on the intake manifold, uses a thermistor to control the signal voltage to the ECM. The ECM applies a reference voltage (4-5.5 volts) on CKT 472 to the sensor. When intake air is cold, the sensor (thermistor) resistance is high. The ECM will then sense a high signal voltage. As the air warms, the sensor resistance becomes less and the voltage drops.

Test Description: Numbers below refer to circled numbers on the diagnostic chart.

1. This step determines if Code 23 is the result of a hard failure or an intermittent condition. Code 23 will set when signal voltage indicates a IAT/MAT temperature less than -30°C and the engine is running for longer than 58 seconds.

2. This test simulates conditions for a Code 25. If the "Scan" tool displays a high temperature, the ECM and wiring are OK.

3. This step checks continuity of CKTs 472 and 469. If CKT 469 is open there may also be a Code 33.

Diagnostic Aids:

If the engine has been allowed to cool to an ambient temperature (overnight), coolant and IAT/MAT temperatures may be checked with a Tech 1 "Scan" tool and should read close to each other.

A Code 23 will result if CKT 472 or 469 becomes open.

If Code 23 is intermittent, refer to "Symptoms."

THROTTLE BODY INJECTION DIAGNOSTIC CHARTS

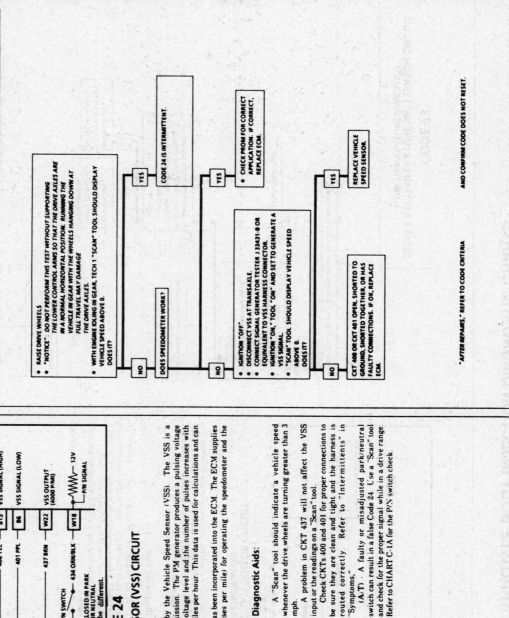

CODE 24
VEHICLE SPEED SENSOR (VSS) CIRCUIT

DISREGARD CODE 24 IF SET WHILE DRIVE WHEELS ARE NOT TURNING. REFER TO "DIAGNOSTIC AIDS" ON FACING PAGE.

- RAISE DRIVE WHEELS
- "NOTICE" - DO NOT PERFORM THIS TEST WITHOUT SUPPORTING THE LOWER CONTROL ARMS SO THAT THE DRIVE AXLES ARE IN A NORMAL HORIZONTAL POSITION. RUNNING THE VEHICLE IN GEAR WITH THE WHEELS HANGING DOWN AT FULL TRAVEL MAY DAMAGE THE DRIVE AXLES.
- WITH ENGINE IDLING IN GEAR, TECH 1 "SCAN" TOOL SHOULD DISPLAY VEHICLE SPEED ABOVE 0.

DOES IT?

NO → DOES SPEEDOMETER WORK?

YES → CODE 24 IS INTERMITTENT.

DOES SPEEDOMETER WORK?

YES → • CHECK PROM FROM CORRECT APPLICATION. IF CORRECT, REPLACE ECM.

NO
- IGNITION "OFF".
- DISCONNECT VSS AT TRANSAXLE.
- CONNECT SIGNAL GENERATOR TESTER J 33431-B OR EQUIVALENT TO VSS HARNESS CONNECTOR.
- IGNITION "ON", "TOOL ON" AND SET TO GENERATE A VSS SIGNAL.
- "SCAN" TOOL SHOULD DISPLAY VEHICLE SPEED ABOVE 0.

DOES IT?

YES → REPLACE VEHICLE SPEED SENSOR.

NO → CKT 400 OR CKT 401 OPEN, SHORTED TO GROUND, SHORTED TOGETHER, OR HAS FAULTY CONNECTIONS. IF OK, REPLACE ECM.

"AFTER REPAIRS," • REFER TO CODE CRITERIA AND CONFIRM CODE DOES NOT RESET.

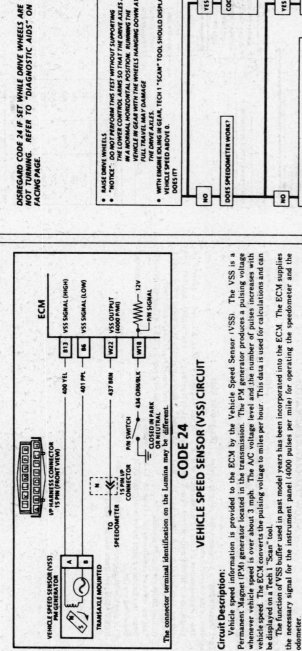

VEHICLE SPEED SENSOR (VSS) PM GENERATOR

V/P HARNESS CONNECTOR 15 PIN (FRONT VIEW)

TRANSAXLE MOUNTED

TO SPEEDOMETER

15 PIN V/P CONNECTOR

ECM

B13	400 YEL	VSS SIGNAL (HIGH)
B6	401 PPL	VSS SIGNAL (LOW)
W22	437 BRN	VSS OUTPUT (4000 P/MI)
W18	434 ORN/BLK	12V / P/N SIGNAL

P/N SWITCH

CLOSED IN PARK OR NEUTRAL

The connector terminal identification on the Lumina may be different.

CODE 24
VEHICLE SPEED SENSOR (VSS) CIRCUIT

Circuit Description:

Vehicle speed information is provided to the ECM by the Vehicle Speed Sensor (VSS). The VSS is a Permanent Magnet (PM) generator located in the transmission. The PM generator produces a pulsing voltage whenever vehicle speed is over about 3 mph. The A/C voltage level and the number of pulses increases with vehicle speed. The ECM converts the pulsing voltage to miles per hour. This data is used for calculations and can be displayed on a Tech 1 "Scan" tool.

The function of VSS buffer used in past model years has been incorporated into the ECM. The ECM supplies the necessary signal for the instrument panel (4000 pulses per mile) for operating the speedometer and the odometer.

Test Description:

Code 24 will set if vehicle speed equals 0 mph when:

- Engine speed is between 1500 and 4400 rpm
- TPS is less than 2%
- Low load condition (low MAP voltage, high manifold vacuum)
- Transmission not in park or neutral
- All above conditions are met for 4 seconds.

These conditions are met during a road load deceleration.

Disregard a Code 24 that sets when the drive wheels are not turning. This can be caused by a faulty park/neutral switch circuit.

The PM generator only produces a signal if the drive wheels are turning greater than 3 mph.

Diagnostic Aids:

A "Scan" tool should indicate a vehicle speed whenever the drive wheels are turning greater than 3 mph.

A problem in CKT 437 will not affect the VSS input or the readings on a "Scan" tool.

Check CKTs 400 and 401 for proper connections to be sure they are clean and tight and the harness is routed correctly. Refer to "Intermittents" in "Symptoms."

(A/T) - A faulty or misadjusted park/neutral switch can result in a false Code 24. Use a "Scan" tool and check for the proper signal while in a drive range. Refer to CHART C-1A for the P/N switch check.

THROTTLE BODY INJECTION DIAGNOSTIC CHARTS

CODE 25

INTAKE AIR TEMPERATURE (IAT) SENSOR CIRCUIT
(HIGH TEMPERATURE INDICATED)

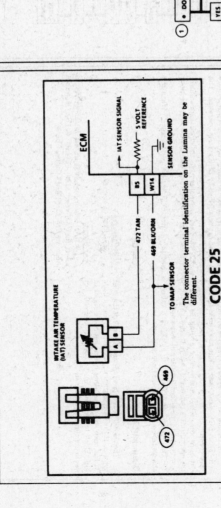

ECM

IAT SENSOR SIGNAL
5 VOLT REFERENCE
SENSOR GROUND

B5
W14

472 TAN
469 BLK/ORN

TO MAP SENSOR

INTAKE AIR TEMPERATURE (IAT) SENSOR

A   B

469
472

The connector terminal identification on the Lumina may be different.

CODE 25

INTAKE AIR TEMPERATURE (IAT) SENSOR CIRCUIT
(HIGH TEMPERATURE INDICATED)

Circuit Description:

The Intake Air Temperature (IAT) sensor, located on the intake manifold, uses a thermistor to control the signal voltage to the ECM. The ECM applies a reference voltage (4-5.5 volts) on CKT 472 to the sensor. When intake air is cold, the sensor (thermistor) resistance is high. Therefore, the ECM will see a high signal voltage. As the air warms, the sensor resistance becomes less and the voltage drops.

Test Description: Numbers below refer to circled numbers on the diagnostic chart.

1. This check determines if the Code 25 is the result of a hard failure or an intermittent condition. Code 25 will set if a IAT/MAT temperature greater than 135°C is detected for a time longer than 2 seconds and the ignition is "ON."

Diagnostic Aids:

If the engine has been allowed to cool to an ambient temperature (overnight), coolant and IAT/MAT temperatures may be checked with a Tech 1 "Scan" tool and should read close to each other.

A Code 25 will result if CKT 472 is shorted to ground.

If Code 25 is intermittent, refer to "Intermittent" in "Symptoms."

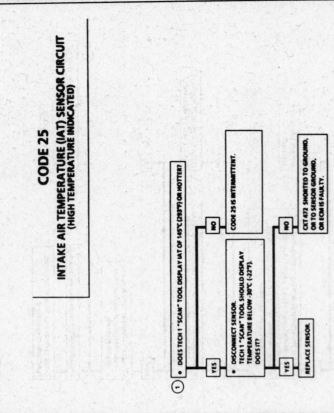

① • DOES TECH 1 "SCAN" TOOL DISPLAY IAT OF 145°C (293°F) OR HOTTER?

YES → • DISCONNECT SENSOR.
TECH 1 "SCAN" TOOL SHOULD DISPLAY TEMPERATURE BELOW -30°C (-22°F).
DOES IT?

NO → CODE 25 IS INTERMITTENT.

YES → REPLACE SENSOR.

NO → CKT 472 SHORTED TO GROUND, OR TO SENSOR GROUND, OR ECM IS FAULTY.

"AFTER REPAIRS," REFER TO CODE CRITERIA AND CONFIRM CODE DOES NOT RESET.

DIAGNOSTIC AID

IAT SENSOR	
TEMPERATURE VS. RESISTANCE VALUES (APPROXIMATE)	
°C	OHMS
°F	

°F	°C	OHMS
210	100	185
160	70	450
100	38	1,800
70	20	3,400
40	4	7,500
20	-7	13,500
0	-18	25,000
-40	-40	100,700

THROTTLE BODY INJECTION DIAGNOSTIC CHARTS

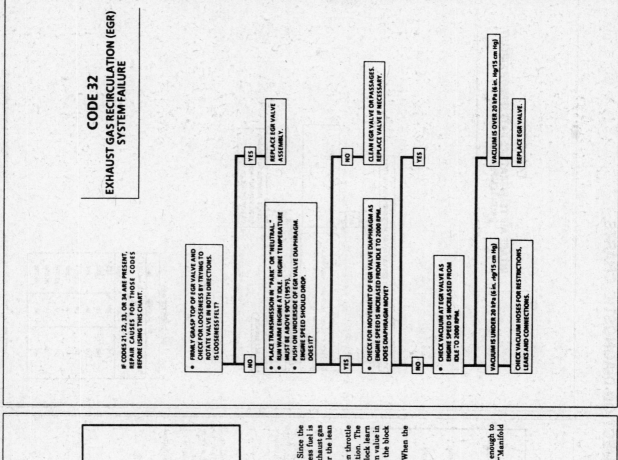

CODE 32

EXHAUST GAS RECIRCULATION (EGR) SYSTEM FAILURE

IF CODES 21, 22, 23, OR 34 ARE PRESENT, REPAIR CAUSES FOR THOSE CODES BEFORE USING THIS CHART.

- FIRMLY GRASP TOP OF EGR VALVE AND CHECK FOR LOOSENESS BY TRYING TO ROTATE VALVE IN BOTH DIRECTIONS. IS LOOSENESS FELT?

YES → REPLACE EGR VALVE ASSEMBLY.

NO

- PLACE TRANSMISSION IN "PARK" OR "NEUTRAL." RUN WARM ENGINE AT IDLE. ENGINE TEMPERATURE MUST BE ABOVE 90°C (195°F).
- PUSH ON UNDERSIDE OF EGR VALVE DIAPHRAGM. ENGINE SPEED SHOULD DROP. DOES IT?

NO → CLEAN EGR VALVE OR PASSAGES. REPLACE VALVE IF NECESSARY.

YES

- CHECK FOR MOVEMENT OF EGR VALVE DIAPHRAGM AS ENGINE SPEED IS INCREASED FROM IDLE TO 2000 RPM. DOES DIAPHRAGM MOVE?

YES → VACUUM IS OVER 20 kPa (6 in. Hg/15 cm Hg) → REPLACE EGR VALVE.

NO

- CHECK VACUUM AT EGR VALVE AS ENGINE SPEED IS INCREASED FROM IDLE TO 2000 RPM.

VACUUM IS UNDER 20 kPa (6 in. Hg/15 cm Hg) → CHECK VACUUM HOSES FOR RESTRICTIONS, LEAKS AND CONNECTORS.

CODE 32

EXHAUST GAS RECIRCULATION (EGR) SYSTEM FAILURE

Circuit Description:

A properly operating EGR system will directly affect the air/fuel requirements of the engine. Since the exhaust gas introduced into the air/fuel mixture is an inert gas (contains very little or no oxygen), less fuel is required to maintain a correct air/fuel ratio. If the EGR system were to become inoperative, the inert exhaust gas would be replaced with air and the air/fuel mixture would be leaner. The ECM would compensate for the lean condition by adding fuel, resulting in higher block learn values.

The engine control system operates within two block learn cells, a closed throttle cell, and an open throttle cell. Since EGR is not used at idle, the closed throttle cell would not be affected by EGR system operation. The open throttle cell is affected by EGR operation and, when the EGR system is operating properly, the block learn values in both cells should be close to being the same. If the EGR system was inoperative, the block learn value in the open throttle cell would change (become higher) to compensate for the resulting lean system, but the block learn value in the closed throttle cell would not change.

This change or difference in block learn values is used to monitor EGR system performance. When the change becomes too great, a Code 32 is set.

Diagnostic Aids:

The Code 32 chart is a functional check of the EGR system. If the EGR system works properly, but a Code 32 has been set, check other items that could result in high block learn values in the open throttle cell, but not in the closed throttle cell.

CHECK:

EGR Passages
Restricted or blocked

MAP Sensor
A MAP sensor may shift in calibration enough to affect fuel delivery. Use CHART C-1D, "Manifold Absolute Pressure (MAP) Output Check."

EGR VALVE

PORTED VACUUM

TO INTAKE

EXHAUST

TBI UNIT

THROTTLE BODY INJECTION DIAGNOSTIC CHARTS

CODE 33

MANIFOLD ABSOLUTE PRESSURE (MAP) SENSOR CIRCUIT
(SIGNAL VOLTAGE HIGH - LOW VACUUM)

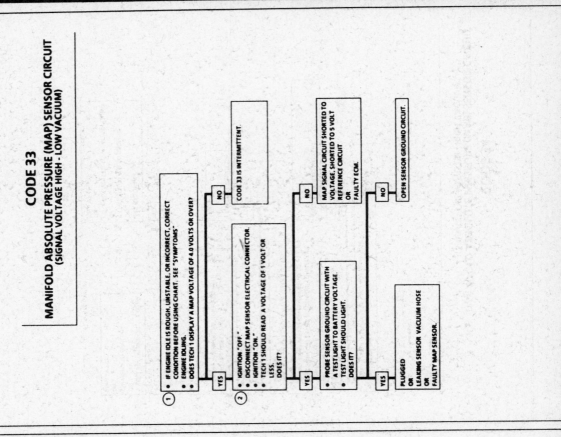

①
- IF ENGINE IDLE IS ROUGH, UNSTABLE, OR INCORRECT, CORRECT CONDITION BEFORE USING CHART. SEE "SYMPTOMS"
- ENGINE IDLING.
- DOES TECH 1 DISPLAY A MAP VOLTAGE OF 4.0 VOLTS OR OVER?

NO → CODE 33 IS INTERMITTENT.

YES ↓

②
- IGNITION "OFF."
- DISCONNECT MAP SENSOR ELECTRICAL CONNECTOR.
- IGNITION "ON."
- TECH 1 SHOULD READ A VOLTAGE OF 1 VOLT OR LESS.
- DOES IT?

NO → MAP SIGNAL CIRCUIT SHORTED TO VOLTAGE, SHORTED TO 5 VOLT REFERENCE CIRCUIT OR FAULTY ECM.

YES ↓

- PROBE SENSOR GROUND CIRCUIT WITH A TEST LIGHT TO BATTERY VOLTAGE.
- TEST LIGHT SHOULD LIGHT.
- DOES IT?

NO → OPEN SENSOR GROUND CIRCUIT.

YES ↓

PLUGGED OR LEAKING SENSOR VACUUM HOSE OR FAULTY MAP SENSOR.

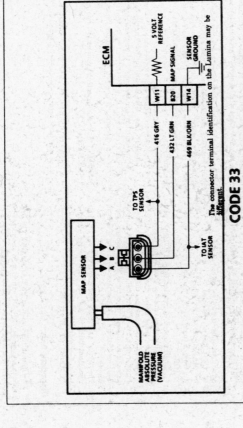

CODE 33

MANIFOLD ABSOLUTE PRESSURE (MAP) SENSOR CIRCUIT
(SIGNAL VOLTAGE HIGH - LOW VACUUM)

Circuit Description:

The Manifold Absolute Pressure (MAP) sensor, located on the air cleaner assembly, responds to changes in manifold pressure (vacuum). The ECM receives this information as a signal voltage that will vary from about 1 to 1.5 volts at closed throttle (idle) to 4.5-4.8 volts at wide open throttle (low vacuum).

If the MAP sensor fails, the ECM will substitute a fixed MAP value and use the Throttle Position Sensor (TPS) to control fuel delivery.

Test Description: Numbers below refer to circled numbers on the diagnostic chart.

1. This step will determine if Code 33 is the result of a hard failure or an intermittent condition.
   A Code 33 will set under the following conditions:
   - MAP signal voltage is too high (low vacuum).
   - TPS less than 2%.
   - These conditions exist longer than 5 seconds.
2. This step simulates conditions for a Code 34. If the ECM recognizes the change, the ECM and CKTs 416 and 432 are OK.

Diagnostic Aids:

With the ignition "ON" and the engine stopped, the manifold pressure is equal to atmospheric pressure and the signal voltage will be high. This information is used by the ECM as an indication of vehicle altitude. Comparison of this reading with a known good vehicle with the same sensor is a good way to check accuracy of a "suspect" sensor. Readings should be the same ± .4 volt.

A Code 33 will result if CKT 469 is open or if CKT 432 is shorted to voltage or to CKT 416.
If Code 33 is intermittent, refer to "Intermittent" in "Symptoms."
- Check all connections.
- Disconnect sensor from bracket and twist sensor (by hand only) to check for intermittent connections. Output changes greater than .1 volt indicates a faulty connector or connection. If OK, replace sensor.

NOTE: Make sure electrical connector remains securely fastened.

- Refer to CHART C-1D, MAP sensor voltage vs. atmospheric pressure for further diagnosis.

THROTTLE BODY INJECTION DIAGNOSTIC CHARTS

CODE 34

MANIFOLD ABSOLUTE PRESSURE (MAP) SENSOR CIRCUIT
(SIGNAL VOLTAGE LOW - HIGH VACUUM)

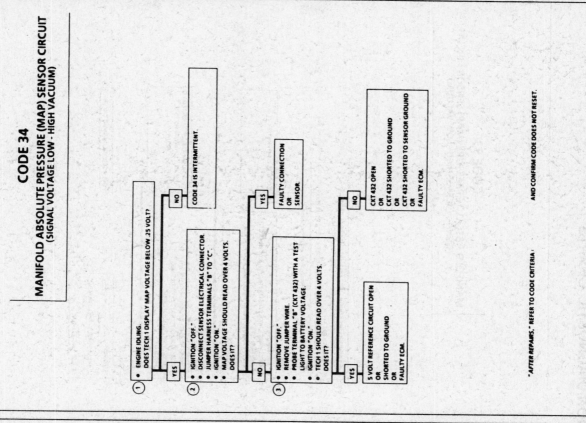

① ENGINE IDLING.
• DOES TECH 1 DISPLAY MAP VOLTAGE BELOW .25 VOLT?

YES / NO → CODE 34 IS INTERMITTENT.

② • IGNITION "OFF."
• DISCONNECT SENSOR ELECTRICAL CONNECTOR.
• JUMPER HARNESS TERMINALS "B" TO "C".
• IGNITION "ON."
• MAP VOLTAGE SHOULD READ OVER 4 VOLTS.
• DOES IT?

YES → FAULTY CONNECTION OR SENSOR.

NO

③ • IGNITION "OFF."
• REMOVE JUMPER WIRE.
• PROBE TERMINAL "B" (CKT 432) WITH A TEST LIGHT TO BATTERY VOLTAGE.
• IGNITION "ON."
• TECH 1 SHOULD READ OVER 4 VOLTS.
• DOES IT?

YES → 5 VOLT REFERENCE CIRCUIT OPEN
OR
SHORTED TO GROUND
OR
FAULTY ECM.

NO → CKT 432 OPEN
OR
CKT 432 SHORTED TO GROUND
OR
CKT 432 SHORTED TO SENSOR GROUND
OR
FAULTY ECM.

*"AFTER REPAIRS," "REFER TO CODE CRITERIA AND CONFIRM CODE DOES NOT RESET.

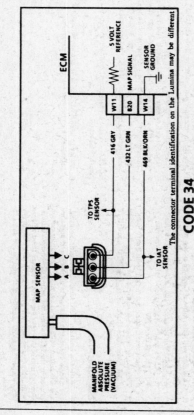

The connector terminal identification on the Lumina may be different

CODE 34

MANIFOLD ABSOLUTE PRESSURE (MAP) SENSOR CIRCUIT
(SIGNAL VOLTAGE LOW - HIGH VACUUM)

Circuit Description:

The Manifold Absolute Pressure (MAP) sensor, located on the air cleaner assembly, responds to changes in manifold pressure (vacuum). The ECM receives this information as a signal voltage that will vary from about 1 to 1.5 volts at closed throttle (idle) to 4.5 - 4.8 volts at wide open throttle (low vacuum).

If the MAP sensor fails, the ECM will substitute a fixed MAP value and use the Throttle Position Sensor (TPS) to control fuel delivery.

Test Description: Numbers below refer to circled numbers on the diagnostic chart.

1. This step determines if Code 34 is the result of a hard failure or an intermittent condition. A Code 34 will set under the following conditions:
   • Code 21 is not detected.
   • MAP signal voltage is too low.
   • Engine speed is less than 1200 rpm.
   OR
   • Engine speed is greater than 1200 rpm and throttle angle is greater than 20%.
   • All conditions above have been present for a period of time greater than .02 second.
2. Jumpering harness terminals "B" to "C" (5 volts to signal circuit) will determine if the sensor is at fault, or if there is a problem with the ECM or wiring.
3. The "Scan" tool may not display 5 volts. The important thing is that the ECM recognizes the voltage as more than 4 volts, indicating that the ECM and CKT 432 are OK.

Diagnostic Aids:

An intermittent open in CKT 432 or CKT 416 will result in a Code 34. If CKT 416 is open or shorted to ground, there may also be a stored Code 22.

With the ignition "ON" and the engine "OFF," the manifold pressure is equal to atmospheric pressure and the signal voltage will be high. This information is used by the ECM as an indication of vehicle altitude.

Comparison of this reading with a known good vehicle with the same sensor is a good way to check accuracy of a "suspect" sensor. Readings should be the same ± 4 volts. Also CHART C-1D can be used to test the MAP sensor. Refer to "Intermittents" in "Symptoms."

• Check all connections.
• Disconnect sensor from bracket and twist sensor (by hand only) to check for intermittent connections. Output changes greater than .1 volt indicates a faulty connector or connection. If OK, replace sensor.

NOTE: Make sure electrical connector remains securely fastened.

• Refer to CHART C-1D. MAP sensor voltage vs. atmospheric pressure for further diagnosis.

THROTTLE BODY INJECTION DIAGNOSTIC CHARTS

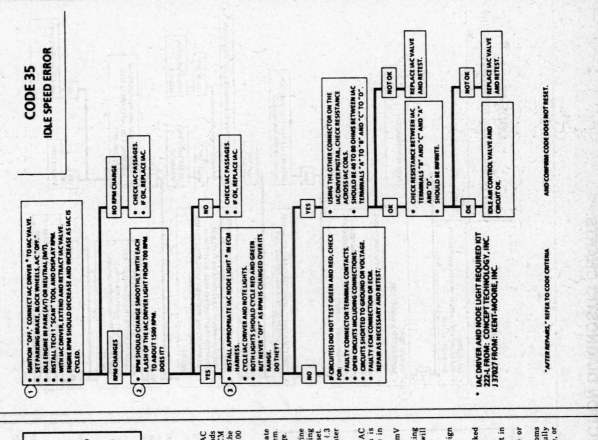

CODE 35
IDLE SPEED ERROR

1
- IGNITION "OFF." CONNECT IAC DRIVER * TO IAC VALVE.
- SET PARKING BRAKE. BLOCK WHEELS. A/C "OFF."
- IDLE ENGINE IN PARK (A/T) OR NEUTRAL (M/T).
- INSTALL TECH 1 "SCAN" TOOL AND DISPLAY RPM.
- WITH IAC DRIVER, EXTEND AND RETRACT IAC VALVE.
- ENGINE RPM SHOULD DECREASE AND INCREASE AS IAC IS CYCLED.

→ RPM CHANGES

→ NO RPM CHANGE
- CHECK IAC PASSAGES.
- IF OK, REPLACE IAC.

2
- RPM SHOULD CHANGE SMOOTHLY WITH EACH FLASH OF THE IAC DRIVER LIGHT FROM 700 RPM TO ABOUT 1500 RPM.
  DOES IT?

→ YES

→ NO
- CHECK IAC PASSAGES.
- IF OK, REPLACE IAC.

3
- INSTALL APPROPRIATE IAC NODE LIGHT * IN ECM HARNESS.
- CYCLE IAC DRIVER AND NOTE LIGHTS.
- BOTH LIGHTS SHOULD CYCLE RED AND GREEN BUT NEVER "OFF" AS RPM IS CHANGED OVER ITS RANGE.
  DO THEY?

→ YES
- USING THE OTHER CONNECTOR ON THE IAC DRIVER PIGTAIL, CHECK RESISTANCE ACROSS IAC COILS.
- SHOULD BE 40 TO 80 OHMS BETWEEN IAC TERMINALS "A" TO "B" AND "C" TO "D".

  → OK
  - CHECK RESISTANCE BETWEEN IAC TERMINALS "B" AND "C" AND "A" AND "D".
  - SHOULD BE INFINITE.

    → OK
    - IDLE AIR CONTROL VALVE AND CIRCUIT OK.

    → NOT OK
    - REPLACE IAC VALVE AND RETEST.

  → NOT OK
  - REPLACE IAC VALVE AND RETEST.

→ NO
- IF CIRCUIT(S) DID NOT TEST GREEN AND RED, CHECK FOR:
  - FAULTY CONNECTOR TERMINAL CONTACTS.
  - OPEN CIRCUITS INCLUDING CONNECTIONS.
  - CIRCUITS SHORTED TO GROUND OR VOLTAGE.
  - FAULTY ECM CONNECTION OR ECM.
  - REPAIR AS NECESSARY AND RETEST.

- IAC DRIVER AND NODE LIGHT REQUIRED KIT 222-L FROM: CONCEPT TECHNOLOGY, INC. J 37027 FROM: KENT-MOORE, INC.

*AFTER REPAIRS, * REFER TO CODE CRITERIA   AND CONFIRM CODE DOES NOT RESET.

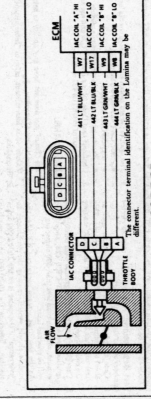

ECM

W7	IAC COIL "A" HI
W17	IAC COIL "A" LO
W3	IAC COIL "B" HI
W8	IAC COIL "B" LO

441 LT BLU/WHT
442 LT BLU/BLK
443 LT GRN/WHT
444 LT GRN/BLK

IAC CONNECTOR

THROTTLE BODY

AIR FLOW

The connector terminal identification on the Lumina may be different.

CODE 35

IDLE SPEED ERROR

Circuit Description:

The ECM controls engine idle speed with the IAC valve. To increase idle speed, the ECM retracts the IAC valve pintle away from its seat, allowing more air to bypass the throttle bore. To decrease idle speed, it extends the IAC valve pintle towards its seats, reducing bypass air flow. A Tech 1 "Scan" tool will read the ECM commands to the IAC valve in counts. Higher the counts indicate more air bypass (higher idle). The lower the counts indicate less air is allowed by bypass (lower idle.) Code 35 will be set when the closed throttle speed is 100 rpm above or below the desired idle speed for 2.5 seconds.

Test Description: Numbers below refer to circled numbers on the diagnostic chart.

1. The IAC tester is used to extend and retract the IAC valve. Valve movement is verified by an engine speed change. If no change in engine speed occurs, the valve can be retested when removed from the throttle body.

2. This step checks the quality of the IAC movement in step 1. Between 700 rpm and about 1500 rpm, the engine speed should change smoothly with each flash of the tester light in both extend and retract. If the IAC valve is retracted beyond the control range (about 1500 rpm), it may take many flashes in the extend position before engine speed will begin to drop. This is normal on certain engines, fully extending IAC may cause engine stall. This may be normal.

3. Steps 1 and 2 verified proper IAC valve operation. This step checks the IAC circuits. Each lamp on the node light should flash red and green while the IAC valve is cycled. While the sequence of color is not important if either light is "OFF" or does not flash red and green, check the circuits for faults beginning with poor terminal contacts.

Diagnostic Aids:

A slow, unstable, or fast idle may be caused by a non-IAC system problem that cannot be overcome by the IAC valve. Out of control range IAC "Scan" tool counts will be above 60 if idle is too low, and zero counts if idle is too high. The following checks should be made to repair a non-IAC system problem:

- **Vacuum Leak (High Idle)** —
  If idle is too high, stop the engine. Fully extend (low) IAC with tester.

Start engine. If idle speed is above 800 rpm, locate and correct vacuum leak including PCV system. Also check for binding of throttle blade or linkage.

- **System too lean (High Air/Fuel Ratio)**
  The idle speed may be too high or too low. Engine speed may vary up and down and disconnecting the IAC valve does not help. Code 44 may be set. "Scan" O₂ voltage will be less than 300 mV (.3 volt). Check for low regulated fuel pressure, water in the fuel or a restricted injector.

- **System too rich (Low Air/Fuel Ratio)**
  The idle speed will be too low. "Scan" tool IAC counts will usually be above 80. System is obviously rich and may exhibit black smoke in exhaust. "Scan" cool O₂ voltage will be fixed above 800 mV (.8 volt). Check for high fuel pressure, leaking or sticking injector. Silicone contaminated O₂ sensor will "Scan" an O₂ voltage slow to respond.

- **Throttle Body**
  Remove IAC valve and inspect bore for foreign material.

- **IAC Valve Electrical Connections**
  IAC valve connections should be carefully checked for proper contact.

- **PCV System**
  An incorrect or faulty PCV system may result in an incorrect idle speed. Refer to "Rough, Unstable, Incorrect Idle or Stalling" in "Symptoms."
  If intermittent poor driveability or idle symptoms are resolved by disconnecting the IAC, carefully recheck connections, valve terminal resistance, or replace IAC.

THROTTLE BODY INJECTION DIAGNOSTIC CHARTS

CODE 42
ELECTRONIC SPARK TIMING (EST) CIRCUIT

1.
- CLEAR CODES.
- IDLE ENGINE FOR 1 MINUTE OR UNTIL CODE 42 SETS.
- DOES CODE 42 SET?

YES → 2 → NO → CODE 42 INTERMITTENT.

2.
- IGNITION "OFF."
- DISCONNECT ECM CONNECTORS.
- IGNITION "ON."
- SET OHMMETER SELECTOR SWITCH IN THE 1000 TO 2000 OHMS RANGE.
- GROUND THE BLACK (-) OHMMETER LEAD.
- PROBE ECM HARNESS EST. CIRCUIT USING THE RED (+) OHMMETER LEAD. THE OHMMETER SHOULD READ LESS THAN 500 OHMS. DOES IT?

YES → 3 → NO → OPEN CKT 423, FAULTY CONNECTION, OR FAULTY IGNITION MODULE.

3.
- PROBE ECM HARNESS CONNECTOR CKT 424 WITH A TEST LIGHT TO BATTERY VOLTAGE AND OBSERVE LIGHT.

LIGHT "OFF" / LIGHT "ON"

3. (continued)
- WITH OHMMETER STILL CONNECTED TO ECM HARNESS CKT 423 AND GROUND AS DESCRIBED IN STEP #2, AGAIN PROBE ECM HARNESS CKT 424 WITH THE TEST LIGHT CONNECTED TO BATTERY VOLTAGE. AS TEST LIGHT CONTACTS CKT 424, RESISTANCE SHOULD SWITCH FROM HUNDREDS TO THOUSANDS OHMS. DOES IT?

NO → DISCONNECT IGNITION MODULE 6-WAY CONNECTOR.

LIGHT "ON" → CKT 424 SHORTED TO GROUND.

LIGHT "OFF" → REPLACE IGNITION MODULE.

4.
- DISCONNECT DIS 6-WAY CONNECTOR. NOTE OHMMETER THAT IS STILL CONNECTED TO CKT 423 AND GROUND. RESISTANCE SHOULD HAVE BECOME VERY HIGH (OPEN CIRCUIT). DOES IT?

YES → CKT 424 OPEN, FAULTY CONNECTIONS, OR FAULTY IGNITION MODULE.

NO → CKT 423 SHORTED TO GROUND.

5.
- RECONNECT ECM AND IDLE ENGINE FOR ONE MINUTE OR UNTIL CODE 42 SETS. DOES CODE SET?

YES → REPLACE ECM.

NO → CODE 42 INTERMITTENT.

"AFTER REPAIRS," REFER TO CODE CRITERIA AND CONFIRM CODE DOES NOT RESET.

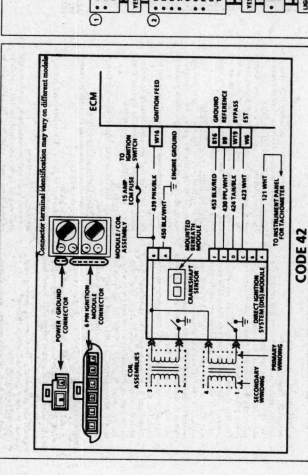

Connector terminal identification may vary on different modules.

CODE 42
ELECTRONIC SPARK TIMING (EST) CIRCUIT

Circuit Description:

The DIS module sends a reference signal to the ECM when the engine is cranking. While the engine speed is under 400 rpm, the DIS module controls the ignition timing. When the system is running on the ignition module (no voltage on the bypass line), the ignition module grounds the EST signal. The ECM expects to sense no voltage on the EST line during this condition. If it senses a voltage, it sets Code 42 and will not enter the EST mode.

When the engine speed exceeds 400 rpm, the ECM applies 5 volts to the bypass line to switch the timing to ECM control (EST). If the bypass line is open or grounded, once the rpm for EST control is reached, the ignition module will not switch to EST mode. This results in low EST voltage and the setting of Code 42. If the EST line is grounded, the ignition module will switch to EST, but because the line is grounded, there will be no EST signal. A Code 42 will be set.

Test Description: Numbers below refer to circled numbers on the diagnostic chart.

1. Code 42 means the ECM has sensed an open or short to ground in the EST or bypass circuits. This test confirms Code 42 and that the fault causing the code is present.

2. Checks for a normal EST ground path through the ignition module. An EST CKT 423, shorted to ground, will also read less than 500 ohms, but this will be checked later.

3. As the test light voltage contacts CKT 424, the module should switch, causing the ohmmeter to "overrange" if the meter is in the 1000-2000 ohms position. Selecting the 10-20,000 ohms position will indicate a reading above 5000 ohms. The important thing is that the module "switched."

4. The module did not switch and this step checks for:
   - EST CKT 423 shorted to ground
   - Bypass CKT 424 open
   - Faulty ignition module connection or module.

5. Confirms that Code 42 is a faulty ECM and not an intermittent in CKT(s) 423 or 424.

Diagnostic Aids:

The "Scan" tool does not have any ability to help diagnose a Code 42 problem.

If Code 42 is intermittent, refer to "Intermittent" in "Symptoms."

THROTTLE BODY INJECTION DIAGNOSTIC CHARTS

CODE 44
OXYGEN SENSOR CIRCUIT (LEAN EXHAUST INDICATED)

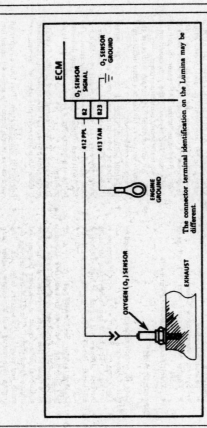

(1)
- RUN WARM ENGINE (75°C/167°F TO 95°C/203°F) AT 1200 RPM.
- DOES TECH 1 INDICATE O₂ SENSOR VOLTAGE FIXED BELOW .35 VOLT (350 mV)?

YES →
- DISCONNECT O₂ SENSOR.
- WITH ENGINE IDLING, TECH 1 SHOULD DISPLAY O₂ SENSOR VOLTAGE BETWEEN .35 VOLT AND .55 VOLT (350 mV AND 550 mV). DOES IT?

NO → CODE 44 IS INTERMITTENT.

YES → CKT 412 SHORTED TO GROUND OR FAULTY ECM.

"AFTER REPAIRS," REFER TO CODE CRITERIA AND CONFIRM CODE DOES NOT RESET.

ECM

O₂ SENSOR SIGNAL | O₂ SENSOR GROUND

B2 | B23

412 PPL | 413 TAN

ENGINE GROUND

OXYGEN (O₂) SENSOR

EXHAUST

The connector terminal identification on the Lumina may be different.

CODE 44
OXYGEN SENSOR CIRCUIT (LEAN EXHAUST INDICATED)

Circuit Description:

The ECM supplies a voltage of about .45 volt between terminals "B2" and "B23". (If measured with a 10 megohm digital voltmeter, this may read as low as .32 volt).

When the O₂ sensor reaches operating temperature, it varies this voltage from about .1 volt (exhaust is lean) to about .9 volt (exhaust is rich).

The sensor is like an open circuit and produces no voltage when it is below 316°C (600°F). An open sensor circuit, or cold sensor, causes "Open Loop" operation.

Test Description: Numbers below refer to circled numbers on the diagnostic chart.

1. Code 44 is set when the O₂ sensor signal voltage on CKT 412 remains below .2 volt for 60 seconds or more and the system is operating in "Closed Loop."

Diagnostic Aids:

Using the Tech 1 "Scan" tool, observe the block learn value at different engine speeds. If the conditions for Code 44 exists, the block learn values will be around 150 or higher.

Check the following possible causes:
- O₂ Sensor A cracked or otherwise damaged O₂ sensor may cause an intermittent Code 44.
- O₂ Sensor Wire. Sensor pigtail may be mispositioned and contacting the exhaust manifold.

Check for ground in wire between connector and sensor.

- Fuel Contamination. Water, even in small amounts, near the in-tank fuel pump inlet can be delivered to the injector. The water causes a lean exhaust and can set a Code 44.
- Fuel Pressure. System will be lean if fuel pressure is too low. It may be necessary to monitor fuel pressure while driving the car at various road speeds and/or loads to confirm. See "Fuel System Diagnosis," CHART A-7.
- Exhaust Leaks. If there is an exhaust leak, the engine can cause outside air to be pulled into the exhaust and past the sensor. Vacuum or crankcase leaks can cause a lean condition.
- If Code 44 is intermittent, refer to "Intermittents" in "Symptoms."

THROTTLE BODY INJECTION DIAGNOSTIC CHARTS

CODE 45
OXYGEN SENSOR CIRCUIT
(RICH EXHAUST INDICATED)

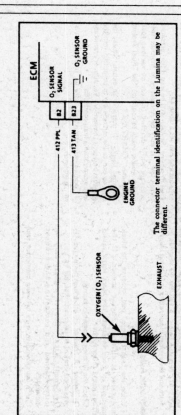

ECM
O₂ SENSOR SIGNAL — B2 — 412 PPL
O₂ SENSOR GROUND — B23 — 413 TAN
ENGINE GROUND

The connector terminal identification on the Lumina may be different.

CODE 45
OXYGEN SENSOR CIRCUIT
(RICH EXHAUST INDICATED)

Circuit Description:

The ECM supplies a voltage of about .45 volt between terminals "B2" and "B23" (If measured with a 10 megohm digital voltmeter, this may read as low as .32 volt). When the O₂ sensor reaches operating temperature, it varies this voltage from about 1 volt (exhaust is lean) to about .9 volt (exhaust is rich).

The sensor is like an open circuit and produces no voltage when it is below 316°C (600°F). An open sensor circuit, or cold sensor, causes "Open Loop" operation.

Test Description: Numbers below refer to circled numbers on the diagnostic chart.

1. Code 45 is set when the O₂ sensor signal voltage on CKT 412 remains above .7 volt under the following conditions:
   - 50 seconds or more.
   - System is operating in "Closed Loop."
   - Engine run time after start is 1 minute or more.
   - Throttle angle is between 3% and 45%.

Diagnostic Aids:

Code 45, or rich exhaust, is most likely caused by one of the following:

- **Fuel Pressure.** System will go rich, if pressure is too high. The ECM can compensate for some increase. However, if it gets too high, a Code 45 will be set. See "Fuel System Diagnosis," CHART A-7.
- **Leaking Injector.** See CHART A-7.
- **HEI Shielding.** An open ground CKT 453 may result in EMI, or induced electrical "noise." The ECM looks at this "noise" as reference pulses. The additional pulses result in a higher than actual engine speed signal. The ECM then delivers too much fuel causing the system to go rich. The engine tachometer will also show higher than actual engine speed, which can help in diagnosing this problem.

- **Canister Purge.** Check for fuel saturation. If full of fuel, check canister hoses. See "Evaporative Emission Control System (EECS)."
- **MAP Sensor.** An output that causes the ECM to sense a higher than normal manifold pressure (low vacuum) can cause the system to go rich. Disconnecting the MAP sensor will allow the ECM to set a fixed value for the MAP sensor. Substitute a different MAP sensor if the rich condition is gone, while the sensor is disconnected.
- **TPS.** An intermittent TPS output will cause the system to operate richly due to a false indication of the engine accelerating.
- **O₂ Sensor Contamination.** Inspect oxygen sensor for silicone contamination from fuel, or use of improper RTV sealant. The sensor may have a white, powdery coating and result in a high but false signal voltage (rich exhaust indication). The ECM will then reduce the amount of fuel delivered to the engine causing a severe surge driveability problem.
- **EGR Valve.** EGR sticking open at idle is usually accompanied by a rough idle and/or stall condition. If Code 45 is intermittent, refer to "Symptoms."
- **Engine Oil Contamination.** Fuel fouled engine oil could cause the O₂ sensor to sense a rich air/fuel mixture and set a Code 45.

---

1. • RUN WARM ENGINE (75°C/167°F TO 95°C/203°F) AT 1200 RPM.
   • DOES TECH 1 DISPLAY O₂ SENSOR VOLTAGE FIXED ABOVE .75 VOLT (750 mv)?

   YES →
   • DISCONNECT O₂ SENSOR AND JUMPER HARNESS CKT 412 TO GROUND.
   • TECH 1 SHOULD DISPLAY O₂ BELOW .35 VOLT (350 mv).
   DOES IT?

   YES → REPLACE ECM.

   NO → REPLACE ECM.

   NO → CODE 45 IS INTERMITTENT.

"AFTER REPAIRS," REFER TO CODE CRITERIA AND CONFIRM CODE DOES NOT RESET.

THROTTLE BODY INJECTION DIAGNOSTIC CHARTS

CHART C-1D

MANIFOLD ABSOLUTE PRESSURE (MAP) OUTPUT CHECK

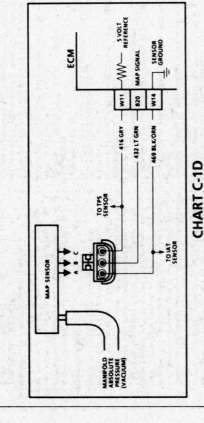

Circuit Description:

The Manifold Absolute Pressure (MAP) sensor measures the changes in the intake manifold pressure which result from engine load (intake manifold vacuum) and rpm changes; and converts these into a voltage output. The ECM sends a 5 volt reference voltage to the MAP sensor. As the manifold pressure changes, the output voltage of the sensor also changes. By monitoring the sensor output voltage, the ECM knows the manifold pressure. A lower pressure (low voltage) output voltage will be about 1 - 2 volts at idle. While higher pressure (high voltage) output voltage will be about 4 - 4.8 at Wide Open Throttle (WOT). The MAP sensor is also used, under certain conditions, to measure barometric pressure, allowing the ECM to make adjustments for different altitudes. The ECM uses the MAP sensor to control fuel delivery and ignition timing.

Test Description: Numbers below refer to circled numbers on the diagnostic chart.

⚠️ **Important**

- Be sure to use the same Diagnostic Test Equipment for all measurements.

1. When comparing Tech 1 readings to a known good vehicle, it is important to compare vehicles that use a MAP sensor having the same color insert or having the same "Hot Stamped" number. See figures on facing page.

2. Applying 34 kPa vacuum to the MAP sensor should cause the voltage to change. Subtract second reading from the first. Voltage value should be greater than 1.5 volts. Upon applying vacuum to the sensor, the change in voltage should be instantaneous. A slow voltage change indicates a faulty sensor.

3. Check vacuum hose to sensor for leaking or restriction. Be sure that no other vacuum devices are connected to the MAP hose.

   NOTE: Make sure electrical connector remains securely fastened.

4. Disconnect sensor from bracket and twist sensor (by hand only) to check for intermittent connection. Output changes greater than .1 volt indicate a faulty connector or connection. If OK, replace sensor.

CHART C-1D

MANIFOLD ABSOLUTE PRESSURE (MAP) OUTPUT CHECK

NOTE: THIS CHART ONLY APPLIES TO MAP SENSORS HAVING GREEN OR BLACK COLOR KEY INSERT (SEE BELOW).

① • IGNITION "ON," ENGINE "OFF –"
   • "SCAN" TOOL SHOULD INDICATE A MAP SENSOR VOLTAGE.
   • COMPARE THIS READING WITH THE READING OF A KNOWN GOOD VEHICLE. SEE FACING PAGE TEST DESCRIPTION, STEP 1.
   • VOLTAGE READING SHOULD BE WITHIN, ± .4 VOLT.
   IS IT?

   NO → REPLACE SENSOR.

② • DISCONNECT AND PLUG VACUUM SOURCE TO MAP SENSOR.
   • CONNECT A HAND VACUUM PUMP TO MAP SENSOR.
   • START ENGINE.
   • NOTE MAP SENSOR VOLTAGE.
   • APPLY 34 kPa (10" Hg) OF VACUUM AND NOTE VOLTAGE CHANGE. SUBTRACT SECOND READING FROM THE FIRST. VOLTAGE VALUE SHOULD BE GREATER THAN 1.5 VOLTS.
   IS IT?

③ NO TROUBLE FOUND. CHECK SENSOR VACUUM SOURCE FOR LEAKAGE OR RESTRICTION. BE SURE THIS SOURCE SUPPLIES VACUUM TO MAP SENSOR ONLY.

   NO → CHECK SENSOR CONNECTION. IF OK, REPLACE SENSOR.

④ CHECK SENSOR CONNECTION. IF OK, REPLACE SENSOR.

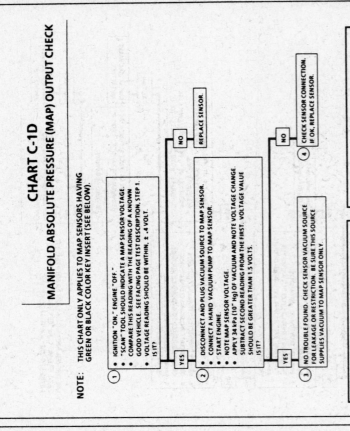

Figure 1 - Color Key Insert

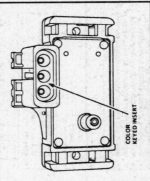

Figure 2 - Hot-Stamped Number

"AFTER REPAIRS," CONFIRM "CLOSED LOOP" OPERATION AND NO "SERVICE ENGINE SOON" LIGHT.

THROTTLE BODY INJECTION DIAGNOSTIC CHARTS

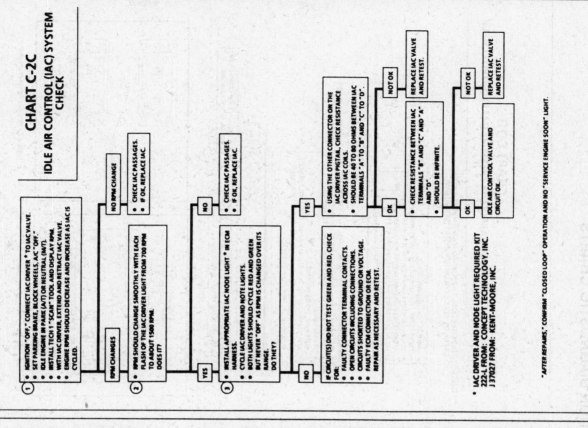

CHART C-2C
IDLE AIR CONTROL (IAC) SYSTEM CHECK

① • IGNITION "OFF." CONNECT IAC DRIVER * TO IAC VALVE.
• SET PARKING BRAKE, BLOCK WHEELS, A/C "OFF."
• IDLE ENGINE IN PARK (A/T) OR NEUTRAL (M/T).
• INSTALL TECH 1 "SCAN" TOOL AND DISPLAY RPM.
• WITH IAC DRIVER, EXTEND AND RETRACT IAC VALVE.
• ENGINE RPM SHOULD DECREASE AND INCREASE AS IAC IS CYCLED.

→ NO RPM CHANGE → CHECK IAC PASSAGES. IF OK, REPLACE IAC.

→ RPM CHANGES

② RPM SHOULD CHANGE SMOOTHLY WITH EACH FLASH OF THE IAC DRIVER LIGHT FROM 700 RPM TO ABOUT 1500 RPM. DOES IT?

→ NO → CHECK IAC PASSAGES. IF OK, REPLACE IAC.

→ YES

③ • INSTALL APPROPRIATE IAC NODE LIGHT * IN ECM HARNESS.
• CYCLE IAC DRIVER AND NOTE LIGHTS.
• BOTH LIGHTS SHOULD CYCLE RED AND GREEN BUT NEVER "OFF" AS RPM IS CHANGED OVER ITS RANGE.
DO THEY?

→ YES → IF CIRCUIT(S) DID NOT TEST GREEN AND RED, CHECK FOR:
• FAULTY CONNECTOR TERMINAL CONTACTS.
• OPEN CIRCUITS INCLUDING CONNECTIONS.
• CIRCUITS SHORTED TO GROUND OR VOLTAGE.
• FAULTY ECM CONNECTION OR ECM.
REPAIR AS NECESSARY AND RETEST.

→ NO → • USING THE OTHER CONNECTOR ON THE IAC DRIVER PIGTAIL, CHECK RESISTANCE ACROSS IAC COILS.
• SHOULD BE 40 TO 80 OHMS BETWEEN IAC TERMINALS "A" TO "B" AND "C" TO "D".

→ NOT OK → REPLACE IAC VALVE AND RETEST.

→ OK → • CHECK RESISTANCE BETWEEN IAC TERMINALS "B" AND "C" AND "A" AND "D".
• SHOULD BE INFINITE.

→ NOT OK → REPLACE IAC VALVE AND RETEST.

→ OK → IDLE AIR CONTROL VALVE AND CIRCUIT OK.

CHART C-2C
IDLE AIR CONTROL (IAC) SYSTEM CHECK

* IAC DRIVER AND NODE LIGHT REQUIRED KIT
222-1 FROM: CONCEPT TECHNOLOGY, INC.
J 37027 FROM: KENT-MOORE, INC.

"AFTER REPAIRS," CONFIRM "CLOSED LOOP" OPERATION AND NO "SERVICE ENGINE SOON" LIGHT.

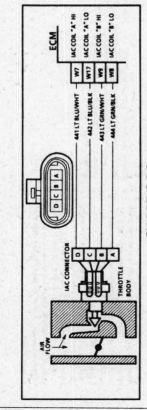

ECM

IAC COIL "A" HI	W7
IAC COIL "A" LO	W17
IAC COIL "B" HI	W9
IAC COIL "B" LO	W8

441 LT BLU/WHT
442 LT BLU/BLK
443 LT GRN/WHT
444 LT GRN/BLK

IAC CONNECTOR — D C B A — THROTTLE BODY

AIR FLOW

CHART C-2C
IDLE AIR CONTROL (IAC) SYSTEM CHECK

Circuit Description:

The ECM controls engine idle speed with the IAC valve. To increase idle speed, the ECM retracts the IAC valve pintle away from its seat, allowing more air to bypass the throttle bore. To decrease idle speed, the ECM commands to the IAC valve pintle towards its seat, reducing bypass air flow. A Tech 1 "Scan" tool will read the ECM commands to the IAC valve in counts. Higher the counts indicate more air bypass (higher idle). The lower the counts indicate less air is allowed to bypass (lower idle).

Test Description: Numbers below refer to circled numbers on the diagnostic chart.

1. The IAC tester is used to extend and retract the IAC valve. Valve movement is verified by an engine speed change. If no change in engine speed occurs, the valve can be retested when removed from the throttle body.

2. This step checks the quality of the IAC movement in step 1. Between 700 rpm and about 1500 rpm, the engine speed should change smoothly with each flash of the tester light in both extend and retract. If the IAC valve is retracted beyond the control range (about 1500 rpm), it may take many flashes in the extend position before engine speed will begin to drop. This is normal on certain engines, fully extending IAC may cause engine stall. This may be normal.

3. Steps 1 and 2 verified proper IAC valve operation while this step checks the IAC circuits. Each lamp on the node light should flash red and green while the IAC valve is cycled. While the sequence of color is not important if either light is "OFF" or does not flash red and green, check the circuits for faults, beginning with poor terminal contacts.

Diagnostic Aids:

• **Vacuum Leak (High Idle)**
A slow, unstable, or fast idle may be caused by a non-IAC system problem that cannot be overcome by a the IAC valve. Out of control range IAC "Scan" tool counts will be above 60 if idle is too low, and zero counts if idle is too high. The following checks should be made to repair a non-IAC system problem.
• **Vacuum Leak (High Idle)**
If idle is too high, stop the engine. Fully extend (low) IAC with tester.

Start engine. If idle speed is above 800 rpm, locate and correct vacuum leak including PCV system. Also check for binding of throttle blade or linkage.
• **System too lean (High Air/Fuel Ratio)**
The idle speed may be too high or too low. Engine speed may vary up and down and disconnecting the IAC valve does not help. Code 44 may be set. "Scan" O₂ voltage will be less than 300 mv (.3 volt). Check for low regulated fuel pressure, water in the fuel or a restricted injector.
• **System too rich (Low Air/Fuel Ratio)**
The idle speed will be too low. "Scan" tool IAC counts will usually be above 80. System is obviously rich and may exhibit black smoke in exhaust.
"Scan" tool O₂ voltage will be fixed over 800 mv (.8 volt).
Check for high fuel pressure, leaking or sticking injector. Silicone contaminated O₂ sensors "Scan" voltage will be slow to respond.
• **Throttle Body**
Remove IAC valve and inspect bore for foreign material.
• **IAC Valve Electrical Connections**
IAC valve connections should be carefully checked for proper contact.
• **PCV System**
Incorrect or faulty PCV system components may result in an incorrect idle speed.
Refer to "Rough, Unstable, Incorrect Idle or Stalling" in "Symptoms."
• If intermittent poor driveability or idle symptoms are resolved by disconnecting the IAC, carefully recheck connections, valve terminal resistance, or replace IAC.

THROTTLE BODY INJECTION DIAGNOSTIC CHARTS

CHART C-8A
TORQUE CONVERTER CLUTCH (TCC) CIRCUIT

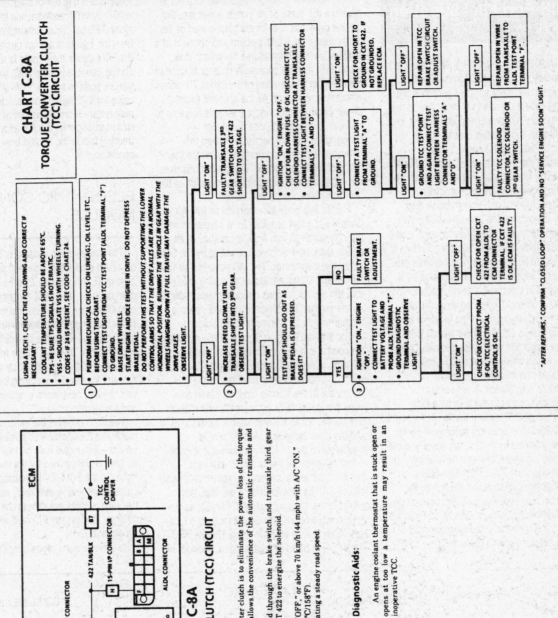

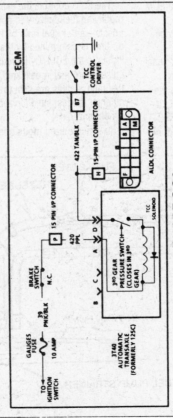

Circuit Description:

The purpose of the automatic transaxle torque converter clutch is to eliminate the power loss of the torque converter when the vehicle is in a cruise condition. This allows the convenience of the automatic transaxle and the fuel economy of a manual transaxle.

Fused ignition voltage is supplied to the TCC solenoid through the brake switch and transaxle third gear apply switch. The ECM will engage TCC by grounding CKT 422 to energize the solenoid.

TCC will engage under the following conditions:

- Vehicle speed is above 56 km/h (35 mph) with A/C "OFF," or above 70 km/h (44 mph) with A/C "ON."
- Engine at normal operating temperature (above 70°C/158°F).
- Throttle position sensor output not changing, indicating a steady road speed.
- Transaxle third gear switch closed.
- Brake switch closed.

Test Description:
Numbers below refer to circled numbers on the diagnostic chart.

1. Light "OFF" confirms transaxle third gear apply switch is open.

2. At approximately 48 km/h (30 mph), the transaxle third gear switch should close. This depends on throttle position. The minimum speed at which the third gear switch will close is approximately 34 km/h (21 mph). Test light will turn "ON" and confirm ignition voltage in the circuit and a closed brake switch.

3. Grounding the diagnostic terminal with the ignition "ON" and the engine "OFF" should light the test light. This test checks the capability of the ECM to control the solenoid.

Diagnostic Aids:

An engine coolant thermostat that is stuck open or opens at too low a temperature may result in an inoperative TCC.

Multi-Port Fuel Injection (MPI)

The Multi-Port Fuel Injection (MPI) system is controlled by an Electronic Control Module (ECM) which monitors engine operations and generates output signals to provide the correct air/fuel mixture, ignition timing and engine idle speed control. Input to the control unit is provided by an oxygen sensor, coolant temperature sensor, detonation sensor, hot film mass sensor and throttle position sensor. The ECM also receives information concerning engine rpm, road speed, transmission gear position, power steering and air conditioning.

The injectors are located, one at each intake port, rather than the single injector found on the earlier throttle body system. The injectors are mounted on a fuel rail and are activated by a signal from the electronic control module. The injector is a solenoid-operated valve which remains open depending on the width of the electronic pulses (length of the signal) from the ECM; the longer the open time, the more fuel is injected. In this manner, the air/fuel mixture can be precisely controlled for maximum performance with minimum emissions.

Fuel is pumped from the tank by a high pressure fuel pump, located inside the fuel tank. It is a positive displacement roller vane pump. The impeller serves as a vapor separator and pre-charges the high pressure assembly. A pressure regulator maintains 28–36 psi (28–50 psi on turbocharged engines) in the fuel line to the injectors and the excess fuel is fed back to the tank. A fuel accumulator is used to dampen the hydraulic line hammer in the system created when all injectors open simultaneously.

The Mass Air Flow (MAF) Sensor is used to measure the mass of air that is drawn into the engine cylinders. It is located just ahead of the air throttle in the intake system and consists of a heated film which measures the mass of air, rather than just the volume. A resistor is used to measure the temperature of the film at 75° above ambient temperature. As the ambient (outside) air temperature rises, more energy is required to maintain the heated film at the higher temperature and the control unit used this difference in required energy to calculate the mass of the incoming air. The control unit uses this information to determine the duration of fuel injection pulse, timing and EGR.

The throttle body incorporates an Idle Air Control (IAC) that provides for a bypass channel through which air can flow. It consists of an orifice and pintle which is controlled by the ECM through a step motor. The IAC provides air flow for idle and allows additional air during cold start until the engine reaches operating temperature. As the engine temperature rises, the opening through which air passes is slowly closed.

The Throttle Position Sensor (TPS) provides the control unit with information on throttle position, in order to determine injector pulse width and hence correct mixture. The TPS is connected to the throttle shaft on the throttle body and consists of as potentiometer with on end connected to a 5 volt source from the ECM and the other to ground. A third wire is connected to the ECM to measure the voltage output from the TPS which changes as the throttle valve angle is changed (accelerator pedal moves). At the closed throttle position, the output is low (approximately 0.4 volts); as the throttle valve opens, the output increases to a maximum 5 volts at Wide Open Throttle (WOT). The TPS can be misadjusted open, shorted, or

loose and if it is out of adjustment, the idle quality or WOT performance may be poor. A loose TPS can cause intermittent bursts of fuel from the injectors and an unstable idle because the ECM thinks the throttle is moving. This should cause a trouble code to be set. Once a trouble code is set, the ECM will use a preset value for TPS and some vehicle performance may return. A small amount of engine coolant is routed through the throttle assembly to prevent freezing inside the throttle bore during cold operation.

ELECTRONIC CONTROL MODULE

The fuel injection system is controlled by an on-board computer, the electronic control module (ECM), usually located in the passenger compartment. The ECM monitors engine operations and environmental conditions (ambient temperature, barometric pressure, etc.) needed to calculate the fuel delivery time (pulse width/injector on-time) of the fuel injector. The fuel pulse may be modified by the ECM to account for special operating conditions, such as cranking, cold starting, altitude, acceleration and deceleration.

The ECM controls the exhaust emissions by modifying fuel delivery to achieve, as nearly as possible an air/fuel ratio of 14.7:1. The injector on-time is determined by the various sensor inputs to the ECM. By increasing the injector pulse, more fuel is delivered, enriching the air/fuel ratio. Pulses are sent to the injector in 2 different modes, synchonized and non-synchronized.

In synchronized mode operation, the injector

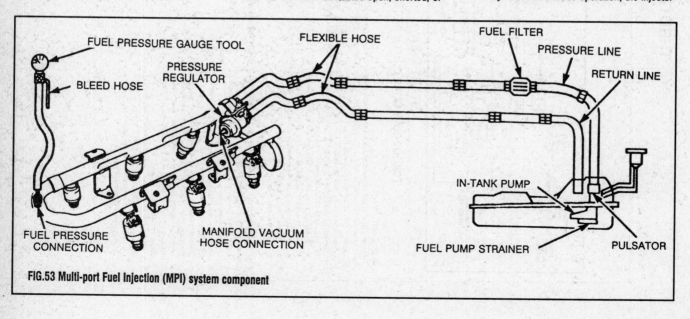

FIG.53 Multi-port Fuel Injection (MPI) system component

is pulsed once for each distributor reference pulse. In nonsynchronized mode operation, the injector is pulsed once every 12.5 milliseconds or 6.25 milliseconds depending on calibration. This pulse time is totally independent of distributor reference.

The ECM constantly monitors the input information, processes this information from various sensors, and generates output commands to the various systems that affect vehicle performance.

The ability of the ECM to recognize and adjust for vehicle variations (engine transmission, vehicle weight, axle ratio, etc.) is provided by a removable calibration unit (PROM) that is programmed to tailor the ECM for the particular vehicle. There is a specific ECM/PROM combination for each specific vehicle, and the combinations are not interchangeable with those of other vehicles.

The ECM also performs the diagnostic function of the system. It can recognize operational problems, alert the driver through the SERVICE ENGINE SOON light, and store a code or codes which identify the problem areas to aid the in making repairs.

➡ Instead of an edgeboard connector, newer ECM's have a header connector which attaches solidly to the ECM case. Like the edgeboard connectors, the header connectors have a different pinout identification for different engine designs.

The ECM consists of 3 parts; a Controller (the ECM without a PROM), a Calibrator called a PROM (Programmable Read Only Memory) and a Cal-Pak.

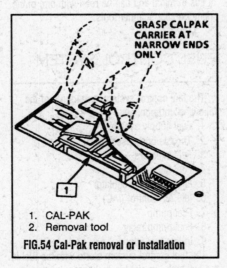

GRASP CALPAK CARRIER AT NARROW ENDS ONLY

1. CAL-PAK
2. Removal tool

FIG.54 Cal-Pak removal or installation

PROM

To allow 1 model of the ECM to be used for many different vehicles, a device called a Calibrator (or PROM) is used. The PROM is located inside the ECM and has information on the vehicle's weight, engine, transmission, axle ratio and other components.

While one ECM part number can be used by many different vehicles, a PROM is very specific and must be used for the right vehicle. For this reason, it is very important to check the latest parts book and or service bulletin information for the correct PROM part number when replacing the PROM.

An ECM used for service (called a controller) comes without a PROM. The PROM from the old ECM must be carefully removed and installed in the new ECM.

Cal-Pak

A device called a Cal-Pak is added to allow fuel delivery if other parts of the ECM are damaged. It has an access door in the ECM, and removal and replacement procedures are the same as with the PROM. If the Cal-Pak is missing, a Code 52 will be set.

Mem-Cal

This assembly contains the functions of the PROM Cal-Pak and the ESC module used on other GM applications. Like the PROM, it contains the calibrations needed for a specific vehicle as well as the back-up fuel control circuitry required if the rest of the ECM becomes damaged or faulty.

Synchronized Mode

In synchronized mode operation, the injector is pulsed once for each distributor reference pulse.

Nonsyncronized Mode

In nonsynchronized mode operation, the injector is pulsed once every 12.5 milliseconds or 6.25 milliseconds depending on calibration. This pulse time is totally independent of distributor reference pulses.

Nonsynchronized mode results only under the following conditions:

1. The fuel pulse width is too small to be delivered accurately by the injector (approximately 1.5 milliseconds)
2. During the delivery of prime pulses (prime pulses charge the intake manifold with fuel during or just prior to engine starting)
3. During acceleration enrichment
4. During deceleration leanout

Starting Mode

When the engine is first turned **ON**, the ECM will turn on the fuel pump relay for 2 seconds

and the fuel pump will build up pressure. The ECM then checks the coolant temperature sensor, throttle position sensor and crank sensor, then the ECM determines the proper air/fuel ratio for starting. This ranges from 1.5:1 at −33°F (−36°C) to 14.7:1 at 201°F (94°C).

The ECM controls the amount of fuel that is delivered in the Starting Mode by changing how long the injectors are turned on and off. This is done by pulsing the injectors for very short times.

Clear Flood Mode

If for some reason the engine should become flooded, provisions have been made to clear this condition. To clear the flood, the driver must depress the accelerator pedal enough to open to wide-open throttle position. The ECM then issues completely turns off the fuel flow. The ECM holds this operational mode as long as the throttle stays in the wide open position and the engine rpm is below 600. If the throttle position becomes less than 62% (2.9mv), the ECM returns to the starting mode. For throttle openings up to 62% (2.9mv) the ECM increases the fuel flow (based on TPS).

Run Mode

▸ SEE FIGS. 30 to 35

There are 2 different run modes. When the engine is first started and the rpm is above 400, the system goes into open loop operation. In open loop operation, the ECM will ignore the signal from the oxygen (O_2) sensor and calculate the injector on-time based upon inputs from the coolant sensor, MAF sensors and MAT sensors.

During open loop operation, the ECM analyzes the following items to determine when the system is ready to go to the closed loop mode.

1. The oxygen sensor varying voltage output. (This is dependent on temperature).
2. The coolant sensor must be above specified temperature.
3. A specific amount of time must elapse after starting the engine. These values are stored in the PROM.

When these conditions have been met, the system goes into closed loop operation In closed loop operation, the ECM will calculate the air/fuel ratio (injector on time) based upon the signal from the oxygen sensor. The ECM will decrease the on-time if the air/fuel ratio is too rich, and will increase the on-time if the air/fuel ratio is too lean.

Acceleration Mode

When the engine is required to accelerate, the opening of the throttle valve(s) causes a rapid increase in Manifold Absolute Pressure (MAP). This rapid increase in MAP causes fuel to condense on the manifold walls. The ECM

senses this increase in throttle angle and MAP, and supplies additional fuel for a short period of time. This prevents the engine from stumbling due to too lean a mixture.

Deceleration Mode

Upon deceleration, a leaner fuel mixture is required to reduce emission of hydrocarbons (HC) and carbon monoxide (CO). To adjust the injection on-time, the ECM uses the decrease in MAP and the decrease in throttle position to calculate a decrease in injector on time. To maintain an idle fuel ratio of 14.7:1, fuel output is momentarily reduced. This is done because of the fuel remaining in the intake manifold. The ECM can cut off the fuel completely for short periods of time.

Battery Voltage Correction Mode

The purpose of battery voltage correction is to compensate for variations in battery voltage to fuel pump and injector response. The ECM compensates by increasing the engine idle rpm.

Battery voltage correction takes place in all operating modes. When battery voltage is low, the spark delivered by the distributor may be low. To correct this low battery voltage problem, the ECM can do any or all of the following:

a. Increase injector on time (increase fuel)

b. Increase idle rpm

c. Increase ignition dwell time

Fuel Cut-off Mode

When the ignition is **OFF**, no fuel will be delivered by the injectors. Fuel will also be cut off if the ECM does not receive a reference pulse from the distributor. To prevent dieseling, fuel delivery is completely stopped as soon as the engine is stopped. The ECM will not allow any fuel supply until it receives distributor reference pulses which prevents flooding.

Converter Protection Mode

In this mode the ECM estimates the temperature of the catalytic converter and then modifies fuel delivery to protect the converter from high temperatures. When the ECM has determined that the converter may overheat, it will cause open loop operation and will enrichen the fuel delivery. A slightly richer mixture will then cause the converter temperature to be reduced.

Fuel Backup Mode

The ECM functions in the fuel backup circuit mode if any one, or any combination, of the following exist:

1. The ECM voltage is lower than 9 volts.
2. The cranking voltage is below 9 volts.
3. The PROM is missing or not functioning.

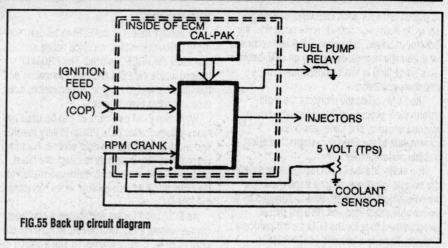

FIG.55 Back up circuit diagram

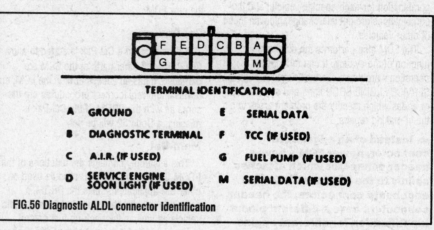

TERMINAL IDENTIFICATION

A	GROUND	E	SERIAL DATA
B	DIAGNOSTIC TERMINAL	F	TCC (IF USED)
C	A.I.R. (IF USED)	G	FUEL PUMP (IF USED)
D	SERVICE ENGINE SOON LIGHT (IF USED)	M	SERIAL DATA (IF USED)

FIG.56 Diagnostic ALDL connector identification

4. The ECM circuit fails to insure the computer operating pulse. The computer operating pulse (COP) is an internal ECM feature designed to inform the fuel backup circuit that the ECM is able to function.

Some engines run erratically in the fuel backup mode, while others (5.0L and 5.7L) seemed to run very well. Code 52 will be set to indicate a missing Cal-Pak. The fuel backup circuit is ignition fed and senses Throttle Position Sensor (TPS), Coolant Temperature Sensor (CTS) and rpm. The fuel backup circuit controls the fuel pump relay and the pulse width of the injectors.

ALDL/Check Connector

The Assembly Line Diagnostic Link (ALDL), is a diagnostic connector located in the passenger compartment, usually under the instrument panel.

The assembly plant were the vehicles originate use these connectors to check the engine for proper operation before it leaves the plant. Vehicles with the ALDL system, enter the Diagnostic mode or the Field Service Mode by connecting or jumping terminal B, the diagnostic TEST terminal to terminal A, or ground circuit.

Vehicles with the check connector, connect or jump terminal TE1, the diagnostic TEST terminal to terminal E1, or ground circuit. This connector is a very useful tool in diagnosing EFI engines. Important information from the ECM is available at this terminal and can be read with one of the many popular scanner tools.

FUEL CONTROL SYSTEM

The fuel control system is made up of the following components:

1. Fuel supply system
2. Throttle body assembly
3. Fuel injectors
4. Fuel rail
5. Fuel pressure regulator
6. Idle Air Control (IAC)
7. Fuel pump
8. Fuel pump relay
9. In-line fuel filter

The fuel control system starts with the fuel in the fuel tank. An electric fuel pump, located in the fuel tank with the fuel gauge sending unit, pumps fuel to the fuel rail through an in-line fuel

filter. The pump is designed to provide fuel at a pressure above the pressure needed by the injectors. A pressure regulator in the fuel rail keeps fuel available to the injectors at a constant pressure. Unused fuel is returned to the fuel tank by a separate line.

In order for the fuel injectors to supply a precise amount of fuel at the command of the ECM, the fuel supply system maintains a constant pressure (approximately 35 psi) drop across the injectors. As manifold vacuum changes, the fuel system pressure regulator controls the fuel supply pressure to compensate. The fuel pressure accumulator used on select models, isolates fuel line noise. The fuel rail is bolted rigidly to the engine and it provides the upper mount for the fuel injectors. It also contains a spring loaded pressure tap for testing the fuel system or relieving the fuel system pressure.

The injectors are controlled by the ECM. They deliver fuel in one of several modes as previously described. In order to properly control the fuel supply, the fuel pump is operated by the ECM through the fuel pump relay and oil pressure switch.

Throttle Body Unit

The throttle body unit has a throttle valve to control the amount of air delivered to the engine. The TPS and IAC valve are also mounted onto the throttle body. The throttle body contains vacuum ports located at, above or below the throttle valve. These vacuum ports generate the vacuum signals needed by various components.

On some vehicles, the engine coolant is directed through the coolant cavity at the bottom of the throttle body to warm the throttle valve and prevent icing.

Fuel Injector

A fuel injector is installed in the intake manifold at each cylinder. Mounting is approximately 70–100mm from the center line of the intake valve on V6 and V8 engine applications. The nozzle spray pattern is on a 25 degree angle. The fuel injector is a solenoid operated device controlled by the ECM. The ECM turns on the solenoid, which opens the valve which allows fuel delivery. The fuel, under pressure, is injected in a conical spray pattern at the opening of the intake valve. The fuel, which is not used by the injectors, passes through the pressure regulator before returning to the fuel tank.

An injector that is partly open, will cause loss of fuel pressure after the engine is shut down, so long crank time would be noticed on some engines. Also dieseling could occur because

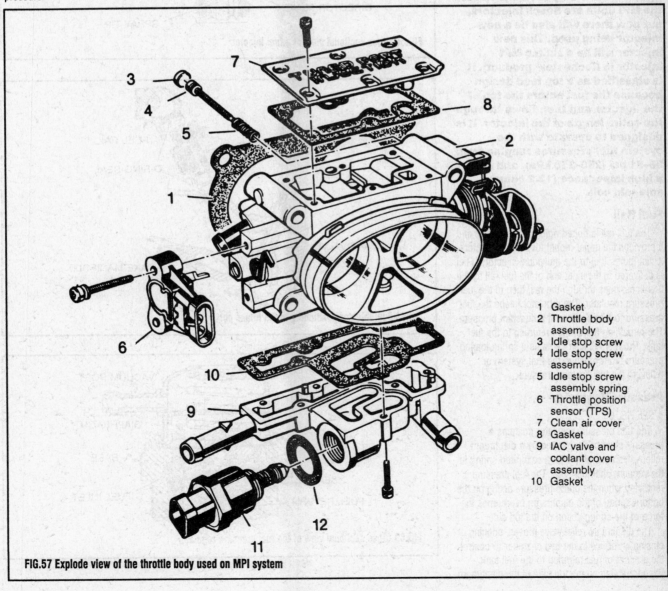

1 Gasket
2 Throttle body assembly
3 Idle stop screw
4 Idle stop screw assembly
5 Idle stop screw assembly spring
6 Throttle position sensor (TPS)
7 Clean air cover
8 Gasket
9 IAC valve and coolant cover assembly
10 Gasket

FIG.57 Explode view of the throttle body used on MPI system

some fuel could be delivered after the ignition is turned to **OFF** position.

There are 2 O-ring seals used. The lower O-ring seals the injector at the intake manifold. The O-rings are lubricated and should be replaced whenever the injector is removed from the intake manifold. The O-rings provide thermal insulation, thus preventing the formation of vapor bubbles and promoting good hot start characteristics. The O-rings also prevent excess injector vibration.

Air leakage at the injector/intake area would create a lean cylinder and a possible driveability problem. A second seal is used to seal the fuel injector at the fuel rail connection. The injectors are identified with an ID number cast on the injector near the top side. Injectors manufactured by Rochester® Products have an **RP** positioned near the top side in addition to the ID number.

➡ **The most widely used Injector for the MPI units are Bosch injectors, but now there will also be a new injector being used. This new injector will be a Multec MPI injector (a Rochester® product). It is classified as a top feed design because the fuel enters the top of the injector and then flows through the entire length of the injector. It is designed to operate with the system fuel pressures ranging from 36–51 psi (250–350 kPa), and uses a high impedance (12.2 ohms) solenoid coil.**

Fuel Rail

The fuel rail is bolted rigidly to the engine and it provides the upper mount for the fuel injectors. It distributes fuel to the individual injectors. Fuel is delivered to the input end of the fuel rail by the fuel lines, goes through the rail, then to the fuel pressure regulator. The regulator keeps the fuel pressure to the injectors at a constant pressure. The remaining fuel is then returned to the fuel tank. The fuel rail also contains a spring loaded pressure tap for testing the fuel system or relieving the fuel system pressure.

Pressure Regulator

◆ SEE FIG. 60

The fuel pressure regulator contains a pressure chamber separated by a diaphragm relief valve assembly with a calibrated spring in the vacuum chamber side. The fuel pressure is regulated when the pump pressure acting on the bottom spring of the diaphragm overcomes the force of the spring action on the top side.

The diaphragm relief valve moves, opening or closing an orifice in the fuel chamber to control the amount of fuel returned to the fuel tank. Vacuum acting on the top side of the diaphragm

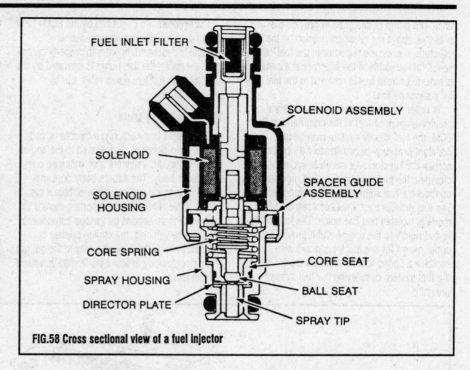

FIG.58 Cross sectional view of a fuel injector

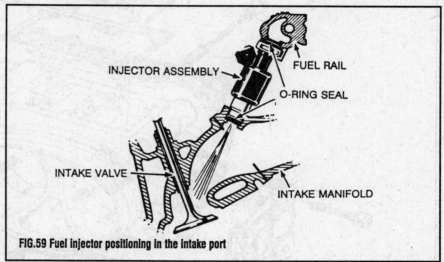

FIG.59 Fuel injector positioning in the intake port

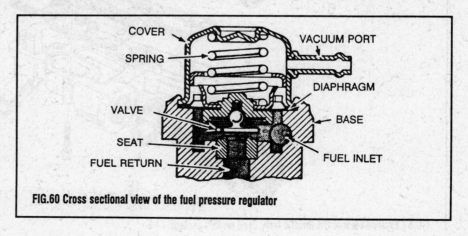

FIG.60 Cross sectional view of the fuel pressure regulator

along with spring pressure controls the fuel pressure. A decrease in vacuum creates an increase in the fuel pressure. An increase in vacuum creates a decrease in fuel pressure.

An example of this is under heavy load conditions the engine requires more fuel flow. The vacuum decreases under a heavy load condition because of the throttle opening. A decrease in the vacuum allows more fuel pressure to the top side of the pressure relief valve, thus increasing the fuel pressure.

The pressure regulator is mounted on the fuel rail and serviced separately. If the pressure is too low, poor performance could result. If the pressure is too high, excessive odor and a Code 45 may result.

Idle Air Control (IAC)

▶ SEE FIG. 61

The purpose of the Idle Air Control (IAC) system is to control engine idle speeds while preventing stalls due to changes in engine load. The IAC assembly, mounted on the throttle body, controls bypass air around the throttle plate. By extending or retracting a conical valve, a controlled amount of air can move around the throttle plate. If rpm is too low, more air is diverted around the throttle plate to increase rpm.

During idle, the proper position of the IAC valve is calculated by the ECM based on battery voltage, coolant temperature, engine load, and engine rpm. If the rpm drops below a specified rate, the throttle plate is closed. The ECM will then calculate a new valve position.

Three different designs are used for the IAC conical valve. The first design used is single taper while the second design used is a dual taper. The third design is a blunt valve. Care should be taken to insure use of the correct design when service replacement is required.

The IAC motor has 255 different positions or steps. The zero, or reference position, is the fully extended position at which the pintle is seated in the air bypass seat and no air is allowed to bypass the throttle plate. When the motor is fully retracted, maximum air is allowed to bypass the throttle plate. When the motor is fully retracted, maximum air is allowed to bypass the throttle plate.

The ECM always monitors how many steps it

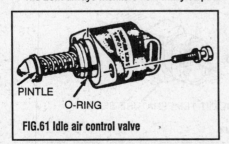

PINTLE
O-RING

FIG.61 Idle air control valve

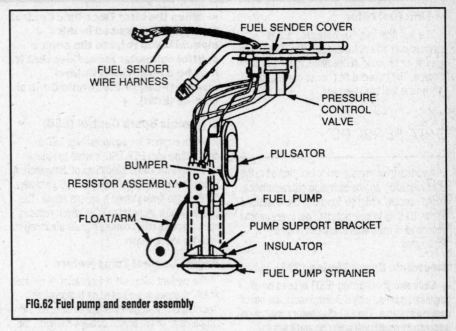

FUEL SENDER COVER

FUEL SENDER WIRE HARNESS

PRESSURE CONTROL VALVE

PULSATOR

BUMPER

RESISTOR ASSEMBLY

FUEL PUMP

FLOAT/ARM

PUMP SUPPORT BRACKET

INSULATOR

FUEL PUMP STRAINER

FIG.62 Fuel pump and sender assembly

has extended or retracted the pintle from the zero or reference position; thus, it always calculates the exact position of the motor. Once the engine has started and the vehicle has reached approximately 40 mph, the ECM will extend the motor 255 steps from whatever position it is in. This will bottom out the pintle against the seat. The ECM will call this position **O** and thus keep its zero reference updated.

The IAC only affects the engine's idle characteristics. If it is stuck fully open, idle speed is too high (too much air enters the throttle bore) If it is stuck closed, idle speed is too low (not enough air entering). If it is stuck somewhere in the middle, idle may be rough, and the engine won't respond to load changes.

Fuel Pump

The fuel is supplied to the system from an in-tank positive displacement roller vane pump. The pump supplies fuel through the in-line fuel filter to the fuel rail assembly. The pump is removed for service along with the fuel gauge sending unit. Once they are removed from the fuel tank, they pump and sending unit can be serviced separately.

Fuel pressure is achieved by rotation of the armature driving the roller vane components. The impeller at the inlet end serves as a vapor separator and a precharger for the roller vane assembly. The unit operates at approximately 3500 rpm.

The pressure relief valve in the fuel pump will control the fuel pump maximum psi to 60–90 psi. The fuel pump delivers more fuel than the engine can consume even under the most extreme conditions. Excess fuel flows through the pressure regulator and back to the tank via

the return line. The constant flow of fuel means that the fuel system is always supplied with cool fuel, thereby preventing the formation of fuel-vapor bubbles (vapor lock).

Fuel Pump Relay Circuit

The fuel pump relay is usually located on the left front inner fender (or shock tower) or on the engine side of the firewall (center cowl). The fuel pump electrical system consists of the fuel pump relay, ignition circuit and the ECM circuits are protected by a fuse. The fuel pump relay contact switch is in the normally open (NO) position.

When the ignition is turned **ON** the ECM will for 2 seconds, supply voltage to the fuel pump relay coil, closing the open contact switch. The ignition circuit fuse can now supply ignition voltage to the circuit which feeds the relay contact switch. With the relay contacts closed, ignition voltage is supplied to the fuel pump. The ECM will continue to supply voltage to the relay coil circuit as long as the ECM receives the rpm reference pulses from the ignition module.

The fuel pump control circuit also includes an engine oil pressure switch with a set of normally open contacts. The switch closes at approximately 4 lbs. of oil pressure and provides a secondary battery feed path to the fuel pump. If the relay fails, the pump will continue to run using the battery feed supplied by the closed oil pressure switch. A failed fuel pump relay will result in extended engine crank times in order to build up enough oil pressure to close the switch and turn on the fuel pump.

In-Line Fuel Filter

The fuel filter is a 10–20 micron and is serviced only as a complete unit. The O-rings are used at all threaded connections to prevent fuel leakage. The threaded flex hoses connect the filter to the fuel tank feed line.

DATA SENSORS

A variety of sensors provide information to the ECM regarding engine operating characteristics. These sensors and their functions are described below. Be sure to take note that not every sensor described is used with every GM engine application.

Electronic Spark Timing (EST)

Electronic spark timing (EST) is used on all engines equipped with HEI distributors and direct ignition systems. The EST distributor contains no vacuum or centrifugal advance and uses a 7-terminal distributor module. It also has 4 wires going to a 4-terminal connector in addition to the connectors normally found on HEI distributors. A reference pulse, indicating both engine rpm and crankshaft position, is sent to the ECM. The ECM determines the proper spark advance for the engine operating conditions and sends an **EST** pulse to the distributor.

The EST system is designed to optimize spark timing for better control of exhaust emissions and for fuel economy improvements. The ECM monitors information from various engine sensors, computes the desired spark timing and changes the timing accordingly. A backup spark advance system is incorporated in the module in case of EST failure.

The basic function of the fuel control system is to control the fuel delivery to the engine. The fuel is delivered to the engine by individual fuel injectors mounted on the intake manifold near each cylinder.

The main control sensor is the oxygen sensor which is located in the exhaust manifold. The oxygen sensor tells the ECM how much oxygen is in the exhaust gas and the ECM changes the air/fuel ratio to the engine by controlling the fuel injectors. The best mixture (ratio) to minimize exhaust emissions is 14.7:1 which allows the catalytic converter to operate the most efficiently. Because of the constant measuring and adjusting of the air/fuel ratio, the fuel injection system is called a **CLOSED LOOP** system.

➡ **When the term Electronic Control Module (ECM) is used in this manual it will refer to the engine control computer regardless that it may be a Powertrain Control Module (PCM) or Electronic Control Module (ECM).**

Electronic Spark Control (ESC)

When engines are equipped with ESC in conjunction with EST, ESC is used to reduce spark advance under conditions of detonation. A knock sensor signals a separate ESC controller to retard the timing when it senses knock. The ESC controller signals the ECM which reduces spark advance until no more signals are received from the knock sensor.

Engine Coolant Temperature

The coolant sensor is a thermister (a resistor which changes value based on temperature) mounted on the engine coolant stream. As the temperature of the engine coolant changes, the resistance of the coolant sensor changes. Low coolant temperature produces a high resistance (100,000 ohms at –40°C/–40°F), while high temperature causes low resistance (70 ohms at 130°C/266°F).

The ECM supplies a 5 volt signal to the coolant sensor and measures the voltage that returns. By measuring the voltage change, the ECM determines the engine coolant temperature. The voltage will be high when the engine is cold and low when the engine is hot. This information is used to control fuel management, IAC, spark timing, EGR, canister purge and other engine operating conditions.

A failure in the coolant sensor circuit should either set a Code 14 or 15. These codes indicate a failure in the coolant temperature sensor circuit. Once the trouble code is set, the ECM will use a default valve for engine coolant temperature.

Intake Air Temperature Sensor (IAT)

The Intake Air Temperature Sensor (IAT) is the same as the Manifold Air temperature Sensor (MAT). General Motors on a few applications just change the name.

Oxygen Sensor

▶ SEE FIG. 64

The exhaust oxygen sensor is mounted in the exhaust system where it can monitor the oxygen content of the exhaust gas stream. The oxygen content in the exhaust reacts with the oxygen sensor to produce a voltage output. This voltage ranges from approximately 100 millivolts (high oxygen — lean mixture) to 900 millivolts (low oxygen — rich mixture).

By monitoring the voltage output of the oxygen sensor, the ECM will determine what fuel mixture command to give to the injector (lean mixture — low voltage — rich command, rich mixture — high voltage — lean command).

Remember that oxygen sensor indicates to the ECM what is happening in the exhaust. It does not cause things to happen. It is a type of gauge: high oxygen content = lean mixture; low oxygen content = rich mixture. The ECM adjust fuel to keep the system working.

The oxygen sensor, if open should set a Code 13. a constant low voltage in the sensor circuit should set a Code 44 while a constant high voltage in the circuit should set a Code 45. Codes 44 and 45 could also be set as a result of fuel system problems.

Manifold Absolute Pressure (MAP) Sensor

The Manifold Absolute Pressure (MAP) sensor measures the changes in the intake manifold pressure which result from engine load and speed changes. The pressure measured by the MAP sensor is the difference between barometric pressure (outside air) and manifold pressure (vacuum). A closed throttle engine coastdown would produce a relatively low MAP value (approximately 20–35 kPa), while wide-open throttle would produce a high value (100 kPa). This high value is produced when the pressure inside the manifold is the same as outside the manifold, and 100% of outside air (or 100 kPa) is being measured. This MAP output is the opposite of what you would measure on a vacuum gauge. The use of this sensor also allows the ECM to adjust automatically for different altitude.

The ECM sends a 5 volt reference signal to the

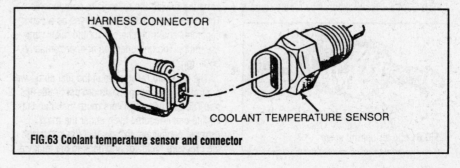

FIG.63 Coolant temperature sensor and connector

HARNESS CONNECTOR

COOLANT TEMPERATURE SENSOR

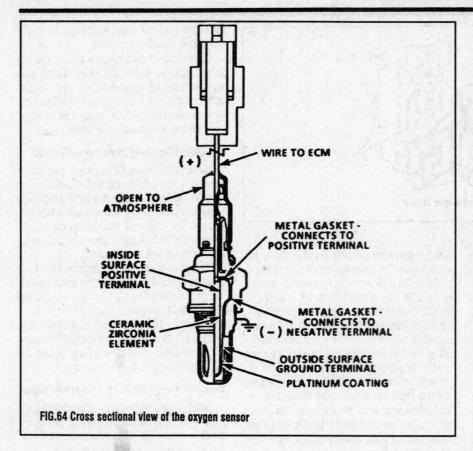

(+)
WIRE TO ECM

OPEN TO ATMOSPHERE

METAL GASKET - CONNECTS TO POSITIVE TERMINAL

INSIDE SURFACE POSITIVE TERMINAL

METAL GASKET - CONNECTS TO (–) NEGATIVE TERMINAL

CERAMIC ZIRCONIA ELEMENT

OUTSIDE SURFACE GROUND TERMINAL

PLATINUM COATING

FIG.64 Cross sectional view of the oxygen sensor

MAP sensor. As the MAP changes, the electrical resistance of the sensor also changes. By monitoring the sensor output voltage the ECM can determine the manifold pressure. A higher pressure, lower vacuum (high voltage) requires more fuel, while a lower pressure, higher vacuum (low voltage) requires less fuel. The ECM uses the MAP sensor to control fuel delivery and ignition timing. A failure in the MAP sensor circuit should set a Code 33 or Code 34.

Manifold Air Temperature Sensor

The Manifold Air Temperature (MAT) sensor is a thermistor mounted in the intake manifold. A thermistor is a resistor which changes resistance based on temperature. Low manifold air temperature produces a high resistance (100,000 ohms at –40°F/–40°C), while high temperature cause low resistance (70 ohms at 266°F/130°C).

The ECM supplies a 5 volt signal to the MAT sensor through a resistor in the ECM and monitors the voltage. The voltage will be high when the manifold air is cold and low when the air is hot. By monitoring the voltage, the ECM calculates the air temperature and uses this data to help determine the fuel delivery and spark advance. A failure in the MAT circuit should set either a Code 23 or Code 25. Once the trouble

code is set, the ECM will use an artificial default value for the MAT and some vehicle performance will return.

Mass Air Flow (MAF) Sensor

The Mass Air Flow (MAF) sensor measures the amount of air which passes through it. The ECM uses this information to determine the operating condition of the engine, to control fuel delivery. A large quantity of air indicates acceleration, while a small quantity indicates deceleration or idle.

This sensor produces a frequency output between 32 and 150 hertz. A scan tool will display air flow in terms of grams of air per second (gm/sec), with a range from 3gm/sec to 150 gm/sec.

Vehicle Speed Sensor (VSS)

➡ **A vehicle equipped with a speed sensor, should not be driven without a the speed sensor connected, as idle quality may be affected.**

The vehicle speed sensor (VSS) is mounted behind the speedometer in the instrument cluster or on the transmission/speedometer drive gear. It provides electrical pulses to the ECM from the speedometer head. The pulses indicate the road

speed. The ECM uses this information to operate the IAC, canister purge, and TCC.

Some vehicles equipped with digital instrument clusters use a Permanent Magnet (PM) generator to provide the VSS signal. The PM generator is located in the transmission and replaces the speedometer cable. The signal from the PM generator drives a stepper motor which drives the odometer. A failure in the VSS circuit should set a Code 24.

Throttle Position Sensor (TPS)

The Throttle Position Sensor (TPS) is connected to the throttle shaft and is controlled by the throttle mechanism. A 5 volt reference signal is sent to the TPS from the ECM. As the throttle valve angle is changed (accelerator pedal moved), the resistance of the TPS also changes. At a closed throttle position, the resistance of the TPS is high, so the output voltage to the ECM will be low (approximately 0.5 volt). As the throttle plate opens, the resistance decreases so that, at wide open throttle, the output voltage should be approximately 5 volts. At closed throttle position, the voltage at the TPS should be less than 1.25 volts.

By monitoring the output voltage from the TPS, the ECM can determine fuel delivery based on throttle valve angle (driver demand). The TPS can either be misadjusted, shorted, open or loose. Misadjustment might result in poor idle or poor wide-open throttle performance. An open TPS signals the ECM that the throttle is always closed, resulting in poor performance. This usually sets a Code 22. A shorted TPS gives the ECM a constant wide-open throttle signal and should set a Code 21. A loose TPS indicates to the ECM that the throttle is moving. This causes intermittent bursts of fuel from the injector and an unstable idle. Once the trouble code is set, the ECM will use an artificial default value for the TBI and some vehicle performance will return.

Crankshaft Sensor

Some systems use a magnetic crankshaft sensor, mounted remotely from the ignition module, which protrudes into the block within approximately 0.050 in. (0.127mm) of the crankshaft reluctor. The reluctor is a special wheel cast into the crankshaft with 7 slots machined into it, 6 of which are equally spaced (60 degrees apart). A seventh slot is spaced approximately 10 degrees from one of the other slots and severs to generate a **SYNC PULSE** signal. As the reluctor rotates as part of the crankshaft, the slots change the magnetic field of the sensor, creating an induced voltage pulse.

Based on the crank sensor pulses, the ignition module sends 2X reference signals to the ECM which are used to indicate crankshaft position and engine speed. The ignition module continues

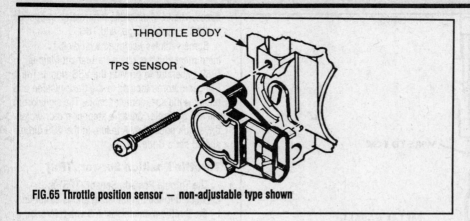

FIG.65 Throttle position sensor — non-adjustable type shown

to send these reference pulses to the ECM at a rate of 1 per each 180 degrees of the crankshaft rotation. This signal is called the 2X reference because it occurs 2 times per crankshaft revolution.

The ignition also sends a second, 1X reference signal to the ECM which occurs at the same time as the **SYNC PULSE** from the crankshaft sensor. This signal is called the 1X reference because it occurs 1 time per crankshaft revolution. The 1X reference and the 2X reference signals are necessary for the ECM to determine when to activate the fuel injectors.

By comparing the time between pulses, the ignition module can recognize the pulse representing the seventh slot (sync pulse) which starts the calculation of the ignition coil sequencing. The second crank pulse following the **SYNC PULSE** signals the ignition module to fire the No. 2–3 ignition coil and the fifth crank pulse signals the module to fire the No. 1–4 ignition coil.

Dual Crank Sensor/Combination Sensor

The dual crank sensor is mounted in a pedestal on the front of the engine near the harmonic balancer. The sensor consists of 2 Hall Effect switches, which depend on 2 metal interrupter rings mounted on the balancer to activate them. Windows in the interrupters activate the hall effect switches as they provide a patch for the magnetic field between the switches transducers and magnets. When one of the hall effect switches is activated, it grounds the signal line to the C3I module, pulling that signal line's (Sync Pulse or Crank) applied voltage low, which is interpreted as a signal.

Because of the way the signal is created by the dual crank sensor, the signal circuit is always either at a high or low voltage (square wave signal). Three crank signal pulses and one **SYNC PULSE** are created during each crankshaft revolution. The crank signal is used by the C3I module to create a reference signal

which is also a square wave signal similar to the crank signal. The reference signal is used to calculate the engine rpm and crankshaft position by the ECM. The **SYNC PULSE** is used by the C3I module to begin the ignition coil firing sequence starting with No. 3–6 coil. The firing sequence begins with this coil because either piston No. 3 or piston No. 6 is now at the correct position in compression stroke for the spark plugs to be fired. Both the crank sensor and the **SYNC PULSE** signals must be received by the ignition module for the engine to start. A misadjusted sensor or bent interrupter ring could cause rubbing of the sensor resulting in potential driveability problems, such as rough idle, poor performance, or a nor start condition.

➡ **Failure to have the correct clearance will damage the crankshaft sensor.**

The dual crank sensor is not adjustable for ignition timing but positioning of the interrupter ring is very important. A clearance of 0.025 in. (0.635mm) is required on either side of the interrupter ring. A dual crank sensor that is damaged, due to mispositioning or a bent

interrupter ring, can result in a hesitation, sag stumble or dieseling condition.

To determine if the dual crank sensor could be at fault, scan the engine rpm with a suitable scan tool, while driving the vehicle. An erratic display indicates that a proper reference pulse has not been received by the ECM, which may be the result of a malfunctioning dual crank sensor.

Air Conditioning Pressure Sensor

The air conditioning (A/C) pressure sensor provides a signal to the electronic control module (ECM) which indicates varying high side refrigerant pressure between approximately 0–450 psi. The ECM used this input to the A/C compressor load on the engine to help control the idle speed with the IAC valve.

The A/C pressure sensor electrical circuit consists of a 5 volt reference line and a ground line, both provided by the ECM and a signal line to the ECM. The signal is a voltage that varies approximately 0.1 volt at 0 psi, to 4.9 volts at 450 psi or more. A problem in the A/C pressure circuits or sensor should set a Code 66 and will make the A/C compressor inoperative.

Non-Air Conditioning Program Input

Vehicles not equipped with air conditioning (A/C) have a circuit connecting the ECM terminal **BC3** to ground, to program to operate without A/C related components connected to it. Vehicles with A/C do not have a wire in ECM **BC3** terminal. If this circuit is open on a non-A/C vehicle it may cause false Codes 26 and/or Code 66. If terminal **BC3** is grounded on A/C equipped vehicles, it will cause the compressor relay to be on whenever the ignition is in the **ON** position.

Detonation (Knock) Sensor

This sensor is a piezoelectric sensor located near the back of the engine (transmission end).

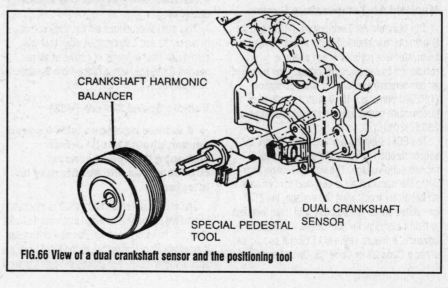

FIG.66 View of a dual crankshaft sensor and the positioning tool

It generates electrical impulses which are directly proportional to the frequency of the knock which is detected. A buffer then sorts these signals and eliminates all except for those frequency range of detonation. This information is passed to the ESC module and then to the ECM, so that the ignition timing advance can be retarded until the detonation stops.

Park/Neutral Switch

➡ **Vehicle should not be driven with the park/neutral switch disconnected as idle quality may be affected in park or neutral and a Code 24 (VSS) may be set.**

This switch indicates to the ECM when the transmission is in **P** or **N**. the information is used by the ECM for control on the torque converter clutch, EGR, and the idle air control valve operation.

Air Conditioning Request Signal

This signal indicates to the ECM that an air conditioning mode is selected at the switch and that the A/C low pressure switch is closed. The ECM controls the A/C and adjusts the idle speed in response to this signal.

Torque Converter Clutch Solenoid

The purpose of the torque converter clutch system is designed to eliminate power loss by the converter (slippage) to increase fuel economy. By locking the converter clutch, a more effective coupling to the flywheel is achieved. The converter clutch is operated by the ECM controlled torque converter clutch solenoid.

Power Steering Pressure Switch

The power steering pressure switch is used so that the power steering oil pressure pump load will not effect the engine idle. Turning the steering wheel increase the power steering oil pressure and pump load on the engine. The power steering pressure switch will close before

the load can cause an idle problem. The ECM will also turn the A/C clutch off when high power steering pressure is detected.

Oil Pressure Switch

The oil pressure switch is usually mounted on the back of the engine, just below the intake manifold. Some vehicles use the oil pressure switch as a parallel power supply, with the fuel pump relay and will provide voltage to the fuel pump, after approximately 4 psi (28 kPa) of oil pressure is reached. This switch will also help prevent engine seizure by shutting off the power to the fuel pump and causing the engine to stop when the oil pressure is lower than 4 psi.

EMISSION CONTROL SYSTEMS

Various components are used to control exhaust emissions from a vehicle. These components are controlled by the ECM based on different engine operating conditions. These components are described in the following paragraphs. Not all components are used on all engines.

Exhaust Gas Recirculation (EGR) System

EGR is a oxides of nitrogen (NOx) control which recycles exhaust gases through the combustion cycle by admitting exhaust gases into the intake manifold. The amount of exhaust gas admitted is adjusted by a vacuum controlled valve in response to engine operating conditions. If the valve is open, the recirculated exhaust gas is released into the intake manifold to be drawn into the combustion chamber.

The integral exhaust pressure modulated EGR valve uses a transducer responsive to exhaust pressure to modulate the vacuum signal to the EGR valve. The vacuum signal is provided by an

EGR vacuum port in the throttle body valve. Under conditions when exhaust pressure is lower than the control pressure, the EGR signal is reduced by an air bleed within the transducer. Under conditions when exhaust pressure is higher than the control pressure, the air bleed is closed and the EGR valve responds to an unmodified vacuum signal. Physical arrangement of the valve components will vary depending on whether the control pressure is positive or negative.

Positive Crankcase Ventilation (PCV) System

A closed Positive Crankcase Ventilation (PCV) system is used to provide more complete scavenging of crankcase vapors. Fresh air from the air cleaner is supplied to the crankcase, mixed with blow-by gases and then passed through a PCV valve into the induction system.

The primary mode of crankcase ventilation control is through the PCV valve which meters the mixture of fresh air and blow-by gases into the induction system at a rate dependent upon manifold vacuum.

To maintain the idle quality, the PCV valve restricts the ventilation system flow whenever intake manifold vacuum is designed to allow excessive amounts of blow-by gases to backflow through the breather assembly into the air cleaner and through the throttle body to be consumed by normal combustion.

Evaporative Emission Control (EEC) Systems

The basic evaporative emission control system used on all vehicles uses the carbon canister storage method. This method transfers fuel vapor to an activated carbon storage device for retention when the vehicle is not operating. A ported vacuum signal is used for purging vapors stored in the canister.

CONTROLLED CANISTER PURGE

The ECM controls a solenoid valve which controls vacuum to the purge valve in the charcoal canister. In open loop, before a specified time has expired and below a specified rpm, the solenoid valve is energized and blocks vacuum to the purge valve. When the system is in closed loop, after a specified time and above a specified rpm, the solenoid valve is de-energized and vacuum can be applied to the purge valve. This releases the collected vapors into the intake manifold. On systems not using an ECM controlled solenoid, a Thermo Vacuum Valve (TVV) is used to control purge. See the appropriate vehicle sections for checking procedures.

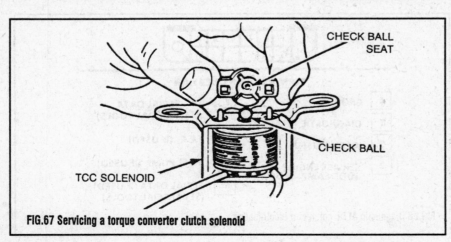

CHECK BALL SEAT

CHECK BALL

TCC SOLENOID

FIG.67 Servicing a torque converter clutch solenoid

Air Management Control

♦ SEE FIGS. 19, 20 and 50

The air management system aids in the reduction of exhaust emissions by supplying air to either the catalytic converter, engine exhaust manifold, or to the air cleaner. The ECM controls the air management system by energizing or de-energizing an air switching valve. Operation of the air switching valve is dependent upon such engine operating characteristics as coolant temperature, engine load, and acceleration (or deceleration), all of which are sensed by the ECM.

PULSAIR REACTOR SYSTEM

The Pulsair Injection Reactor (PAIR) system utilizes exhaust pressure pulsations to draw air into the exhaust system. Fresh air from the clean side of the air cleaner supplies filtered air to avoid dirt build-up on the check valve seat. The air cleaner also serves as a muffler for noise reduction. The internal mechanism of the Pulsair valve reacts to 3 distinct conditions.

The firing of the engine creates a pulsating flow of exhaust gases which are of positive (+) or negative (–) pressure. This pressure or vacuum is transmitted through external tubes to the Pulsair valve.

1. If the pressure is positive, the disc is forced to the closed position and no exhaust gas is allowed to flow past the valve and into the air supply line.

2. If there is a negative pressure (vacuum) in the exhaust system at the valve, the disc will open, allowing fresh air to mix with the exhaust gases.

3. Due to the inertia of the system, the disc ceases to follow the pressure pulsations at high engine rpm. At this point, the disc remains closed, preventing any further fresh air flow.

Catalytic Converter

Of all emission control devices available, the catalytic converter is the most effective in reducing tailpipe emissions. The major tailpipe pollutants are hydrocarbons (HC), carbon monoxide (CO), and oxides of nitrogen (NOx).

SERVICE PRECAUTIONS

When working around any part of the fuel system, take precautionary steps to prevent fire and/or explosion:

• Disconnect negative terminal from battery (except when testing with battery voltage is required).

• When ever possible, use a flashlight instead of a drop light.

• Keep all open flame and smoking material out of the area.

• Use a shop cloth or similar to catch fuel when opening a fuel system.

• Relieve fuel system pressure before servicing.

• Use eye protection.

• Always keep a dry chemical (class B) fire extinguisher near the area.

➡ **Due to the amount of fuel pressure in the fuel lines, before doing any work to the fuel system, the fuel system should be de-pressurized.**

Electrostatic Discharge Damage

Electronic components used in the control system are often design to carry very low voltage and are very susceptible to damage caused by electrostatic discharge. It is possible for less than 100 volts of static electricity to cause damage to some electronic components. By comparison it takes as much as 4000 volts for a person to even feel the zap of a static discharge.

There are several ways for a person to become statically charged. The most common methods of charging are by friction and induction. An example of charging by friction is a person sliding across a car seat, in which a charge as much as 25000 volts can build up. Charging by induction occurs when a person with well insulated shoes stands near a highly charged object and momentarily touches ground. Charges of the same polarity are drained off, leaving the person highly charged with the opposite polarity. Static charges of either type can cause damage, therefore, it is important to use care when handling and testing electronic components.

➡ **To prevent possible electrostatic discharge damage to the ECM, do not touch the connector pins or soldered components on the circuit board. When handling a PROM, Mem-Cal or Cal-Pak, do not touch the component leads and remove the integrated circuit from the carrier.**

ECM LEARNING ABILITY

The ECM has a learning capability. If the battery is disconnected the learning process has to begin all over again. A change may be noted in the vehicle's performance. To teach the ECM, insure the vehicle is at operating temperature and drive at part throttle, with moderate acceleration and idle conditions, until performance returns.

ALDL/CHECK CONNECTOR

The Assembly Line Diagnostic Link (ALDL), is a diagnostic connector located in the passenger compartment, usually under the instrument panel.

The assembly plant were the vehicles originate use these connectors to check the engine for proper operation before it leaves the plant. Vehicles with the ALDL system, enter the Diagnostic mode or the Field Service Mode by connecting or jumping terminal B, the diagnostic TEST terminal to terminal A, or ground circuit. Vehicles with the check connector, connect or jump terminal TE1, the diagnostic TEST terminal to terminal E1, or ground circuit. This connector is a very useful tool in diagnosing EFI engines. Important information from the ECM is available at this terminal and can be read with one of the many popular scanner tools.

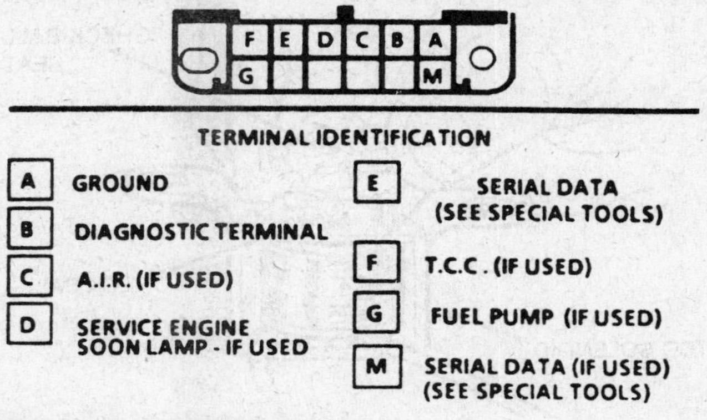

TERMINAL IDENTIFICATION

A GROUND	E SERIAL DATA (SEE SPECIAL TOOLS)
B DIAGNOSTIC TERMINAL	F T.C.C. (IF USED)
C A.I.R. (IF USED)	G FUEL PUMP (IF USED)
D SERVICE ENGINE SOON LAMP - IF USED	M SERIAL DATA (IF USED) (SEE SPECIAL TOOLS)

FIG.68 Diagnostic ALDL connector identification

READING CODES AND DIAGNOSTIC MODES

This information is able to be read by putting the ECM into 1 of 4 different modes. These modes are entered by inserting a specific amount of resistance between the ALDL connector terminals A and B. The modes and resistances needed to enter these modes are as follows:

DIAGNOSTIC MODES — 0 OHMS

When 0 resistance is between terminals A and B of the ALDL connector, the diagnostic mode is entered. There are 2 positions to this mode. One with the engine **OFF**, but the ignition **ON**; the other is when the engine is running called Field Service Mode.

If the diagnostic mode is entered with the engine in the **OFF** position, trouble codes will flash and the idle air control motor will pulsate in and out. Also, the relays and solenoids are energized with the exception of the fuel pump and injector.

As a bulb and system check, the SERVICE ENGINE SOON light will come on with the ignition switch **ON** and the engine not running. When the engine is started, the SERVICE ENGINE SOON light will turn off. If the SERVICE ENGINE SOON light remains on, the self-diagnostic system has detected a problem.

If the B terminal is then grounded with the ignition **ON**, engine not running, each trouble code will flash and repeat 3 times. If more than 1 problem has been detected, each trouble code will flash 3 times. Trouble codes will flash in numeric order (lowest number first). The trouble code series will repeat as long as the B terminal is grounded.

A trouble code indicates a problem in a given circuit (Code 14, for example, indicates a problem in the coolant sensor circuit; this includes the coolant sensor, connector harness, and ECM). The procedure for pinpointing the problem can be found in diagnosis. Similar charts are provided for each code.

Also in this mode all ECM controlled relays and solenoids except the fuel pump relay. This allows checking the circuits which may be difficult to energize without driving the vehicle and being under particular operating conditions. The IAC valve will move to its fully extended position on most vehicles, block the idle air passage. This is useful in checking the minimum idle speed.

FIELD SERVICE MODE — 0 OHMS

When the ALDL connector terminal B is grounded with the engine running, the ECM goes into the field service mode. In this mode, the SERVICE ENGINE SOON light flashes closed or open loop and indicates the rich/lean status of the engine. The ECM runs the engine at a fixed ignition timing advanced above the base setting.

The SERVICE ENGINE SOON light will show whether the system is in Open loop or Closed loop. In Open loop the SERVICE ENGINE SOON light flashes 2 times and one half times per second. In Closed loop the light flashes once per second. Also in closed loop, the light will stay OUT most of the time if the system is too lean. It will stay ON most of the time if the system is too rich. In either case the Field Service mode check, which is part of the Diagnostic circuit check, will lead you into choosing the correct diagnostic chart to refer to.

BACK-UP MODE — 3.9 KILO-OHMS

The backup mode is entered by applying 3.9 kilo-ohms resistance between terminals A and B of the ALDL connector with the ignition switch in the **ON** position. The ALDL scanner tool can now read 5 of the 20 parameters on the data stream. These parameters are as mode status, oxygen sensor voltage, rpm, block learn and idle air control. There are 2 ways to enter the backup mode. Using a scan tool is one way; putting a 3.9 kilo-ohms resistor across terminals A and B of the ALDL is another.

SPECIAL MODE — 10 KILO-OHMS

This special mode is entered by applying a 10K ohms resistor across terminals A and B. When this happens the ECM does the following:

1. Allows all of the serial data to be read.
2. Bypasses all timers.
3. Add a calibrated spark advance.
4. Enables the canister purge solenoid on some engines.
5. Idles at 1000 rpm fixed idle air control and fixed base pulse width on the injector.
6. Forces the idle air control to reset at part throttle (approximately 2000 rpm).
7. Disables the park/neutral restrict functions

OPEN OR ROAD TEST MODE — 20 KILO-OHMS

The system is in this mode during normal operation and is used by a scan tool to extract data while driving the vehicle.

ALDL SCAN TESTER INFORMATION

An ALDL display unit (ALDL tester, scanner, monitor, etc), allows a you to read the engine control system information from the ALDL connector under the instrument panel. It can provide information faster than a digital voltmeter or ohmmeter can. The scan tool does not diagnose the exact location of the problem. The tool supplies information about the ECM, the information that it is receiving and the commands that it is sending plus special information such as integrator and block learn.

To use an ALDL display tool you should understand thoroughly how an engine control system operates.

An ALDL scanner or monitor puts a fuel injection system into a special test mode. This mode commands an idle speed of 1000 rpm. The idle quality cannot be evaluated with a tester plugged in. Also the test mode commands a fixed spark with no advance. On vehicles with Electronic Spark Control (ESC), there will be a fixed spark, but it will be advanced. On vehicles with ESC, there might be a serious spark knock, this spark knock could be bad enough so as not being able to road test the vehicle in the ALDL test mode. Be sure to check the tool manufacturer for instructions on special test modes which should overcome these limitations.

When a tester is used with a fuel injected engine, it bypasses the timer that keeps the system in Open loop for a certain period of time. When all Closed loop conditions are met, the engine will go into Closed loop as soon as the vehicle is started. This means that the air management system will not function properly and air may go directly to the converter as soon as the engine is started.

These tools cannot diagnose everything. They do not tell where a problem is located in a circuit. The diagnostic charts to pinpoint the problems must still be used. These tester's do not let a you know if a solenoid or relay has been turned on. They only tell the you the ECM command. To find out if a solenoid has been turned on, check it with a suitable test light or digital voltmeter, or see if vacuum through the solenoid changes.

SCAN TOOLS FOR INTERMITTENTS

In some scan tool applications, the data update rate may make the tool less effective than a voltmeter, such as when trying to detect an intermittent problem which lasts for a very short time. Some scan tools have a snapshot function which stores several seconds or even minutes of operation to located an intermittent problem. Scan tools allow one to manipulate the wiring harness or components under the hood with the engine not running while observing the scan tool's readout.

The scan tool can be plugged in and observed while driving the vehicle under the condition when the SERVICE ENGINE SOON light turns on momentarily or when the engine driveability is momentarily poor. If the problem seems to be related to certain parameters that can be checked on the scan tool, they should be checked while driving the vehicle. If there does not seem to be any correlation between the problem and any specific circuit, the scan tool can be checked on each position. Watching for a period of time to see if there is any change in

the reading that indicates intermittent operation.

The scan tool is also an easy way to compare the operating parameters of a poorly operating engine with typical scan data for the vehicle being serviced or those of a known good engine. For example, a sensor may shift in value but not set a trouble code. Comparing the sensor's reading with those of a known good parameters may uncover the problem.

The scan tool has the ability to save time in diagnosis and prevent the replacement of good parts. The key to using the scan tool successfully for diagnosis lies in the ability to understand the system he is trying to diagnose as well as an understanding of the scan tool's operation and limitations.

CLEARING TROUBLE CODES

When the ECM detects a problem with the system, the SERVICE ENGINE SOON light will come on and a trouble code will be recorded in the ECM memory. If the problem is intermittent, the SERVICE ENGINE SOON light will go out after 10 seconds, when the fault goes away. However the trouble code will stay in the ECM memory until the battery voltage to the ECM is removed. Removing the battery voltage for 10 seconds will clear all trouble codes. Do this by disconnecting the ECM harness from the positive battery terminal pigtail for 10 seconds with the key in the **OFF** position, or by removing the ECM fuse for 10 seconds with the key **OFF**.

➡ **To prevent ECM damage, the key must be OFF when disconnecting and reconnecting ECM power.**

INTEGRATOR AND BLOCK LEARN

The integrator and block learn functions of the ECM are responsible for making minor adjustments to the air/fuel ratio on the fuel injected GM vehicles. These small adjustments are necessary to compensate for pinpoint air leaks and normal wear.

The integrator and block learn are 2 separate ECM memory functions which control fuel delivery. The integrator makes a temporary change and the block learn makes a more permanent change. Both of these functions apply only while the engine is in CLOSED LOOP. They represent the on-time of the injector. Also, integrator and block learn controls fuel delivery on the fuel injected engines as does the MC solenoid dwell on the CCC carbureted engines.

INTEGRATOR

Integrator is the term applied to a means of temporary change in fuel delivery. Integrator is displayed through the ALDL data line and monitored with a scanner as a number between 0 and 255 with an average of 128. The integrator monitors the oxygen sensor output voltage and adds and subtracts fuel depending on the lean or rich condition of the oxygen sensor. When the integrator is displaying 128, it indicates a neutral condition. This means that the oxygen sensor is seeing results of the 14.7:1 air/fuel mixture burned in the cylinders.

➡ **An air leak in the system (a lean condition) would cause the oxygen sensor voltage to decrease while the integrator would increase (add more fuel) to temporarily correct for the lean condition. If this happened the injector pulse width would increase.**

BLOCK LEARN

Although the integrator can correct fuel delivery over a wide range, it is only for a temporary correction. Therefore, another control called block learn was added. Although it cannot make as many corrections as the integrator, it does so for a longer period of time. It gets its name from the fact that the operating range of the engine for any given combinations of rpm and load is divided into 16 cell or blocks.

The computer has a given fuel delivery stored in each block. As the operating range gets into a given block the fuel delivery will be based on what value is stored in the memory in that block. Again, just like the integrator, the number represents the on-time of the injector. Also, just like the integrator, the number 128 represents no correction to the value that is stored in the cell or block. When the integrator increases or decreases, block learn which is also watching the integrator will make corrections in the same direction. As the block learn makes corrections, the integrator correction will be reduced until finally the integrator will return to 128 if the block learn has corrected the fuel delivery.

BLOCK LEARN MEMORY

Block learn operates on 1 of 2 types of memories depending on application, non-volatile and volatile. The non-volatile memories retain the value in the block learn cells even when the ignition switch is turned **OFF**. When the engine is restarted, the fuel delivery for a given block will be based on information stored in memory.

The volatile memories lose the numbers stored in the block learn cells when the ignition is turned to the **OFF** position. Upon restarting, the block learn starts at 128 in every block and corrects from that point as necessary.

INTEGRATOR/BLOCK LEARN LIMITS

Both the integrator and block learn have limits which will vary from engine to engine. If the mixture is off enough so that the block learn reaches the limit of its control and still cannot correct the condition, the integrator would also go to its limit of control in the same direction and the engine would then begin to run poorly. If the integrators and block learn are close to or at their limits of control, the engine hardware should be checked to determine the cause of the limits being reached, vacuum leaks, sticking injectors, etc.

If the integrator is lied to, for example, if the oxygen sensor lead was grounded (lean signal) the integrator and block learn would add fuel to the engine to cause it to run rich. However, with the oxygen sensor lead grounded, the ECM would continue seeing a lean condition eventually setting a Code 44 and the fuel control system would change to open loop operations.

CLOSED LOOP FUEL CONTROL

The purpose of closed loop fuel control is to precisely maintain an air/fuel mixture 14.7:1. When the air/fuel mixture is maintained at 14.7:1, the catalytic converter is able to operate at maximum efficiency which results in lower emission levels.

Since the ECM controls the air/fuel mixture, it needs to check its output and correct the fuel mixture for deviations from the ideal ratio. The oxygen sensor feeds this output information back to the ECM.

ENGINE PERFORMANCE DIAGNOSIS

Engine performance diagnosis procedures are guides that will lead to the most probable causes of engine performance complaints. They consider the components of the fuel, ignition, and mechanical systems that could cause a particular complaint, and then outline repairs in a logical sequence.

It is important to determine if the SERVICE ENGINE SOON light is on or has come on for a short interval while driving. If the SERVICE ENGINE SOON light has come on, the Computer Command Control System should be checked for stored **TROUBLE CODES** which may indicate the cause for the performance complaint.

All of the symptoms can be caused by worn out or defective parts such as spark plugs,

ignition wiring, etc. If time and/or mileage indicate that parts should be replaced, it is recommended that it be done.

➡ **Before checking any system controlled by the Electronic Fuel Injection (EFI) system, the Diagnostic Circuit Check must be performed or misdiagnosis may occur. If the complaint involves the SERVICE ENGINE SOON light, go directly to the Diagnostic Circuit Check.**

Basic Troubleshooting

➡ **The following explains how to activate the trouble code signal light in the instrument cluster and gives an explanation of what each code means. This is not a full system troubleshooting and isolation procedure.**

Before suspecting the system or any of its components as faulty, check the ignition system including distributor, timing, spark plugs and wires. Check the engine compression, air cleaner, and emission control components not controlled by the ECM. Also check the intake manifold, vacuum hoses and hose connectors for leaks.

The following symptoms could indicate a possible problem with the system:
1. Detonation
2. Stalls or rough idle-cold
3. Stalls or rough idle-hot
4. Missing
5. Hesitation
6. Surges
7. Poor gasoline mileage
8. Sluggish or spongy performance
9. Hard starting-cold
10. Objectionable exhaust odors (that rotten egg smell)
11. Cuts out
12. Improper idle speed

As a bulb and system check, the SERVICE ENGINE SOON light will come on when the ignition switch is turned to the **ON** position but the engine is not started. The SERVICE ENGINE SOON light will also produce the trouble code or codes by a series of flashes which translate as follows. When the diagnostic test terminal under the dash is grounded, with the ignition in the **ON** position and the engine not running, the SERVICE ENGINE SOON light will flash once, pause, then flash twice in rapid succession. This is a Code 12, which indicates that the diagnostic system is working. After a long pause, the Code 12 will repeat itself 2 more times. The cycle will then

repeat itself until the engine is started or the ignition is turned off.

When the engine is started, the SERVICE ENGINE SOON light will remain on for a few seconds, then turn off. If the SERVICE ENGINE SOON light remains on, the self-diagnostic system has detected a problem. If the test terminal is then grounded, the trouble code will flash 3 times. If more than 1 problem is found, each trouble code will flash 3 times. Trouble codes will flash in numerical order (lowest code number to highest). The trouble codes series will repeat as long as the test terminal is grounded.

A trouble code indicates a problem with a given circuit. For example, trouble Code 14 indicates a problem in the cooling sensor circuit. This includes the coolant sensor, its electrical harness, and the ECM. Since the self-diagnostic system cannot diagnose every possible fault in the system, the absence of a trouble code does not mean the system is trouble-free. To determine problems within the system which do not activate a trouble code, a system performance check must be made.

In the case of an intermittent fault in the system, the SERVICE ENGINE SOON light will go out when the fault goes away, but the trouble code will remain in the memory of the ECM. Therefore, it a trouble code can be obtained even though the SERVICE ENGINE SOON light is not on, the trouble code must be evaluated. It must be determined if the fault is intermittent or if the engine must be at certain operating conditions (under load, etc.) before the SERVICE ENGINE SOON light will come on. Some trouble codes will not be recorded in the ECM until the engine has been operated at part throttle for about 5–18 minutes.

INTERMITTENT SERVICE ENGINE SOON LIGHT

An intermittent open in the ground circuit would cause loss of power through the ECM and intermittent SERVICE ENGINE SOON light operation. When the ECM loses ground, distributor ignition is lost. An intermittent open in the ground circuit would be described as an engine miss.

Therefore, an intermittent SERVICE ENGINE SOON light, no code stored and a driveability comment described as similar to a miss will require checking the grounding circuit and the Code 12 circuit as it originates at the ignition coil.

UNDERVOLTAGE TO THE ECM

An undervoltage condition below 9 volts will cause the SERVICE ENGINE SOON light to come on as long as the condition exist.

Therefore, an intermittent SERVICE ENGINE SOON light, no code stored and a driveability comment described as similar to a miss will require checking the grounding circuit, Code 12 circuit and the ignition feed circuit to terminal C of the ECM. This does nor eliminate the necessity of checking the normal vehicle electrical system for possible cause such as a loose battery cable.

OVERVOLTAGE TO THE ECM

The ECM will also shut off when the power supply rises above 16 volts. The overvoltage condition will also cause the SERVICE ENGINE SOON to come on as long as this condition exist.

A momentary voltage surge in a vehicle's electrical system is a common occurrence. These voltage surges have never presented any problems because the entire electrical system acted as a shock absorber until the surge dissipated. Voltage surges or spikes in the vehicle's electrical system have been known, on occasion, to exceed 100 volts.

The system is a low voltage (between 9 and 16 volts) system and will not tolerate these surges. The ECM will be shut off by any surge in excess of 16 volts and will come back on, only after the surge has dissipated sufficiently to bring the voltage under 16 volts.

A surge will usually occur when an accessory requiring a high voltage supply is turned off or down. The voltage regulator in the vehicle's charging system cannot react to the changes in the voltage demands quickly enough and surge occurs. The driver should be questioned to determine which accessory circuit was turned off that caused the SERVICE ENGINE SOON light to come on.

Therefore, intermittent SERVICE ENGINE SOON light operation, with no trouble code stored, will require installation of a diode in the appropriate accessory circuit.

TPS OUTPUT CHECK TEST

Due to the varied application of components, a general procedure is outlined. For the exact procedure for the vehicle being service use Code 21 or 22 chart the appropriate engine.

WITH SCAN TOOL

1. Use a suitable scan tool to read the TPS voltage.

2. With the ignition switch **ON** and the engine **OFF**, the TPS voltage should be less than 1.25 volts.

3. If the voltage reading is higher than specified, replace the throttle position sensor.

WITHOUT SCAN TOOL

1. Remove air cleaner. Disconnect the TPS harness from the TPS.

2. Using suitable jumper wires, connect a digital voltmeter J–29125–A or equivalent to the correct TPS terminals A and B.

3. With the ignition **ON** and the engine running, The TPS voltage should be 0.3–1.0 volts at base idle to approximately 4.5 volts at wide open throttle.

4. If the reading on the TPS is out of specification, check the minimum idle speed before replacing the TPS.

5. If the voltage reading is correct, remove the voltmeter and jumper wires and reconnect the TPS connector to the sensor.

6. Reinstall the air cleaner.

FUEL SYSTEM PRESSURE

Testing

When the ignition switch is turned **ON**, the in-tank fuel pump is energized for as long as the engine is cranking or running and the control unit is receiving signals from the HEI distributor or DIS. If there are no reference pulses, the control unit will shut off the fuel pump within 2 seconds. The pump will deliver fuel to the fuel rail and injectors, then the pressure regulator where the system pressure is controlled to maintain 26–46 psi.

1. Connect pressure gauge J–34730–1, or equivalent, to fuel pressure test point on the fuel rail. Wrap a rag around the pressure tap to absorb any leakage that may occur when installing the gauge.

2. Turn the ignition **ON** and check that pump pressure is 24–40 psi. This pressure is controlled by spring pressure within the regulator assembly.

3. Start the engine and allow it to idle. The fuel pressure should drop to 28–32 psi due to the lower manifold pressure.

➡ **The idle pressure will vary somewhat depending on barometric pressure. Check for a drop in pressure indicating regulator control, rather than specific values.**

4. On turbocharged vehicles, use a low pressure air pump to apply air pressure to the regulator to simulate turbocharger boost pressure. Boost pressure should increase fuel pressure 1 lb. for every lb. of boost. Again, look for changes rather than specific pressures. The maximum fuel pressure should not exceed 46 psi.

5. If the fuel pressure drops, check the operation of the check valve, the pump coupling connection, fuel pressure regulator valve and the injectors. A restricted fuel line or filter may also cause a pressure drip. To check the fuel pump output, restrict the fuel return line and run 12 volts to the pump. The fuel pressure should rise to approximately 75 psi with the return line restricted.

❋❋ CAUTION

Before attempting to remove or service any fuel system component, it is necessary to relieve the fuel system pressure.

CRANKSHAFT SENSOR

Inspection

1. Disconnect the negative battery cable.

2. Rotate the harmonic balancer using a 28mm socket and pull on the handle until the interrupter ring fills the sensor slots and edge of the interrupter window is aligned with the edge of the deflector on the pedestal.

3. Insert feeler gauge adjustment tool J–36179 or equivalent into the gap between the sensor and the interrupter on each side of the interrupter ring.

4. If the gauge will not slide past the sensor on either side of the interrupter ring, the sensor is out of adjustment or the interrupter ring is bent.

5. The clearance should be checked again, at 3 positions around the interrupter ring

approximately 120 degrees apart.

6. If found out of adjustment, the sensor should be removed and inspected for potential damage.

MPI SYSTEM DIAGNOSTIC CHARTS

To properly diagnosis driveability problems you need to use the following charts. Make certain the charts cover the engine your car has. If your check engine light is not lit, check for engine stored engine codes. If any codes are stored write them down for reference later. Clear the codes as described earlier. Road test the vehicle to see if any of the codes return. Never try to fix a code problem until you're sure that it comes back. It may have been a old code from years ago that was never cleared or a code that was set do to a rain storm, battery jump, etc.

After clearing any codes and checking that they do not return. If the car drives fine your finished. But if there are no codes and the car runs poorly you'll need to check the symptoms charts. The problem is most likely not the computer or the devices it controls but the ignition system or engine mechanical.

If you do have a code(s) that returns start with the lowest code and follow the proper chart. You must follow every step of the chart and not jump from test to test or you'll never be certain to find and fix the real problem.

Start with the lowest to highest code chart, making sure to use the charts for your engine. If you have a 50 series code, like code 54. Always check those out first. They are rare but usually indicate a problem with the computer itself or its ability to test itself properly.

➡ **Component repair and replacement are covered in Section 5 Fuel System, this section will only deal with the testing of the system for both driveabilities and emission problems.**

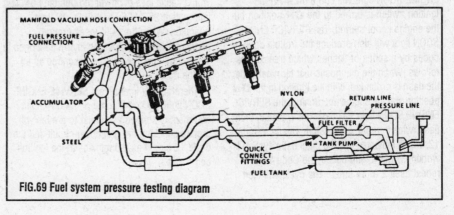

FIG.69 Fuel system pressure testing diagram

MULTI-PORT FUEL INJECTION DIAGNOSTIC CHARTS

CODE 13
OXYGEN SENSOR CIRCUIT (OPEN CIRCUIT)

① ENGINE AT NORMAL OPERATING TEMPERATURE (ABOVE 80°C/176°F).
- **RUN ENGINE ABOVE 1200 RPM FOR TWO MINUTES.**
- **DOES "SCAN" TOOL INDICATE "CLOSED LOOP"?**

YES → CODE 13 IS INTERMITTENT. IF NO ADDITIONAL CODES WERE STORED, REFER TO "DIAGNOSTIC AIDS" ON FACING PAGE.

NO ↓

② DISCONNECT O₂ SENSOR.
- **JUMPER HARNESS CKT 412 (ECM SIDE) TO GROUND.**
- **"SCAN" TOOL SHOULD DISPLAY O₂ VOLTAGE BELOW .2 VOLT (200 mV) WITH ENGINE RUNNING. DOES IT?**

YES → FAULTY O₂ SENSOR CONNECTION OR SENSOR.

NO ↓

③ REMOVE JUMPER.
- **IGNITION "ON", ENGINE "OFF".**
- **CHECK VOLTAGE OF CKT 412 (ECM SIDE) AT O₂ SENSOR HARNESS CONNECTOR USING A DVM.**

LESS THAN .3 VOLT (300 mV)	OVER .6 VOLT (600 mV)	.3-.6 VOLT (300 - 600 mV)
OPEN CKT 412 OR FAULTY ECM CONNECTION OR FAULTY ECM.	OPEN CKT 450 OR FAULTY CONNECTION OR FAULTY ECM.	FAULTY ECM.

CLEAR CODES AND CONFIRM "CLOSED LOOP" OPERATION AND NO "SERVICE ENGINE SOON" LIGHT.

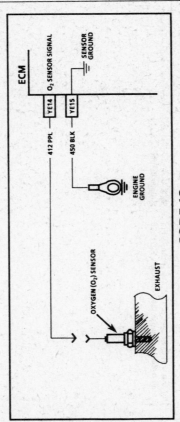

CODE 13
OXYGEN SENSOR CIRCUIT (OPEN CIRCUIT)
3.1L (VIN T)

Circuit Description:

The ECM supplies a voltage of about .45 volt between terminals "YE14" and "YE15". (If measured with a 10 megohm digital voltmeter, this may read as low as .32 volt.) The O₂ sensor varies the voltage within a range of about 1 volt if the exhaust is rich, down through about .10 volt if exhaust is lean.

The sensor is like an open circuit and produces no voltage when it is below 315°C (600°F). An open sensor circuit or cold sensor causes "Open Loop" operation.

Test Description: Numbers below refer to circled numbers on the diagnostic chart.

1. Code 13 will set:
   - Engine at normal operating temperature.
   - At least 2 minutes engine time after start.
   - O₂ signal voltage steady between .35 and .55 volt.
   - Throttle position sensor signal above 4%.
   - All conditions must be met for about 60 seconds.

   If the conditions for a Code 13 exist, the system will not go "Closed Loop."

2. This will determine if the sensor is at fault or the wiring or ECM is the cause of the Code 13.

3. In doing this test use only a high impedance digital volt ohmmeter. This test checks the continuity of CKTs 412 and 450 because if CKT 450 is open the ECM voltage on CKT 412 will be over .6 volt (600 mV).

Diagnostic Aids:

Normal "Scan" voltage varies between 100 mV to 999 mV (.1 and 1.0 volt) while in "Closed Loop." Code 13 sets in one minute if voltage remains between .35 and .55 volt, but the system will go "Open Loop" in about 15 seconds. Refer to "Intermittents" Section

MULTI-PORT FUEL INJECTION DIAGNOSTIC CHARTS

CODE 14
COOLANT TEMPERATURE SENSOR CIRCUIT
(HIGH TEMPERATURE INDICATED)

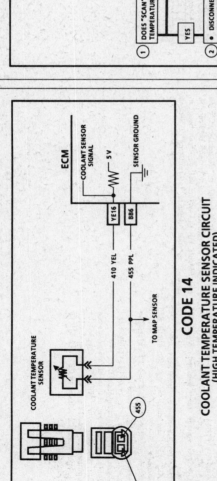

ECM

COOLANT SENSOR SIGNAL

5 V

SENSOR GROUND

YE16

BB6

410 YEL

455 PPL

TO MAP SENSOR

COOLANT TEMPERATURE SENSOR

455

410

CODE 14
COOLANT TEMPERATURE SENSOR CIRCUIT
(HIGH TEMPERATURE INDICATED)
3.1L (VIN T)

Circuit Description:

The Coolant Temperature Sensor (CTS) uses a thermistor to control the signal voltage to the ECM. The ECM applies a voltage on CKT 410 to the sensor. When the engine is cold, the sensor (thermistor) resistance is high, therefore the ECM will see high signal voltage.

As the engine warms, the sensor resistance becomes less, and the voltage drops. At normal engine operating temperature (85°C to 95°C), the voltage will measure about 1.5 to 2.0 volts.

Test Description: Numbers below refer to circled numbers on the diagnostic chart.

1. Code 14 will set if:
   - Signal voltage indicates a coolant temperature above 135°C (275°F) for 3 seconds.

2. This test will determine if CKT 410 is shorted to ground which will cause the conditions for Code 14.

Diagnostic Aids:

Check harness routing for a potential short to ground in CKT 410. "Scan" tool displays engine temperature in degrees centigrade. After engine is started, the temperature should rise steadily to about 90°C, then stabilize when thermostat opens. Refer to "Intermittents" Section

---

(1) DOES "SCAN" TOOL DISPLAY COOLANT TEMPERATURE OF 130°C (266°F) OR HIGHER?

YES →

NO → CODE 14 IS INTERMITTENT. IF NO ADDITIONAL CODES WERE STORED, REFER TO "DIAGNOSTIC AIDS" ON FACING PAGE.

(2) DISCONNECT SENSOR.
"SCAN" TOOL SHOULD DISPLAY TEMPERATURE BELOW -30°C (-22°F).
DOES IT?

YES → REPLACE SENSOR.

NO → CKT 410 SHORTED TO GROUND,
OR
CKT 410 SHORTED TO SENSOR GROUND CIRCUIT
OR
FAULTY ECM.

DIAGNOSTIC AID

COOLANT SENSOR
TEMPERATURE VS. RESISTANCE VALUES
(APPROXIMATE)

°F	°C	OHMS
210	100	185
160	70	450
100	38	1,800
70	20	3,400
40	4	7,500
20	-7	13,500
0	-18	25,000
-40	-40	100,700

CLEAR CODES AND CONFIRM "CLOSED LOOP" OPERATION AND NO "SERVICE ENGINE SOON" LIGHT.

MULTI-PORT FUEL INJECTION DIAGNOSTIC CHARTS

CODE 15

COOLANT TEMPERATURE SENSOR CIRCUIT
(LOW TEMPERATURE INDICATED)
(PORT)

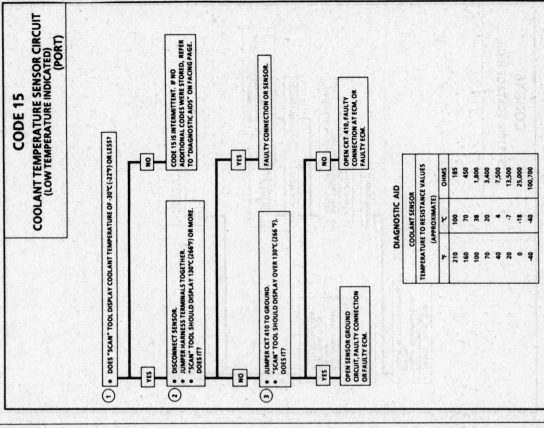

DIAGNOSTIC AID

COOLANT SENSOR TEMPERATURE TO RESISTANCE VALUES (APPROXIMATE)		
°F	°C	OHMS
210	100	185
160	70	450
100	38	1,800
70	20	3,400
40	4	7,500
20	-7	13,500
0	-18	25,000
-40	-40	100,700

① • DOES "SCAN" TOOL DISPLAY COOLANT TEMPERATURE OF -30°C (-22°F) OR LESS?

    YES → ② • DISCONNECT SENSOR.
                 • JUMPER HARNESS TERMINALS TOGETHER.
                 • "SCAN" TOOL SHOULD DISPLAY 130°C (266°F) OR MORE.
                 DOES IT?

           NO → ③ • JUMPER CKT 410 TO GROUND.
                      • "SCAN" TOOL SHOULD DISPLAY OVER 130°C (266°F).
                      DOES IT?

                      YES → OPEN SENSOR GROUND CIRCUIT, FAULTY CONNECTION OR FAULTY ECM.

                      NO → OPEN CKT 410, FAULTY CONNECTION AT ECM, OR FAULTY ECM.

NO → CODE 15 IS INTERMITTENT. IF NO ADDITIONAL CODES WERE STORED, REFER TO "DIAGNOSTIC AIDS" ON FACING PAGE.

                YES → FAULTY CONNECTION OR SENSOR.

CLEAR CODES AND CONFIRM "CLOSED LOOP" OPERATION AND NO "SERVICE ENGINE SOON" LIGHT.

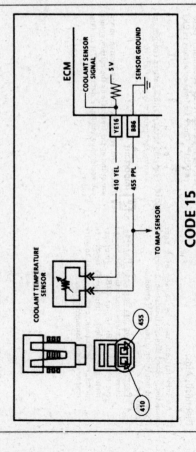

CODE 15

COOLANT TEMPERATURE SENSOR CIRCUIT
(LOW TEMPERATURE INDICATED)
3.1L (VIN T)

Circuit Description:

The Coolant Temperature Sensor (CTS) uses a thermistor to control the signal voltage to the ECM. The ECM applies a voltage on CKT 410 to the sensor. When the engine is cold the sensor (thermistor) resistance is high, therefore, the ECM will see high signal voltage.

As the engine warms, the sensor resistance becomes less and the voltage drops. At normal engine operating temperature (85°C to 95°C), the voltage will measure about 1.5 to 2.0 volts at the ECM.

Test Description: Numbers below refer to circled numbers on the diagnostic chart.

1. Code 15 will set if:
   • Signal voltage indicates a coolant temperature less than -39°C (-38°F) for 3 seconds.

2. This test simulates a Code 14. If the ECM recognizes the low signal voltage, (high temperature) and the "Scan" reads 130°C, the ECM and wiring are OK.

3. This test will determine if CKT 410 is open. There should be 5 volts present at sensor connector, if measured with a DVOM.

Diagnostic Aids:

A "Scan" tool reads engine temperature in degrees centigrade. After engine is started the temperature should rise steadily to about 90°C then stabilize when thermostat opens.

A faulty connection, or an open in CKT 410 or 455 will result in a Code 15.

If Code 23 or 33 is also set, check CKT 455 for faulty wiring or connections. Check terminals at sensor for good contact. Refer to "Intermittents" Section'.

MULTI-PORT FUEL INJECTION DIAGNOSTIC CHARTS

CODE 16
SYSTEM VOLTAGE HIGH

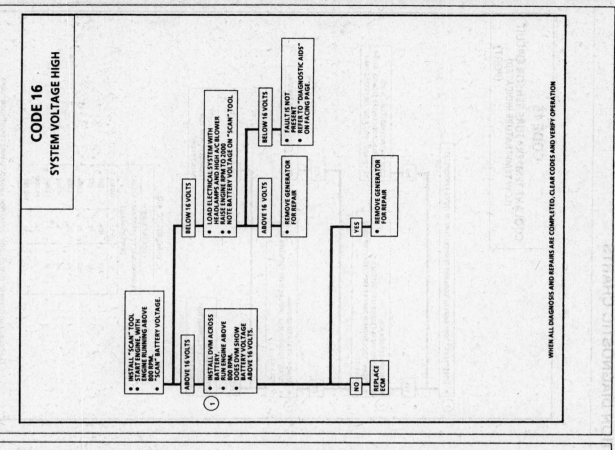

- INSTALL "SCAN" TOOL
- START ENGINE, WITH ENGINE RUNNING ABOVE 800 RPM.
- "SCAN" BATTERY VOLTAGE.

ABOVE 16 VOLTS

- INSTALL DVM ACROSS BATTERY.
- RUN ENGINE ABOVE 800 RPM.
- DOES DVM SHOW BATTERY VOLTAGE ABOVE 16 VOLTS.

BELOW 16 VOLTS

- LOAD ELECTRICAL SYSTEM WITH HEADLAMPS AND HIGH A/C BLOWER
- RAISE ENGINE RPM TO 2000
- NOTE BATTERY VOLTAGE ON "SCAN" TOOL

ABOVE 16 VOLTS

- REMOVE GENERATOR FOR REPAIR

BELOW 16 VOLTS

- FAULT IS NOT PRESENT REFER TO "DIAGNOSTIC AIDS" ON FACING PAGE.

(1)

NO

REPLACE ECM

YES

REMOVE GENERATOR FOR REPAIR

WHEN ALL DIAGNOSIS AND REPAIRS ARE COMPLETED, CLEAR CODES AND VERIFY OPERATION

ECM

BC16		BATTERY FEED
BB1		
BA6		IGN FEED
YE7		QDM
YE12		3-6 VOLTS
BA8		SERIAL DATA

→TO FUEL PUMP RELAY
ORN 440
ORN 440
PNK/BLK 439
BRN/WHT 419
WHT/BLK 451

IGN FUSE
10 AMP

450 BLK/WHT

BATT FUSE 20 AMP
IGN SWITCH
SES LIGHT
GAGE FUSE
10 AMP

BATTERY JUNCTION BOX
TO B+
TO IGN SWITCH

FUSIBLE LINK

Battery +

ORN 461
→TO DIS

ALDL CONNECTOR

B	A
M	

4-7-89

CODE 16
SYSTEM VOLTAGE HIGH
3300 (VIN N) "A" CARLINE (PORT)

Circuit Description:

The ECM monitors battery or system voltage on CKT 440 to terminals "BC16" and "BB1". If the ECM detects voltage above 16 volts for more than 10 seconds, it will turn the SES light "ON" and set Code 16 in memory.

Test Description: Numbers below refer to circled numbers on the diagnostic chart.

1. Test generator output to determine proper operation of the voltage regulator. Run engine at moderate speed and measure voltage across the battery. If over 16 volts, repair generator.

Diagnostic Aids:

An intermittent may be caused by a poor connection, rubbed through insulation, a wire broken inside the insulation or poor ECM grounds. Check For:

- **Poor Connection or Damaged Harness.** Inspect ECM harness connectors for backed out terminal "BC16" or "BB1", improper mating, broken locks, improperly formed or damaged terminals, poor terminal to wire connection and damaged harness.

- **Intermittent Test.** If connections and harness checks OK, monitor battery voltage display while moving related connectors. If the failure is induced, the battery voltage will abruptly change. This may help to isolate the location of the malfunction. An engine stall while manipulating the harness indicates that the ECM has lost voltage at terminal "BC16" or "BB1". Check for loose connectors in CKT 440.

Note: Charging battery with a battery charger and starting the engine may set a Code 16.

Important

- If ECM and sensor grounds are located on the same stud at the transaxle as the battery ground you could have improper data to ECM or false codes.

MULTI-PORT FUEL INJECTION DIAGNOSTIC CHARTS

CODE 21
THROTTLE POSITION SENSOR (TPS) CIRCUIT
(SIGNAL VOLTAGE HIGH)

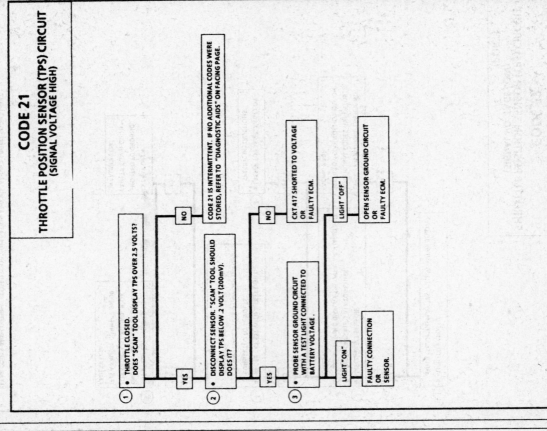

1. THROTTLE CLOSED.
DOES "SCAN" TOOL DISPLAY TPS OVER 2.5 VOLTS?

YES — 2. DISCONNECT SENSOR. "SCAN" TOOL SHOULD DISPLAY TPS BELOW .2 VOLT (200mV). DOES IT?

YES — 3. PROBE SENSOR GROUND CIRCUIT WITH A TEST LIGHT CONNECTED TO BATTERY VOLTAGE.

LIGHT "ON" → FAULTY CONNECTION OR SENSOR.

LIGHT "OFF" → OPEN SENSOR GROUND CIRCUIT OR FAULTY ECM.

NO (from 2) → CKT 417 SHORTED TO VOLTAGE OR FAULTY ECM.

NO (from 1) → CODE 21 IS INTERMITTENT. IF NO ADDITIONAL CODES WERE STORED, REFER TO "DIAGNOSTIC AIDS" ON FACING PAGE.

CLEAR CODES AND CONFIRM "CLOSED LOOP" OPERATION AND NO "SERVICE ENGINE SOON" LIGHT.

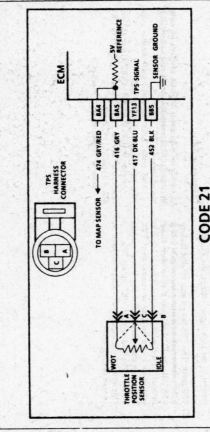

TPS HARNESS CONNECTOR

ECM

TO MAP SENSOR ← 474 GRY/RED — BA4
416 GRY — BA5 — 5V REFERENCE
417 DK BLU — YF13 — TPS SIGNAL
452 BLK — BB5 — SENSOR GROUND

THROTTLE POSITION SENSOR — WOT / IDLE

CODE 21
THROTTLE POSITION SENSOR (TPS) CIRCUIT
(SIGNAL VOLTAGE HIGH)
3.1L (VIN T)

Circuit Description:

The Throttle Position Sensor (TPS) provides a voltage signal that changes relative to the throttle blade.
Signal voltage will vary from about .29 at idle to about 4.8 volts at wide open throttle.
The TPS signal is one of the most important inputs used by the ECM for fuel control and for most of the ECM control outputs.

Test Description: Numbers below refer to circled numbers on the diagnostic chart.

1. Code 21 will set if:
   - Engine is running.
   - TPS signal voltage is greater than 3.8 volts.
   - Air flow is less than 17 GM/sec.
   - All conditions met for 10 seconds.
   - TPS check: The TPS has an auto zeroing feature. If the voltage reading is within the range of 0.29 to 0.98 volt, the ECM will use that value as closed throttle. If the voltage reading is out of the auto zero range on an existing or replacement TPS, make sure the cruise control and throttle cables are not being held open.

2. With the TPS sensor disconnected, the TPS voltage should go low if the ECM and wiring are OK.

3. Probing CKT 452 with a test light checks the 5 volts return circuit, because a faulty 5 volts return will cause a Code 21.

Diagnostic Aids:

A "Scan" tool reads throttle position in volts. Voltage should increase at a steady rate as throttle is moved toward WOT.
Also, some "Scan" tools will read throttle angle 0% = closed throttle, 100% = WOT.
An open in CKT 452 will result in a Code 21.
Refer to "Intermittents" Section

MULTI-PORT FUEL INJECTION DIAGNOSTIC CHARTS

CODE 22

THROTTLE POSITION SENSOR (TPS) CIRCUIT
(SIGNAL VOLTAGE LOW)
(PORT)

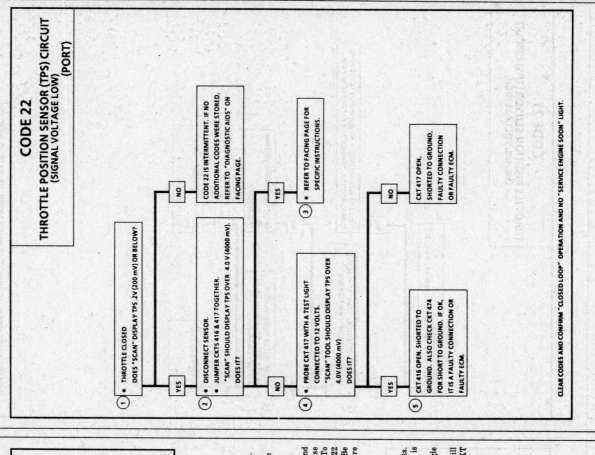

1.
- THROTTLE CLOSED
- DOES "SCAN" DISPLAY TPS .2V (200 mV) OR BELOW?

YES / NO

NO → CODE 22 IS INTERMITTENT. IF NO ADDITIONAL CODES WERE STORED, REFER TO "DIAGNOSTIC AIDS" ON FACING PAGE.

2.
- DISCONNECT SENSOR.
- JUMPER CKTS 416 & 417 TOGETHER.
- "SCAN" SHOULD DISPLAY TPS OVER 4.0 V (4000 mV).
  DOES IT?

YES → (3) • REFER TO FACING PAGE FOR SPECIFIC INSTRUCTIONS.

NO

4.
- PROBE CKT 417 WITH A TEST LIGHT CONNECTED TO 12 VOLTS.
- "SCAN" TOOL SHOULD DISPLAY TPS OVER 4.0V (4000 mV)
  DOES IT?

NO → CKT 417 OPEN, SHORTED TO GROUND, FAULTY CONNECTION OR FAULTY ECM.

5.
- CKT 416 OPEN, SHORTED TO GROUND. ALSO CHECK CKT 474 FOR SHORT TO GROUND. IF OK, IT IS A FAULTY CONNECTION OR FAULTY ECM.

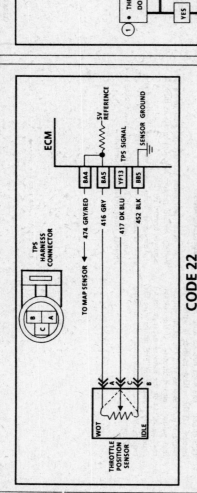

CODE 22

THROTTLE POSITION SENSOR (TPS) CIRCUIT
(SIGNAL VOLTAGE LOW)
3.1L (VIN T)   (PORT)

Circuit Description:

The Throttle Position Sensor (TPS) provides a voltage signal that changes relative to the throttle blade.

Signal voltage will vary from about .29 at idle to about 4.8 volts at wide open throttle.

The TPS signal is one of the most important inputs used by the ECM for fuel control and for most of the ECM control outputs.

Test Description: Numbers below refer to circled numbers on the diagnostic chart.

1. Code 22 will set if
   - Engine running
   - TPS signal voltage is less than about .2 volt for 3 seconds.

2. Simulates Code 21: (high voltage) if the ECM recognizes the high signal voltage, the ECM and wiring are OK.

3. TPS check: The TPS has an auto zeroing feature. If the voltage reading is within the range of 0.29 to 0.98 volt, the ECM will use that value as closed throttle. If the voltage reading is out of the auto zero range on an existing or replacement TPS, make sure the cruise control and throttle cables are not being held open. If "OK" replace TPS.

4. This simulates a high signal voltage to check for an open in CKT 417.

5. CKTs 416 and 474 share a common sensor ground buffered reference signal. If either of these circuits is shorted to ground, Code 22 will set. To determine if the MAP sensor is causing the 22 problem, disconnect it to see if Code 22 resets. Be sure TPS is connected and clear codes before testing.

Diagnostic Aids:

A "Scan" tool reads throttle position in volts. Voltage should increase at a steady rate as throttle is moved toward WOT.

Also, some "Scan" tools will read: throttle angle 0% = closed throttle, 100% = WOT.

An open or short to ground in CKT 416 or 417 will result in a Code 22. Also, a short to ground in CKT 474 will result in a Code 22.

Refer to "Intermittents" Section

CLEAR CODES AND CONFIRM "CLOSED LOOP" OPERATION AND NO "SERVICE ENGINE SOON" LIGHT.

MULTI-PORT FUEL INJECTION DIAGNOSTIC CHARTS

CODE 23

MANIFOLD AIR TEMPERATURE (MAT) SENSOR CIRCUIT
(LOW TEMPERATURE INDICATED)
(PORT)

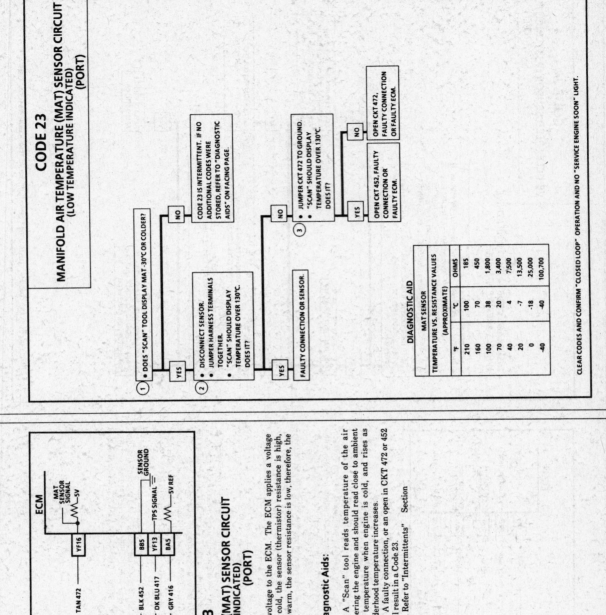

CODE 23

MANIFOLD AIR TEMPERATURE (MAT) SENSOR CIRCUIT
(LOW TEMPERATURE INDICATED)
3.1L (VIN T)
(PORT)

Circuit Description:

The MAT sensor uses a thermistor to control the signal voltage to the ECM. The ECM applies a voltage (about 5 volts) on CKT 472 to the sensor. When the air is cold, the sensor (thermistor) resistance is high, therefore the ECM will see a high signal voltage. If the air is warm, the sensor resistance is low, therefore, the ECM will see a low voltage.

Test Description: Numbers below refer to circled numbers on the diagnostic chart.

1. Code 23 will set if:
   - A signal voltage indicates a manifold air temperature below −35°C (−31°F) for 3 seconds.
   - Time since engine start is 4 minutes or longer.
   - No VSS.
2. A Code 23 will set, due to an open sensor, wire, or connection. This test will determine if the wiring and ECM are OK.
3. This will determine if the signal CKT 472 or the sensor ground return CKT 452 is open.

Diagnostic Aids:

A "Scan" tool reads temperature of the air entering the engine and should read close to ambient air temperature when engine is cold, and rises as underhood temperature increases.

A faulty connection, or an open in CKT 472 or 452 will result in a Code 23.

Refer to "Intermittents" Section

DIAGNOSTIC AID

MAT SENSOR
TEMPERATURE VS. RESISTANCE VALUES
(APPROXIMATE)

°F	°C	OHMS
210	100	185
160	70	450
100	38	1,800
70	20	3,400
40	4	7,500
20	−7	13,500
0	−18	25,000
−40	−40	100,700

CLEAR CODES AND CONFIRM "CLOSED LOOP" OPERATION AND NO "SERVICE ENGINE SOON" LIGHT.

MULTI-PORT FUEL INJECTION DIAGNOSTIC CHARTS

CODE 24

VEHICLE SPEED SENSOR (VSS) CIRCUIT (PORT)

VEHICLE SPEED SENSOR (VSS)

TRANS. MOUNTED

TO CRUISE CONTROL

TO I/P SPEEDOMETER

I/P HARNESS CONNECTOR 15 - WAY (FRONT VIEW)

ECM

BB9	PPL 401	VSS SIGNAL (LOW)
BB10	YEL 400	VSS SIGNAL (HIGH)
BC1	RED 381	VSS OUTPUT (2000 P/MI)
BB11	BRN 437	VSS OUTPUT (4000 P/MI)
BD16	434 ORN/BLK	P/N SIGNAL 12V

P/N SWITCH — CLOSED IN PARK OR NEUTRAL

15-WAY I/P CONNECTOR

CODE 24
VEHICLE SPEED SENSOR (VSS) CIRCUIT (PORT)
3.1L (VIN T)

Circuit Description:

Vehicle speed information is provided to the ECM by the Vehicle Speed Sensor (VSS), which is a permanent magnet (PM) generator and it is mounted in the transaxle. The PM generator produces a pulsing voltage, whenever vehicle speed is over about 3 mph. The A/C voltage level and the number of pulses increases with vehicle speed. The ECM then converts the pulsing voltage to mph which is used for calculations, and the mph can be displayed with a "Scan" tool.

The function of VSS buffer used in past model years has been incorporated into the ECM. The ECM then supplies the necessary signal for the instrument panel (4000 pulses per mile) for operating the speedometer and the odometer. If the vehicle is equipped with cruise control, the ECM also provides a signal (2000 pulses per mile) to the cruise control module

Test Description:
Numbers below refer to circled numbers on the diagnostic chart.

1. Code 24 will set if vehicle speed equals 0 mph when:
   - Engine speed is between 2200 and 4400 rpm
   - TPS is less than 2%
   - Low load condition (low air flow)
   - Not in park or neutral
   - All conditions met for 5 seconds

   These conditions are met during a road load deceleration. Disregard Code 24 that sets when drive wheels are not turning.
   - The PM generator only produces a signal if drive wheels are turning greater than 3 mph.

2. CKTs 400, 401 and 437 are OK if the speedometer works properly. Code 24 is being caused by a faulty ECM, faulty Mem-Cal or an incorrect Mem-Cal.

Diagnostic Aids:

"Scan" should indicate a vehicle speed whenever the drive wheels are turning greater than 3 mph.

A problem in CKT 437 or 381 will not affect the VSS input or the readings on a "Scan."

Check CKTs 400 and 401 for proper connections to be sure they're clean and tight and the harness is routed correctly. Refer to "Intermittents" Section

(A/T) A faulty or misadjusted park/neutral switch can result in a false Code 24. Use a "Scan" and check for proper signal while in drive 3T40 or overdrive 4T60. Refer to CHART C-1A for P/N switch diagnosis check.

DISREGARD CODE 24 IF SET WHILE DRIVE WHEELS ARE NOT TURNING.

1. - RAISE DRIVE WHEELS
   - **"NOTICE":** *DO NOT PERFORM THIS TEST WITHOUT SUPPORTING THE DRIVE AXLES ARE IN A NORMAL HORIZONTAL POSITION. RUNNING THE VEHICLE IN GEAR WITH THE WHEELS HANGING DOWN AT FULL TRAVEL MAY DAMAGE THE DRIVE AXLES.*
   - WITH ENGINE IDLING IN GEAR, "SCAN" TOOL SHOULD DISPLAY VEHICLE SPEED ABOVE 0.

   DOES IT?

   NO → DOES SPEEDOMETER WORK?

   YES → CODE 24 IS INTERMITTENT. IF NO ADDITIONAL CODES WERE STORED, REFER TO "DIAGNOSTIC AIDS" ON FACING PAGE.

   (NO branch) →
   - IGNITION "OFF"
   - DISCONNECT VSS HARNESS CONNECTOR AT TRANSAXLE.
   - CONNECT SIGNAL GENERATOR TESTER J 33431-B OR EQUIVALENT TO VSS HARNESS CONNECTOR.
   - IGNITION "ON." TOOL "ON" AND SET TO GENERATE A VSS SIGNAL.
   - "SCAN" TOOL SHOULD DISPLAY VEHICLE SPEED ABOVE 0.

   DOES IT?

   YES → 2. CHECK PROM FOR CORRECT APPLICATION. IF OK, REPLACE ECM.

   NO → CKT 400 OR 401 OPEN, SHORTED TO GROUND, SHORTED TOGETHER, FAULTY CONNECTIONS, OR FAULTY ECM.

   YES → REPLACE VEHICLE SPEED SENSOR.

CLEAR CODES AND CONFIRM "CLOSED LOOP" OPERATION AND NO "SERVICE ENGINE SOON" LIGHT.

MULTI-PORT FUEL INJECTION DIAGNOSTIC CHARTS

CODE 25

MANIFOLD AIR TEMPERATURE (MAT) SENSOR CIRCUIT
(HIGH TEMPERATURE INDICATED)
(PORT)

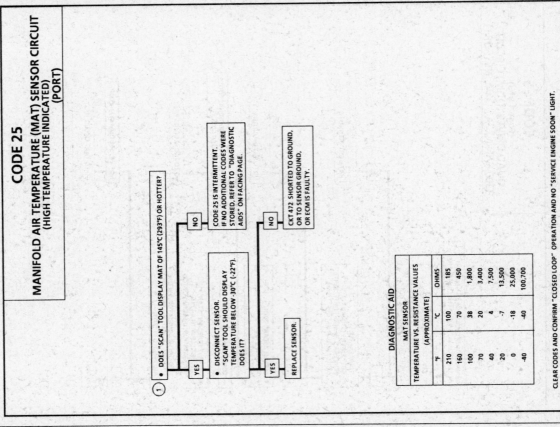

1 • DOES "SCAN" TOOL DISPLAY MAT AT 145°C (293°F) OR HOTTER?

YES

• DISCONNECT SENSOR. "SCAN" TOOL SHOULD DISPLAY TEMPERATURE BELOW -30°C (-22°F). DOES IT?

NO → CODE 25 IS INTERMITTENT. IF NO ADDITIONAL CODES WERE STORED, REFER TO "DIAGNOSTIC AIDS" ON FACING PAGE.

YES → REPLACE SENSOR.

NO → CKT 472 SHORTED TO GROUND, OR TO SENSOR GROUND, OR ECM IS FAULTY.

DIAGNOSTIC AID

MAT SENSOR
TEMPERATURE VS. RESISTANCE VALUES
(APPROXIMATE)

°F	°C	OHMS
210	100	185
160	70	450
100	38	1,800
70	20	3,400
40	4	7,500
20	-7	13,500
0	-18	25,000
-40	-40	100,700

CLEAR CODES AND CONFIRM "CLOSED LOOP" OPERATION AND NO "SERVICE ENGINE SOON" LIGHT.

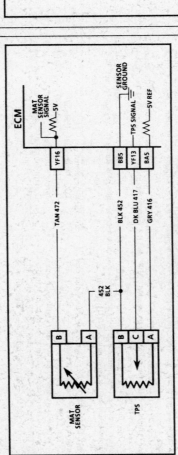

MAT SENSOR

TPS

CODE 25

MANIFOLD AIR TEMPERATURE (MAT) SENSOR CIRCUIT
(HIGH TEMPERATURE INDICATED)
(PORT)
3.1L (VIN T)

Circuit Description:

The Manifold Air Temperature (MAT) sensor uses a thermistor to control the signal voltage to the ECM. The ECM applies a voltage (about 5 volts) on CKT 472 to the sensor. When manifold air is cold, the sensor (thermistor) resistance is high, therefore, the ECM will see a high signal voltage. As the air warms, the sensor resistance becomes less, and the voltage drops.

Test Description: Numbers below refer to circled numbers on the diagnostic chart.

1. Code 25 will set if:
   • Signal voltage indicates a manifold air temperature greater than 145°C (293°F) for 3 seconds.
   • Time since engine start is 4 minutes or longer.
   • A vehicle speed is present.

Diagnostic Aids:

A "Scan" tool reads temperature of the air entering the engine and should read close to ambient air temperature when engine is cold and rises as underhood temperature increases.

A short to ground in CKT 472 will result in a Code 25.

Refer to "Intermittents" Section

MULTI-PORT FUEL INJECTION DIAGNOSTIC CHARTS

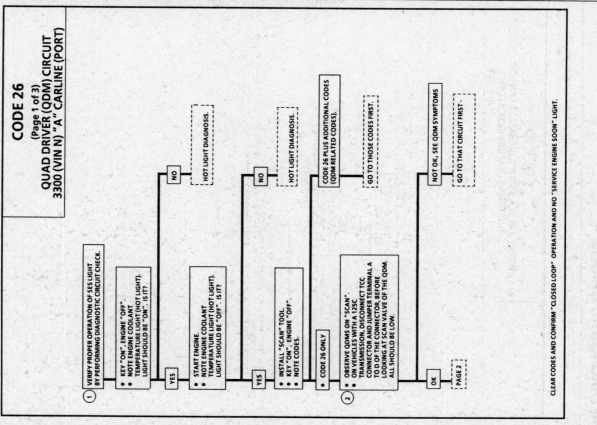

CODE 26
(Page 1 of 3)
QUAD DRIVER (QDM) CIRCUIT
3300 (VIN N) "A" CARLINE (PORT)

**125C TRANS ONLY

Circuit Description:

Quad-driver modules (QDM) are used to control the components shown in the illustration above. When the ECM is commanding a component "ON", the QDM closes the switch completing the circuit to ground.

Each QDM has a sense line and a fault line. When a component is commanded "ON", the voltage potential on the sense line is low, and when the component is commanded "OFF" the voltage potential on the sense line is high.

Code 26 will set when the ECM is commanding a component "ON" and the voltage potential on the sense line is high, or if the component is commanded "OFF" and the voltage potential on the sense line is low. QDM number 3 will not set a code 26.

On vehicles with a 125C transmission, the QDM status on the Tech 1 will read HI until the second gear switch is closed. To simulate driving in second gear and change the QDM status to low, disconnect TCC connector and jumper terminals A and D together.

Test Description: Numbers below refer to circled numbers on the diagnostic chart.

1. The ECM does not know which controlled circuit caused the Code 26 so this chart will go through each of the circuits to determine which is at fault. This test checks the "Service Engine Soon" light driver and the "Service Engine Soon" light circuit.

2. QDM symptoms:
   - TCC - Inoperative - Code 39.
   - Hot Light - "ON" all the time/"OFF" during bulb check.
   - Coolant fan on all the time or won't come "ON" at all,
   - Poor driveability due to 100% canister purge.

MULTI-PORT FUEL INJECTION DIAGNOSTIC CHARTS

CODE 26
(Page 2 of 3)
QUAD DRIVER (QDM) CIRCUIT
3300 (VIN N) (PORT)

CIRCUIT NOT ISOLATED BY PRIOR STEPS
(VOLTAGE TEST)

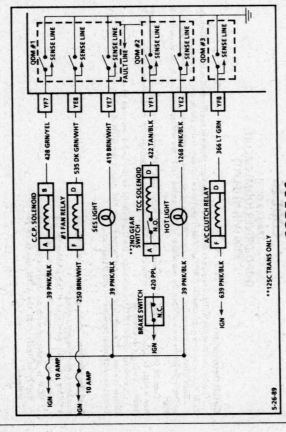

③ CIRCUIT NOT ISOLATED BY PRIOR STEPS
(VOLTAGE TEST).
- KEY "ON," ENGINE "OFF."
- DIAGNOSTIC TERMINAL NOT GROUNDED.
- BACKPROBE ECM QDM TERMINAL(S) FOR VOLTAGE WITH DVM.
- ALL TERMINALS SHOULD BE B + EXCEPT "YE7", "YE2" WHICH WILL BE NEAR 0 VOLTS.

- GROUND DIAGNOSTIC TERMINAL.
ALL SHOULD BE NEAR 0 VOLTS EXCEPT
"YE7," WHICH WILL BE TOGGLING
BETWEEN B + AND 0 VOLTS.

| OK | NOT OK → SEE PAGE 3 |

| OK → SEE "DIAGNOSTIC AIDS" ON FACING PAGE. | NOT OK → SEE PAGE 3 |

CLEAR CODES AND CONFIRM "CLOSED LOOP" OPERATION AND NO "SERVICE ENGINE SOON" LIGHT.

CODE 26
(Page 2 of 3)
QUAD-DRIVER (QDM) CIRCUIT
3300 (VIN N) "A" CARLINE (PORT)

5-26-89

**125C TRANS ONLY

Circuit Description:

Quad-driver modules (QDM) are used to control the components shown in the illustration above. When the ECM is commanding a component "ON", the QDM closes the switch completing the circuit to ground.

Each QDM has a sense line and a fault line. When a component is commanded "ON" the voltage potential on the sense line is low and when the component is commanded "OFF" the voltage potential on the sense line is high.

Code 26 will set when the ECM is commanding a component "ON" and the voltage potential on the sense line is high, or if the component is commanded "OFF" and the voltage potential on the sense line is low. QDM number 3 will not set a code 26.

On vehicles with a 125C transmission, the QDM status on the Tech 1 will read HI until the second gear switch is closed. To simulate driving in second gear and change the QDM status to low, disconnect TCC connector and jumper terminals A and D together.

Test Description: Numbers below refer to circled numbers on the diagnostic chart.

3. This test will determine which circuit is out of specifications. All circuits EXCEPT "YE7", the SES light and "YE2", the "hot light" should be B+ when key is "ON", engine not running. The diagnostic test terminal is not grounded.

Diagnostic Aids:

Monitor the voltage at each terminal while moving related harness connectors, including ECM harness. If the failure is induced, the voltage will change. This may help locate the intermittent. Check for bent pins at ECM and ECM connector terminals. If code re-occurs with no apparent connector problem, replace ECM.

MULTI-PORT FUEL INJECTION DIAGNOSTIC CHARTS

CODE 26
(Page 3 of 3)
QUAD DRIVER CIRCUIT
3300 (VIN N) "A" CARLINE (PORT)

CIRCUIT ISOLATED FROM PRIOR CHARTS

(4)
- USE FACING PAGE WIRING DIAGRAM FOR SPECIFIC TERMINALS TO BE TESTED.
- RECONNECT ECM, IF APPLICABLE.
- KEY "ON", ENGINE "OFF". DIAGNOSTIC TEST TERMINAL (DTT) GROUNDED.
- REMOVE CONN. FROM RELAY/SOL. IN AFFECTED CIRCUIT.
- PLACE TEST LIGHT ACROSS TERMS. FOR B + AND ECM DRIVER CIRCUIT.
- LIGHT SHOULD BE "ON", IS IT?

NO →
- CONNECT TEST LIGHT FROM B + CIRCUIT TO GROUND.
- NOTE LIGHT.

"ON" →
- DISCONNECT ECM CONNECTOR.
- CHECK FOR OPEN IN DRIVER CIRCUIT.

NOT OK → REPAIR OPEN.

OK → ECM CONN. OR ECM.

"OFF" → REPAIR OPEN IN B + CIRCUIT.

YES →
- REMOVE JUMPER AT DTT.
- NOTE LIGHT.

"ON" →
- DISCONNECT ECM CONNECTOR.
- NOTE LIGHT.

"ON" → REPAIR GROUNDED CIRCUIT.

"OFF" → REPLACE ECM.

"OFF" → CHECK FOR POOR CONNECTIONS. IF OK, REPLACE COMPONENT.

CLEAR CODES AND CONFIRM "CLOSED LOOP" OPERATION AND NO "SERVICE ENGINE SOON" LIGHT

Wiring Diagram

QDM #1 — SENSE LINE — YF7 — 428 GRN/YEL — C.C.P. SOLENOID A / B — 39 PNK/BLK — IGN — 10 AMP

SENSE LINE — YE8 — 535 DK GRN/WHT — #1 FAN RELAY F / D — 250 BRN/WHT — GN — 10 AMP

SENSE LINE — YE7 — 419 BRN/WHT — SES LIGHT — 39 PNK/BLK

FAULT LINE

QDM #2 — SENSE LINE — YF1 — 422 TAN/BLK — **2ND GEAR SWITCH** A / D TCC SOLENOID N.O. — 39 PNK/BLK — IGN

BRAKE SWITCH N.C. — 420 PPL

SENSE LINE — YE2 — 1268 PNK/BLK — HOT LIGHT — 39 PNK/BLK

QDM #3 — SENSE LINE — YF8 — 366 LT GRN — A/C CLUTCH RELAY F / D — 639 PNK/BLK — IGN

**125C TRANS ONLY

CODE 26
(PAGE 3 OF 3)
QUAD-DRIVER (QDM) CIRCUIT
3300 (VIN N) (PORT)

Circuit Description:

Quad-driver modules (QDM) are used to control the components shown in the illustration above. When the ECM is commanding a component "ON", the QDM closes the switch completing the circuit to ground.

Each QDM has a sense line and a fault line. When a component is commanded "ON", the voltage potential on the sense line is low and when the component is commanded "OFF" the voltage potential on the sense line is high.

Code 26 will set when the ECM is commanding a component "ON" and the voltage potential on the sense line is high, or if the component is commanded "OFF" and the voltage potential on the sense line is low. QDM number 3 will not set a code 26.

On vehicles with a 125C transmission, the QDM status on the Tech 1 will read HI until the second gear switch is closed. To simulate driving in second gear and change the QDM status to low, disconnect TCC connector and jumper terminals A and D together.

Test Description: Numbers below refer to circled numbers on the diagnostic chart.

4. This test will determine if the problem is the circuit or the component. As the factory installed ECM is protected with an internal fuse, it is highly unlikely that the ECM needs to be replaced.

MULTI-PORT FUEL INJECTION DIAGNOSTIC CHARTS

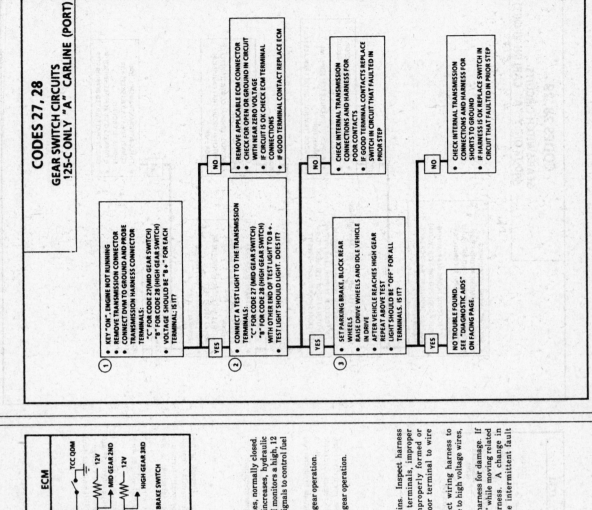

CODES 27, 28
GEAR SWITCH CIRCUITS
3300 (VIN N) 125-C ONLY "A" CARLINE (PORT)

Circuit Description:

The gear switches are located inside the transaxle. They are pressure operated switches, normally closed. The ECM supplies 12 volts through each selected circuit to the switch. As road speed increases, hydraulic pressure applies the specific gear clutches and the gear switch opens. At this time, the ECM monitors a high, 12 volt potential, and interprets this to indicate that gear is applied. The ECM uses the gear signals to control fuel delivery (and TCC).

Code 27 will set if
- CKT 108 indicates ground or closed switch for 10 seconds when vehicle is in 3rd gear operation.
- CKT 108 indicates an open (drive) when the engine is first started.

Code 28 will set if
- CKT 581 indicates ground or closed switch for 10 seconds when vehicle is in 3rd gear operation.
- CKT 581 indicates an open (drive) when the engine is first started.

Test Description: Numbers below refer to circled numbers on the diagnostic chart.
1. Must use a DVM. A test light will not light due to the very low current being supplied by the ECM.
2. Checks to see if circuit is grounded through the switch.
3. Checks for a good, properly operating switch and checks circuit within transaxle for an improper ground.

Diagnostic Aids:

An intermittent may be caused by a poor connection, mis-routed harness, rubbed through wire insulation, or a wire broken inside the insulation.

Check For:
- **Poor Connection at ECM pins.** Inspect harness connectors for backed out terminals, improper mating, broken locks, improperly formed or damaged terminals, and poor terminal to wire connection.
- **Mis-routed Harness** Inspect wiring harness to insure that it is not too close to high voltage wires, such as spark plug leads.
- **Damaged Harness** Inspect harness for damage. If harness appears OK, "Scan" while moving related connectors and wiring harness. A change in display would indicate the intermittent fault location.

6-1-88

MULTI-PORT FUEL INJECTION DIAGNOSTIC CHARTS

CODES 28, 29
GEAR SWITCH CIRCUITS
440-T4 ONLY "A" CARLINE (PORT)

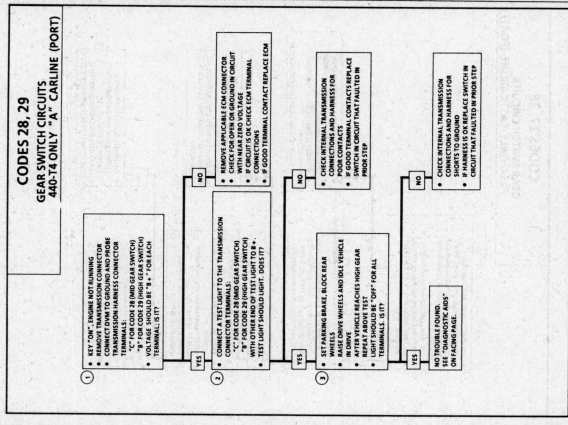

1
- KEY "ON", ENGINE NOT RUNNING
- REMOVE TRANSMISSION CONNECTOR
- CONNECT DVM TO GROUND AND PROBE TRANSMISSION HARNESS CONNECTOR TERMINALS:
  "C" FOR CODE 28 (MID GEAR SWITCH)
  "B" FOR CODE 29 (HIGH GEAR SWITCH)
- VOLTAGE SHOULD BE "B+" FOR EACH TERMINAL. IS IT?

2
- CONNECT A TEST LIGHT TO THE TRANSMISSION CONNECTOR TERMINALS:
  "C" FOR CODE 28 (MID GEAR SWITCH)
  "B" FOR CODE 29 (HIGH GEAR SWITCH)
- WITH OTHER END OF TEST LIGHT TO B+.
- TEST LIGHT SHOULD LIGHT. DOES IT?

3
- SET PARKING BRAKE, BLOCK REAR WHEELS
- RAISE DRIVE WHEELS AND IDLE VEHICLE IN DRIVE
- AFTER VEHICLE REACHES HIGH GEAR REPEAT TEST
- LIGHT SHOULD BE "OFF" FOR ALL TERMINALS. IS IT?

NO (from 1)
- REMOVE APPLICABLE ECM CONNECTOR
- CHECK FOR OPEN OR GROUND IN CIRCUIT WITH NEAR ZERO VOLTAGE
- IF CIRCUIT IS OK CHECK ECM TERMINAL CONNECTIONS
- IF GOOD TERMINAL CONTACT REPLACE ECM

NO (from 2)
- CHECK INTERNAL TRANSMISSION CONNECTIONS AND HARNESS FOR POOR CONTACTS
- IF GOOD TERMINAL CONTACTS REPLACE SWITCH IN CIRCUIT THAT FAULTED IN PRIOR STEP

NO (from 3)
- CHECK INTERNAL TRANSMISSION CONNECTIONS AND HARNESS FOR SHORTS TO GROUND
- IF HARNESS IS OK REPLACE SWITCH IN CIRCUIT THAT FAULTED IN PRIOR STEP

YES (from 3)
- NO TROUBLE FOUND. SEE "DIAGNOSTIC AIDS" ON FACING PAGE.

CODES 28, 29
GEAR SWITCH CIRCUITS
3300 (VIN N) 440-T4 ONLY "A" CARLINE (PORT)

Circuit Description:

The gear switches are located inside the transaxle. They are pressure operated switches, normally closed. The ECM supplies 12 volts through each selected circuit to the switch. As road speed increases, hydraulic pressure applies the specific gear clutches and the gear switch opens. At this time, the ECM monitors a high, 12 volt potential, and interprets this to indicate that gear is applied. The ECM uses the gear signals to control fuel delivery (and TCC).

Code 28 will set if
- CKT 108 indicates ground or closed switch for 10 seconds when vehicle is in 4th gear operation.
- CKT 108 indicates an open (drive) when the engine is first started.

Code 29 will set if
- CKT 446 indicates ground or closed switch for 10 seconds when vehicle is in 4th gear operation.
- CKT 446 indicates an open (drive) when the engine is first started.

Test Description: Numbers below refer to circled numbers on the diagnostic chart.
1. Must use a DVM. A test light will not light due to the very low current being supplied by the ECM.
2. Checks to see if circuit is grounded through the switch.
3. Checks for a good, properly operating switch and checks circuit within transaxle for an improper ground.

Diagnostic Aids:

An intermittent may be caused by a poor connection, mis-routed harness, rubbed through wire insulation, or a wire broken inside the insulation.

Check For:
- Poor Connection at ECM pins. Inspect harness connectors at ECM pins. Inspect harness connectors for backed out terminals, improper mating, broken locks, improperly formed or damaged terminals, and poor terminal to wire connection.
- Mis-routed Harness. Inspect wiring harness to insure that it is not too close to high voltage wires, such as spark plug leads.
- Damaged Harness. Inspect harness for damage. If harness appears OK, "Scan" while moving related connectors and wiring harness. A change in display would indicate the intermittent fault location.

MULTI-PORT FUEL INJECTION DIAGNOSTIC CHARTS

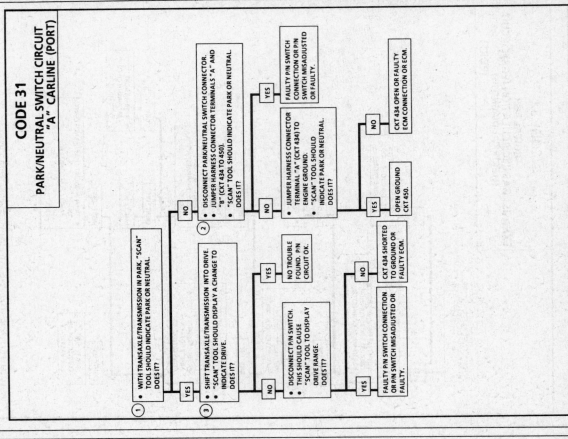

CODE 31
PARK/NEUTRAL SWITCH CIRCUIT "A" CARLINE (PORT)

① WITH TRANSAXLE/TRANSMISSION IN PARK, "SCAN" TOOL SHOULD INDICATE PARK OR NEUTRAL. DOES IT?

③ SHIFT TRANSAXLE/TRANSMISSION INTO DRIVE. "SCAN" TOOL SHOULD DISPLAY A CHANGE TO INDICATE DRIVE. DOES IT?

DISCONNECT PARK/NEUTRAL SWITCH CONNECTOR. JUMPER HARNESS CONNECTOR TERMINALS "A" AND "B" (CKT 434 TO 450). "SCAN" TOOL SHOULD INDICATE PARK OR NEUTRAL. DOES IT?

JUMPER HARNESS CONNECTOR TERMINAL "A" (CKT 434) TO ENGINE GROUND. "SCAN" TOOL SHOULD INDICATE PARK OR NEUTRAL. DOES IT?

FAULTY P/N SWITCH CONNECTION OR P/N SWITCH MISADJUSTED OR FAULTY.

CKT 434 OPEN OR FAULTY ECM CONNECTION OR ECM.

OPEN GROUND CKT 450.

DISCONNECT P/N SWITCH. THIS SHOULD CAUSE "SCAN" TOOL TO DISPLAY DRIVE RANGE. DOES IT?

NO TROUBLE FOUND. P/N CIRCUIT OK.

CKT 434 SHORTED TO GROUND OR FAULTY ECM.

FAULTY P/N SWITCH CONNECTION OR P/N SWITCH MISADJUSTED OR FAULTY.

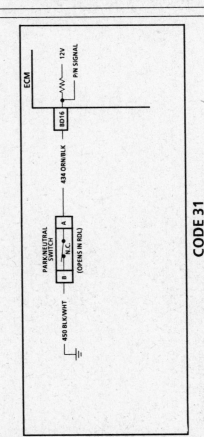

CODE 31
PARK/NEUTRAL SWITCH CIRCUIT
3300 (VIN N) "A" CARLINE (PORT)

Circuit Description:

The park/neutral switch contacts are a part of the neutral start switch and are closed to ground in park or neutral and open in drive ranges.

The ECM supplies ignition voltage through a current limiting resistor to CKT 434 and senses a closed switch when the voltage on CKT 434 drops to less than one volt.

The ECM uses the P/N signal as one of the inputs to control:

- Idle Speed (IAC)
- Vehicle Speed Sensor Diagnostics (VSS)
- Spark Advance

Code 31 will set if:

- CKT 434 indicates an open for 3 consecutive starts

or if:

- CKT 434 indicates a ground
- No Code 38
- Transmission is in high gear
- TCC is locked (4-speed only)
- VSS greater than 45 mph and TPS less than 15% (.94 volt) – 3 speed only
- Above conditions are met for 12 seconds

Test Description: Numbers below refer to circled numbers on the diagnostic chart.

1. Checks for a closed switch to ground in park position. Different makes of "Scan" tools will read P/N differently. Refer to "Tool Operator's" manual for type of display used for a specific tool.

2. Checks for an open switch in drive range.

3. Be sure "Scan" indicates drive, even while wiggling shifter, to test for an intermittent or misadjusted switch in drive or overdrive range.

MULTI-PORT FUEL INJECTION DIAGNOSTIC CHARTS

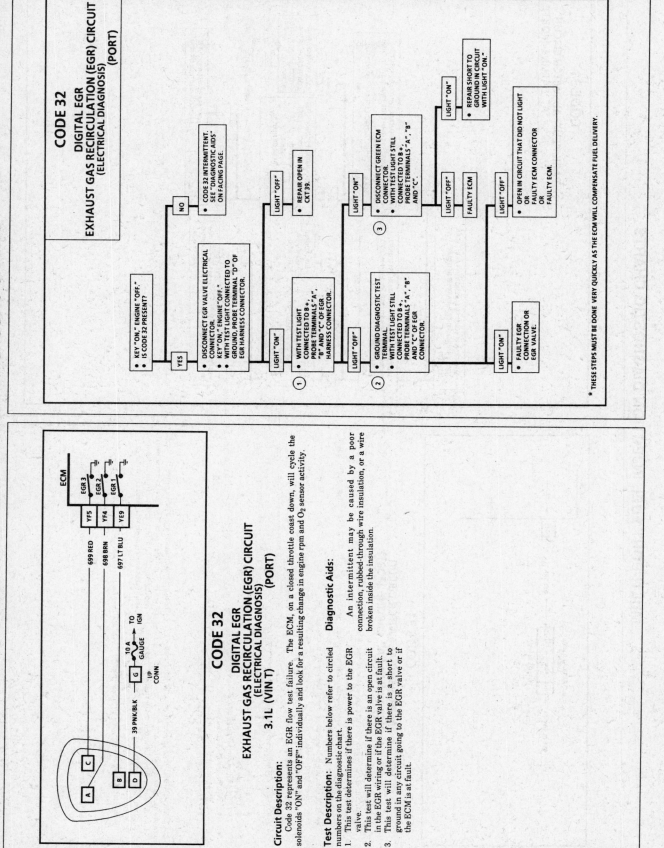

CODE 32

DIGITAL EGR

EXHAUST GAS RECIRCULATION (EGR) CIRCUIT

(ELECTRICAL DIAGNOSIS)

3.1L (VIN T)

Circuit Description:

Code 32 represents an EGR flow test failure. The ECM, on a closed throttle coast down, will cycle the solenoids "ON" and "OFF" individually and look for a resulting change in engine rpm and O₂ sensor activity.

Test Description: Numbers below refer to circled numbers on the diagnostic chart.

1. This test determines if there is power to the EGR valve.

2. This test will determine if there is an open circuit in the EGR wiring or if the EGR valve is at fault.

3. This test will determine if there is a short to ground in any circuit going to the EGR valve or if the ECM is at fault.

Diagnostic Aids:

An intermittent may be caused by a poor connection, rubbed-through wire insulation, or a wire broken inside the insulation.

MULTI-PORT FUEL INJECTION DIAGNOSTIC CHARTS

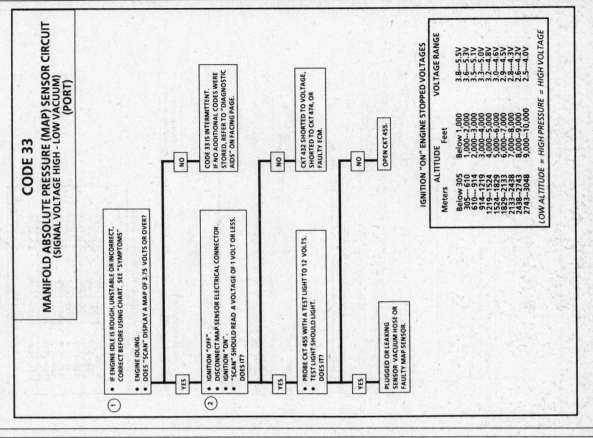

CODE 33

MANIFOLD ABSOLUTE PRESSURE (MAP) SENSOR CIRCUIT
(SIGNAL VOLTAGE HIGH - LOW VACUUM)
(PORT)

(1)
- IF ENGINE IDLE IS ROUGH, UNSTABLE OR INCORRECT, CORRECT BEFORE USING CHART. SEE "SYMPTOMS"
- ENGINE IDLING.
- DOES "SCAN" DISPLAY A MAP OF 3.75 VOLTS OR OVER?

YES | NO

NO → CODE 33 IS INTERMITTENT. IF NO ADDITIONAL CODES WERE STORED, REFER TO "DIAGNOSTIC AIDS" ON FACING PAGE.

(2)
- IGNITION "OFF".
- DISCONNECT MAP SENSOR ELECTRICAL CONNECTOR.
- IGNITION "ON".
- "SCAN" SHOULD READ A VOLTAGE OF 1 VOLT OR LESS. DOES IT?

YES | NO

NO → CKT 432 SHORTED TO VOLTAGE, SHORTED TO CKT 474, OR FAULTY ECM.

- PROBE CKT 455 WITH A TEST LIGHT TO 12 VOLTS.
- TEST LIGHT SHOULD LIGHT. DOES IT?

YES | NO

NO → OPEN CKT 455.

PLUGGED OR LEAKING SENSOR VACUUM HOSE OR FAULTY MAP SENSOR.

IGNITION "ON" ENGINE STOPPED VOLTAGES

ALTITUDE		VOLTAGE RANGE
Meters	Feet	
Below 305	Below 1,000	3.8—5.5V
305—610	1,000—2,000	3.6—5.3V
610—914	2,000—3,000	3.5—5.1V
914—1219	3,000—4,000	3.3—5.0V
1219—1524	4,000—5,000	3.2—4.8V
1524—1829	5,000—6,000	3.0—4.6V
1829—2133	6,000—7,000	2.9—4.5V
2133—2438	7,000—8,000	2.8—4.3V
2438—2743	8,000—9,000	2.6—4.2V
2743—3048	9,000—10,000	2.5—4.0V

LOW ALTITUDE = HIGH PRESSURE = HIGH VOLTAGE

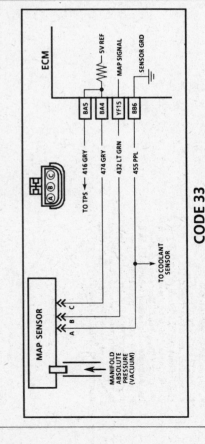

ECM

5V REF — BA5
MAP SIGNAL — BA4
— YF15
SENSOR GRD — BB6

TO TPS ← 416 GRY
474 GRY
432 LT GRN
455 PPL

MAP SENSOR

A B C

MANIFOLD ABSOLUTE PRESSURE (VACUUM)

TO COOLANT SENSOR

CODE 33

MANIFOLD ABSOLUTE PRESSURE (MAP) SENSOR CIRCUIT
(SIGNAL VOLTAGE HIGH - LOW VACUUM)
3.1L (VIN T) (PORT)

Circuit Description:

The Manifold Absolute Pressure (MAP) sensor responds to changes in manifold pressure (vacuum). The ECM receives this information as a signal voltage that will vary from about 1–1.5 volts at idle (high vacuum) to 4–4.5 volts at wide open throttle (low vacuum).

Test Description: Numbers below refer to circled numbers on the diagnostic chart.

1. Code 33 will set when:
   - Engine running
   - Codes 21 or 22 not detected.
   - Manifold pressure greater than 74 kPa (A/C "OFF") 83.4 kPa (A/C "ON").
   - Throttle angle less than 2%
   - Conditions met for 4.8 seconds

   Engine misfire or a low unstable idle may set Code 33.

2. With the MAP sensor disconnected, the ECM should see a low voltage if the ECM and wiring are OK.

Diagnostic Aids:

If idle is rough or unstable, refer to "Symptoms" Section for items which can cause an unstable idle.

An open in CKT 455 or the connection will result in a Code 33.

Ignition "ON" engine "OFF", voltages should be within the values shown in the table on the chart. Also, CHART C-1D can be used to test the MAP sensor.

Refer to "Intermittents" Section

MULTI-PORT FUEL INJECTION DIAGNOSTIC CHARTS

CODE 34

MANIFOLD ABSOLUTE PRESSURE (MAP) SENSOR CIRCUIT
(SIGNAL VOLTAGE LOW - HIGH VACUUM)
(PORT)

①
- IGNITION "OFF" FOR 10 SECONDS
- START ENGINE AND IMMEDIATELY NOTE MAP VALUE ON "SCAN".
  DOES "SCAN" DISPLAY MAP BELOW .25 VOLT?

| YES | NO |

NO → CODE 34 IS INTERMITTENT. IF NO ADDITIONAL CODES WERE STORED, REFER TO "DIAGNOSTIC AIDS" ON FACING PAGE.

②
- IGNITION "OFF".
- DISCONNECT SENSOR ELECTRICAL CONNECTOR.
- JUMPER HARNESS TERMINALS "B" TO "C".
- IGNITION "ON".
- MAP VOLTAGE SHOULD READ OVER 4 VOLTS.
  DOES IT?

| YES | NO |

YES → FAULTY CONNECTION OR SENSOR.

③
- IGNITION "OFF".
- REMOVE JUMPER WIRE.
- PROBE TERMINAL "B" (CKT 432) WITH A LIGHT TO 12 VOLTS.
- IGNITION "ON".
- "SCAN" SHOULD READ OVER 4 VOLTS.
  DOES IT?

| NO | YES |

NO → CKT 432 OPEN OR SHORTED TO GROUND OR FAULTY ECM.

YES → CKT 474 OPEN OR SHORTED TO GROUND OR FAULTY ECM.

IGNITION "ON" ENGINE STOPPED VOLTAGES

ALTITUDE		VOLTAGE RANGE
Meters	Feet	
Below 305	Below 1,000	3.8---5.5V
305---610	1,000---2,000	3.6---5.3V
610---914	2,000---3,000	3.5---5.1V
914---1219	3,000---4,000	3.3---5.0V
1219---1524	4,000---5,000	3.2---4.8V
1524---1829	5,000---6,000	3.0---4.6V
1829---2133	6,000---7,000	2.9---4.5V
2133---2438	7,000---8,000	2.8---4.3V
2438---2743	8,000---9,000	2.6---4.2V
2743---3048	9,000---10,000	2.5---4.0V

LOW ALTITUDE = HIGH PRESSURE = HIGH VOLTAGE

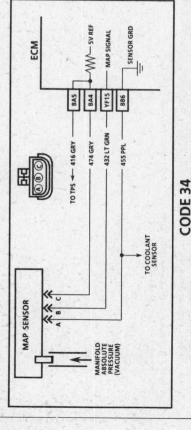

ECM
5V REF
MAP SIGNAL
SENSOR GRD

BA5 — 416 GRY — TO TPS
BA4 — 474 GRY
YF15 — 432 LT GRN
BB6 — 455 PPL — TO COOLANT SENSOR

A B C

MAP SENSOR
A B C

MANIFOLD ABSOLUTE PRESSURE (VACUUM)

CODE 34

MANIFOLD ABSOLUTE PRESSURE (MAP) SENSOR CIRCUIT
(SIGNAL VOLTAGE LOW - HIGH VACUUM)
3.1L (VIN T) (PORT)

Circuit Description:

The Manifold Absolute Pressure (MAP) sensor responds to changes in manifold pressure (vacuum). The ECM receives this information as a signal voltage that will vary from about 1-1.5 volts at idle (high vacuum) to 4-4.5 volts at wide open throttle (low vacuum).

Test Description: Numbers below refer to circled numbers on the diagnostic chart.

1. Code 34 will set if:
   - Engine rpm less than 600
   - Code 21 not detected.
   - Manifold pressure reading less than 13 kPa
   - Conditions met for 1 second

   or
   - Engine rpm greater than 600
   - Throttle angle over 20%
   - Manifold pressure less than 13 kPa
   - Conditions met for 1 second

2. This test to see if the sensor is at fault for the low voltage, or if there is an ECM or wiring problem.

3. This simulates a high signal voltage to check for an open in CKT 432. If the test light is bright during this test, CKT 432 is probably shorted to ground. If "Scan" reads over 4 volts at this test, CKT 474 can be checked by measuring the voltage at terminal "C" (should be 5 volts).

Diagnostic Aids:

An intermittent open in CKTs 432 or 474 will result in a Code 34.

Ignition "ON" engine "OFF" voltages should be within the values shown in the table on the chart. Also CHART C-1D can be used to test MAP sensor.

Refer to "Intermittents" Section

MULTI-PORT FUEL INJECTION DIAGNOSTIC CHARTS

CODE 34
MASS AIR FLOW (MAF) SENSOR CIRCUIT
(GM/SEC LOW)
"A" CARLINE (PORT)

(1) CLEAR CODES.
START AND IDLE ENGINE FOR AT LEAST 1 MINUTE OR UNTIL CODE 34 SETS.
DOES CODE SET?

- **YES** ↓
- **NO** → CODE 34 IS INTERMITTENT, REFER TO "DIAGNOSTIC AIDS" ON FACING PAGE.

(2) • IGNITION "OFF".
• DISCONNECT MAF SENSOR ELECTRICAL CONNECTOR.
• IGNITION "ON". ENGINE STOPPED.
• CONNECT VOLTMETER BETWEEN HARNESS CONNECTOR TERMINAL "A" AND GROUND.
• SHOULD READ 4-6 VOLTS.
DOES IT?

- **YES** ↓
- **NO** ↓
  - LESS THAN 4 VOLTS → CKT 492 OPEN, SHORTED TO GROUND, OR FAULTY ECM CONNECTIONS OR FAULTY ECM.
  - OVER 6 VOLTS → CKT 492 SHORTED TO VOLTAGE OR FAULTY ECM.

(3) • CONNECT TEST LIGHT BETWEEN HARNESS CONNECTOR TERMINALS "B" AND "C".
• TEST LIGHT SHOULD BE "ON".
IS IT?

- **YES** → FAULTY MAF SENSOR CONNECTION OR SENSOR.
- **NO** ↓

• CONNECT TEST LIGHT BETWEEN HARNESS CONNECTOR TERMINAL "C" AND CHASSIS GROUND.
• TEST LIGHT SHOULD BE "ON".
IS IT?

- **YES** → OPEN CKT 450
- **NO** → OPEN CKT 439

CLEAR CODES AND CONFIRM "CLOSED LOOP" OPERATION AND NO "SERVICE ENGINE SOON" LIGHT.

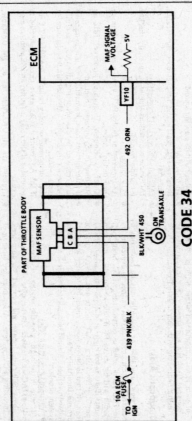

ECM

MAF SIGNAL VOLTAGE — 5V

YF10

492 ORN

PART OF THROTTLE BODY

MAF SENSOR

C B A

BLK/WHT 450 — ON TRANSAXLE

439 PNK/BLK

10A ECM FUSE

TO IGN

CODE 34
MASS AIR FLOW (MAF) SENSOR CIRCUIT
(GM/SEC LOW)
3300 (VIN N) "A" CARLINE (PORT)

Circuit Description:

The mass air flow (MAF) sensor measures the flow of air which passes through it in a given time. The ECM uses this information to monitor the operating condition of the engine for fuel delivery calculations. A large quantity of air movement indicates acceleration, while a small quantity indicates deceleration or idle.

The MAF sensor produces a frequency signal which cannot be easily measured. The sensor can be diagnosed using the procedures on this chart.

Code 34 will set when of the following conditions exists:

- Engine running
- If MAF sensor signal frequency is less than 960 Hz

Note: If the MAF sensor signal frequency is too low (Code 34 is set), a substitute value for airflow is calculated based on engine rpm, TPS, and IAC motor position.

Test Description: Numbers below refer to circled numbers on the diagnostic chart.

1. This step checks to see if ECM recognizes a problem.
2. A voltage reading at sensor harness connector terminal "A" of less than 4 or over 6 volts indicates a fault in CKT 492 or poor connection.
3. Verifies that both ignition voltage and a good ground circuit are available.

Diagnostic Aids:

An intermittent may be caused by a poor connection, mis-routed harness, rubbed through wire insulation, or a wire broken inside the insulation.

Check For:
- **Poor connection** at ECM pin "YF10". Inspect harness connectors for backed out terminals, improper mating, broken locks, improperly formed or damaged terminals, and poor terminal to wire connection.
- **Mis-routed Harness.** Inspect MAF sensor harness to insure that it is not too close to high voltage wires, such as spark plug leads.
- **Damaged Harness.** Inspect harness for damage. If harness appears OK, "Scan" while moving related connectors and wiring harness. A change in display would indicate the intermittent fault location.

MULTI-PORT FUEL INJECTION DIAGNOSTIC CHARTS

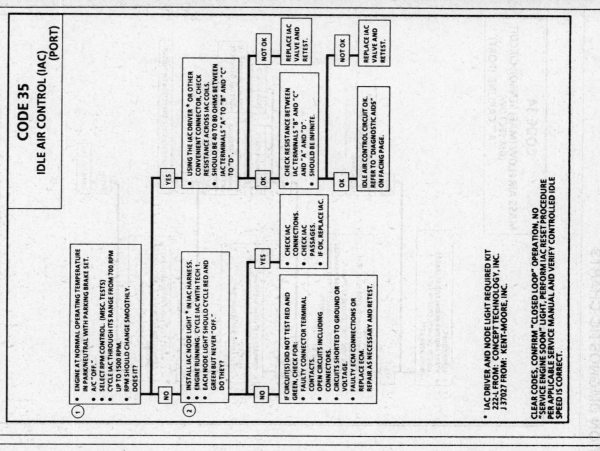

CODE 35

IDLE AIR CONTROL (IAC)
(PORT)

1. • ENGINE AT NORMAL OPERATING TEMPERATURE IN PARK/NEUTRAL WITH PARKING BRAKE SET.
   • A/C "OFF."
   • SELECT RPM CONTROL (MISC. TESTS)
   • CYCLE IAC THROUGH ITS RANGE FROM 700 RPM UP TO 1500 RPM.
   • RPM SHOULD CHANGE SMOOTHLY.
   DOES IT?

2. • INSTALL IAC NODE LIGHT * IN IAC HARNESS.
   • ENGINE RUNNING. CYCLE IAC WITH TECH 1.
   • EACH NODE LIGHT SHOULD CYCLE RED AND GREEN BUT NEVER "OFF."
   DO THEY?

NO → IF CIRCUIT(S) DID NOT TEST RED AND GREEN, CHECK FOR:
• FAULTY CONNECTOR TERMINAL CONTACTS.
• OPEN CIRCUITS INCLUDING CONNECTORS.
• CIRCUITS SHORTED TO GROUND OR VOLTAGE.
• FAULTY ECM CONNECTIONS OR REPLACE ECM.
REPAIR AS NECESSARY AND RETEST.

YES → • CHECK IAC CONNECTIONS.
• CHECK IAC PASSAGES.
• IF OK, REPLACE IAC.

YES → • USING THE IAC DRIVER * OR OTHER CONVENIENT CONNECTOR, CHECK RESISTANCE ACROSS IAC COILS.
• SHOULD BE 40 TO 80 OHMS BETWEEN IAC TERMINALS "A" TO "B" AND "C" TO "D".

NOT OK → REPLACE IAC VALVE AND RETEST.

OK → • CHECK RESISTANCE BETWEEN IAC TERMINALS "B" AND "C" AND "A" AND "D".
• SHOULD BE INFINITE.

NOT OK → REPLACE IAC VALVE AND RETEST.

OK → IDLE AIR CONTROL CIRCUIT OK. REFER TO "DIAGNOSTIC AIDS" ON FACING PAGE.

* IAC DRIVER AND NODE LIGHT REQUIRED KIT 222-L FROM: CONCEPT TECHNOLOGY, INC. J 37027 FROM: KENT-MOORE, INC.

CLEAR CODES, CONFIRM "CLOSED LOOP" OPERATION, NO "SERVICE ENGINE SOON" LIGHT, PERFORM IAC RESET PROCEDURE PER APPLICABLE SERVICE MANUAL AND VERIFY CONTROLLED IDLE SPEED IS CORRECT.

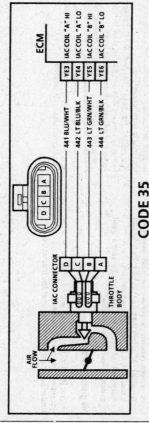

ECM

YE3	IAC COIL "A" HI
YE4	IAC COIL "A" LO
YE5	IAC COIL "B" HI
YE6	IAC COIL "B" LO

441 BLU/WHT
442 LT BLU/BLK
443 LT GRN/WHT
444 LT GRN/BLK

IAC CONNECTOR
D C B A

THROTTLE BODY

AIR FLOW

CODE 35

IDLE AIR CONTROL (IAC)
(PORT)
3.1L (VIN T)

Circuit Description:

Code 35 will set when the closed throttle engine speed is 200 rpm above or below the desired (commanded) idle speed for 50 seconds. Review the "General Description" of the IAC operation

Test Description: Numbers below refer to circled numbers on the diagnostic chart.

1. The Tech 1 rpm control mode is used to extend and retract the IAC valve. The valve should move smoothly within the specified range. If the idle speed is commanded (IAC extended) too low (below 700 rpm), the engine may stall. This may be normal and would not indicate a problem. Retracting the IAC beyond its controlled range (above 1500 rpm) will cause a delay before the rpm's start dropping. This too is normal.

2. This test uses the Tech 1 to command the IAC controlled idle speed. The ECM issues commands to obtain commanded idle speed. the node lights each should flash red and green to indicate a good circuit as the ECM issues commands. While the sequence of color is not important if either light is "OFF" or does not flash red and green, check the circuits for faults, beginning with poor terminal contacts.

Diagnostic Aids:

A slow, unstable, or fast idle may be caused by a non-IAC system problem that cannot be overcome by the IAC system. Out of control range IAC "Scan" tool counts will be above 60 if idle is too low, and zero counts if idle is too high. If idle speed is above 600-700 rpm in drive with an A/T, locate and correct vacuum leak. If rpm is below spec, check for foreign material around throttle plates. The following checks should be made to repair a non-IAC system problem:

• **Vacuum Leak (High Idle)**
If idle is too high, stop the engine. Start engine. If idle speed is above 800 rpm, locate and correct vacuum leak including PCV system. Also check for binding of throttle blade or linkage.

• **System too lean (High Air/Fuel Ratio)**
The idle speed may be too high or too low. Engine speed may vary up and down and disconnecting the IAC valve does not help. Code 44 may be set. "Scan" O₂ voltage will be less than 300 mV (.3 volt). Check for low regulated fuel pressure, water in the fuel or a restricted injector.

• **System too rich (Low Air/Fuel Ratio)**
The idle speed will be too low. "Scan" tool IAC counts will usually be above 80. System is obviously rich and may exhibit black smoke in exhaust.
"Scan" tool O₂ voltage will be fixed above 800 mV (.8 volt).
Check for high fuel pressure, leaking or sticking injector. Silicone contaminated O₂ sensors "Scan" voltage will be slow to respond.

• **Throttle Body**
Remove IAC valve and inspect bore for foreign material.

• **IAC Valve Electrical Connections**
IAC valve connections should be carefully checked for proper contact.

• **PCV Valve**
An incorrect or faulty PCV valve may result in an incorrect idle speed.
Refer to "Rough, Unstable, Incorrect Idle or Stalling" in "Symptoms" Section
If intermittent poor driveability or idle symptoms are resolved by disconnecting the IAC, carefully recheck connections, valve terminal resistance, or replace IAC.
A/C compressor or relay failure. See CHART C-10 if the A/C control relay drive circuit is shorted to ground or if the relay is faulty, an idle problem may exist.
If above are all OK, refer to "Rough, Unstable, Incorrect Idle, or Stalling" in "Symptoms" Section

MULTI-PORT FUEL INJECTION DIAGNOSTIC CHARTS

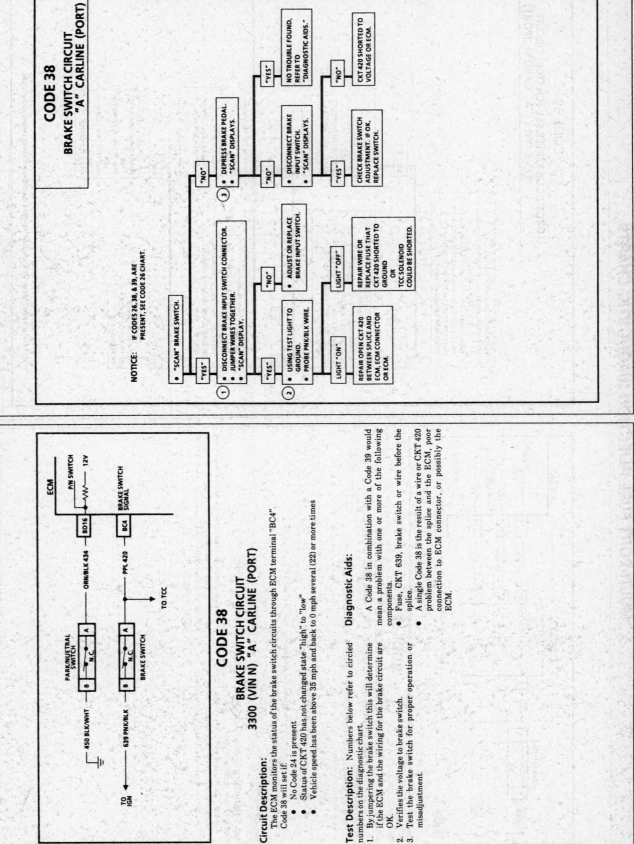

CODE 38

BRAKE SWITCH CIRCUIT "A" CARLINE (PORT)

CODE 38
BRAKE SWITCH CIRCUIT
3300 (VIN N) "A" CARLINE (PORT)

Circuit Description:

The ECM monitors the status of the brake switch circuits through ECM terminal "BC4".
Code 38 will set if:

- No Code 24 is present
- Status of CKT 420 has not changed state "high" to "low"
- Vehicle speed has been above 35 mph and back to 0 mph several (22) or more times

Test Description: Numbers below refer to circled numbers on the diagnostic chart.

1. By jumpering the brake switch this will determine if the ECM and the wiring for the brake circuit are OK.
2. Verifies the voltage to brake switch.
3. Test the brake switch for proper operation or misadjustment.

Diagnostic Aids:

A Code 38 in combination with a Code 39 would mean a problem with one or more of the following components.

- Fuse, CKT 639, brake switch or wire before the splice.
- A single Code 38 is the result of a wire or CKT 420 problem between the splice and the ECM, poor connection to ECM connector, or possibly the ECM.

MULTI-PORT FUEL INJECTION DIAGNOSTIC CHARTS

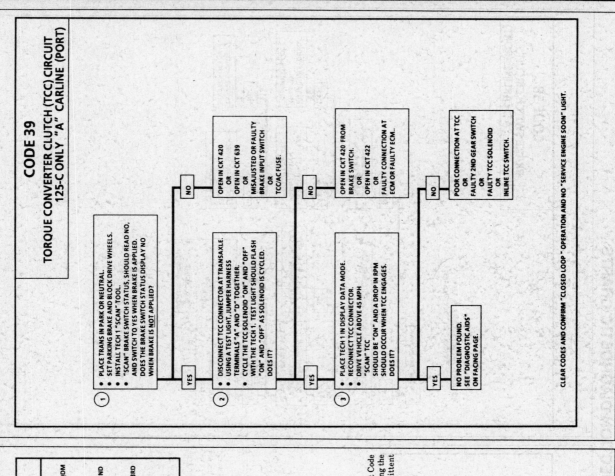

CODE 39
TORQUE CONVERTER CLUTCH (TCC) CIRCUIT
125-C ONLY "A" CARLINE (PORT)

(1)
- PLACE TRANS IN PARK OR NEUTRAL.
- SET PARKING BRAKE AND BLOCK DRIVE WHEELS.
- INSTALL TECH 1 "SCAN" TOOL.
- "SCAN" BRAKE SWITCH STATUS, SHOULD READ NO, AND SWITCH TO YES WHEN BRAKE IS APPLIED.

DOES THE BRAKE SWITCH STATUS DISPLAY NO WHEN BRAKE IS NOT APPLIED?

NO →
OPEN IN CKT 420
OR
OPEN IN CKT 639
OR
MISADJUSTED OR FAULTY BRAKE INPUT SWITCH
OR
TCC/AC FUSE.

(2)
- DISCONNECT TCC CONNECTOR AT TRANSAXLE.
- USING A TEST LIGHT, JUMPER HARNESS TERMINALS "A" AND "D" TOGETHER.
- CYCLE THE TCC SOLENOID "ON" AND "OFF" WITH THE TECH 1. TEST LIGHT SHOULD FLASH "ON" AND "OFF" AS SOLENOID IS CYCLED.

DOES IT?

NO →
OPEN IN CKT 420 FROM BRAKE SWITCH.
OR
OPEN IN CKT 422
OR
FAULTY CONNECTION AT ECM OR FAULTY ECM.

(3)
- PLACE TECH 1 IN DISPLAY DATA MODE.
- RECONNECT TCC CONNECTOR.
- DRIVE VEHICLE ABOVE 45 MPH "SCAN" TCC.

SHOULD BE "ON" AND A DROP IN RPM SHOULD OCCUR WHEN TCC ENGAGES. DOES IT?

NO →
POOR CONNECTION AT TCC
OR
FAULTY 2ND GEAR SWITCH
OR
FAULTY TCC SOLENOID
OR
INLINE TCC SWITCH.

YES →
NO PROBLEM FOUND. SEE "DIAGNOSTIC AIDS" ON FACING PAGE.

CLEAR CODES AND CONFIRM "CLOSED LOOP" OPERATION AND NO "SERVICE ENGINE SOON" LIGHT.

CODE 39
TORQUE CONVERTER CLUTCH (TCC) CIRCUIT
3300 (VIN N) 125-C ONLY "A" CARLINE (PORT)

Circuit Description:
The ECM controls the TCC operation by ground CKT 422 through a quad driver.
Code 39 will set when:
- No Code 28 is present
- Brake is not applied
- TCC is commanded by the ECM
- Transaxle is in high gear
- The engine speed to vehicle speed ratio does not indicate that TCC is engaged
- All of the above for a time is greater than 15 seconds

Test Description: Numbers below refer to circled numbers on the diagnostic chart.
1. Checks TCC/AC fuse and brake switch.
2. Checks ECM for proper operation.
3. Checks the internal switches in the transaxle.

Diagnostic Aids:
A poor connection can cause an intermittent Code 39. Using a DVM connected to the circuit, moving the wire(s) or connector(s) would cause an intermittent signal to dim.

MULTI-PORT FUEL INJECTION DIAGNOSTIC CHARTS

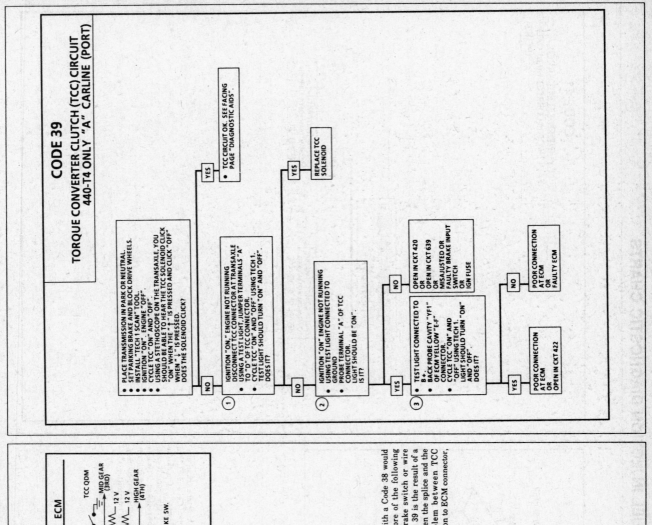

CODE 39

TORQUE CONVERTER CLUTCH (TCC) CIRCUIT
440-T4 ONLY "A" CARLINE (PORT)

- PLACE TRANSMISSION IN PARK OR NEUTRAL.
- SET PARKING BRAKE AND BLOCK DRIVE WHEELS.
- INSTALL "TECH 1" SCAN" TOOL.
- IGNITION "ON", ENGINE "OFF".
- IGNITION TCC "ON" AND "OFF".
- USING A STETHOSCOPE ON THE TRANSAXLE, YOU SHOULD BE ABLE TO HEAR THE TCC SOLENOID CLICK "ON" WHEN THE "↑" IS PRESSED AND CLICK "OFF" WHEN ".↓." IS PRESSED.
- DOES THE SOLENOID CLICK?

NO → (1)

YES → • TCC CIRCUIT OK. SEE FACING PAGE "DIAGNOSTIC AIDS".

(1)
- IGNITION "ON", ENGINE NOT RUNNING
- DISCONNECT TCC CONNECTOR AT TRANSAXLE
- USING A TEST LIGHT, JUMPER TERMINALS "A" TO "D" OF TCC CONNECTOR.
- CYCLE TCC "ON" AND "OFF" USING TECH 1. TEST LIGHT SHOULD TURN "ON" AND "OFF". DOES IT?

NO → (2)

YES → REPLACE TCC SOLENOID

(2)
- IGNITION "ON" ENGINE NOT RUNNING
- USING TEST LIGHT CONNECTED TO GROUND
- PROBE TERMINAL "A" OF TCC CONNECTOR.
- LIGHT SHOULD BE "ON".
- IS IT?

NO → OPEN IN CKT 420 OR OPEN IN CKT 639 OR MISADJUSTED OR FAULTY BRAKE INPUT SWITCH OR IGN FUSE

YES → (3)

(3)
- TEST LIGHT CONNECTED TO B+.
- BACK PROBE CAVITY "YF1" OF ECM YELLOW "E-F" CONNECTOR.
- CYCLE TCC "ON" AND "OFF" USING TECH 1. LIGHT SHOULD TURN "ON" AND "OFF". DOES IT?

NO → POOR CONNECTION AT ECM OR FAULTY ECM

YES → POOR CONNECTION AT ECM OR OPEN IN CKT 422

ECM

TCC QDM
MID GEAR (3RD)
12 V
12 V
HIGH GEAR (4TH)
BRAKE SW.

YF1
BD14
BD13
BC4

422 TAN/BLK
108 DK GRN
446 LT BLU
420 PPL

TCC (LOCATED IN TRANSAXLE)

D
C N.C.
B N.C.
A

420 PPL

BRAKE SWITCH
B
N.C.
A

10 AMP

639 PNK/BLK

TO IGN

4-27-89

CODE 39

TORQUE CONVERTER CLUTCH (TCC) CIRCUIT
3300 (VIN N) 440-T4 ONLY "A" CARLINE (PORT)

Circuit Description:

The ECM controls TCC operation by grounding CKT 422 through the quad-driver.

Code 39 will set when

- No Code 28 & 29 is present
- Brake switch is closed, "OFF"
- TCC is commanded by the ECM
- Vehicle is in high gear (4th)
- The engine speed to vehicle speed ratio does not indicate that TCC is engaged
- All of the above for a time greater than 15 seconds

Test Description: Numbers below refer to circled numbers on the diagnostic chart.

1. Checks fuse, brake switch and B + circuit to the TCC solenoid.
2. Checks availability of B + on CKT 420.
3. Checks the ECM for proper operation.

Diagnostic Aids:

A Code 39 in combination with a Code 38 would mean a problem with one or more of the following components. Fuse, CKT 639, brake switch or wire before the splice. A single Code 39 is the result of a wire or CKT 420 problem between the splice and the TCC solenoid, CKT 422 problem between TCC connector, solenoid and ECM, poor connection to ECM connector, or possibly the ECM.

MULTI-PORT FUEL INJECTION DIAGNOSTIC CHARTS

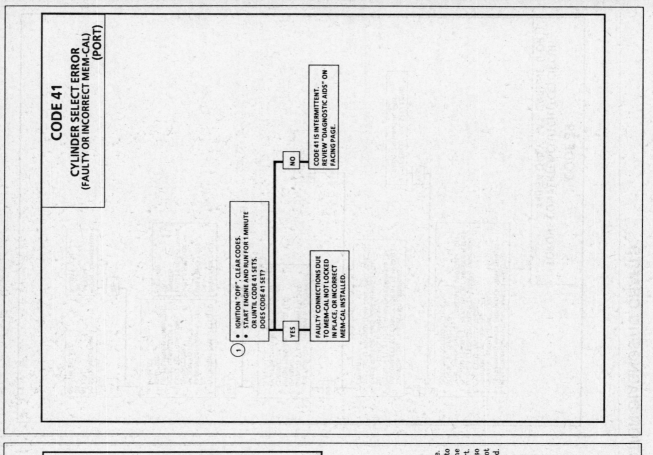

CODE 41
CYLINDER SELECT ERROR
(FAULTY OR INCORRECT MEM-CAL)
(PORT)

1
- IGNITION "OFF", CLEAR CODES.
- START ENGINE AND RUN FOR 1 MINUTE OR UNTIL CODE 41 SETS.
DOES CODE 41 SET?

YES
FAULTY CONNECTIONS DUE TO MEM-CAL NOT LOCKED IN PLACE, OR INCORRECT MEM-CAL INSTALLED.

NO
CODE 41 IS INTERMITTENT. REVIEW "DIAGNOSTIC AIDS" ON FACING PAGE.

ACCESS COVER

MEM-CAL

ECM ASSEMBLY

9-21-87

CODE 41
CYLINDER SELECT ERROR
(FAULTY OR INCORRECT MEM-CAL)
(PORT)
3.1L (VIN T)

Test Description: Numbers below refer to circled numbers on the diagnostic chart.
1. The ECM used for this engine can also be used for other engines, and the difference is in the Mem-Cal. If a Code 41 sets, the incorrect Mem-Cal has been installed, or it is faulty and must be replaced.

Diagnostic Aids:

Check Mem-Cal to be sure locking tabs are secure. Also check the pins on both the Mem-Cal and ECM to assure they are making proper contact. Check the Mem-Cal part number to assure it is the correct part. If the Mem-Cal is faulty it must be replaced. It is also possible that the ECM is faulty, however, it should not be replaced until all of the above have been checked. For additional information, refer to "Intermittents"

MULTI-PORT FUEL INJECTION DIAGNOSTIC CHARTS

CODE 42
ELECTRONIC SPARK TIMING (EST) CIRCUIT (PORT)

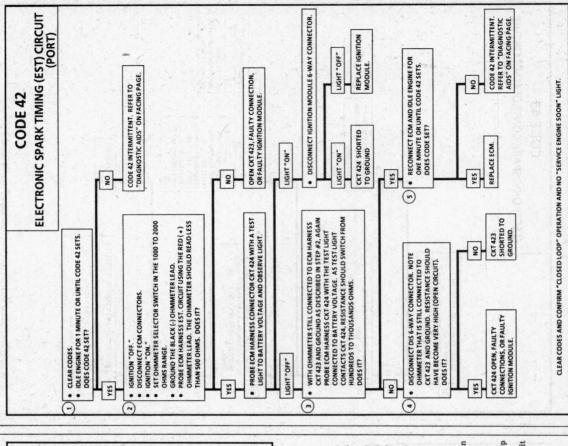

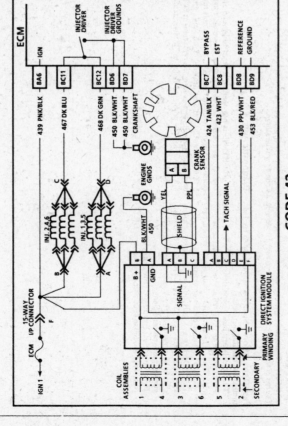

CODE 42
ELECTRONIC SPARK TIMING (EST) CIRCUIT 3.1L (VIN T)

Circuit Description:

When the system is running on the ignition module, that is, no voltage on the bypass line, the ignition module grounds the EST signal. The ECM expects to see no voltage on the EST line during this condition. If it sees a voltage, it sets Code 42 and will not go into the EST mode.

When the rpm for EST is reached (about 200 rpm), and bypass voltage applied, the EST should no longer be grounded in the ignition module so the EST voltage should be varying.

If the bypass line is open or grounded, the ignition module will not switch to EST mode, so the EST voltage will be low and Code 42 will be set.

If the EST line is grounded, the ignition module will switch to EST, but because the line is grounded, there will be no EST signal. A Code 42 will be set.

Test Description: Numbers below refer to circled numbers on the diagnostic chart.

1. Code 42 means the ECM has seen an open or short to ground in the EST or bypass circuits. This test confirms Code 42 and that the fault causing the code is present.

2. Checks for a normal EST ground path through the ignition module. An EST CKT 423 shorted to ground will also read less than 500 ohms; however, this will be checked later.

3. As the test light voltage touches CKT 424, the module should switch causing the ohmmeter to "overrange" if the meter is in the 1000-2000 ohms position. Selecting the 10-20,000 ohms position will indicate above 5000 ohms. The important thing is that the module "switched."

4. The module did not switch and this step checks for:

- EST CKT 423 shorted to ground
- Bypass CKT 424 open
- Faulty ignition module connection or module

5. Confirms that Code 42 is a faulty ECM and not an intermittent in CKTs 423 or 424.

Diagnostic Aids:

The "Scan" tool does not have any ability to help diagnose a Code 42 problem.

A Mem-Cal not fully seated in the ECM can result in a Code 42.

Refer to "Intermittents" Section

MULTI-PORT FUEL INJECTION DIAGNOSTIC CHARTS

CODE 43
ELECTRONIC SPARK CONTROL (ESC) CIRCUIT (PORT)

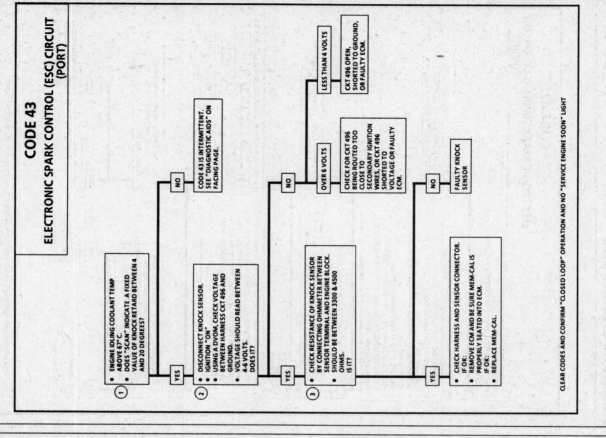

CLEAR CODES AND CONFIRM "CLOSED LOOP" OPERATION AND NO "SERVICE ENGINE SOON" LIGHT

1.
- ENGINE IDLING COOLANT TEMP ABOVE 67° C.
- DOES "SCAN" INDICATE A FIXED VALUE OF KNOCK RETARD BETWEEN 4 AND 20 DEGREES?

NO → CODE 43 IS INTERMITTENT. SEE "DIAGNOSTIC AIDS" ON FACING PAGE.

YES ↓

2.
- DISCONNECT KNOCK SENSOR.
- IGNITION "ON"
- USING A DVOM, CHECK VOLTAGE BETWEEN HARNESS CKT 496 AND GROUND.
- VOLTAGE SHOULD READ BETWEEN 4-6 VOLTS.
- DOES IT?

NO → OVER 6 VOLTS → CHECK FOR CKT 496 BEING ROUTED TOO CLOSE TO SECONDARY IGNITION WIRES, OR CKT 496 SHORTED TO VOLTAGE OR FAULTY ECM.

NO → LESS THAN 4 VOLTS → CKT 496 OPEN, SHORTED TO GROUND, OR FAULTY ECM.

YES ↓

3.
- CHECK RESISTANCE OF KNOCK SENSOR BY CONNECTING OHMMETER BETWEEN SENSOR TERMINAL AND ENGINE BLOCK.
- SHOULD BE BETWEEN 3300 & 4500 OHMS.
- IS IT?

NO → FAULTY KNOCK SENSOR

YES →
- CHECK HARNESS AND SENSOR CONNECTOR.
- IF OK:
- REMOVE ECM AND BE SURE MEM-CAL IS PROPERLY SEATED INTO ECM.
- IF OK:
- REPLACE MEM-CAL.

CODE 43
ELECTRONIC SPARK CONTROL (ESC) CIRCUIT (PORT)
3.1L (VIN T)

ECM

KNOCK SIGNAL TO MEM-CAL — 5V

YF9 — 496 DK BLU — KNOCK SENSOR

YE16 — COOLANT SENSOR INPUT

BC8 — EST SIGNAL

Circuit Description:

The knock sensor is used to detect engine detonation and the ECM will retard the electronic spark timing based on the signal being received. The circuitry within the knock sensor causes the ECM 5 volts to be pulled down so that, under a no knock condition, CKT 496 would measure about 2.5 volts. The knock sensor produces an A/C signal which rides on the 2.5 volts DC voltage. The amplitude and signal frequency is dependent upon the knock level.

If CKT 496 becomes open or shorted to ground, the voltage will either go above 4.8 volts or below .64 volts. If either of these conditions are met for about 10 seconds, a Code 43 will be stored.

Test Description: Numbers below refer to circled numbers on the diagnostic chart.

1. This step determines if conditions for Code 43 still exist (voltage on CKT 496 above 4.8 volts or below .64 volts). The system is designed to retard the spark 15° if either condition exists.
2. The ECM has a 5 volt pull up resistor, which applies 5 volts to CKT 496. The 5 volt signal should be present at the knock sensor terminal during these test conditions.
3. This step determines if the knock sensor resistance is 3300 to 4500 ohms the sensor is OK.

Diagnostic Aids:

If CKT 496 is not open or shorted to ground and the voltage reading is below 4 volts, the most likely cause is an open circuit in the ECM. It is possible that a faulty Mem-Cal could be drawing the 5 volt signal down, and it should be replaced, if a replacement ECM did not correct the problem. Refer to "Intermittents" Section

MULTI-PORT FUEL INJECTION DIAGNOSTIC CHARTS

CODE 44
OXYGEN SENSOR CIRCUIT
(LEAN EXHAUST INDICATED)
(PORT)

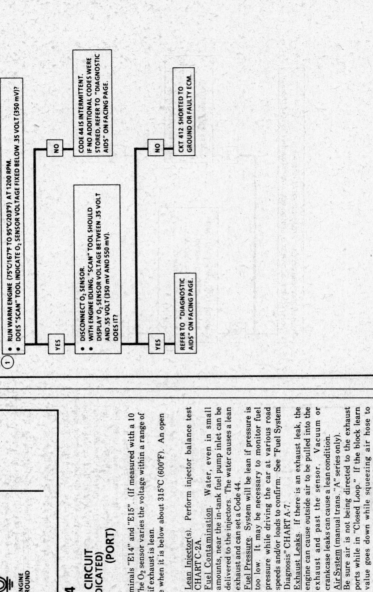

1. • RUN WARM ENGINE (75°C/167°F TO 95°C/203°F) AT 1200 RPM.
   • DOES "SCAN" TOOL INDICATE O_2 SENSOR VOLTAGE FIXED BELOW .35 VOLT (350 mV)?

YES →
• DISCONNECT O_2 SENSOR.
• WITH ENGINE IDLING, "SCAN" TOOL SHOULD DISPLAY O_2 SENSOR VOLTAGE BETWEEN .35 VOLT AND .55 VOLT (350 mV AND 550 mV). DOES IT?

NO → CODE 44 IS INTERMITTENT. IF NO ADDITIONAL CODES WERE STORED, REFER TO "DIAGNOSTIC AIDS" ON FACING PAGE.

YES → REFER TO "DIAGNOSTIC AIDS" ON FACING PAGE.

NO → CKT 412 SHORTED TO GROUND OR FAULTY ECM.

CLEAR CODES AND CONFIRM "CLOSED LOOP" OPERATION AND NO "SERVICE ENGINE SOON" LIGHT.

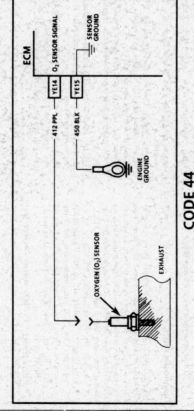

ECM — O_2 SENSOR SIGNAL — SENSOR GROUND
YE14 — YE15
412 PPL — 450 BLK
ENGINE GROUND
OXYGEN (O_2) SENSOR
EXHAUST

CODE 44
OXYGEN SENSOR CIRCUIT
(LEAN EXHAUST INDICATED)
(PORT)
3.1L (VIN T)

Circuit Description:

The ECM supplies a voltage of about .45 volt between terminals "E14" and "E15". (If measured with a 10 megohm digital voltmeter, this may read as low as .32 volt). The O_2 sensor varies the voltage within a range of about 1 volt if the exhaust is rich, down through about .10 volt if exhaust is lean.

The sensor is like an open circuit and produces no voltage when it is below about 315°C (600°F). An open sensor circuit or cold sensor causes "Open Loop" operation.

Test Description: Numbers below refer to circled numbers on the diagnostic chart.

1. Code 44 is set when the O_2 sensor signal voltage on CKT 412.
   • No Code 33 or 34 detected.
   • Remains below .2 volt for 60 seconds or more.
   • And the system is operating "Closed Loop."

Diagnostic Aids:

Using the "Scan," observe the block learn values at different rpm and air flow conditions. The "Scan" also displays the block cells, so the block learn values can be checked in each of the cells to determine when the Code 44 may have been set. If the conditions for Code 44 exist, the block learn values will be around 150.

• Idle Air Control (IAC)Valve. A faulty IAC circuit can set a Code 44. Use Chart C-2B to verify proper operation of IAC valve.
• O_2 Sensor Wire. Sensor pigtail may be mispositioned and contacting the exhaust manifold.
• Check for intermittent ground in wire between connector and sensor.

• Lean Injector(s). Perform injector balance test CHART C-2A.
• Fuel Contamination. Water, even in small amounts, near the in-tank fuel pump inlet can be delivered to the injectors. The water causes a lean exhaust and can set a Code 44.
• Fuel Pressure. System will be lean if pressure is too low. It may be necessary to monitor fuel pressure while driving the car at various road speeds and/or loads to confirm. See "Fuel System Diagnosis" CHART A-7.
• Exhaust Leaks. If there is an exhaust leak, the engine can cause outside air to be pulled into the exhaust and past the sensor. Vacuum or crankcase leaks can cause a lean condition.
• Air System (manual trans. "A" series only). Be sure air is not being directed to the exhaust ports while in "Closed Loop." If the block learn value goes down while squeezing air hose to exhaust ports, refer to CHART C-6.
• If the above are OK, it is a faulty oxygen sensor.

MULTI-PORT FUEL INJECTION DIAGNOSTIC CHARTS

CODE 45
OXYGEN SENSOR CIRCUIT
(RICH EXHAUST INDICATED) (PORT)

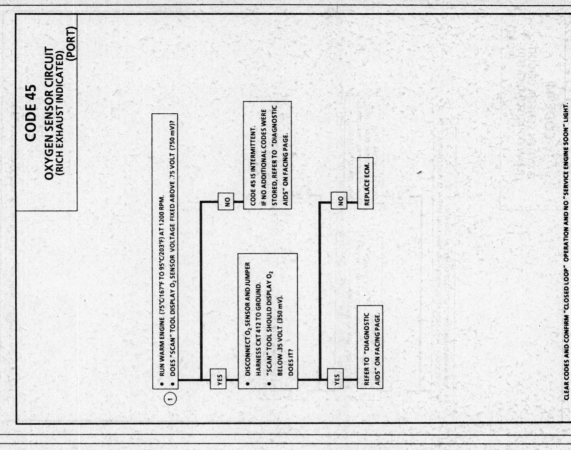

- RUN WARM ENGINE (75°C/167°F TO 95°C/203°F) AT 1200 RPM.
- DOES "SCAN" TOOL DISPLAY O₂ SENSOR VOLTAGE FIXED ABOVE .75 VOLT (750 mV)?

NO
- CODE 45 IS INTERMITTENT. IF NO ADDITIONAL CODES WERE STORED, REFER TO "DIAGNOSTIC AIDS" ON FACING PAGE.

YES
- DISCONNECT O₂ SENSOR AND JUMPER HARNESS CKT 412 TO GROUND.
- "SCAN" TOOL SHOULD DISPLAY O₂ BELOW .35 VOLT (350 mV).
- DOES IT?

NO
- REPLACE ECM.

YES
- REFER TO "DIAGNOSTIC AIDS" ON FACING PAGE.

(1) CLEAR CODES AND CONFIRM "CLOSED LOOP" OPERATION AND NO "SERVICE ENGINE SOON" LIGHT.

CODE 45
OXYGEN SENSOR CIRCUIT
(RICH EXHAUST INDICATED) (PORT)
3.1L (VIN T)

ECM — O₂ SENSOR SIGNAL — YE14 — 412 PPL
SENSOR GROUND — YE15 — 450 BLK — ENGINE GROUND

OXYGEN (O₂) SENSOR — EXHAUST

Circuit Description:

The ECM supplies a voltage of about .45 volt between terminals "E14" and "E15." (If measured with a 10 megohm digital voltmeter, this may read as low as .32 volt). The O₂ sensor varies the voltage within a range of about 1 volt if the exhaust is rich, down through about .10 volt if exhaust is lean.

The sensor is like an open circuit and produces no voltage when it is below about 315°C (600°F). An open sensor circuit or cold sensor causes "Open Loop" operation.

Test Description: Numbers below refer to circled numbers on the diagnostic chart.

1. Code 45 is set when the O₂ sensor signal voltage or CKT 412.
   - No Codes 33 or 34 detected.
   - Remains above .7 volt for 30 seconds, and in "Closed Loop."
   - Engine time after start is 1 minute or more.
   - Throttle angle between 3% and 45%.

Diagnostic Aids:

Using the "Scan," observe the block learn values at different rpm and air flow conditions. The "Scan" also displays the block cells, so the block learn values can be checked in each of the cells to determine when the Code 45 may have been set. If the conditions for Code 45 exist, the block learn values will be around 115.
- Check for short to voltage on CKT 412.
- **Fuel Pressure.** System will go rich if pressure is too high. The ECM can compensate for some increase. However, if it gets too high, a Code 45 may be set. See "Fuel System Diagnosis" CHART A-7.
- **Rich Injector.** Perform injector balance test Chart C-2A.

- **Leaking Injector.** See CHART A-7.
- Check for fuel contaminated oil.
- **HEI Shielding.** An open ground CKT 453 (ignition system reflow) may result in EMI, or induced electrical "noise." The ECM looks at this "noise" as reference pulses. The additional pulses result in a higher than actual engine speed signal. The ECM then delivers too much fuel, causing system to go rich. Engine tachometer will also show higher than actual engine speed, which can help in diagnosing this problem.
- **Canister Purge.** Check for fuel saturation. If full of fuel, check canister control and hoses. See "Canister Purge." Section "C3"
- Check for leaking fuel pressure regulator diaphragm by checking vacuum line to regulator for fuel.
- **TPS.** An intermittent TPS output will cause the system to go rich, due to a false indication of the engine accelerating.
- **EGR.** An EGR staying open (especially at idle) will cause the O₂ sensor to indicate a rich exhaust, and this could result in a Code 45.

MULTI-PORT FUEL INJECTION DIAGNOSTIC CHARTS

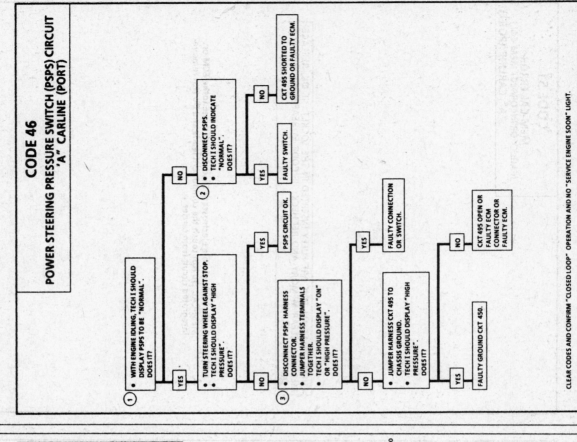

CODE 46
POWER STEERING PRESSURE SWITCH (PSPS) CIRCUIT "A" CARLINE (PORT)

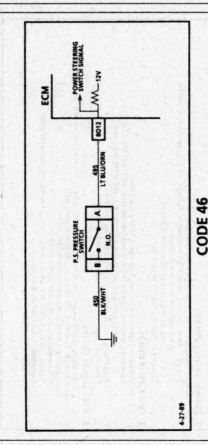

4-27-89

CODE 46
POWER STEERING PRESSURE SWITCH (PSPS) CIRCUIT
3300 (VIN N) "A" CARLINE (PORT)

Circuit Description:

The power steering pressure switch is normally open, and CKT 495 will be near battery voltage.

Turning the steering wheel increases power steering oil pressure and its load on an idling engine. The pressure switch will close before the load can cause an idle problem.

Closing the switch causes CKT 495 to read less than 1 volt. The electronic control module (ECM) will increase the idle air rate and disengage the A/C clutch.

- A pressure switch that will not close, or an open CKT 495 or 450, may cause the engine to stop when power steering loads are high.
- A switch that will not open, or a CKT 495 shorted to ground, may affect idle quality and will cause the A/C relay to be de-energized.

To set a Code 46, the following conditions must be met:
- Closed power steering switch. "LO" (low voltage potential)
- Vehicle speed is greater than 40 mph
- Both conditions existing for a time greater than 25 seconds

Test Description: Numbers below refer to circled numbers on the diagnostic chart.

1. Different makes of "Scan" tools may display the state of this switch in different ways. Refer to "Scan" tool operator's manual to determine how this input is indicated.

2. Checks to determine if CKT 495 is shorted to ground.

3. This should simulate a closed switch.

MULTI-PORT FUEL INJECTION DIAGNOSTIC CHARTS

CODE 51
MEM-CAL ERROR
(FAULTY OR INCORRECT MEM-CAL)
"A" CARLINE (PORT)

CHECK THAT ALL PINS ARE FULLY INSERTED IN THE SOCKET. IF OK, REPLACE MEM-CAL, CLEAR MEMORY AND RECHECK. IF CODE 51 REAPPEARS, REPLACE ECM.

NOTICE: To prevent possible Electrostatic Discharge damage to the ECM or MEM-CAL, Do Not touch the component leads, and Do Not remove integrated circuit from carrier.

CODE 48
MISFIRE DIAGNOSIS
3300 (VIN N) "A" CARLINE (PORT)

If multiple codes are set, go to the lowest code first.
Repairing for a Code 13, 44, or 45 may correct Code 48.

Test Description:

Code 48 will set if the following:
- TPS is between .58 and .93 volts
- Rpm is between 1500 and 2500
- Mph is between 50 and 60
- O_2 cross counts greater than 32-125C and 26-440 T_4
- All of the above for 30 seconds

O_2 Sensor Test:

Code 48 could be set if the O_2 sensor is degraded and cannot travel over the full rich to lean voltage range. This narrowed range could allow O_2 cross counts to be above the value necessary to set the code.

- WITH "SCAN" TOOL INSTALLED, VERIFY ENGINE IS AT NORMAL OPERATING TEMPERATURE AND IN "CLOSED LOOP".

- ENGINE IDLING IN PARK.
  SELECT O_2 SENSOR POSITION ON "SCAN".
  RAPIDLY FLASH THE THROTTLE FROM IDLE TO NEAR WIDE OPEN THROTTLE AND BACK WHILE OBSERVING O_2 VOLTAGE.
  REPEAT IF NECESSARY TO CONFIRM VOLTAGE RANGE, AND "CLOSED LOOP".

VOLTAGE EXCEEDS 250-750 mV RANGE.

O_2 SENSOR OK. SEE "DIAGNOSTIC AIDS".

VOLTAGE REMAINS WITHIN 250-750 mV RANGE.

REPLACE O_2 SENSOR.

Diagnostic Aids:

1. Ignition system checks:
Remove each spark plug and inspect (fouled, cracked, worn)
Fouled -- check ignition wires (high resistance, damage, poor connections, grounds)
check coil and module operation
check basic engine problem (see 3 below)
Cracked or worn -- replace as necessary

2. Fuel system checks:
Restricted fuel system (injectors, fuel pump, lines, and filter)
Injectors -- perform injector balance test (see Section "6E3" CHART C-2)
verify each injector circuit with tool J-34730-2 or equivalent
Fuel Pump -- verify proper fuel pressure and fuel quality
Lines and Filter -- verify no restrictions in lines or filter

3. Basic Engine Checks:
Unless spark plug(s) inspection identifies a specific cylinder(s), road test vehicle under test conditions to reverify Code 48 prior to engine disassembly.
Basic engine (valves, compression, camshaft, lifters)
Compression -- check rings, pistons, valves
Valves -- check for burned, weak springs, broken parts, worn or loose guide
Camshaft -- check for worn or broken
Lifters -- check for worn, broken

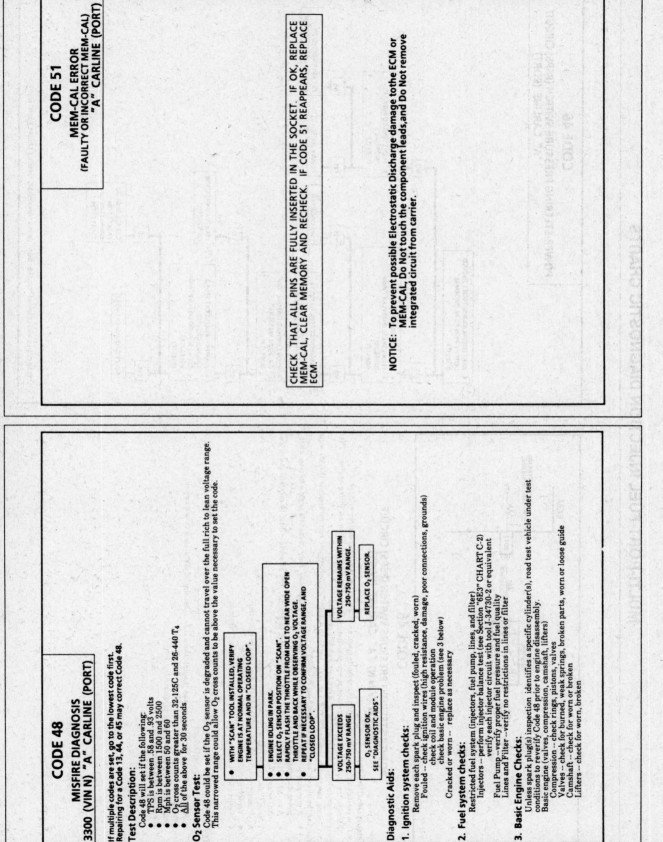

MULTI-PORT FUEL INJECTION DIAGNOSTIC CHARTS

CODE 61
DEGRADED OXYGEN SENSOR

IF A CODE 61 IS STORED IN MEMORY THE ECM HAS DETERMINED THE OXYGEN SENSOR IS CONTAMINATED OR DEGRADED, BECAUSE THE VOLTAGE CHANGE TIME IS SLOW OR SLUGGISH.

THE ECM PERFORMS THE OXYGEN SENSOR RESPONSE TIME TEST WHEN:

COOLANT TEMPERATURE IS GREATER THAN 85°C.

MAT TEMPERATURE IS GREATER THAN 10°C.

IN CLOSED LOOP.

IN DECEL FUEL CUT-OFF MODE.

IF A CODE 61 IS STORED THE OXYGEN SENSOR SHOULD BE REPLACED. A CONTAMINATED SENSOR CAN BE CAUSED BY FUEL ADDITIVES, SUCH AS SILICON, OR BY USE OF NON-GM APPROVED LUBRICANTS OR SEALANTS. SILICON CONTAMINATION IS USUALLY INDICATED BY A WHITE POWDERY SUBSTANCE ON THE SENSOR FINS.

CLEAR CODES AND CONFIRM "CLOSED LOOP" OPERATION AND NO "SERVICE ENGINE SOON" LIGHT.

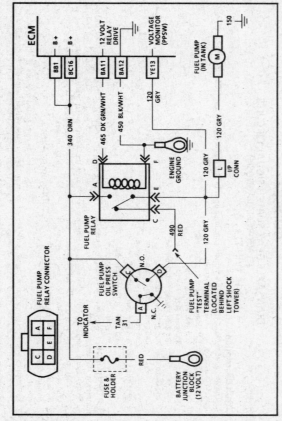

CODE 54
FUEL PUMP CIRCUIT
(LOW VOLTAGE)   (PORT)
3.1L (VIN T)

Circuit Description:

The status of the fuel pump CKT 120 is monitored by the ECM at terminal "YE13" and is used to compensate fuel delivery based on system voltage. This signal is also used to store a trouble code if the fuel pump relay is defective or fuel pump voltage is lost while the engine is running. There should be about 12 volts on CKT 120 for 2 seconds after the ignition is turned or any time references pulses are being received by the ECM.

Code 54 will set if the voltage at terminal "YE13" is less than 4 volts for 4 second since the last reference pulse was received. This code is designed to detect a faulty relay, causing extended crank time, and the code will help the diagnosis of an engine that "Cranks But Will Not Run."

If a fault is detected during start-up, the "Service Engine Soon" light will stay "ON" until the ignition is cycled "OFF." However, if the voltage is detected below 4 volts with the engine running, the light will only remain "ON" while the condition exists.

MULTI-PORT FUEL INJECTION DIAGNOSTIC CHARTS

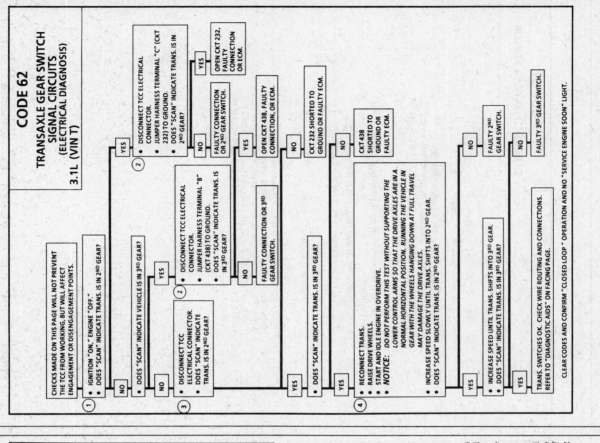

CODE 62

TRANSAXLE GEAR SWITCH SIGNAL CIRCUITS (ELECTRICAL DIAGNOSIS)
3.1L (VIN T)

- CHECKS MADE ON THIS PAGE WILL NOT PREVENT THE TCC FROM WORKING, BUT WILL AFFECT ENGAGEMENT OR DISENGAGEMENT POINTS.

1.
- IGNITION "ON," ENGINE "OFF."
- DOES "SCAN" INDICATE TRANS. IS IN 2ND GEAR?

- DISCONNECT TCC ELECTRICAL CONNECTOR.
- JUMPER HARNESS TERMINAL "C" (CKT 232) TO GROUND.
- DOES "SCAN" INDICATE TRANS. IS IN 2ND GEAR?

YES — OPEN CKT 232, FAULTY CONNECTION OR ECM.

NO — FAULTY CONNECTION OR 2ND GEAR SWITCH.

- DOES "SCAN" INDICATE VEHICLE IS IN 3RD GEAR?

3.
- DISCONNECT TCC ELECTRICAL CONNECTOR.
- DOES "SCAN" INDICATE TRANS. IS IN 2ND GEAR?

- DISCONNECT TCC ELECTRICAL CONNECTOR.
- JUMPER HARNESS TERMINAL "B" (CKT 438) TO GROUND.
- DOES "SCAN" INDICATE TRANS. IS IN 3RD GEAR?

YES — OPEN CKT 438, FAULTY CONNECTION, OR ECM.

NO — FAULTY CONNECTION OR 3RD GEAR SWITCH.

- DOES "SCAN" INDICATE TRANS. IS IN 3RD GEAR?

YES — CKT 232 SHORTED TO GROUND OR FAULTY ECM.

NO — CKT 438 SHORTED TO GROUND OR FAULTY ECM.

4.
- RECONNECT TRANS.
- RAISE DRIVE WHEELS.
- START AND IDLE ENGINE IN OVERDRIVE.
- **NOTICE:** DO NOT PERFORM THIS TEST WITHOUT SUPPORTING THE LOWER CONTROL ARMS SO THAT THE DRIVE AXLES ARE IN A NORMAL HORIZONTAL POSITION. RUNNING THE VEHICLE IN GEAR WITH THE WHEELS HANGING DOWN AT FULL TRAVEL MAY DAMAGE THE DRIVE AXLES.
- INCREASE SPEED SLOWLY UNTIL TRANS. SHIFTS INTO 2ND GEAR.
- DOES "SCAN" INDICATE TRANS. IS IN 2ND GEAR?

YES
- INCREASE SPEED UNTIL TRANS. SHIFTS INTO 3RD GEAR.
- DOES "SCAN" INDICATE TRANS. IS IN 3RD GEAR?

NO — FAULTY 2ND GEAR SWITCH.

YES — TRANS. SWITCHES OK. CHECK WIRE ROUTING AND CONNECTIONS. REFER TO "DIAGNOSTIC AIDS" ON FACING PAGE.

NO — FAULTY 3RD GEAR SWITCH.

CLEAR CODES AND CONFIRM "CLOSED LOOP" OPERATION AND NO "SERVICE ENGINE SOON" LIGHT.

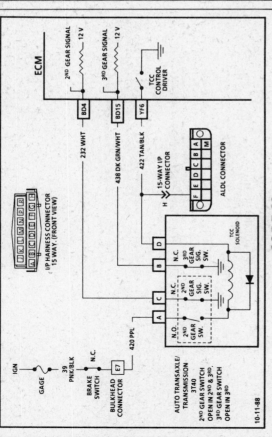

ECM

2ND GEAR SIGNAL — 12 V
3RD GEAR SIGNAL — 12 V
TCC CONTROL DRIVER

BD4
BD15
YF6

232 WHT
438 DK GRN/WHT
422 TAN/BLK

I/P HARNESS CONNECTOR 15 WAY. (FRONT VIEW)

IGN
GAGE
39 PNK/BLK
BRAKE SWITCH — N.C.
BULKHEAD CONNECTOR E7
420 PPL

15-WAY I/P CONNECTOR
ALDL CONNECTOR

TCC SOLENOID

N.C. 2ND GEAR SIG. SW.
N.C. 3RD GEAR SIG. SW.
N.O. 2ND GEAR SW.

AUTO TRANSAXLE/ TRANSMISSION 3T40
2ND GEAR SWITCH OPEN IN 2ND & 3RD.
3RD GEAR SWITCH OPEN IN 3RD

10-11-88

CODE 62

TRANSAXLE GEAR SWITCH SIGNAL CIRCUITS (ELECTRICAL DIAGNOSIS)
3.1L (VIN T)

Circuit Description:
The 2nd gear signal switch in this vehicle should be open in 2nd gear. The ECM uses this 2nd gear signal to disengage the TCC when downshifting.

The 3rd gear switch should be open in 3rd gear.

1st Gear = 2nd gear switch open
2nd gear signal switch closed
3rd gear signal switch closed

2nd Gear = 2nd gear switch closed
2nd gear signal switch opens
3rd gear signal switch closed

3rd Gear = 2nd gear switch closed
2nd gear signal switch opens
3rd gear signal switch opens

Test Description: Numbers below refer to circled numbers on the diagnostic chart.

1. Some "Scan" tools display the state of these switches in different ways. Be familiar with the type of tool being used. Since both switches should be in the closed state during this test, the tool should read the same for either the 2nd or 3rd gear switch.

2. Determines whether the switch or signal circuit is open. The circuit can be checked for an open by measuring the voltage (with a voltmeter) at the TCC connector (should be about 12 volts).

3. Because the switch(s) should be grounded in this step, disconnecting the TCC connector should cause the "Scan" switch state to change.

4. The switch state should change when the vehicle shifts into 2nd gear.

Diagnostic Aids:

If vehicle is road tested because of a TCC related problem, be sure the switch states do not change while in 3rd gear because the TCC will disengage. If switches change state, carefully check wire routing and connections.

MULTI-PORT FUEL INJECTION DIAGNOSTIC CHARTS

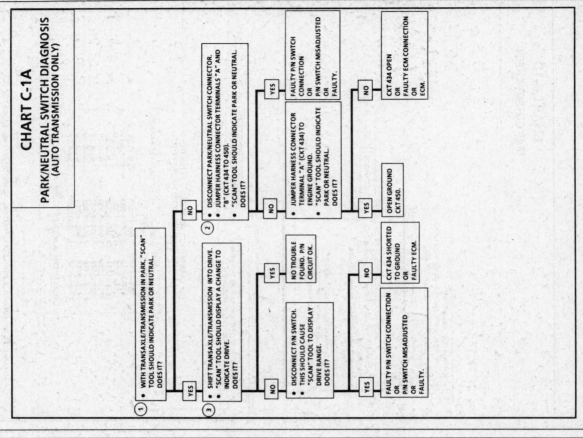

CHART C-1A
PARK/NEUTRAL SWITCH DIAGNOSIS
(AUTO TRANSMISSION ONLY)

① WITH TRANSAXLE/TRANSMISSION IN PARK, "SCAN" TOOL SHOULD INDICATE PARK OR NEUTRAL. DOES IT?

③ SHIFT TRANSAXLE/TRANSMISSION INTO DRIVE. "SCAN" TOOL SHOULD DISPLAY A CHANGE TO INDICATE DRIVE. DOES IT?

DISCONNECT P/N SWITCH. THIS SHOULD CAUSE "SCAN" TOOL TO DISPLAY DRIVE RANGE. DOES IT?

NO TROUBLE FOUND. P/N CIRCUIT OK.

FAULTY P/N SWITCH CONNECTION OR P/N SWITCH MISADJUSTED OR FAULTY.

CKT 434 SHORTED TO GROUND OR FAULTY ECM.

② DISCONNECT PARK/NEUTRAL SWITCH CONNECTOR. JUMPER HARNESS CONNECTOR TERMINALS "A" AND "B" (CKT 434 TO 450). "SCAN" TOOL SHOULD INDICATE PARK OR NEUTRAL. DOES IT?

JUMPER HARNESS CONNECTOR TERMINAL "A" (CKT 434) TO ENGINE GROUND. "SCAN" TOOL SHOULD INDICATE PARK OR NEUTRAL. DOES IT?

FAULTY P/N SWITCH CONNECTION OR P/N SWITCH MISADJUSTED OR FAULTY.

OPEN GROUND CKT 450.

CKT 434 OPEN OR FAULTY ECM CONNECTION OR ECM.

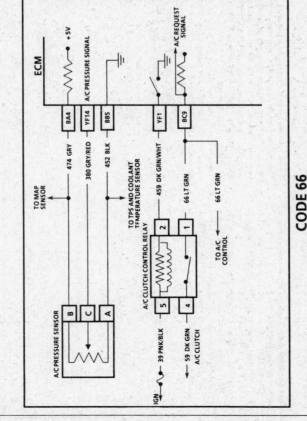

CODE 66
A/C PRESSURE SENSOR CIRCUIT
3.1L (VIN T) "J" CARLINE (PORT)

Circuit Description:

The A/C pressure sensor responds to changes in A/C refrigerant system high side pressure. This input indicates how much load the A/C compressor is putting on the engine and is one of the factors used by the ECM to determine IAC valve position for idle speed control. The circuit consists of a 5 volts reference and a ground, both provided by the ECM, and a signal line to the ECM. The signal is a voltage which is proportional to the pressure. The sensor's range of operation is 0 to 450 psi. At 0 psi, the signal will be about .1 volt, varying up to about 4.9 volts at 450 psi or above. Code 66 sets if the voltage is above 4.9 volts or below .1 volt 5 seconds or more. The A/C compressor is disabled by the ECM if Code 66 is present, or if pressure is above or below calibrated values described in Section "C10".

Test Description: Numbers below refer to circled numbers on the diagnostic chart.

1. This step checks the voltage signal being received by the ECM from the A/C pressure sensor. The normal operating range is between .1 volt and 4.9 volts.

2. Checks to see if the high voltage signal is from a shorted sensor or a short to voltage in the circuit. Normally, disconnecting the sensor would make a normal circuit go to near zero volt.

3. Checks to see if low voltage signal is from the sensor or the circuit. Jumpering the sensor signal CKT 380 to 5 volts, checks the circuit, connections, and ECM.

4. This step checks to see if the low voltage signal was due to an open in the sensor circuit or the 5 volts reference circuit since the prior step eliminated the pressure sensor.

Diagnostic Aids:

Code 66 sets when signal voltage falls outside the normal possible range of the sensor and is not due to a refrigerant system problem. If problem is intermittent, check for opens or shorts in harness or poor connections. If OK, replace A/C pressure sensor. If Code 66 re-sets, replace ECM.

MULTI-PORT FUEL INJECTION DIAGNOSTIC CHARTS

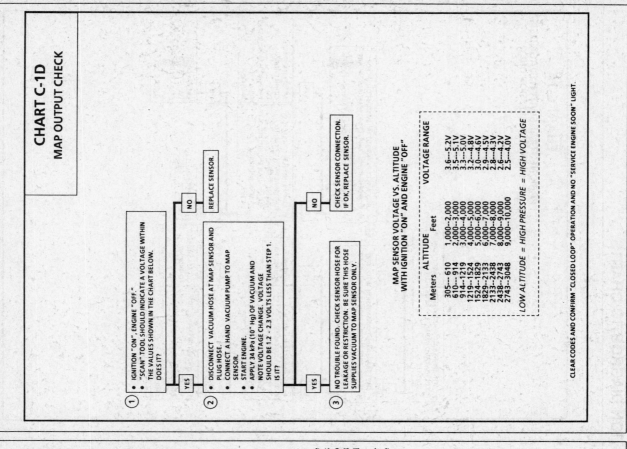

CHART C-1D
MAP OUTPUT CHECK

① IGNITION "ON", ENGINE "OFF."
• "SCAN" TOOL SHOULD INDICATE A VOLTAGE WITHIN THE VALUES SHOWN IN THE CHART BELOW. DOES IT?

YES →

② • DISCONNECT VACUUM HOSE AT MAP SENSOR AND PLUG HOSE.
• CONNECT A HAND VACUUM PUMP TO MAP SENSOR.
• START ENGINE.
• APPLY 34 kPa (10" Hg) OF VACUUM AND NOTE VOLTAGE CHANGE. VOLTAGE SHOULD BE 1.2 - 2.3 VOLTS LESS THAN STEP 1. IS IT?

NO → REPLACE SENSOR.

YES →

③ NO TROUBLE FOUND. CHECK SENSOR HOSE FOR LEAKAGE OR RESTRICTION. BE SURE THIS HOSE SUPPLIES VACUUM TO MAP SENSOR ONLY.

NO → CHECK SENSOR CONNECTION. IF OK, REPLACE SENSOR.

MAP SENSOR VOLTAGE VS. ALTITUDE WITH IGNITION "ON" AND ENGINE "OFF"

ALTITUDE		VOLTAGE RANGE
Meters	Feet	
305—610	1,000—2,000	3.6—5.2V
610—914	2,000—3,000	3.5—5.1V
914—1219	3,000—4,000	3.3—5.0V
1219—1524	4,000—5,000	3.2—4.8V
1524—1829	5,000—6,000	3.0—4.6V
1829—2133	6,000—7,000	2.9—4.5V
2133—2438	7,000—8,000	2.8—4.3V
2438—2743	8,000—9,000	2.6—4.2V
2743—3048	9,000—10,000	2.5—4.0V

LOW ALTITUDE = HIGH PRESSURE = HIGH VOLTAGE

CLEAR CODES AND CONFIRM "CLOSED LOOP" OPERATION AND NO "SERVICE ENGINE SOON" LIGHT.

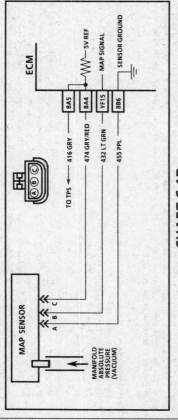

CHART C-1D
MAP OUTPUT CHECK
3.1L (VIN T)

Circuit Description:
The Manifold Absolute Pressure (MAP) sensor measures manifold pressure (vacuum) and sends that signal to the ECM. The MAP sensor is mainly used for fuel calculation, when the ECM is running in the throttle body backup mode. The MAP sensor is also used to determine the barometric pressure and to help calculate fuel delivery.

Test Description: Numbers below refer to circled numbers on the diagnostic chart.

1. Checks MAP sensor output voltage to the ECM. This voltage, without engine running, represents a barometer reading to the ECM.

2. Applying 34 kPa (10 inches Hg) vacuum to the MAP sensor should cause the voltage to be 1.2 volts less than the voltage at Step I. Upon applying vacuum to the sensor, the change in voltage should be instantaneous.

A slow voltage change indicates a faulty sensor. The engine must be running in this step or the "Scanner" will not indicate a change in voltage. It is normal for the "Service Engine Soon" light to come "ON" and for the system to set a Code 33 during this step. Make sure the code is cleared when this test is completed.

3. Check vacuum hose to sensor for leaking or restriction. Be sure no other vacuum devices are connected to the MAP hose.

MULTI-PORT FUEL INJECTION DIAGNOSTIC CHARTS

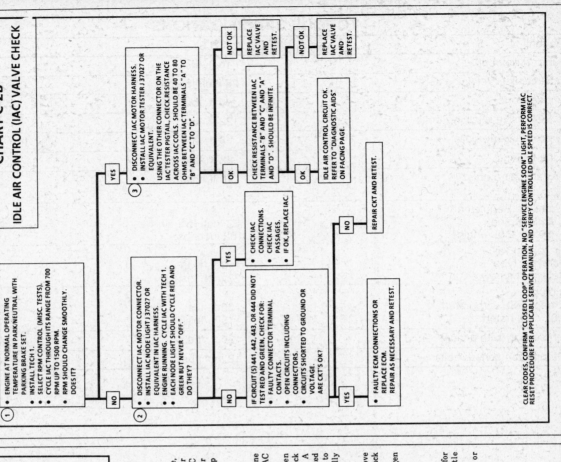

CHART C-2B
IDLE AIR CONTROL (IAC) VALVE CHECK

①
- ENGINE AT NORMAL OPERATING TEMPERATURE IN PARK/NEUTRAL WITH PARKING BRAKE SET.
- INSTALL TECH 1.
- SELECT RPM CONTROL (MISC. TESTS).
- CYCLE IAC THROUGH ITS RANGE FROM 700 RPM UP TO 1500 RPM.
- RPM SHOULD CHANGE SMOOTHLY. DOES IT?

②
- DISCONNECT IAC MOTOR CONNECTOR. INSTALL IAC NODE LIGHT J 37027 OR EQUIVALENT IN IAC HARNESS.
- ENGINE RUNNING. CYCLE IAC WITH TECH 1. EACH NODE LIGHT SHOULD CYCLE RED AND GREEN BUT NEVER "OFF." DO THEY?

③
- DISCONNECT IAC MOTOR HARNESS.
- INSTALL IAC MOTOR TESTER J 37027 OR EQUIVALENT.
USING THE OTHER CONNECTOR ON THE IAC TESTER PIGTAIL, CHECK RESISTANCE ACROSS IAC COILS. SHOULD BE 40 TO 80 OHMS BETWEEN IAC TERMINALS "A" TO "B" AND "C" TO "D."

NOT OK → REPLACE IAC VALVE AND RETEST.

OK → CHECK RESISTANCE BETWEEN IAC TERMINALS "B" AND "C" AND "A" AND "D". SHOULD BE INFINITE.

NOT OK → REPLACE IAC VALVE AND RETEST.

OK → IDLE AIR CONTROL CIRCUIT OK. REFER TO "DIAGNOSTIC AIDS" ON FACING PAGE.

YES (from ②) →
- CHECK IAC CONNECTIONS.
- CHECK IAC PASSAGES.
- IF OK, REPLACE IAC.

NO (from ②) → IF CIRCUIT (S) 441, 442, 443, OR 444 DID NOT TEST RED AND GREEN, CHECK FOR:
- FAULTY CONNECTOR TERMINAL CONTACTS.
- OPEN CIRCUITS INCLUDING CONNECTORS.
- CIRCUITS SHORTED TO GROUND OR VOLTAGE.
ARE CKT'S OK?

YES →
- FAULTY ECM CONNECTIONS OR REPLACE ECM. REPAIR AS NECESSARY AND RETEST.

NO → REPAIR CKT AND RETEST.

CLEAR CODES, CONFIRM "CLOSED LOOP" OPERATION, NO "SERVICE ENGINE SOON" LIGHT, PERFORM IAC RESET PROCEDURE PER APPLICABLE SERVICE MANUAL AND VERIFY CONTROLLED IDLE SPEED IS CORRECT.

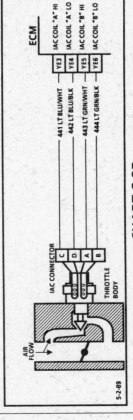

ECM

441 LT BLU/WHT	YE3	IAC COIL "A" HI
442 LT BLU/BLK	YE4	IAC COIL "A" LO
443 LT GRN/WHT	YE5	IAC COIL "B" HI
444 LT GRN/BLK	YE6	IAC COIL "B" LO

IAC CONNECTOR — C, D, A, B

THROTTLE BODY

AIR FLOW

5-2-89

CHART C-2B
IDLE AIR CONTROL (IAC) VALVE CHECK
3300 (VIN N) "A" CARLINE (PORT)

Circuit Description:
The ECM controls idle rpm with the IAC valve. To increase idle rpm, the ECM retracts the IAC pintle, allowing more air to bypass the throttle plate. To decrease rpm, it extends the IAC pintle valve, reducing air flow through the IAC valve port in the throttle body. A "Scan" tool will read the ECM commands to the IAC valve in counts. The higher the counts, the more air allowed (higher idle). The lower the counts, the less air allowed (lower idle). The ECM learns a new IAC position every time the ignition is cycled when in closed loop and the transmission is in drive. This is to control engine speed at different idle conditions.

Test Description: Numbers below refer to circled numbers on the diagnostic chart.
1. The Tech 1 is used to extend and retract the IAC valve. Valve movement is verified by an engine speed change.
2. This test checks all wires, connectors, and ECM.
3. This test check for shorted or open IAC valve coils.

Diagnostic Aids:
A slow, unstable idle may be caused by a system problem that cannot be overcome by the IAC. "Scan" counts will be above 60 counts, if idle speed is too low. If idle speed is too high, IAC counts will be "0".

- System lean (High Air/Fuel Ratio)
Idle speed may be too high or too low. Engine speed may vary up and down, disconnecting IAC does not help. May set Code 44.
"Scan" and/or voltmeter will read an oxygen sensor output less than 300 mV (.3 volt). Check for low regulated fuel pressure or water in fuel. A lean exhaust, with an oxygen sensor output fixed above 800 mV (.8 volt) indicates rich exhaust to ECM), will be a contaminated sensor, usually silicone. This may also set Code 45.
- System rich (Low Air/Fuel Ratio)
Idle speed too low. "Scan" counts usually above 80. System obviously rich and may exhibit black smoke exhaust.
"Scan" tool and/or voltmeter will read an oxygen sensor signal fixed above 800 mV (.8 volt).
Check:
  - High fuel pressure
  - Injector leaking or sticking
  - Throttle Body - Remove IAC and inspect bore for foreign material or evidence of IAC pintle dragging the bore.
- Refer to "Rough, Unstable, Incorrect Idle or Stalling" in "Symptoms" Section

TORQUE SPECIFICATIONS

Component	U.S.	Metric
AIR pump pulley bolts:	10 ft. lbs.	13 Nm
Charcoal canister retaining screws:	25 inch lbs.	2.8 Nm
Coolant sensors:	15 ft. lbs.	20 Nm
Digital EGR valve retaining bolts:	22 ft. lbs.	30 Nm
EGR valve retaining bolts:	16 ft. lbs.	22 Nm
Fuel Line Fittings:	22 ft. lbs.	30 Nm
Fuel rail attaching nuts:	20 ft. lbs.	27 Nm
Fuel Pressure Regulator:		
2.5L engine:	22 inch lbs.	2.5 Nm
Except 2.5L engine:	102 inch lbs.	11.5 Nm
Idle air control valve:		
Screw-in type:	13 ft. lbs.	18 Nm
Retaining screws:	27 inch lbs.	3 Nm
Spark plugs:		
Except 2.8L carburated	20 ft. lbs.	27 Nm
2.8L carburated	15 ft. lbs.	17 Nm
Oxygen sensor (with anti-sieze):	30 ft. lbs.	41 Nm
Throttle position sensor bolts:	18 inch lbs.	2 Nm

5

FUEL
SYSTEM

CARBURETED FUEL SYSTEM

Mechanical Fuel Pump

Mechanical fuel pumps are used on 6–2.8L engines. The pump has a vapor return line for both emission control purposes and to reduce the likelihood of vapor lock.

REMOVAL & INSTALLATION

All Models

The fuel pump is located at the left side of the engine.

1. Disconnect the negative cable at the battery. Raise and support the car.

2. Remove the pump shields and the oil filter, if so equipped.

3. Disconnect the inlet hose from the pump. Disconnect the vapor return hose, if equipped.

4. Loosen the fuel line at the carburetor, then disconnect the outlet pipe from the pump.

5. Remove the two mounting bolts and remove the pump from the engine.

6. To install, place a new gasket on the pump and install the pump on the engine. Tighten the two mounting bolts alternately and evenly.

7. Install the pump outlet pipe. This is easier if the pipe is disconnected from the carburetor. Tighten the fitting while backing up the pump nut with another wrench. Install the pipe at the carburetor.

8. Install the inlet and vapor hoses. Install the shields (if equipped) and oil filter. Lower the car, connect the negative battery cable, start the engine, and check for leaks.

TESTING THE FUEL PUMP

To determine if the pump is in good condition, tests for both volume and pressure should be performed. The tests are made with the pump installed. Never replace a fuel pump without first performing these simple tests.

Be sure that the fuel filter has been changed at the specified interval. If in doubt, install a new filter first.

Pressure Test

1. Disconnect the fuel line at the carburetor and connect a fuel pump pressure gauge. Fill the carburetor float bowl with gasoline.

2. Start the engine and check the pressure

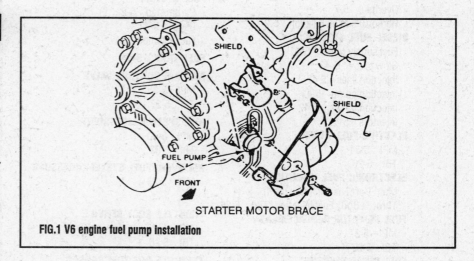

FIG.1 V6 engine fuel pump installation

with the engine at idle. If the pump has a vapor return hose, squeeze it off so that an accurate reading can be obtained. Pressure should measure 6.0–7.5 psi.

3. If the pressure is incorrect, replace the pump. If it is okay, go on to the volume test.

Volume Test

1. Disconnect the pressure gauge. Run the fuel line into a graduated container.

2. Run the engine at idle until one pint of gasoline has been pumped. One pint should be delivered in 30 seconds or less. There is normally enough fuel in the carburetor float bowl to perform this test, but refill it if necessary.

3. If the delivery rate is below the minimum, check the lines for restrictions or leaks, then replace the pump.

Carburetor

The Rochester E2SE is used on all 1982 and later A-body cars. It is a two barrel, two stage carburetor of downdraft design used in conjunction with the Computer Command Control system of fuel control. The carburetor has special design features for optimum air/fuel mixture control during all ranges of engine operation.

MODEL IDENTIFICATION

General Motors Rochester carburetors are identified by their model code. The first number

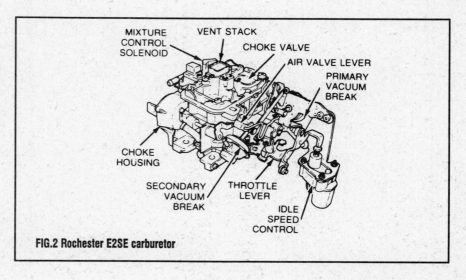

FIG.2 Rochester E2SE carburetor

indicates the number of barrels, while one of the last letters indicates the type of choke used. These are V for the manifold mounted choke coil, C for the choke coil mounted in the carburetor body, and E for electric choke, also mounted on the carburetor. Model codes ending in A indicate an altitude compensation carburetor.

FLOAT ADJUSTMENT

♦ SEE FIGS. 4 and 5

1. Remove the air horn from the throttle body.

2. Use your fingers to hold the retainer in place, and to push the float down into light contact with the needle.

3. Measure the distance from the toe of the float (furthest from the hinge) to the top of the carburetor (gasket removed).

4. To adjust, remove the float and gently bend the arm to specification. After adjustment, check the float alignment in the chamber.

PUMP ADJUSTMENT

E2SE carburetors have a non-adjustable pump lever. No adjustments are either necessary or possible.

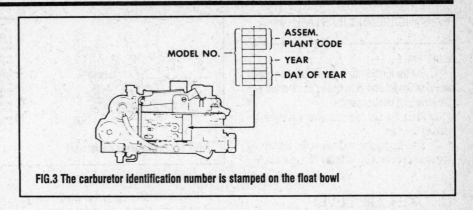

FIG.3 The carburetor identification number is stamped on the float bowl

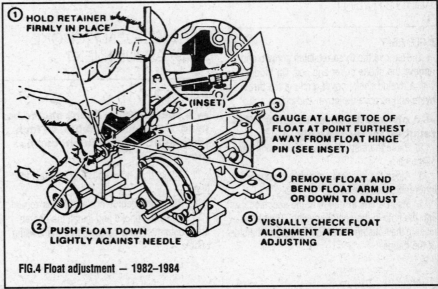

① HOLD RETAINER FIRMLY IN PLACE

② PUSH FLOAT DOWN LIGHTLY AGAINST NEEDLE

③ GAUGE AT LARGE TOE OF FLOAT AT POINT FURTHEST AWAY FROM FLOAT HINGE PIN (SEE INSET)

④ REMOVE FLOAT AND BEND FLOAT ARM UP OR DOWN TO ADJUST

⑤ VISUALLY CHECK FLOAT ALIGNMENT AFTER ADJUSTING

(INSET)

FIG.4 Float adjustment — 1982–1984

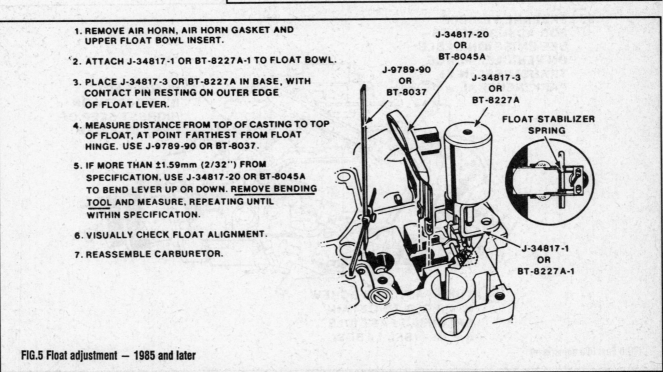

1. REMOVE AIR HORN, AIR HORN GASKET AND UPPER FLOAT BOWL INSERT.

2. ATTACH J-34817-1 OR BT-8227A-1 TO FLOAT BOWL.

3. PLACE J-34817-3 OR BT-8227A IN BASE, WITH CONTACT PIN RESTING ON OUTER EDGE OF FLOAT LEVER.

4. MEASURE DISTANCE FROM TOP OF CASTING TO TOP OF FLOAT, AT POINT FARTHEST FROM FLOAT HINGE. USE J-9789-90 OR BT-8037.

5. IF MORE THAN ±1.59mm (2/32") FROM SPECIFICATION, USE J-34817-20 OR BT-8045A TO BEND LEVER UP OR DOWN. REMOVE BENDING TOOL AND MEASURE, REPEATING UNTIL WITHIN SPECIFICATION.

6. VISUALLY CHECK FLOAT ALIGNMENT.

7. REASSEMBLE CARBURETOR.

J-34817-20 OR BT-8045A

J-9789-90 OR BT-8037

J-34817-3 OR BT-8227A

FLOAT STABILIZER SPRING

J-34817-1 OR BT-8227A-1

FIG.5 Float adjustment — 1985 and later

FAST IDLE ADJUSTMENT

▶ SEE FIG. 6

1. Set the ignition timing and curb idle speed, and disconnect and plug hoses as directed on the emission control decal.

2. Place the fast idle screw on the highest step of the cam.

3. Start the engine and adjust the engine speed to specification with the fast idle screw.

CHOKE COIL LEVER ADJUSTMENT

▶ SEE FIG. 7

1. Remove the three retaining screws and remove the choke cover and coil. On models with a riveted choke cover, drill out the three rivets and remove the cover and choke coil.

➡ **A choke stat cover retainer kit is required for reassembly.**

2. Place the fast idle screw on the high step of the cam.

3. Close the choke by pushing in on the intermediate choke lever.

4. Insert a drill or gauge of the specified size into the hole in the choke housing. The choke lever in the housing should be up against the side of the gauge.

5. If the lever does not just touch the gauge, bend the intermediate choke rod to adjust.

FAST IDLE CAM (CHOKE ROD) ADJUSTMENT

▶ SEE FIG. 8

➡ **A special angle gauge should be used. If it is not available, an inch (milimeter) measurement can be made.**

1. Adjust the choke coil lever and fast idle first.

2. Rotate the degree scale until it is zeroed.

3. Close the choke and install the degree scale onto the choke plate. Center the leveling bubble.

4. Rotate the scale so that the specified degree is opposite the scale pointer.

5. Place the fast idle screw on the second step of the cam (against the high step). Close the choke by pushing in the intermediate lever.

6. Bend the fast idle cam rod at the U to adjust the angle to specifications.

AIR VALVE ROD ADJUSTMENT

1. Seat the vacuum diaphragm with an outside vacuum source. Tape over the purge bleed hole if present.

2. Close the air valve.

3. Insert the specified gauge between the rod and the end of the slot in the plunger.

4. Bend the rod to adjust the clearance.

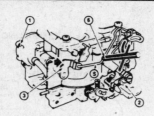

① IF RIVETED, DRILL OUT AND REMOVE RIVETS. REMOVE CHOKE COVER AND STAT ASSEMBLY.
② PLACE FAST IDLE SCREW ON HIGH STEP OF FAST IDLE CAM.
③ PUSH ON INTERMEDIATE CHOKE LEVER UNTIL CHOKE VALVE IS CLOSED.
④ INSERT .085" (2.18mm) PLUG GAGE IN HOLE.
⑤ EDGE OF LEVER SHOULD JUST CONTACT SIDE OF GAGE.
⑥ SUPPORT AT 'S' AND BEND INTERMEDIATE CHOKE LINK TO ADJUST

FIG.7 Choke stat lever adjustment

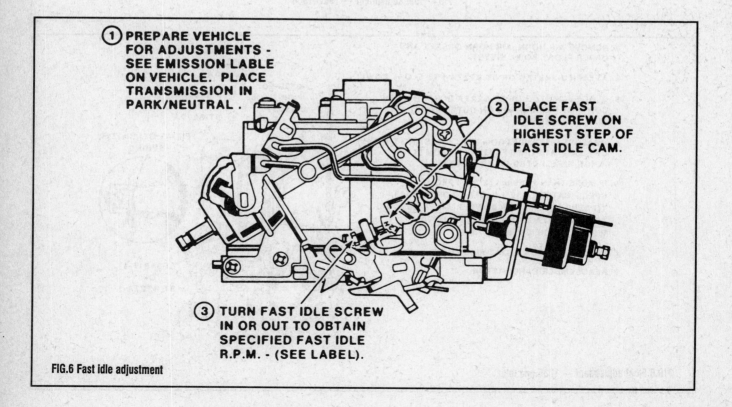

① **PREPARE VEHICLE FOR ADJUSTMENTS - SEE EMISSION LABLE ON VEHICLE. PLACE TRANSMISSION IN PARK/NEUTRAL.**

② **PLACE FAST IDLE SCREW ON HIGHEST STEP OF FAST IDLE CAM.**

③ **TURN FAST IDLE SCREW IN OR OUT TO OBTAIN SPECIFIED FAST IDLE R.P.M. - (SEE LABEL).**

FIG.6 Fast idle adjustment

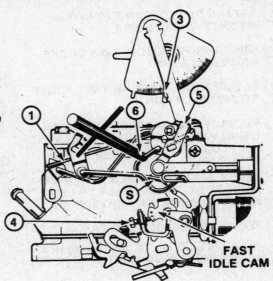

① ATTACH RUBBER BAND TO INTER-MEDIATE CHOKE LEVER.

② OPEN THROTTLE TO ALLOW CHOKE VALVE TO CLOSE.

③ SET UP ANGLE GAGE AND SET ANGLE TO SPECIFICATIONS.

④ PLACE FAST IDLE SCREW ON SECOND STEP OF CAM AGAINST RISE OF HIGH STEP.

⑤ PUSH ON CHOKE SHAFT LEVER TO OPEN CHOKE VALVE AND TO MAKE CONTACT WITH BLACK CLOSING TANG.

⑥ SUPPORT AT "S" AND ADJUST BY BENDING FAST IDLE CAM LINK UNTIL BUBBLE IS CENTERED.

FIG.8 Fast idle cam (choke rod) adjustment

PRIMARY SIDE VACUUM BREAK ADJUSTMENT

▶ SEE FIG. 11

1. Follow Steps 1–4 of the Fast Idle Cam Adjustment.
2. Seat the choke vacuum diaphragm with an outside vacuum source.

3. Push in on the intermediate choke lever to close the choke valve, and hold closed during adjustment.
4. Adjust by using a 1/8 in. (3mm) hex wrench to turn the screw in the rear cover until the bubble is centered.
5. After adjusting, apply RTV silicone sealant over the screw to seal the setting.

SECONDARY VACUUM BREAK ADJUSTMENT

▶ SEE FIG. 12

1. Follow Steps 1–4 of the Fast Idle Cam Adjustment.
2. Seat the choke vacuum diaphragm with an outside vacuum source.

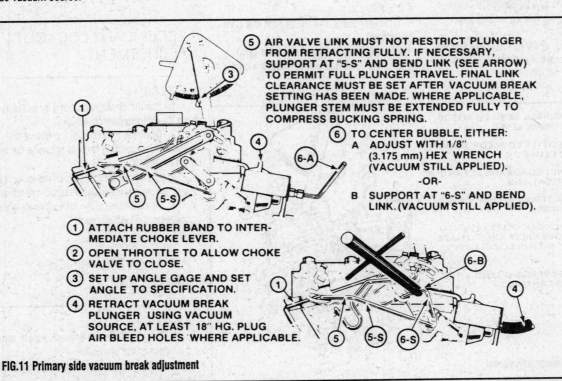

⑤ AIR VALVE LINK MUST NOT RESTRICT PLUNGER FROM RETRACTING FULLY. IF NECESSARY, SUPPORT AT "5-S" AND BEND LINK (SEE ARROW) TO PERMIT FULL PLUNGER TRAVEL. FINAL LINK CLEARANCE MUST BE SET AFTER VACUUM BREAK SETTING HAS BEEN MADE. WHERE APPLICABLE, PLUNGER STEM MUST BE EXTENDED FULLY TO COMPRESS BUCKING SPRING.

⑥ TO CENTER BUBBLE, EITHER:
A ADJUST WITH 1/8" (3.175 mm) HEX WRENCH (VACUUM STILL APPLIED).
   -OR-
B SUPPORT AT "6-S" AND BEND LINK. (VACUUM STILL APPLIED).

① ATTACH RUBBER BAND TO INTER-MEDIATE CHOKE LEVER.

② OPEN THROTTLE TO ALLOW CHOKE VALVE TO CLOSE.

③ SET UP ANGLE GAGE AND SET ANGLE TO SPECIFICATION.

④ RETRACT VACUUM BREAK PLUNGER USING VACUUM SOURCE, AT LEAST 18" HG. PLUG AIR BLEED HOLES WHERE APPLICABLE.

FIG.11 Primary side vacuum break adjustment

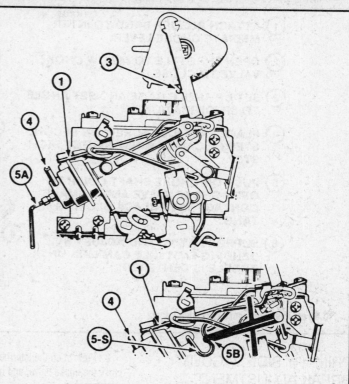

① ATTACH RUBBER BAND TO INTER-MEDIATE CHOKE LEVER.

② OPEN THROTTLE TO ALLOW CHOKE VALVE TO CLOSE.

③ SET UP ANGLE GAGE AND SET ANGLE TO SPECIFICATION.

④ RETRACT VACUUM BREAK PLUNGER USING VACUUM SOURCE, AT LEAST 18" HG. PLUG AIR BLEED HOLES WHERE APPLICABLE.

WHERE APPLICABLE, PLUNGER STEM MUST BE EXTENDED FULLY TO COM-PRESS PLUNGER BUCKING SPRING.

⑤ TO CENTER BUBBLE, EITHER:

A. ADJUST WITH 1/8" (3.175 mm) HEX WRENCH (VACUUM STILL APPLIED)

-OR-

B. SUPPORT AT "5-S", BEND LINK (VACUUM STILL APPLIED)

FIG.12 Secondary side vacuum break adjustment

3. Push in on the intermediate choke lever to close the choke valve, and hold closed during adjustment. Make sure the plunger spring is compressed and seated, if present.

4. Adjust by using a 1/8 in. (3mm) hex wrench to turn the screw in the rear cover until the bubble is centered.

5. After adjusting, apply RTV silicone sealant over the screw to seal the setting.

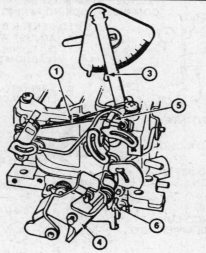

① ATTACH RUBBER BAND TO INTER-MEDIATE CHOKE LEVER.

② OPEN THROTTLE TO ALLOW CHOKE VALVE TO CLOSE.

③ SET UP ANGLE GAGE AND SET ANGLE TO SPECIFICATIONS.

④ HOLD THROTTLE LEVER IN WIDE OPEN POSITION.

⑤ PUSH ON CHOKE SHAFT LEVER TO OPEN CHOKE VALVE AND TO MAKE CONTACT WITH BLACK CLOSING TANG.

⑥ ADJUST BY BENDING TANG UNTIL BUBBLE IS CENTERED.

FIG.13 Choke unloader adjustment

CHOKE UNLOADER ADJUSTMENT

▶ SEE FIG. 13

1. Follow Steps 1–4 of the Fast Idle Cam Adjustment.

2. Hold the primary throttle wide open.

3. If the engine is warm, close the choke valve by pushing in on the intermediate choke lever.

4. Bend the unloader tang until the bubble is centered.

SECONDARY LOCKOUT ADJUSTMENT

▶ SEE FIG. 14

1. Pull the choke wide open by pushing out on the intermediate choke lever.

2. Open the throttle until the end of the secondary actuating lever is opposite the toe of the lockout lever.

3. Gauge clearance between the lockout lever and secondary lever should be as specified.

4. To adjust, bend the lockout lever where it contacts the fast idle cam.

AIR VALVE SPRING ADJUSTMENT

▶ SEE FIG. 15

1. To gain access to the lock screw, remove the intermediate choke link.

2. Using a 3/32 in. hex wrench, loosen the lock screw.

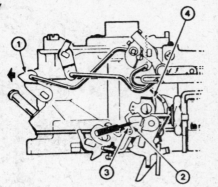

1. HOLD CHOKE VALVE WIDE OPEN BY PUSHING DOWN ON INTERMEDIATE CHOKE LEVER.

2. OPEN THROTTLE LEVER UNTIL END OF SECONDARY ACTUATING LEVER IS OPPOSITE TOE OF LOCKOUT LEVER.

3. GAGE CLEARANCE - DIMENSION SHOULD BE .025".

4. IF NECESSARY TO ADJUST, BEND LOCKOUT LEVER TANG CONTACTING FAST IDLE CAM.

FIG.14 Secondary lockout adjustment

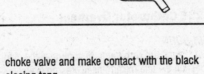

1. IF NECESSARY, REMOVE INTER-MEDIATE CHOKE LINK, TO GAIN ACCESS TO LOCK SCREW.

2. LOOSEN LOCK SCREW USING 3/32" (2.381mm) HEX WRENCH.

3. TURN TENSION-ADJUSTING SCREW ↻ UNTIL AIR VALVE OPENS SLIGHTLY.

TURN ADJUSTING SCREW ↺ UNTIL AIR VALVE JUST CLOSES. CONTINUE ↺ SPECIFIED NUMBER OF TURNS.

4. TIGHTEN LOCK SCREW.

5. APPLY LITHIUM BASE GREASE TO LUBRICATE PIN AND SPRING CONTACT AREA.

FIG.15 Air valve spring adjustment

3. Turn the adjusting screw clockwise until the air valve opens slightly, then turn the screw counterclockwise until the valve closes and continue the number of specified turns.

4. Tighten the lock screw and apply lithium grease to the pin and the spring contact area.

CHOKE LINK/FAST IDLE CAM ADJUSTMENT

1. Connect a rubber band to the intermediate choke lever, then open the throttle valve to allow the choke valve to close.

2. Set up the angle gauge and the angle to specifications.

3. Position the fast idle screw on the second step of the fast idle cam (against the rise of the high step).

4. Turn the choke lever shaft to open the choke valve and make contact with the black closing tang.

5. Support at the **S** point and bend the fast idle cam link until the bubble is centered.

REMOVAL & INSTALLATION

1. Remove the air cleaner and gasket.

2. Disconnect the fuel pipe and all vacuum lines.

3. Tag and disconnect all electrical connections.

4. If equipped with an Automatic Transaxle, disconnect the downshift cable.

5. If equipped with cruise control, disconnect the linkage.

6. Unscrew the carburetor mounting bolts and remove the carburetor.

7. Inspect the EFE heater for damage. Be sure that the throttle body and EFE mating surfaces are clean.

8. Install the carburetor and tighten the nuts alternately to the proper specifications.

9. Installation of the remaining components is in the reverse order of removal.

Carburetor Overhaul

Efficient carburetion depends greatly on careful cleaning and inspection during overhaul, since dirt, gum, water, or varnish in or on the carburetor parts are often responsible for poor performance.

Overhaul your carburetor in a clean, dust-free area. Carefully disassemble the carburetor, referring often to the exploded views and directions packaged with the rebuilding kit. Keep all similar and look-alike parts segregated during disassembly and cleaning to avoid accidental interchange during assembly. Make a note of all jet sizes.

When the carburetor is disassembled, wash all parts (except diaphragms, electric choke units, pump plunger, and any other plastic, leather, fiber, or rubber parts) in clean carburetor solvent. Do not leave parts in the solvent any longer than is necessary to sufficiently loosen the deposits. Excessive cleaning may remove the special finish from the float bowl and choke valve bodies, leaving these parts unfit for service. Rinse all parts in clean solvent and blow them dry with compressed air or allow them to air dry. Wipe clean all cork, plastic, leather, and fiber parts with a clean, lint-free cloth.

Blow out all passages and jets with compressed air and be sure that there are no restrictions or blockages. Never use wire or similar tools to clean jets, fuel passages, or air bleeds. Clean all jets and valves separately to avoid accidental interchange.

Check all parts for wear or damage. If wear or damage is found, replace the defective parts. Especially check the following:

1. Check the float needle and seat for wear. If wear is found, replace the complete assembly.

2. Check the float hinge pin for wear and the float(s) for dents or distortion. Replace the float if fuel has leaked into it.

3. Check the throttle and choke shaft bores for wear or an out-of-round condition. Damage or wear to the throttle arm, shaft, or shaft bore will often require replacement of the throttle body. These parts require a close tolerance of fit; wear may allow air leakage, which could affect starting and idling.

➡ **Throttle shafts and bushings are not included in overhaul kits. They can be purchases separately.**

4. Inspect the idle mixture adjusting needles for burrs or grooves. Any such condition requires replacement of the needle, since you will not be able to obtain a satisfactory idle.

5. Test the accelerator pump check valves. They should pass air one way but not the other. Test for proper seating by blowing and sucking on the valve. Replace the valve check ball and spring as necessary. If the valve is satisfactory, wash the valve parts again to remove breath moisture.

6. Check the bowl cover for warped surfaces with a straightedge.

7. Closely inspect the accelerator pump plunger for wear and damage, replacing as necessary.

8. After the carburetor is assembled, check the choke valve for freedom of operation.

Carburetor overhaul kits are recommended for each overhaul. These kits contain all gaskets and new parts to replace those which deteriorate most rapidly. Failure to replace all parts supplied with the kit (especially gaskets) can result in poor performance later.

Some carburetor manufacturers supply overhaul kits for three basic types: minor repair; major repair; and gasket kits. Basically, they contain the following:

Minor Repair Kits:
• All gaskets
• Float needle valve
• All diagrams
• Spring for the pump diaphragm

Major Repair Kits:
• All jets and gaskets
• All diaphragms
• Float needle valve
• Pump ball valve
• Float
• Complete intermediate rod
• Intermediate pump lever
• Some cover holddown screws and washers

Gasket Kits:
• All gaskets

After cleaning and checking all components, reassemble the carburetor, using new parts and referring to the exploded view. When reassembling, make sure that all screws and jets are tight in their seats, but do not overtighten as the tips will be distorted. Tighten all screws gradually, in rotation. Do not tighten needle valves into their seats; uneven jetting will result. Always use new gaskets. Be sure to adjust the float level when reassembling.

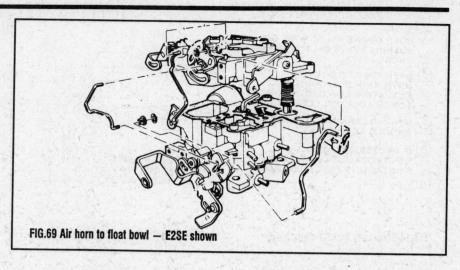

FIG.69 Air horn to float bowl — E2SE shown

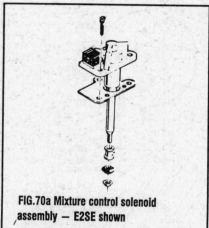

FIG.70a Mixture control solenoid assembly — E2SE shown

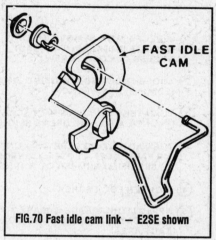

FIG.70 Fast idle cam link — E2SE shown

FAST IDLE CAM

E2SE Carburetor Overhaul

AIR HORN

1. Invert the carburetor, then remove the plug covering the idle mixture needle as previously described.

2. Install the carburetor in a suitable holding stand.

3. Remove the primary and secondary vacuum break assemblies. Be sure to take note of the linkage positions for installation.

4. Remove the three screws from the mixture control solenoid. Remove the mixture control solenoid with gasket and discard the gasket.

5. Remove the two screws from the vent stack and remove the vent stack. Remove the intermediate choke shaft link retainer at the choke lever and discard it.

6. Remove the choke link and bushing from choke lever and save the bushing.

7. Remove the retainer and bushing from the fast idle cam link and discard the retainer.

➡ **Do not remove fast idle cam screw and cam from the float bowl. If removed, the cam might not operate properly when reassembled. If needed, a replacement float bowl will include a secondary locknut lever, fast idle cam, and cam screw.**

8. Remove the retainer from the pump link. Do not remove the screw attaching the pump lever to the air horn assembly. When reassembled, the screw might not hold properly.

9. Remove the seven screw assemblies of various length that retain the air horn to the carburetor and remove the air horn assembly. Tilt the air horn to disconnect fast idle cam link from the slot in fast idle cam and the pump link from the hole in the pump lever.

10. Remove the cam link from the choke lever. Be sure to line up the "squirt" on link with slot in lever.

11. Invert the air horn and remove the TPS actuator plunger. The TPS adjusting screw and plug should not be removed.

12. Remove the stakings that holds the TPS plunger seal retainer and pump stem seal retainer.

13. Remove the retainers and seals and discard them.

14. Further disassembly of the air horn is not required for cleaning purposes. The choke valve and choke valve screws, the air valve and air valve shaft should not be removed.

➡ **Do not turn the secondary metering rod adjusting screw. The rod could come out of jet and possibly cause damage.**

FLOAT BOWL

1. Remove the accelerator pump, air horn gasket and pump return spring.

2. Remove the Throttle Position Sensor (TPS) assembly and spring. Inspect the TPS connector wires for broken insulation, which could cause grounding of the TPS.

3. Remove the upper insert and the hinge pin. Remove the float and lever assembly with the float stabilizing spring if used. Remove the float needle and pull clip.

4. Remove the lower insert, if used.

5. Remove the float needle seat and seat gasket.

6. Remove the jet and lean mixture needle assembly.

➡ **Do not remove or change the preset adjustment of calibration needle in the metering jet unless the Computer Command Control system performance check requires it.**

7. Remove the pump discharge spring guide, using a suitable slide hammer puller only.

➡ **Do not pry the guide. Damage could occur to the sealing surfaces, and could require replacement of the float bowl.**

9. Remove the spring and check ball, by inverting the bowl and catching them as they fall.

10. Remove the fuel inlet nut and the fuel filter spring.

11. Remove the fuel filter assembly and discard it. Remove the filter gasket and discard it.

CHOKE ASSEMBLY AND THROTTLE BODY

1. Remove the choke cover as follows:

a. Use a 5/32 in. (4 mm) drill bit to remove the heads (only) from the rivets.

b. Remove the choke cover retainers. Remove the remaining pieces of rivets, using drift and small hammer.

c. Remove the electric choke cover and stat assembly.

2. Remove the stat lever screw, Stat lever, intermediate choke shaft, lever and link assembly.

3. Remove the two screws and the choke housing.

4. Remove the four screws, and the throttle body assembly from the inverted float bowl.

5. Remove the gasket, pump link and line up the "squirt" on link with the slot in the lever.

6. Count and make a record of the number of turns needed to lightly bottom the idle

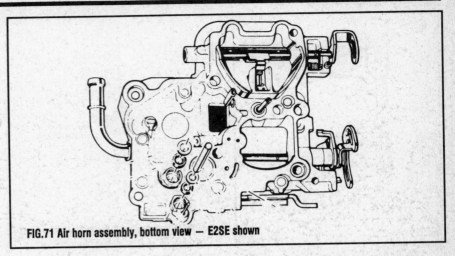
FIG.71 Air horn assembly, bottom view — E2SE shown

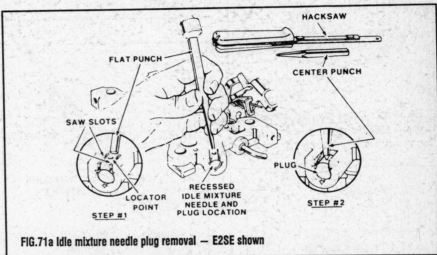
FIG.71a Idle mixture needle plug removal — E2SE shown

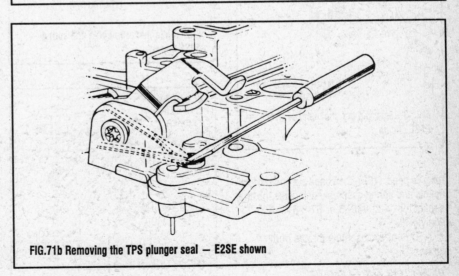
FIG.71b Removing the TPS plunger seal — E2SE shown

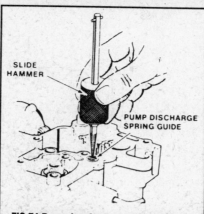

FIG.72 Lean mixture adjusting needle and tool — E2SE shown

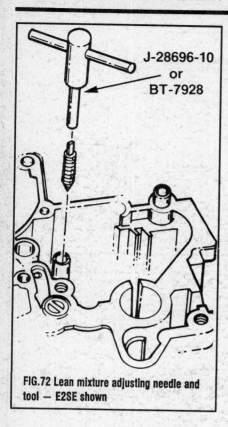

FIG.73 Removing the choke cover rivets — E2SE shown

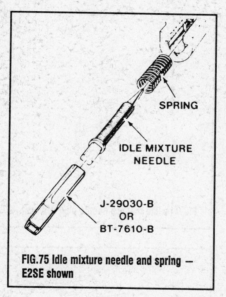

FIG.74 Removing the pump discharge spring guide with special slide hammer — E2SE shown

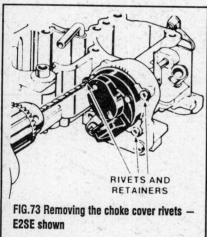

FIG.75 Idle mixture needle and spring — E2SE shown

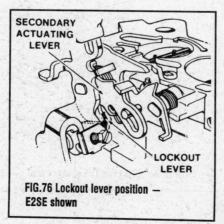

FIG.76 Lockout lever position — E2SE shown

mixture needle (69), then back out and remove needle and spring assembly using idle mixture socket tool J–29030–B or BT–7610–B or equivalent.

7. Do not disassemble throttle body further.

INSPECTION AND CLEANING

1. Place the metal parts in immersion carburetor cleaner.

➡ Do not immerse idle stop solenoid, mixture control solenoid, throttle lever actuator, TPS, electric choke, rubber and plastic parts, diaphragms, and pump in the cleaner, as they may be damaged. Plastic bushing in throttle lever will withstand normal cleaning.

2. Blow dry the parts with shop air. Be sure all fuel and air passages are free of burrs and dirt. Do not pass drill bits or wires through jets and passages.

3. Be sure to check the mating surfaces of casting for damage. Replace if necessary. Check for holes in levers for wear or out-of-round conditions. Check the bushings for damage and excessive wear. Replace if necessary.

CARBURETOR REASSEMBLY

1. Install the mixture needle and spring assembly using idle mixture socket tool J–29030–B or BT–7610–B or equivalent. Lightly bottom the needle and back it out the number of turns recorded during removal, as a preliminary adjustment. Refer to idle mixture adjustment procedure in this section for the final idle mixture adjustment.

2. Install the pump link and a new gasket on the inverted float bowl.

3. Install the throttle body to the float bowl assembly and finger tighten the four retaining screws. If the secondary actuating lever engages the lockout lever, and linkage moves without binding, tighten retaining screws.

4. If the float bowl assembly was replaced, stamp or engrave the model number on the new float bowl in same location as on old bowl.

5. Place the throttle body and float bowl together on a suitable carburetor holding stand.

6. Install the choke housing on the throttle body, with the retaining screws.

7. Install the intermediate choke shaft, lever and link assembly.

8. Install the choke stat lever on the intermediate choke shaft. The intermediate choke lever must be upright.

9. Install the choke lever attaching screw in the shaft.

10. Install the gasket on the fuel inlet nut and install the new filter assembly in the nut.

11. Install the filter spring and then install the fuel inlet nut. Tighten the fuel inlet nut to 18 ft. lbs. (24 Nm).

✽✽ CAUTION

Tightening beyond this limit may damage gasket and could cause a fuel leak, which might result in personal injury.

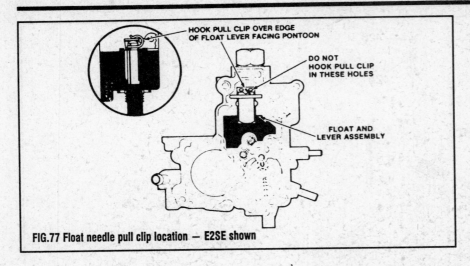

FIG.77 Float needle pull clip location — E2SE shown

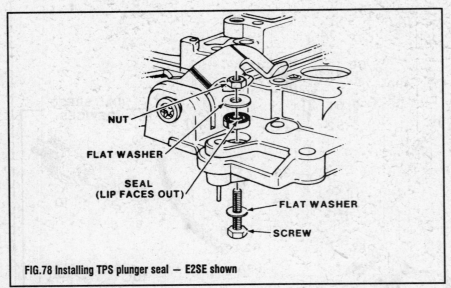

FIG.78 Installing TPS plunger seal — E2SE shown

12. Install the pump discharge ball and spring.

13. Install a new spring guide and tap it until the top is flush with the bowl casting.

14. Install the needle seat with gasket. If used, lower the insert.

15. Install the jet and lean mixture needle assembly. Using lean mixture adjusting tool J–28696–10 or BT–7928 or equivalent, lightly bottom the lean mixture needle. Back it out 2¹/₂ turns, as a preliminary adjustment.

➡ **Only adjust the lean mixture needle screw if it was removed or touched during disassembly or if the Computer Command Control system performance check, made before disassembly, indicated an incorrect lean mixture needle setting:**

16. Bend the float lever upward slightly at the notch.

17. If used, install the float stabilizing spring on float. Install the hinge pin in float lever, with ends toward the pump well.

18. Install the needle with pull clip assembly on the edge of the float lever. Install the float and lever assembly in float bowl.

➡ **Adjust the float level using Float Level T-Scale J-9789–90 or BT-8037 or equivalent.**

19. Install the upper insert over the hinge pin, with the top flush with the bowl. Install the TPS spring and the TPS assembly. The parts must be below the surface of the bowl.

20. Install the gasket over the dowels. Install the spring and pump assembly.

21. Install a new pump stem seal with the lip facing outside of carburetor and install the retainer. Be sure to stake it at new locations.

22. Install a new TPS actuator plunger seal with the lip facing outside of carburetor and install the retainer. Be sure to stake it at new locations.

23. Install the TPS plunger through the seal in the air horn. Use lithium base grease, liberally to pin, if used, where contacted by spring.

24. Install the fast idle cam link in the choke lever. Be sure to line-up the "squirt" on link with slot in lever.

25. Rotate the cam to the highest position. The lower end of the fast idle cam link goes in cam slot, and the pump link end goes into the hole in the lever.

26. Hold the pump down, and than lower the air horn assembly onto the float bowl. Be sure to guide the pump stem through the seal.

27. Install the one of the air horn retaining screws, finger tight to hold the air horn in place.

28. Install the cam link in the slot of the cam. Install a new bushing and retainer to the link, with the large end of bushing facing the retainer. Check for freedom of movement.

29. Install the rest of the air horn retaining screws.

30. Install the spacer and a new seal, lightly coat the seal with automatic transmission fluid. Assemble the seal on the solenoid stem, touching the spacer.

31. Install a new retainer and a new gasket on the air horn. Install the mixture control solenoid lining up the stem with the recess in the bowl.

32. Install the solenoid retaining screws. Install the vent stack, with two retaining screws, (unless lean mixture needle requires on-vehicle adjustment).

33. Install a new retainer on the pump link. Adjust the air valve spring, if adjustable.

34. Install the bushing on the choke link. With the intermediate choke lever upright, install the link in the choke lever hole. Install the new link retainer.

35. The following procedures is for reassembly of any small components that have been removed from the carburetor, if part replacement is necessary or for any other reason.

   a. Install the idle stop solenoid, retainer and nut to the secondary side vacuum break bracket. Bend the retainer tab to secure nut.

   b. Install the bushing to the link and the link to the vacuum break plunger. Install the retainer to the link.

   c. Rotate the assembly, insert the end of the link in the upper slot of the choke lever. Install the bracket screws.

   d. Install the idle speed device, retainer and nut to the primary side vacuum break bracket. Bend the retainer tab to secure the nut.

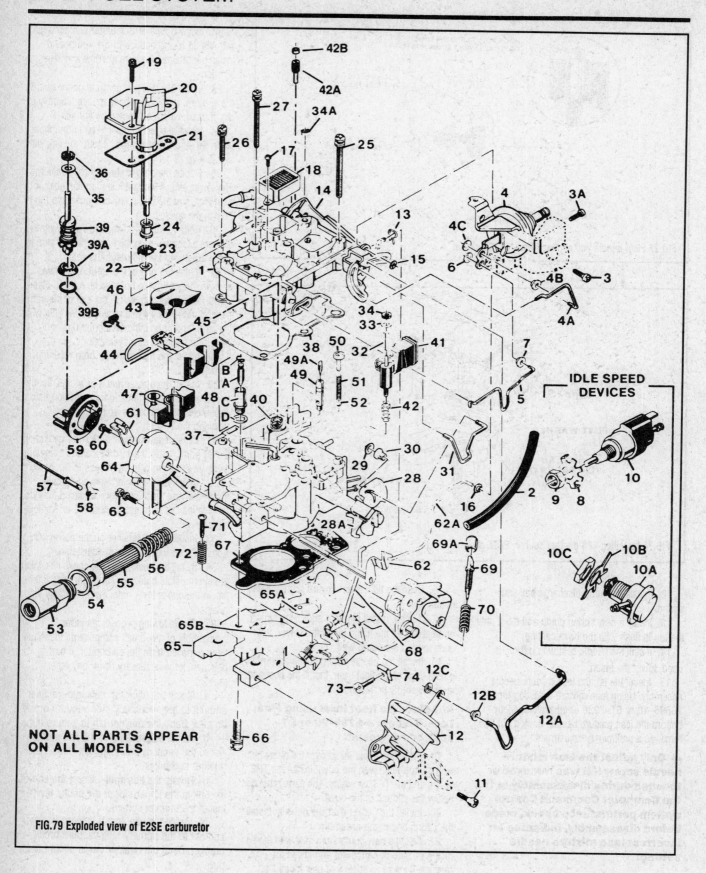

IDLE SPEED DEVICES

NOT ALL PARTS APPEAR ON ALL MODELS

FIG.79 Exploded view of E2SE carburetor

AIR HORN PARTS

1. MIXTURE CONTROL (M/C) SOLENOID
2. SCREW ASSEMBLY-SOLENOID ATTACHING
3. GASKET-M/C SOLENOID TO AIR HORN
4. SPACER-M/C SOLENOID
5. SEAL-M/C SOLENOID TO FLOAT BOWL
6. RETAINER-M/C SOLENOID SEAL
7. AIR HORN ASSEMBLY
8. GASKET-AIR HORN TO FLOAT BOWL
9. SCREW-AIR HORN TO FLOAT BOWL (SHORT)
10. SCREW-AIR HORN TO FLOAT BOWL (LONG)
11. SCREW-AIR HORN TO FLOAT BOWL (LARGE)
12. VENT STACK AND SCREEN ASSEMBLY
13. SCREW-VENT STACK ATTACHING
14. SEAL-PUMP STEM
15. RETAINER-PUMP STEM SEAL
16. SEAL-T.P.S. PLUNGER
17. RETAINER-T.P.S. PLUNGER SEAL
18. PLUNGER-T.P.S. ACTUATOR

CHOKE PARTS

19. VACUUM BREAK AND BRACKET ASSEMBLY- PRIMARY
20. HOSE-VACUUM BREAK PRIMARY
21. TEE-VACUUM BREAK
22. SOLENOID-IDLE SPEED
23. RETAINER-IDLE SPEED SOLENOID
24. NUT-IDLE SPEED SOLENOID ATTACHING
25. SCREW-VACUUM BREAK BRACKET ATTACHING
26. LINK-AIR VALVE
27. BUSHING-AIR VALVE LINK
28. RETAINER-AIR VALVE LINK
29. LINK-FAST IDLE CAM
29A LINK-FAST IDLE CAM
29B RETAINER-LINK
29C BUSHING-LINK
30. HOSE-VACUUM BREAK
31. INTERMEDIATE CHOKE SHAFT/LEVER/LINK ASSEMBLY
32. BUSHING-INTERMEDIATE CHOKE LINK
33. RETAINER-INTERMEDIATE CHOKE LINK
34. VACUUM BREAK AND LINK ASSEMBLY-SECONDARY
35. SCREW-VACUUM BREAK ATTACHING
36. ELECTRIC CHOKE-COVER AND COIL ASSEMBLY
37. SCREW-CHOKE LEVER ATTACHING
38. CHOKE COIL LEVER ASSEMBLY
39. CHOKE HOUSING
40. SCREW-CHOKE HOUSING ATTACHING
41. CHOKE COVER RETAINER KIT
67. SCREW-VACUUM BREAK BRACKET ATTACHING

FLOAT BOWL PARTS

42. NUT-FUEL INLET
43. GASKET-FUEL INLET NUT
44. FILTER-FUEL INLET
45. SPRING-FUEL FILTER
46. FLOAT AND LEVER ASSEMBLY
47. HINGE PIN-FLOAT
48. UPPER INSERT-FLOAT BOWL
48A LOWER INSERT-FLOAT BOWL
49. NEEDLE AND SEAT ASSEMBLY
50. SPRING-PUMP RETURN
51. PUMP PLUNGER ASSEMBLY
52. PRIMARY METERING JET ASSEMBLY
53. RETAINER-PUMP DISCHARGE BALL
54. SPRING-PUMP DISCHARGE
55. BALL-PUMP DISCHARGE
56. SPRING-T.P.S. ADJUSTING
57. SENSOR-THROTTLE POSITION (TPS)
58. FLOAT BOWL ASSEMBLY
59. GASKET-FLOAT BOWL

THROTTLE BODY PARTS

60. RETAINER-PUMP LINK
61. LINK-PUMP
62. THROTTLE BODY ASSEMBLY
63. CLIP-CAM SCREW
64. SCREW-FAST IDLE CAM
65. IDLE NEEDLE AND SPRING ASSEMBLY
66. SCREW-THROTTLE BODY TO FLOAT BOWL
68. SCREW-IDLE STOP
69. SPRING-IDLE STOP SCREW
70. GASKET-INSULATOR FLANGE

FIG.79 Exploded view of E2SE carburetor

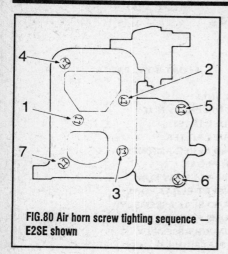

FIG.80 Air horn screw tighting sequence — E2SE shown

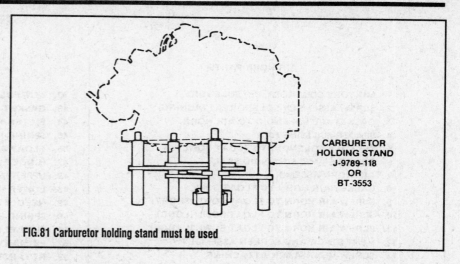

FIG.81 Carburetor holding stand must be used

e. Install the bushing to the vacuum break link. Install the link to vacuum break plunger. Install the retainer to the link and the bushing to the air valve link. Install the link to the plunger and the retainer to the link.

36. Rotate the vacuum break assembly (primary side) and insert the end of the air valve link into the air valve lever and the vacuum break link into the lower slot of the choke lever.

37. Install the bracket screws, vacuum hose between the throttle body tube and the vacuum break assembly.

38. Install the choke thermostat lever. Install the choke cover and thermostat assembly in the choke housing.

39. If the thermostat has a "trap" (box-shaped pick-up tang), the trap surrounds the lever.

40. Line up the notch in the cover with projection on the housing flange. Install the retainers and rivets with rivet tool. If necessary, use an adapter. Adjust the choke as previously described.

E2ME Carburetor Overhaul

In many cases, necessary service can be carried out and completed without removing the carburetor from the engine. The information that follows pertains to a complete overhaul. The carburetor first must be removed from the engine. A complete overhaul includes disassembly, through cleaning, inspection and replacement of all gaskets, diaphragms, seals, worn or damaged parts, and adjustment of individual systems.

Refer to exploded view for parts identification. Always replace internal gaskets that are removed. Base gasket should be inspected and replaced, only if damaged.

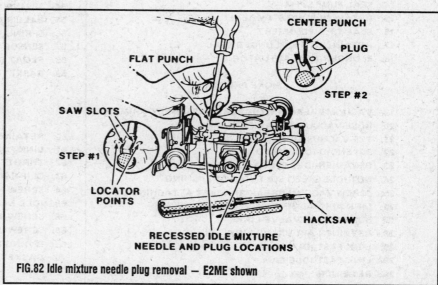

FIG.82 Idle mixture needle plug removal — E2ME shown

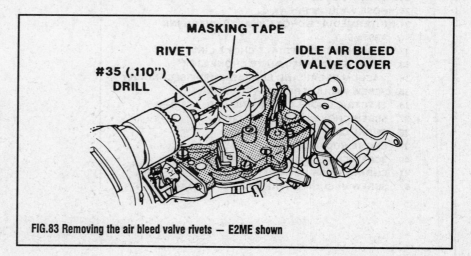

FIG.83 Removing the air bleed valve rivets — E2ME shown

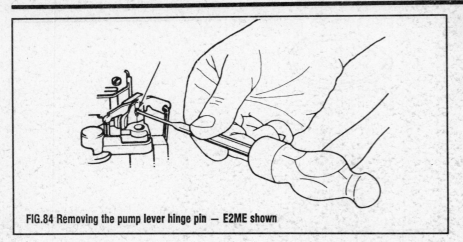

FIG.84 Removing the pump lever hinge pin — E2ME shown

※※ CAUTION

For the next operation, safety glasses must be worn to protect eyes from possible metal shaving damage.

4. Lift off cover and remove any pieces of rivet still inside tower. Use shop air to blow out any remaining chips.

5. Remove idle air bleed valve from the air horn.

6. Remove and discard O-ring seals from valve. New O-ring seals are required for reassembly. The idle air bleed valve is serviced as a complete assembly only.

➡ **Before performing any service on the carburetor, it is essential that it be placed on a suitable holding fixture, such as Tool J–9789–118, BY–30–15 or equivalent. Without the use of the holding fixture, it is possible to damage throttle valves or other parts of the carburetor.**

IDLE SPEED SOLENOID REMOVAL

Remove the attaching screws, then remove the Idle Speed Solenoid. The Idle Speed Solenoid should not be immersed in any carburetor cleaner, and should always be removed before complete carburetor overhaul, as carburetor cleaner will damage the internal components.

IDLE MIXTURE NEEDLE PLUG REMOVAL

1. Use hacksaw to make two parallel cuts in the throttle body, one on each side of the locator points near one idle mixture needle plug. The distance between the cuts will depend on the size of the punch to be used. Cuts should reach down to the steel plug, but should but extend more than $1/8$ in. beyond the locator points.

2. Place a flat punch at a point near the ends of the saw marks in the throttle body. Hold the punch at a 45° angle, and drive it into the throttle body until the casting breaks away, exposing the hardened steel plug. The plug will break, rather than remaining intact. Remove all the loose pieces.

3. Repeat the procedure for the other idle mixture needle plug.

IDLE AIR BLEED VALVE REMOVAL

1. Cover internal bowl vents and air inlets to the bleed valve with masking tape.

2. Carefully align a $7/64$ in. drill bit on rivet head. Drill only enough to remove head of each rivet holding the idle air bleed valve cover.

3. Use a suitably sized punch to drive out the remainder of the rivet from the castings. Repeat procedure with other rivet.

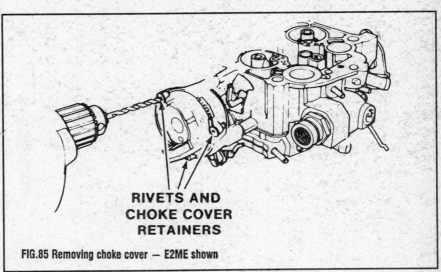

RIVETS AND CHOKE COVER RETAINERS

FIG.85 Removing choke cover — E2ME shown

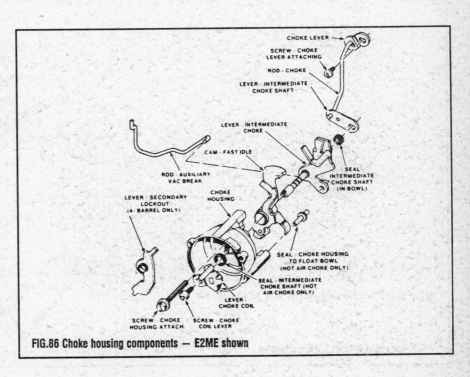

FIG.86 Choke housing components — E2ME shown

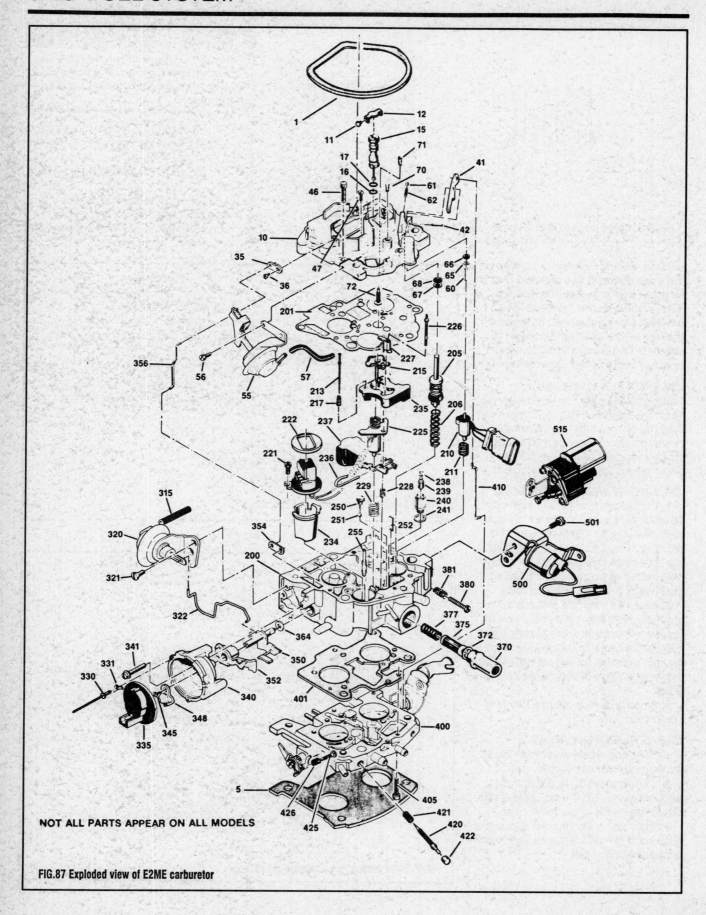

NOT ALL PARTS APPEAR ON ALL MODELS

FIG.87 Exploded view of E2ME carburetor

1	Gasket - Air Cleaner	237	Float
5	Gasket - Flange	238	Pull Clip - Float Needle
10	Air Horn Assembly	239	Needle - Float
11	Rivet - Cover Attaching	240	Seat - Float Needle
12	Cover - Air Bleed Valve	241	Gasket - Float Needle Seat
15	Air Bleed Valve Assembly	250	Plug - Pump Discharge (Retainer)
16	O-ring - Air Bleed Valve - Lower	251	Ball - Pump Discharge
17	O-ring - Air Bleed Valve - Upper	252	Baffle - Pump Well
35	Lever - Choke	255	Primary Metering Jet Assembly
36	Screw - Choke Lever Attaching	315	Hose - Secondary Side (Rear) Vacuum Break
41	Lever - Pump	320	Vacuum Break Assembly - Secondary Side (Rear)
42	Pin - Pump Lever Hinge	321	Screw - Secondary Side (Rear) Vacuum Break Assembly Attaching
46	Screw Assembly - Air Horn to Float Bowl	322	Link - Secondary Side (Rear) Vacuum Break to Choke
47	Screw - Air Horn to Float Bowl (countersunk)	330	Rivet - Choke Cover Attaching
55	Vacuum Break Assembly - Primary Side (Front)	331	Retainer - Choke Cover
56	Screw - Primary Side (Front) Vacuum Break Assembly Attaching	335	Electric Choke Cover and Stat Assembly
		340	Choke Housing Assembly
57	Hose - Primary Side (Front) Vacuum Break	341	Screw and Washer Assembly - Choke Housing to Float Bowl
60	Plunger - Sensor Actuator	345	Screw - Choke Stat Lever Attaching
61	Plug - TPS Adjusting Screw	348	Lever - Choke Stat
62	Screw - TPS Adjusting	350	Intermediate Choke Shaft, Lever and Link Assembly
65	Retainer - TPS Seal	352	Fast Idle Cam Assembly
66	Seal - TPS Plunger	354	Lever - Intermediate Choke
67	Retainer - Pump Stem Seal	356	Link - Choke
68	Seal - Pump Stem	364	Seal - Intermediate Choke Shaft
70	Plug - Solenoid Adjusting Screw	370	Nut - Fuel Inlet
71	Plug - Solenoid Stop Screw	372	Gasket - Fuel Inlet Nut
72	Screw - Solenoid Stop (Rich Mixture)	375	Filter - Fuel Inlet
200	Float Bowl Assembly	377	Spring - Fuel Filter
201	Gasket - Air Horn to Float Bowl	380	Screw - Throttle Stop
205	Pump Assembly	381	Spring - Throttle Stop Screw
206	Spring - Pump Return	400	Throttle Body Assembly
210	Sensor - Throttle Position (TPS)	401	Gasket - Float Bowl to Throttle Body
211	Spring - Sensor Adjusting	405	Screw Assembly - Float Bowl to Throttle Body
213	Rod - Primary Metering	410	Link - Pump
215	Plunger - Solenoid	420	Needle - Idle Mixture
217	Spring - Primary Metering Rod (E2M, E4M only)	421	Spring - Idle Mixture Needle
221	Screw - Solenoid Connector Attaching	422	Plug - Idle Mixture Needle
222	Gasket - Solenoid Connector to Air Horn	425	Screw - Fast Idle Adjusting
225	Mixture Control Solenoid Assembly	426	Spring - Fast Idle Adjusting Screw
226	Screw - Solenoid Adjusting (Lean Mixture)	500	Solenoid and Bracket Assembly
227	Stop - Rich Limit	501	Screw - Bracket Attaching
228	Spring - Solenoid Adjusting Screw	515	Idle Speed Control Assembly
229	Spring - Solenoid Return		
234	Insert - Aneroid Cavity		
235	Insert - Float Bowl		
236	Hinge Pin - Float Description - E4ME		

FIG.87 Exploded view of E2ME carburetor

AIR HORN REMOVAL

1. Remove upper choke lever from the end of choke shaft by removing retaining screw. Rotate upper choke lever to remove choke rod from slot in lever.

2. Remove choke rod from lower lever inside the float bowl casting. Remove rod by holding lower lever outward with small screwdriver and twisting rod counterclockwise.

3. Remove secondary metering rods by removing the small screw in the top of the metering rod hanger. Lift upward on the metering rod hanger until the secondary metering rods are completely out of the air horn. Metering rods may be disassembled from the hanger by rotating the ends out of the holes in the end of the hanger.

4. Remove pump link retainer and remove link from pump lever.

➡ **Do not attempt to remove the lever, as damage to the air horn could result.**

5. Remove front vacuum break hose from tube on float bowl.

6. Remove eleven air horn-to-bowl screws; then remove the two countersunk attaching screws located next to the venturi. If used, remove secondary air baffle deflector from beneath the two center air horn screws.

7. Remove air horn from float bowl by lifting it straight up. The air horn gasket should remain on the float bowl for removal later.

➡ **When removing air horn from float bowl, use care to prevent damaging the mixture control solenoid connector, Throttle Position Sensor (TPS) adjustment lever, and the small tubes protruding from the air horn. These tubes are permanently pressed into the air horn casting. DO NOT remove them.**

8. Remove front vacuum break bracket attaching screws. The vacuum break assembly may now be removed from the air valve dashpot rod, and the dashpot rod from the air valve lever.

➡ **Do not place vacuum break assembly in carburetor cleaner, as damage to vacuum break will occur.**

9. Remove Throttle Position Sensor (TPS) plunger by pushing plunger down through seal in air horn.

10. Remove TPS seal and pump plunger stem seal by inverting air horn and using a small screwdriver to remove staking holding seal retainers in place. Remove and discard retainers and seals.

➡ **Use care in removing the TPS plunger seal retainer and pump plunger stem seal retainer to prevent damage to air horn casting. New seals and retainers are required for reassembly.**

11. Invert air horn, and use Tool J–28696–4, BT–7967A, or equivalent, to remove rich mixture stop screw and spring.

12. Use a suitable punch to drive the lean mixture screw plug and rich mixture stop screw plug out of the air horn. Discard the plugs.

13. Further disassembly of the air horn is not required for cleaning purposes.

The choke valve and choke valve screws, the air valves and air valve shaft should not be removed. However, if it is necessary to replace the air valve closing springs or center plastic eccentric cam, a repair kit is available. Instructions for assembly are included in the repair kit.

FLOAT BOWL DISASSEMBLY

1. Remove solenoid metering rod plunger by lifting straight up.

2. Remove air horn gasket by lifting it from the dowel locating pins on float bowl. Discard gasket.

3. Remove pump plunger from pump well.

4. Remove staking holding Throttle Position Sensor (TPS) in bowl as follows:

a. Lay a flat tool or metal piece across bowl casting to protect gasket sealing surface.

b. Use a small screwdriver to depress TPS sensor lightly and hold against spring tension.

c. Observing safety precautions, pry upward with a small chisel or equivalent to remove bowl staking, making sure prying force is exerted against the metal piece and not against the bowl casting. Use care not to damage the TPS sensor.

d. Push up from bottom on electrical connector and remove TPS and connector assembly from bowl. Use care in removing sensor and connector assembly to prevent damage to this critical electrical part.

e. Remove spring from bottom of TPS well in float bowl.

5. Remove plastic bowl insert from float bowl.

6. Carefully lift each metering rod out of the guided metering jet, checking to be sure the return spring is removed with each metering rod.

➡ **Use extreme care when handling these critical parts to avoid damage to the metering rod and spring.**

7. Remove the mixture control solenoid from the float bowl as follows:

a. Remove screw attaching solenoid connector to float bowl. Do not remove solenoid connector from float bowl until called for in text.

b. Use Tool J–28696–10, BT–7928, or equivalent, to remove lean mixture (solenoid) screw. Do not remove plunger return spring or connector and wires from the solenoid body. The mixture control solenoid, with plunger and connector, is only serviced as a complete assembly.

c. Remove rubber gasket from top of solenoid connector and discard.

d. Remove solenoid screw tension spring (next to float hanger pin).

8. Remove float assembly and float needle by pulling up on retaining pin. Remove needle and seat and gasket using set remover Tool J–22769, BT–3006M, or equivalent.

9. Remove large mixture control solenoid tension spring from boss on bottom of float bowl located between guided metering jets.

10. If necessary, remove the primary main metering jets using special Tool J–28696–4, BT–7928, or equivalent.

➡ **Use care installing tool on jet, to prevent damage to the metering rod guide (upper area), and locating tool over vertical float sections on lower area of jet. Also, no attempt should be made to remove the secondary metering jets (metering orifice plates). These jets are fixed and, if damaged, entire bowl replacement is required.**

11. Remove pump discharge check ball retainer and turn bowl upside down, catching discharge ball as if falls.

12. Remove secondary air baffle, if replaced is required.

13. Remove pump well fill slot baffle only if necessary.

CHOKE DISASSEMBLY

The tamper-resistant choke cover is used to discourage unnecessary readjustment of the choke thermostatic cover and coil assembly. However, if it is necessary to remove the cover and coil assembly during normal carburetor disassembly for cleaning and normal carburetor disassembly for cleaning and overhaul, the procedures below should be followed.

1. Support float bowl and throttle body, as an assembly, on a suitable holding fixture such as Tool J–9789–118, BT–30–15, or equivalent.

2. Carefully align a $\frac{5}{32}$ in. drill (0.159 in.) on rivet head and drill only enough to remove rivet head. Drill the two remaining rivet heads, then

use a drift and small hammer to drive the remainder of the rivets out of the choke housing.

➡ **Use care in drilling to prevent damage to the choke cover or housing.**

3. Remove the two conventional retainers, retainer with tab, and choke cover assembly from choke housing.

4. Remove choke housing assembly from float bowl by removing retaining screw and washer inside the choke housing. The complete choke assembly can be removed from the float bowl by sliding outward.

5. Remove secondary throttle valve lock-out lever from float bowl.

6. Remove lower choke lever from inside float bowl cavity by inverting bowl.

7. To disassemble intermediate choke shaft from choke housing, remove coil lever retaining screw at end of shaft inside the choke housing. Remove thermostatic coil lever from flats on intermediate choke shaft.

8. Remove intermediate choke shaft from the choke housing by sliding it outward. The fast idle cam can now be removed from the intermediate choke shaft. Remove the cup seal from the float bowl cleaning purposes. DO NOT ATTEMPT TO REMOVE THE INSERT.

9. Remove fuel inlet nut, gasket, check valve, filter assembly and spring. Discard Check valve filter assembly and gasket.

10. Remove three throttle body-to-bowl attaching screws and lockwashers and remove throttle body assembly.

11. Remove throttle body-to-bowl insulator gasket.

THROTTLE BODY DISASSEMBLY

Place throttle body assembly on carburetor holding fixture to avoid damage to throttle valves.

1. Remove pump rod from the throttle lever by rotating the rod until the tang on the rod aligns with the slot in the lever.

2. Use Tool J–29030–B, BT–7610B, or equivalent, to remove idle mixture needles for thorough throttle body cleaning.

3. Further disassembly of the throttle body is not required for cleaning purposes. The throttle valve screws are permanently staked in place and should not be removed. The throttle body is serviced as a complete assembly.

CARBURETOR REASSEMBLY

1. Install the lower end of the pump rod in the throttle lever by aligning the tang on the rod with the slot in the lever. The end of the rod should point outward toward the throttle lever.

2. Install idle mixture needles and springs using Tool J–29030–B, BT07610B, or equivalent. Lightly seat each needle and then turn counterclockwise the number of speified turns,

the final idle mixture adjustment is made on the vehicle.

3. If a new float bowl assembly is used, stamp or engrave the model number on the new float bowl. Install new throttle body-to-bowl insulator gasket over two locating dowels on bowl.

4. Install throttle body making certain throttle body is properly located over dowels on float bowl. Install three throttle body-to-bowl screws and lockwashers and tighten evenly and securely.

5. Place carburetor on proper holding fixture such as J–9789–118, BT–30–15 or equivalent.

6. Install fuel inlet filter spring, a new check valve filter assembly, new gasket and inlet nut. Tighten nut to 18 ft. lbs. (24 Nm).

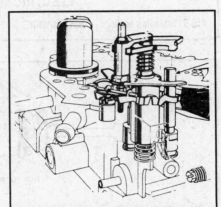

FIG.88 Installing mixture control solenoid, using special gauging tool — E2ME shown

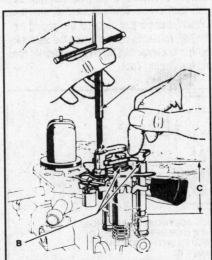

B PLUNGER CONTACTING SOLENOID STOP AND GAGING TOOL
C GAGING DIMENSION 1.304"

FIG.89 Adjusting solenoid (lean mixture) screw using special gauge — E2ME shown

➡ **When Installing a service replacement filter, make sure the filter is the type that includes the check valve to meet government safety standard. New service replacement filters with check valve meet this requirement. When properly installed, the hole in the filter faces toward the inlet nut. Ribs on the closed end of the filter element prevent it from being installed incorrectly, unless forced. Tightening beyond the specified torque can damage the nylon gasket.**

7. Install a new cup seal into the insert on the side of the float bowl for the intermediate choke shaft. The lip on the cup seal faces outward.

8. Install the secondary throttle valve lock-out lever on the boss of the float bowl, with the recess hole in the lever facing inward.

9. Install the fast idle cam on the intermediate choke shaft (steps on cam face downward).

10. Carefully install fast idle cam and intermediate choke shaft assembly in the choke housing. Install the thermostatic coil lever on the flats on the intermediate choke shaft. Inside thermostatic choke coil lever is properly aligned when both inside and outside levers face toward the fuel inlet. Install inside lever retaining screw into the end of the intermediate choke shaft.

11. Install lower choke rod (inner) lever into cavity in float bowl.

12. Install choke housing to bowl, sliding intermediate choke shaft into lower (inner) lever. Tool J–23417, BT–6911 or equivalent, can be used to hold the lower choke lever in correct position while installing the choke housing. The intermediate choke shaft lever and fast idle cam are in correct position when the tang on lever is beneath the fast idle cam.

13. Install choke housing retaining screws and washers. Check linkage for freedom of movement. Do not install choke cover and coil assembly until inside coil lever is adjusted.

14. If removed, install air baffle in secondary side of float bowl with notches toward the top. Top edge of baffle must be flush with bowl casting.

15. If removed, install baffle inside of the pump well with slot toward the bottom.

16. Install pump discharge check ball and retainer screw in the passage next to the pump well.

17. If removed, carefully install primary main metering jets in bottom of float bowl using Tool J–28696–4, BT–7928, or equivalent.

➡ **Use care in installing jets to prevent damage to metering rod guide.**

18. Install large mixture control solenoid tension spring over boss on bottom of float bowl.

19. Install needle seat assembly, with gasket, using seat installer J–22769, BT–3006M, or equivalent.

20. To make adjustment easier, carefully bend float arm before assembly.

21. Install float needle onto float arm by sliding float lever under needle pull clip. Proper installation of the needle pull clip is to hook the clip over the edge of the float on the float arm facing the float pontoon.

22. Install float hinge pin into float arm with end of loop of pin facing pump well. Install float assembly by aligning needle in the seat, and float hinge pin into locating channels in float bowl. DO NOT install float needle pull clip into holes in float arm.

23. Make a float level adjustment as necessary.

24. Install mixture control solenoid screw tension spring between raised bosses next to float hanger pin.

25. Install mixture control solenoid and connector assembly as follows:

   a. Install new rubber gasket on top of solenoid connector.

   b. Install solenoid carefully in the float chamber, aligning pin on end of solenoid with hole in raised boss at bottom of bowl. Align solenoid connector wires to fit in slot in bowl.

   c. Install lean mixture (solenoid) screw through hole in solenoid bracket and tension spring in bowl, engaging first six screw threads to assure proper thread engagement.

   d. Install mixture control solenoid gaging Tool J–33815–1, BT–8253–A, or equivalent over the throttle side metering jet rod guide, and temporarily install solenoid plunger.

   e. Holding the solenoid plunger against the Solenoid Stop, use Tool J–28696–10, BT–

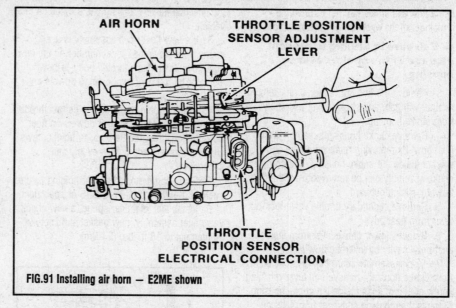

FIG.91 Installing air horn — E2ME shown

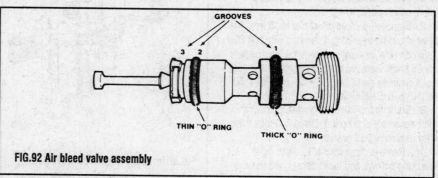

FIG.92 Air bleed valve assembly

7928, or equivalent, to turn the lean mixture (solenoid) screw slowly clockwise, until the solenoid plunger just contacts the gaging tool. The adjustment is correct when the solenoid plunger is contacting BOTH the Solenoid Stop and the Gaging Tool.

   f. Remove solenoid plunger and gaging tool.

26. Install connector attaching screw, but DO NOT overtighten, as that could cause damage to the connector.

27. Install Throttle Position Sensor return spring in bottom of well in float bowl.

28. Install Throttle Position Sensor and connector assembly in float bowl by aligning groove in electrical connector with slot in float bowl casting. Push down on connector and sensor assembly so that connector and wires are located below bowl casting surface.

29. Install plastic bowl insert over float valve, pressing downward until properly seated (flush with bowl casting surface).

30. Slide metering rod return spring over metering rod tip until small end of spring stops against shoulder on rod. Carefully install metering rod and spring assembly through holding in plastic bowl insert and gently lower the metering rod into the guided metering jet, until large end of spring seats on the recess on end of jet guide.

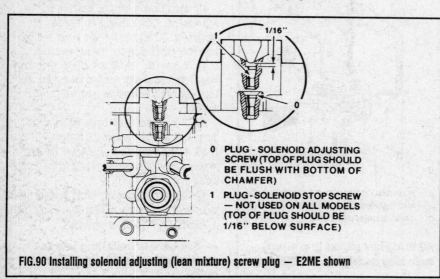

FIG.90 Installing solenoid adjusting (lean mixture) screw plug — E2ME shown

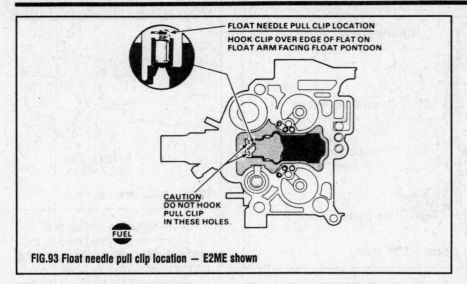

FLOAT NEEDLE PULL CLIP LOCATION

HOOK CLIP OVER EDGE OF FLAT ON
FLOAT ARM FACING FLOAT PONTOON

CAUTION:
DO NOT HOOK
PULL CLIP
IN THESE HOLES.

FIG.93 Float needle pull clip location — E2ME shown

✳✳ CAUTION

Do not force metering rod down in jet. Use extreme care when handling these critical parts to avoid damage to rod and spring. If service replacement metering rods, springs and jets are installed, they must be installed in matched sets.

31. Install pump return spring in pump well.

32. Install pump plunger assembly in pump well.

33. Holding down on pump plunger assembly against return spring tension, install air horn gasket by aligning pump plunger stem with hole in gasket, and aligning holes in gasket over TPS plunger, solenoid plunger return spring metering rods, solenoid attaching screw and electrical connector. Position gasket over the two dowel locating pins on the float bowl.

34. Holding down on air horn gasket and pump plunger assembly, install the solenoid-metering rod plunger in the solenoid, aligning slot in end of plunger with solenoid attaching screw. Be sure plunger arms engage top of each metering.

35. If a service replacement Mixture Control Solenoid package is installed, the solenoid and plunger MUST be installed as a matched set.

AIR HORN ASSEMBLY

1. If removed, install TPS adjustment screw in air horn using Tool J–28696–10, BT–7967A, or equivalent. Final adjustment of the Throttle Position Sensor is made on the vehicle.

2. Inspect the air valve shaft pin for lubrication. Apply a liberal quantity of lithium base grease to the air valve shaft pin, especially in the area contacted by the air valve spring.

3. Install new pump plunger and TPS plunger seals and retainers in air horn casting. The lip on the seal faces outward, away from the air horn mounting surface. Lightly stake seal retainer in three places, choosing locations different from the original stakings.

4. Install rich mixture stop screw and rich authority adjusting spring from bottom side of the air horn. Use Tool J–2869–4, BT–7967A, or equivalent, to bottom the stop screw lightly, then back out 1/4 turn. Final adjustment procedure will be covered later in this section.

5. Install TPS actuator plunger in the seal.

6. Carefully lower the air horn assembly onto the float bowl while positioning the TPS Adjustment Lever over the TPS sensor and guiding pump plunger stem through the seal in the air horn casting. To ease installation, insert a thin screwdriver between the air horn gasket and float bowl to raise the TPS Adjustment Lever, positioning it over the TPS sensor.

7. Make sure that the bleed tubes and accelerating well tubes are positioned properly through the holes in the air horn gasket. Do not force the air horn assembly onto the bowl, but lower it lightly into place over the two dowel locating pins.

8. Install two long air horn screws and lockwashers, nine short screws and lockwashers and two countersunk screws located next to the carburetor venturi area. Install secondary air baffle beneath the No. 3 and 4 screws. Tighten all screws evenly and securely.

9. Install air valve rod into slot in the lever on the end of the air valve shaft. Install the other end of the rod in hole in front vacuum break plunger. Install front vacuum break and bracket assembly on the air horn, using two attaching screws. Tighten screw securely. Connect pump link to pump lever and install retainer.

→ **Use care installing the roll pin to prevent damage to the pump lever bearing surface and casting bosses.**

10. Install two secondary metering rods into the secondary metering rod hanger (upper end of rods point toward each other). Install secondary metering rod holder, with rods, onto air valve cam follower. Install retaining screw and tighten securely. Work air valves up and down several times to make sure they remove freely in both directions.

11. Connect choke rod into lower choke lever inside bowl cavity. Install choke rod in slot in upper choke lever, and position lever on end of choke shaft, making sure flats on end of shaft align with flats in lever. Install attaching screw and tighten securely. When properly installed, the number on the lever will face outward.

12. Adjust the rich mixture stop screw:

a. Insert external float gaging Tool J–34935–1,BT–8420A, or equivalent, in the vertical D-shaped vent hole in the air horn casting (next to the idle air bleed valve) and allow it to float freely.

b. Read (at eye level) the mark on the gauge, in inches, that lines up with the tip of the air horn casting.

c. Lightly press down on gage, and again read and record the mark on the gauge that lines up with the top of the air horn casting.

d. Subtract gauge UP dimension, found in Step b, from gage DOWN dimension, found in Step c, and record the difference in inches. This difference in dimension is the total solenoid plunger travel.

e. Insert Tool J–28696–10, BT–7928, or equivalent, in the access hole in the air horn, and adjust the rich mixture stop screw to obtain $\frac{4}{32}$ in. total solenoid plunger travel.

13. With the solenoid plunger travel correctly set, install the plugs supplied in the service kit into the air horn to retain the setting and prevent fuel vapor loss:

a. Install the plug, hollow end down, into the access hole to the lean mixture (solenoid) screw and use a suitably sized punch to drive the plug into the air horn until top of plug is even with the lower edge of the hole chamber.

b. In a similar manner, install the plug over the rich mixture screw access hole and drive the plug into place so that the tip of the plug is $\frac{1}{16}$ in. below the surface of the air horn casting.

14. Install the Idle Air Bleed Valve as follows:

a. Lightly coat two new O-ring seals with automatic transmission fluid, to aid in their installation on the idle air bleed valve body. The thick seal goes in the upper groove and the thin seal goes in the lower groove.

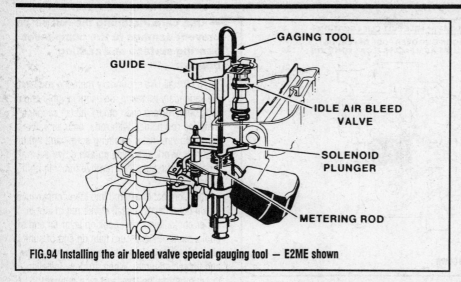

FIG.94 Installing the air bleed valve special gauging tool — E2ME shown

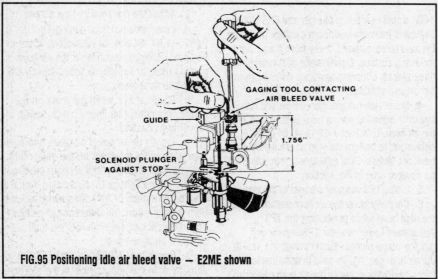

FIG.95 Positioning idle air bleed valve — E2ME shown

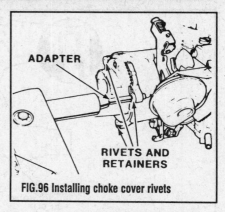

FIG.96 Installing choke cover rivets

brake and on the tube on the float bowl.

18. Position the idle speed solenoid and bracket assembly on the float bowl, retaining it with two large countersunk screws.

19. Perform the Choke Rod-Fast Idle Cam Adjustment, Primary (Front) Vacuum Break Adjustment, Air Valve Rod Adjustment-Front, Unloader Adjustment and the Secondary Lockout Adjustment as previously described.

20. Reinstall the carburetor on the vehicle with a new flange gasket.

Carburetor Adjustments

PRELIMINARY CHECKS

The following should be observed before attempting any adjustments.

1. Thoroughly warm the engine. If the engine is cold, be sure that it reaches operating temperature.

2. Check the torque of all carburetor mounting nuts and assembly screws. Also check the intake manifold-to-cylinder head bolts. If air is leaking at any of these points, any attempts at adjustment will inevitably lead to frustration.

3. Check the manifold heat control valve (if used) to be sure that it is free.

4. Check and adjust the choke as necessary.

5. Adjust the idle speed and mixture. If the mixture screws are capped, don't adjust them unless all other causes of rough idle have been eliminated. If any adjustments are performed that might possible change the idle speed or mixture, adjust the idle and mixture again when you are finished.

Before you make any carburetor adjustments make sure that the engine is in tune. Many problems which are thought to be carburetor related can be traced to an engine which is simply out-of-tune. Any trouble in these areas will have symptoms like those of carburetor problems.

b. Install the idle air bleed valve in the air horn, making sure that there is proper thread engagement.

c. Insert idle air bleed valve gaging Tool J–33815–2, BT–8353B, or equivalent, in throttle side D-shaped vent hole of the air horn casting. The upper end of the tool should be positioned over the open cavity next to the idle air bleed valve.

d. Hold the gauging tool down lightly so that the solenoid plunger is against the solenoid stop, then adjust the idle air bleed valve so that the gauging tool will pivot over and just contact the top of the valve.

e. Remove the gauging tool.

f. The final adjustment of the idle air bleed valve is made on the vehicle to obtain idle mixture control.

15. Perform the Air Valve Spring Adjustment and Choke coil Lever Adjustment as previously described.

16. Install the cover and coil assembly in the choke housing, as follows:

a. Place the cam follower on the highest step of the fast idle cam.

b. Install the thermostatic cover and coil assembly in the choke housing, making sure the coil tang engages the inside coil pickup lever. Ground contact for the electric choke is provided by a metal plate located at the rear of the choke cover assembly. DO NOT install a choke cover gasket between the electric choke assembly and the choke housing.

c. A choke cover retainer kit is required to attach the choke cover to the choke housing. Follow the instructions found in the kit and install the proper retainer and rivets using a suitable blind rivet tool.

d. It may be necessary to use an adapter (tube) if the installing tool interferes with the electrical connector tower on the choke cover.

17. Install the hose on the front vacuum

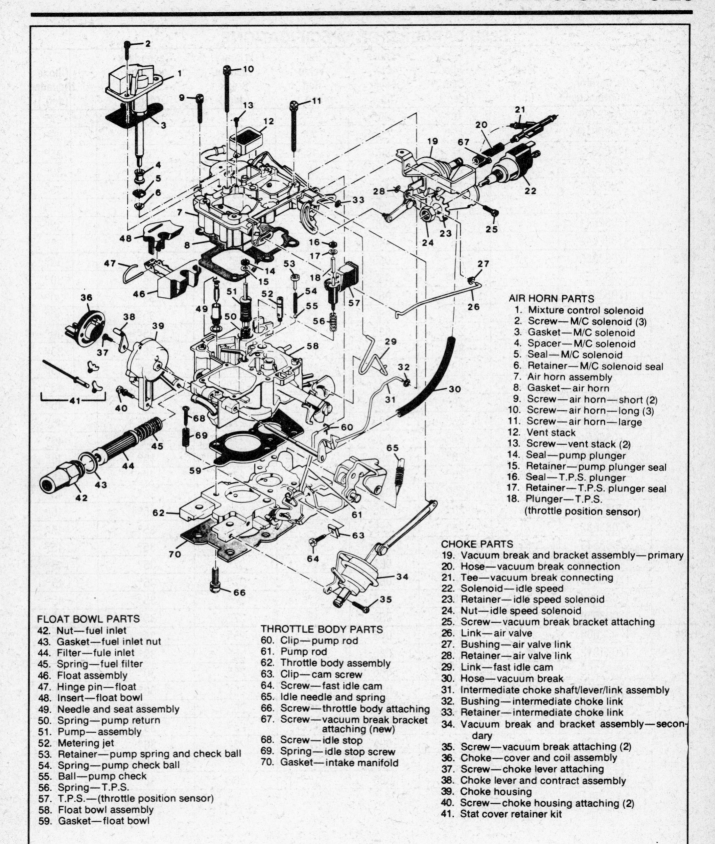

AIR HORN PARTS
1. Mixture control solenoid
2. Screw—M/C solenoid (3)
3. Gasket—M/C solenoid
4. Spacer—M/C solenoid
5. Seal—M/C solenoid
6. Retainer—M/C solenoid seal
7. Air horn assembly
8. Gasket—air horn
9. Screw—air horn—short (2)
10. Screw—air horn—long (3)
11. Screw—air horn—large
12. Vent stack
13. Screw—vent stack (2)
14. Seal—pump plunger
15. Retainer—pump plunger seal
16. Seal—T.P.S. plunger
17. Retainer—T.P.S. plunger seal
18. Plunger—T.P.S.
    (throttle position sensor)

CHOKE PARTS
19. Vacuum break and bracket assembly—primary
20. Hose—vacuum break connection
21. Tee—vacuum break connecting
22. Solenoid—idle speed
23. Retainer—idle speed solenoid
24. Nut—idle speed solenoid
25. Screw—vacuum break bracket attaching
26. Link—air valve
27. Bushing—air valve link
28. Retainer—air valve link
29. Link—fast idle cam
30. Hose—vacuum break
31. Intermediate choke shaft/lever/link assembly
32. Bushing—intermediate choke link
33. Retainer—intermediate choke link
34. Vacuum break and bracket assembly—secondary
35. Screw—vacuum break attaching (2)
36. Choke—cover and coil assembly
37. Screw—choke lever attaching
38. Choke lever and contract assembly
39. Choke housing
40. Screw—choke housing attaching (2)
41. Stat cover retainer kit

FLOAT BOWL PARTS
42. Nut—fuel inlet
43. Gasket—fuel inlet nut
44. Filter—fule inlet
45. Spring—fuel filter
46. Float assembly
47. Hinge pin—float
48. Insert—float bowl
49. Needle and seat assembly
50. Spring—pump return
51. Pump—assembly
52. Metering jet
53. Retainer—pump spring and check ball
54. Spring—pump check ball
55. Ball—pump check
56. Spring—T.P.S.
57. T.P.S.—(throttle position sensor)
58. Float bowl assembly
59. Gasket—float bowl

THROTTLE BODY PARTS
60. Clip—pump rod
61. Pump rod
62. Throttle body assembly
63. Clip—cam screw
64. Screw—fast idle cam
65. Idle needle and spring
66. Screw—throttle body attaching
67. Screw—vacuum break bracket attaching (new)
68. Screw—idle stop
69. Spring—idle stop screw
70. Gasket—intake manifold

FIG.37 Exploded view of the E2SE carburetor

E2SE CARBURETOR SPECIFICATIONS

Year	Carburetor Identification	Float Level (in.)	Fast Idle Cam (deg.)	Choke Coil Lever (in.)	Air Valve Rod (deg.)	Primary Vacuum Break (deg.)	Secondary Vacuum Break (deg.)	Choke Unloader (deg.)
1982	17082196	5/16	18°	.096	—	21°	19°	27°
	17082316	1/4	17°	.090	10	26°	34°	35°
	17082317	1/4	17°	.090	10	29°	35°	35°
	17082320	1/4	25°	.142	10	30°	35°	33°
	17082321	1/4	25°	.142	10	29°	35°	35°
	17082640	1/4	17°	.090	10	26°	34°	35°
	17082641	1/4	17°	.090	10	29°	35°	35°
	17082642	1/4	25°	.142	10	30°	35°	33°
1983	17083356	13/32	22°	.085	1°	25°	35°	30°
	17083357	13/32	22°	.085	1°	25°	35°	30°
	17083358	13/32	22°	.085	1°	25°	35°	30°
	17083359	13/32	22°	.085	1°	25°	35°	30°
	17083368	1/8	22°	.085	1°	25°	35°	30°
	17083370	1/8	22°	.085	1°	25°	35°	30°
	17083450	1/8	28°	.085	1°	27°	35°	45°
	17083451	1/8	28°	.085	1°	27°	35°	45°
	17083452	1/8	28°	.085	1°	27°	35°	45°
	17083453	1/8	28°	.085	1°	27°	35°	45°
	17083454	1/8	28°	.085	1°	27°	35°	45°
	17083455	1/8	28°	.085	1°	27°	35°	45°
	17083456	1/8	28°	.085	1°	27°	35°	45°
	17083630	1/4	28°	.085	1°	27°	35°	45°
	17083631	1/4	28°	.085	1°	27°	35°	45°
	17083632	1/4	28°	.085	1°	27°	35°	45°
	17083633	1/4	28°	.085	1°	27°	35°	45°
	17083634	1/4	28°	.085	1°	27°	35°	45°
	17083635	1/4	28°	.085	1°	27°	35°	45°
	17083636	1/4	28°	.085	1°	27°	35°	45°
	17083650	1/8	28°	.085	1°	27°	35°	45°
1984	17072683	9/32	28°	.085	1°	25°	35°	45°
	17074812	9/32	28°	.085	1°	25°	35°	45°
	17084356	9/32	22°	.085	1°	25°	30°	30°
	17084357	9/32	22°	.085	1°	25°	30°	30°
	17084358	9/32	22°	.085	1°	25°	30°	30°
	17084359	9/32	22°	.085	1°	25°	30°	30°
	17084368	1/8	22°	.085	1°	25°	30°	30°
	17084370	1/8	22°	.085	1°	25°	30°	30°
	17084430	11/32	15°	.085	1°	26°	38°	42°

E2SE CARBURETOR SPECIFICATIONS

Year	Carburetor Identification	Float Level (in.)	Fast Idle Cam (deg.)	Choke Coil Lever (in.)	Air Valve Rod (deg.)	Primary Vacuum Break (deg.)	Secondary Vacuum Break (deg.)	Choke Unloader (deg.)
1984	17084431	11/32	15°	.085	1°	26°	38°	42°
	17084434	11/32	15°	.085	1°	26°	38°	42°
	17084435	11/32	15°	.085	1°	26°	38°	42°
	17084452	5/32	28°	.085	1°	25°	35°	45°
	17084453	5/32	28°	.085	1°	25°	35°	45°
	17084455	5/32	28°	.085	1°	25°	35°	45°
	17084456	5/32	28°	.085	1°	25°	35°	45°
	17084458	5/32	28°	.085	1°	25°	35°	45°
	17084532	5/32	28°	.085	1°	25°	35°	45°
	17084534	5/32	28°	.085	1°	25°	35°	45°
	17084535	5/32	28°	.085	1°	25°	35°	45°
	17084537	5/32	28°	.085	1°	25°	35°	45°
	17084538	5/32	28°	.085	1°	25°	35°	45°
	17084540	5/32	28°	.085	1°	25°	35°	45°
	17084542	1/8	28°	.085	1°	25°	35°	45°
	17084632	9/32	28°	.085	1°	25°	35°	45°
	17084633	9/32	28°	.085	1°	25°	35°	45°
	17084635	9/32	28°	.085	1°	25°	35°	45°
	17084636	9/32	28°	.085	1°	25°	35°	45°
1985	17084534	5/32	28°	.085	1°	25°	35°	45°
	17084535	5/32	28°	.085	1°	25°	35°	45°
	17084540	5/32	28°	.085	1°	25°	35°	45°
	17084542	1/8	28°	.085	1°	25°	35°	45°
	17085356	1/8	22°	.085	1°	25°	30°	30°
	17085357	9/32	22°	.085	1°	25°	30°	30°
	17085358	1/8	22°	.085	1°	25°	30°	30°
	17085359	9/32	22°	.085	1°	25°	30°	30°
	17085368	1/8	22°	.085	1°	25°	30°	30°
	17085369	9/32	22°	.085	1°	25°	30°	30°
	17085370	1/8	22°	.085	1°	25°	30°	30°
	17085371	9/32	22°	.085	1°	25°	30°	30°
	17085452	5/32	28°	.085	1°	28°	35°	45°
	17085453	5/32	28°	.085	1°	28°	35°	45°
	17085458	5/32	28°	.085	1°	28°	35°	45°
1986	17084534	5/32	28°	.085	1°	25°	35°	45°
	17084535	5/32	28°	.085	1°	25°	35°	45°
	17084540	5/32	28°	.085	1°	25°	35°	45°
	17084542	5/32	28°	.085	1°	25°	35°	45°

THROTTLE BODY FUEL INJECTION SYSTEM

Some engines are equipped with throttle body electronic fuel injection. The computer (ECM) is in complete control of fuel metering under all driving conditions. The proper amount of fuel is injected directly into the intake manifold. An electric fuel pump located in the fuel tank maintains a constant fuel pressure between 9 and 13 psi. This electrical fuel pump is controlled by an electric fuel pump relay.

The emission section of the book contains detailed descriptions of this system its function and its testing. This section will just deal with the component replacement and adjustment procedures for your throttle body injection components. If your car has several fuel injectors located at the head or in the intake manifold, your car have multi-port injection. The multi-port injected cars are cover later in this section.

Electric Fuel Pump

The electric fuel pumps are attached to the fuel sending unit, which is located in the fuel tank.

※※ CAUTION

Before opening any part of the fuel system, the pressure must be relieved. Follow the procedure below to relieve the pressure:

RELIEVING THE FUEL SYSTEM PRESSURE

1. Remove the fuel pump fuse from the fuse panel.
2. Start the engine and let it run until all fuel in the line is used.
3. Crank the starter an additional three seconds to relieve any residual pressure.
4. With the ignition OFF, replace the fuse.

REMOVAL & INSTALLATION

1. Relieve fuel system pressure.
2. Drain the fuel tank.
3. Disconnect wiring from the tank.
4. Remove the ground wire retaining screw from under the body.

5. Disconnect all hoses from the tank.
6. Support the tank on a jack and remove the retaining strap nuts.
7. Lower the tank and remove it.
8. Remove the fuel gauge/pump retaining ring using a spanner wrench such as tool J–24187.
9. Remove the gauge unit and the pump.
10. Installation is the reverse of removal. Always replace the O-ring under the gauge/pump retaining ring.

TESTING THE FUEL PUMP

Pressure Test

1. Relive the fuel system pressure.
2. On TBI equipped engines, disconnect the fuel line from the EFI, then connect the fuel line to a pressure gauge.

➡ **If the system is equipped with a fuel return hose, squeeze it off so that an accurate reading can be obtained.**

3. On the TBI equipped engines, connect a jumper wire from the positive battery terminal to the **G** terminal of the ALCL unit or on the carbureted engines, start the engine, then check the fuel pressure.
4. The fuel pressure on the TBI unit is 9–13 psi.

➡ **If the pressures do not indicate correctly, check the fuel line for restrictions or the pump for malfunctions.**

Volume Test

This test should be completed after the pressure test has been performed.

1. Disconnect the pressure gauge from the fuel line and connect a flexible tube from the fuel line to an unbreakable container.

➡ **If the engine is equipped with a fuel return line, squeeze off the line to obtain an accurate reading.**

2. Connect a jumper wire from the positive battery cable to the **G** terminal of the ALCL unit.
3. In 15 seconds, the fuel pump should supply 1/2 pint of fuel.

➡ **If the fuel volume is below minimum, check the fuel line for restrictions.**

4. After testing, reconnect the fuel line to the EFI unit.

Throttle Body

REMOVAL & INSTALLATION

1. Relieve the fuel system pressure as described above.
2. Remove the air cleaner.
3. Disconnect all wiring from the unit.
4. Disconnect the linkage from the unit.
5. Mark and disconnect the vacuum lines from the unit.
6. Follow the CAUTION under the fuel Pressure Test above, then disconnect the fuel feed and return lines from the unit.
7. Unbolt and remove the unit.
8. Installation is the reverse of removal. Torque the TBI attaching bolts to 10–15 ft. lbs.; the fuel lines to 19 ft. lbs.

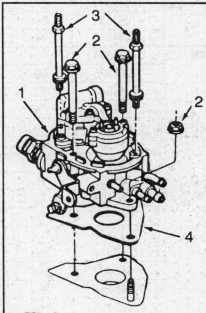

1. TBI unit
2. Bolts and nut—tighten to 18 N·m (13 ft. lbs.)
3. Stud—tighten to 5 N·m (45 in. lbs.)
4. Gasket

FIG.16 Remove the model 300 TBI unit — 2.5L 1985–86 shown

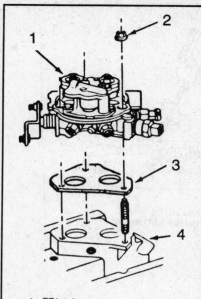

1. TBI unit
2. Nut-tighten to 25 N·m (18 ft. lbs.)
3. Gasket
4. Engine inlet manifold

FIG.17 Removing the model 220 TBI unit — 2.8L shown

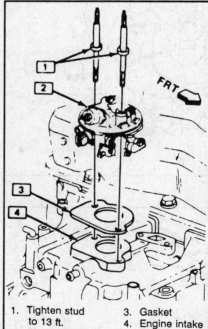

1. Tighten stud to 13 ft. lbs. (18 Nm)
2. TBI unit
3. Gasket
4. Engine intake manifold

FIG.18 Removing the model 700 TBI unit — 2.5L 1987 and newer

Injector

REPLACEMENT

♦ SEE FIGS. 19 to 24

1. Relieve fuel system pressure as described above.
2. Remove the air cleaner.
3. Disconnect the injector by squeezing the two tabs together and pulling straight up.
4. Remove the fuel meter cover by removing the five attaching bolts; note the positions of the two short bolts.

✳✳ CAUTION

Do not remove the four screws securing the pressure regulator to the meter cover. The pressure regulator includes a large spring under heavy tension.

5. Using a small pliers, grasp the center collar of the injector, between the terminals and remove it with a gentle, upward, twisting motion.
6. Installation is the reverse of removal. Always use new O-ring coated with clean automatic transmission fluid. Make sure all O-rings and steel washers are properly located. Make sure that the injector is fully seated with its locating lug mated with its notch and the electrical terminals parallel with the throttle shaft in the throttle body. Apply thread compound to the first three threads of the fuel meter cover bolts.

Idle Air Control (IAC) Valve

REMOVAL & INSTALLATION

1. Remove the air cleaner.
2. Disconnect the electrical connection from the idle air control assembly.
3. Remove the idle air control assembly from the throttle body.

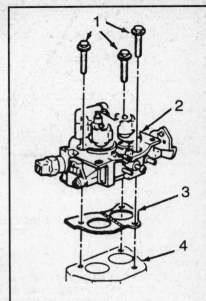

1. Bolt
2. TBI unit
3. Gasket must be installed with stripe facing up
4. Engine intake manifold

FIG.19 Model 220 TBI unit

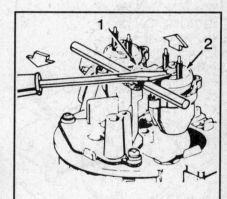

1. Fuel meter cover gasket
2. Removing fuel injector

FIG.20 Removing the fuel injector from the model 220 TBI

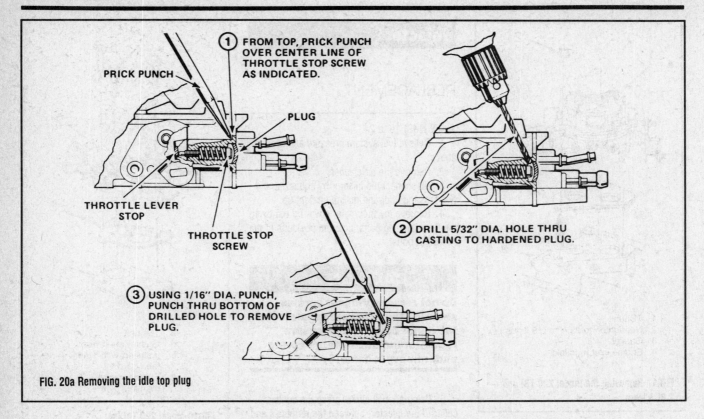

① FROM TOP, PRICK PUNCH OVER CENTER LINE OF THROTTLE STOP SCREW AS INDICATED.

PRICK PUNCH

PLUG

THROTTLE LEVER STOP

THROTTLE STOP SCREW

② DRILL 5/32" DIA. HOLE THRU CASTING TO HARDENED PLUG.

③ USING 1/16" DIA. PUNCH, PUNCH THRU BOTTOM OF DRILLED HOLE TO REMOVE PLUG.

FIG. 20a Removing the idle top plug

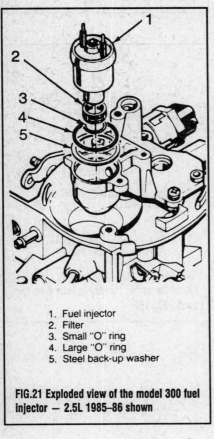

1. Fuel injector
2. Filter
3. Small "O" ring
4. Large "O" ring
5. Steel back-up washer

FIG.21 Exploded view of the model 300 fuel injector — 2.5L 1985–86 shown

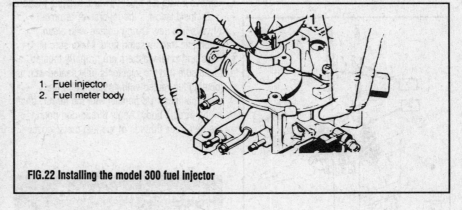

1. Fuel injector
2. Fuel meter body

FIG.22 Installing the model 300 fuel injector

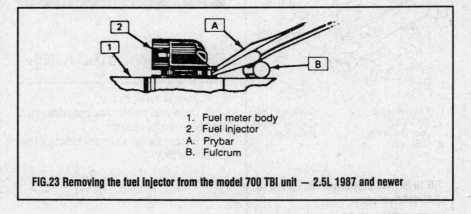

1. Fuel meter body
2. Fuel injector
A. Prybar
B. Fulcrum

FIG.23 Removing the fuel injector from the model 700 TBI unit — 2.5L 1987 and newer

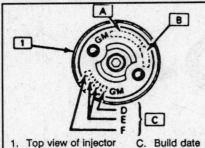

1. Top view of injector
A. Part identification number
B. Vendor identification
C. Build date
D. Year
E. Day
F. Month

FIG.24 Model 220 fuel injector part number location — 2.8L shown

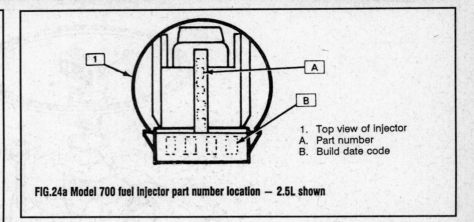

1. Top view of injector
A. Part number
B. Build date code

FIG.24a Model 700 fuel injector part number location — 2.5L shown

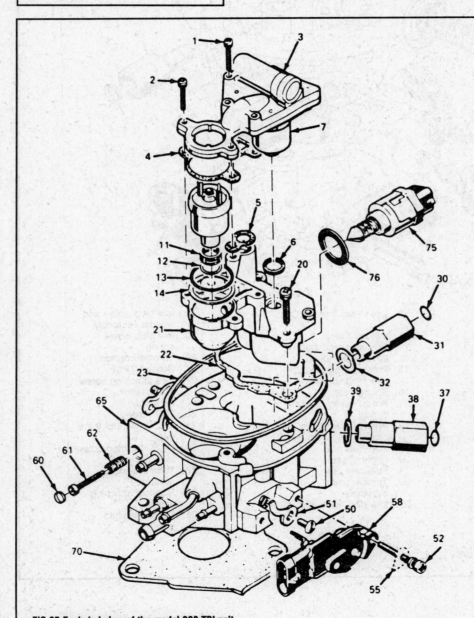

1. Screw & washer assembly
2. Screw & washer assembly
3. Fuel meter cover assembly
4. Gasket—fuel meter cover
5. Gasket—fuel meter outlet
6. Dust seal—pressure regulator
7. Pressure regulator
11. Filter—fuel injector nozzle
12. Lower "O" ring
13. Upper "O" ring
14. Back-up washer—fuel injector
20. Screw & washer assembly
21. Fuel meter body assembly
22. Gasket—fuel meter body
23. Gasket—air filter
30. Fuel return line "O" ring
31. Nut—fuel return
32. Gasket—fuel return nut
37. Fuel inlet line "O" ring
38. Nut—fuel inlet
39. Gasket—fuel inlet nut
50. Screw—TPS lever attaching
51. Lever—TPS
52. Screw & washer assembly
55. Retainer—TPS attaching screw
58. Sensor—throttle position
60. Plug—idle stop screw
61. Screw—throttle stop
62. Spring—throttle stop screw
65. Throttle body assembly
70. Gasket—flange mounting
75. Idle air control assembly
76. Gasket—IAC to throttle body

FIG.25 Exploded view of the model 300 TBI unit

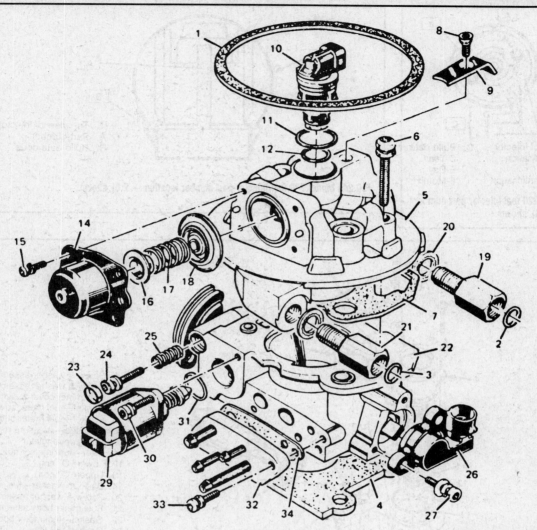

1. Air filter gasket
2. Fuel line inlet nut O-ring
3. Fuel line outlet nut O-ring
4. Flange gasket
5. Fuel meter assembly
6. Fuel meter body attaching screw and washer assembly
7. Fuel meter body-to-throttle body gasket
8. Injector retainer screw
9. Injector retainer
10. Fuel injector
11. Upper fuel injector O-ring
12. Lower fuel injector O-ring
13. Injector filter
14. Pressure regulator cover assembly
15. Pressure regulator attaching screw
16. Spring seat
17. Pressure regulator spring
18. Pressure regulator diaphragm assembly
19. Fuel inlet nut
20. Fuel nut seal
21. Fuel inlet nut
22. Throttle body assembly
23. Idle stop screw plug
24. Idle stop screw and washer assembly
25. Idle stop screw spring
26. Throttle Position Sensor (TPS)
27. TPS attaching screw and washer assembly
28. TPS screw
29. Idle Air Control Valve (IAC)
30. IACV attaching screw
31. IACV O-ring
32. Tube module assembly
33. Manifold attaching screw
34. Tubes manifold gasket

FIG.26 Exploded view of the model 700 TBI unit

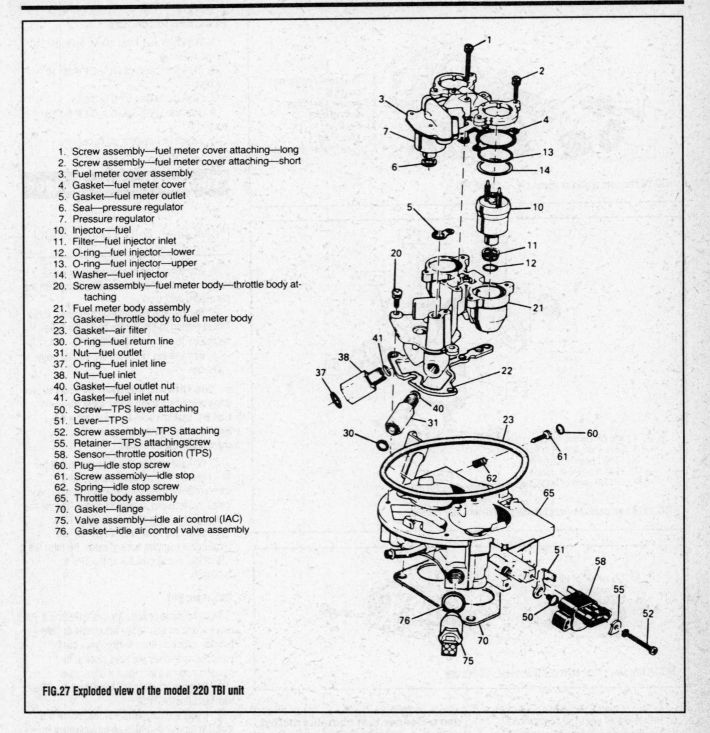

1. Screw assembly—fuel meter cover attaching—long
2. Screw assembly—fuel meter cover attaching—short
3. Fuel meter cover assembly
4. Gasket—fuel meter cover
5. Gasket—fuel meter outlet
6. Seal—pressure regulator
7. Pressure regulator
10. Injector—fuel
11. Filter—fuel injector inlet
12. O-ring—fuel injector—lower
13. O-ring—fuel injector—upper
14. Washer—fuel injector
20. Screw assembly—fuel meter body—throttle body attaching
21. Fuel meter body assembly
22. Gasket—throttle body to fuel meter body
23. Gasket—air filter
30. O-ring—fuel return line
31. Nut—fuel outlet
37. O-ring—fuel inlet line
38. Nut—fuel inlet
40. Gasket—fuel outlet nut
41. Gasket—fuel inlet nut
50. Screw—TPS lever attaching
51. Lever—TPS
52. Screw assembly—TPS attaching
55. Retainer—TPS attachingscrew
58. Sensor—throttle position (TPS)
60. Plug—idle stop screw
61. Screw assembly—idle stop
62. Spring—idle stop screw
65. Throttle body assembly
70. Gasket—flange
75. Valve assembly—idle air control (IAC)
76. Gasket—idle air control valve assembly

FIG.27 Exploded view of the model 220 TBI unit

➡ **Before installing a new idle air control valve, measure the distance that the valve is extended. This measurement should be made from motor housing to end of the cone. The distance should be no greater than 1¹/₈ in. (28mm). If the cone is extended too far damage to the valve may result. The IAC valve pintle may also be retracted by** using IAC/ISC Motor Tester J–37027/BT–8256K. It is recommended not to push or pull on the IAC pintle. The force required to move the pintle of a new valve should not cause damage. Do not soak the IAC valve in any liquid cleaner or solvent as damage may result.

4. Be sure to identify the replacement idle air control valve and replace with an identical part. The IAC valve pintle shape and diameter are designed for specific applications.

➡ **Shiny spots on the pintle or seat are normal and do not indicate misalignment or bend in the shaft.**

5. Install the new idle air control valve and torque the valve to 13 ft. lbs.

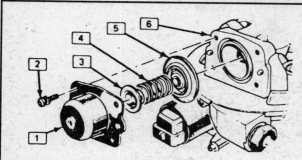

1. Pressure regulator cover
2. Screw assembly
3. Spring seat
4. Spring
5. Diaphragm
6. Fuel meter assembly

FIG.28 Pressure regulator assembly — model 700

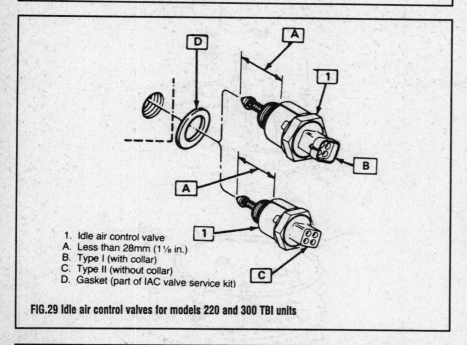

1. Idle air control valve
A. Less than 28mm (1⅛ in.)
B. Type I (with collar)
C. Type II (without collar)
D. Gasket (part of IAC valve service kit)

FIG.29 Idle air control valves for models 220 and 300 TBI units

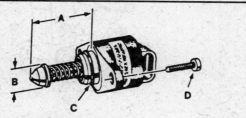

A. Distance of pintle extension
B. Diameter of pintle
C. IAC valve O-ring
D. IAC valve attaching screw

FIG.30 Idle air control valve for the model 700 TBI unit

6. Reconnect all electrical connections.
7. The base idle will not be correct unit the ECM resets the IAC.

➡ **Be sure to clean the IAC valve O-ring sealing surface, pintle valve seat and air passage. Use a suitable carburetor cleaner (be sure it is safe to use on systems equipped with a oxygen sensor) and a parts cleaning brush to remove the carbon deposits. Do not use a cleaner that contains methyl ethyl ketone. It is an extremely strong solvent and not necessary for this type of deposits. Shiny spots on the pintle or on the seat are normal and do not indicate a misalignment or a bent pintle shaft. If the air passage has heavy deposits, remove the throttle body for a complete cleaning. Replace the IAC O-ring with a new one.**

Resetting Procedure

1. If a repair has been made, reset the IAC before retesting.
2. Turn the ignition switch **OFF** for 10 seconds.
3. Start the engine for 5 seconds.
4. Turn the ignition switch **OFF** for 10 seconds.
5. Retest IAC system, as necessary.

Throttle Position Sensor

REMOVAL & INSTALLATION

1. Disconnect the negative battery cable. Remove the air cleaner assembly along with the necessary duct work.
2. Remove the TPS attaching screws. If the TPS is riveted to the throttle body, it will be necessary to drill out the rivets.
3. Remove the TPS from the throttle body assembly.

➡ **The throttle position sensor is an electrical component and should not be immersed in any type of liquid solvent or cleaner, as damage may result.**

4. With the throttle valve closed, install the TPS onto the throttle shaft. Rotate the TPS counterclockwise to align the mounting holes. Install the retaining screws or rivets. Torque the retaining screws to 18 inch lbs. (2.0 Nm).
5. Install the air cleaner assembly and connect the negative battery cable. Perform the TPS output check and adjust the TPS if applicable.

Adjustment

Not all vehicle provide for this adjustment. All newer vehicles don't have adjustable throttle position sensors. If the sensor your car is equipped with does not have slots at the mounting screws then its not adjustable.

1. Remove air cleaner. Disconnect the TPS harness from the TPS.
2. Using suitable jumper wires, connect a digital voltmeter J–34029–A or equivalent from the TPS connector center terminal B to the outside terminal A. A suitable ALDL scanner can also be used to read the TPS output voltage.
3. With the ignition **ON** and the engine stopped, The TPS voltage should be less than 1.25 volts.
4. If the reading on the TPS is not within the specified range, rotate the TPS until 0.48 ± .06 volts are obtained. If this specified voltage cannot be obtained, replace the TPS.

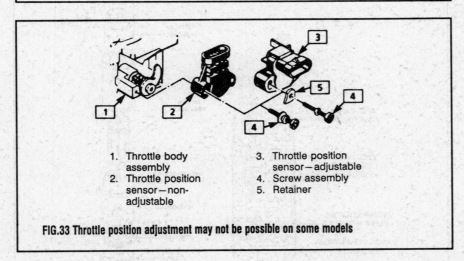

1. Throttle position sensor
2. Screw & washer
3. TPS pick up lever
4. Screw
5. Lever
6. Throttle body assembly

FIG.31 Throttle position sensor for model 300 TBI unit

1. Fuel meter assembly
2. Throttle body assembly
3. Throttle position sensor
4. TPS attaching screw and washer assembly

FIG.32 Throttle position sensor for model 700 TBI unit

1. Throttle body assembly	3. Throttle position sensor — adjustable
2. Throttle position sensor — non-adjustable	4. Screw assembly
	5. Retainer

FIG.33 Throttle position adjustment may not be possible on some models

5. If the voltage reading is correct, remove the voltmeter and jumper wires and reconnect the TPS connector to the sensor. Re-install the air cleaner.

IDLE SPEED ADJUSTMENT

This procedure should be performed only when the throttle body parts have been replaced.

Newer models may not provide for this adjustment as the computer is responsible for idle control.

➡ **The following procedure requires the use of a special tool.**

1. Remove the air cleaner and gasket.
2. Plug the vacuum port on the TBI marked THERMAC.
3. If the car is equipped with a tamper resistant plug cover the throttle stop screw, the TBI unit must be removed as instructed above, to remove the plug.

4. Remove the throttle valve cable from the throttle control bracket to allow access to the throttle stop screw.

5. Connect a tachometer to the engine.

6. Start the engine and run it to normal operating temperature.

7. Install tool J–33047 into the idle air passage of the throttle body. Be sure that the tool is fully seated and that no air leaks exist.

8. Using a #20 Torx bit, turn the minimum air screw until the engine rpm is 675–725 with auto. trans. or 725–825 with manual trans. The AT should be in Park; the MT in neutral.

9. Stop the engine and remove the special tool.

10. Install the cable on the throttle body.

11. Use RTV sealant to cover the throttle stop screw.

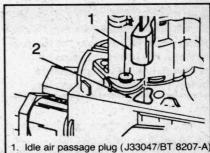

1. Idle air passage plug (J33047/BT 8207-A)
2. Idle air passage

FIG.34 Plug the passage of the throttle body as shown — 2.5L shown

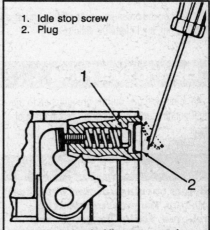

1. Idle stop screw
2. Plug

FIG.35 Unpluging the idle stop screw plug — model 220 TBI unit shown. New cars do not provide for this adjustment

MULTI PORT FUEL INJECTION

The system is controlled by the ECM which is in complete control of the fuel delivery during normal driving conditions. For a complete detailed description of operation and system testing see Section 4 on Emission Systems. This section contains replacement and adjustment of components.

The intake manifold functions like that of a diesel, to let air into the engine. The fuel is injected by separate injectors mounted over the intake valves; the injectors operate on every revolution of the crankshaft.

Of the various sensors which receive both temperature and barometric pressure information, the Mass Air Flow sensor (mounted between the air cleaner and the throttle body) measures the volume and temperature of the air moving through the intake manifold.

❉❉ CAUTION

Before opening any part of the fuel system, the pressure must be relieved. Follow the procedure below to relieve the pressure:

The fuel pressure release fitting is located at the top rear of the fuel injection rail.

1. Remove the cap from the pressure release fitting, then connect a flexible tube to the fitting and place the other end in an unbreakable container.

➡ **Place a shop towel around the fitting to collect any excess fuel from spilling.**

2. Open the pressure release fitting and bleed off the fuel, then close the fitting.

Electric Fuel Pump

The electric fuel pumps are attached to the fuel sending unit, which is located in the fuel tank.

❉❉ CAUTION

Before opening any part of the fuel system, the pressure must be relieved. Follow the procedure below to relieve the pressure:

RELIEVING THE FUEL SYSTEM PRESSURE

1. Remove the fuel pump fuse from the fuse panel.
2. Start the engine and let it run until all fuel in the line is used.
3. Crank the starter an additional three seconds to relieve any residual pressure.
4. With the ignition OFF, replace the fuse.

REMOVAL & INSTALLATION

1. Relieve fuel system pressure.
2. Drain the fuel tank.
3. Disconnect wiring from the tank.
4. Remove the ground wire retaining screw from under the body.
5. Disconnect all hoses from the tank.
6. Support the tank on a jack and remove the retaining strap nuts.
7. Lower the tank and remove it.
8. Remove the fuel gauge/pump retaining

ring using a spanner wrench such as tool J–24187.
9. Remove the gauge unit and the pump.
10. Installation is the reverse of removal. Always replace the O-ring under the gauge/pump retaining ring.

TESTING THE FUEL PUMP

Pressure Test

1. Relive the fuel system pressure.
2. On MPI equipped engines, disconnect the fuel line from the EFI, then connect the fuel line to a pressure gauge.

➡ **If the system is equipped with a fuel return hose, squeeze it off so that an accurate reading can be obtained.**

3. On the MPI equipped engines, connect a jumper wire from the positive battery terminal to the **G** terminal of the ALCL unit or on the carbureted engines, start the engine, then check the fuel pressure.

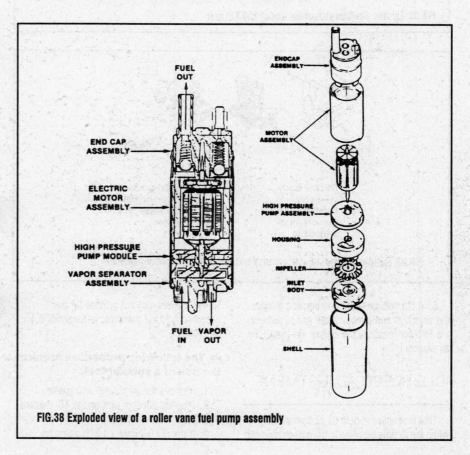

FIG.38 Exploded view of a roller vane fuel pump assembly

4. The fuel pressure should be about 34–46 psi.

➡ **If the pressures do not indicate correctly, check the fuel line for restrictions or the pump for malfunctions.**

Volume Test

This test should be completed after the pressure test has been performed.

1. Disconnect the pressure gauge from the fuel line and connect a flexible tube from the fuel line to an unbreakable container.

➡ **If the engine is equipped with a fuel return line, squeeze off the line to obtain an accurate reading.**

2. Connect a jumper wire from the positive battery cable to the **G** terminal of the ALCL unit.

3. In 15 seconds, the fuel pump should supply ½ pint of fuel.

➡ **If the fuel volume is below minimum, check the fuel line for restrictions.**

4. After testing, reconnect the fuel line to the EFI unit.

Throttle Body

The throttle body is located at the front of the engine and is attached to the intake plenum.

REMOVAL & INSTALLATION

1. Disconnect the negative battery cable.
2. Drain the coolant from the cooling system until the level is below the throttle body.
3. Remove the air inlet duct, the vacuum hoses and the coolant hoses from the throttle body.
4. Remove the Idle Air Control (IAC) and the Throttle Position Sensor (TPS) electrical connectors from the throttle body.
5. Remove the throttle and the cruise control (if equipped) cables.
6. Remove the mounting bolts and the throttle body.
7. To install, reverse the removal procedures and refill the cooling system.

Plenum

The Plenum is the top portion of the intake manifold. This portion must be removed before servicing the injector system.

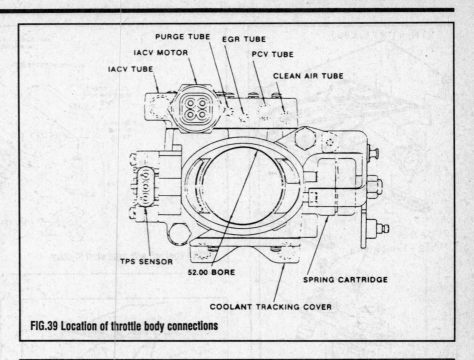

FIG.39 Location of throttle body connections

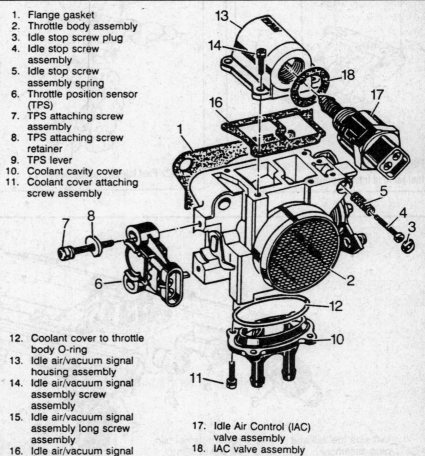

1. Flange gasket
2. Throttle body assembly
3. Idle stop screw plug
4. Idle stop screw assembly
5. Idle stop screw assembly spring
6. Throttle position sensor (TPS)
7. TPS attaching screw assembly
8. TPS attaching screw retainer
9. TPS lever
10. Coolant cavity cover
11. Coolant cover attaching screw assembly
12. Coolant cover to throttle body O-ring
13. Idle air/vacuum signal housing assembly
14. Idle air/vacuum signal assembly screw assembly
15. Idle air/vacuum signal assembly long screw assembly
16. Idle air/vacuum signal assembly gasket
17. Idle Air Control (IAC) valve assembly
18. IAC valve assembly gasket

FIG.40 Exploded view of a multi-port throttle body — 3.8L engine shown

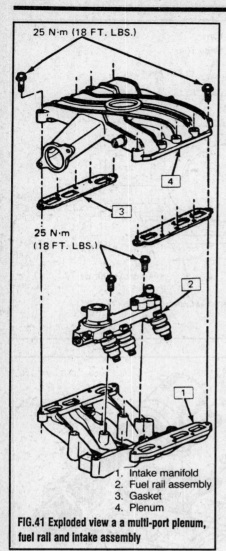

25 N·m (18 FT. LBS.)

25 N·m (18 FT. LBS.)

1. Intake manifold
2. Fuel rail assembly
3. Gasket
4. Plenum

FIG.41 Exploded view a a multi-port plenum, fuel rail and intake assembly

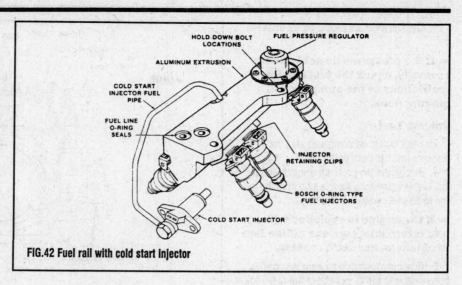

HOLD DOWN BOLT LOCATIONS

FUEL PRESSURE REGULATOR

ALUMINUM EXTRUSION

COLD START INJECTOR FUEL PIPE

FUEL LINE O-RING SEALS

INJECTOR RETAINING CLIPS

BOSCH O-RING TYPE FUEL INJECTORS

COLD START INJECTOR

FIG.42 Fuel rail with cold start injector

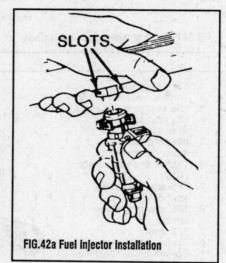

SLOTS

FIG.42a Fuel injector installation

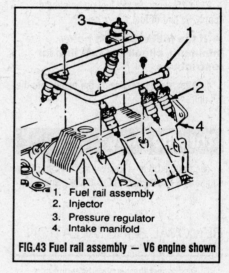

1. Fuel rail assembly
2. Injector
3. Pressure regulator
4. Intake manifold

FIG.43 Fuel rail assembly — V6 engine shown

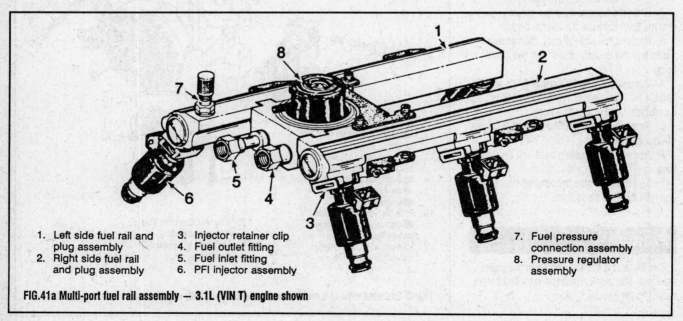

1. Left side fuel rail and plug assembly
2. Right side fuel rail and plug assembly
3. Injector retainer clip
4. Fuel outlet fitting
5. Fuel inlet fitting
6. PFI injector assembly
7. Fuel pressure connection assembly
8. Pressure regulator assembly

FIG.41a Multi-port fuel rail assembly — 3.1L (VIN T) engine shown

REMOVAL & INSTALLATION

1. Disconnect the negative battery cable.
2. Tag and disconnect the vacuum lines.
3. Remove the EGR to plenum nuts.
4. Remove the two throttle body bolts.
5. Remove the throttle cable bracket bolts.
6. Remove the ignition wire plastic shield bolts.
7. Remove the plenum bolts.
8. Remove the plenum and gaskets from the engine.
9. To install reverse steps 1 through 8. Torque the plenum bolts to 16 ft. lbs.

Fuel Rail

REMOVAL & INSTALLATION

1. Disconnect the negative battery cable.
2. Relieve the fuel system pressure.
3. Remove the intake manifold plenum, as required.
4. Disconnect the fuel feed and return lines at the fuel rail. Use a backup wrench, as required, to support the fuel rail tube fittings.
5. Remove the fuel line O-rings and discard.
6. Disconnect the vacuum line at the pressure regulator, as required.
7. Disconnect the fuel injector electrical connectors.
8. Remove the fuel rail attaching bolts. Remove the fuel rail assembly. Note the location and routing of vacuum hoses around the fuel rail before removing the rail.
9. Remove the injector O-ring seal from the spray tip end of each injector. Discard the O-rings.

To install:

10. Lubricate new injector O-ring seals with engine oil and install on the spray tip end of each injector.
11. Install the fuel rail assembly into the intake manifold. Tilt the rail assembly to install the injectors. Install the fuel rail attaching bolts and fuel rail bracket bolts. Tighten fuel rail attaching bolts.
12. Connect the injector electrical connectors. Rotate the injectors, as required, to prevent stretching the wire harness.
13. If disconnected, connect the vacuum line to the pressure regulator.
14. Install new O-rings on the fuel feed and return lines. Connect the fuel lines.
15. Temporarily, connect the negative battery cable.

16. Turn the ignition switch to the **ON** position for 2 seconds, then turn to the **OFF** position for 10 seconds. Again, turn the ignition switch to the **ON** position and check for fuel leaks.
17. Disconnect the negative battery cable.
18. Install the intake manifold plenum.
19. Tighten the fuel filler cap.
20. Connect the negative battery cable.
21. If equipped with the 3.1L (VIN T) engine, perform the Idle Learn Procedure.

Intake Plenum and Runners

REMOVAL & INSTALLATION

This is a special procedure for cars equipped with the 3.1L (VIN T) Engine.

1. Disconnect the negative battery cable.
2. Remove the air inlet duct at the throttle body and crankcase vent pipe at the valve cover grommet.
3. Disconnect the vacuum harness connector from the throttle body.
4. Remove the throttle cable bracket bolt.
5. Remove the throttle body attaching bolts. Remove the throttle body and gasket. Discard the gasket.
6. Remove the EGR transfer tube-to-plenum bolts. Remove the EGR transfer tube and gasket. Discard the gasket.
7. Remove the air conditioning compressor-to-plenum bracket attaching hardware. Remove the bracket.
8. Remove the plenum bolts and studs. Remove the plenum and gaskets. Discard the gaskets.

To install:

➡ **Use care in cleaning old gasket material from machined aluminum surfaces. Sharp tool may damage gasket surfaces.**

9. Carefully, remove old gasket material from gasket sealing surfaces.
10. Install new plenum gaskets.
11. Install the plenum. Install the plenum bolts and studs. Tighten to 18 ft. lbs. (25 Nm).
12. Install the air conditioning compressor-to-plenum bracket and attaching hardware.
13. Install the EGR transfer tube with a new gasket. Install the EGR transfer tube bolts.
14. Install a new throttle body gasket. Install the throttle body and attaching bolts.

15. Install the throttle cable bracket bolt.
16. Connect the vacuum harness connector to the throttle body.
17. Connect the air inlet duct to the throttle body and crankcase vent pipe to the valve cover grommet.
18. Connect the negative battery cable.
19. With the ignition switch in the **OFF** position, ensure that the movement of the accelerator is free.
20. Perform Idle Learn Procedure.

Fuel Injectors

REMOVAL & INSTALLATION

1. Disconnect the negative battery cable.
2. Relieve fuel system pressure.
3. Remove the intake plenum and, if equipped, remove the runners.
4. Refer to the Fuel Rail, Removal and Installation procedures in this section and remove the fuel rail.
5. Rotate the injector retaining clip to the release position.
6. Remove the injector from the fuel rail assembly.
7. Remove the O-rings from both ends of the injector and discard.

To install:

➡ **When replacing fuel injectors, be sure the new injector is the same part number as the one removed from the engine.**

8. Lubricate new injector O-rings with engine oil and install on the injectors.

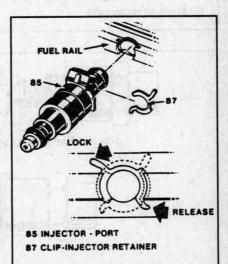

85 INJECTOR - PORT
87 CLIP-INJECTOR RETAINER

FIG. 43a Fuel injector installation

9. If new injector retainers are supplied in the kit, install on the injector.

10. Install injector into fuel rail injector socket with the electrical connectors facing out.

11. Rotate the injector clip to the locked position.

12. Install the fuel rail assembly.

13. Check for fuel leaks by performing the following:

a. Temporarily connect the negative battery cable.

b. Turn the ignition switch to the **ON** position for 2 seconds. Turn the ignition switch to the **OFF** position for 10 seconds. Again turn the ignition switch to the **ON** position and check for fuel leaks.

c. Disconnect the negative battery cable.

14. Install the plenum assembly.

15. Tighten the fuel filler cap.

16. Connect the negative battery cable.

Idle Air Control Valve

REMOVAL AND INSTALLATION

The idle air control valve is mounted to the throttle body and controls the bypass air around

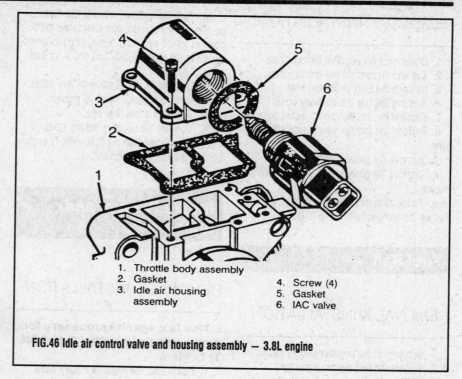

1. Throttle body assembly
2. Gasket
3. Idle air housing assembly
4. Screw (4)
5. Gasket
6. IAC valve

FIG.46 Idle air control valve and housing assembly — 3.8L engine

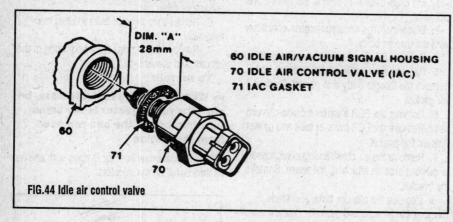

DIM. "A"
28mm

60 IDLE AIR/VACUUM SIGNAL HOUSING
70 IDLE AIR CONTROL VALVE (IAC)
71 IAC GASKET

FIG.44 Idle air control valve

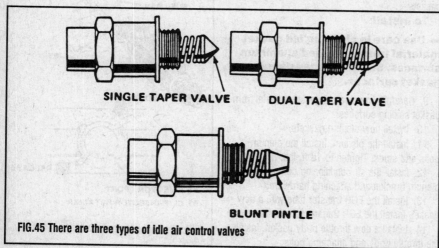

SINGLE TAPER VALVE   DUAL TAPER VALVE

BLUNT PINTLE

FIG.45 There are three types of idle air control valves

the throttle plate; it is used to control the engine idle speed, to prevent stalls due to changes in the engine load.

1. Remove the electrical connector from the Idle Air Control (IAC) valve assembly.

2. Unscrew the IAC from the throttle body and discard the gasket.

➡ **Do not remove the thread locking compound from the threads.**

3. To install, use a new gasket and reverse the removal procedures.

Cold Start Valve

REMOVAL & INSTALLATION

The cold start valve (not controlled by the ECM) provides additional fuel during the starting mode to improve cold start ups.

1. Disconnect the negative battery cable.

2. Remove the IAC pipe and the engine mount strut brace.

3. Remove the fuel line from the fuel rail, the electrical connector from the valve and the valve retaining bolt.

4. Pull the cold start valve from the fuel rail.

5. To install, use new O-rings and reverse steps 1 through 4.

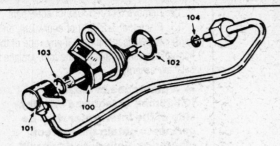

FIG.47 Cold start valve assembly

100 VALVE - COLD START
101 TUBE AND BODY ASSEMBLY
102 O-RING SEAL - VALVE
103 O-RING SEAL - BODY
104 O-RING SEAL - TUBE

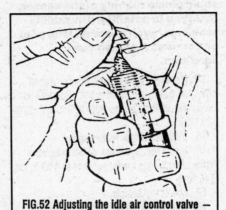

FIG.52 Adjusting the idle air control valve — type 2 without a collar at electrical connector end

ADJUSTMENT

Cold Start Valve Assembly

This procedure is to be performed ONLY when installing the Cold Start Valve Assembly.

1. Turn the cold start valve completely into the body, until it seats.
2. Back out the valve one complete turn, until the electrical connector is at the top.
3. Bend the body tang forward to limit the rotation to less than a full turn.
4. Coat the new O-ring with engine oil and install it into the fuel rail.

Throttle Position Sensor (TPS)

REMOVAL & INSTALLATION

1. Disconnect the negative battery cable.
2. Disconnect the TPS electrical connector.
3. Remove the 2 mounting screws.

4. Remove the TPS and, if equipped, TPS seal from the throttle body.

To Install:

5. Place the TPS in position. Align the TPS lever with the TPS drive lever on the throttle body.
6. Install the 2 TPS mounting screws.
7. Connect the electrical connector.
8. Connect the negative battery cable.

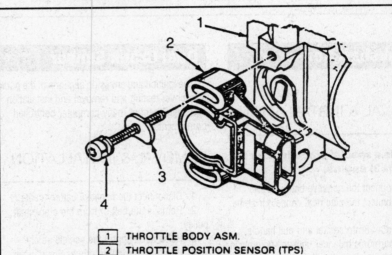

1	THROTTLE BODY ASM.
2	THROTTLE POSITION SENSOR (TPS)
3	RETAINER (2)
4	SCREW (2) 2 N·m (18 IN. LBS.)

FIG.48 Throttle position sensor assembly — adjustable type with slots

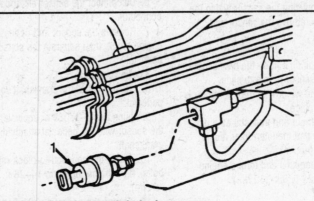

FIG.49 Power steering pressure switch simply unscrews

Mass Air Flow Sensor

REMOVAL & INSTALLATION

1. Disconnect the negative battery cable.
2. Disconnect the electrical connector at the MAF.
3. Loosen the clamps on the air inlet ducts.
4. Remove the air inlet ducts and remove the MAF sensor.
5. Installation is just the reverse of the above steps. Take note that this is an expensive and fragile sensor. If it was defective try and find the cause so the new one will not be damaged by the same problem, espically no air filter, broken screen, defective charging system, etc.

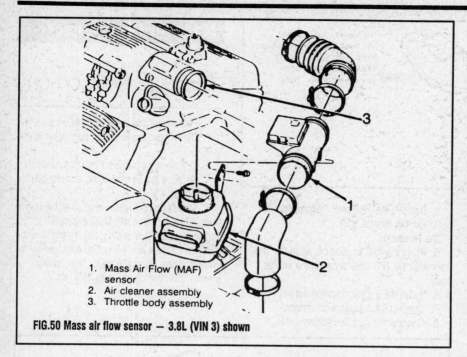

1. Mass Air Flow (MAF) sensor
2. Air cleaner assembly
3. Throttle body assembly

FIG.50 Mass air flow sensor — 3.8L (VIN 3) shown

Crankshaft Sensor

REMOVAL & INSTALLATION

➡ **This is a special procedure for the 3.8L (VIN 3) engine.**

1. Disconnect the negative battery cable.
2. Disconnect the electrical connector at the sensor.
3. Using a 28mm socket and pull handle, rotate the harmonic balancer until any window in the interrupter is aligned with the crank sensor.
4. Loosen the pinch bolt on the sensor pedestal until the sensor is free to slide.
5. Remove the pedestal to the engine mounting bolts.
6. While manipulating the sensor within the pedestal, carefully remove the sensor and pedestal as a unit.

To install:

7. Loosen the pinch bolt on the new sensor pedestal until the sensor is free to slide.
8. Verify that the window in the interrupter is still in the correct place.
9. Install the sensor and pedestal as a unit while making sure that the interrupter ring is aligned within the proper slot.
10. Install the pedestal and torque engine mounting bolts to 22 ft. lbs. (30 Nm).

Dual Crank Sensor

The ignition and emission sections of the book also cover testing and removal and installation and adjustment of many computer controlled components.

REMOVAL & INSTALLATION

1. Disconnect the negative battery cable.
2. Remove the belt(s) from the crankshaft pulley.
3. Raise and support the vehicle safely.
4. Remove the right front wheel and inner fender access cover.
5. Remove the crankshaft harmonic balancer retaining bolt, then remove the harmonic balancer.
6. Disconnect the sensor electrical connector.
7. Remove the sensor and pedestal from the engine block, then separate the sensor from the pedestal.

To install:

8. Loosely install the crankshaft sensor to the pedestal.
9. Using tool J–37089 or equivalent, position the sensor with the pedestal attached, on the crankshaft.
10. Install the pedestal-to-block retaining bolts. Tighten and torque to 14–28 ft. lbs. (20–40 Nm).
11. Torque the pedestal pinch bolt 30–35 inch lbs. (20–40 Nm).

12. Remove tool J–37089 or equivalent.
13. Place tool J–37089 or equivalent, on the harmonic balancer and turn. If any vane of the harmonic balancer touches the tool, replace the balancer assembly.

➡ **A clearance of 0.025 in. (0.635mm) is required on either side of the interrupter ring. Be certain to obtain the correct clearance. Failure to do so will damage the sensor. A misadjusted sensor of bent interrupter ring could cause rubbing of the sensor, resulting in potential driveability problems, such as rough idle, poor performance, or a no start condition.**

14. Install the balancer on the crankshaft. Install the balancer retaining bolt. Tighten and torque the retaining bolt to 200–239 ft. lbs. (270–325 Nm).
15. Install the inner fender shield.
16. Install the right front wheel assembly. Tighten and torque the wheel nuts to 100 ft. lbs. (140 Nm).
17. Lower the vehicle.
18. Install the belt(s).
19. Reconnect the negative battery cable.

Minimum Idle Speed

ADJUSTMENTS

The engine should be at normal operating temperature before making this adjustment. Newer engines do not provide for this adjustment as the idle is completely computer controlled. If the computer cannot control the

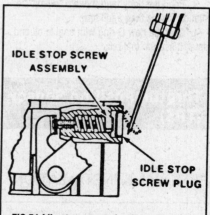

IDLE STOP SCREW ASSEMBLY

IDLE STOP SCREW PLUG

FIG.51 Idle stop screw plug removal — if equipped

idle, the most likely cause a defective idle air control valve. Test the IAC valve, check the engine mechanical for basic tune-up, vacuum leaks, proper compression and the rest of the fuel control system. The least likely item bad is the computer itself, unless someone has recently working on the computer or the electrical system. For models that are adjustable following the following procedures:

1. Using an awl, pierce the idle stop screw plug (located on the side of the throttle body) and remove it by prying it from the housing.

2. Using a jumper wire, ground the diagnostic lead of the IAC motor.

3. Turn on the ignition, DO NOT start the engine and wait for 30 seconds, then disconnect the IAC electrical connector. Remove the diagnostic lead ground lead and start the engine. Allow the system to go to closed loop.

4. Adjust the idle set screw to 550 rpm for the automatic transaxle (in Drive) or 650 rpm for the manual transaxle (in Neutral).

5. Turn the ignition Off and reconnect the IAC motor lead.

6. Using a voltmeter, adjust the TPS to 0.55 $\pm$ 0.1 volt and secure the TPS.

7. Recheck the setting, then start the engine and check for proper idle operation.

8. Seal the idle stop screw with silicone sealer.

DIESEL FUEL SYSTEM

The diesel injection pump is mounted on top of the engine. It is gear driven by the camshaft and turns at camshaft speed. A light pressure rotary pump injects a metered amount of fuel into each cylinder at the precise time. Fuel delivery lines are the same length to prevent any difference in timing, from cylinder to cylinder. The timing advance is also controlled by the fuel pump. Engine rpm is controlled by the rotary fuel metering valve.

The fuel filter is located between the fuel pump and the injection pump at the left rear of the engine.

An electric fuel pump is used which is located at the front of the engine next to the fuel heater. Excess fuel returns to the tank via the fuel return line.

➡ **Because of the exacting nature of the diesel injection system all major repairs should be referred to your local GM dealer**

Fuel Supply Pump

REMOVAL & INSTALLATION

1. Disconnect the negative battery terminal.
2. Remove the air cleaner.
3. Unplug the electrical connection.
4. Using a 3/4 in. wrench to support the inlet fitting, use a 5/8 in. wrench to unscrew the inlet tube.
5. Remove the outlet tube.
6. Installation is the reverse of removal. After the pump has been replaced disconnect the fuel line at the filter. Turn the ignition on and bleed the lines. If the pump runs with a clicking sound, or air bubbles show up in the fuel, check the line for leaks. Check all connections to be sure they are dry. When the clicking noise disappears, tighten the line.

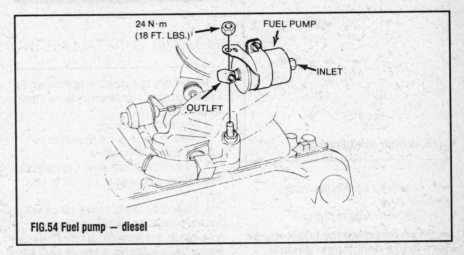

FIG.54 Fuel pump — diesel

Injection Pump

REMOVAL & INSTALLATION

1. Remove the air cleaner.
2. Remove the crankcase ventilation filter and pipes from the valve cover and air crossover.
3. Remove the air crossover and install special cover J–29657 or its equal. Remove the fuel lines, filter and fuel pump as an assembly. Cap all line openings.
4. Disconnect the throttle cable. Remove the return spring.
5. Remove the throttle and TV detent cables from the intake manifold brackets.
6. Disconnect the fuel return line from the injection pump.
7. Disconnect the injection line clamps, closest to the pump.
8. Disconnect the injection lines from the pump. Cap all openings. Carefully reposition the fuel lines.
9. Remove the two bolts retaining the injection pump.

10. Remove the pump. Discard the pump to adapter O-ring.

11. Installation is the reverse of removal, with the following recommendations. Position the number one cylinder to the firing position. Install a new O-ring, then install the pump fully, seating it by hand. If a new or intermediate adapter plate is used, set the pump at the center slots on the mounting flange. If the original adapter is used align the pump timing mark and the adapter mark. Torque the pump bolts to 35 ft. lbs.

Injector

REMOVAL & INSTALLATION

➡ **When the lines are disconnected use a back-up wrench on the upper injection nozzle hex. It may also be necessary to jack up the engine to gain access to the back bank of injectors.**

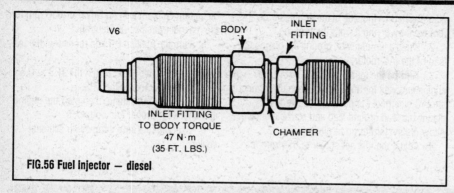

FIG.56 Fuel injector — diesel

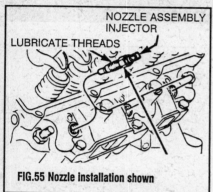

FIG.55 Nozzle installation shown

1. Remove the fuel injection lines as described below.
2. Remove the injector nozzles.

➡ **When replacing the injectors, be sure to use new copper gaskets.**

3. Installation is the reverse of removal.
When reinstalling the injectors special lubricant (GM part 9985462 or its equal) must be applied to the nozzle threads. Torque the injectors to 25 ft. lbs. Make sure the copper gasket is installed on the nozzle.

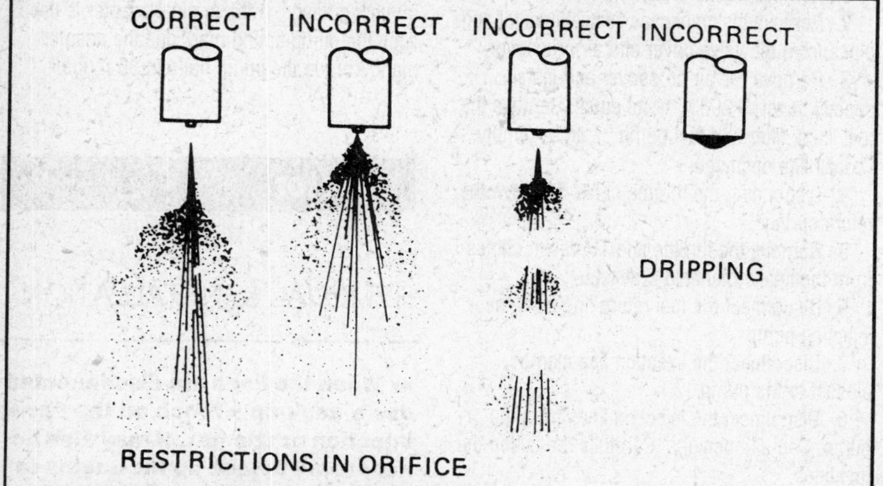

Fuel Pump Lines

REMOVAL & INSTALLATION

All lines may be removed without moving the injection pump. It is not necessary to use a back-up wrench.
1. Remove the air cleaner.
2. Remove the filters and pipes from the valve covers and air crossover.
3. Remove the air crossover. Cap the intake manifold with special cover J–29657 or its equal.
4. Remove the injection pump line clamps. Remove the injection pump lines. Cap open lines, nozzles and pump fittings. Use a back-up wrench on the nozzle hex to prevent a fuel leak.
5. Installation is the reverse of removal.

Diesel Idle Speed

ADJUSTMENT

1. Apply the parking brake, then place the transaxle in Park and block the drive wheels.
2. Start the engine and allow it to reach operating temperature, then turn it Off.
3. Remove the air cleaner cover and the MAP sensor retainer, then move the MAP sensor (with the leads and the hoses attached) aside.
4. Remove the air cleaner assembly and install tool J–26996–1 on the intake manifold.
5. Clean the rpm counter on the front cover and the crankshaft balancer rim. Install the magnetic pickup probe tool J–26925 into the rpm counter, then connect the power leads to the battery.
6. If equipped with A/C, disconnect the compressor clutch lead from the compressor. If equipped with cruise control, remove the servo cable retainer and disconnect the servo throttle cable from the servo blade.
7. Make sure all of the electrical accessories are turned Off.
8. Start the engine and place the transaxle in Drive, then check the slow idle speed reading.
9. Turn Off the engine and unplug the engine coolant temperature sensor connector.
10. Start the engine and place the transaxle in Drive, then check the fast idle speed (allow the plunger to extend by opening the throttle slightly.
11. Connect the engine coolant temperature sensor connector and recheck and/or reset the slow idle speed.
12. Turn Off the engine and reconnect the A/C compressor lead, if equipped.
13. To complete the installation, reverse the removal procedures.

Diesel Injection Timing

CHECKING

➡ **A special diesel timing meter is needed to check injection timing. There are a few variations of this meter, but the type desirable here uses a signal through a glow plug probe to determine combustion timing. The meter picks up the engine speed in RPM and the crankshaft position from the crankshaft balancer. This tool is**

CORRECT   INCORRECT   INCORRECT   INCORRECT

DRIPPING

RESTRICTIONS IN ORIFICE

FIG.57 Check fuel injector for proper spray patterns

available at automotive supply houses and from tool jobbers, and is the counterpart to a gasoline engine timing light, coupled with a tachometer. An intake manifold cover is also needed. **The marks on the pump and adapter flange will normally be aligned within 0.050 in. (1.27mm).**

1. Place the transmission shift lever in Park, apply the parking brake and block the rear wheels.

2. Start the engine and let it run at idle until fully warm. Shut off the engine.

➡ **If the engine is not allowed to completely warm up, the probe may soot up, causing incorrect timing readings.**

3. Remove the air cleaner assembly and carefully install cover J–26996–1. This cover over the intake is important. Disconnect the EGR valve hose.

4. Clean away all dirt from the engine probe holder (RPM counter) and the crankshaft balancer rim.

5. Clean the lens on both ends of the glow plug probe and clean the lens in the photoelectric pickup. Use a tooth pick to scrape the carbon from the combustion chamber side of the glow plug probe, then look through the probe to make sure it's clean. Cleanliness is crucial for accurate readings.

6. Install the probe into the crankshaft RPM counter (probe holder) on the engine front cover.

7. Remove the glow plug from No. 1 cylinder. Install the glow plug probe in the glow plug opening, and torque to 8 ft. lbs.

8. Set the timing meter offset selector to **A** (20).

9. Connect the battery leads, red to positive, black to negative.

10. Disconnect the two-lead connector at the generator.

11. Start the engine. Adjust the engine RPM to the speed specified on the emissions control decal.

12. Observe the timing reading, then observe it again in 2 minutes. When the readings stabilize over the 2 minutes intervals, compare that final stabilized reading to the one specified on the emissions control decal. The timing reading will be an ATDC (After Top Dead Center) reading when set to specifications.

13. Disconnect the timing meter and install the removed glow plug, torquing it to 15 ft. lbs.

14. Connect the generator two-lead connection.

15. Install the air cleaner assembly and connect the EGR valve hose.

INJECTION TIMING ADJUSTING

1. Shut off the engine.

2. Note the relative position of the marks on the pump flange and either the pump intermediate adapter.

3. Loosen the nuts or bolts holding the pump to a point where the pump can just be rotated. You may need a wrench with a slight offset to clear the fuel return line.

4. Rotate the pump to the left to advance the timing and to the right to retard the timing. The width of the mark on the intermediate adaptor is about $2/3°$. Move the pump the amount that is needed and tighten the pump retaining nuts to 35 ft. lbs.

5. Start the engine and recheck the timing as described earlier. Reset the timing if necessary.

6. Reset the fast and curb idle speeds.

➡ **Wild needle fluctuations on the timing meter indicate a cylinder not firing properly. Correction of this condition must be made prior to adjusting the timing.**

7. If after resetting the timing, the timing marks are far apart and the engine still runs poorly, the dynamic timing could still be off. It is possible that a malfunctioning cylinder will cause incorrect timing. If this occurs, it is essential that timing be checked in cylinder 1 or 4. If different timing exists between cylinders, try both positions to determine which timing works best.

Diesel Vacuum Regulator Valve

ADJUSTMENT

1. Disconnect the EGR valve pipe assembly from the air crossover, then remove the air crossover.

2. Disconnect the throttle cable and the TV cable from the pump throttle lever.

3. Loosen the vacuum regulator valve-to-injection pump bolts.

4. Install tool BT–7944 or J–26701–15 to the injection pump throttle lever, then place angle gauge tool BT–7704 or J–26701 on the adapter.

➡ **It may be necessary to file the tool so that it can fit on the pump's thicker throttle lever.**

5. Move the throttle lever to the wide open position and set the angle gauge to 0°.

6. Center the bubble in the level, then set the gauge to 49°. Rotate the throttle lever so that the bubble is centered.

7. Attach a vacuum source to port **A** and the vacuum gauge to port **B**, then apply 22 in.Hg vacuum to port **A**.

8. Rotate the vacuum valve clockwise until 10.3–10.9 in.Hg vacuum is obtained.

9. Tighten the vacuum bolts, then remove the vacuum source and the gauge.

10. Connect the throttle cable and the TV cables to the pump throttle lever, then remove the intake manifold screens.

11. Install the air crossover and the EGR valve pipe assembly to the crossover. Torque the bolts to 19 ft. lbs.

Glow Plugs

➡ **A burned out Fast Glow glow plug may bulge then break off and drop into the pre-chamber when the glow plug is removed. When this occurs the cylinder head must be removed and the pre-chamber removed from the head to remove the broken tip. When installing a glow plug, apply lubricant 1052771 or equivalent to the threads only when the engine is equipped with aluminum cylinder heads. It is important that the pre-chamber be fully installed flush to the surface of the cylinder head. If this is not done, cylinder head gasket or piston damage can occur. When servicing the right rear glow plugs, it may be necessary to follow the procedures below.**

REMOVAL & INSTALLATION

1. Remove the engine support strut (see above figure).

2. Rotate the intermediate steering shaft so that the steering gear stub shaft clamp bolt is in the up position and remove the clamp bolt. Then disconnect the intermediate shaft from the stub shaft.

✳✳ CAUTION

Failure to disconnect the intermediate shaft from the rack and pinion stub shaft can result in damage to the steering gear and/or intermediate shaft. This damage can cause loss of steering control which could result in a vehicle crash with possible bodily injury.

3. Place a floor jack under the front crossmember of the cradle and raise the jack until the jack just starts to raise the car.

4. Remove the front two body mount bolts with the lower cushions and retainers. Then remove the cushions from the bolts.

The removal of any one body mount requires the loosening of the adjacent body mounts to permit the cradle to separate from the body. Take care to prevent breaking the plastic fan shroud, or damaging frame attachments such as steering hoses and brake pipes, during replacement of body mounts.

When installing a body mount, take care to ensure that the body is seated properly in the frame mounting hole; otherwise, direct metal to metal contact will result between the frame and the body. The tube spacer should be in all bolt-in-body mounts. The insulator and metal washer should be positioned to prevent contact with the frame rail. Do not overtighten the body mount; a collapsed tube spacer or stripped bolt may result.

Proper clamping by the mount depends on clean dry surfaces. If the body mount bolt doesn't screw in smoothly, it may be necessary to run a tap through the cage nut in the body to remove foreign material. Take care to ensure that the tap does not punch through the underbody.

Whenever the body is going to be moved in relation to the cradle, the intermediate shaft should be disconnected from the rack and pinion steering gear stub shaft.

✳✳ CAUTION

Failure to disconnect the intermediate shaft from the rack and pinion steering gear stub shaft can result in damage to the steering gear and/or intermediate shaft. This damage can cause loss of steering control which could result in a vehicle crash with possible bodily injury.

5. Thread the body mount bolts with retainers a minimum of three turns into the cage nuts so that the bolts retain cradle movement.

6. Release the floor jack slowly until the crossmember contacts the body mount bolt retainers. As the jack is being lowered, watch and correct any interference with hoses, lines, pipes and cables.

✳✳ CAUTION

**Do not place your hands between the crossmember and body mount to remove objects or correct interference while the jack is lowering.
Do not lower the cradle without it being restrained as possible damage can occur to the body and underhood items.**

7. Reverse the procedure for installation. Torque the intermediate steering shaft clamp bolt to 46 ft. lbs. and the body mount bolts to 77 ft. lbs.

FUEL TANK

REMOVAL & INSTALLATION

1. Disconnect the negative cable at the battery. Raise and support the car.

2. Drain the tank. There is no drain plug; remaining fuel in the tank must be siphoned through the fuel feed line (the line to the fuel pump), because of the restrictor in the filler neck.

3. Disconnect the hose and the vapor return hose from the level sending unit fittings.

4. Remove the ground wire screw.

5. Unplug the level sending unit electrical connector.

6. Disconnect the vent hose.

7. Unbolt the support straps, and lower and remove the tank.

8. To install reverse steps 1 through 7.

SENDING UNIT REPLACEMENT

The fuel gauge sending unit is attached to the fuel pump on cars with an electric intank pump. The following procedure is for pump and sending unit removal and installation. If the vehicle as a pump mounted on the engine the basic steps will still lead you through sending unit replacement. Be extremely cautious of sparks or flame when working around the fuel pump. NEVER apply battery power to a used fuel pump out of the fuel tank.

1. Relieve the fuel system pressure, then disconnect the negative battery cable.

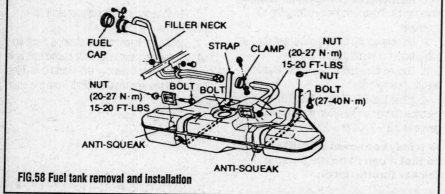

FIG.58 Fuel tank removal and installation

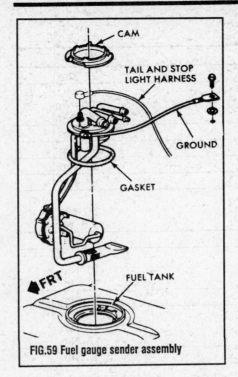

FIG.59 Fuel gauge sender assembly

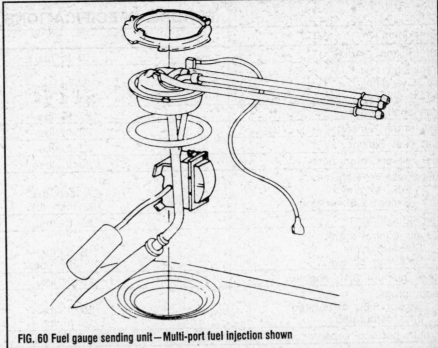

FIG. 60 Fuel gauge sending unit — Multi-port fuel injection shown

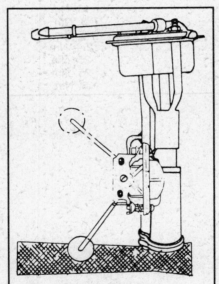

FIG. 61 Sending unit and fuel pump — Multi-port fuel injection shown

2. Raise and support the vehicle safely. Drain the fuel tank.

3. Disconnect wiring from the tank, then remove the ground wire retaining screw from under the body.

4. Disconnect all hoses from the tank.

5. Support the tank on a jack and remove the retaining strap nuts.

6. Lower the tank and remove it from the vehicle.

7. Remove the fuel gauge/pump retaining ring using a suitable spanner wrench.

8. Remove the gauge unit and the pump.

To install:

9. Install the gauge unit and the pump.

10. Install the fuel gauge/pump retaining ring using a suitable spanner.

11. Raise the tank and and install it to the vehicle.

12. Support the tank on a jack stand and install the retaining strap nuts.

13. Connect the hoses to the tank.

14. Connect the electrical connectors and the ground wire, if equipped.

15. Lower the vehicle.

16. Fill the fuel tank.

17. Turn the ignition switch to the **ON** position for 2 seconds, then turn to the **OFF** position for 10 seconds. Turn the ignition switch back to the **ON** position and check for fuel leaks.

TORQUE SPECIFICATIONS

Component	U.S.	Metric
C3I Ignition module:	19 ft. lbs.	25 Nm
Crankshaft bolt		
3.3L engine:	220 ft. lbs.	300 Nm
3.8L engine:	220 ft. lbs.	300 Nm
Crankshaft sensor:	22 ft. lbs.	30 Nm
Dual crank sensor:	22 ft. lbs.	30 Nm
Fuel Line Fittings:	22 ft. lbs.	30 Nm
Fuel rail attaching nuts:	20 ft. lbs.	27 Nm
Fuel Pressure Regulator:		
2.5L engine:	22 inch lbs.	2.5 Nm
Except 2.5L engine:	102 inch lbs.	11.5 Nm
Fuel tank straps:	26 ft. lbs.	35 Nm
Idle air control valve:		
Screw-in type:	13 ft. lbs.	18 Nm
Retaining screws:	27 inch lbs.	3 Nm
Intake plenum 3.1L engine:	18 ft. lbs.	25 Nm
Spark plugs:		
Except 2.8L carburated	20 ft. lbs.	27 Nm
2.8L carburated	15 ft. lbs.	17 Nm
Throttle position sensor:	18 inch lbs.	2 Nm
TBI components:		
Fuel line nuts:	20 ft. lbs.	18 Nm
Idle air control valve:	27 inch lbs.	3 Nm
Injector retainer:	27 inch lbs.	3 Nm
Pressure regulator cover:	21 inch lbs.	2.4 Nm
Throttle body bolts:	18 ft. lbs.	25 Nm
Throttle body bolts:	18 ft. lbs.	25 Nm
Tube module assembly:	27 inch lbs.	3 Nm

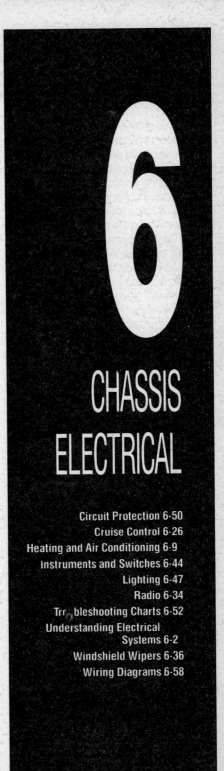

6

CHASSIS ELECTRICAL

BASIC ELECTRICITY

At the rate which both import and domestic manufacturers are incorporating electronic control systems into their production lines, it won't be long before every new vehicle is equipped with one or more on-board computer. These electronic components (with no moving parts) should theoretically last the life of the vehicle, provided nothing external happens to damage the circuits or memory chips.

While it is true that electronic components should never wear out, in the real world malfunctions do occur. It is also true that any computer-based system is extremely sensitive to electrical voltages and cannot tolerate careless or haphazard testing or service procedures. An inexperienced individual can literally do major damage looking for a minor problem by using the wrong kind of test equipment or connecting test leads or connectors with the ignition switch ON. When selecting test equipment, make sure the manufacturers instructions state that the tester is compatible with whatever type of electronic control system is being serviced. Read all instructions carefully and double check all test points before installing probes or making any test connections.

The following section outlines basic diagnosis techniques for dealing with computerized automotive control systems. Along with a general explanation of the various types of test equipment available to aid in servicing modern electronic automotive systems, basic repair techniques for wiring harnesses and connectors is given. Read the basic information before attempting any repairs or testing on any computerized system, to provide the background of information necessary to avoid the most common and obvious mistakes that can cost both time and money. Although the replacement and testing procedures are simple in themselves, the systems are not, and unless one has a thorough understanding of all components and their function within a particular computerized control system, the logical test sequence these systems demand cannot be followed. Minor malfunctions can make a big difference, so it is important to know how each component affects the operation of the overall electronic system to find the ultimate cause of a problem without replacing good components unnecessarily. It is not enough to use the correct test equipment; the test equipment must be used correctly.

Safety Precautions

✳ CAUTION

Whenever working on or around any computer based microprocessor control system, always observe these general precautions to prevent the possibility of personal injury or damage to electronic components.

• Never install or remove battery cables with the key ON or the engine running. Jumper cables should be connected with the key OFF to avoid power surges that can damage electronic control units. Engines equipped with computer controlled systems should avoid both giving and getting jump starts due to the possibility of serious damage to components from arcing in the engine compartment when connections are made with the ignition ON.

• Always remove the battery cables before charging the battery. Never use a high output charger on an installed battery or attempt to use any type of "hot shot" (24 volt) starting aid.

• Exercise care when inserting test probes into connectors to insure good connections without damaging the connector or spreading the pins. Always probe connectors from the rear (wire) side, NOT the pin side, to avoid accidental shorting of terminals during test procedures.

• Never remove or attach wiring harness connectors with the ignition switch ON, especially to an electronic control unit.

• Do not drop any components during service procedures and never apply 12 volts directly to any component (like a solenoid or relay) unless instructed specifically to do so. Some component electrical windings are designed to safely handle only 4 or 5 volts and can be destroyed in seconds if 12 volts are applied directly to the connector.

• Remove the electronic control unit if the vehicle is to be placed in an environment where temperatures exceed approximately 176°F (80°C), such as a paint spray booth or when arc or gas welding near the control unit location in the car.

• When possible use a flashlight instead of a drop light.

• Do not allow extension cords for power tools or drop lights to lie on or across any of the vehicle wiring.

• NEVER use an external power supply to retain component memory when working on the instrument panel or inside the car, if the car is equipped with an air bag.

• Leave electronic components in the package until you are ready to install them and never touch the connector pins.

• Touch the metal of the car often when servicing electronic components to remove and static charge that may build on your body. This charge will damage electronic components if you touch them.

ORGANIZED TROUBLESHOOTING

When diagnosing a specific problem, organized troubleshooting is a must. The complexity of a modern automobile demands that you approach any problem in a logical, organized manner. There are certain troubleshooting techniques that are standard:

1. Establish when the problem occurs. Does the problem appear only under certain conditions? Were there any noises, odors, or other unusual symptoms?

2. Isolate the problem area. To do this, make some simple tests and observations; then eliminate the systems that are working properly. Check for obvious problems such as broken wires, dirty connections or split or disconnected vacuum hoses. Always check the obvious before assuming something complicated is the cause.

3. Test for problems systematically to determine the cause once the problem area is isolated. Are all the components functioning properly? Is there power going to electrical switches and motors? Is there vacuum at vacuum switches and/or actuators? Is there a mechanical problem such as bent linkage or loose mounting screws? Doing careful, systematic checks will often turn up most causes on the first inspection without wasting time checking components that have little or no relationship to the problem.

4. Test all repairs after the work is done to make sure that the problem is fixed. Some causes can be traced to more than one component, so a careful verification of repair work is important to pick up additional malfunctions that may cause a problem to reappear or a different problem to arise. A blown fuse, for example, is a simple problem that may require more than another fuse to repair. If you

don't look for a problem that caused a fuse to blow, for example, a shorted wire may go undetected.

Experience has shown that most problems tend to be the result of a fairly simple and obvious cause, such as loose or corroded connectors or air leaks in the intake system; making careful inspection of components during testing essential to quick and accurate troubleshooting. Special, hand held computerized testers designed specifically for diagnosing the EEC-IV system are available from a variety of aftermarket sources, as well as from the vehicle manufacturer, but care should be taken that any test equipment being used is designed to diagnose that particular computer controlled system accurately without damaging the control unit (ECU) or components being tested.

➡ **Pinpointing the exact cause of trouble in an electrical system can sometimes only be accomplished by the use of special test equipment. The following describes commonly used test equipment and explains how to put it to best use in diagnosis. In addition to the information covered below, the manufacturer's instructions booklet provided with the tester should be read and clearly understood before attempting any test procedures.**

TEST EQUIPMENT

Jumper Wires

Jumper wires are simple, yet extremely valuable, pieces of test equipment. Jumper wires are merely wires that are used to bypass sections of a circuit. The simplest type of jumper wire is merely a length of multistrand wire with an alligator clip at each end. Jumper wires are usually fabricated from lengths of standard automotive wire and whatever type of connector (alligator clip, spade connector or pin connector) that is required for the particular vehicle being tested. The well equipped tool box will have several different styles of jumper wires in several different lengths. Some jumper wires are made with three or more terminals coming from a common splice for special purpose testing. In cramped, hard-to-reach areas it is advisable to have insulated boots over the jumper wire terminals in order to prevent accidental grounding, sparks, and possible fire, especially when testing fuel system components.

Jumper wires are used primarily to locate open electrical circuits, on either the ground (–) side of the circuit or on the hot (+) side. If an electrical component fails to operate, connect the jumper wire between the component and a good ground. If the component operates only with the jumper installed, the ground circuit is open. If the ground circuit is good, but the component does not operate, the circuit between the power feed and component is open. You can sometimes connect the jumper wire directly from the battery to the hot terminal of the component, but first make sure the component uses 12 volts in operation. Some electrical components, such as fuel injectors, are designed to operate on about 4 volts and running 12 volts directly to the injector terminals can burn out the wiring. By inserting an inline fuseholder between a set of test leads, a fused jumper wire can be used for bypassing open circuits. Use a 5 amp fuse to provide protection against voltage spikes. When in doubt, use a voltmeter to check the voltage input to the component and measure how much voltage is being applied normally. By moving the jumper wire successively back from the lamp toward the power source, you can isolate the area of the circuit where the open is located. When the component stops functioning, or the power is cut off, the open is in the segment of wire between the jumper and the point previously tested.

❋❋ CAUTION

Never use jumpers made from wire that is of lighter gauge than used in the circuit under test. If the jumper wire is of too small gauge, it may overheat and possibly melt. Never use jumpers to bypass high resistance loads (such as motors) in a circuit. Bypassing resistances, in effect, creates a short circuit which may, in turn, cause damage and fire. Never use a jumper for anything other than temporary bypassing of components in a circuit.

12 Volt Test Light

The 12 volt test light is used to check circuits and components while electrical current is flowing through them. It is used for voltage and ground tests. Twelve volt test lights come in different styles but all have three main parts; a ground clip, a probe, and a light. The most commonly used 12 volt test lights have pick-type probes. To use a 12 volt test light, connect the ground clip to a good ground and probe

wherever necessary with the pick. The pick should be sharp so that it can penetrate wire insulation to make contact with the wire, without making a large hole in the insulation. The wrap-around light is handy in hard to reach areas or where it is difficult to support a wire to push a probe pick into it. To use the wrap around light, hook the wire to probed with the hook and pull the trigger. A small pick will be forced through the wire insulation into the wire core.

❋❋ CAUTION

Do not use a test light to probe electronic ignition spark plug or coil wires. Never use a pick-type test light to probe wiring on computer controlled systems unless specifically instructed to do so. Any wire insulation that is pierced by the test light probe should be taped and sealed with silicone after testing.

Like the jumper wire, the 12 volt test light is used to isolate opens in circuits. But, whereas the jumper wire is used to bypass the open to operate the load, the 12 volt test light is used to locate the presence of voltage in a circuit. If the test light glows, you know that there is power up to that point; if the 12 volt test light does not glow when its probe is inserted into the wire or connector, you know that there is an open circuit (no power). Move the test light in successive steps back toward the power source until the light in the handle does glow. When it does glow, the open is between the probe and point previously probed.

➡ **The test light does not detect that 12 volts (or any particular amount of voltage) is present; it only detects that some voltage is present. It is advisable before using the test light to touch its terminals across the battery posts to make sure the light is operating properly.**

Self-Powered Test Light

The self-powered test light usually contains a 1.5 volt penlight battery. One type of self-powered test light is similar in design to the 12 volt test light. This type has both the battery and the light in the handle and pick-type probe tip. The second type has the light toward the open tip, so that the light illuminates the contact point. The self-powered test light is dual purpose piece of test equipment. It can be used to test for either open or short circuits when power is isolated from the circuit (continuity test). A powered test light should not be used on any computer

controlled system or component unless specifically instructed to do so. Many engine sensors can be destroyed by even this small amount of voltage applied directly to the terminals.

Open Circuit Testing

To use the self-powered test light to check for open circuits, first isolate the circuit from the vehicle's 12 volt power source by disconnecting the battery or wiring harness connector. Connect the test light ground clip to a good ground and probe sections of the circuit sequentially with the test light. (start from either end of the circuit). If the light is out, the open is between the probe and the circuit ground. If the light is on, the open is between the probe and end of the circuit toward the power source.

Short Circuit Testing

By isolating the circuit both from power and from ground, and using a self-powered test light, you can check for shorts to ground in the circuit. Isolate the circuit from power and ground. Connect the test light ground clip to a good ground and probe any easy-to-reach test point in the circuit. If the light comes on, there is a short somewhere in the circuit. To isolate the short, probe a test point at either end of the isolated circuit (the light should be on). Leave the test light probe connected and open connectors, switches, remove parts, etc., sequentially, until the light goes out. When the light goes out, the short is between the last circuit component opened and the previous circuit opened.

➡ **The 1.5 volt battery in the test light does not provide much current. A weak battery may not provide enough power to illuminate the test light even when a complete circuit is made (especially if there are high resistances in the circuit). Always make sure that the test battery is strong. To check the battery, briefly touch the ground clip to the probe; if the light glows brightly the battery is strong enough for testing. Never use a self-powered test light to perform checks for opens or shorts when power is applied to the electrical system under test. The 12 volt vehicle power will quickly burn out the 1.5 volt light bulb in the test light.**

Voltmeter

A voltmeter is used to measure voltage at any point in a circuit, or to measure the voltage drop across any part of a circuit. It can also be used to check continuity in a wire or circuit by indicating current flow from one end to the other. Voltmeters usually have various scales on the meter dial and a selector switch to allow the selection of different voltages. The voltmeter has a positive and a negative lead. To avoid damage to the meter, always connect the negative lead to the negative (–) side of circuit (to ground or nearest the ground side of the circuit) and connect the positive lead to the positive (+) side of the circuit (to the power source or the nearest power source). Note that the negative voltmeter lead will always be black and that the positive voltmeter will always be some color other than black (usually red). Depending on how the voltmeter is connected into the circuit, it has several uses.

voltmeter can be connected either in parallel or in series with a circuit and it has a very high resistance to current flow. When connected in parallel, only a small amount of current will flow through the voltmeter current path; the rest will flow through the normal circuit current path and the circuit will work normally. When the voltmeter is connected in series with a circuit, only a small amount of current can flow through the circuit. The circuit will not work properly, but the voltmeter reading will show if the circuit is complete or not.

Available Voltage Measurement

Set the voltmeter selector switch to the 20V position and connect the meter negative lead to the negative post of the battery. Connect the positive meter lead to the positive post of the battery and turn the ignition switch ON to provide a load. Read the voltage on the meter or digital display. A well charged battery should register over 12 volts. If the meter reads below 11.5 volts, the battery power may be insufficient to operate the electrical system properly. This test determines voltage available from the battery and should be the first step in any electrical trouble diagnosis procedure. Many electrical problems, especially on computer controlled systems, can be caused by a low state of charge in the battery. Excessive corrosion at the battery cable terminals can cause a poor contact that will prevent proper charging and full battery current flow.

Normal battery voltage is 12 volts when fully charged. When the battery is supplying current to one or more circuits it is said to be "under load". When everything is off the electrical system is under a "no-load" condition. A fully charged battery may show about 12.5 volts at no load; will drop to 12 volts under medium load; and will drop even lower under heavy load. If the battery is partially discharged the voltage decrease under heavy load may be excessive, even though the battery shows 12 volts or more at no load. When allowed to discharge further, the battery's available voltage under load will decrease more severely. For this reason, it is important that the battery be fully charged during all testing procedures to avoid errors in diagnosis and incorrect test results.

Voltage Drop

When current flows through a resistance, the voltage beyond the resistance is reduced (the larger the current, the greater the reduction in voltage). When no current is flowing, there is no voltage drop because there is no current flow. All points in the circuit which are connected to the power source are at the same voltage as the power source. The total voltage drop always equals the total source voltage. In a long circuit with many connectors, a series of small, unwanted voltage drops due to corrosion at the connectors can add up to a total loss of voltage which impairs the operation of the normal loads in the circuit.

INDIRECT COMPUTATION OF VOLTAGE DROPS

1. Set the voltmeter selector switch to the 20 volt position.
2. Connect the meter negative lead to a good ground.
3. Probe all resistances in the circuit with the positive meter lead.
4. Operate the circuit in all modes and observe the voltage readings.

DIRECT MEASUREMENT OF VOLTAGE DROPS

1. Set the voltmeter switch to the 20 volt position.
2. Connect the voltmeter negative lead to the ground side of the resistance load to be measured.
3. Connect the positive lead to the positive side of the resistance or load to be measured.
4. Read the voltage drop directly on the 20 volt scale.

Too high a voltage indicates too high a resistance. If, for example, a blower motor runs too slowly, you can determine if there is too high a resistance in the resistor pack. By taking voltage drop readings in all parts of the circuit, you can isolate the problem. Too low a voltage drop indicates too low a resistance. If, for example, a blower motor runs too fast in the MED and/or LOW position, the problem can be isolated in the resistor pack by taking voltage drop readings in all parts of the circuit to locate a possibly shorted resistor. The maximum allowable voltage drop under load is critical, especially if there is more than one high resistance problem in a circuit because all voltage drops are cumulative. A small drop is normal due to the resistance of the conductors.

HIGH RESISTANCE TESTING

1. Set the voltmeter selector switch to the 4 volt position.

2. Connect the voltmeter positive lead to the positive post of the battery.

3. Turn on the headlights and heater blower to provide a load.

4. Probe various points in the circuit with the negative voltmeter lead.

5. Read the voltage drop on the 4 volt scale. Some average maximum allowable voltage drops are:

FUSE PANEL — 7 volts

IGNITION SWITCH — 5 volts

HEADLIGHT SWITCH — 7 volts

IGNITION COIL (+) — 5 volts

ANY OTHER LOAD — 1.3 volts

➡ **Voltage drops are all measured while a load is operating; without current flow, there will be no voltage drop.**

Ohmmeter

The ohmmeter is designed to read resistance (ohms) in a circuit or component. Although there are several different styles of ohmmeters, all will usually have a selector switch which permits the measurement of different ranges of resistance (usually the selector switch allows the multiplication of the meter reading by 10, 100, 1,000, and 10,000). A calibration knob allows the meter to be set at zero for accurate measurement. Since all ohmmeters are powered by an internal battery (usually 9 volts), the ohmmeter can be used as a self-powered test light. When the ohmmeter is connected, current from the ohmmeter flows through the circuit or component being tested. Since the ohmmeter's internal resistance and voltage are known values, the amount of current flow through the meter depends on the resistance of the circuit or component being tested.

The ohmmeter can be used to perform continuity test for opens or shorts (either by observation of the meter needle or as a self-powered test light), and to read actual resistance in a circuit. It should be noted that the ohmmeter is used to check the resistance of a component or wire while there is no voltage applied to the circuit. Current flow from an outside voltage source (such as the vehicle battery) can damage the ohmmeter, so the circuit or component should be isolated from the vehicle electrical system before any testing is done. Since the ohmmeter uses its own voltage source, either lead can be connected to any test point.

➡ **When checking diodes or other solid state components, the ohmmeter leads can only be connected one way in order to measure current flow in a single direction. Make sure the positive (+) and negative (–) terminal connections are as described in the test procedures to verify the one-way diode operation.**

In using the meter for making continuity checks, do not be concerned with the actual resistance readings. Zero resistance, or any resistance readings, indicate continuity in the circuit. Infinite resistance indicates an open in the circuit. A high resistance reading where there should be none indicates a problem in the circuit. Checks for short circuits are made in the same manner as checks for open circuits except that the circuit must be isolated from both power and normal ground. Infinite resistance indicates no continuity to ground, while zero resistance indicates a dead short to ground.

RESISTANCE MEASUREMENT

The batteries in an ohmmeter will weaken with age and temperature, so the ohmmeter must be calibrated or "zeroed" before taking measurements. To zero the meter, place the selector switch in its lowest range and touch the two ohmmeter leads together. Turn the calibration knob until the meter needle is exactly on zero.

➡ **All analog (needle) type ohmmeters must be zeroed before use, but some digital ohmmeter models are automatically calibrated when the switch is turned on. Self-calibrating digital ohmmeters do not have an adjusting knob, but its a good idea to check for a zero readout before use by touching the leads together. All computer controlled systems require the use of a digital ohmmeter with at least 10 meagohms impedance for testing. Before any test procedures are attempted, make sure the ohmmeter used is compatible with the electrical system or damage to the on-board computer could result.**

To measure resistance, first isolate the circuit from the vehicle power source by disconnecting the battery cables or the harness connector. Make sure the key is OFF when disconnecting any components or the battery. Where necessary, also isolate at least one side of the circuit to be checked to avoid reading parallel resistances. Parallel circuit resistances will always give a lower reading than the actual resistance of either of the branches. When measuring the resistance of parallel circuits, the total resistance will always be lower than the smallest resistance in the circuit. Connect the meter leads to both sides of the circuit (wire or component) and read the actual measured ohms on the meter scale. Make sure the selector switch is set to the proper ohm scale for the circuit being tested to avoid misreading the ohmmeter test value.

✳✳✳ WARNING

Never use an ohmmeter with power applied to the circuit. Like the self-powered test light, the ohmmeter is designed to operate on its own power supply. The normal 12 volt automotive electrical system current could damage the meter!

Ammeters

An ammeter measures the amount of current flowing through a circuit in units called amperes or amps. Amperes are units of electron flow which indicate how fast the electrons are flowing through the circuit. Since Ohms Law dictates that current flow in a circuit is equal to the circuit voltage divided by the total circuit resistance, increasing voltage also increases the current level (amps). Likewise, any decrease in resistance will increase the amount of amps in a circuit. At normal operating voltage, most circuits have a characteristic amount of amperes, called "current draw" which can be measured using an ammeter. By referring to a specified current draw rating, measuring the amperes, and comparing the two values, one can determine what is happening within the circuit to aid in diagnosis. An open circuit, for example, will not allow any current to flow so the ammeter reading will be zero. More current flows through a heavily loaded circuit or when the charging system is operating.

An ammeter is always connected in series with the circuit being tested. All of the current that normally flows through the circuit must also flow through the ammeter; if there is any other path for the current to follow, the ammeter reading will not be accurate. The ammeter itself has very little resistance to current flow and therefore will not affect the circuit, but it will measure current draw only when the circuit is closed and electricity is flowing. Excessive current draw can blow fuses and drain the battery, while a reduced current draw can cause motors to run slowly, lights to dim and other

components to not operate properly. The ammeter can help diagnose these conditions by locating the cause of the high or low reading.

Multimeters

Different combinations of test meters can be built into a single unit designed for specific tests. Some of the more common combination test devices are known as Volt/Amp testers, Tach/Dwell meters, or Digital Multimeters. The Volt/Amp tester is used for charging system, starting system or battery tests and consists of a voltmeter, an ammeter and a variable resistance carbon pile. The voltmeter will usually have at least two ranges for use with 6, 12 and 24 volt systems. The ammeter also has more than one range for testing various levels of battery loads and starter current draw and the carbon pile can be adjusted to offer different amounts of resistance. The Volt/Amp tester has heavy leads to carry large amounts of current and many later models have an inductive ammeter pickup that clamps around the wire to simplify test connections. On some models, the ammeter also has a zero-center scale to allow testing of charging and starting systems without switching leads or polarity. A digital multimeter is a voltmeter, ammeter and ohmmeter combined in an instrument which gives a digital readout. These are often used when testing solid state circuits because of their high input impedance (usually 10 megohms or more).

The tach/dwell meter combines a tachometer and a dwell (cam angle) meter and is a specialized kind of voltmeter. The tachometer scale is marked to show engine speed in rpm and the dwell scale is marked to show degrees of distributor shaft rotation. In most electronic ignition systems, dwell is determined by the control unit, but the dwell meter can also be used to check the duty cycle (operation) of some electronic engine control systems. Some tach/dwell meters are powered by an internal battery, while others take their power from the car battery in use. The battery powered testers usually require calibration much like an ohmmeter before testing.

Special Test Equipment

A variety of diagnostic tools are available to help troubleshoot and repair computerized engine control systems. The most sophisticated of these devices are the console type engine analyzers that usually occupy a garage service bay, but there are several types of aftermarket electronic testers available that will allow quick circuit tests of the engine control system by plugging directly into a special connector located in the engine compartment or under the dashboard. Several tool and equipment manufacturers offer simple, hand held testers

that measure various circuit voltage levels on command to check all system components for proper operation. Although these testers usually cost about $300–500, consider that the average computer control unit (or ECM) can cost just as much and the money saved by not replacing perfectly good sensors or components in an attempt to correct a problem could justify the purchase price of a special diagnostic tester the first time it's used.

These computerized testers can allow quick and easy test measurements while the engine is operating or while the car is being driven. In addition, the on-board computer memory can be read to access any stored trouble codes; in effect allowing the computer to tell you where it hurts and aid trouble diagnosis by pinpointing exactly which circuit or component is malfunctioning. In the same manner, repairs can be tested to make sure the problem has been corrected. The biggest advantage these special testers have is their relatively easy hookups that minimize or eliminate the chances of making the wrong connections and getting false voltage readings or damaging the computer accidentally.

➡ **It should be remembered that these testers check voltage levels in circuits; they don't detect mechanical problems or failed components if the circuit voltage falls within the preprogrammed limits stored in the tester PROM unit. Also, most of the hand held testes are designed to work only on one or two systems made by a specific manufacturer.**

A variety of aftermarket testers are available to help diagnose different computerized control systems. Owatonna Tool Company (OTC), for example, markets a device called the OTC Monitor which plugs directly into the assembly line diagnostic link (ALDL). The OTC tester makes diagnosis a simple matter of pressing the correct buttons and, by changing the internal PROM or inserting a different diagnosis cartridge, it will work on any model from full size to subcompact, over a wide range of years. An adapter is supplied with the tester to allow connection to all types of ALDL links, regardless of the number of pin terminals used. By inserting an updated PROM into the OTC tester, it can be easily updated to diagnose any new modifications of computerized control systems.

Wiring Harnesses

The average automobile contains about 1/2 mile of wiring, with hundreds of individual connections. To protect the many wires from

damage and to keep them from becoming a confusing tangle, they are organized into bundles, enclosed in plastic or taped together and called wire harnesses. Different wiring harnesses serve different parts of the vehicle. Individual wires are color coded to help trace them through a harness where sections are hidden from view.

A loose or corroded connection or a replacement wire that is too small for the circuit will add extra resistance and an additional voltage drop to the circuit. A ten percent voltage drop can result in slow or erratic motor operation, for example, even though the circuit is complete. Automotive wiring or circuit conductors can be in any one of three forms:

1. Single strand wire
2. Multistrand wire
3. Printed circuitry

Single strand wire has a solid metal core and is usually used inside such components as alternators, motors, relays and other devices. Multistrand wire has a core made of many small strands of wire twisted together into a single conductor. Most of the wiring in an automotive electrical system is made up of multistrand wire, either as a single conductor or grouped together in a harness. All wiring is color coded on the insulator, either as a solid color or as a colored wire with an identification stripe. A printed circuit is a thin film of copper or other conductor that is printed on an insulator backing. Occasionally, a printed circuit is sandwiched between two sheets of plastic for more protection and flexibility. A complete printed circuit, consisting of conductors, insulating material and connectors for lamps or other components is called a printed circuit board. Printed circuitry is used in place of individual wires or harnesses in places where space is limited, such as behind instrument panels.

Wire Gauge

Since computer controlled automotive electrical systems are very sensitive to changes in resistance, the selection of properly sized wires is critical when systems are repaired. The wire gauge number is an expression of the cross section area of the conductor. The most common system for expressing wire size is the American Wire Gauge (AWG) system.

Wire cross section area is measured in circular mils. A mil is $1/1000$ in. (0.001 in. [0.0254mm]); a circular mil is the area of a circle one mil in diameter. For example, a conductor $1/4$ in. (6mm) in diameter is 0.250 in. or 250 mils. The circular mil cross section area of the wire is 250 squared (250^2) or 62,500 circular mils. Imported car models usually use metric wire gauge designations, which is simply

the cross section area of the conductor in square millimeters (mm^2).

Gauge numbers are assigned to conductors of various cross section areas. As gauge number increases, area decreases and the conductor becomes smaller. A 5 gauge conductor is smaller than a 1 gauge conductor and a 10 gauge is smaller than a 5 gauge. As the cross section area of a conductor decreases, resistance increases and so does the gauge number. A conductor with a higher gauge number will carry less current than a conductor with a lower gauge number.

➡ **Gauge wire size refers to the size of the conductor, not the size of the complete wire. It is possible to have two wires of the same gauge with different diameters because one may have thicker insulation than the other.**

12 volt automotive electrical systems generally use 10, 12, 14, 16 and 18 gauge wire. Main power distribution circuits and larger accessories usually use 10 and 12 gauge wire. Battery cables are usually 4 or 6 gauge, although 1 and 2 gauge wires are occasionally used. Wire length must also be considered when making repairs to a circuit. As conductor length increases, so does resistance. An 18 gauge wire, for example, can carry a 10 amp load for 10 feet without excessive voltage drop; however if a 15 foot wire is required for the same 10 amp load, it must be a 16 gauge wire.

An electrical schematic shows the electrical current paths when a circuit is operating properly. It is essential to understand how a circuit works before trying to figure out why it doesn't. Schematics break the entire electrical system down into individual circuits and show only one particular circuit. In a schematic, no attempt is made to represent wiring and components as they physically appear on the vehicle; switches and other components are shown as simply as possible. Face views of harness connectors show the cavity or terminal locations in all multi-pin connectors to help locate test points.

If you need to backprobe a connector while it is on the component, the order of the terminals must be mentally reversed. The wire color code can help in this situation, as well as a keyway, lock tab or other reference mark.

➡ **Wiring diagrams are not included in this book. As trucks have become more complex and available with longer option lists, wiring diagrams have grown in size and complexity. It has become almost impossible to provide a readable reproduction of a wiring diagram in a book this size. Information on ordering wiring diagrams from the vehicle manufacturer can be found in the owner's manual.**

WIRING REPAIR

Soldering is a quick, efficient method of joining metals permanently. Everyone who has the occasion to make wiring repairs should know how to solder. Electrical connections that are soldered are far less likely to come apart and will conduct electricity much better than connections that are only "pig-tailed" together. The most popular (and preferred) method of soldering is with an electrical soldering gun. Soldering irons are available in many sizes and wattage ratings. Irons with higher wattage ratings deliver higher temperatures and recover lost heat faster. A small soldering iron rated for no more than 50 watts is recommended, especially on electrical systems where excess heat can damage the components being soldered.

There are three ingredients necessary for successful soldering; proper flux, good solder and sufficient heat. A soldering flux is necessary to clean the metal of tarnish, prepare it for soldering and to enable the solder to spread into tiny crevices. When soldering, always use a resin flux or resin core solder which is non-corrosive and will not attract moisture once the job is finished. Other types of flux (acid core) will leave a residue that will attract moisture and cause the wires to corrode. Tin is a unique metal with a low melting point. In a molten state, it dissolves and alloys easily with many metals. Solder is made by mixing tin with lead. The most common proportions are 40/60, 50/50 and 60/40, with the percentage of tin listed first. Low priced solders usually contain less tin, making them very difficult for a beginner to use because more heat is required to melt the solder. A common solder is 40/60 which is well suited for all-around general use, but 60/40 melts easier, has more tin for a better joint and is preferred for electrical work.

Soldering Techniques

Successful soldering requires that the metals to be joined be heated to a temperature that will melt the solder—usually 360–460°F (182–238°C). Contrary to popular belief, the purpose of the soldering iron is not to melt the solder itself, but to heat the parts being soldered to a temperature high enough to melt the solder when it is touched to the work. Melting flux-cored solder on the soldering iron will usually destroy the effectiveness of the flux.

➡ **Soldering tips are made of copper for good heat conductivity, but must be "tinned" regularly for quick transference of heat to the project and to prevent the solder from sticking to the iron. To "tin" the iron, simply heat it and touch the flux-cored solder to the tip; the solder will flow over the hot tip. Wipe the excess off with a clean rag, but be careful as the iron will be hot.**

After some use, the tip may become pitted. If so, simply dress the tip smooth with a smooth file and "tin" the tip again. An old saying holds that "metals well cleaned are half soldered." Flux-cored solder will remove oxides but rust, bits of insulation and oil or grease must be removed with a wire brush or emery cloth. For maximum strength in soldered parts, the joint must start off clean and tight. Weak joints will result in gaps too wide for the solder to bridge.

If a separate soldering flux is used, it should be brushed or swabbed on only those areas that are to be soldered. Most solders contain a core of flux and separate fluxing is unnecessary. Hold the work to be soldered firmly. It is best to solder on a wooden board, because a metal vise will only rob the piece to be soldered of heat and make it difficult to melt the solder. Hold the soldering tip with the broadest face against the work to be soldered. Apply solder under the tip close to the work, using enough solder to give a heavy film between the iron and the piece being soldered, while moving slowly and making sure the solder melts properly. Keep the work level or the solder will run to the lowest part and favor the thicker parts, because these require more heat to melt the solder. If the soldering tip overheats (the solder coating on the face of the tip burns up), it should be retinned. Once the soldering is completed, let the soldered joint stand until cool. Tape and seal all soldered wire splices after the repair has cooled.

Wire Harness and Connectors

The on-board computer (ECM) wire harness electrically connects the control unit to the various solenoids, switches and sensors used by the control system. Most connectors in the engine compartment or otherwise exposed to the elements are protected against moisture and dirt which could create oxidation and deposits on the

terminals. This protection is important because of the very low voltage and current levels used by the computer and sensors. All connectors have a lock which secures the male and female terminals together, with a secondary lock holding the seal and terminal into the connector. Both terminal locks must be released when disconnecting ECM connectors.

These special connectors are weather-proof and all repairs require the use of a special terminal and the tool required to service it. This tool is used to remove the pin and sleeve terminals. If removal is attempted with an ordinary pick, there is a good chance that the terminal will be bent or deformed. Unlike standard blade type terminals, these terminals cannot be straightened once they are bent. Make certain that the connectors are properly seated and all of the sealing rings in place when connecting leads. On some models, a hinge-type flap provides a backup or secondary locking feature for the terminals. Most secondary locks are used to improve the connector reliability by retaining the terminals if the small terminal lock tangs are not positioned properly.

Molded-on connectors require complete replacement of the connection. This means splicing a new connector assembly into the harness. All splices in on-board computer systems should be soldered to insure proper contact. Use care when probing the connections or replacing terminals in them as it is possible to short between opposite terminals. If this happens to the wrong terminal pair, it is possible to damage certain components. Always use jumper wires between connectors for circuit checking and never probe through weatherproof seals.

Open circuits are often difficult to locate by sight because corrosion or terminal misalignment are hidden by the connectors. Merely wiggling a connector on a sensor or in the wiring harness may correct the open circuit condition. This should always be considered when an open circuit or a failed sensor is indicated. Intermittent problems may also be caused by oxidized or loose connections. When using a circuit tester for diagnosis, always probe connections from the wire side. Be careful not to damage sealed connectors with test probes.

All wiring harnesses should be replaced with identical parts, using the same gauge wire and connectors. When signal wires are spliced into a harness, use wire with high temperature insulation only. With the low voltage and current levels found in the system, it is important that the best possible connection at all wire splices be made by soldering the splices together. It is seldom necessary to replace a complete harness. If replacement is necessary, pay close attention to insure proper harness routing.

Secure the harness with suitable plastic wire clamps to prevent vibrations from causing the harness to wear in spots or contact any hot components.

➡ **Weatherproof connectors cannot be replaced with standard connectors. Instructions are provided with replacement connector and terminal packages. Some wire harnesses have mounting indicators (usually pieces of colored tape) to mark where the harness is to be secured.**

In making wiring repairs, it's important that you always replace damaged wires with wires that are the same gauge as the wire being replaced. The heavier the wire, the smaller the gauge number. Wires are color-coded to aid in identification and whenever possible the same color coded wire should be used for replacement. A wire stripping and crimping tool is necessary to install solderless terminal connectors. Test all crimps by pulling on the wires; it should not be possible to pull the wires out of a good crimp.

Wires which are open, exposed or otherwise damaged are repaired by simple splicing. Where possible, if the wiring harness is accessible and the damaged place in the wire can be located, it is best to open the harness and check for all possible damage. In an inaccessible harness, the wire must be bypassed with a new insert, usually taped to the outside of the old harness.

When replacing fusible links, be sure to use fusible link wire, NOT ordinary automotive wire. Make sure the fusible segment is of the same gauge and construction as the one being replaced and double the stripped end when crimping the terminal connector for a good contact. The melted (open) fusible link segment of the wiring harness should be cut off as close to the harness as possible, then a new segment spliced in as described. In the case of a damaged fusible link that feeds two harness wires, the harness connections should be replaced with two fusible link wires so that each circuit will have its own separate protection.

➡ **Most of the problems caused in the wiring harness are due to bad ground connections. Always check all vehicle ground connections for corrosion or looseness before performing any power feed checks to eliminate the chance of a bad ground affecting the circuit.**

Repairing Hard Shell Connectors

Unlike molded connectors, the terminal contacts in hard shell connectors can be replaced. Weatherproof hard-shell connectors

with the leads molded into the shell have non-replaceable terminal ends. Replacement usually involves the use of a special terminal removal tool that depress the locking tangs (barbs) on the connector terminal and allow the connector to be removed from the rear of the shell. The connector shell should be replaced if it shows any evidence of burning, melting, cracks, or breaks. Replace individual terminals that are burnt, corroded, distorted or loose.

➡ **The insulation crimp must be tight to prevent the insulation from sliding back on the wire when the wire is pulled. The insulation must be visibly compressed under the crimp tabs, and the ends of the crimp should be turned in for a firm grip on the insulation.**

The wire crimp must be made with all wire strands inside the crimp. The terminal must be fully compressed on the wire strands with the ends of the crimp tabs turned in to make a firm grip on the wire. Check all connections with an ohmmeter to insure a good contact. There should be no measurable resistance between the wire and the terminal when connected.

Mechanical Test Equipment

Vacuum Gauge

Most gauges are graduated in inches of mercury (in.Hg), although a device called a manometer reads vacuum in inches of water (in. H_2O). The normal vacuum reading usually varies between 18 and 22 in.Hg at sea level. To test engine vacuum, the vacuum gauge must be connected to a source of manifold vacuum. Many engines have a plug in the intake manifold which can be removed and replaced with an adapter fitting. Connect the vacuum gauge to the fitting with a suitable rubber hose or, if no manifold plug is available, connect the vacuum gauge to any device using manifold vacuum, such as EGR valves, etc. The vacuum gauge can be used to determine if enough vacuum is reaching a component to allow its actuation.

Hand Vacuum Pump

Small, hand-held vacuum pumps come in a variety of designs. Most have a built-in vacuum gauge and allow the component to be tested without removing it from the vehicle. Operate the pump lever or plunger to apply the correct amount of vacuum required for the test specified in the diagnosis routines. The level of vacuum in inches of Mercury (in.Hg) is indicated on the

pump gauge. For some testing, an additional vacuum gauge may be necessary.

Intake manifold vacuum is used to operate various systems and devices on late model vehicles. To correctly diagnose and solve problems in vacuum control systems, a vacuum source is necessary for testing. In some cases, vacuum can be taken from the intake manifold when the engine is running, but vacuum is normally provided by a hand vacuum pump.

These hand vacuum pumps have a built-in vacuum gauge that allow testing while the device is still attached to the component. For some tests, an additional vacuum gauge may be necessary.

HEATER AND AIR CONDITIONING

Refer to Section 1 for discharging and charging of the air conditioning system.

The heating system provides heating, ventilation and defrosting for the windshield and side windows. The heater core is a heat exchanger supplied with coolant from the engine cooling system. Temperature is controlled by the temperature valve which moves an air door that directs air flow through the heater core for more heat or bypasses the heater core for less heat.

Vacuum actuators control the mode doors which direct air flow to the outlet ducts. The mode selector on the control panel directs engine vacuum to the actuators. The position of the mode doors determines whether air flows from the floor, panel, defrost or panel and defrost ducts (bi-level mode).

Blower Motor

REMOVAL & INSTALLATION

◆ SEE FIGS. 1-3

➡ **This procedure is for all cars, with or without air conditioning.**

1. Disconnect the negative cable at the battery.
2. Working inside the engine compartment, disconnect the blower motor electrical leads.
3. Remove the motor retaining screws, and remove the blower motor.
4. Reverse the removal process to install.

Heater Core

REMOVAL & INSTALLATION

Cars Without Air Conditioning

1. Disconnect the negative battery cable and drain the cooling system.

❄ CAUTION

When draining the coolant, keep in mind that cats and dogs are

attracted by the ethylene glycol antifreeze, and are quite likely to drink any that is left in an uncovered container or in puddles on the ground. This will prove fatal in sufficient quantity. Always drain the coolant into a sealable container. Coolant should be reused unless it is contaminated or several years old.

3. Disconnect the heater hoses from the heater core inlet and outlet connections in the engine compartment.
4. Blow residual coolant from the heater core using shop air.
5. Working inside the vehicle, remove the lower instrument panel sound insulator panel.
6. Remove the heater floor outlet duct screws or clips and remove the duct.
7. Remove the heater core cover by removing the attaching screws and clips.
8. Remove the heater core cover.
9. Remove the heater core retaining straps and remove the heater core.

To install:

10. Position the heater core in the housing and install the retaining straps.
11. Position the heater core cover on the housing and install the attaching screws and clips.
12. Install the floor outlet duct and attaching screws or clips.
13. Install the lower instrument panel sound insulator panel.
14. Working in the engine compartment, connect the heater core inlet and outlet hoses.
15. Fill the cooling system.
16. Start the engine and check for coolant leaks. Allow the engine to warm up sufficiently to confirm the proper operation of the heater. Recheck for leaks. Fill the cooling system.

Cars With Air Conditioning

1. Drain the cooling system.

❄ CAUTION

When draining the coolant, keep in mind that cats and dogs are

attracted by the ethylene glycol antifreeze, and are quite likely to drink any that is left in an uncovered container or in puddles on the ground. This will prove fatal in sufficient quantity. Always drain the coolant into a sealable container. Coolant should be reused unless it is contaminated or several years old.

2. On the diesel, raise and support the car on jackstands.
3. Disconnect the hoses at the core.
4. On the diesel, remove the instrument panel lower sound absorber.
5. Remove the heater duct and lower side covers.
6. Remove the lower heater outlet.
7. Remove the two housing cover-to-air valve housing clips.
8. Remove the housing cover.
9. Remove the core restraining straps.
10. Remove the core tubing retainers and lift out the core.
11. Reverse the above process to install the heater core.

Control Head

REMOVAL & INSTALLATION

1. Disconnect the negative battery cable.
2. Remove the radio knobs (if equipped) and the clock set knob (if equipped).
3. Remove the instrument bezel retaining screws.
4. Pull the bezel out to disconnect the rear defogger switch and the remote mirror control (if equipped).
5. Remove the instrument panel.
6. Remove the control head to dash screws and pull the head out.
7. Disconnect the electrical connectors and/or control cable(s) (if equipped), then remove the control head.
8. To install, reverse steps 1 through 7.

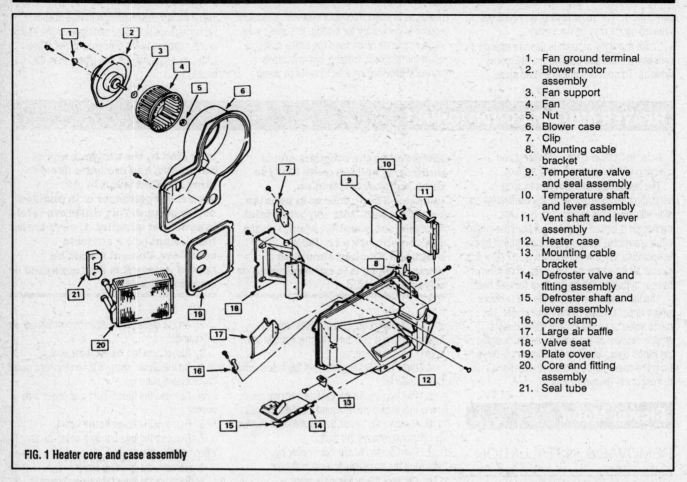

1. Fan ground terminal
2. Blower motor assembly
3. Fan support
4. Fan
5. Nut
6. Blower case
7. Clip
8. Mounting cable bracket
9. Temperature valve and seal assembly
10. Temperature shaft and lever assembly
11. Vent shaft and lever assembly
12. Heater case
13. Mounting cable bracket
14. Defroster valve and fitting assembly
15. Defroster shaft and lever assembly
16. Core clamp
17. Large air baffle
18. Valve seat
19. Plate cover
20. Core and fitting assembly
21. Seal tube

FIG. 1 Heater core and case assembly

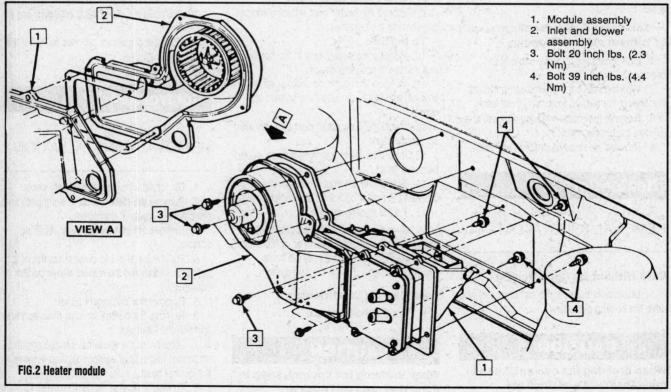

1. Module assembly
2. Inlet and blower assembly
3. Bolt 20 inch lbs. (2.3 Nm)
4. Bolt 39 inch lbs. (4.4 Nm)

VIEW A

FIG.2 Heater module

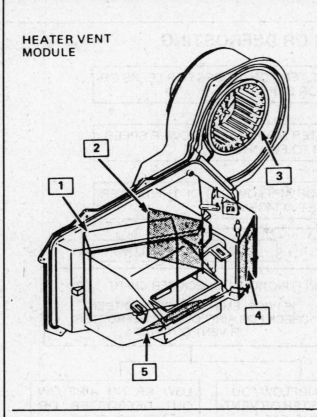

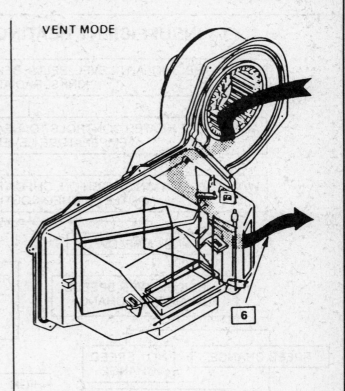

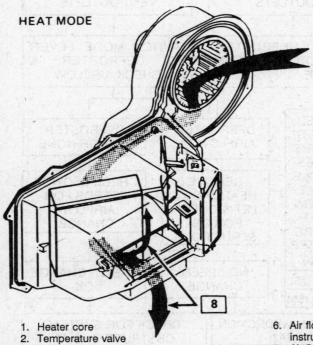

HEATER VENT MODULE

VENT MODE

HEAT MODE

DEFROST MODE

1. Heater core
2. Temperature valve
3. Blower
4. Vent valve
5. Defrost valve

6. Air flow through the instrument panel
7. Air flow to the windshield and heater outlet

8. Air flow to the windshield and heater outlet

FIG.3 Heater module air flow pattern

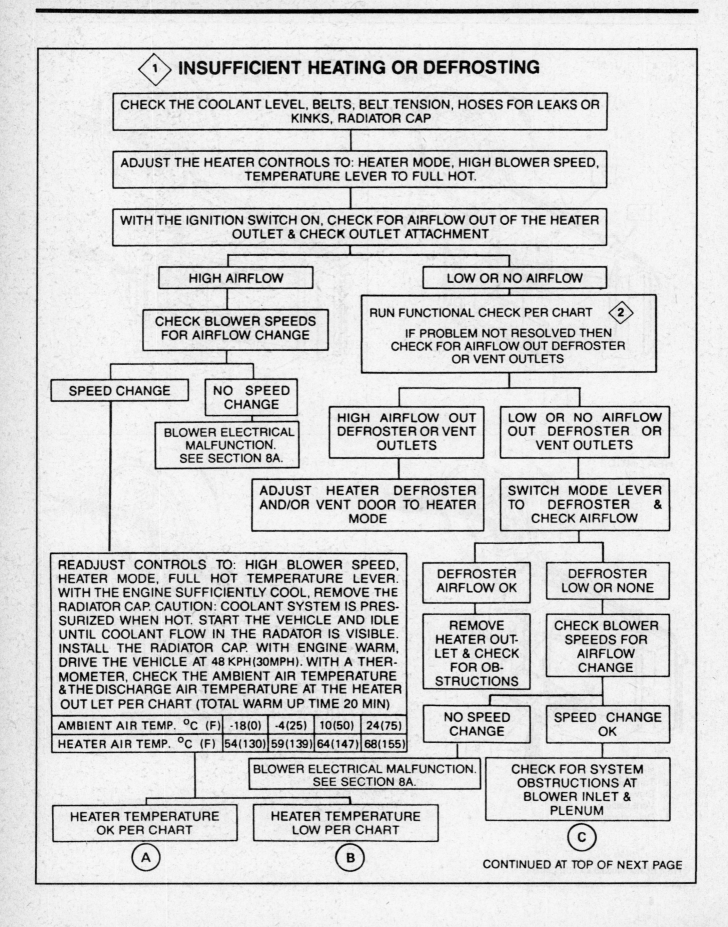

① **INSUFFICIENT HEATING OR DEFROSTING**

CHECK THE COOLANT LEVEL, BELTS, BELT TENSION, HOSES FOR LEAKS OR KINKS, RADIATOR CAP

ADJUST THE HEATER CONTROLS TO: HEATER MODE, HIGH BLOWER SPEED, TEMPERATURE LEVER TO FULL HOT.

WITH THE IGNITION SWITCH ON, CHECK FOR AIRFLOW OUT OF THE HEATER OUTLET & CHECK OUTLET ATTACHMENT

HIGH AIRFLOW

LOW OR NO AIRFLOW

CHECK BLOWER SPEEDS FOR AIRFLOW CHANGE

RUN FUNCTIONAL CHECK PER CHART ② IF PROBLEM NOT RESOLVED THEN CHECK FOR AIRFLOW OUT DEFROSTER OR VENT OUTLETS

SPEED CHANGE

NO SPEED CHANGE

BLOWER ELECTRICAL MALFUNCTION. SEE SECTION 8A.

HIGH AIRFLOW OUT DEFROSTER OR VENT OUTLETS

LOW OR NO AIRFLOW OUT DEFROSTER OR VENT OUTLETS

ADJUST HEATER DEFROSTER AND/OR VENT DOOR TO HEATER MODE

SWITCH MODE LEVER TO DEFROSTER & CHECK AIRFLOW

READJUST CONTROLS TO: HIGH BLOWER SPEED, HEATER MODE, FULL HOT TEMPERATURE LEVER. WITH THE ENGINE SUFFICIENTLY COOL, REMOVE THE RADIATOR CAP. CAUTION: COOLANT SYSTEM IS PRESSURIZED WHEN HOT. START THE VEHICLE AND IDLE UNTIL COOLANT FLOW IN THE RADATOR IS VISIBLE. INSTALL THE RADIATOR CAP. WITH ENGINE WARM, DRIVE THE VEHICLE AT 48 KPH(30MPH). WITH A THERMOMETER, CHECK THE AMBIENT AIR TEMPERATURE & THE DISCHARGE AIR TEMPERATURE AT THE HEATER OUT LET PER CHART (TOTAL WARM UP TIME 20 MIN)

AMBIENT AIR TEMP. °C (F)	-18(0)	-4(25)	10(50)	24(75)
HEATER AIR TEMP. °C (F)	54(130)	59(139)	64(147)	68(155)

DEFROSTER AIRFLOW OK

DEFROSTER LOW OR NONE

REMOVE HEATER OUTLET & CHECK FOR OBSTRUCTIONS

CHECK BLOWER SPEEDS FOR AIRFLOW CHANGE

NO SPEED CHANGE

SPEED CHANGE OK

BLOWER ELECTRICAL MALFUNCTION. SEE SECTION 8A.

CHECK FOR SYSTEM OBSTRUCTIONS AT BLOWER INLET & PLENUM

HEATER TEMPERATURE OK PER CHART

HEATER TEMPERATURE LOW PER CHART

Ⓐ

Ⓑ

Ⓒ

CONTINUED AT TOP OF NEXT PAGE

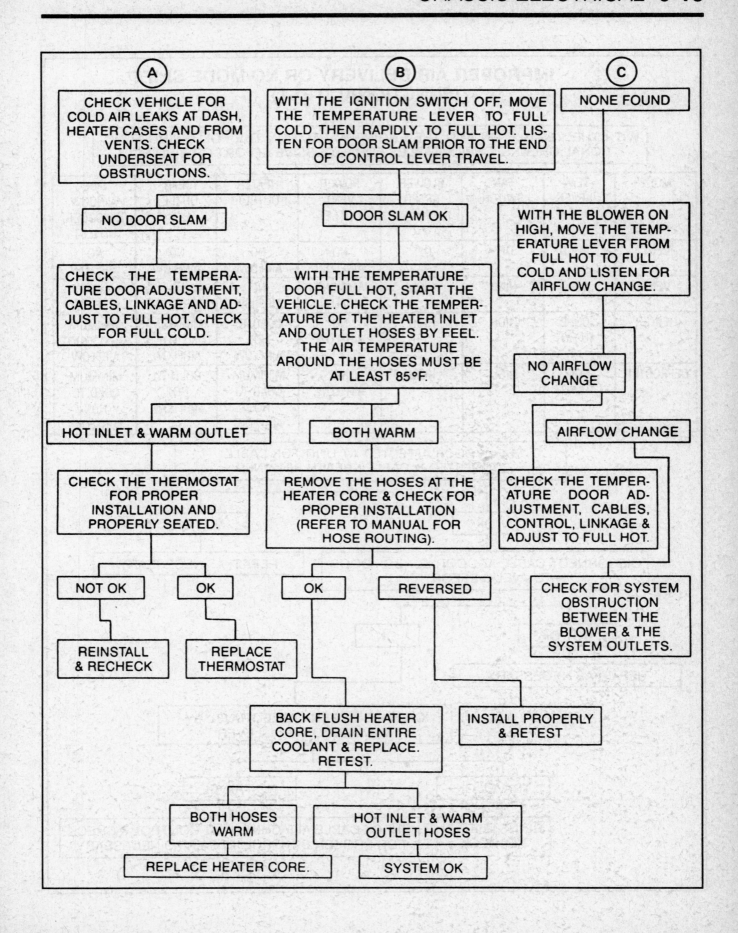

A

CHECK VEHICLE FOR COLD AIR LEAKS AT DASH, HEATER CASES AND FROM VENTS. CHECK UNDERSEAT FOR OBSTRUCTIONS.

B

WITH THE IGNITION SWITCH OFF, MOVE THE TEMPERATURE LEVER TO FULL COLD THEN RAPIDLY TO FULL HOT. LISTEN FOR DOOR SLAM PRIOR TO THE END OF CONTROL LEVER TRAVEL.

C

NONE FOUND

NO DOOR SLAM

DOOR SLAM OK

WITH THE BLOWER ON HIGH, MOVE THE TEMPERATURE LEVER FROM FULL HOT TO FULL COLD AND LISTEN FOR AIRFLOW CHANGE.

CHECK THE TEMPERATURE DOOR ADJUSTMENT, CABLES, LINKAGE AND ADJUST TO FULL HOT. CHECK FOR FULL COLD.

WITH THE TEMPERATURE DOOR FULL HOT, START THE VEHICLE. CHECK THE TEMPERATURE OF THE HEATER INLET AND OUTLET HOSES BY FEEL. THE AIR TEMPERATURE AROUND THE HOSES MUST BE AT LEAST 85°F.

NO AIRFLOW CHANGE

HOT INLET & WARM OUTLET

BOTH WARM

AIRFLOW CHANGE

CHECK THE THERMOSTAT FOR PROPER INSTALLATION AND PROPERLY SEATED.

REMOVE THE HOSES AT THE HEATER CORE & CHECK FOR PROPER INSTALLATION (REFER TO MANUAL FOR HOSE ROUTING).

CHECK THE TEMPERATURE DOOR ADJUSTMENT, CABLES, CONTROL, LINKAGE & ADJUST TO FULL HOT.

NOT OK

OK

OK

REVERSED

CHECK FOR SYSTEM OBSTRUCTION BETWEEN THE BLOWER & THE SYSTEM OUTLETS.

REINSTALL & RECHECK

REPLACE THERMOSTAT

BACK FLUSH HEATER CORE, DRAIN ENTIRE COOLANT & REPLACE. RETEST.

INSTALL PROPERLY & RETEST

BOTH HOSES WARM

HOT INLET & WARM OUTLET HOSES

REPLACE HEATER CORE.

SYSTEM OK

IMPROPER AIR DELIVERY OR NO MODE SHIFT (FUNCTIONAL TEST)

WITH THE VEHICLE ON AND THE ENGINE WARM, RUN THE FOLLOWING FUNC-TIONAL CHECKS. CHECK CABLES FOR EXCESSIVE EFFORT OR BINDING.

MODE	TEMP LEVER	FAN SWITCH	BLOWER SPEED	POWER VENT OUTLET	HEATER OUTLET	DEFR. OUTLET	SIDE WINDOW DEFOGGER OUTLET
VENT	COLD	OFF	OFF	NO AIRFLOW	NO AIRFLOW	NO AIRFLOW	NO AIRFLOW
VENT	COLD	HIGH	HIGH	AMBIENT AIRFLOW	NO AIRFLOW	NO AIRFLOW	NO AIRFLOW
HEATER	COLD TO HOT	HIGH	HIGH	NO AIRFLOW	COLD TO HOT AIRFLOW	MINIMUM COLD TO HOT AIRFLOW	MINIMUM COLD TO HOT AIRFLOW
DEFROSTER	COLD TO HOT	HIGH	HIGH	NO AIRFLOW	MINIMUM COLD TO HOT AIRFLOW	COLD TO HOT AIRFLOW	MINIMUM COLD TO HOT AIRFLOW

CHECK DOOR AFFECTED AT UNIT FOR CABLE CONNECTED & CABLE SHEATH RETAINED

OK

NOT OK

DISCONNECT CABLE AT DOOR &CHECK DOOR TRAVEL & EFFORT

REPAIR AS NECESSARY

NOT OK

OK

REPAIR AS NECESSARY

CHECK BOWDEN CABLE TRAVEL BY MOVING CONTROL LEVER

TRAVEL OK

NO TRAVEL

REINSTALL & RECHECK

CHECK CABLE ATTACHMENT AT CONTROL & CHECK FOR BROKEN CONTROL. REPAIR AS NECESSARY.

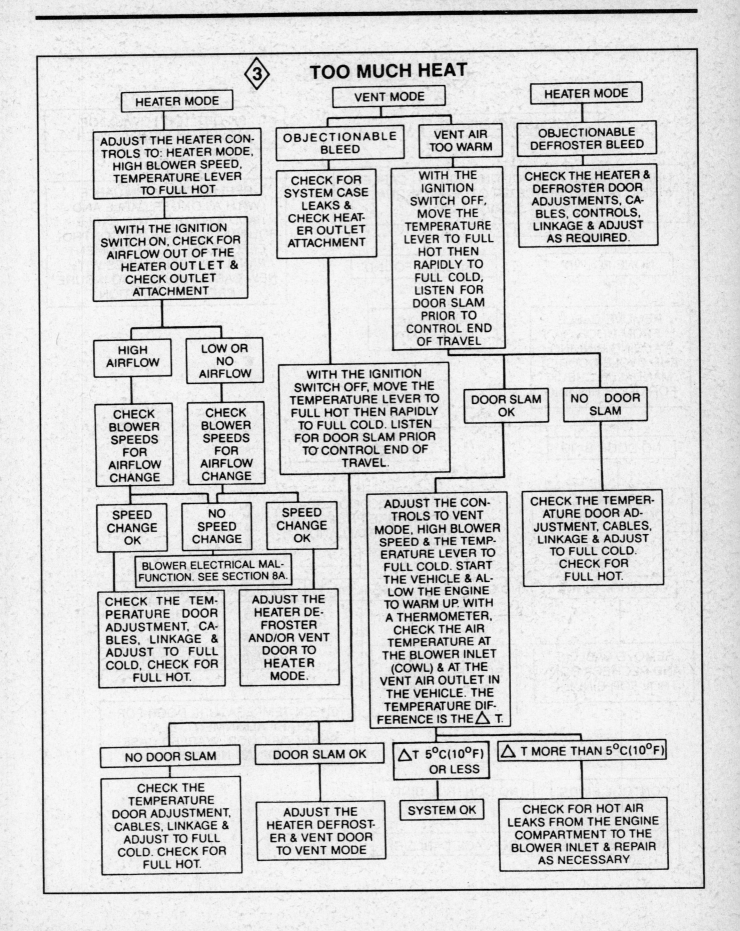

③ **TOO MUCH HEAT**

HEATER MODE

ADJUST THE HEATER CONTROLS TO: HEATER MODE, HIGH BLOWER SPEED, TEMPERATURE LEVER TO FULL HOT

WITH THE IGNITION SWITCH ON, CHECK FOR AIRFLOW OUT OF THE HEATER OUTLET & CHECK OUTLET ATTACHMENT

HIGH AIRFLOW

LOW OR NO AIRFLOW

CHECK BLOWER SPEEDS FOR AIRFLOW CHANGE

CHECK BLOWER SPEEDS FOR AIRFLOW CHANGE

SPEED CHANGE OK

NO SPEED CHANGE

SPEED CHANGE OK

BLOWER ELECTRICAL MALFUNCTION. SEE SECTION 8A.

CHECK THE TEMPERATURE DOOR ADJUSTMENT, CABLES, LINKAGE & ADJUST TO FULL COLD, CHECK FOR FULL HOT.

ADJUST THE HEATER DEFROSTER AND/OR VENT DOOR TO HEATER MODE.

VENT MODE

OBJECTIONABLE BLEED

CHECK FOR SYSTEM CASE LEAKS & CHECK HEATER OUTLET ATTACHMENT

WITH THE IGNITION SWITCH OFF, MOVE THE TEMPERATURE LEVER TO FULL HOT THEN RAPIDLY TO FULL COLD. LISTEN FOR DOOR SLAM PRIOR TO CONTROL END OF TRAVEL.

VENT AIR TOO WARM

WITH THE IGNITION SWITCH OFF, MOVE THE TEMPERATURE LEVER TO FULL HOT THEN RAPIDLY TO FULL COLD, LISTEN FOR DOOR SLAM PRIOR TO CONTROL END OF TRAVEL

DOOR SLAM OK

NO DOOR SLAM

ADJUST THE CONTROLS TO VENT MODE, HIGH BLOWER SPEED & THE TEMPERATURE LEVER TO FULL COLD. START THE VEHICLE & ALLOW THE ENGINE TO WARM UP. WITH A THERMOMETER, CHECK THE AIR TEMPERATURE AT THE BLOWER INLET (COWL) & AT THE VENT AIR OUTLET IN THE VEHICLE. THE TEMPERATURE DIFFERENCE IS THE △ T.

HEATER MODE

OBJECTIONABLE DEFROSTER BLEED

CHECK THE HEATER & DEFROSTER DOOR ADJUSTMENTS, CABLES, CONTROLS, LINKAGE & ADJUST AS REQUIRED.

CHECK THE TEMPERATURE DOOR ADJUSTMENT, CABLES, LINKAGE & ADJUST TO FULL COLD. CHECK FOR FULL HOT.

NO DOOR SLAM

CHECK THE TEMPERATURE DOOR ADJUSTMENT, CABLES, LINKAGE & ADJUST TO FULL COLD. CHECK FOR FULL HOT.

DOOR SLAM OK

ADJUST THE HEATER DEFROSTER & VENT DOOR TO VENT MODE

△T 5°C(10°F) OR LESS

SYSTEM OK

△ T MORE THAN 5°C(10°F)

CHECK FOR HOT AIR LEAKS FROM THE ENGINE COMPARTMENT TO THE BLOWER INLET & REPAIR AS NECESSARY

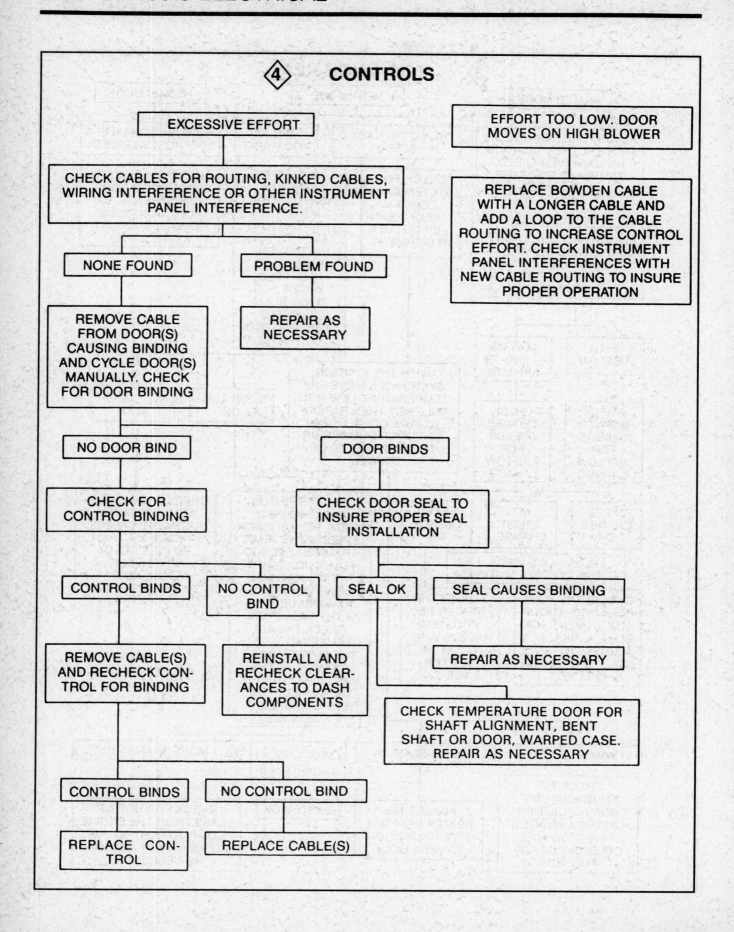

◆4◆ **CONTROLS**

EXCESSIVE EFFORT

EFFORT TOO LOW. DOOR MOVES ON HIGH BLOWER

CHECK CABLES FOR ROUTING, KINKED CABLES, WIRING INTERFERENCE OR OTHER INSTRUMENT PANEL INTERFERENCE.

REPLACE BOWDEN CABLE WITH A LONGER CABLE AND ADD A LOOP TO THE CABLE ROUTING TO INCREASE CONTROL EFFORT. CHECK INSTRUMENT PANEL INTERFERENCES WITH NEW CABLE ROUTING TO INSURE PROPER OPERATION

NONE FOUND

PROBLEM FOUND

REMOVE CABLE FROM DOOR(S) CAUSING BINDING AND CYCLE DOOR(S) MANUALLY. CHECK FOR DOOR BINDING

REPAIR AS NECESSARY

NO DOOR BIND

DOOR BINDS

CHECK FOR CONTROL BINDING

CHECK DOOR SEAL TO INSURE PROPER SEAL INSTALLATION

CONTROL BINDS

NO CONTROL BIND

SEAL OK

SEAL CAUSES BINDING

REMOVE CABLE(S) AND RECHECK CONTROL FOR BINDING

REINSTALL AND RECHECK CLEARANCES TO DASH COMPONENTS

REPAIR AS NECESSARY

CHECK TEMPERATURE DOOR FOR SHAFT ALIGNMENT, BENT SHAFT OR DOOR, WARPED CASE. REPAIR AS NECESSARY

CONTROL BINDS

NO CONTROL BIND

REPLACE CONTROL

REPLACE CABLE(S)

BLOWER NOISE

CHECK ALL ELECTRICAL CONNECTIONS AND GROUNDS FOR PROPER CONNECTIONS
IF IN DOUBT, USE A VOLTMETER TO CHECK FOR CONSTANT VOLTAGE
AT THE BLOWER MOTOR.

SIT IN THE VEHICLE WITH THE DOORS AND WINDOWS CLOSED. WITH THE IGNITION ON
AND THE ENGINE OFF, START WITH THE BLOWER ON HIGH, IN VENT MODE AND THE
TEMPERATURE LEVER ON FULL COLD. CYCLE THROUGH BLOWER SPEEDS, MODES AND
TEMPERATURE DOOR POSITIONS TO FIND WHERE THE NOISE OCCURS AND WHERE THE
NOISE DOES NOT OCCUR. TRY TO DEFINE THE TYPE OF NOISE: AIR RUSH, WHINE,
TICK/CLICK, SQUEAL/SCREECH, FLUTTER, RUMBLE OR SCRAPING NOISE. CHART
BELOW SHOULD BE COMPLETELY FILLED IN AT COMPLETION.

A CONSTANT AIR RUSH NOISE IS TYPICAL OF ALL SYSTEMS ON HIGH BLOWER. SOME
SYSTEMS AND MODES (USUALLY DEFROSTER) MAY BE WORSE THAN OTHERS. CHECK
ANOTHER VEHICLE IF POSSIBLE (SAME MODEL) TO DETERMINE IF THE NOISE IS
TYPICAL OF THE SYSTEM AS DESIGNED.

INDICATE THE TYPE OF NOISE AND WHERE IT OCCURS:

	VENT		HEATER		DEFROST	
	FULL COLD	FULL HOT	FULL COLD	FULL HOT	FULL COLD	FULL HOT
LOW BLOWER						
M2						
M3						
HIGH BLOWER						

A—WHINE, B—CLICK/TICK, C—SQUEAL/SCREECH, D—FLUTTER, E—RUMBLE,
F—SCRAPING, G—AIR RUSH, H—OTHER, DESCRIBE _____

1. NOISE IS CONSTANT
BUT LESSENS WITH
BLOWER SPEED REDUC-
TION. TYPICAL NOISES
ARE WHINE, TICK/CLICK
FLUTTER OR
SCRAPING NOISE.

2. NOISE IS AT START-UP
ONLY OR IS INTERMITTANT.
MAY OCCUR AT COLD AM-
BIENTS AND LOW BLOWER
SPEEDS. TYPICAL NOISE
IS AN OBJECTIONABLE
SQUEAL/SCREECH.

3. NOISE IS CONSTANT AT HIGH
BLOWER SPEEDS WITH SOME
DOOR COMBINATIONS BUT CAN
BE ELIMINATED AT LOWER
BLOWER SPEEDS OR WITH
OTHER DOOR COMBINATIONS.
TYPICAL NOISES ARE
FLUTTER OR RUMBLE

 L

M

CONTINUED AT TOP OF NEXT PAGE

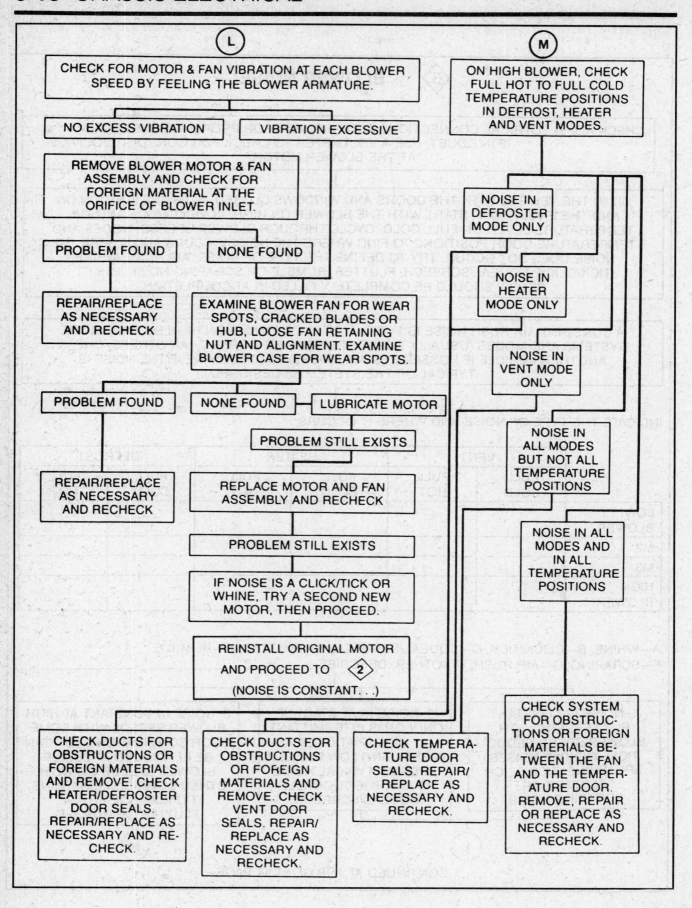

(L)

CHECK FOR MOTOR & FAN VIBRATION AT EACH BLOWER SPEED BY FEELING THE BLOWER ARMATURE.

NO EXCESS VIBRATION

VIBRATION EXCESSIVE

REMOVE BLOWER MOTOR & FAN ASSEMBLY AND CHECK FOR FOREIGN MATERIAL AT THE ORIFICE OF BLOWER INLET.

PROBLEM FOUND

NONE FOUND

REPAIR/REPLACE AS NECESSARY AND RECHECK

EXAMINE BLOWER FAN FOR WEAR SPOTS, CRACKED BLADES OR HUB, LOOSE FAN RETAINING NUT AND ALIGNMENT. EXAMINE BLOWER CASE FOR WEAR SPOTS.

PROBLEM FOUND

NONE FOUND

LUBRICATE MOTOR

REPAIR/REPLACE AS NECESSARY AND RECHECK

PROBLEM STILL EXISTS

REPLACE MOTOR AND FAN ASSEMBLY AND RECHECK

PROBLEM STILL EXISTS

IF NOISE IS A CLICK/TICK OR WHINE, TRY A SECOND NEW MOTOR, THEN PROCEED.

REINSTALL ORIGINAL MOTOR AND PROCEED TO ⟨2⟩

(NOISE IS CONSTANT. . .)

(M)

ON HIGH BLOWER, CHECK FULL HOT TO FULL COLD TEMPERATURE POSITIONS IN DEFROST, HEATER AND VENT MODES.

NOISE IN DEFROSTER MODE ONLY

NOISE IN HEATER MODE ONLY

NOISE IN VENT MODE ONLY

NOISE IN ALL MODES BUT NOT ALL TEMPERATURE POSITIONS

NOISE IN ALL MODES AND IN ALL TEMPERATURE POSITIONS

CHECK DUCTS FOR OBSTRUCTIONS OR FOREIGN MATERIALS AND REMOVE. CHECK HEATER/DEFROSTER DOOR SEALS. REPAIR/REPLACE AS NECESSARY AND RE-CHECK.

CHECK DUCTS FOR OBSTRUCTIONS OR FOREIGN MATERIALS AND REMOVE. CHECK VENT DOOR SEALS. REPAIR/REPLACE AS NECESSARY AND RECHECK.

CHECK TEMPERA-TURE DOOR SEALS. REPAIR/REPLACE AS NECESSARY AND RECHECK.

CHECK SYSTEM FOR OBSTRUCTIONS OR FOREIGN MATERIALS BE-TWEEN THE FAN AND THE TEMPER-ATURE DOOR. REMOVE, REPAIR OR REPLACE AS NECESSARY AND RECHECK.

AIR CONDITIONER

The heater and air conditioning systems are controlled manually or electronically. The systems differ mainly in the way air temperature and the routing of air flow are controlled. The manual system controls air temperature through a cable-actuated lever and air flow through a vacuum switching valve and vacuum actuators. With Electronic Climate Control (ECC) systems, both temperature and air flow are controlled by the BCM through the Climate Control Panel (CCP).

There are 2 types of compressors used on front wheel drive car air conditioning systems. The HR-6 compressor, used on Cycling Clutch Orifice Tube (CCOT) systems, is a 6 cylinder axial compressor consisting of 3 double-ended pistons actuated by a swash plate shaft assembly. The compressor cycles on and off according to system demands. The compressor driveshaft is driven by the serpentine belt when the electro-magnetic clutch is engaged.

The V-5 compressor, used on Variable Displacement Orifice Tube (VDOT) systems, is designed to meet the demands of the air conditioning system without cycling. The compressor employs a variable angle wobble plate controlling the displacement of 5 axially oriented cylinders. Displacement is controlled by a bellows actuated control valve located in the rear head of the compressor. The electro-magnetic compressor clutch connects the compressor shaft to the serpentine drive belt when the coil is energized.

Service Valve Locations

Refer to Section 1 for discharging and charging of the air conditioning system.

The high-side service valve is normally located in the refrigerant line near the discharge fitting of the compressor.

The low-side service valve is normally located on the accumulator or in the condenser-to-evaporator refrigerant line.

Compressor

REMOVAL & INSTALLATION

♦ SEE FIGS. 4 & 5
1. Disconnect the negative battery cable.

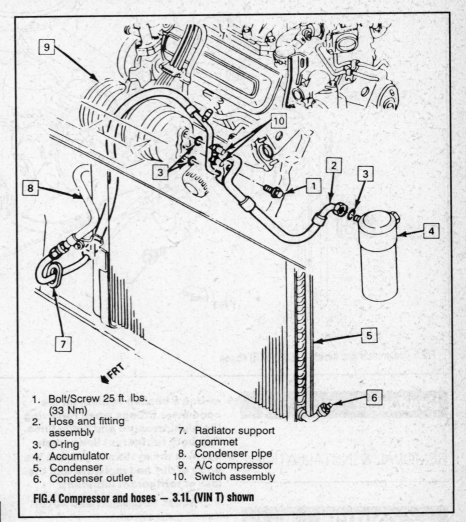

1. Bolt/Screw 25 ft. lbs. (33 Nm)
2. Hose and fitting assembly
3. O-ring
4. Accumulator
5. Condenser
6. Condenser outlet
7. Radiator support grommet
8. Condenser pipe
9. A/C compressor
10. Switch assembly

FIG.4 Compressor and hoses — 3.1L (VIN T) shown

2. Disconnect the electrical connectors from the compressor.
3. Properly discharge the air conditioning system.
4. Remove the coupled hose assembly from the rear of the compressor. Discard the O-rings.

➡ **Cap the refrigerant lines when opening the system to prevent the entry of dirt and moisture and the loss of refrigerant lubricant.**

5. Release the drive belt tension and remove the belt from the compressor.
6. Remove the compressor attaching bolts.
7. Remove the compressor.
8. Drain and measure the refrigerant oil from the compressor. Discard the old oil.

To Install:

9. If the compressor is to be replaced, drain the oil from the new compressor and discard. Add new refrigerant oil equivalent to the amount that was drained from the compressor upon removal.
10. Position the compressor in the vehicle.
11. Install the compressor attaching bolts.
12. Install new O-rings to the coupled hose assembly. Lubricate the O-rings with refrigerant oil.
13. Install the coupled hose assembly to the back of the compressor.
14. Install the drive belt.
15. Connect the electrical connectors to the compressor.
16. Evacuate, recharge and leak test the system.
17. Connect negative battery cable.

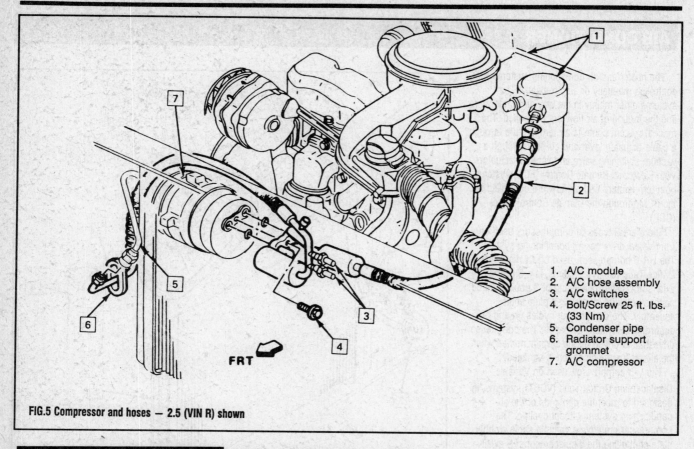

1. A/C module
2. A/C hose assembly
3. A/C switches
4. Bolt/Screw 25 ft. lbs. (33 Nm)
5. Condenser pipe
6. Radiator support grommet
7. A/C compressor

FIG.5 Compressor and hoses — 2.5 (VIN R) shown

Condenser

REMOVAL & INSTALLATION

❋❋ CAUTION

Some vehicles are equipped with the Supplemental Inflatable Restraint or air bag system. The air bag system must be disabled before performing service on or around the air bag, instrument panel components, wiring and sensors. Failure to follow safety and disabling procedures could result in accidental air bag deployment, possible personal injury and unnecessary air bag system repairs.

1. Properly discharge the air conditioning system.
2. Disconnect the high-pressure and liquid lines at the condenser fittings. Discard the O-rings.

➡ **Use a backup wrench on the condenser fittings when removing the high-pressure and liquid lines. Cap both refrigerant lines when opening the system to prevent the entry of dirt and moisture and the loss of refrigerant lubricant.**

3. Remove the condenser attaching bolts from the center support.
4. Remove the engine strut bracket and upper radiator support. Lean radiator back.
5. Remove the condenser.

To install:
6. Position the condenser in the vehicle.

➡ **If replacing the condenser or if the original condenser was flushed during service, add 1 fluid oz. (30ml) of refrigerant lubricant to the system.**

7. Install the upper radiator support and engine strut bracket.
8. Install the condenser attaching bolts.
9. Replace the condenser fitting O-rings. Lubricate the O-rings with refrigerant oil.
10. Connect the condenser high-pressure and liquid lines.

➡ **Use a backup wrench on the condenser fittings when tightening lines.**

11. Evacuate, charge and leak test the system.

Blower Motor

REMOVAL & INSTALLATION

♦ SEE FIG. 7

EXCEPT 1991–92 CENTURY AND CUTLASS CIERA AND CRUISER

1. Disconnect the negative battery cable.
2. Disconnect the electrical connections at the blower motor.
3. Remove the bolts attaching the blower motor to the evaporator case.
4. Remove the blower motor.

➡ **If equipped with 2.8L or 3.1L MPI engines, it may be necessary to rotate the alternator away in order to completely remove the blower motor.**

To install:
5. Position the blower motor in the evaporator case and install the attaching bolts.
6. Connect the electrical connectors at the blower motor.

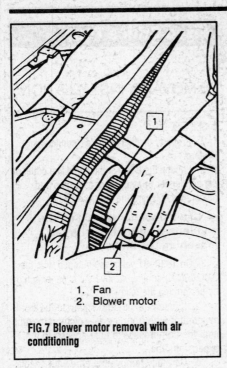

1. Fan
2. Blower motor

FIG.7 Blower motor removal with air conditioning

7. Connect the negative battery cable.

1991–92 CENTURY AND CUTLASS CIERA AND CRUISER

1. Disconnect the negative battery cable.
2. Remove the wiper arms.
3. Remove the cowl panel.
4. Disconnect the blower motor electrical connector and vent tube.
5. Remove the blower motor attaching screws.
6. Remove the fan retaining nut from the blower motor shaft through the plenum opening.
7. Remove the fan from the blower motor while removing the blower motor from the vehicle.

To install:
8. Holding the fan through the plenum opening, position the blower motor in the evaporator housing while installing the fan to the blower motor.
9. Install the fan retaining nut to the blower motor shaft through the plenum opening.
10. Install the blower motor attaching screws.
11. Connect the electrical connector and vent tube.
12. Install the cowl panel.
13. Install the wiper arms.
14. Connect the negative battery cable.

Blower Motor Resistor/Power Module

REMOVAL & INSTALLATION

1. Disconnect the negative battery cable.
2. Disconnect the electrical connector at the resistor.
3. Remove the resistor attaching screws.
4. Remove the resistor from the evaporator case.

To install:
5. Position the resistor in the evaporator case. Install the attaching screws.
6. Connect the electrical connector.
7. Connect the negative battery cable.

Evaporator

REMOVAL & INSTALLATION

❄❄ CAUTION

Some vehicles are equipped with the Supplemental Inflatable Restraint or air bag system. The air bag system must be disabled before performing service on or around the air bag, instrument panel components, wiring and sensors. Failure to follow safety and disabling procedures could result in accidental air bag deployment, possible personal injury and unnecessary air bag system repairs.

1. Disconnect the negative battery cable.
2. Remove the air cleaner.
3. Properly discharge the air conditioning system.
4. Disconnect the module electrical connectors, disconnect the harness straps and move the harness aside.
5. Remove the heater hose routing bracket from the back of the cover.
6. Disconnect the liquid line at the evaporator inlet and low pressure line at the evaporator outlet.

➡ Cap the refrigerant lines when opening the system to prevent the entry of dirt and moisture and the loss of refrigerant lubricant.

7. Remove the blower motor resistor from the top of the cover.
8. Disconnect the blower motor electrical connector.
9. If equipped with the 2.8L MPI engine, remove the alternator bracket bolts, alternator rear brace bolt, alternator pivot bolt and move the alternator away from the module.
10. Remove the evaporator core.

To install:
➡ If replacing the evaporator or if the original evaporator was flushed during service, add 2–3 fluid oz. (60–90ml) of refrigerant lubricant to the system.

11. Clean the old gasket material from the cowl.
12. Install the evaporator core in the module.
13. Apply permagum sealer to the case and install the cover using a new gasket.
14. Install the cover attaching screws.
15. If equipped with the 2.8L MPI engine, position the alternator and install the pivot bolts, rear brace bolt and alternator bracket bolts.
16. Connect the blower motor electrical connector.
17. Install the resistor to the top of the cover.
18. Install new O-rings to the liquid and low pressure lines. Lubricate O-rings with refrigerant oil.
19. Connect the liquid line at the evaporator inlet and low pressure line at the evaporator outlet.
20. Install the heater hose routing bracket to the cover.
21. Route the cowl harness in the straps and connect the module electrical connectors.
22. Evacuate, recharge and leak test the system.
23. Connect the negative battery cable.

Evaporator Core

REMOVAL & INSTALLATION

1. Disconnect the negative battery cable.
2. Discharge the A/C system.

❄ CAUTION

When discharging, evacuating and charging the A/C system, please refer to Section 1 and be aware of all precautions of handling refrigerant.

3. Remove the module's rubber seal and screen.

4. Remove the right windshield wiper arm.

5. Remove the diagnostic connector, the high blower relay and the thermostatic switch.

6. Disconnect the electrical connectors from the module.

7. Remove the module's top cover.

8. Remove the accumulator bracket screws.

9. Disconnect and tape the refrigerant lines at the accumulator and liquid line.

10. Remove the evaporator core.

11. When installing, use new sealing material. When connecting the refrigerant lines, use new O-rings dipped in clean refrigerant oil and charge the A/C system. Refer to Section 1 for proper charging procedure.

Accumulator

REMOVAL & INSTALLATION

1. Disconnect the negative battery cable.

2. Properly discharge the air conditioning system.

3. Disconnect the low-pressure lines at the inlet and outlet fittings on the accumulator.

➡ Cap the refrigerant lines when opening the system to prevent the entry of dirt and moisture and the loss of refrigerant lubricant.

4. Disconnect the pressure cycling switch connection and remove the switch, as required.

5. Loosen the lower strap bolt and spread the strap. Turn the accumulator and remove.

6. Drain and measure the oil in the accumulator. Discard the old oil.

To install:

7. Add new oil equivalent to the amount drained from the old accumulator. Add an additional 2–3 oz. (60–90ml) of oil to compensate for the oil retained by the accumulator dessicant.

8. Position the accumulator in the securing bracket and tighten the clamp bolt.

9. Install new O-rings at the inlet and outlet connections on the accumulator. Lubricate the O-rings with refrigerant oil.

10. Connect the low-pressure inlet and outlet lines.

11. Evacuate, charge and leak test the system.

12. Connect the negative battery cable.

Refrigerant Lines

REMOVAL & INSTALLATION

▶ SEE FIG. 8

1. Disconnect the negative battery cable.

2. Properly discharge the air conditioning system.

3. Disconnect the refrigerant line connectors, using a backup wrench as required.

4. Remove refrigerant line support or routing brackets, as required.

5. Remove refrigerant line.

To install:

6. Position new refrigerant line in place, leaving protective caps installed until ready to connect.

7. Install new O-rings on refrigerant line connector fittings. Lubricate with refrigerant oil.

8. Connect refrigerant line, using a backup wrench, as required.

9. Install refrigerant line support or routing brackets, as required.

10. Evacuate, recharge and leak test the system.

11. Connect the negative battery cable.

Fixed Orifice Tube

REMOVAL & INSTALLATION

▶ SEE FIG. 9

1. Properly discharge the air conditioning system.

2. Loosen the fitting at the liquid line outlet on the condenser or evaporator inlet pipe and disconnect. Discard the O-ring.

➡ Use a backup wrench on the condenser outlet fitting when loosening the lines.

3. On 1990–91 vehicles equipped with the 2.0L (VIN K) engine, remove the expansion tube by performing the following:

a. Loosen the nut and separate the front evaporator tube from the rear evaporator tube near the compressor to gain access to the expansion tube.

b. Carefully remove the tube with needle-nose pliers or special tool J–26549D.

c. Inspect the tube for contamination or metal cuttings.

4. Carefully, remove the fixed orifice tube from the tube fitting in the evaporator inlet line.

5. In the event that the restricted or plugged orifice tube is difficult to remove, perform the following:

a. Remove as much of the impacted residue as possible.

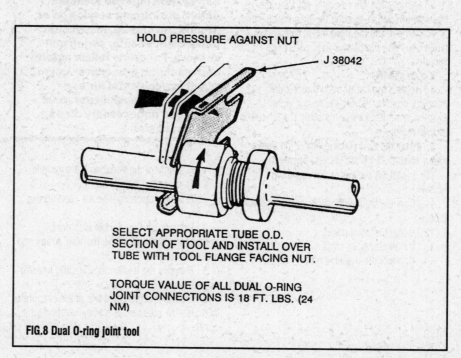

HOLD PRESSURE AGAINST NUT

J 38042

SELECT APPROPRIATE TUBE O.D. SECTION OF TOOL AND INSTALL OVER TUBE WITH TOOL FLANGE FACING NUT.

TORQUE VALUE OF ALL DUAL O-RING JOINT CONNECTIONS IS 18 FT. LBS. (24 NM)

FIG.8 Dual O-ring joint tool

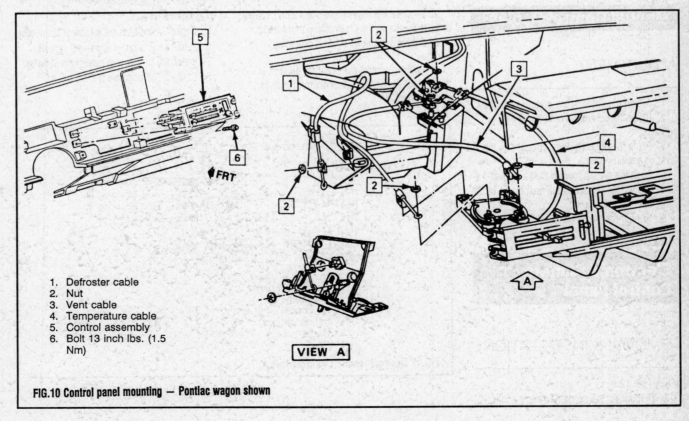

1. Expansion (orifice) tube
2. O-ring
3. Short screen (outlet-install towards evaporator)
4. Long screen (inlet-install towards condenser)

FIG.9 Orifice tube and location

b. Using a hair dryer, epoxy drier or equivalent, carefully apply heat approximately 1/4 in. (6mm) from the dimples on the inlet pipe. Do not overheat the pipe.

➡ **If the system has a pressure switch near the orifice tube, it should be removed prior to heating the pipe to avoid damage to the switch.**

c. While applying heat, use special tool J 26549–C or equivalent to grip the orifice tube. Use a turning motion along with a push-pull motion to loosen the impacted orifice tube and remove it.

6. Swab the inside of the evaporator inlet pipe with R-11 to remove any remaining residue.

7. Add 1 oz. of 525 viscosity refrigerant oil to the system.

8. Lubricate the new O-ring and orifice tube with refrigerant oil and insert into the inlet pipe.

➡ **Ensure that the new orifice tube is inserted in the inlet tube with the smaller screen end first.**

9. Connect the evaporator inlet pipe with the condenser outlet fitting.

➡ **Use a backup wrench on the condenser outlet fitting when tightening the lines.**

10. Evacuate, recharge and leak test the system.

Manual Control Head

REMOVAL & INSTALLATION

▶ SEE FIGS. 10 & 11

1. Disconnect the negative battery cable.
2. Remove the hush panel, as required.
3. Remove the instrument panel trim plate.
4. Remove the control head attaching screws and pull the control head out.
5. Disconnect the electrical and vacuum connectors at the back of the control head. Disconnect the temperature control cable.
6. Remove the control head.

To install:

7. Position control head near the mounting location. Connect the electrical and vacuum connectors and cables to the back of the control head. Connect the temperature control.
8. Install the control head and attaching screws.
9. Install the instrument panel trim plate.
10. Install the hush panel, if removed.
11. Connect the negative battery cable.

1. Defroster cable
2. Nut
3. Vent cable
4. Temperature cable
5. Control assembly
6. Bolt 13 inch lbs. (1.5 Nm)

VIEW A

FIG.10 Control panel mounting — Pontiac wagon shown

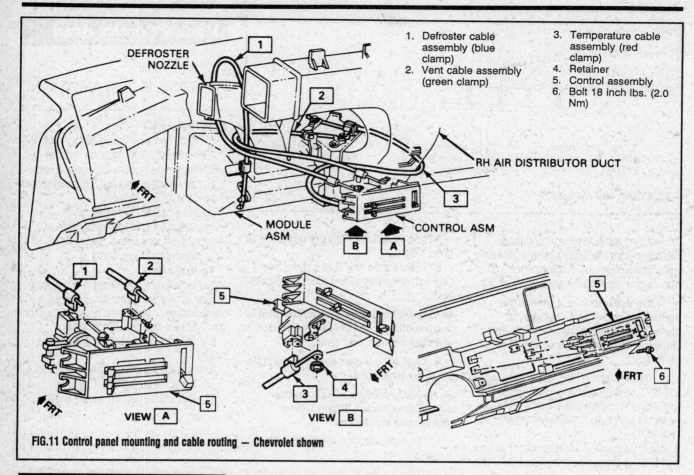

1. Defroster cable assembly (blue clamp)
2. Vent cable assembly (green clamp)
3. Temperature cable assembly (red clamp)
4. Retainer
5. Control assembly
6. Bolt 18 inch lbs. (2.0 Nm)

FIG.11 Control panel mounting and cable routing — Chevrolet shown

Manual Control Cables

ADJUSTMENT

1. Attach the cable to the control assembly.
2. Place the control lever in the **OFF** position.
3. Place the opposite loop of cable on the lever or actuator post.
4. Push the sheath toward the lever until the lever or actuator seats and the lash is out of the cable and control.
5. Tighten the screw to secure the cable.

Electronic Climate Control Panel

REMOVAL & INSTALLATION

◆ SEE FIG. 12

1. Disconnect the negative battery cable.

2. Remove the instrument panel trim plate(s) to gain access to the electronic control panel.
3. Remove the control panel attaching screws.
4. Pull the control panel out far enough to disconnect the electrical connector. Remove control panel.

To install:

5. Connect control panel electrical connector.
6. Install control panel attaching screws.
7. Install the instrument panel trim plate(s).
8. Connect the negative battery cable.

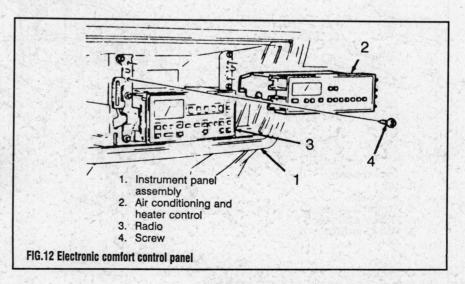

1. Instrument panel assembly
2. Air conditioning and heater control
3. Radio
4. Screw

FIG.12 Electronic comfort control panel

High-Pressure Compressor Cut-Off Switch

The function of the switch is to protect the engine from overheating in the event of excessively high compressor head pressure and to deenergize the compressor clutch before the high pressure relief valve discharge pressure is reached. The switch is mounted on the back of the compressor or on the refrigerant hose assembly near the back of the compressor. Servicing a switch mounted on the back of the compressor requires that the system be discharged. Switches mounted on the coupled hose assembly are mounted on Schrader-type valves and do not require discharging the system to be serviced.

REMOVAL & INSTALLATION

➡ SEE FIG. 6

Compressor-Mounted Switch

➡ **The system must be discharged in order to service the high pressure relief switch mounted to the back of the compressor.**

1. Disconnect the negative battery cable.
2. Properly discharge the air conditioning system.
3. Remove the coupled hose assembly at the rear of the compressor.
4. Disconnect the electrical connector.
5. Remove the switch retaining ring using internal snapring pliers.
6. Remove the switch from the compressor. Discard the O-ring.

To install:

7. Lubricate a new O-ring with refrigerant oil. Insert into the switch cavity.
8. Lubricate the control switch housing with clean refrigerant oil and insert the switch until it bottoms in the cavity.
9. Install the switch retaining snapring with the high point of the curved sides adjacent to the switch housing. Ensure that the retaining ring is properly seated in the switch cavity retaining groove.
10. Connect the electrical connector.
11. Lubricate new coupled hose assembly O-rings with refrigerant oil. Install on the hose assembly fittings.
12. Connect the coupled hose assembly to the compressor.

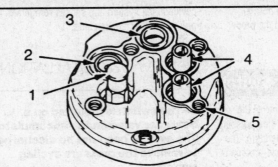

FIG.6 Compressor high and low pressure switch locations — 2.8L (VIN W) shown

1. Pressure relief valve
2. Discharge port
3. Suction port
4. Control switches
5. Mounting boss

13. Evacuate, recharge and leak test the system.
14. Connect the negative battery cable.
15. Operate the system to ensure proper operation and leak test the switch.

Refrigerant Line-Mounted Switch

➡ **The switch is mounted on a Schrader-type valve and does not require that the system be discharged.**

1. Disconnect the negative battery cable.
2. Disconnect the electrical connector.
3. Remove the switch from the coupled hose assembly. Discard the O-ring.

To install:

4. Lubricate a new O-ring with refrigerant oil.
5. Install the O-ring on the switch and install the switch.
6. Connect the electrical connector.
7. Connect the negative battery cable.

Low-Pressure Compressor Cut-Off Switch

The function of the switch is to protect the compressor by deenergizing the compressor in the event of a low-charge condition. The switch may be mounted at the back of the compressor or on the coupled hose assembly near the compressor. Servicing the valve requires discharging the system.

REMOVAL & INSTALLATION

1. Disconnect the negative battery cable.
2. Properly discharge the air conditioning system.

3. Disconnect the electrical connector(s).
4. If the switch is mounted to the rear head of the compressor, remove the coupled hose assembly to gain access to the switch. Remove the switch.
5. If the switch is mounted to the coupled hose assembly, remove the switch from its mounting position.

To install:

6. Install the switch.
7. Lubricate new O-rings with refrigerant oil.
8. If the switch is mounted to the rear head of the compressor, install the switch. Install new O-rings on the coupled hose assembly and install the assembly to the back of the compressor.
9. If the switch is mounted on the coupled hose assembly, install the switch.
10. Connect the electrical connector(s).
11. Evacuate, charge and leak test the system.
12. Connect the negative battery cable.

Idle Speed Power Steering Pressure Switch

Engine idle speed is maintained by cutting off the compressor when high power steering loads are imposed at idle. The switch is located on the pinion housing portion of the steering rack.

REMOVAL & INSTALLATION

1. Disconnect the negative battery cable.
2. Disconnect the electrical connector.
3. Remove the switch.

To install:

4. Install the switch.
5. Connect the electrical connector.
6. Connect the negative battery cable.

7. Allow the engine to come to normal operating temperature and confirm the proper operation of the switch.

Pressure Cycling Switch

The pressure cycling switch controls the refrigeration cycle by sensing low-side pressure as an indicator of evaporator temperature. The pressure cycling switch is the freeze-protection device in the system and senses refrigerant pressure on the suction side.

REMOVAL & INSTALLATION

➡ **The switch is mounted on a Schrader valve on the accumulator. The system need not be discharged to remove the pressure cycling switch.**

1. Disconnect the negative battery cable.
2. Disconnect the electrical connector.
3. Remove the switch and O-ring seal. Discard the O-ring.
   To install:
4. Install a new O-ring. Lubricate with refrigerant oil.
5. Install the switch to the accumulator.
6. Connect the electrical connector.
7. Connect the negative battery cable.

CRUISE CONTROL SYSTEMS

General Description

Cruise Control is a speed control system which maintains a desired vehicle speed under normal driving conditions. Steep grades — either up or down — may cause some variation in the set speed. Speed is maintained only by mechanically holding the throttle open or releasing it; the system cannot apply braking to slow the vehicle.

Most systems use vacuum to operate a throttle servo unit. The servo unit maintains a desired speed by trapping vacuum when the servo is at the desired position. The position of the servo and the vehicle speed are overseen by the controller or cruise control module (CCM); this unit controls the input or release of vacuum within the servo, thus adjusting the throttle to maintain speed.

The some models usually older ones may use an Electro–Motor Cruise System. The EMC uses an electric motor and connecting strap to vary the throttle angle according to directions from the CCM. The system is completely independent of vacuum and allows smoother throttle transitions.

Although the systems vary widely across GM's model line (component location, circuitry, interaction of computers, etc.) all cruise control units share certain common traits:

• The system will not engage until the vehicle exceeds a minimum speed, usually 25 mph.

• The system provides several modes of operation including cruise, coast, resume/accelerate; most allow "tap up" and "tap down", an incremental increase or decrease in set speed.

• All have a system **ON/OFF** switch; the system must be turned **ON** before it will engage. Many have a pilot light on the dash which illuminates when the cruise control is engaged.

• All systems will disconnect if the brake and/or clutch pedal is depressed when the system is engaged. The vacuum–sustained systems release vacuum as well as interrupting the electrical signal to the controller.

• The accelerator may be depressed at any time to override the chosen cruising speed. If the system receives no new orders, it will remember the previous cruising speed and return to it when the driver finishes accelerating.

• Failures in the cruise control may stem from electrical, mechanical and/or vacuum problems within the cruise control system or any combination of these.

➡ **The use of the speed control is not recommended when driving conditions do not permit maintaining a constant speed. These conditions may include heavy or varying traffic, winding roads or slippery surfaces.**

The main parts of the vacuum systems are the mode control switches, the controller (which may be the ECM, BCM, instrument panel cluster or a cruise controller module), servo unit, vehicle speed sensor, vacuum supply, electrical and vacuum release switches, and electrical harness. The EMC system includes an electric motor in place of the vacuum servo unit and related hoses.

SYSTEM OPERATION

For any of the following conditions to occur, the vehicle must be moving above 25 mph and the cruise control system switch must be switched **ON**. If either of these basics change, the system will cease to operate.

Set and Coast

When the vehicle is at the desired speed, engage the SET/COAST button momentarily. This button is usually at the end of the stalk and is pushed inward to engage it. Vehicle speed will be maintained within 1 mph of the speed the vehicle was traveling when the button was pushed. The system will maintain this speed until:

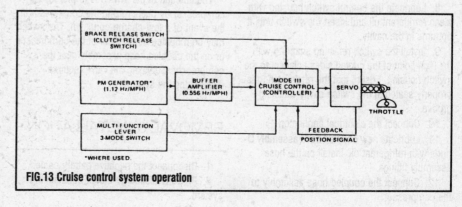

FIG.13 Cruise control system operation

• The brake or clutch pedals move enough to disengage the system.

• A system control switch is used to send a new message to the controller.

• The system switch is turned **OFF**.

• The ignition is switched **OFF**.

If only the brake or clutch pedal is moved, the system disconnects the cruise function but remembers the set speed and can return to it. Pushing a system control button or turning the system off removes memory of the previous speed.

Once the vehicle is holding the desired speed, the SET/COAST button may be used to slow the vehicle. Holding the button in will disconnect the system as long as the button is held. Once the car has slowed to the new desired speed, releasing the button will cause the system to hold the new, slower speed.

If the driver accelerates beyond the set cruising speed, pushing the SET/COAST button causes the system to maintain the new higher speed. If the button is not engaged at the higher speed, the system will maintain the previous set speed after the vehicle slows.

Resume and Accelerate

The RESUME/ACCEL switch is used after braking to tell the system to return to the previous speed. The switch must be moved momentarily into engagement — less than one second for most systems. If held too long, the system enters the ACCEL mode.

The ACCEL mode, when engaged, will accelerate the vehicle from the present set speed; when the switch is released, the new (higher) speed will be set and maintained.

Tap–Up and Tap–Down

Many of the GM systems are programmed to obey momentary signals from the SET/COAST and RESUME/ACCEL switches. If the SET/COAST switch is tapped or engaged for less than one second, the controller will reduce the car speed by 1 mph per tap. Similarly, if the RESUME/ACCEL switch is momentarily engaged, the set speed will increase by 1 mph per tap. This is a particularly handy function for fine tuning vehicle speed to prevailing limits, weather or traffic conditions.

If either switch is held too long, the system enters either the COAST or ACCEL mode. When the driver next releases the switch, the system will note and maintain the new speed.

SYSTEM COMPONENTS

Vacuum Servo Unit

The servo operates the throttle in response to signals from the controller. The servo consists of a vacuum operated diaphragm, a normally open solenoid valve to vent the diaphragm chamber to atmosphere, a normally closed solenoid valve to connect the diaphragm chamber to the vacuum source, and a variable inductance position sensor. Under normal operating conditions, the controller reacts to 3 vehicle or system states.

STEADY CRUISE STATE

Both vacuum and vent valves are closed or sealed. The servo has a constant vacuum on the diaphragm and places no flow requirements on the vacuum source. Vacuum is trapped in diaphragm chamber.

VEHICLE LOSING SPEED

The controller energizes the vacuum solenoid, opening the vacuum valve to the vacuum source. This increases the vacuum level in the servo to increase the throttle opening. The vent remains closed.

VEHICLE GAINING SPEED

The controller de-energizes the vent solenoid, opening the vent valve to the atmosphere. This reduces vacuum in the servo and allows the throttle return spring to decrease the throttle opening. The vacuum inlet valve remains closed. When the controller senses an over or underspeed condition, it will pulse the opening of the vent or vacuum valve. The controller pulse

will be repeated, as required, until the speed correction brings the vehicle to the set speed.

Under normal road conditions, the vacuum valve will remain in a completely open position when vehicle speed has dropped 5 mph below set speed. Likewise, if vehicle speed is 3 or more mph over the set speed, such as down a steep grade, the vent will go into full open position.

When the cruise system is on and operating with no input from the driver through the control switches, no correction to the speed will be made until the vehicle deviates $\pm 1/2$ mph from the set speed.

The servo incorporates a steel core which moves within a coil. Its resulting variable inductance provides a continuous voltage signal to the controller. The servo position signal is constantly compared to the vehicle speed signal. This comparison determines if the pulses issued have corrected the speed error or if additional pulses are required. This comparison is also used to lengthen the average pulse when it is not enough to compensate for the speed error, such as a steep grade.

EMC Controller/Actuator

The Electro–Motor Cruise Control eliminates the vacuum servo and incorporates the controller and actuator into a single unit. The

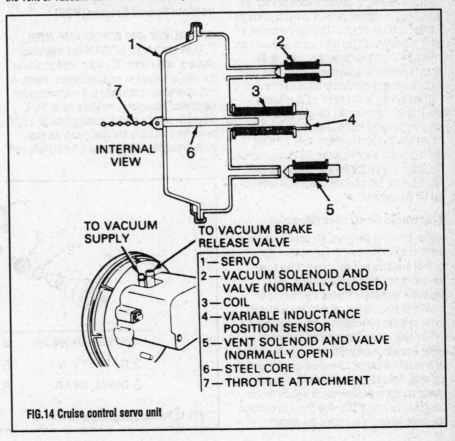

TO VACUUM SUPPLY

TO VACUUM BRAKE RELEASE VALVE

INTERNAL VIEW

1 — SERVO
2 — VACUUM SOLENOID AND VALVE (NORMALLY CLOSED)
3 — COIL
4 — VARIABLE INDUCTANCE POSITION SENSOR
5 — VENT SOLENOID AND VALVE (NORMALLY OPEN)
6 — STEEL CORE
7 — THROTTLE ATTACHMENT

FIG.14 Cruise control servo unit

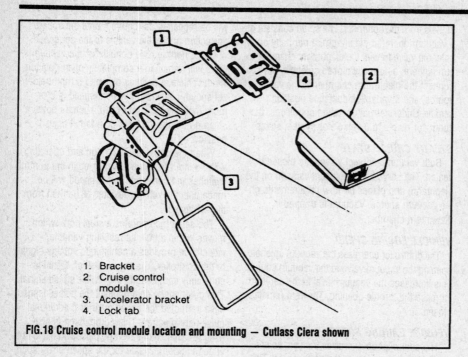

1. Bracket
2. Cruise control module
3. Accelerator bracket
4. Lock tab

FIG.18 Cruise control module location and mounting — Cutlass Ciera shown

control assembly consists of the electronic controller board, a solenoid operated clutch, the drum gear and strap (connected to the throttle linkage) and a stepper motor with 3-phase wiring and 4-pole stator.

When the vehicle speed is set or changed, the controller assembly adjusts throttle position by activating the stepper motor. The motor provides rotation in either direction through the use of 3 drive transistors. As the rotor turns, a pinion gear drives the drum gear assembly, causing the strap to wind or unwind on the drum. The strap pulls or releases the throttle linkage accordingly.

If the system is turned off or deactivated for any reason, the controller de-energizes the solenoid operated clutch. The spring on the clutch arm pushes the pinion away from the drum gear and a spring within the drum unwinds the strap. The throttle linkage is released and returns to the idle position until a new speed is set by the operator.

Electronic Controller (Module)

The controller interprets the position of the servo or electric motor, the position of the control switches and the output of the speed sensor. In response to these inputs, the controller electrically signals the opening or closing of the vent and vacuum solenoid valves in the servo or the rotation of the actuator motor.

The control functions may be performed by either a separate controller (stand alone system) or through the engine control module (integrated system). The stand alone controller uses a quartz crystal to produce clock signals for the integrated circuits within. The ECU can perform the same functions to control the system.

Integrated systems also receive input from the neutral safety switch; many of these systems receive a throttle position signal instead of servo position signal. Cadillac products with DFI employ a vacuum bleed within the servo and do not use a servo position sensor.

Vehicle Speed Sensor (VSS)

OPTICAL VSS AND BUFFER AMPLIFIER

There are 2 types of VSS buffer amplifiers; single or dual output. The optic head portion of the VSS is located in the speedometer frame. A reflective blade is attached to the speedometer cable/head assembly. The blade spins like a propeller, with its blades passing through a light beam from a LED in the optic head. As each blade enters the LED light beam, light is reflected back to a photocell in the optic head, causing a low power speed signal to be sent to the buffer for amplification and signal conditioning. The switching transistor within the buffer provides the 2000 pulses per mile (0.556 Hz/mph) speed signal to the ECM and/or cruise control module.

PM GENERATOR

This device supplies the vehicle speed input to the controller on some cars. Vehicle speed information is provided to the controller by a permanent magnet (PM) generator driven by the transmission/transaxle. The PM generator produces an AC sine wave signal of 4000 pulses per mile or a signal frequency of 1.112 Hz/mph. The signal is received by the buffer amplifier. Through use of an integrator and Schmitt Trigger, the signal is converted to square wave DC. The buffer amplifier contains a divider circuit which can develop a 2000 pulse (0.556 Hz/mph) as well as the 4000 pulse signal. Since cruise control is not the only function requiring VSS input, these two signals are sent to various control units on the vehicle. Depending on the model, the speed signal may be used by the speedometer, the suspension control module or even the radio volume controller.

Vacuum Accumulator

Found on most systems except those with diesel engines, the familiar ball-shaped vacuum accumulator is used to maintain satisfactory cruise control performance in vehicles with low manifold vacuum at normal road speeds. The accumulator is connected to the intake manifold through a one-way check valve and "stores" the high vacuum level that is available during periods of low engine loading. The system operates on accumulator vacuum when higher than manifold vacuum.

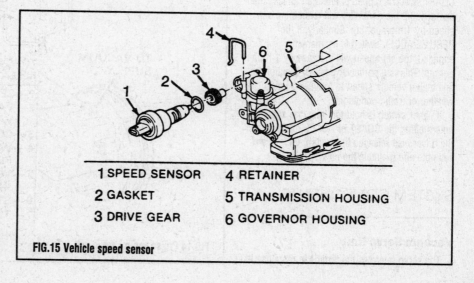

1 SPEED SENSOR	4 RETAINER
2 GASKET	5 TRANSMISSION HOUSING
3 DRIVE GEAR	6 GOVERNOR HOUSING

FIG.15 Vehicle speed sensor

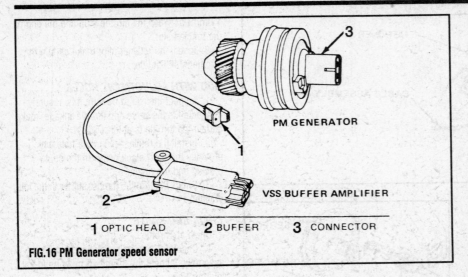

PM GENERATOR

VSS BUFFER AMPLIFIER

1 OPTIC HEAD   **2** BUFFER   **3** CONNECTOR

FIG.16 PM Generator speed sensor

System Service Precautions

❋ CAUTION

Many vehicles are equipped with SIR or air bag systems. Before performing any diagnosis or repair procedures, you must follow the safety and disarming procedures. Failure to safely disable the system may result in air bag deployment, possible injury or un-needed repairs.

- Never disconnect any electrical connection with the ignition switch **ON** unless instructed to do so in a test.
- Always wear a grounded wrist static strap when servicing any control module or component labeled with a Electrostatic Discharge (ESD) sensitive device symbol.
- Avoid touching module connector pins.
- Leave new components and modules in the shipping package until ready to install them.
- Always touch a vehicle ground after sliding across a vehicle seat or walking across vinyl or carpeted floors to avoid static charge damage.
- Never allow welding cables to lie on, near or across any vehicle electrical wiring.
- Do not allow extension cords for power tools or droplights to lie on, near or across any vehicle electrical wiring.
- Do not operate the cruise control or the engine with the drive wheels off the ground unless specifically instructed to do so by a test procedure.

Electric Brake Release Switch and Vacuum Release Valve

REMOVAL & INSTALLATION

1. At the brake switch, remove either the 2 electrical connectors or the electrical connector and the vacuum hose.
2. Remove the switch from the retainer.
3. Remove the tubular retainer from the brake pedal mounting bracket.

To Install:

4. Install the tubular retainer to the brake pedal mounting bracket.
5. Press the brake pedal and install the release switch into the retainer until fully seated in the clips.
6. Connect the wiring and/or vacuum lines. Adjust the switch.

Adjustment

1. Depress the brake pedal and check that the release switch is fully seated in the clips.
2. Slowly pull the brake pedal back to the at-rest position; the switch and valve assembly will move within the clips to the adjusted position.
3. Measure pedal travel and check switch engagement. The electric brake release switch contacts must open at $1/8$–$1/2$ in. (3–13mm) of pedal travel when measured at the centerline of the pedal pad. The brake lights should illuminate after another $3/16$ in. (5mm) of travel. The vacuum release should engage at $5/8$–1 in. (16–25mm) of pedal travel.

Vacuum Servo Unit

REMOVAL & INSTALLATION

▶ SEE FIG. 20
1. Disconnect the electrical connector and vacuum hoses at the servo.
2. Disconnect the actuating chain, cable or rod from the servo.

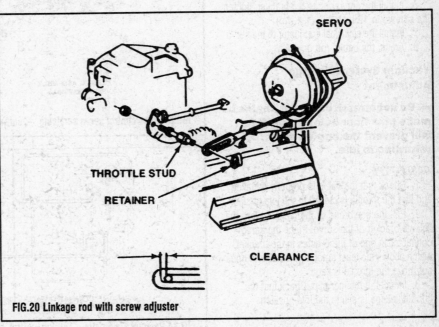

SERVO

THROTTLE STUD

RETAINER

CLEARANCE

FIG.20 Linkage rod with screw adjuster

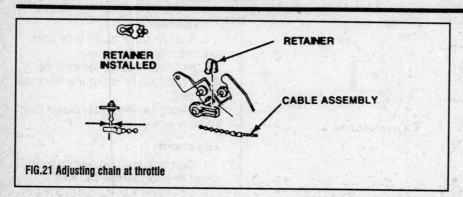

FIG.21 Adjusting chain at throttle

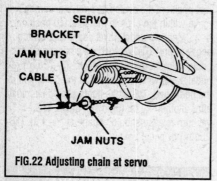

FIG.22 Adjusting chain at servo

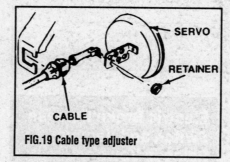

FIG.19 Cable type adjuster

3. Remove the screws holding the vacuum servo and solenoid unit to the bracket and remove the unit.

To Install:

4. Connect the large diameter brake release vacuum line to the servo unit. Connect the vacuum hose from the vacuum control valve to the servo unit.

5. Connect the actuating chain, rod or cable to the servo.

6. Install the servo unit to the bracket; tighten the screws to 12 inch lbs. (1.4 Nm).

7. Install the electrical connector to the servo.

8. Adjust the cable, rod or chain.

Vacuum System Linkage Adjustment

➡ **Do not stretch cables or chains to make pins fit or holes align. This will prevent the engine from returning to idle.**

CABLE TYPE

1. Check that the cable is properly installed and that the throttle is closed to the idle position.

2. Pull the servo end of the cable toward the linkage bracket of the servo. Place the servo connector in one of the 6 holes in the bracket which allows the least amount of slack and does not move the throttle linkage.

3. Install the retainer clip. Check that the throttle linkage is still in the idle position.

ROD WITH SCREW ADJUSTER

1. Inspect the rod assembly for proper attachment to the servo and throttle stud. Make certain the throttle is at idle.

2. Adjust the slotted bracket or the rod to obtain a clearance of 0.02–0.04 in. (0.5–1.0mm) between the throttle stud and the end of the bracket slot.

3. Install the retainer clip; make certain the throttle is still at idle.

ROD WITH ADJUSTMENT HOLES

1. Inspect the rod to be sure it is securely connected to the servo and throttle linkage; make certain the throttle is at idle.

2. Install the retainer pin in the hole which provides the least slack between the servo bracket and the retainer.

3. Check the throttle; it must still be in the idle position.

CHAIN AND CABLE

Chain at Throttle

1. Check for proper installation of cable assembly. Inspect the throttle; it must be in the idle position.

2. Install the chain in the swivel so that the slack does not exceed 1/2 the diameter of the ball stud.

3. Install the retainer on the swivel and make sure the throttle has not move from idle.

Chain at Servo

1. Check for proper installation of cable assembly. Inspect the throttle; it must be in the idle position.

2. Install the cable on the third link of the chain; adjust the jam nuts of the servo until there is no noticeable slack in the chain.

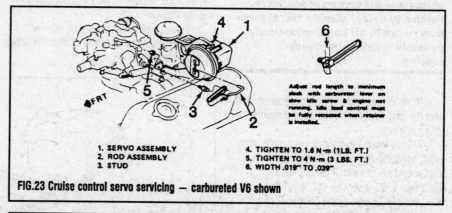

1. SERVO ASSEMBLY
2. ROD ASSEMBLY
3. STUD
4. TIGHTEN TO 1.6 N·m (1LB. FT.)
5. TIGHTEN TO 4 N·m (3 LBS. FT.)
6. WIDTH .019" TO .039"

FIG.23 Cruise control servo servicing — carbureted V6 shown

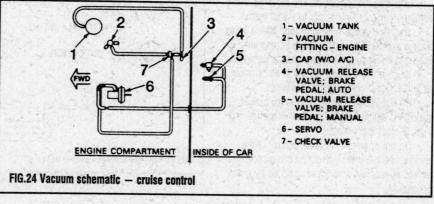

1 – VACUUM TANK
2 – VACUUM FITTING – ENGINE
3 – CAP (W/O A/C)
4 – VACUUM RELEASE VALVE; BRAKE PEDAL; AUTO
5 – VACUUM RELEASE VALVE; BRAKE PEDAL; MANUAL
6 – SERVO
7 – CHECK VALVE

FIG.24 Vacuum schematic — cruise control

3. Tighten the jam nuts and check that the throttle has not moved out of the idle position.

Electro–Motor Cruise Module and Motor Unit

REMOVAL & INSTALLATION

◆ SEE FIG. 25

1. Disconnect the negative battery cable.
2. Disconnect the throttle cable from the module ribbon.
3. Remove the retaining screws from the module and remove the module.
4. Disconnect the electrical harness from the module.

➡ **Do not attempt the repair the module.**

To install:

5. Connect the wiring connector to the module.
6. Install the module and secure the retaining screws.
7. Connect the cable to the module ribbon. Make certain the ribbon is not twisted; it must be flat and vertical.
8. Adjust the cable as needed.

CABLE ADJUSTMENT

1. Unlock the cable conduit (sheath) lock at the engine bracket.
2. For gasoline engines, move the cable conduit until the throttle plate just begins to open; move the cable in the opposite direction enough to close the throttle but no more. Hold this position.

3. For diesel engines, move the cable conduit until the injection pump lever moves off the idle stop screw, then move the conduit just enough to return the lever to the idle stop screw. Hold this position.
4. While holding the cable exactly in position, press down firmly on the cable conduit lock until it snaps in place. Do not let go of the cable until firmly locked.
5. Inspect the throttle linkage for proper idle position; if either the throttle plate or injection pump lever is not at idle (fully released), readjust the cable.

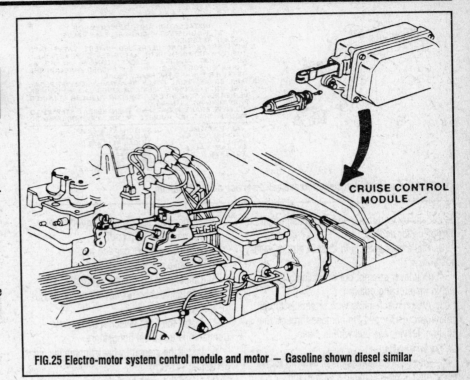

FIG.25 Electro-motor system control module and motor — Gasoline shown diesel similar

Multi–Function Lever with Set/Coast and Resume/Accel

REMOVAL & INSTALLATION

◆ SEE FIG. 27

1. Disconnect the negative battery terminal.
2. Disconnect cruise control switch connector at the base of steering column. it may

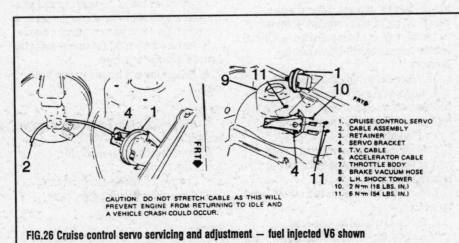

1. CRUISE CONTROL SERVO
2. CABLE ASSEMBLY
3. RETAINER
4. SERVO BRACKET
5. T.V. CABLE
6. ACCELERATOR CABLE
7. THROTTLE BODY
8. BRAKE VACUUM HOSE
9. L.H. SHOCK TOWER
10. 2 N·m (18 LBS. IN.)
11. 6 N·m (54 LBS. IN.)

CAUTION: DO NOT STRETCH CABLE AS THIS WILL PREVENT ENGINE FROM RETURNING TO IDLE AND A VEHICLE CRASH COULD OCCUR.

FIG.26 Cruise control servo servicing and adjustment — fuel injected V6 shown

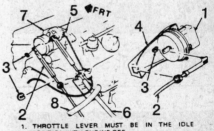

1. THROTTLE LEVER MUST BE IN THE IDLE POSITION WITH ENGINE OFF.
2. PULL SERVO ASSEMBLY END OF CABLE TOWARD THE SERVO BLADE.
3. IF HOLE IN SERVO BLADE LINES UP WITH CABLE PIN, INSTALL PIN IN THAT HOLE AND INSTALL RETAINER.
4. IF HOLE DOES NOT ALIGN WITH THE PIN, INSTALL PIN IN THE NEXT HOLE AWAY FROM SERVO ASSEMBLY.

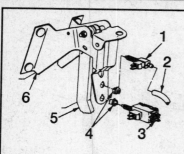

INSTALLATION AND ADJUSTMENT OF SELF-ADJUSTING VACUUM RELEASE VALVE
1. INSTALL RETAINER.
2. WITH BRAKE PEDAL DEPRESSED, INSERT VALVE INTO TUBULAR RETAINER UNTIL VALVE SEATS ON RETAINER. NOTE THAT AUDIBLE "CLICKS" CAN BE HEARD AS THREADED PORTION OF VALVE IS PUSHED THROUGH THE RETAINER TOWARD THE BRAKE PEDAL.
3. PULL BRAKE PEDAL FULLY REARWARD AGAINST PEDAL STOP UNTIL AUDIBLE "CLICK" SOUNDS CAN NO LONGER BE HEARD. VALVE WILL BE MOVED IN TUBULAR RETAINER PROVIDING ADJUSTMENT.
4. RELEASE BRAKE PEDAL AND THEN REPEAT STEP #3 TO ASSURE THAT NO AUDIBLE "CLICK" SOUNDS REMAIN.

1—VALVE ASSEMBLY · VACUUM RELEASE
2—HOSE · VACUUM RELEASE VALVE TO SERVO
3—SWITCH · STOP LAMP AND CRUISE ELECTRICAL RELEASE
4—RETAINER
5—BRAKE PEDAL
6—BRAKE PEDAL MOUNTING BRACKET

FIG.27 Cruise control vacuum release valve service and adjustment

be necessary to remove an under dash panel or trim piece for access.

3. Make sure lever is in **CENTER** or **OFF** position.

4. Pull lever straight out of retaining clip within the steering column.

5. Attach mechanic's wire or similar to the connector; gently pull the harness through the column, leaving the pull wire in place.

To install:

6. Place the transmission selector in **LOW** or **1**. Attach the mechanic's wire to the connector. Gently pull the harness into place, checking that the harness is completely clear of any moving or movable components such as tilt-column, telescoping column, brake pedal linkage, etc.

7. Position the lever and push it squarely into the retainer until it snaps in place.

8. Remove the mechanics' wire and connect the cruise control harness connector.

9. Reinstall any panels or insulation which were removed for access.

10. Connect the negative battery terminal.

Set/Coast And Resume/ Accel Switches on Wheel

REMOVAL & INSTALLATION

❄ CAUTION

If equipped with air bag (SIR) system, the system must be fully disabled before performing repairs. Follow safety procedures in Section 10. Failure to disarm the system can result in personal injury and/or property damage.

1. Disconnect the negative battery cable.
2. Remove the horn pad.
3. Remove the retainer and nut.
4. Remove the steering wheel.
5. Disconnect the electrical connectors.
6. Remove the horn switch if necessary.

To install:

7. Install the horn switch if necessary. Connect the electrical connectors.

8. Install the steering wheel; tighten the nut to 30 ft. lbs. (41 Nm).

9. Install the retainer and clip.

10. Install the horn pad.

11. Connect the negative battery cable.

Speed Sensor

REMOVAL & INSTALLATION

OPTICAL TYPE WITH BUFFER

1. Disconnect the negative battery cable.
2. To gain access to the sensor and buffer behind the speedometer, the instrument cluster must be partially removed. When doing so, disconnect the harness connector at the rear of the cluster; if the cluster is pulled too far outward with the harness attached, both may be damaged.
3. Disconnect the amplifier connector.
4. Remove the speed sensor attaching screw and remove the sensor through the opening in the base of the instrument panel.

To install:

5. Route the sensor wire connector and harness through the opening in the base of the instrument panel.

6. Install the sensor on its bracket and install the retaining screw.

7. Connect the amplifier connector.

8. Reinstall the instrument cluster and connect the electrical harness.

9. Connect the negative battery cable.

PERMANENT MAGNET TYPE

1. Disconnect the wiring harness from the speed sensor. If the sensor also contains the speedometer cable, remove the cable.

2. Remove the retainer clip.

3. Carefully lift the sensor out of the transmission.

4. Remove the O-ring.

To install:

5. Lubricate a new O-ring with appropriate transmission fluid and install the ring on the sensor.

6. Install the sensor and secure the retaining clip.

7. Connect the speedometer cable if it was removed; connect the wiring harness. Make certain the harness is routed clear of moving or hot components.

Vacuum Reservoir

REMOVAL & INSTALLATION

Disconnect the vacuum line, remove the retaining screws and remove the reservoir. When reinstalling, tighten the retaining screws to 53 inch lbs. (6 Nm).

Cruise Control Module

REMOVAL & INSTALLATION

◆ SEE FIG.28

1. Disconnect the negative battery cable.
2. The cruise control module is located on a bracket mounted above the accelerator pedal. Disconnect the wiring harness from the module.
3. Remove the bracket and module assembly from the accelerator bracket.
4. Release the lock tab and remove the module.

To install:

5. Fit the module to its bracket and secure the lock tab.

6. Install the module assembly to the accelerator bracket.

7. Connect the module wiring harness.

8. Connect the negative battery cable.

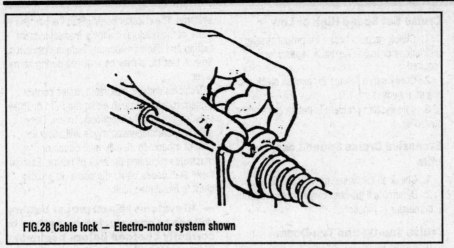

FIG.28 Cable lock — Electro-motor system shown

3. Engage system by momentarily depressing the SET button and releasing at approximately 50 mph; remove foot from accelerator.) Vehicle should maintain speed.

4. Push the RESUME/ACCEL switch and hold. Vehicle should accelerate at a controlled rate. Release slide to engage system at cruise speed of approximately 55 mph. System should now be set at this new speed and vehicle should maintain that speed.

5. Depress brake pedal about ½ in. (13mm); indicator light, if equipped, should go out, confirming action of electric brake release switch, and vehicle should start to slow down. Allow the vehicle to slow to approximately 45 mph, using brakes if desired.

6. Momentarily push RESUME/ACCEL switch and release. Vehicle should accelerate at a controlled rate and resume previously set speed of about 55 mph and maintain that speed. The indicator light (if equipped) should come on when slide switch is released.

Cruise Control Basic Tests

car to highway speed. Depress the SET switch button and release. System should remain inoperative.

2. Set cruise control system switch to **ON**.

PRELIMINARY CHECKS

Improper operation can be caused by any combination of mechanical, electrical and vacuum problems. In resolving any cruise system operating problem, always insure there are no bare, broken, or disconnected wires or any pinched, damaged, or disconnected vacuum hoses. The servo and throttle linkage should operate freely and smoothly.

Since any problem in this system may be due to one or more causes, a quick visual inspection should always be made before beginning extended diagnosis. This can be done by eliminating an obvious vacuum, mechanical or electrical problem. Start the engine and use a finger or vacuum gauge to confirm vacuum at the servo. Check the related fuse(s) and look for loose or corroded harness connectors. Inspect the brake and clutch switches for loose wires or hoses; check that the switch plunger moves smoothly and is not stuck in the disconnect position. Inspect the throttle linkage from the servo for binding, breakage or excess slack.

➡ **If the speedometer is not operating correctly, vehicles using optic vehicle speed sensors will not provide the correct speed signal to the cruise control module.**

ROAD TEST

1. With the cruise control switch **OFF**, drive

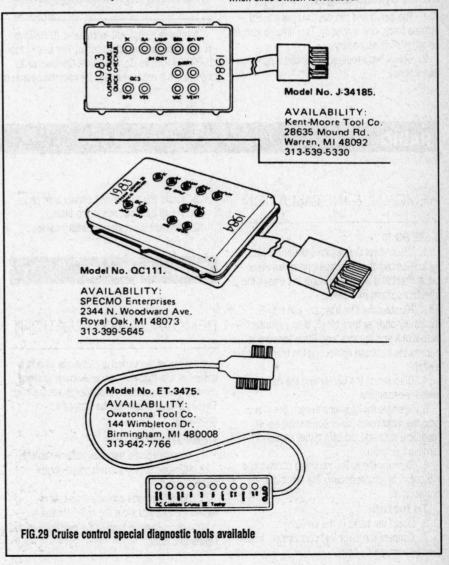

Model No. J-34185.

AVAILABILITY:
Kent-Moore Tool Co.
28635 Mound Rd.
Warren, MI 48092
313-539-5330

Model No. QC111.

AVAILABILITY:
SPECMO Enterprises
2344 N. Woodward Ave.
Royal Oak, MI 48073
313-399-5645

Model No. ET-3475.

AVAILABILITY:
Owatonna Tool Co.
144 Wimbleton Dr.
Birmingham, MI 480008
313-642-7766

FIG.29 Cruise control special diagnostic tools available

7. Depress SET/COAST button and hold. Indicator light (if equipped) should go out. Coast to 50 mph. with button pressed.

8. Release SET/COAST button to engage system at 50 mph; vehicle should maintain the new speed.

9. Check the tap-down feature. Depress SET/COAST button for less than 1/2 second (tap). Vehicle speed should drop about 1 mph. Tap the button a couple more times to check incremental speed decreases.

10. Check the tap-up feature. Actuate RESUME/ACCEL for less than 1/2 second (tap). Vehicle speed should increase about 1 mph. Tap the switch a couple more times to check incremental speed increases.

11. If all functional conditions are met during this test, the regular driver may not be familiar with the correct operation of the cruise control system.

Cruise System Surges

1. The servo and throttle linkages should operate freely and smoothly. This linkage should be adjusted if necessary.

2. Check hose routing for pinches, leaks or restrictions.

Cruise Set Speed High or Low

1. Check vacuum hoses for proper routing, restrictions or leaks. Adjust or replace as required.

2. Check servo linkage for excess slack and adjust, if necessary.

3. If no system problem is noted, replace the controller.

Excessive Cruise Speed Loss On Hills

1. Check all the hoses for vacuum leaks.

2. Determine if the check valve to the vacuum accumulator is functional.

Cruise Tap-Up and Tap-Down

If all other functions of cruise control are operating correctly except tap-up and/or tap-down, the controller is faulty.

SYSTEM TESTING

A reliable digital volt–ohmmeter (DVOM) is required for testing all systems. The use of tool J–34185, Cruise Control Quick Checker or its equivalent is recommended for vacuum operated systems. The checker connects to the harness in place of the module; it allows manual system testing and can considerably reduce diagnostic time. A test lamp may be required during some tests.

Vehicles with an integrated cruise control system running through either the ECM or BCM must be put into the diagnostic mode. Once engaged, the diagnostic mode will allow the control module to display fault codes or messages regarding the area of failure. Each of these fault codes direct the use a diagnostic chart to isolate the fault.

➡ **All systems rely on proper battery voltage to operate. Insure battery is correctly charged before beginning diagnostics. Do not allow battery to drain during extended testing. Turn system switch or ignition switch OFF when not actively testing the system. Involved testing and special tools are required for most testing. This would be best left to a professional shop with the necessary test equipment, as the cost involed for the tools is usually more than the cost of the repairs.**

RADIO

REMOVAL & INSTALLATION

◆ SEE FIG.30

1. Disconnect the negative battery cable.

2. Remove the instrument panel insulator panel mounting screws enough to remove the steering column trim cover.

3. Remove the ash tray, the ash tray assembly and the fuse block, then separate the fuse block and the ash tray. Push forward to access the cigarette lighter and the rear defogger switch.

4. Disconnect the lighter and the defogger switch connectors.

5. Remove the cigarette lighter, the glove box, the instrument panel center trim panel mounting nuts and the trim panel enough to remove the radio.

6. Remove the radio mounting screws and the radio, by disconnecting the electrical connectors.

To install:

6. Install the radio in the vehicle.

7. Connect the electrical connectors. Install the radio attaching bolts.

8. Install the instrument cluster trim plate.

9. Install the accessory trim plate.

10. Connect the negative battery cable.

Power Antenna

REMOVAL & INSTALLATION

Because of the varied applications of power antennas, the following general power antenna removal and installation procedures are outlined. These removal steps can be altered as necessary.

FRONT MOUNTED TYPE

1. Disconnect the negative battery cable.

2. Remove the instrument panel sound absorber pad.

3. Disconnect the antenna lead-in and harness connector from the relay assembly.

4. Apply masking tape to the rear edge of the fender and door.

5. If required, remove the inner to outer fender retaining screws.

6. If required, raise the vehicle and support it safely; then remove the associated front wheel assembly.

7. Remove the lower rocker panel retaining screws, lower fender to body retaining bolt and remove the lower rocker panel, as required.

8. Remove the inner splash shield from the fender, as required.

9. Remove the upper antenna retaining nut, using an appropriately tool.

10. Remove the antenna to bracket retaining bolts, then remove the antenna.

To install:

11. Fit the antenna into position, then loosely install the antenna gasket and upper nut.

12. Loosely install the antenna to bracket retaining bolts.

13. Tighten the upper antenna retaining nut, using the appropriately tool, then tighten the antenna to bracket retaining bolts.

14. Complete installation in the reverse order of the removal procedure.

15. Apply silicone grease to the harness connector before reconnecting.

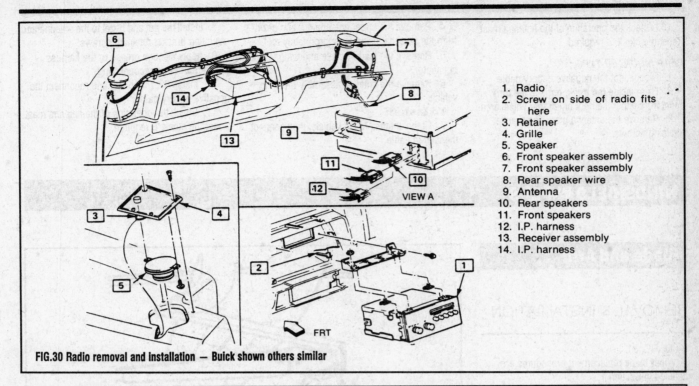

1. Radio
2. Screw on side of radio fits here
3. Retainer
4. Grille
5. Speaker
6. Front speaker assembly
7. Front speaker assembly
8. Rear speaker wire
9. Antenna
10. Rear speakers
11. Front speakers
12. I.P. harness
13. Receiver assembly
14. I.P. harness

VIEW A

FRT

FIG.30 Radio removal and installation — Buick shown others similar

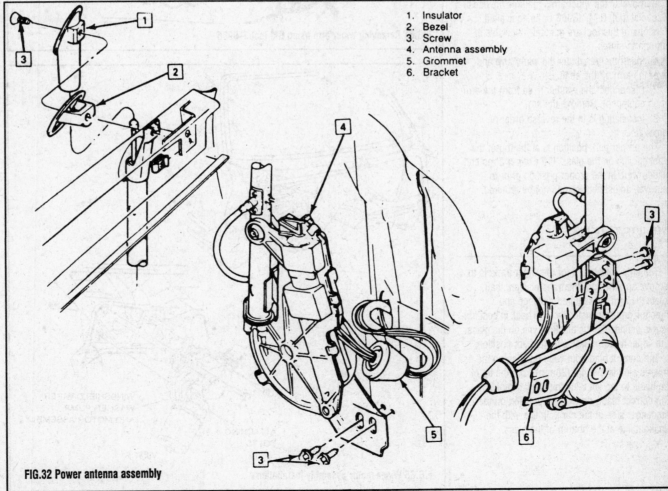

1. Insulator
2. Bezel
3. Screw
4. Antenna assembly
5. Grommet
6. Bracket

FIG.32 Power antenna assembly

16. Check the operation of the antenna mast. Reset the clock, if required.

REAR MOUNTED TYPE

1. Disconnect the negative battery cable.
2. From inside the trunk, remove the trim panel from either the right or left rear wheel area.
3. Remove the antenna mounting bracket retaining screws.

4. Remove the upper antenna nut and bezel from the antenna, using an appropriately tool.
5. Remove the lead-in cable and wiring connector.
6. Remove the antenna assembly from the vehicle.

To install:
7. Fit the antenna to the vehicle, then connect the lead-in cable.

8. Install the nut and bezel to the antenna and mounting bracket retaining screws.
9. Apply silicone grease to the harness connector before reconnecting.
10. Install the trim panel and reconnect the negative battery cable.
11. Check the operation of the antenna mast. Reset the clock, if required.

WINDSHIELD WIPERS

Blade and Arm

REMOVAL & INSTALLATION

◆ SEE FIG. 31

Wiper blade replacement procedures are detailed in Section 1.

Removal of the wiper arms requires the use of a special tool, G.M. J8966 or its equivalent. Versions of this tool are generally available in auto parts stores.

1. Insert the tool under the wiper arm and lever the arm off the shaft.
2. Disconnect the washer hose from the arm (if so equipped). Remove the arm.
3. Installation is in the reverse order of removal.

The proper park position is at the top of the blackout line on the glass. If the wiper arms and blades were in the proper position prior to removal, adjustment should not be required.

ADJUSTMENT

The only adjustment for the wiper arms is to remove an arm from the transmission shaft, rotate the arm the required distance and direction and then install the arm back in position so it is in line with the blackout line on the glass. The wiper motor must be in the park position.

The correct blade-out wipe position on the driver's side is $1\frac{3}{32}$ in. (28mm) from the tip of the blade to the left windshield pillar molding. The correct blade-down wipe position on the passenger side of the car is in line with the blackout line at the bottom of the glass.

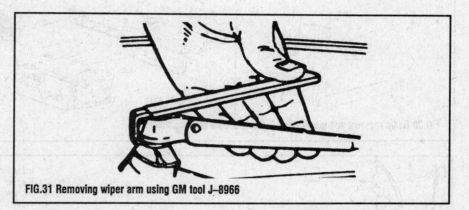
FIG.31 Removing wiper arm using GM tool J–8966

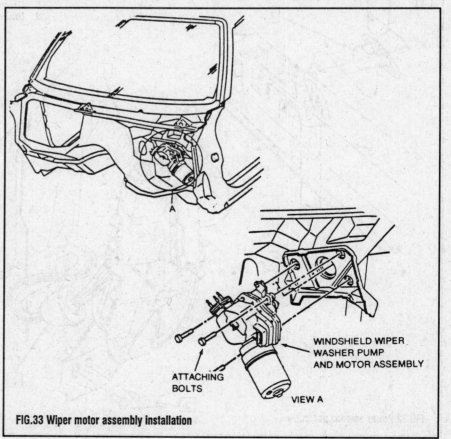

WINDSHIELD WIPER WASHER PUMP AND MOTOR ASSEMBLY

ATTACHING BOLTS

VIEW A

FIG.33 Wiper motor assembly installation

Wiper Motor

REMOVAL & INSTALLATION

▶ SEE FIGS. 33 & 34

1. Disconnect the negative battery cable.
2. Remove the wiper arms.
3. Remove the cowl cover.
4. Loosen (but do not remove) the drive link-to-crank arm attaching nuts and detach the drive link from the motor crank arm.
5. Disconnect the wiper motor electrical connector.
6. Remove the wiper motor attaching bolts.
7. Remove the wiper motor, guiding the crank arm through the hole.

To install:

8. Insert the wiper motor, guiding the crank arm through the hole.
9. Guide the crank arm through the opening in the body and then tighten the mounting bolts to 4–6 ft. lbs.
10. Install the drive link to the crank arm with the motor in the park position.
11. Install the wiper motor attaching bolts.
12. Connect the electrical connectors.

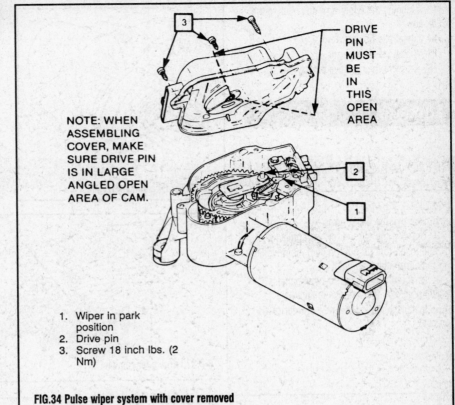

DRIVE PIN MUST BE IN THIS OPEN AREA

NOTE: WHEN ASSEMBLING COVER, MAKE SURE DRIVE PIN IS IN LARGE ANGLED OPEN AREA OF CAM.

1. Wiper in park position
2. Drive pin
3. Screw 18 inch lbs. (2 Nm)

FIG.34 Pulse wiper system with cover removed

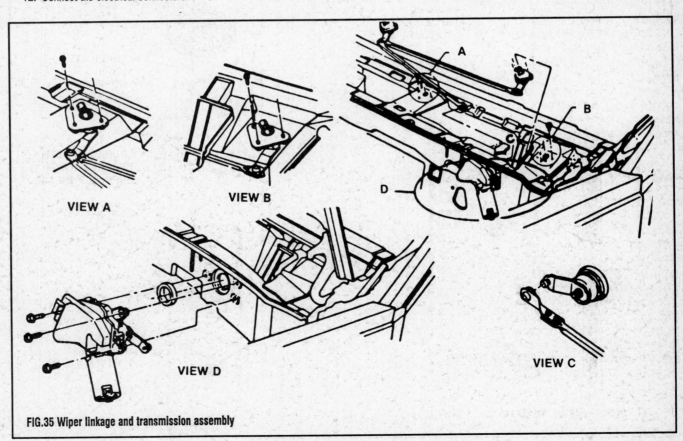

VIEW A

VIEW B

VIEW D

VIEW C

A

B

C

D

FIG.35 Wiper linkage and transmission assembly

13. Connect the wiper arm drive link to the crank arm.

14. Install the cowl cover.

15. Install the wiper arms.

16. Connect the negative battery cable.

Linkage

REMOVAL & INSTALLATION

▶ SEE FIGS. 35-41

1. Remove the wiper arms.

2. Remove the shroud top vent grille.

3. Loosen (but do not remove) the drive link-to-crank arm attaching nuts.

4. Unscrew the linkage-to-cowl panel retaining screws and remove the linkage.

5. Installation is in the reverse order of removal.

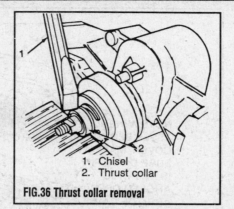
1. Chisel
2. Thrust collar

FIG.36 Thrust collar removal

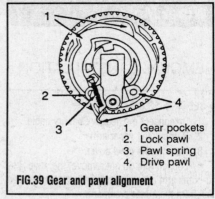
1. Gear pockets
2. Lock pawl
3. Pawl spring
4. Drive pawl

FIG.39 Gear and pawl alignment

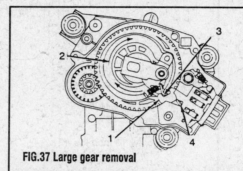
1. Latch arm (must be out of the way when the gear is removed)
2. Rotation
3. Drive pawl
4. Relay slot

FIG.37 Large gear removal

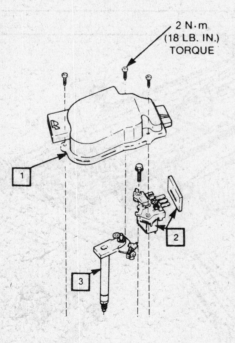

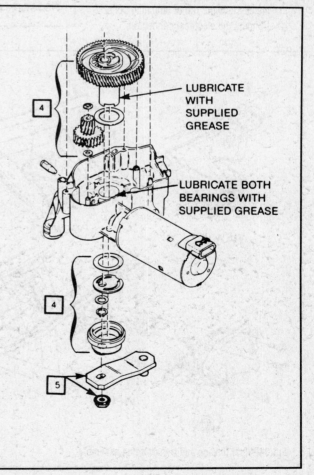

2 N·m
(18 LB. IN.)
TORQUE

LUBRICATE WITH SUPPLIED GREASE

LUBRICATE BOTH BEARINGS WITH SUPPLIED GREASE

1. Cover
2. Park switch
3. Drive shaft package
4. Gear package
5. Crank arm

FIG.38 Wiper assembly explode view

SWITCH MODE TERMINAL #		MIST	OFF	PULSE	LO	HI †	WASH
PULSE	1	C	C	C	C	C	C
	2	B(+)	—	B(+)	B(+)	—	*B(+)
	3	B(+)	B(+)	—	B(+)	—	*B(+)
	4	—	—	—	—	—	—
	5	—	—	—	—	—	—
	6	10-12V	10-12V	10-12V	10-12V	10-12V	B(+)
	7	GROUND	GROUND	GROUND	GROUND	GROUND	GROUND
	8	C	C	C	C	C	C
	9	—	—	—	—	B(+)	—
STANDARD	1	▨	C	▨	C	C	C
	2	▨	—	▨	B(+)	—	*B(+)
	3	▨	B(+)	▨	B(+)	—	*B(+)
	4	▨	—	▨	—	—	—
	5	▨	—	▨	—	—	—
	6	▨	—	▨	—	—	B(+)
	7	▨	GROUND	▨	GROUND	GROUND	GROUND
	8	▨	C	▨	C	C	C
	9	▨	—	▨	—	B(+)	—

C = CONTINUITY   † TERMINALS #2 & #3 CONNECTED TOGETHER.   *EXCEPT ON HI.

FIG.40 Wiper and washer switch check chart — 6000 wagon shown

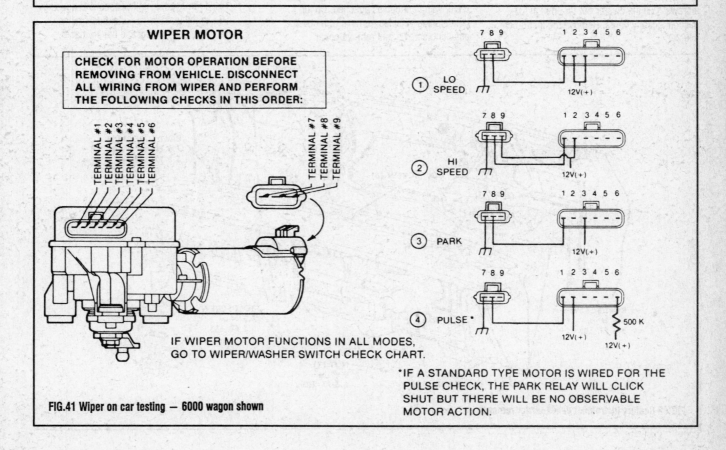

WIPER MOTOR

CHECK FOR MOTOR OPERATION BEFORE REMOVING FROM VEHICLE. DISCONNECT ALL WIRING FROM WIPER AND PERFORM THE FOLLOWING CHECKS IN THIS ORDER:

TERMINAL #1
TERMINAL #2
TERMINAL #3
TERMINAL #4
TERMINAL #5
TERMINAL #6

TERMINAL #7
TERMINAL #8
TERMINAL #9

IF WIPER MOTOR FUNCTIONS IN ALL MODES, GO TO WIPER/WASHER SWITCH CHECK CHART.

① LO SPEED   12V(+)

② HI SPEED   12V(+)

③ PARK   12V(+)

④ PULSE *   500 K   12V(+)   12V(+)

*IF A STANDARD TYPE MOTOR IS WIRED FOR THE PULSE CHECK, THE PARK RELAY WILL CLICK SHUT BUT THERE WILL BE NO OBSERVABLE MOTOR ACTION.

FIG.41 Wiper on car testing — 6000 wagon shown

INSTRUMENTS AND SWITCHES

Instrument Cluster

REMOVAL & INSTALLATION

Century

1. Disconnect the negative battery cable.
2. Disconnect the speedometer cable and pull it through the firewall.
3. Remove the left side hush panel retaining screws and nut.
4. Remove the right side hush panel retaining screws and nut.
5. Remove the shift indicator cable clip.
6. Remove the steering column trim plate.
7. Put the gear selector in **L**. Remove the retaining screws and gently pull out the instrument panel trim plate.
8. Disconnect the parking brake cable at the lever by pushing it forward and sliding it from its slot.
9. Unbolt and lower the steering column.
10. Remove the gauge cluster retaining screws. Pull the cluster out far enough to disconnect any wires. Remove the instrument cluster.

To Install:

11. Install the gauge cluster, connect the electrical connectors and install the retaining screws.
12. Position the steering column and install the retaining bolts.
13. Connect the parking brake cable at the lever.
14. Put the gear selector in **L**. Install the instrument panel trim plate.
15. Install the steering column trim plate.
16. Install the shift indicator cable clip.
17. Install the right side hush panel retaining screws and nut.
18. Install the left side hush panel retaining screws and nut.
19. Pull the speedometer cable through the firewall and connect to the speedometer.
20. Connect the negative battery cable.

Celebrity

1. Disconnect the negative battery cable.
2. Remove instrument panel hush panel.
3. Remove vent control housing, as required.
4. On non-air conditioning vehicles, remove steering column trim cover screws and lower cover with vent cables attached. On air conditioning vehicles, remove trim cover attaching screws and remove cover.
5. Remove instrument cluster trim pad.
6. Remove ash tray, retainer and fuse block, disconnect wires as necessary.
7. Remove headlight switch knob and instrument panel trim plate. Disconnect electrical connectors of any accessory switches in trim plate.
8. Remove cluster assembly and disconnect speedometer cable, **PRNDL** and cluster electrical connectors.

To install:

9. Install cluster assembly and connect speedometer cable, **PRNDL** and cluster electrical connectors.
10. Install headlight switch knob and instrument panel trim plate. Connect electrical connectors of any accessory switches in trim plate.
11. Install ash tray, retainer and fuse block, connect electrical connectors.
12. Install instrument cluster trim pad.
13. On non-air conditioned vehicles, raise the cover with vent cables attached and install steering column trim cover screws. On air conditioned vehicles, install trim cover and attaching screws.
14. If removed, install vent control housing.
15. Install instrument panel hush panel.
16. Connect the negative battery cable.

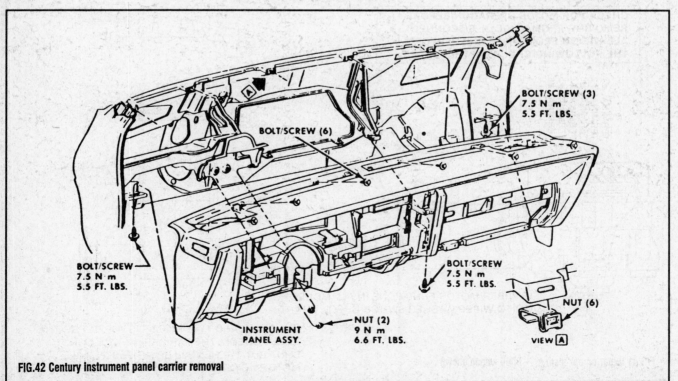

FIG.42 Century instrument panel carrier removal

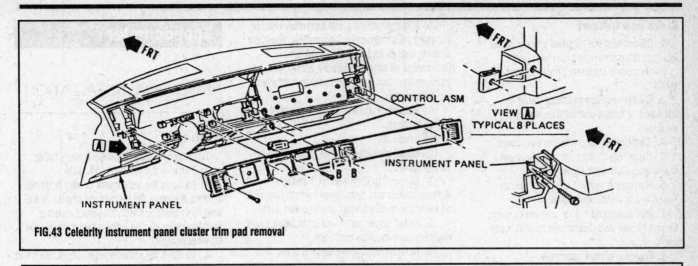

FIG.43 Celebrity instrument panel cluster trim pad removal

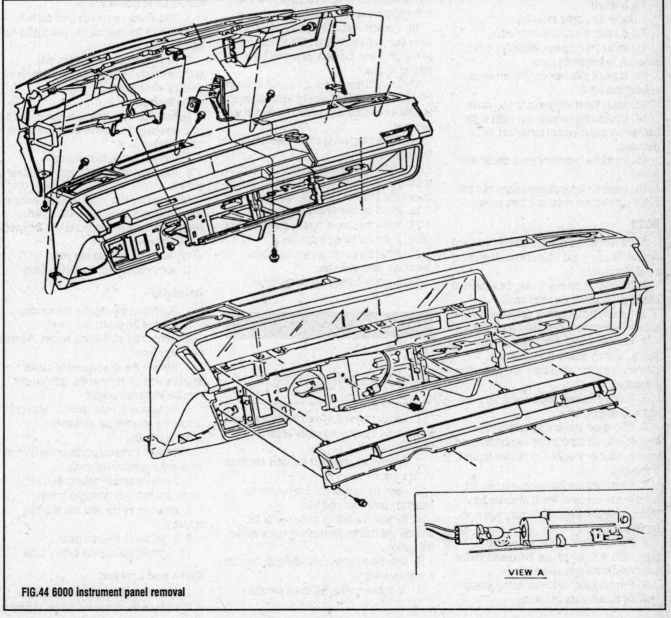

FIG.44 6000 instrument panel removal

Ciera and Cruiser

1. Disconnect the negative battery cable. Remove left instrument panel trim pad.

2. Remove instrument panel cluster trim cover.

3. Disconnect speedometer cable at transaxle or cruise control transducer, if equipped.

4. Remove steering column trim cover.

5. Disconnect shift indicator clip from steering column shift bowl.

6. Remove 4 screws attaching cluster assembly to instrument panel.

7. Pull assembly out far enough to reach behind cluster and disconnect speedometer cable.

8. Remove cluster assembly.

To install:

9. Install the cluster assembly.

10. Connect the speedometer cable.

11. Install the 4 screws attaching cluster assembly to instrument panel.

12. Connect shift indicator clip to steering column shift bowl.

13. Install the steering column trim cover.

14. Connect the speedometer cable at the transaxle or cruise control transducer, if equipped.

15. Install the instrument panel cluster trim cover.

16. Install the left instrument panel trim pad.

17. Connect the negative battery cable.

6000

1. Disconnect the negative battery cable, and remove the center and left side lower instrument panel trim plate.

2. Remove the screws holding the instrument cluster to the instrument panel carrier.

3. Remove the instrument cluster lens to gain access to the speedometer head and gauges.

4. Remove right side and left side hush panels, steering column trim cover and disconnect parking brake cable and vent cables, if equipped.

5. Remove steering column retaining bolts and drop steering column.

6. Disconnect temperature control cable, inner-to-outer air conditioning wire harness and inner-to-outer air conditioning vacuum harness, if equipped.

7. Disconnect chassis harness behind left lower instrument panel and ECM connectors behind glove box. Disconnect instrument panel harness at cowl.

8. Remove center instrument panel trim plate, radio, if equipped, and disconnect neutral switch and brake light switch.

9. Remove upper and lower instrument panel retaining screws, nuts and bolts.

10. Pull instrument panel assembly out far enough to disconnect ignition switch, headlight dimmer switch and turn signal switch. Disconnect all other accessory wiring and vacuum lines necessary to remove instrument panel assembly.

11. Remove instrument panel assembly with wiring harness.

To install:

12. Install instrument panel assembly with wiring harness.

13. Connect ignition switch, headlight dimmer switch and turn signal switch. Connect all other accessory wiring and vacuum lines.

14. Install upper and lower instrument panel retaining screws, nuts and bolts.

15. Connect neutral switch and brake light switch. Install the radio, if equipped, and install center instrument panel trim plate.

16. Connect chassis harness behind left lower instrument panel and ECM connectors behind glove box. Connect instrument panel harness at cowl.

17. Connect temperature control cable, inner-to-outer air conditioning wire harness and inner-to-outer air conditioning vacuum harness, if equipped.

18. Raise the steering column and install retaining bolts.

19. Install right side and left side hush panels, steering column trim cover and connect parking brake cable and vent cables, if equipped.

20. Install the instrument cluster lens.

21. Install the screws holding the instrument cluster to the instrument panel carrier.

22. Install the center and left side lower instrument panel trim plate.

23. Connect the negative battery cable.

Console

REMOVAL & INSTALLATION

1. Remove the shifter knob from the shifter by removing the retaining screw at the back of the knob.

2. Remove the screws at the sides and front of the console.

3. Open the console box and remove the retaining screw inside the box.

4. Remove the ashtray at the rear of the console and remove the retaining screw behind the ashtray.

5. Slide the console rearward slightly, then lift it over the shifter.

6. To install, reverse the above process.

Speedometer

REMOVAL & INSTALLATION

Century

1. Disconnect the negative battery cable.

2. Remove the left side trim plate.

3. Remove the instrument cluster housing screws. Remove the instrument cluster. If the vehicle is equipped with tilt-wheel steering, working room can be gained by removing the tilt-wheel cover.

4. Remove the speedometer lens screws and remove the speedometer lens.

5. Disconnect the speedometer cable by pushing in on the retaining clip and pulling back on the cable.

6. Remove the screws holding the speedometer to the instrument and remove the speedometer assembly.

To install:

7. Install the speedometer assembly and the screws holding the speedometer assembly to the instrument panel.

8. Connect the speedometer cable.

9. Install the speedometer lens and retaining screws.

10. Install the instrument cluster housing and retaining screws. If equipped with tilt-wheel steering and the tilt-wheel cover was removed, replace the cover.

11. Install the left side trim plate.

12. Connect the negative battery cable.

Celebrity

1. Disconnect the negative battery cable.

2. Remove the cluster trim panel.

3. Remove the cluster lens screws. Remove the cluster lens.

4. Remove the speedometer-to-cluster attaching screws. Remove the speedometer from the instrument cluster.

5. Disconnect the speedometer cable and remove the speedometer assembly.

To install:

6. Position the speedometer assembly and connect the speedometer cable.

7. Install the speedometer-to-instrument cluster and install the attaching screws.

8. Install the cluster lens and attaching screws.

9. Install the cluster trim panel.

10. Connect the negative battery cable.

Ciera and Cruiser

1. Disconnect the negative battery cable.

2. Remove the instrument cluster assembly.

3. Remove the vehicle speed sensor screw from the rear of the speedometer. Remove the vehicle speed sensor, if equipped.

4. Remove the speedometer lens screws and remove the speedometer lens. Remove the bezel.

5. Remove the screw that holds the speedometer to the instrument cluster.

6. Remove the speedometer head by pulling forward. Disconnect the speedometer cable by prying gently on the retainer and pulling the speedometer cable from the speedometer head.

To install:

7. Position the speedometer head and connect the speedometer cable.

8. Install the screw that holds the speedometer to the instrument cluster.

9. Install the speedometer lens and attaching screws. Install the bezel.

10. Install the vehicle speed sensor and the attaching screw at the rear of the speedometer.

11. Install the instrument cluster assembly.

12. Connect the negative battery cable.

6000

1. Disconnect the negative battery cable.

2. Remove the center and left lower trim plates.

3. Remove the screws holding the instrument cluster assembly to the dash assembly. Remove the instrument cluster.

4. Remove the instrument cluster lens screws. Remove the instrument cluster lens.

5. Remove the screws holding the speedometer to the instrument cluster. Remove the speedometer.

6. Disconnect the speedometer cable from the rear of the speedometer.

To install:

7. Connect the speedometer cable at the rear of the speedometer.

8. Install speedometer and the screws holding the speedometer to the instrument cluster.

9. Install the instrument cluster lens and attaching screws.

10. Install the instrument cluster and the screws holding the instrument cluster assembly to the dash assembly.

11. Install the center and left lower trim plates.

12. Connect the negative battery cable.

Speedometer Cable

REMOVAL & INSTALLATION

➡ **Removing the instrument cluster will give better access to the speedometer cable.**

⬧ **SEE FIG. 45**

1. Remove the instrument cluster.

2. Slide the cable out from the casing. If the cable is broken, the casing will have to be unscrewed from the transaxle and the broken piece removed from that end.

3. Before installing a new cable, slip a piece of cable into the speedometer and spin it between your fingers in the direction of normal rotation. If the mechanism sticks or binds, the speedometer should be repaired or replaced.

4. Inspect the casing. If it is cracked, kinked, or broken, the casing should be replaced.

5. Slide a new cable into the casing, engaging the transaxle end securely. Sometimes it is easier to unscrew the casing at the transaxle end, install the cable into the transaxle fitting, and screw the casing back into place. Install the instrument cluster.

Wiper Switch

REMOVAL & INSTALLATION

1986 and early

⬧ SEE FIGS. 40 to 49

1. Disconnect the negative battery cable.

2. Remove the steering wheel, the cover and the lock plate assembly.

3. Remove the turn signal actuator arm, the lever and the hazard flasher button.

4. Remove the turn signal switch screws, the lower steering column trim panel and the steering column bracket bolts.

5. Disconnect the turn signal switch and the wiper switch connectors.

6. Pull the turn signal rearward 6–8 in. (152–203mm), then remove the key buzzer switch and the cylinder lock.

7. Remove and pull the steering column housing rearward, then remove the housing cover screw.

8. Remove the wiper switch pivot and the switch.

9. To install, reverse the removal procedures.

1987 and later

1. Disconnect the negative battery cable.

2. Remove the steering wheel and turn signal switch. It may be necessary to first remove the column mounting nuts and remove the 4 bracket-to-mast jacket screws, then separate the bracket from the mast jacket to allow the connector clip on the ignition switch to be pulled from the column assembly.

3. Tag and disconnect the washer/wiper switch lower connector.

4. Remove the screws attaching the column housing to the mast jacket. Be sure to note the position of the dimmer switch actuator rod for reassembly in the same position. Remove the column housing and switch as an assembly.

➡ **Certain tilt and travel columns are equipped with a removable plastic cover on the column housing. This provides access to the wiper switch without removing the entire column housing.**

5. Turn upside down and use a drift to remove the pivot pin from the washer/wiper switch. Remove the switch.

To install:

6. Place the switch into position in the housing. Install the pivot pin.

7. Position the housing onto the mast jacket and attach by installing the screws. Install the dimmer switch actuator rod in the same position as noted when removed. Check switch operation.

8. Reconnect lower end of the switch assembly.

9. Install the ignition switch connector clip to the column assembly.

10. Install the mast jacket to the bracket.

11. If removed, install the column mounting nuts and the retaining bolts.

12. Install the turn signal switch and steering wheel.

13. Connect the negative battery cable.

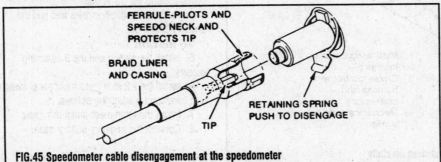

FERRULE-PILOTS AND SPEEDO NECK AND PROTECTS TIP

BRAID LINER AND CASING

RETAINING SPRING PUSH TO DISENGAGE

TIP

FIG.45 Speedometer cable disengagement at the speedometer

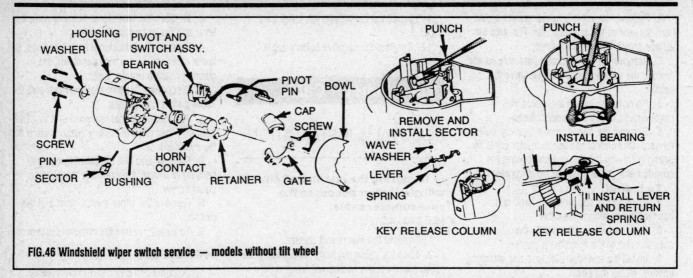

FIG.46 Windshield wiper switch service — models without tilt wheel

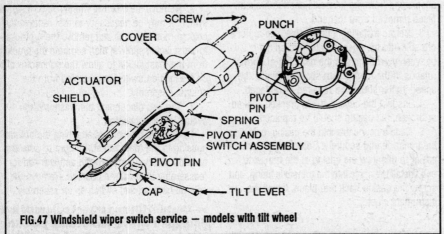

FIG.47 Windshield wiper switch service — models with tilt wheel

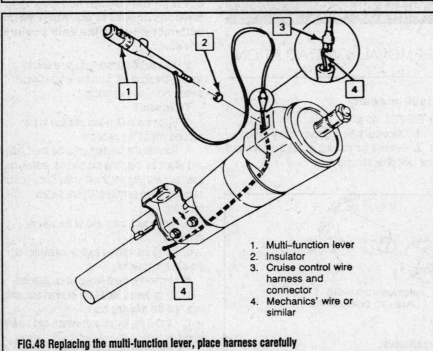

1. Multi–function lever
2. Insulator
3. Cruise control wire harness and connector
4. Mechanics' wire or similar

FIG.48 Replacing the multi-function lever, place harness carefully

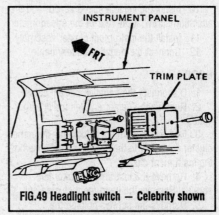

FIG.49 Headlight switch — Celebrity shown

Headlight Switch

♦ SEE FIGS. 49 and 50

REMOVAL & INSTALLATION

Century

1. Disconnect the negative battery cable.
2. Remove the instrument panel trim plate.
3. Remove the left side instrument panel switch trim panel by removing the 3 screws and gently rocking the panel out.
4. Remove the three screws and pull the switch straight out.

To install:

5. Install the switch and the 3 attaching screws.
6. Install the left side instrument panel switch trim panel and 3 attaching screws.
7. Install the instrument panel trim plate.
8. Connect the negative battery cable.

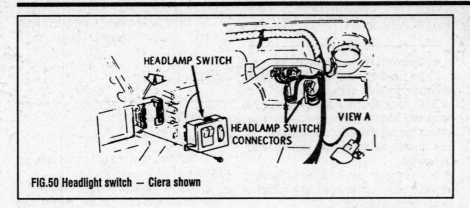

FIG.50 Headlight switch — Ciera shown

Celebrity

1. Disconnect the negative battery cable.
2. Remove the headlight switch knob.
3. Remove the instrument panel trim pad.
4. Unbolt the switch mounting plate from the instrument panel carrier.
5. Disconnect the wiring from the switch.
6. Remove the switch.

To install:

7. Install the switch.
8. Connect the wiring to the switch.
9. Install the bolts attaching the switch mounting plate to the instrument panel carrier.
10. Install the instrument panel trim pad.
11. Install the headlight switch knob.
12. Connect the negative battery cable.

Ciera and Cruiser

1. Disconnect the negative battery cable.
2. Remove the left side instrument panel trim pad.
3. Unbolt the switch from the instrument panel.
4. Pull the switch rearward and remove it.

To install:

5. Install the switch and connect the electrical connectors.
6. Install the bolts attaching the switch to the instrument panel.
7. Install the left side instrument panel trim pad.
8. Connect the negative battery cable.

6000

1. Disconnect the negative battery cable.
2. Remove the steering column trim cover and headlight rod and knob by reaching behind the instrument panel and depressing the lock tab.
3. Remove the left instrument panel trim plate.
4. Unbolt and remove the switch and bracket assembly from the instrument panel.
5. Loosen the bezel and remove the switch from the bracket.

To install:

6. Install the switch to the bracket and install the bezel.

7. Install the switch and bracket assembly to the instrument panel and install the attaching bolts.
8. Install the left instrument panel trim plate.
9. Install the headlight rod and knob. Install the steering column trim cover.
10. Connect the negative battery cable.

Dimmer Switch

REMOVAL & INSTALLATION

1. Disconnect the negative battery cable.
2. Remove the steering wheel. Remove the trim cover.
3. Remove the turn signal switch assembly.
4. Remove the ignition switch stud and screw. Remove the ignition switch.
5. Remove the dimmer switch actuator rod by sliding it from the switch assembly.
6. Remove the dimmer switch bolts and remove the dimmer switch.

To install:

7. Install the dimmer switch and attaching bolts.
8. Install the dimmer switch actuator rod by sliding it into the switch assembly.
9. Adjust the dimmer switch by depressing the switch slightly and inserting a $\frac{3}{32}$ in. drill bit into the adjusting hole. Push the switch up to remove any play and tighten the dimmer switch adjusting screw.
10. Install the ignition switch, stud and screw.
11. Install the turn signal switch assembly.
12. Install the trim cover. Install the steering wheel.
13. Connect the battery negative cable.

Combination Switch

REMOVAL & INSTALLATION

1. Disconnect the negative battery cable. Remove the steering wheel and trim cover.
2. Loosen the cover screws. Pry the cover upward and remove it from the shaft.
3. Position U-shaped lock plate compressing tool J–23653–C on the end of the steering shaft and compress the lockplate by turning the shaft nut clockwise. Pry the wire snapring from the shaft groove.
4. Remove the tool and lift the lock plate off the shaft.
5. Slip the canceling cam, upper bearing preload spring and thrust washer off the shaft.
6. Remove the turn signal lever. Push the flasher knob in and unscrew it. Remove the button retaining screw and remove the button, spring and knob.
7. Pull the switch connector out the mast jacket and tape the upper part to facilitate switch removal. Attach a long piece of wire to the turn signal switch connector. When installing the turn signal switch, feed this wire through the column first, and then use this wire to pull the switch connector into position. If equipped with tilt-wheel, place the turn signal and shifter housing in the lowest position and remove the harness cover.
8. Remove the 3 switch mounting screws. Remove the switch by pulling it straight up while guiding the wiring harness cover through the column.

To install:

9. Install the replacement switch by working the connector and cover down through the housing and under the bracket. If equipped with tilt-wheel, work the connector down through the housing, under the bracket and install the harness cover.
10. Install the switch mounting screws and the connector on the mast jacket bracket. Install the column-to-dash trim plate.
11. Install the flasher knob and the turn signal lever.
12. With the turn signal lever in the middle position and the flasher knob out, slide the thrust washer, upper bearing preload spring and canceling cam onto the shaft.
13. Position the lock plate on the shaft and press it down until a new snapring can be inserted in the shaft groove. Always use a new snapring when assembling.
14. Install the cover and the steering wheel. Connect the battery negative cable.

Clock

REMOVAL & INSTALLATION

1. Remove the instrument panel cluster bezel.
2. Remove the clock retaining screws and remove the clock.

Back-up Light Switch

REMOVAL & INSTALLATION

Column Mounted

1. Working from underneath the dashboard, locate the back-up light switch on the steering column and remove the wiring harness.
2. Then pull downward and remove the switch from the steering column.

To install:

3. Apply the parking brake and place the gear select lever in neutral.
4. Align the actuator on the switch with the hole in the shift tube.
5. Position the rearward portion of the switch (connector side) to fit into the cutout in the lower jacket.
6. Push up on the front of the switch, the two tangs on the housing back will snap into place in the rectangular holes in the jacket.
7. Adjust the switch by moving the gear selector to park. The main housing and the back should ratchet, providing proper switch adjustment.

Rear Defogger System

All systems operate on 12 volts. An instrument panel mounted switch with an integral indicator lamp is used to turn the system ON.

Certain conditions such as outside temperature, vehicle speed, atmospheric pressure and even the number of passengers inside the vehicle affects the length of time required to remove fog from the glass.

The defogger is designed to turn OFF after approximately 10 minutes of operation. If the defogger is turn ON again, it will only operate for approximately 5 minutes. You can however, turn the system OFF before the time is up by turning the defogger switch or ignition switch OFF.

REMOVAL & INSTALLATION

1. Disconnect the negative battery cable.
2. Remove the left side instrument panel or accessory trim plate, as required.
3. On some vehicles, it may be necessary to remove the steering column collar, steering column opening filler and cluster trim plate.
4. Remove the ash tray and sound insulator, as required.
5. On some vehicles, it may be necessary to remove the radio control knobs, air conditioning/heater control and/or cables.
6. Remove the rear defogger control retaining screws or clip and remove the switch.
7. Disconnect the switch electrical connector.

To install:

8. Reconnect the electrical connector to the switch.
9. Fit the switch to the instrument panel and install the retaining screws.
10. Install the instrument panel or trim plate.
11. Reconnect the negative battery cable.

GRID LINE

♦ SEE FIGS. 51 to 53

Testing

1. Start the engine and pull out the defogger switch knob.
2. Using a test lamp, ground the end and touch the probe to each grid line. The test lamp should operate as indicated.
3. If the test lamp remains bright at both ends of the grid lines, check for a loose ground.

➡ **The range zones may vary slightly from 1 glass to another; but, the test lamp brilliance will decrease proportionately as it is moved from left to right on the grid line.**

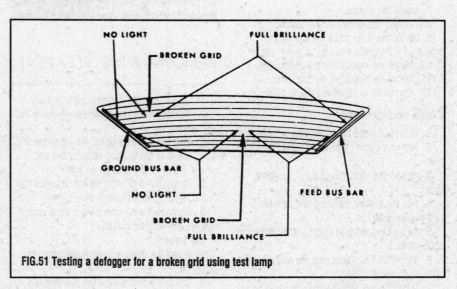

FIG.51 Testing a defogger for a broken grid using test lamp

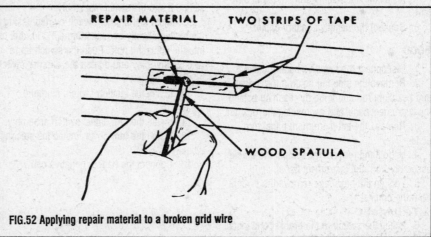

FIG.52 Applying repair material to a broken grid wire

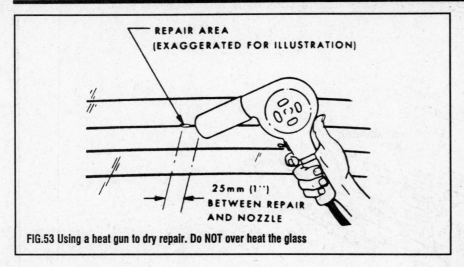

FIG.53 Using a heat gun to dry repair. Do NOT over heat the glass

3. Clean the area to be repaired. Buff with steel wool and wipe clean with a damped cloth with alcohol.

4. Position a strip of tape above and below the grid line area to be repair.

5. Repair the grid line break using defogger repair kit (Part 1052858 or equivalent) and follow the manufacturer's instructions.

6. After the grid line has been repaired, carefully remove the strips of tape.

7. Apply heat, using a heat gun, to the repaired area for approximately 1–2 minutes. A minimum temperature of 300°F (149°C) is required.

➡ **To avoid damage to the interior trim, protect the trim near the area to be repair. Allow the repair materials to cure for at least 24 hours. Do not operate the unit until such time.**

8. Test the rear defogger operation to verified proper operation.

4. If an abnormal reading is observed by the test lamp on any grid line, place the test lamp probe on the left of that bus bar and move the probe toward the right until the test lamp goes out. This will indicate a break in the continuity on that grid line.

Repair

1. Locate the break(s) on the grid line(s) and mark the outside of the glass, using a grease pencil.

2. Disconnect the negative battery cable.

LIGHTING

Take care not to squeeze the bulbs too tightly, they can break in you hand and give a very bad cut. If the bulbs are stuck, spray them with penetrating oil and allow them to soak for a few minutes. There are also tools on the market for gripping and removing bulbs.

Headlights

REMOVAL & INSTALLATION

1. Remove the headlamp trim panel attaching screws.

2. Remove the headlamp bulb retaining screws. Do not touch the two headlamp aiming screws, at the top and side of the retaining ring, or the headlamp aim will have to be readjusted.

3. Pull the bulb and ring forward the separate them. Unplug the electrical connector from the rear of the bulb.

4. Plug the new bulb into the electrical connector. Install the bulb into the retaining ring and install the ring and bulb. Install the trim panel.

Signal and Marker Lights

REMOVAL & INSTALLATION

1. Remove the headlight bezel mounting screws and the bezel.

2. Disconnect the twist lock socket from the lens housing.

3. Remove the parking light housing.

➡ **To remove the bulb, turn the twist lock socket at the rear of the housing) counterclockwise 1/4 turn, then remove the socket with the bulb; replace the bulb if defective.**

4. To install, reverse the removal procedures.

Side Marker Lights

REMOVAL & INSTALLATION

1. Remove the marker light housing screws and the housing.

2. Disconnect the twist lock socket from the lens housing.

➡ **To remove the bulb, turn the twist lock socket (at the rear of the housing) counterclockwise 1/4 turn, then remove the socket with the bulb; replace the bulb if defective.**

3. To install, reverse the removal procedures.

Rear Turn Signal, Brake and Parking Lights

REMOVAL & INSTALLATION

1. Remove the tail light panel screws and the panel.

2. Disconnect the twist lock socket from the lens housing.

➡ **To remove the bulb, turn the twist lock socket (at the rear of the housing) counterclockwise 1/4 turn, then remove the socket with the bulb; replace the bulb if defective.**

3. To install, reverse the removal procedures.

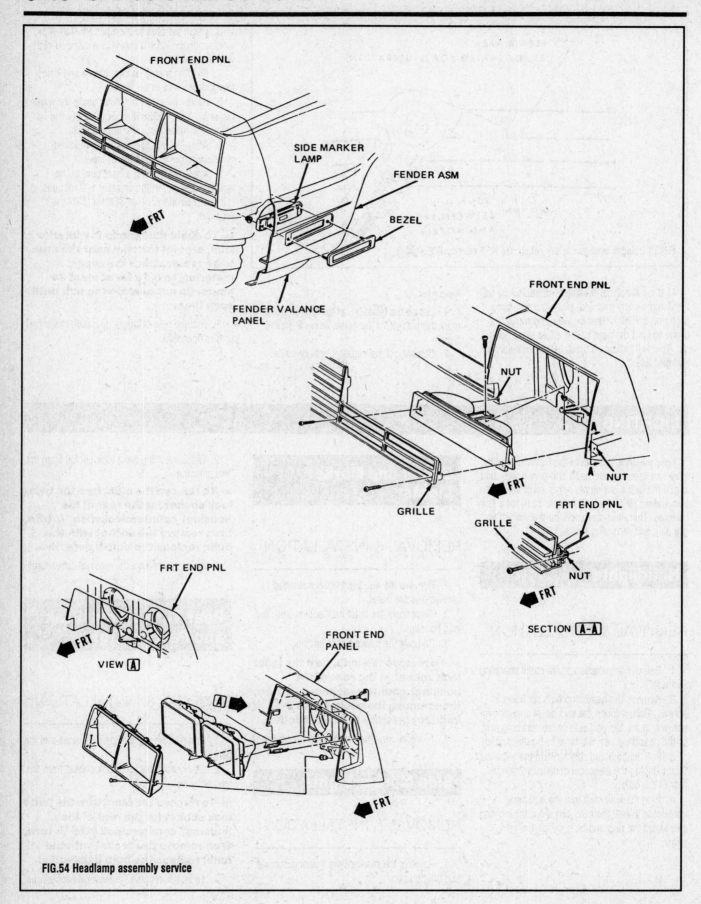

FIG.54 Headlamp assembly service

APPLICATION	BULB NO.	QUANTITY	RATING CANDLEPOWER
FRONT LAMPS			
Headlamp — Inner—Std.	4651	2	50W
— Inner—Halogen	H4651	2	50W
— Outer	4652	2	60/40W
Park	194NA	2	1.5CP
Park & Turn Signal	2057NA	2	1.5/24
Sidemarker	194	2	2
REAR LAMPS			
Backup — Sedan	2057	2	2/32
— Wagon	1156	2	32
License	194	1	2
Sidemarker	194	2	2
Tail — Sedan	194	2	2
Tail, Stop & Turn Signal	2057	4	2/32
High Mounted Stop — Sedan	1156	1	32
— Wagon	557	2	21
	212-2	1	12
INTERIOR ILLUMINATION			
A/C — Heater Control	194	1	2
Ash Tray	168	1	3
Auto Trans — Console	168	1	3
Courtesy Lamp — Front	194	2	2
— Console	212-2	1	6
Dome Lamp	561	1	12
Glove Box	194	1	2
Instrument Cluster	161/194	2/3	1/2
Luggage Compt. — Sedan	1003		
— Wagon	561	1	12
Radio Dial Exc. Graphic Equalizer	194	1	2
Graphic Equalizer	37	2	0.5
Reading Lamp	906	2	6
Underhood Lamp	93	1	15
WARNING LIGHTS & INDICATORS			
Brake	194	1	2
Service Engine Soon	194	1	2
Choke	194	1	2
High Beam	194	1	2
Low Fuel	194	1	2
Oil	194	1	2
Seat Belts	194	1	2
Tailgate Ajar	194	1	2
Temperature	194	1	2
Turn Signal	194	2	2
Upshift	194	1	2
Volts	194	1	2

TRAILER WIRING

Wiring the car for towing is fairly easy. There are a number of good wiring kits available and these should be used, rather than trying to design your own. All trailers will need brake lights and turn signals as well as tail lights and side marker lights. Most states require extra marker lights for overly wide trailers. Also, most states have recently required back-up lights for trailers, and most trailer manufacturers have been building trailers with back-up lights for several years.

Additionally, some Class I, most Class II and just about all Class III trailers will have electric brakes.

Add to this number an accessories wire, to operate trailer internal equipment or to charge the trailer's battery, and you can have as many as seven wires in the harness.

Determine the equipment on your trailer and buy the wiring kit necessary. The kit will contain all the wires needed, plus a plug adapter set which included the female plug, mounted on the bumper or hitch, and the male plug, wired into, or plugged into the trailer harness.

When installing the kit, follow the manufacturer's instructions. The color coding of the wires is standard throughout the industry.

One point to note, some domestic vehicles, and most imported vehicles, have separate turn signals. On most domestic vehicles, the brake lights and rear turn signals operate with the same bulb. For those vehicles with separate turn signals, you can purchase an isolation unit so that the brake lights won't blink whenever the turn signals are operated, or, you can go to your local electronics supply house and buy tour diodes to wire in series with the brake and turn signal bulbs. Diodes will isolate the brake and turn signals. The choice is yours. The isolation units are simple and quick to install, but far more expensive than the diodes. The diodes, however, require more work to install properly, since they require the cutting of each bulb's wire and soldering in place of the diode.

One final point, the best kits are those with a spring loaded cover on the vehicle mounted socket. This cover prevents dirt and moisture from corroding the terminals. Never let the vehicle socket hang loosely. Always mount it securely to the bumper or hitch.

➡ **For more information on towing a trailer please refer to Section 1.**

CIRCUIT PROTECTION

Fuses

Fuses (located on a swing down unit near the steering column or in the glove box) protect all the major electrical systems in the car. In case of an electrical overload, the fuse melts, breaking the circuit and stopping the flow of electricity.

If a fuse blows, the cause should be investigated and corrected before the installation of a new fuse. This, however, is easier to say than to do. Because each fuse protects a limited number of components, your job is narrowed down somewhat. Begin your investigation by looking for obvious fraying, loose connections, breaks in insulation, etc. Use the techniques outlined at the beginning of this section. Electrical problems are almost always a real headache to solve, but if you are patient and persistent, and approach the problem logically (that is, don't start replacing electrical components randomly), you will eventually find the solution.

The amperage of each fuse and the circuit it protects are marked on the fusebox, which is located under the left side (driver's side) of the instrument panel and pulls down for easy access.

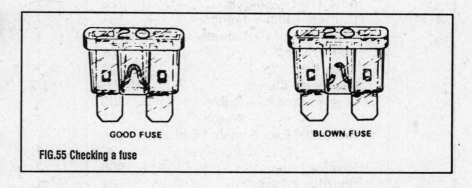

GOOD FUSE   BLOWN FUSE

FIG.55 Checking a fuse

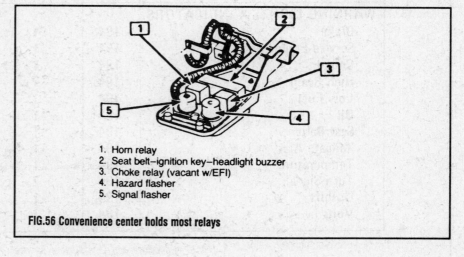

1. Horn relay
2. Seat belt–ignition key–headlight buzzer
3. Choke relay (vacant w/EFI)
4. Hazard flasher
5. Signal flasher

FIG.56 Convenience center holds most relays

Fusible Links

The fuse link is a short length of special, Hypalon (high temperature) insulated wire, integral with the engine compartment wiring harness and should not be confused with standard wire. It is several wire gauges smaller than the circuit which it protects. Under no circumstances should a fuse link replacement repair be made using a length of standard wire cut from bulk stock or from another wiring harness.

To repair any blown fuse link use the following procedure:

1. Determine which circuit is damaged, its location and the cause of the open fuse link. If the damaged fuse link is one of three fed by a common No. 10 or 12 gauge feed wire, determine the specific affected circuit.

2. Disconnect the negative battery cable.

3. Cut the damaged fuse link from the wiring harness and discard it. If the fuse link is one of three circuits fed by a single feed wire, cut it out of the harness at each splice end and discard it.

4. Identify and procure the proper fuse link and butt connectors for attaching the fuse link to the harness.

5. To repair any fuse link in a 3-link group with one feed:

   a. After cutting the open link out of the harness, cut each of the remaining undamaged fuse links close to the feed wire weld.

   b. Strip approximately 1/2 in. (13mm) of insulation from the detached ends of the two good fuse links, Then insert two wire ends into one end of a butt connector and carefully push one stripped end of the replacement fuse link into the same end of the butt connector and crimp all three firmly together.

➡ **Care must be taken when fitting the three fuse links into the butt connector as the internal diameter is a snug fit for three wires. Make sure to use a proper crimping tool. Pliers, side cutter, etc. will not apply the proper crimp to retain the wires and withstand a pull test.**

   c. After crimping the butt connector to the three fuse links, cut the weld portion from the feed wire and strip approximately 1/2 in. (13mm) of insulation from the cut end. Insert the stripped end into the open end of the butt connector and crimp very firmly.

   d. To attach the remaining end of the replacement fuse link, strip approximately 1/2 in. (13mm) of insulation from the wire end of the circuit from which the blown fuse link was removed, and firmly crimp a butt connector or

equivalent to the stripped wire. Then, insert the end of the replacement link into the other end of the butt connector and crimp firmly.

   e. Using rosin core solder with a consistency of 60 percent tin and 40 percent lead, solder the connectors and the wires at the repairs and insulate with electrical tape.

6. To replace any fuse link on a single circuit in a harness, cut out the damaged portion, strip approximately 1/2 in. (13mm) of insulation from the two wire ends and attach the appropriate replacement fuse link to the stripped wire ends with two proper size butt connectors. Solder the connectors and wires and insulate with tape.

7. To repair any fuse link which has an eyelet terminal on one end such as the charging circuit, cut off the open fuse link behind the weld, strip approximately 1/2 in. (13mm) of insulation from the cut end and attach the appropriate new eyelet fuse link to the cut stripped wire with an appropriate size butt connector. Solder the connectors and wires at the repair and insulate with tape.

8. Connect the negative battery cable to the battery and test the system for proper operation.

➡ **Do not mistake a resistor wire for a fuse link. The resistor wire is generally longer and has print stating, "Resistor-don't cut or splice".**

When attaching a single No. 16, 17, 18 or 20 gauge fuse link to a heavy gauge wire, always double the stripped wire end of the fuse link before inserting and crimping it into the butt connector for positive wire retention.

Circuit Breakers

The headlights are protected by a circuit breaker in the headlamp switch. If the circuit breaker trips, the headlights will either flash on and off, or stay off altogether. The circuit breaker rests automatically after the overload is removed.

The windshield wipers are also protected by a circuit breaker. If the motor overheats, the circuit breaker will trip, remaining off until the motor cools or the overload is removed. One common cause of overheating is operation of the wipers in heavy snow.

The circuit breakers for the power door locks and power windows are located in the fuse box.

Flashers

The hazard flasher is located in the convenience center', under the dash, on the left side kick panel. The horn relay and the buzzer assembly may be found here also. The turn signal flasher is installed in a clamp attached to the base of the steering column support inside the car. In all cases, replacement is made by unplugging the old unit and plugging in a new one.

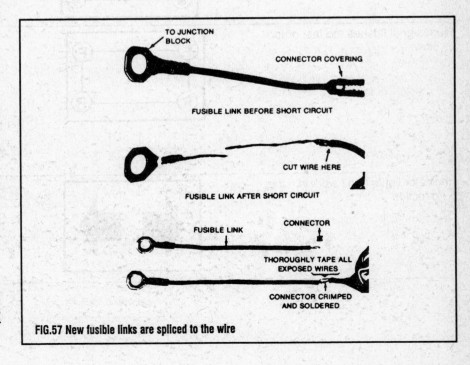

FIG.57 New fusible links are spliced to the wire

Troubleshooting Basic Turn Signal and Flasher Problems

Most problems in the turn signals or flasher system can be reduced to defective flashers or bulbs, which are easily replaced. Occasionally, problems in the turn signals are traced to the switch in the steering column, which will require professional service.

F = Front   R = Rear   ● = Lights off   o = Lights on

Problem		Solution
Turn signals light, but do not flash		• Replace the flasher
No turn signals light on either side		• Check the fuse. Replace if defective. • Check the flasher by substitution • Check for open circuit, short circuit or poor ground
Both turn signals on one side don't work		• Check for bad bulbs • Check for bad ground in both housings
One turn signal light on one side doesn't work		• Check and/or replace bulb • Check for corrosion in socket. Clean contacts. • Check for poor ground at socket
Turn signal flashes too fast or too slow		• Check any bulb on the side flashing too fast. A heavy-duty bulb is probably installed in place of a regular bulb. • Check the bulb flashing too slow. A standard bulb was probably installed in place of a heavy-duty bulb. • Check for loose connections or corrosion at the bulb socket
Indicator lights don't work in either direction		• Check if the turn signals are working • Check the dash indicator lights • Check the flasher by substitution

Troubleshooting Basic Turn Signal and Flasher Problems

Most problems in the turn signals or flasher system can be reduced to defective flashers or bulbs, which are easily replaced. Occasionally, problems in the turn signals are traced to the switch in the steering column, which will require professional service.

F = Front   R = Rear   ● = Lights off   o = Lights on

Problem		Solution

One indicator light doesn't light		· On systems with 1 dash indicator:
		  See if the lights work on the same side. Often the filaments have been reversed in systems combining stoplights with taillights and turn signals.
		  Check the flasher by substitution
		· On systems with 2 indicators:
		  Check the bulbs on the same side
		  Check the indicator light bulb
		  Check the flasher by substitution

Troubleshooting Basic Lighting Problems

Problem	Cause	Solution
Lights		
One or more lights don't work, but others do	· Defective bulb(s) · Blown fuse(s) · Dirty fuse clips or light sockets · Poor ground circuit	· Replace bulb(s) · Replace fuse(s) · Clean connections · Run ground wire from light socket housing to car frame
Lights burn out quickly	· Incorrect voltage regulator setting or defective regulator · Poor battery/alternator connections	· Replace voltage regulator · Check battery/alternator connections
Lights go dim	· Low/discharged battery · Alternator not charging · Corroded sockets or connections · Low voltage output	· Check battery · Check drive belt tension; repair or replace alternator · Clean bulb and socket contacts and connections · Replace voltage regulator
Lights flicker	· Loose connection · Poor ground · Circuit breaker operating (short circuit)	· Tighten all connections · Run ground wire from light housing to car frame · Check connections and look for bare wires
Lights "flare"—Some flare is normal on acceleration—if excessive, see "Lights Burn Out Quickly"	· High voltage setting	· Replace voltage regulator
Lights glare—approaching drivers are blinded	· Lights adjusted too high · Rear springs or shocks sagging · Rear tires soft	· Have headlights aimed · Check rear springs/shocks · Check/correct rear tire pressure

Troubleshooting Basic Lighting Problems

Problem	Cause	Solution
Turn Signals		
Turn signals don't work in either direction	• Blown fuse • Defective flasher • Loose connection	• Replace fuse • Replace flasher • Check/tighten all connections
Right (or left) turn signal only won't work	• Bulb burned out • Right (or left) indicator bulb burned out • Short circuit	• Replace bulb • Check/replace indicator bulb • Check/repair wiring
Flasher rate too slow or too fast	• Incorrect wattage bulb • Incorrect flasher	• Flasher bulb • Replace flasher (use a variable load flasher if you pull a trailer)
Indicator lights do not flash (burn steadily)	• Burned out bulb • Defective flasher	• Replace bulb • Replace flasher
Indicator lights do not light at all	• Burned out indicator bulb • Defective flasher	• Replace indicator bulb • Replace flasher

Troubleshooting Basic Dash Gauge Problems

Problem	Cause	Solution
Coolant Temperature Gauge		
Gauge reads erratically or not at all	• Loose or dirty connections • Defective sending unit • Defective gauge	• Clean/tighten connections • Bi-metal gauge: remove the wire from the sending unit. Ground the wire for an instant. If the gauge registers, replace the sending unit. • Magnetic gauge: disconnect the wire at the sending unit. With ignition ON gauge should register COLD. Ground the wire; gauge should register HOT.
Ammeter Gauge—Turn Headlights ON (do not start engine). Note reaction		
Ammeter shows charge Ammeter shows discharge Ammeter does not move	• Connections reversed on gauge • Ammeter is OK • Loose connections or faulty wiring • Defective gauge	• Reinstall connections • Nothing • Check/correct wiring • Replace gauge

Troubleshooting Basic Dash Gauge Problems

Problem	Cause	Solution
Oil Pressure Gauge		
Gauge does not register or is inaccurate	• On mechanical gauge, Bourdon tube may be bent or kinked	• Check tube for kinks or bends preventing oil from reaching the gauge
	• Low oil pressure	• Remove sending unit. Idle the engine briefly. If no oil flows from sending unit hole, problem is in engine.
	• Defective gauge	• Remove the wire from the sending unit and ground it for an instant with the ignition ON. A good gauge will go to the top of the scale.
	• Defective wiring	• Check the wiring to the gauge. If it's OK and the gauge doesn't register when grounded, replace the gauge.
	• Defective sending unit	• If the wiring is OK and the gauge functions when grounded, replace the sending unit
All Gauges		
All gauges do not operate	• Blown fuse	• Replace fuse
	• Defective instrument regulator	• Replace instrument voltage regulator
All gauges read low or erratically	• Defective or dirty instrument voltage regulator	• Clean contacts or replace
All gauges pegged	• Loss of ground between instrument voltage regulator and car	• Check ground
	• Defective instrument regulator	• Replace regulator
Warning Lights		
Light(s) do not come on when ignition is ON, but engine is not started	• Defective bulb	• Replace bulb
	• Defective wire	• Check wire from light to sending unit
	• Defective sending unit	• Disconnect the wire from the sending unit and ground it. Replace the sending unit if the light comes on with the ignition ON.
Light comes on with engine running	• Problem in individual system	• Check system
	• Defective sending unit	• Check sending unit (see above)

Troubleshooting the Heater

Problem	Cause	Solution
Blower motor will not turn at any speed	• Blown fuse • Loose connection • Defective ground • Faulty switch • Faulty motor • Faulty resistor	• Replace fuse • Inspect and tighten • Clean and tighten • Replace switch • Replace motor • Replace resistor
Blower motor turns at one speed only	• Faulty switch • Faulty resistor	• Replace switch • Replace resistor
Blower motor turns but does not circulate air	• Intake blocked • Fan not secured to the motor shaft	• Clean intake • Tighten security
Heater will not heat	• Coolant does not reach proper temperature • Heater core blocked internally • Heater core air-bound • Blend-air door not in proper position	• Check and replace thermostat if necessary • Flush or replace core if necessary • Purge air from core • Adjust cable
Heater will not defrost	• Control cable adjustment incorrect • Defroster hose damaged	• Adjust control cable • Replace defroster hose

Troubleshooting Basic Windshield Wiper Problems

Problem	Cause	Solution
Electric Wipers		
Wipers do not operate— Wiper motor heats up or hums	• Internal motor defect • Bent or damaged linkage • Arms improperly installed on linking pivots	• Replace motor • Repair or replace linkage • Position linkage in park and reinstall wiper arms
Electric Wipers		
Wipers do not operate— No current to motor	• Fuse or circuit breaker blown • Loose, open or broken wiring • Defective switch • Defective or corroded terminals • No ground circuit for motor or switch	• Replace fuse or circuit breaker • Repair wiring and connections • Replace switch • Replace or clean terminals • Repair ground circuits
Wipers do not operate— Motor runs	• Linkage disconnected or broken	• Connect wiper linkage or replace broken linkage
Vacuum Wipers		
Wipers do not operate	• Control switch or cable inoperative • Loss of engine vacuum to wiper motor (broken hoses, low engine vacuum, defective vacuum/fuel pump) • Linkage broken or disconnected • Defective wiper motor	• Repair or replace switch or cable • Check vacuum lines, engine vacuum and fuel pump • Repair linkage • Replace wiper motor
Wipers stop on engine acceleration	• Leaking vacuum hoses • Dry windshield • Oversize wiper blades • Defective vacuum/fuel pump	• Repair or replace hoses • Wet windshield with washers • Replace with proper size wiper blades • Replace pump

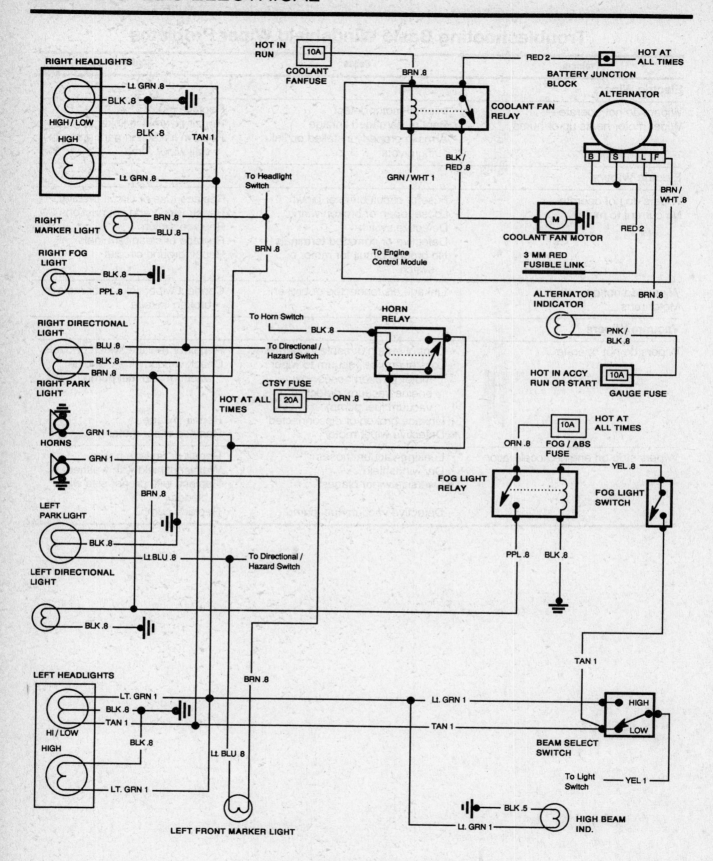

External front lighting system — 1982-90 Celebrity

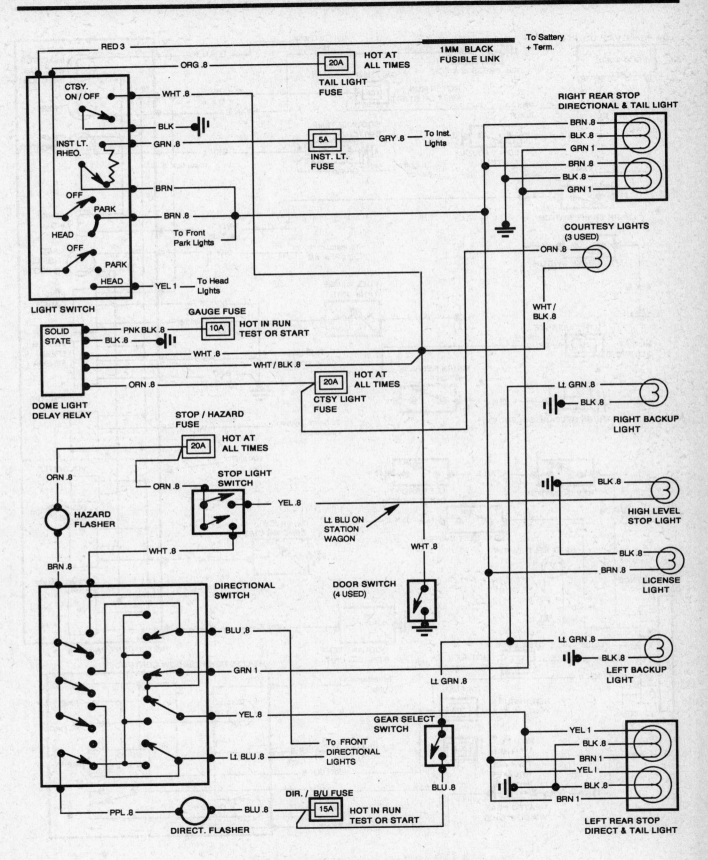

External rear lighting system — 1982–90 Celebrity

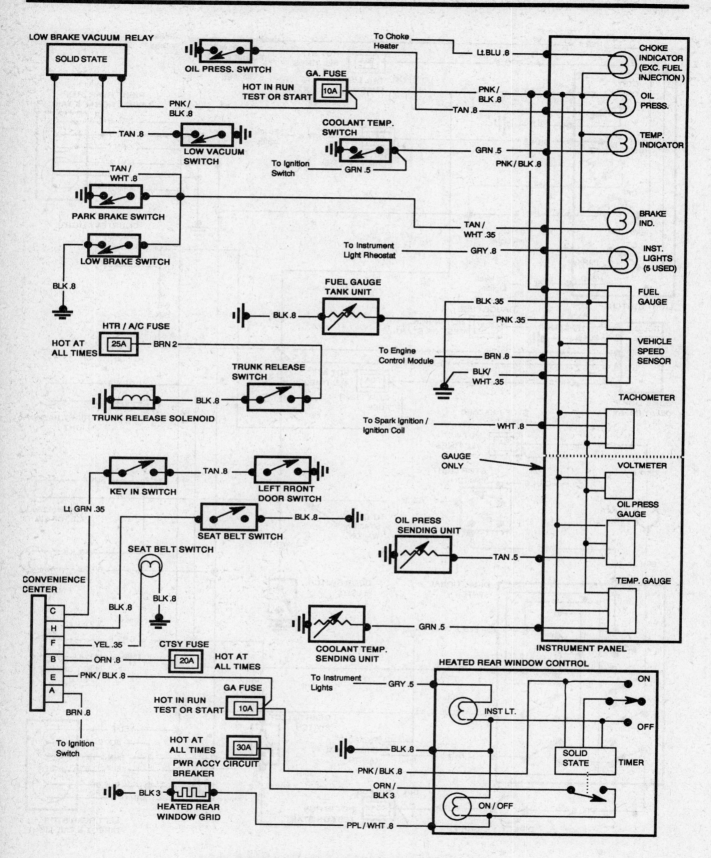

Instrument panel and lighting system — 1982-85 Celebrity

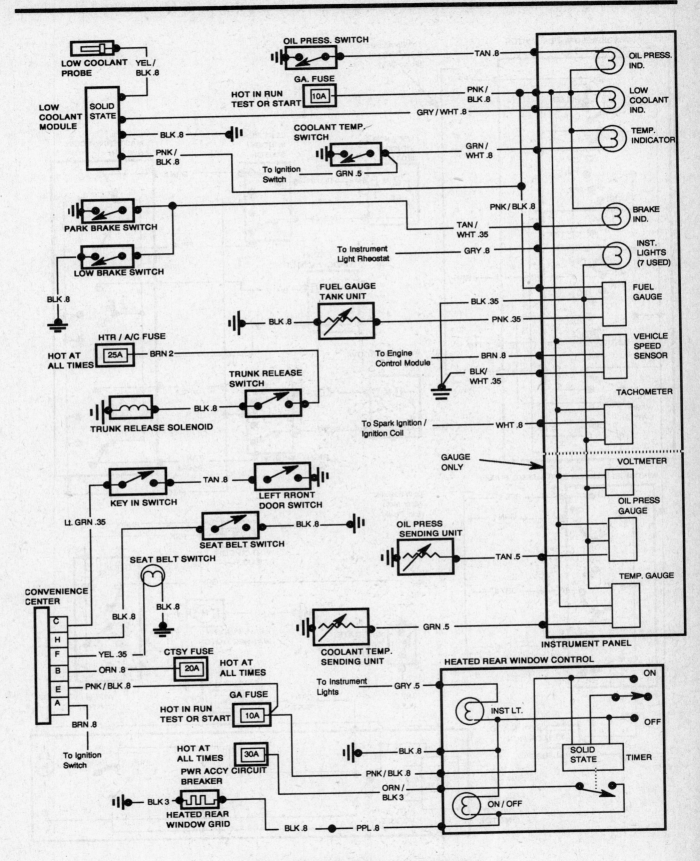

Instrument panel and lighting system — 1986–90 Celebrity

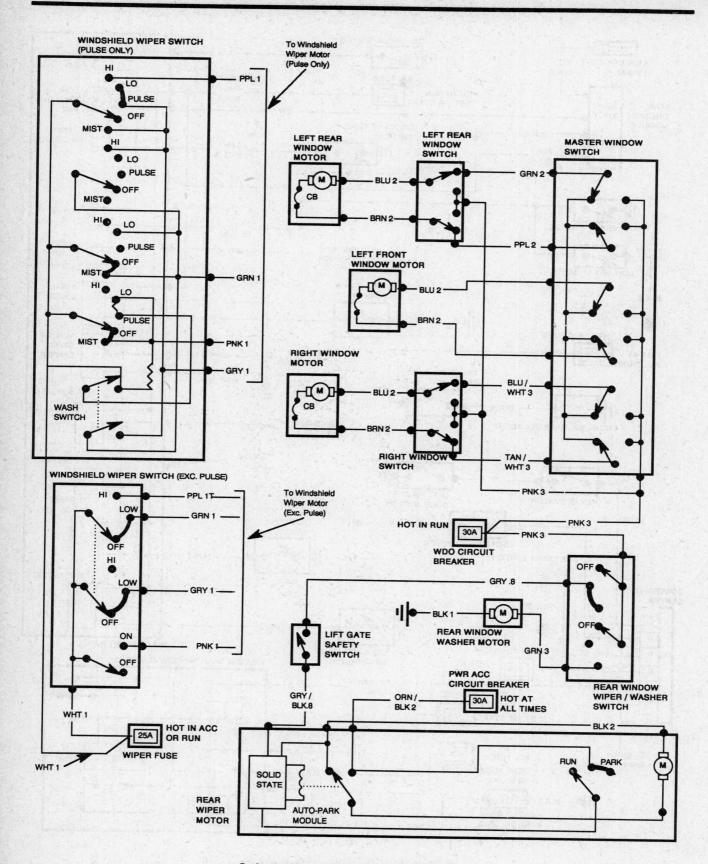

Dash controls and accessories — 1982-90 Celebrity

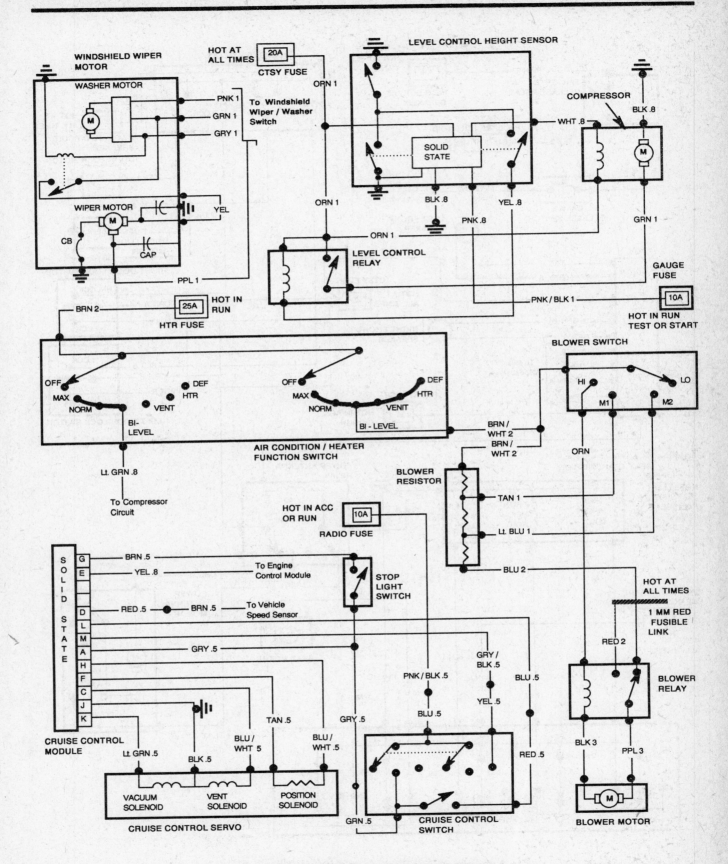

Dash controls and accessories — 1982–90 Celebrity (continued)

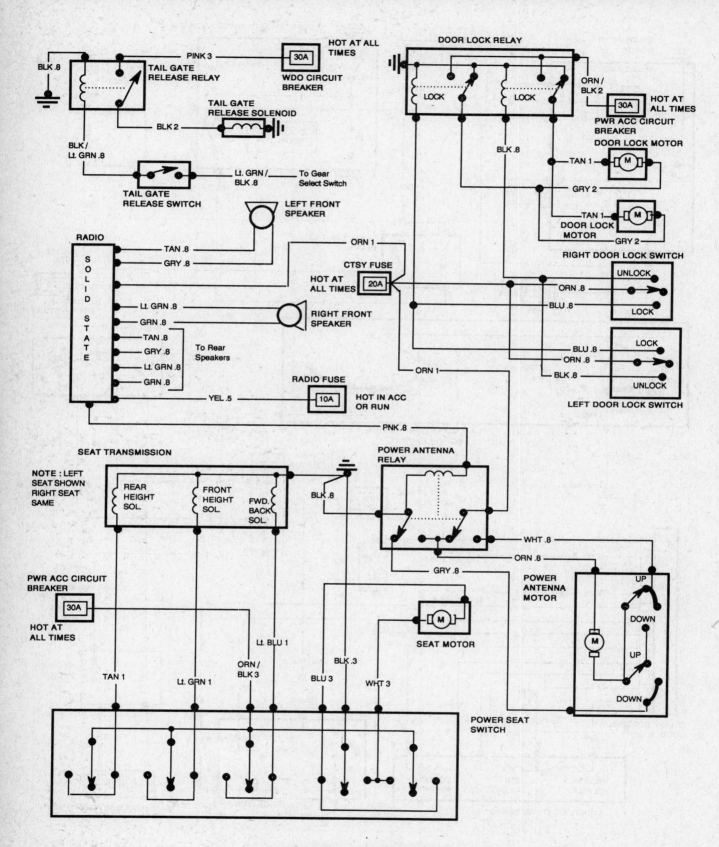

Power accessories — 1982–86 Celebrity

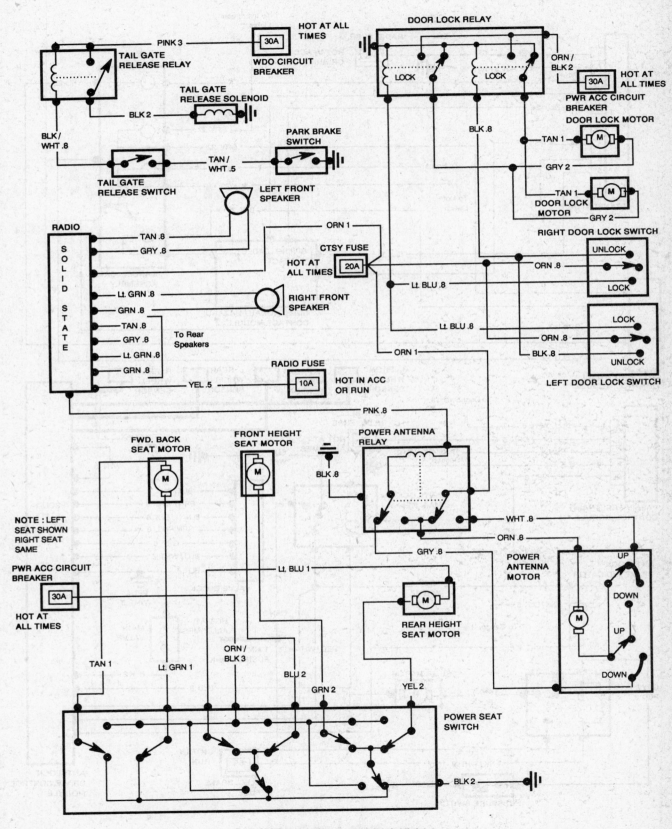

Power accessories — 1986-90 Celebrity

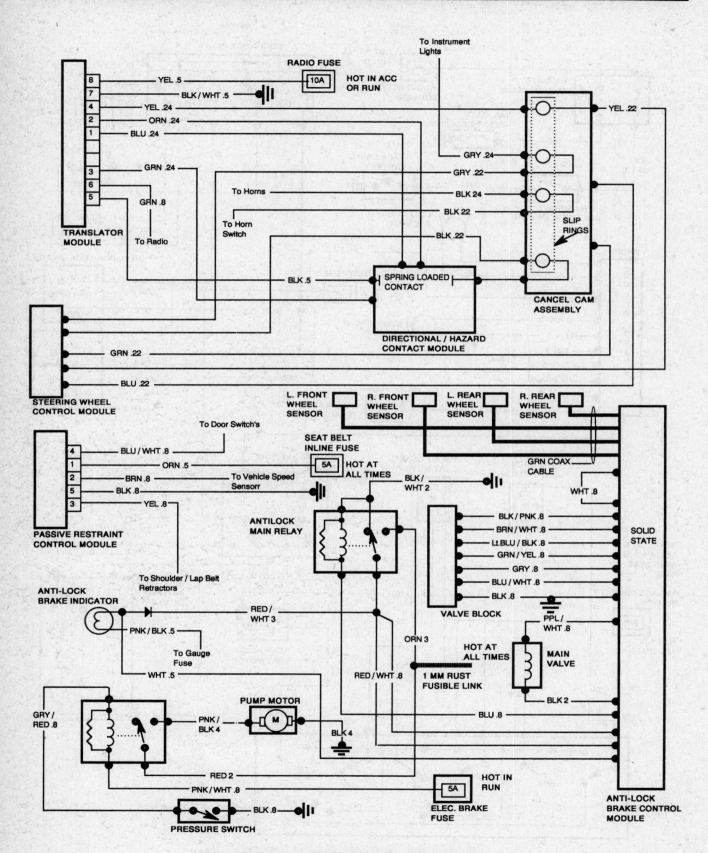

Anti-lock brake system and dash accessories — 1986-90 Celebrity

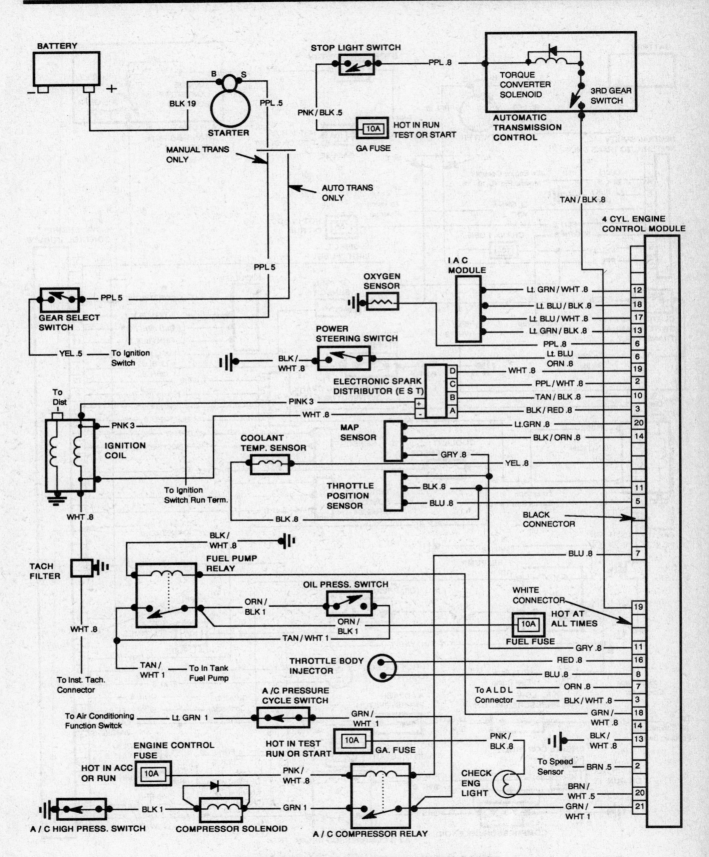

Engine control system 4-cylinder engine — 1982–86 Celebrity

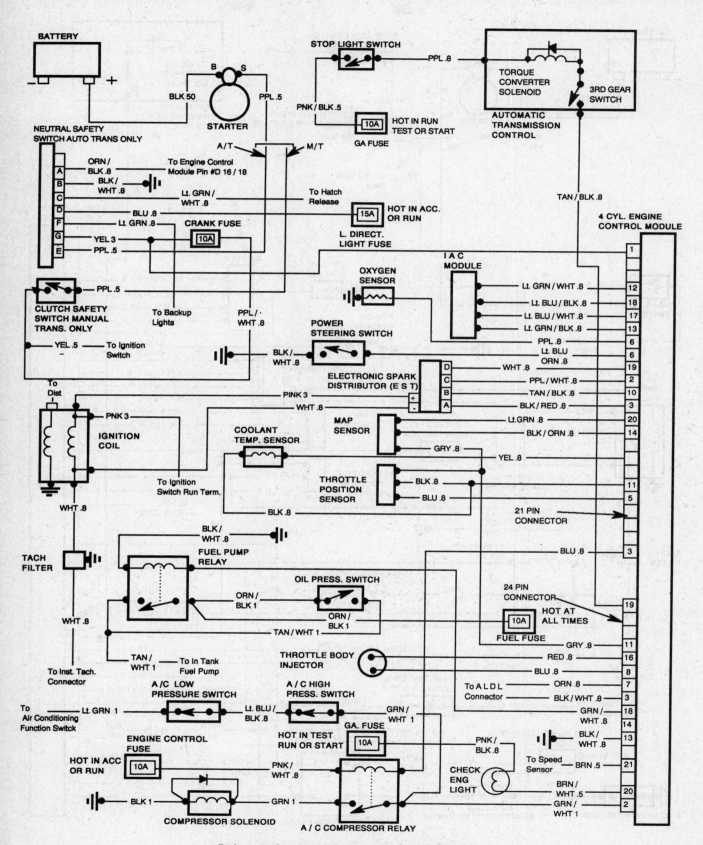

Engine control system 4-cylinder engine — 1987–90 Celebrity

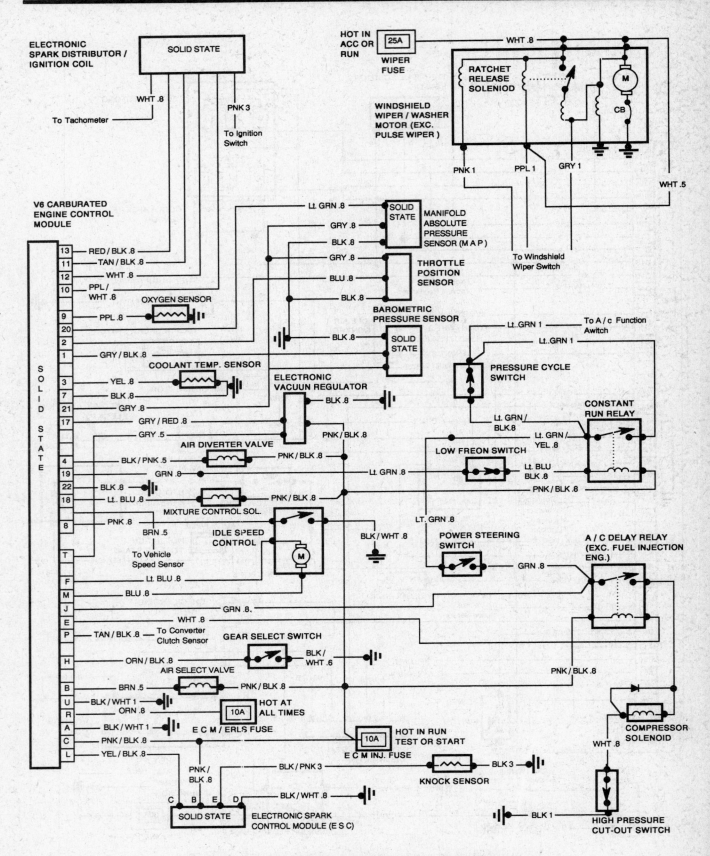

Engine control system (carbureted) 6-cylinder engine — 1982–86 Celebrity

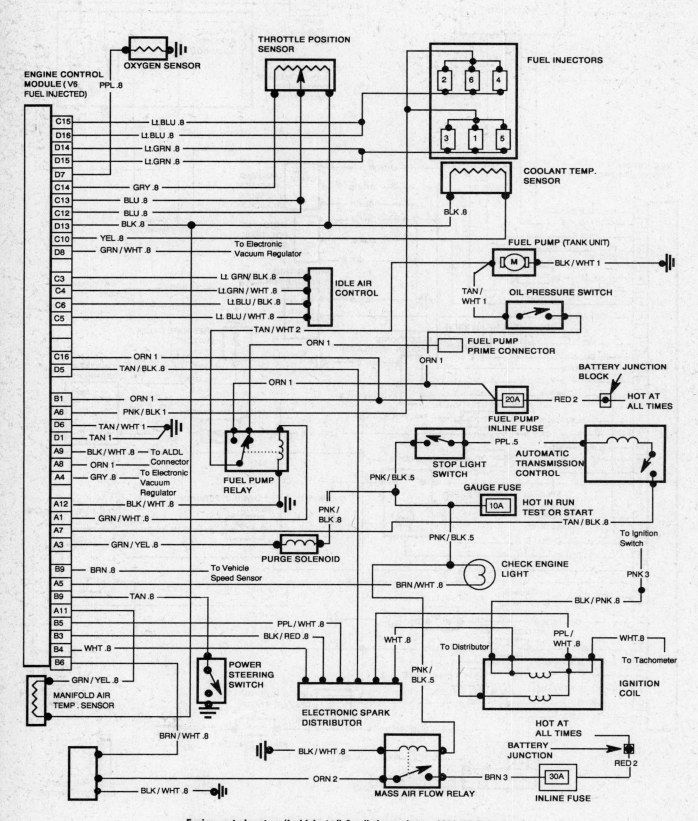

Engine control system (fuel injected) 6-cylinder engine — 1982–86 Celebrity

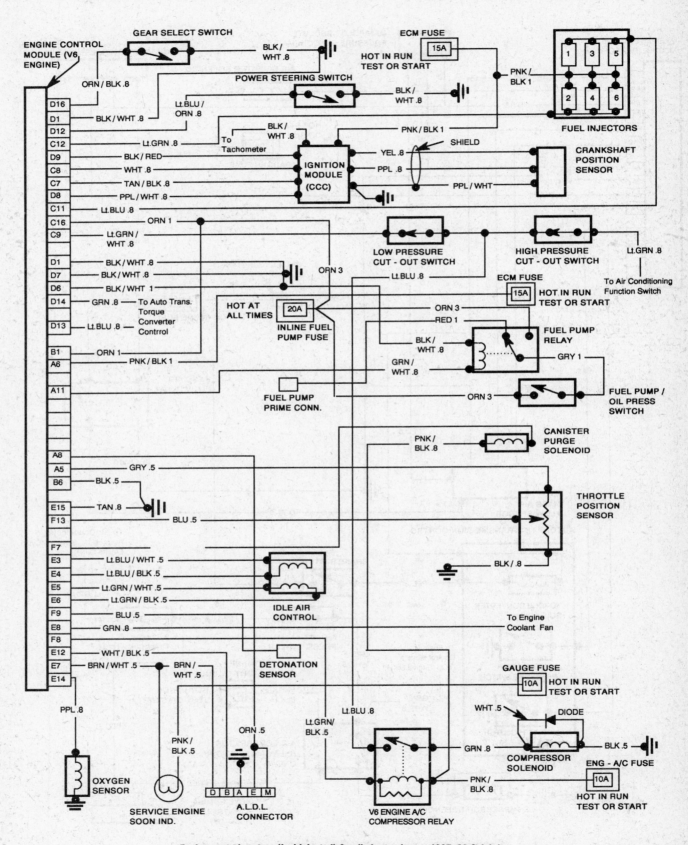

Engine control system (fuel injected) 6-cylinder engine — 1987–90 Celebrity

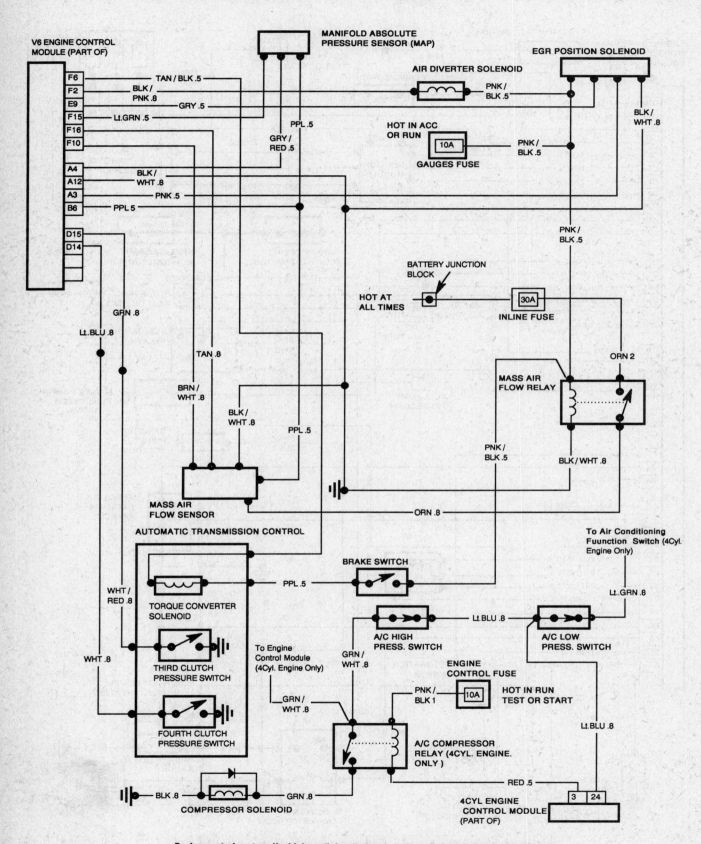

Engine control system (fuel injected) 6-cylinder engine — 1987–90 Celebrity (continued)

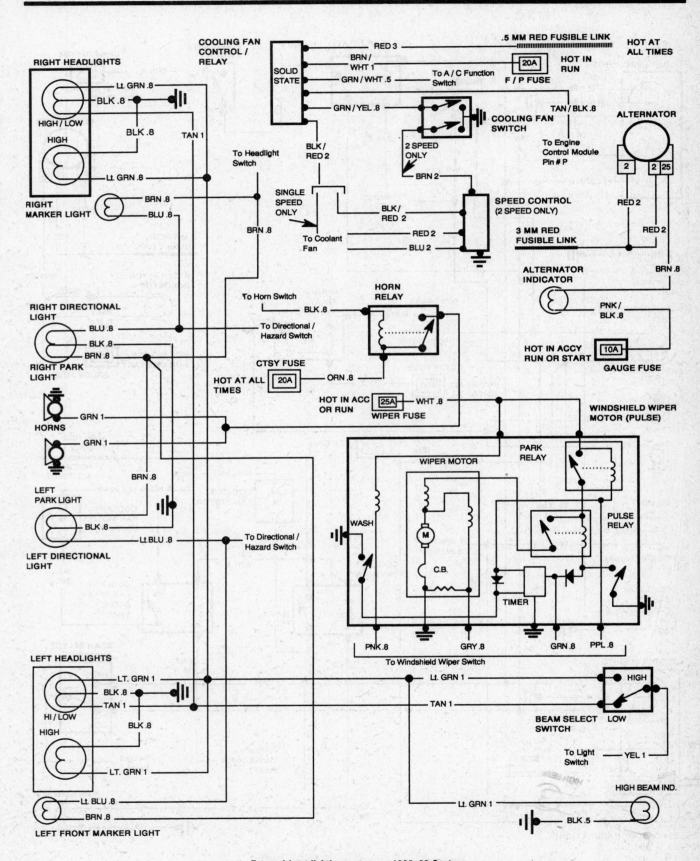

External front lighting system — 1982–89 Century

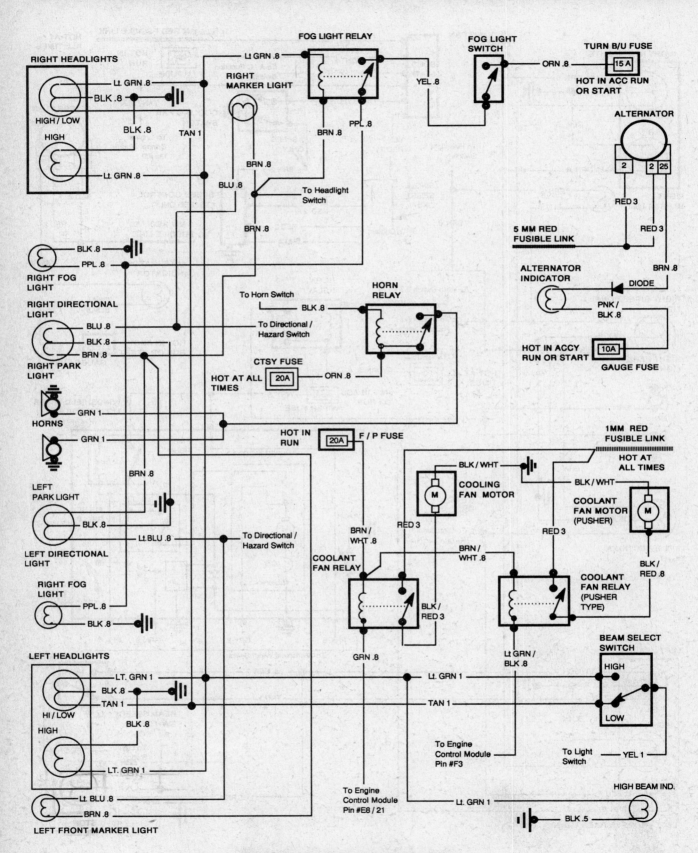

External front lighting system — 1990-92 Century

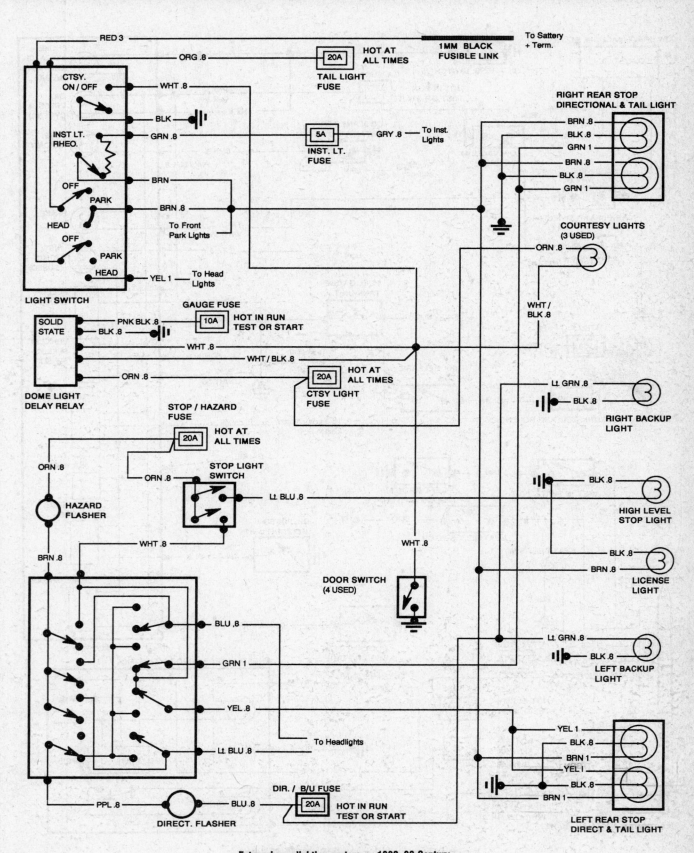

External rear lighting system — 1982–90 Century

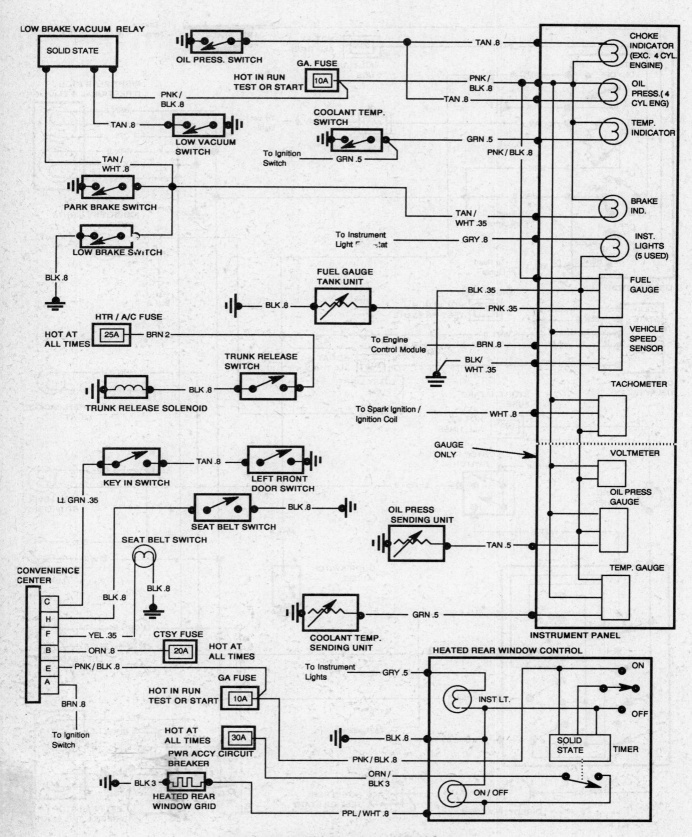

Instrument panel and lighting system — 1982–89 Century

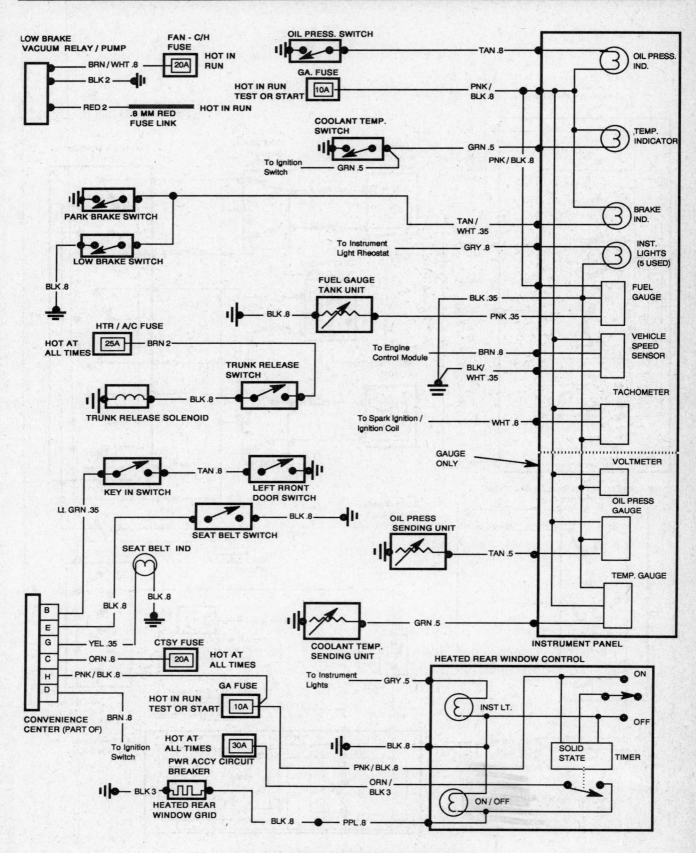

Instrument panel and lighting system — 1990-92 Century

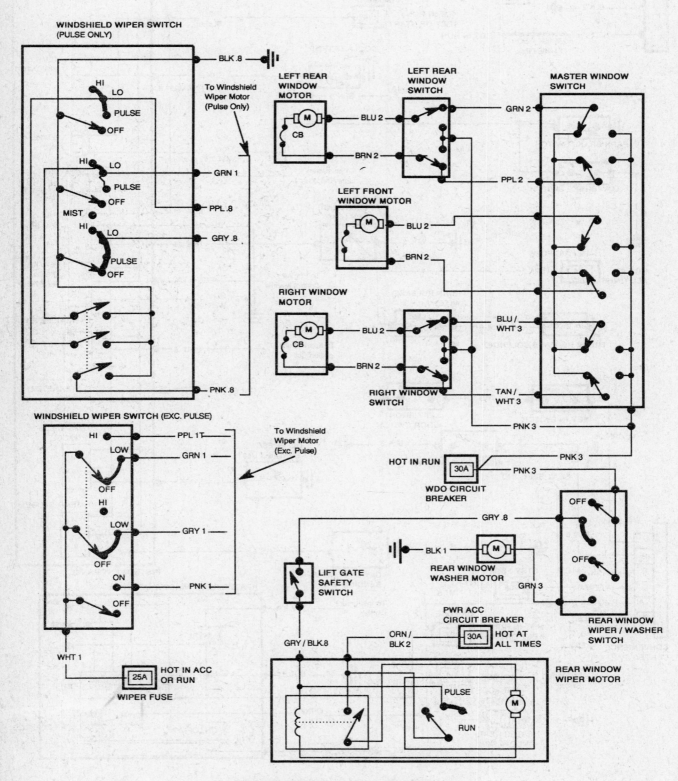

Dash controls and accessories — 1982–89 Century

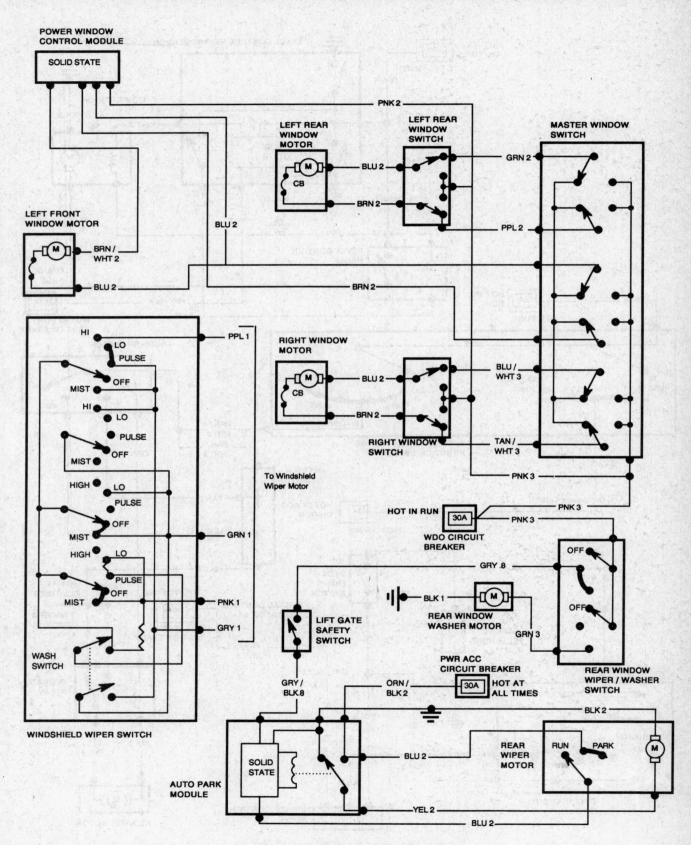

Dash controls and accessories — 1990–92 Century

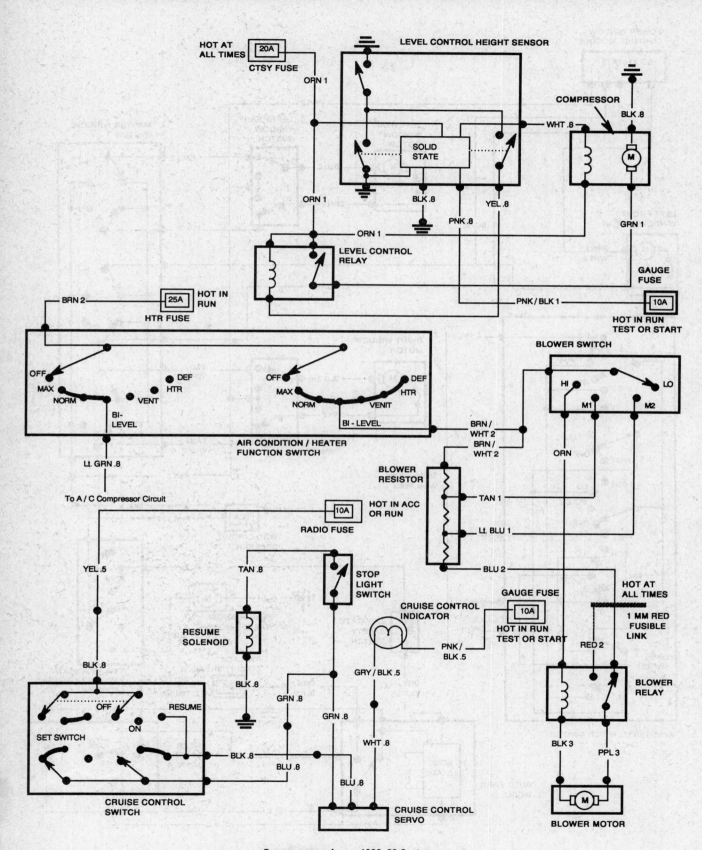

Power accessories — 1982–89 Century

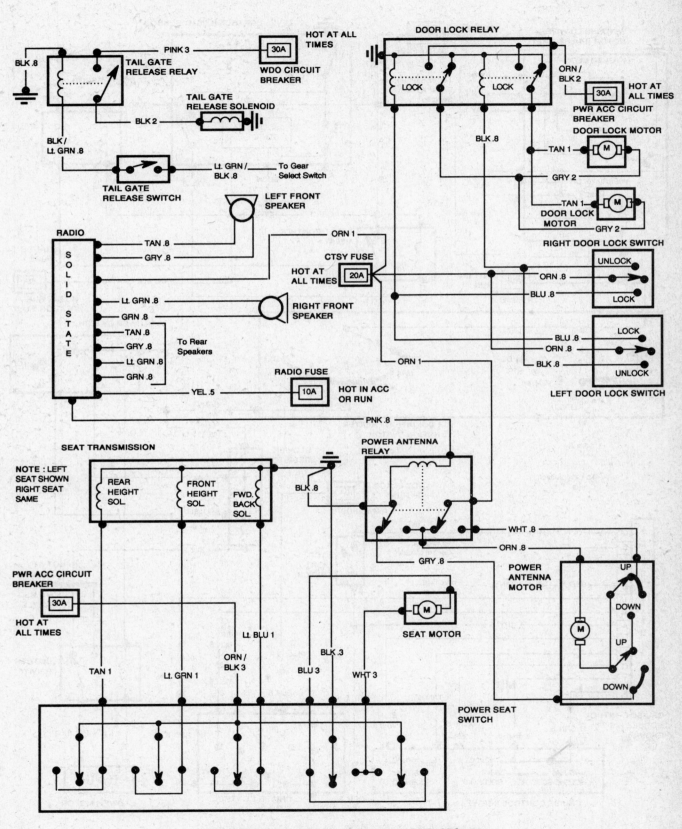

Power accessories, seat and door assembly — 1982-92 Century

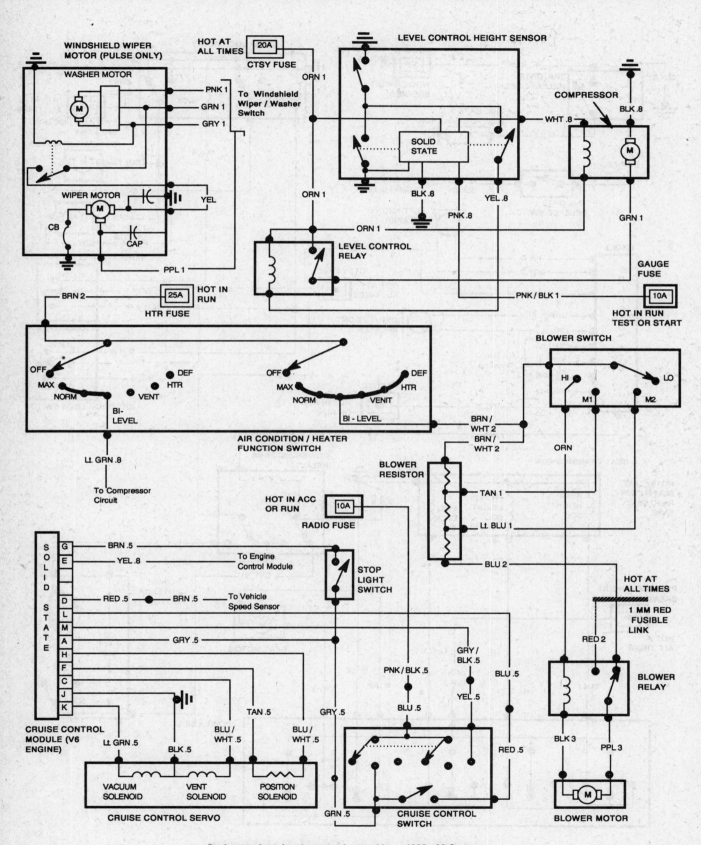

Dash controls and cruise control assembly — 1982– 92 Century

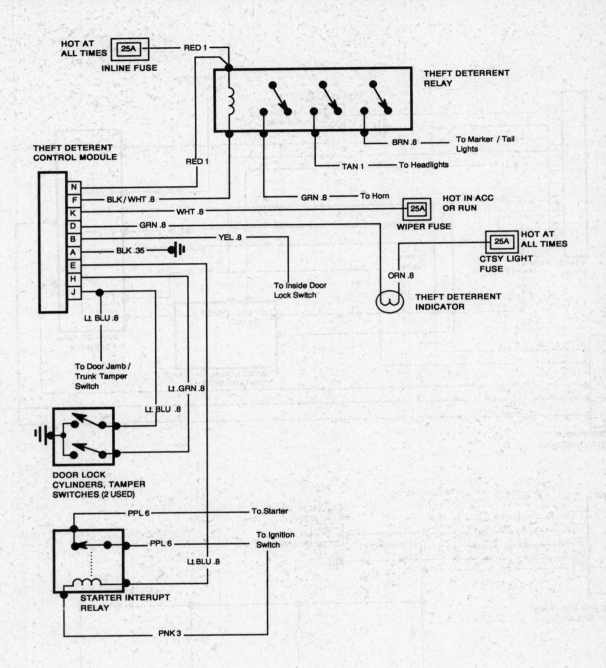

HOT AT
ALL TIMES — 25A — RED 1
INLINE FUSE

**THEFT DETERRENT
RELAY**

BRN .8 — To Marker / Tail
Lights

**THEFT DETERENT
CONTROL MODULE**

RED 1

TAN 1 — To Headlights

N

F — BLK / WHT .8

K — WHT .8

GRN .8 — To Horn

HOT IN ACC
OR RUN

25A

D — GRN .8

WIPER FUSE

B

A — BLK .35

YEL .8

25A — HOT AT
ALL TIMES

E

H

To Inside Door
Lock Switch

**CTSY LIGHT
FUSE**

J

ORN .8

Lt. BLU .8

**THEFT DETERRENT
INDICATOR**

To Door Jamb /
Trunk Tamper
Switch

Lt .GRN .8

Lt. BLU .8

**DOOR LOCK
CYLINDERS, TAMPER
SWITCHES (2 USED)**

PPL 6 — To.Starter

PPL 6 — To Ignition
Switch

Lt.BLU .8

**STARTER INTERUPT
RELAY**

PNK 3

Theft controller unit

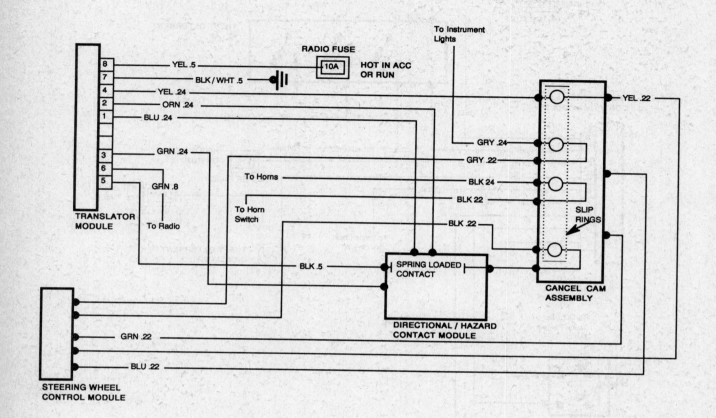

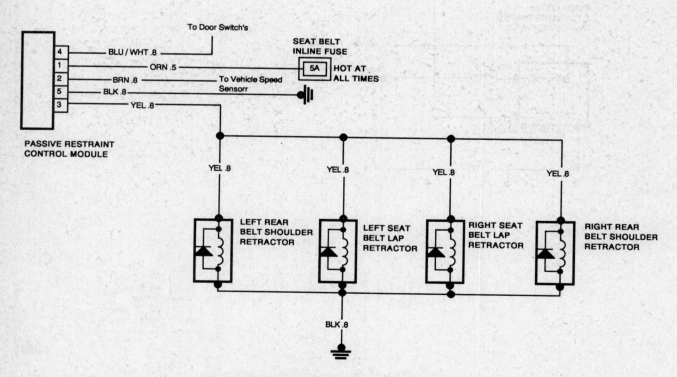

Passive restraint controller, seat belt assembly

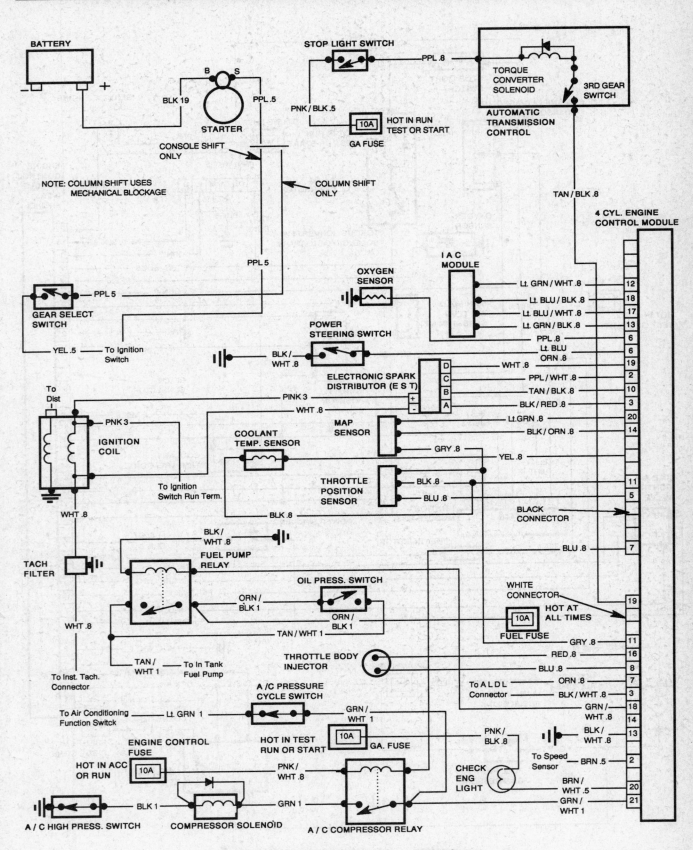

Engine control system 4-cylinder engine — 1982–89 Century

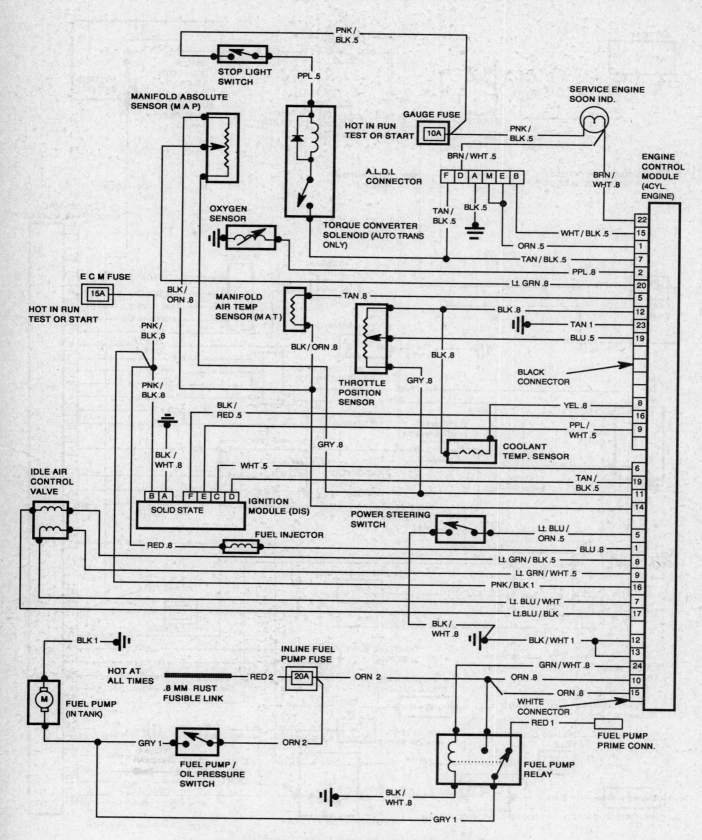

Engine control system 4-cylinder engine — 1990–92 Century

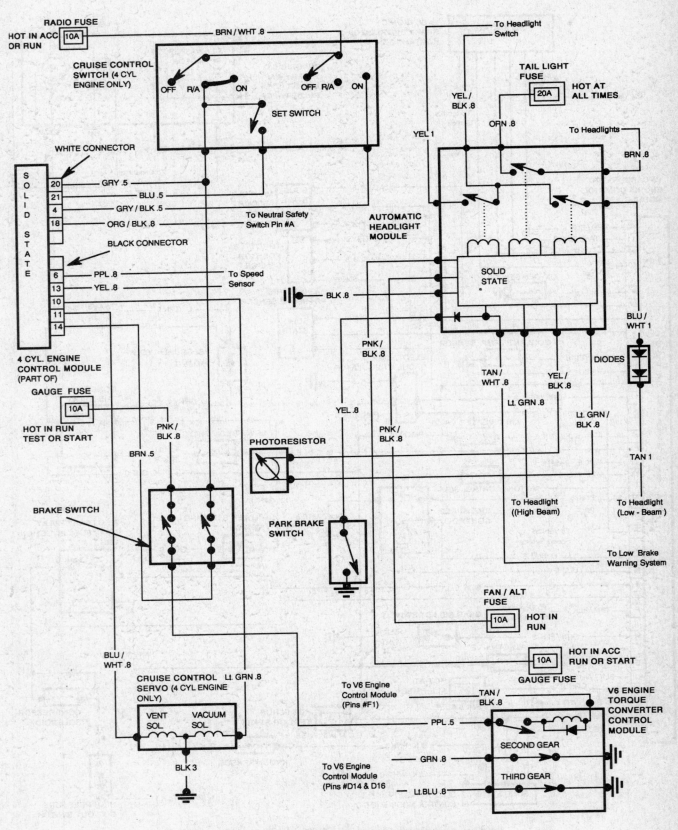

Engine control system 4-cylinder engine — 1990–92 Century (continued)

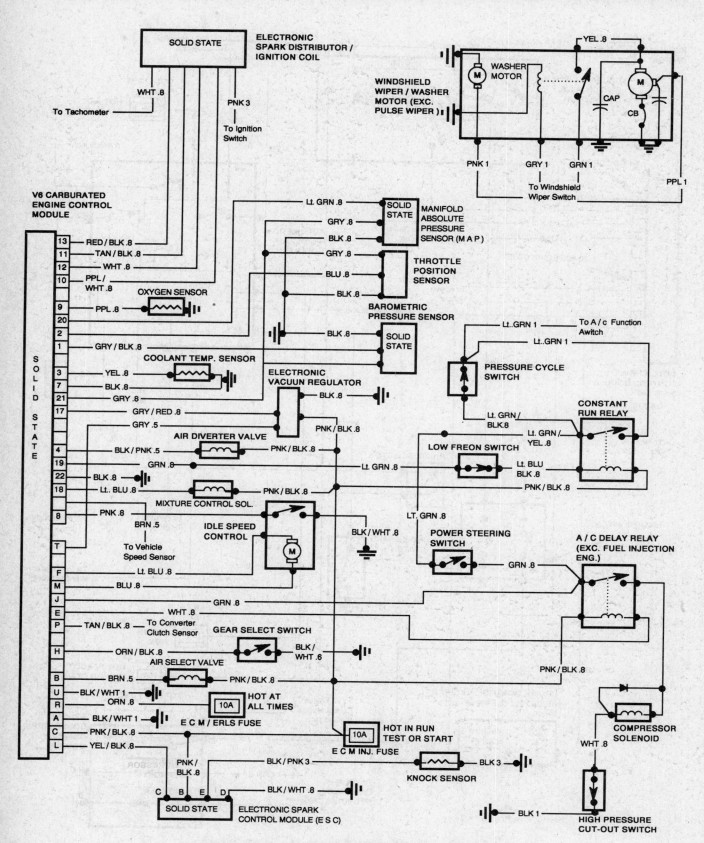

Engine control system (carbureted) 6-cylinder engine — Century

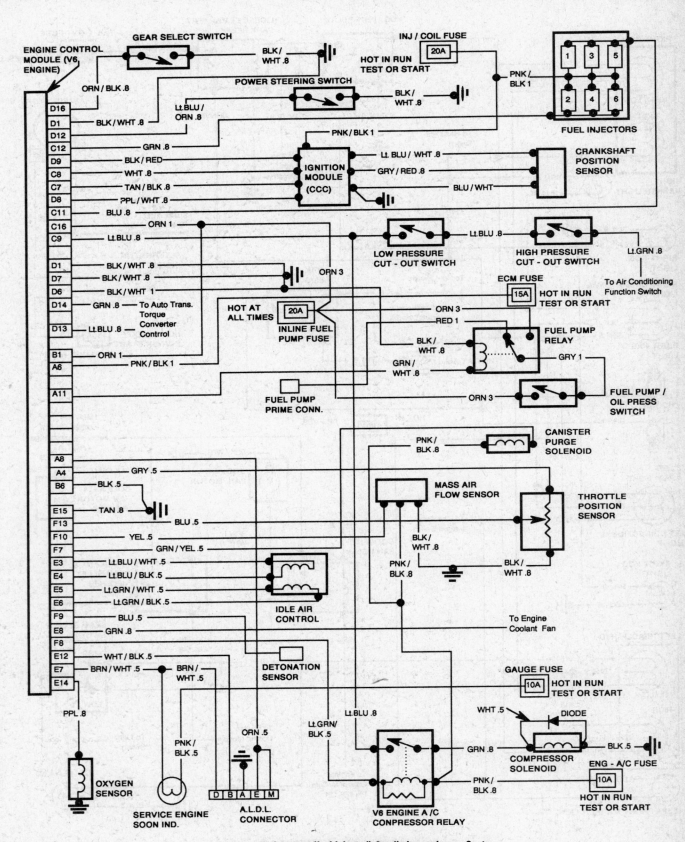

Engine control system (fuel injected) 6-cylinder engine — Century

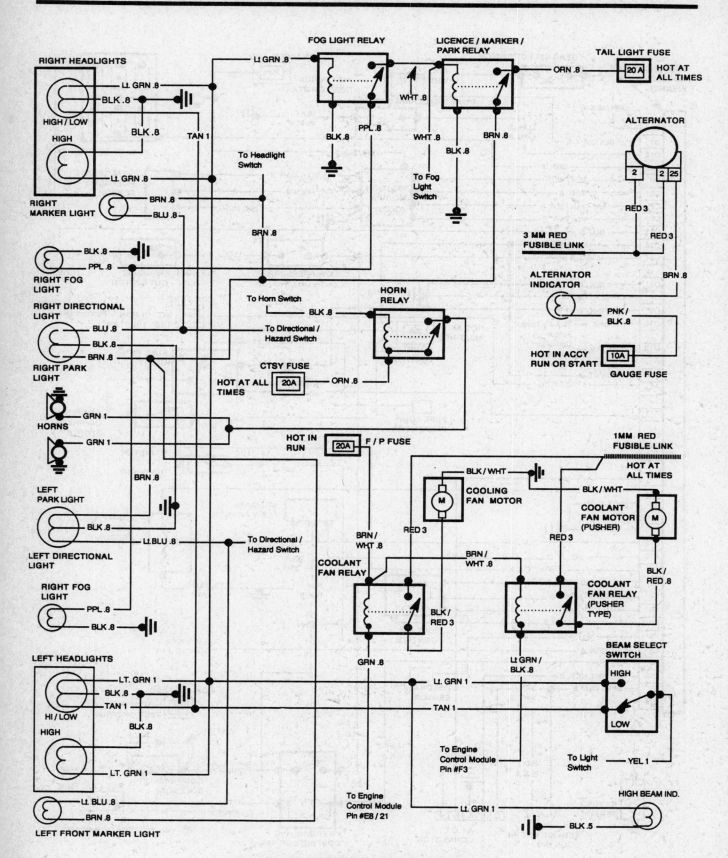

External front lighting system — 1982–89 Cutlass

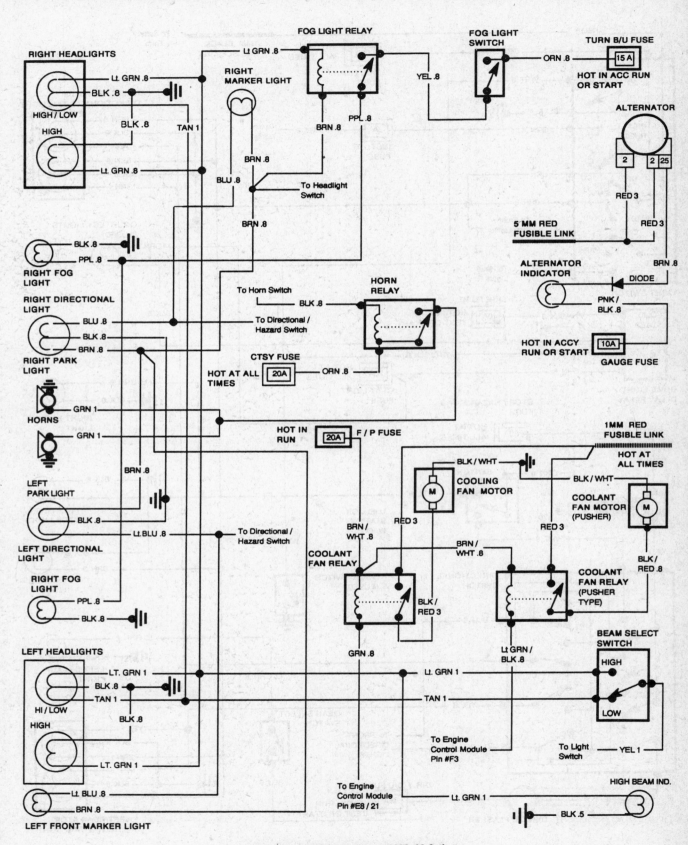

External front lighting system — 1990–92 Cutlass

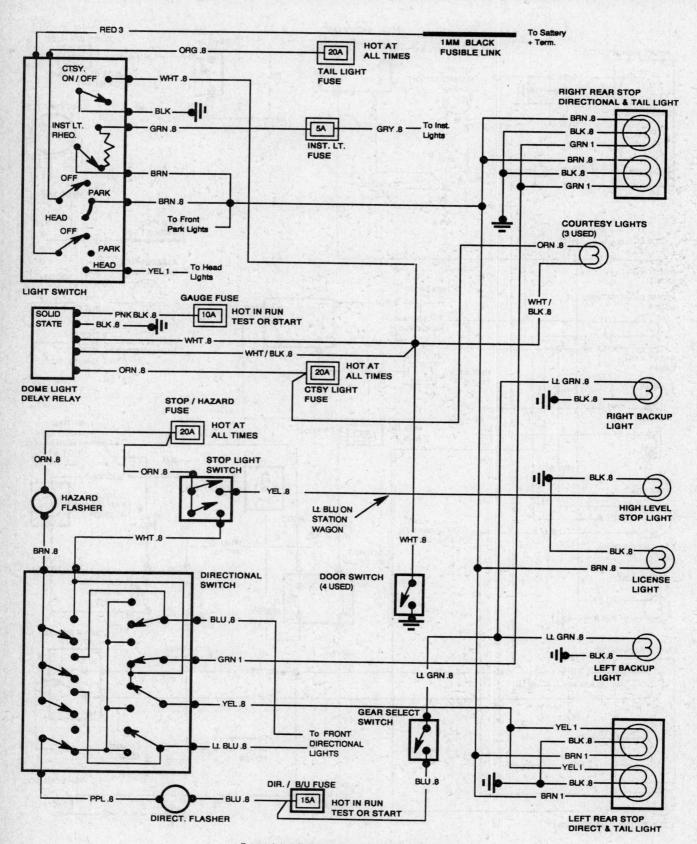

External rear lighting system — 1982–92 Cutlass

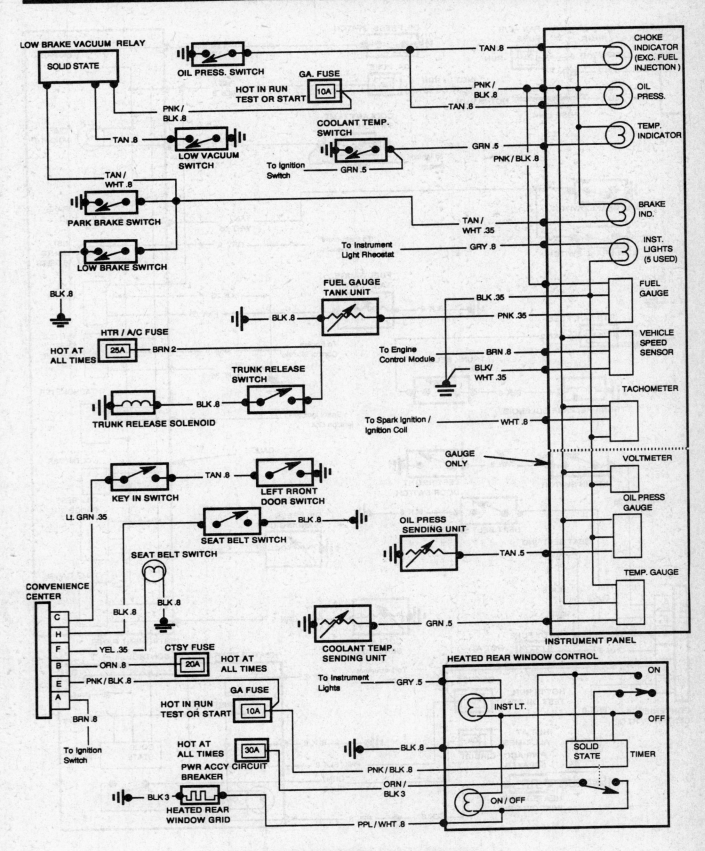

Instrument panel and lighting system — 1982–89 Cutlass

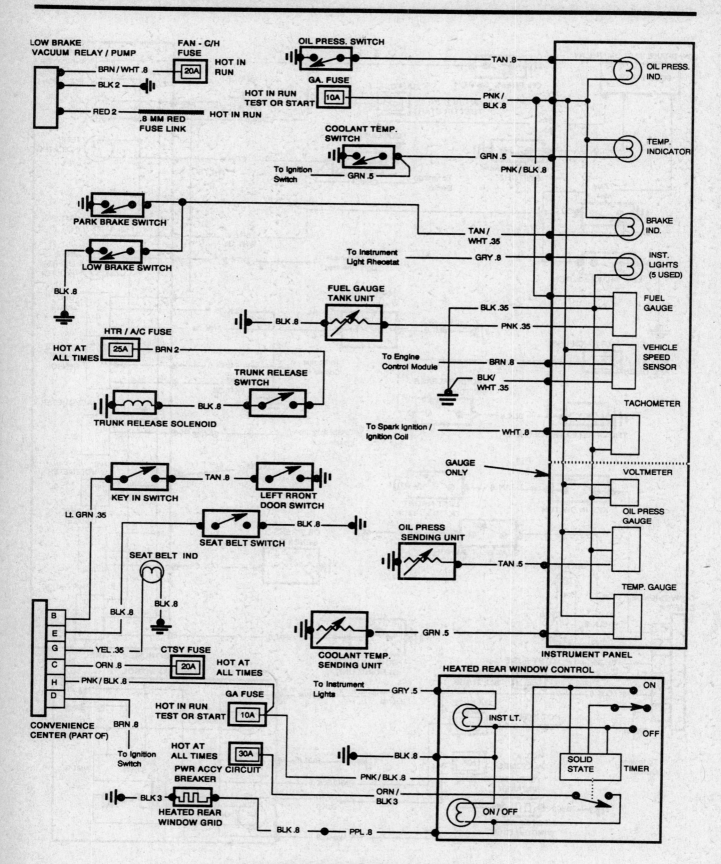

Instrument panel and lighting system — 1990–92 Cutlass

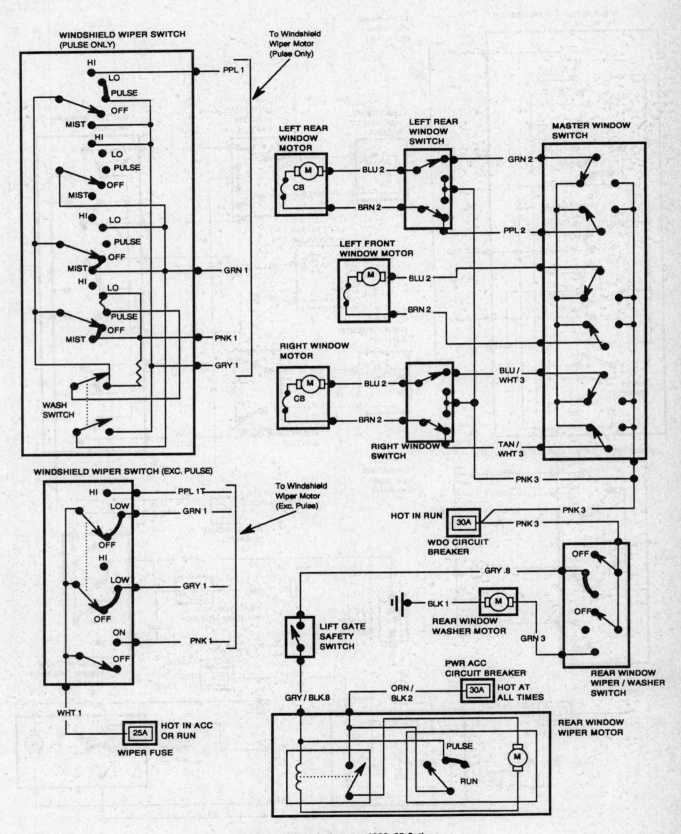

Dash controls and wipers — 1982–85 Cutlass

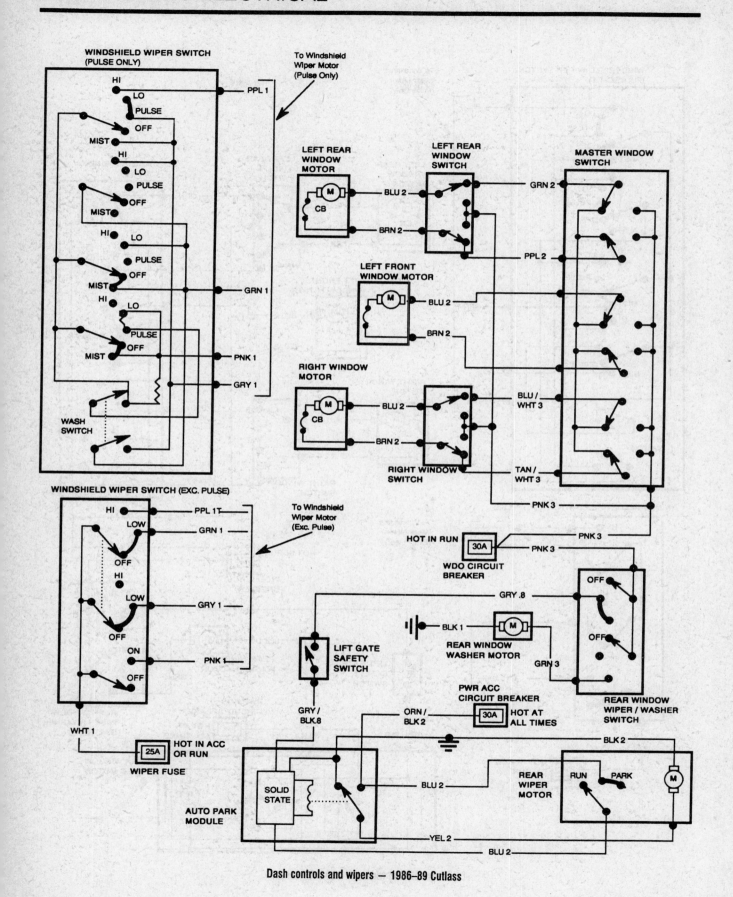

Dash controls and wipers — 1986–89 Cutlass

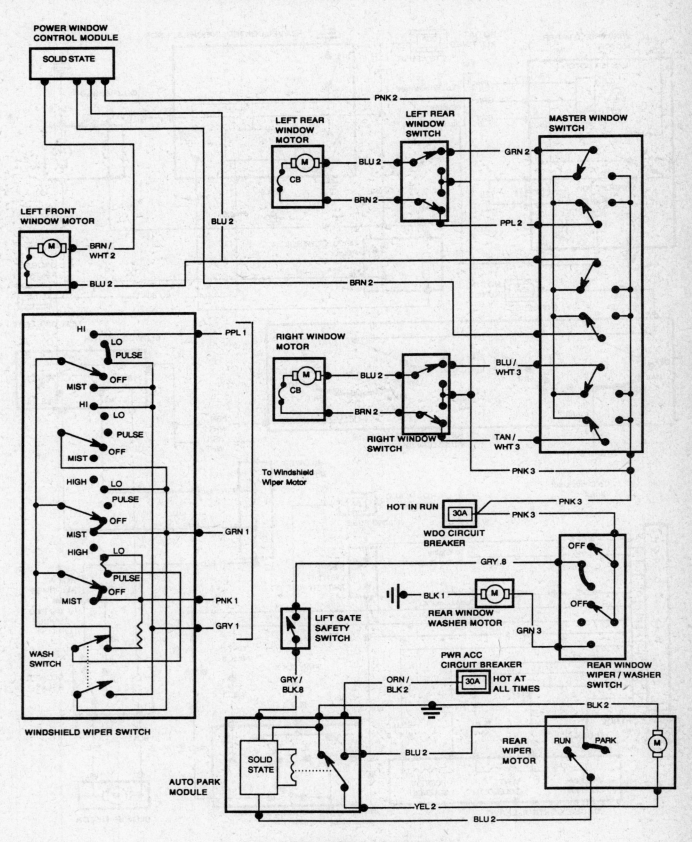

Dash controls and wipers — 1990–92 Cutlass

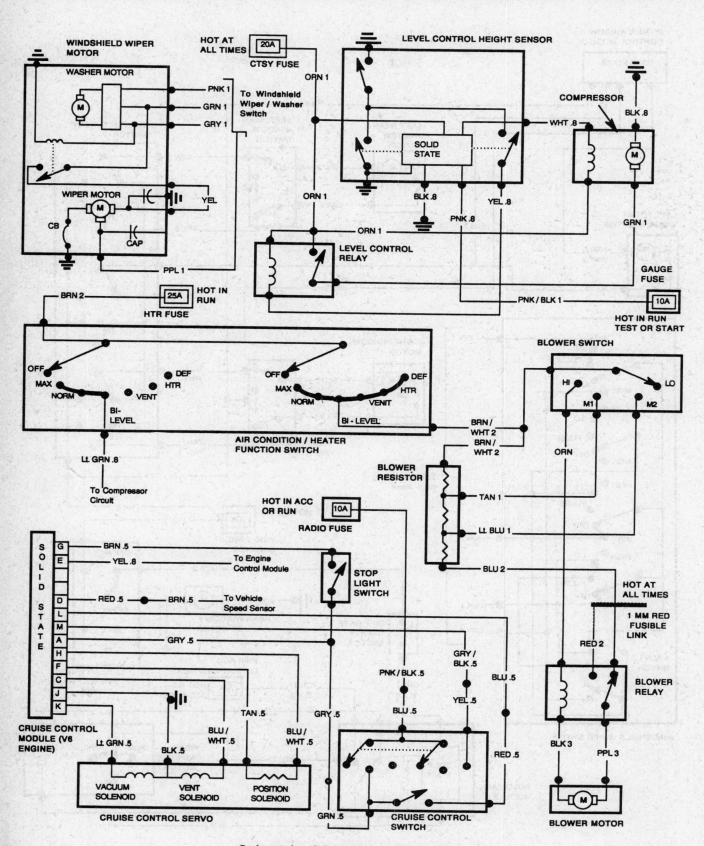

Dash controls and accessories — 1990–92 Cutlass

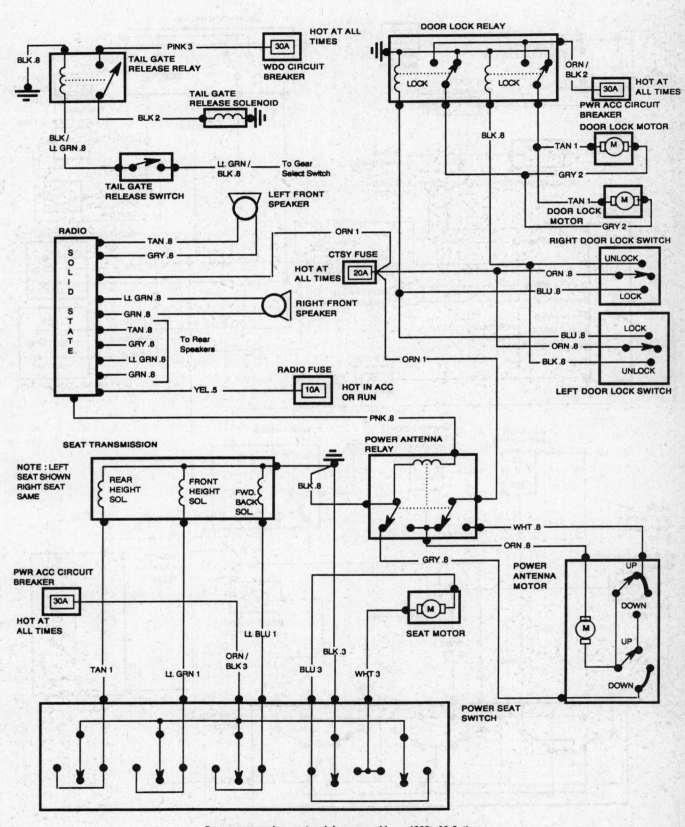

Power accessories, seat and door assembly — 1982– 89 Cutlass

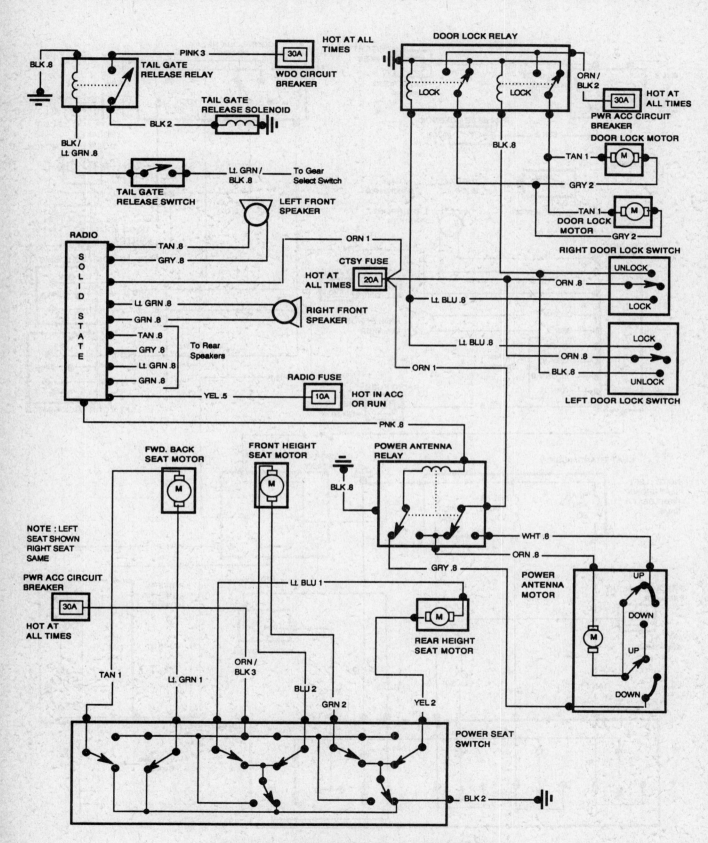

Power accessories, seat and door assembly — 1989–92 Cutlass

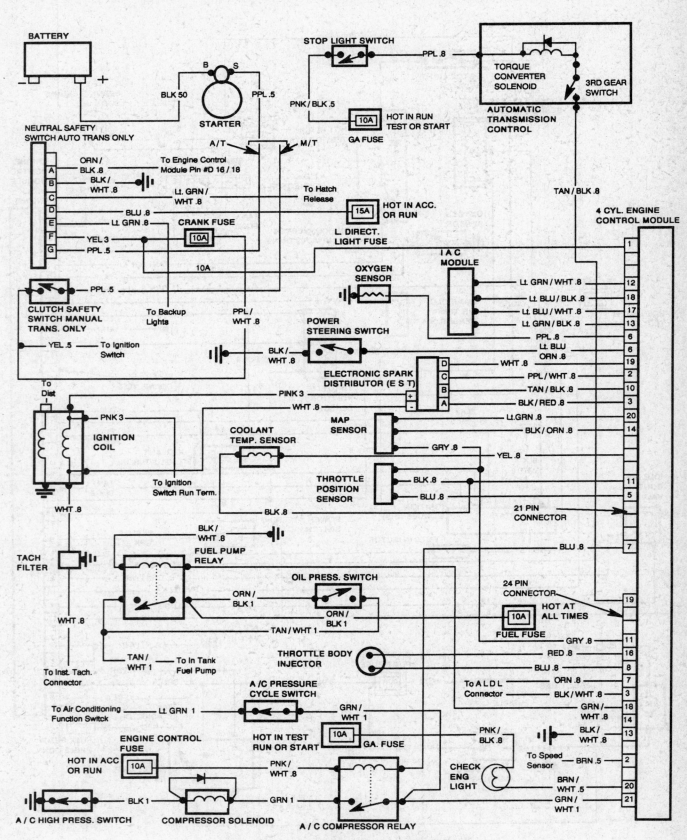

Engine control system 4-cylinder engine — 1982–89 Cutlass

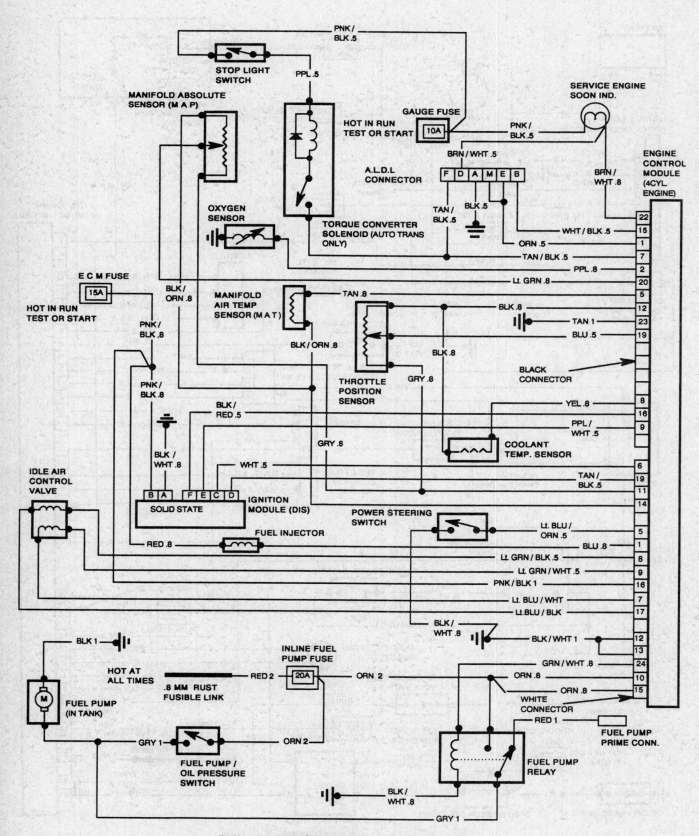

Engine control system 4-cylinder engine — 1990–92 Cutlass

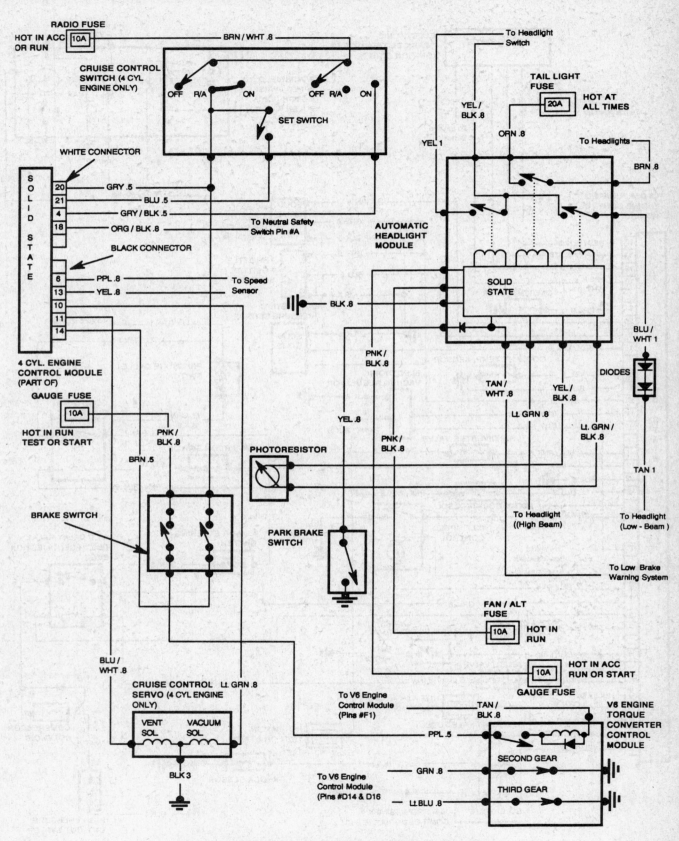

Engine control system 4-cylinder engine — 1990-92 Cutlass (continued)

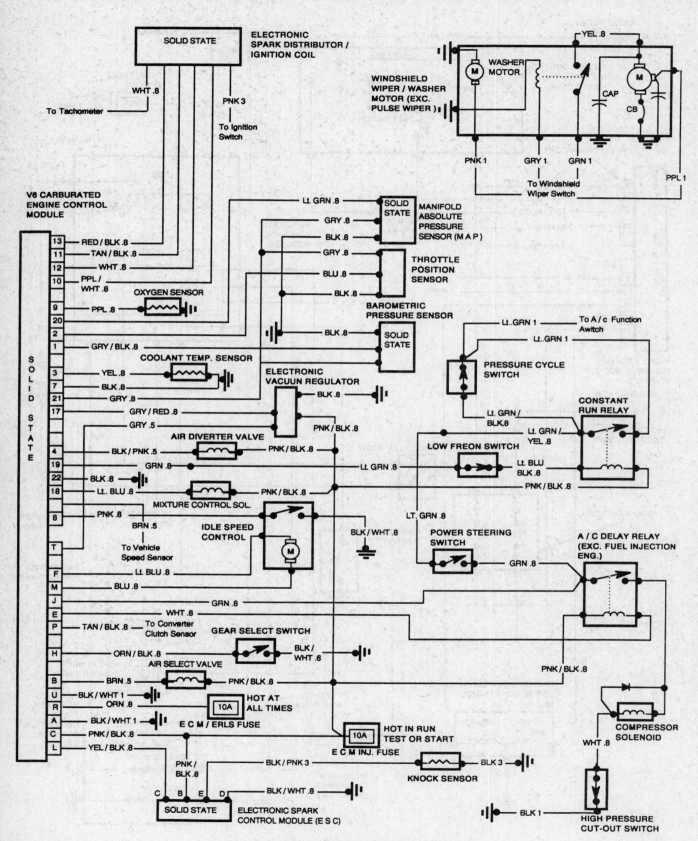

Engine control system (carbureted) 6-cylinder engine — Cutlass

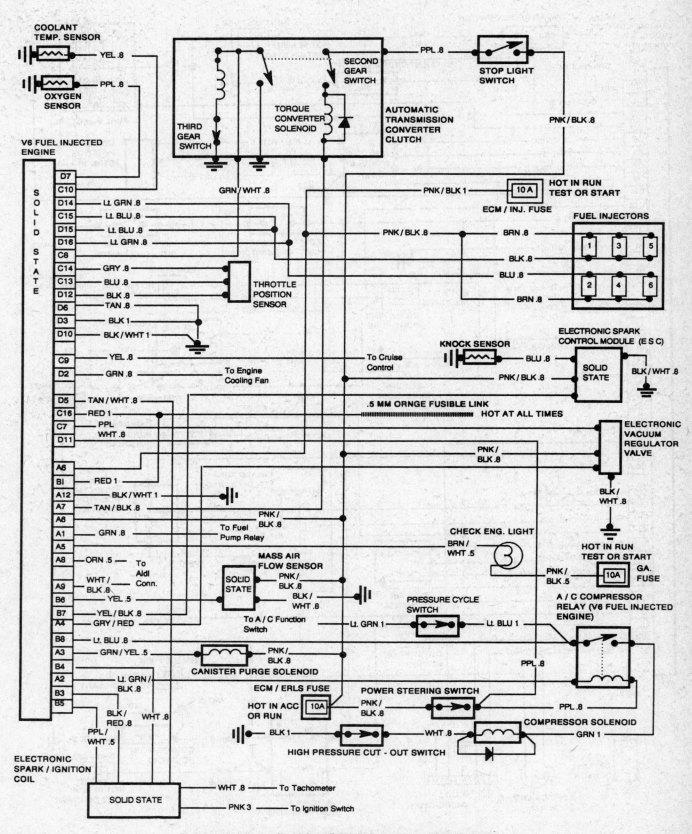

Engine control system (fuel injected) 6-cylinder engine — 1982–89 Cutlass

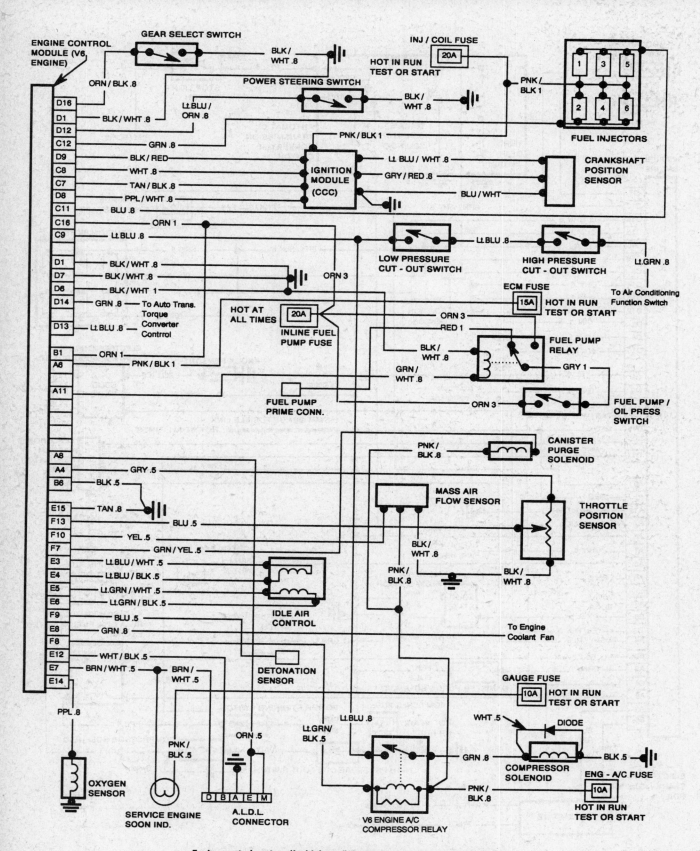

Engine control system (fuel injected) 6-cylinder engine — 1989–92 Cutlass

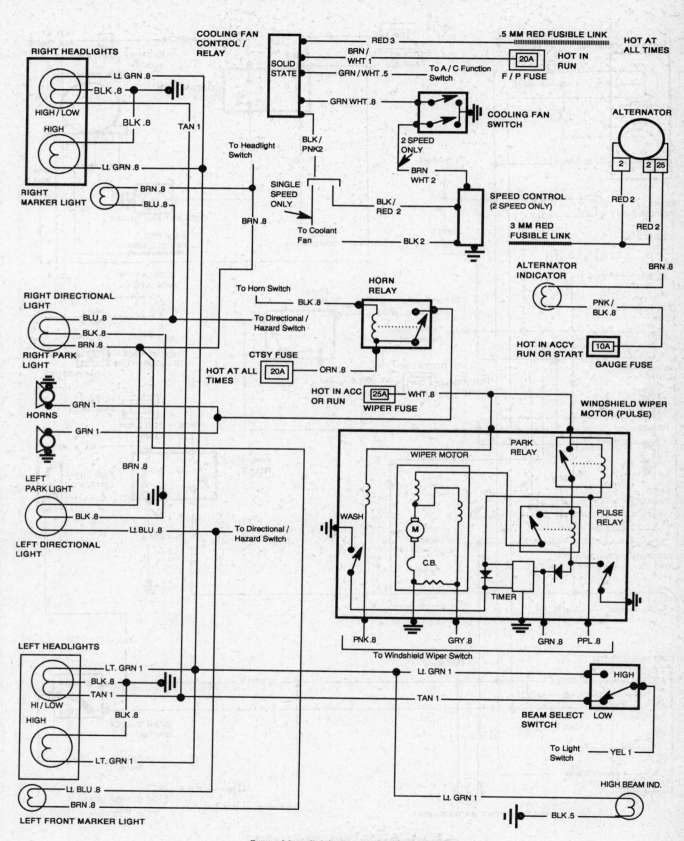

External front lighting system – 1982–85 6000

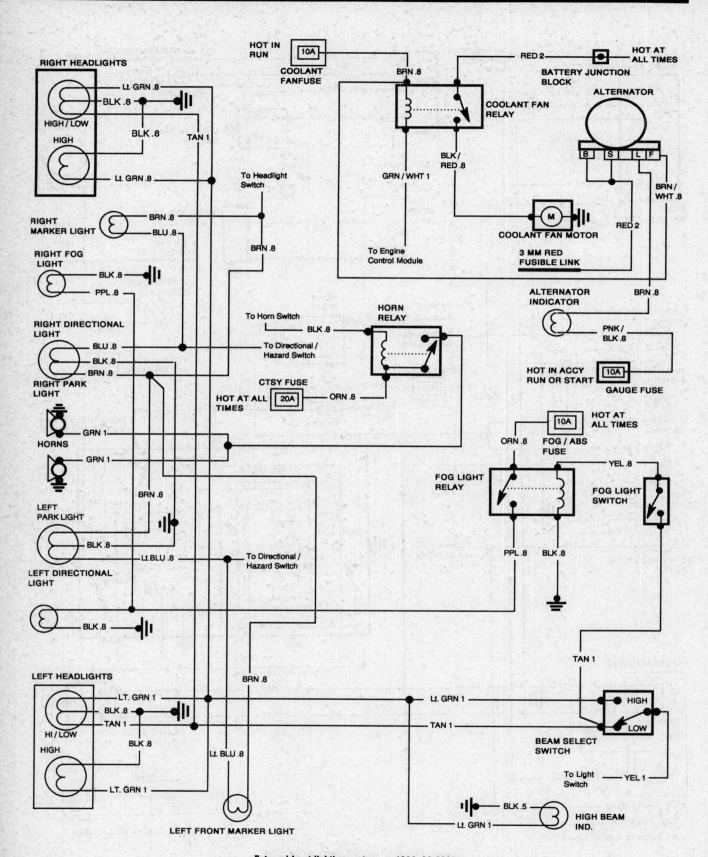

External front lighting system — 1986–92 6000

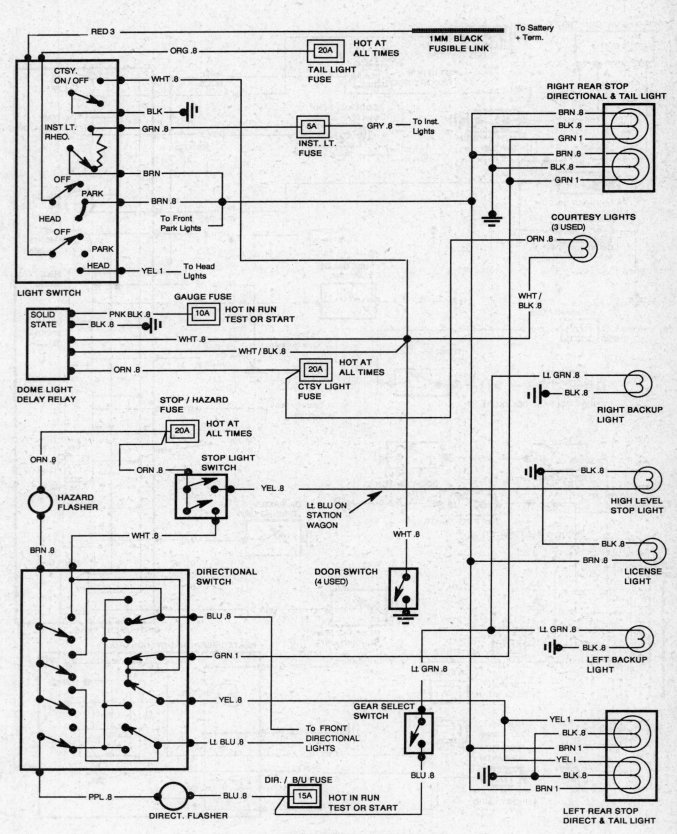

External rear lighting system — 1982–92 6000

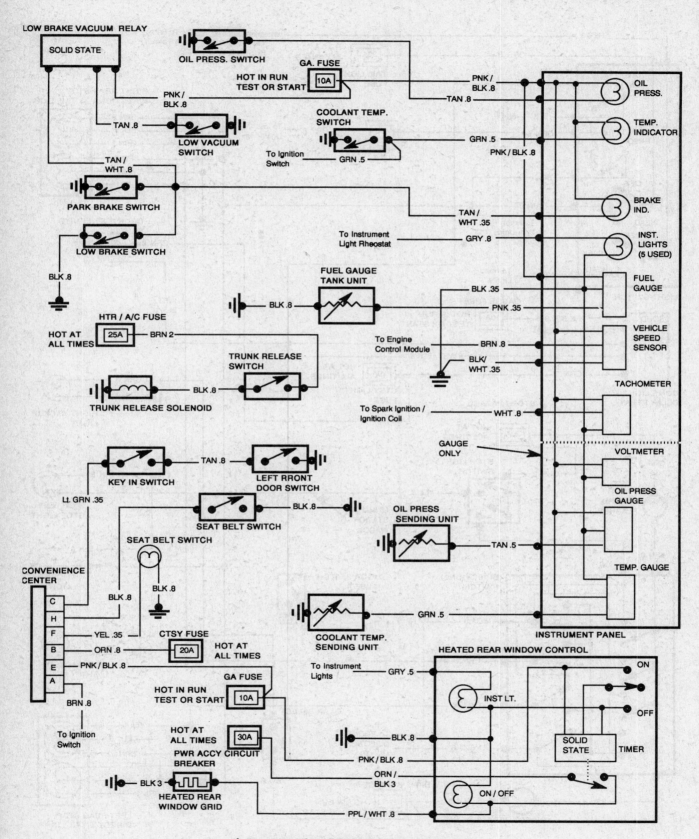

Instrument panel and lighting system — 1982–85 6000

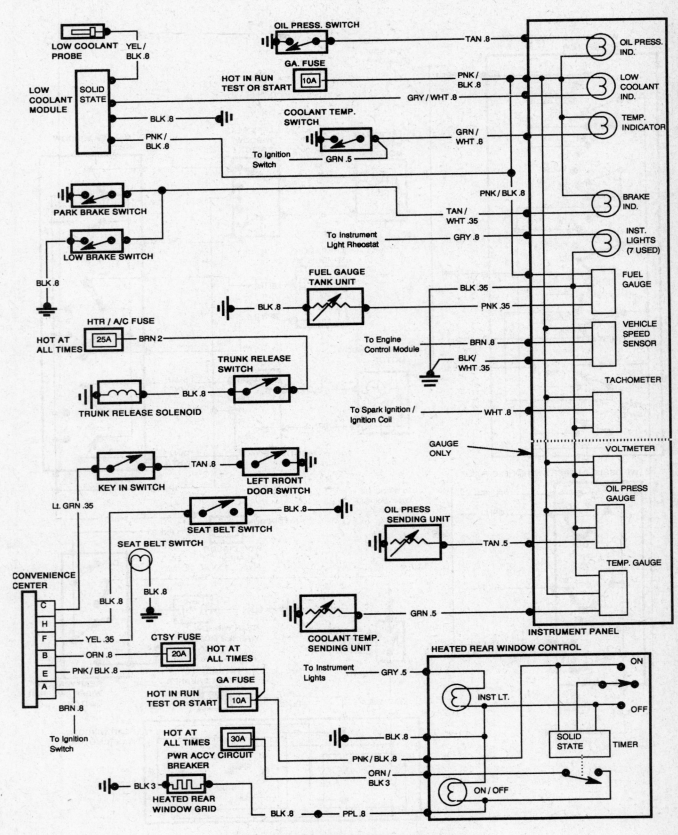

Instrument panel and lighting system – 1986-92 6000

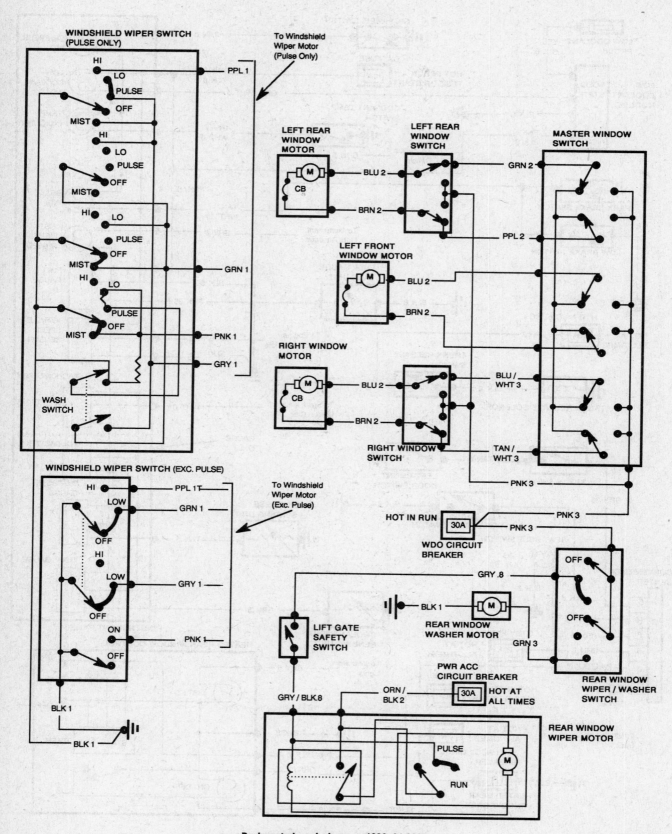

Dash controls and wipers — 1982-84 6000

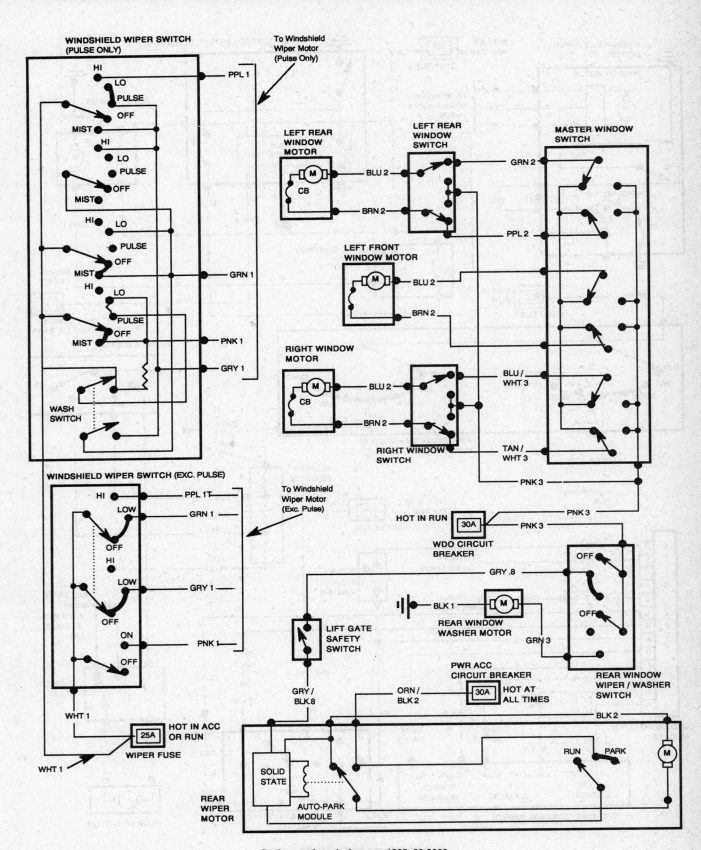

Dash controls and wipers — 1985–92 6000

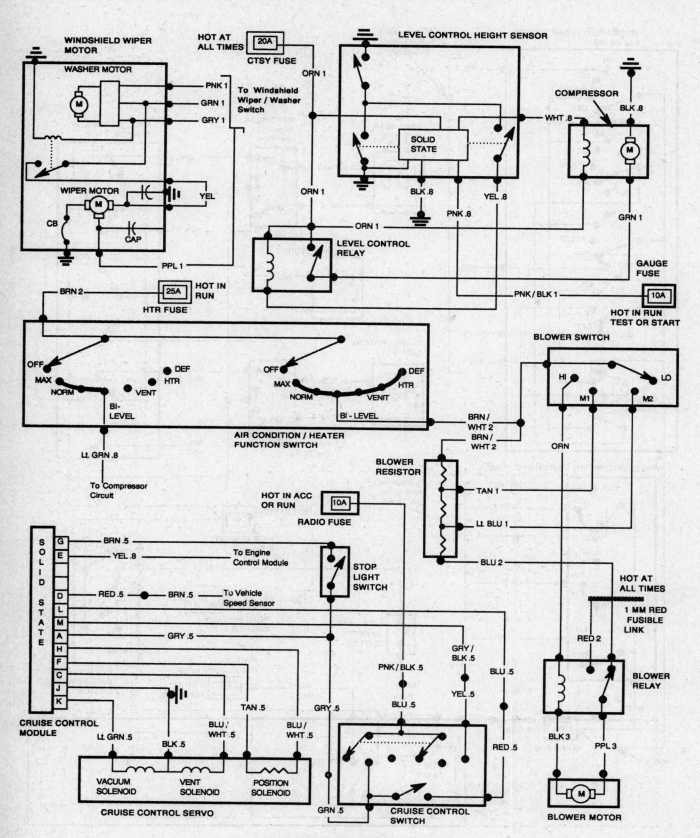

Dash controls and cruise control — 6000

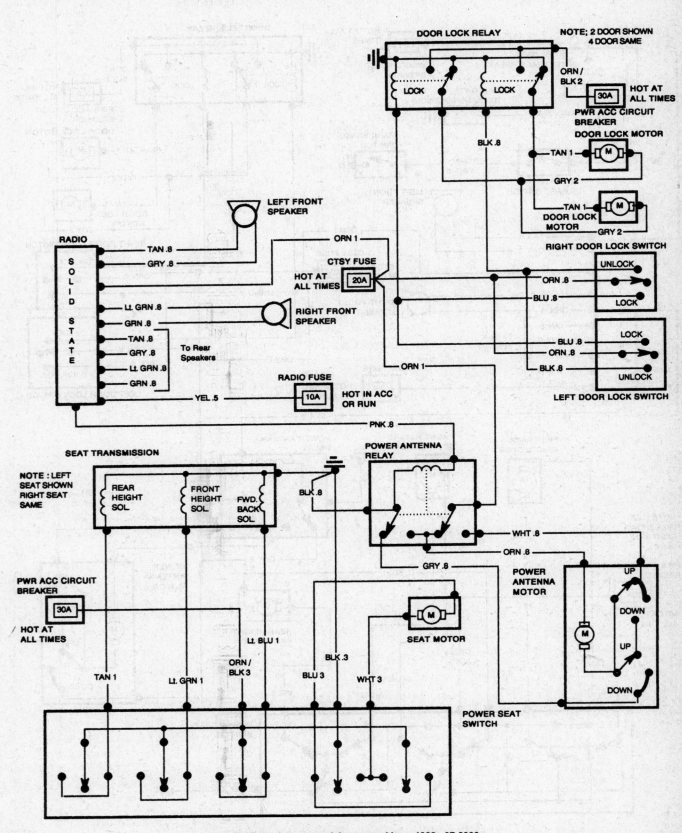

Power accessories, seat and door assembly — 1982– 87 6000

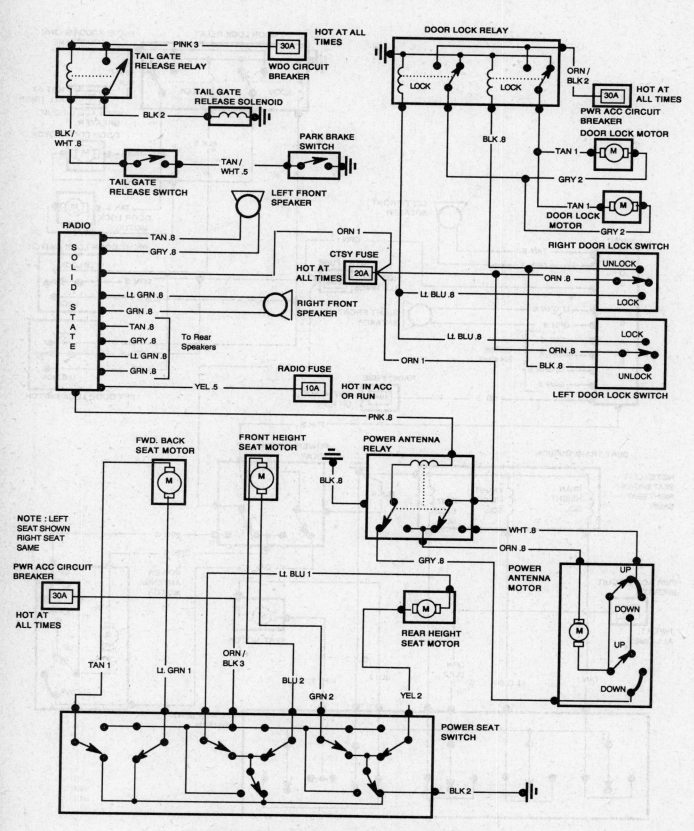

Power accessories, seat and door assembly — 1988–92 6000

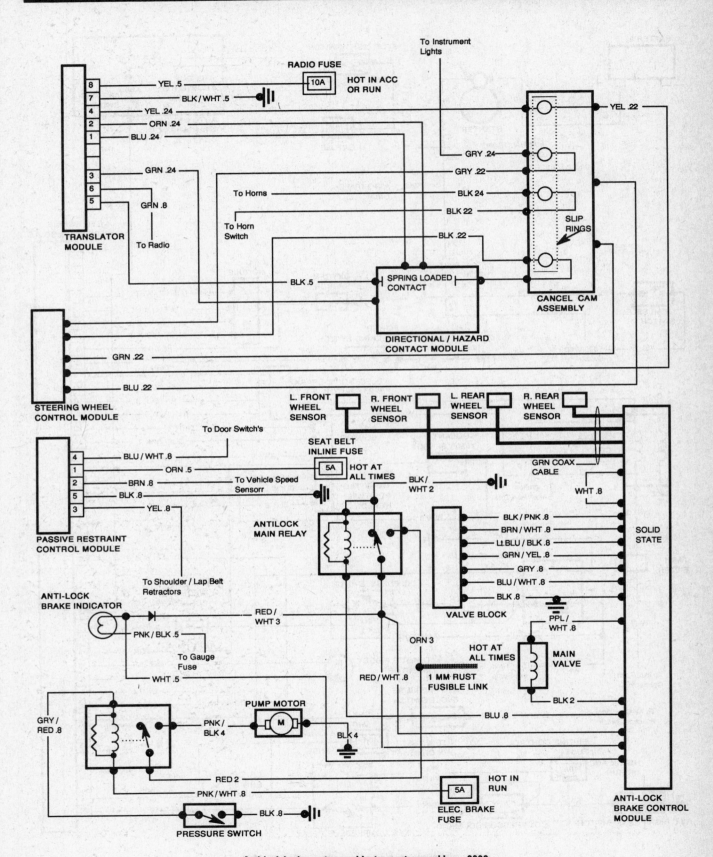

Anti-lock brake system and instrument assembly — 6000

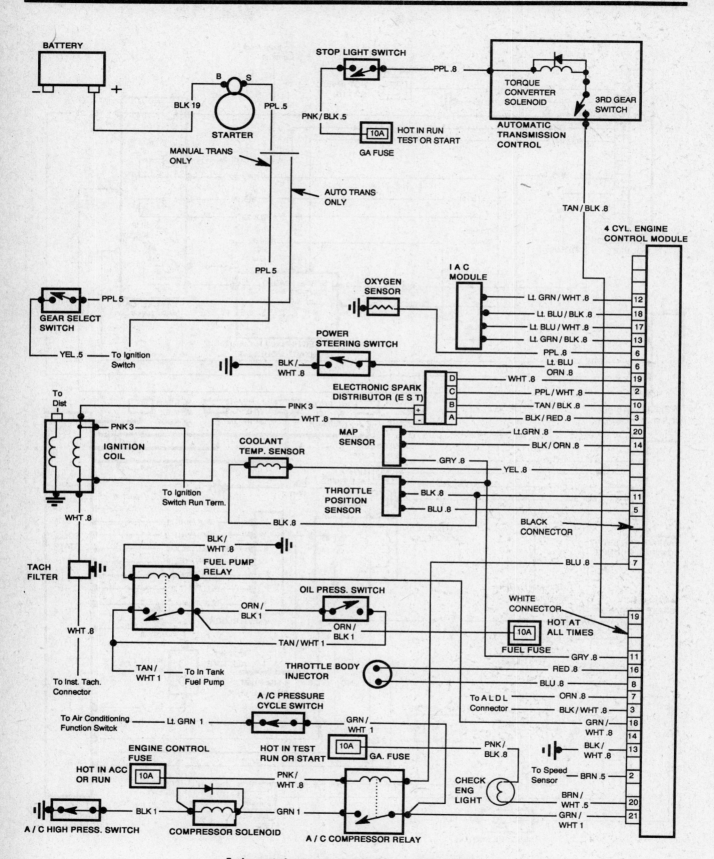

Engine control system 4-cylinder engine — 1982–88 6000

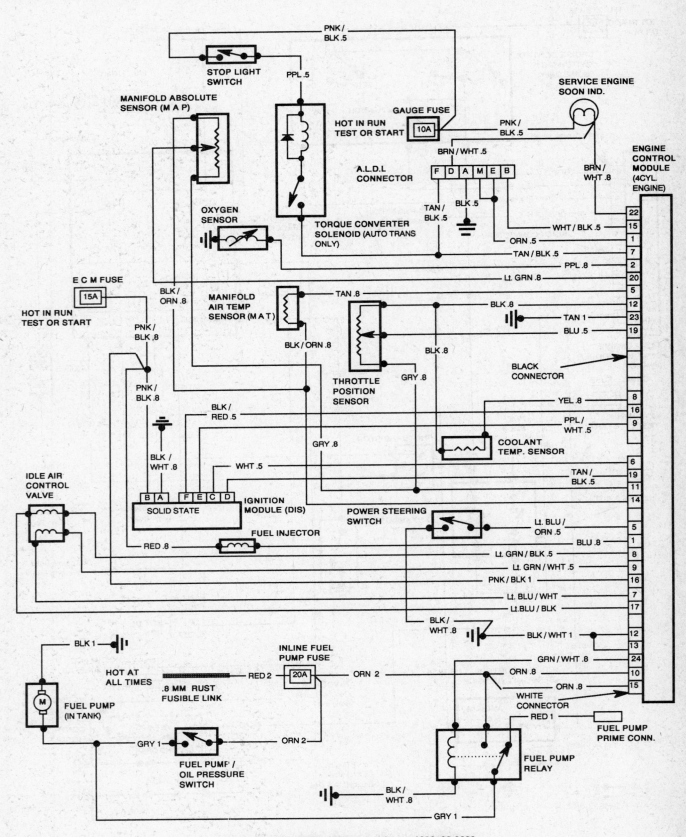

Engine control system 4-cylinder engine — 1989–92 6000

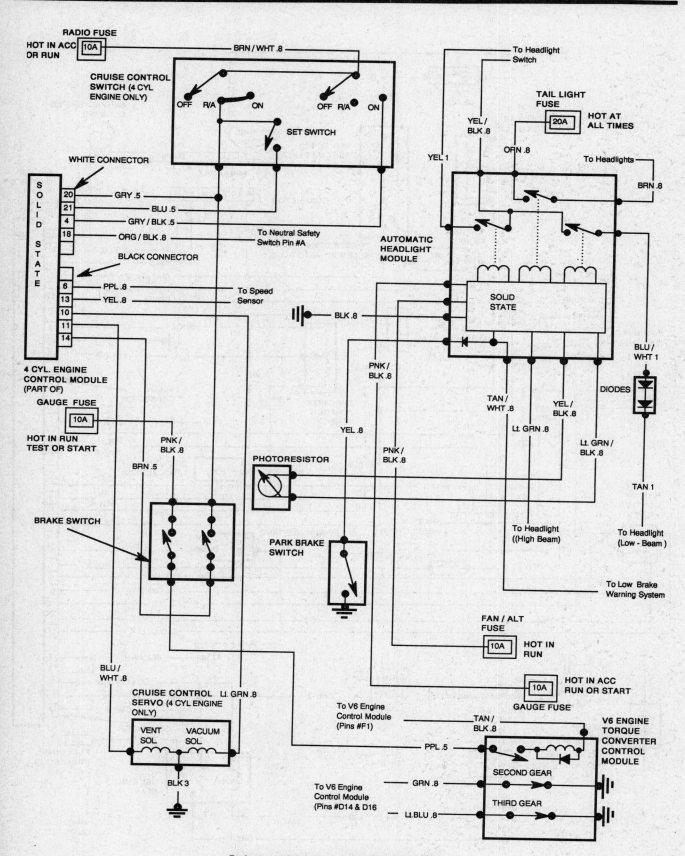

Engine control system — 1999–92 6000 (continued)

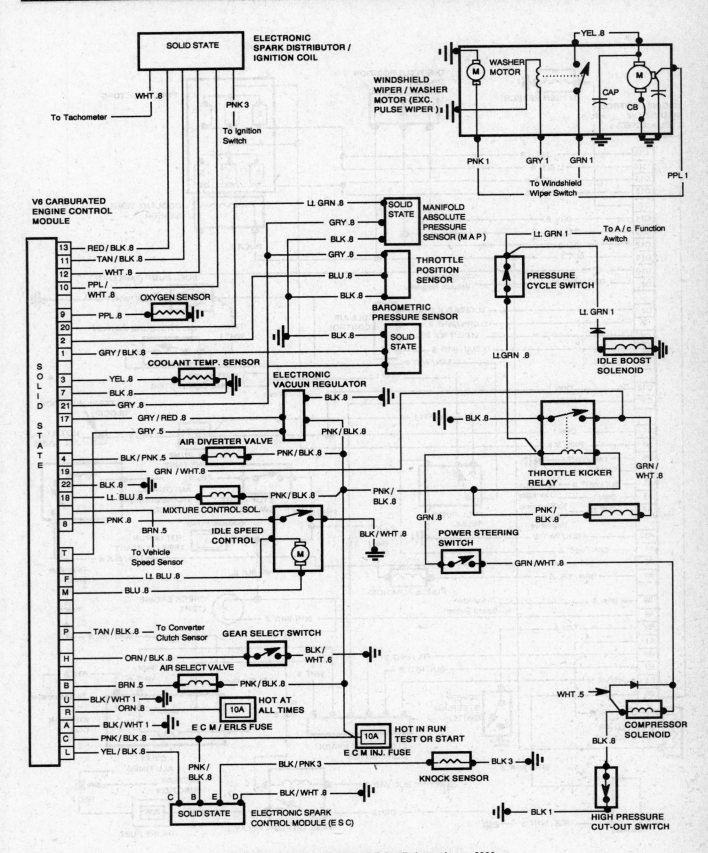

Engine control system (carbureted) 6-cylinder engine — 6000

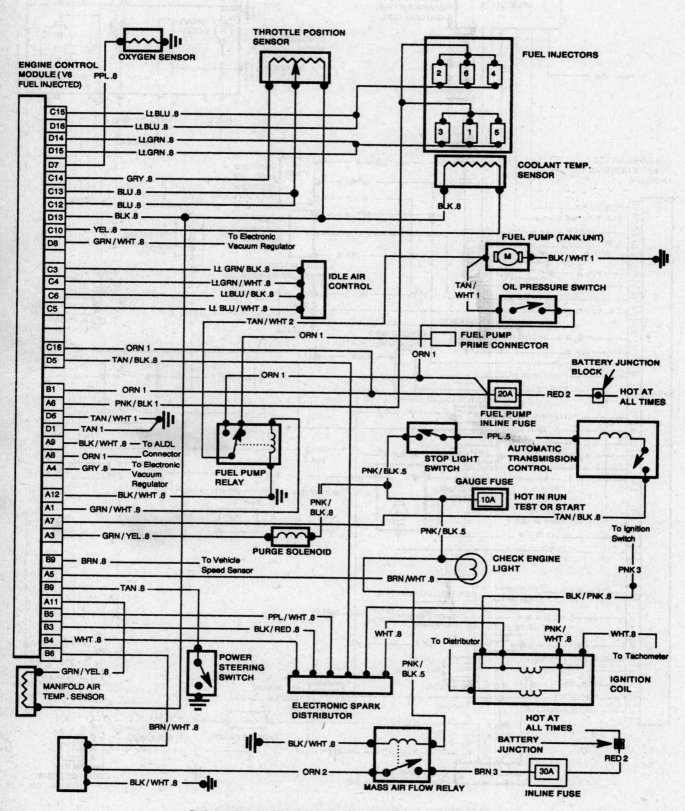

Engine control system (fuel injected) 6-cylinder engine – 1982–89 6000

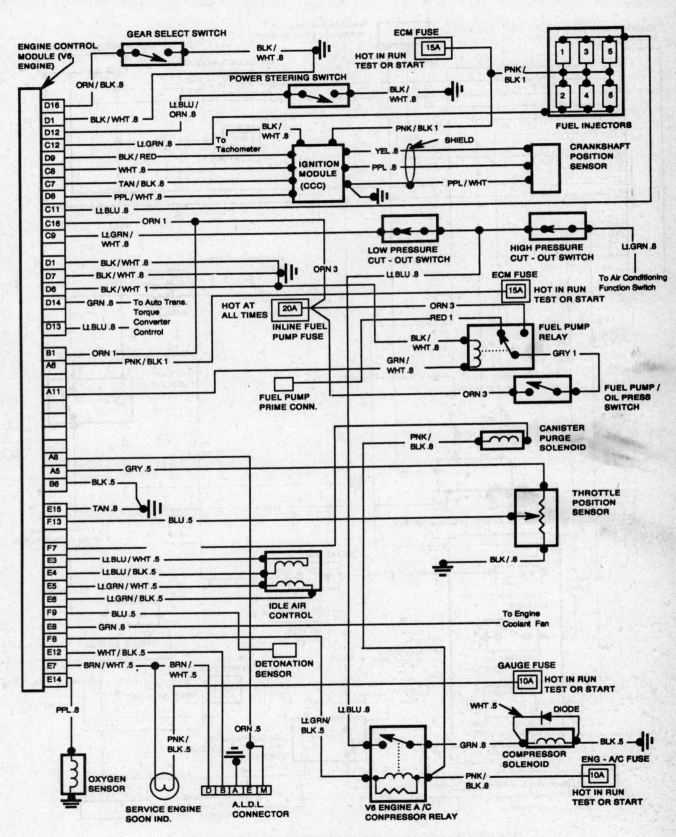

Engine control system (fuel injected) 6-cylinder engine – 1989–92 6000

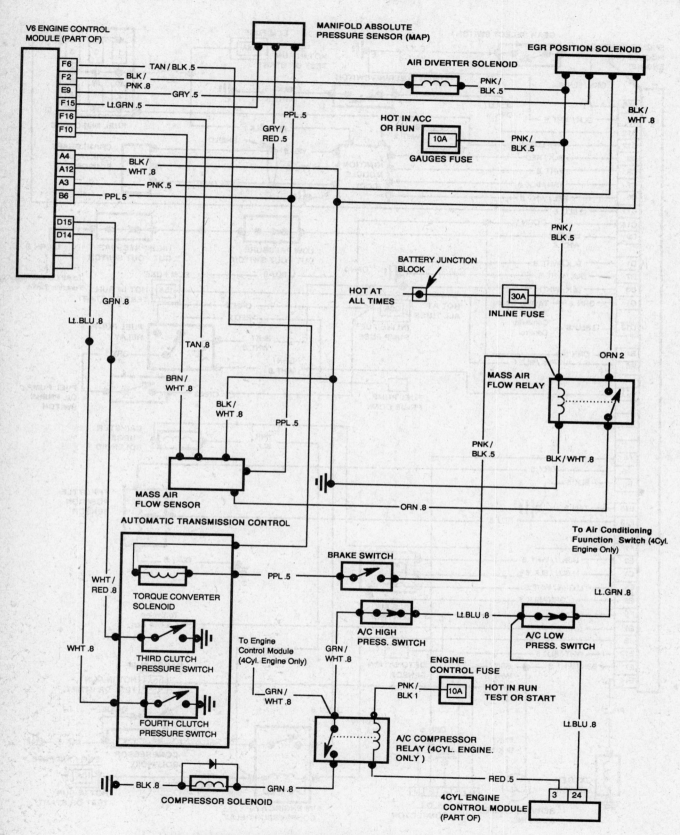

Engine control system (fuel injected) 6-cylinder engine — 1989–92 6000 (continued)

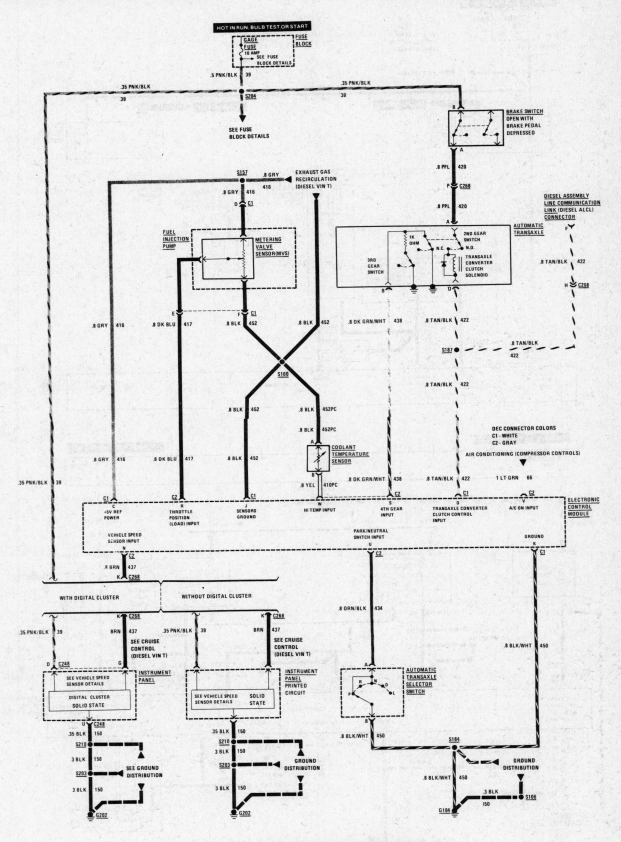

Diesel engine fuel control system — 4.3L (VIN T) Diesel engine

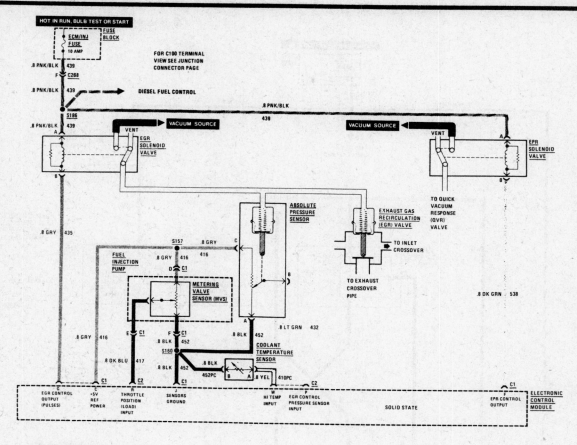

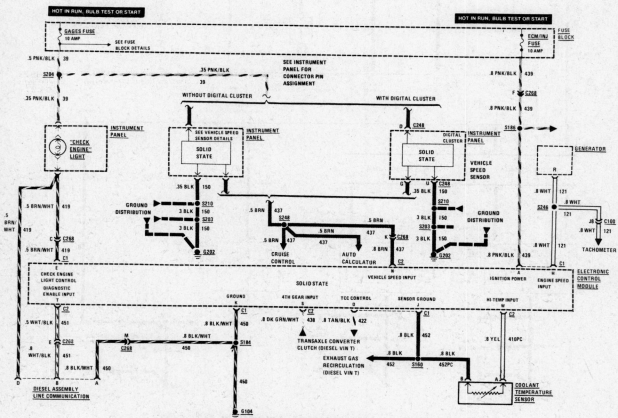

Diesel engine fuel control system — 4.3L (VIN T) Diesel engine (continued)

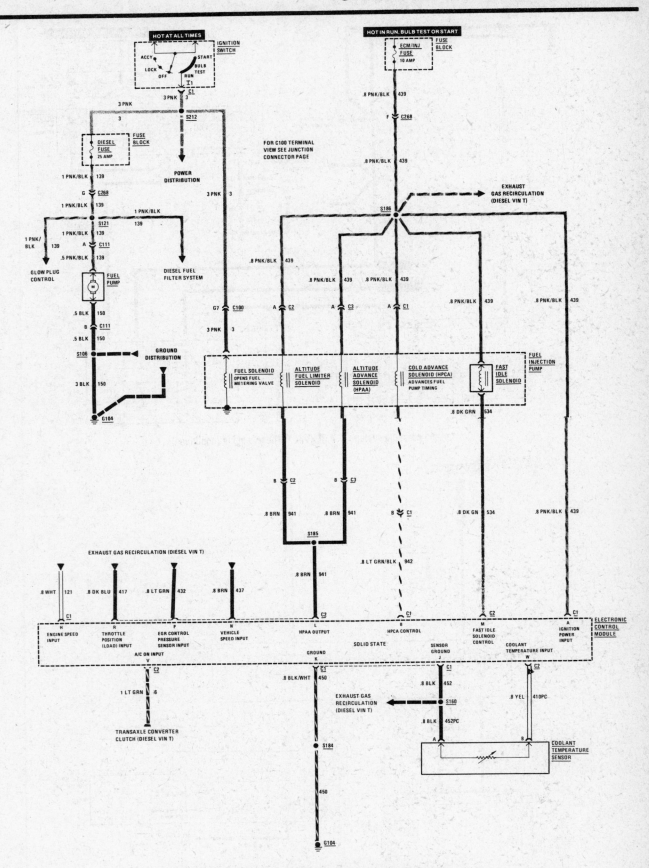

Diesel engine fuel control system — 4.3L (VIN T) Diesel engine (continued)

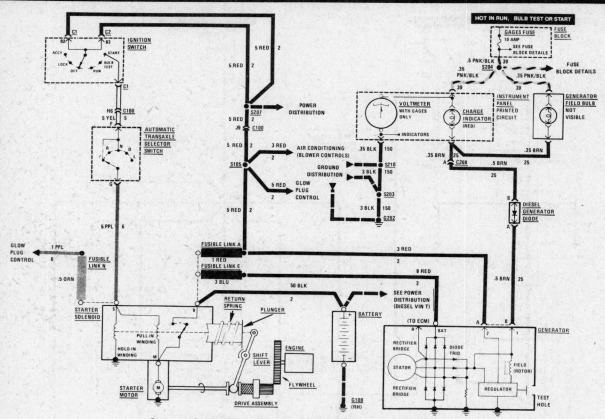

Starter and charging system — 4.3L (VIN T) Diesel engine (continued)

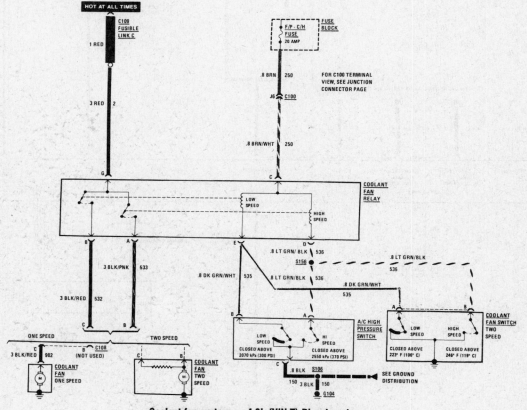

Coolant fan system — 4.3L (VIN T) Diesel engine

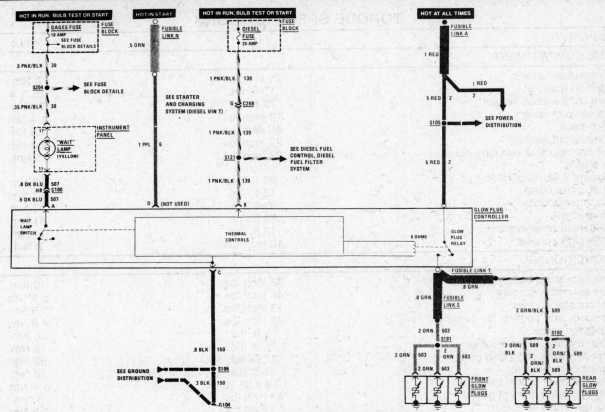

Glow plug control system — 4.3L (VIN T) Diesel engine

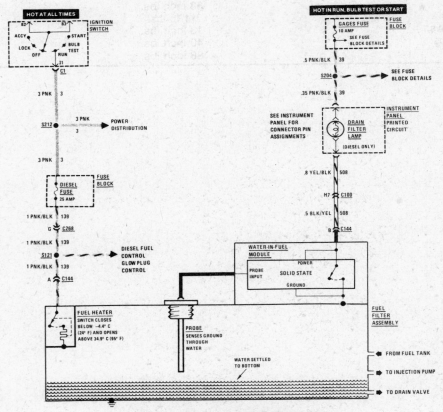

Fuel filter system — 4.3L (VIN T) Diesel engine

TORQUE SPECIFICATIONS

Component	U.S.	Metric
ENGINE COMPARTMENT		
C3I Crankshaft sensor:	71 inch lbs.	8 Nm
C3I Ignition module:	19 ft. lbs.	25 Nm
Coolant temperature sensor:	22 ft. lbs.	30 Nm
Crusie servo bracket:	12 inch lbs.	1.4 Nm
DIS Coil pack:	40 inch lbs.	4.5 Nm
DIS Crankshaft sensor:	20 inch lbs.	2.3 Nm
Idle air control valve retaining screw:	27 inch lbs.	3 Nm
Spark plugs:		
Except 2.8L carburated	20 ft. lbs.	27 Nm
2.8L carburated	15 ft. lbs.	17 Nm
Starter through bolts:	32 ft. lbs.	43 Nm
Steering wheel:	30 ft. lbs.	41 Nm
TCC solenoid retaining screws:	10 ft. lbs.	14 Nm
TPS retaining screws:	18 inch lbs.	2 Nm
AIR CONDITIONING		
Accumulator strap bolt:	88 inch lbs.	10 Nm
Air inlet assembly screws:	48 inch lbs.	5.4 Nm
Blower resistor screws:	13 inch lbs.	1.5 Nm
Compressor and cooling fan switches:	42 inch lbs.	4.8 Nm
Compressor brace:	22 ft. lbs.	30 Nm
Compressor bracket to engine:	25 ft. lbs.	18 Nm
Compressor front mounting bolts:	37 ft. lbs.	50 Nm
Compressor to bracket:	25 ft. lbs.	18 Nm
Condenser lower bracket bolt:	12.5 inch lbs.	1.4 Nm
Condenser lower bracket nut:	53 inch lbs.	6 Nm
Control assembly screws:	13 inch lbs.	1.5 Nm
Coupled hose assembly:	25 ft. lbs.	33 Nm
Defroster duct screws:	13 inch lbs.	1.5 Nm
Heater pipe clips:	88 inch lbs.	10 Nm
Liquid line filter nuts:	11 ft. lbs.	15 Nm
Outlet (all) duct screws:	13 inch lbs.	1.5 Nm
Refrigent hose clamps:	40 inch lbs.	4.5 Nm
Vaccum tank bolts:	88 inch lbs.	10 Nm

7
DRIVE
TRAIN

MANUAL TRANSAXLE

General Information

Transaxle is the term used to identify a unit which combines the transmission and drive axle into one component. All 1982–86 models were equipped with MT-125 manual four speed transaxles. In 1987–88 Muncie five speed transaxles were used. The 4-speed transaxles use cable actuated clutches while the five speed clutches are hydraulically controlled utilizing a clutch master and slave cylinder.

All forward gears in this design are in constant mesh. Final drive from the transmission is taken from the output gear, which is an integral part of the output shaft; the output gear transfers power to the differential ring gear and differential assembly. The differential is of conventional design.

The 4-speed transaxle assembly is a constant mesh design, combined with a differential unit and assembled in a single case; the forward gears are in constant mesh. For ease of shifting and gear selecting, synchronizers with blocker rings are controlled by shifting forks. A sliding idler gear arrangement is used for reverse gear.

The components consists of: an aluminum transaxle case, an aluminum clutch cover, input gear (shaft), output gear (shaft) and the differential assembly. Preloaded tapered roller bearings support the input gear, output gear and differential. Selective shims, used to establish the correct preload, are located beneath the right hand bearing cups.

The halfshafts which are attached to the front wheels, are turned by the differential and ring gear which are controlled by the final output gear.

The differential, consisting of a set of 4 gears, is a conventional arrangement that divides the torque between the halfshafts, allowing them to rotate at different speeds. Of the 4 gear set, 2 are known as differential side gears and the others are differential pinion gears.

The differential pinion gears, mounted on a differential pinion shaft, are free to rotate on the shaft. The pinion shaft, placed in the differential case bore, is at a right angle to the drive axle shaft.

The Hydra-Matic Muncie 282 (HM–282) transaxle is a 5 speed unit. The gearing provides for 5 synchronized forward speeds, a reverse speed, a final drive with differential output and speedometer drive.

The input and output gear clusters are nested very close together, requiring extremely tight tolerances of shafts, gears and synchronizers.

The input shaft is supported by a roller bearing in the clutch and differential housing and a ball bearing in the transaxle case.

The output shaft is supported by a roller bearing in the clutch and differential housing and a combination ball-and-roller bearing in the transaxle case.

The differential case is supported by opposed tapered roller bearings which are under preload.

The speed gears are supported by roller bearings. A bushing supports the reverse idler gear.

Manual 4 Speed Transaxle Troubleshooting Chart

Condition	Cause	Correction
Noise is the same in drive or coast	a) Road noise b) Tire noise c) Front wheel bearing noise d) Incorrect drive axle angle (Standing Height)	a) Road test on a smooth road b) Select a different tire design c) Repair front wheel bearing d) Adjust vehicle height
Noise changes on a different type of road	a) Road noise b) Tire noise	a) Road test on a smooth road b) Select a different tire design
Noise tone lowers as vehicle speed is lowered	a) Tire noise	a) Select a different tire design
Noise is produced with engine running vehicle stopped and/or driving	a) Engine noise b) Transaxle noise c) Exhaust noise	a) Determine engine problem and repair it b) Determine transaxle problem and repair it c) Determine exhaust problem and repair it
A knock at low speed	a) Worn drive axle joints b) Worn side gear hub counterbore	a) Replace worn drive axle joints b) Replace differential assembly
Noise most pronounced on turns	a) Differential gear noise	a) Replace differential gear(s) or assembly
Clunk on acceleration or deceleration	a) Loose engine mounts b) Worn differential pinion shaft in case or side gear hub counterbore in case worn oversize c) Worn or damaged drive axle inboard joints	a) Tighten or replace loose engine mounts b) Replace differential pinion shaft or assembly c) Replace inboard drive axle joint

Manual 4 Speed Transaxle Troubleshooting Chart (cont.)

Condition	Cause	Correction
Clicking noise in turns	a) Worn or damaged outboard joint	a) Replace damaged outboard joint
Vibration	a) Rough wheel bearing b) Damaged drive axle shaft c) Out of round tires d) Tire unbalance e) Worn joint in drive axle shaft f) Incorrect drive axle angle	a) Replace damaged wheel bearing b) Replace axle shaft c) Replace the tires d) Balance the tires e) Replace worn drive axle joint f) Adjust vehicle height
Noisy in Neutral with engine running	a) Damaged input gear bearings	a) Replace input gear bearings
Noisy in First only	a) Damaged or worn first-speed constant mesh gears b) Damaged or worn 1-2 synchronizer	a) Replace damaged 1st gears b) Replace damaged 1-2 synchronizer
Noisy in Second only	a) Damaged or worn second-speed constant mesh gears b) Damaged or worn 1-2 synchronizer	a) Replace damaged 2nd gears b) Replace damaged 1-2 synchronizer
Rattle noise in 2nd gear while making left turn	a) Bent reverse fork	a) Replace bent reverse fork
Noisy in Third only	a) Damaged or worn third-speed constant mesh gears b) Damaged or worn 3-4 synchronizer	a) Replace damaged 3rd gears b) Replace damaged 3-4 synchronizer
Noisy in High Gear	a) Damaged 3-4 synchronizer b) Damaged 4th speed gear or output gear	a) Replace damaged 3-4 synchronizer b) Replace damaged 4th gear
Noisy in Reverse only	a) Worn or damaged reverse idler gear or idler bushing b) Worn or damaged 1-2 synchronizer sleeve	a) Replace damaged reverse idler gear or bushing b) Replace damaged 1-2 synchronizer sleeve
Noisy in All Gears	a) Insufficient lubricant b) Damaged or worn bearings c) Worn or damaged input gear (shaft) and/or output gear (shaft)	a) Add lubricant b) Replace damaged bearings c) Replace damaged input and/or output gear/shaft
Slips out of Gear	a) Worn or improperly adjusted linkage b) Transmission loose on engine housing c) Shift linkage does not work freely; binds d) Bent or damaged cables e) Input gear bearing retainer broken or loose f) Dirt between clutch cover and engine housing g) Stiff shift lever seal h) Worn shift fork	a) Replace or adjust linkage b) Tighten transaxle housing bolts c) Replace, lubricate or adjust linkage d) Replace damaged cables e) Replace or tighten input gear bearing retainer f) Remove dirt between clutch cover and engine housing g) Replace or lubricate shift lever seal h) Replace worn shift fork
Leaks Lubricant	a) Axle shaft seals b) Excessive amount of lubricant in transmission c) Loose or broken input gear (shaft) bearing retainer d) Input gear bearing retainer ''O'' ring and/or lip seal damaged e) Lack of sealant between case and clutch cover or loose clutch cover f) Shift lever seal leaks	a) Replace axle shaft seals b) Remove excessive lubricant c) Replace or tighten input gear bearing retainer d) Replace O-ring or seal e) Add sealant between case and cover or tighten cover f) Replace shift lever seal.

Muncie HM 282 5-Speed Manual Transaxle

Condition	Cause	Correction
A knock at low speeds	a) Drive axle CV or TRI-POT joints worn b) Side gear hub counterbore worn	a) Replace CV or joints b) Replace hub counterbore
Noise most pronounced on turns	a) Differential gear noise	a) Check and repair or replace gear
Clunk on acceleration or deceleration	a) Engine mounts loose b) Drive axle inboard TRI-POT joints worn c) Differential pinion shaft in case worn d) Side gear hub counterbore in case worn oversize	a) Replace mounts b) Replace joints c) Replace shaft d) Repair or replace hub counterbore
Vibration	a) Wheel bearing rough b) Drive axle shaft bent c) Tires out-of-round d) Tire unbalance e) CV joint in drive axle shaft worn f) Drive axle angle (trim height) incorrect	a) Replace bearing b) Replace shaft c) Replace tire d) Balance tire e) Replace CV joint f) Adjust angle
Noisy in neutral with engine running	a) Input gear bearings worn b) Clutch release bearing worn	a) Replace bearings b) Replace bearings
Noisy in 1st only	a) 1st speed constant-mesh gears chipped, scored or worn b) 1/2 synchronizer worn	a) Replace gears b) Replace synchronizer
Noisy in 2nd only	a) 2nd speed constant-mesh gears chipped, scored or worn b) 1/2 synchronizer worn	a) Replace gears b) Replace synchronizer
Noisy in 3rd only	a) 3rd gear constant-mesh gears chipped, scored or worn b) 3/4 synchronizer worn	a) Replace gears b) Replace synchronizer
Noisy in 4th only	a) 4th gear or output gear chipped, scored or worn b) 3/4 synchronizer worn	a) Replace gears b) Replace synchronizer
Noisy in 5th only	a) 5th speed gear or output gears chipped, scored or worn b) 5th gear synchronizer worn	a) Replace gears b) Replace synchronizer
Noisy in reverse only	a) Reverse idler gear, idler gear bushing, input or output gear(s) chipped, scored or worn	a) Replace gear(s) and/or bushings
Noisy in all gears	a) Insufficient lubricant b) Bearings worn c) Input gear (shaft) and/or output gear (shaft) worn, chipped or scored	a) Add lubricant b) Replace bearings c) Replace gear(s)
Slips out of gear	a) Linkage worn or improperly adjusted b) Shift linkage does not work freely; binds c) Cables bent or worn d) Input gear bearing retainer broken or loose e) Shift fork worn or bent	a) Replace and/or adjust linkage b) Repair or replace linkage c) Replace cables d) Repair or replace retainer e) Replace shift fork

Muncie HM 282 5-Speed Manual Transaxle

Condition	Cause	Correction
Leaks lubricant	a) Fluid level indicator not seated in fill port, causing fluid leakage at vent plug	a) Seat fluid level indicator
	b) Axle shaft seals worn	b) Replace seals
	c) Excessive amount of lubricant in transaxle	c) Remove excessive fluid
	d) Input gear (shaft) bearing retainer loose or broken	d) Repair or replace retainer
	e) Input gear bearing worn and/or lip seal damaged	e) Replace bearing and/or lip seal
	f) Worn shift lever seal leaks	f) Replace seal
	g) Lack of sealant between case and clutch cover or loose clutch cover	g) Repair case and/or cover

Transaxle Identification

The transaxle identification stamp is located at the center top of the case. The transaxle identification tag is located on the left side near the left side cover.

Adjustments

SHIFT LINKAGE

MT-125

1. Disconnect the negative battery cable. Remove the shifter boot, the console and retainer inside the car. Shift into first gear, then loosen the shift cable mounting nuts at the transaxle.

2. Install two No. 22 drill bits, or two 5/32 in. (4mm) rods, into the two alignment holes in the shifter assembly to hold it in first gear.

3. Place the transaxle into first gear by pushing the rail selector shaft down just to the point of feeling the resistance of the inhibitor spring. Then rotate the shift lever all the way counterclockwise.

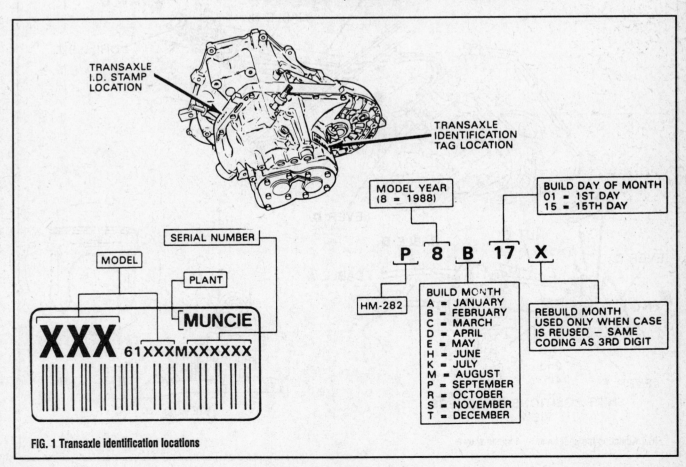

FIG. 1 Transaxle identification locations

4. Install the stud, with the cable attached, into the slotted area of the select lever, while gently pulling on the lever to remove all lash.

5. Remove the two drill bits or pins from the shifter.

6. Check the shifter for proper operation. It may be necessary to fine tune the adjustment after road testing.

SHIFTER SHAFT WASHER

If a hang-up is experienced in the 1–2 gear range and the shift cables are properly adjusted, it may be necessary to change the shift selector washer.

1. From the end of the housing, remove the reverse inhibitor fitting spring and washer.

2. Position the shifter shaft into the **2nd** gear position.

3. Measure the end of housing-to-end of shifter shaft (dimension **A**).

4. On the opposite end of the shaft, apply a load of 8.8–13.3 lbs. (4–6 Kg) and measure the end of housing-to-end of shifter shaft (dimension **B**).

5. Subtract dimension **B** from dimension **A** and secure dimension **C**.

6. Using the dimension **C** and shifter shaft selective washer chart, select the correct shim washer to be used on the reinstallation.

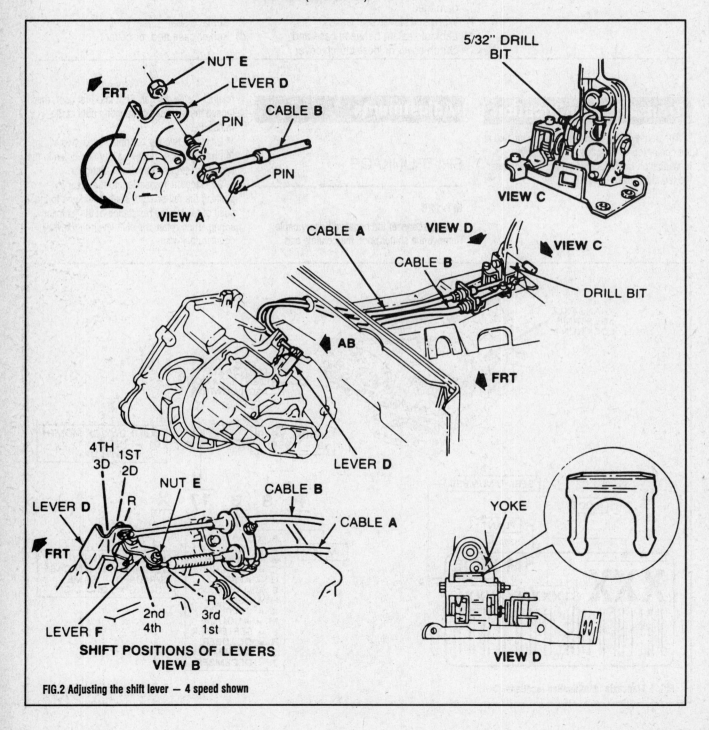

FIG.2 Adjusting the shift lever — 4 speed shown

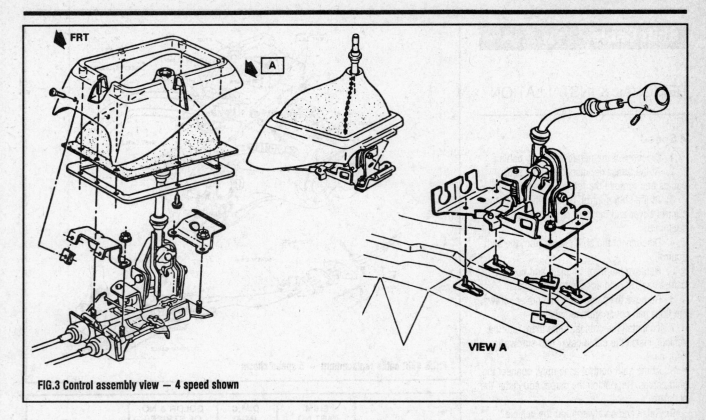

FIG.3 Control assembly view — 4 speed shown

FRT

A

VIEW A

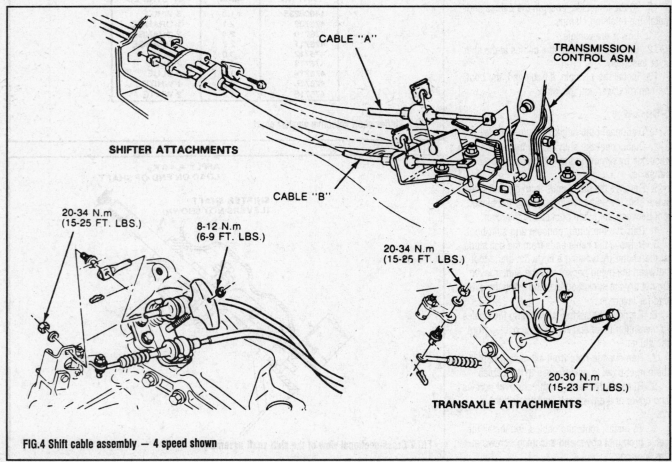

CABLE "A"

TRANSMISSION CONTROL ASM

SHIFTER ATTACHMENTS

CABLE "B"

20-34 N.m
(15-25 FT. LBS.)

8-12 N.m
(6-9 FT. LBS.)

20-34 N.m
(15-25 FT. LBS.)

20-30 N.m
(15-23 FT. LBS.)

TRANSAXLE ATTACHMENTS

FIG.4 Shift cable assembly — 4 speed shown

Shift Cable

REMOVAL & INSTALLATION

4 Speed

1. Disconnect the negative battery cable.
2. At the transaxle, disconnect the shift cables and remove the retaining clamp.
3. At the shift control, remove the knob, the control cover and the boot or console (if equipped).
4. Disconnect the shift cables from the shift control.
5. Remove the front sill plate and pull the carpet back to gain access to the cables.
6. Remove the cable grommet cover screws, the floor pan cover and the cables.
7. To install the cables, route them into the vehicle, install the cable cover and screws (at floor pan).
8. At the shift control assembly, connect the shift cables. Reposition the carpet and install the sill plate.
9. Raise and safely support the vehicle.
10. At the transaxle, position the cables and install the retaining clamps.
11. Lower the vehicle.
12. Connect and adjust the cables at the shift lever assembly.
13. Install the console, if equipped, the boot, the control cover and the knob.

5-Speed

1. Disconnect the negative battery cable.
2. Disconnect the shift cables from the transaxle by removing the cable clamp at the transaxle.
3. Remove the cable ends from the ball studs at the shift levers by twisting a large flat blade tool between the nylon socket and the lever.
4. Remove the knob, console and shift boot.
5. Remove the cable ends from the ball studs of the shifter by twisting a large flat blade tool between the nylon socket and the shifter lever. Do not pry the socket off the stud using the cable end for leverage.
6. Remove the spring clip holding the cables to the shifter base and remove the cables from the shifter.
7. Remove the right front sill plate and pull the carpet back to gain access to the cables.
8. Remove the cable grommet cover screws and cover at the floor pan and remove the cables.
9. To install, route the cables and install the cable grommet cover and attaching screws at the floor pan.

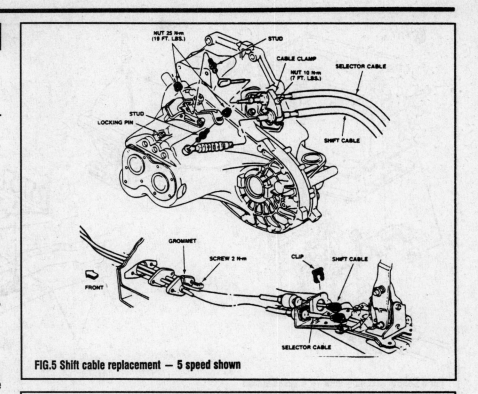

FIG.5 Shift cable replacement — 5 speed shown

SHIM PART NO.	DIM C (MM)	COLOR & NO OF STRIPES
14008235	1.8	3 WHITE
476709	2.1	1 ORANGE
476710	2.4	2 ORANGE
476711	2.7	3 ORANGE
476712	3.0	1 BLUE
476713	3.3	2 BLUE
476714	3.6	3 BLUE
476715	3.9	1 WHITE
476716	4.2	2 WHITE

FIG.6 Shifter shaft selective washer chart

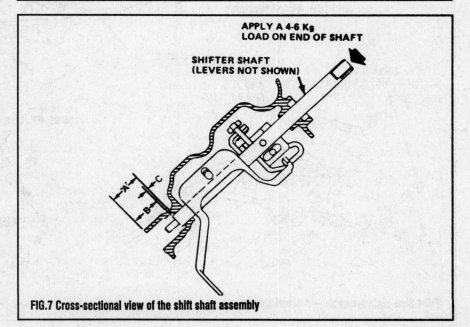

FIG.7 Cross-sectional view of the shift shaft assembly

10. Install the shift cables at the control assembly. Snap the cable ends onto the ball studs using the channel locks.

11. Reposition the carpet and install the sill plate.

12. Raise and support the vehicle safely.

13. Route the cables to the transaxle.

14. Lower the vehicle.

15. Position the cables and install the retaining clamps at the transaxle. Connect the cables to the shift levers.

16. Install the shift boot, console and knob.

17. Connect the negative battery cable.

Neutral Safety/Back-up Light Switch

REMOVAL & INSTALLATION

1. Remove the shifter knob from the shifter by removing the retaining screw at the back of the knob.

2. Remove the screws at the sides and front of the console.

3. Open the console box and remove the retaining screw inside the box.

4. Remove the ashtray at the rear of the console and remove the retaining screw behind the ashtray.

5. Slide the console rearward slightly, then lift it over the shifter.

6. Disconnect the wiring harness at the back-up light switch.

7. Remove the switch from the base of the shifter.

8. Reverse steps 1 through 7 to install the switch.

Transaxle

REMOVAL & INSTALLATION

1982–83

MT-125

1. Disconnect the negative battery cable from the transaxle case.

2. Remove the two transaxle strut bracket bolts on the left side of the engine compartment, if equipped.

3. Remove the top four engine-to-transaxle bolts, and the one at the rear near the firewall.

The one at the rear is installed from the engine side.

4. Loosen the engine-to-transaxle bolt near the starter, but do not remove.

5. Disconnect the speedometer cable at the transaxle, or at the speed control transducer on cars so equipped.

6. Remove the retaining clip and washer from the shift linkage at the transaxle. Remove the clips holding the cables to the mounting bosses on the case.

7. Support the engine with a lifting chain.

8. Unlock the steering column and raise and support the car. Drain the transaxle. Remove the two nuts attaching the stabilizer bar to the left lower control arm. Remove the four bolts which attach the left retaining plate to the engine cradle. The retaining plate covers and holds the stabilizer bar.

9. Loosen the four bolts holding the right stabilizer bracket.

10. Disconnect and remove the exhaust pipe and crossover if necessary.

11. Pull the stabilizer bar down on the left side.

12. Remove the four nuts and disconnect the front and rear transaxle mounts from the engine cradle. Remove the two rear center crossmember bolts.

13. Remove the three right side front cradle attaching bolts. They are accessible under the splash shield.

14. Remove the top bolt from the lower front transaxle shock absorber if equipped.

15. Remove the left front wheel. Remove the front cradle-to-body bolts on the left side, and the rear cradle-to-body bolts.

16. Pull the left side driveshaft from the transaxle using G. M. special tool J-28468 or the equivalent. The right side axle shaft will simply disconnect from the cage. When the transaxle is removed, the right shaft can be swung out of the way. A boot protector should be used when disconnecting the driveshafts.

17. Swing the cradle to the left side. Secure out of the way, outboard of the fender well.

18. Remove the flywheel and starter shield bolts, and remove the shields.

19. Remove the two transaxle extension bolts from the engine-to-transaxle bracket, if equipped.

20. Place a jack under the transaxle case. Remove the last engine-to-transaxle bolt. Pull the transaxle to the left, away from the engine, then down and out from under the car.

To install:

21. Place the transaxle on a jack and raise it into position. Position the right axle shaft into its bore as the transaxle is bolted to the engine.

22. Swing the cradle into position and install the cradle-to-body bolts immediately. Be sure to guide the left axle shaft into place as the cradle is moved back into position.

23. Install the two transaxle extension bolts into the engine-to-transaxle bracket.

24. Install the lower engine-to-transaxle bolts.

25. Install the flywheel to starter shield and retaining bolts.

26. Remove the boot protectors from the driveshafts.

27. Install the top bolt to the lower front transaxle shock absorber.

28. Install the four nuts and connect the front and rear transaxle mounts to the engine cradle. Install the two rear center crossmember bolts.

29. Install the stabilizer bar.

30. Install the exhaust pipe and crossover.

31. Install the four bolts holding the right stabilizer bracket.

32. Install the two nuts attaching the stabilizer bar to the left lower control arm. Install the four bolts which attach the left retaining plate to the engine cradle.

33. Remove the transaxle jack, disconnect the engine lifting chain and lower the vehicle.

34. Fill the transaxle with the recommended fluid.

35. Install the retaining clip and washer to the shift linkage at the transaxle. Install the clips holding the cables to the mounting bosses on the case.

36. Connect the speedometer cable at the transaxle, or at the speed control transducer on cars so equipped.

37. Tighten the engine-to-transaxle bolt near the starter.

38. Install the top four engine-to-transaxle bolts, and the one at the rear near the firewall. The one at the rear is installed from the engine side.

39. Remove the two transaxle strut bracket bolts on the left side of the engine compartment, if equipped.

40. Connect the negative battery cable to the transaxle case.

1984–86

MT-125

1. Disconnect the battery ground cable from the transaxle and support it with a wire.

2. Disconnect the horn's electrical lead and remove the horn's mounting bolt. Remove the air cleaner.

3. Support the clutch pedal upward against the bumper stop to release the pawl from the quadrant. Disconnect the clutch cable from the release lever at the transaxle.

4. Lift the locking pawl away from the quadrant and slide the cable out to the right side of the quadrant.

5. At the right side of the cowl, disconnect the cable retainer-to-upper stud nuts. Disconnect the cable from the transaxle bracket and remove the cable.

6. If equipped with a V6 engine, disconnect the fuel lines and clamps from the clutch cable bracket, then remove the exhaust crossover pipe.

7. At the transaxle, remove the shift linkage retaining clips and the shift cable retaining clips from the transaxle bosses.

8. Disconnect the speedometer cable at the transaxle. Remove the top engine-to-transaxle bolts.

9. Install and support the engine with tool J–22825–1. Raise the vehicle and drain the transaxle fluid.

10. Install the drive axle boot protector tool J–33162 to the drive axle boot. Remove the left front wheel and tire assembly.

11. Turn the steering wheel so that the intermediate shaft-to-steering gear stub shaft is in the upward position, then remove the bolt.

12. Position a floor jack under the engine to act as a support. Remove the power steering pressure line brackets.

13. Remove the steering gear mounting bolts, then support the steering gear. Disconnect the drive line vibration absorber, the front stabilizer from the left side lower control arm and the left side lower ball joint from the steering knuckle.

14. Remove both sides of the stabilizer bar reinforcements.

15. Using a 1/2 in. drill bit, drill through the spot weld (located between the rear holes of the left side front stabilizer bar mounting).

16. Disconnect the engine/transaxle mounts from the cradle. Remove the crossmember side bolts and the left side body bolts.

17. Remove the left side and the front crossmember assembly.

18. Using tools J–33008, J–29794 and J–261901, remove the left drive axle from the transaxle and the support.

➡ **The right drive axle can be removed when the transaxle is removed from the vehicle.**

19. Remove the flywheel/starter shield bolts. Connect a transaxle jack to the transaxle, then remove the last engine-to-transaxle bolt.

20. Slide the transaxle away from the engine, lower the jack and move the transaxle away from the vehicle.

To install:

21. Place the transaxle on a jack and raise it into position. Position the right axle shaft into its bore as the transaxle is bolted to the engine.

22. Swing the cradle into position and install the cradle-to-body bolts immediately. Be sure to guide the left axle shaft into place as the cradle is moved back into position.

23. Install the flywheel/starter shield and bolts.

24. Install the left side and front crossmember assembly.

25. Install the crossmember side bolts and the left side body bolts.

26. Connect the engine/transaxle mounts to the cradle.

27. Connect the left side lower ball joint to the steering knuckle.

28. Connect the front stabilizer to the left lower control arm.

29. Connect the drive line vibration absorber.

30. Install the stabilizer bar reinforcements, and the steering gear.

31. Install the power steering pressure line brackets.

32. Turn the steering wheel so that the intermediate shaft-to-steering gear stub shaft is in the upward position, then install the bolt.

33. Remove the drive axle boot protector tool J–33162 from the drive axle boot. Install the left front wheel and tire assembly.

34. Remove the engine support tool J–22825–1. Lower the vehicle and fill the transaxle with fluid.

35. Connect the speedometer cable at the transaxle. Install the top engine-to-transaxle bolts.

36. Install the shift linkage retaining clips and the shift cable retaining clips to the transaxle bosses.

37. If equipped with a V6 engine, connect the fuel lines and clamps to the clutch cable bracket, then install the exhaust crossover pipe.

38. At the right side of the cowl, connect the cable retainer-to-upper stud nuts. Install the cable to the transaxle bracket.

39. Lift the locking pawl away from the quadrant and slide the cable into the right side of the quadrant.

40. Connect the clutch cable to the release lever at the transaxle. Return the clutch pedal to its normal position.

41. Connect the horn's electrical lead and install the mounting bolt. Install the air cleaner.

42. Connect the battery ground cable to the transaxle.

1987–88

MUNCIE

1. Disconnect the negative battery cable.

2. Remove the air cleaner and air intake duct assembly.

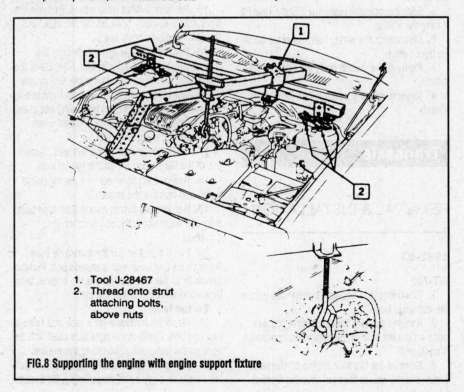

1. Tool J-28467
2. Thread onto strut attaching bolts, above nuts

FIG.8 Supporting the engine with engine support fixture

3. Remove the sound insulator from inside the car.

4. Remove the clutch master cylinder push rod from the clutch pedal.

5. Remove the clutch slave cylinder from the transaxle.

6. Disconnect the exhaust crossover pipe.

7. Disconnect the shift cables at the transaxle.

8. Install the engine support fixture J–28467.

9. Remove the top engine to transaxle bolts.

10. Raise the car and suitably support it.

11. Remove the L.H. and R.H. front wheel and tire.

12. Install the drive axle boot seal protectors, Tool J–34754.

13. Remove the L.H. side frame and disconnect the rear transaxle mount from the bracket.

14. Drain the transaxle.

15. Disengage the R.H. and L.H. drive axles from the transaxle.

16. Remove the clutch housing cover bolts.

17. Disconnect the speedometer cable.

18. Attach a jack to the transaxle case.

19. Remove the remaining transaxle to engine bolts.

20. Slide the transaxle away from the engine. Carefully lower the jack while guiding the R.H. drive axle out of the transaxle.

To install:

21. Place the transaxle on a jack and guide it into the vehicle, position the right drive axle shaft into its bore as the transaxle is being installed. The R.H. shaft CANNOT be readily installed after the transaxle is connected to the engine.

22. Install the transaxle to engine bolts.

23. After the transaxle is fastened to the engine and the left drive axle is installed at the transaxle, position the left side frame and install the frame to body bolts.

24. Connect the transaxle to the front and rear mounts.

25. Connect the speedometer cable.

26. Install the clutch housing cover bolts.

27. Remove the drive axle boot seal protectors, Tool J–34754.

28. Fill the transaxle with the proper fluid.

29. Install the left side frame and connect the rear transaxle mount to the bracket (if not already done).

30. Install the left and right front wheel and tire.

31. Remove the jack and safety supports and lower the car.

32. Install the top engine to transaxle bolts.

33. Remove the engine support fixture J–28467.

34. Connect the shift cables at the transaxle.

35. Connect the exhaust crossover pipe.

36. Install the clutch slave cylinder to the transaxle.

37. Install the clutch master cylinder push rod from the clutch pedal.

38. Install the sound insulator inside the car.

39. Install the air intake duct assembly and the air cleaner.

40. Connect the negative battery cable.

1989–92

4-SPEED

1. Disconnect the negative battery cable. Drain the transaxle.

2. Remove the 2 transaxle strut bracket bolts on the left side of the engine compartment, if equipped.

3. If equipped with a V6 engine, disconnect the fuel lines and fuel line clamps at the clutch cable bracket, as required.

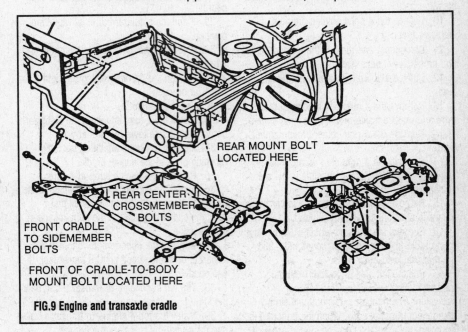

FIG.9 Engine and transaxle cradle

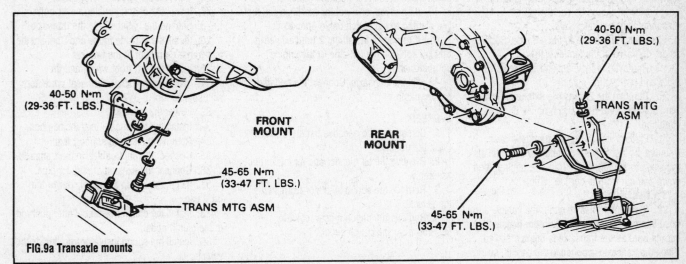

FIG.9a Transaxle mounts

4. Remove the top 4 engine-to-transaxle bolts and the one at the rear near the firewall. The one at the rear is installed from the engine side.

5. Loosen the engine-to-transaxle bolt near the starter but do not remove.

6. Disconnect the speedometer cable at the transaxle or at the speed control transducer, if equipped.

7. Remove the retaining clip and washer from the shift linkage at the transaxle. Remove the clips holding the cables to the mounting bosses on the case.

8. Support the engine with a lifting chain.

9. Unlock the steering column. Raise and safely support the vehicle. Drain the transaxle. Remove the 2 nuts attaching the stabilizer bar to the left lower control arm. Remove the 4 bolts which attach the left retaining plate to the engine cradle. The retaining plate covers holds the stabilizer bar.

10. Loosen the 4 bolts holding the right stabilizer bracket.

11. Disconnect and remove the exhaust pipe and crossover, if necessary.

12. Pull the stabilizer bar down on the left side.

13. Remove the 4 nuts and disconnect the front and rear transaxle mounts from the engine cradle. Remove the 2 rear center crossmember bolts.

14. Remove the 3 right side front cradle attaching bolts. They are accessible under the splash shield.

15. Remove the top bolt from the lower front transaxle shock absorber, if equipped.

16. Remove the left front wheel. Remove the front cradle-to-body bolts on the left side, and the rear cradle-to-body bolts.

17. Pull the left side driveshaft from the transaxle using special tool J–28468 or equivalent. The right side halfshaft will simply disconnect from the case. When the transaxle is removed, the right shaft can be swung aside. A boot protector should be used when disconnecting the driveshafts.

18. Swing the cradle to the left side. Secure aside, outboard of the fender well.

19. Remove the flywheel and starter shield bolts and remove the shields.

20. Remove the 2 transaxle extension bolts from the engine-to-transaxle bracket, if equipped.

21. Place a jack under the transaxle case. Remove the last engine-to-transaxle bolt. Pull the transaxle to the left, away from the engine, then down and out from under the vehicle.

To install:

22. Place the transaxle under the vehicle and raise into position. Position the right halfshaft into its bore as the transaxle is being installed. When the transaxle is bolted to the engine, swing the cradle into position and install the cradle-to-body bolts immediately. Be sure to guide the left halfshaft into place as the cradle is moved back into position.

23. If removed, install the 2 transaxle extension bolts to the engine-to-transaxle bracket.

24. Install flywheel, starter shield and attaching bolts.

25. Install the front cradle-to-body bolts on the left side and the rear cradle-to-body bolts. Install the left front wheel.

26. If removed, install the top bolt to the lower front transaxle shock absorber.

27. Install the 3 right side front cradle attaching bolts.

28. Connect the front and rear transaxle mounts to the engine cradle and install the 4 nuts. Install the 2 rear center crossmember bolts.

29. Place the stabilizer bar in its mounting position.

30. Install and connect the exhaust pipe and crossover.

31. Tighten the 4 bolts holding the right stabilizer bracket.

32. Lower the vehicle.

33. Install the 2 nuts attaching the stabilizer bar to the left side lower control arm.

34. Install the 4 bolts attaching the left retaining plate to the engine cradle.

35. Remove the engine support fixture.

36. Install the clips holding the cables to the mounting bosses on the case. Install the retaining clip and washer to the shift linkage at the transaxle.

37. Connect the speedometer cable at the transaxle or at the speed control transducer, if equipped.

38. Tighten the engine-to-transaxle bolt near the starter.

39. Install the top 4 engine-to-transaxle bolts and the one at the rear near the firewall.

40. If removed, connect the fuel lines and fuel line clamps to the clutch cable bracket.

41. If removed, install the 2 transaxle strut bracket bolts on the left side of the engine compartment.

42. Fill the transaxle. Connect the negative battery cable.

5-SPEED

1. Disconnect the negative battery cable. Drain the transaxle.

2. Remove the air cleaner and air intake duct assembly.

3. Remove the sound insulator from inside the vehicle.

4. Remove the clutch master cylinder pushrod from the clutch pedal.

5. Remove the clutch slave cylinder from the transaxle.

6. Disconnect the exhaust crossover pipe.

7. Disconnect the shift cables at the transaxle.

8. Install the engine support fixture J–28467.

9. Remove the top engine-to-transaxle bolts.

10. Raise and safely support the vehicle.

11. Install the halfshaft boot seal protectors with special tool J–34754.

12. Remove the left front wheel and tire.

13. Remove the left side frame and disconnect the rear transaxle mount from the bracket.

14. Drain the transaxle.

15. Disengage the halfshafts from the transaxle.

16. Remove the clutch housing cover bolts.

17. Disconnect the speedometer cable.

18. Attach a jack to the transaxle case.

19. Remove the remaining transaxle-to-engine bolts.

20. Slide the transaxle away from the engine. Carefully lower the jack while guiding the right halfshaft from the transaxle.

To install:

21. Place the transaxle into position in the vehicle. When installing the transaxle, position the right halfshaft shaft into its bore as the transaxle is being installed. The right shaft cannot be readily installed after the transaxle is connected to the engine.

22. After the transaxle is fastened to the engine and the left halfshaft is installed at the transaxle, position the left side frame and install the frame to body bolts.

23. Connect the transaxle to the front and rear mounts.

24. Install the remaining transaxle-to-engine bolts.

25. Remove the jack.

26. Connect the speedometer cable.

27. Install the clutch housing cover bolts.

28. Engage the halfshafts to the transaxle.

29. Install the left side frame and Connect the rear transaxle mount to the bracket.

30. Install the left front wheel and tire.

31. Install the halfshaft boot seal protectors with special tool J–34754.

32. Lower the vehicle.

33. Install the top engine-to-transaxle bolts.

34. Remove the engine support fixture.

35. Connect the shift cables to the transaxle.

36. Connect the exhaust crossover pipe.

37. Install the clutch slave cylinder to the transaxle.

38. Install the clutch master cylinder pushrod to the clutch pedal.

39. Install the sound insulator from inside the vehicle.

40. Install the air cleaner and air intake duct assembly.

41. Connect the negative battery cable.

MT-125 Transaxle Overhaul

The following procedure is for the 4 speed transaxle, expect some applications. For the Celebrity with 4 cylinder engine from 1984 and newer with a 4 speed follow procedures for Munice 4-speed transaxle.

TRANSAXLE CASE DISSASSEMBLY

1. Place the transmission so that it is resting on the bell housing.

2. Drive the spring pin from the shifter shaft arm assembly and the shifter shaft, then remove the shifter shaft arm assembly.

3. Remove the five extension housing-to-case bolts and the extension housing.

4. Press down on the speedometer gear retainer, then remove the gear and the retainer from the mainshaft.

5. Remove the snaprings from the shifter shaft, then the Reverse shifter shaft cover, the shifter shaft detent cap, the spring, the ball and the interlock lock pin.

6. Pull the Reverse lever shaft outward to disengage the Reverse idler, then remove the idler shaft with the gear attached.

7. Remove the Reverse gear snapring, the Reverse countershaft gear and the gears.

8. Turn the case on its side and remove the clutch gear bearing retainer bolts, the retainer and the gasket.

9. Remove the clutch gear ball bearing-to-bell housing snapring, then the bell housing-to-case bolts.

10. Turn the case so that it rests on the bell housing, then expand the mainshaft bearing snapring and remove the case by lifting it off the mainshaft.

➡ **Make sure that the mainshaft assembly, the countergear and shifter shaft assembly stay with the bell housing.**

11. Lift the entire mainshaft assembly complete with shifter forks and countergear from the bell housing.

ASSEMBLY

1. Using a press, install the shielded ball bearing to the clutch gear shaft with the snapring groove up.

2. Install the snapring on the clutch gear shaft. Place the pilot bearings into the clutch gear cavity, using heavy grease to hold them in place.

3. Assemble the clutch gear to the mainshaft and the detent lever to the shift shaft with the roll pin.

4. Position the 1st-2nd gear shifter so that it engages the detent lever.

5. Assemble the 3rd-4th gear shifter fork to the detent bushing and slide the assembly on the shift shaft to place it below the 1st-2nd shifter fork arm.

6. Install the shifter assembly to the synchronizer sleeve grooves on the mainshaft.

5. With the front of the bell housing resting on wooden blocks, place a thrust washer over the hole for the countergear shaft. The thrust washer must be placed in the holes in the bellhousing.

6. Mesh the countershaft gears to the mainshaft gears and install this assembly into the bellhousing.

7. Turn the bellhousing on its side, then install the snapring to the ball bearing on the clutch gear and the bearing retainer to the bell housing. Use sealant on the four retaining bolts.

8. Turn the bell housing (so that it is resting on the blocks) and install the Reverse lever to the case using grease to hold it in place. When installing the Reverse lever, the screwdriver slot should be parallel to the front of the case.

9. Install the Reverse lever snapring and the roller bearing-to-countergear opening with the snapring groove inside of the case.

10. Using rubber cement, install the gasket on the bell housing. Before installing the case, make sure the synchronizers are in the Neutral position, the detent bushing slot is facing outward and the Reverse lever is flush with the inside wall of the case.

11. Expand the snapring in the mainshaft case opening and let it slide over the bearing.

12. Install the interlock lock pin with locking compound to hold the shifter shaft in place and the idler shaft so it engages with the Reverse lever inside the shaft.

13. Install the cover over the screwdriver arm to hold the Reverse lever in place.

14. Install the detent ball, the spring and the cap in the case, then the Reverse gear (with the chamfer on the gear teeth facing up). Push the Reverse gear onto the splines and secure with a snapring.

15. Install the smaller Reverse gear on the countergear shaft (with the shoulder resting against the countergear bearing) and secure with a snapring.

16. Install the snapring, the thrust washer and the Reverse idler gear (with the gear teeth chamfer facing down) to the idler shaft, then secure with the thrust washer and the snapring.

17. Install the shifter shaft snaprings and engage the speedometer gear retainer in the hole in the mainshaft (with the retainer loop toward the front), then slide the speedometer gear over the mainshaft and into position.

➡ **Before installation, heat the gear to 175°F; use an oven or heat lamp, not a torch.**

18. Place the extension housing and the gasket on the case, then loosely install the two pilot bolts (one in the top right hand corner and the other in the bottom left hand corner) and the other three bolts. The pilot bolts must be installed in the right holes to prevent splitting the case.

19. Assemble the shifter shaft arm over the shifter shaft, align with the drilled hole near the end of the shaft, then drive the spring pin into the shifter shaft arm and shaft.

20. Turn the case on its side and loosely install the two pilot bolts through the bell housing and then the four retaining bolts.

MAINSHAFT DISASSEMBLY

1. Separate the shift shaft assembly and countergear from the mainshaft.

2. Remove the clutch gear and the blocking ring from the mainshaft; make sure you don't lose any of the clutch gear roller bearings.

3. Remove the 3rd-4th gear synchronizer hub snapring and the hub, using an arbor press (if necessary).

4. Remove the blocking ring and the 3rd speed gear. Using an arbor press and press plates, remove the ball bearing from the rear of the mainshaft. Remove the remaining parts from the mainshaft keeping them in order for later reassembly.

ASSEMBLY

1. With the rear of the mainshaft turned up, install the 2nd speed gear with the clutching teeth facing upward; the rear face of the gear will butt against the flange of the mainshaft.

2. Install a blocking ring (with the clutching teeth down) over the 2nd speed gear.

3. Install the 1st-2nd synchronizer assembly (with the fork slot down), then press it onto the splines on the mainshaft until it bottoms.

➡ **Make sure the notches of the blocking ring align with the keys of the synchronizer assembly.**

4. Install the synchronizer hub-to-mainshaft snapring, then install a blocking ring (with the notches facing down) so they align with the keys of the 1st-2nd gear synchronizer assembly.

5. Install the 1st speed gear (with the clutching teeth down), then the rear ball bearing (with the snapring groove down) and press it into place on the mainshaft.

6. Turn the mainshaft up and install the 3rd speed gear (with the clutching teeth facing up); the front face of the gear will butt against the flange on the mainshaft.

7. Install a blocking ring (with the clutching teeth facing down) over the synchronizer surface of the 3rd speed gear.

8. Install the 3rd-4th gear synchronizer assembly (with the fork slot facing down); make sure the notches of the blocking ring align with the keys of the synchronizer assembly.

9. Install the synchronizer hub-to-mainshaft snapring and a blocking ring (with the notches facing down) so that they align with the keys of the 3rd-4th gear synchronizer assembly.

SYNCHRONIZER KEYS AND SPRINGS REPLACEMENT

1. The synchronizer hubs and the sliding sleeves are an assembly which should be kept together as an assembly; the keys and the springs can be replaced.

2. Mark the position of the hub and the sleeve for reassembly.

3. Push the hub from the sliding sleeve; the keys will fall out and the springs can be easily removed.

4. Place the new springs in position (with one on each side of the hub) so that the three keys are engaged by both springs.

5. Place and hold the keys in position, then slide the sleeve into the hub aligning the marks made during disassembly.

EXTENSION OIL SEAL REPLACEMENT

1. Pry the oil seal and drive the bushing from rear of the extension housing.

2. Coat the inside diameter of the seal and bushing with transmission fluid and install them.

DRIVE GEAR BEARING OIL SEAL REPLACEMENT

Pry out the old seal and install a new one making sure that it bottoms properly in its bore.

Muncie 4-Speed Overhaul

BEFORE DISASSEMBLY

When servicing the transaxle it is important to be aware of cleanliness. Before disassembling the transaxle, the outside should be throughly cleaned, preferably with a high-pressure spray cleaning equipment. Dirt entering the unit may negate all the effort and time spent on the overhaul.

During inspection and reassembly, all parts should be cleaned with solvent and dried with compressed air. Lubricate the seals with transaxle fluid and use petroleum jelly to hold the thrust washers; this will ease the assembly of the seals and not leave harmful residues in the system. Do not use solvent on neoprene seals, if they are to be reused.

Before installing bolts into aluminum parts, dip the threads into clean transmission fluid. Anti-seize compound may be used to prevent galling the aluminum or seizing. Be sure to use a torque wrench to prevent stripping the threads. Be especially careful when installing the seals, the smallest nick can cause a leak. Aluminum parts are very susceptible to damage; great care should be used when handling them. Reusing

snaprings is not recommended but should they be: compress the internal ones and compress the external ones.

TRANSAXLE DISASSEMBLY

1. Secure the transaxle to a work stand.

2. Remove the clutch cover-to-transaxle bolts. Using a plastic hammer, carefully tap the clutch cover from the transaxle case.

3. Remove the ring gear/differential assembly.

4. Move the shifter shaft into the **N** position; the shifter should move freely and not be engaged in any gear.

5. At the shifter shaft, bend back the lock tab and remove the bolt. Remove the shifter shaft and the shift fork shaft from the synchronizer forks.

6. Disengage the reverse shift fork from the guide pin and interlock bracket, then, remove the reverse shift fork.

7. Remove the reverse idler gear shaft lock bolt and the gear/shaft/spacer assembly.

8. Remove the detent shift lever and interlock assembly. Do not remove the shift forks from the synchronizer or the detent spring.

9. Grasp both the input and output shafts and lift them (as an assembly) from the case.

➡ **When removing the input/output shaft assembly, note the position of the shift forks for reassembly purposes.** **The terms right hand and left hand refer to the installed positions on the vehicle. Right hand refers to the end nearest the clutch (passenger side); left hand refers to the end farthest from the clutch (drivers side).**

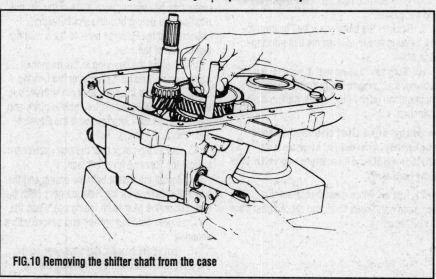

FIG.10 Removing the shifter shaft from the case

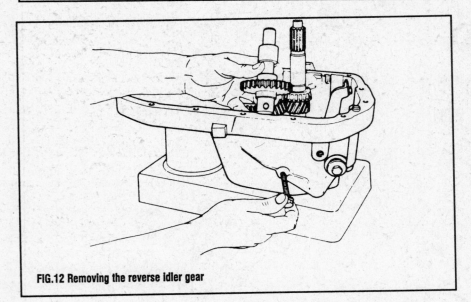

FIG.11 Removing the reverse fork

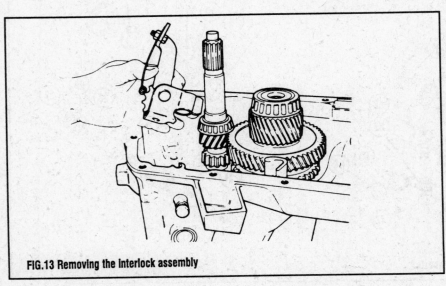

FIG.12 Removing the reverse idler gear

FIG.13 Removing the interlock assembly

INPUT SHAFT DISASSEMBLY

1. From the input shaft, remove (slide) the left hand bearing and the 4th gear.

2. Remove the brass blocker ring and the snapring from the 3–4 synchronizer.

3. Using a shop press and support plates (behind the 3rd gear), press the 3rd gear and 3–4 synchronizer from the input shaft.

4. Using the input shaft right hand bearing remover tool or equivalent, press the right hand bearing from the shaft.

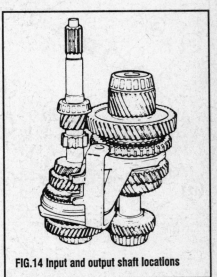

FIG.14 Input and output shaft locations

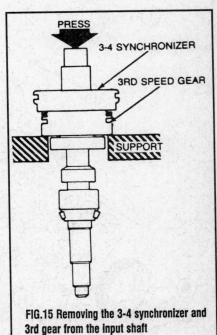

PRESS

3-4 SYNCHRONIZER

3RD SPEED GEAR

SUPPORT

FIG.15 Removing the 3-4 synchronizer and 3rd gear from the input shaft

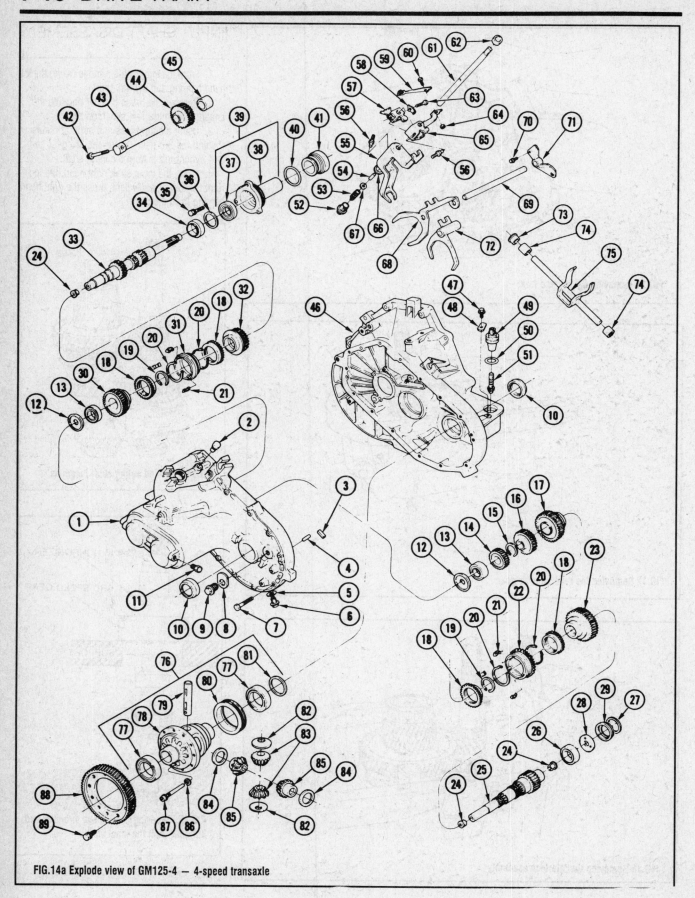

FIG.14a Explode view of GM125-4 — 4-speed transaxle

1. Case assembly
2. Vent assembly
3. Magnet
4. Pin
5. Washer
6. Drain screw
7. Bolt
8. Fill plug washer
9. Fill plug
10. Axle shaft seal
11. Plug
12. Oil shield
13. Bearing assembly
14. 4th output gear
15. 3rd output gear retaining ring
16. 3rd output gear
17. 2nd output gear
18. Synchronizer blocking ring
19. Synchronizer blocking ring retainer
20. Synchronizer blocking ring spring
21. Synchronizer key
22. Synchronizer assembly
23. 1st output gear
24. Oil shield sleeve
25. Output gear
26. Output bearing assembly
27. Output bearing adjustment shim
28. Output bearing oil shield
29. Output bearing oil shield retainer
30. 4th input gear
31. Synchronizer assembly
32. 3rd input gear
33. Input cluster gear
34. Input bearing assembly
35. Screw
36. Input gear bearing assembly shim
37. Input gear seal assembly
38. Input gear seal assembly
39. Input gear bearing retainer assembly
40. Input gear bearing retainer seal
41. Clutch release bearing assembly
42. Reverse idler screw and washer
43. Reverse idler shaft
44. Reverse idler gear assembly
45. Reverse idler shaft
46. spacer
46. Clutch and differential housing
47. Screw
48. Speedo gear fitting retainer
49. Speedo driven gear sleeve
50. Speedo gear sleeve seal
51. Speedo driven gear
52. Reverse inhibitor spring seat
53. Reverse inhibitor spring
54. Pin
55. Reverse shift lever
56. Reverse lever locating stud
57. Lever assembly detent
58. Lock detent lever washer
59. Detent spring
60. Bolt
61. Shift shaft
62. Shift shaft seal assembly
63. Bolt
64. Nut
65. Shift interlock
66. Shift shaft shim
67. Reverse inhibitor spring washer
68. 3rd/4rd shift fork
69. Shift shaft fork
70. Screw
71. Oil guide
72. 1st/2nd shift fork
73. Clutch fork shaft seal assembly
74. Clutch fork shaft bearing
75. Clutch fork shaft assembly
76. Differential assembly
77. Differential bearing assembly
78. Differential case
79. Differential pinion shaft
80. Speedo drive gear
81. Differential bearing adjustment shim
82. Pinion thrust washer
83. Differential Pinion gear
84. Side gear thrust washer
85. Differential side gear
86. Lockwasher
87. Pinion shaft screw
88. Differential ring gear
89. Bolt

FIG.14a Explode view of GM125-4 — 4-speed transaxle

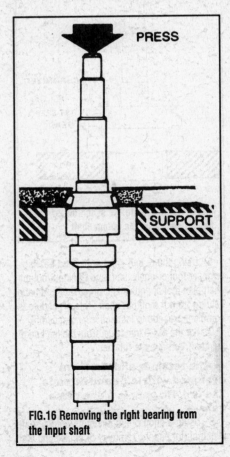

FIG.16 Removing the right bearing from the input shaft

INSPECTION

1. Check the input shaft bearing surfaces for scoring and/or wear; if necessary, replace the shaft.

2. Check the input shaft splines for wear; if necessary, replace the shaft.

3. Inspect the bearings for scoring, wear and/or damage; if necessary, replace them.

4. Check the gears and synchronizer parts for damage and/or excessively worn teeth; if necessary, replace them.

ASSEMBLY

1. Using the input shaft right hand bearing installer tool or equivalent and a shop press, press the right hand bearing onto the input shaft.

2. Position the 3rd gear onto the shaft (aligned with the 3–4 synchronizer), the brass blocker ring onto the gear cone and the 3–4 synchronizer. Using a deep socket or a piece of pipe, position it on the synchronizer hub (not the sleeve) and press the synchronizer hub onto the shaft.

3. Install the snapring (beveled edges away from synchronizer) to secure the 3–4 synchronizer.

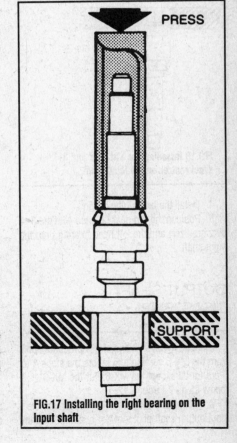

FIG.17 Installing the right bearing on the input shaft

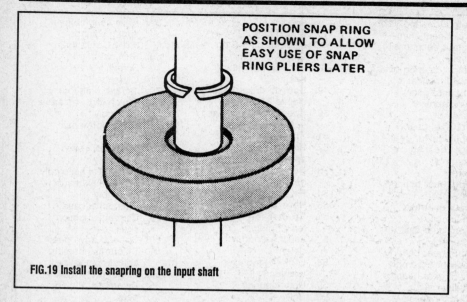

POSITION SNAP RING
AS SHOWN TO ALLOW
EASY USE OF SNAP
RING PLIERS LATER

FIG.19 Install the snapring on the input shaft

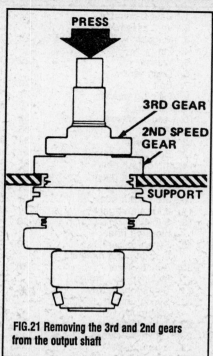

FIG.21 Removing the 3rd and 2nd gears
from the output shaft

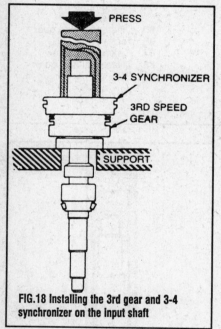

FIG.18 Installing the 3rd gear and 3-4
synchronizer on the input shaft

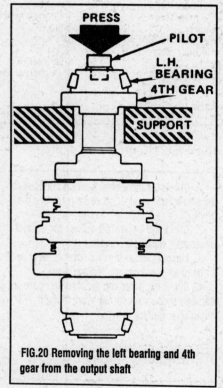

FIG.20 Removing the left bearing and 4th
gear from the output shaft

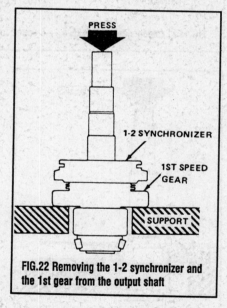

FIG.22 Removing the 1-2 synchronizer and
the 1st gear from the output shaft

4. Install the brass blocker ring.

5. Position the 4th gear (aligned with the 3–4 synchronizer) and the left hand bearing onto the input shaft.

OUTPUT SHAFT DISASSEMBLY

There are two variations of this procedure one from the MX-6 version and others the steps 1 to 6 are for all except the MX-6. For the MX-6 follow steps 7 through 12.

1. Except MX-6, by using a shop press, the input/output shaft pilot tool (for bearing removal) or equivalent, and support plates (behind the 4th gear), press the 4th gear and the left hand bearing from the output shaft.

2. Remove the 3rd gear snapring.

3. Move the 1–2 synchronizer into the 1st gear position and allow the press to support the 2nd gear. Press the 2nd and 3rd gears from the output shaft. Remove the brass blocker ring.

4. Remove the 1–2 synchronizer snapring.

5. Place press plates behind the 1st gear and press the 1st gear/1–2 synchronizer from the output shaft.

6. Using the output shaft right hand bearing remover tool or equivalent, and the input/output shaft pilot tool or equivalent, press the right hand bearing from the output shaft. This procedure is complete precede to inspection and assembly.

7. For the MX-6 transaxle, from the left end of the shaft, remove the retainer.

➡ **The retainer and shaft are designed with left hand threads. The 3rd/4th gear is a one piece gear.**

8. Using a shop press, the input/output shaft pilot tool (for bearing removal) or equivalent, and

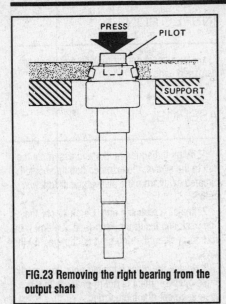

FIG.23 Removing the right bearing from the output shaft

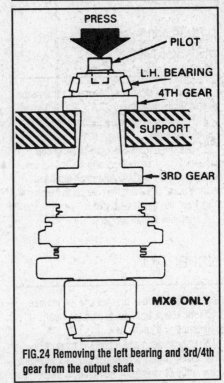

FIG.24 Removing the left bearing and 3rd/4th gear from the output shaft

INSPECTION

1. Check the output shaft bearing surfaces for scoring and/or wear; if necessary, replace the shaft.

2. Check the output shaft splines for wear; if necessary, replace the shaft.

3. Inspect the bearings for scoring, wear and/or damage; if necessary, replace them.

4. Check the gears and synchronizer parts for damage and/or excessively worn teeth; if necessary, replace them.

ASSEMBLY

Steps 1 to 7 are for all except the MX-6. For the MX-6 follow steps 8 through 14.

1. Except on the MX-6, by using a shop press and the input/output shaft pilot tool or equivalent, press the right hand bearing onto the output shaft.

2. Position the 1st gear onto the shaft (aligned with the 1–2 synchronizer), the brass blocker ring onto the gear cone and the 1–2 synchronizer. Using a deep socket or a piece of pipe, position it on the synchronizer hub (not the sleeve) and press the synchronizer hub onto the shaft.

support plates (behind the 4th gear), press the 3rd/4th gear and the left hand bearing from the output shaft.

9. Remove the 2nd gear and the brass blocker ring from the output shaft.

10. Remove the 1–2 synchronizer snapring.

11. Using a shop press and press plates (behind the 1st gear), press the 1st gear and the 1–2 synchronizer from the output shaft.

12. Using the output shaft right hand bearing remover tool or equivalent, and the input/output shaft pilot tool or equivalent, press the right hand bearing from the output shaft.

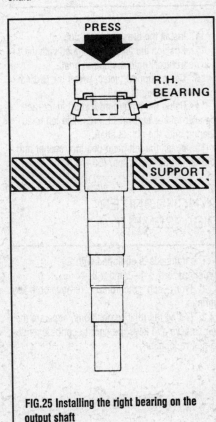

FIG.25 Installing the right bearing on the output shaft

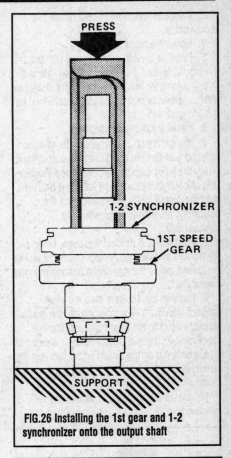

FIG.26 Installing the 1st gear and 1-2 synchronizer onto the output shaft

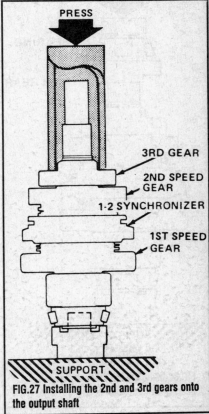

FIG.27 Installing the 2nd and 3rd gears onto the output shaft

3. Install the snapring to secure the 1–2 synchronizer.

4. Install the brass blocker ring.

5. Position the 2nd gear (aligned with the 1–2 synchronizer) and press the 3rd gear (aligned with the 4th gear hub) onto the output shaft; use a deep socket or a piece of pipe, positioned on the 3rd gear hub.

6. Install the 3rd gear snapring.

7. Using support plates, press the 4th gear (aligned with the 3rd gear) onto the output shaft. Using the input/output shaft inner race installer tool or equivalent, install the left hand bearing onto the output shaft. This completes the assembly, precede to transaxle case disassembly.

8. For the MX-6 model transaxles, using a shop press and the input/output shaft pilot tool or equivalent, press the right hand bearing onto the output shaft.

9. Position the 1st gear onto the shaft (aligned with the 1–2 synchronizer), the brass blocker ring onto the gear cone and the 1–2 synchronizer. Using a deep socket or a piece of pipe, position it on the synchronizer hub (not the sleeve) and press the synchronizer hub onto the shaft.

10. Install the snapring to secure the 1–2 synchronizer.

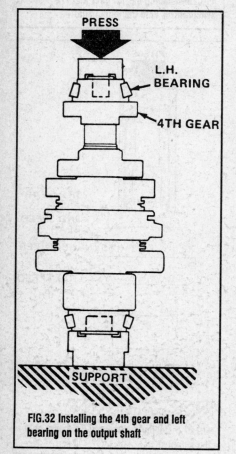

FIG.32 Installing the 4th gear and left bearing on the output shaft

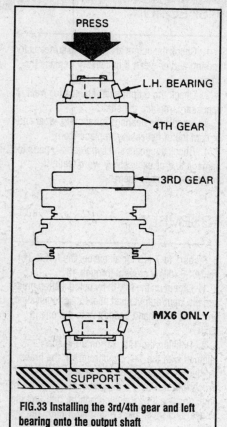

FIG.33 Installing the 3rd/4th gear and left bearing onto the output shaft

11. Install the brass blocker ring.

12. Position the 2nd gear (aligned with the 1–2 synchronizer) onto the output shaft.

13. Using support plates, press the 3rd/4th gear onto the output shaft.

14. Using the input/output shaft inner race installer tool or equivalent, press the left hand bearing onto the output shaft.

15. Install the left hand bearing retainer and torque it to 37–55 ft. lbs. (50–75 Nm).

SYNCHRONIZER DISASSEMBLY

The transaxle is equipped with 2 synchronizers: a 1–2 and a 3–4.

1. From each synchronizer, remove both key springs.

2. Noting the relative positions, separate the hub, sleeve and keys; be sure to scribe the hub-to-sleeve location.

INSPECTION

Clean, inspect and/or replace any worn or damaged parts.

ASSEMBLY

1. Align the scribe marks and assemble the hub to the sleeve; the extruded hub lip should be directed away from the sleeve's shift fork groove.

2. Install a retaining ring. Carefully pry the ring back and insert the keys (one at a time); be sure to position the ring so it is captured by the keys.

3. Install the other retaining ring; be sure the ring's open segment is out of phase with the open segment of the other ring.

TRANSAXLE CASE DISASSEMBLY

1. From the exterior of the case, remove the reverse inhibitor fitting.

2. From inside the case, remove the spring and pilot/spacer.

3. Using the transaxle case bearing cup remover tool or equivalent, and a slide hammer puller, press the input/output shaft left hand bearing cups and the differential side bearing cups from the transaxle case.

4. Remove the oil slingers.

INSPECTION

1. At the interlock bracket and the reverse shift fork, check both guide pins for wear; replace them, if necessary.

2. Check, clean and install the magnet.

3. Using a gasket remover tool or equivalent, remove the sealant from the mating surfaces; be careful not to gouge or damage the aluminum surfaces, for leaks can result.

ASSEMBLY

1. Using the transaxle case bearing cup installer tool or equivalent, install the differential side bearing cups into the transaxle case.

2. Install the oil slingers.

3. Using the axle shaft seal and bearing cup installer tool or equivalent, install the input/output shaft left hand bearing cups into the transaxle case.

4. Inside the case, install the spring and pilot/spacer.

5. Outside the case, install the reverse inhibitor fitting.

CLUTCH COVER DISASSEMBLY

1. Using the transaxle case bearing cup remover tool or equivalent, remove the differential side bearing cup/shim and the input/output shafts right hand bearing cup. From the back of the input bearing cup, remove the shim. From the back of the output shaft bearing cup, remove the oil shield, the shim and the retainer.

2. Remove the input gear bearing retainer bolts and tap the sleeve.

3. From the sleeve, remove the external and internal oil rings.

4. Remove the plastic oil scoop.

➡ **If it is necessary to replace the clutch for shaft or bushing, do not break the weld on the clutch fork to remove it.**

5. Using the clutch shaft bushing installer/remover tool or equivalent, remove the shaft bushings and slide the clutch shaft from the case at a slight angle.

INSPECTION

1. Check, clean and install the magnet.

2. Using a gasket remover tool or equivalent, remove the sealant from the mating surfaces; be careful not to gouge or damage the aluminum surfaces, for leaks can result.

ASSEMBLY

1. Install a new clutch fork shaft seal and the clutch fork shaft.

2. Install the plastic oil scoop.

3. On the bearing retainer, install a new oil ring.

4. Install the bearing retainer and torque the bolts to 7 ft. lbs. (9 Nm).

5. Using the right hand input shaft seal and bearing cup installer tool or equivalent, install the new internal oil seal and the bearing cups.

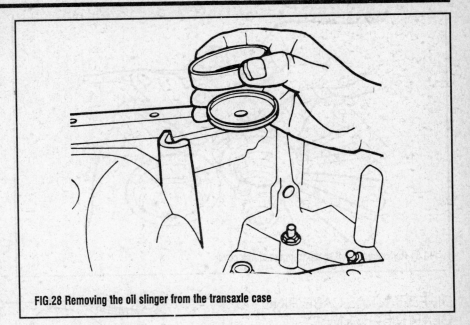

FIG.28 Removing the oil slinger from the transaxle case

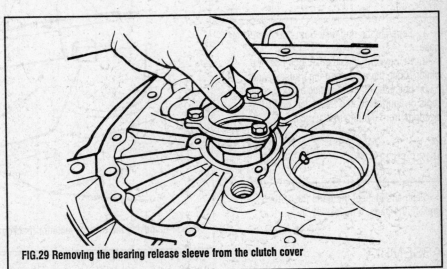

FIG.29 Removing the bearing release sleeve from the clutch cover

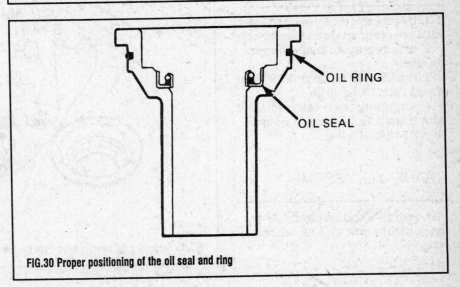

OIL RING

OIL SEAL

FIG.30 Proper positioning of the oil seal and ring

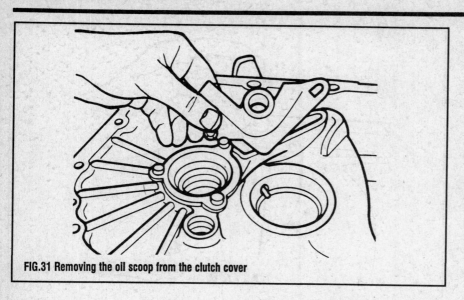

FIG.31 Removing the oil scoop from the clutch cover

2. Grasp both shafts (as an assembly) and carefully lower them into the case; be careful not to nick the gears.

3. Using a guide pin tool or equivalent, position the interlock bracket on it; be sure the bracket engages the shifting forks fingers.

4. Using a straight edge, position it on both sides of the interlock, to determine if the detent is out alignment with the interlock.

➡ **The straight edge should rest on both sides of the interlock without interference from the detent paddle.**

5. If interference is noted on either sides, perform the following procedures:

a. With the alignment pin still in position, place the detent and interlock assembly in a

DIFFERENTIAL CASE/RING GEAR DISASSEMBLY

1. Separate the ring gear from the differential case.

2. Remove the pinion shaft lock bolt, the pinion shaft, the gears and the thrust washers.

3. Using the differential side bearing puller leg tools or equivalent, and the puller, press the bearings from the differential case.

INSPECTION

Clean and inspect the parts for damage; replace the parts, if necessary.

ASSEMBLY

1. Using the cone installer tool or equivalent, install the side bearings into the differential case.

2. Install the gears and thrust washers into the case.

3. Install the pinion shaft and lock bolt; torque the lock bolt to 7 ft. lbs. (9 Nm).

4. Attach the ring gear to the differential case, apply sealant to the ring gear bolts and torque them to 54 ft. lbs. (73 Nm).

TRANSAXLE ASSEMBLY

1. Position the input and output shafts on a bench, mesh the gears and install both shift forks.

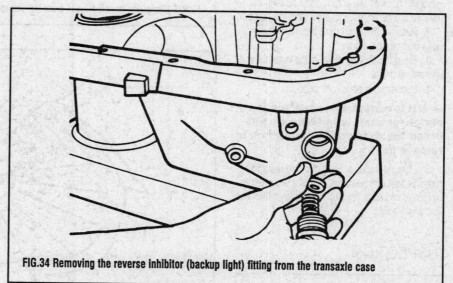

FIG.34 Removing the reverse inhibitor (backup light) fitting from the transaxle case

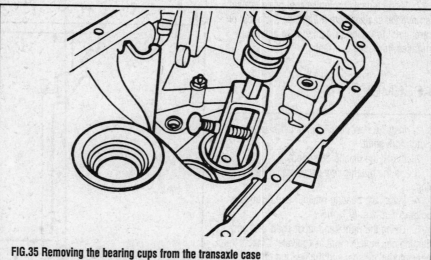

FIG.35 Removing the bearing cups from the transaxle case

DRIVE TRAIN **7-23**

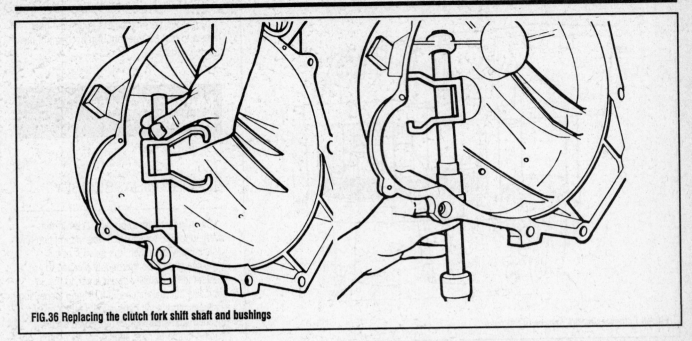

FIG.36 Replacing the clutch fork shift shaft and bushings

vise. Using light pressure, press the detent paddle into alignment.

b. Loosen the detent spring-to-interlock nut; the detent spring is slotted beneath the nut and will seek proper alignment.

c. While exerting thumb pressure on the spring, tighten the detent spring-to-interlock nut.

d. Using a straight edge, recheck the detent alignment.

6. Position the detent shift lever into the interlock.

7. Through the interlock bracket and the detent shift lever, install the shifter shaft; do not extend it any further at this time.

8. Onto the guide pin, install the reverse shift fork; be sure the fork engages with the interlock bracket.

9. Install the reverse idler gear and shaft into position; be sure the shaft's long end points upward and the gear teeth (large chamfered ends) are facing upward. Install the spacer onto the shaft.

➡ **The reverse idler shaft's flat faces the input gear (shaft).**

10. Through the reverse shift fork, install the shifter shaft until it pilots into the inhibitor spring spacer. Remove the dummy shaft. With the shaft in the **N** position, install the bolt and lock

through the detent shift lever. Bend the lock tab over the bolt head.

11. Through the synchronizer forks and into the case bore, install the fork shaft.

12. Carefully install the ring gear/differential assembly into the case. Install the magnet.

13. To adjust the transaxle for the correct shim sizes, perform the following procedures:

a. Place the transaxle case into holding fixture tool or equivalent.

b. With the left hand bearing races installed in the case, place the input shaft, output shaft and differential assemblies into their installed positions. Position the right hand bearing races onto their respective bearings.

c. Using the shim selector set or equivalent, position a gauge on the input bearing, output bearing and differential bearing; sure the bearing races fit smoothly into the bores of the gauge tools.

d. On top of the output shaft gauge, install the oil shield retainer.

e. Carefully assemble the clutch cover over the gauges and onto the case, using the spacers provided evenly around the perimeter. Retain the assembly with the bolts provided.

f. Alternately and gradually, tighten the cover-to-case bolts to 10 ft. lbs. (13 Nm); this will compress the gauge sleeves.

g. Rotate each gauge to seat the bearings. Rotate the differential case through 3 revolutions in each direction.

h. With the gauges compressed, the gap between the outer sleeve and the base pad is larger than the correct preload shim at each location. Carefully compare the gap to the available shims. Determine the largest shim that

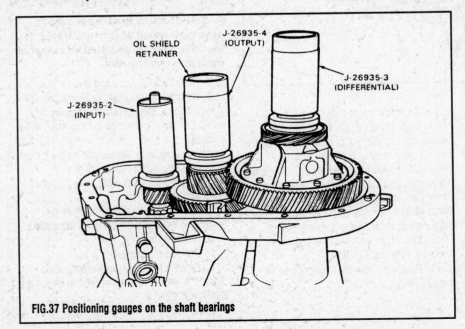

FIG.37 Positioning gauges on the shaft bearings

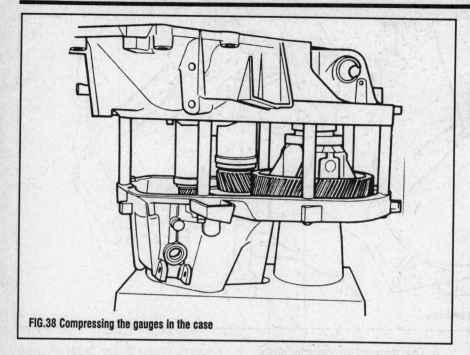

FIG.38 Compressing the gauges in the case

FIG.39 Measuring for shim gap

can be placed into the gap and drawn through without binding. Then, use the next size smaller on the output shaft and differential or reassembly. On the input shaft, use a shim 2 sizes smaller. If endplay occurs, use the next larger shim size.

i. When each of the 3 shims have been selected, remove the clutch cover, spacers and gauges.

j. Place the selected shims into their respective clutch cover bores and add the metal shield. Using the right hand input shaft seal and bearing cup installer tool or equivalent, install the bearing cups on the input shaft. Using the transaxle case bearing cup installer tool or

equivalent, install the bearing cups onto the output shaft. Using the axle shaft seal and bearing cup installer tool or equivalent, install the bearing cup onto the differential side.

14. Using anaerobic sealant (not RTV), apply a thin bead onto the clutch cover. Using the dowel pins, install the clutch cover onto the transaxle case. Using a plastic hammer, gently tap the cover to insure the parts are seated.

15. Install the clutch cover-to-case bolts and torque to 16 ft. lbs. (21 Nm).

16. Torque the idler shaft lock bolt to 16 ft. lbs. (21 Nm).

17. Move the shift shaft through the gear ranges to test for freedom of movement of the internal parts.

Muncie 5-Speed Overhaul

BEFORE DISASSEMBLY

Cleanliness is an important factor in the overhaul of the transaxle. Before attempting any disassembly operation, the exterior of the transaxle should be thoroughly cleaned to prevent the possibility of dirt entering the transaxle internal mechanism. During inspection and reassembly, all parts should be thoroughly cleaned with cleaning fluid and then air dried. Wiping cloths or rags should not be used to dry parts. All oil passages should be blown out and checked to make sure that they are not obstructed. Small passages should be checked with tag wire. All parts should be inspected to determine which parts are to be replaced.

TRANSAXLE DISASSEMBLY

External Transaxle Mounted Linkage

♦ SEE FIG. 42

1. Remove the nut using a 21mm socket and driver.

➡ **Do not allow the lever to move during removal of the nut. Use a 3/8 in. drive ratchet to hold the external shift lever by the slot.**

2. Remove the washer and lever.

3. Remove the pivot pin. Depending on the type of linkage, this pin may be removed by using a hammer and punch to drive it out of the bracket (replace with part number 14091786) or removing a retaining clip and sliding the pin out of the bracket, which may be reused.

4. Remove the pivot using a 3/16 in. punch and hammer.

5. Remove the pin and collar. Note the position of the slot in the collar for installation.

6. Remove the bolts.

7. Remove the bracket.

8. Remove the fluid level indicator and washer. A wrench may be needed to loosen the fluid level indicator.

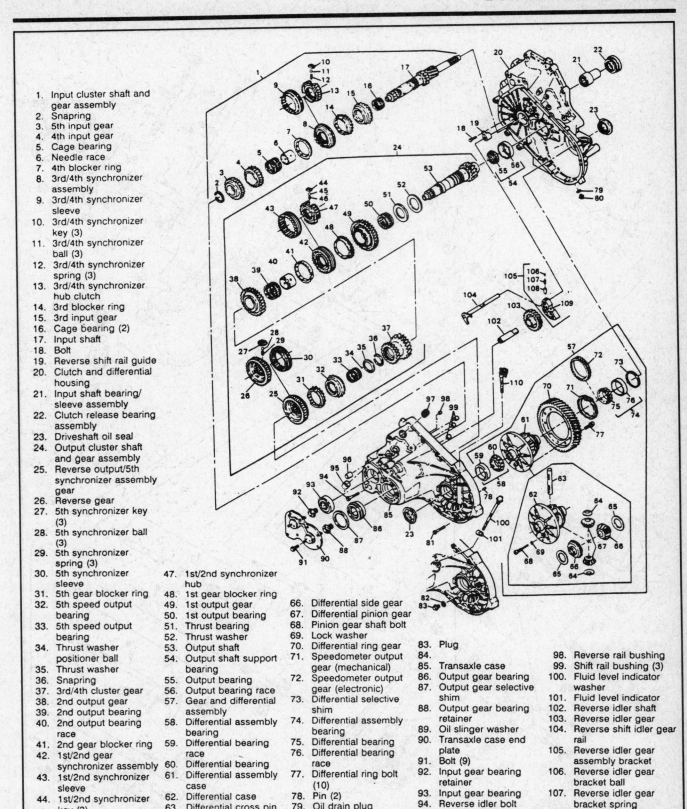

1. Input cluster shaft and gear assembly
2. Snapring
3. 5th input gear
4. 4th input gear
5. Cage bearing
6. Needle race
7. 4th blocker ring
8. 3rd/4th synchronizer assembly
9. 3rd/4th synchronizer sleeve
10. 3rd/4th synchronizer key (3)
11. 3rd/4th synchronizer ball (3)
12. 3rd/4th synchronizer spring (3)
13. 3rd/4th synchronizer hub clutch
14. 3rd blocker ring
15. 3rd input gear
16. Cage bearing (2)
17. Input shaft
18. Bolt
19. Reverse shift rail guide
20. Clutch and differential housing
21. Input shaft bearing/sleeve assembly
22. Clutch release bearing assembly
23. Driveshaft oil seal
24. Output cluster shaft and gear assembly
25. Reverse output/5th synchronizer assembly gear
26. Reverse gear
27. 5th synchronizer key (3)
28. 5th synchronizer ball (3)
29. 5th synchronizer spring (3)
30. 5th synchronizer sleeve
31. 5th gear blocker ring
32. 5th speed output bearing
33. 5th speed output bearing
34. Thrust washer positioner ball
35. Thrust washer
36. Snapring
37. 3rd/4th cluster gear
38. 2nd output gear
39. 2nd output bearing
40. 2nd output bearing race
41. 2nd gear blocker ring
42. 1st/2nd gear synchronizer assembly
43. 1st/2nd synchronizer sleeve
44. 1st/2nd synchronizer key (3)
45. 1st/2nd synchronizer ball (3)
46. 1st/2nd synchronizer spring (3)

47. 1st/2nd synchronizer hub
48. 1st gear blocker ring
49. 1st output gear
50. 1st output bearing
51. Thrust bearing
52. Thrust washer
53. Output shaft
54. Output shaft support bearing
55. Output bearing
56. Output bearing race
57. Gear and differential assembly
58. Differential assembly bearing
59. Differential bearing race
60. Differential bearing
61. Differential assembly case
62. Differential case
63. Differential cross pin
64. Pinion gear thrust washer
65. Side gear thrust washer
66. Differential side gear
67. Differential pinion gear
68. Pinion gear shaft bolt
69. Lock washer
70. Differential ring gear
71. Speedometer output gear (mechanical)
72. Speedometer output gear (electronic)
73. Differential selective shim
74. Differential assembly bearing
75. Differential bearing
76. Differential bearing race
77. Differential ring bolt (10)
78. Pin (2)
79. Oil drain plug
80. Washer
81. Transaxle case bolt (15)
82. Washer

83. Plug
84.
85. Transaxle case
86. Output gear bearing
87. Output gear selective shim
88. Output gear bearing retainer
89. Oil slinger washer
90. Transaxle case end plate
91. Bolt (9)
92. Input gear bearing retainer
93. Input gear bearing
94. Reverse idler bolt
95. Detent lever bushing
96. Sliding sleeve bushing
97. Shift shaft needle bearing

98. Reverse rail bushing
99. Shift rail bushing (3)
100. Fluid level indicator washer
101. Fluid level indicator
102. Reverse idler shaft
103. Reverse idler gear
104. Reverse shift idler gear rail
105. Reverse idler gear assembly bracket
106. Reverse idler gear bracket ball
107. Reverse idler gear bracket spring
108. Reverse idler gear detent bracket sleeve
109. Reverse idler gear bracket

FIG.40 Transaxle exploded view — 5 Speed

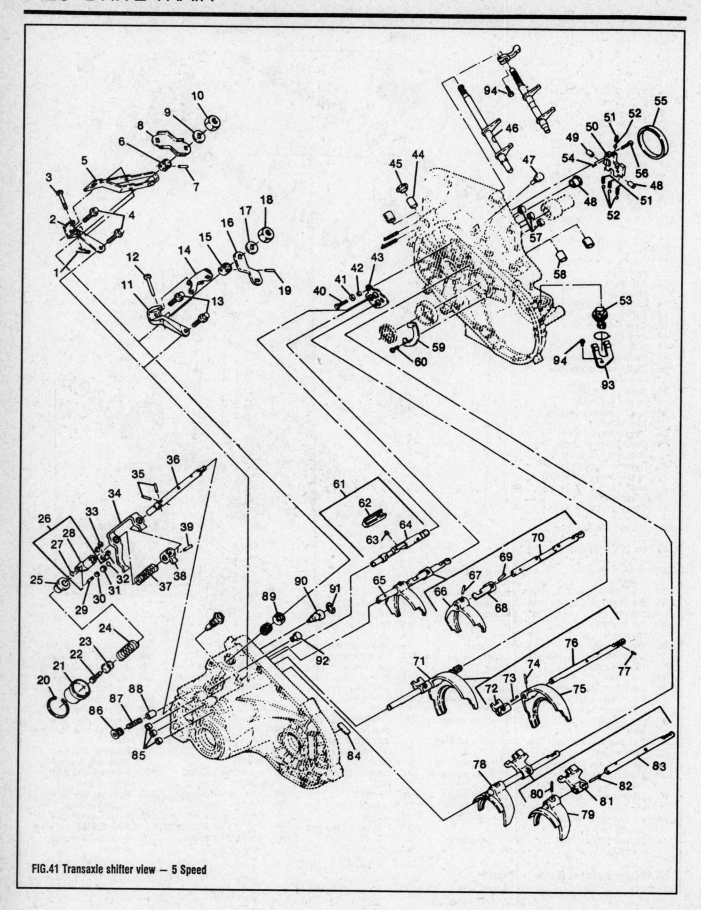

FIG.41 Transaxle shifter view — 5 Speed

1. Selector pin retainer
2. Selector lever retainer
3. Selector lever pilot pin
4. Bolt (2)
5. Selector lever
6. Shift shaft collar
7. Spring pin
8. Shift lever
9. Washer
10. Nut
11. Selector lever retainer
12. Selector lever pivot pin
13. Bolt (2)
14. Selector lever
15. Shift shaft collar
16. Shift lever
17. Washer
18. Nut
19. Spring pin
20. Snapring
21. Shift shaft cover
22. Bolt
23. 5th detent outer spring seat
24. Spring
25. 5th detent inner spring seat
26. Detent assembly lever
27. Detent pin retainer
28. Detent lever
29. Detent lever pin
30. Detent lever spacer
31. Detent lever roller
32. Detent pin retainer
33. Detent roller (4)
34. Reverse lever
35. Detent lever rollers pin (2)
36. Shift shaft
37. 3rd/4th bias spring
38. Shift lever
39. Roll pin
40. Bolt (3)
41. Flat washer (3)
42. Spacer (3)
43. Shift interlock plate
44. Outer clutch fork bushing
45. Clutch fork seal
46. Clutch fork shaft
47. Breather assembly
48. Reverse shift rail bushing
49. Interlock pin (2)
50. Detent holder
51. Detent spring (4)
52. Detent ball (4)
53. Speedometer signal assembly
54. Spring pin
55. Detent holder cover
56. Bolt (2)
57. Shift rail bushings (3)
58. Inner clutch fork bushing
59. Output bearing race retainer
60. Bolt (2)
61. Reverse shift assembly rail
62. 5th/reverse shift gate
63. Gear disengage roller
64. Reverse shift shaft
65. 3rd/4th shift assembly rail
66. 3rd/4th shift shift fork
67. Fork retainer pin
68. 3rd/4th select lever
69. Lever retainer pin
70. 3rd/4th shift shaft
71. 1st/2nd shift assembly rail
72. 1st/2nd select lever
73. Lever retainer pin
74. Fork retainer pin
75. 1st/2nd shift fork
76. 1st/2nd shift shaft
77. Lock pin
78. 5th shift assembly rail
79. 5th shift fork
80. Fork retainer pin
81. 5th shift lever
82. Lever retainer pin
83. 5th shift shaft
84. Chip collector magnet
85. Shift rail plug (3)
86. Bolt
87. Sliding sleeve spring
88. Sliding sleeve
89. Shift shaft seal
90. Plug
91. Snapring
92. Stud
93. Speedometer signal assembly retainer
94. Bolt

FIG.41 Transaxle shifter view — 5 Speed

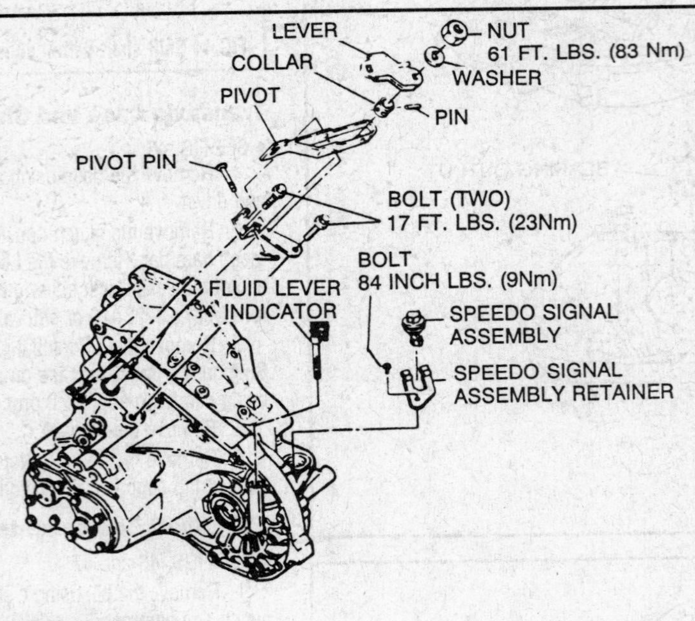

FIG.42 External transaxle linkage

9. Remove the electronic speedometer signal assembly, retainer and bolt using a 10mm socket and driver.

Shift Rail Detent/Clutch and Differential Housing

♦ SEE FIG. 43

1. Remove the bearing.

2. Remove the detent holder cover. Puncture the cover in the middle and pry off. Discard this part and replace it with part number 14082039.

3. Remove the bolts and interlock plate (early transaxles). If the detent holder is not 18mm thick, interlock plate kit must be used.

4. Remove the holder, detent, springs and interlock pins.

5. Remove the balls and detent.

6. Remove the bushing by prying loose (2 small pry bars in the slots). Two allen wrenches work well to pry this bushing.

Shift Shaft Detent/Transaxle Housing

♦ SEE FIG. 44

1. Remove the snapring.

2. Remove the cover using a soft faced hammer.

3. Remove screw and outer spring seat using a 5mm bit and driver.

4. Remove the 5th/reverse bias spring and inner spring seat.

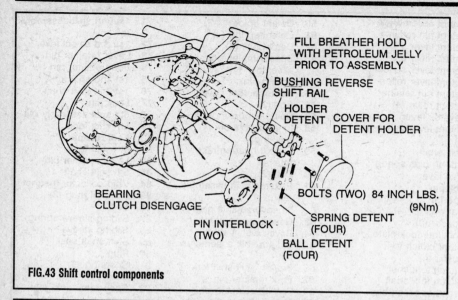

FILL BREATHER HOLD WITH PETROLEUM JELLY PRIOR TO ASSEMBLY

BUSHING REVERSE SHIFT RAIL

HOLDER DETENT

COVER FOR DETENT HOLDER

BEARING CLUTCH DISENGAGE

BOLTS (TWO) 84 INCH LBS. (9Nm)

PIN INTERLOCK (TWO)

SPRING DETENT (FOUR)

BALL DETENT (FOUR)

FIG.43 Shift control components

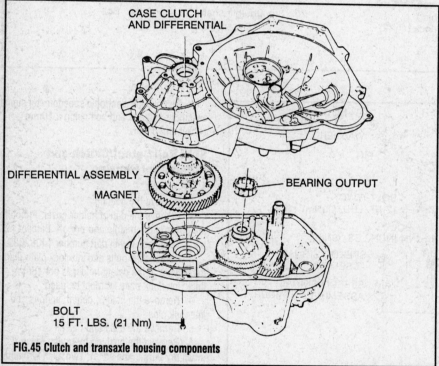

CASE CLUTCH AND DIFFERENTIAL

DIFFERENTIAL ASSEMBLY

MAGNET

BEARING OUTPUT

BOLT 15 FT. LBS. (21 Nm)

FIG.45 Clutch and transaxle housing components

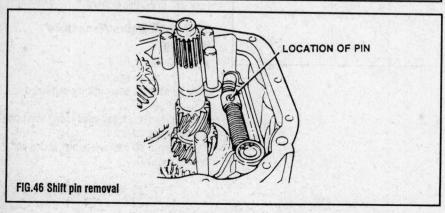

LOCATION OF PIN

FIG.46 Shift pin removal

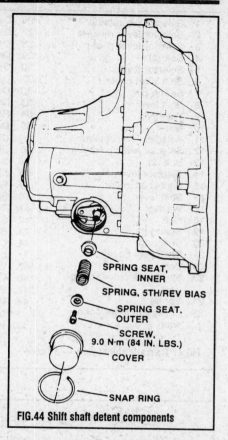

SPRING SEAT, INNER

SPRING, 5TH/REV BIAS

SPRING SEAT, OUTER

SCREW, 9.0 N·m (84 IN. LBS.)

COVER

SNAP RING

FIG.44 Shift shaft detent components

Transaxle Case and Clutch Housing

▶ SEE FIG. 45

1. Remove the bolts using a 13mm socket and driver.

2. Remove the clutch housing using a soft faced hammer. Remove the Loctite®518 anaerobic sealer with either a liquid gasket remover or J–28410 or equivalent, scraper.

3. Remove the differential gear assembly. Support the transaxle case on a workbench top, being careful to support it properly.

4. Remove the magnet.

5. Remove the bearing. Note the position of the bearing cage for installation.

Shift Shaft Components

▶ SEE FIGS. 46 and 47

1. Remove the pin using a size ³⁄₁₆ in. (5mm) punch and hammer.

2. Remove the shift shaft assembly. This assembly consists of shaft, rollers and pins, 1st/2nd bias spring, shift and reverse levers. Take care not to lose the detent rollers.

Gear Cluster Support Components

▶ SEE FIGS. 48 and 49

➡ **Engage the gear cluster in 4th and reverse by pushing down on the 3rd/4th gear rail and reverse gear rail.**

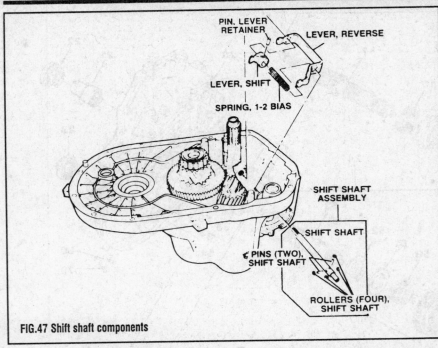

FIG.47 Shift shaft components

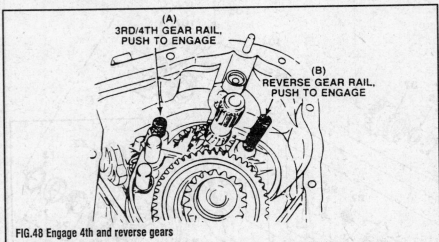

FIG.48 Engage 4th and reverse gears

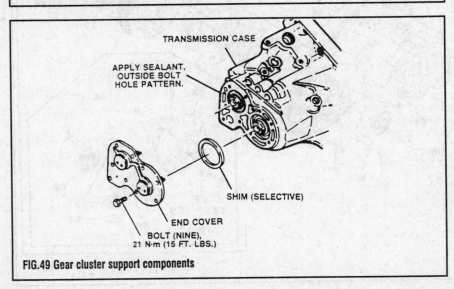

FIG.49 Gear cluster support components

1. Remove the bolts using a 13mm socket and driver.
2. Remove the cover. Tap gently with a soft faced hammer.
3. Remove the selective shim.
4. Remove the oil shield.
5. Remove the retainer, output gear cluster using tool J–36031 or equivalent.
6. Remove the retainer, input gear cluster using tool J–36031 or equivalent. These retainers must not be reused.
7. Return the transaxle to **N**.

Gear Clusters

◆ SEE FIG. 50

1. Position tool J–36182–1 and J–36182–2 or equivalent, in the hydraulic press.
2. Position the transaxle case/gear cluster assembly on tool J–36182–1 and –2 or equivalent. Align the shift rail and shaft pilots to the fixture.
3. Position tool J–36185 or equivalent, on the shaft support bearings and pilots. Using a hydraulic press, separate the shaft and gear clusters from the transaxle case.
4. After this operation, the input and output shaft bearings should be discarded. Remove the gear clusters from the pallets, as an entire assembly.

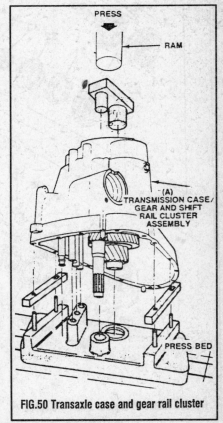

FIG.50 Transaxle case and gear rail cluster

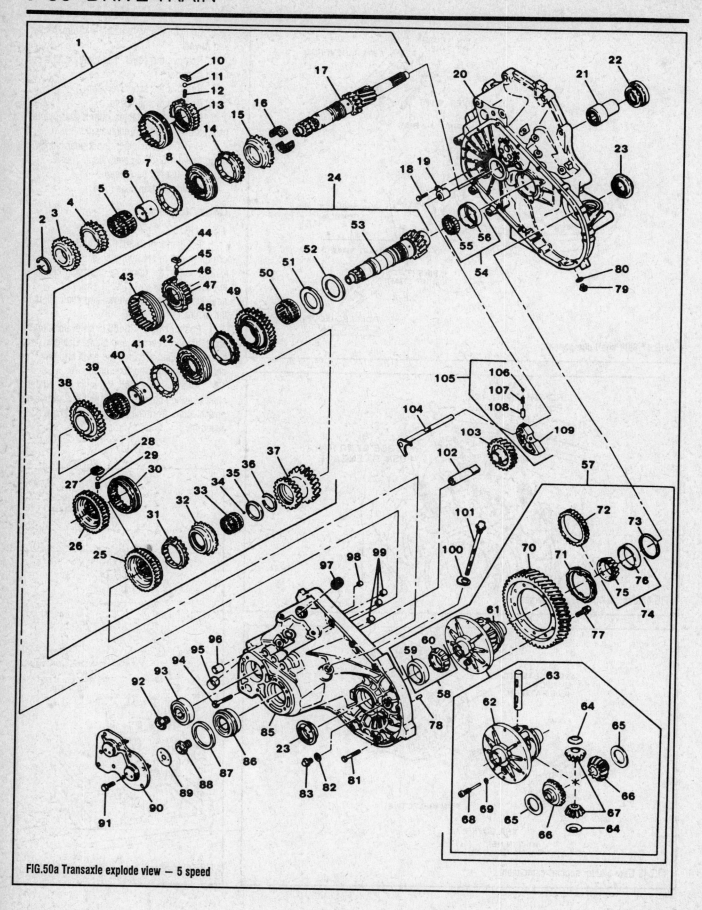

FIG.50a Transaxle explode view — 5 speed

1. Input cluster shaft and gear assembly
2. Snapring
3. Fifth input gear
4. Fourth input gear
5. Bearing cage
6. Needle race
7. Blocker 4th ring
8. Synchronizer assembly 3rd/4th
9. Synchronizer sleeve 3rd/4th
10. Synchronizer key 3rd/4th
11. Synchronizer ball 3rd/4th
12. Synchronizer spring 3rd/4th
13. Synchronizer hub 3rd/4th
14. Blocker ring 3rd
15. Thrid input gear
16. Cage bearing
17. Input shaft
18. M6 bolt
19. Reverse shaft guide shift rail
20. Clutch and differential housing
21. Input shaft bearing/ sleeve assembly
22. Clutch release bearing
23. Oil drive axle seal
24. Output cluster shaft and seal assembly
25. Reverse output/5th synchronizer assembly
26. Reverse gear

27. 5th synchronizer key
28. 5th synchronizer ball
29. 5th synchronizer spring
30. 5th synchronizer sleeve
31. 5th gear blocker ring
32. 5th output gear
33. 5th output gear bearing
34. Thrust washer positioner ball
35. Thrust washer
36. Snapring
37. 3rd/4th cluster gear
38. 2nd output gear
39. 2nd output gear bearing
40. 2nd output gear bearing race
41. 2nd gear blocker ring
42. 1st/2nd synchronizer assembly
43. 1st/2nd synchronizer sleeve
44. 1st/2nd synchronizer key
45. 1st/2nd synchronizer ball
46. 1st/2nd synchronizer spring
47. 1st/2nd synchronizer hub
48. 1st gear blocker ring
49. 1st output gear
50. 1st output gear bearing
51. Bearing thrust
52. Thrust washer

53. Output shaft
54. Output shaft support bearing
55. Output bearing
56. Output bearing race
57. Gear and differential assembly
58. Differential assembly bearing
59. Bearing race
60. Differential bearing
61. Differential case assembly
62. Differential case
63. Differential cross pin
64. Thrust pinion gear washer
65. Thrust side gear washer
66. Differential side gear
67. Differential pinion gear
68. Pinion gear shaft bolt
69. Lockwasher
70. Ring gear
71. Speedo output mech.
72. Speedo output elec.
73. Differential selective shim
74. Differential bearing assembly
75. Differential bearing
76. Differential bearing race
77. Ring bolts (10)
78. Pins
79. Oil drain plug
80. Washer
81. M8 bolts

82. Washer
83. Plug
84. Blank
85. Transaxle case
86. Output gear bearing
87. Output gear selective shim
88. Output gear bearing retainer
89. Oil slinger washer
90. End plate
91. M8 Bolt
92. Input gear bearing retainer
93. Input gear bearing
94. M8 bolt
95. Detent lever bushing
96. Slide sleeve bushing
97. Shift shaft bearings needle
98. Reverse rail bushing
99. Shift rail bushings
100. Fluid indicator washer
101. Fluid indicator
102. Reverse idler shaft
103. Reverse idler gear
104. Reverse shift idler gear rail
105. Reverse idler bracket assembly
106. Reverse idler bracket ball
107. Reverse idler bracket spring
108. Reverse idler bracket detent sleeve
109. Reverse idler gear bracket

FIG.50a Transaxle explode view — 5 speed

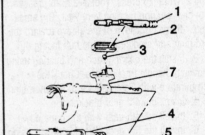
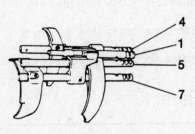
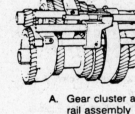

A. Gear cluster and shift rail assembly
1. Reverse rail
2. Shift gate
3. Roller
4. 3rd/4th rail
5. 1st/2nd rail
6. Interlock pin
7. 5th rail

FIG.51 Shift rail assembly

Gear Clusters and Shift Rails

♦ SEE FIG. 51

➡ **This should be done on a workbench after taking the gear clusters off the pallet.**

1. Remove the 1/2 shift rail assembly and lock pin.
2. Remove the 3/4 rail assembly.
3. Remove the 5th rail assembly.
4. Remove the reverse rail assembly, consisting of the shift gate and disengage roller.

➡ **Be careful not to lose both the lock pin and the gear disengage roller, as they are small parts.**

UNIT DISASSEMBLY AND ASSEMBLY

♦ SEE FIGS. 52 to 74

➡ **The following components will require heating prior to installation during assembly procedures. A suggested heating oven is a toaster oven (used as a kitchen appliance). Heat the races, gear assembly and speedometer gear (electronic) for 7–10 minutes at 250°F (120°C). Heat the speedometer gear (mechanical) in hot tap water for 5 minutes. Heat the gear cluster for a minimum of 20 minutes at 250°F (120°C).**

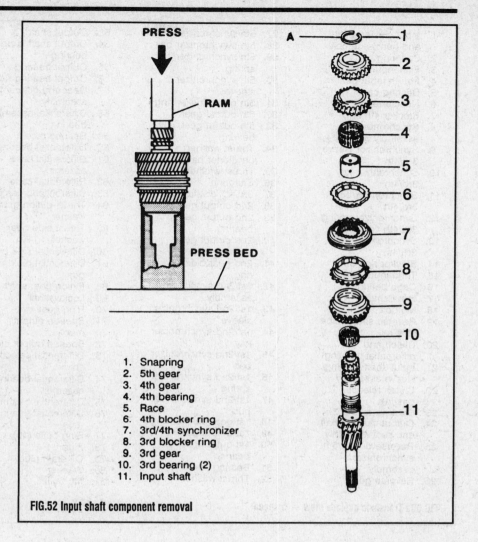

1. Snapring
2. 5th gear
3. 4th gear
4. 4th bearing
5. Race
6. 4th blocker ring
7. 3rd/4th synchronizer
8. 3rd blocker ring
9. 3rd gear
10. 3rd bearing (2)
11. Input shaft

FIG.52 Input shaft component removal

INPUT SHAFT DISASSEMBLY

➡ **Identify blocker ring for 3rd gear and blocker ring for 4th gear. Do not mix.**

1. Remove the snapring and discard, if stretched.
2. Remove the gear, bearing, race, blocker ring, synchronizer assembly and gear using tool J–36183, J–36184 or equivalent and a hydraulic press.
3. Remove the 3rd gear bearing.

INSPECTION

1. Clean parts with solvent and air dry.
2. Inspect shaft, spline wear for cracks.
3. Inspect gear teeth for scuffed, nicked, burred or broken teeth.

4. Inspect bearings for roughness of rotation, burred or pitted condition.
5. Inspect bearing races for scoring, wear or overheating.
6. Inspect snaprings for nicks, distortion or wear.
7. Inspect synchronizers assembly for wear.

ASSEMBLY

1. Install the 3rd gear bearing, 3rd gear (cone up) and blocker ring.

➡ **When pressing the 3rd/4th synchronizer assembly, start press operation, stop before tangs engage. Lift and rotate the 3rd gear into the synchronizer tangs. Continue to press until seated. Be sure all shavings are removed.**

2. Install the 3/4 synchronizer, using tool J–22912–01, J–36183, J–36184 or equivalent

and a hydraulic press. Tool J–22828 presses 4th gear bearing race on very well. The small outer diameter groove of the sleeve toward the 3rd gear and small end of the hub facing 4th.

3. Install the bearing race and bearing using gloves to handle the hot race. Check the temperature with Tempilstick® or thermometer.
4. Install the 4th gear blocker ring.
5. Install the 4th gear with the cone down.
6. Install the 5th gear (flat side down) using tool J–36183, J–36184 or equivalent and a hydraulic press.
7. Install the snapring.

OUTPUT SHAFT DISASSEMBLY

➡ **Identify the blocker ring for 5th gear, blocker ring for 2nd gear and blocker ring for 1st gear. Do not mix.**

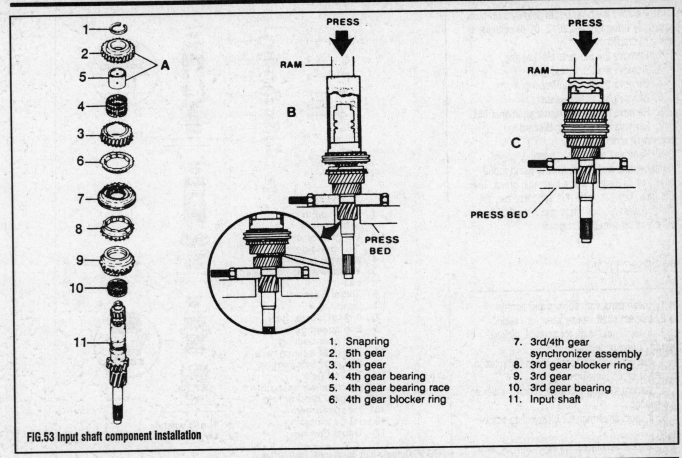

1. Snapring
2. 5th gear
3. 4th gear
4. 4th gear bearing
5. 4th gear bearing race
6. 4th gear blocker ring
7. 3rd/4th gear synchronizer assembly
8. 3rd gear blocker ring
9. 3rd gear
10. 3rd gear bearing
11. Input shaft

FIG.53 Input shaft component installation

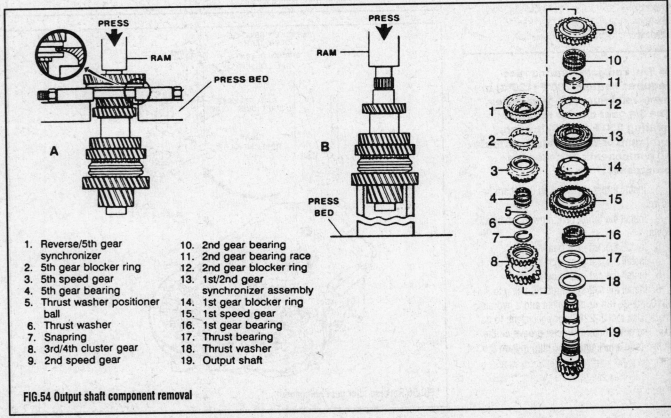

1. Reverse/5th gear synchronizer
2. 5th gear blocker ring
3. 5th speed gear
4. 5th gear bearing
5. Thrust washer positioner ball
6. Thrust washer
7. Snapring
8. 3rd/4th cluster gear
9. 2nd speed gear
10. 2nd gear bearing
11. 2nd gear bearing race
12. 2nd gear blocker ring
13. 1st/2nd gear synchronizer assembly
14. 1st gear blocker ring
15. 1st speed gear
16. 1st gear bearing
17. Thrust bearing
18. Thrust washer
19. Output shaft

FIG.54 Output shaft component removal

1. Remove the reverse/5th gear synchronizer assembly using tool J–22912–01 or equivalent and a hydraulic press.
2. Remove the 5th gear blocker ring.
3. Remove the 5th speed gear.
4. Remove the 5th gear bearing.
5. Remove the thrust washer.
6. Remove the thrust washer positioner ball.
7. Remove the snapring. Discard the snapring if stretched.
8. Remove the 1st gear, bearing, caged thrust bearing and thrust washer using tool J–36183 or equivalent and a hydraulic press. The 2nd gear, bearing, race, 1/2 synchronizer, 1st and 2nd gear blocker rings and 3/4 gear cluster will press off with the 1st gear.

INSPECTION

1. Clean parts with solvent and air dry.
2. Inspect shaft, spline wear for cracks.
3. Inspect gear teeth for scuffed, nicked, burred or broken teeth.
4. Inspect bearings for roughness of rotation, burred or pitted condition.
5. Inspect bearing races for scoring, wear or overheating.
6. Inspect snaprings for nicks, distortion or wear.
7. Inspect synchronizers assembly for wear.

ASSEMBLY

➡ **The 2nd gear bearing race requires heating 250°F (120°C) in oven, minimum of 7–10 minutes. The 3/4 gear cluster requires heating 250°F (120°C) in oven, minimum of 20 minutes. Lubricate all components as assembly progresses.**

1. Install thrust washer with the chamfer down.
2. Install the thrust bearing with the needles down.
3. Install the 1st gear bearing.
4. Install the 1st gear with the cone up.
5. Install the 1st gear blocker ring.
6. Install the 1/2 synchronizer using tool J–36183, J–36184 or equivalent and a hydraulic press. Use tool J–22828 or equivalent, to do this. The small outer diameter groove on the sleeve (and small end of the hub) toward the 1st gear.

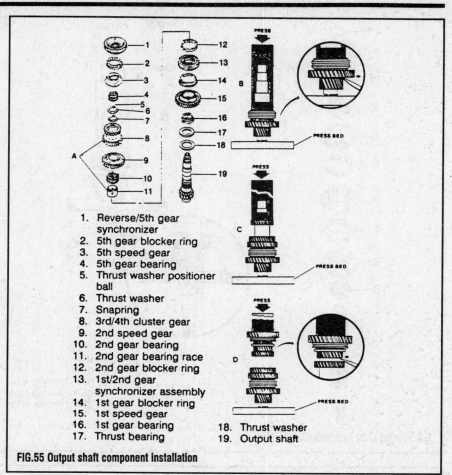

1. Reverse/5th gear synchronizer
2. 5th gear blocker ring
3. 5th speed gear
4. 5th gear bearing
5. Thrust washer positioner ball
6. Thrust washer
7. Snapring
8. 3rd/4th cluster gear
9. 2nd speed gear
10. 2nd gear bearing
11. 2nd gear bearing race
12. 2nd gear blocker ring
13. 1st/2nd gear synchronizer assembly
14. 1st gear blocker ring
15. 1st speed gear
16. 1st gear bearing
17. Thrust bearing
18. Thrust washer
19. Output shaft

FIG.55 Output shaft component installation

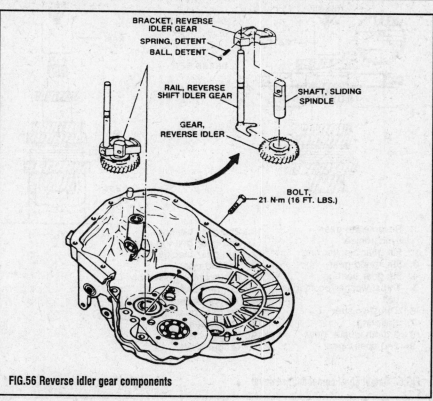

FIG.56 Reverse idler gear components

➡ **When pressing the 1/2 synchronizer assembly, start press operation, stop before tangs engage. Lift and rotate the 1st gear and 1st gear blocker ring, to engage the blocker ring tangs. Continue to press until seated. Be sure all the shavings are removed.**

7. Install the 2nd gear bearing race (be careful handling the hot bearing race), 2nd gear bearing and 2nd gear (cone down).

8. Install the 3rd/4th gear cluster (be careful when handling hot cluster gear) using tool J–36183 or equivalent and a hydraulic press. The large outer diameter gear down.

9. Install the snapring, thrust washer positioning ball (retain with petroleum jelly) and slotted thrust washer. Align the inner diameter slot with the ball.

10. Install the 5th gear bearing and the 5th gear with the cone up.

11. Install the 5th gear blocker ring.

12. Install the reverse/5th gear synchronizer assembly using tool J–36183, J–36184 or equivalent and hydraulic press.

➡ **When pressing the reverse/5th synchronizer, start press operation, stop before tangs engage. Lift and rotate the 5th gear and 5th gear blocker ring (thrust washer must stay down), engaging tangs. Continue to press until seated. Be sure all shavings are removed.**

REVERSE IDLER GEAR DISASSEMBLY

1. Remove the bolt using a 13mm socket and driver.

2. Remove the shift rail, gear, shaft and bracket.

3. Remove the shift rail, detent ball and spring.

INSPECTION

1. Clean parts with solvent and air dry.

2. Inspect gear teeth for scuffed, nicked, burred or broken teeth.

3. Inspect bushings for roughness, burred, scores or overheating.

4. Inspect shaft for scoring, wear or overheating.

ASSEMBLY

1. Lubricate all components as assembly progresses.

2. Assemble spring and ball in bracket.

3. Install the shaft in the bracket assembly.

4. Install the gear on the shaft with the slot on the gear toward the threaded hole in the shaft.

5. Install the reverse idler gear assembly.

6. Install sealer to the bolt threads and install the bolt. Torque to 16 ft. lbs. (21 Nm).

TRANSAXLE CASE DISASSEMBLY

➡ **Remove the bearings and bushings only if there is evidence of damage or a mating part is being replaced.**

1. Remove the snapring.

2. Remove the plug.

3. Remove the sliding sleeve screw, sliding sleeve spring and sliding sleeve.

4. Remove the sliding sleeve bushing using tool J–36034 and J–36190 or equivalent and a hammer.

5. Remove the detent lever.

6. Remove the bushing shift detent lever using tool J–36039 and J–36190 or equivalent and a hammer.

7. Remove the shift shaft seal using a small suitable tool.

8. Remove the bearing shift shaft using tool J–36027 and J–36190 or equivalent and a hammer.

9. Remove the axle seal using a punch and hammer.

10. Remove the differential case support outer race using tool J–36181 and J–8092 or equivalent and a hammer.

11. Remove the shift rails plugs using a punch and a hammer.

12. Remove the input shaft support bearing. Remember that these bearings are not to be reused.

13. Remove the output shaft support bearing using a hammer.

14. Remove the 3 shift rail bushings using tool J–36029 or equivalent, (small end of J–36029–2 or equivalent adapter in bushing) and J–36190 or equivalent and a hammer. Make sure the tool is positioned to clear the case.

15. Remove the reverse shift rail bushing using tool J–36032 and J–23907 or equivalent.

16. Remove the stud using a 13mm socket and driver.

INSPECTION

1. Clean with solvent and air dry.

2. Inspect the case bearing race bore for wear, scratches or grooves.

3. Inspect the case bushings for scores, burrs, roundness or evidence of overheating.

4. Inspect case for cracks, threaded openings for damaged threads, mounting faces for nicks, burrs or scratches.

ASSEMBLY

1. Install the shift shaft bearing using tool J–36189 and J–36190 or equivalent and a hammer.

2. Install the shift shaft seal using tool J–35823 or equivalent and a hammer.

3. Install the 3 shift rail bushings using tool J–36029 or equivalent, (place new bushing on –2 adapter and retain between the –1 and –2 tool parts) and J–36190 or equivalent and a hammer.

4. Install the reverse rail bushing using tool J–36030 and J–36190 or equivalent and a hammer.

5. Install the differential carrier support outer race using tool J–26938 or equivalent and a hammer.

6. Install the axle seal using tool J–26938 or equivalent and a hammer.

7. Install the plugs even with the bore surface using suitable socket and hammer.

8. Install the detent lever bushing using tool J–36039 or equivalent and a hammer.

9. Install the detent lever.

10. Install the sliding sleeve bushing using tool J–36034 and J–36190 or equivalent and a hammer.

11. Install the sliding sleeve, spring and screw. Use sealer on the screw and tighten to 32 ft. lbs. (44 Nm).

12. Install the plug and snapring with the flat side up.

13. Install the stud with the chamfer end out and tighten to 15 ft. lbs. (21 Nm).

CLUTCH AND DIFFERENTIAL HOUSING DISASSEMBLY

1. Remove the bolts and retainer using a 10mm socket and driver.

2. Remove the output shaft race using tool J–36038 and J–23907 or equivalent and a hammer.

3. Remove the bolts, washers, spacer and plate using a 10mm socket and driver.

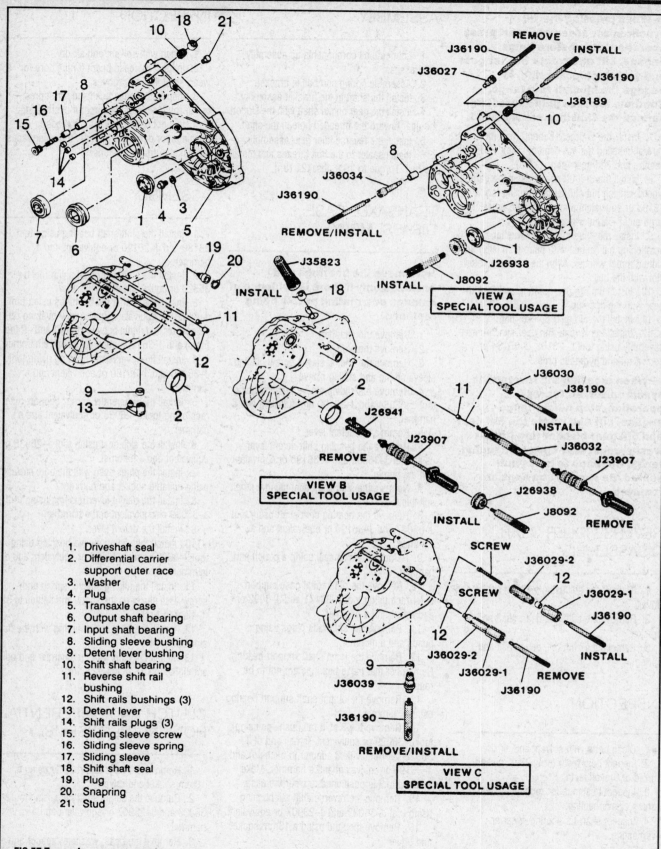

1. Driveshaft seal
2. Differential carrier
   support outer race
3. Washer
4. Plug
5. Transaxle case
6. Output shaft bearing
7. Input shaft bearing
8. Sliding sleeve bushing
9. Detent lever bushing
10. Shift shaft bearing
11. Reverse shift rail
    bushing
12. Shift rails bushings (3)
13. Detent lever
14. Shift rails plugs (3)
15. Sliding sleeve screw
16. Sliding sleeve spring
17. Sliding sleeve
18. Shift shaft seal
19. Plug
20. Snapring
21. Stud

FIG.57 Transaxle case components

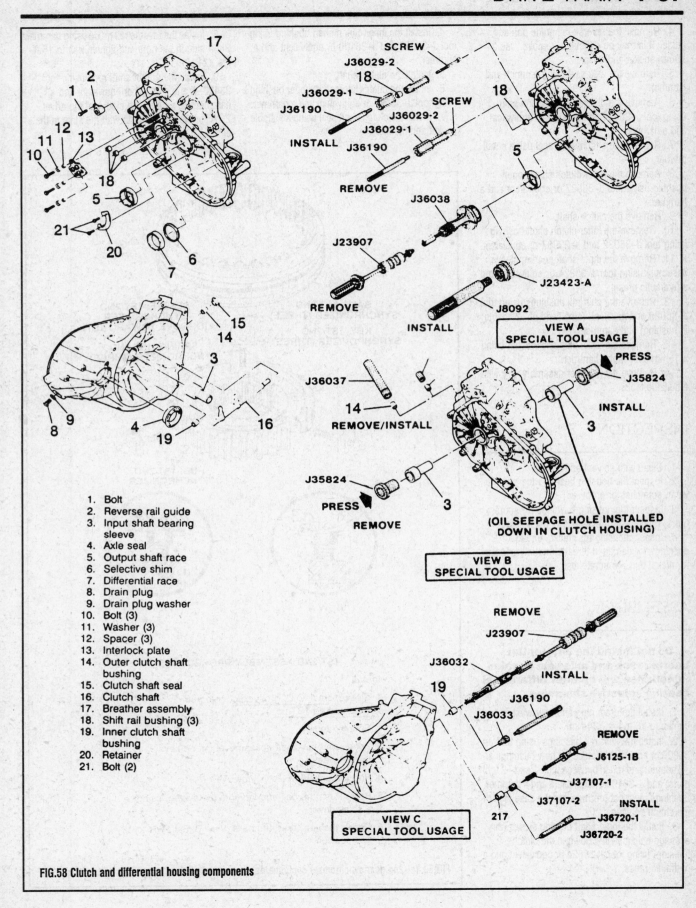

1. Bolt
2. Reverse rail guide
3. Input shaft bearing sleeve
4. Axle seal
5. Output shaft race
6. Selective shim
7. Differential race
8. Drain plug
9. Drain plug washer
10. Bolt (3)
11. Washer (3)
12. Spacer (3)
13. Interlock plate
14. Outer clutch shaft bushing
15. Clutch shaft seal
16. Clutch shaft
17. Breather assembly
18. Shift rail bushing (3)
19. Inner clutch shaft bushing
20. Retainer
21. Bolt (2)

FIG.58 Clutch and differential housing components

4. Remove the reverse rail guide bolt and guide. This may be difficult to remove. Use a 10mm socket and driver.

5. Remove the axle seal using a punch and hammer.

6. Remove the differential race and shim using tool J–36181 and J–8092 or equivalent and a hammer.

7. Remove the clutch shaft seal using small pry bar.

8. Remove the outer clutch shaft upper bushing using tool J–36037 or equivalent and a hammer.

9. Remove the clutch shaft.

10. Remove the inner clutch shaft bushing using tool J–36032 and J–23907 or equivalent.

11. Remove the input shaft bearing sleeve assembly using tool J–35824 or equivalent and a hydraulic press.

12. Remove the shift rail bushings using tool J–36029 or equivalent, (small end of –2 adapter in bushing) and hammer.

13. Remove the drain plug and washer using a 15mm socket and hammer.

14. Remove the breather assembly. Pry with a suitable tool.

INSPECTION

1. Clean with solvent and air dry.

2. Inspect the housing bearing race bore for wear, scratches or grooves.

3. Inspect the housing bushings for scores, burrs, roundness or evidence of overheating.

4. Inspect housing for cracks, threaded openings for damaged threads, mounting faces for nicks, burrs or scratches.

ASSEMBLY

➡ **Do not install the differential bearing race and axle seal or shim. Installation will be after differential bearing selective shimming.**

1. Install the drain plug and new washer and tighten to 18 ft. lbs. (24 Nm).

2. Install the shift rail bushings using tool J–36029 or equivalent, (place the new bushings on –2 adapter and retain between the –1 and –2 tool parts) and J–36190 or equivalent and a hammer. Bushings must not protrude into the case side of the clutch housing.

3. Install the input shaft bearing sleeve (oil seepage hole installed down in the clutch housing) using tool J–35824 or equivalent and a hydraulic press.

4. Install the inner clutch shaft bushing using tool J–36033 and J–36190 or equivalent and a hammer.

5. Install the clutch shaft.

6. Install the outer clutch shaft upper bushing using tool J–36037 or equivalent and a hammer.

7. Install the clutch shaft seal using a suitable socket and hammer.

8. Install the reverse rail guide using hammer. Short side in the bore and tighten bolt to 15 ft. lbs. (21 Nm).

9. Install the output shaft race using tool J–23423–A and J–8092 or equivalent and a hammer. Be sure to use side A of the driver.

2. Align the race cutouts with the slots in the case.

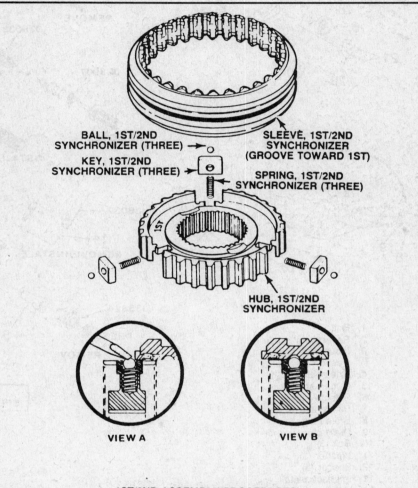

1ST/2ND ASSEMBLY PROCEDURES

Install

1. Sleeve, small O.D. groove up, onto hub. side marked 1ST up.

2. Spring into key.

3. Spring and key assemblies bevel cut on keys toward sleeve.

4. Position assembly as in View A.

5. Balls. Push the ball and key into the sleeve, using a screwdriver.

6. Center the hub, keys and balls. View B. Balls will "click" into position.

FIG.59 1st/2nd gear synchronizer components

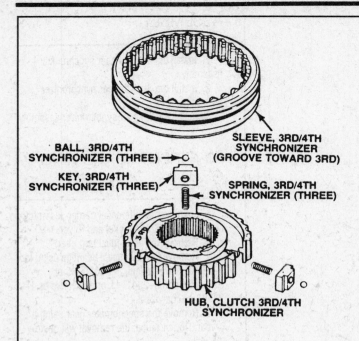

VIEW C

VIEW D

BALL, 3RD/4TH
SYNCHRONIZER (THREE)

KEY, 3RD/4TH
SYNCHRONIZER (THREE)

SLEEVE, 3RD/4TH
SYNCHRONIZER
(GROOVE TOWARD 3RD)

SPRING, 3RD/4TH
SYNCHRONIZER (THREE)

HUB, CLUTCH 3RD/4TH
SYNCHRONIZER

3RD/4TH ASSEMBLY PROCEDURES

Install

1. Sleeve, small O.D. groove up, onto hub,
   side marked 3RD up. Align the ball and spring pockets.

2. Spring into key.

3. Spring and key assemblies, stepped side of keys
   toward sleeve.

4. Position assemblys as in View C.

5. Balls. Push the ball and key into the sleeve, using a small
   screwdriver.

6. Center the hub, keys and balls. View D. Balls will "click"
   into position.

FIG.60 3rd/4th gear synchronizer components

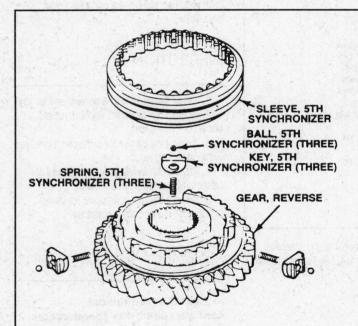

VIEW E

VIEW F

SLEEVE, 5TH
SYNCHRONIZER

BALL, 5TH
SYNCHRONIZER (THREE)

KEY, 5TH
SYNCHRONIZER (THREE)

SPRING, 5TH
SYNCHRONIZER (THREE)

GEAR, REVERSE

5TH ASSEMBLY PROCEDURES

Install

1. Spring into key.

2. Spring and key assemblies, teeth on keys out into slots
   on gear.

3. Sleeve, teeth up. Align the ball and spring pockets.

4. Position assembly as in View E.

5. Balls. Push the ball and key into the sleeve, using a small
   screwdriver.

6. Center the sleeve, keys and balls. View F. Balls will
   "click" into position.

FIG.61 5th gear synchronizer components

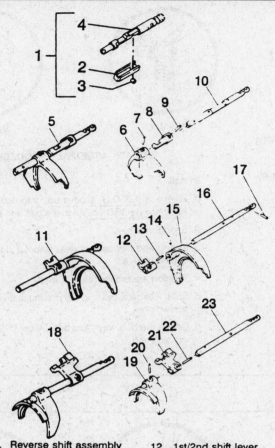

1. Reverse shift assembly rail
2. 5th/reverse shift gate
3. Gear disengage roller
4. Reverse shift shaft
5. 3rd/4th shift assembly rail
6. 3rd/4th shift shaft fork
7. Fork retainer pin
8. 3rd/4th select lever
9. Lever retainer pin
10. 3rd/4th shift shaft
11. 1st/2nd shift assembly rail

12. 1st/2nd shift lever
13. Lever retainer pin
14. Fork retainer pin
15. 1st/2nd shift fork
16. 1st/2nd shift shaft
17. Lock pin
18. 5th shift assembly rail
19. 5th shift fork
20. Fork retainer pin
21. 5th shift lever
22. Lever retainer pin
23. 5th shift shaft

FIG.62 Shift rail and fork assemblies

10. Install the retainer and bolts and tighten to 15 ft. lbs. (21 Nm). Use Loctite® 242 on the bolt.

11. Install the interlock plate, spacers, washers and bolts. Use Loctite® 242 and torque bolts to 15 ft. lbs. (21 Nm).

12. Install the breather assembly using a hammer.

SYNCHRONIZERS DISASSEMBLY

1. Place the 1–2, 3–4 and 5th speed synchronizers in separate shop towels, wrap the assemblies and press against the inner hub.

2. Mark the sleeve and hub for installation.

INSPECTION

1. Clean the assembly with solvent and air dry.

2. Inspect the synchronizer teeth for wear, scuffed, nicked, burred or broken teeth.

3. Inspect the synchronizer keys for wear or distortion.

4. Inspect the synchronizer balls and springs for distortion, cracks or wear.

ASSEMBLY

1. Install the 1st/2nd gear synchronizer assembly.

2. Install the 3rd/4th gear synchronizer assembly.

3. Install the 5th gear synchronizer assembly.

DIFFERENTIAL AND RING GEAR

1. Remove the differential carrier assembly bolts using a 15mm socket and driver.

2. Remove the differential ring gear.

3. Remove the differential bearings using tool J–22888 or equivalent, J–22888–35 or equivalent and J–2241–11 or equivalent or J–23598 or equivalent.

4. Remove the speedometer gear using a prybar. Do not reuse; the removal will destroy the gear.

5. Remove the differential cross pin locking bolt and washer.

6. Remove the differential cross pin.

7. Remove the differential pinion gear and washer, differential side gear and side gear thrust washer. Identify the parts for same installation.

INSPECTION

1. Clean the parts with a solvent and air dry.

2. Inspect the gears for scuffed, nicked, burred or broken teeth.

3. Inspect the carrier for distortion, bores out of round or scoring.

4. Inspect the bearings for roughness of rotation, burred or pitted condition.

5. Inspect the thrust washers for wear, scuffed, nicked or burred condition.

ASSEMBLY

➡ **Heat the mechanical configuration nylon speedometer drive gear in hot tap water for 5 minutes prior to installation. Heat the electronic configuration steel speedometer drive gear in an oven at 250°F (120°C) for 7–10 minutes prior to installation. Do not reuse bolts.**

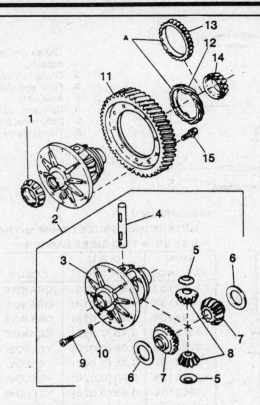

1. Differential bearing
2. Differential assembly carrier
3. Differential carrier
4. Differential cross pin
5. Pinion gear thrust washer
6. Side gear thrust washer
7. Differential side gear
8. Differential pinion gear
9. Screw
10. Lock washer
11. Differential ring gear
12. Speedometer gear (mechanical)
13. Speedometer gear (electronic)
14. Differential bearing
15. Bolt (10)

FIG.63 Differential and ring gear assembly

1. Install the speedometer gear and allow to cool.

2. Install the differential bearings using tool J–22919 or equivalent and a hydraulic press.

3. Install the differential side gear and side gear thrust washer and differential pinion gear and pinion gear side thrust washer.

4. Install the differential cross pin.

5. Install the differential cross locking bolt and washer. Torque to 84 inch lbs. (9 Nm).

6. Install the differential ring gear with the identification chamfer to the carrier.

7. Install new bolts and torque to 61 ft. lbs. (83 Nm).

DIFFERENTIAL ASSEMBLY SELECTIVE SHIM PRELOAD PROCEDURE

1. Install tool J–26935 or equivalent, to the clutch housing and transaxle housing.

2. Measure the largest shim possible on tool J–26935–3; use the shim 2 sizes larger.

3. Install the selective shim.

4. Install the differential bearing race using tool J–26938 or equivalent and J–8092 or equivalent and a hammer.

5. Install the driveshaft seal using tool J–8092 or equivalent and a hammer.

TRANSAXLE ASSEMBLY

Gear/Shift Rail Assemblies and Support Components

1. Position the gear cluster/shift rail assembly on tool J–36182–1 or equivalent. Align the shift rail and shaft pilots to the fixture.

2. Install the transaxle case. Align the bearing bores in the case with the shaft pilots.

3. Install the new output shaft bearing using tool J–35824 or equivalent and a hydraulic press.

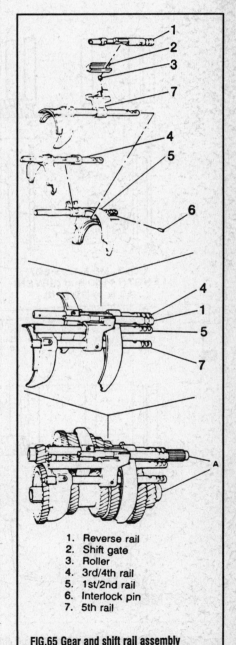

1. Reverse rail
2. Shift gate
3. Roller
4. 3rd/4th rail
5. 1st/2nd rail
6. Interlock pin
7. 5th rail

FIG.65 Gear and shift rail assembly

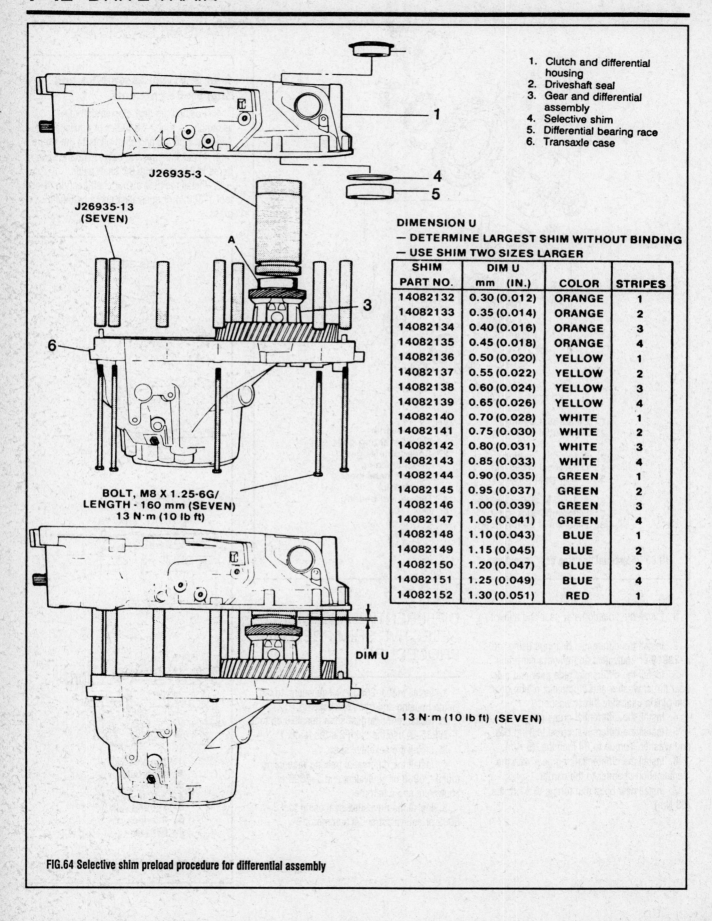

1. Clutch and differential housing
2. Driveshaft seal
3. Gear and differential assembly
4. Selective shim
5. Differential bearing race
6. Transaxle case

J26935-3

J26935-13 (SEVEN)

A

BOLT, M8 X 1.25-6G/ LENGTH - 160 mm (SEVEN) 13 N·m (10 lb ft)

DIMENSION U

— **DETERMINE LARGEST SHIM WITHOUT BINDING**

— **USE SHIM TWO SIZES LARGER**

SHIM PART NO.	DIM U mm (IN.)	COLOR	STRIPES
14082132	0.30 (0.012)	ORANGE	1
14082133	0.35 (0.014)	ORANGE	2
14082134	0.40 (0.016)	ORANGE	3
14082135	0.45 (0.018)	ORANGE	4
14082136	0.50 (0.020)	YELLOW	1
14082137	0.55 (0.022)	YELLOW	2
14082138	0.60 (0.024)	YELLOW	3
14082139	0.65 (0.026)	YELLOW	4
14082140	0.70 (0.028)	WHITE	1
14082141	0.75 (0.030)	WHITE	2
14082142	0.80 (0.031)	WHITE	3
14082143	0.85 (0.033)	WHITE	4
14082144	0.90 (0.035)	GREEN	1
14082145	0.95 (0.037)	GREEN	2
14082146	1.00 (0.039)	GREEN	3
14082147	1.05 (0.041)	GREEN	4
14082148	1.10 (0.043)	BLUE	1
14082149	1.15 (0.045)	BLUE	2
14082150	1.20 (0.047)	BLUE	3
14082151	1.25 (0.049)	BLUE	4
14082152	1.30 (0.051)	RED	1

DIM U

13 N·m (10 lb ft) (SEVEN)

FIG.64 Selective shim preload procedure for differential assembly

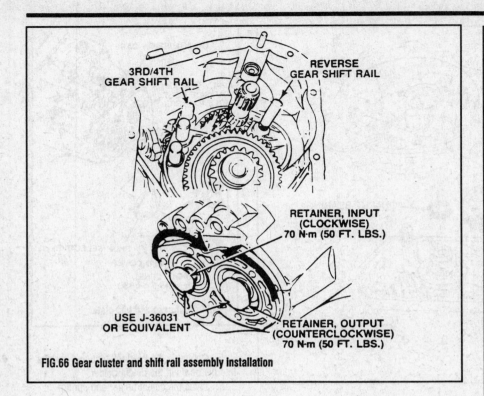

FIG.66 Gear cluster and shift rail assembly installation

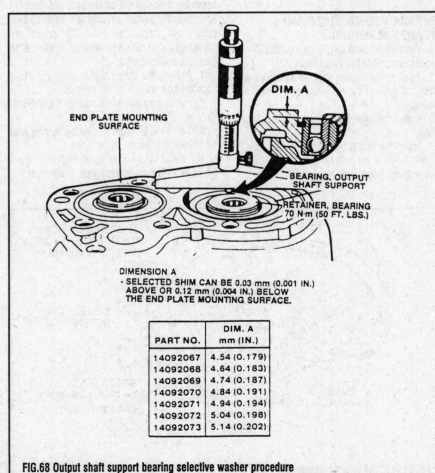

DIMENSION A
- SELECTED SHIM CAN BE 0.03 mm (0.001 IN.)
ABOVE OR 0.12 mm (0.004 IN.) BELOW
THE END PLATE MOUNTING SURFACE.

PART NO.	DIM. A mm (IN.)
14092067	4.54 (0.179)
14092068	4.64 (0.183)
14092069	4.74 (0.187)
14092070	4.84 (0.191)
14092071	4.94 (0.194)
14092072	5.04 (0.198)
14092073	5.14 (0.202)

FIG.68 Output shaft support bearing selective washer procedure

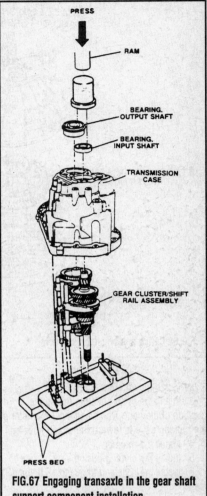

FIG.67 Engaging transaxle in the gear shaft support component installation

4. Install the new input shaft bearing using tool J–35824 or equivalent and a hydraulic press. Push the rails to engage and hold the transaxle in 4th and reverse gear. The bearings must be seated.

5. Install the new input and output retainers using tool J–36031 or equivalent and torque to 50 ft. lbs. (70 Nm). Return the transaxle to **N**.

Shift Shaft

1. Assemble the pins and rollers on the shift shaft. Retain with petroleum jelly.

2. Install the shift shaft assembly. Tap in with a light hammer and align the hole in the shaft with the hole in the shift lever.

3. Install the lever retainer pin using a $\frac{3}{16}$ in. (5mm) punch and a hammer. Install pin till it is even with the surface of the shift lever.

Clutch and Differential Housing

1. Apply sealant, part number 1052942 or equivalent, to the outside of the bolt hole pattern of the gear case flange.

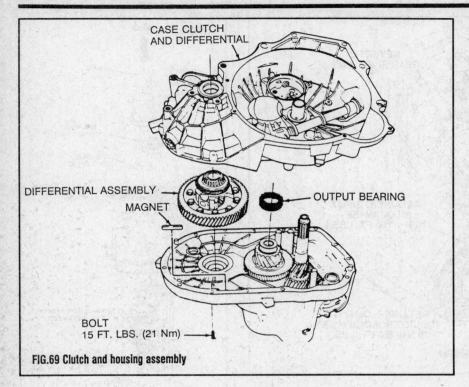

FIG.69 Clutch and housing assembly

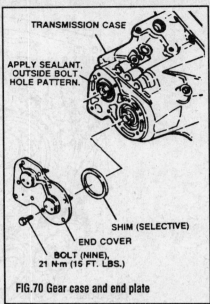

FIG.70 Gear case and end plate

2. Install the differential.

3. Install the output bearing noting the position of the cage. The small inner diameter of the bearing cage is toward the clutch housing.

4. Install the magnet.

5. Install the clutch housing.

6. Install the bolts and torque to 15 ft. lbs. (21 Nm).

OUTPUT SHAFT SUPPORT BEARING SELECTIVE SHIM PROCEDURE

➡ **Be sure that the output bearing is seated in the bore by tapping the bearing into the case. Be sure that the bearing retainer is properly torqued. Selected shim can be 0.001 in. (0.03mm) above, or 0.004 in. (0.12mm) below the end plate mounting surface.**

1. Using tool J–26900–19 metric dial depth gauge or equivalent, measure the distance between the end plate mounting surface and the outer race of the output shaft bearing.

2. Select the proper shim.

TRANSAXLE CASE END PLATE

1. Apply sealant, part number 1052942 or equivalent, to the outside of the end plate bolt hole pattern of the case.

2. Install the selective shim.

3. Install the oil shield.

4. Install the end cover plate.

5. Install the bolts and torque to 15 ft. lbs. (21 Nm).

SHIFT RAIL DETENT/CLUTCH AND DIFFERENTIAL HOUSING

1. Position the shift rails to expose the interlock notches in the **N** position.

2. Position the reverse shift rail to allow the detent ball to sit in the notch and on the reverse bushing.

3. Install the reverse bushing using a suitable socket.

4. Install the detent balls. Place them in the notched areas of the shift rails. Retain the ball positions with petroleum jelly.

5. Assemble the interlock pins and springs into the bores in the detent holder.

6. Install the detent holder and spring assembly. Position the detent balls over the springs using a small suitable tool. After all the detent balls are positioned over the springs, pry the reverse shift rail up to allow its detent ball to enter the spring pocket.

7. Position the detent holder using a pry to align the bolt holes with the threads.

8. Install the bolts and torque to 84 inch lbs. (9 Nm).

9. Install the protective cover by tapping with a hammer until seated in the bore.

10. Install the bearing. Apply high temperature grease to the inside of the bore.

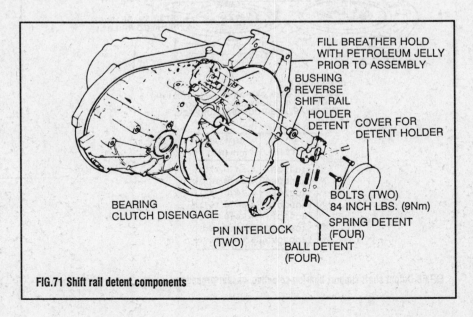

FIG.71 Shift rail detent components

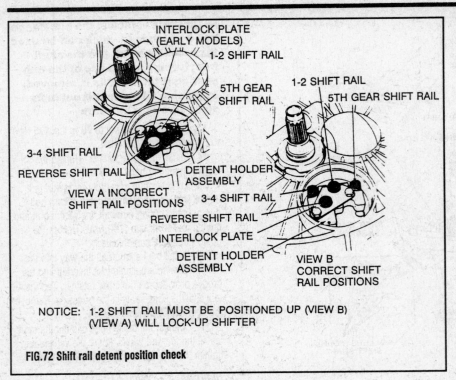

FIG.72 Shift rail detent position check

INTERLOCK PLATE (EARLY MODELS)

1-2 SHIFT RAIL

5TH GEAR SHIFT RAIL

1-2 SHIFT RAIL

5TH GEAR SHIFT RAIL

3-4 SHIFT RAIL

REVERSE SHIFT RAIL

DETENT HOLDER ASSEMBLY

VIEW A INCORRECT SHIFT RAIL POSITIONS

3-4 SHIFT RAIL

REVERSE SHIFT RAIL

INTERLOCK PLATE

DETENT HOLDER ASSEMBLY

VIEW B CORRECT SHIFT RAIL POSITIONS

NOTICE: 1-2 SHIFT RAIL MUST BE POSITIONED UP (VIEW B)
(VIEW A) WILL LOCK-UP SHIFTER

SHIFT SHAFT DETENT/TRANSAXLE HOUSING

◆ SEE FIG. 44

1. Install the inner spring seat.
2. Install the 5th/reverse bias spring.
3. Install the outer spring seat.
4. Install the spring screw and torque to 84 inch lbs. (9 Nm). Use a small amount of thread sealant, part number 11052624 or equivalent, to the screw.
5. Install the protective cover using a hammer. Position to below the snapring groove.
6. Install the snapring.

EXTERNAL TRANSAXLE MOUNTED LINKAGE

◆ SEE FIG. 42

1. Install the bracket.
2. Install the bolts and torque to 17 ft. lbs. (23 Nm).
3. Install the collar and pin using a punch and a hammer.
4. Install the pivot.
5. Install a new pin.
6. Install the lever.

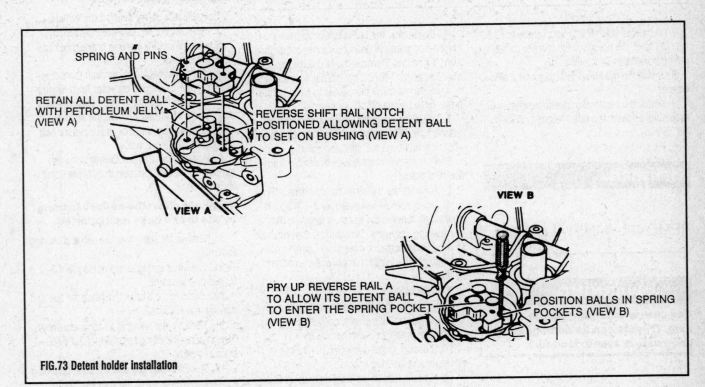

FIG.73 Detent holder installation

SPRING AND PINS

RETAIN ALL DETENT BALL WITH PETROLEUM JELLY (VIEW A)

REVERSE SHIFT RAIL NOTCH POSITIONED ALLOWING DETENT BALL TO SET ON BUSHING (VIEW A)

VIEW A

VIEW B

PRY UP REVERSE RAIL A TO ALLOW ITS DETENT BALL TO ENTER THE SPRING POCKET (VIEW B)

POSITION BALLS IN SPRING POCKETS (VIEW B)

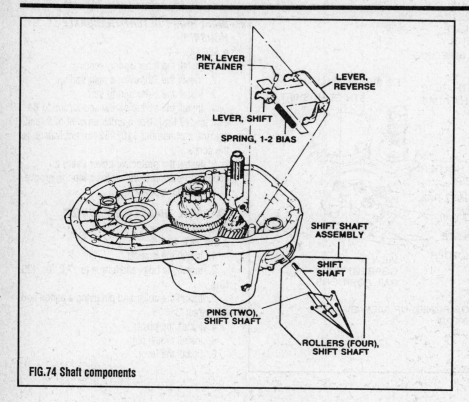

PIN, LEVER
RETAINER

LEVER,
REVERSE

LEVER, SHIFT

SPRING, 1-2 BIAS

SHIFT SHAFT
ASSEMBLY

SHIFT
SHAFT

PINS (TWO),
SHIFT SHAFT

ROLLERS (FOUR),
SHIFT SHAFT

FIG.74 Shaft components

7. Install the washer and nut. Torque to 61 ft. lbs. (83 Nm). Do not allow the lever to move during installation of the nut.

8. Install the fluid level indicator and a new washer.

9. Install the electronic speedometer sensor assembly, retainer and bolt. Torque to 84 inch lbs. (9 Nm).

Halfshafts

REMOVAL & INSTALLATION

❄ WARNING

Use care when removing the drive axle. Tri-pots can be damaged if the drive axle is over extended.

EXCEPT REAR AXLE — 6000 STE AWD

1. Remove the hub nut and discard. A new hub nut must be used for reassembly.

2. Raise and safely support the vehicle. Remove the wheel and tire assembly.

3. Install an halfshaft boot seal protector onto the seal.

4. Disconnect the brake hose clip from the Mcpherson strut but do not disconnect the hose from the caliper. Remove the brake caliper from the spindle and support the caliper with a length of wire. Do not allow the caliper to hang by the brake hose unsupported.

5. Mark the camber alignment cam bolt for reassembly. Remove the cam bolt and the upper attaching bolt from the strut and spindle.

6. Pull the steering knuckle assembly from the strut bracket.

7. Remove the halfshaft from the transaxle.

8. Using spindle remover tool J–28733 or equivalent, remove the halfshaft from the hub and bearing assembly. Do not allow the halfshaft to hang unsupported. If necessary, support using a length of wire in order to prevent component damage.

To install:

9. If a new halfshaft is to be installed, a new knuckle seal should be installed first along with a boot seal protector when necessary.

10. Loosely install the halfshaft into the transaxle and steering knuckle.

11. Loosely attach the steering knuckle to the suspension strut.

12. The halfshaft is an interference fit in the steering knuckle. Press the axle into place, then install the hub nut. When the shaft begins to turn with the hub, insert a drift through the caliper into one of the cooling slots in the rotor to keep it from turning.

→ **On some vehicles, the hub flange has a notch in it which can be used to prevent the hub and the shaft from turning, when one of the hub bearing retainer bolts is removed, by placing a longer bolt put in its place through the notch**

13. Tighten the hub nut to 70 ft. lbs. (95 Nm) to completely seat the shaft.

14. Install the brake caliper. Tighten the caliper mounting bolts to 30 ft. lbs. (41 Nm).

15. Load the hub assembly by lowering it onto a jackstand. Align the camber cam bolt marks made during removal, install the bolt and tighten to 140 ft. lbs. (190 Nm). Tighten the upper nut to the same value.

16. Install the halfshaft all the way into the transaxle using a suitable tool inserted into the groove provided on the inner retainer. Tap the tool until the shaft seats in the transaxle. Remove the boot seal protector.

17. Connect the brake hose clip the the strut. Install the tire and wheel, lower the vehicle and tighten the hub nut to 192 ft. lbs. (261 Nm).

REAR AXLE — 6000 STE AWD

1. Raise and safely support the vehicle.

2. Remove the tire and wheel assembly.

3. Disconnect the parking brake cable end from the bracket.

4. Insert a suitable tool through the caliper into the rotor to prevent the rotor from turning.

5. Remove the shaft nut and washer using special tool J–34826. Discard the shaft nut.

6. Remove the anti-lock brake sensor bolt and move the sensor aside.

7. Remove the 2 brake caliper bolts and remove the caliper. Support the caliper using a length of wire.

→ **Do not allow the caliper to hang by the brake hose unsupported.**

8. Remove the rotor from the hub and bearing assembly.

9. Install leaf spring compression tool J–33432 or equivalent.

10. Remove the 3 bolts mounting the hub and bearing to the knuckle.

11. Remove the hub and bearing assembly from the knuckle using special tool J–28733–A or equivalent.

12. Remove the bolts and nut plate attaching the lower strut mount to the knuckle. Scribe the position of the upper bolt prior removing.

13. Install a suitable CV-boot protector to prevent damage to the boot.

14. Swing the knuckle downward and away from the driveshaft.

15. Remove the drive axle from the differential using a suitable slide hammer.

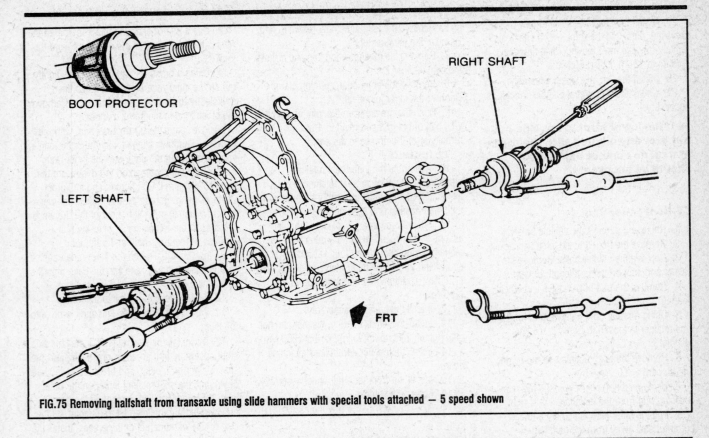

FIG.75 Removing halfshaft from transaxle using slide hammers with special tools attached — 5 speed shown

To install:

16. Install the drive axle to the differential. Ensure positive engagement by pulling outward on the inner axle end. Grasp the housing only. Do not grasp and pull on the axle shaft.

17. Swing the knuckle up to the lower strut mount.

18. Position the nut plate and install the lower strut mount bolts to the knuckle. Align the top bolt with scribe marks before tightening the bolts. Tighten the bolts to 148 ft. lbs. (200 Nm).

19. Remove the CV boot protector.

20. Install the hub and bearing assembly to the knuckle and axle spline.

21. Install the hub and bearing attaching bolts. Tighten to 61 ft. lbs. (84 Nm).

22. Remove the leaf spring compression tool.

23. Install the rotor to hub and bearing assembly.

24. Install the brake caliper to the rotor and install the retaining bolts. Tighten the bolts to 38 ft. lbs. (51 Nm).

25. Install the anti-lock brake sensor to the knuckle and install the retaining bolt. Using a non-ferrous feeler gauge, adjust the sensor gap to 0.028 in. (0.7mm). Tighten the adjustment screw to 19 inch lbs. (2.2 Nm).

26. Connect the parking brake cable end into the bracket.

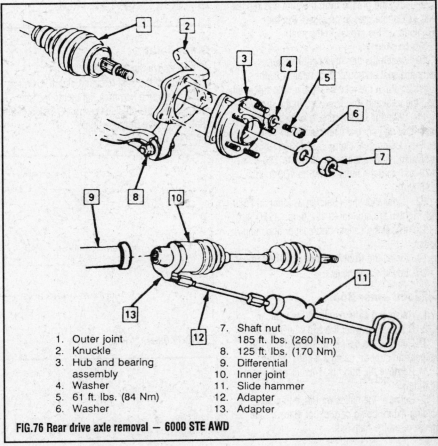

1. Outer joint
2. Knuckle
3. Hub and bearing assembly
4. Washer
5. 61 ft. lbs. (84 Nm)
6. Washer
7. Shaft nut 185 ft. lbs. (260 Nm)
8. 125 ft. lbs. (170 Nm)
9. Differential
10. Inner joint
11. Slide hammer
12. Adapter
13. Adapter

FIG.76 Rear drive axle removal — 6000 STE AWD

27. Install the shaft washer and new torque prevailing nut. Hold the rotor with a suitable to prevent the axle from turning while tightening. Tighten to 185 ft. lbs. (260 Nm).

28. Install the tire and wheel assembly.

29. Check the rear wheel camber. Adjust as necessary.

➡ **If the lower strut to knuckle bolts are properly aligned with the scribe marks, no camber adjustment should be necessary.**

30. Lower the vehicle.

CV-Boot Outer Boot

1. Raise and support the vehicle safely.

2. Remove the front tire and wheel assembly.

3. Remove the caliper bolts. Remove the caliper and support using a length of wire.

4. Remove the hub nut, washer and wheel bearing.

5. Using a brass drift, lightly tap around the seal retainer to loosen it. Remove the seal retainer.

6. Remove the seal retaining clamp or ring and discard.

7. Using snapring pliers, remove the race retaining ring from the halfshaft.

8. Pull the outer joint assembly and the outboard seal away from the halfshaft.

9. Flush the grease from the joint and repack with half of the grease provided. Put the remainder of the grease in the seal.

To install:

10. Assemble the inner seal retainer, outboard seal and outer seal retainer to the halfshaft. Push the joint assembly onto the shaft until the retaining ring is seated in the groove.

11. Slide the outboard seal onto the joint assembly and secure using the outer seal retainer. Using seal clamp tool J–35910 or equivalent, torque the outer clamp to 130 ft. lbs. (176 Nm) and the inner clamp to 100 ft. lbs. (136 Nm).

12. Install the wheel bearing, washer and hub nut. Tighten the hub nut to 192 ft. lbs. (260 Nm).

13. Install the caliper and caliper attaching bolts.

14. Install the front tire and wheel assembly.

15. Lower the vehicle.

CV Joint Inner Boot

1. Raise and safely support the vehicle.

2. Remove the front tire and wheel assembly.

3. Remove the caliper bolts. Remove the caliper and support using a length of wire.

4. Remove the hub nut, washer and wheel bearing.

5. Remove the halfshaft. Place in a suitable holding fixture being careful not place undue pressure on the halfshaft.

6. Remove the joint assembly retaining ring. Remove the joint assembly.

7. Remove the race retaining ring and remove the seal retainer.

8. Remove the inner seal retaining clamp. Remove the inner joint seal.

9. Flush the grease from the joint and repack with half of the grease provided. Put the remainder of the grease in the seal.

To install:

10. Assemble the inner seal retainer, outboard seal and outer seal retainer to the halfshaft. Push the joint assembly onto the shaft until the retaining ring is seated in the groove.

11. Slide the outboard seal onto the joint assembly and secure using the outer seal retainer. Using seal clamp tool J–35910 or equivalent, torque the outer clamp to 130 ft. lbs. (176 Nm) and the inner clamp to 100 ft. lbs. (136 Nm).

12. Install the halfshaft assembly.

13. Install the wheel bearing, washer and hub nut. Tighten the hub nut to 192 ft. lbs. (260 Nm).

14. Install the caliper and caliper attaching bolts.

15. Install the front tire and wheel assembly.

16. Lower the vehicle.

CV-JOINT OVERHAUL

Outer Joint

1. Remove the axle shaft.

2. Cut off the seal retaining clamp. Using a brass drift and a hammer, lightly tap the seal retainer from the outside toward the inside of the shaft to remove from the joint.

3. Use a pair of snapring pliers to spread the retaining ring apart. Pull the axle shaft from the joint.

4. Using a brass drift and a hammer, lightly tap on the inner race cage until it has tilted sufficiently to remove one of the balls. Remove the other balls in the same manner.

5. Pivot the cage 90 degrees and, with the cage ball windows aligned with the outer joint windows, lift out the cage and the inner race.

6. The inner race can be removed from the cage by pivoting it 90 degrees and lifting out. Clean all parts thoroughly and inspect for wear.

7. To install, put a light coat of the grease provided in the rebuilding kit onto the ball grooves of the inner race and outer joint.

8. Install the balls into the inner race cage.

9. Install the inner race into the cage onto the axle joint.

10. Install the axle shaft into the joint.

11. Install a new seal retainer and clamp onto the joint.

12. To install the seal retainer, install the axle shaft assembly into an arbor press. Support the seal retainer on blocks, and press the axle shaft down until the seal retainer seats on the outer joint. When assembling, apply half the grease provided in the rebuilding kit to the joint; fill the seal (boot) with the rest of the grease. Install the axle shaft.

Inner Joint

1. The joint seal is removed in the same manner as the outer joint seal. Follow Steps 1-3 of the outer joint procedure.

2. To disassemble the inner joint, remove the ball retaining ring from the joint. Pull the cage and inner race from the joint. The balls will come out with the race.

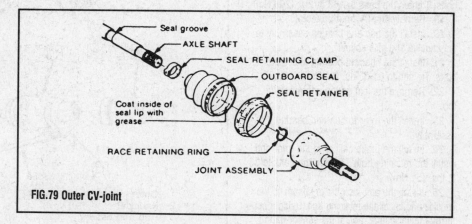

FIG.79 Outer CV-joint

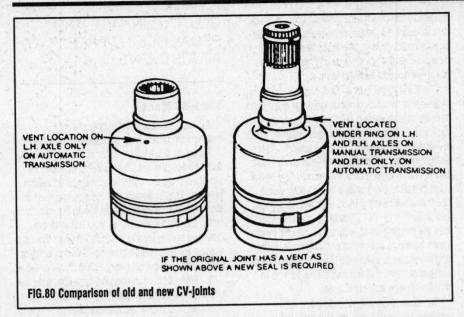

FIG.80 Comparison of old and new CV-joints

(labels within figure:) VENT LOCATION ON L.H. AXLE ONLY ON AUTOMATIC TRANSMISSION. — VENT LOCATED UNDER RING ON L.H. AND R.H. AXLES ON MANUAL TRANSMISSION AND R.H. ONLY. ON AUTOMATIC TRANSMISSION — IF THE ORIGINAL JOINT HAS A VENT AS SHOWN ABOVE A NEW SEAL IS REQUIRED.

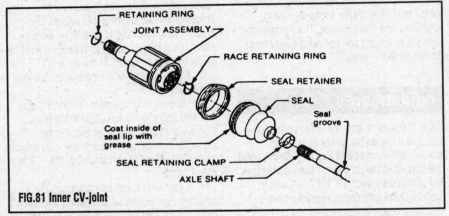

FIG.81 Inner CV-joint

(labels within figure:) RETAINING RING — JOINT ASSEMBLY — RACE RETAINING RING — SEAL RETAINER — SEAL — Seal groove — Coat inside of seal lip with grease — SEAL RETAINING CLAMP — AXLE SHAFT

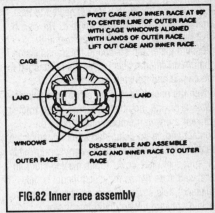

FIG.82 Inner race assembly

(labels within figure:) PIVOT CAGE AND INNER RACE AT 90° TO CENTER LINE OF OUTER RACE WITH CAGE WINDOWS ALIGNED WITH LANDS OF OUTER RACE. LIFT OUT CAGE AND INNER RACE. — CAGE — LAND — LAND — WINDOWS — OUTER RACE — DISASSEMBLE AND ASSEMBLE CAGE AND INNER RACE TO OUTER RACE

3. Center the inner race lobes in the cage windows, pivot the race 90 degrees, and lift the race from the cage.

4. Reverse steps 1, 2 and 3 to assembly the joint. The inner joint seal retainer must be pressed onto the joint. See Step 12 of the outer joint procedure.

Driveshaft

The procedure for replacing the driveshaft on the Pontiac 6000 AWD is covered in detail under Automatic Transaxle Driveshaft removal and installation.

CLUTCH

✽✽ CAUTION

The clutch driven disc contains asbestos, which has been determined to be a cancer causing agent. Never clean clutch surfaces with compressed air! Avoid inhaling any dust from any clutch surface! When cleaning clutch surfaces, use a commercially available brake cleaning fluid.

Understanding the Clutch

The purpose of the clutch is to disconnect and connect engine power from the transmission. A car at rest requires a lot of engine torque to get all that weight moving. An internal combustion engine does not develop a high starting torque (unlike steam engines), so it must be allowed to operate without any load until it builds up enough torque to move the car. Torque increases with engine rpm. The clutch allows the engine to build up torque by physically disconnecting the engine from the transmission, relieving the engine of any load or resistance. The transfer of engine power to the transmission (the load) must be smooth and gradual; if it weren't, drive line components would wear out or break quickly. This gradual power transfer is made possible by gradually releasing the clutch pedal. The clutch disc and pressure plate are the connecting link between the engine and transmission. When the clutch pedal is released, the disc and plate contact each other (clutch engagement), physically joining the engine and transmission. When the pedal is pushed in, the disc and plate separate (the clutch is disengaged), disconnecting the engine from the transmission.

The clutch assembly consists of the flywheel, the clutch disc, the clutch pressure plate, the throwout bearing and fork, the actuating linkage and the pedal. The flywheel and clutch pressure

plate (driving members) are connected to the engine crankshaft and rotate with it. The clutch disc is located between the flywheel and pressure plate, and splined to the transmission shaft. A driving member is one that is attached to the engine and transfers engine power to a driven member (clutch disc) on the transmission shaft. A driving member (pressure plate) rotates (drives) a driven member (clutch disc) on contact and, in so doing, turns the transmission shaft. There is a circular diaphragm spring within the pressure plate cover (transmission side). In a relaxed state (when the clutch pedal is fully released), this spring is convex; that it, it is dished outward toward the transmission. Pushing in the clutch pedal actuates an attached linkage rod. Connected to the other end of this rod is the throwout bearing fork. The throwout bearing is attached to the fork. When the clutch pedal is depressed, the clutch linkage pushes the fork and bearing forward to contact the diaphragm spring of the pressure plate. The outer edges of the spring are secured to the pressure plate and are pivoted on rings so that when the center of the spring is compressed by the throwout bearing, the outer edges bow outward and, by so doing, pull the pressure plate in the same direction — away from the clutch disc. This action separates the disc from the plate, disengaging the clutch and allowing the transmission to be shifted into another gear. A coil type clutch return spring attached to the clutch pedal arm permits full release of the pedal. Releasing the pedal pulls the throwout bearing away from the diaphragm spring resulting in a reversal of spring position. As bearing pressure is gradually released from the spring center, the outer edges of the spring bow outward, pushing the pressure plate into closer contact with the clutch disc. As the disc and plate move closer together, friction between the two increases and slippage is reduced until, when full spring pressure is applied (by fully releasing the pedal), The speed of the disc and plate are the same. This stops all slipping, creating a direct connection between the plate and disc which results in the transfer of power from the engine to the transmission. The clutch disc is now rotating with the pressure plate at engine speed and, because it is splined to the transmission shaft, the shaft now turns at the same engine speed. Understanding clutch operation can be rather difficult at first; if you're still confused after reading this, consider the following analogy. The action of the diaphragm spring can be compared to that of an oil can bottom. The bottom of an oil can is shaped very much like the clutch diaphragm spring and pushing in on the can bottom and then releasing it produces a similar effect. As mentioned earlier, the clutch pedal return spring permits full

release of the pedal and reduces linkage slack due to wear. As the linkage wears, clutch free-pedal travel will increase and free-travel will decrease as the clutch wears. Free-travel is actually throwout bearing lash.

The diaphragm spring type clutches used are available in two different designs: flat diaphragm springs or bent spring. The bent fingers are bent back to create a centrifugal boost ensuring quick re-engagement at higher engine speeds. This design enables pressure plate load to increase as the clutch disc wears and makes low pedal effort possible even with a heavy-duty clutch. The throwout bearing used with the bent finger design is 1 1/4 in. (31.75mm) long and is shorter than the bearing used with the flat finger design. These bearings are not interchangeable. If the longer bearing is used with the bent finger clutch, free-pedal travel will not exist. This results in clutch slippage and rapid wear.

The transmission varies the gear ratio between the engine and rear wheels. It can be shifted to change engine speed as driving conditions and loads change. The transmission allows disengaging and reversing power from the engine to the wheels.

Adjustments

On 1982–86 models the only service adjustment necessary on the clutch is to maintain the correct pedal free play. Clutch pedal free play, or throwout bearing lash, decreases with driven disc wear. On 1987 and newer models a hydraulic clutch system provides automatic clutch adjustment.

CLUTCH LINKAGE AND PEDAL HEIGHT/FREE-PLAY ADJUSTMENT

1982–86 Models

All cars use a self-adjusting clutch mechanism which may be checked as follows:

As the clutch friction material wears, the cable must be lengthened. This is accomplished by simply pulling the clutch pedal up to its rubber bumper. This action forces the pawl against its stop and rotates it out of mesh with the quadrant teeth, allowing the cable to play out until the quadrant spring load is balanced against the load applied by the release bearing. This adjustment procedure is required every 5,000 miles or less.

1. With engine running and brake on, hold the clutch pedal approximately 1/2 in. (13mm) from floor mat and move shift lever between first and reverse several times. If this can be done smoothly without clashing into reverse, the clutch is fully releasing. If shift is not smooth, clutch is not fully releasing and linkage should be inspected and corrected as necessary.

2. Check clutch pedal bushings for sticking or excessive wear.

3. Have an assistant sit in the driver's seat and fully apply the clutch pedal to the floor. Observe the clutch fork lever travel at the transaxle. The end of the clutch fork lever should have a total travel of approximately 1.5–1.7 in. (38–43mm).

4. If fork lever is not correct, check the adjusting mechanism by depressing the clutch pedal and looking for pawl to firmly engage with the teeth in the quadrant.

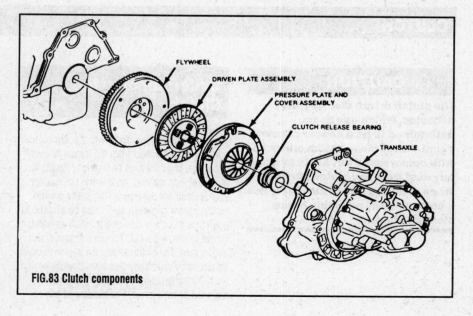

FIG.83 Clutch components

FLYWHEEL

DRIVEN PLATE ASSEMBLY

PRESSURE PLATE AND COVER ASSEMBLY

CLUTCH RELEASE BEARING

TRANSAXLE

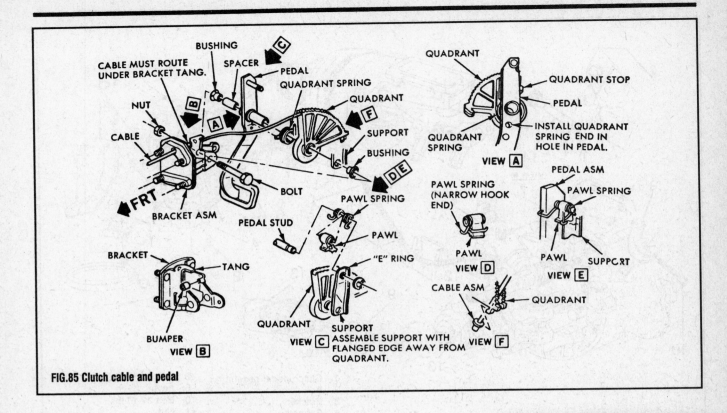

FIG. 85 Clutch cable and pedal

Clutch Cable

REMOVAL

1. Support the clutch pedal upward against the bumper stop to release the pawl from the quadrant. Disconnect the end of the cable from the clutch release lever at the transaxle. Be careful to prevent the cable from snapping rapidly toward the rear of the car. The quadrant in the adjusting mechanism can be damaged by allowing the cable to snap back.

2. Disconnect the clutch cable from the quadrant. Lift the locking pawl away from the quadrant, then slide the cable out on the right side of the quadrant.

3. From the engine side of the cowl disconnect the two upper nuts holding the cable retainer to the upper studs. Disconnect the cable from the bracket mounted to the transaxle, and remove the cable.

4. Inspect the clutch cable for frayed wires, kinks, worn ends and excessive friction. If any of these conditions exist, replace the cable.

INSTALLATION

1. With the gasket in position on the two upper studs, position a new cable with the retaining flange against the bracket.

2. Attach the end of the cable to the quadrant, being sure to route the cable underneath the pawl.

3. Attach the two upper nuts to the retainer mounting studs, and torque to specifications.

4. Attach the cable to the bracket mounted to the transaxle.

5. Support the clutch pedal upward against the bumper stop to release the pawl from the quadrant. Attach the outer end of the cable to the clutch release lever. Be sure not to yank on the cable, since overloading the cable could damage the quadrant.

6. Check clutch operation and adjust by lifting the clutch pedal up to allow the mechanism to adjust the cable length. Depress the pedal slowly several times to set the pawl into mesh with quadrant teeth.

Driven Disc and Pressure Plate

REMOVAL & INSTALLATION

1. On 1987 and newer models disconnect the negative battery cable, remove the hush panel from inside the vehicle then disconnect the clutch master cylinder push rod from the clutch pedal.

2. Remove the transaxle.

3. Mark the pressure plate assembly and the flywheel so that they can be assembled in the same position. They were balanced as an assembly at the factory.

4. Loosen the attaching bolts one turn at a time until spring tension is relieved.

5. Support the pressure plate and remove the bolts. Remove the pressure plate and clutch disc. Do not disassemble the pressure plate assembly; replace it if defective.

6. Inspect the flywheel, clutch disc, pressure plate, throwout bearing and the clutch fork and pivot shaft assembly for wear. Replace the parts as required. If the flywheel shows any signs of overheating, or if it is badly grooved or scored, it should be replaced.

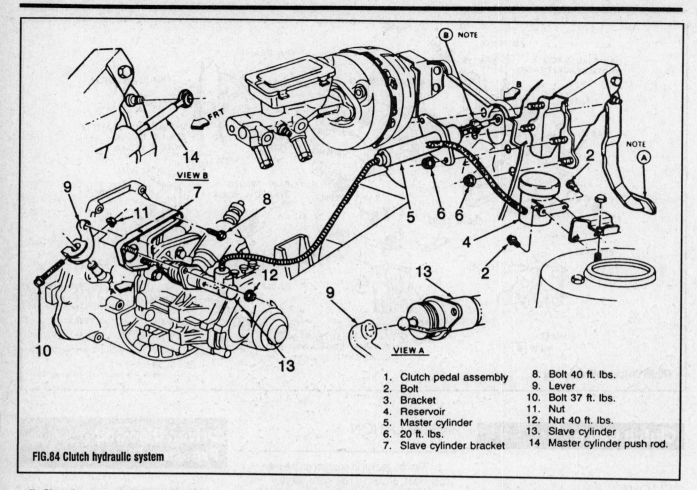

1. Clutch pedal assembly
2. Bolt
3. Bracket
4. Reservoir
5. Master cylinder
6. 20 ft. lbs.
7. Slave cylinder bracket
8. Bolt 40 ft. lbs.
9. Lever
10. Bolt 37 ft. lbs.
11. Nut
12. Nut 40 ft. lbs.
13. Slave cylinder
14 Master cylinder push rod.

FIG.84 Clutch hydraulic system

7. Clean the pressure plate and flywheel mating surfaces thoroughly. Position the clutch disc and pressure plate into the installed position, and support with a dummy shaft or clutch aligning tool. The clutch plate is assembled with the damper springs offset toward the transaxle. One side of the factory supplied clutch disc is stamped "Flywheel side".

8. Install the pressure plate-to-flywheel bolts. Tighten them gradually in a crisscross pattern.

9. Lubricate the outside groove and the inside recess of the release bearing with high temperature grease. Wipe off any excess. Install the release bearing.

10. Install the transaxle.

11. On 1987 and newer models connect the clutch master cylinder push rod to the clutch pedal and install the retaining clip.

12. On 1987 and newer models, if equipped with cruise control, check the switch adjustment at the clutch pedal bracket.

➡ When adjusting the cruise control switch, do not exert an upward force on the clutch pedal pad of more than 20 lbs. or damage to the master cylinder push rod retaining ring may result.

13. On 1987 and newer models, install the hush panel and reconnect the negative battery cable.

Clutch Master and Slave Cylinder

➡ The clutch hydraulic system is serviced as a complete unit, it has been bled of air and filled with fluid.

REMOVAL & INSTALLATION

1. Disconnect the negative battery cable.
2. Remove the hush panel from inside the vehicle.
3. Remove the clutch master cylinder retaining nuts at the front of the dash.
4. Remove the slave cylinder retaining nuts at the transaxle.
5. Remove the hydraulic system as a unit from the vehicle.

6. Install the slave cylinder to the transmission support bracket aligning the push rod into the pocket on the clutch fork outer lever. Tighten the retaining nuts evenly to prevent damage to the slave cylinder. Torque the nuts to 40 ft. lbs.

➡ Do not remove the plastic push rod retainer from the slave cylinder. The straps will break on the first clutch pedal application.

7. Position the clutch master cylinder to the front of the dash. Torque the nuts evenly to 20 ft. lbs.

8. Remove the pedal restrictor from the push rod. Lube the push rod bushing on the clutch pedal. Connect the push rod to the clutch pedal and install the retaining clip.

9. If equipped with cruise control, check the switch adjustment at the clutch pedal bracket.

➡ When adjusting the cruise control switch, do not exert an upward force on the clutch pedal pad of more than 20 lbs. or damage to the master cylinder push rod retaining ring may result.

10. Install the hush panel.

11. Press the clutch pedal down several times. This will break the plastic retaining straps on the slave cylinder push rod. Do not remove the plastic button on the end of the push rod.

12. Connect the negative battery cable.

OVERHAUL

This is a tedious, time consuming job. You can save yourself a lot of trouble by buying a rebuilt master cylinder from your dealer or parts supply house. The small difference in price between a rebuilding kit and a rebuilt part usually makes it more economical, in terms of time and work, to buy the rebuilt part.

1. Remove the master cylinder.

2. Remove the reservoir cover and drain the fluid.

3. Remove the pushrod and the rubber boot on non-power models.

4. Unbolt the proportioners and the failure warning switch from the side of the master cylinder body. Discard the O-rings found under the proportioners. Use new ones on installation. There may or may not be an O-ring under the original equipment failure warning switch. If there is, discard it. In either case, use a new O-ring upon assembly.

5. Clamp the master cylinder body in a vise, taking care not to crush it. Depress the primary piston with a wooden dowel and remove the lock ring with a pair of snaping pliers.

6. The primary and secondary pistons can be removed by applying compressed air into one of the outlets at the end of the cylinder and plugging the other three outlets. The primary piston must be replaced as an assembly if the seals are bad. The secondary piston seals are replaceable. Install these new seals with the lips facing outwards.

7. Inspect the bore for corrosion. If any corrosion is evident, the master cylinder body must be replaced. Do not attempt to polish the bore with crocus cloth, sandpaper or anything else. The body is aluminum; polishing the bore won't work.

8. To remove the failure warning switch piston assembly, remove the allen head plug from the end of the bore and withdraw the

assembly with a pair of needlenosed pliers. The switch piston assembly seals are replaceable.

9. The reservoir can be removed from the master cylinder if necessary. Clamp the body in a vise by its mounting flange. Use a pry bar to remove the reservoir. If the reservoir is removed, remove the reservoir grommets and discard them. The quick take-up valves under the grommets are accessible after the retaining snaprings are removed. Use snapring pliers; no other tool will work.

10. Clean all parts in denatured alcohol and allow to air dry. Do not use anything else to clean and do not wipe dry with a rag, which will leaves bits of lint behind. Inspect all parts for corrosion or wear. Generally, it is best to replace all rubber parts whenever the master cylinder is disassembled and replace any metal part which shows any sign of wear or corrosion.

11. Lubricate all parts with fresh brake fluid before assembly.

12. Install the quick take-up valves into the master cylinder body and secure with the snaprings. Make sure the snaprings are properly seated in their grooves. Lubricate the new reservoir grommets with fresh brake fluid and press them into the master cylinder.

13. Install the reservoir into the grommets by placing the reservoir on its lid and pressing the master cylinder body down onto it with a rocking motion.

14. Lubricate the switch piston assembly. Install new O-rings and retainers on the piston. Install the piston assembly into the master cylinder and secure with the plug, using a new O-ring on the plug. Torque is 40–140 inch lbs. (5–16 Nm.).

15. Assemble the new secondary piston seals onto the piston. Lubricate the parts, then install the spring, spring retainer and secondary piston into the cylinder. Install the primary piston, depress and install the lock ring.

16. Install new O-rings on the proportioners and the failure warning switch. Install the proportioners and torque to 18–30 ft. lbs. (25–40 Nm.). Install the failure warning switch and torque to 15–50 inch lbs. (2–6 Nm.).

17. Clamp the master cylinder body upright into a vise by one of the mounting flanges. Fill the reservoir with fresh fluid. Pump the piston

with a dowel until fluid squirts from the outlet ports. Continue pumping until the expelled fluid is free of air bubbles.

18. Install the master cylinder and bleed the clutch. Check the clutch system for proper operation.

BLEEDING THE HYDRAULIC CLUTCH SYSTEM

Bleeding air from the system is necessary any time part of the system has been disconnected, or the fluid level in the reservoir has been allowed to fall so low that air has been drawn into the master cylinder.

✳✳ CAUTION

Never under any circumstance use fluid that has been bled from the system as it could be contaminated with air or moisture.

1. Clean the cap then remove the cap and diaphragm and fill the reservoir to the top with certified DOT 3 brake fluid.

2. Fully loosen the bleed screw which is in the slave cylinder body next to the inlet connection. Fluid will now begin to move from the master cylinder down the tube to the slave. It is important that for efficient gravity fill, the reservoir must be filled at all times.

3. At this point bubbles will be noticeable at the bleed screw outlet showing air is being expelled. When the slave is full, a steady stream of fluid will come from the slave outlet. At this point, tighten the bleed screw.

4. Install the diaphragm and cap to the reservoir. The fluid in the reservoir should be level with the step.

5. The hydraulic system should now be fully bled and should release the clutch. Check the vehicle by starting, then push the clutch pedal to the floor and selecting reverse gear. There should be no grinding of gears, if there is, the hydraulic system still contains air. If so, bleed the system again.

AUTOMATIC TRANSAXLE

Understanding Automatic Transmissions

The automatic transmission allows engine torque and power to be transmitted to the rear wheels within a narrow range of engine operating speeds. The transmission will allow the engine to turn fast enough to produce plenty of power and torque at very low speeds, while keeping it at a sensible rpm at high vehicle speeds. The transmission performs this job entirely without driver assistance. The transmission uses a light fluid as the medium for the transmission of power. This fluid also works in the operation of various hydraulic control circuits and as a lubricant. Because the transmission fluid performs all of these three functions, trouble within the unit can easily travel from one part to another. For this reason, and because of the complexity and unusual operating principles of the transmission, a very sound understanding of the basic principles of operation will simplify troubleshooting.

THE TORQUE CONVERTER

The torque converter replaces the conventional clutch. It has three functions:

1. It allows the engine to idle with the vehicle at a standstill, even with the transmission in gear.

2. It allows the transmission to shift from range to range smoothly, without requiring that the driver close the throttle during the shift.

3. It multiplies engine torque to an increasing extent as vehicle speed drops and throttle opening is increased. This has the effect of making the transmission more responsive and reduces the amount of shifting required.

The torque converter is a metal case which is shaped like a sphere that has been flattened on opposite sides. It is bolted to the rear end of the engine's crankshaft. Generally, the entire metal case rotates at engine speed and serves as the engine's flywheel.

The case contains three sets of blades. One set is attached directly to the case. This set forms the torus or pump. Another set is directly connected to the output shaft, and forms the turbine. The third set is mounted on a hub which, in turn, is mounted on a stationary shaft through

a one-way clutch. This third set is known as the stator.

A pump, which is driven by the converter hub at engine speed, keeps the torque converter full of transmission fluid at all times. Fluid flows continuously through the unit to provide cooling.

Under low speed acceleration, the torque converter functions as follows:

The torus is turning faster than the turbine. It picks up fluid at the center of the converter and, through centrifugal force, slings it outward. Since the outer edge of the converter moves faster than the portions at the center, the fluid picks up speed.

The fluid then enters the outer edge of the turbine blades. It then travels back toward the center of the converter case along the turbine blades. In impinging upon the turbine blades, the fluid loses the energy picked up in the torus.

If the fluid were now to immediately be returned directly into the torus, both halves of the converter would have to turn at approximately the same speed at all times, and torque input and output would both be the same.

In flowing through the torus and turbine, the fluid picks up two types of flow, or flow in two separate directions. It flows through the turbine blades, and it spins with the engine. The stator, whose blades are stationary when the vehicle is being accelerated at low speeds, converts one type of flow into another. Instead of allowing the fluid to flow straight back into the torus, the stator's curved blades turn the fluid almost 90° toward the direction of rotation of the engine. Thus the fluid does not flow as fast toward the torus, but is already spinning when the torus picks it up. This has the effect of allowing the torus to turn much faster than the turbine. This difference in speed may be compared to the difference in speed between the smaller and larger gears in any gear train. The result is that engine power output is higher, and engine torque is multiplied.

As the speed of the turbine increases, the fluid spins faster and faster in the direction of engine rotation. As a result, the ability of the stator to redirect the fluid flow is reduced. Under cruising conditions, the stator is eventually forced to rotate on its one-way clutch in the direction of engine rotation. Under these conditions, the torque converter begins to behave almost like a solid shaft, with the torus and turbine speeds being almost equal.

THE PLANETARY GEARBOX

The ability of the torque converter to multiply engine torque is limited. Also, the unit tends to be more efficient when the turbine is rotating at relatively high speeds. Therefore, a planetary gearbox is used to carry the power output of the turbine to the driveshaft.

Planetary gears function very similarly to conventional transmission gears. However, their construction is different in that three elements make up one gear system, and, in that all three elements are different from one another. The three elements are: an outer gear that is shaped like a hoop, with teeth cut into the inner surface; a sun gear, mounted on a shaft and located at the very center of the outer gear; and a set of three planet gears, held by pins in a ring-like planet carrier, meshing with both the sun gear and the outer gear. Either the outer gear or the sun gear may be held stationary, providing more than one possible torque multiplication factor for each set of gears. Also, if all three gears are forced to rotate at the same speed, the gearset forms, in effect, a solid shaft.

Most modern automatics use the planetary gears to provide either a single reduction ratio of about 1.8:1, or two reduction gears: a low of about 2.5:1, and an intermediate of about 1.5:1. Bands and clutches are used to hold various portions of the gearsets to the transmission case or to the shaft on which they are mounted. Shifting is accomplished, then, by changing the portion of each planetary gearset which is held to the transmission case or to the shaft.

THE SERVOS AND ACCUMULATORS

The servos are hydraulic pistons and cylinders. They resemble the hydraulic actuators used on many familiar machines, such as bulldozers. Hydraulic fluid enters the cylinder, under pressure, and forces the piston to move to engage the band or clutches.

The accumulators are used to cushion the engagement of the servos. The transmission fluid must pass through the accumulator on the way to the servo. The accumulator housing contains a thin piston which is sprung away from the discharge passage of the accumulator. When fluid passes through the accumulator on the way to the servo, it must move the piston against

spring pressure, and this action smooths out the action of the servo.

THE HYDRAULIC CONTROL SYSTEM

The hydraulic pressure used to operate the servos comes from the main transmission oil pump. This fluid is channeled to the various servos through the shift valves. There is generally a manual shift valve which is operated by the transmission selector lever and an automatic shift valve for each automatic upshift the transmission provides: i.e., 2-speed automatics have a low/high shift valve, while 3-speeds have a 1–2 valve, and a 2–3 valve.

There are two pressures which effect the operation of these valves. One is the governor pressure which is affected by vehicle speed. The other is the modulator pressure which is affected by intake manifold vacuum or throttle position. Governor pressure rises with an increase in vehicle speed, and modulator pressure rises as the throttle is opened wider. By responding to these two pressures, the shift valves cause the upshift points to be delayed with increased throttle opening to make the best use of the engine's power output.

Most transmissions also make use of an auxiliary circuit for downshifting. This circuit may be actuated by the throttle linkage or the vacuum line which actuates the modulator, or by a cable or solenoid. It applies pressure to a special downshift surface on the shift valve or valves.

The transmission modulator also governs the line pressure, used to actuate the servos. In this way, the clutches and bands will be actuated with a force matching the torque output of the engine.

Identification

All models use a 125C or 440-T4 automatic transmission. The 125C is equipped with a torque converter clutch (TCC) which under certain conditions mechanically couples the engine to the transaxle for greater power transfer efficiency and increased fuel mileage. The 440-T4 provides an overdrive feature, for greater fuel efficiency. A cable operated throttle valve linkage is used. Automatic transaxle operation is provided through a conventional three element torque converter, a compound planetary gear set, and a dual sprocket and drive link assembly.

No overhaul procedures are given in this book because of the complexity of the transaxle. Transaxle removal and installation, adjustment, and halfshaft removal, installation, and overhaul procedures are covered.

Pan and Filter

REMOVAL & INSTALLATION

1. Raise and support the vehicle on jackstands.
2. Loosen the pan bolts and drain the fluid.
3. Remove the pan and the filter.
4. Clean the gasket mounting surfaces.
5. To install, use a new gasket and filter, then reverse the removal procedures. Refill the transaxle. Torque the pan bolts to 10 ft. lbs.

Adjustments

The only adjustment required on the 125C transaxle is the shift linkage (cable) adjustment. The neutral start switch and throttle valve are self-adjusting. The transaxle has only one band, with no provision for periodic adjustment. Pan removal, fluid and filter changes are covered in Section 1.

T.V. CABLE

1. Depress and hold down the metal adjustment tab at the engine end of the TV cable.

2. Move the slider up until it stops against the fitting.
3. Release the adjusting tab.

SHIFT LINKAGE

1. Place the shift lever into Neutral.
2. Disconnect the shift cable from the transaxle lever. Place the transaxle lever in Neutral, by moving the lever clockwise to the Low (L) detent, then counterclockwise through the Second (S) and Drive (D) detents to the Neutral detent.
3. Attach and torque the shift cable to the pin on the transaxle lever. Check the shift operation.

❋❋ CAUTION

Any inaccuracies in shift linkage adjustments may result in premature failure of the transmission due to operation without the controls in full detent. Such operation results in reduced fluid pressure and in turn, partial engagement of the affected clutches. Partial engagement of the clutches, with sufficient pressure to permit apparently normal vehicle operation will result in failure of the clutches and/or other internal parts after only a few miles of operation.

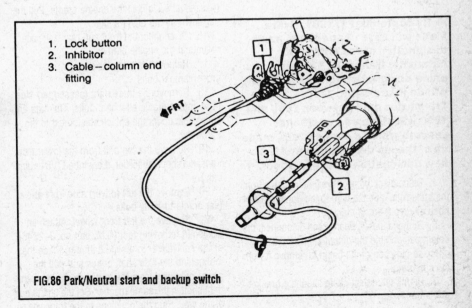

1. Lock button
2. Inhibitor
3. Cable—column end fitting

FIG.86 Park/Neutral start and backup switch

Neutral Safety/Back-Up Light Switch

REMOVAL & INSTALLATION

1. Remove the shifter knob from the shifter by removing the retaining screw at the back of the knob.

2. Remove the screws at the sides and front of the console.

3. Open the console box and remove the retaining screw inside the box.

4. Remove the ashtray at the rear of the console and remove the retaining screw behind the ashtray.

5. Slide the console rearward slightly, then lift it over the shifter.

6. Disconnect the wiring harness at the back-up light switch.

7. Remove the switch from the base of the shifter.

8. Reverse steps 1 through 7 to install the switch.

Transaxle

REMOVAL & INSTALLATION

125C

➡ **By September 1, 1991, Hydra-Matic will have changed the name designation of the THM 125C automatic transaxle. The new name designation for this transaxle will be Hydra-Matic 3T40. Transaxles built between 1989 and 1990 will serve as transitional years in which a dual system, made up of the old designation and the new designation will be in effect.**

1. Disconnect the negative battery cable from the transaxle. Tape the wire to the upper radiator hose to keep it out of the way.

2. Remove the air cleaner and disconnect the detent cable. Slide the detent cable in the opposite direction of the cable to remove it from the carburetor.

3. Unbolt the detent cable attaching bracket at the transaxle.

4. Pull up on the detent cable cover at the transaxle until the cable is exposed. Disconnect the cable from the rod.

5. Remove the two transaxle strut bracket bolts at the transaxle, if equipped.

6. Remove all the engine-to-transaxle bolts except the one near the starter. The one nearest the firewall is installed from the engine side; you will need a short handled box wrench or ratchet to reach it.

7. Loosen, but do not remove the engine-to-transaxle bolt near the starter.

8. Disconnect the speedometer cable at the upper and lower coupling. On cars with cruise control, remove the speedometer cable at the transducer.

9. Remove the retaining clip and washer from the shift linkage at the transaxle. Remove the two shift linkage at the transaxle. Remove the two shift linkage bracket bolts.

10. Disconnect and plug the two fluid cooler lines at the transaxle. These are inch-size fittings; use a back-up wrench to avoid twisting the lines.

11. Install an engine holding chain or hoist. Raise the engine enough to take its weight off the mounts.

12. Unlock the steering column and raise the car.

13. Remove the two nuts holding the anti-sway (stabilizer) bar to the left lower control arm (driver's side).

14. Remove the four bolts attaching the covering plate over the stabilizer bar to the engine cradle on the left side (driver's side).

15. Loosen but do not remove the four bolts holding the stabilizer bar bracket to the right side (passenger's side) of the engine cradle. Pull the bar down on the driver's side.

16. Disconnect the front and rear transaxle mounts at the engine cradle.

17. Remove the two rear center crossmember bolts.

18. Remove the three right (passenger) side front engine cradle attaching bolts. The nuts are accessible under the splash shield next to the frame rail.

19. Remove the top bolt from the lower front transaxle shock absorber, if equipped (V6 engine only).

20. Remove the left (driver) side front and rear cradle-to-body bolts.

21. Remove the left front wheel. Attach an axle shaft removing tool (G.M. part no. J–28468 or the equivalent) to a slide hammer. Place the tool behind the axle shaft cones and pull the cones out away from the transaxle. Remove the right shaft in the same manner. Set the shafts out of the way. Plug the openings in the transaxle to prevent fluid leakage and the entry of dirt.

22. Swing the partial engine cradle to the left (driver) side and wire it out of the way outboard of the fender well.

23. Remove the four torque converter and starter shield bolts. Remove the two transaxle extension bolts from the engine-to-transaxle bracket.

24. Attach a transaxle jack to the case.

25. Use a felt pen to matchmark the torque converter and flywheel. Remove the three torque converter-to-flywheel bolts.

26. Remove the transaxle-to-engine bolt near the starter. Remove the transaxle by sliding it to the left, away from the engine.

27. To install, place the transaxle on a jack and raise it into the vehicle. As the transaxle is installed, slide the right axle shaft into the case.

28. Align the matchmarks and connect the torque converter to the flywheel. Install the transaxle-to-engine bolt near the starter.

29. Install the engine-to-transaxle bracket extension bolts. Install the torque converter and starter shield bolts.

30. Install the partial engine cradle.

31. Install the left axle shaft.

32. Install the drivers side front and rear cradle to body bolts.

33. Install the top bolt tr the lower front transaxle shock absorber, if equipped (V6 engine only).

34. Install the three right (passenger) side front engine cradle attaching bolts.

35. Install the two rear center crossmember bolts.

36. Connect the front and rear transaxle mounts at the engine cradle.

37. Install the stabilizer bar. Tighten the four bolts holding the stabilizer bar bracket to the right side (passenger's side) of the engine cradle.

➡ **To aid in stabilizer bar installation, a pry hole has been provided in the engine cradle.**

38. Install the four bolts attaching the covering plate over the stabilizer bar to the engine cradle on the left side (driver's side).

39. Install the two nuts holding the anti-sway (stabilizer) bar to the left lower control arm (driver's side).

40. Lower the vehicle and remove the engine support device.

41. Connect the two fluid cooler lines at the transaxle.

42. Install the two shift linkage bracket bolts.

43. Connect the two shift linkages at the transaxle and install the retaining clips and washers.

44. Connect the speedometer cable at the upper and lower coupling. On cars with cruise control, connect the speedometer cable at the transducer.

45. Tighten the engine-to-transaxle bolt near the starter.

46. Install all remaining engine-to-transaxle bolts. The one nearest the firewall is installed from the engine side; you will need a short handled box wrench or ratchet to reach it.

47. Install the two transaxle strut bracket bolts at the transaxle, if equipped.

48. Install the detent cable and air cleaner.

49. Connect the negative battery cable to the transaxle.

440-T4

➡ **By September 1, 1991, Hydra-Matic will have changed the name designation of the THM 440-T4 automatic transaxle. The new name designation for this transaxle will be Hydra-Matic 4T60. Transaxles built between 1989 and 1990 will serve as transitional years in which a dual system, made up of the old designation and the new designation will be in effect.**

1. Disconnect the negative battery cable.

2. Remove the air cleaner and disconnect the TV cable at the throttle body.

3. Disconnect the shift linkage at the transaxle.

4. Remove the engine support fixture tool J–28467 or equivalent.

5. Disconnect all electrical connectors.

6. Remove the 3 bolts from the transaxle to the engine.

7. Disconnect the vacuum line at the modulator.

8. Raise and safely support the vehicle.

9. Remove the left front wheel and tire assembly.

10. Remove the left side ball joint from the steering knuckle.

11. Disconnect the brake line bracket at the strut.

➡ **A halfshaft seal protector tool J–34754 should be modified and installed on any halfshaft prior to service procedures on or near the halfshaft. Failure to do so could result in seal damage or joint failure.**

12. Remove the halfshafts from the transaxle.

13. Disconnect the pinch bolt at the intermediate steering shaft. Failure to do so could cause damage to the steering gear.

14. Remove the frame to stabilizer bolts.

15. Remove the stabilizer bolts at the control arm.

16. Remove the left front frame assembly.

17. Disconnect the speedometer cable or wire connector from the transaxle.

18. Remove the extension housing to engine block support bracket.

19. Disconnect the cooler pipes.

20. Remove the converter cover and converter-to-flywheel bolts.

21. Remove all of the remaining transaxle-to-engine bolts except one.

22. Position a jack under the transaxle.

23. Remove the remaining transaxle-to-engine bolt and remove the transaxle.

To install:

24. Install the transaxle in the vehicle. Install the engine-to-transaxle bolt accessible from under the vehicle. Tighten to 55 ft. lbs. (75 Nm).

25. Install all of the remaining transaxle-to-engine bolts. Tighten to 55 ft. lbs. (75 Nm).

26. Remove the jack.

27. Install the converter-to-flywheel bolts and the converter cover.

28. Connect the cooler pipes.

29. Install the extension housing to engine block support bracket.

30. Connect the speedometer cable or wire connector to the transaxle.

31. Install the left front frame assembly.

32. Install the stabilizer bolts at the control arm.

33. Install the frame-to-stabilizer bolts.

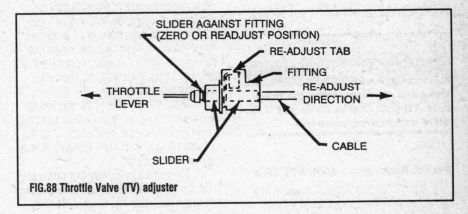

FIG.88 Throttle Valve (TV) adjuster

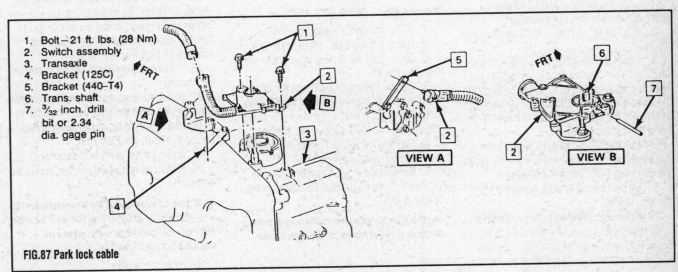

1. Bolt – 21 ft. lbs. (28 Nm)
2. Switch assembly
3. Transaxle
4. Bracket (125C)
5. Bracket (440–T4)
6. Trans. shaft
7. $^{3}/_{32}$ inch drill bit or 2.34 dia. gage pin

FIG.87 Park lock cable

34. Connect the pinch bolt at the intermediate steering shaft.

35. Install the halfshafts to the transaxle.

36. Connect the brake line bracket at the strut.

37. Install the left side ball joint to the steering knuckle.

38. Install the left front wheel and tire assembly.

39. Lower the vehicle.

40. Connect the vacuum line at the modulator.

41. Install the 3 bolts from the transaxle to the engine.

42. Connect all electrical connectors.

43. Remove the engine support tool.

44. Connect the shift linkage to the transaxle.

45. Connect the TV cable at the throttle body and adjust as necessary. Install the air cleaner.

46. Connect the negative battery cable.

Halfshafts

♦ SEE FIG. 75

REMOVAL & INSTALLATION

❊❊ CAUTION

Use care when removing the drive axle. Tri-pots can be damaged if the drive axle is over-extended.

Except Rear Axle – 6000 STE AWD

1. Remove the hub nut and discard. A new hub nut must be used for reassembly.

2. Raise and safely support the vehicle. Remove the wheel and tire assembly.

3. Install an halfshaft boot seal protector onto the seal.

4. Disconnect the brake hose clip from the Mcpherson strut but do not disconnect the hose from the caliper. Remove the brake caliper from the spindle and support the caliper with a length of wire. Do not allow the caliper to hang by the brake hose unsupported.

5. Mark the camber alignment cam bolt for reassembly. Remove the cam bolt and the upper attaching bolt from the strut and spindle.

6. Pull the steering knuckle assembly from the strut bracket.

7. Remove the halfshaft from the transaxle.

8. Using spindle remover tool J–28733 or equivalent, remove the halfshaft from the hub and bearing assembly. Do not allow the halfshaft

to hang unsupported. If necessary, support using a length of wire in order to prevent component damage.

To install:

9. If a new halfshaft is to be installed, a new knuckle seal should be installed first along with a boot seal protector when necessary.

10. Loosely install the halfshaft into the transaxle and steering knuckle.

11. Loosely attach the steering knuckle to the suspension strut.

12. The halfshaft is an interference fit in the steering knuckle. Press the axle into place, then install the hub nut. When the shaft begins to turn with the hub, insert a drift through the caliper into one of the cooling slots in the rotor to keep it from turning.

➡ **On some vehicles, the hub flange has a notch in it which can be used to prevent the hub and the shaft from turning, when one of the hub bearing retainer bolts is removed, by placing a longer bolt put in its place through the notch**

13. Tighten the hub nut to 70 ft. lbs. (95 Nm) to completely seat the shaft.

14. Install the brake caliper. Tighten the caliper mounting bolts to 30 ft. lbs. (41 Nm).

15. Load the hub assembly by lowering it onto a jackstand. Align the camber cam bolt marks made during removal, install the bolt and tighten to 140 ft. lbs. (190 Nm). Tighten the upper nut to the same value.

16. Install the halfshaft all the way into the transaxle using a suitable tool inserted into the groove provided on the inner retainer. Tap the tool until the shaft seats in the transaxle. Remove the boot seal protector.

17. Connect the brake hose clip the the strut. Install the tire and wheel, lower the vehicle and tighten the hub nut to 192 ft. lbs. (261 Nm).

Rear Axle – 6000 STE AWD

1. Raise and safely support the vehicle.

2. Remove the tire and wheel assembly.

3. Disconnect the parking brake cable end from the bracket.

4. Insert a suitable tool through the caliper into the rotor to prevent the rotor from turning.

5. Remove the shaft nut and washer using special tool J–34826. Discard the shaft nut.

6. Remove the anti-lock brake sensor bolt and move the sensor aside.

7. Remove the 2 brake caliper bolts and remove the caliper. Support the caliper using a length of wire.

➡ **Do not allow the caliper to hang by the brake hose unsupported.**

8. Remove the rotor from the hub and bearing assembly.

9. Install leaf spring compression tool J–33432 or equivalent.

10. Remove the 3 bolts mounting the hub and bearing to the knuckle.

11. Remove the hub and bearing assembly from the knuckle using special tool J–28733–A or equivalent.

12. Remove the bolts and nut plate attaching the lower strut mount to the knuckle. Scribe the position of the upper bolt prior removing.

13. Install a suitable CV-boot protector to prevent damage to the boot.

14. Swing the knuckle downward and away from the driveshaft.

15. Remove the drive axle from the differential using a suitable slide hammer.

To install:

16. Install the drive axle to the differential. Ensure positive engagement by pulling outward on the inner axle end. Grasp the housing only. Do not grasp and pull on the axle shaft.

17. Swing the knuckle up to the lower strut mount.

18. Position the nut plate and install the lower strut mount bolts to the knuckle. Align the top bolt with scribe marks before tightening the bolts. Tighten the bolts to 148 ft. lbs. (200 Nm).

19. Remove the CV boot protector.

20. Install the hub and bearing assembly to the knuckle and axle spline.

21. Install the hub and bearing attaching bolts. Tighten to 61 ft. lbs. (84 Nm).

22. Remove the leaf spring compression tool.

23. Install the rotor to hub and bearing assembly.

24. Install the brake caliper to the rotor and install the retaining bolts. Tighten the bolts to 38 ft. lbs. (51 Nm).

25. Install the anti-lock brake sensor to the knuckle and install the retaining bolt. Using a non-ferrous feeler gauge, adjust the sensor gap to 0.028 in. (0.7mm). Tighten the adjustment screw to 19 inch lbs. (2.2 Nm).

26. Connect the parking brake cable end into the bracket.

27. Install the shaft washer and new torque prevailing nut. Hold the rotor with a suitable to prevent the axle from turning while tightening. Tighten to 185 ft. lbs. (260 Nm).

28. Install the tire and wheel assembly.

29. Check the rear wheel camber. Adjust as necessary.

➡ **If the lower strut to knuckle bolts are properly aligned with the scribe marks, no camber adjustment should be necessary.**

30. Lower the vehicle.

OVERHAUL

Inner And Outer Boots

OUTER BOOT

1. Raise and support the vehicle safely.
2. Remove the front tire and wheel.
3. Remove the caliper bolts and wire the caliper off to the side.
4. Remove the hub nut, washer and wheel bearing.
5. Using a brass drift, lightly tap around the seal retainer to loosen it. Remove the seal retainer.
6. Remove the seal retaining clamp or ring and discard.
7. Using snapring pliers, remove the race retaining ring from the axle shaft.
8. Pull the outer joint assembly and the outboard seal away from the axle shaft.
9. Installation is the reverse of the removal procedure. Pack the joint assembly with half of the grease provided. Put the remainder of the grease in the seal.

INNER BOOT

1. Raise and support the vehicle safely.
2. Remove the front tire and wheel.
3. Remove the caliper bolts and wire the caliper off to the side of the vehicle.
4. Remove the hub nut, washer and wheel bearing.
5. Remove the front drive axle as outlined earlier in this section: Place in a suitable holding fixture being careful not place undue pressure on the axle shaft.
6. Remove the joint assembly retaining ring. Remove the joint assembly.

7. Remove the race retaining ring and remove the seal retainer.
8. Remove the inner seal retaining clamp. Remove the inner joint seal.
9. Installation is the reverse of the removal procedure. Pack the joint assembly with half of the grease provided. Place remainder of the grease in the seal.

Driveshaft

The procedure for replacing the driveshaft on the Pontiac 6000 AWD is covered in detail under Automatic Transaxle Driveshaft removal and installation.

REMOVAL & INSTALLATION

6000 SE AWD

ORIGINAL DRIVESHAFT

1. Raise and safely support the vehicle.

➡ **The relationship between the center bearing support and the floor pan must be maintained. Established at the assembly plant, the relationship has an influence on the front joint stoke capacity and remains constant for the vehicle, regardless of the driveshaft installed.**

2. Scribe the transmission output shaft flange opposite the "painted" marking on the front driveshaft. The rear pinion flange must be scribed opposite the "painted" marking on the rear driveshaft. Scribe the center support

mounting plate to floor pan of the vehicle.

3. Remove the 4 bolts connecting the rear driveshaft to the rear axle pinion flange.

➡ **Do not loosen, remove or disconnect the 4 bolts adjacent to the center double cardan joint. Disturbing these fasteners may result in a vibration.**

4. With the aid of an assistant, support the driveshaft while performing the following:
   a. Remove the 3 nuts retaining the center bearing support to the underbody of the vehicle.
   b. Remove the 4 bolts connecting the front driveshaft to the transaxle output shaft flange.
   c. Remove the driveshaft from the vehicle.

To install:

5. With the aid of an assistant, perform the following:
   a. Install the driveshaft to the vehicle.
   b. Align the rear driveshaft flange to the rear axle pinion flange, aligning the scribe marks.

➡ **The center mount plate must be reinstalled at the scribed position so that the front CV joint is correctly located within its travel limits.**

   c. Loosely install the nuts to the center bearing support and bolts to the rear axle pinion flange. Tighten the rear driveshaft flange to the rear axle pinion flange bolts to 40 ft. lbs. (54 Nm).
   d. Install the bolts to the front driveshaft-to-transmission output flange, using the reference marks to align the front flange

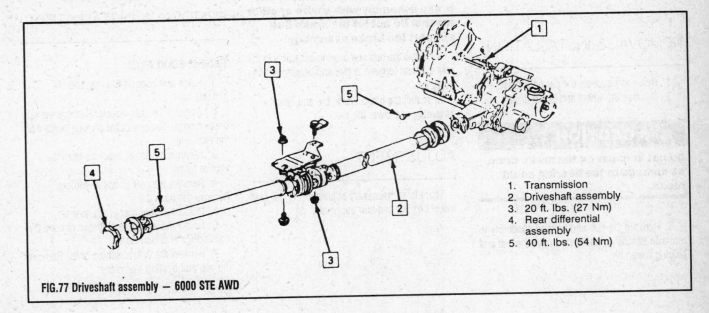

1. Transmission
2. Driveshaft assembly
3. 20 ft. lbs. (27 Nm)
4. Rear differential assembly
5. 40 ft. lbs. (54 Nm)

FIG.77 Driveshaft assembly — 6000 STE AWD

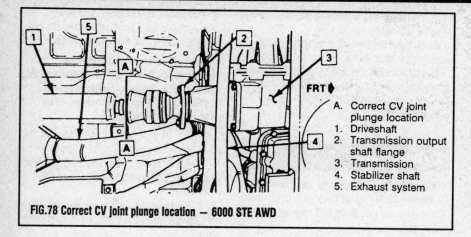

A. Correct CV joint plunge location
1. Driveshaft
2. Transmission output shaft flange
3. Transmission
4. Stabilizer shaft
5. Exhaust system

FRT↑

FIG.78 Correct CV joint plunge location — 6000 STE AWD

position and center bracket location. Tighten the center bearing support bolts using the scribed reference marks to 25 ft. lbs. (34 Nm); nuts to 20 ft. lbs. (27 Nm). Tighten the front propeller shaft-to-transmission output flange bolts to 40 ft. lbs. (54 Nm).

6. Remove the support and lower the vehicle.

NEW DRIVESHAFT

1. Remove the original driveshaft from the vehicle.

To Install:

2. Using a dial indicator, measure and mark the bolt hole corresponding to the high point of radial runout on both the transmission output flange and rear axle pinion flange.

3. Transfer the center bearing bracket from the old driveshaft to the new driveshaft assembly.

4. With the aid of an assistant, perform the following:

a. Install the driveshaft to the vehicle.

b. Align the point marks supplied on the flanges of the propeller shaft to the scribe marks made during removal.

c. Loosely install the nuts to the center bearing support and bolts to the rear axle pinion flange. Tighten the rear driveshaft flange to the rear axle pinion flange bolts to 40 ft. lbs. (54 Nm).

d. Push the propeller shaft forward until a click is heard. Temporarily install a 23mm thick spacer between the output flange and the front driveshaft flange. Clamp in this position.

5. Install the remaining center bracket nuts. Tighten to 20 ft. lbs. (27 Nm).

6. Remove the spacer, extend the front CV joint to meet the output flange and tighten the bolts. Tighten the front propeller shaft-to-transmission output flange bolts to 40 ft. lbs. (54 Nm).

7. Verify correct location of the front CV joint plunge.

8. Remove the supports. Lower the vehicle.

REAR AXLE

Hub and Bearing Assembly

REMOVAL & INSTALLATION

1. Raise and support the car on a hoist.
2. Remove the wheel and brake drum.

✳✳ CAUTION

Do not hammer on the brake drum as damage to the bearing could result.

3. Remove the hub and bearing assembly to rear axle attaching bolts and remove the hub and bearing assembly.

➡ **The bolts which attach the hub and bearing assembly also support the brake assembly. When removing these bolts, support the brake assembly with a wire or other means. Do not let the brake line support the brake assembly.**

4. Install the hub and bearing assembly to the rear axle and torque the hub and bearing bolts to 45 ft. lbs.

5. Install the brake drum, tire and wheel assembly and lower the car.

ADJUSTMENT

There is no necessary adjustment to the rear wheel bearing and hub assembly.

Axle Housing

REMOVAL & INSTALLATION

Except 6000 AWD

1. Raise and support the rear end on jackstands.

2. Remove the rear wheels. Remove the rear brake drums. Disconnect the parking brake from the rear axle.

3. Remove the brake brackets from the vehicle frame.

4. Remove the rear shock absorbers. Remove the track bar.

5. Disconnect the rear brake hoses.

6. Lower the axle assembly and remove the coil springs and insulators.

7. Remove the hub attaching bolts. Remove the hub and bearing assembly.

8. Remove the control arm bracket attaching bolts. Remove the control arms. Lower the axle from the vehicle.

9. To install:

10. Install the control arms and bracket bolts.

11. Install the hub and bearing assemblies and bracket bolts.

12. Install the coil springs and insulators.

13. Raise the axle into the vehicle.

14. Connect the rear brake hoses.

15. Install the shock absorbers and track bar.

16. Install the brake brackets to the vehicle frame.

17. Connect the parking brake, install the brake drums and rear wheels.

18. Remove the safety stands and lower the vehicle.

Rear Axle — 6000 STE AWD

1. Raise and safely support the vehicle.

2. Remove the tire and wheel assembly.

3. Disconnect the parking brake cable end from the bracket.

4. Insert a suitable tool through the caliper into the rotor to prevent the rotor from turning.

5. Remove the shaft nut and washer using special tool J–34826. 8. Discard the shaft nut.

6. Remove the anti-lock brake sensor bolt and move the sensor aside.

7. Remove the 2 brake caliper bolts and remove the caliper. Support the caliper using a length of wire.

➡ **Do not allow the caliper to hang by the brake hose unsupported.**

8. Remove the rotor from the hub and bearing assembly.

9. Install leaf spring compression tool J–33432 or equivalent.

10. Remove the 3 bolts mounting the hub and bearing to the knuckle.

11. Remove the hub and bearing assembly from the knuckle using special tool J–28733–A or equivalent.

12. Remove the bolts and nut plate attaching the lower strut mount to the knuckle. Scribe the position of the upper bolt prior removing.

13. Install a suitable CV-boot protector to prevent damage to the boot.

14. Swing the knuckle downward and away from the driveshaft.

15. Remove the drive axle from the differential using a suitable slide hammer.

To install:

16. Install the drive axle to the differential. Ensure positive engagement by pulling outward on the inner axle end. Grasp the housing only. Do not grasp and pull on the axle shaft.

17. Swing the knuckle up to the lower strut mount.

18. Position the nut plate and install the lower strut mount bolts to the knuckle. Align the top bolt with scribe marks before tightening the bolts. Tighten the bolts to 148 ft. lbs. (200 Nm).

19. Remove the CV boot protector.

20. Install the hub and bearing assembly to the knuckle and axle spline.

21. Install the hub and bearing attaching bolts. Tighten to 61 ft. lbs. (84 Nm).

22. Remove the leaf spring compression tool.

23. Install the rotor to hub and bearing assembly.

24. Install the brake caliper to the rotor and install the retaining bolts. Tighten the bolts to 38 ft. lbs. (51 Nm).

25. Install the anti-lock brake sensor to the knuckle and install the retaining bolt. Using a non-ferrous feeler gauge, adjust the sensor gap to 0.028 in. (0.7mm). Tighten the adjustment screw to 19 inch lbs. (2.2 Nm).

26. Connect the parking brake cable end into the bracket.

27. Install the shaft washer and new torque prevailing nut. Hold the rotor with a suitable to prevent the axle from turning while tightening. Tighten to 185 ft. lbs. (260 Nm).

28. Install the tire and wheel assembly.

29. Check the rear wheel camber. Adjust as necessary.

➡ **If the lower strut to knuckle bolts are properly aligned with the scribe marks, no camber adjustment should be necessary.**

30. Lower the vehicle.

Differential Carrier

REMOVAL & INSTALLATION

6000 SE AWD

1. Disconnect the negative battery cable.

2. Disconnect the air pressure from the Electronic Level Control (ELC) system.

3. Raise and safely support the vehicle.

4. Drain the lubricant from the differential carrier housing.

5. Remove the tire and wheel assemblies.

➡ **Mark the relationship of the driveshaft to the rear axle pinion flange prior to removal of the driveshaft from the rear axle pinion flange to ensure proper driveshaft alignment.**

6. Disconnect the rear driveshaft at the rear axle pinion flange.

7. Remove the rear axle assembly.

8. Remove the rear axle shafts.

9. Disconnect the rear axle remote vent hose.

10. Remove the 3 bolts attaching the differential carrier assembly to the rear axle assembly.

11. Remove the differential carrier assembly from the rear axle assembly.

To install:

12. Position the differential carrier in the rear axle assembly.

13. Install the 3 differential carrier retaining bolts. Tighten to 60 ft. lbs. (82 Nm).

14. Connect the rear axle remote vent hose and clamp.

15. Install the rear axle shafts.

16. Install the rear axle assembly in the vehicle.

➡ **The driveshaft must be installed using the reference mark made during removal of the driveshaft.**

17. Connect the rear driveshaft to the rear axle pinion flange.

18. Install the tire and wheel assemblies.

19. Fill the differential carrier housing with 1.9 qts. (1.8L) of SAE 80W–90 weight gear lubricant.

20. Remove the axle assembly supporting device.

21. Lower the vehicle.

22. Connect the negative battery cable.

23. Check the rear camber and align, as necessary.

Troubleshooting the Manual Transmission

Problem	Cause	Solution
Transmission shifts hard	• Clutch adjustment incorrect • Clutch linkage or cable binding • Shift rail binding	• Adjust clutch • Lubricate or repair as necessary • Check for mispositioned selector arm roll pin, loose cover bolts, worn shift rail bores, worn shift rail, distorted oil seal, or extension housing not aligned with case. Repair as necessary.
	• Internal bind in transmission caused by shift forks, selector plates, or synchronizer assemblies • Clutch housing misalignment • Incorrect lubricant • Block rings and/or cone seats worn	• Remove, dissemble and inspect transmission. Replace worn or damaged components as necessary. • Check runout at rear face of clutch housing • Drain and refill transmission • Blocking ring to gear clutch tooth face clearance must be 0.030 inch or greater. If clearance is correct it may still be necessary to inspect blocking rings and cone seats for excessive wear. Repair as necessary.
Gear clash when shifting from one gear to another	• Clutch adjustment incorrect • Clutch linkage or cable binding • Clutch housing misalignment • Lubricant level low or incorrect lubricant • Gearshift components, or synchronizer assemblies worn or damaged	• Adjust clutch • Lubricate or repair as necessary • Check runout at rear of clutch housing • Drain and refill transmission and check for lubricant leaks if level was low. Repair as necessary. • Remove, disassemble and inspect transmission. Replace worn or damaged components as necessary.
Transmission noisy	• Lubricant level low or incorrect lubricant • Clutch housing-to-engine, or transmission-to-clutch housing bolts loose • Dirt, chips, foreign material in transmission • Gearshift mechanism, transmission gears, or bearing components worn or damaged • Clutch housing misalignment	• Drain and refill transmission. If lubricant level was low, check for leaks and repair as necessary. • Check and correct bolt torque as necessary • Drain, flush, and refill transmission • Remove, disassemble and inspect transmission. Replace worn or damaged components as necessary. • Check runout at rear face of clutch housing

Troubleshooting the Manual Transmission

Problem	Cause	Solution
Jumps out of gear	• Clutch housing misalignment	• Check runout at rear face of clutch housing
	• Gearshift lever loose	• Check lever for worn fork. Tighten loose attaching bolts.
	• Offset lever nylon insert worn or lever attaching nut loose	• Remove gearshift lever and check for loose offset lever nut or worn insert. Repair or replace as necessary.
	• Gearshift mechanism, shift forks, selector plates, interlock plate, selector arm, shift rail, detent plugs, springs or shift cover worn or damaged	• Remove, disassemble and inspect transmission cover assembly. Replace worn or damaged components as necessary.
	• Clutch shaft or roller bearings worn or damaged	• Replace clutch shaft or roller bearings as necessary
Jumps out of gear (cont.)	• Gear teeth worn or tapered, synchronizer assemblies worn or damaged, excessive end play caused by worn thrust washers or output shaft gears	• Remove, disassemble, and inspect transmission. Replace worn or damaged components as necessary.
	• Pilot bushing worn	• Replace pilot bushing
Will not shift into one gear	• Gearshift selector plates, interlock plate, or selector arm, worn, damaged, or incorrectly assembled	• Remove, disassemble, and inspect transmission cover assembly. Repair or replace components as necessary.
	• Shift rail detent plunger worn, spring broken, or plug loose	• Tighten plug or replace worn or damaged components as necessary
	• Gearshift lever worn or damaged	• Replace gearshift lever
	• Synchronizer sleeves or hubs, damaged or worn	• Remove, disassemble and inspect transmission. Replace worn or damaged components.
Locked in one gear—cannot be shifted out	• Shift rail(s) worn or broken, shifter fork bent, setscrew loose, center detent plug missing or worn	• Inspect and replace worn or damaged parts
	• Broken gear teeth on countershaft gear, clutch shaft, or reverse idler gear	• Inspect and replace damaged part
	Gearshift lever broken or worn, shift mechanism in cover incorrectly assembled or broken, worn damaged gear train components	• Disassemble transmission. Replace damaged parts or assemble correctly.

Troubleshooting Basic Clutch Problems

Problem	Cause
Excessive clutch noise	Throwout bearing noises are more audible at the lower end of pedal travel. The usual causes are: • Riding the clutch • Too little pedal free-play • Lack of bearing lubrication A bad clutch shaft pilot bearing will make a high pitched squeal, when the clutch is disengaged and the transmission is in gear or within the first 2″ of pedal travel. The bearing must be replaced. Noise from the clutch linkage is a clicking or snapping that can be heard or felt as the pedal is moved completely up or down. This usually requires lubrication. Transmitted engine noises are amplified by the clutch housing and heard in the passenger compartment. They are usually the result of insufficient pedal free-play and can be changed by manipulating the clutch pedal.
Clutch slips (the car does not move as it should when the clutch is engaged)	This is usually most noticeable when pulling away from a standing start. A severe test is to start the engine, apply the brakes, shift into high gear and SLOWLY release the clutch pedal. A healthy clutch will stall the engine. If it slips it may be due to: • A worn pressure plate or clutch plate • Oil soaked clutch plate • Insufficient pedal free-play
Clutch drags or fails to release	The clutch disc and some transmission gears spin briefly after clutch disengagement. Under normal conditions in average temperatures, 3 seconds is maximum spin-time. Failure to release properly can be caused by: • Too light transmission lubricant or low lubricant level • Improperly adjusted clutch linkage
Low clutch life	Low clutch life is usually a result of poor driving habits or heavy duty use. Riding the clutch, pulling heavy loads, holding the car on a grade with the clutch instead of the brakes and rapid clutch engagement all contribute to low clutch life.

Troubleshooting Basic Automatic Transmission Problems

Problem	Cause	Solution
Fluid leakage	• Defective pan gasket	• Replace gasket or tighten pan bolts
	• Loose filler tube	• Tighten tube nut
	• Loose extension housing to transmission case	• Tighten bolts
	• Converter housing area leakage	• Have transmission checked professionally
Fluid flows out the oil filler tube	• High fluid level	• Check and correct fluid level
	• Breather vent clogged	• Open breather vent
	• Clogged oil filter or screen	• Replace filter or clean screen (change fluid also)
	• Internal fluid leakage	• Have transmission checked professionally
Transmission overheats (this is usually accompanied by a strong burned odor to the fluid)	• Low fluid level	• Check and correct fluid level
	• Fluid cooler lines clogged	• Drain and refill transmission. If this doesn't cure the problem, have cooler lines cleared or replaced.
	• Heavy pulling or hauling with insufficient cooling	• Install a transmission oil cooler
	• Faulty oil pump, internal slippage	• Have transmission checked professionally
Buzzing or whining noise	• Low fluid level	• Check and correct fluid level
	• Defective torque converter, scored gears	• Have transmission checked professionally
No forward or reverse gears or slippage in one or more gears	• Low fluid level	• Check and correct fluid level
	• Defective vacuum or linkage controls, internal clutch or band failure	• Have unit checked professionally
Delayed or erratic shift	• Low fluid level	• Check and correct fluid level
	• Broken vacuum lines	• Repair or replace lines
	• Internal malfunction	• Have transmission checked professionally

Lockup Torque Converter Service Diagnosis

Problem	Cause	Solution

No lockup	• Faulty oil pump
	• Sticking governor valve
	• Valve body malfunction
	   (a) Stuck switch valve
	   (b) Stuck lockup valve
	   (c) Stuck fail-safe valve
	• Failed locking clutch
	• Leaking turbine hub seal
	• Faulty input shaft or seal ring
		• Replace oil pump
		• Repair or replace as necessary
		• Repair or replace valve body or its internal components as necessary
		
		• Replace torque converter
		• Replace torque converter
		• Repair or replace as necessary

Will not unlock	• Sticking governor valve
	• Valve body malfunction
	   (a) Stuck switch valve
	   (b) Stuck lockup valve
	   (c) Stuck fail-safe valve
		• Repair or replace as necessary
		• Repair or replace valve body or its internal components as necessary

Stays locked up at too low a speed in direct	• Sticking governor valve
	• Valve body malfunction
	   (a) Stuck switch valve
	   (b) Stuck lockup valve
	   (c) Stuck fail-safe valve
		• Repair or replace as necessary
		• Repair or replace valve body or its internal components as necessary

Locks up or drags in low or second	• Faulty oil pump
	• Valve body malfunction
	   (a) Stuck switch valve
	   (b) Stuck fail-safe valve
		• Replace oil pump
		• Repair or replace valve body or its internal components as necessary

Sluggish or stalls in reverse	• Faulty oil pump
	• Plugged cooler, cooler lines or fittings
	• Valve body malfunction
	   (a) Stuck switch valve
	   (b) Faulty input shaft or seal ring
		• Replace oil pump as necessary
		• Flush or replace cooler and flush lines and fittings
		• Repair or replace valve body or its internal components as necessary

Loud chatter during lockup engagement (cold)	• Faulty torque converter • Failed locking clutch • Leaking turbine hub seal	• Replace torque converter • Replace torque converter • Replace torque converter
Vibration or shudder during lockup engagement	• Faulty oil pump • Valve body malfunction • Faulty torque converter • Engine needs tune-up	• Repair or replace oil pump as necessary • Repair or replace valve body or its internal components as necessary • Replace torque converter • Tune engine
Vibration after lockup engagement	• Faulty torque converter • Exhaust system strikes underbody • Engine needs tune-up • Throttle linkage misadjusted	• Replace torque converter • Align exhaust system • Tune engine • Adjust throttle linkage

Lockup Torque Converter Service Diagnosis

Problem	Cause	Solution
Vibration when revved in neutral Overheating: oil blows out of dip stick tube or pump seal	• Torque converter out of balance • Plugged cooler, cooler lines or fittings • Stuck switch valve	• Replace torque converter • Flush or replace cooler and flush lines and fittings • Repair switch valve in valve body or replace valve body
Shudder after lockup engagement	• Faulty oil pump • Plugged cooler, cooler lines or fittings • Valve body malfunction • Faulty torque converter • Fail locking clutch • Exhaust system strikes underbody • Engine needs tune-up • Throttle linkage misadjusted	• Replace oil pump • Flush or replace cooler and flush lines and fittings • Repair or replace valve body or its internal components as necessary • Replace torque converter • Replace torque converter • Align exhaust system • Tune engine • Adjust throttle linkage

Transmission Fluid Indications

The appearance and odor of the transmission fluid can give valuable clues to the overall condition of the transmission. Always note the appearance of the fluid when you check the fluid level or change the fluid. Rub a small amount of fluid between your fingers to feel for grit and smell the fluid on the dipstick.

If the fluid appears:	It indicates:
Clear and red colored	• Normal operation
Discolored (extremely dark red or brownish) or smells burned	• Band or clutch pack failure, usually caused by an overheated transmission. Hauling very heavy loads with insufficient power or failure to change the fluid, often result in overheating. Do not confuse this appearance with newer fluids that have a darker red color and a strong odor (though not a burned odor).
Foamy or aerated (light in color and full of bubbles)	• The level is too high (gear train is churning oil) • An internal air leak (air is mixing with the fluid). Have the transmission checked professionally.
Solid residue in the fluid	• Defective bands, clutch pack or bearings. Bits of band material or metal abrasives are clinging to the dipstick. Have the transmission checked professionally.
Varnish coating on the dipstick	• The transmission fluid is overheating

TORQUE SPECIFICATIONS

Component	U.S.	Metric
Clutch Assembly:		
Clutch master cylinder:	15-25 ft. lbs.	20-34 Nm
Clutch pedal to bracket:	20-25 ft. lbs.	28-34 Nm
Clutch release lever:	30-45 ft. lbs.	40-60 Nm
Clutch slave cylinder:	14-20 ft. lbs.	18-26 Nm
4 Speed Transaxle:		
Case to cover bolts:	16 ft. lbs.	21 Nm
Front support strut:	48 ft. lbs.	65 Nm
Input shaft right bearing retainer:	7 ft. lbs.	9 Nm
Pinion shaft lock bolt:	7 ft. lbs.	9 Nm
Output shaft left bearing retainer:	45 ft. lbs.	65 Nm
Rear mount through bolt nut:	80 ft. lbs.	108 Nm
Reverse idler shaft lock bolt:	16 ft. lbs.	21 Nm
Reverse inhibitor fitting:	26 ft. lbs.	35 Nm
Ring gear bolts:	54 ft. lbs.	73 Nm
Shift control mount nuts:	18 ft. lbs.	24 Nm
Transaxle to engine:	47-62 ft. lbs.	65-85 Nm
5 Speed Transaxle:		
Clutch housing to gear housing:	15 ft. lbs.	21 Nm
Control box to case:	11-16 ft. lbs.	15-22 Nm
Dentent spring retaining bolt:	15-21 ft. lbs.	21-29 Nm
Differential gear:	61 ft. lbs.	83 Nm
Differential pin:	84 inch lbs.	9 Nm
End plate to gear housing:	15 ft. lbs.	21 Nm
Fluid drain plug:	18 ft. lbs.	24 Nm
Flywheel:	44-60 ft. lbs.	60-80 Nm
Front strut to frame:	50 ft. lbs.	68 Nm
Front strut to transaxle:	40 ft. lbs.	54 Nm
Input shaft bearing support:	50 ft. lbs.	70 Nm
Input/output shaft retaining nuts:	87-101 lbs.	118-137 Nm
Interlock plate:	15 ft. lbs.	21 Nm
Neutral Switch:	3 ft. lbs.	4-5 Nm
Output bearing race:	15 ft. lbs.	21 Nm
Output shaft bearing support:	50 ft. lbs.	70 Nm
Pressure plate to flywheel:	14-18 ft. lbs.	18-24 Nm
Rear cover:	11-16 lbs.	15-22 Nm
Rear mount through bolt nut:	80 lbs.	108 Nm
Reverse idler shaft bolt:	22-33 lbs.	30-45 Nm
Reverse shift bracket:	11-16 ft. lbs.	15-22 Nm
Ring gear bolts:	73-79 lbs.	98-107 Nm
Shift control mount nuts:	18 lbs.	24 Nm
Transaxle case to clutch housing:	22-33 lbs.	30-45 Nm
Transaxle to engine:	60 lbs.	75 Nm

8

SUSPENSION AND STEERING

WHEELS

Front and Rear Wheel

REMOVAL & INSTALLATION

There are many different aftermarket wheels that can be installed on your car. The procedures given in this manual are for the factory original wheels. Take care if your car as other than factory wheels for their correct installation, too. Pay attention to any special washers, spacers or adapters that may have come with aftermarket wheels.

1. When removing a wheel, loosen all the lug nuts at least one full turn, before jacking up the car.
2. Raise and safely support the car.
3. Finish removing the already loosened lug nuts. Sometimes applying slight pressure on wheel toward car will make it easy to screw them off by hand.
4. Remove the wheel, take care on some drum brakes the drum could slide off.
5. If the wheel is stuck on the hub place at least to lug nuts back on. Only screw them on two or three turns, don't allow them to touch the wheel.
6. Lower the vehicle back on the ground and rock it side to side. This is safer than shaking a vehicle that is on a jack. After the wheel pops loose, repeat Steps 2 through 5.

To install:
7. Place wheel on car, hand tighten all lug nuts. If studs or nuts are rusty, now is a good time to place some light lubricate on them.
8. After all nuts are hand tighten, finished tighten until snug by skipping every other nut. This is called a star pattern, because on a five lug car it makes a star design.
9. After all nuts are very snug, lower the vehicle.
10. Finishing tightening with a torque wrench to 100 ft. lbs., or on aftermarket wheels what ever they recommend.

❋❋ WARNING

Warning: Uneven tightening of wheel lug nuts can cause early disc brake pad and rotor wear.

Inspection

Wheels can be distorted or bent and not effect dry road handling to a noticeable degree. Out of round wheels will show up as uneven tire wear, or make it difficult to balance the tires. Without special tools it is difficult to check wheel radial runout. It would be best to ask the shop that balances the tires for you to do this. But a good visual inspection will usually reveal any problems.

Look for any bends, cracks or bends. Not repairs can be made to a wheel. If a wheel has any repair marks like welds or patches it should be discarded. Steel wheels that have slight bends where the tire meets the wheel doesn't mean the wheel is bad. Many times this is cause by the tire changing machine and can be hammered back into shape. This will only work on steel wheels not alloy or aluminum. If a wheel had a little bend in this area and had been repair it should be rebalanced and placed in a tank of water to check for leaks.

Another way to check for leaks where the wheel and tire meet is to lay the wheel flat on the ground. Place dish detergent and water solution around the wheel and wait a few minutes. If there is a slow leak you will see subs. Flip the tire over and repeat this procedure. If a leak is found the tire must be removed from the wheel. The the tire bead and wheel rim cleaned, lubricated and reassembled. Always recheck to make sure the leak is fixed.

Wheel Studs

REMOVAL & INSTALLATION

▶ SEE FIGS. 1 to 3
1. Raise and safely support the car.
2. Remove the brake assembly components.
3. Remove the hub assembly.
4. Remove the damaged stud using a C-clamp and pressing it out the back. Hammering can be done if there is no bearing assembly to be damaged.
5. Install the new stud by inserting in hole.

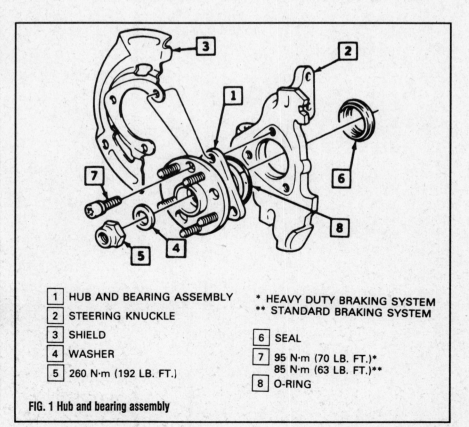

1	HUB AND BEARING ASSEMBLY	
2	STEERING KNUCKLE	
3	SHIELD	
4	WASHER	
5	260 N·m (192 LB. FT.)	

* HEAVY DUTY BRAKING SYSTEM
** STANDARD BRAKING SYSTEM

6	SEAL
7	95 N·m (70 LB. FT.)*
	85 N·m (63 LB. FT.)**
8	O-RING

FIG. 1 Hub and bearing assembly

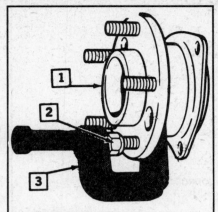

1. HUB AND BEARING ASSEMBLY REMOVED FROM VEHICLE
2. WHEEL NUT INSTALLED ON WHEEL STUD
3. WHEEL STUD REMOVING TOOL J-6627-A

FIG.2 Removing the wheel lug stud

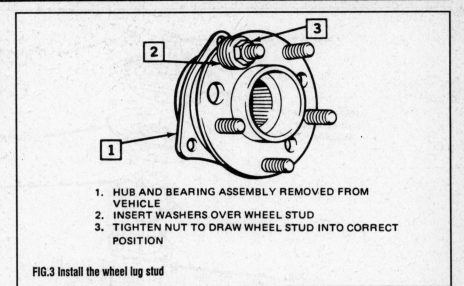

1. HUB AND BEARING ASSEMBLY REMOVED FROM VEHICLE
2. INSERT WASHERS OVER WHEEL STUD
3. TIGHTEN NUT TO DRAW WHEEL STUD INTO CORRECT POSITION

FIG.3 Install the wheel lug stud

6. Place washers on stud, install nut and tighten evenly to pull stud into place.

7. Make certain stud doesn't turn in hub or it will strip out the hole. If stud doesn't fit very tight you'll need to replace the hub, too.

8. Reinstall the hub and brake components.
9. Install the wheel following instruction given earlier and lower vehicle.

FRONT SUSPENSION

The A-Bodies use a MacPherson strut front suspension design. A MacPherson strut combines the functions of a shock absorber and an upper suspension member (upper arm) into one unit. The strut is surrounded by a coil spring, which provides normal front suspension functions.

The strut bolts to the body shell at its upper end, and to the steering knuckle at the lower end. The strut pivots with the steering knuckle by means of a sealed mounting assembly at the upper end which contains a preloaded, non-adjustable bearing.

The steering knuckle is connected to the chassis at the lower end by a conventional lower control arm, and pivots in the arm in a preloaded ball joint of standard design. The knuckle is fastened to the ball joint stud by means of a castellated nut and cotter pin.

Advantages of the MacPherson strut design, aside from its relative simplicity, include reduced weight and friction, minimal intrusion into the engine and passenger compartments, and ease of service.

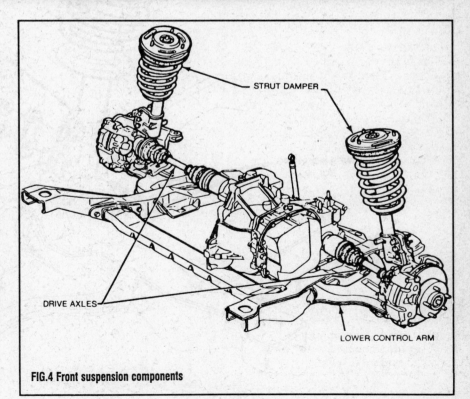

FIG.4 Front suspension components

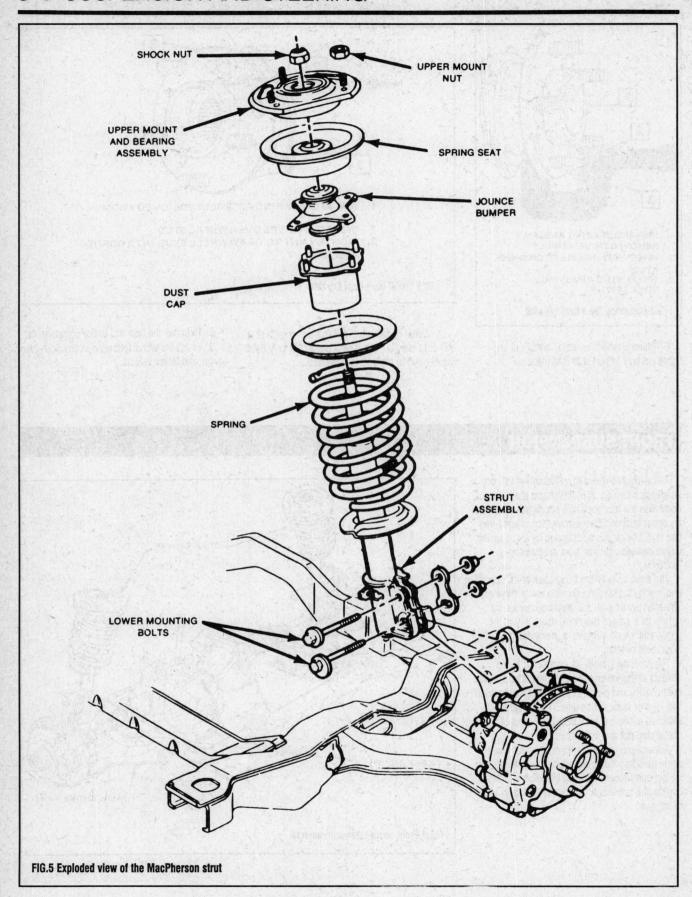

FIG.5 Exploded view of the MacPherson strut

MacPherson Struts Springs and Shock Absorbers

TESTING

The function of the shock absorber is to dampen harsh spring movement and provide a means of dissipating the motion of the wheels so that the shocks encountered by the wheels are not totally transmitted to the body and, therefore, to you and your passengers. As the wheel moves up and down, the shock absorber shortens and lengthens, thereby imposing a restraint on movement by its hydraulic action.

A good way to see if your shock absorbers are functioning correctly is to push one corner of the car until it is moving up and down for almost the full suspension travel, then release it and watch its recovery. If the car bounces slightly about one more time and comes to a rest, the shock is all right. If the car continues to bounce excessively, the shocks will probably require replacement.

REMOVAL & INSTALLATION

1. Remove the top strut-to-body mounting nuts.
2. Loosen the wheel nuts, then raise and support the vehicle on jackstands.
3. Remove the brake line clip from the strut, then the wheel and the tire assembly.
4. Install the boot protector tool J–28712 (Double-Offset joint) or J–33162 (Tri-Pot joint) over the drive axle boot.

➡ **If equipped with a Tri-Pot Joint, disconnect the drive axle from the transaxle before separating the strut from the steering knuckle.**

5. Before separating the strut from the steering knuckle, perform the following:
   a. Refer to view A, then using a sharp tool, scribe the steering knuckle along the lower outboard strut radius.
   b. Refer to view B, then scribe the strut flange on the inboard side, along the curve of the steering knuckle.
   c. Refer to view C, then using a chisel, mark the strut-to-steering knuckle interface.
6. Remove the steering knuckle-to-strut bolts.
7. Remove the strut.

To install:
8. Install the strut to the body. Tighten the upper nuts hand tight.
9. Place a jack under the lower arm. Raise the arm and install the lower strut-to-knuckle bolts. Align the strut-to-steering knuckle marks made during removal. Tighten the strut-to-knuckle bolts to 140 ft. lbs. (190 Nm), and the strut-to-body nuts to 18 ft. lbs. (24 Nm).
10. Install the brake hose clip on the strut.
11. Install the wheel and lower the car.

➡ **If a new strut damper has been installed, the front end will have to be realigned.**

OVERHAUL

A MacPherson strut compressor tool J–26584 or the equivalent must be used.
1. Clamp the strut compressor in a vise.
2. Install the strut in the compressor. Install the compressor adapters, if used.
3. Compress the spring approximately ½ in. (13mm). Do not bottom the spring or the strut rod.
4. Remove the strut shaft top nut and the top mount and bearing assembly from the strut.
5. Unscrew the compressor until all spring tension is relieved. Remove the spring.
6. Place the strut into the compressor. Rotate the strut until the spindle mounting flange is facing out, away from the compressor.
7. Place the spring on the strut. Make sure it is properly seated on the strut bottom plate.
8. Install the strut assembly on the spring. Install the compressor adapters, if used.
9. Tighten the strut compressor until it just contacts the spring seat, or the adapters if a tool with adapters is being used.
10. Thread on alignment rod tool J–26584–27 (1982–83) or J–34013–27 (1984–88), onto the strut damper shaft, hand tight.
11. Compress the spring until approximately 1½ in. (38mm) of the damper rod can be pulled up through the top spring seat. Do not compress the spring until it bottoms.
12. Remove the alignment rod and install the top mount and nut. Tighten the nut to 65 ft. lbs. (88 Nm.).
13. Unscrew the compressor and remove the strut.

Lower Ball Joints

➡ SEE FIGS. 7 to 9

INSPECTION

1. Raise and safely support the car.
2. Grasp the tire at top and bottom and move the top to the tire in and out.
3. Observe for any horizontal movement of the knuckle relative to the control arm.
4. Ball joints must be replaced if there is any looseness in the ball joint and should be replaced if the seal is damaged. The ball joint may check good with a bad seal, but will not last long due to dirt and water entering the joint.

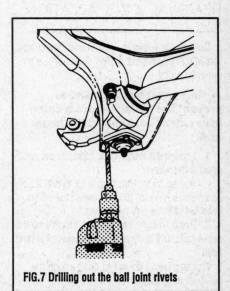

FIG.7 Drilling out the ball joint rivets

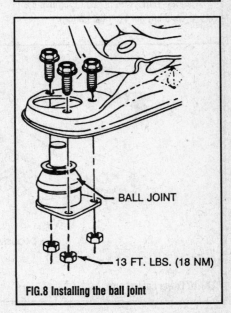

BALL JOINT

13 FT. LBS. (18 NM)

FIG.8 Installing the ball joint

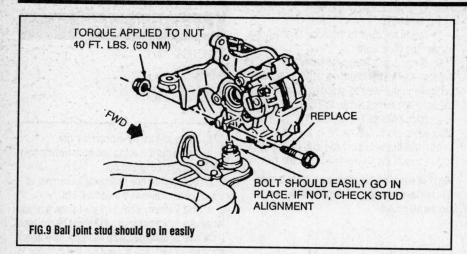

TORQUE APPLIED TO NUT
40 FT. LBS. (50 NM)

FWD

REPLACE

BOLT SHOULD EASILY GO IN
PLACE. IF NOT, CHECK STUD
ALIGNMENT

FIG.9 Ball joint stud should go in easily

REMOVAL & INSTALLATION

Only one ball joint is used in each lower arm. The MacPherson strut design does not use an upper ball joint.

➡ Care must be exercised to prevent the halfshafts from being over extended. Support the lower arm.

1. Loosen the wheel nuts, raise the car, and remove the wheel.

2. Use an 1/8 in. (3mm) drill bit to drill a hole approximately 1/4 in. (6mm) deep in the center of each of the three ball joint rivets.

3. Use a 1/2 in. (13mm) drill bit to drill off the rivet heads. Drill only enough to remove the rivet head.

Warning: Take care not to drill through the halfshaft dust boots.

4. Use a hammer and punch to remove the rivets. Drive them out from the bottom.

5. Loosen the ball joint pinch bolt in the steering knuckle.

6. Remove the ball joint.

7. Install the new ball joint in the control arm. Tighten the bolts supplied with the replacement joint to 13 ft. lbs. (18 Nm).

8. Install the ball stud into the knuckle pinch bolt fitting. It should go in easily; if not, check the stud alignment. Install the pinch bolt from the rear to the front. Tighten to 40 ft. lbs. (50 Nm) for for 1982–84 or 33 ft. lbs. (45 Nm) for 1985–88.

9. Install the wheel and lower the car.

Stabilizer Bar

REMOVAL & INSTALLATION

1. Raise and support the vehicle on jackstands.

2. Remove the two nuts attaching the stabilizer bar to the left lower control arm. Remove the four bolts which attach the left retaining plate to the engine cradle. The retaining plate covers and holds the stabilizer bar.

3. Loosen the four bolts holding the right stabilizer bracket.

4. Disconnect and remove the exhaust pipe and crossover if necessary.

5. Pull the stabilizer bar down on the left side.

6. Reverse steps 1 through 5 to install the stabilizer bar

➡ To aid in stabilizer bar installation, a pry hole has been provided in the engine cradle.

7. Install the stabilizer bar attachment. Tighten to 35 ft. lbs.

Lower Control Arm

REMOVAL & INSTALLATION

1. Loosen the wheel nuts, raise the car, and remove the wheel.

2. Remove the stabilizer bar from the control arm.

3. Remove the ball joint pinch bolt in the steering knuckle.

4. Remove the control arm pivot bolts and the control arm.

5. To install, insert the control arm into its fittings. Install the pivot bolts from the rear to the front. Tighten the bolts to 66 ft. lbs. (90 Nm).

6. Insert the ball stud into the knuckle pinch bolt fitting. It should go in easily; if not, check the ball joint stud alignment.

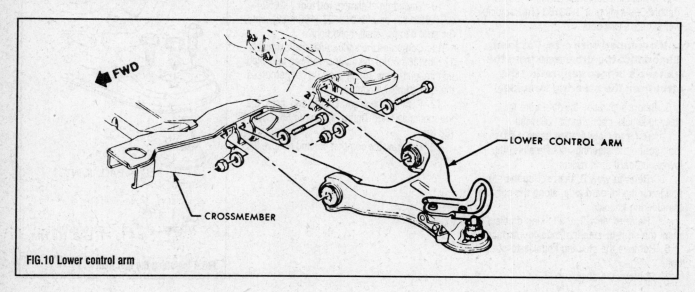

FWD

LOWER CONTROL ARM

CROSSMEMBER

FIG.10 Lower control arm

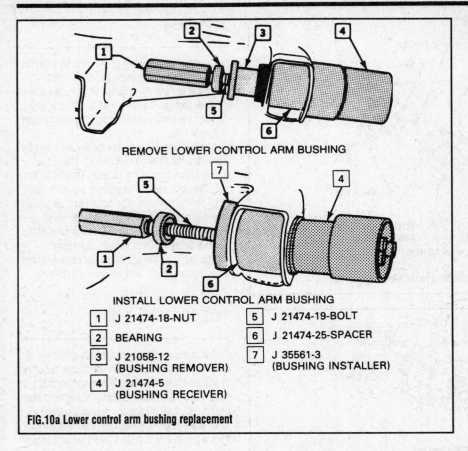

REMOVE LOWER CONTROL ARM BUSHING

INSTALL LOWER CONTROL ARM BUSHING

1	J 21474-18-NUT	5	J 21474-19-BOLT
2	BEARING	6	J 21474-25-SPACER
3	J 21058-12 (BUSHING REMOVER)	7	J 35561-3 (BUSHING INSTALLER)
4	J 21474-5 (BUSHING RECEIVER)		

FIG.10a Lower control arm bushing replacement

7. Install the pinch bolt from the rear to the front. Tighten to 40 ft. lbs. (50 Nm) for 1982–84 or 33 ft. lbs. (45 Nm) for 1985–92.

8. Install the stabilizer bar clamp. Tighten to 33 ft. lbs. (45 Nm).

9. Install the wheel and lower the car.

Knuckle

REMOVAL & INSTALLATION

1. Remove the hub nut.

2. Raise the front of the car. Remove the wheel and tire.

3. Install an axle shaft boot seal protector, GM special tool No. J–28712 or equivalent, onto the seal.

4. Disconnect the brake hose clip from the MacPherson strut, but do not disconnect the hose from the caliper. Remove the brake caliper, rotor and shield from the spindle, and hang the caliper out of the way by a length of wire. Do not allow the caliper to hang by the brake hose.

5. Mark the camber alignment cam bolt for reassembly. Remove the cam bolt and the upper attaching bolt from the strut and spindle.

6. Pull the steering knuckle assembly from the strut bracket.

Prior to installation, a new knuckle seal should be installed on the steering knuckle.

7. Loosely attach the steering knuckle to the suspension strut, then install the rotor and the hub nut. When the shaft begins to turn with the hub, insert a drift through the caliper into one of the cooling slots in the rotor to keep it from turning. Insert a long bolt in the hub flange to prevent the shaft from turning. Tighten the hub nut to 70 ft. lbs.

8. Tighten the brake caliper bolts to 30 ft. lbs.

9. Load the hub assembly by lowering it onto a jackstand. Align the camber cam bolt marks made during removal, install the bolt and tighten to 140 ft. lbs. Tighten the upper nut to the same value.

10. Remove the boot seal protector.

11. Connect the brake hose clip to the strut. Install the tire and wheel, lower the car, and tighten the hub nut to 225 ft. lbs. (1981–82); 185 ft. lbs. (1983–92).

Front Hub and Bearing

REMOVAL AND INSTALLATION

The front wheel bearings are sealed, non-adjustable units which require no periodic attention. They are bolted to the steering knuckle by means of an integral flange.

You will need a special tool to pull the bearing free of the halfshaft tool J–28733 or the equivalent. You should also use a halfshaft boot protector tool J–28712 (Double-Offset joint) or J–33162 (Tri-Pot joint) to protect the parts from damage.

1. Remove the wheel cover, loosen the hub nut, and raise and support the car. Remove the front wheel.

2. Install the boot cover, tool J–28712 (Double–Offset joint) or J–33162 (Tri–Pot joint).

3. Remove and discard the hub nut. Be sure to use a new one on assembly, not the old one.

4. Remove the brake caliper and rotor:

   a. Remove the allen head caliper mounting bolts;

   b. Remove the caliper from the knuckle and suspend from a length of wire. Do not allow the caliper to hang from the brake hose. Pull the rotor from the knuckle.

5. Remove the three hub and bearing attaching bolts and remove the hub. If the old bearing is to be reused, match mark the bolts and holes for installation. The brake rotor splash shield will have to come off, too.

6. Attach a puller, tool J–28733 or the equivalent, and remove the bearing. If corrosion is present, make sure the bearing is loose in the knuckle before using the puller.

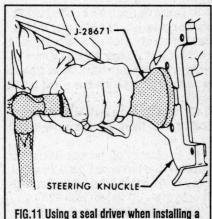

FIG.11 Using a seal driver when installing a new seal into the knuckle

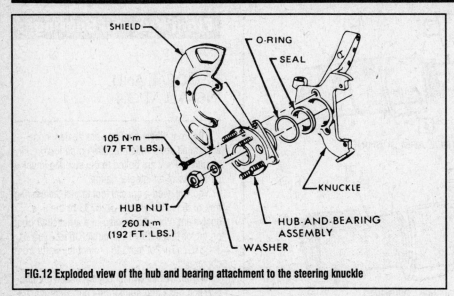

FIG.12 Exploded view of the hub and bearing attachment to the steering knuckle

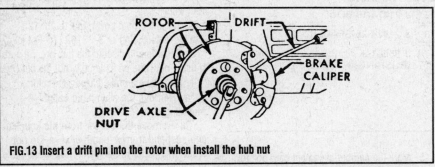

FIG.13 Insert a drift pin into the rotor when install the hub nut

7. Clean the mating surfaces of all dirt and corrosion. Check the knuckle bore and knuckle seal for damage. If a new bearing is to be installed, remove the old knuckle seal and install a new one. Grease the lips of the new seal before installation; install with a seal driver made for the purpose, tool J–28671 (1982–84) or J–34657 (1985–92).

8. Push the bearing onto the halfshaft. Install a new washer and hub nut.

9. Tighten the new hub nut on the halfshaft until the bearing is seated. If the rotor and hub start to rotate as the hub nut is tightened, insert a drift through the caliper and into the rotor cooling fins to prevent rotation. Do not apply full torque to the hub nut at this time — just seat the bearing.

10. Install the brake shield and the bearing retaining bolts. Tighten the bolts evenly to 63 ft. lbs. (85 Nm).

11. Install the caliper and rotor. Be sure that the caliper hose isn't twisted. Install the caliper bolts and tighten to 28 ft. lbs. (38 Nm) for 1982–84 or 38 ft. lbs. (51 Nm) for 1985–92.

12. Install the wheel. Lower the car. Tighten the hub nut to 214 ft. lbs. (290 Nm) for '82 or 192 ft. lbs. (260 Nm) for 1983–92.

Front End Alignment

Only camber and toe are adjustable on these cars; caster is preset and non-adjustable.

CAMBER

Camber is the inward or outward tilt from the vertical, measured in degrees, of the front wheels at the top. An outward tilt gives the wheel positive camber, an inward tilt is called negative camber. Proper camber is critical to assure even tire wear.

Camber angle is adjusted on the A-Bodies by loosening the through bolts which attach the MacPherson strut to the steering knuckle in or out. The bolts must be tightened to 140 ft. lbs. (190 Nm) afterwards. The bolts must be seated properly between the inner and outer guide surfaces on the strut flange. Measurement of the camber angle requires special alignment equipment; thus the adjustment of camber is not a do-it-yourself job, and not covered here.

TOE

Toe is the amount, measured in a fraction of a millimeter, that the wheels are closer together at one end than the other. Toe-in means that the front wheels are closer together at the front than the rear; toe-out means the rear of the front wheels are closer together than the front. A-Body cars are designed to have a slight amount of toe-in.

Toe is adjusted by turning the tie rods. It must be checked after camber has been adjusted, but it can be adjusted without disturbing the camber setting. you can make this adjustment without special equipment if you make very careful measurements. The wheels must be straight ahead.

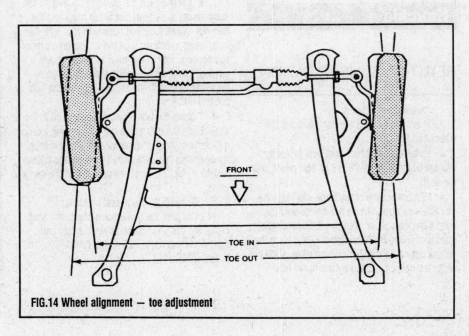

FIG.14 Wheel alignment — toe adjustment

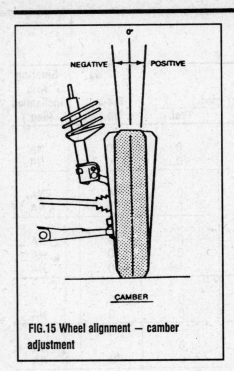

FIG.15 Wheel alignment — camber adjustment

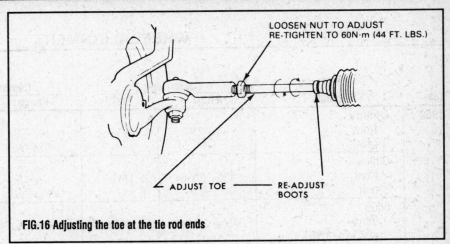

FIG.16 Adjusting the toe at the tie rod ends

1. Toe can be determined by measuring the distance between the centers of the tire treads, at the front of the tire and at the rear. If the tread pattern makes this impossible, you can measure between the edges of the wheel rims, but make sure to move the car forward and measure in a couple of places to avoid errors caused by bent rims or wheel runout.

2. If the measurement is not within specifications, loosen the nuts at the steering knuckle end of the tie rod, and remove the tie rod boot clamps. Rotate the tie rods to align the toe to specifications. Rotate the tie rods evenly, or the steering wheel will be crooked when you're done.

3. When the adjustment is correct, tighten the nuts to 44 ft. lbs. (60 Nm). Adjust the boots and tighten the clamps.

✳✳ WARNING

If out of adjustment enough a tire can wear out in only a few miles. It is advisable to have a front end alignment professional done after replacing steering or suspension components to avoid costly tire wear.

WHEEL ALIGNMENT

Year	Models	Caster (deg.) Range	Pref.	Camber (deg.) Range	Pref.	Toe-in (in.)	Steering Axis Inclination (deg.)
1982	All	1–3	2	$-1/2$–$1/2$	0	0	14.5
1983	All	1–3	2	$-1/2$–$1/2$	0	0	NA
1984	All	1–3	2	$-1/2$–$1/2$	0	0	NA
1985	All	1–3	2	$-1/2$–$1/2$	0	0	NA
1986	All	$3/4$–$2^{3}/4$	$1^{3}/4$	$-1/2$–$1/2$	0	0	NA
1987	All	$3/4$–$2^{3}/4$	$1^{3}/4$	$-1/2$–$1/2$	0	0	NA
1988	Celebrity front	$-^{23}/32$–$2^{23}/32$	$1^{23}/32$	$-1/2$–$1/2$	0	0	NA
	rear	—	—		0	0	NA
	Century front	$-3/4$–$2^{3}/4$	$1^{3}/4$	$-1/2$–$1/2$	0	0	NA
	rear	—	—	$-^{5}/16$–$^{5}/16$	0	0	NA
	Cutlass front	$1^{1}/2$–$2^{1}/2$	2	$3/16$–$1^{3}/16$	$^{11}/16$	0	NA
	rear	—	—	—	0	0	NA
	6000 front	$-^{23}/32$–$2^{23}/32$	$1^{23}/32$	$-1/2$–$1/2$	0	0	NA
	rear	—	—		0	0	NA

WHEEL ALIGNMENT

Year	Models	Caster (deg.)		Camber (deg.)		Toe-in (in.)	Steering Axis Inclination (deg.)
		Range	Pref.	Range	Pref.		
1989	Century						
	front	$-3/4$–$2^3/4$	$1^3/4$	$-1/2$–$1/2$	0	0	NA
	rear	—	—	$-5/16$–$5/16$	0	0	NA
	Cutlass						
	front	$1^5/16$–$2^5/16$	$1^{13}/16$	$-1/2$–$1/2$	0	0	NA
	rear	—	—	$-5/16$–$5/16$	0	0	NA
	6000						
	front	$1^1/16$–$2^{11}/16$	$1^{11}/16$	$-1/2$–$1/2$	0	0	NA
	rear exc. AWD	—	—	$-1/4$–$1/4$	0	0	NA
	rear AWD	—	—	-1–$1/2$	$-1/2$	0	NA
1990	Century						
	front	$-3/4$–$2^3/4$	$1^3/4$	$-1/2$–$1/2$	0	0	NA
	rear	—	—	$-5/16$–$5/16$	0	0	NA
	Celebrity						
	front	$1^1/16$–$2^{11}/16$	$1^1/16$	$-1/2$–$1/2$	0	0	NA
	rear	—	—	$-5/16$–$5/16$	0	0	NA
	Cutlass						
	front	$1^1/2$–$2^1/2$	2	$3/16$–$1^3/16$	$11/16$	0	NA
	rear 14″ wheel	—	—	$-3/8$–$5/8$	$1/8$	0	NA
	rear exc. 14″ wheel	—	—	$-11/16$–$5/16$	$-3/16$	0	NA
	6000						
	front	$1^1/16$–$2^{11}/16$	$1^{11}/16$	$-1/2$–$1/2$	0	0	NA
	rear exc. AWD	—	—	$-1/4$–$1/4$	0	0	NA
	rear AWD	—	—	-1–$1/2$	$-1/2$	0	NA
1991	Century						
	front	$1^1/16$–$2^{11}/16$	$1^{11}/16$	$-1/2$–$1/2$	0	0	NA
	rear	—	—	$-5/16$–$5/16$	0	0	NA
	Cutlass						
	front	$1^5/16$–$2^5/16$	$1^{13}/16$	$3/16$–$1^3/16$	$11/16$	0	NA
	rear			$-11/16$–$5/16$	$-3/16$	0	NA
	6000						
	front	$1^1/16$–$2^{11}/16$	$1^{11}/16$	$-1/2$–$1/2$	0	0	NA
	rear	—	—	$-5/16$–$5/16$	0	0	NA
1992	Century						
	front	$1^1/16$–$2^{11}/16$	$1^{11}/16$	$-1/2$–$1/2$	0	0	NA
	rear	—	—	$-5/16$–$5/16$	0	0	NA
	Cutlass						
	front	$1^5/16$–$2^5/16$	$1^{13}/16$	$3/16$–$1^3/16$	$11/16$	0	NA
	rear	—	—	$-11/16$–$5/16$	$-3/16$	0	NA
	6000						
	front	$1^1/16$–$2^{11}/16$	$1^{11}/16$	$-1/2$–$1/2$	0	0	NA
	rear	—	—	$-5/16$–$5/16$	0	0	NA

REAR SUSPENSION

Rear suspension consists of a solid rear axle tube containing an integral, welded-in stabilizer bar, coil springs, shock absorbers, a lateral track bar, and trailing arms. The trailing arms (control arms) are welded to the axle, and pivot at the frame. Fore and after movement is controlled by the trailing arms; lateral movement is controlled by the track bar. A permanently lubricated and sealed hub and bearing assembly is bolted to each end of the axle tube, it is a non-adjustable unit which must be replaced as an assembly if defective.

Coil Springs

♦ SEE FIGS. 17 and 18

REMOVAL & INSTALLATION

✱✱ CAUTION

The coil springs are under a considerable amount of tension. Be very careful when removing or installing them; they can exert enough force to cause very serious injuries.

1. Raise and support the car on a hoist. Do not use twin-post hoist. The swing arc of the axle may cause it to slip from the hoist when the bolts are removed. If a suitable hoist is not available, raise and support the car on jackstands, and use a jack under the axle.

2. Support the axle with a jack that can be raised and lowered.

3. Remove the brake hose attaching brackets (right and left), allowing the hoses to hang freely. Do not disconnect the hoses.

4. Remove the track bar attaching bolts from the rear axle.

5. Remove both shock absorber lower attaching bolts from the axle.

6. Lower the axle. Remove the coil spring and insulator.

7. To install, position the spring and insulator on the axle. The leg on the upper coil of the spring must be parallel to the axle, facing the left hand side of the car.

8. Install the shock absorber bolts. Tighten to 43 ft. lbs. (58 Nm) for 1982–84 or 35 ft. lbs. (47 Nm) for 1985–92. Install the track bar, tightening

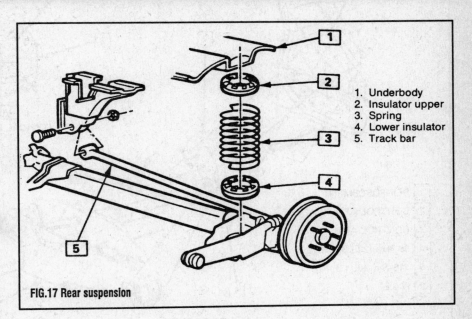

FIG.17 Rear suspension

1. Underbody
2. Insulator upper
3. Spring
4. Lower insulator
5. Track bar

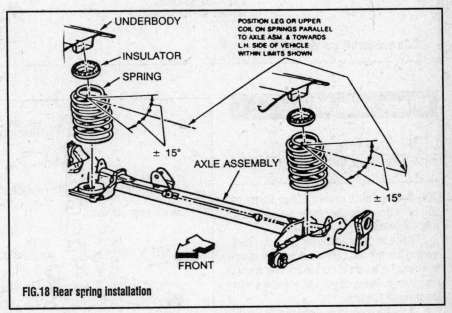

FIG.18 Rear spring installation

to 44 ft. lbs. (60 Nm). Install the brake line brackets. Tighten to 8 ft. lbs. (11 Nm).

Track Bar

REMOVAL & INSTALLATION

1. Raise the vehicle on a hoist and support the rear axle.

2. Remove the nut and bolt from both the axle and body attachments and remove the bar.

3. To install: Position the track bar at the axle mounting bracket and loosely install the bolt and nut.

4. Place the other end of the track bar into the body reinforcement and install the bolt and nut. Torque the nut at the axle bracket to 44 ft. lbs. (60 Nm). Torque the nut at the body reinforcement to 35 ft. lbs. (47 Nm).

5. Remove the rear axle support and lower the vehicle.

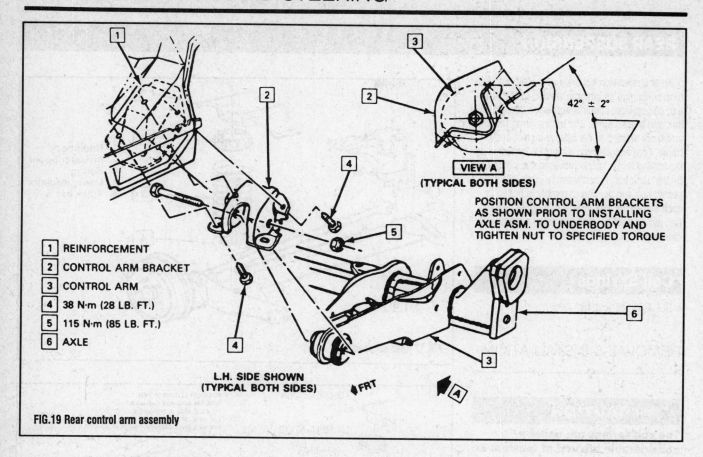

1 REINFORCEMENT
2 CONTROL ARM BRACKET
3 CONTROL ARM
4 38 N·m (28 LB. FT.)
5 115 N·m (85 LB. FT.)
6 AXLE

42° ± 2°

VIEW A
(TYPICAL BOTH SIDES)

POSITION CONTROL ARM BRACKETS
AS SHOWN PRIOR TO INSTALLING
AXLE ASM. TO UNDERBODY AND
TIGHTEN NUT TO SPECIFIED TORQUE

L.H. SIDE SHOWN
(TYPICAL BOTH SIDES)

FRT

A

FIG.19 Rear control arm assembly

Shock Absorbers

REMOVAL & INSTALLATION

1. Open the hatch or trunk lid, remove the trim cover if present, and remove the upper shock absorber nut.

2. Raise and support the car at a convenient working height if you desire. It is not necessary to remove the weight of the car from the shock absorbers, however, so you can leave the car on the ground if you prefer.

3. If the car is equipped with superlift shock absorbers, disconnect the air line.

4. Remove the lower attaching bolt and remove the shock.

5. If new shock absorbers are being installed, repeatedly compress them while inverted and extend them in their normal upright position. This will purge them of air.

6. Install the shocks in the reverse order of removal. Tighten the lower mount nut and bolt to 43 ft. lbs. (58 Nm) for 1982–84 or 38 ft. lbs. (51 Nm) for 1985–92, the upper to 13 ft. lbs. (17 Nm) for 1982–83 or 28 ft. lbs. (37 Nm) for 1984–92.

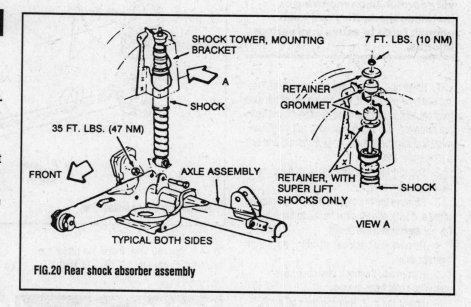

SHOCK TOWER, MOUNTING BRACKET

7 FT. LBS. (10 NM)

A

SHOCK

35 FT. LBS. (47 NM)

FRONT

AXLE ASSEMBLY

RETAINER
GROMMET

RETAINER, WITH
SUPER LIFT
SHOCKS ONLY

SHOCK

VIEW A

TYPICAL BOTH SIDES

FIG.20 Rear shock absorber assembly

TESTING

Visually inspect the shock absorber. If there is evidence of leakage and the shock absorber is covered with oil, the shock is defective and should be replaced.

If there is no sign of excessive leakage (a small amount of weeping is normal) bounce the car at one corner by pressing down on the fender or bumper and releasing. When you have the car bouncing as much as you can, release the fender or bumper. The car should stop bouncing after the first rebound. If the bouncing continues past

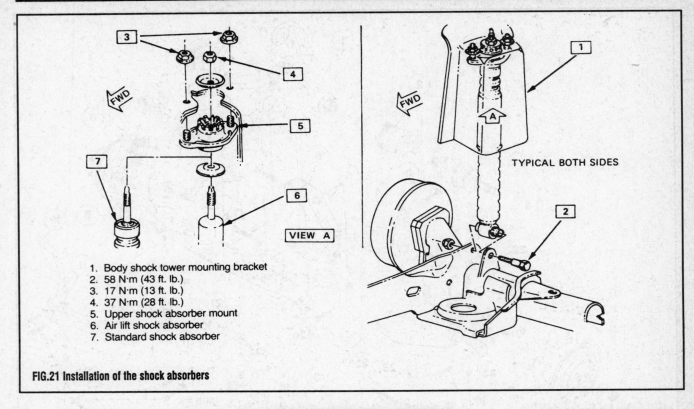

1. Body shock tower mounting bracket
2. 58 N·m (43 ft. lb.)
3. 17 N·m (13 ft. lb.)
4. 37 N·m (28 ft. lb.)
5. Upper shock absorber mount
6. Air lift shock absorber
7. Standard shock absorber

FIG.21 Installation of the shock absorbers

the center point of the bounce more than once, the shock absorbers are worn and should be replaced.

Rear Hub and Bearing

REMOVAL & INSTALLATION

1. Loosen the wheel lug nuts. Raise and support the car and remove the wheel.

2. Remove the brake drum. Removal procedures are covered in the next section, if needed.

➡ **Do not hammer on the brake drum to remove; damage to the bearing will result.**

3. Remove the four hub and bearing retaining bolts and remove the assembly from the axle.

4. Installation is the reverse. Hub and bearing bolt torque is 45 ft. lbs. (60 Nm).

Rear Axle – 6000 STE AWD

REMOVAL & INSTALLATION

1. Raise and safely support the vehicle.
2. Remove the tire and wheel assembly.
3. Disconnect the parking brake cable end from the bracket.
4. Insert a suitable tool through the caliper into the rotor to prevent the rotor from turning.
5. Remove the shaft nut and washer using special tool J–34826. Discard the shaft nut.
6. Remove the anti-lock brake sensor bolt and move the sensor aside.
7. Remove the 2 brake caliper bolts and remove the caliper. Support the caliper using a length of wire.

➡ **Do not allow the caliper to hang by the brake hose unsupported.**

8. Remove the rotor from the hub and bearing assembly.
9. Install leaf spring compression tool J–33432 or equivalent.
10. Remove the 3 bolts mounting the hub and bearing to the knuckle.

11. Remove the hub and bearing assembly from the knuckle using special tool J–28733–A or equivalent.
12. Remove the bolts and nut plate attaching the lower strut mount to the knuckle. Scribe the position of the upper bolt prior removing.
13. Install a suitable CV-boot protector to prevent damage to the boot.
14. Swing the knuckle downward and away from the driveshaft.
15. Remove the drive axle from the differential using a suitable slide hammer.

To Install:

16. Install the drive axle to the differential. Ensure positive engagement by pulling outward on the inner axle end. Grasp the housing only. Do not grasp and pull on the axle shaft.
17. Swing the knuckle up to the lower strut mount.
18. Position the nut plate and install the lower strut mount bolts to the knuckle. Align the top bolt with scribe marks before tightening the bolts. Tighten the bolts to 148 ft. lbs. (200 Nm).
19. Remove the CV boot protector.
20. Install the hub and bearing assembly to the knuckle and axle spline.
21. Install the hub and bearing attaching bolts. Tighten to 61 ft. lbs. (84 Nm).
22. Remove the leaf spring compression tool.
23. Install the rotor to hub and bearing assembly.

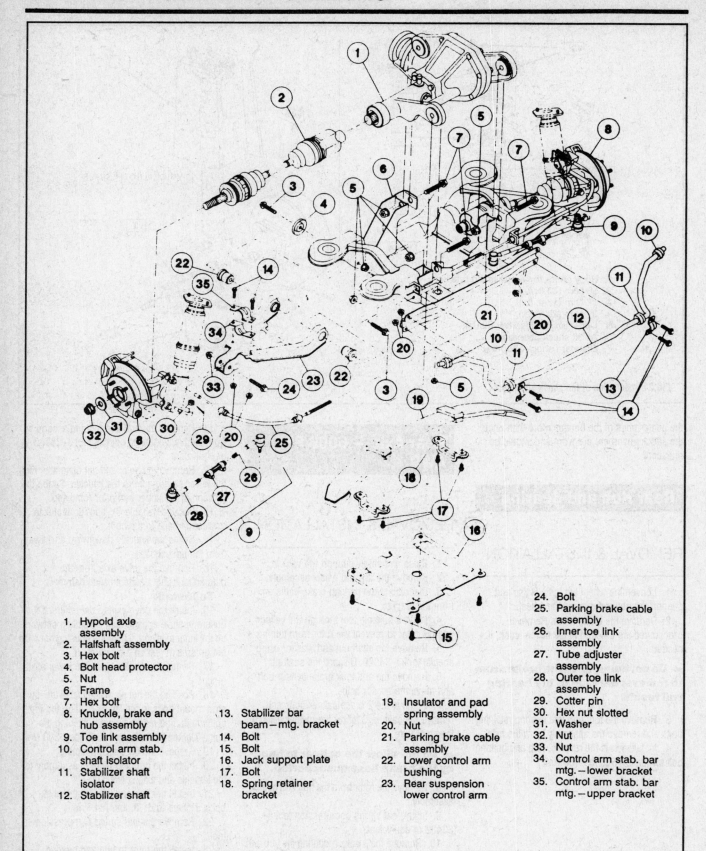

FIG.22 Rear axle assembly — 6000 STE AWD

1. Hypoid axle assembly
2. Halfshaft assembly
3. Hex bolt
4. Bolt head protector
5. Nut
6. Frame
7. Hex bolt
8. Knuckle, brake and hub assembly
9. Toe link assembly
10. Control arm stab. shaft isolator
11. Stabilizer shaft isolator
12. Stabilizer shaft
13. Stabilizer bar beam—mtg. bracket
14. Bolt
15. Bolt
16. Jack support plate
17. Bolt
18. Spring retainer bracket
19. Insulator and pad spring assembly
20. Nut
21. Parking brake cable assembly
22. Lower control arm bushing
23. Rear suspension lower control arm
24. Bolt
25. Parking brake cable assembly
26. Inner toe link assembly
27. Tube adjuster assembly
28. Outer toe link assembly
29. Cotter pin
30. Hex nut slotted
31. Washer
32. Nut
33. Nut
34. Control arm stab. bar mtg.—lower bracket
35. Control arm stab. bar mtg.—upper bracket

24. Install the brake caliper to the rotor and install the retaining bolts. Tighten the bolts to 38 ft. lbs. (51 Nm).

25. Install the anti-lock brake sensor to the knuckle and install the retaining bolt. Using a non-ferrous feeler gauge, adjust the sensor gap to 0.028 in. (0.7mm). Tighten the adjustment screw to 19 inch lbs. (2.2 Nm).

26. Connect the parking brake cable end into the bracket.

27. Install the shaft washer and new torque prevailing nut. Hold the rotor with a suitable to prevent the axle from turning while tightening. Tighten to 185 ft. lbs. (260 Nm).

28. Install the tire and wheel assembly.

29. Check the rear wheel camber. Adjust as necessary.

➡ **If the lower strut to knuckle bolts are properly aligned with the scribe marks, no camber adjustment should be necessary.**

30. Lower the vehicle.

STEERING

The A-Body cars use an aluminum-housed Saginaw manual rack and pinion steering gear as standard equipment. The pinion is supported by and turns in a sealed ball bearing at the top and a pressed-in roller bearing at the bottom. The rack moves in bushings pressed into each end of the rack housing.

Wear compensation occurs through the action of an adjuster spring which forces the rack against the pinion teeth. This adjuster eliminates the need for periodic pinion preload adjustments. Preload is adjustable only at overhaul.

The inner tie rod assemblies are both threaded and staked to the rack. A special joint is used, allowing both rocking and rotating motion of the tie rods. The inner tie rod assemblies are lubricated for life and require no periodic attention.

Any service other than replacement of the outer tie rods or the boots requires removal of the unit from the car.

The optional power rack and pinion steering gear is an integral unit, and shares most features with the manual gear. A rotary control valve directs the hydraulic fluid to either side of the rack piston. The integral rack piston is attached to the rack and converts the hydraulic pressure into left or right linear motion. A vane-type constant displacement pump with integral reservoir provides hydraulic pressure. No in-car adjustments are necessary or possible on the system, except for periodic belt tension checks and adjustments for the pump.

Steering Wheel

❊❊ CAUTION

If car is equipped with an air bag, do not service steering wheel, or dash components. Extreme danger of air bag deployment even with battery removed! Serious injury could occur.

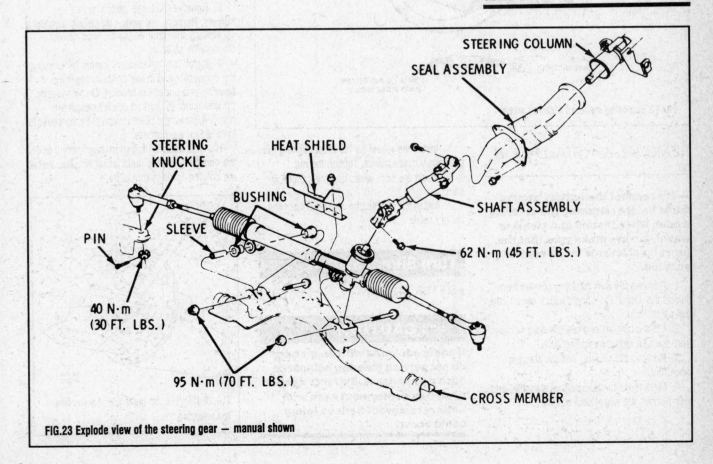

FIG.23 Explode view of the steering gear — manual shown

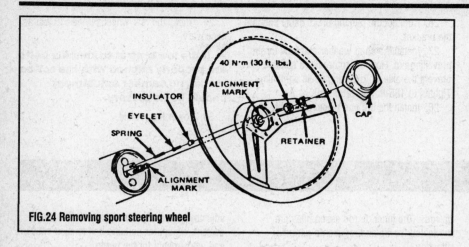

FIG.24 Removing sport steering wheel

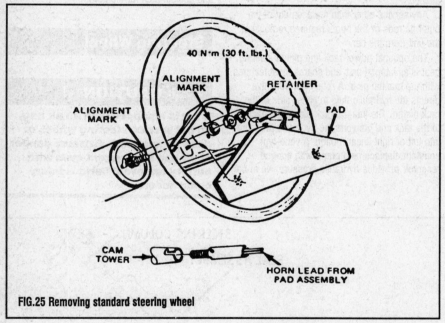

FIG.25 Removing standard steering wheel

REMOVAL & INSTALLATION

➡ **Disconnect the battery ground cable before removing the steering wheel. When installing a steering wheel, always make sure that the turn signal lever is in the neutral position.**

1. Remove the trim retaining screws from behind the wheel. On wheels with a center cap, pull off the cap.

2. Lift the trim off and pull the horn wires from the turn signal canceling cam.

3. Remove the retainer and the steering wheel nut.

4. Mark the wheel-to-shaft relationship, and then remove the wheel with a puller.

5. Install the wheel on the shaft aligning the previously made marks. Tighten the nut.

6. Insert the horn wires into the canceling cam.

7. Install the center trim and reconnect the battery cable.

Turn Signal Switch

♦ SEE FIGS. 24 to 28

❊❊❊ CAUTION

If car is equipped with an air bag, do not service steering column or dash components. Extreme danger of air bag deployment even with battery removed! Serious injury could occur.

REMOVAL & INSTALLATION

1. Remove the steering wheel as previously outlined. Remove the trim cover.

2. Loosen the cover screws. Pry the cover off with a screwdriver, and lift the cover off the shaft.

3. Position the U-shaped lockplate compressing tool on the end of the steering shaft and compress the lock plate by turning the shaft nut clockwise. Pry the wire snapring out of the shaft groove.

4. Remove the tool and lift the lock plate off the shaft.

5. Slip the canceling cam, upper bearing preload spring, and thrust washer off the shaft.

6. Remove the turn signal lever. Push the flasher knob in and unscrew it. Remove the button retaining screw and remove the button, spring and knob.

7. Pull the switch connector out the mast jacket and tape the upper part to facilitate switch removal. Attach a long piece of wire to the turn signal switch connector. When installing the turn signal switch, feed this wire through the column first, and then use this wire to pull the switch connector into position. On tilt wheels, place the turn signal and shifter housing in low position and remove the harness cover.

8. Remove the three switch mounting screws. Remove the switch by pulling it straight up while guiding the wiring harness cover through the column.

9. Install the replacement switch by working the connector and cover down through the housing and under the bracket. On tilt models, the connector is worked down through the housing, under the bracket, and then the cover is installed on the harness.

10. Install the switch mounting screws and the connector on the mast jacket bracket. Install the column-to-dash trim plate.

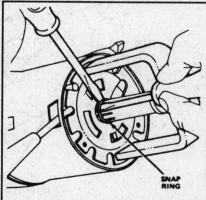

FIG.26 Depress the lockplate and remove the snapring

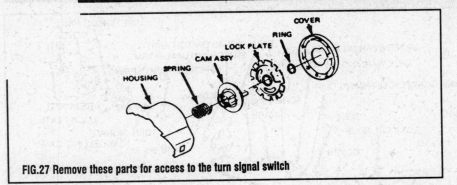

FIG.27 Remove these parts for access to the turn signal switch

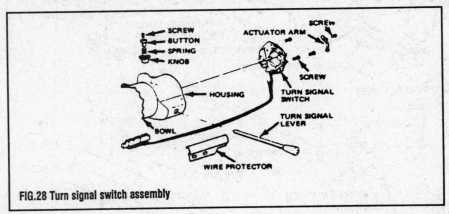

FIG.28 Turn signal switch assembly

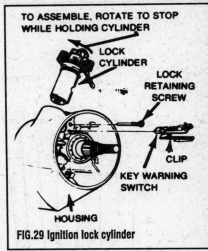

FIG.29 Ignition lock cylinder

11. Install the flasher knob and the turn signal lever.

12. With the turn signal lever in neutral and the flasher know out, slide the thrust washer, upper bearing preload spring, and canceling cam onto the shaft.

13. Position the lock plate on the shaft and press it down until a new snapring can be inserted in the shaft groove. Always use a new snapring when assembling.

14. Install the cover and the steering wheel.

Ignition Switch

▶ SEE FIGS. 26 to 30

✳✳ CAUTION

If car is equipped with an air bag, do not service steering column or dash components. Extreme danger of air bag deployment even with battery removed! Serious injury could occur.

REMOVAL & INSTALLATION

The switch is located inside the channel section of the brake pedal support and is completely inaccessible without first lowering the steering column. The switch is actuated by a rod and rack assembly. A gear on the end of the lock cylinder engages the toothed upper end of the rod.

1. Lower the steering column; be sure to properly support it.

2. Put the switch in the Off-Unlocked position. With the cylinder removed, the rod is in Lock when it is in the next to the uppermost detent. Off-Unlocked is two detents from the top.

3. Remove the two switch screws and remove the switch assembly.

4. Before installing, place the new switch in Off-Unlocked position and make sure the lock cylinder and actuating rod are in Off-Unlocked (third detent from the top) position.

5. Install the activating rod into the switch and assemble the switch on the column. Tighten the mounting screws. Use only the specified screws since overlength screws could impair the collapsibility of the column.

6. Reinstall the steering column.

Ignition Lock Cylinder

✳✳ CAUTION

If car is equipped with an air bag, do not service steering column or dash components. Extreme danger of air bag deployment even with battery removed! Serious injury could occur.

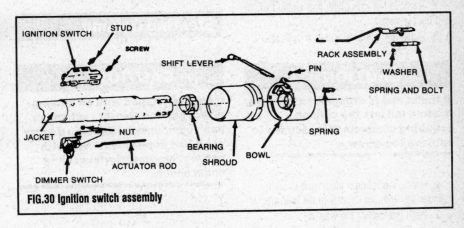

FIG.30 Ignition switch assembly

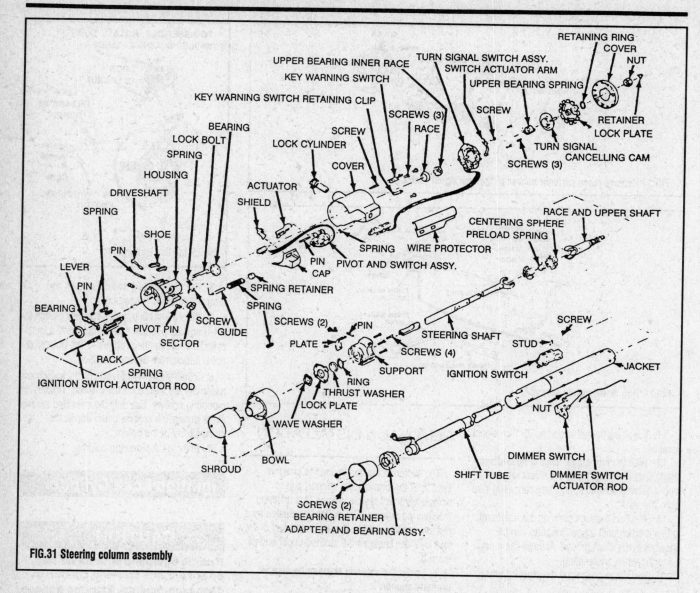

FIG.31 Steering column assembly

REMOVAL & INSTALLATION

1. Place the lock in the Run position.
2. Remove the lock plate, turn signal switch and buzzer switch.
3. Remove the screw and lock cylinder.

✳✳ CAUTION

If the screw is dropped on removal, it could fall into the column, requiring complete disassembly to retrieve the screw.

4. Rotate the cylinder clockwise to align cylinder key with the keyway in the housing.
5. Push the lock all the way in.

6. Install the screw. Tighten the screw to 14 inch lb. for adjustable columns and 25 inch lb. for standard columns.

Steering Column

✳✳ CAUTION

If car is equipped with an air bag, do not service steering column or dash components. Extreme danger of air bag deployment even with battery removed! Serious injury could occur.

➡ **Once the steering column is removed from the car, the column is extremely susceptible to damage. Dropping the column assembly on its end could collapse the steering shaft or loosen the plastic injections which maintain column rigidity. Leaning on the column assembly could cause the jacket to bend or deform. Any of the above damage could impair the column's collapsible design. If it is necessary to remove the steering wheel, use a standard wheel puller. Under no condition should the end of the shaft be hammered upon, as hammering could loosen the plastic injection which maintains column rigidity.**

REMOVAL & INSTALLATION

1. Disconnect the negative battery cable.

2. If column repairs are to be made, remove the steering wheel.

3. Remove the nuts and bolts attaching the flexible coupling to the bottom of the steering column. Remove the safety strap and bolt if equipped.

4. Remove the steering column trim shrouds and column covers.

5. Disconnect all wiring harness connectors. Remove the dust boot mounting screws and column mounting bracket bolts.

6. Lower the column to clear the mounting bracket and carefully remove from the car.

To Install:

7. Install the column into the vehicle and raise it into the mounting bracket.

8. Loosely install the column mounting bolts and connect all wiring harness connectors.

9. Tighten the column mounting bolts and install the trim shrouds and column covers.

10. Install and tighten the nuts and bolts in the flexible coupling at the bottom of the steering shaft.

11. Install the steering wheel and connect the battery cable.

Steering Linkage

▶ SEE FIGS. 32 and 33

REMOVAL & INSTALLATION

Tie Rod Ends

1. Loosen the jam nut on the steering rack (inner tie rod).

2. Remove the tie rod end nut. Separate the tie rod end from the steering knuckle using a puller tool J–6627 or BT–7101.

3. Unscrew the tie rod end, counting the number of turns.

4. To install, screw the tie rod end onto the steering rack (inner tie rod) the same number of turns as counted for removal. This will give approximately correct toe.

5. Install the tie rod end into the knuckle. Install the nut and tighten to 40 ft. lbs. (1982–84) or 30 ft. lbs. (1985–92).

6. If the toe must be adjusted, use pliers to expand the boot clamp. Turn the inner tie rod to adjust. Replace the clamp.

7. Tighten the jam nut to 44 ft. lbs.

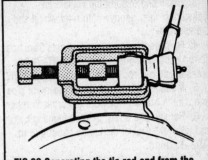

FIG.32 Separating the tie rod end from the knuckle with a puller

Power Rack and Pinion Steering Gear

REMOVAL & INSTALLATION

1. Raise the intermediate shaft seal and remove intermediate shaft-to-stub shaft pinch bolt.

2. If equipped with power steering, remove the air cleaner and disconnect the pressure hoses from the steering gear.

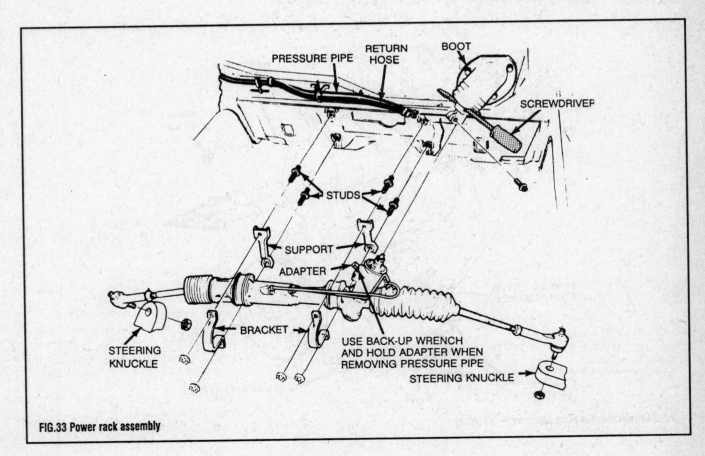

FIG.33 Power rack assembly

3. Raise and support the vehicle on jackstands, then remove both front wheel and tire assemblies.

4. Remove the cotter pins and nuts from both tie rod ends. Using tool J–6627 or BT–7101, press the tie rod ends from the steering knuckle.

5. If equipped with an Air Management pipe, remove the bracket bolt from the crossmember.

6. Remove the 2 rear cradle mounting bolts and lower the rear of the cradle about 4–5 in. (102–127mm).

❄ WARNING

If the rear of the cradle is lowered to far, the engine components nearest the cowl may be damaged.

7. If equipped, remove the rack and pinion heat shield.

8. Remove the rack and pinion mounting bolts, then the gear assembly through the left wheel opening.

9. To install:

10. Install the gear assembly through the left wheel opening and install the mounting bolts.

11. Install the heat shield.

12. Raise the rear of the cradle and install the mounting bolts.

13. Install the bracket bolt to the crossmember under the air management pipe.

14. Install the tie rod ends to the steering knuckles, install the retaining nuts and insert new cotter pins.

15. Install the front wheels and lower the vehicle.

16. Install the high pressure hoses to the steering gear and install the air cleaner.

17. Install the intermediate shaft seal and the intermediate shaft-to-stub shaft pinch bolt.

➡ **If equipped with power steering, reconnect the pressure hoses and bleed the system.**

Power Steering Pump

REMOVAL & INSTALLATION

Gasoline Engines

All models use integral rack and pinion power steering. A pump delivers hydraulic pressure through two hoses to the steering gear itself.

1. Remove the hoses at the pump and tape the openings shut to prevent contamination.

Position the disconnected lines in a raised position to prevent leakage.

2. Remove the pump belt.

3. On the four cylinder, remove the radiator hose clamp bolt. On the 6-2.8L, disconnect the negative battery cable, disconnect the electrical connector at the blower motor, drain the cooling system, and remove the heater hose at the water pump. On the 6-3.0L, remove the alternator. On any model if access appears easier if removing a component such as the alternator, then that should be considered.

4. Loosen the retaining bolts and any braces, and remove the pump.

5. Install the pump on the engine with the retaining bolts handtight.

6. Connect and tighten the hose fittings.

7. Refill the pump with fluid and bleed the system.

8. Install the pump belt on the pulley and adjust the tension.

9. Remove the tape and install the power steering pump hoses.

Diesel Engine

1. Remove the drive belt.

2. Siphon the fluid from the power steering reservoir.

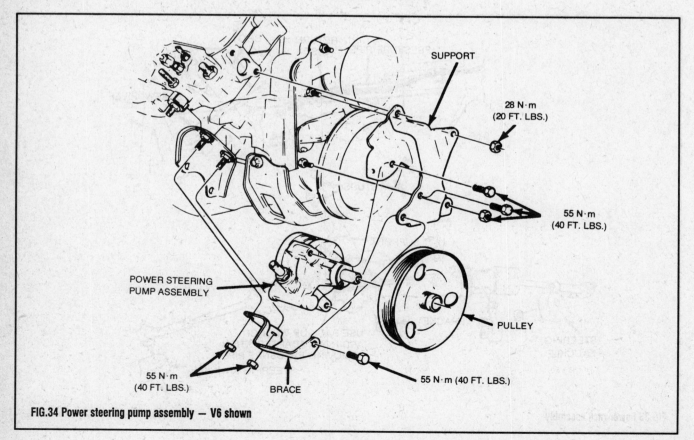

FIG.34 Power steering pump assembly — V6 shown

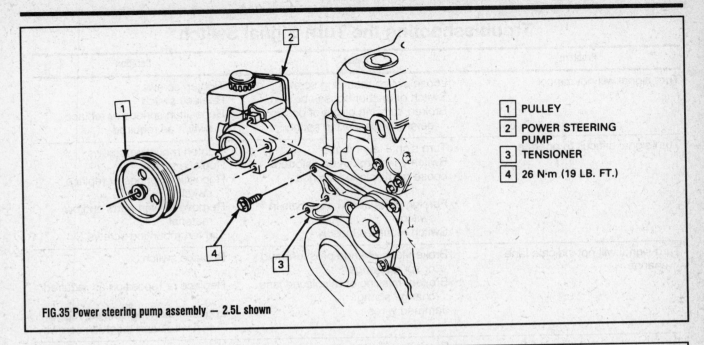

FIG.35 Power steering pump assembly — 2.5L shown

1	PULLEY
2	POWER STEERING PUMP
3	TENSIONER
4	26 N·m (19 LB. FT.)

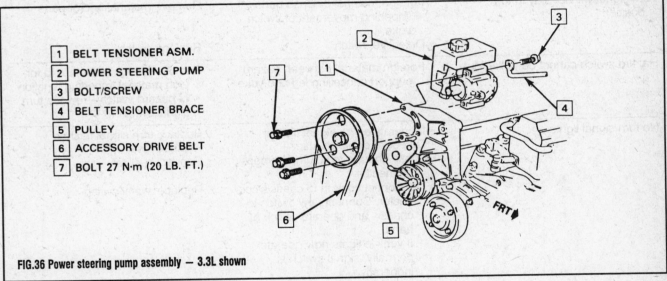

FIG.36 Power steering pump assembly — 3.3L shown

1	BELT TENSIONER ASM.
2	POWER STEERING PUMP
3	BOLT/SCREW
4	BELT TENSIONER BRACE
5	PULLEY
6	ACCESSORY DRIVE BELT
7	BOLT 27 N·m (20 LB. FT.)

➡ On some models, it may be necessary to remove the right front wheel.

3. Disconnect the hoses from the pump.
4. Remove the three bolts from the front of the pump through the access holes in the pulley.
5. Remove the two nuts holding the lower brace to the engine. Remove the brace.
6. Remove the pump.

7. To install, reverse steps 1 through 6. Torque the brace nuts to 40 ft. lbs.; the pump bolt to 40 ft. lbs.

BLEEDING

1. Fill the fluid reservoir.
2. Let the fluid stand undisturbed for two minutes, then crank the engine for about two seconds. Refill reservoir if necessary.
3. Repeat Steps 1 and 2 above until the fluid level remains constant after cranking the engine.
4. Raise the front of the car until the wheels are off the ground, then start the engine. Increase the engine speed to about 1,500 rpm.
5. Turn the wheels lightly against the stops to the left and right, checking the fluid level and refilling if necessary.

Troubleshooting the Turn Signal Switch

Problem	Cause	Solution
Turn signal will not cancel	• Loose switch mounting screws • Switch or anchor bosses broken • Broken, missing or out of position detent, or cancelling spring	• Tighten screws • Replace switch • Reposition springs or replace switch as required
Turn signal difficult to operate	• Turn signal lever loose • Switch yoke broken or distorted • Loose or misplaced springs • Foreign parts and/or materials in switch • Switch mounted loosely	• Tighten mounting screws • Replace switch • Reposition springs or replace switch • Remove foreign parts and/or material • Tighten mounting screws
Turn signal will not indicate lane change	• Broken lane change pressure pad or spring hanger • Broken, missing or misplaced lane change spring • Jammed wires	• Replace switch • Replace or reposition as required • Loosen mounting screws, reposition wires and retighten screws
Turn signal will not stay in turn position	• Foreign material or loose parts impeding movement of switch yoke • Defective switch	• Remove material and/or parts • Replace switch
Hazard switch cannot be pulled out	• Foreign material between hazard support cancelling leg and yoke	• Remove foreign material. No foreign material impeding function of hazard switch—replace turn signal switch.
No turn signal lights	• Inoperative turn signal flasher • Defective or blown fuse • Loose chassis to column harness connector • Disconnect column to chassis connector. Connect new switch to chassis and operate switch by hand. If vehicle lights now operate normally, signal switch is inoperative • If vehicle lights do not operate, check chassis wiring for opens, grounds, etc.	• Replace turn signal flasher • Replace fuse • Connect securely • Replace signal switch • Repair chassis wiring as required

Troubleshooting the Turn Signal Switch (cont.)

Problem	Cause	Solution
Instrument panel turn indicator lights on but not flashing	• Burned out or damaged front or rear turn signal bulb • If vehicle lights do not operate, check light sockets for high resistance connections, the chassis wiring for opens, grounds, etc. • Inoperative flasher • Loose chassis to column harness connection • Inoperative turn signal switch • To determine if turn signal switch is defective, substitute new switch into circuit and operate switch by hand. If the vehicle's lights operate normally, signal switch is inoperative.	• Replace bulb • Repair chassis wiring as required • Replace flasher • Connect securely • Replace turn signal switch • Replace turn signal switch
Stop light not on when turn indicated	• Loose column to chassis connection • Disconnect column to chassis connector. Connect new switch into system without removing old.	• Connect securely • Replace signal switch
Stop light not on when turn indicated (cont.)	Operate switch by hand. If brake lights work with switch in the turn position, signal switch is defective. • If brake lights do not work, check connector to stop light sockets for grounds, opens, etc.	• Repair connector to stop light circuits using service manual as guide
Turn indicator panel lights not flashing	• Burned out bulbs • High resistance to ground at bulb socket • Opens, ground in wiring harness from front turn signal bulb socket to indicator lights	• Replace bulbs • Replace socket • Locate and repair as required
Turn signal lights flash very slowly	• High resistance ground at light sockets • Incorrect capacity turn signal flasher or bulb • If flashing rate is still extremely slow, check chassis wiring harness from the connector to light sockets for high resistance • Loose chassis to column harness connection • Disconnect column to chassis connector. Connect new switch into system without removing old. Operate switch by hand. If flashing occurs at normal rate, the signal switch is defective.	• Repair high resistance grounds at light sockets • Replace turn signal flasher or bulb • Locate and repair as required • Connect securely • Replace turn signal switch

Troubleshooting the Turn Signal Switch (cont.)

Problem	Cause	Solution
Hazard signal lights will not flash— turn signal functions normally	• Blow fuse • Inoperative hazard warning flasher • Loose chassis-to-column harness connection • Disconnect column to chassis connector. Connect new switch into system without removing old. Depress the hazard warning lights. If they now work normally, turn signal switch is defective. • If lights do not flash, check wiring harness "K" lead for open between hazard flasher and connector. If open, fuse block is defective	• Replace fuse • Replace hazard warning flasher in fuse panel • Conect securely • Replace turn signal switch • Repair or replace brown wire or connector as required

Troubleshooting the Power Steering Pump

Problem	Cause	Solution
Chirp noise in steering pump	• Loose belt	• Adjust belt tension to specification
Belt squeal (particularly noticeable at full wheel travel and stand still parking)	• Loose belt	• Adjust belt tension to specification
Growl noise in steering pump	• Excessive back pressure in hoses or steering gear caused by restriction	• Locate restriction and correct. Replace part if necessary.
Growl noise in steering pump (particularly noticeable at stand still parking)	• Scored pressure plates, thrust plate or rotor • Extreme wear of cam ring	• Replace parts and flush system • Replace parts
Groan noise in steering pump	• Low oil level • Air in the oil. Poor pressure hose connection.	• Fill reservoir to proper level • Tighten connector to specified torque. Bleed system by operating steering from right to left— full turn.
Rattle noise in steering pump	• Vanes not installed properly • Vanes sticking in rotor slots	• Install properly • Free up by removing burrs, varnish, or dirt
Swish noise in steering pump	• Defective flow control valve	• Replace part
Whine noise in steering pump	• Pump shaft bearing scored	• Replace housing and shaft. Flush system.
Low pump pressure	• Flow control valve stuck or inoperative • Pressure plate not flat against cam ring	• Remove burrs or dirt or replace. Flush system. • Correct

Troubleshooting the Power Steering Pump (cont.)

Problem	Cause	Solution
Hard steering or lack of assist	• Loose pump belt • Low oil level in reservoir **NOTE:** Low oil level will also result in excessive pump noise • Steering gear to column misalignment • Lower coupling flange rubbing against steering gear adjuster plug • Tires not properly inflated	• Adjust belt tension to specification • Fill to proper level. If excessively low, check all lines and joints for evidence of external leakage. Tighten loose connectors. • Align steering column • Loosen pinch bolt and assemble properly • Inflate to recommended pressure
Foaming milky power steering fluid, low fluid level and possible low pressure	• Air in the fluid, and loss of fluid due to internal pump leakage causing overflow	• Check for leaks and correct. Bleed system. Extremely cold temperatures will cause system aeriation should the oil level be low. If oil level is correct and pump still foams, remove pump from vehicle and separate reservoir from body. Check welsh plug and body for cracks. If plug is loose or body is cracked, replace body.
Momentary increase in effort when turning wheel fast to right or left	• Low oil level in pump • Pump belt slipping • High internal leakage	• Add power steering fluid as required • Tighten or replace belt • Check pump pressure. (See pressure test)
Steering wheel surges or jerks when turning with engine running especially during parking	• Low oil level • Loose pump belt • Steering linkage hitting engine oil pan at full turn • Insufficient pump pressure	• Fill as required • Adjust tension to specification • Correct clearance • Check pump pressure. (See pressure test). Replace flow control valve if defective.
Steering wheel surges or jerks when turning with engine running especially during parking (cont.)	• Sticking flow control valve	• Inspect for varnish or damage, replace if necessary
Excessive wheel kickback or loose steering	• Air in system	• Add oil to pump reservoir and bleed by operating steering. Check hose connectors for proper torque and adjust as required.
Low pump pressure	• Extreme wear of cam ring • Scored pressure plate, thrust plate, or rotor • Vanes not installed properly • Vanes sticking in rotor slots • Cracked or broken thrust or pressure plate	• Replace parts. Flush system. • Replace parts. Flush system. • Install properly • Freeup by removing burrs, varnish, or dirt • Replace part

TORQUE SPECIFICATIONS

Component	English	Metric
Brake line brackets:	8 ft. lbs.	11 Nm
Caliper retaining bolts:	38 ft. lbs.	51 Nm
Front crossmember-to-body bolts:	103 ft. lbs.	140 Nm
Halfshaft end nut:	184-192 ft. lbs.	250-260 Nm
Lower ball pinch bolt:	33 ft. lbs.	45 Nm
Lower control arm bolts:	61 ft. lbs.	83 Nm
MacPherson strut shaft nut:	65 ft. lbs.	85 Nm
MacPherson strut to fender:	18 ft. lbs.	24 Nm
MacPherson strut to knuckle:	140 ft. lbs.	190 Nm
Rear Shock mount to frame:	16 ft. lbs.	22 Nm
Rear Shock to lower mount:	44 ft. lbs.	59 Nm
Rear Shock to upper mount:	16 ft. lbs.	22 Nm
Rear axle top bolt 6000 AWD:	148 ft. lbs.	200 Nm
Rear control arm-to-bracket:	84 ft. lbs.	115 Nm
Rear control bracket-to-underbody:	28 ft. lbs.	38 Nm
Rear hub and bearing assembly:	44 ft. lbs.	60 Nm
Rear jack pad mounting bolts:	18 ft. lbs.	25 Nm
Rear track bar at brace or underbody:	35 ft. lbs.	47 Nm
Spring retention plate bolts:	15 ft. lbs.	20 Nm
Steering column mounting bolts:	18 ft. lbs.	25 Nm
Steering rack mounting bolts:	59 ft. lbs.	80 Nm
Steering wheel retaining nut:	30 ft. lbs.	41 Nm
Tie rod adjustment jam nut:	45 ft. lbs.	60 Nm
Tie rod nut:	43 ft. lbs.	58 Nm
Wheel nuts:	100 ft. lbs.	140 Nm

9

BRAKES

BRAKE SYSTEM OPERATION

UNDERSTANDING THE BRAKE SYSTEM

Hydraulic System

A hydraulic system is used to actuate the brakes. The system transports the power required to force the frictional surfaces of the braking system together from the pedal to the individual braking units at each wheel. A hydraulic system is used for three reasons. First, fluid under pressure can be carried to all parts of the automobile by small hoses, some of which are flexible, without taking up a significant amount of room or posing routine problems. Second, liquid is non-compressible; a hydraulic system can transport force without modifying or reducing that force. Third, a great mechanical advantage can be given to the brake pedal end of the system, and the foot pressure required to actuate the brakes can be reduced by making the surface area of the master cylinder pistons smaller than that of any of the pistons in the wheel cylinders or calipers.

The master cylinder consists of a fluid reservoir, a double cylinder and a piston assembly. Double type master cylinders are designed to separate the front and rear braking systems hydraulically in case of a leak.

Steel lines carry the brake fluid to a point on the vehicle's frame near each of the vehicle's wheels. The fluid is then carried to the slave cylinder by flexible tubes in order to allow for suspension and steering movements.

In drum brake systems, the slave cylinders are called wheel cylinders. Each wheel cylinder contains two pistons, one at either end, which push outward in opposite directions.

In disc brake systems, the slave cylinders are part of the calipers. One large cylinder is used to force the brake pads against the disc. All slave cylinder pistons employ some type of seal, usually made of rubber, to minimize the leakage of fluid around the piston. A rubber dust boot seals the outer end of the cylinder against dust and dirt. The boot fits around the outer end of the piston on disc brake calipers and around the brake actuating rod on wheel cylinders.

The hydraulic system operates as follows: When at rest, the entire system, from the pistons in the master cylinder to those in the wheel cylinders or calipers, is full of brake fluid. Upon application of the brake pedal, fluid trapped in front of the master cylinder pistons is forced through the lines to the slave cylinders. Here, it forces the pistons outward, in the case of drum brakes, and inward toward the disc, in the case of disc brakes. The motion of the pistons is opposed by return springs mounted outside the cylinders in drum brakes.

Upon release of the brake pedal, a spring located inside the master cylinder immediately returns the master cylinder pistons to the normal position. The pistons contain check valves and the master cylinder has compensating ports drilled in it. These are uncovered as the pistons reach their normal position. The piston check valves allow fluid to flow toward the wheel cylinders or calipers as the master cylinder pistons withdraw. Then, as the return springs force the shoes into the released position, the excess fluid returns to the master cylinder fluid reservoir through the compensating ports. It is during the time the pedal is in the released position that any fluid that has leaked out of the system will be replaced through the compensating ports.

Dual circuit master cylinders employ two pistons, located one behind the other, in the same cylinder. The primary piston is actuated by fluid trapped between the two pistons. If a leak develops in front of the secondary piston, it moves forward until it bottoms against the front of the master cylinder and the fluid trapped between the pistons will operate the rear brakes. If the rear brakes develop a leak, the primary piston will move forward until direct contact with the secondary piston takes place and it will force the secondary piston to actuate the front brakes. In either case, the brake pedal moves farther when the brakes are applied and less braking power is available.

All dual circuit systems use a distributor switch to warn the driver when only half of the brake system is operational. This switch is located in a valve body which is mounted on the master cylinder. A hydraulic piston receives pressure from both circuits, each circuit's pressure being applied to one end of the piston. When the pressures are in balance, the piston remains stationary. When one circuit has a leak, however, the greater pressure in that circuit during application of the brakes will push the piston to one side, closing the distributor switch and activating the brake warning light.

In disc brake systems, this valve body also contains a metering valve and, in some cases, a proportioning valve. The metering valve keeps pressure from traveling to the disc brakes on the front wheels until the brake shoes on the rear wheels have contacted the drums, ensuring that the front brakes will never be used alone. The proportioning valve throttles the pressure to the rear brakes so as to avoid rear wheel lock-up during very hard braking.

These valves may be tested by removing the lines to the front and rear brake systems and installing special brake pressure testing gauge. Front and rear system pressures are then compared as the pedal is gradually depressed. Specifications vary with the manufacturer and design of the brake systems.

Brake warning lights may be tested by depressing the brake pedal and holding it while opening one of the wheel cylinder bleeder screws. If this does not cause the light to go on, substitute a new lamp, make continuity checks, and finally, replace the switch as necessary.

The hydraulic system may be checked for leaks by applying pressure to the pedal gradually and steadily. If the pedal sinks very slowly to the floor, the system has a leak. This is not to be confused with a springy or spongy feel due to the compression of air within the lines. If the system leaks, there will be a gradual change in the position of the pedal with a constant pressure.

Check for leaks along all lines and at wheel cylinder. If no external leaks are apparent, the problem is inside the master cylinder.

Disc Brakes

Instead of the traditional expanding brakes that press outward against a circular drum, disc brake systems utilize a cast iron disc with brake pads positioned on either side of it. Braking effect is achieved in a manner similar to the way you would squeeze a spinning phonograph record between your fingers. The disc (rotor) is a one-piece casting with cooling fins between the two braking surfaces. This enables air to circulate between the braking surfaces making them less sensitive to heat buildup and more resistant to fade. Dirt and water do not affect braking action since contaminants are thrown off by the centrifugal action of the rotor or scraped off by the pads. Also, the equal clamp action of the two brake pads tends to ensure uniform, straightline stops. All disc brakes are self-adjusting.

Drum Brakes

Drum brakes employ two brake shoes mounted on a stationary backing plate. These shoes are positioned inside a circular cast iron drum which rotates with the wheel assembly. The shoes are held in place by springs; this allows them to slide toward the drums (when they are applied) while keeping the linings and drums in alignment. The shoes are actuated by a wheel cylinder which is mounted at the top of the backing plate. When the brakes are applied, hydraulic pressure forces the wheel cylinder's two actuating links outward. Since these links bear directly against the top of the brake shoes, the tops of the shoes are then forced outward against the inner side of the drum. This action forces the bottoms of the two shoes to contact the brake drum by rotating the entire assembly slightly (known as servo action). When pressure within the wheel cylinder is relaxed, return springs pull the shoes back away from the drum.

The drum brakes are designed to self-adjust during application when the car is moving in reverse. This motion causes both shoes to rotate very slightly with the drum, rocking an adjusting lever, thereby causing rotation of the adjusting screw by means of an actuating lever.

Power Brake Boosters

Power brakes operate just as standard brake systems except in the actuation of the master cylinder pistons. A vacuum diaphragm is located on the front of the master cylinder and assists the driver in applying the brakes, reducing both the effort and travel he must put into moving the brake pedal.

The vacuum diaphragm housing is connected to the intake manifold by a vacuum hose. A check valve is placed at the point where the hose enters the diaphragm housing, so that during periods of low manifold vacuum brake assist vacuum will not be lost.

Depressing the brake pedal closes off the vacuum source and allows atmospheric pressure to enter on one side of the diaphragm. This causes the master cylinder pistons to move and apply the brakes. When the brake pedal is released, vacuum is applied to both sides of the diaphragm, the return springs return the diaphragm and master cylinder pistons to the released position. If the vacuum fails, the brake pedal rod will butt against the end of the master cylinder actuating rod and direct mechanical application will occur as the pedal is depressed.

The hydraulic and mechanical problems that apply to conventional brake systems also apply to power brakes and should be checked if the following tests do not reveal the problem.

The hydraulic and mechanical problems that apply to conventional brake systems also apply to power brakes and should be checked if the following tests do not reveal the problem.

Test for a system vacuum leak as described below:

1. Operate the engine at idle with the transaxle in Neutral without touching the brake pedal for at least one minute.

2. Turn off the engine and wait one minute.

3. Test for the presence of assist vacuum by depressing the brake pedal and releasing it several times. Light application will produce less and less pedal travel, if vacuum was present. If there is no vacuum air is leaking into the system.

Test for system operation as follows:

1. Pump the brake pedal (with engine off) until the supply vacuum is entirely gone.

2. Put a light, steady pressure on the pedal.

3. Start the engine and operate it at idle with the transaxle in Neutral. If the system is operating, the brake pedal should fall toward the floor if constant pressure is maintained on the pedal. Power brake systems may be tested for hydraulic leaks just as ordinary systems are tested, except that the engine should be idling with the transaxle in neutral throughout the test.

THE BRAKING SYSTEM

The A-Body cars have a diagonally split hydraulic system. This differs from conventional practice in that the left front and right rear brakes are on one hydraulic circuit, and the right front and left rear are on the other.

A diagonally split system necessitates the use of a special master cylinder design. The A-Body master cylinder incorporates the functions of a standard tandem master cylinder, plus a warning light switch and proportioning valves. Additionally, the master cylinder is designed with a quick take-up feature which provides a large volume of fluid to the brakes at low pressure when the brakes are initially applied. The lower pressure fluid acts to quickly fill the large displacement requirements of the system.

The front disc brakes are single piston sliding caliper units. Fluid pressure acts equally against the piston and the bottom of the piston bore in the caliper. This forces the piston outward until the pad contacts the caliper to slide over, carrying the other pad into contact with the other side of the rotor. The disc brakes are self-adjusting.

Rear drum brakes are conventional duo-servo

units. A dual piston wheel cylinder mounted to the top of the backing plate, actuates both brake shoes. Wheel cylinder force to the shoes is supplemented by the tendency of the shoes to wrap into the drum (servo action). An actuating link, pivot and lever serve to automatically engage the adjuster as the brakes are applied when the car is moving in reverse. Provisions for manual adjustment are also provided. The rear brakes also serve as the parking brakes; linkage is mechanical. Vacuum boost is an option. The booster is a conventional tandem vacuum unit.

Adjustments

DISC BRAKES

The front disc brakes are self-adjusting. No adjustments are either necessary or possible.

DRUM BRAKES

The drum brakes are designed to self-adjust when applied with the car moving in reverse. however, they can also be adjusted manually. This manual adjustment should also be performed whenever the linings are replaced.

➡ **Never adjust the parking brake cable, until after the regular service brakes have been adjusted.**

1. Use a punch to knock out the stamped area on the brake drum. If this is done with the drum installed on the car, the drum must then be removed to clean out all metal pieces. After adjustments are complete, obtain a hole cover from your dealer (Part no. 4874119 or the equivalent) to present entry of dirt and water into the brakes.

2. Use an adjusting tool especially made for the purpose to turn the brake adjusting screw star wheel.

➡ **Keep turning the drum as you are adjusting it or you may over tighten the shoes against the drum. It is extremely difficult to back the adjustment off if over tighten.**

3. Expand the shoes until there is a slight drag. No tighter than if the drum can just barely be turned by hand.

3. Back off the adjusting screw a few notches, if too tight. If the shoes still are dragging lightly, back off the adjusting screw one or two additional notches. If the brakes still drag, the parking brake adjustment is incorrect or the parking brake is applied. Fix and start over.

4. Install the hole cover into the drum.

5. Check the parking brake adjustment.

On some models, no marked area or stamped area is present on the drum. In this case, a hole must be drilled in the backing plate:

1. All backing plates have two round flat areas in the lower half through which the parking brake cable is installed. Drill a 1/2 in. (13mm) hole into the round flat area on the backing plate opposite the parking brake cable. This will allow access to the star wheel.

2. After drilling the hole, remove the drum and remove all metal particles. Install a hole plug (Part no. 4874119 or the equivalent) to prevent the entry of water or dirt.

Another option on these models is simply to remove the drum, adjust the shoe and try the drum on. If the drum fit is still loose adjust the shoes out slightly more and repeat. Using this method you'll find you need to make the drum a very sung fit, due to a ridge that forms on the outer edge of the drum.

Brake Light Switch

REMOVAL & INSTALLATION

1. Disconnect the wiring connectors from the brake light switch.

2. Unscrew the brake light switch from the tubular retaining clip.

3. Insert the new switch into the retainer until the switch body seats against the clip.

4. Connect the wiring connectors.

5. Pull the brake pedal rearward against the internal pedal stop. The switch will be moved in the tubular clip providing proper adjustment.

Master Cylinder

REMOVAL & INSTALLATION

1. If your car does not have power brakes, disconnect the master cylinder pushrod at the brake pedal inside the car. The pushrod is retained to the brake pedal by a clip; there is a washer under the clip, and a spring washer on the other side of the pushrod.

2. Unplug the electrical connector from the master cylinder.

3. Place a number of cloths or a container under the master cylinder to catch the brake fluid. Disconnect the brake tubes from the

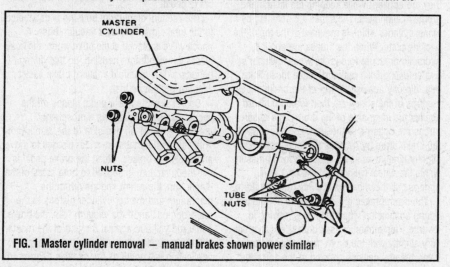

FIG. 1 Master cylinder removal — manual brakes shown power similar

FIG. 1a Keep the master cylinder area clean, only use clean new fluid

master cylinder; use a flare nut wrench if one is available. Tape over the open ends of the tubes.

➡ Brake fluid eats paint. Wipe up any spilled fluid immediately, then flush the area with clean water.

4. Remove the two nuts attaching the master cylinder to the booster or firewall.

5. Remove the master cylinder.

6. To install, attach the master cylinder to the firewall or the booster with the nuts. Torque to 29 ft. lbs. (40 Nm) for 1982–84 or 22 ft. lbs. (27 Nm) for 1985–88.

7. Reconnect the pushrod to the brake pedal with non-power brakes.

8. Remove the tape from the lines and connect to the master cylinder. Torque to 12 ft. lbs. (17 Nm) for 1982–84 or 18 ft. lbs. (24 Nm) for 1985–88. Connect the electrical lead.

9. Bleed the brakes.

OVERHAUL

This is a tedious, time consuming job. You can save yourself a lot of trouble by buying a rebuilt master cylinder from your dealer or parts supply house. The small difference in price between a rebuilding kit and a rebuilt part usually makes it more economical, in terms of time and work, to buy the rebuilt part.

1. Remove the master cylinder.

2. Remove the reservoir cover and drain the fluid.

3. Remove the pushrod and the rubber boot on non-power models.

4. Unbolt the proportioners and the failure warning switch from the side of the master cylinder body. Discard the O-rings found under the proportioners. Use new ones on installation. There may or may not be an O-ring under the original equipment failure warning switch. If there is, discard it. In either case, use a new O-ring upon assembly.

5. Clamp the master cylinder body in a vise, taking care not to crush it. Depress the primary piston with a wooden dowel and remove the lock ring with a pair of snapring pliers.

6. The primary and secondary pistons can be removed by applying compressed air into one of the outlets at the end of the cylinder and plugging the other three outlets. The primary piston must be replaced as an assembly if the seals are bad. The secondary piston seals are replaceable. Install these new seals with the lips facing outwards.

7. Inspect the bore for corrosion. If any corrosion is evident, the master cylinder body must be replaced. Do not attempt to polish the bore with crocus cloth, sandpaper or anything else. The body is aluminum; polishing the bore won't work.

8. To remove the failure warning switch piston assembly, remove the allen head plug from the end of the bore and withdraw the assembly with a pair of needlenose pliers. The switch piston assembly seals are replaceable.

9. The reservoir can be removed from the master cylinder if necessary. Clamp the body in a vise by its mounting flange. Use a pry bar to remove the reservoir. If the reservoir is removed, remove the reservoir grommets and discard them. The quick take-up valves under the grommets are accessible after the retaining snaprings are removed. Use snapring pliers; no other tool will work.

10. Clean all parts in denatured alcohol and allow to air dry. Do not use anything else to clean

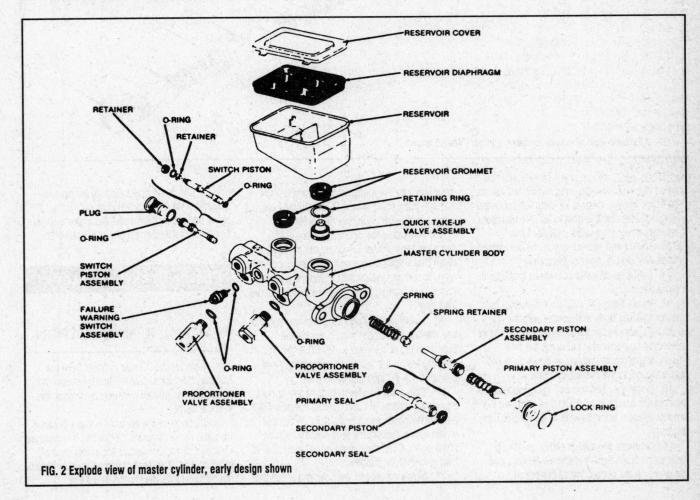

FIG. 2 Explode view of master cylinder, early design shown

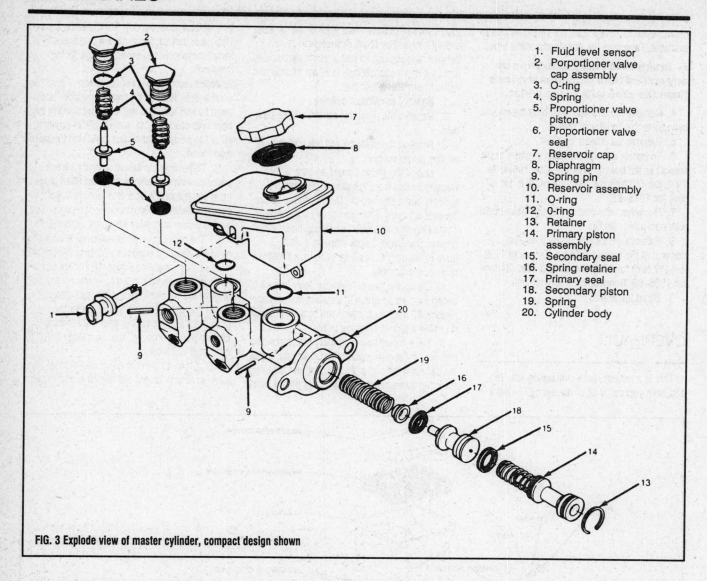

1. Fluid level sensor
2. Porportioner valve cap assembly
3. O-ring
4. Spring
5. Proportioner valve piston
6. Proportioner valve seal
7. Reservoir cap
8. Diaphragm
9. Spring pin
10. Reservoir assembly
11. O-ring
12. 0-ring
13. Retainer
14. Primary piston assembly
15. Secondary seal
16. Spring retainer
17. Primary seal
18. Secondary piston
19. Spring
20. Cylinder body

FIG. 3 Explode view of master cylinder, compact design shown

and do not wipe dry with a rag, which will leaves bits of lint behind. Inspect all parts for corrosion or wear. Generally, it is best to replace all rubber parts whenever the master cylinder is disassembled and replace any metal part which shows any sign of wear or corrosion.

11. Lubricate all parts with clean brake fluid before assembly.

12. Install the quick take-up valves into the master cylinder body and secure with the snaprings. Make sure the snaprings are properly seated in their grooves. Lubricate the new reservoir grommets with clean brake fluid and press them into the master cylinder.

13. Install the reservoir into the grommets by placing the reservoir on its lid and pressing the master cylinder body down onto it with a rocking motion.

14. Lubricate the switch piston assembly with clean brake fluid. Install new O-rings and retainers on the piston. Install the piston

assembly into the master cylinder and secure with the plug, using a new O-ring on the plug. Torque is 40–140 inch lbs. (5–16 Nm).

15. Assemble the new secondary piston seals onto the piston. Lubricate the parts with clean brake fluid, then install the spring, spring retainer and secondary piston into the cylinder. Install the primary piston, depress and install the lock ring.

16. Install new O-rings on the proportioners and the failure warning switch. Install the proportioners and torque to 18–30 ft. lbs. (25–40 Nm). Install the failure warning switch and torque to 15–50 inch lbs. (2–6 Nm).

17. Clamp the master cylinder body upright into a vise by one of the mounting flanges. Fill the reservoir with fresh brake fluid. Pump the piston with a dowel until fluid squirts from the outlet ports. Continue pumping until the expelled fluid is free of air bubbles.

18. Install the master cylinder and bleed the

brakes. Check the brake system for proper operation. Do not move the car until a "hard" brake pedal is obtained and the brake system has been thoroughly checked for soundness.

Power Brake Booster

REMOVAL & INSTALLATION

1. Remove the master cylinder from the booster. It is not necessary to disconnect the lines from the master cylinder. Just move the cylinder aside.

2. Disconnect the vacuum booster pushrod from the brake pedal inside the car. It is retained by a bolt. A spring washer lies under the bolt head, and a flat washer goes on the other side of the pushrod eye, next to the pedal arm.

FIG. 3a Check outside of master cylinder and brake lines for signs of leaks. Signs of dirt build up around brake lines is sometimes a sign of slight leakage

3. Remove the four attaching nuts from inside the car. Remove the booster.

4. Install the booster on the firewall. Tighten the mounting nuts to 22 ft. lbs. (30 Nm) for 1982–84 or 15 ft. lbs. (21 Nm) for 1985–88.

5. Connect the pushrod to the brake pedal.

6. Install the master cylinder. Mounting torque is 29 ft. lbs. (40 Nm) for 1982–84 or 22 ft. lbs. (27 Nm) for 1985–88.

OVERHAUL

This job is not difficult, but requires a number of special tools which are expensive, especially if they're to be used only once. Generally, it's better to leave this job to your dealer, or buy a rebuilt vacuum booster and install it yourself.

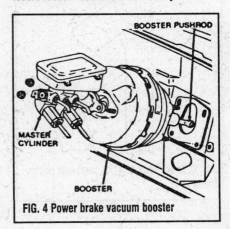

FIG. 4 Power brake vacuum booster

Hydro-Boost

Hydro-Boost differs from conventional power brake systems, in that it operates from power steering pump fluid pressure rather than intake manifold vacuum.

The Hydro-Boost unit contains a spool valve with an open center which controls the strength of the pump pressure when braking occurs. A lever assembly controls the valve's position. A boost piston provides the force necessary to operate the conventional master cylinder on the front of the booster.

A reserve of at least two assisted brake applications is supplied by an pneumatic accumulator. The accumulator is an integral part of the Hydro-Boost II unit. The brakes can be applied manually if the reserve system is depleted.

All system checks, tests and troubleshooting procedure are the same for the two systems.

1. Turn the engine off and pump the brake pedal 4 or 5 times to deplete the accumulator.

2. Remove the nuts from the master cylinder, then move the master cylinder away from the booster, with brake lines still attached.

3. Remove the hydraulic lines from the booster.

4. Remove the retainer and washer at the brake pedal.

5. Remove the attaching nuts retaining the booster fastened to the cowl and the booster.

6. To install, place the booster into position, reconnect the hydraulic lines, reconnect the booster rod to the brake pedal and torque the booster-to-cowl nuts to 15 ft. lbs., and the master cylinder-to-booster nuts to 20 ft. lbs. Bleed the power steering and hydro-booster system.

Proportioning Valves and Failure Warning Switch

These parts are installed in the master cylinder body. No separate proportioning or metering valve is used. Replacement of these parts requires disassembly of the master cylinder.

Brake Hoses

Brake hoses are rubber covered flex hoses designed to transmit brake pressure from the metal tubes running along the frame to the calipers in front and wheel cylinders in the rear.

The calipers and wheel cylinders are unsprung (ride along with the wheels) and the metal brake lines coming from the master cylinder are suspended by the vehicle's springs, along with the frame and body. The flex hoses permit the hydraulic force of the brake fluid to be transmitted to the wheels even though they are moving up and down in relation to the frame. The flexing can cause the hoses to wear, especially if the surface of a hose should rub against the frame or a suspension component. Inspect the hoses frequently and replace them if the rubber cover has cracked or deteriorated, or if there is any sign of leakage.

REMOVAL & INSTALLATION

Front

1. Remove the through bolt that fastens the hose to the caliper. Remove the washers, noting that there is one on either side of the fitting at the caliper end of the hose, and disconnect the hose.

2. If there is a clip retaining the connection at the frame, remove it. Then, unscrew the flare fitting located on the pipe running along the frame, using a backup wrench on the flats of the fitting at the end of the brake hose. Remove the brake line.

3. Install in reverse order, using new washers and torqueing the connection at the caliper to 33 ft. lbs. Bleed the system.

Rear

1. Remove the clips at either end of the hose. Unscrew the flared fitting located on the pipe running along the frame, using a backup wrench on the flats of the fitting at the end of the brake hose. Do the same with the flared fitting on the wheel cylinder end.

2. Install in reverse order. Bleed the system.

Bleeding

The purpose of bleeding the brakes is to expel air trapped in the hydraulic system. The system must be bled whenever the pedal feels spongy, indicating that compressible air has entered the system. It must also be bled whenever the system has been opened or repaired. You will need a helper for this job.

✳ CAUTION

Never reuse brake fluid which has been bled from the brake system. Brake fluid should be changed every few years. It wears out due to moisture being absorbed which lowers the boiling point.

➡ **Old brake fluid is often the cause of spongy brakes returning a week or so after bleeding the system. If all parts check good. Change the fluid by repeated bleeding.**

1. The sequence for bleeding is right rear, left front, left rear and right front. If the car has power brakes, remove the vacuum by applying the brakes several times. Do not run the engine while bleeding the brakes.

2. Clean all the bleeder screws. You may want to give each one a shot of penetrating solvent to loosen it up; seizure is a common problem with bleeder screws, which then break off, sometimes requiring replacement of the part to which they are attached.

3. Fill the master cylinder with DOT 3 brake fluid.

➡ **Brake fluid absorbs moisture from the air. Don't leave the master cylinder or the fluid container uncovered any longer than necessary. Be careful handling the fluid, it eats paint.**

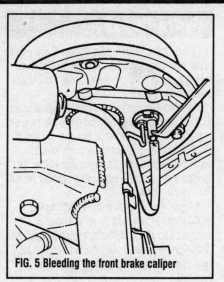

FIG. 5 Bleeding the front brake caliper

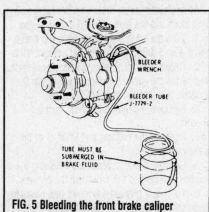

FIG. 5 Bleeding the front brake caliper

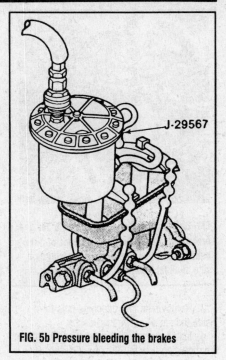

FIG. 5b Pressure bleeding the brakes

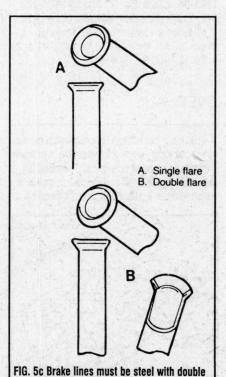

FIG. 5c Brake lines must be steel with double flared ends

A. Single flare
B. Double flare

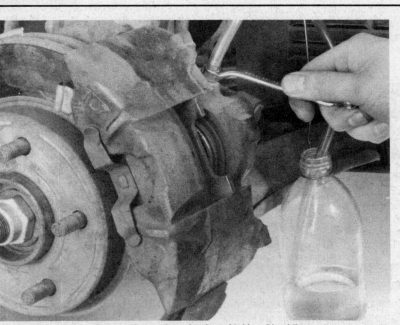
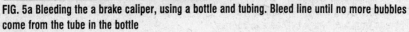

FIG. 5a Bleeding the a brake caliper, using a bottle and tubing. Bleed line until no more bubbles come from the tube in the bottle

Check the level of the fluid often when bleeding, and refill the reservoirs as necessary. Don't let them run dry, or you will have to repeat the process.

4. Attach a length of clear vinyl tubing to the bleeder screw on the wheel cylinder. Insert the other end of the tube into a clear, clean jar half filled with brake fluid.

5. Have your assistant slowly depress the brake pedal. As this is done, open the bleeder screw $1/3$–$1/2$ of a turn and allow the fluid to run through the tube. Then close the bleeder screw before the pedal reaches the end of its travel. Have your assistant slowly release the pedal. Repeat this process until no air bubbles appear in the expelled fluid.

6. Repeat the procedure on the other three brakes, checking the level of fluid in the master cylinder reservoir often.

After you're done, there should be no in the brake pedal feel. If there is, either there is still air in the line, in which case the process should be repeated or there is a leak somewhere, which of course must be corrected before the car is moved.

FRONT DISC BRAKES

❄ CAUTION

Brake shoes contain asbestos, which has been determined to be a cancer causing agent. Never clean the brake surfaces with compressed air! Avoid inhaling any dust from any brake surface! When cleaning brake surfaces, use a commercially available brake cleaning fluid.

Brake Pads

INSPECTION

The pad thickness should be inspected every time that the tires are removed for rotation. The outer pad can be checked by looking in at each end, which is the point at which the highest rate of wear occurs. The inner pad can be checked by looking down through the inspection hole in the top of the caliper. If the thickness of the pad is worn to within 0.030 in. (0.76mm) of the rivet at either end of the pad, all the pads should be replaced. This is the factory recommended measurement; your state's automobile inspection laws may not agree with this.

➡ **Always replace all pads on both front wheels at the same time. Failure to do so will result in uneven braking action and premature wear.**

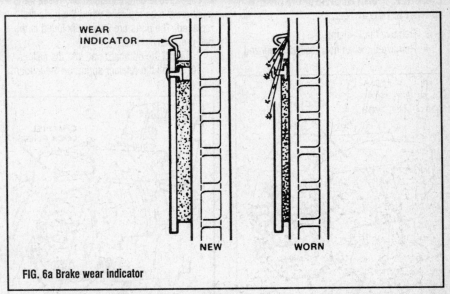

FIG. 6a Brake wear indicator

FIG. 7 The brake pads can be inspected with wheel removed, by looking through the caliper opening

REMOVAL & INSTALLATION

◆ SEE FIGS. 7 to 18

1. Siphon ⅔ of the brake fluid from the master cylinder reservoir. Loosen the wheel lug nuts and raise the car. Remove the wheel.

2. Position a C-clamp across the caliper so that it presses on the pads and tighten it until the caliper bottoms in its bore.

➡ **If you haven't removed some brake fluid from the master cylinder, it will overflow when the piston is retracted.**

3. Remove the C-clamp.

4. Remove the allen head caliper mounting bolts. Inspect the bolts for corrosion and replace as necessary.

5. Remove the caliper from the steering knuckle and suspend it from the body of the car with a length of wire. Do not allow the caliper to hang by its hose.

6. Remove the pad retaining springs and the pads from the caliper.

7. Remove the plastic sleeves and the rubber bushings from the mounting bolt holes.

8. Install new sleeves and bushings. Lubricate the sleeves with a light coating of silicone grease before installation. These parts must always be replaced when the pads are replaced. The parts are usually included in the pad replacement kits.

9. Install the outboard pad into the caliper.

10. Install the retainer spring on the inboard pad. A new spring should be included in the pad replacement kit.

11. Install the new inboard into the caliper. The retention lugs fit into the piston.

12. Use a large pair of slip joint pliers to bend the outer pad ears down over the caliper.

13. Install the caliper onto the steering knuckle. Tighten the mounting bolts to 28 ft. lbs. (38 Nm) for 1982–84 or 40 ft. lbs. (51 Nm) for 1985–92. Install the wheel and lower the car. Fill the master cylinder to its proper level with fresh brake fluid meeting DOT 3 specifications. Since the brake hose wasn't disconnected it isn't really necessary to bleed the brakes, although most mechanics do this as a matter of course.

Brake Caliper

REMOVAL & INSTALLATION

1. Follow Steps 1, 2 and 3 of the pad replacement procedure.

2. Before removing the caliper mounting bolts, remove the bolt holding the brake hose to the caliper.

3. Remove the allen head caliper mounting bolts. Inspect them for corrosion and replace them if necessary.

4. Install the caliper and brake pads over the rotor. Mounting bolt torque is 28 ft. lbs. (38 Nm) for 1982–84 or 40 ft. lbs. (51 Nm) for 1985–92 for the caliper.

5. Install the brake hose to the caliper. The brake hose fitting should be tightened to 33 ft. lbs. (45 Nm).

6. Install the wheel and tire and lower the vehicle.

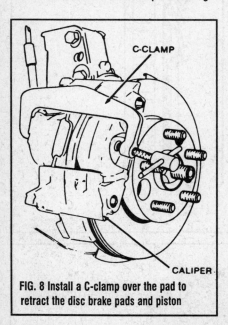

FIG. 8 Install a C-clamp over the pad to retract the disc brake pads and piston

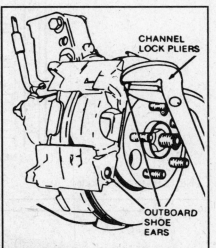

FIG. 9 Bend the outboard pad ears into place with a large pair of slip joint pliers

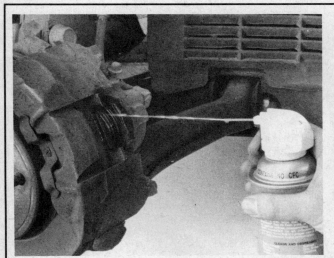

FIG. 10 First step in brake repair is to clean the brake components with proper brake cleaning chemicals, to avoid dry brake dust

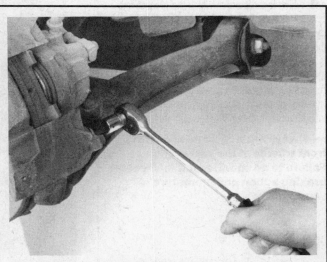

FIG. 11 Remove caliper retaining bolts. Make certain socket or hex is a perfect fit. Use one lugnut to keep rotor from falling off

FIG. 12 Remove caliper and support with clothes hanger. Don't allow to hang from brake hose. Outboard pad is sometimes a very tight

FIG. 13 When removing the inboard pad note the location and direction of the retaining pins

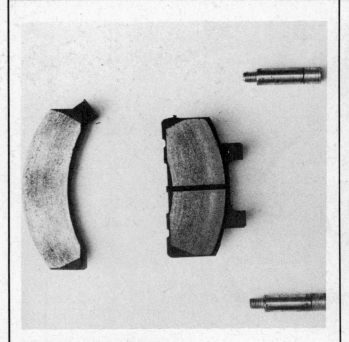

FIG. 14 Front disc pads and caliper pins

FIG. 15 Front piston can be pressed back into caliper using slip-joint pliers or a C-clamp. Remove 1/3 the fluid from the master cylinder

FIG. 16 Install caliper taking care not to kink brake hose

FIG. 17 Clean, lubricate and install caliper retaining pins

FIG. 18 Your completed disc brake replacement should be bled and road tested

OVERHAUL

1. Remove the caliper.
2. Remove the pads.
3. Place some cloths or a slat of wood in front of the piston. Remove the piston by applying compressed air to the fluid inlet fitting. Use just enough air pressure to ease the piston from the bore.

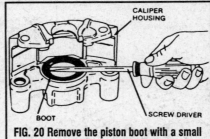
FIG. 20 Remove the piston boot with a small flat tool

✳✳ CAUTION

Do not try to catch the piston with your fingers, which can result in serious injury.

4. Remove the piston boot with a screwdriver, working carefully so that the piston bore is not scratched.
5. Remove the bleeder screw.

6. Inspect the piston for scoring, nicks, corrosion, wear, etc., and damaged or worn chrome plating. Replace the piston if any defects are found.
7. Remove the piston seal from the caliper bore groove using a piece of pointed wood or plastic. Do not use a screwdriver, which will damage the bore. Inspect the caliper bore for nicks, corrosion and so on. Very light wear can be cleaned up with crocus cloth. Use finger

pressure to rub the crocus cloth around the circumference of the bore; do not slide it in and out. More extensive wear or corrosion warrants replacement of the part.

8. Clean any parts which are to be reused in denatured alcohol. Dry them with compressed or allow to air dry. Don't wipe the parts dry with a cloth, which will leave behind bits of lint.
9. Lubricate the new seal, provided in the repair kit, with clean brake fluid. Install the seal in its groove, making sure it is fully seated and not twisted.
10. Install the new dust boot on the piston. Lubricate the bore of the caliper with clean brake fluid and insert the piston into its bore. Position the boot in the caliper housing and seat with a seal driver of the appropriate size, or G.M. tool N. J–29077.
11. Install the bleeder screw, tightening to 110 inch lbs. (13 Nm) for 1982–84 or 120 inch lbs. (14 Nm) for 1985–92. Do not overtighten.
12. Install the pads, the caliper and bleed the brakes.

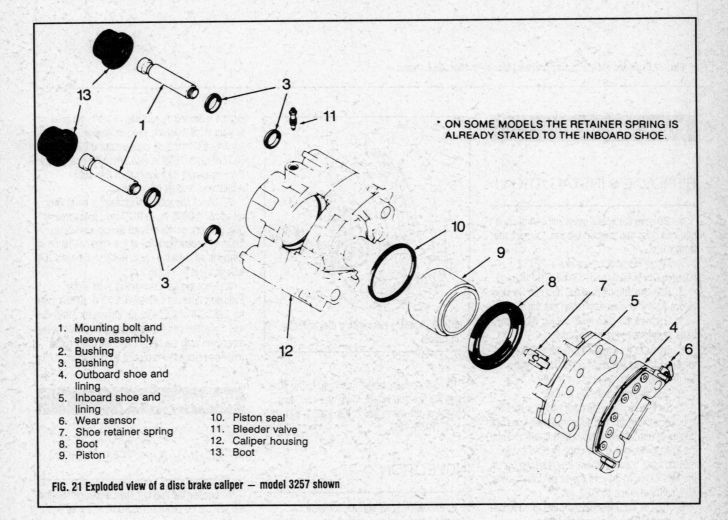

* ON SOME MODELS THE RETAINER SPRING IS ALREADY STAKED TO THE INBOARD SHOE.

1. Mounting bolt and sleeve assembly
2. Bushing
3. Bushing
4. Outboard shoe and lining
5. Inboard shoe and lining
6. Wear sensor
7. Shoe retainer spring
8. Boot
9. Piston
10. Piston seal
11. Bleeder valve
12. Caliper housing
13. Boot

FIG. 21 Exploded view of a disc brake caliper — model 3257 shown

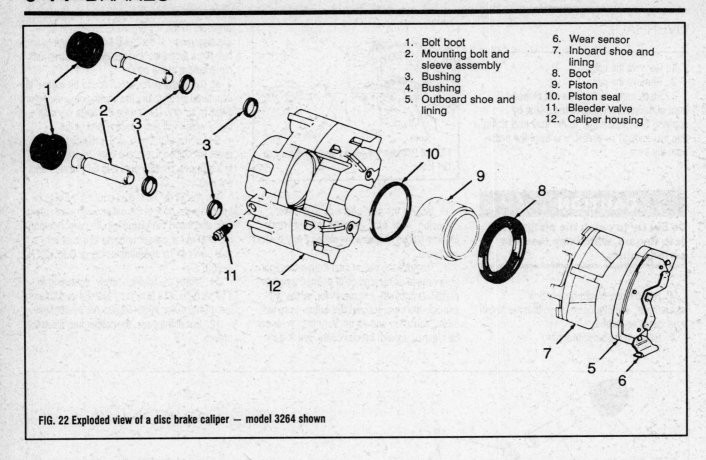

1. Bolt boot
2. Mounting bolt and sleeve assembly
3. Bushing
4. Bushing
5. Outboard shoe and lining
6. Wear sensor
7. Inboard shoe and lining
8. Boot
9. Piston
10. Piston seal
11. Bleeder valve
12. Caliper housing

FIG. 22 Exploded view of a disc brake caliper — model 3264 shown

Brake Disc (Rotor)

REMOVAL & INSTALLATION

1. Remove the wheel cover, loosen the hub nut, and raise and support the car. Remove the front wheel.

2. Install the boot cover, tool J–28712 (Double-Offset joint) or J–33162 (Tri-Pot joint).

3. Remove and discard the hub nut. Be sure to use a new one on assembly, not the old one.

4. Remove the allen head caliper mounting bolts and remove the brake caliper.

5. Remove the caliper from the knuckle and suspend from a length of wire. Do not allow the caliper to hang from the brake hose.

6. Pull the rotor from the knuckle.

7. To install, place the rotor onto the steering knuckle, then install the hub nut. When the shaft begins to turn with the hub, insert a drift through the caliper into one of the cooling slots in the rotor to keep it from turning. Insert a long bolt in the hub flange to prevent the shaft from turning. Tighten the hub nut to 70 ft. lbs.

8. Tighten the brake caliper bolts to 30 ft. lbs.

9. Remove the boot seal protector.

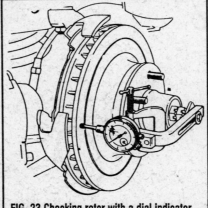

FIG. 23 Checking rotor with a dial indicator for runout

10. Connect the brake hose clip to the strut. Install the tire and wheel, lower the car, and tighten the hub nut to 225 ft. lbs. (1981–82); 185 ft. lbs. (1983–92).

INSPECTION

1. Check the rotor surface for wear or scoring. Deep scoring, grooves or rust pitting

can be removed by refacing, a job to be referred to your local machine shop or garage. Minimum thickness is stamped on the rotor 0.030 in. (0.76mm) or 0.972 in. (24.7mm) for heavy duty. If the rotor will be thinner than this after refinishing, it must be replaced.

2. Check the rotor parallelism; it must vary less than 0.0005 in. (0.0127mm) measured at four or more points around the circumference. Make all measurements at the same distance in from the edge of the rotor. Refinish the rotor if it fails to meet this specification.

3. Measure the disc runout with a dial indicator. If runout exceeds 0.002 in. (0.051mm) for 1982–84 or 0.004 in. (0.10mm) for 1985–88 and the wheel bearings are OK (if runout is being measured with the disc on the car), the rotor must be refaced or replaced as necessary.

Wheel Bearing

REMOVAL & INSTALLATION

1. Loosen the hub nut, then raise and support the vehicle on jackstands. Remove the wheel and tire assembly.

2. Using tool J–28712 (Double-Offset Joint) or J–33162 (Tri-Pot Joint), install it over the drive axle joint boot.

3. Remove the hub nut, the caliper (support it on a wire) and the rotor.

4. Remove the hub/bearing assembly-to-steering knuckle mounting bolts and the bearing assembly, then the splash shield.

➡ **If the bearing assembly is to be reused, mark the assembly and the steering knuckle so that the assembly can be reinstalled in the same position. To prevent damage to the bearing, DO NOT use heat or a hammer.**

5. Install tool J–28733 to the bearing assembly and press the assembly from the drive axle.

6. Remove the steering knuckle seal from the inboard side and cut it off the drive axle.

➡ **On the 1985 and later models with a standard bearing, it will be necessary to remove the steering knuckle from the vehicle. Disconnect the stabilizer bar from the lower control arm, using tool J–29330, separate the ball joint from the steering knuckle, then disconnect the steering knuckle from the strut. Support the drive axle (out of the way) on a wire. Using a brass drift, drive the inner knuckle seal from the steering knuckle.**

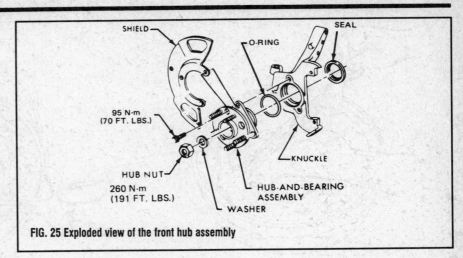

FIG. 25 Exploded view of the front hub assembly

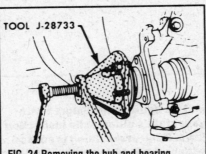

FIG. 24 Removing the hub and bearing assembly

7. Clean the gasket and the seal mounting surfaces.

8. Using tool J–28671 (1982–84) or J–34657 (1985–88 heavy duty), install the new steering knuckle seal from the outboard side; use tool J–34658 (1985–88 standard duty) to install the seal from the inboard side. Grease the lip of the seal with wheel bearing grease.

9. Install a new O-ring between the steering knuckle and the bearing assembly.

10. To complete the installation, reverse the removal procedures. Torque the bearing assembly-to-steering knuckle bolts to 63 ft. lbs. (85 Nm) for 1982–85 standard duty or 77 ft. lbs. (104 Nm) for 1985–88 heavy duty.

11. Install the hub/bearing assembly-to-drive axle nut and partially torque to 74 ft. lbs. (100 Nm), then lower the vehicle and torque the hub nut to 214 ft. lbs. (289 Nm) for 1982 or 192 ft. lbs. (260 Nm) for 1983–88.

REAR DRUM BRAKES

✷✷ CAUTION

Brake shoes contain asbestos, which has been determined to be a cancer causing agent. Never clean the brake surfaces with compressed air! Avoid inhaling any dust from any brake surface! When cleaning brake surfaces, use a commercially available brake cleaning fluid.

Brake Drums

REMOVAL & INSTALLATION

1. Loosen the wheel lug nuts. Raise and support the car. Mark the relationship of the wheel to the axle and remove the wheel.

2. Mark the relationship of the drum to the axle and remove the drum. If it cannot be slipped off easily, check to see that the parking brake is fully released. If so, the brake shoes are probably locked against the drum. See the "Adjustment" section earlier in this section for details on how to back off the adjuster.

3. Installation is the reverse. Be sure to align the matchmarks made during removal. Lug nut torque is 102 ft. lbs. (140 Nm).

INSPECTION

1. After removing the brake drum, wipe out the accumulated dust with a damp cloth.

✷✷ WARNING

Do not blow the brake dust out of the drums with compressed air or lung-power. Brake linings contain asbestos, a known cancer causing substance. Dispose of the cloth used to clean the parts after use.

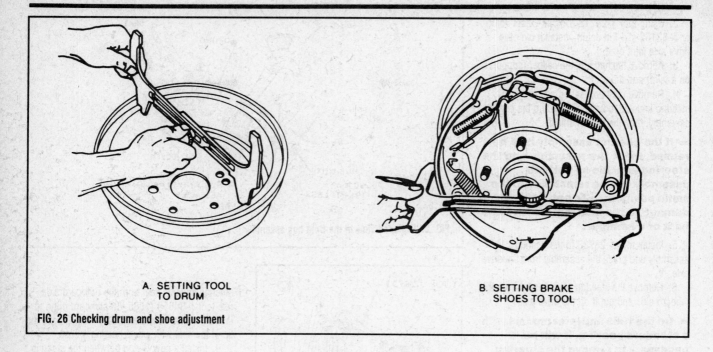

A. SETTING TOOL TO DRUM

B. SETTING BRAKE SHOES TO TOOL

FIG. 26 Checking drum and shoe adjustment

2. Inspect the drums for cracks, deep grooves, roughness, scoring, or out-of-roundness. Replace any drum which is cracked; do not try to weld it up.

3. Smooth any slight scores by polishing the friction surface with fine emery cloth. Heavy or extensive scoring will cause excessive lining wear and should be removed from the drum through resurfacing, a job to be referred to your local machine shop or garage. The maximum finished diameter of the drums is 7.894 in. (200.5mm) for 1982–84 or 8.92 in. (226.57mm) for 1985–88. The drum must be replaced if the diameter is 7.929 in. (201.40mm) for 1982–84 or 8.95 in. (227.33mm) for 1985 or newer.

Brake Shoes

▶ SEE FIGS. 27 to 47

INSPECTION

After removing the brake drum, inspect the brake shoes. If the lining is worn down to within $1/_{32}$ in. (0.8mm) of a rivet, the shoes must be replaced.

➡ **This figure may disagree with your state's automobile inspection laws. If the brake lining is soaked with brake fluid or grease, it must be replaced. If this is the case, the brake drum should be sanded with crocus cloth to remove all traces of brake fluid, and the wheel cylinders should be rebuilt. Clean all grit from the friction surface of the drum before replacing it.**

If the lining is chipped, cracked or otherwise damaged, it must be replaced with a new lining.

➡ **Always replace the brake linings in sets of two on both ends of the axle. Never replace just one shoe or both shoes on one side.**

Check the condition of the shoes, retracting springs and holddown springs for signs of overheating. If the shoes or springs have a slight blue color, this indicates overheating, then replacement of the shoes and springs is recommended. The wheel cylinders should be rebuilt as a precaution against future problems.

REMOVAL & INSTALLATION

1. Loosen the lug nuts on the wheel to be serviced, raise and support the car, and remove the wheel and brake drum.

➡ **It is not really necessary to remove the hub and wheel bearing assembly from the axle, but it does make the job easier. If you can work with the hub and bearing assembly in place, skip down to Step 3.**

2. Remove the four hub and bearing assembly retaining bolts and remove the assembly from the axle.

3. Remove the return springs from the shoes with a pair of needle nose pliers. There are also special brake spring pliers for this job.

4. Remove the hold down springs by gripping them with a pair of pliers, then pressing down and turning 90°. There are special tools to grab and turn these parts, but pliers work fairly well.

5. Remove the shoe holddown pins from behind the brake backing plate. They will simply slide out once the holddown spring tension is relieved.

6. Lift up the actuator lever for the self-adjusting mechanism and remove the actuating link. Remove the actuator lever, pivot and the pivot return spring.

7. Spread the shoes apart to clear the wheel cylinder pistons, then remove the parking brake strut and spring.

8. If the hub and bearing assembly is still in place, spread the shoes far enough apart to clear it.

9. Disconnect the parking brake cable from the lever. Remove the shoes, still connected by their adjusting screw spring, from the car.

FIG. 27 Discard the metal retaining clips; they are only used to retain drums on the assembly line

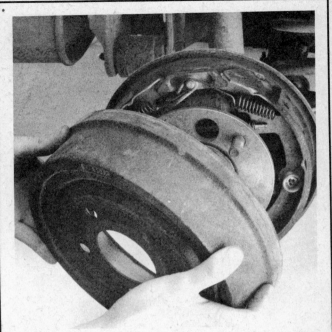

FIG. 28 Slide drum off carefully to avoid creating brake dust

FIG. 29 First step in brake repair is to clean the brake components with proper brake cleaning chemicals, to avoid dry brake dust

FIG. 30 Removing return springs

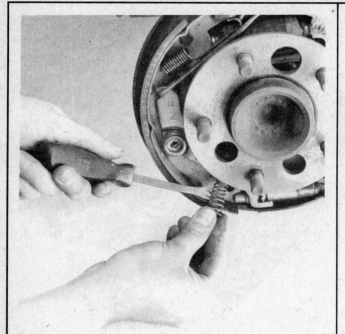

FIG. 31 Removing self-adjuster lever anti-rattle spring

FIG. 32 Pull back on parking brake lever to allow enough room to remove from anchor

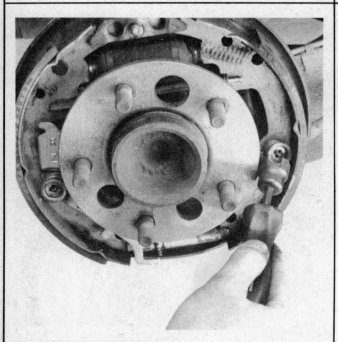

FIG. 33 Removing hold-down springs

FIG. 34 Remove brake shoes; note that parking brake lever is still attached to secondary brake shoe

FIG. 35 Twist brake shoe assembly around and remove parking brake lever

FIG. 36 Keep brake components in order for easy installation

FIG. 37 Clean and lubricate the backing plate

FIG. 38 Install new brake shoes, make certain adjuster spring does NOT touch starwheel

FIG. 39 Install the parking brake lever on secondary shoe

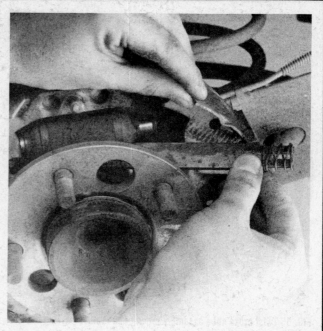

FIG. 40 Insert parking brake strut rod, spring end toward primary shoe

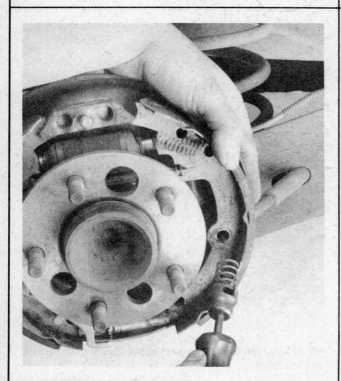

FIG. 41 Install the hold-down springs

FIG. 42 Install the self-adjuster lever

FIG. 43 Install the return springs

FIG. 44 Check all components for proper seating and arrangement before installing drum and adjusting

10. With the shoes removed, note the position of the adjusting spring, then remove the spring and adjusting screw.

11. Remove the C-clip from the parking brake lever and the lever from the secondary shoe.

12. Use a damp cloth to remove all dirt and dust from the backing plate and brake parts.

13. Check the wheel cylinder by carefully pulling the lower edges of the wheel cylinder boots away from the cylinders. If there is excessive leakage, the inside of the cylinder will be moist with fluid. If leakage exists, a wheel cylinder overhaul is in order. Do not delay, because brake failure could result.

➡ **A small amount of fluid will be present to act as a lubricant or the wheel cylinder pistons. Fluid spilling from the boot center hole, after the piston is removed, indicates cup leakage and the necessity for cylinder overhaul.**

14. Check the backing plate attaching bolts to make sure that they are tight. Use fine emery cloth to clean all rust and dirt from the shoe contact surfaces on the plate.

15. Lubricate the fulcrum end of the parking brake lever with brake grease specially made for the purpose. Install the lever on the secondary shoe and secure with the C-clip.

16. Install the adjusting screw and spring on the shoes, connecting them together. The coils of the spring must not be over the star wheel on the adjuster. The left and right hand springs are not interchangeable. Do not mix them up.

17. Lubricate the shoe contact surfaces on the backing plate with the brake grease. Be certain when you are using this stuff that none of it actually gets on the linings or drums. Apply the same grease to the point where the parking brake cable contacts the plate. Use the grease sparingly.

18. Spread the shoe assemblies apart and connect the parking brake cable. Install the shoes on the backing plate, engaging the shoes at the top temporarily with the wheel cylinder pistons. Make sure that the star wheel on the adjuster is lined up with the adjusting hole in the backing plate, if the hole is back there.

19. Spread the shoes apart slightly and install the parking brake strut and spring. Make sure that the end of the strut without the spring engages the parking brake lever. The end with the spring engages the primary shoe (the one with the shorter lining).

20. Install the actuator pivot, lever and return spring. Install the actuating link in the shoe retainer. Lift up the actuator lever and hook the link into the lever.

21. Install the holddown pins through the back of the plate, install the lever pivots and holddown springs. Install the shoe return springs with a pair of pliers. Be very careful not to stretch or otherwise distort these springs.

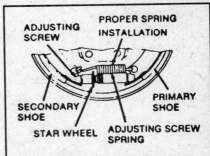

FIG. 45 Proper spring installation with the coils over adjuster body and not touching the star wheel. The star wheel movement must not be stopped by the spring

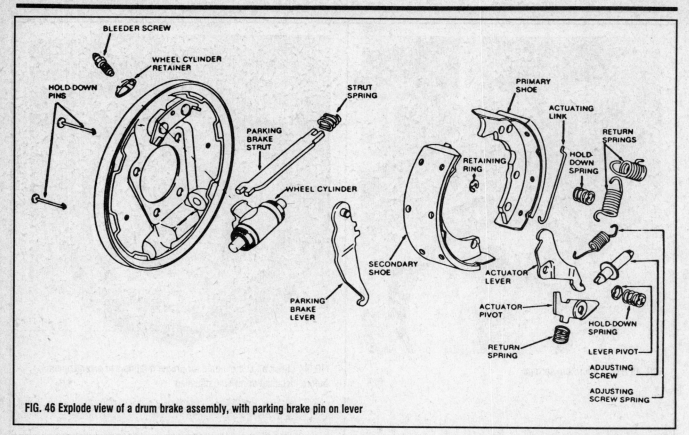

FIG. 46 Explode view of a drum brake assembly, with parking brake pin on lever

1. Return spring
2. Return spring
3. Hold down spring
4. Lever pivot
5. Hold down pin
6. Actuator link
7. Actuator lever
8. Lever return spring
9. Parking brake strut
10. Strut spring
11. Primary (small) shoe & lining
12. Secondary (larger) shoe & lining
13. Adjusting screw spring
14. Socket
15. Pivot nut
16. Adjusting screw
17. Retaining ring
18. Pin
19. Parking brake lever
20. Bleeder valve
21. Bolt
22. Boot
23. Piston
24. Seal
25. Spring assembly
26. Wheel cylinder
27. Backing plate

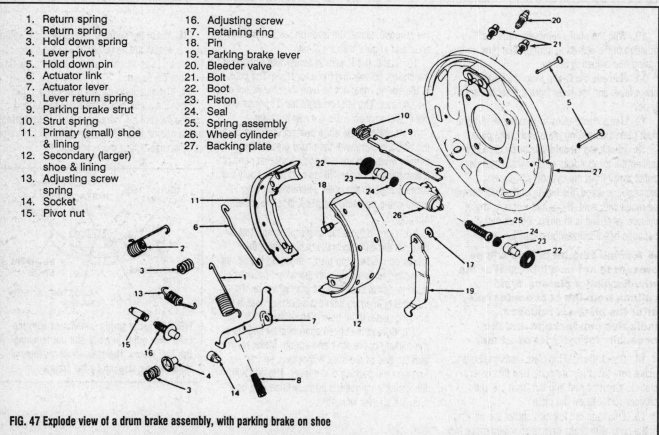

FIG. 47 Explode view of a drum brake assembly, with parking brake on shoe

22. Take a look at everything. Make sure the linings are in the right place, the self-adjusting mechanism is correctly installed and the parking brake parts are all hooked up. if in doubt, remove the other wheel and take a look at that one for comparison.

23. Measure the width of the linings, then measure the inside width of the drum. Adjust the linings by means of the adjuster so that the drum will fit onto the linings.

24. Install the hub and bearing assembly onto the axle if removed. Tighten the retaining bolts to 45 ft. lbs. (60 Nm).

25. Install the drum and wheel. Adjust the brakes. Be sure to install a rubber hole cover in the knock-out hole after the adjustment is complete. Adjust the parking brake.

26. Lower the car and check the pedal for any sponginess or lack of a "hard" feel. Check the braking action and the parking brake. The brakes must not be applied severely immediately after installation. They should be used moderately for the first 200 miles of city driving or 1000 miles of highway driving, to allow the linings to conform to the shape of the drum.

Wheel Cylinders

◆ SEE FIGS. 48 to 50

REMOVAL & INSTALLATION

1. Loosen the wheel lug nuts, raise and support the car, and remove the wheel. Remove the drum and brake shoes. Leave the hub and wheel bearing assembly in place.

2. Remove any dirt from around the brake line fitting. Disconnect the brake line.

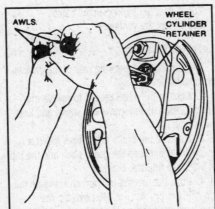

FIG. 48 Remove the wheel cylinder retainer from the backing plate with a pair of awls or punches. Wear eye protection

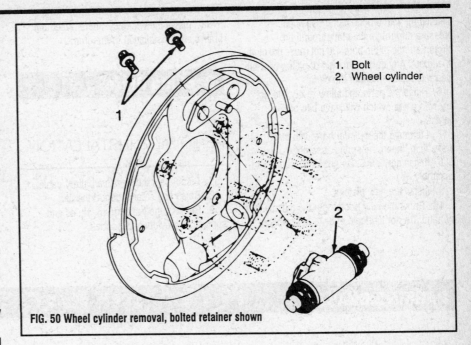

1. Bolt
2. Wheel cylinder

FIG. 50 Wheel cylinder removal, bolted retainer shown

3. If the wheel cylinder is retained with #6 torx head bolts simply remove the bolts. If retained with clips, remove the wheel cylinder retainer by using two awls or punches with a tip diameter of 1/8 in. (3mm) or less. Insert the awls or punches into the access slots between the wheel cylinder pilot and retainer locking tabs. Bend both tabs away simultaneously. Remove the wheel cylinder from the backing plate.

To install:

4. If retained with bolts simply install wheel cylinder and tighten bolts to 15 ft. lbs. (20 Nm). If retained with clips, position the wheel cylinder against the backing plate and hold it in place with a wooden block between the wheel cylinder and the hub and bearing assembly.

5. Install a new retainer over the wheel cylinder abutment on the rear of the backing plate by pressing it into place with an 1 1/8 in. 12-point socket and an extension.

6. Install a new bleeder screw into the wheel cylinder. Install brake line and torque to 10–15 ft. lbs. (14–20 Nm).

7. Install the brake shoes and drum. Adjust the brakes.

8. Install the tire and wheel assembly.

9. Lower the vehicle.

10. Bleed the brake system.

11. Install a new retainer over the wheel cylinder abutment on the rear of the backing plate by pressing it into place with a 1 1/8 in. 12-point socket and an extension.

12. Install a new bleeder screw into the wheel cylinder. Install the brake line and tighten to 12.5 ft. lbs. (17 Nm) for 1982–84 or 18 ft. lbs. (24 Nm) for 1985 and newer.

13. The rest of installation is the reverse of removal. After the drum is installed, bleed the brakes.

OVERHAUL

As is the case with master cylinders, overhaul kits are available for the wheel cylinders. And, as is the case with master cylinders, it is usually more profitable to simply buy new or rebuilt wheel cylinders rather rebuilding them. When rebuilding wheel cylinders, avoid getting any contaminants in the system. Always install new high quality brake fluid; the use of improper fluid will swell and deteriorate the rubber parts.

1. Remove the wheel cylinders.

2. Remove the rubber boots from the cylinder ends. Discard the boots.

3. Remove and discard the pistons and cups.

4. Wash the cylinder and metal parts in denatured alcohol.

❊❊ CAUTION

Never use mineral based solvents to clean the brake parts.

5. Allow the parts to air dry and inspect the cylinder bore for corrosion or wear. Light corrosion can be cleaned up with crocus cloth; use finger pressure and rotate the cloth around the circumference of the bore. Do not move the cloth in and out. Any deep corrosion can be

cleaned up with crocus cloth; use finger pressure and rotate the cloth around the circumference of the bore. Do not move the cloth in and out. Any deep corrosion or pitting or wear warrants replacement of the parts.

6. Rinse the parts and allow to dry. Do not dry with a rag, which will leave bits of line behind.

7. Lubricate the cylinder bore with clean brake fluid. Insert the spring assembly.

8. Install new cups. Do not lubricate prior to assembly.

9. Install the new pistons.

10. Press the new boots onto the cylinders by hand. Do not lubricate prior to assembly.

11. Install the wheel cylinders. Bleed the brakes after installation of the drum.

Backing Plate

REMOVAL & INSTALLATION

1. Disconnect the negative battery cable.
2. Raise and safely support the car.
3. Remove the brake drum, shoes and springs as previously described.

4. Remove the brake line from the wheel cylinder.

5. Remove the parking brake cable.

6. Remove the hub and bearing assembly.

7. Remove the backing plate.

To Install:

8. Install the backing plate to axle.

9. Install the hub and bearing assembly.

10. Install the parking brake cable.

11. Install the wheel cylinder and brake line, following procedures given earlier.

12. Install the brake components, shoes, spring, etc..

13. Adjust and bleed the rear brakes.

14. Adjust the parking brake cables.

PARKING BRAKE

Cables

REMOVAL & INSTALLATION
▶ SEE FIGS. 51 to 52

Front Cable

1. Raise and safely support the vehicle.
2. Loosen the equalizer nut.
3. Disconnect the front cable from the connector and equalizer.
4. Remove the clip at the frame.
5. Remove the cable from the hanger.
6. Lower the vehicle.

7. Remove the 3 screws and 1 nut and lower the driver's side sound insulator panel.

8. Remove the carpet finish molding. Lift the carpet.

9. Remove the cable retaining clip at the lever assembly.

10. Depress the retaining tangs and remove the cable and casing from the lever assembly.

11. Remove the cable from the retaining clips.

12. Remove the grommet retainer from the floor pan.

13. Unseat the grommet and pull the cable through the floor pan.

To install:

14. Insert the cable through the floor pan and grommet.

15. Seat the grommet. Install the grommet retainer to the floor pan.

16. Fasten the cable in the retaining clips.

17. Connect the cable and casing to the lever assembly. Seat the retaining tangs.

18. Install the cable retaining clip at the lever assembly.

19. Place the carpet into position. Install the carpet finish molding.

20. Install the driver's side sound insulator panel and attaching screws and nuts.

21. Raise and safely support the vehicle.

22. Fasten the cable to the hanger.

23. Install the clip to the frame.

24. Connect the front cable to the equalizer and connector.

25. Adjust the parking brake cable.

26. Lower the vehicle.

Left Rear Cable

1. Raise and support the rear of the vehicle on jackstands.

2. Loosen the equalizer nut to relieve the cable tension, then remove the wheel and tire assembly.

3. Remove the brake drum, then insert a screwdriver between the brake shoe and the top of the brake adjuster bracket.

4. Push the bracket forward and release the top adjuster bracket rod. Remove the rear holddown spring, the actuator lever and the lever return spring.

5. Remove the adjuster screw spring and the top rear brake shoe return spring.

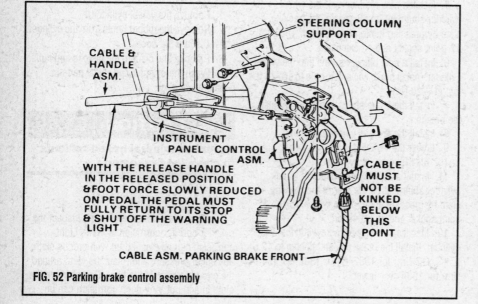

FIG. 52 Parking brake control assembly

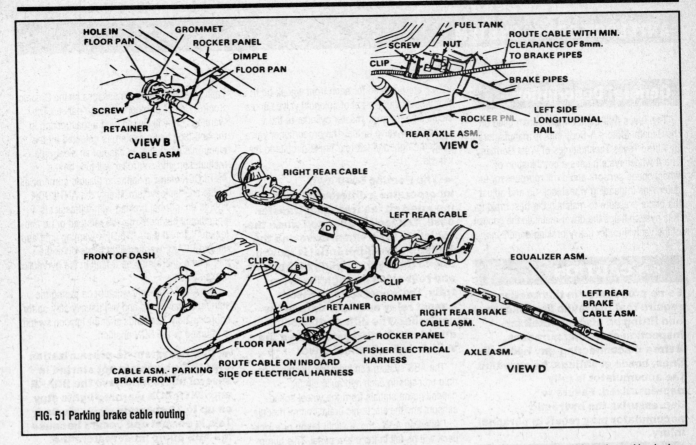

FIG. 51 Parking brake cable routing

6. Remove the parking brake cable from the parking brake lever.

7. Depress the conduit fitting retaining tangs and remove the fitting from the backing plate.

8. Back off the equalizer nut and remove the left cable from the equalizer.

9. Depress the conduit fitting retaining tangs and remove the fitting from the axle bracket.

To install:

10. Install the cable through the rear of the backing plate. Seat the retaining tangs in the backing plate.

11. Connect the cable to the parking brake lever.

12. Install the brake drum, tire and wheel.

13. Connect the cable at the equalizer and connector.

14. Adjust the regular service brake shoes, then adjust the parking brake cable.

15. Lower the vehicle.

Right Rear Cable

1. Raise and support the rear of the vehicle on jackstands.

2. Loosen the equalizer nut to relieve the cable tension, then remove the wheel and tire assembly.

3. Remove the brake drum, then insert a screwdriver between the brake shoe and the top of the brake adjuster bracket.

4. Push the bracket forward and release the top adjuster bracket rod. Remove the rear holddown spring, the actuator lever and the lever return spring.

5. Remove the adjuster screw spring and the top rear brake shoe return spring.

6. Remove the parking brake cable from the parking brake lever.

7. Depress the conduit fitting retaining tangs and remove the fitting from the backing plate.

8. Remove the cable button end from the connector.

9. Depress the conduit fitting retaining tangs and remove the fitting from the axle bracket.

To install:

10. Install the cable through the rear of the backing plate. Seat the retaining tangs in the backing plate.

11. Connect the cable to the parking brake lever.

12. Install the brake drum, tire and wheel.

13. Connect the cable at the equalizer and connector.

14. Adjust the regular service brake, then adjust the parking brake cable.

15. Lower the vehicle.

ADJUSTMENT

1. Raise and support the car with both rear wheels off the ground.

2. Depress the parking brake pedal exactly three ratchet clicks.

3. Loosen the equalizer locknut, then tighten the adjusting nut until the left rear wheel can just be turned backward using two hands, but is locked in forward rotation.

4. Tighten the locknut.

5. Release the parking brake. Rotate the rear wheels; there should be no drag.

6. Lower the car.

ANTI-LOCK BRAKE SYSTEM

General Description

The Teves Anti-Lock Brake System used on the General Motors A-Body cars is manufactured by Alfred Teves Technologies of West Germany. The 4 wheel system uses a combination of wheel speed sensors and a microprocessor to determine impending wheel lock-up and adjust the brake pressure to maintain the best braking. This system helps the driver maintain the control of the vehicle under heavy braking conditions.

✳✳ CAUTION

Some procedures in this section require that hydraulic lines, hoses and fitting be disconnected for inspection or testing purposes. Before disconnecting any hydraulic lines, hoses or fittings, be sure that the accumulator is fully depressurized. Failure to depressurize the hydraulic accumulator may result in personal injury.

➡ **The use of rubber hoses or parts other than those specified for the ABS system may lead to functional problems and/or impaired braking or ABS function. Install all components included in repair kits for this system. Lubricate rubber pats with clean fresh brake fluid to ease assembly. Do not use lubricated shop air to clean or dry components; damage to rubber parts may result.**

SYSTEM OPERATION

Under normal driving conditions the Anti-lock system functions the same as a standard brake system. The primary difference is that the power assist for normal braking is provided by the booster portion of the hydraulic unit through the use of pressurized brake fluid.

If a wheel locking tendency is noted during a brake application, the ABS system will modulate hydraulic pressure in the individual wheel circuits to prevent any wheel from locking. A separate hydraulic line and 2 specific solenoid valves are provided for each front wheel; both rear wheels share a set of solenoid valves and a single pipe from the master cylinder to the proportioner valve or tee. The proportioner valve splits the right and left rear brake circuits to the wheels.

➡ **The Pontiac 6000 AWD incorporates a differential lock mounted on the transaxle transfer case. The lock is engaged when the vehicle is in all wheel drive and the transfer case differential is locked. Due to the rigid coupling of the front and rear axles through the drive train, the wheel speed sensors cannot relay accurate data to the controller. The differential lock disables the ABS system when the vehicle is in all wheel drive.**

The ABS system can increase, decrease or hold pressure in each hydraulic circuit depending on signals from the wheel speed sensors and the electronic brake control module.

During an ABS stop, a slight bump or a kick-back will be felt in the brake pedal. This bump will be followed by a series of short pulsations which occur in rapid succession. The brake pedal pulsations will continue until there is no longer a need for the anti-lock function or until the vehicle is stopped. A slight ticking or popping noise may be heard during brake applications with anti-lock. This noise is normal and indicates that the anti-lock system is being used.

During anti-lock stops on dry pavement, the tires may make intermittent chirping noises as they approach lock-up. These noises are considered normal as long as the wheel does not truly lock or skid. When the anti-lock system is being used, the brake pedal may rise even as the brakes are being applied. This is normal. Maintaining a constant force on the pedal will provide the shortest stopping distance.

Vehicles equipped with the Anti-lock Brake System may be stopped by applying normal force to the brake pedal. Although there is no need to push the brake pedal beyond the point where it stops or holds the vehicle, applying more force causes the pedal to travel toward the floor. This extra brake travel is normal.

Anti-lock Warning Light

Vehicles equipped with the Anti-lock Brake System have an amber warning light in the instrument panel marked ANTILOCK. Additionally, some models using this system will flash other ABS related messages on the Graphic Control Center or other message panels. The warning light will illuminate if a malfunction in the anti-lock brake system is detected by the electronic controller. In case of an electronic malfunction, the controller will turn on the ANTILOCK warning light and disable some or all of the anti-lock system. If only the ANTILOCK light is on, normal braking with full assist is operational but there may be reduced or no anti-lock function. If the ANTILOCK warning light and the red BRAKE warning light come on at the same time, there may be a fault in the hydraulic brake system.

The ANTILOCK light will turn on during the starting of the engine and will usually stay on for approximately 3 seconds after the ignition switch is returned to the RUN position.

➡ **Due to system de-pressurization over time, a vehicle not started in several hours may have the BRAKE and ANTILOCK warning lights stay on up to 30 seconds when started. This is normal and occurs because the ABS pump must restore the correct pressure within the hydraulic accumulator; both lamps will remain on while this recharging is completed.**

Brake System Warning Light

The Anti-lock Brake System uses a 2 circuit design so that some braking capacity is still available if hydraulic pressure is lost in 1 circuit. A BRAKE warning light is located on the instrument cluster and is designed to alert the driver of conditions that could result in reduced braking ability. Certain models may display brake related messages on screens or other panels; these messages supplement the brake warning light.

The BRAKE warning light should turn on briefly during engine starting and should remain on whenever the parking brake is not fully released. Additionally, the BRAKE warning lamp will illuminate if a sensor detects low brake fluid, if the pressure switch detects low accumulator pressure or if certain on-board computers run a self-check of the dashboard and instruments.

If the BRAKE warning light stays on longer than 30 seconds after starting the engine, or comes on and stays on while driving, there may be a malfunction in the brake hydraulic system.

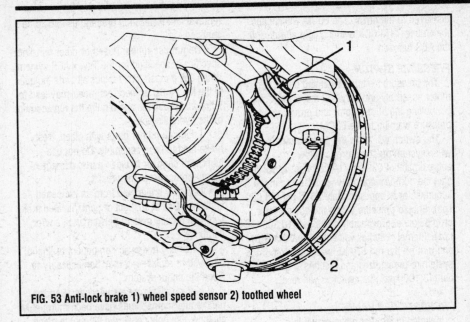

FIG. 53 Anti-lock brake 1) wheel speed sensor 2) toothed wheel

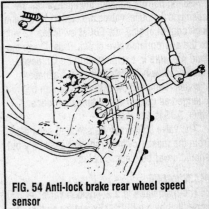

FIG. 54 Anti-lock brake rear wheel speed sensor

SYSTEM COMPONENTS

Electronic Brake Control Module (EBCM)

The EBCM monitors the speed of each wheel and the electrical status of the hydraulic unit. The EBCM's primary functions are to detect wheel lockup, control the brake system while in anti-lock mode and monitor the system for proper electrical operation. When 1 or more wheels approach lockup during a stop, the EBCM will command appropriate valve positions to modulate brake fluid pressure and provide optimum braking. It will continue to command pressure changes in the system until a locking tendency is no longer noted.

The EBCM is a separate computer used exclusively for control of the Anti-lock brake system. The unit also controls the retention and display of the ABS trouble codes when in the diagnostic mode. As the EBCM monitors the system or performs a self–check, it can react to a fault by disabling all or part of the ABS system and illuminating the amber ANTILOCK warning light. The EBCM is located on the right side of the dashboard, generally behind the glove box.

Wheel Speed Sensors

A wheel speed sensor at each wheel transmits speed information to the EBCM by generating a small AC voltage relative to the wheel speed. The voltage is generated by magnetic induction caused by passing a toothed sensor ring past a stationary sensor. The signals are transmitted through a pair of wires which are shielded against interference. The EBCM then calculates wheel speed for each wheel based on the frequency of the AC voltage received from the sensor.

Hydraulic Components

The ABS uses an integrated hydraulic unit mounted on the firewall or cowl. This unit functions as a brake master cylinder and brake booster. Additionally, the hydraulic unit provides brake fluid pressure modulation for each of the individual wheel circuits as required during braking. The hydraulic unit consists of several individual components.

MASTER CYLINDER/BOOSTER ASSEMBLY

This portion of the hydraulic unit contains the valves and pistons necessary to develop hydraulic pressure within the brake lines. Pressure in the booster servo circuit is controlled by a spool valve which opens in response to the amount of force applied to the brake pedal. The rate at which the vehicle decelerates depends on the type of road surface and the pressure applied to the brake pedal.

The master cylinder portion uses a 3–circuit configuration during normal braking; individual circuits are provided for each front wheel while a shared circuit is used for the rear wheels. The 3 circuits are isolated so that a leak or malfunction in one will allow continued braking on the others.

The master cylinder/booster is a non–serviceable component and should never be disassembled.

VALVE BLOCK

The valve block is attached to the right side of the hydraulic unit and includes the 6 solenoid valves used to modulate pressures in the 3 circuits during anti-lock braking. Each circuit is equipped with an inlet and outlet valve.

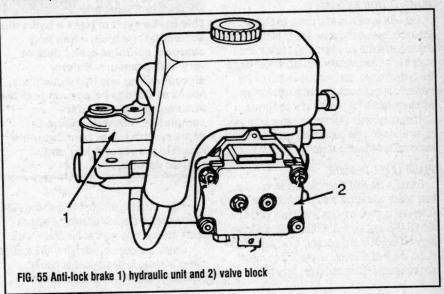

FIG. 55 Anti-lock brake 1) hydraulic unit and 2) valve block

During normal braking, the inlet valves are open and the outlet valves are closed. When anti-lock control begins, the EBCM switches 12 volts to the appropriate valve circuit. This allows the fluid pressure in each circuit to be increased, decreased or held constant as the situation dictates. The position of the valves can be changed as quickly as 15 times per second when ABS is engaged.

The valve block may be serviced separately from the master cylinder/booster assembly but should never be disassembled.

MAIN VALVE

The main valve is a 2–position valve controlled by the EBCM. Except for testing, the valve is open only during ABS stops. When open, the valve allows pressurized brake fluid from the booster servo into the master cylinder front brake circuits to prevent excessive pedal travel.

The main valve is not serviceable as a component; the master cylinder/booster assembly must be replaced.

ACCUMULATOR

The hydraulic accumulator is used to store brake fluid at high pressure so that a supply of pressurized fluid is available for ABS operation and to provide power assist. The accumulator uses a rubber diaphragm to separate high–pressure nitrogen gas from the brake fluid.

Nitrogen in the accumulator is pre–charged to approximately 870 psi (6000 kpa). During normal operation, the pump and motor assembly charges the accumulator with brake fluid to an operation range of 2000–2600 psi (13,800–18,000 kpa).

Because of the high pressures in the system, it is extremely important to observe all safety and pressure reduction precautions before performing repairs or diagnosis.

PUMP/MOTOR ASSEMBLY

The ABS system uses a pump and motor assembly located on the left side of the hydraulic unit to pressurize fluid from the reservoir and store it in the accumulator. When pressure within the system drops, the pressure switch on the hydraulic unit grounds the pump motor relay which energizes the pump motor and pump.

The pump/motor assembly is serviceable only as an assembly; the pump must never be disconnected from the motor.

FLUID LEVEL SENSOR

Found in the fluid reservoir, this sensor is a float which operates 2 reed switches when low fluid level is detected. One switch will cause the red BRAKE warning light to illuminate; the other signals the EBCM and possibly other computers of the low fluid situation. Depending on model and equipment, other messages may be

displayed to the driver. The EBCM will engage the amber ANTILOCK warning light and disable the ABS function.

PRESSURE SWITCH

The pressure switch is mounted on the pump/motor assembly and serves 2 major functions, controlling the pump/motor and providing low pressure warning to the EBCM.

The switch will allow the pump/motor to run when system pressure drops below approximately 2030 psi (14,000 kpa) and will shut the pump/motor off when pressure in the accumulator is approximately 2610 psi (18,000 kpa). Should pressure within the accumulator drop below approximately 1500 psi (10,300 kpa), internal switches will both signal the EBCM and turn on the red BRAKE warning lamp. If the system re-pressurizes and reaches at least 1900 psi (13,100 kpa), the switches will reset.

PROPORTIONER VALVE

Included in the rear brake circuit is a proportioner valve or tee assembly which limits brake pressure build–up at the rear brake calipers. Since the front brakes do the majority of the braking, less pressure is required for the rear brakes under certain conditions. The proportioner valve improves front–to–rear brake balance during normal braking.

Troubleshooting

SERVICE PRECAUTIONS

❄❄ CAUTION

This brake system uses a hydraulic accumulator which, when fully charged, contains brake fluid at very high pressure. Before disconnecting any hydraulic lines, hoses or fittings be certain that the accumulator pressure is completely relieved. Failure to depressurize the accumulator may result in personal injury and/or vehicle damage.

• If the vehicle is equipped with air bag (SIR) system, always properly disable the system before commencing work on the ABS system.
• Certain components within the ABS system are not intended to be serviced or repaired individually. Only those components with

removal and installation procedures should be serviced.
• Do not use rubber hoses or other parts not specifically specified for the Teves ABS system. When using repair kits, replace all parts included in the kit. Partial or incorrect repair may lead to functional problems and require the replacement of the hydraulic unit.
• Lubricate rubber parts with clean, fresh brake fluid to ease assembly. Do not use lubricated shop air to clean parts; damage to rubber components may result.
• Use only brake fluid from an unopened container. Use of suspect or contaminated brake fluid can reduce system performance and/or durability.
• When any hydraulic component or line is removed or replaced, it may be necessary to bleed the entire system.
• A clean repair area is essential. Perform repairs after components have been thoroughly cleaned; use only denatured alcohol to clean components. Do not allow ABS components to come into contact with any substance containing mineral oil; this includes used shop rags.
• Remove the lock pin before disconnecting Connector Position Assurance (CPA) connectors in the harnesses.
• The EBCM is a microprocessor similar to other computer units in the vehicle. Insure that the ignition switch is **OFF** before removing or installing controller harnesses. Avoid static electricity discharge at or near the Controller.
• Never disconnect any electrical connection with the ignition switch **ON** unless instructed to do so in a test.
• Always wear a grounded wrist strap when servicing any control module or component labeled with a Electrostatic Discharge (ESD) symbol.
• Avoid touching module connector pins.
• Leave new components and modules in the shipping package until ready to install them.
• To avoid static discharge, always touch a vehicle ground after sliding across a vehicle seat or walking across carpeted or vinyl floors.
• Never allow welding cables to lie on, near or across any vehicle electrical wiring.
• Do not allow extension cords for power tools or droplights to lie on, near or across any vehicle electrical wiring.

DEPRESSURIZING THE HYDRAULIC UNIT

The ABS pump/motor assembly will keep the accumulator charged to a pressure between approximately 2000 psi (13,800 kpa) and 2600 psi (18,000 kpa) any time the ignition is in the

ON or RUN position. The pump/motor cannot operate if the ignition is OFF or if a battery cable is disconnected.

1. With the ignition OFF or the negative battery cable disconnected, pump the brake pedal a minimum of 25 times using at least 50 lbs. of pedal force each time.

2. A definite increase in pedal effort will be felt as the accumulator becomes discharged.

3. After the increased pedal effort occurs, continue with 5–10 additional brake applications to release any remaining pressure.

VISUAL INSPECTION

Before any system diagnosis is begun, the brake system should be inspected visually for common faults which could disable the ABS or cause a code to set. Check the vehicle carefully for any sign of: binding parking brake or faulty parking brake switch, low brake fluid, system fluid leaks including pump/motor area, failed fuses or fusible links, failed ABS relay, loose or damaged wiring including connectors, harnesses, and insulation wear. Check the mounting and function of the brake calipers at each wheel. Carefully inspect the multi–pin connectors at the EBCM for pushouts or poor connections.

FUNCTIONAL CHECK

Once the visual check has been performed, perform the functional check to determine if the problem is truly ABS related or arising from common faults.

DISPLAYING ABS TROUBLE CODES

➡ **The 1st generation system found on the 6000 AWD does not display trouble codes; diagnosis is performed through symptom analysis and circuit testing.**

Only certain ABS malfunctions will cause the EBCM to store diagnostic trouble codes. Failures causing a code will generally involve wheel speed sensors, main valve or the inlet and outlet valves. Conditions affecting the pump/motor assembly, the accumulator, pressure switch or fluid level sensor usually do not cause a code to set.

The EBCM will store trouble codes in a non-volatile memory. These codes remain in memory until erased through use of the correct procedure. The codes are NOT erased by disconnecting the EBCM, disconnecting the battery cable or turning off the ignition. Always be sure to clear the codes from the memory after repairs are made. To read stored ABS trouble codes:

1. Turn ignition switch to ON. Allow the pump to charge the accumulator; if fully discharged, dash warning lights may stay on up to 30 seconds. If ANTI-LOCK warning light does not go off within 30 seconds, note it.

2. Turn ignition switch to OFF.

3. Remove the cover from the ALDL connector. Enter the diagnostic mode by using a jumper wire to connect pins H and A or to connect pin H to body ground.

4. Turn the ignition switch to ON and count the light flashes for the first digit of the first code. The ANTI-LOCK light should illuminate for 4

seconds before beginning to flash. If, after 4 seconds, the light turns off and stays off, no codes are stored.

5. The light will pause for 3 seconds between the first and second digits of the first code and then continue flashing. When counting flashes, count only the ON pulses.

6. When the EBCM is finished transmitting the second digit of the first code, the ANTI-LOCK light will remain on. This last, constant ON should not be counted as a flash. Record the 2-digit code.

7. Without turning the ignition switch OFF, disconnect the jumper from pin H and reconnect it. If an additional code is present, it will be displayed in similar fashion to the first. Record the second code.

8. Repeat the disconnection and reconnection of pin H without changing the ignition switch until no more codes are displayed. The system is capable of storing and displaying 7 codes; the ANTI-LOCK warning light will stay on continuously when all codes have been displayed.

9. After recording each code, remove the jumper from the ALDL, replace the cover and proceed.

➡ **The ABS trouble codes are not specifically designated current or history codes. If the ANTI-LOCK light is on before entering the ABS diagnostic mode, at least 1 of the stored codes is current. It is impossible to tell which code is current. If the ANTI-LOCK light is off before entering the diagnostic mode, none of the codes are current.**

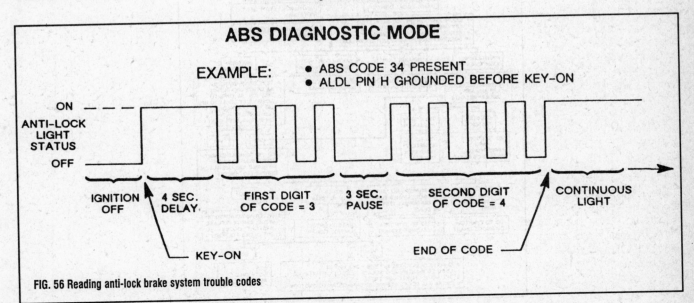

FIG. 56 Reading anti-lock brake system trouble codes

INTERMITTENTS

Although the ABS trouble codes stored by the EBCM are not identified as current or history codes, these codes may still be useful in diagnosing intermittent conditions.

If an intermittent condition is being diagnosed:

1. Obtain an accurate description of the circumstances in which the failure occurs.

2. Display and clear any ABS trouble codes which may be present in the EBCM.

3. Test drive the vehicle, attempting to duplicate the failure condition exactly.

4. After duplicating the condition(s), stop the vehicle and display any ABS codes which have set.

5. If no codes have been stored, refer to the Symptom Diagnosis Charts. A good description of vehicle behavior can be helpful in determining a most likely circuit.

Most intermittent problems are caused by faulty electrical connections or wiring. Always check for poor mating of connector halves or terminals not fully seated in connector bodies, deformed or damaged terminals and poor terminal to wire connections.

Most failures within the ABS will disable the anti-lock function for the entire ignition cycle, even if the fault clears before the next key–off occurrence. There are 3 situations which will allow the ABS to re–engage if the condition corrects during the ignition cycle. Each of these will illuminate 1 or both dash warning lights.

• Low system voltage: If the EBCM detects low voltage, the ANTI-LOCK warning lamp is illuminated. If correct minimum voltage is restored to the EBCM, normal ABS function resumes.

• Low brake fluid level: Once detected by the fluid level sensor, this condition illuminates both the BRAKE and ANTI-LOCK warning lights; when the sensor indicates acceptable fluid level, the normal ABS function resumes.

• Low accumulator pressure: Should the accumulator lose or not develop correct pressure, both the BRAKE and ANTI-LOCK warning lights will illuminate. Full function is restored when the correct pressure is achieved.

• Any condition interrupting power to either the EBCM or hydraulic unit may cause the warning lights to come on intermittently. These circuits include the main relay, main relay fuse, EBCM fuse, pump motor relay and all related wiring.

CLEARING TROUBLE CODES

Stored ABS trouble codes should not be cleared until all repairs are completed. The control module will not allow any codes to be cleared until all have been read. After reading each stored code, drive the vehicle at a speed over 18 mph.

Re-read the system; if codes are still present, not all codes were read previously or additional repair is needed.

➡ **In the following diagnostic charts, certain special tools may be required. Use of the J–35592 Pinout box or equivalent is required to avoid damage to the connectors at the EBCM; use of J–35604 pressure gauge and J–35604–88 adapter (or equivalents) will be required to measure accumulator pressure.**
The use of a high-impedance multi-meter (DVM or DVOM) is required at all times.

TEVES ANTI-LOCK BRAKE FUNCTIONAL CHECK

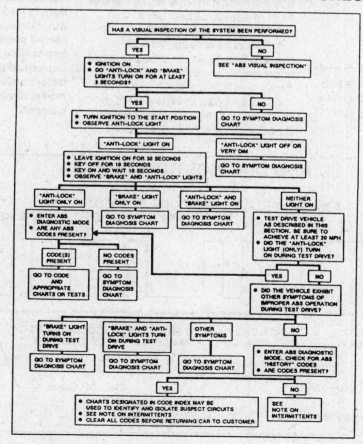

DIFFERENTIAL LOCK CONNECTOR FACES

CHART 15

ABS WIRING SCHEMATIC

CHART 16

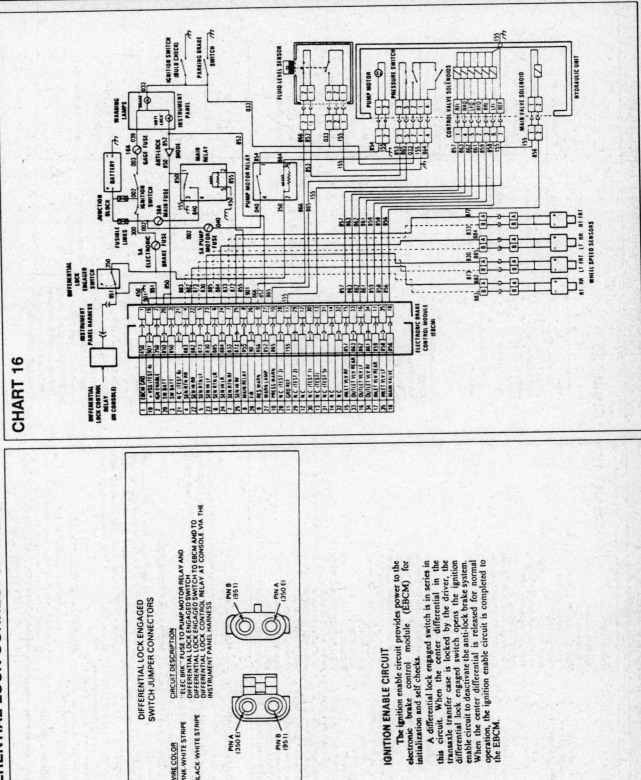

DIFFERENTIAL LOCK ENGAGED SWITCH JUMPER CONNECTORS

CIRCUIT DESCRIPTION

"ELEC BRK" FUSE TO PUMP MOTOR RELAY AND
DIFFERENTIAL LOCK ENGAGED SWITCH
DIFFERENTIAL LOCK ENGAGED SWITCH TO EBCM AND TO
DIFFERENTIAL LOCK CONTROL RELAY AT CONSOLE VIA THE
INSTRUMENT PANEL HARNESS

CIRCUIT NUMBER	WIRE COLOR
350	PINK-WHITE STRIPE
951	BLACK-WHITE STRIPE

IGNITION ENABLE CIRCUIT

The ignition enable circuit provides power to the electronic brake control module (EBCM) for initialization and self checks.

A differential lock engaged switch is in series in this circuit. When the center differential in the transaxle transfer case is locked by the driver, the differential lock engaged switch opens the ignition enable circuit to deactivate the anti-lock brake system. When the center differential is released for normal operation, the ignition enable circuit is completed to the EBCM.

PRE-DIAGNOSIS INSPECTION

CHART 20

ITEM	INSPECT FOR:	CORRECTIVE ACTION
BRAKE FLUID RESERVOIR AND HYDRAULIC UNIT	– LOW FLUID LEVEL – EXTERNAL LEAKS	– FILL RESERVOIR – REPAIR LEAKS AS REQUIRED
PARKING BRAKE	– FULLY RELEASED – IMPROPERLY ADJUSTED	– RELEASE PARKING BRAKE – ADJUST CABLE
BATTERY	ADEQUATE CHARGE	– CHARGE OR REPLACE BATTERY AS REQUIRED – SERVICE CHARGING SYSTEM AS REQUIRED
FUSES • 5 AMP ELECTRONIC BRAKE FUSE – LOCATED IN CONVENIENCE CENTER	– BLOWN FUSE	– REPLACE FUSE AND VERIFY OPERATION
• 10 AMP GAGES FUSE – LOCATED IN FUSE BLOCK	– BLOWN FUSE	– REPLACE FUSE AND VERIFY OPERATION
• 30 AMP MAIN RELAY FUSE – LOCATED ON MAIN RELAY BRACKET	– BLOWN FUSE	– REPLACE FUSE AND VERIFY OPERATION
• 30 AMP PUMP MOTOR FUSE – LOCATED ON PUMP MOTOR RELAY BRACKET	– BLOWN FUSE	– REPLACE FUSE AND VERIFY OPERATION
CONNECTORS • MAIN RELAY • PUMP MOTOR RELAY • PRESSURE SWITCH • PUMP MOTOR • MAIN VALVE • VALVE BLOCK • FLUID LEVEL SENSOR • ELECTRONIC BRAKE CONTROL MODULE (EBCM) • 4 SENSOR CONNECTORS	– PROPER ENGAGEMENT OF CONNECTOR – LOOSE WIRES IN CONNECTOR	– PROPERLY ENGAGE CONNECTORS – REPAIR LOOSE WIRES
CONNECTORS (WITH ALL WHEEL DRIVE) • DIFFERENTIAL LOCK ENGAGED SWITCH CONNECTOR AT TRANSAXLE TRANSFER CASE • DIFFERENTIAL LOCK ENGAGED SWITCH JUMPER CONNECTOR TO EBCM WIRING HARNESS AT LEFT SIDE OF DASH PANEL	– PROPER ENGAGEMENT OF CONNECTOR – LOOSE WIRES IN CONNECTOR	– PROPERLY ENGAGE CONNECTORS – REPAIR LOOSE WIRES

ABS CIRCUIT INDEX

CHART 19

CIRCUIT NUMBER	WIRE COLOR	CIRCUIT LOCATION
002	RED	IGNITION ENABLE
003	PINK	IGNITION ENABLE
033	TAN-WHITE STRIPE	"BRAKE" WARNING LAMP
039	PINK-BLACK STRIPE	"BRAKE" WARNING LAMP
040	RED-WHITE STRIPE	PUMP MOTOR
155	BLACK	MAIN RELAY; PUMP MOTOR; VALVE BLOCK AND MAIN VALVE; "BRAKE" WARNING LAMP
300	ORANGE	IGNITION ENABLE
350	PINK-WHITE STRIPE	IGNITION ENABLE: PUMP MOTOR
450	BLACK-WHITE STRIPE	IGNITION ENABLE: MAIN RELAY
640	RED-WHITE STRIPE	MAIN RELAY
850	ORANGE SPLICED TO PINK-WHITE	MAIN RELAY: "ANTILOCK" WARNING LAMP
852	BROWN-RED STRIPE	"ANTILOCK" WARNING LAMP
853	LT. BLUE-ORANGE STRIPE	EBCM LOOP
854	RED	PUMP MOTOR
855	DARK BLUE	MAIN RELAY
856	PURPLE-WHITE STRIPE	VALVE BLOCK AND MAIN VALVE
857	BLACK-PINK STRIPE	VALVE BLOCK AND MAIN VALVE
858	DRK GREEN-YELLOW STRIPE	VALVE BLOCK AND MAIN VALVE
859	GRAY	VALVE BLOCK AND MAIN VALVE
861	BROWN-WHITE STRIPE	VALVE BLOCK AND MAIN VALVE
862	LIGHT BLUE-BLACK STRIPE	VALVE BLOCK AND MAIN VALVE
863	DARK BLUE-WHITE STRIPE	VALVE BLOCK AND MAIN VALVE
864	GRAY-RED STRIPE	PUMP MOTOR
865	PURPLE	EBCM LOOP
866	LIGHT GREEN	EBCM LOOP
901	RED-DOUBLE YELLOW STRIPE	EBCM TO EBCM CONNECT CIRCUIT
830	GREEN COAXIAL CABLE	WHEEL SPEED SENSOR
873	GREEN COAXIAL CABLE	WHEEL SPEED SENSOR
884	GREEN COAXIAL CABLE	WHEEL SPEED SENSOR
885	GREEN COAXIAL CABLE	WHEEL SPEED SENSOR
833	GREEN COAXIAL CABLE	WHEEL SPEED SENSOR
872	GREEN COAXIAL CABLE	WHEEL SPEED SENSOR
882	GREEN COAXIAL CABLE	WHEEL SPEED SENSOR
883	GREEN COAXIAL CABLE	WHEEL SPEED SENSOR

IGNITION ENABLE POWER CIRCUIT

When the ignition switch is "ON" the battery supplies a 12 volt signal to the EBCM through the junction block, fusible link, ignition switch, circuit 300 to the 5 amp electronic brake fuse in the convenience center, circuit 350E to the differential lock engaged switch, and circuit 951 to EBCM pin 2. The ignition enable circuit also supplies a 12 volt signal to the anti-lock brake system pump relay through a branch of circuit 350E, and to the differential lock control relay in the console through circuit 951.

When the ignition switch is turned to the "RUN" position, the "ANTI-LOCK" warning lamp will turn on for 3 to 5 seconds. If there is no voltage at EBCM pin 2, the anti-lock function will be disabled and the "ANTI-LOCK" warning lamp will remain on.

IGNITION ENABLE GROUND CIRCUIT

Circuit 450 grounds the EBCM to the main relay bracket through EBCM pin 1.

MAIN RELAY CIRCUIT

The main relay supplies switched battery power to the electronic brake control module (EBCM) to operate the main vlave, solenoid valve, logic circuits and some self checks.

MAIN RELAY COIL CIRCUIT

The EBCM supplies 12 volts to the main relay coil through pin 8 of the EBCM and circuit 855 after the ignition switch is turned on, refer to "Ignition Enable Circuit" in this section. The main relay coil is grounded to the main relay bracket through circuit 450.

MAIN RELAY GROUND CIRCUIT

If the ignition system is on and power is not supplied to the main relay coil, circuit 850 will be grounded to the main relay bracket through circuit 155 and the "ANTI-LOCK" warning lamp will light, refer to "ANTI-LOCK Warning Lamp Circuit".

WARNING AND INDICATOR LAMP SEQUENCES

CHART 22

WARNING/INDICATOR LAMP	COLOR	IGNITION "ON"	CRANKING*	RUNNING*	MOVING*	BRAKING*	STOPPED*	IDLE*	"LOCK-NORMAL" SWITCH MOVED TO "LOCK"	"LOCK-NORMAL" SWITCH MOVED TO "NORMAL"
"BRAKE"	RED	OFF	ON	OFF	OFF	OFF	OFF	OFF	OFF	OFF
"ANTI-LOCK"	AMBER	ON, THEN OFF	ON	ON, THEN OFF	OFF	OFF	OFF	OFF	ON	ON, THEN OFF
"LOCK NORMAL" SWITCH	AMBER	OFF	OFF	OFF	OFF	OFF	OFF	OFF	FLASH	OFF
"LOCK"	AMBER	OFF	OFF	OFF	OFF	OFF	OFF	OFF	OFF, THEN ON	ON, THEN OFF

* "LOCK-NORMAL" SWITCH SET TO "NORMAL"

NORMAL SEQUENCE

1. WITH IGNITION "ON", "ANTILOCK" WARNING LAMP WILL COME ON FOR 3.5 SECONDS IF ACCUMULATOR IS CHARGED. "ANTILOCK" WARNING LAMP MAY STAY ON FOR UP TO 30 SECONDS IF ACCUMULATOR IS DISCHARGED.
2. "BRAKE" AND "ANTILOCK" WARNING LAMPS WILL TURN ON DURING CRANKING.
3. IMMEDIATELY AFTER THE ENGINE STARTS, "ANTILOCK" WARNING LAMP WILL BE ON FOR 3.5 SECONDS.
4. WHEN "LOCK NORMAL" SWITCH IS MOVED TO "LOCK," AMBER SWITCH INDICATOR LAMP WILL FLASH.
5. THE "LOCK" AND "ANTILOCK" LAMPS WILL TURN ON WHEN THE TRANSFER CASE DIFFERENTIAL VACUUM ACTUATED LOCK LOCKS THE DIFFERENTIAL.
6. WHEN "LOCK NORMAL" SWITCH IS MOVED BACK TO "NORMAL," "ANTILOCK" WARNING LAMP WILL REMAIN ON FOR 3.5 SECONDS AND THEN GO OFF. SWITCH INDICATOR LAMP WILL IMMEDIATELY STOP FLASHING AND REMAIN OFF.
7. THE "LOCK" INDICATOR LAMP WILL GO OFF WHEN THE TRANSFER CASE DIFFERENTIAL SPRING MECHANISM UNLOCKS THE DIFFERENTIAL.
8. ALL FOUR LAMPS WILL REMAIN OFF AT ALL OTHER TIMES.

PRE-DIAGNOSIS INSPECTION (CONTINUED)

CHART 21

ITEM	INSPECT FOR:	CORRECTIVE ACTION
GROUNDS • BODY GROUNDS – LOCATED ON MAIN RELAY BRACKET • HYDRAULIC UNIT GROUND – ON HYDRAULIC UNIT	– LOOSE CONNECTIONS – BROKEN EYELETS – CORROSION	– TIGHTEN CONNECTIONS – REPAIR WIRE OR EYELET – CLEAN CONTACT SURFACES
JUNCTION BLOCK	– CORROSION – LOOSE JUNCTION BLOCK OR CONNECTIONS – BROKEN WIRES	– CLEAN CONTACT SURFACES – TIGHTEN CONNECTIONS – REPAIR OR REPLACE WIRES AS NECESSARY

LOW OR SPONGY PEDAL

CHART 24

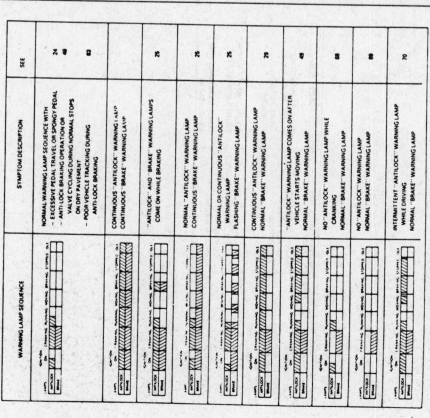

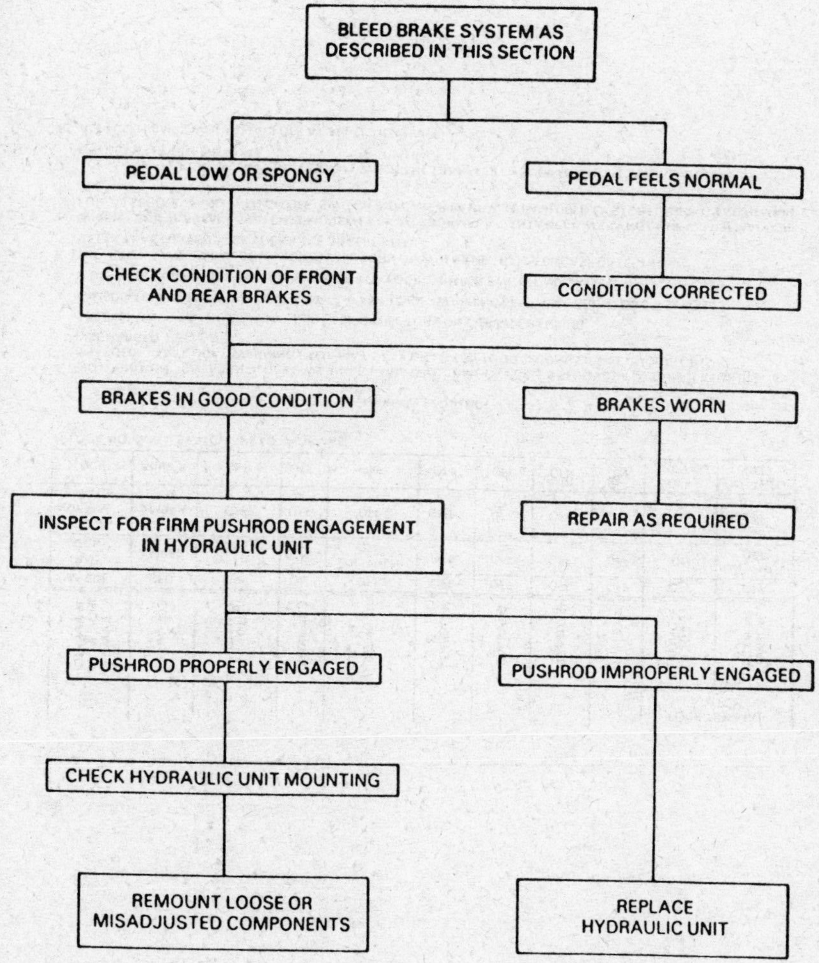

- BLEED BRAKE SYSTEM AS DESCRIBED IN THIS SECTION
- PEDAL FEELS NORMAL
- PEDAL LOW OR SPONGY
- CHECK CONDITION OF FRONT AND REAR BRAKES
- CONDITION CORRECTED
- BRAKES WORN
- BRAKES IN GOOD CONDITION
- REPAIR AS REQUIRED
- INSPECT FOR FIRM PUSHROD ENGAGEMENT IN HYDRAULIC UNIT
- PUSHROD IMPROPERLY ENGAGED
- PUSHROD PROPERLY ENGAGED
- CHECK HYDRAULIC UNIT MOUNTING
- REPLACE HYDRAULIC UNIT
- REMOUNT LOOSE OR MISADJUSTED COMPONENTS

WARNING AND INDICATOR LAMP SYMPTOM INDEX

CHART 23

WARNING LAMP SEQUENCE	SYMPTOM DESCRIPTION	SEE
	NORMAL WARNING LAMP SEQUENCE WITH - EXCESSIVE PEDAL TRAVEL OR SPONGY PEDAL - ANTI-LOCK BRAKING OPERATION OR VALVE CYCLING DURING NORMAL STOPS ON DRY PAVEMENT - POOR VEHICLE TRACKING DURING ANTI-LOCK BRAKING	24 49 63
	CONTINUOUS "ANTILOCK" WARNING LAMP CONTINUOUS "BRAKE" WARNING LAMP	
	"ANTILOCK" AND "BRAKE" WARNING LAMPS COME ON WHILE BRAKING	25
	NORMAL "ANTILOCK" WARNING LAMP CONTINUOUS "BRAKE" WARNING LAMP	25
	NORMAL OR CONTINUOUS "ANTILOCK" WARNING LAMP FLASHING "BRAKE" WARNING LAMP	25
	CONTINUOUS "ANTILOCK" WARNING LAMP NORMAL "BRAKE" WARNING LAMP	29
	"ANTILOCK" WARNING LAMP COMES ON AFTER VEHICLE STARTS MOVING NORMAL "BRAKE" WARNING LAMP	49
	NO "ANTILOCK" WARNING LAMP WHILE CRANKING NORMAL "BRAKE" WARNING LAMP	66
	NO "ANTILOCK" WARNING LAMP NORMAL "BRAKE" WARNING LAMP	68
	INTERMITTENT "ANTILOCK" WARNING LAMP WHILE DRIVING NORMAL "BRAKE" WARNING LAMP	70

LAMP STATUS
- SHADED AREAS: LAMP ON
- BLANK AREAS (NO SHADING): LAMP OFF
- PARTIALLY SHADED AREAS: LAMP ON FOR PART OF TEST PERIOD

ENERGY UNIT: FUNCTIONAL CHECK (CONTINUED)

CHART 26

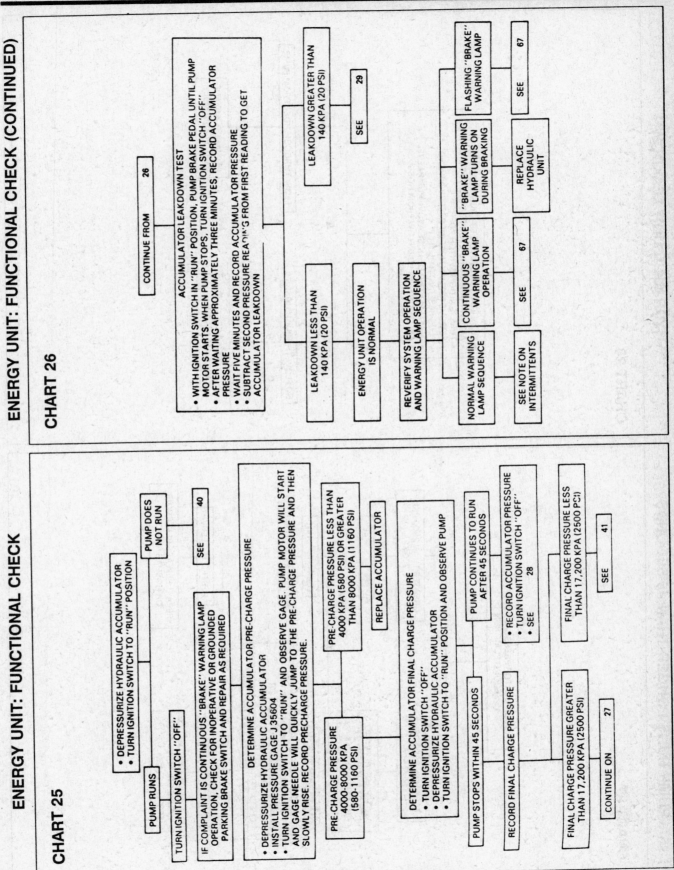

CONTINUE FROM 26

ACCUMULATOR LEAKDOWN TEST
- WITH IGNITION SWITCH IN "RUN" POSITION, PUMP BRAKE PEDAL UNTIL PUMP MOTOR STARTS. WHEN PUMP STOPS, TURN IGNITION SWITCH "OFF".
- AFTER WAITING APPROXIMATELY THREE MINUTES, RECORD ACCUMULATOR PRESSURE
- WAIT FIVE MINUTES AND RECORD ACCUMULATOR PRESSURE
- SUBTRACT SECOND PRESSURE READING FROM FIRST READING TO GET ACCUMULATOR LEAKDOWN

LEAKDOWN GREATER THAN 140 KPA (20 PSI)

SEE 29

LEAKDOWN LESS THAN 140 KPA (20 PSI)

ENERGY UNIT OPERATION IS NORMAL

REVERIFY SYSTEM OPERATION AND WARNING LAMP SEQUENCE

NORMAL WARNING LAMP SEQUENCE

"BRAKE" WARNING LAMP TURNS ON DURING BRAKING

CONTINUOUS "BRAKE" WARNING LAMP OPERATION

FLASHING "BRAKE" WARNING LAMP

SEE 67

SEE 67

REPLACE HYDRAULIC UNIT

SEE NOTE ON INTERMITTENTS

ENERGY UNIT: FUNCTIONAL CHECK

CHART 25

- DEPRESSURIZE HYDRAULIC ACCUMULATOR
- TURN IGNITION SWITCH TO "RUN" POSITION

PUMP RUNS

PUMP DOES NOT RUN

SEE 40

TURN IGNITION SWITCH "OFF"

IF COMPLAINT IS CONTINUOUS "BRAKE" WARNING LAMP OPERATION, CHECK FOR INOPERATIVE OR GROUNDED PARKING BRAKE SWITCH AND REPAIR AS REQUIRED

DETERMINE ACCUMULATOR PRE-CHARGE PRESSURE
- DEPRESSURIZE HYDRAULIC ACCUMULATOR
- INSTALL PRESSURE GAGE J 35604
- TURN IGNITION SWITCH TO "RUN" AND OBSERVE GAGE. PUMP MOTOR WILL START AND GAGE NEEDLE WILL QUICKLY JUMP TO THE PRE-CHARGE PRESSURE AND THEN SLOWLY RISE. RECORD PRECHARGE PRESSURE.

PRE-CHARGE PRESSURE 4000-8000 KPA (580-1160 PSI)

PRE-CHARGE PRESSURE LESS THAN 4000 KPA (580 PSI) OR GREATER THAN 8000 KPA (1160 PSI)

REPLACE ACCUMULATOR

DETERMINE ACCUMULATOR FINAL CHARGE PRESSURE
- TURN IGNITION SWITCH "OFF"
- DEPRESSURIZE HYDRAULIC ACCUMULATOR
- TURN IGNITION SWITCH TO "RUN" POSITION AND OBSERVE PUMP

PUMP STOPS WITHIN 45 SECONDS

PUMP CONTINUES TO RUN AFTER 45 SECONDS

- RECORD ACCUMULATOR PRESSURE
- TURN IGNITION SWITCH "OFF"
- SEE 28

RECORD FINAL CHARGE PRESSURE

FINAL CHARGE PRESSURE GREATER THAN 17,200 KPA (2500 PSI)

FINAL CHARGE PRESSURE LESS THAN 17,200 KPA (2500 PSI)

SEE 41

CONTINUE ON 27

HYDRAULIC UNIT LEAKDOWN

CHART 28

- TURN IGNITION SWITCH TO "RUN" POSITION
- ALLOW PUMP TO RUN FOR 60 SECONDS MAXIMUM
- TURN IGNITION SWITCH "OFF"
- REMOVE RETURN HOSE AT RESERVOIR AND PLUG RESERVOIR OUTLET
- HOLD FREE END OF HOSE ABOVE PUMP LEVEL AND LOOK FOR FLUID FLOW FROM HOSE FOR FIVE MINUTES

FLOW THROUGH HOSE FROM PUMP

REPLACE PUMP AND MOTOR ASSEMBLY

NO FLOW THROUGH HOSE

REPLACE HYDRAULIC UNIT

PUMP RUNS LONGER THAN 45 SECONDS

CHART 27

ACCUMULATOR PRESSURE AFTER 45 SECOND PUMP RUN

GREATER THAN 2500 PSI. (17,200 KPA.)

SEE **41**

LESS THAN 2500 PSI. (17,200 KPA.)

WITH PUMP RUNNING, INSPECT ENTIRE SYSTEM FOR EXTERNAL LEAKAGE

LEAKAGE FOUND

REPAIR AS REQUIRED

NO LEAKAGE FOUND

- TURN IGNITION SWITCH "OFF"
- DEPRESSURIZE ACCUMULATOR
- REMOVE RETURN HOSE FROM PUMP
- CHECK FOR OBSTRUCTED FLUID FLOW THROUGH HOSE FROM RESERVOIR

RESTRICTED FLOW

REPAIR/REPLACE RESERVOIR OR HOSE AS REQUIRED

FLUID FLOWS FREELY

- INSTALL RETURN HOSE
- SEE **29**

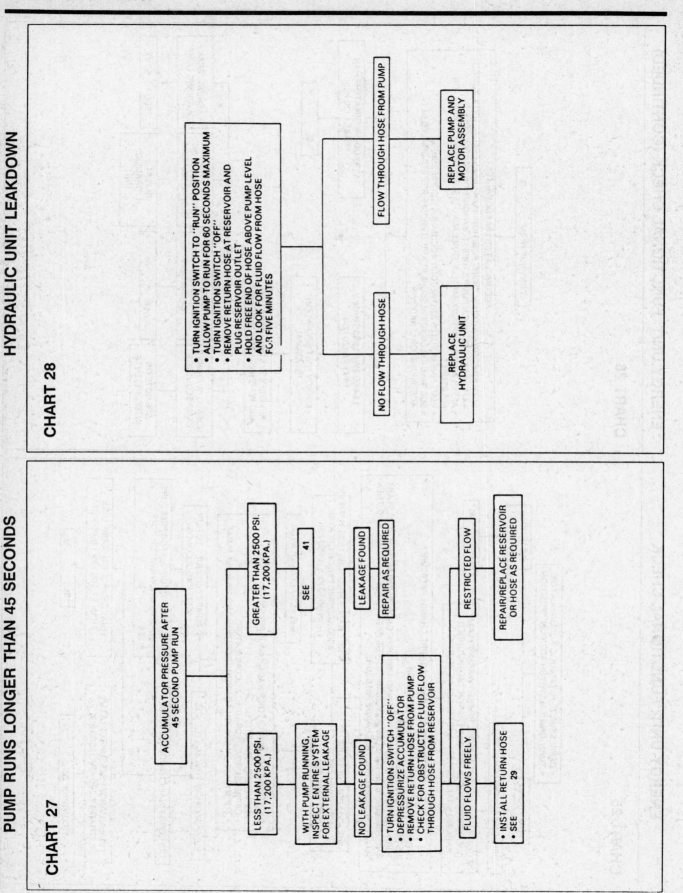

IGNITION ENABLE CIRCUIT SCHEMATIC

CHART 30

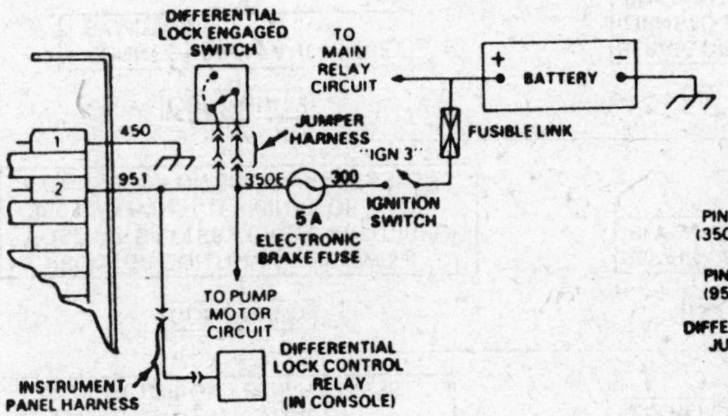

BATTERY

FUSIBLE LINK

IGNITION SWITCH

JUMPER HARNESS "IGN 3"

300

350E

ELECTRONIC BRAKE FUSE 5A

DIFFERENTIAL LOCK CONTROL RELAY (IN CONSOLE)

TO MAIN RELAY CIRCUIT

DIFFERENTIAL LOCK ENGAGED SWITCH

450

951

TO PUMP MOTOR CIRCUIT

INSTRUMENT PANEL HARNESS

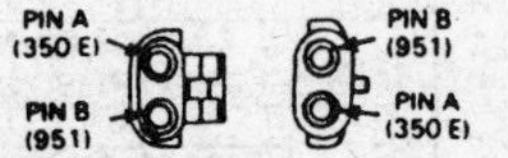

PIN B (951) PIN A (350 E)

PIN A (350 E) PIN B (951)

DIFFERENTIAL LOCK ENGAGED SWITCH JUMPER HARNESS CONNECTORS

PIN OUT CHECKS

CHART 29

- CONNECT J 35592 TO 35-PIN EBCM HARNESS CONNECTOR.
- PERFORM CHECKS WITH HIGH IMPEDANCE DIGITAL MULTIMETER J 34029-A OR EQUIVALENT
- ALL CHECKS ARE MADE WITH ENGINE OFF

CIRCUIT TO BE TESTED	IGNITION SWITCH POSITION	MULTIMETER SCALE/RANGE	MEASURE BETWEEN PIN NUMBERS	SPECIFICATION	IF RESULT NOT WITHIN SPECIFICATION, SEE
IGNITION ENABLE	RUN	20 DCV	2(+),1(-)*	10 V MINIMUM	32 and 33
MAIN RELAY GROUND	OFF	200 Ω	1,3	CONTINUITY	35
MAIN RELAY COIL	OFF	200 Ω	1,20	CONTINUITY	36
	OFF	200 Ω	1,8	45-105 Ω	36

BEFORE PERFORMING THIS TEST: • REMOVE GAGE FUSE FROM FUSE BOX • PLACE FUSED JUMPER BETWEEN J 35592 PINS 2 & 8

MAIN RELAY POWER	ON	20 DCV	3(+),1(-)	10 V MINIMUM	37
	ON	20 DCV	20(+),1(-)	10 V MINIMUM	

BEFORE PROCEEDING: • REMOVE JUMPER FROM PINS 2 & 8 • INSTALL GAGE FUSE

EBCM SWITCH LOOP	OFF	200 Ω	9,10	LESS THAN 5 Ω	44
	OFF	200 Ω	1,9	NO CONTINUITY	45
RR SENSOR RESISTANCE	OFF	2k Ω	4,22	800-1400 Ω	47
LF SENSOR RESISTANCE	OFF	2k Ω	6,23	800-1400 Ω	48
LR SENSOR RESISTANCE	OFF	2k Ω	6,24	800-1400 Ω	49
RF SENSOR RESISTANCE	OFF	2k Ω	7,25	800-1400 Ω	50
MAIN VALVE SOLENOID	OFF	200 Ω	11,18	2-5 Ω	56
VALVE BLOCK GROUND	OFF	200 Ω	1,11	LESS THAN 2 Ω	58
RF INLET VALVE	OFF	200 Ω	11,15	5-7 Ω	59
LF INLET VALVE	OFF	200 Ω	11,35	5-7 Ω	60
REAR INLET VALVE	OFF	200 Ω	11,17	5-7 Ω	61
RF OUTLET VALVE	OFF	200 Ω	11,34	3-5 Ω	62
LF OUTLET VALVE	OFF	200 Ω	11,16	3-5 Ω	63
REAR OUTLET VALVE	OFF	200 Ω	11,33	3-5 Ω	64

*(+) OR (-) INDICATES MULTI-METER POLARITY

IF ALL TEST RESULTS ARE WITHIN SPECIFICATION, RECONNECT EBCM AND VERIFY CONTINUOUS "ANTILOCK" WARNING LAMP OPERATION
- IF NORMAL OPERATION RESUMES, SEE NOTE ON INTERMITTENTS
- IF LAMP REMAINS ON, SEE 69

CHECKING IGNITION ENABLE CIRCUIT

CHART 31

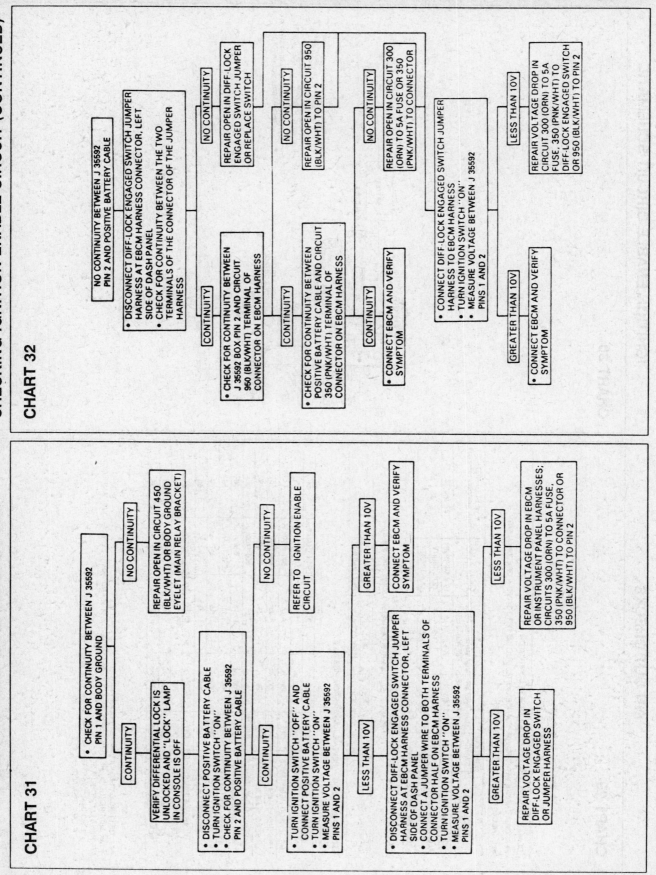

CHECKING IGNITION ENABLE CIRCUIT (CONTINUED)

CHART 32

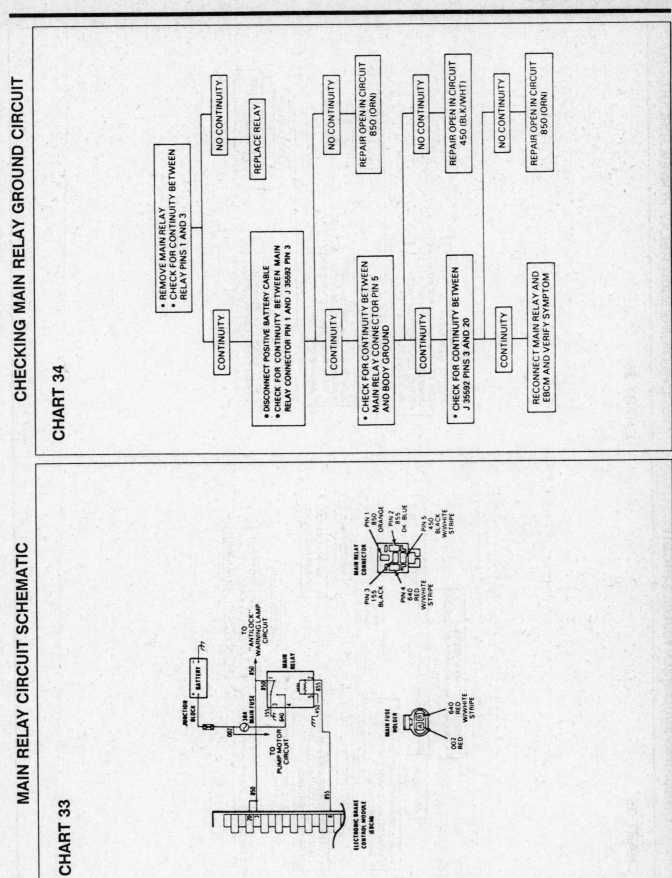

CHECKING MAIN RELAY GROUND CIRCUIT

CHART 34

MAIN RELAY CIRCUIT SCHEMATIC

CHART 33

CHECKING MAIN RELAY POWER CIRCUIT

CHART 36

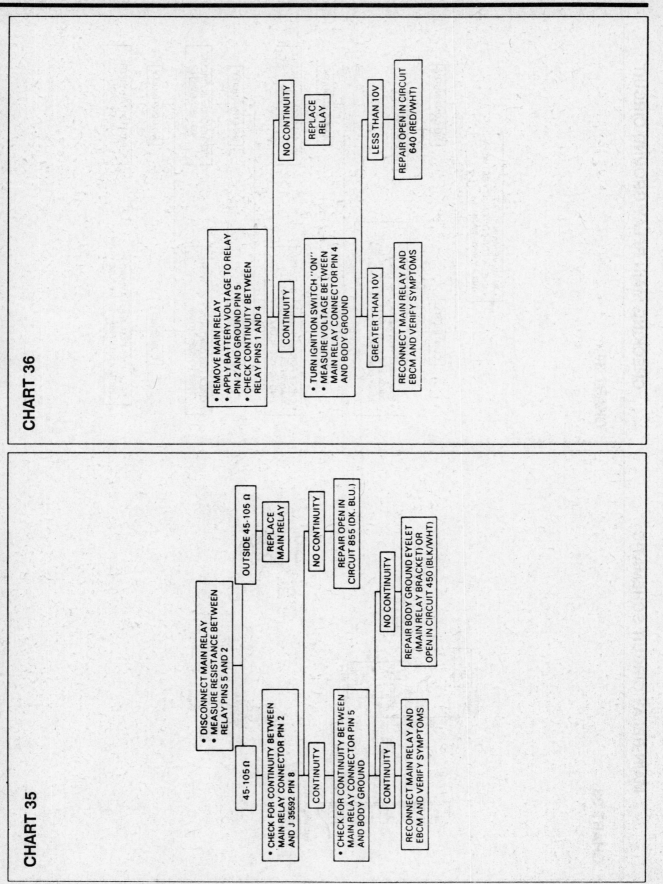

- REMOVE MAIN RELAY
- APPLY BATTERY VOLTAGE TO RELAY PIN 2 AND GROUND PIN 5
- CHECK CONTINUITY BETWEEN RELAY PINS 1 AND 4

NO CONTINUITY → REPLACE RELAY

CONTINUITY
- TURN IGNITION SWITCH "ON"
- MEASURE VOLTAGE BETWEEN MAIN RELAY CONNECTOR PIN 4 AND BODY GROUND

LESS THAN 10V → REPAIR OPEN IN CIRCUIT 640 (RED/WHT)

GREATER THAN 10V → RECONNECT MAIN RELAY AND EBCM AND VERIFY SYMPTOMS

CHECKING MAIN RELAY COIL CIRCUIT

CHART 35

- DISCONNECT MAIN RELAY
- MEASURE RESISTANCE BETWEEN RELAY PINS 5 AND 2

OUTSIDE 45-105 Ω → REPLACE MAIN RELAY

45-105 Ω
- CHECK FOR CONTINUITY BETWEEN MAIN RELAY CONNECTOR PIN 2 AND J 35592 PIN 8

NO CONTINUITY → REPAIR OPEN IN CIRCUIT 855 (DK. BLU.)

CONTINUITY
- CHECK FOR CONTINUITY BETWEEN MAIN RELAY CONNECTOR PIN 5 AND BODY GROUND

NO CONTINUITY → REPAIR BODY GROUND EYELET (MAIN RELAY BRACKET) OR OPEN IN CIRCUIT 450 (BLK/WHT)

CONTINUITY → RECONNECT MAIN RELAY AND EBCM AND VERIFY SYMPTOMS

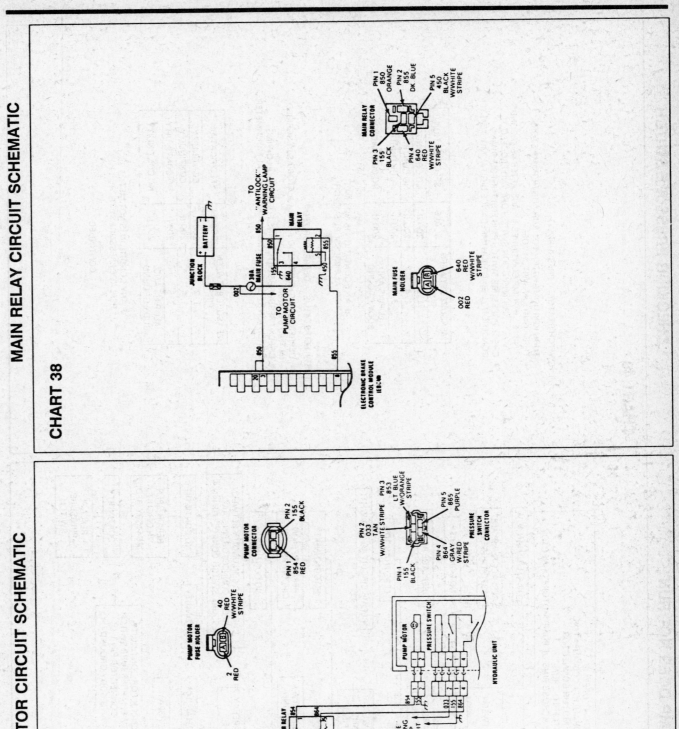

MAIN RELAY CIRCUIT SCHEMATIC

CHART 38

PUMP MOTOR CIRCUIT SCHEMATIC

CHART 37

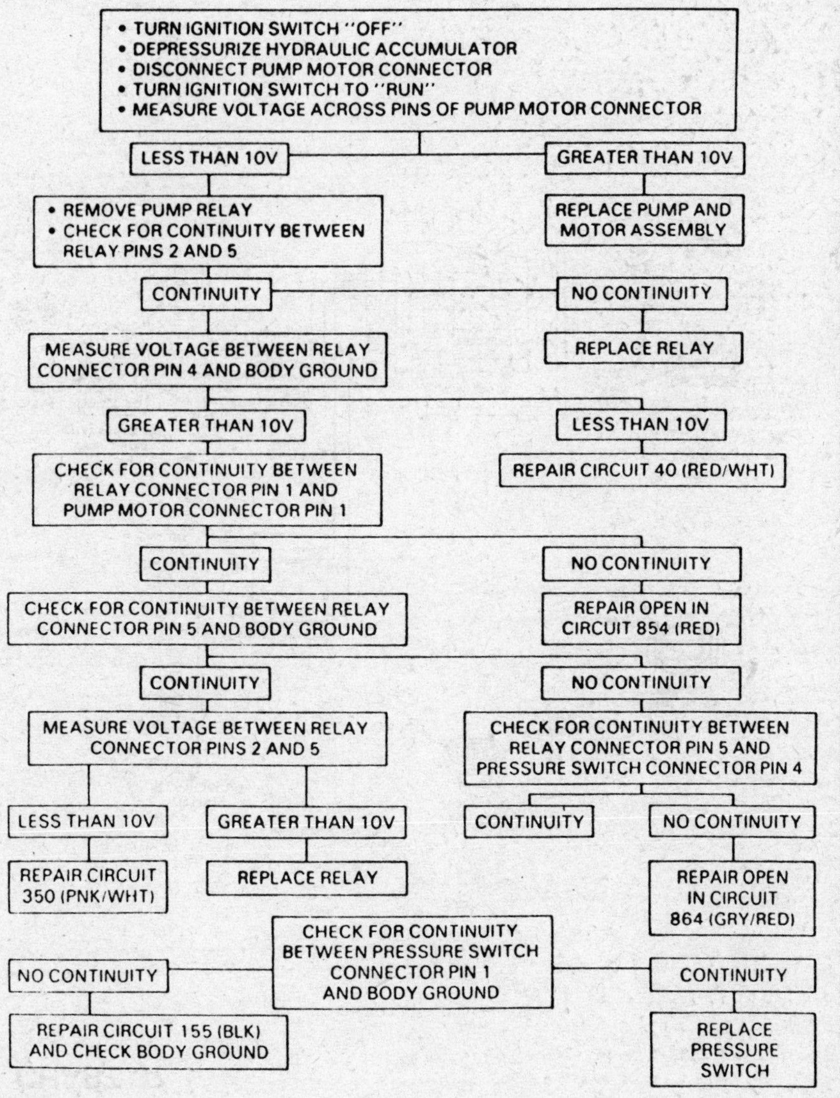

CHECKING PRESSURE SWITCH

CHART 40

I. SWITCH STATUS — PRESSURIZED
- TURN IGNITION SWITCH TO "RUN" UNTIL PUMP STOPS
- TURN IGNITION SWITCH TO "RUN"
- TURN IGNITION SWITCH "OFF"
  NOTE: IF PUMP CONTINUES TO RUN AFTER 45 SECONDS, TURN IGNITION SWITCH OFF AND PROCEED
- CHECK PRESSURE SWITCH PINS FOR THE FOLLOWING CONDITIONS USING HIGH IMPEDANCE DIGITAL MULTIMETER

MEASURE BETWEEN PINS	SCALE	SPECIFICATION
1, 2	200 Ω	NO CONTINUITY
1, 4	200 Ω	NO CONTINUITY
3, 5	200 Ω	CONTINUITY
ALL PINS AND BODY GROUND	200 Ω	NO CONTINUITY

IF ANY CONDITION IS NOT MET, REPLACE PRESSURE SWITCH

II. SWITCH STATUS — DEPRESSURIZED
- DEPRESSURIZE HYDRAULIC ACCUMULATOR AS DESCRIBED IN THIS SECTION
- CHECK PRESSURE SWITCH PINS FOR THE FOLLOWING CONDITIONS USING HIGH IMPEDANCE DIGITAL MULTIMETER

MEASURE BETWEEN PINS	SCALE	SPECIFICATION
1, 2	200 Ω	CONTINUITY
1, 4	200 Ω	CONTINUITY
3, 5	200 Ω	NO CONTINUITY
ALL PINS AND BODY GROUND	200 Ω	NO CONTINUITY

IF ANY CONDITION IS NOT MET, REPLACE PRESSURE SWITCH

CONTINUED

PUMP DOES NOT RUN

CHART 39

- TURN IGNITION SWITCH "OFF"
- DEPRESSURIZE HYDRAULIC ACCUMULATOR
- DISCONNECT PUMP MOTOR CONNECTOR
- TURN IGNITION SWITCH TO "RUN"
- MEASURE VOLTAGE ACROSS PINS OF PUMP MOTOR CONNECTOR

- GREATER THAN 10V → REPLACE PUMP AND MOTOR ASSEMBLY
- LESS THAN 10V →
  - REMOVE PUMP RELAY
  - CHECK FOR CONTINUITY BETWEEN RELAY PINS 2 AND 5
    - NO CONTINUITY → REPLACE RELAY
    - CONTINUITY → MEASURE VOLTAGE BETWEEN RELAY CONNECTOR PIN 4 AND BODY GROUND
      - LESS THAN 10V → REPAIR CIRCUIT 40 (RED/WHT)
      - GREATER THAN 10V → CHECK FOR CONTINUITY BETWEEN RELAY CONNECTOR PIN 1 AND PUMP MOTOR CONNECTOR PIN 1
        - NO CONTINUITY → REPAIR OPEN IN CIRCUIT 854 (RED)
        - CONTINUITY → CHECK FOR CONTINUITY BETWEEN RELAY CONNECTOR PIN 5 AND BODY GROUND
          - NO CONTINUITY → CHECK FOR CONTINUITY BETWEEN RELAY CONNECTOR PIN 5 AND PRESSURE SWITCH CONNECTOR PIN 4
            - NO CONTINUITY → REPAIR OPEN IN CIRCUIT 864 (GRY/RED)
            - CONTINUITY → CHECK FOR CONTINUITY BETWEEN PRESSURE SWITCH CONNECTOR PIN 1 AND BODY GROUND
              - CONTINUITY → REPLACE PRESSURE SWITCH
              - NO CONTINUITY → REPAIR CIRCUIT 155 (BLK) AND CHECK BODY GROUND
          - CONTINUITY → MEASURE VOLTAGE BETWEEN RELAY CONNECTOR PINS 2 AND 5
            - GREATER THAN 10V → REPLACE RELAY
            - LESS THAN 10V → REPAIR CIRCUIT 350 (PNK/WHT)

EBCM LOOP CIRCUIT SCHEMATIC

CHART 42

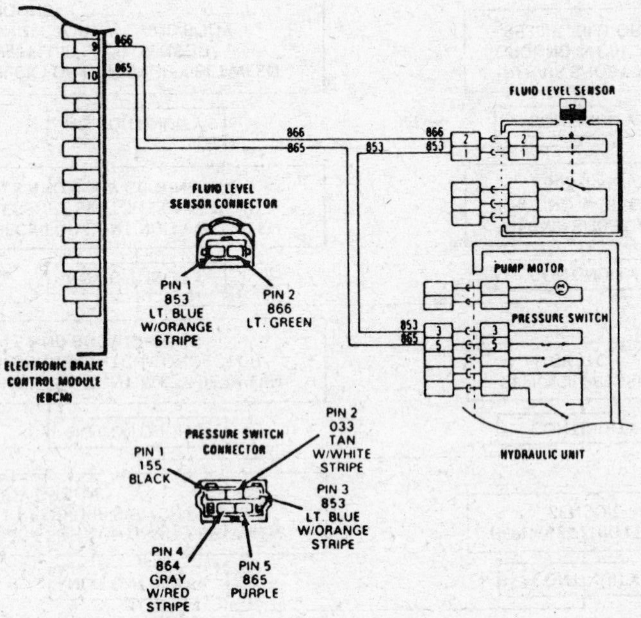

FLUID LEVEL SENSOR

PUMP MOTOR

PRESSURE SWITCH

HYDRAULIC UNIT

FLUID LEVEL SENSOR CONNECTOR

PIN 2 866 LT. GREEN

PIN 1 853 LT. BLUE W/ORANGE STRIPE

PRESSURE SWITCH CONNECTOR

PIN 2 033 TAN W/WHITE STRIPE

PIN 3 853 LT. BLUE W/ORANGE STRIPE

PIN 5 865 PURPLE

PIN 1 155 BLACK

PIN 4 864 GRAY W/RED STRIPE

ELECTRONIC BRAKE CONTROL MODULE (EBCM)

CHECKING PRESSURE SWITCH (CONTINUED)

CHART 41

III. SWITCH THRESHOLDS

- DEPRESSURIZE HYDRAULIC ACCUMULATOR
- INSTALL J 35604-A
- CONNECT PRESSURE SWITCH CONNECTOR AND TURN IGNITION SWITCH TO "RUN" UNTIL PUMP STOPS
- USING HIGH IMPEDANCE DIGITAL MULTIMETER J 34029-A OR EQUIVALENT, MONITOR FOR CONTINUITY BETWEEN PRESSURE SWITCH PINS AS SHOWN BELOW WHILE SLOWLY BLEEDING OFF ACCUMULATOR PRESSURE BY PUMPING THE BRAKE PEDAL. CONTINUITY SHOULD BE GAINED OR LOST AS INDICATED.
- PRESSURIZE SYSTEM BETWEEN EACH TEST BY RECONNECTING PRESSURE SWITCH AND TURNING IGNITION SWITCH TO "RUN" UNTIL PUMP STOPS

MEASURE BETWEEN PINS	SWITCH STATUS	PRESSURE RANGE
1, 4	CONTINUITY SHOULD BE GAINED AT:	1980-2080 PSI (13,650-14,350 KPA)
1, 2	CONTINUITY SHOULD BE GAINED AT:	1500-1550 PSI (10,350-10,700 KPA)
3, 5	CONTINUITY SHOULD BE LOST AT:	1500-1550 PSI (10,350-10,700 KPA)

IF ANY CONDITION IS NOT MET, REPLACE PRESSURE SWITCH

- DEPRESSURIZE HYDRAULIC ACCUMULATOR AS DESCRIBED IN THIS SECTION
- WITH IGNITION "OFF," CONNECT PRESSURE SWITCH CONNECTOR
- TURN IGNITION TO "RUN" AND OBSERVE GAGE. "ANTILOCK" LAMP, "BRAKE" LAMP AND PUMP MOTOR EVENTS SHOULD OCCUR AT PRESSURES INDICATED IN CHART BELOW

EVENT	PRESSURE
"ANTILOCK" LAMP TURNS OFF	1900-1975 PSI (13,100-13,600 KPA)
"BRAKE" LAMP TURNS OFF	1900-1975 PSI (13,100-13,600 KPA)
PUMP MOTOR STOPS	2550-2670 PSI (17,580-18,400 KPA)

IF ANY CONDITION IS NOT MET, REPLACE PRESSURE SWITCH

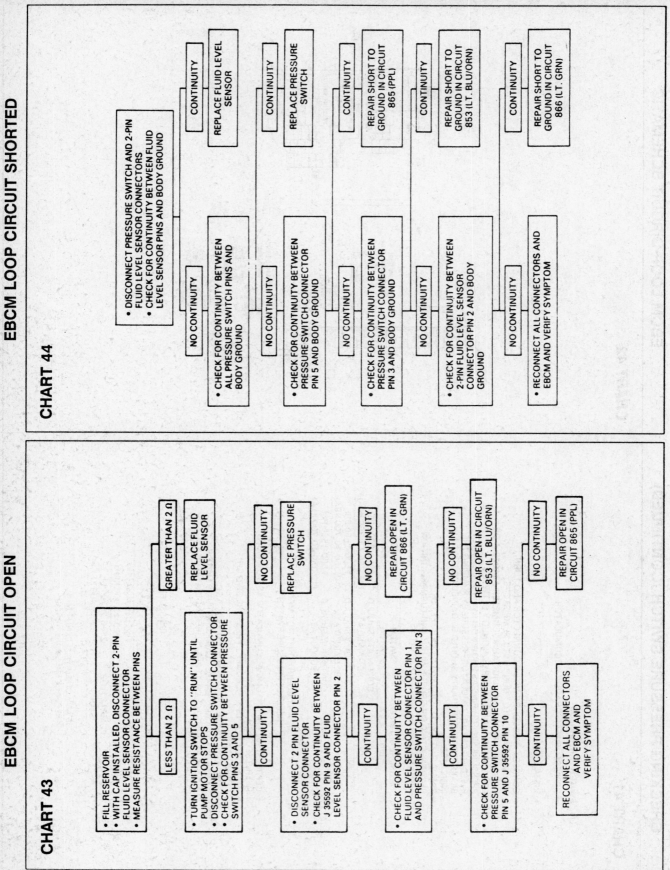

EBCM LOOP CIRCUIT OPEN

CHART 43

- FILL RESERVOIR
- WITH CAP INSTALLED, DISCONNECT 2-PIN FLUID LEVEL SENSOR CONNECTOR
- MEASURE RESISTANCE BETWEEN PINS

GREATER THAN 2 Ω → REPLACE FLUID LEVEL SENSOR

LESS THAN 2 Ω

- TURN IGNITION SWITCH TO "RUN" UNTIL PUMP MOTOR STOPS
- DISCONNECT PRESSURE SWITCH CONNECTOR
- CHECK FOR CONTINUITY BETWEEN PRESSURE SWITCH PINS 3 AND 5

NO CONTINUITY → REPLACE PRESSURE SWITCH

CONTINUITY

- DISCONNECT 2 PIN FLUID LEVEL SENSOR CONNECTOR
- CHECK FOR CONTINUITY BETWEEN J 35592 PIN 9 AND FLUID LEVEL SENSOR CONNECTOR PIN 2

NO CONTINUITY → REPAIR OPEN IN CIRCUIT 866 (LT. GRN)

CONTINUITY

- CHECK FOR CONTINUITY BETWEEN FLUID LEVEL SENSOR CONNECTOR PIN 1 AND PRESSURE SWITCH CONNECTOR PIN 3

NO CONTINUITY → REPAIR OPEN IN CIRCUIT 853 (LT. BLU/ORN)

CONTINUITY

- CHECK FOR CONTINUITY BETWEEN PRESSURE SWITCH CONNECTOR PIN 5 AND J 35592 PIN 10

NO CONTINUITY → REPAIR OPEN IN CIRCUIT 865 (PPL)

CONTINUITY

- RECONNECT ALL CONNECTORS AND EBCM AND VERIFY SYMPTOM

EBCM LOOP CIRCUIT SHORTED

CHART 44

- DISCONNECT PRESSURE SWITCH AND 2-PIN FLUID LEVEL SENSOR CONNECTORS
- CHECK FOR CONTINUITY BETWEEN FLUID LEVEL SENSOR PINS AND BODY GROUND

CONTINUITY → REPLACE FLUID LEVEL SENSOR

NO CONTINUITY

- CHECK FOR CONTINUITY BETWEEN ALL PRESSURE SWITCH PINS AND BODY GROUND

CONTINUITY → REPLACE PRESSURE SWITCH

NO CONTINUITY

- CHECK FOR CONTINUITY BETWEEN PRESSURE SWITCH CONNECTOR PIN 5 AND BODY GROUND

CONTINUITY → REPAIR SHORT TO GROUND IN CIRCUIT 865 (PPL)

NO CONTINUITY

- CHECK FOR CONTINUITY BETWEEN PRESSURE SWITCH CONNECTOR PIN 3 AND BODY GROUND

CONTINUITY → REPAIR SHORT TO GROUND IN CIRCUIT 853 (LT. BLU/ORN)

NO CONTINUITY

- CHECK FOR CONTINUITY BETWEEN 2-PIN FLUID LEVEL SENSOR CONNECTOR PIN 2 AND BODY GROUND

CONTINUITY → REPAIR SHORT TO GROUND IN CIRCUIT 866 (LT. GRN)

NO CONTINUITY

- RECONNECT ALL CONNECTORS AND EBCM AND VERIFY SYMPTOM

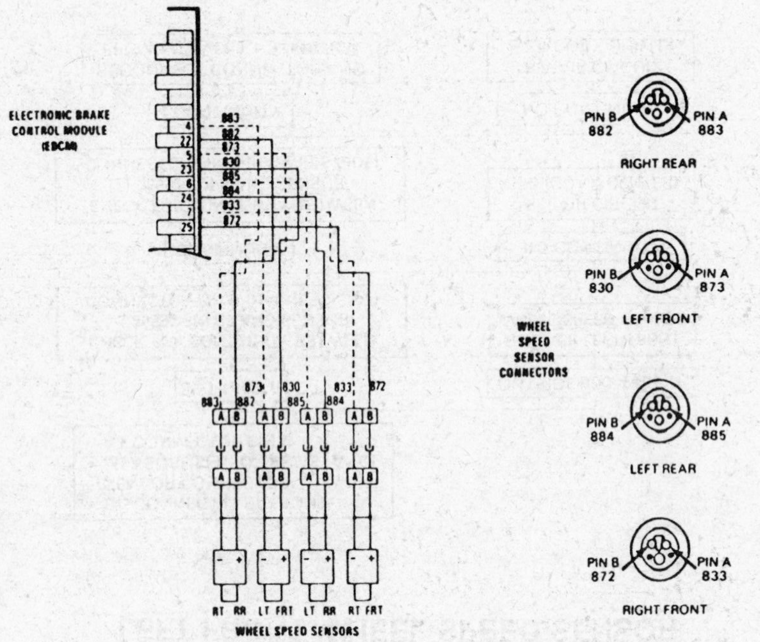

RESISTANCE CHECK

CHART 46

RIGHT REAR WHEEL SPEED SENSOR

- DISCONNECT RIGHT REAR SENSOR CONNECTOR
- MEASURE SENSOR RESISTANCE AT CONNECTOR PINS

↓

800-1400 Ω → CHECK FOR CONTINUITY BETWEEN BREAK-OUT BOX PIN 22 AND SENSOR CONNECTOR PIN B (HARNESS SIDE)

OUTSIDE 800-1400 Ω → REPLACE RIGHT REAR WHEEL SPEED SENSOR

CONTINUITY → CHECK FOR CONTINUITY BETWEEN BREAK-OUT BOX PIN 4 AND SENSOR CONNECTOR PIN A (HARNESS SIDE)

NO CONTINUITY → REPAIR CIRCUIT 882 (COAX CENTER)

CONTINUITY → RECONNECT CONNECTOR AND EBCM AND VERIFY SYMPTOM

NO CONTINUITY → REPAIR CIRCUIT 883 (COAX SHIELD)

WHEEL SPEED SENSOR CIRCUIT SCHEMATIC

CHART 45

PIN A 883 / PIN B 882 — RIGHT REAR

PIN A 873 / PIN B 830 — LEFT FRONT

PIN A 885 / PIN B 884 — LEFT REAR

PIN A 833 / PIN B 872 — RIGHT FRONT

WHEEL SPEED SENSOR CONNECTORS

ELECTRONIC BRAKE CONTROL MODULE (EBCM)

WHEEL SPEED SENSORS

RT FRT LT FRT LT RR RT RR

RESISTANCE CHECK

CHART 48

LEFT REAR WHEEL SPEED SENSOR

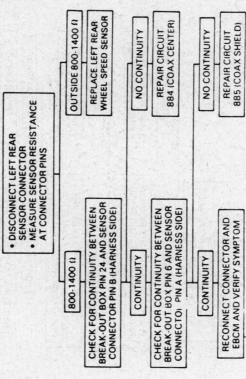

- DISCONNECT LEFT REAR SENSOR CONNECTOR
- MEASURE SENSOR RESISTANCE AT CONNECTOR PINS

800-1400 Ω	OUTSIDE 800-1400 Ω

REPLACE LEFT REAR WHEEL SPEED SENSOR

CHECK FOR CONTINUITY BETWEEN BREAK-OUT BOX PIN 24 AND SENSOR CONNECTOR PIN B (HARNESS SIDE)

CONTINUITY	NO CONTINUITY

REPAIR CIRCUIT 884 (COAX CENTER)

CHECK FOR CONTINUITY BETWEEN BREAK-OUT BOX PIN 6 AND SENSOR CONNECTOR PIN A (HARNESS SIDE)

CONTINUITY	NO CONTINUITY

REPAIR CIRCUIT 885 (COAX SHIELD)

RECONNECT CONNECTOR AND EBCM AND VERIFY SYMPTOM

RESISTANCE CHECK

CHART 47

LEFT FRONT WHEEL SPEED SENSOR

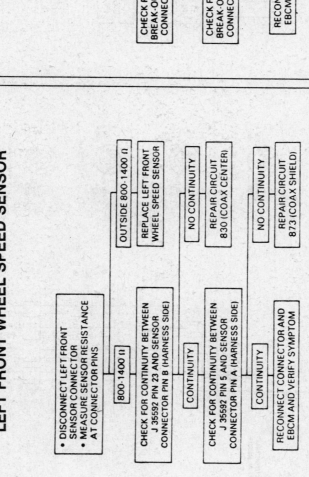

- DISCONNECT LEFT FRONT SENSOR CONNECTOR
- MEASURE SENSOR RESISTANCE AT CONNECTOR PINS

800-1400 Ω	OUTSIDE 800-1400 Ω

REPLACE LEFT FRONT WHEEL SPEED SENSOR

CHECK FOR CONTINUITY BETWEEN J 35592 PIN 23 AND SENSOR CONNECTOR PIN B (HARNESS SIDE)

CONTINUITY	NO CONTINUITY

REPAIR CIRCUIT 830 (COAX CENTER)

CHECK FOR CONTINUITY BETWEEN J 35592 PIN 5 AND SENSOR CONNECTOR PIN A (HARNESS SIDE)

CONTINUITY	NO CONTINUITY

REPAIR CIRCUIT 873 (COAX SHIELD)

RECONNECT CONNECTOR AND EBCM AND VERIFY SYMPTOM

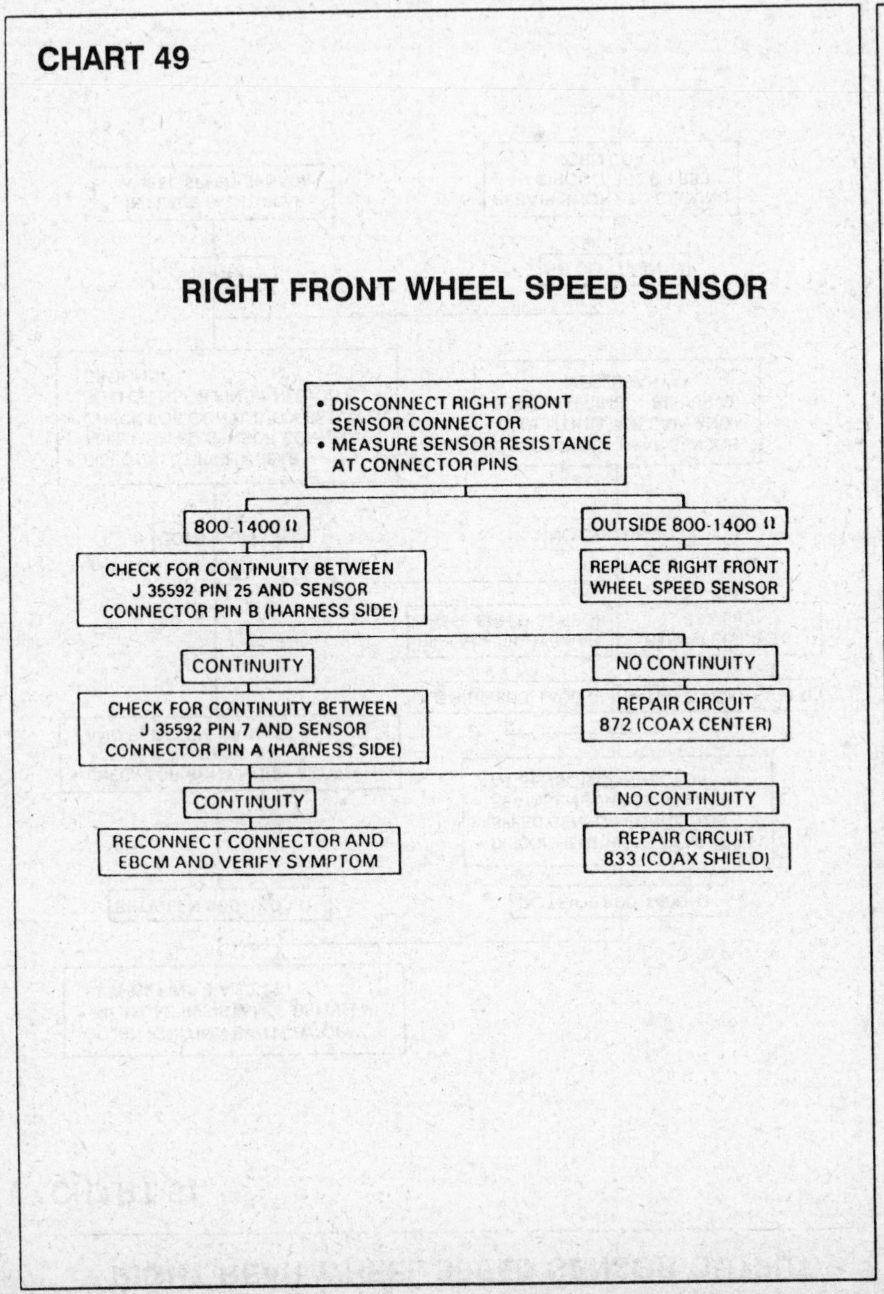

CHECKING WHEEL SPEED SENSOR OUTPUT

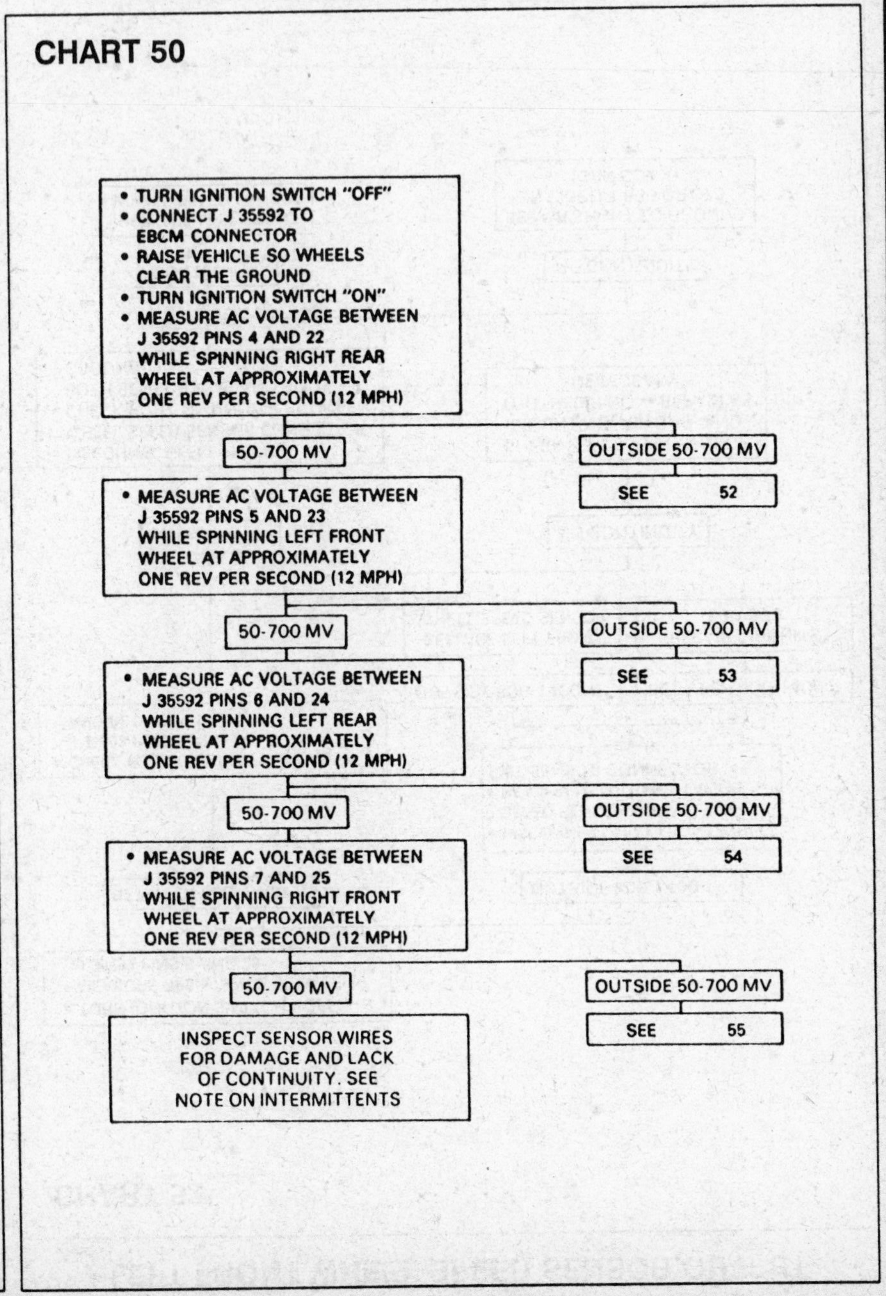

CHART 50

- TURN IGNITION SWITCH "OFF"
- CONNECT J 35592 TO EBCM CONNECTOR
- RAISE VEHICLE SO WHEELS CLEAR THE GROUND
- TURN IGNITION SWITCH "ON"
- MEASURE AC VOLTAGE BETWEEN J 35592 PINS 4 AND 22 WHILE SPINNING RIGHT REAR WHEEL AT APPROXIMATELY ONE REV PER SECOND (12 MPH)

→ 50-700 MV

→ OUTSIDE 50-700 MV → SEE 52

- MEASURE AC VOLTAGE BETWEEN J 35592 PINS 5 AND 23 WHILE SPINNING LEFT FRONT WHEEL AT APPROXIMATELY ONE REV PER SECOND (12 MPH)

→ 50-700 MV

→ OUTSIDE 50-700 MV → SEE 53

- MEASURE AC VOLTAGE BETWEEN J 35592 PINS 6 AND 24 WHILE SPINNING LEFT REAR WHEEL AT APPROXIMATELY ONE REV PER SECOND (12 MPH)

→ 50-700 MV

→ OUTSIDE 50-700 MV → SEE 54

- MEASURE AC VOLTAGE BETWEEN J 35592 PINS 7 AND 25 WHILE SPINNING RIGHT FRONT WHEEL AT APPROXIMATELY ONE REV PER SECOND (12 MPH)

→ 50-700 MV

→ OUTSIDE 50-700 MV → SEE 55

INSPECT SENSOR WIRES FOR DAMAGE AND LACK OF CONTINUITY. SEE NOTE ON INTERMITTENTS

RESISTANCE CHECK

CHART 49

RIGHT FRONT WHEEL SPEED SENSOR

- DISCONNECT RIGHT FRONT SENSOR CONNECTOR
- MEASURE SENSOR RESISTANCE AT CONNECTOR PINS

→ 800-1400 Ω

→ OUTSIDE 800-1400 Ω → REPLACE RIGHT FRONT WHEEL SPEED SENSOR

CHECK FOR CONTINUITY BETWEEN J 35592 PIN 25 AND SENSOR CONNECTOR PIN B (HARNESS SIDE)

→ CONTINUITY

→ NO CONTINUITY → REPAIR CIRCUIT 872 (COAX CENTER)

CHECK FOR CONTINUITY BETWEEN J 35592 PIN 7 AND SENSOR CONNECTOR PIN A (HARNESS SIDE)

→ CONTINUITY

→ NO CONTINUITY → REPAIR CIRCUIT 833 (COAX SHIELD)

RECONNECT CONNECTOR AND EBCM AND VERIFY SYMPTOM

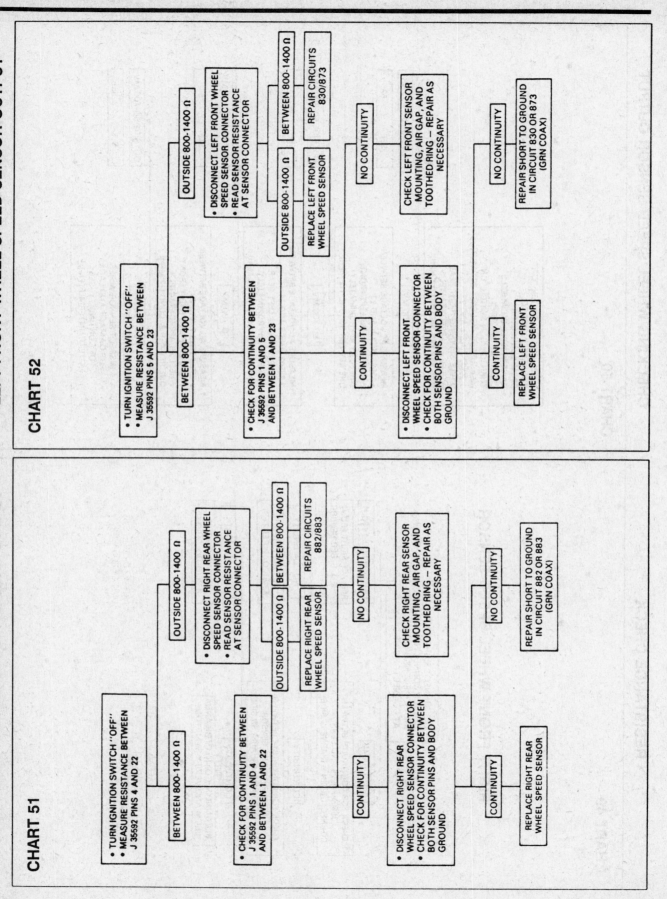

LEFT FRONT WHEEL SPEED SENSOR OUTPUT

CHART 52

- TURN IGNITION SWITCH "OFF"
- MEASURE RESISTANCE BETWEEN J 35592 PINS 5 AND 23

→ BETWEEN 800-1400 Ω
- CHECK FOR CONTINUITY BETWEEN J 35592 PINS 1 AND 5 AND BETWEEN 1 AND 23

→ OUTSIDE 800-1400 Ω
- DISCONNECT LEFT FRONT WHEEL SPEED SENSOR CONNECTOR
- READ SENSOR RESISTANCE AT SENSOR CONNECTOR

→ BETWEEN 800-1400 Ω
REPAIR CIRCUITS 830/873

→ OUTSIDE 800-1400 Ω
REPLACE LEFT FRONT WHEEL SPEED SENSOR

→ CONTINUITY
- DISCONNECT LEFT FRONT WHEEL SPEED SENSOR CONNECTOR
- CHECK FOR CONTINUITY BETWEEN BOTH SENSOR PINS AND BODY GROUND

→ NO CONTINUITY
CHECK LEFT FRONT SENSOR MOUNTING, AIR GAP, AND TOOTHED RING — REPAIR AS NECESSARY

→ CONTINUITY
REPLACE LEFT FRONT WHEEL SPEED SENSOR

→ NO CONTINUITY
REPAIR SHORT TO GROUND IN CIRCUIT 830 OR 873 (GRN COAX)

RIGHT REAR WHEEL SPEED SENSOR OUTPUT

CHART 51

- TURN IGNITION SWITCH "OFF"
- MEASURE RESISTANCE BETWEEN J 35592 PINS 4 AND 22

→ BETWEEN 800-1400 Ω
- CHECK FOR CONTINUITY BETWEEN J 35592 PINS 1 AND 4 AND BETWEEN 1 AND 22

→ OUTSIDE 800-1400 Ω
- DISCONNECT RIGHT REAR WHEEL SPEED SENSOR CONNECTOR
- READ SENSOR RESISTANCE AT SENSOR CONNECTOR

→ BETWEEN 800-1400 Ω
REPAIR CIRCUITS 882/883

→ OUTSIDE 800-1400 Ω
REPLACE RIGHT REAR WHEEL SPEED SENSOR

→ CONTINUITY
- DISCONNECT RIGHT REAR WHEEL SPEED SENSOR CONNECTOR
- CHECK FOR CONTINUITY BETWEEN BOTH SENSOR PINS AND BODY GROUND

→ NO CONTINUITY
CHECK RIGHT REAR SENSOR MOUNTING, AIR GAP, AND TOOTHED RING — REPAIR AS NECESSARY

→ CONTINUITY
REPLACE RIGHT REAR WHEEL SPEED SENSOR

→ NO CONTINUITY
REPAIR SHORT TO GROUND IN CIRCUIT 882 OR 883 (GRN COAX)

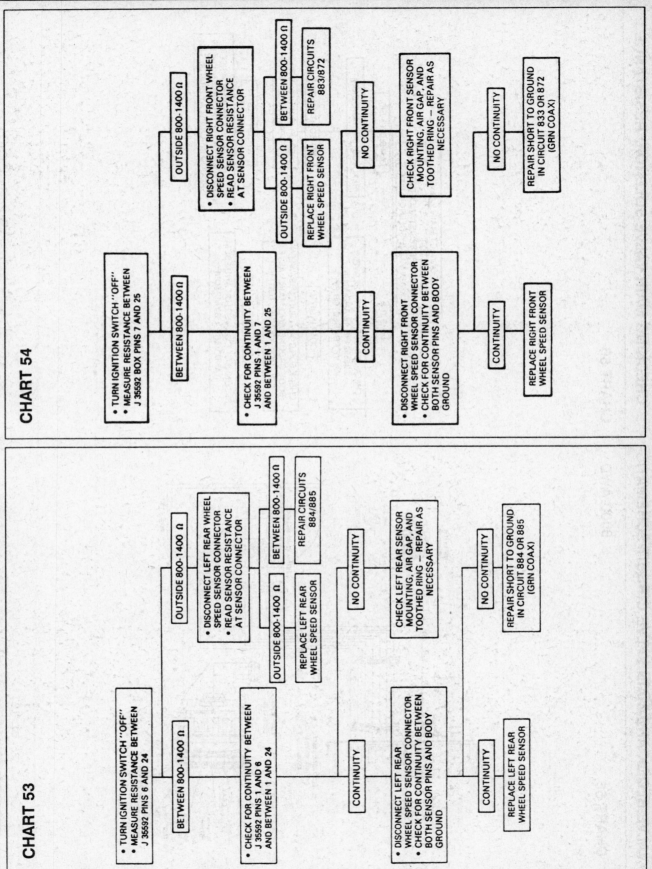

RIGHT FRONT WHEEL SPEED SENSOR OUTPUT

CHART 54

- TURN IGNITION SWITCH "OFF"
- MEASURE RESISTANCE BETWEEN J 35592 BOX PINS 7 AND 25

BETWEEN 800-1400 Ω

OUTSIDE 800-1400 Ω

- DISCONNECT RIGHT FRONT WHEEL SPEED SENSOR CONNECTOR
- READ SENSOR RESISTANCE AT SENSOR CONNECTOR

OUTSIDE 800-1400 Ω

BETWEEN 800-1400 Ω

REPLACE RIGHT FRONT WHEEL SPEED SENSOR

REPAIR CIRCUITS 883/872

- CHECK FOR CONTINUITY BETWEEN J 35592 PINS 1 AND 7 AND BETWEEN 1 AND 25

CONTINUITY

NO CONTINUITY

- DISCONNECT RIGHT FRONT WHEEL SPEED SENSOR CONNECTOR
- CHECK FOR CONTINUITY BETWEEN BOTH SENSOR PINS AND BODY GROUND

CHECK RIGHT FRONT SENSOR MOUNTING, AIR GAP, AND TOOTHED RING — REPAIR AS NECESSARY

CONTINUITY

NO CONTINUITY

REPLACE RIGHT FRONT WHEEL SPEED SENSOR

REPAIR SHORT TO GROUND IN CIRCUIT 833 OR 872 (GRN COAX)

LEFT REAR WHEEL SPEED SENSOR OUTPUT

CHART 53

- TURN IGNITION SWITCH "OFF"
- MEASURE RESISTANCE BETWEEN J 35592 PINS 6 AND 24

BETWEEN 800-1400 Ω

OUTSIDE 800-1400 Ω

- DISCONNECT LEFT REAR WHEEL SPEED SENSOR CONNECTOR
- READ SENSOR RESISTANCE AT SENSOR CONNECTOR

OUTSIDE 800-1400 Ω

BETWEEN 800-1400 Ω

REPLACE LEFT REAR WHEEL SPEED SENSOR

REPAIR CIRCUITS 884/885

- CHECK FOR CONTINUITY BETWEEN J 35592 PINS 1 AND 6 AND BETWEEN 1 AND 24

CONTINUITY

NO CONTINUITY

- DISCONNECT LEFT REAR WHEEL SPEED SENSOR CONNECTOR
- CHECK FOR CONTINUITY BETWEEN BOTH SENSOR PINS AND BODY GROUND

CHECK LEFT REAR SENSOR MOUNTING, AIR GAP, AND TOOTHED RING — REPAIR AS NECESSARY

CONTINUITY

NO CONTINUITY

REPLACE LEFT REAR WHEEL SPEED SENSOR

REPAIR SHORT TO GROUND IN CIRCUIT 884 OR 885 (GRN COAX)

VALVE BLOCK AND MAIN VALVE CIRCUIT SCHEMATIC

CHECKING MAIN VALVE SOLENOID RESISTANCE

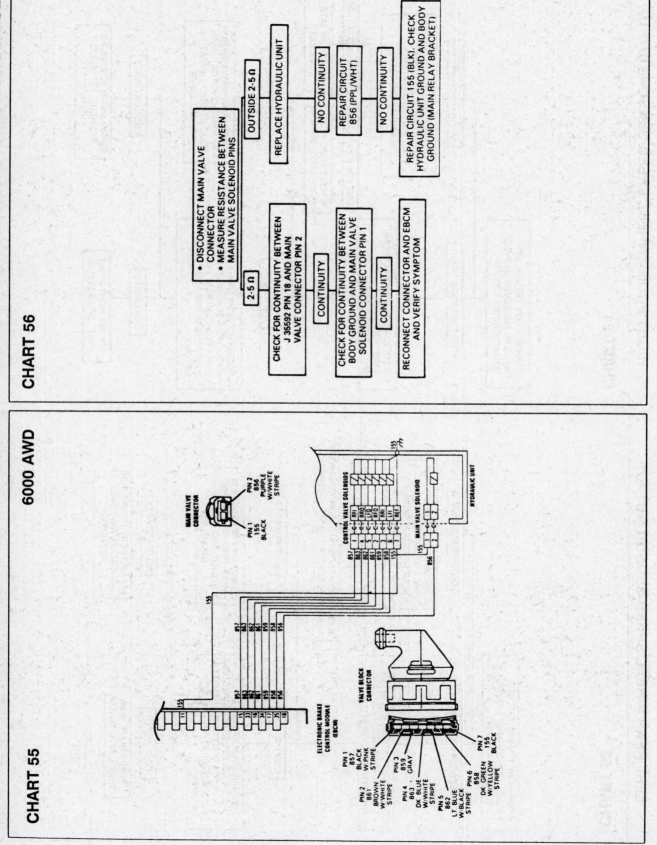

CHART 55

6000 AWD

CHART 56

RIGHT FRONT INLET VALVE RESISTANCE

CHART 58

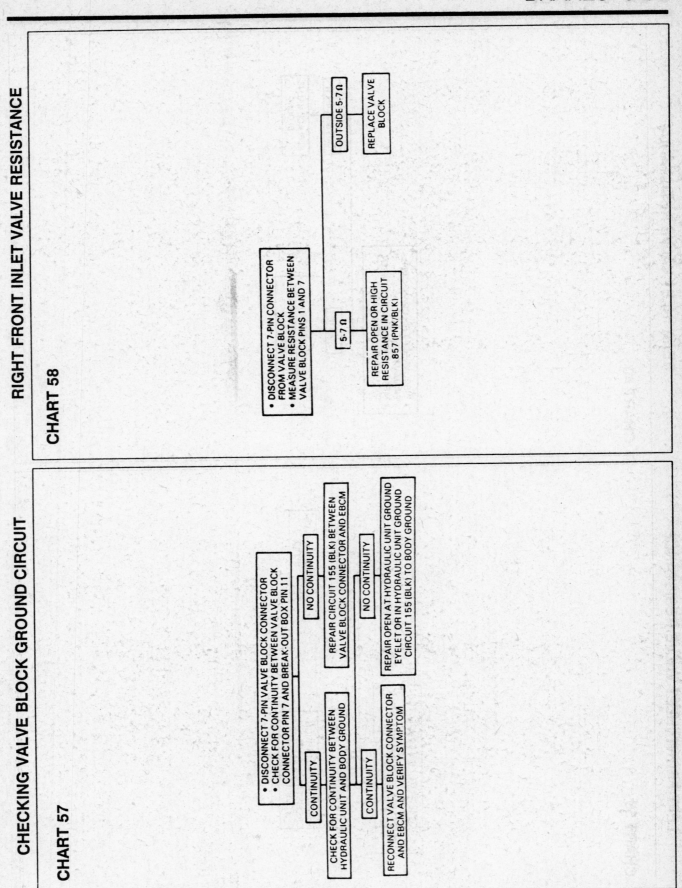

- DISCONNECT 7-PIN CONNECTOR FROM VALVE BLOCK
- MEASURE RESISTANCE BETWEEN VALVE BLOCK PINS 1 AND 7

5-7 Ω

REPAIR OPEN OR HIGH RESISTANCE IN CIRCUIT 857 (PNK/BLK)

OUTSIDE 5-7 Ω

REPLACE VALVE BLOCK

CHECKING VALVE BLOCK GROUND CIRCUIT

CHART 57

- DISCONNECT 7-PIN VALVE BLOCK CONNECTOR
- CHECK FOR CONTINUITY BETWEEN VALVE BLOCK CONNECTOR PIN 7 AND BREAK-OUT BOX PIN 11

NO CONTINUITY

REPAIR CIRCUIT 155 (BLK) BETWEEN VALVE BLOCK CONNECTOR AND EBCM

CONTINUITY

CHECK FOR CONTINUITY BETWEEN HYDRAULIC UNIT AND BODY GROUND

NO CONTINUITY

REPAIR OPEN AT HYDRAULIC UNIT GROUND EYELET OR IN HYDRAULIC UNIT GROUND CIRCUIT 155 (BLK) TO BODY GROUND

CONTINUITY

RECONNECT VALVE BLOCK CONNECTOR AND EBCM AND VERIFY SYMPTOM

LEFT FRONT INLET VALVE RESISTANCE

CHART 59

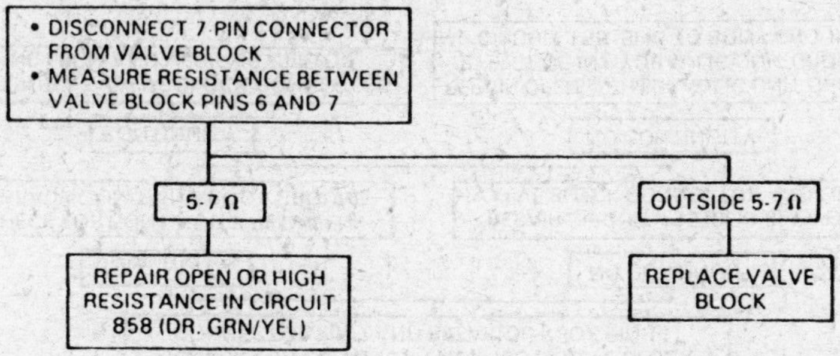

- DISCONNECT 7-PIN CONNECTOR FROM VALVE BLOCK
- MEASURE RESISTANCE BETWEEN VALVE BLOCK PINS 6 AND 7

| 5-7 Ω | OUTSIDE 5-7 Ω |

REPAIR OPEN OR HIGH RESISTANCE IN CIRCUIT 858 (DR. GRN/YEL)

REPLACE VALVE BLOCK

REAR INLET VALVE RESISTANCE

CHART 60

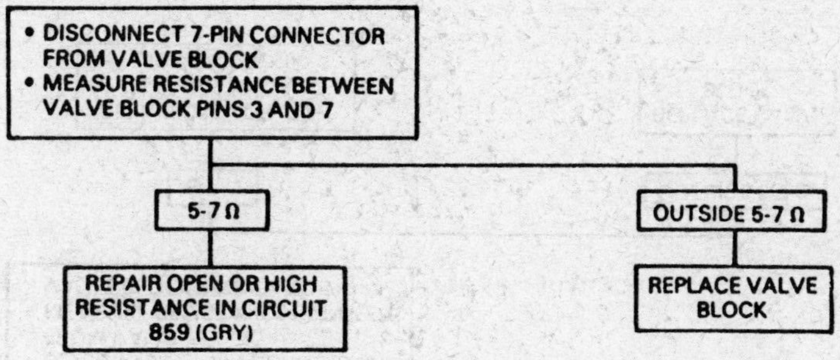

- DISCONNECT 7-PIN CONNECTOR FROM VALVE BLOCK
- MEASURE RESISTANCE BETWEEN VALVE BLOCK PINS 3 AND 7

| 5-7 Ω | OUTSIDE 5-7 Ω |

REPAIR OPEN OR HIGH RESISTANCE IN CIRCUIT 859 (GRY)

REPLACE VALVE BLOCK

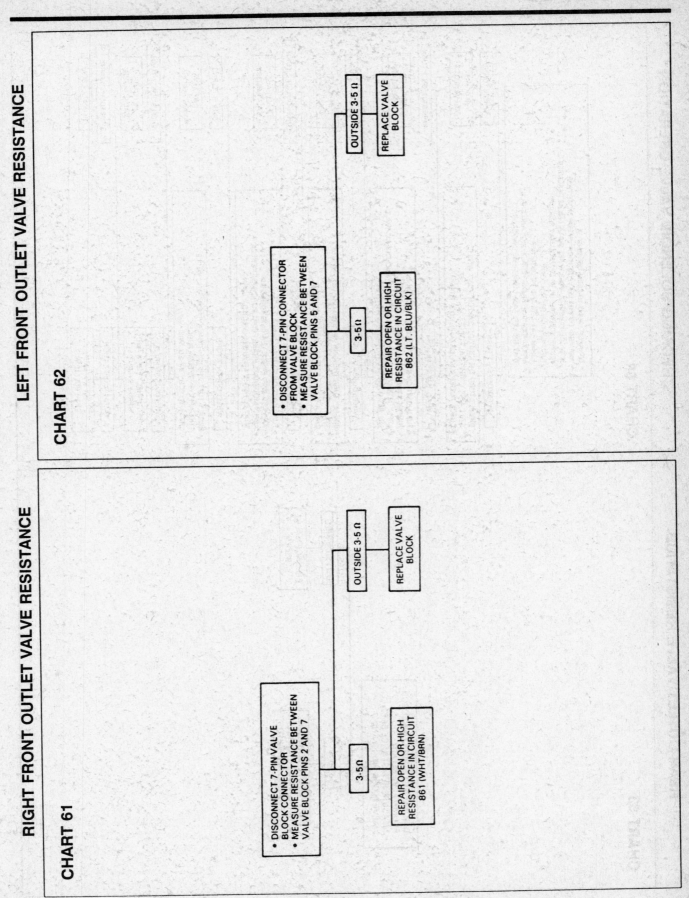

RIGHT FRONT OUTLET VALVE RESISTANCE

CHART 61

- DISCONNECT 7-PIN VALVE BLOCK CONNECTOR
- MEASURE RESISTANCE BETWEEN VALVE BLOCK PINS 2 AND 7

3-5 Ω

REPAIR OPEN OR HIGH RESISTANCE IN CIRCUIT 861 (WHT/BRN)

OUTSIDE 3-5 Ω

REPLACE VALVE BLOCK

LEFT FRONT OUTLET VALVE RESISTANCE

CHART 62

- DISCONNECT 7-PIN CONNECTOR FROM VALVE BLOCK
- MEASURE RESISTANCE BETWEEN VALVE BLOCK PINS 5 AND 7

3-5 Ω

REPAIR OPEN OR HIGH RESISTANCE IN CIRCUIT 862 (LT. BLU/BLK)

OUTSIDE 3-5 Ω

REPLACE VALVE BLOCK

REAR OUTLET VALVE RESISTANCE

CHART 63

CHECKING SOLENOID VALVE OPERATION

CHART 64

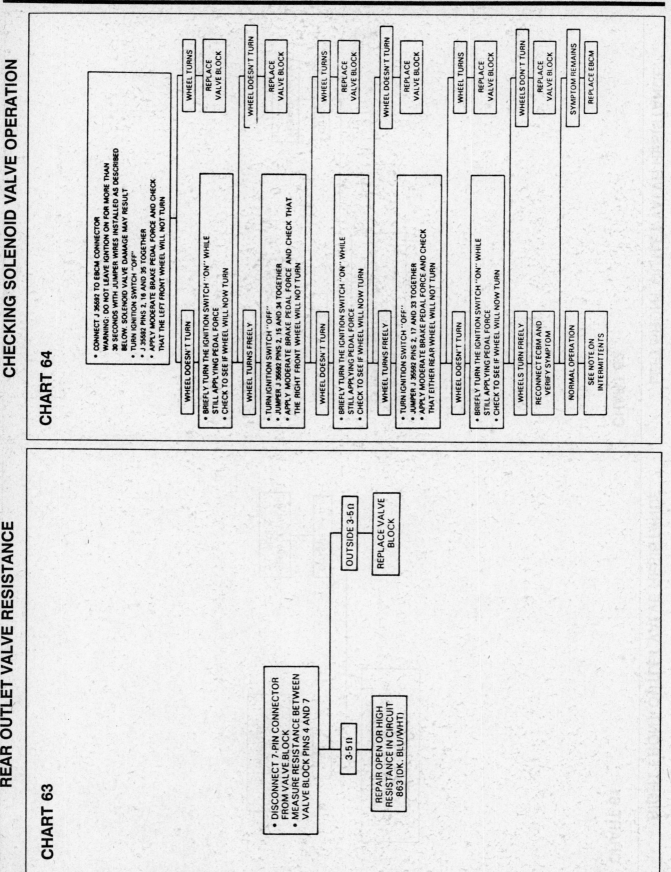

CHART 63

- DISCONNECT 7-PIN CONNECTOR FROM VALVE BLOCK
- MEASURE RESISTANCE BETWEEN VALVE BLOCK PINS 4 AND 7

3-5 Ω → REPAIR OPEN OR HIGH RESISTANCE IN CIRCUIT 863 (DK. BLU/WHT)

OUTSIDE 3-5 Ω → REPLACE VALVE BLOCK

CHART 64

- CONNECT J 35592 TO EBCM CONNECTOR
  WARNING: DO NOT LEAVE IGNITION ON FOR MORE THAN 30 SECONDS WITH JUMPER WIRES INSTALLED AS DESCRIBED BELOW. SOLENOID VALVE DAMAGE MAY RESULT
- TURN IGNITION SWITCH "OFF"
- J 35592 PINS 2, 16 AND 35 TOGETHER
- APPLY MODERATE BRAKE PEDAL FORCE AND CHECK THAT THE LEFT FRONT WHEEL WILL NOT TURN

WHEEL DOESN'T TURN
- BRIEFLY TURN THE IGNITION SWITCH "ON" WHILE STILL APPLYING PEDAL FORCE
- CHECK TO SEE IF WHEEL WILL NOW TURN
  - WHEEL TURNS
  - WHEEL DOESN'T TURN → REPLACE VALVE BLOCK

WHEEL TURNS FREELY
- TURN IGNITION SWITCH "OFF"
- JUMPER J 35592 PINS 2, 15 AND 34 TOGETHER
- APPLY MODERATE BRAKE PEDAL FORCE AND CHECK THAT THE RIGHT FRONT WHEEL WILL NOT TURN
  - WHEEL DOESN'T TURN → REPLACE VALVE BLOCK

WHEEL DOESN'T TURN
- BRIEFLY TURN THE IGNITION SWITCH "ON" WHILE STILL APPLYING PEDAL FORCE
- CHECK TO SEE IF WHEEL WILL NOW TURN
  - WHEEL TURNS
  - WHEEL DOESN'T TURN → REPLACE VALVE BLOCK

WHEEL TURNS FREELY
- TURN IGNITION SWITCH "OFF"
- JUMPER J 35592 PINS 2, 17 AND 33 TOGETHER
- APPLY MODERATE BRAKE PEDAL FORCE AND CHECK THAT EITHER REAR WHEEL WILL NOT TURN
  - WHEEL DOESN'T TURN → REPLACE VALVE BLOCK

WHEEL DOESN'T TURN
- BRIEFLY TURN THE IGNITION SWITCH "ON" WHILE STILL APPLYING PEDAL FORCE
- CHECK TO SEE IF WHEEL WILL NOW TURN
  - WHEELS TURN FREELY
  - WHEELS DON'T TURN → REPLACE VALVE BLOCK

- RECONNECT ECBM AND VERIFY SYMPTOM
  - NORMAL OPERATION → SEE NOTE ON INTERMITTENTS
  - SYMPTOM REMAINS → REPLACE EBCM

CHECKING BRAKE WARNING LAMP CIRCUIT

CHART 66

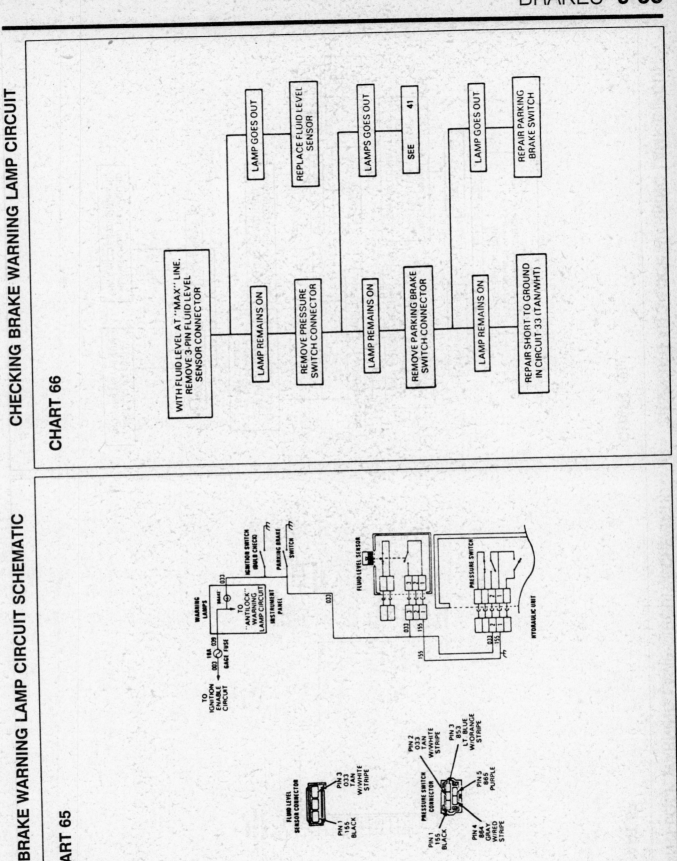

BRAKE WARNING LAMP CIRCUIT SCHEMATIC

CHART 65

CHECKING ANTI-LOCK WARNING LAMP CIRCUIT

CHART 68

ANTI-LOCK WARNING LAMP CIRCUIT SCHEMATIC

CHART 67

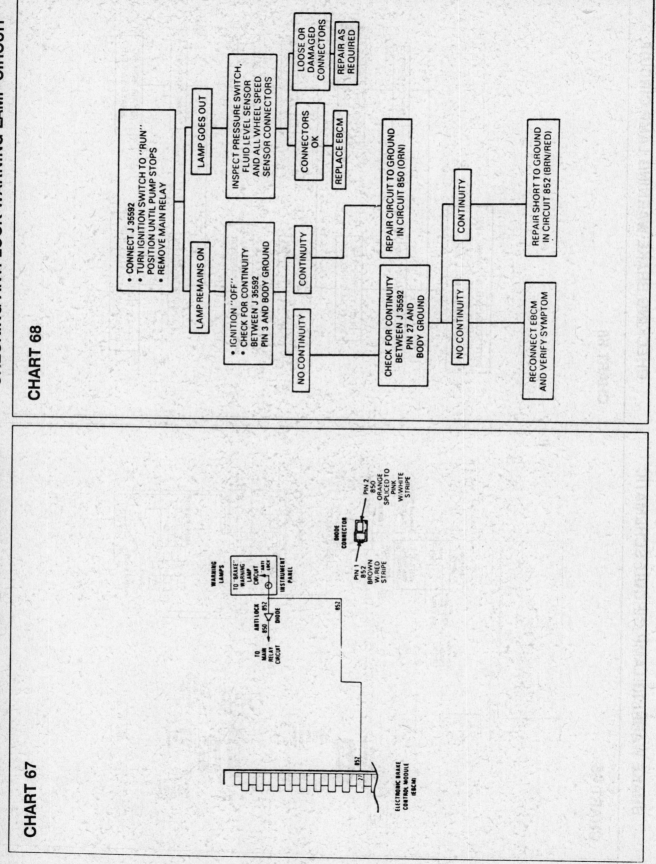

ANTI-LOCK WARNING LAMP INOPERATIVE

CHART 70

CHECKING DIODE CIRCUIT

CHART 69

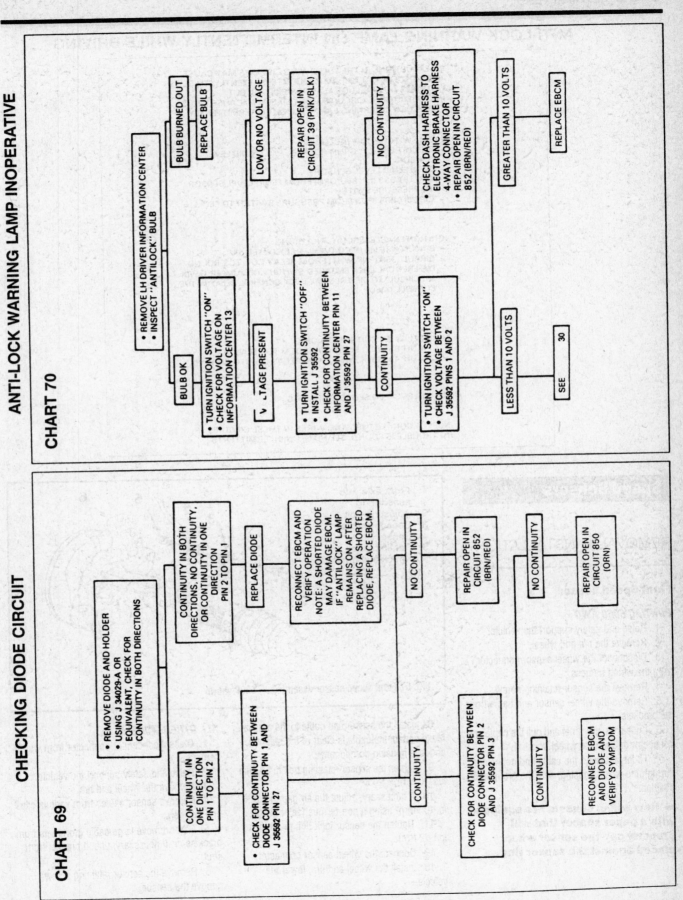

ANTI-LOCK WARNING LAMP ON INTERMITTENTLY WHILE DRIVING

INTERRUPTIONS IN THE FOLLOWING CIRCUITS MAY CAUSE THE "ANTILOCK" LAMP TO LIGHT INTERMITTENTLY. THIS LIST DOES NOT INCLUDE ALL POSSIBILITIES, BUT INCLUDES THOSE CIRCUITS MOST LIKELY TO CAUSE THE "ANTILOCK" WARNING LAMP TO LIGHT INTERMITTENTLY.

- EBCM SWITCH LOOP, INCLUDING
  - CIRCUIT 866 (LT. GRN) FROM EBCM TO FLUID LEVEL SENSOR
  - 2-PIN FLUID LEVEL SENSOR
  - CIRCUIT 853 (LT. BLU/ORN) FROM FLUID LEVEL SENSOR TO PRESSURE SWITCH
  - CIRCUIT 865 (PPL) FROM PRESSURE SWITCH TO EBCM

- IGNITION ENABLE CIRCUIT, INCLUDING
  - BRAKE FUSE (#5 IN CONVENIENCE CENTER 5A)
  - CIRCUIT 350 (PNK/WHT) FROM RELAY COIL TO GROUND
  - DIFFERENTIAL LOCK ENGAGED SWITCH AND JUMPER (AWD)
  - 951 CIRCUIT TO DIFFERENTIAL LOCK CONTROL RELAY IN THE CONSOLE (AWD)

- MAIN RELAY CIRCUITS, INCLUDING
  - CIRCUIT 855 (DK. BLU) FROM EBCM TO RELAY COIL
  - CIRCUIT 450 (BLK/WHT) FROM RELAY COIL TO GROUND

- ALL WHEEL SPEED SENSOR CIRCUITS

INSPECT CONNECTORS AND WIRES IN THESE CIRCUITS. IF NO TROUBLE IS FOUND, SEE NOTE ON INTERMITTENTS

Speed Sensors

REMOVAL & INSTALLATION

Front Speed Sensor

PONTIAC 6000 AWD

1. Raise and safely support the vehicle.
2. Remove the tire and wheel.
3. Disconnect the wheel sensor connector from the wiring harness.
4. Remove the sensor retaining screw.
5. Remove the wheel sensor and cable from the brackets.
6. Unseat the grommet and pull the cable and connector through the wheel housing.
7. To install, insert the cable and connector through the wheel housing; seat the grommet in position.

➡ **New wheel sensors are equipped with a paper spacer that will properly gap the sensor when placed against the sensor ring.**

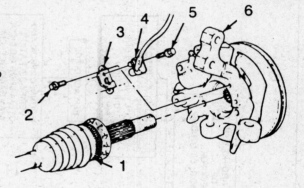

1. Front axle with sensor ring
2. Adjusting bolt
3. Sensor bracket
4. Sensor
5. Retaining bolt
6. Knuckle and hub

FIG. 57 Front speed sensor assembly — 6000 shown

8. Install the sensor and cable to the bracket. Make certain the cable is clear of the steering and axle housing components.
9. Tighten the sensor retaining bolt to 53 inch lbs. (6 Nm).
10. If necessary, adjust the air gap to 0.028 in. (0.7mm) using a non-ferrous feeler gauge.
11. Tighten the sensor lock bolt to 18 inch lbs. (2 Nm).
12. Connect the wheel sensor connector.
13. Install the wheel and tire; lower the vehicle.

ALL OTHER MODELS

1. Disconnect sensor connector from wiring harness.
2. Raise and safely support the vehicle.
3. Remove the wheel and tire.
4. Remove sensor cables from various clips and retainers.
5. Either remove large cable grommets from brackets or, if necessary, unbolt bracket from strut.
6. Remove the sensor retaining screw; remove the sensor.

7. To install, coat the sensor body with anti–corrosion compound GM 1052856 or equivalent where the sensor will contact the knuckle.

8. Install the sensor. Tighten the mounting bolt to 106 inch lbs. (12 Nm).

9. Position and install the cable in grommets, clips and retainers. Cables must be secure in the retainers and clear of moving parts. Cable must not be pulled too tight.

10. Connect sensor to wiring harness.

11. Install wheel and tire; lower the vehicle.

Rear Speed Sensor

PONTIAC 6000 AWD

1. Disconnect the speed sensor connector in the front corner of the trunk compartment. If the right rear connector is to be disconnected, the spare wheel and tire must be removed.

2. Release the cable grommet. Carefully work the sensor cable and connector through the hole in the body panel.

3. Raise and safely support the vehicle.

4. Remove the wheel and tire.

5. Remove the sensor mounting bolt; remove the sensor from the caliper. Slide the grommets out of the slots in the brackets and cable guide.

6. If the old sensor is to be reused, remove the paper spacer and any debris from the face of the sensor.

7. Install the sensor and tighten the retaining bolt to 80 inch lbs. (9 Nm). If reusing the old sensor, adjust the air gap.

➡ **New wheel sensors are equipped with a paper spacer that will properly gap the sensor when placed against the sensor ring.**

8. Install the grommets in position on the brackets and cable guide.

9. Route the cable to avoid contact with moving suspension components. work the connector and cable up through the hole in the underbody, then fit the grommet into position in the hole.

10. Install the wheel and tire. Lower the vehicle.

11. Connect the wheel sensor connector to the wiring harness.

12. Install the spare wheel and tire if removed; secure the trunk carpet.

Air Gap Adjustment

➡ **Only the front and rear sensors on the Pontiac 6000 AWD are adjustable. On all other vehicles, the gap may be checked but is not adjustable.**

PONTIAC 6000 AWD

1. Raise and safely support the vehicle.

2. Remove the wheel and tire.

3. Loosen the sensor adjustment bolt for the front or rear sensor.

4. Inspect the face of the sensor for abnormal wear or damage. If necessary, replace the sensor.

➡ **New sensors come with a paper spacer which will properly gap the sensor when placed against the speed sensor ring.**

5. If the sensor is to be reused, clean the face of the sensor of all traces of the paper spacer, dirt, dust, etc.

6. Reposition the sensor; adjust the air gap to 0.028 in. (0.7mm) using a non–ferrous feeler gauge.

7. Tighten the adjustment screw to 18 inch lbs. (2 Nm).

8. Install the wheel and tire. Lower the vehicle.

ALL OTHER MODELS

1. Disconnect the sensor connector located in the trunk on most models. Disengage the retaining clips and grommets holding the sensor wire harness.

2. Raise and safely support the vehicle.

3. Remove the wheel and tire.

4. Remove the sensor retaining bolt and remove the sensor.

5. To install, the surfaces of the sensor which contact the knuckle must be coated with an anti–corrosion compound such as 1052856 or equivalent. This coating must be applied any time the sensor is removed.

6. To install, position the sensor and install the retaining bolt. Tighten the bolt to 80–100 inch lbs. (9–12 Nm).

7. Install the sensor harness into the clips and grommets. Correct cable placement is critical to avoid contact or stretching damage during suspension movement.

8. If the sensor connector is not in the trunk, connect the harnesses. Install the wheel and tire. Lower the vehicle.

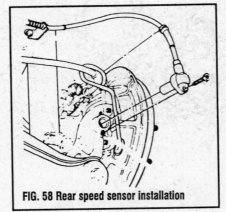

FIG. 58 Rear speed sensor installation

9. If the wiring harness connector is in the trunk, connect the wiring.

REMOVAL & INSTALLATION

Pontiac 6000 AWD

1. Depressurize the hydraulic accumulator.

2. With the key **OFF**, disconnect the negative battery cable.

3. Remove the wire clip from the return hose fitting and remove the return hose from the pump. Pull the return hose fitting out of the pump housing.

4. Remove the pressure hose bolt from the pump; remove the hose and O-rings from the pump.

5. Remove the pump mounting bolt; separate the energy unit from the energy unit from the hydraulic unit.

6. Using 2 wrenches, disconnect the brake lines from the valve block and the hydraulic unit.

7. Disconnect the pushrod from the brake pedal.

8. Push the dust boot forward, off the rear half of the pushrod. Unscrew the 2 halves of the pushrod.

9. Remove the 2 hydraulic unit mounting bolts from the pushrod bracket.

10. Remove the hydraulic unit from the pushrod bracket. The front half of the pushrod will remain locked into the hydraulic unit.

To Install:

11. Mount the hydraulic unit to the pushrod bracket and install the mounting bolts. Tighten the bolts to 37 ft. lbs. (50 Nm).

12. Thread the 2 parts of the pushrod together and reposition the dust boot.

13. Connect the pushrod to the brake pedal; tighten the nut to 27 ft. lbs. (37 Nm).

14. Using 2 wrenches, connect the brake lines to the hydraulic unit and the valve block. Tighten to 11 ft. lbs (20 Nm).

15. Connect the energy unit to the pump unit and install the pump mounting bolt.

16. Install the pressure hose and O-rings to the pump; install the hose bolt and tighten it to 15 ft. lbs. (20 Nm).

17. Push the return hose fitting into the pump body and connect the return hose to the pump.

18. Install the wire clip to the return hose fitting.

19. Connect the wiring to the hydraulic unit.

20. Connect the negative battery cable.

21. Bleed the brake system.

All Other Models

1. With ignition switch **OFF**, disconnect the negative battery cable.
2. Depressurize the hydraulic accumulator.
3. Disconnect all electrical connections at the hydraulic unit.
4. Remove the cross-car brace if equipped.
5. Remove the pump bolt and move pump/motor assembly to allow access to the brake lines.

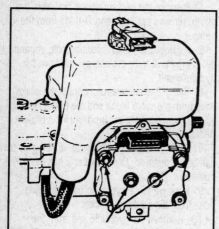

FIG. 59 Remove the fasteners from the positions shown by arrows only, other fasteners must NOT be disturbed

6. Using 2 wrenches, disconnect the brake lines from the hydraulic unit and valve body.
7. Push the dust boot forward, past the hex on the pushrod, and separate the pushrod into 2 sections by unscrewing it.
8. Remove the hydraulic unit mounting bolts at the pushrod bracket. Remove the hydraulic unit from the car; part of the pushrod may remain with the unit.

To Install:

9. Position the hydraulic unit and install new retaining bolts at the pushrod bracket. Tighten the bolts to 37 ft. lbs. (50 Nm).
10. From inside car, thread pushrod halves together and tighten. Reposition the dust boot and connect the pushrod to the brake pedal.
11. Install the brake lines to the valve block; tighten to 106 inch lbs. (12 Nm).
12. Position the pump/motor assembly on the hydraulic unit. Install the mounting bolt and tighten to 10 ft. lbs. (13 Nm).
13. Install the cross-car brace if one was removed.
14. Connect the electrical harness to the hydraulic unit.
15. Connect the negative battery cable.
16. Bleed the brake system.

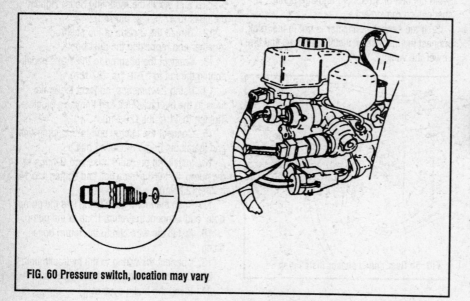

FIG. 60 Pressure switch, location may vary

Valve Block Assembly

REMOVAL & INSTALLATION

1. With the ignition **OFF** disconnect the negative battery cable.
2. Depressurize the accumulator.
3. For Pontiac 6000 AWD, remove the hydraulic unit. For all other models, drain or remove the brake fluid from the reservoir.
4. Disconnect the electrical harness running to the valve block.
5. It may be necessary on some models to disconnect the brake lines from the bottom of the valve block.
6. At the valve block, remove the 3 nuts or 2 nuts and 1 bolt with hex faces only. Remove the valve block assembly and O-rings by sliding the valve block off of the studs. Recover any O-rings or gaskets from the mounting points and/or the fluid line ports.

➡ **Do not attempt to disassemble the valve block by removing the bolts with the recessed drive heads; the unit cannot be overhauled or repaired.**

To install:

7. Lubricate the O-rings with brake fluid.
8. Install the valve block and O-rings onto the master cylinder body.
9. Install the 3 nuts or 2 nuts and 1 bolt; tighten to 18 ft. lbs. (25 Nm).
10. Connect the brake lines to the bottom of the valve block if they were removed.
11. Reinstall the hydraulic unit if it was removed.
12. Connect the wiring harnesses.
13. Refill the system or reservoir to the correct level.
14. Connect the negative battery cable.
15. Bleed the brake system.

Pressure Warning Switch

REMOVAL & INSTALLATION

1. Disconnect the negative battery cable.
2. Depressurize the accumulator.
3. Disconnect the electrical connector from the pressure/warning switch.

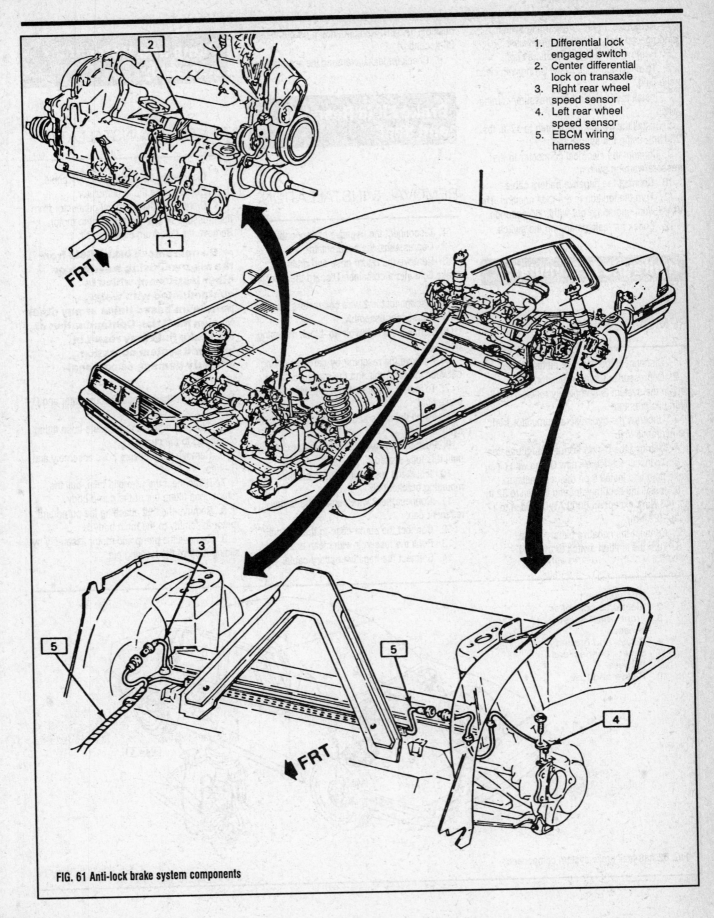

1. Differential lock engaged switch
2. Center differential lock on transaxle
3. Right rear wheel speed sensor
4. Left rear wheel speed sensor
5. EBCM wiring harness

FIG. 61 Anti-lock brake system components

4. Remove the pressure/warning switch using special tool J–35804 or equivalent.

5. Remove the O-ring from the switch.

6. To install, lubricate a new O-ring with clean brake fluid.

7. Install the O-ring on the pressure/warning switch.

8. Install the switch and tighten to 17 ft. lbs. (23 Nm). using the special tool.

9. Connect the electrical connector to the pressure/warning switch.

10. Connect the negative battery cable.

11. Turn the ignition to the **ON** position. The BRAKE light should go out within 60 seconds.

12. Check for leakage around the switch.

Hydraulic Accumulator

REMOVAL & INSTALLATION

1. Disconnect the negative battery cable.

2. Depressurize the accumulator. Make certain the system is completely relieved of all hydraulic pressure.

3. Unscrew the hydraulic accumulator from the hydraulic unit.

4. Remove the O-ring from the accumulator.

5. To install, lubricate a new O-ring with clean brake fluid and install it on the accumulator.

6. Install the accumulator and tighten to 32 ft. lbs. (43 Nm), except on 6000 AWD tighten to 17 ft. lbs. (23 Nm).

7. Connect the negative battery cable.

8. Turn the ignition switch to the **ON**

position. The BRAKE light should go out within 60 seconds.

9. Check for leakage around the accumulator.

Brake Fluid Reservoir and Seal

REMOVAL & INSTALLATION

1. Disconnect the negative battery cable.

2. Depressurize the accumulator.

3. Remove the return hose and drain the brake fluid into a container. Discard the fluid properly.

4. Disconnect the 2 wire connectors from the fluid level sensor assembly.

5. Remove the reservoir–to–block mounting bolt.

6. Remove the reservoir by carefully prying between the reservoir and the master cylinder.

7. To install, lubricate the seals with clean brake fluid.

8. Install the seals and O-ring into the master cylinder body.

9. Push the reservoir into the master cylinder until it is fully seated.

10. Install the reservoir to valve block mounting bracket bolt.

11. Connect the 2 wire connectors to the reservoir cap.

12. Connect the sump hose to the reservoir.

13. Refill the reservoir with clean brake fluid.

14. Connect the negative battery cable.

Pump and Motor Assembly

REMOVAL & INSTALLATION

1. Disconnect the negative battery cable.

2. Depressurize the accumulator.

3. Disconnect the electrical connector from the pressure switch and the electric motor. Remove the fluid from the reservoir.

➡ **Do not remove brake fluid from the reservoir using a syringe or other instrument which is contaminated with water, petroleum based fluids or any other foreign material. Contamination of the brake fluid may result in impaired system operation, property damage or personal injury.**

4. Remove the hydraulic accumulator and O-ring.

5. Disconnect the high pressure hose fitting connected to the pump.

6. Remove the pressure hose assembly and O-rings.

7. Disconnect the wire clip then, pull the return hose fitting out of the pump body.

8. Remove the bolt attaching the pump and motor assembly to the main body.

9. Remove the pump and motor assembly by sliding it off of the locating pin.

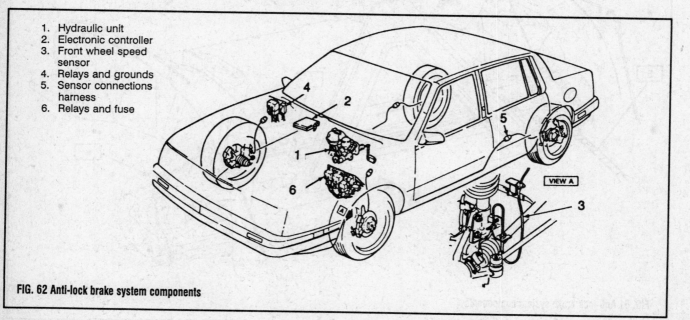

1. Hydraulic unit
2. Electronic controller
3. Front wheel speed sensor
4. Relays and grounds
5. Sensor connections harness
6. Relays and fuse

FIG. 62 Anti-lock brake system components

➡ **Replace the Insulators if damaged or deteriorated.**

10. To install, position the pump and motor assembly to the main body.

11. Install the bolt attaching the pump and motor assembly to the main body.

12. Connect the pressure hose assembly.

13. Connect the return hose and fitting into the pump body. Install the wire clip.

14. Install the bolt, O-rings and fitting of the high pressure hose to the pump assembly.

15. Connect the electrical connector to the pump motor.

16. Connect the negative battery cable.

Filling and Bleeding the System

SYSTEM FILLING

➡ **Do not allow the pump to run more than 60 seconds at 1 time. If the pump must run longer, allow the pump to cool several minutes between 60 second runs.**

With the ignition **OFF** and the negative battery cable disconnected, discharge the pressure within the accumulator. Remove the cap from the reservoir; fill the reservoir to the correct level with DOT 3 fluid.

➡ **Use only DOT 3 brake fluid from a clean, sealed container. Use of DOT 5 silicone fluid is not recommended. Internal damage to the pump components may result.**

SYSTEM BLEEDING

Front and/or rear brake circuits should be bled using pressure bleeding equipment. The pressure bleeder must be of the diaphragm type and must have a rubber diaphragm between the air supply and brake fluid. If necessary, the front brakes may be bled manually; manual bleeding is not recommended for the rear brakes.

FRONT BRAKE CIRCUIT

✳✳ CAUTION

Do not move vehicle until a firm brake pedal is achieved. Failure to obtain firm brake pedal may result in personal injury and/or property damage

1. With the ignition switch **OFF**, disconnect the negative battery cable.

2. Depressurize the accumulator.

3. Remove the reservoir cap or disconnect the wiring sensor from the fluid level sensor and remove the sensor.

4. Install the special tool No. J–35798 in place of the cap or sensor.

5. Attach the brake bleeder to the adapter tool No. J–35798 and charge to 20 psi (138 kPa).

5. Attach a bleeder hose to 1 front bleeder valve and submerge the other end in a container of clean brake fluid.

6. Open the bleeder valve.

7. Allow the fluid to flow from the bleeder until no air bubbles are seen in the brake fluid.

8. Close the bleeder valve.

9. Repeat Steps 4–7 on the other front bleeder valve.

10. Check the fluid level and adjust as necessary.

11. Remove the brake bleeding equipment and adapters, install the cap or sensor.

REAR BRAKE CIRCUIT

✳✳ CAUTION

Do not move vehicle until a firm brake pedal is achieved. Failure to obtain firm brake pedal may result in personal injury and/or property damage

1. With the ignition switch **OFF**, disconnect the negative battery cable.

2. Depressurize the accumulator.

3. Check the fluid level in the reservoir and fill as necessary.

4. Turn the ignition switch **ON** and allow the system to charge. (Listen for the pump motor; it will stop when the system is charged.)

2. Attach a bleeder hose to 1 of the rear bleeder valves and submerge the other end in a container of clean brake fluid.

3. Open the bleeder valve.

4. With the ignition **ON**, slightly depress the brake pedal for at least 10 seconds.

5. Allow the fluid to flow from the bleeder until no air bubbles are seen in the brake fluid. Repeat the Step above if necessary.

6. Close the bleeder valve.

7. Repeat Steps 2–6 on the other rear bleeder valve.

8. Depressurize the system. Inspect the reservoir fluid level and adjust as necessary.

Brake Specifications

Model	Lug Nut Torque (ft. lb.)	Master Cylinder Bore	Bake Disc		Brake Drum			Minimum Lining Thickness	
			Minimum Thickness	Maximum Run-Out	Diameter	Max Machine O/S	Max Wear Limit	Front	Rear
All	102	0.874	0.830 ② ③	0.0005	7.874	7.900	7.930	①	①

① Minimum lining thickness is to ¹⁄₃₂ of rivet
② *Minimum lining thickness is as recommended by the manufacturer. Because of variations in state inspection regulations, the minimum allowable thickness may be different than recommended by the manufacturer.*
③ Heavy Duty: 0.972

BRAKE SPECIFICATIONS

(All specifications in inches)

Year	Model	Master Cylinder Bore	Brake Disc			Brake Drum			Minimum Lining Thickness	
			Original Thickness	Minimum Thickness	Maximum Runout	Original Inside Diameter	Max. Wear Limit	Maximum Machine O/S	Front	Rear
1982	All	0.874	NA	0.815	0.004	7.879	7.899	7.899	0.030	①
1983	All	0.874	NA	0.815	0.004	7.879	7.899	7.899	0.030	①
1984	All exc. HD	0.874	NA	0.815	0.004	8.863	8.883	8.883	0.030	①
	All HD	0.944	NA	0.957	0.004	8.863	8.883	8.883	0.030	①
1985	All exc. HD	0.874	NA	0.815	0.004	8.863	8.883	8.920	0.030	①
	All HD	0.944	NA	0.957	0.004	8.863	8.920	8.920	0.030	①
1986	All exc. HD	0.874	NA	0.815	0.004	8.863	8.877	8.877	0.030	①
	All HD	0.944	NA	0.957	0.004	8.863	8.883	8.877	0.030	①
1987	All exc. HD	0.874	NA	0.815	0.004	8.863	8.877	8.877	0.030	①
	All HD	0.944	NA	0.957	0.004	8.863	8.883	8.877	0.030	①
	Century r/disc	—	NA	0.681	0.003	—	—	—	—	0.030
	6000 r/disc	—	NA	0.429	0.004	—	—	—	—	0.030
1988	All exc. HD									
	wagon	0.874	NA	0.815	0.004	8.863	8.877	8.877	0.030	①
	sedan	0.874	NA	0.815	0.004	8.863	8.920	8.920	0.030	①
	All HD									
	wagon	0.944	NA	0.957	0.004	8.863	8.877	8.877	0.030	①
	sedan	0.874	NA	0.957	0.004	8.863	8.920	8.920	0.030	①
	Century r/disc	—	NA	0.681	0.003	—	—	—	—	0.030
	6000 r/disc	—	NA	0.429	0.004	—	—	—	—	0.030
1989	All exc. HD									
	wagon	0.874	NA	0.815	0.004	8.863	8.877	8.877	0.030	①
	sedan	0.874	NA	0.815	0.004	8.863	8.920	8.920	0.030	①
	rear disc	—	NA	0.681	0.003	—	—	—	—	0.030
	All HD									
	wagon	0.944	NA	0.957	0.004	8.863	8.877	8.877	0.030	①
	sedan	0.874	NA	0.957	0.004	8.863	8.920	8.920	0.030	①
	rear disc	—	NA	0.681	0.003	—	—	—	—	0.030
1990	All exc. HD									
	wagon	0.874	NA	0.815	0.004	8.863	8.877	8.877	0.030	①
	sedan	0.874	NA	0.815	0.004	8.863	8.920	8.920	0.030	①
	rear disc	—	NA	0.681	0.003	—	—	—	—	0.030
	All HD									
	wagon	0.944	NA	0.957	0.004	8.863	8.877	8.877	0.030	①
	sedan	0.874	NA	0.957	0.004	8.863	8.920	8.920	0.030	①
	rear disc	—	NA	0.681	0.003	—	—	—	—	0.030
1991	All exc. HD									
	wagon	0.874	NA	0.815	0.004	8.863	8.877	8.877	0.030	①
	sedan	0.874	NA	0.815	0.004	8.863	8.920	8.920	0.030	①
	rear disc	—	NA	0.681	0.003	—	—	—	—	0.030
	All HD									
	wagon	0.944	NA	0.957	0.004	8.863	8.877	8.877	0.030	①
	sedan	0.874	NA	0.957	0.004	8.863	8.920	8.920	0.030	①
	rear disc	—	NA	0.681	0.003	—	—	—	—	0.030

BRAKE SPECIFICATIONS
(All specifications in inches)

Year	Model	Master Cylinder Bore	Brake Disc			Brake Drum			Minimum Lining Thickness	
			Original Thickness	Minimum Thickness	Maximum Runout	Original Inside Diameter	Max. Wear Limit	Maximum Machine O/S	Front	Rear
1992	All exc. HD									
	wagon	0.874	NA	0.815	0.004	8.863	8.877	8.877	0.030	①
	sedan	0.874	NA	0.815	0.004	8.863	8.920	8.920	0.030	①
	rear disc	—	NA	0.681	0.003	—	—	—	—	0.030
	All HD									
	wagon	0.944	NA	0.957	0.004	8.863	8.877	8.877	0.030	①
	sedan	0.874	NA	0.957	0.004	8.863	8.920	8.920	0.030	①
	rear disc	—	NA	0.681	0.003	—	—	—	—	0.030

① 0.030 in. over rivet head or 0.062 in. over bonded shoe

Troubleshooting the Brake System

Problem	Cause	Solution
Low brake pedal (excessive pedal travel required for braking action.)	• Excessive clearance between rear linings and drums caused by inoperative automatic adjusters	• Make 10 to 15 alternate forward and reverse brake stops to adjust brakes. If brake pedal does not come up, repair or replace adjuster parts as necessary.
	• Worn rear brakelining	• Inspect and replace lining if worn beyond minimum thickness specification
	• Bent, distorted brakeshoes, front or rear	• Replace brakeshoes in axle sets
	• Air in hydraulic system	• Remove air from system. Refer to Brake Bleeding.
Low brake pedal (pedal may go to floor with steady pressure applied.)	• Fluid leak in hydraulic system	• Fill master cylinder to fill line; have helper apply brakes and check calipers, wheel cylinders, differential valve tubes, hoses and fittings for leaks. Repair or replace as necessary.
	• Air in hydraulic system	• Remove air from system. Refer to Brake Bleeding.
	• Incorrect or non-recommended brake fluid (fluid evaporates at below normal temp).	• Flush hydraulic system with clean brake fluid. Refill with correct-type fluid.
	• Master cylinder piston seals worn, or master cylinder bore is scored, worn or corroded	• Repair or replace master cylinder
Low brake pedal (pedal goes to floor on first application—o.k. on subsequent applications.)	• Disc brake pads sticking on abutment surfaces of anchor plate. Caused by a build-up of dirt, rust, or corrosion on abutment surfaces	• Clean abutment surfaces

Troubleshooting the Brake System (cont.)

Problem	Cause	Solution
Fading brake pedal (pedal height decreases with steady pressure applied.)	· Fluid leak in hydraulic system	· Fill master cylinder reservoirs to fill mark, have helper apply brakes, check calipers, wheel cylinders, differential valve, tubes, hoses, and fittings for fluid leaks. Repair or replace parts as necessary.
	· Master cylinder piston seals worn, or master cylinder bore is scored, worn or corroded	· Repair or replace master cylinder
Spongy brake pedal (pedal has abnormally soft, springy, spongy feel when depressed.)	· Air in hydraulic system	· Remove air from system. Refer to Brake Bleeding.
	· Brakeshoes bent or distorted	· Replace brakeshoes
	· Brakelining not yet seated with drums and rotors	· Burnish brakes
	· Rear drum brakes not properly adjusted	· Adjust brakes
Decreasing brake pedal travel (pedal travel required for braking action decreases and may be accompanied by a hard pedal.)	· Caliper or wheel cylinder pistons sticking or seized	· Repair or replace the calipers, or wheel cylinders
	· Master cylinder compensator ports blocked (preventing fluid return to reservoirs) or pistons sticking or seized in master cylinder bore	· Repair or replace the master cylinder
	· Power brake unit binding internally	· Test unit according to the following procedure: (a) Shift transmission into neutral and start engine (b) Increase engine speed to 1500 rpm, close throttle and fully depress brake pedal (c) Slow release brake pedal and stop engine (d) Have helper remove vacuum check valve and hose from power unit. Observe for backward movement of brake pedal. (e) If the pedal moves backward, the power unit has an internal bind—replace power unit
Grabbing brakes (severe reaction to brake pedal pressure.)	· Brakelining(s) contaminated by grease or brake fluid	· Determine and correct cause of contamination and replace brakeshoes in axle sets
	· Parking brake cables incorrectly adjusted or seized	· Adjust cables. Replace seized cables.
	· Incorrect brakelining or lining loose on brakeshoes	· Replace brakeshoes in axle sets
	· Caliper anchor plate bolts loose	· Tighten bolts
	· Rear brakeshoes binding on support plate ledges	· Clean and lubricate ledges. Replace support plate(s) if ledges are deeply grooved. Do not attempt to smooth ledges by grinding.
	· Incorrect or missing power brake reaction disc	· Install correct disc
	· Rear brake support plates loose	· Tighten mounting bolts

Troubleshooting the Brake System (cont.)

Problem	Cause	Solution
Chatter or shudder when brakes are applied (pedal pulsation and roughness may also occur.)	• Brakeshoes distorted, bent, contaminated, or worn • Caliper anchor plate or support plate loose • Excessive thickness variation of rotor(s)	• Replace brakeshoes in axle sets • Tighten mounting bolts • Refinish or replace rotors in axle sets
Noisy brakes (squealing, clicking, scraping sound when brakes are applied.)	• Bent, broken, distorted brakeshoes • Excessive rust on outer edge of rotor braking surface	• Replace brakeshoes in axle sets • Remove rust
Hard brake pedal (excessive pedal pressure required to stop vehicle. May be accompanied by brake fade.)	• Loose or leaking power brake unit vacuum hose • Incorrect or poor quality brake-lining • Bent, broken, distorted brakeshoes • Calipers binding or dragging on mounting pins. Rear brakeshoes dragging on support plate. • Caliper, wheel cylinder, or master cylinder pistons sticking or seized • Power brake unit vacuum check valve malfunction • Power brake unit has internal bind	• Tighten connections or replace leaking hose • Replace with lining in axle sets • Replace brakeshoes • Replace mounting pins and bushings. Clean rust or burrs from rear brake support plate ledges and lubricate ledges with molydisulfide grease. **NOTE:** If ledges are deeply grooved or scored, do not attempt to sand or grind them smooth—replace support plate. • Repair or replace parts as necessary • Test valve according to the following procedure: (a) Start engine, increase engine speed to 1500 rpm, close throttle and immediately stop engine (b) Wait at least 90 seconds then depress brake pedal (c) If brakes are not vacuum assisted for 2 or more applications, check valve is faulty • Test unit according to the following procedure: (a) With engine stopped, apply brakes several times to exhaust all vacuum in system (b) Shift transmission into neutral, depress brake pedal and start engine (c) If pedal height decreases with foot pressure and less pressure is required to hold pedal in applied position, power unit vacuum system is operating normally. Test power unit. If power unit exhibits a bind condition, replace the power unit.

Troubleshooting the Brake System (cont.)

Problem	Cause	Solution
Hard brake pedal (excessive pedal pressure required to stop vehicle. May be accompanied by brake fade.)	• Master cylinder compensator ports (at bottom of reservoirs) blocked by dirt, scale, rust, or have small burrs (blocked ports prevent fluid return to reservoirs). • Brake hoses, tubes, fittings clogged or restricted • Brake fluid contaminated with improper fluids (motor oil, transmission fluid, causing rubber components to swell and stick in bores • Low engine vacuum	• Repair or replace master cylinder **CAUTION:** Do not attempt to clean blocked ports with wire, pencils, or similar implements. Use compressed air only. • Use compressed air to check or unclog parts. Replace any damaged parts. • Replace all rubber components, combination valve and hoses. Flush entire brake system with DOT 3 brake fluid or equivalent. • Adjust or repair engine
Dragging brakes (slow or incomplete release of brakes)	• Brake pedal binding at pivot • Power brake unit has internal bind • Parking brake cables incorrrectly adjusted or seized • Rear brakeshoe return springs weak or broken • Automatic adjusters malfunctioning • Caliper, wheel cylinder or master cylinder pistons sticking or seized • Master cylinder compensating ports blocked (fluid does not return to reservoirs).	• Loosen and lubricate • Inspect for internal bind. Replace unit if internal bind exists. • Adjust cables. Replace seized cables. • Replace return springs. Replace brakeshoe if necessary in axle sets. • Repair or replace adjuster parts as required • Repair or replace parts as necessary • Use compressed air to clear ports. Do not use wire, pencils, or similar objects to open blocked ports.
Vehicle moves to one side when brakes are applied	• Incorrect front tire pressure • Worn or damaged wheel bearings • Brakelining on one side contaminated • Brakeshoes on one side bent, distorted, or lining loose on shoe • Support plate bent or loose on one side • Brakelining not yet seated with drums or rotors • Caliper anchor plate loose on one side • Caliper piston sticking or seized • Brakelinings water soaked • Loose suspension component attaching or mounting bolts • Brake combination valve failure	• Inflate to recommended cold (reduced load) inflation pressure • Replace worn or damaged bearings • Determine and correct cause of contamination and replace brakelining in axle sets • Replace brakeshoes in axle sets • Tighten or replace support plate • Burnish brakelining • Tighten anchor plate bolts • Repair or replace caliper • Drive vehicle with brakes lightly applied to dry linings • Tighten suspension bolts. Replace worn suspension components. • Replace combination valve

Troubleshooting the Brake System (cont.)

Problem	Cause	Solution
Noisy brakes (squealing, clicking, scraping sound when brakes are applied.) (cont.)	• Brakelining worn out—shoes contacting drum of rotor	• Replace brakeshoes and lining in axle sets. Refinish or replace drums or rotors.
	• Broken or loose holdown or return springs	• Replace parts as necessary
	• Rough or dry drum brake support plate ledges	• Lubricate support plate ledges
	• Cracked, grooved, or scored rotor(s) or drum(s)	• Replace rotor(s) or drum(s). Replace brakeshoes and lining in axle sets if necessary.
	• Incorrect brakelining and/or shoes (front or rear).	• Install specified shoe and lining assemblies
Pulsating brake pedal	• Out of round drums or excessive lateral runout in disc brake rotor(s)	• Refinish or replace drums, re-index rotors or replace

TORQUE SPECIFICATIONS

Component	English	Metric
Brake hose fitting to caliper:	33 ft. lbs.	45 Nm
Brake line-to-wheel cylinder:	13 ft. lbs.	17 Nm
Brake lines-to-master cylinder:	13-15 ft. lbs.	17-20 Nm
Brake pedal pivot bolt:	25 ft. lbs.	34 Nm
Bleeder screw:		
Caliper screw:	80-140 inch lbs.	9-16 Nm
Wheel cylinder screw:	10-15 ft. lbs.	14-18 Nm
Caliper mounting bolts:	38 ft. lbs.	51 Nm
Failure warning switch:	15-50 inch lbs.	2-6 Nm
Master cylinder retaining nuts:	20 ft. lbs.	27 Nm
Master cylinder piston plug:	80-140 inch lbs.	5-16 Nm
Power booster mounting nuts:	20 ft. lbs.	28 Nm
Proportioner valves:	18-30 ft. lbs.	25-40 Nm
Rear hub & bearing retaining bolts:	38 ft. lbs.	51 Nm
Wheel cylinder mounting bolt:	15 ft. lbs.	20 Nm
Wheel lug nuts:	100 ft. lbs.	140 Nm
Anti-Lock Brake Components:		
Bleeder valve:	65 inch lbs.	7 Nm
Brake pipes to the modulator:	13 ft. lbs.	17 Nm
Front speed sensor:		
Except 6000 AWD:	106 inch lbs.	12 Nm
6000 AWD:	53 inch lbs.	6 Nm
Lock bolt:	18 inch lbs.	2 Nm
Hydraulic modulator solenoid bolts:	39 inch lbs.	5 Nm
Hydraulic modulator to mount:	38 ft. lbs.	52 Nm
Rear speed sensor:	80 inch lbs.	9 Nm
Vacuum booster nuts:	20 ft. lbs.	27 Nm

10

BODY

EXTERIOR

Doors

♦ SEE FIGS. 1 to 6

REMOVAL & INSTALLATION

1. Open the door and support it securely.
2. On doors equipped with power operated components, proceed as follows.

   a. Remove the door trim panel, insulator pad (if so equipped) and inner panel water deflector.

   b. Disconnect the wiring harness from all components in door.

   c. Remove rubber conduit from door, then remove wire harness from door through conduit access hole.
3. Tape the area around the door pillar and body pillar (below the upper hinge) with cloth backed body tape.

❄❄ CAUTION

Before performing the following step, cover the door spring with a towel to prevent the spring from flying out and possibly causing personal injury or damaging the car.

4. Insert a long flat-bladed lever underneath the pivot point of the hold-open link and over top of the spring. The lever should be positioned so as not to apply pressure to the hold-open link. Cover spring with shop cloth and lift screwdriver to disengage spring. Spring can also be removed using tool No. J–28625, door hinge spring compressor tool, or equivalent. Proceed as follows:

   a. Install two jaws of tool over spring. Jaw with slot slides over spring at hold-open link. Jaw with hole fits over spring at bubble on door hinge pillar.

   b. Install bolt to jaws of tool and tighten to compress spring.

   c. Remove tool and spring from door hinge assembly. Do not remove spring from tool.
5. If replacement hinge pin barrel clips are not available, save the clips as follows:

   a. Using two small flat-bladed tools, spread each clip just enough to move clip over recess, toward the pointed end of the pin.

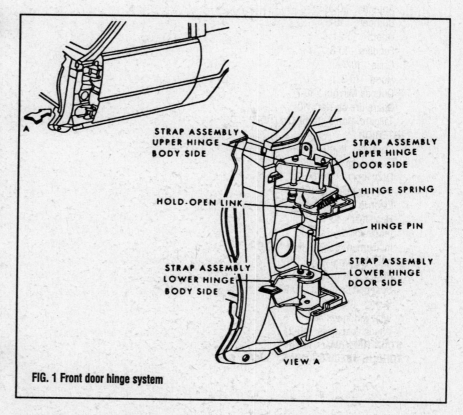

FIG. 1 Front door hinge system

Labels: STRAP ASSEMBLY UPPER HINGE BODY SIDE — STRAP ASSEMBLY UPPER HINGE DOOR SIDE — HINGE SPRING — HOLD-OPEN LINK — HINGE PIN — STRAP ASSEMBLY LOWER HINGE BODY SIDE — STRAP ASSEMBLY LOWER HINGE DOOR SIDE — VIEW A

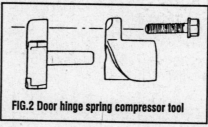

FIG.2 Door hinge spring compressor tool

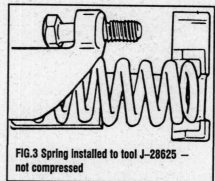

FIG.3 Spring installed to tool J–28625 — not compressed

   b. As pin is removed, clip will ride the shank of the pin and fall free.

   c. Reinstall clips onto pins before installing the door.
6. With the aid of an assistant, to support the door, remove the lower hinge pin using soft headed hammer and locking type pliers. Assistant can aid in removal of hinge pins by raising and lowering rear of door.
7. Insert 1¼ in. x 1½ in. bolt into upper hole of lower hinge to maintain door attachment during upper hinge pin removal.
8. Remove upper hinge pin in same manner as lower. Remove screw from lower hinge and remove door from body.

➡ **Before installing door, replace hinge pin clips or reuse old clips as explained in the removal procedure.**

9. With the aid of an assistant, position the door and insert a small bolt in the upper hole of the lower hinge.
10. The upper hinge pin is installed with the pointed end up. The lower hinge pin is installed with the pointed end down. With the door in the full open position, install the upper hinge pin using locking type pliers and a soft-headed hammer. Use a drift punch and hammer to complete installation.

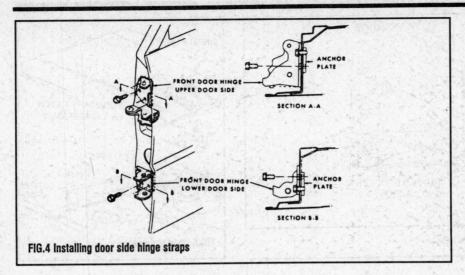

FIG.4 Installing door side hinge straps

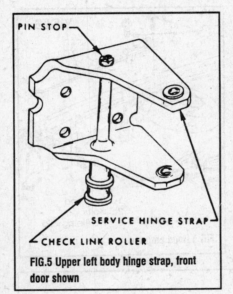

FIG.5 Upper left body hinge strap, front door shown

11. Remove the screw from the lower hinge and install the lower hinge pin. Use of tool No. J–28625 or equivalent is the recommended method for installing the hinge spring.

➡ **If spring is installed before installing upper hinge pin, hinge bushings may be damaged.**

12. If spring was removed using a screwdriver, install as follows:

    a. Place spring in tool No. J–28625 or equivalent.

    b. Place tool and spring in a bench vise.

    c. Compress tool in vise and install bolt until spring is fully compressed.

    d. Remove tool (with compressed spring) from vise and install in proper position in door upper hinge. Slot in one jaw of tool fits over hold-open link. Hole on other jaw fits over bubble on hinge.

    e. Remove bolt from tool to install the spring.

    f. Remove the tool from the door hinge (tool will fall out in three pieces). Open and close door to check for proper operation of the spring.

➡ **If tool No. J–28625 or equivalent was used to remove spring, follow steps d, e and f to install the spring.**

13. Remove the tape from the door and body pillars.

14. On doors with power operated components, install the wire harness to the door through conduit access hole and install the rubber conduit to the door.

15. Connect the wiring harness to each component in the door.

16. Install the inner panel water deflector.

17. Install the insulator pad and the door trim panel.

STRIKER ADJUSTMENT

◆ SEE FIG. 7

The striker has provisions for fore and aft adjustment only.

1. Insert tool No. J–23457, BT7107 or equivalent into the star shaped recess in the head of the striker and loosen the bolt.

2. Shift striker as required, then tighten the bolt 34–46 ft. lbs.

Hood

REMOVAL & INSTALLATION

◆ SEE FIGS. 9 to 11

1. Raise the hood. Install protective coverings over the fenders, to prevent damage to paint and moldings when removing or installing the hood.

2. Disconnect the underhood lamp wire.

3. Mark the position of the hinge on the hood to Lid in alignment when hood is reinstalled.

4. With the hood supported, remove the hinge to hood screws on each side of the hood.

5. Remove the hood.

To Install:

6. Align the hood with the marks made during removal.

7. Install the hood to hinge screws on each side of the hood and torque to 20 ft. lbs.

8. Connect the underhood lamp wire.

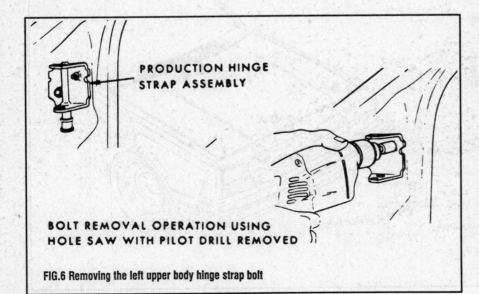

FIG.6 Removing the left upper body hinge strap bolt

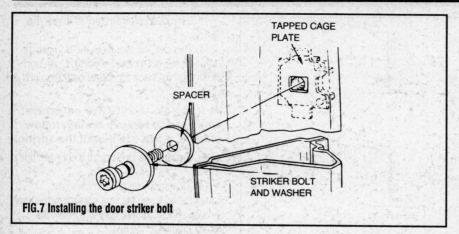

FIG.7 Installing the door striker bolt

TAPPED CAGE PLATE

SPACER

STRIKER BOLT AND WASHER

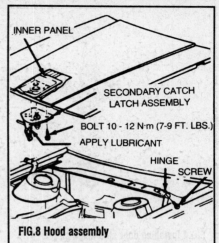

INNER PANEL

SECONDARY CATCH LATCH ASSEMBLY

BOLT 10 - 12 N·m (7-9 FT. LBS.)

APPLY LUBRICANT

HINGE

SCREW

FIG.8 Hood assembly

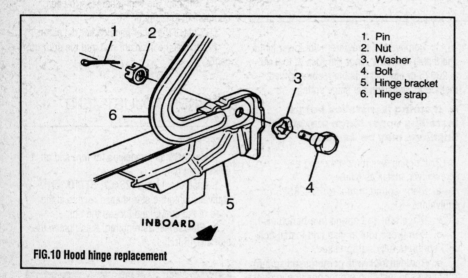

1. Pin
2. Nut
3. Washer
4. Bolt
5. Hinge bracket
6. Hinge strap

INBOARD

FIG.10 Hood hinge replacement

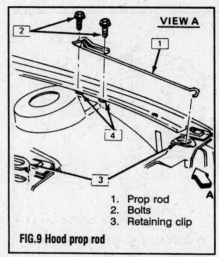

VIEW A

1. Prop rod
2. Bolts
3. Retaining clip

FIG.9 Hood prop rod

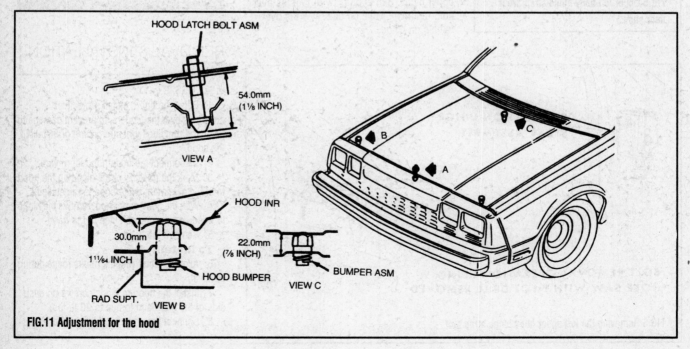

HOOD LATCH BOLT ASM

54.0mm (1 1/8 INCH)

VIEW A

HOOD INR

30.0mm
1 11/64 INCH

HOOD BUMPER

RAD SUPT. VIEW B

22.0mm (7/8 INCH)

BUMPER ASM

VIEW C

B

C

A

FIG.11 Adjustment for the hood

ALIGNMENT

Fore and aft adjustment made be made at the hinge-to-hood attaching screws. Vertical adjustment at the front may be made by adjusting the rubber bumpers up or down.

Trunk Lid

REMOVAL & INSTALLATION

♦ SEE FIGS. 12 to 15

1. Prop the lid open and place protective covering along the edges of the rear compartment opening to prevent damage to the painted areas.
2. Where necessary, disconnect the wiring harness from the lid.
3. Mark the location of the hinge strap attaching bolts to lid.
4. While a helper supports the lid, remove the hinge to lid bolts and remove the lid.
5. Reverse steps 1 through 4 to install the lid.
6. Torque the hinge-to-lid attaching bolts to 20 ft. lbs.

ADJUSTMENT

Fore and aft adjustment of the lid assembly is controlled by the hinge-to-lid attaching bolts. To adjust the lid, loosen the hinge-to-lid attaching bolts and shift the lid to the desired position; then tighten the bolts to 20 ft. lbs.

Lift Gate/Hatch

REMOVAL & INSTALLATION

1. Open and support the lift gate in the full open position.

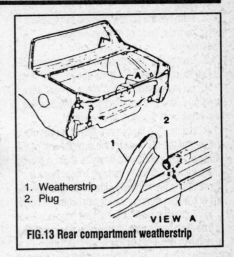

1. Weatherstrip
2. Plug

FIG.13 Rear compartment weatherstrip

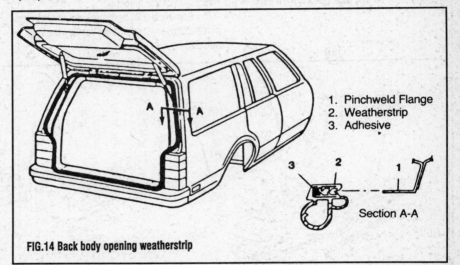

1. Pinchweld Flange
2. Weatherstrip
3. Adhesive

Section A-A

FIG.14 Back body opening weatherstrip

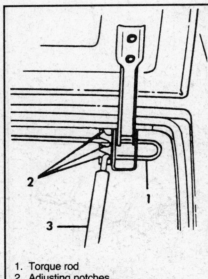

1. Torque rod
2. Adjusting notches
3. Length of ⅜" inside diameter pipe

FIG. 12 Trunk torque rod adjustment

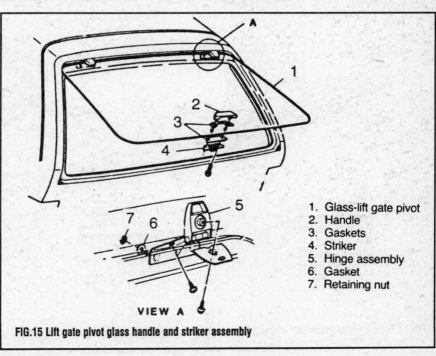

1. Glass-lift gate pivot
2. Handle
3. Gaskets
4. Striker
5. Hinge assembly
6. Gasket
7. Retaining nut

VIEW A

FIG.15 Lift gate pivot glass handle and striker assembly

2. Remove the lid and body side retaining clips from the ends of the gas support assemblies.

3. Disengage the attachment at each end of the support and remove from body.

4. On styles with heated glass or rear wiper-washer system, disconnect the wiring harness and hose from the washer assembly.

5. Using a $\frac{5}{32}$ in. (4mm) diameter rod, place the end of the rod against the pointed end of the hinge pin; then strike rod firmly to shear retaining clip tabs and drive pin through hinge. Repeat operation on the opposite side hinge and with the aid of a helper remove the lift gate from the body.

6. To install, reverse the above process. Prior to installing hinge pins, install new retaining clips in notches provided in hinge pins. Position retaining clips so that tabs point toward head of pin.

Bumpers

REMOVAL & INSTALLATION

Front

1. Remove the 4 retaining screws in each of the head light bezels and remove the bezels.

2. Raise the car and support it securely.

3. Remove the 6 push-on retainers from the bottom of the bumper and remove the 6 screws holding the retainer to each fender.

4. Remove the 4 push-on retainers from the outer molding and partially remove the outer molding from the fenders.

5. Remove the 2 sheet metal screws from the center bumper retainer, then remove the front bumper.

6. Remove the 8 retaining screws and bolts from the impact bar and remove the impact bar from its reinforcements.

7. To install, reverse steps 1 through 6.

Rear

1. Remove the 2 push-on retainer clips from each end of the molding, then remove the molding.

2. Remove the 4 wing nuts and electrical connectors from each of the tail lamp assemblies and remove the left and right tail lamp assemblies.

3. Remove the 5 wing nuts, disconnect the electrical connector and remove the backup light assembly.

4. Open the trunk and remove the 2 retaining nuts from the left and right side reflectors, then remove the reflectors.

5. Remove the 7 retaining pins from the valance panel and remove the panel.

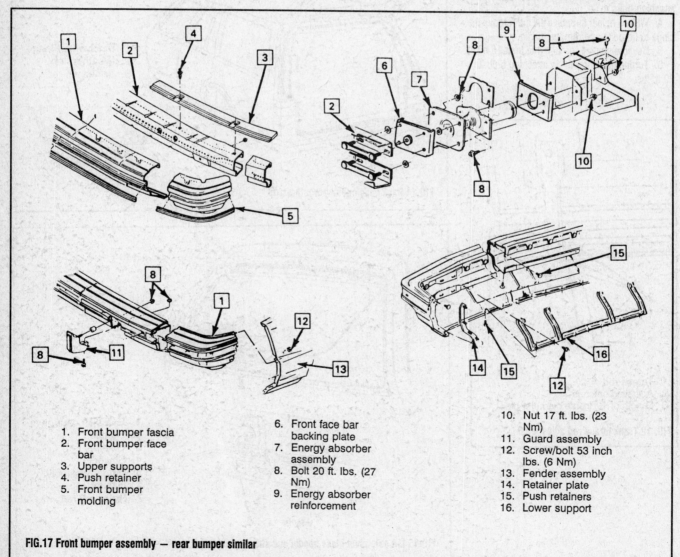

1. Front bumper fascia
2. Front bumper face bar
3. Upper supports
4. Push retainer
5. Front bumper molding
6. Front face bar backing plate
7. Energy absorber assembly
8. Bolt 20 ft. lbs. (27 Nm)
9. Energy absorber reinforcement
10. Nut 17 ft. lbs. (23 Nm)
11. Guard assembly
12. Screw/bolt 53 inch lbs. (6 Nm)
13. Fender assembly
14. Retainer plate
15. Push retainers
16. Lower support

FIG.17 Front bumper assembly — rear bumper similar

6. Disconnect the electrical connector and remove the 8 retaining nuts, 4 retaining bolts and 11 retaining pins from the rear bumper and remove the bumper.

7. Disconnect the electrical connector, and remove the 8 retaining nuts from the impact bar and energy absorber.

8. Remove the 8 retaining clips and remove the impact bar from the mounting support bracket.

9. To install, reverse steps 1 through 8.

Grille

REMOVAL & INSTALLATION

1. Remove the 8 retaining screws from the grille assembly.

2. Remove the grille from the front end panel.

3. To install; position the grille in the front end panel and install the retaining screws.

Mirrors

REMOVAL & INSTALLATION

Standard

1. Remove the door trim panel and detach the inner panel water deflector. With the glass in the down position, pull out the front portion of the glass run weather strip.

2. Remove the attaching bolts and screws from the front glass run channel lower retainer to filler and rotate retainer rearward.

3. Remove the noise control patch to gain access to the 7mm screw at the belt and remove the screw.

4. Remove the filler attaching screws at the top front of the window frame and remove the mirror and filler from the door.

5. Remove the attaching nuts from the mirror base studs and remove the mirror.

6. To install, reverse steps 1 through 5. Be sure that the mirror gasket is aligned.

Manual Remote Control

1. Remove the mirror remote control escutcheons and door trim panel. Detach the inner panel water deflector.

➡ **Right side remote mirror may require detaching part of the instrument panel.**

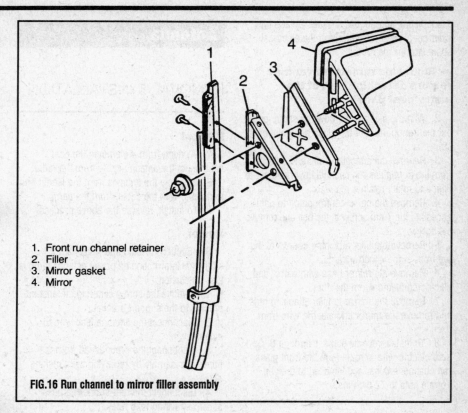

1. Front run channel retainer
2. Filler
3. Mirror gasket
4. Mirror

FIG.16 Run channel to mirror filler assembly

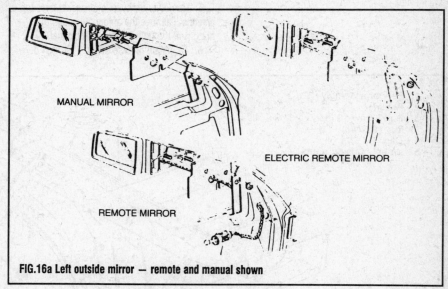

MANUAL MIRROR

ELECTRIC REMOTE MIRROR

REMOTE MIRROR

FIG.16a Left outside mirror — remote and manual shown

2. With the glass in the down position, pull out the front portion of the glass run weather strip.

3. Remove the attaching bolts and screws from the front glass run channel lower retainer to filler and rotate retainer rearward.

4. Remove the noise control patch to gain access to the 7mm screw at the belt and remove the screw.

5. Remove the filler attaching screws at the top front of the window frame.

6. Remove the mirror base with mirror and cable assembly from the door.

7. Remove the mirror to filler attaching nuts and remove the mirror and cable from filler.

8. To install, reverse steps 1 through 6. Be sure cable is routed around front glass run channel retainer and installed to clip. Torque nuts to 72 inch lbs.

Electric Remote Control

1. Remove the mirror remote control

escutcheons and door trim panel. Detach the inner panel water deflector and the electrical connector for the mirror.

➡ **Right side remote mirror may require detaching part of the instrument panel.**

2. With the glass in the down position, pull out the front portion of the glass run weather strip.

3. Remove the attaching bolts and screws from the front glass run channel lower retainer to filler and rotate retainer rearward.

4. Remove the noise control patch to gain access to the 7mm screw at the belt and remove the screw.

5. Remove the filler attaching screws at the top front of the window frame.

6. Remove the mirror base with mirror and electric connector from the door.

7. Remove the mirror to filler attaching nuts and remove the mirror and electric wire from filler.

8. To install, reverse steps 1 through 6. Be sure electric wire is routed around front glass run channel retainer and installed to the clip. Torque nuts to 72 inch lbs.

Antenna

REMOVAL & INSTALLATION

Manual

1. Working from underneath the dash, disconnect the antenna cable from the radio.

2. Unscrew the antenna from the fender and remove it, with the cable, from the car.

3. To install, reverse the above process.

Power

See Section 6 Radio and Antenna, for additional information on power antenna removal and installation.

1. Remove the screw securing the antenna bracket to the support bracket.

2. Disconnect the antenna lead wire to antenna wire.

3. Disconnect the ground lead from the harness assembly by removing the attaching screw.

4. Disconnect the rear quarter harness assembly wiring feed relay.

5. Remove nut, bezel and gasket over top of antenna. Remove the antenna through the bottom of the hole in the quarter panel.

6. To install, reverse steps 1 through 5.

Fenders

REMOVAL & INSTALLATION

1. Disconnect the negative battery cable.

2. It may be easier to service the fender with the hood removed.

3. Remove the wiper arms.

4. Remove the cowl vent panel to gain access to the upper fender-to-cowl bolts.

➡

Warning: ♦ An outer fender panel with plastic inner panel may be used. Care must be taken in handling the unsupported fender due to the lack of rigidity prior to installation.

5. Disconnect and remove the headlamp wire connector.

6. Disconnect and remove the side marker lamp connector.

7. Remove the rocker panel molding, as necessary.

8. Remove the wheelhouse panel bolts.

9. Remove the screws attaching the front end panel to the fender.

10. With the fender removed carefully remove the molding and name plates.

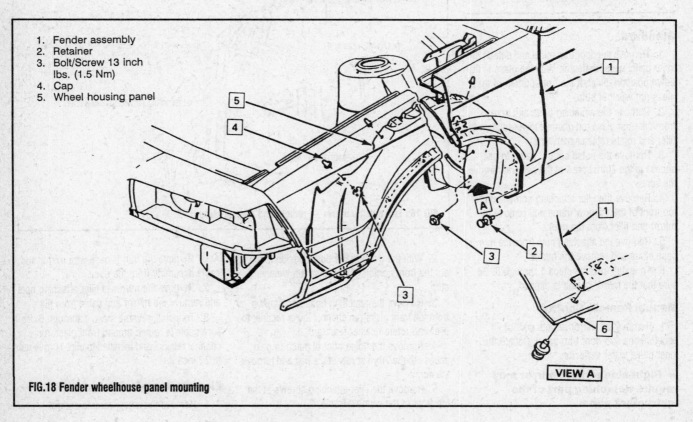

1. Fender assembly
2. Retainer
3. Bolt/Screw 13 inch lbs. (1.5 Nm)
4. Cap
5. Wheel housing panel

FIG.18 Fender wheelhouse panel mounting

To Install:

11. Transfer fender moldings and nameplates to new fender.

➡ **If the fender is not primed or undercoated as you desire it may be better to have this procedure done to the fender before installation.**

12. Install the fender assembly and tighten attaching bolts to 88 inch lbs. (10 Nm).

13. Install the lower valance if removed and tighten bolts to 18 inch lbs. (2 Nm).

14. Install the wheelhouse panel and the rocker panel if used.

15. Install the headlamp and marker lamp wiring and connectors.

16. Install the cowl vent panel and wiper arms.

17. Install the hood if removed and connect the battery cable.

INTERIOR

Instrument Cluster

There is additional information on instrument panel and switches in Section 6 covering electrical components.

REMOVAL & INSTALLATION

Century

1. Disconnect the negative battery cable.

2. Disconnect the speedometer cable and pull it through the firewall.

3. Remove the left side hush panel retaining screws and nut.

4. Remove the right side hush panel retaining screws and nut.

5. Remove the shift indicator cable clip.

6. Remove the steering column trim plate.

7. Put the gear selector in **L**. Remove the retaining screws and gently pull out the instrument panel trim plate.

8. Disconnect the parking brake cable at the lever by pushing it forward and sliding it from its slot.

9. Unbolt and lower the steering column.

10. Remove the gauge cluster retaining screws. Pull the cluster out far enough to disconnect any wires. Remove the instrument cluster.

To Install:

11. Install the gauge cluster, connect the electrical connectors and install the retaining screws.

12. Position the steering column and install the retaining bolts.

13. Connect the parking brake cable at the lever.

14. Put the gear selector in **L**. Install instrument panel trim plate.

15. Install the steering column trim plate.

16. Install the shift indicator cable clip.

17. Install the right side hush panel retaining screws and nut.

18. Install the left side hush panel retaining screws and nut.

19. Pull the speedometer cable through the firewall and connect to the speedometer.

20. Connect the negative battery cable.

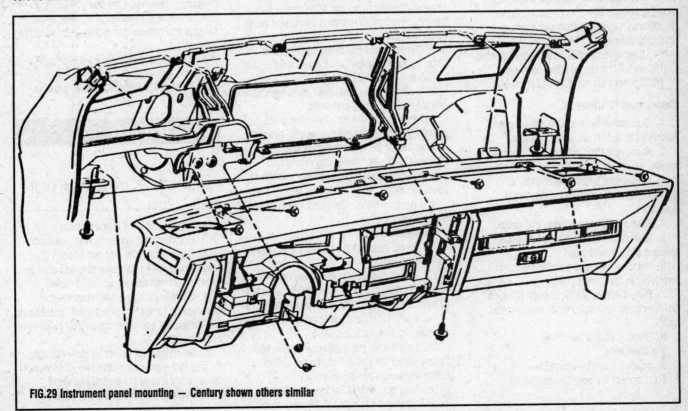

FIG.29 Instrument panel mounting — Century shown others similar

Celebrity

1. Disconnect the negative battery cable.
2. Remove instrument panel hush panel.
3. Remove vent control housing, as required.
4. On non-air conditioning vehicles, remove steering column trim cover screws and lower cover with vent cables attached. On air conditioning vehicles, remove trim cover attaching screws and remove cover.
5. Remove instrument cluster trim pad.
6. Remove ash tray, retainer and fuse block, disconnect wires as necessary.
7. Remove headlight switch knob and instrument panel trim plate. Disconnect electrical connectors of any accessory switches in trim plate.
8. Remove cluster assembly and disconnect speedometer cable, **PRNDL** and cluster electrical connectors.

To install:
9. Install cluster assembly and connect speedometer cable, **PRNDL** and cluster electrical connectors.
10. Install headlight switch knob and instrument panel trim plate. Connect electrical connectors of any accessory switches in trim plate.
11. Install ash tray, retainer and fuse block, connect electrical connectors.
12. Install instrument cluster trim pad.
13. On non-air conditioned vehicles, raise the cover with vent cables attached and install steering column trim cover screws. On air conditioned vehicles, install trim cover and attaching screws.
14. If removed, install vent control housing.
15. Install instrument panel hush panel.
16. Connect the negative battery cable.

Ciera and Cruiser

1. Disconnect the negative battery cable. Remove left instrument panel trim pad.
2. Remove instrument panel cluster trim cover.
3. Disconnect speedometer cable at transaxle or cruise control transducer, if equipped.
4. Remove steering column trim cover.
5. Disconnect shift indicator clip from steering column shift bowl.
6. Remove 4 screws attaching cluster assembly to instrument panel.
7. Pull assembly out far enough to reach behind cluster and disconnect speedometer cable.
8. Remove cluster assembly.

To install:
9. Install the cluster assembly.
10. Connect the speedometer cable.

11. Install the 4 screws attaching cluster assembly to instrument panel.
12. Connect shift indicator clip to steering column shift bowl.
13. Install the steering column trim cover.
14. Connect the speedometer cable at the transaxle or cruise control transducer, if equipped.
15. Install the instrument panel cluster trim cover.
16. Install the left instrument panel trim pad.
17. Connect the negative battery cable.

6000

1. Disconnect the negative battery cable, and remove the center and left side lower instrument panel trim plate.
2. Remove the screws holding the instrument cluster to the instrument panel carrier.
3. Remove the instrument cluster lens to gain access to the speedometer head and gauges.
4. Remove right side and left side hush panels, steering column trim cover and disconnect parking brake cable and vent cables, if equipped.
5. Remove steering column retaining bolts and drop steering column.
6. Disconnect temperature control cable, inner-to-outer air conditioning wire harness and inner-to-outer air conditioning vacuum harness, if equipped.
7. Disconnect chassis harness behind left lower instrument panel and ECM connectors behind glove box. Disconnect instrument panel harness at cowl.
8. Remove center instrument panel trim plate, radio, if equipped, and disconnect neutral switch and brake light switch.
9. Remove upper and lower instrument panel retaining screws, nuts and bolts.
10. Pull instrument panel assembly out far enough to disconnect ignition switch, headlight dimmer switch and turn signal switch. Disconnect all other accessory wiring and vacuum lines necessary to remove instrument panel assembly.
11. Remove instrument panel assembly with wiring harness.

To install:
12. Install instrument panel assembly with wiring harness.
13. Connect ignition switch, headlight dimmer switch and turn signal switch. Connect all other accessory wiring and vacuum lines.
14. Install upper and lower instrument panel retaining screws, nuts and bolts.
15. Connect neutral switch and brake light switch. Install the radio, if equipped, and install center instrument panel trim plate.
16. Connect chassis harness behind left lower instrument panel and ECM connectors

behind glove box. Connect instrument panel harness at cowl.
17. Connect temperature control cable, inner-to-outer air conditioning wire harness and inner-to-outer air conditioning vacuum harness, if equipped.
18. Raise the steering column and install retaining bolts.
19. Install right side and left side hush panels, steering column trim cover and connect parking brake cable and vent cables, if equipped.
20. Install the instrument cluster lens.
21. Install the screws holding the instrument cluster to the instrument panel carrier.
22. Install the center and left side lower instrument panel trim plate.
23. Connect the negative battery cable.

Console

REMOVAL & INSTALLATION

1. Remove the shifter knob from the shifter by removing the retaining screw at the back of the knob.
2. Remove the screws at the sides and front of the console.
3. Open the console box and remove the retaining screw inside the box.
4. Remove the ashtray at the rear of the console and remove the retaining screw behind the ashtray.
5. Slide the console rearward slightly, then lift it over the shifter.
6. To install, reverse the above process.

Door Panels

REMOVAL & INSTALLATION

1. Remove all door inside handles.
2. Remove door inside locking rod knob.
3. Remove screws inserted through door armrest and pull handle assembly into door inner panel or armrest hanger support bracket.
4. On styles with remote control mirror assemblies, remove remote mirror escutcheons and disengage end of mirror control cable from escutcheons.
5. On styles with power window controls located in the door trim assembly, disconnect the wire harness at the switch assembly.
6. Remove the remote control handle escutcheons screws.

7. On styles with integral armrests, remove the screws inserted through the pull cup into the armrest hanger support.

8. Remove screws and plastic retainers from the perimeter of the door trim pad using tool BT–7323A or equivalent and a screwdriver. To remove the door trim panel, push trim upward and outboard to disengage it from the door inner panel at the belt line.

9. On styles with courtesy lamps located in the lower area of the trim panel, disconnect the wiring harness at the lamp assembly.

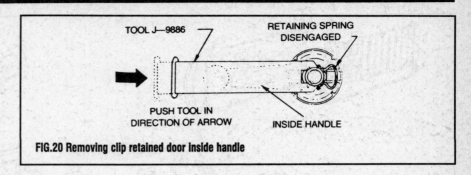

FIG.20 Removing clip retained door inside handle

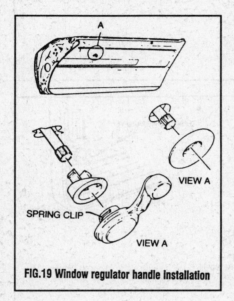

FIG.19 Window regulator handle installation

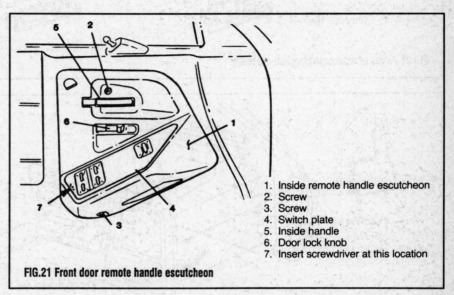

1. Inside remote handle escutcheon
2. Screw
3. Screw
4. Switch plate
5. Inside handle
6. Door lock knob
7. Insert screwdriver at this location

FIG.21 Front door remote handle escutcheon

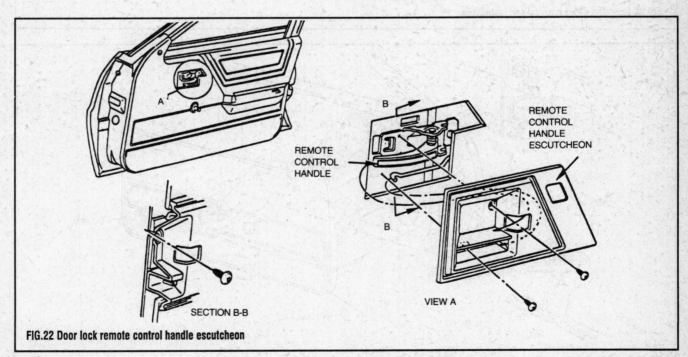

FIG.22 Door lock remote control handle escutcheon

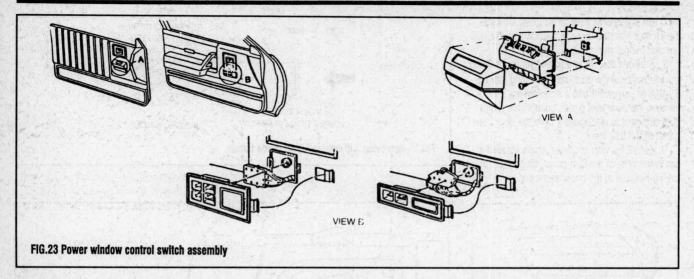

VIEW A

VIEW B

FIG.23 Power window control switch assembly

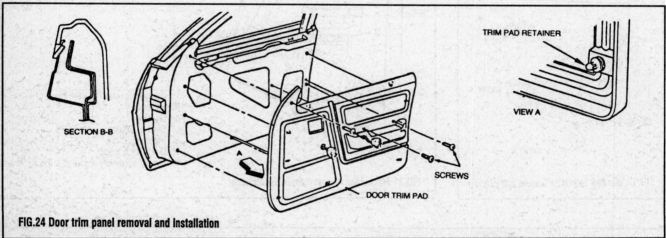

SECTION B-B

TRIM PAD RETAINER

VIEW A

SCREWS

DOOR TRIM PAD

FIG.24 Door trim panel removal and installation

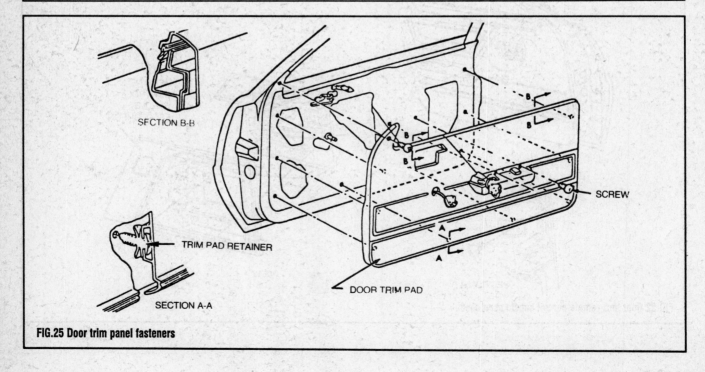

SECTION B-B

TRIM PAD RETAINER

SECTION A-A

SCREW

DOOR TRIM PAD

FIG.25 Door trim panel fasteners

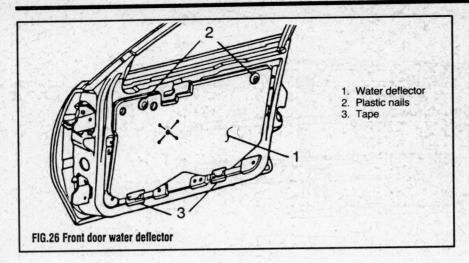

FIG.26 Front door water deflector

1. Water deflector
2. Plastic nails
3. Tape

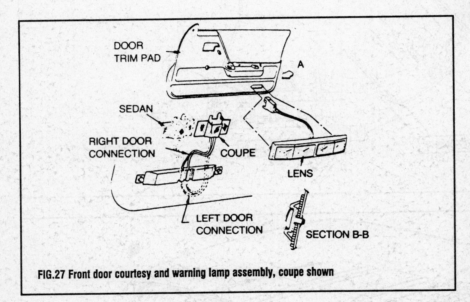

DOOR
TRIM PAD

A

SEDAN

RIGHT DOOR
CONNECTION

COUPE

LENS

LEFT DOOR
CONNECTION

SECTION B-B

FIG.27 Front door courtesy and warning lamp assembly, coupe shown

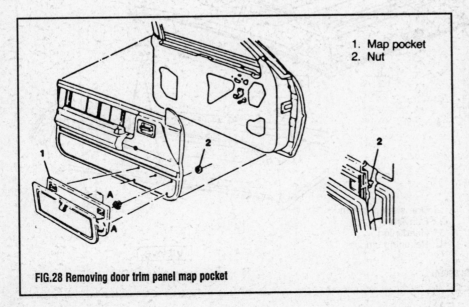

1. Map pocket
2. Nut

FIG.28 Removing door trim panel map pocket

➡ **Before installing the door trim panel, check that all trim retainers are securely installed to the panel and are not damaged. Replace damaged retainers as required.**

10. Connect electrical components where present.

11. To install the door trim panel, pull door inside handle inward; then position the trim panel to the inner panel, inserting door handle through hole in panel.

12. Position the trim panel to the door inner panel so trim retainers are aligned with the attaching holes in the panel and tap the retainers into the holes with a clean rubber mallet. Install all previously removed items.

Headliner

♦ SEE FIGS. 30 to 32

REMOVAL & INSTALLATION

1. Disconnect the negative battery cable.
2. Remove the dome lamp, courtesy lamp, coat hooks and sunvisors.
3. Remove the quarter upper trim finishing panels using tool J–24595–C.
4. Remove the rear seat roof mounted shoulder belt retainers, as needed.
5. Remove the windshield pillar upper side roof rail and garnish moldings.
6. Remove the headlining hook and loop strips along the front and on the sear using tool J–2772–C.
7. Push in the retainers and retainers from rear of the headliner, on wagons.
8. Remove assembly through the right front door opening.

To install:

9. Care must be taken not to over flex new liner when installing. Load the rear portion of the lining diagonally through the right front door opening.

10. Align the headlining with holes for

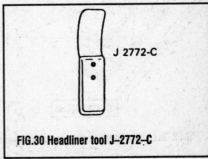

J 2772-C

FIG.30 Headliner tool J–2772–C

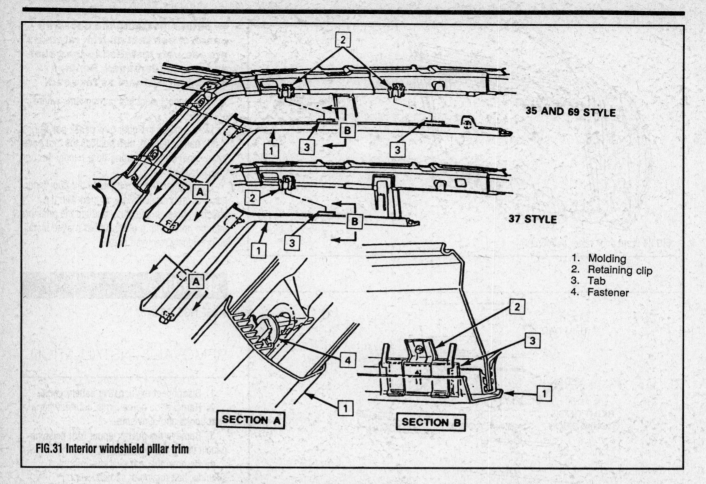

35 AND 69 STYLE

37 STYLE

1. Molding
2. Retaining clip
3. Tab
4. Fastener

SECTION A

SECTION B

FIG.31 Interior windshield pillar trim

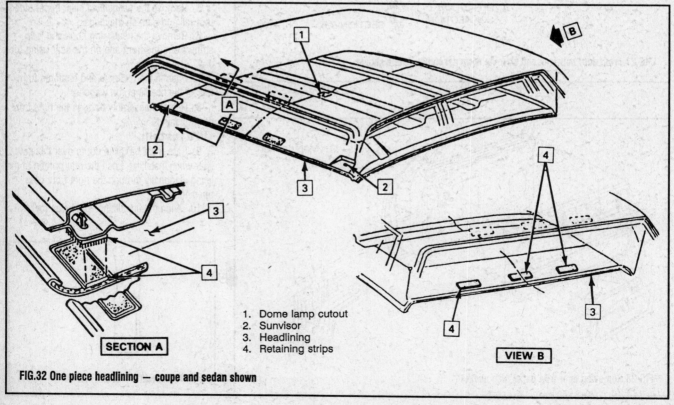

1. Dome lamp cutout
2. Sunvisor
3. Headlining
4. Retaining strips

SECTION A

VIEW B

FIG.32 One piece headlining — coupe and sedan shown

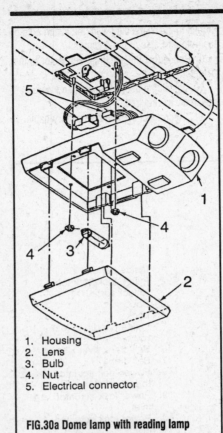

1. Housing
2. Lens
3. Bulb
4. Nut
5. Electrical connector

FIG.30a Dome lamp with reading lamp

sunvisors and interior lamps. Press into place along areas with hook and loop strips.

11. Install the retainers and push-in retainers to the rear of the headlining, on wagons.

12. Install the sunvisors and interior lamps.

13. Install the windshield pillar upper and side roof rail garnish moldings.

14. Install the rear shoulder belt retainers, if needed.

15. Install the quarter trim finishing panels.

16. Install the coat hooks.

17. Make certain no wires for lamps are pinched or installed incorrectly.

18. Connect the negative battery cable.

Door Locks

REMOVAL & INSTALLATION

1. Raise door window. Remove door trim panel and inner panel water deflector.

2. Disengage the inside lock rod, the inside handle to lock rod, the lock cylinder to lock rod and the power lock actuator rod (power locks only) from the lock assembly.

3. On 2AG19 styles, remove the screw

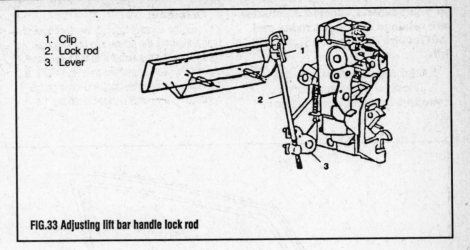

1. Clip
2. Lock rod
3. Lever

FIG.33 Adjusting lift bar handle lock rod

holding door ajar switch to lock and disconnect the connector from the lock.

4. Remove the lock screws and lower the lock to disengage the outside handle to lock rod. Remove the lock from the door.

5. To install, first install the spring clips to the lock assembly, then reverse steps 1 through 4. Torque the door lock attaching screws to 80–100 inch lbs.

Power Lock Actuator

REMOVAL & INSTALLATION

1. Disconnect the negative battery cable.

2. Remove the door trim panel and water deflector.

3. Raise the window.

4. Locate the rivets holding the actuator. Drive out the rivets center pins, then drill out the rivets using a 1/4 in. (6mm) drill bit.

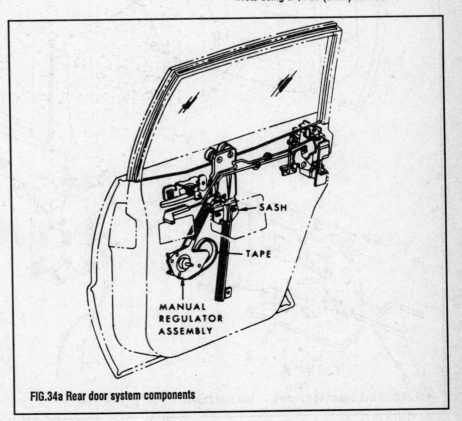

SASH

TAPE

MANUAL REGULATOR ASSEMBLY

FIG.34a Rear door system components

➡ **Some vehicle's door lock actuator are retained with ³⁄₁₆ in. rivets and will require the use of a ³⁄₁₆ in. drill bit.**

5. Remove the actuator from the lock rod.

6. Disconnect the actuator electrical connector and remove the actuator from the door.

To install:

7. Fit the actuator through the door access hole and install the actuator to the lock rod.

8. Fastened the actuator to the inner panel using ¹⁄₄ x ¹⁄₂ in. aluminum peel type rivets. If rivets are not available, install U-clips on the regulator at the metal retainer locations. Be certain to install the clips with the clinch nuts on the outboard side of the retainers.

9. Reconnect the electrical connector to the actuator.

10. Install the door trim panel and water deflector, as required.

11. Reconnect the negative battery cable.

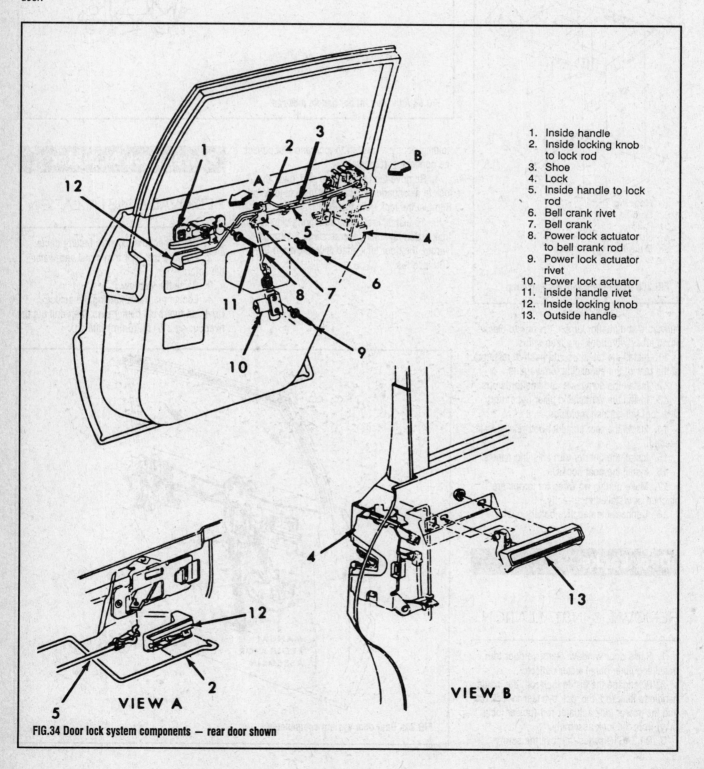

1. Inside handle
2. Inside locking knob to lock rod
3. Shoe
4. Lock
5. Inside handle to lock rod
6. Bell crank rivet
7. Bell crank
8. Power lock actuator to bell crank rod
9. Power lock actuator rivet
10. Power lock actuator
11. inside handle rivet
12. Inside locking knob
13. Outside handle

VIEW A

VIEW B

FIG.34 Door lock system components — rear door shown

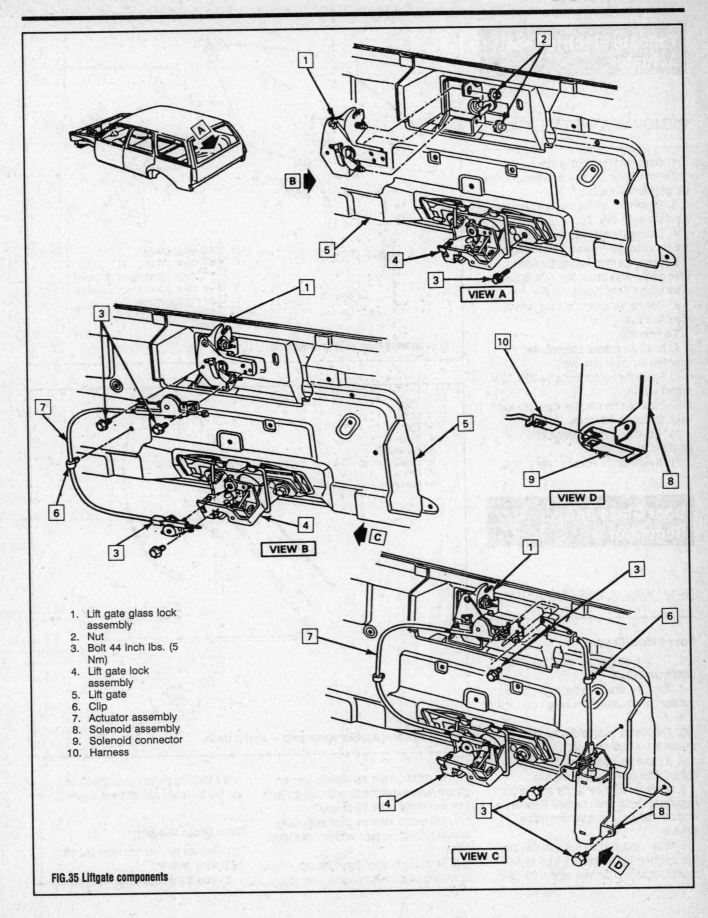

1. Lift gate glass lock
   assembly
2. Nut
3. Bolt 44 inch lbs. (5
   Nm)
4. Lift gate lock
   assembly
5. Lift gate
6. Clip
7. Actuator assembly
8. Solenoid assembly
9. Solenoid connector
10. Harness

FIG.35 Liftgate components

Tailgate Electric Lock Actuator

REMOVAL & INSTALLATION

1. Disconnect the negative battery cable.

2. Open the tailgate as a door, then position the glass fully upwards.

3. Remove the tailgate handle, inner trim panel and water deflector.

4. Remove the right side access hole cover and disconnect the actuator electrical connector.

5. Locate the rivets holding the actuator. Drive out the rivets center pins, then drill out the rivets using a ¼ in. (6mm) drill bit.

6. Remove the actuator and rod from the upper lock lever.

To install:

7. Install the actuator assembly and reconnect the upper lock lever.

8. Secure the actuator using ¼–20 x 7/16 in. screws and nuts.

9. Reconnect the electrical connector and install the access hole cover.

10. Install the water deflector, inner trim panel and tailgate handle.

11. Reconnect the negative battery cable.

Door Glass and Regulator

REMOVAL & INSTALLATION

Door Glass (Coupe)

1. Remove the door trim panel and inner panel water deflector.

2. Raise the window to the full up position and tape glass to door frame using cloth-backed tape.

3. Remove the bolts holding the lower sash channel to the regulator sash.

4. Remove the rubber down stop at the bottom of the door by pulling carefully.

5. Attach the regulator handle and run the regulator to the full down position. Remove the regulator sash by rotating 90° and pulling outboard.

6. While supporting the glass, remove the tape and lower the window to the full down position. Disengage the front edge of the glass

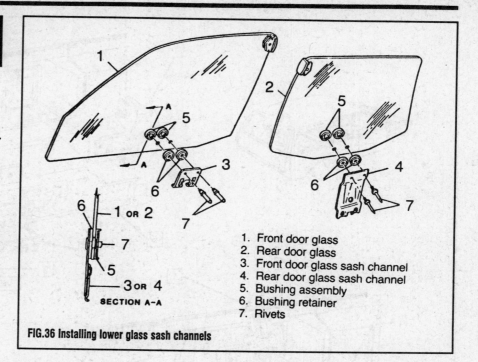

FIG.36 Installing lower glass sash channels

1. Front door glass
2. Rear door glass
3. Front door glass sash channel
4. Rear door glass sash channel
5. Bushing assembly
6. Bushing retainer
7. Rivets

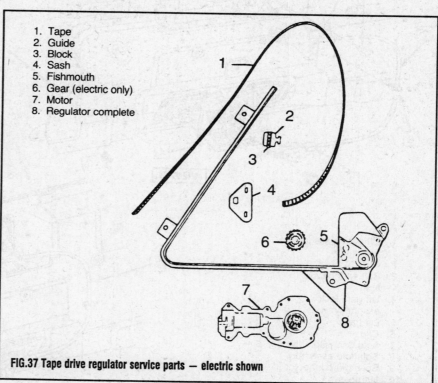

1. Tape
2. Guide
3. Block
4. Sash
5. Fishmouth
6. Gear (electric only)
7. Motor
8. Regulator complete

FIG.37 Tape drive regulator service parts — electric shown

from the glass run channel retainer. Slide the glass forward and tilt slightly to remove the guide from the retainer in the run channel.

7. Using care, raise the glass while tilting forward and remove glass inboard of the upper frame.

8. To install, reverse steps 1 through 7. Use liquid soap solution on the rubber down stop before installing the trim parts, check the window for proper operation and alignment.

Door Glass (Sedan)

1. Remove the door trim panel and inner panel water deflector.

2. Raise the window to the full up position

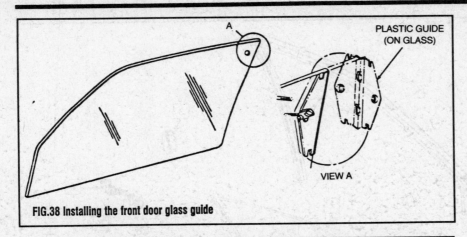

FIG.38 Installing the front door glass guide

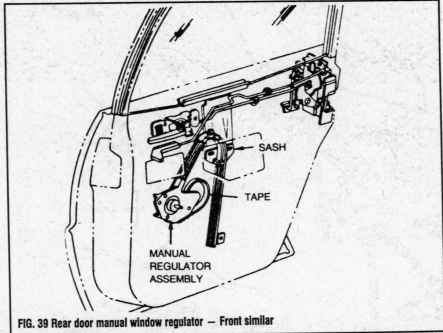

FIG. 39 Rear door manual window regulator — Front similar

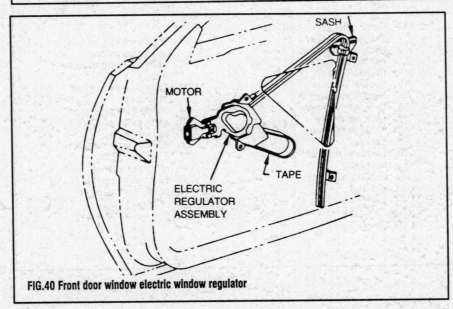

FIG.40 Front door window electric window regulator

and tape glass to door frame using cloth-backed tape.

3. Remove the bolts holding the lower sash channel to the regulator sash.

4. Attach the regulator handle and run the regulator to the full down position.

5. While supporting the glass, remove the tape and lower the window to the half down position.

6. Wrap tape around the blade of tool BT–7323A or equivalent. Insert tool between the guide and glass at the fastener and carefully pry apart.

7. Using care, raise the glass while tilting forward and remove glass inboard of the upper frame.

8. Remove guide from the rear of the run channel weatherstrip metal retainer and discard guide.

9. Replace guide on glass in the following manner:

   a. Heat guide with hot air gun or soak in hot water for about one minute.

   b. Install guide to glass by aligning to hole in glass and carefully press guide together at fastener location.

10. Install glass and lower about halfway.

11. With one hand on bottom edge, rotate glass rearward to snap guide into retainer.

12. To complete installation, reverse the remainder of the removal process.

Regulator

1. Remove the door trim panel and inner panel water deflector.

2. Raise the window to the full up position and tape glass to door frame using cloth-backed tape.

3. Remove the lower sash bolts.

4. Punch out center pins of regulator rivet. Drill out rivets using $1/4$ in. (6mm) drill bit.

5. For manual regulators, remove the regulator through the rear access hole. For electric regulator, remove the glass as stated previously. Move the regulator and motor assembly rearward and remove the electric connector. Remove the regulator and motor assembly through the rear access hole.

6. To install, use hand rivet tool J–29002 or equivalent and install the regulator to the inner panel using $1/4$ in. x $1/2$ in. aluminum peel type rivets, part No. 9436175 or equivalent.

7. If hand rivet tool is not available, install U-clips on regulator at three attaching locations. Be sure to install clips with cinch nuts on outboard side of retainers.

8. Slide the regulator through the rear access hole and align the regulator attaching clips with the holes in the inner panel. Attach regulator metal retainers with $1/4$ in.–20 x $1/2$ in. screws. Attach housing part of regulator with $1/4$ in.–20 x

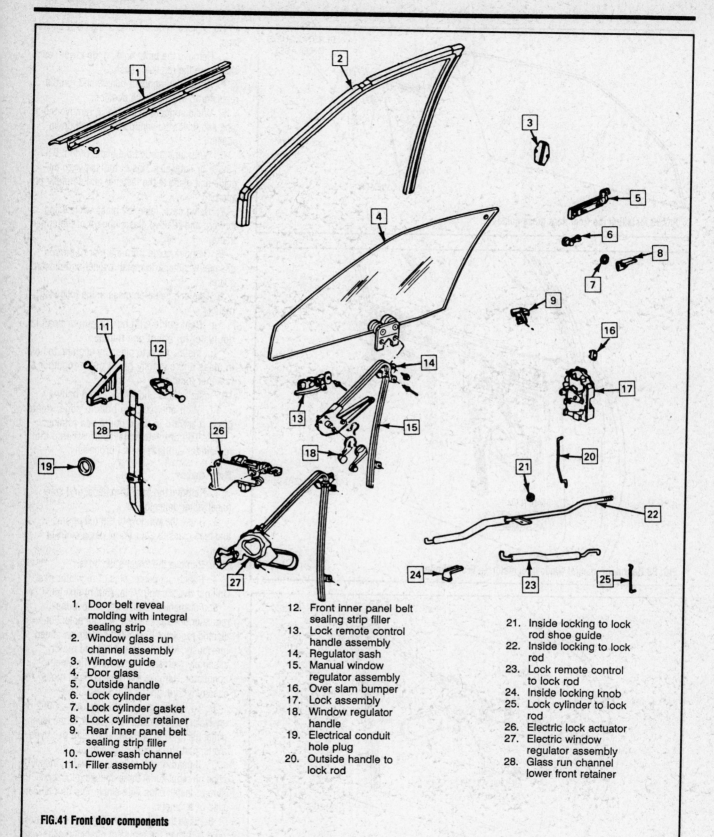

1. Door belt reveal molding with integral sealing strip
2. Window glass run channel assembly
3. Window guide
4. Door glass
5. Outside handle
6. Lock cylinder
7. Lock cylinder gasket
8. Lock cylinder retainer
9. Rear inner panel belt sealing strip filler
10. Lower sash channel
11. Filler assembly
12. Front inner panel belt sealing strip filler
13. Lock remote control handle assembly
14. Regulator sash
15. Manual window regulator assembly
16. Over slam bumper
17. Lock assembly
18. Window regulator handle
19. Electrical conduit hole plug
20. Outside handle to lock rod
21. Inside locking to lock rod shoe guide
22. Inside locking to lock rod
23. Lock remote control to lock rod
24. Inside locking knob
25. Lock cylinder to lock rod
26. Electric lock actuator
27. Electric window regulator assembly
28. Glass run channel lower front retainer

FIG.41 Front door components

½ in. screws into ¼ in. nuts with integral washers! Torque bolts 90–125 inch lbs.

9. Install the lower sash bolts.

10. Remove the tape from the door glass and frame.

11. Install the inner panel water deflector and door trim panel.

Electric Window Motor

REMOVAL & INSTALLATION

1. Remove the door trim panel and inner panel water deflector.

2. Raise the window to the full up position and tape glass to door frame using cloth-backed tape.

3. Remove the lower sash bolts.

4. Punch out center pins of regulator rivet. Drill out rivets using ¼ in. (6mm) drill bit.

5. Move regulator and motor assembly rearward and remove electrical connector.

6. With the regulator in the door, drill out the regulator to motor rivets using a 3/16 in. (5mm) drill bit and remove the motor.

7. To install, reverse steps 1 through 6. Use 3/16 in. rivets or 3/16 in. nuts and bolts to install the motor to the regulator.

Windshield

♦ SEE FIGS. 42 to 47

➡ **Bonded windshields require special tools and procedures to ensure the windshield will be removed without being broken. Also it may be very difficult to provide a quite windshield air seal or water tight seal. For this reason it is recommended you refer to a qualified technician.**

❊❊ CAUTION

If you work on any vehicle glass always wear eye protection and gloves, to reduce the risk of injury.

REMOVAL & INSTALLATION

When replacing the windshield check for the reason it was damaged in the first place. The cause of the crack may be an obstruction or high spot around the flange. This could cause the replacement to crack, especially after temperature changes when the windshield needs to flex and can't.

When a windshield is broken, the glass may have already fallen or been removed from the weatherstriping. Other times it is necessary to remove a cracked windshield that is still intact. In this case, it is a good idea to crisscross the glass with strips of tape before removing it, this will help hold the glass together and minimize the risk of injury.

If a crack extends to the edge of the glass, mark the point where the crack meets the weather strip. Later examine the window flange at this point for the possible cause of the windshield crack.

The higher temperature of the work area, the more pliable the weather strip will be. The more pliable the weather strip the easier the windshield can be removed.

There are 2 methods of removing the windshield depending on the method of windshield replacement chosen. When using the short method of installation, it is important to cut the glass from the urethane adhesive as close to the glass as possible. THis is due to the fact that the urethane adhesive will be used to provide a base for the replacement windshield. When using the extended method, all the urethane adhesive must be removed from the pinchweld flange so the process of cutting the window from the adhesive is less critical.

Glass Removal

➡ **The following procedure requires the use of the urethane glass sealant remover or hot knife tool J–24709–1 or equivalent and/or tool J–24402–A or equivalent.**

1. Place the protective covering around the area will the glass will be removed.

2. Remove the wiper arms, cowl vent grille,

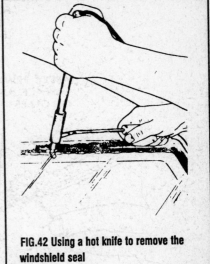

FIG.42 Using a hot knife to remove the windshield seal

windshield supports, rear view mirror and the interior garnish moldings.

➡ **If equipped with the radio antenna embedded in the windshield, disconnect the electrical connector at the base of the windshield.**

3. Remove the exterior reveal molding from the urethane adhesive by prying one end of the molding from the adhesive.

❊❊ CAUTION

If you work on any vehicle glass always wear eye protection and gloves, to reduce the risk of injury.

4. Using the urethane glass sealant remover (hot knife) J–24709 and the glass sealant remover tool J–24402–A or equivalents, cut the windshield from the urethane adhesive. If the

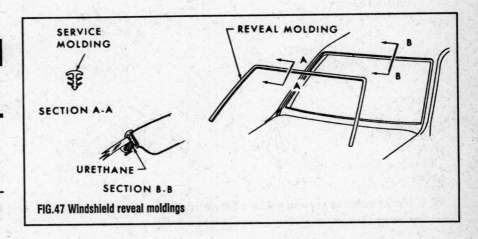

FIG.47 Windshield reveal moldings

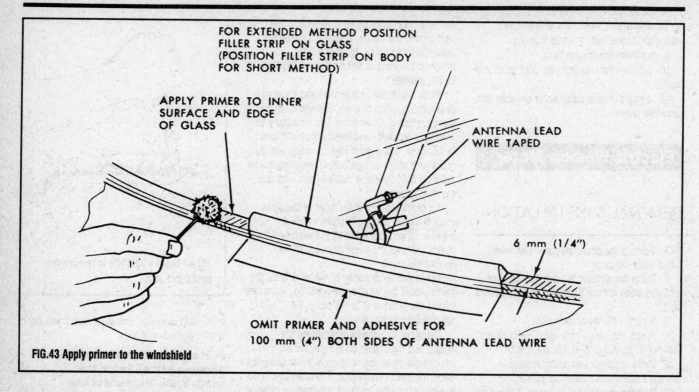

FOR EXTENDED METHOD POSITION
FILLER STRIP ON GLASS
(POSITION FILLER STRIP ON BODY
FOR SHORT METHOD)

APPLY PRIMER TO INNER
SURFACE AND EDGE
OF GLASS

ANTENNA LEAD
WIRE TAPED

6 mm (1/4")

OMIT PRIMER AND ADHESIVE FOR
100 mm (4") BOTH SIDES OF ANTENNA LEAD WIRE

FIG.43 Apply primer to the windshield

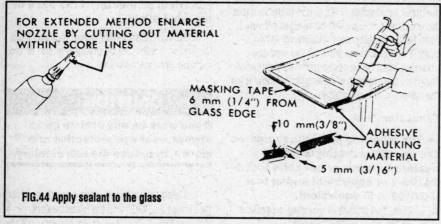

FOR EXTENDED METHOD ENLARGE
NOZZLE BY CUTTING OUT MATERIAL
WITHIN SCORE LINES

MASKING TAPE
6 mm (1/4") FROM
GLASS EDGE

10 mm(3/8")

ADHESIVE
CAULKING
MATERIAL

5 mm (3/16")

FIG.44 Apply sealant to the glass

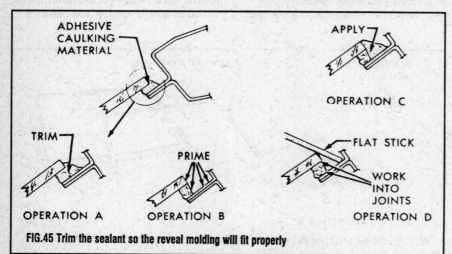

ADHESIVE
CAULKING
MATERIAL

APPLY

OPERATION C

TRIM

PRIME

FLAT STICK

WORK
INTO
JOINTS

OPERATION A   OPERATION B   OPERATION D

FIG.45 Trim the sealant so the reveal molding will fit properly

short method of replacement is to be used, keep the knife as close to the glass as possible in order to leave a base for the replacement glass.

5. With the help of an assistant, remove the glass.

6. If the original glass is to be reinstalled, place it on a protected bench or make a holding device. Remove any remaining adhesive with a razor blade. Any remaining traces of adhesive material can be removed with denatured alcohol or lacquer thinner.

➡ **DO NOT use any petroleum based solvents, this will prevent the adhesion of the new material. Don't allow solvents to contact the plastic or any non-glass areas to avoid discoloration.**

Inspection

Check the opening for the new glass. If a reason why the windshield broke is not known look carefully around the edges for a reason. Inspection the flange for any imperfections.

Check the replacement glass for chips or cracks. Small chips can be grounded off, restoring a smooth edge to the glass and minimizing concentrations of pressure that may cause breakage. Don't remove any more than necessary, you must maintain the original shape of the glass and the proper clearance between the glass and the flange opening.

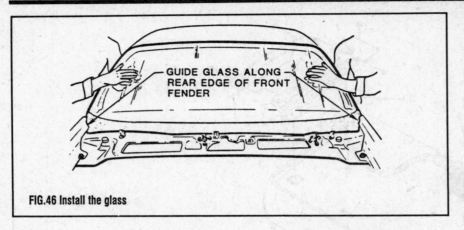

GUIDE GLASS ALONG REAR EDGE OF FRONT FENDER

FIG.46 Install the glass

Short method Installation

1. Using masking tape, apply the tape across the windshield pillar-to-windshield opening, then cut the tape and remove the windshield.

2. Using an alcohol dampened cloth, clean the metal flange surrounding the windshield opening. Allow the alcohol to air dry.

3. Using pinchweld primer, found in the installation service kits, apply to pinchweld area. Don't let any of the primer touch the exposed paint, it will damage the finish.. Allow primer to dry.

4. Cut the tip of the adhesive cartridge 3/16 in. (5mm) from end of tip.

5. Apply adhesive first in and around the spacer blocks. Apply a smooth continuous bead into the gap between the glass edge and the sheet metal. Use a flat tool to paddle the material into position as necessary. Be sure the adhesive contacts the entire edge of the glass and extends to fill the gap between the glass and the solidified urethane base.

6. With aid from a helper, position the glass on the filler strips against the 2 support spacers.

➡ **The vehicle must remain at room temperature for at least 6 hours. If can't be driven during the time.**

7. Spray a mist of water onto the urethane. Water will assist in the curing process. A mist, don't hose it down. Then dry the area where the reveal molding will contact the body glass.

8. Install new reveal moldings. Remove the protective tape covering the butyl adhesive on the underside of the molding. Push the molding caps onto each end of one of the reveal moldings. Press the lip of the molding into the eruethane adhesive while holding it against the edge of the windshield. Take care to seat the moldings in the corners. The lip must fully contact the adhesive and the gap must be entirely coverd by the crown of the molding. Slide the molding caps onto the adjacent

moldings. Use tape to hold the molding in position until the adhesive cures.

9. Install the wiper arms, cowling and interior garnish moldings.

Extended method Installation

1. Using GM Strip Filler No. 20146247 or equivalent, install the sealing strip onto the pinchweld flange. The joint of the molding should be located a the bottom center of the molding.

2. Using masking tape, apply the tape across the windshield pillar-to-windshield opening, then cut the tape and remove the windshield.

3. Using an alcohol dampened cloth, clean the metal flange surrounding the windshield opening. Allow the alcohol to air dry.

4. Using pinchweld primer, found in the installation service kits, apply to pinchweld area. Don't let any of the primer touch the exposed paint, it will damage the finish.. Allow primer to dry.

5. With aid from a helper, position the glass on the filler strips against the 2 support spacers.

6. Cut the tip of the adhesive cartridge 3/8 in. (10mm) from end of tip.

7. Apply adhesive first in and around the spacer blocks. Apply a smooth continuous bead into the gap between the glass edge and the sheet metal. Use a flat tool to paddle the material into position as necessary. Be sure the adhesive contacts the entire edge of the glass and extends to fill the gap between the glass and the solidified urethane base.

➡ **The vehicle must remain at room temperature for at least 6 hours. If can't be driven during the time.**

8. Spray a mist of water onto the urethane. Water will assist in the curing process. A mist, don't hose it down. Then dry the area where the reveal molding will contact the body glass.

9. Install the reveal molding onto the windshield and remove the masking tape from the inner surface of the glass.

10. Press the lip of the molding into the

urethane adhesive while holding it against the edge of the windshield. Take care to seat the molding in the corners. The lip must fully contact the adhesive adhesive and the gap must be entirely coverd by the crown of the molding. Slide the molding caps onto the adjacent moldings. Use tape to hold the molding in position until the adhesive cures.

11. Install the wiper arms, cowling and interior garnish moldings.

Inside Rear View Mirror

REPLACEMENT

The inside rear view mirror is permanently attached to the windshield. Should replacement become necessary, refer to your local dealer or a qualified technician for service.

Seats

REMOVAL & INSTALLATION

Front

1. Position the seat in the full forward position. If the car is equipped with six-way power seats, place the seat in the full forward and up position. When necessary to gain access to the adjuster-to-floor pan attaching nuts, remove the adjuster rear foot covers and or carpet retainers.

2. Remove the track covers where necessary; then remove the adjuster-to-floor pan rear attaching nuts. Position the seat in the full rearward position.

3. Remove the adjuster front foot covers; then remove the adjuster to floor pan front attaching nuts. Tilt the seat rearward and disconnect the feed wire connector.

4. Remove the seat assembly from the car.

5. To install, reverse steps 1 through 4 and check for proper seat operation. Torque the bolts to 40 ft. lbs.

Rear

1. Push the lower forward edge of the seat cushion rearward.

2. Lift upward and pull forward on the seat cushion frame to disengage the cushion frame wires from the retainers on the rear seat pan.

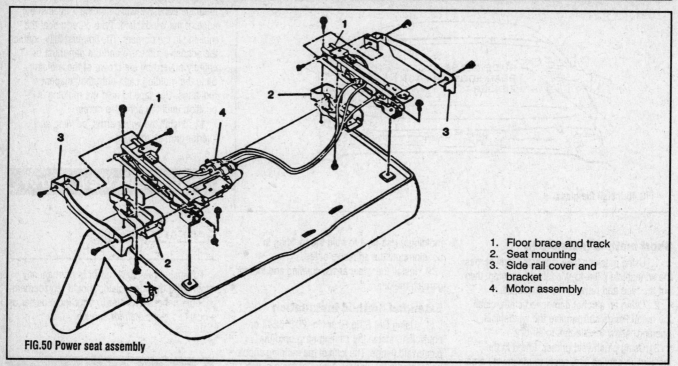

1. Floor brace and track
2. Seat mounting
3. Side rail cover and bracket
4. Motor assembly

FIG.50 Power seat assembly

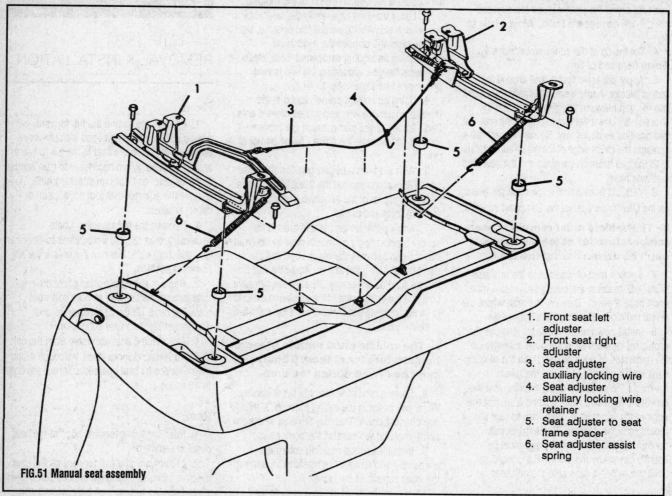

1. Front seat left adjuster
2. Front seat right adjuster
3. Seat adjuster auxiliary locking wire
4. Seat adjuster auxiliary locking wire retainer
5. Seat adjuster to seat frame spacer
6. Seat adjuster assist spring

FIG.51 Manual seat assembly

3. Remove the lower seat cushion from the vehicle.

4. At the bottom of the seatback, remove the anchor bolts securing the rear seat wire retainers.

5. Grasp the bottom of the seatback and swing toward to disengage the offsets on the upper frame bar from the hangers.

6. Lift the seatback upward and remove from vehicle.

7. To install, reverse the above process. Torque the bolts to 40 ft. lbs.

Power Seat Motor

REMOVAL & INSTALLATION

1. Position the seat in the full forward position. If the car is equipped with six-way power seats, place the seat in the full forward and up position. When necessary to gain access to the adjuster-to-floor pan attaching nuts, remove the adjuster rear foot covers and or carpet retainers.

2. Remove the track covers where necessary; then remove the adjuster-to-floor pan rear attaching nuts. Position the seat in the full rearward position.

3. Remove the adjuster front foot covers; then remove the adjuster to floor pan front attaching nuts. Tilt the seat rearward and disconnect the feed wire connector.

4. Remove the seat assembly from the car.

5. Place the seat up side down on a clean surface.

6. Disconnect the vertical and horizontal drive cables from the motor.

7. Remove the retainer nut from the motor support bracket.

8. Remove the motor from the seat.

To install:

9. Position the motor in the motor support bracket.

10. Connect the vertical and horizontal drive cables.

11. Place the seat into the vehicle and connect the feed wire.

12. Position the seat in the position that makes installation of the retaining nuts easiest. Install the adjuster to floor pan attaching nuts and torque to 15–21 ft.lbs. Install the foot covers.

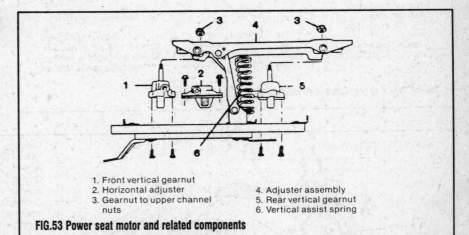

1. Front vertical gearnut
2. Horizontal adjuster
3. Gearnut to upper channel nuts
4. Adjuster assembly
5. Rear vertical gearnut
6. Vertical assist spring

FIG.53 Power seat motor and related components

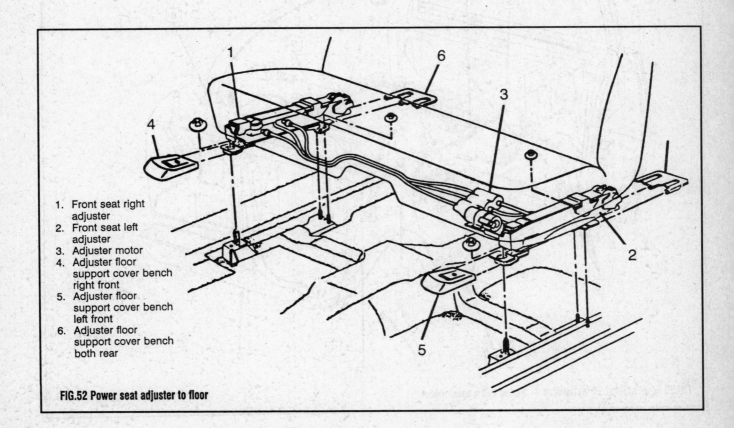

1. Front seat right adjuster
2. Front seat left adjuster
3. Adjuster motor
4. Adjuster floor support cover bench right front
5. Adjuster floor support cover bench left front
6. Adjuster floor support cover bench both rear

FIG.52 Power seat adjuster to floor

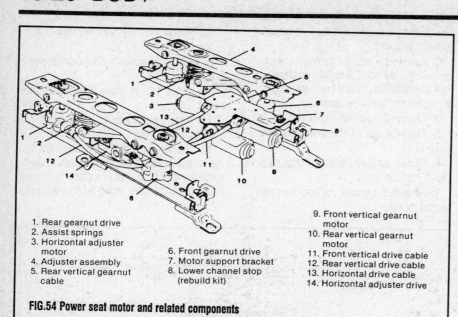

1. Rear gearnut drive
2. Assist springs
3. Horizontal adjuster motor
4. Adjuster assembly
5. Rear vertical gearnut cable

6. Front gearnut drive
7. Motor support bracket
8. Lower channel stop (rebuild kit)

9. Front vertical gearnut motor
10. Rear vertical gearnut motor
11. Front vertical drive cable
12. Rear vertical drive cable
13. Horizontal drive cable
14. Horizontal adjuster drive

FIG.54 Power seat motor and related components

Seat Belts

REMOVAL & INSTALLATION

Floor mount

1. Remove the cover from the anchor plate.
2. Remove the cover from the floor mounted retractor assembly.
3. Disconnect wiring from assembly, as needed.
4. Remove assembly.
5. To install; reverse removal and tighten retaining bolts to 31 ft. lbs. (42 Nm).

Outboard belts and retractors

1. Remove door trim panel.

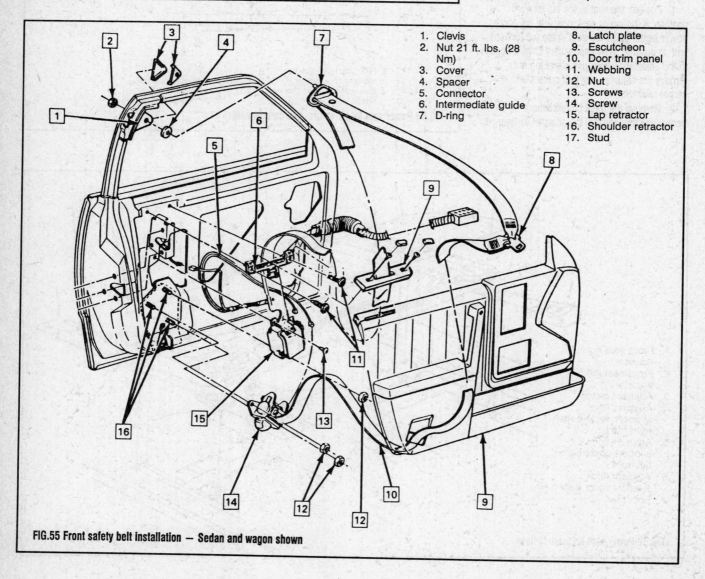

1. Clevis
2. Nut 21 ft. lbs. (28 Nm)
3. Cover
4. Spacer
5. Connector
6. Intermediate guide
7. D-ring

8. Latch plate
9. Escutcheon
10. Door trim panel
11. Webbing
12. Nut
13. Screws
14. Screw
15. Lap retractor
16. Shoulder retractor
17. Stud

FIG.55 Front safety belt installation — Sedan and wagon shown

2. Remove screws securing intermediate guide to door.

3. Remove the intermediate guide.

4. Disconnect electrical connectors.

5. Remove the nut securing the lap retractor.

6. Remove the lap retractor.

7. Remove the nut and screw securing the shoulder retractor.

8. Remove the shoulder retractor.

9. Remove or lower window as necessary.

10. Remove the cover, nut and spacer from D-ring and remove the D-ring.

To Install:

11. Install the D-ring, torque bolt to 21 ft. lbs (28 Nm).

12. Install the covers to D-ring.

13. Install the shoulder retractor and tighten to 31 ft. lbs. (42 Nm).

14. Install the lap retractor and tighten to 31 ft. lbs. (42 Nm).

15. Connect the electrical connectors.

16. Install the intermediate guide, tighten to 44 inch lbs. (5 Nm).

17. Install the door trim panels.

SEAT BELT TORQUE CHART

	PART NAME	TYPE	THREAD	LENGTH	TORQUE N·m	TORQUE Ft-Lb
	BOLT	1	M12-1.75	36 mm	35-48	26-35
	BOLT	2	M12-1.75	25 mm	35-48	26-35
	BOLT	3	M12-1.75	30 mm	35-48	26-35
	BOLT	4	M8-1.25	20 mm	20-24	15-17
	BOLT	5	M12-1.75	39 mm	35-48	26-35
	BOLT	6	M12-1.75	35 mm	35-48	26-35
	BOLT	7	M12-1.75	43 mm	35-48	26-35
	BOLT	8	M12-1.75	31 mm	35-48	26-35
	BOLT	9	M12-1.75	49 mm	35-48	26-35
	STUD	10	M6-1.00	15 mm	N/A	N/A
	BOLT	11	M12-1.75	53 mm	35-48	26-35
	NUT	12	M12-1.75		35-48	26-35
	NUT	13	M10-1.50		40-55	30-41
	NUT	14	M6-1.00		10-14	7-10
	NUT	15	M8-1.25		18-25	14-19
	STUD	16	M8-1.25	13 mm	N/A	N/A
	BOLT	18	5/16-18	1.25 N.S.	20-24	15-17
	BOLT	19	5/16-18	8.75 N.S.	20-24	15-17
	NUT	20	M6-1.00		9-12	7-9
	NUT	21	M10-1.50		30-40	22-30

Hood, Trunk Lid, Hatch Lid, Glass and Doors

Problem	Possible Cause	Correction
HOOD/TRUNK/HATCH LID		
Improper closure.	• Striker and latch not properly aligned.	• Adjust the alignment.
Difficulty locking and unlocking.	• Striker and latch not properly aligned.	• Adjust the alignment.
Uneven clearance with body panels.	• Incorrectly installed hood or trunk lid.	• Adjust the alignment.
WINDOW/WINDSHIELD GLASS		
Water leak through windshield	• Defective seal. • Defective body flange.	• Fill sealant • Correct.
Water leak through door window glass.	• Incorrect window glass installation. • Gap at upper window frame.	• Adjust position. • Adjust position.
Water leak through quarter window.	• Defective seal. • Defective body flange.	• Replace seal. • Correct.
Water leak through rear window.	• Defective seal. • Defective body flange.	• Replace seal. • Correct.
FRONT/REAR DOORS		
Door window malfunction.	• Incorrect window glass installation. • Damaged or faulty regulator.	• Adjust position. • Correct or replace.
Water leak through door edge.	• Cracked or faulty weatherstrip.	• Replace.
Water leak from door center.	• Drain hole clogged. • Inadequate waterproof skeet contact or damage.	• Remove foreign objects. • Correct or replace.
Door hard to open.	• Incorrect latch or striker adjustment.	• Adjust.
Door does not open or close completely.	• Incorrect door installation. • Defective door check strap. • Door check strap and hinge require grease.	• Adjust position. • Correct or replace. • Apply grease.
Uneven gap between door and body.	• Incorrect door installation.	• Adjust position.
Wind noise around door.	• Improperly installed weatherstrip. • Improper clearance between door glass and door weatherstrip. • Deformed door.	• Repair or replace. • Adjust. • Repair or replace.

How to Remove Stains from Fabric Interior

For best results, spots and stains should be removed as soon as possible. Never use gasoline, lacquer thinner, acetone, nail polish remover or bleach. Use a 3' x 3" piece of cheesecloth. Squeeze most of the liquid from the fabric and wipe the stained fabric from the outside of the stain toward the center with a lifting motion. Turn the cheesecloth as soon as one side becomes soiled. When using water to remove a stain, be sure to wash the entire section after the spot has been removed to avoid water stains. Encrusted spots can be broken up with a dull knife and vacuumed before removing the stain.

Type of Stain	How to Remove It
Surface spots	Brush the spots out with a small hand brush or use a commercial preparation such as K2R to lift the stain.
Mildew	Clean around the mildew with warm suds. Rinse in cold water and soak the mildew area in a solution of 1 part table salt and 2 parts water. Wash with upholstery cleaner.
Water stains	Water stains in fabric materials can be removed with a solution made from 1 cup of table salt dissolved in 1 quart of water. Vigorously scrub the solution into the stain and rinse with clear water. Water stains in nylon or other synthetic fabrics should be removed with a commercial type spot remover.
Chewing gum, tar, crayons, shoe polish (greasy stains)	Do not use a cleaner that will soften gum or tar. Harden the deposit with an ice cube and scrape away as much as possible with a dull knife. Moisten the remainder with cleaning fluid and scrub clean.
Ice cream, candy	Most candy has a sugar base and can be removed with a cloth wrung out in warm water. Oily candy, after cleaning with warm water, should be cleaned with upholstery cleaner. Rinse with warm water and clean the remainder with cleaning fluid.
Wine, alcohol, egg, milk, soft drink (non-greasy stains)	Do not use soap. Scrub the stain with a cloth wrung out in warm water. Remove the remainder with cleaning fluid.
Grease, oil, lipstick, butter and related stains	Use a spot remover to avoid leaving a ring. Work from the outisde of the stain to the center and dry with a clean cloth when the spot is gone.
Headliners (cloth)	Mix a solution of warm water and foam upholstery cleaner to give thick suds. Use only foam—liquid may streak or spot. Clean the entire headliner in one operation using a circular motion with a natural sponge.
Headliner (vinyl)	Use a vinyl cleaner with a sponge and wipe clean with a dry cloth.
Seats and door panels	Mix 1 pint upholstery cleaner in 1 gallon of water. Do not soak the fabric around the buttons.
Leather or vinyl fabric	Use a multi-purpose cleaner full strength and a stiff brush. Let stand 2 minutes and scrub thoroughly. Wipe with a clean, soft rag.
Nylon or synthetic fabrics	For normal stains, use the same procedures you would for washing cloth upholstery. If the fabric is extremely dirty, use a multi-purpose cleaner full strength with a stiff scrub brush. Scrub thoroughly in all directions and wipe with a cotton towel or soft rag.

TORQUE SPECIFICATIONS

Component	U.S.	Metric
Adjuster to seat frame bolt:	18 ft. lbs.	24 Nm
Air deflector:	80 inch lbs.	9 Nm
Bumper to absorber bolts:	18-25 ft. lbs.	24-34 Nm
Doors hinge to body:	15-20 ft. lbs.	20-28 Nm
Fender bolts lower:	89 inch lbs.	10 Nm
Fender bolts upper:	18 ft. lbs.	25 Nm
Folding second Seatback lock striker to back support:	34 ft. lbs.	46 Nm
Front seat center armrest:	106 inch lbs.	12 Nm
Front seatbelt to anchor plate:	31 ft. lbs.	42 Nm
Front seatbelt to rocker:	31 ft. lbs.	42 Nm
High mounted stop light:	49 inch lbs.	5.5 Nm
Hood hinge to hood bolts:	24 ft. lb	33 Nm
Interia lock to seat back panel:	89 inch lbs.	10 Nm
Interia lock to seat bottom frame:	89 inch lbs.	10 Nm
Lockout plate to seat bottom:	106 inch lbs.	12 Nm
Luggage carrier deck lid:	13 inch lbs.	1.5 Nm
Luggage carrier rail:	13 inch lbs.	1.5 Nm
Outer seatback hinge upper and lower bolts:	18 ft. lbs.	24 Nm
Outer slat retaining nuts:	49 inch lbs.	5.5 Nm
Outside mirror retaining nuts:	80 inch lbs.	9 Nm
Pivot glass bolts:	80 inch lbs.	9 Nm
Pivot glass lock, solenoid and actuator:	53 inch lbs.	6 Nm
Pivot glass screws to deflector:	80 inch lbs.	9 Nm
Pivot glass stricker to glass assembly:	80 inch lbs.	9 Nm
Rear compartment lid lock and solenoid screws:	53 inch lbs.	6 Nm
Rear seat cushion retainer to floor pan:	89 inch lbs.	10 Nm
Rear seatback frame to floor pan:	89 inch lbs.	10 Nm
Rear seatbelt to anchor plate:	31 ft. lbs.	42 Nm
Recliner to seatback bolt:	13 ft. lbs.	18 Nm
Reclining seatback actuator assembly to back frame:	13 ft. lbs.	18 Nm
Reclining seatback actuator assembly to cushion frame:	13 ft. lbs.	18 Nm
Reveal molding to liftgate:	80 inch lbs.	9 Nm
Seat adjuster to floor bolt:	18 ft. lbs.	24 Nm
Seat bottom to back frame:	89 inch lbs.	10 Nm
Seat motor and trans. support:	106 inch lbs.	12 Nm
Seatback frame to cushion:	34 ft. lbs.	46 Nm
Seatback lock assembly screw:	106 inch lbs.	12 Nm
Seatback lock striker and inner side bar stop:	34 ft. lbs.	46 Nm
Trunk lid retaining bolts:	18 ft. lbs.	25 Nm

GLOSSARY

AIR/FUEL RATIO: The ratio of air to gasoline by weight in the fuel mixture drawn into the engine.

AIR INJECTION: One method of reducing harmful exhaust emissions by injecting air into each of the exhaust ports of an engine. The fresh air entering the hot exhaust manifold causes any remaining fuel to be burned before it can exit the tailpipe.

ALTERNATOR: A device used for converting mechanical energy into electrical energy.

AMMETER: An instrument, calibrated in amperes, used to measure the flow of an electrical current in a circuit. Ammeters are always connected in series with the circuit being tested.

AMPERE: The rate of flow of electrical current present when one volt of electrical pressure is applied against one ohm of electrical resistance.

ANALOG COMPUTER: Any microprocessor that uses similar (analogous) electrical signals to make its calculations.

ARMATURE: A laminated, soft iron core wrapped by a wire that converts electrical energy to mechanical energy as in a motor or relay. When rotated in a magnetic field, it changes mechanical energy into electrical energy as in a generator.

ATMOSPHERIC PRESSURE: The pressure on the Earth's surface caused by the weight of the air in the atmosphere. At sea level, this pressure is 14.7 psi at 32°F (101 kPa at 0°C).

ATOMIZATION: The breaking down of a liquid into a fine mist that can be suspended in air.

AXIAL PLAY: Movement parallel to a shaft or bearing bore.

BACKFIRE: The sudden combustion of gases in the intake or exhaust system that results in a loud explosion.

BACKLASH: The clearance or play between two parts, such as meshed gears.

BACKPRESSURE: Restrictions in the exhaust system that slow the exit of exhaust gases from the combustion chamber.

BAKELITE: A heat resistant, plastic insulator material commonly used in printed circuit boards and transistorized components.

BALL BEARING: A bearing made up of hardened inner and outer races between which hardened steel balls roll.

BALLAST RESISTOR: A resistor in the primary ignition circuit that lowers voltage after the engine is started to reduce wear on ignition components.

BEARING: A friction reducing, supportive device usually located between a stationary part and a moving part.

BIMETAL TEMPERATURE SENSOR: Any sensor or switch made of two dissimilar types of metal that bend when heated or cooled due to the different expansion rates of the alloys. These types of sensors usually function as an on/off switch.

BLOWBY: Combustion gases, composed of water vapor and unburned fuel, that leak past the piston rings into the crankcase during normal engine operation. These gases are removed by the PCV system to prevent the buildup of harmful acids in the crankcase.

BRAKE PAD: A brake shoe and lining assembly used with disc brakes.

BRAKE SHOE: The backing for the brake lining. The term is, however, usually applied to the assembly of the brake backing and lining.

BUSHING: A liner, usually removable, for a bearing; an anti-friction liner used in place of a bearing.

BYPASS: System used to bypass ballast resistor during engine cranking to increase voltage supplied to the coil.

CALIPER: A hydraulically activated device in a disc brake system, which is mounted straddling the brake rotor (disc). The caliper contains at least one piston and two brake pads. Hydraulic pressure on the piston(s) forces the pads against the rotor.

CAMSHAFT: A shaft in the engine on which are the lobes (cams) which operate the valves. The camshaft is driven by the crankshaft, via a belt, chain or gears, at one half the crankshaft speed.

CAPACITOR: A device which stores an electrical charge.

CARBON MONOXIDE (CO): A colorless, odorless gas given off as a normal byproduct of combustion. It is poisonous and extremely dangerous in confined areas, building up slowly to toxic levels without warning if adequate ventilation is not available.

CARBURETOR: A device, usually mounted on the intake manifold of an engine, which mixes the air and fuel in the proper proportion to allow even combustion.

CATALYTIC CONVERTER: A device installed in the exhaust system, like a muffler, that converts harmful byproducts of combustion into carbon dioxide and water vapor by means of a heat-producing chemical reaction.

CENTRIFUGAL ADVANCE: A mechanical method of advancing the spark timing by using fly weights in the distributor that react to centrifugal force generated by the distributor shaft rotation.

CHECK VALVE: Any one-way valve installed to permit the flow of air, fuel or vacuum in one direction only.

CHOKE: A device, usually a movable valve, placed in the intake path of a carburetor to restrict the flow of air.

CIRCUIT: Any unbroken path through which an electrical current can flow. Also used to describe fuel flow in some instances.

CIRCUIT BREAKER: A switch which protects an electrical circuit from overload by opening the circuit when the current flow exceeds a predetermined level. Some circuit breakers must be reset manually, while most reset automatically

COIL (IGNITION): A transformer in the ignition circuit which steps up the voltage provided to the spark plugs.

COMBINATION MANIFOLD: An assembly which includes both the intake and exhaust manifolds in one casting.

COMBINATION VALVE: A device used in some fuel systems that routes fuel vapors to a charcoal storage canister instead of venting them into the atmosphere. The valve relieves fuel tank pressure and allows fresh air into the tank as the fuel level drops to prevent a vapor lock situation.

COMPRESSION RATIO: The comparison of the total volume of the cylinder and combustion chamber with the piston at BDC and the piston at TDC.

CONDENSER: 1. An electrical device which acts to store an electrical charge, preventing voltage surges.
2. A radiator-like device in the air conditioning system in which refrigerant gas condenses into a liquid, giving off heat.

CONDUCTOR: Any material through which an electrical current can be transmitted easily.

CONTINUITY: Continuous or complete circuit. Can be checked with an ohmmeter.

COUNTERSHAFT: An intermediate shaft which is rotated by a mainshaft and transmits, in turn, that rotation to a working part.

CRANKCASE: The lower part of an engine in which the crankshaft and related parts operate.

CRANKSHAFT: The main driving shaft of an engine which receives reciprocating motion from the pistons and converts it to rotary motion.

CYLINDER: In an engine, the round hole in the engine block in which the piston(s) ride.

CYLINDER BLOCK: The main structural member of an engine in which is found the cylinders, crankshaft and other principal parts.

CYLINDER HEAD: The detachable portion of the engine, fastened, usually, to the top of the cylinder block, containing all or most of the combustion chambers. On overhead valve engines, it contains the valves and their operating parts. On overhead cam engines, it contains the camshaft as well.

DEAD CENTER: The extreme top or bottom of the piston stroke.

DETONATION: An unwanted explosion of the air/fuel mixture in the combustion chamber caused by excess heat and compression, advanced timing, or an overly lean mixture. Also referred to as "ping".

DIAPHRAGM: A thin, flexible wall separating two cavities, such as in a vacuum advance unit.

DIESELING: A condition in which hot spots in the combustion chamber cause the engine to run on after the key is turned off.

DIFFERENTIAL: A geared assembly which allows the transmission of motion between drive axles, giving one axle the ability to turn faster than the other.

DIODE: An electrical device that will allow current to flow in one direction only.

DISC BRAKE: A hydraulic braking assembly consisting of a brake disc, or rotor, mounted on an axle, and a caliper assembly containing, usually two brake pads which are activated by hydraulic pressure. The pads are forced against the sides of the disc, creating friction which slows the vehicle.

DISTRIBUTOR: A mechanically driven device on an engine which is responsible for electrically firing the spark plug at a predetermined point of the piston stroke.

DOWEL PIN: A pin, inserted in mating holes in two different parts allowing those parts to maintain a fixed relationship.

DRUM BRAKE: A braking system which consists of two brake shoes and one or two wheel cylinders, mounted on a fixed backing plate, and a brake drum, mounted on an axle, which revolves around the assembly. Hydraulic action applied to the wheel cylinders forces the shoes outward against the drum, creating friction, slowing the vehicle.

DWELL: The rate, measured in degrees of shaft rotation, at which an electrical circuit cycles on and off.

ELECTRONIC CONTROL UNIT (ECU): Ignition module, amplifier or igniter. See Module for definition.

ELECTRONIC IGNITION: A system in which the timing and firing of the spark plugs is controlled by an electronic control unit, usually called a module. These systems have no points or condenser.

ENDPLAY: The measured amount of axial movement in a shaft.

ENGINE: A device that converts heat into mechanical energy.

EXHAUST MANIFOLD: A set of cast passages or pipes which conduct exhaust gases from the engine.

FEELER GAUGE: A blade, usually metal, of precisely predetermined thickness, used to measure the clearance between two parts. These blades usually are available in sets of assorted thicknesses.

F-HEAD: An engine configuration in which the intake valves are in the cylinder head, while the camshaft and exhaust valves are located in the cylinder block. The camshaft operates the intake valves via lifters and pushrods, while it operates the exhaust valves directly.

FIRING ORDER: The order in which combustion occurs in the cylinders of an engine. Also the order in which spark is distributed to the plugs by the distributor.

FLATHEAD: An engine configuration in which the camshaft and all the valves are located in the cylinder block.

FLOODING: The presence of too much fuel in the intake manifold and combustion chamber which prevents the air/fuel mixture from firing, thereby causing a no-start situation.

FLYWHEEL: A disc shaped part bolted to the rear end of the crankshaft. Around the outer perimeter is affixed the ring gear. The starter drive engages the ring gear, turning the flywheel, which rotates the crankshaft, imparting the initial starting motion to the engine.

FOOT POUND (ft.lb. or sometimes, ft. lbs.): The amount of energy or work needed to raise an item weighing one pound, a distance of one foot.

FUSE: A protective device in a circuit which prevents circuit overload by breaking the circuit when a specific amperage is present. The device is constructed around a strip or wire of a lower amperage rating than the circuit it is designed to protect. When an amperage higher than that stamped on the fuse is present in the circuit, the strip or wire melts, opening the circuit.

GEAR RATIO: The ratio between the number of teeth on meshing gears.

GENERATOR: A device which converts mechanical energy into electrical energy.

HEAT RANGE: The measure of a spark plug's ability to dissipate heat from its firing end. The higher the heat range, the hotter the plug fires.

HUB: The center part of a wheel or gear.

HYDROCARBON (HC): Any chemical compound made up of hydrogen and carbon. A major pollutant formed by the engine as a byproduct of combustion.

HYDROMETER: An instrument used to measure the specific gravity of a solution.

INCH POUND (in.lb. or sometimes, in. lbs.): One twelfth of a foot pound.

INDUCTION: A means of transferring electrical energy in the form of a magnetic field. Principle used in the ignition coil to increase voltage.

INJECTION PUMP: A device, usually mechanically operated, which meters and delivers fuel under pressure to the fuel injector.

INJECTOR: A device which receives metered fuel under relatively low pressure and is activated to inject the fuel into the engine under relatively high pressure at a predetermined time.

INPUT SHAFT: The shaft to which torque is applied, usually carrying the driving gear or gears.

INTAKE MANIFOLD: A casting of passages or pipes used to conduct air or a fuel/air mixture to the cylinders.

JOURNAL: The bearing surface within which a shaft operates.

KEY: A small block usually fitted in a notch between a shaft and a hub to prevent slippage of the two parts.

MANIFOLD: A casting of passages or set of pipes which connect the cylinders to an inlet or outlet source.

MANIFOLD VACUUM: Low pressure in an engine intake manifold formed just below the throttle plates. Manifold vacuum is highest at idle and drops under acceleration.

MASTER CYLINDER: The primary fluid pressurizing device in a hydraulic system. In automotive use, it is found in brake and hydraulic clutch systems and is pedal activated, either directly or, in a power brake system, through the power booster.

MODULE: Electronic control unit, amplifier or igniter of solid state or integrated design which controls the current flow in the ignition primary circuit based on input from the pick- up coil. When the module opens the primary circuit, the high secondary voltage is induced in the coil.

NEEDLE BEARING: A bearing which consists of a number (usually a large number) of long, thin rollers.

OHM:(Ω) The unit used to measure the resistance of conductor to electrical flow. One ohm is the amount of resistance that limits current flow to one ampere in a circuit with one volt of pressure.

OHMMETER: An instrument used for measuring the resistance, in ohms, in an electrical circuit.

OUTPUT SHAFT: The shaft which transmits torque from a device, such as a transmission.

OVERDRIVE: A gear assembly which produces more shaft revolutions than that transmitted to it.

OVERHEAD CAMSHAFT (OHC): An engine configuration in which the camshaft is mounted on top of the cylinder head and operates the valves either directly or by means of rocker arms.

OVERHEAD VALVE (OHV): An engine configuration in which all of the valves are located in the cylinder head and the camshaft is located in the cylinder block. The camshaft operates the valves via lifters and pushrods.

OXIDES OF NITROGEN (NOx): Chemical compounds of nitrogen produced as a byproduct of combustion. They combine with hydrocarbons to produce smog.

OXYGEN SENSOR: Used with the feedback system to sense the presence of oxygen in the exhaust gas and signal the computer which can reference the voltage signal to an air/fuel ratio.

PINION: The smaller of two meshing gears.

PISTON RING: An open ended ring which fits into a groove on the outer diameter of the piston. Its chief function is to form a seal between the piston and cylinder wall. Most automotive pistons have three rings: two for compression sealing; one for oil sealing.

PRELOAD: A predetermined load placed on a bearing during assembly or by adjustment.

PRIMARY CIRCUIT: Is the low voltage side of the ignition system which consists of the ignition switch, ballast resistor or resistance wire, bypass, coil, electronic control unit and pick-up coil as well as the connecting wires and harnesses.

PRESS FIT: The mating of two parts under pressure, due to the inner diameter of one being smaller than the outer diameter of the other, or vice versa; an interference fit.

RACE: The surface on the inner or outer ring of a bearing on which the balls, needles or rollers move.

REGULATOR: A device which maintains the amperage and/or voltage levels of a circuit at predetermined values.

RELAY: A switch which automatically opens and/or closes a circuit.

RESISTANCE: The opposition to the flow of current through a circuit or electrical device, and is measured in ohms. Resistance is equal to the voltage divided by the amperage.

RESISTOR: A device, usually made of wire, which offers a preset amount of resistance in an electrical circuit.

RING GEAR: The name given to a ring-shaped gear attached to a differential case, or affixed to a flywheel or as part a planetary gear set.

ROLLER BEARING: A bearing made up of hardened inner and outer races between which hardened steel rollers move.

ROTOR: 1. The disc-shaped part of a disc brake assembly, upon which the brake pads bear; also called, brake disc.
2. The device mounted atop the distributor shaft, which passes current to the distributor cap tower contacts.

SECONDARY CIRCUIT: The high voltage side of the ignition system, usually above 20,000 volts. The secondary includes the ignition coil, coil wire, distributor cap and rotor, spark plug wires and spark plugs.

SENDING UNIT: A mechanical, electrical, hydraulic or electromagnetic device which transmits information to a gauge.

SENSOR: Any device designed to measure engine operating conditions or ambient pressures and temperatures. Usually electronic in nature and designed to send a voltage signal to an on-board computer, some sensors may operate as a simple on/off switch or they may provide a variable voltage signal (like a potentiometer) as conditions or measured parameters change.

SHIM: Spacers of precise, predetermined thickness used between parts to establish a proper working relationship.

SLAVE CYLINDER: In automotive use, a device in the hydraulic clutch system which is activated by hydraulic force, disengaging the clutch.

SOLENOID: A coil used to produce a magnetic field, the effect of which is to produce work.

SPARK PLUG: A device screwed into the combustion chamber of a spark ignition engine. The basic construction is a conductive core inside of a ceramic insulator, mounted in an outer conductive base. An electrical charge from the spark plug wire travels along the conductive core and jumps a preset air gap to a grounding point or points at the end of the conductive base. The resultant spark ignites the fuel/air mixture in the combustion chamber.

SPLINES: Ridges machined or cast onto the outer diameter of a shaft or inner diameter of a bore to enable parts to mate without rotation.

TACHOMETER: A device used to measure the rotary speed of an engine, shaft, gear, etc., usually in rotations per minute.

THERMOSTAT: A valve, located in the cooling system of an engine, which is closed when cold and opens gradually in response to engine heating, controlling the temperature of the coolant and rate of coolant flow.

TOP DEAD CENTER (TDC): The point at which the piston reaches the top of its travel on the compression stroke.

TORQUE: The twisting force applied to an object.

TORQUE CONVERTER: A turbine used to transmit power from a driving member to a driven member via hydraulic action, providing changes in drive ratio and torque. In automotive use, it links the driveplate at the rear of the engine to the automatic transmission.

TRANSDUCER: A device used to change a force into an electrical signal.

TRANSISTOR: A semi-conductor component which can be actuated by a small voltage to perform an electrical switching function.

TUNE-UP: A regular maintenance function, usually associated with the replacement and adjustment of parts and components in the electrical and fuel systems of a vehicle for the purpose of attaining optimum performance.

TURBOCHARGER: An exhaust driven pump which compresses intake air and forces it into the combustion chambers at higher than atmospheric pressures. The increased air pressure allows more fuel to be burned and results in increased horsepower being produced.

VACUUM ADVANCE: A device which advances the ignition timing in response to increased engine vacuum.

VACUUM GAUGE: An instrument used to measure the presence of vacuum in a chamber.

VALVE: A device which control the pressure, direction of flow or rate of flow of a liquid or gas.

VALVE CLEARANCE: The measured gap between the end of the valve stem and the rocker arm, cam lobe or follower that activates the valve.

VISCOSITY: The rating of a liquid's internal resistance to flow.

VOLTMETER: An instrument used for measuring electrical force in units called volts. Voltmeters are always connected parallel with the circuit being tested.

WHEEL CYLINDER: Found in the automotive drum brake assembly, it is a device, actuated by hydraulic pressure, which, through internal pistons, pushes the brake shoes outward against the drums.

MASTER
INDEX